RAND McNALLY

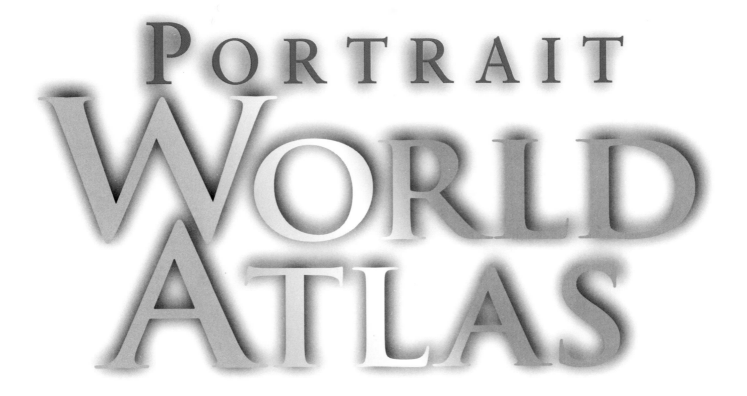

PORTRAIT WORLD ATLAS

TABLE OF CONTENTS

Chairman, President, and CEO,
Rand McNally and Company
Henry J. Feinberg

Vice President and General Manager,
Map & Atlas Publishing
Jayne L. Fenton

Director, Reference Business
Kendra L. Ensor

Editors
Kathryn Martin O'Neil
Brett R. Gover
Ann T. Natunewicz

Art Direction and Design
John C. Nelson
Peggy R. Hogan
Jamie O'Neal

Writers
Donald V. Beaulieu
Catherine C. VanPatten

Marketing
Amy C. Krouse
JoEllen A. Klein

Photo Research
Feldman and Associates, Inc.

Manufacturing
Terry D. Rieger

Cartography Directors
V. Patrick Healy
Jon M. Leverenz

Cartography (U.S.)
Robert K. Argersinger
Barbara Benstead-Strassheim
David M. Bukala
Kerry B. Chambers
Marzee L. Eckhoff
Julie A. Geyer
Winifred V. Farbman
Susan K. Hudson
Elizabeth A. Hunt
William R. Karbler
Brian M. Lash
Nina Lusterman
Gwynn A. Lloyd
Erik J. Pedersen
Thomas F. Vitacco
David R. Walters
Richard A. Wanzo
James Wooden
David C. Zapenski

Cartography (U.K.)
Craig Asquith

Cartography (Italy)
Giovanni Baselli
Ubaldo Uberti

Photo Credits   (l=left, r=right, c=center, t=top, b=bottom)

Jacket
© Joe Cornish/Tony Stone Images (background); © J. Lotter Gurling/Tom Stack & Associates (t r); © Tom Till/Tom Till Photography (c l); © Will & Deni McIntyre/Tony Stone Images (b l); © Andris Apse/Panoramic Images (b r); © PhotoDisc (tulips and polar bear); © TravelPix/FPG International (Great Barrier Reef); © David Muench/David Muench Photography (Lake Superior); © Boyd Norton (Ngorongoro Crater)

Contents
© Ken Ross/FPG International, v (t); © William Wheeler/Dave Houser Photography, v (t c); © Telegraph Colour Library/FPG International, v (b l); © C. Bowman/Picture Perfect, v (b c); © Jerry Sieve/Adstock Photos, v (b r); © Bob Grant/Comstock, vi (t); © Dave Bartruff/Artistry International, vi (b); © Franco Salmoiraghi/Photo Resource Hawaii Stock Photography, vii; © Dewitt Jones/Tony Stone Images, viii (t); © Robert Frerck/Odyssey Productions, viii (b); © Chad Ehlers/International Stock, ix (t); © James Strachan/Tony Stone Images, ix (b); © Arakaki-Argelia/International Stock, x (t); © Galen Rowell/Mountain Light, x (b); © Eye Ubiquitous/Art Directors & TRIP Photo Library, xi (t); © Tom Till/Tom Till Photography, xi (b); © David Muench/David Muench Photography, xii (t); © Tom Till/Tom Till Photography, xii (b); © David Muench/David Muench Photography, xiii (t); © Galen Rowell/Mountain Light, xiii (b); © Greg Vaughn/Tom Stack & Associates, xiv (t); © Boyd Norton, xiv (b); © TravelPix/FPG International, xv (t); © Kevin Schafer/Kevin Schafer Photography, xv (b); © Blaine Harrington, xvi (t); © Brian Lawrence/Uniphoto, xvi (b)

Portrait World Atlas
Copyright © 1998 by Rand McNally and Company

Published and printed in the United States of America.

Rand McNally and Company.
   Portrait world atlas.
     p.   cm.
   Includes index.
   ISBN 0-528-83995-0
   1. Atlases.   I. Title.
G1021 .R43 1998 <G&M>
912—DC21
                        98-8663
                          CIP
                        MAPS

HOW TO USE THE ATLAS

What is an Atlas?

A set of maps bound together is called an atlas. Abraham Ortelius' *Theatrum orbis terrarum*, published in 1570, is considered to be the first modern "atlas," although it was not referred to as such for almost 20 years. In 1589, Gerardus Mercator (*figure 1*) coined the term when he named his collection of maps after Atlas, the mythological Titan who carried Earth on his shoulders as punishment for warring against Zeus. Since then, the definition of "atlas" has been expanded, and atlases often include additional geographic information in diagrams, tables, and text.

figure 1

Latitude and Longitude

The terms "latitude" and "longitude" refer to the grid of horizontal and vertical lines found on most maps and globes. Any point on Earth can be located by its precise latitude and longitude coordinates.

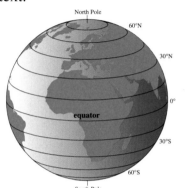
figure 2

The imaginary horizontal line that circles Earth halfway between the North and South poles is called the equator; it represents 0° latitude and lies 90° from either pole. The other lines of latitude, or parallels, measure distances north or south from the equator (*figure 2*). The imaginary vertical line that measures 0° longitude runs through the Greenwich Observatory in the United Kingdom, and is called the Prime Meridian. The other lines of longitude, or meridians, measure distances east or west from the prime meridian (*figure 3*), up to a maximum of 180°. Lines of latitude and longitude cross each other, forming a grid (*figure 4*).

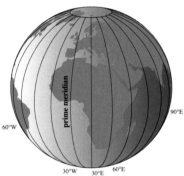
figure 3

Map Projections

Every cartographer is faced with the problem of transforming the curved surface of Earth onto a flat plane with a minimum of distortion. The systematic transformation of locations on Earth (a spherical surface) to locations on a map (a flat surface) is called projection.

figure 4

It is not possible to represent on a flat map the spatial relationships of angle, distance, direction, and area that only a globe can show faithfully. As a result, projections inevitably involve some distortion. On large-scale maps representing a few square miles, the distortion is generally negligible. But on maps depicting large countries, continents, or the entire world, the amount of distortion can be significant. On maps which use the Mercator Projection (*figure 5*), for example, distortion increases with distance from the equator. Thus the island of Greenland appears larger than the entire continent of South America,

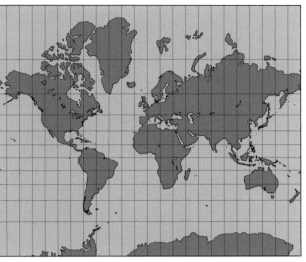
figure 5

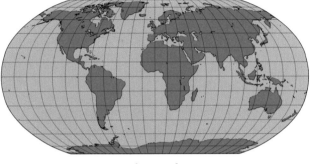
figure 6

although South America is in fact nine time larger. In contrast, the Robinson Projection (*figure 6*) renders the world's major land areas in generally correct proportion to one another, although distortion is still apparent in areas such as Antarctica, which is actually smaller than all of the continents except Europe and Australia.

There are an infinite number of possible map projections, all of which distort one or more of the characteristics of the globe in varying degrees. The projection that a cartographer chooses depends on the size and location of the area being projected and the purpose of the map. In this atlas, most of the maps are drawn on projections that give a consistent or only slightly distorted area scale, good land and ocean shape, parallels that are parallel, and as consistent a linear scale as possible throughout the projection.

Map Scale

The scale of a map is the relationship between distances or areas shown on the map and the corresponding distances or areas on Earth's surface. Large-scale maps show relatively small areas in greater detail than do small-scale maps, such as those of individual continents or of the world.

There are three different ways to express scale. Most often scale is given as a fraction, such as 1:10,000,000, which means that the ratio of distances on the map to actual distances on Earth is 1 to 10,000,000. Scale can also be expressed as a phrase, such as "One inch represents approximately ten million miles." Finally, scale can be illustrated via a bar scale on which various distances are labeled (*figure 7*). Any of these three scale expressions can be used to calculate distances on a map.

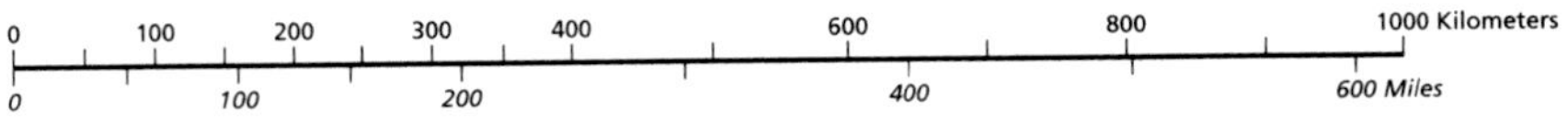

| 0 | 100 | 200 | 300 | 400 | | 600 | | 800 | | 1000 Kilometers |
| 0 | | 100 | | 200 | | | 400 | | | 600 Miles |

figure 7

Measuring Distances

Using a bar scale, it is possible to calculate the distance between any two points on a map. To find the approximate distance between São Paulo and Rio de Janeiro, Brazil, for example, follow these steps:

1) Lay a piece of paper on the right-hand page of the "Eastern Brazil" map found on pages 88-89, lining up its edge with the city dots for São Paulo and Rio de Janeiro. Make a mark on the paper next to each dot *(figure 8)*.

2) Place the paper along the scale bar found below the map, and position the first mark at 0. The second mark falls about a quarter of the way between the 200-mile tick and the 300-mile tick, indicating that the distance separating the two cities is approximately 225 miles *(figure 9)*.

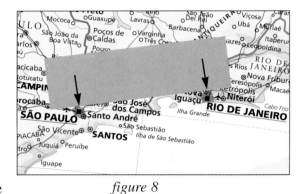

figure 8

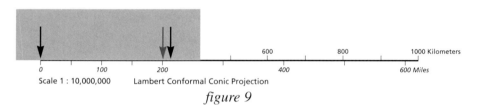

figure 9

3) To confirm this measurement, make a third pencil mark (shown in red in *figure 9*) at the 200-mile tick. Slide the paper to the left so that this mark lines up with 0. The Rio de Janeiro mark now falls about halfway between the 0 tick and the 50-mile tick. Thus, São Paulo and Rio de Janeiro are indeed approximately 225 (200 + 25) miles apart.

Using the Index to Find Places

One of the most important purposes of an atlas is to help the reader locate cities, towns, and geographic features such as rivers, lakes, and mountains. This atlas uses a "bingo key" indexing system. In the index, found on pages I•1 through I•64, every entry is assigned an alpha-numeric code that consists of a letter and a number. This code relates to the red letters and numbers that run along the perimeter of each map. To locate places or features, follow the steps outlined in this example for the city of Bratsk, Russia.

1) Look up Bratsk in the index. The entry *(figure 10)* contains the following information: the place name (Bratsk), the name of the country (Russia) in which Bratsk is located, the map reference key (C18) that corresponds to Bratsk's location on the map, and the page number (32) of the map on which Bratsk can be found.

Brassey, Banjaran, mts., Malay	A10	50
Brass Islands, is., V.I.U.S.	o7	104b
Brasstown Bald, mtn., Ga., U.S.	B2	116
Bratca, Rom.	C9	26
Bratislava, Slov.	H13	16
Bratislava, state, Slov.	H13	16
Bratsk, Russia	C18	32
Bratskoe vodohranilisce, res., Russia	C18	32

figure 10

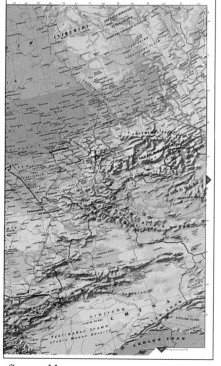

figure 11

2) Turn to the Northwestern Asia map on pages 32-33. Look along either the left or right-hand margin for the red letter "C"—the letter code given for Bratsk. The "C" denotes a band that arcs horizontally across the map, between the grid lines representing 55° and 60° North latitude. Then, look along either the top or bottom margin for the red number "18"—the numerical part of the code given for Bratsk. The "18" denotes a widening vertical band, between the grid lines representing 100° and 105° East longitude, which angles from the top center of the map to right-hand edge.

3) Using your finger, follow the horizontal "C" band and the vertical "18" band to the area where they overlap *(figure 11)*. Bratsk lies within this overlap area.

Physical Maps and Political Maps

Most of the maps in the *Portrait World Atlas* are physical maps, like the one shown in *figure 12*, emphasizing terrain, landforms, and elevation. Political maps, as in *figure 13*, emphasize countries and other political units over topography. The atlas includes political maps of the world and each of the continents except Antarctica.

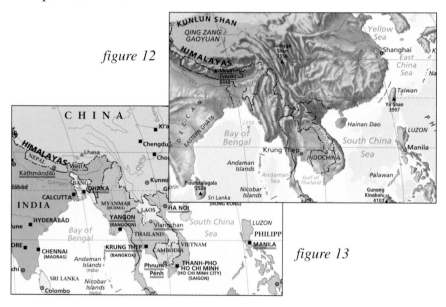

figure 12

figure 13

How Maps Show Topography

The physical maps in this atlas use two techniques to depict Earth's topography. Variations in elevation are shown through a series of colors called hypsometric tints. Areas below sea level appear as a dark green; as the elevation rises, the tints move successively through lighter green, yellow, and orange. Similarly, variations in ocean depth are represented by bathymetric tints. The shallowest areas appear as light blue; darker tints of blue indicate greater depths. The hypsometric/bathymetric scale that accompanies each map identifies, in feet and meters, all of the elevation and depth categories that appear on the map.

Principal landforms, such as mountain ranges and valleys, are rendered in shades of gray, a technique known as shaded relief. The combination of hypsometric tints and shaded relief provides the map reader with a three-dimensional picture of Earth's surface *(figure 14)*.

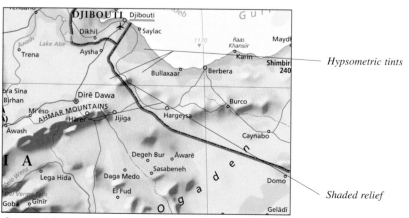

figure 14

Masterpieces of Nature

A landscape artist would have a difficult time painting a single portrait that captures the essence of our planet. From the thunderous tumble of Africa's Victoria Falls to the iridescent coral of Australia's Great Barrier Reef to the cake-layered mesas of the United States' Grand Canyon, the world's geographic terrain is infinitely varied, multi-hued, and wondrous—and impossible to capture at a glance.

An intimate, close-up portrait of Earth must include such vast expanses as Asia's mighty Himalayas and such singularly unique sites as Northern Ireland's fantastic Giant's Causeway, the biggest or tallest or longest natural wonders along with those that are simply stunningly unique. While no listing of the world's wonders is complete, certain geographic features on each continent stand out for their magnificent beauty and enormity—not just as geographic marvels but as important places in the human culture and mythology of the people who experience them. Together these great mountains, rivers, lakes, deserts, canyons, waterfalls, fjords, volcanic craters, reefs, and rock formations—pinpointed on the maps within this atlas—create a detailed portrait of our planet's landscape and represent its greatest works of art.

Mount Everest

A pyramid-shaped colossus serrated by glaciers and blasted by wind and snow, Mount Everest is the pinnacle of the planet, actually jutting into the jet stream, marked by a ribbon of ice particles whirling eastward off the summit. The 29,028-foot (8,848-meter) peak crowns the world's youngest and highest mountains, Asia's mighty Himalayas, which means "abode of snow" in the Sanskrit language. Glaciers carved severe features into Everest and other megaliths of the Himalayan Range, forming along the Nepal-Tibet border a massive skyline of dramatic peaks that seem to be cleaved from Earth like chiseled shards of ice.

The summit of Everest was actually once the seafloor. The Himalayas today separate the Indian subcontinent from the rest of Asia, but until 180 million years ago an ocean divided the two land masses. The Indo-Australian crustal plate on which India sits migrated northward, where it collided with the Eurasian plate, crushing the seafloor and buckling it—along with rocky layers of the ocean bottom—toward the skies.

Everest has always been venerated: The mountain is Chomolungma, "goddess mother of the world," to Tibetans in the north, while Nepalis to the south call it Sagarmatha, "goddess of the sky." But Everest is never so revered as by climbers, for whom the tallest mountain in the world is an irresistible lure. Mere mortals have climbed two thirds of the way up through Earth's atmosphere: Edmund Hillary and Tenzing Norgay are credited with the first ascent in 1953, though it's widely held that George Mallory and Andrew Irvine summited in 1924 before disappearing on their descent. Since then, adventurers have conquered the peak in new and creative ways. Japanese climber Yuichiro Miura summited in 1970 and then descended the mountain on skis, breaking many bones. Reinhold Messner and Peter Habeler first scaled the peak without bottled oxygen in 1978. In 1990 Australian Tim McCartney-Snape repeated the feat, but began from sea level, at the Bay of Bengal.

More than 700 people have reached Everest's summit, but for every five who have succeeded, one has died in the attempt. Some die from falls or avalanches; others succumb to cold, altitude sickness, and oxygen deprivation above 25,000 feet in the Death Zone. "Life of mountains," said Anatoli Boukreev, a Kazakhstani guide who narrowly survived a deadly 1996 Everest storm, but died on Annapurna in 1997, "is stronger than life of people." *(page 55)*

Other Remarkable Mountains

1 *Cerro Aconcagua, Argentina:* The tallest peak in the Western Hemisphere, this steep, 22,831-foot (6,959-meter) glacially sculpted massif in the central Andes was a sacred burial site in Pre-Colombian times. *(page 90)*

2 *K2, Pakistan/China:* Teetering above the Karakoram Range, the world's second-tallest mountain (28,251 feet, 8,611 meters) has claimed the lives of almost as many climbers as have reached its summit. *(page 57)*

3 *Kilimanjaro, Tanzania:* The almost perfect cone of this snowcapped volcanic peak (19,340 feet, 5,895 meters), the highest in Africa, soars above the Serengeti Plain. *(page 67)*

4 *Mount Elbrus, Russia:* Europe's highest point, Elbrus' twin-peaked volcanic cone (18,510 feet, 5,642 meters) is 5,000 feet taller than neighboring peaks. *(page 56)*

5 *Mount Fuji, Japan:* Rising majestically from almost sea level to 12,388 feet (3,776 meters), Japan's highest mountain, Fuji-san, is a stratovolcano built on the remains of older volcanoes. *(page 41)*

6 *Mount McKinley, United States:* Known as the Great One, or "Denali," to the Athabascan people of Alaska, the tallest peak in North America rises dramatically from 2,000 feet (610 meters) at its lowlands base to 20,320 feet (6,194 meters) at its summit. *(page 140)*

At 13,796 feet (4,260 meters) above sea level, the snow-capped crown of Mauna Kea floats like a mirage over the balmy valhalla of the Big Island of Hawaii. A paradox of fire and ice, Mauna Kea was the only glaciated spot in the tropical Pacific during the last Ice Age, and even today Lake Waiau, located inside a volcanic cinder cone near the peak, is fed entirely by permafrost, a frozen Ice Age remnant still melting below the surface. Starkly beautiful, this dormant volcano's rounded slopes were molded into an inverted bowl by repeated eruptions of fast-flowing lava. Its peak is flanked by an arresting moonscape of cinder cones and red lava fields—the Apollo astronauts actually test-drove the lunar rover here in a crater called Moon Valley.

These cinder cones near the summit, representing smaller volcanoes, are an ideal site for the world's largest astronomy telescopes. At the Mauna Kea Observatories the atmosphere is extremely dry and stable, making for accurate measurements of infrared radiation. The skies are dark and cloud-free, with one of the world's best proportions of clear nights. A tropical inversion cloud layer near the summit separates the atmosphere atop the peak from the wetter maritime air at lower elevations and from atmospheric pollutants.

Many consider Mauna Kea the tallest mountain on Earth: It measures nearly 32,000 feet (9,750 meters) from base to summit, but 18,200 of those feet are below sea level. Ancient Hawaiians believed Mauna Kea was the home of the snow goddess Poliahu, whose tempestuous sister Pele resided in Mauna Loa, an active volcano across the island. The sister goddesses sparred perpetually over a human love interest, and the saddle between the two mountains became their battlefield. Prudently, islanders avoided that area and settled on the coast below.

In a precursor of the Ironman Triathlon, natives would run up Mauna Kea, grab as much snow as they could carry, and race back down to the ocean. The runner who arrived with enough snow to make a snowball was declared the winner. Today, visitors pay homage to the mountain by skiing its snowy summit, then sunbathing on its beaches below, in the shadow of this volcanic peak forged by fire from below and shaped by ice from above. *(page 78)*

Mauna Kea

Canyons

Grand Canyon

Each year, five million pilgrims gape at the Grand Canyon's labyrinthine landscape of mesas and spires, its cathedrals of sandstone and shale. They marvel at its pink, red, white, and gold terraces of cake-layered strata a mile (1.6 kilometers) deep. But this intricately eroded chasm was not initially destined to become a tourist mecca. Early explorers of the U.S. Southwest deemed the impassable gorge a "horrible abyss" and "grave of the world." Until a local miner offered in an 1886 Flagstaff, Arizona, newspaper ad to "conduct parties thereto at any time," very few people had any good reason to travel there. But John Hance's modest advertisement opened up to tourists two billion years of geological history laid bare as the Colorado River sliced through northern Arizona's Kaibab Plateau. At the rate of about one inch (2.5 centimeters) every 80 years, the river eroded red Mesozoic mudstone, then creamy Paleozoic limestone, down to dark Precambrian schist in the lower gorge. Side tributaries, along with rain, wind, and frost, gradually broadened the gorge to 18 miles (29 kilometers) wide and 277 miles (446 kilometers) long.

Visitors today—up to 20,000 each day in the summer—descend the Grand Canyon's hiking paths on foot or muleback, soar over the canyon by plane, or merely peer over the precarious edge in an attempt to comprehend its magnificence. Since 1919, most of the canyon has been designated a national park, whose directors work diligently to cope with growing numbers of tourists while fulfilling the mandate of Theodore Roosevelt: "Keep it for your children...and for all who come after you, as the one great sight which every American...should see." *(page 133)*

An immense landscape of steep gorges and rugged badlands isolated from the rest of Mexico for many centuries, Copper Canyon, or "Barranca del Cobre," is the homeland of the Tarahumara Indians. In the seventeenth century, the Tarahumara fled northwestern Mexico's desert plains near present-day Chihuahua to escape enslavement by the Spanish. They settled in Copper Canyon, which burrows along the western slope of the Sierra Madre Occidental Range. Here the Urique River has sculpted sinuous ravines and veined ridges of red volcanic rock into a series of boulder-strewn trenches deeper than the Grand Canyon in places and four times the area. The canyon's arid upper slopes stand in marked contrast with tropical

Copper Canyon

vegetation in its lower depths, and it is named for its rich resources—ancient copper mines that pockmark the region. The land has also yielded, over the course of four centuries, more than a billion dollars' worth of gold.

The only practical means of entering Copper Canyon is a railroad that has traversed the area since the 1960s. There are no paved roads, and the Tarahumara travel the canyon by running along hundreds of miles of switchback trails (their traditional means of hunting deer is running the animals to death). Copper Canyon remains today a harsh, intractable wilderness that retains a mystic hold on the Mexican imagination. "This great Mexican abyss," wrote author Carlos Fuentes, "bears witness to the two extremes of creation, birth and death." *(page 100)*

Other Impressive Canyons and Gorges

1 **Black Canyon of the Gunnison River, United States:** Even its river's namesake, Captain John Gunnison, never entered this gloomy, 2,000-foot-deep (608-meter-deep) canyon in southwestern Colorado, which is deeper in places than it is wide. *(page 132)*

2 **Colca Canyon, Peru:** More than 10,000 feet (3,222 meters) deep, the Andes' Colca is the world's deepest canyon and home of the Andean condor, the world's largest bird, with a wingspan of ten feet (three meters). *(page 84)*

3 **Daryal Gorge, Georgia:** The 5,900-foot-tall (1,794-meter-tall) granite cliffs of this gorge, called the Gates of the Caucasus in Roman times, frame the major pass through the imposing Caucasus Mountains. Greek mythology claims that Prometheus was chained to the mountain above it. *(page 56)*

4 **Grand Canyon of the Verdon River, France:** Carving through limestone pocked with subterranean caves and sinkholes, the Verdon River has created France's longest, deepest, and most scenic canyon, with walls only 650 feet (200 meters) apart in places. *(page 18)*

5 **Tiger Leaping Gorge, China:** This narrow, 9,850-foot (2,994-meter) gorge along the Jinsha River (the Upper Yangtze) in Yunnan Province was named for a hunted tiger of Chinese legend who escaped death by leaping across the chasm. *(page 36)*

6 **Vikos Canyon, Greece:** Its sheer, almost vertical cliffs of brilliant white limestone rise 4,000 feet (1,216 meters) above the Voidomatis River in the Pindus Mountains of northwestern Greece. *(page 28)*

When the Spanish conquistadors explored this South American waterway in 1541, they allegedly encountered a fierce tribe of giant female warriors, which they likened to the Amazons of Greek myth. Truth or exaggeration, the Spanish could not have bestowed a more apt name upon this formidable body of water, artery of the South American continent. The Amazon is unrivaled in physical magnitude among all rivers in the world: More than six million cubic feet (168,000 cubic meters) of water—one fifth of all the flowing water on Earth—discharge through the river's mouth every second. The drainage basin of the Amazon and its thousand tributaries covers 2.7 million square miles (6.9 million square kilometers). Through Brazil the river runs so wide and deep that ocean-going freighters can sail upriver thousands of miles to Iquitos, Peru.

Amazon River

The Amazon's waters originate just below the peaks of the Andes in northern Peru, where small streams cascade down steep gorges and eventually form a flow a mile (1.6 kilometers) wide. From there the river moves languidly through dense jungle; during the rainy season it spills into secondary channels and lakes, drenching an enormous floodplain. This abundant ecosystem supports some truly Amazonian species, including the 30-foot-long (nine-meter-long) anaconda, the 110-pound (50-kilogram) capybara rodent, and a giant water lily that spans up to six feet (two meters) across. The Amazon rain forest has also been home to hundreds of indigenous groups of people, though many have been displaced by logging, farming, and cattle-grazing. The subsequent harm from these activities on the rain forest, river, and even on the global environment and climate suggests that the Amazon is not just the artery of a continent but of Earth itself. *(pages 84-85)*

Other Great Rivers

1 **Congo River, Central Africa:** Its drainage basin, the second largest in the world, straddles the equator and draws on such diverse sources that the river's output into the Atlantic is constant year-round. *(page 66)*

2 **Ganges River, India:** Considered sacred by Hindus, the Ganges flows from the Himalayas to create the world's largest delta, which forms 250 miles (400 kilometers) inland and fans 200 miles (320 kilometers) wide. *(page 55)*

3 **Mississippi River, United States:** Combined with its major tributary, the Missouri River, the Mississippi is the fourth-longest river in the world, with a catchment that collects four-fifths of the rainfall between North America's Rocky and Appalachian Mountain Ranges. *(pages 108-109)*

4 **Ob-Irtysh Rivers, Russia:** The sixth-longest river system in the world, western Siberia's Ob and Irtysh Rivers descend from ancient glaciers and alpine lakes high in the Altay (Altaj) Mountains to converge and flow into the Gulf of Ob at the Arctic Circle. *(page 32)*

5 **Volga River, Russia:** The longest river in Europe, the Volga forms a busy waterway with a network of canals connecting the Caspian, Baltic, and Black Seas. *(page 32)*

6 **Yangtze River, China:** The longest river in Asia and the deepest river in the world is 600 feet (183 meters) deep in the spectacular Yichang Gorges. One in 13 people in the world lives within the basin of the Yangtze, and the Three Gorges Dam, scheduled for completion in 2009, will displace more than a million people. *(page 42)*

Nile River

The longest river in the world, the fabled Nile stretches 4,145 miles (6,671 kilometers) across Africa, a distance greater than the span between Chicago and London. From Khartoum, Sudan, where the White Nile (issuing from Lake Victoria) and the Blue Nile (flowing from Lake Tana on the Ethiopian Plateau) meet, the river flows north through Egypt to the Mediterranean Sea, creating a verdant floodplain of dark, rich soil and lush vegetation up to 20 miles (32 kilometers) wide through the Nubian and Arabian Deserts.

But the true source of the Nile's legend is its delta—the seedbed of Egyptian culture and nurturer of one of the world's most ancient civilizations. Here desert nomads settled 7,000 years ago to escape the advancing sands and arid climate. They farmed, raised animals, fished, and, around 3,000 B.C., founded the city of Memphis, capital of the ancient Egyptian civilization that flourished for three millennia. "Egypt," wrote the ancient Greek historian Herodotus, "is the gift of the Nile."

Little wonder that the Egyptians worshiped the Nile as a god, albeit a mercurial one. Every year the retreating floodwaters deposited a layer of nutrient-rich mud that fertilized their crops, but occasional high floods threatened their settlements, and droughts provoked famines. Modern Egyptians have averted some of the river's wrath by building the Aswan High Dam in the 1960s; its reservoir, Lake Nasser, provides year-round irrigation. But the dam also prevents silt from fertilizing the soil of the floodplain, which only emphasizes the godlike powers of this ribboned oasis bisecting an otherwise barren, arid land. *(page 63)*

Sahara Desert

Arabs call the sterile sun-seared terrain of the Sahara Desert "bahr bila maa," or "ocean without water." Covering a third of the African continent, the desert receives less than three inches (7.6 centimeters) of rainfall a year. Other environments may be drier, but at 3.5 million square miles (9.1 million square kilometers) the Sahara is by far the largest hot desert on Earth.

Great expanses of shifting, rippled sand dunes known as ergs cover only 20 percent of the Sahara, although the Grand Erg de Bilma, which straddles the Niger and Chad border, is almost the size of Spain. The rest of the desert comprises rock-and-gravel plateaus and plains corrugated with wind-scoured mountains and craggy gorges. The Sahara raises millions of tons of dust clouds a year, which are carried away on atmospheric winds as far as the Southeastern United States; these dust clouds make for blinding windstorms and magnify heat like a greenhouse. A person walking the long distances between oases in the summer sun would need four gallons of water a day to replenish lost fluids in temperatures that have soared to 130 degrees Fahrenheit (54 degrees Celsius).

The Sahara is not uninhabited. Nomadic Tuaregs, desert-dwelling camel drivers who once controlled the trans-Saharan caravan trade between the Mediterranean and Central Africa, make their home here. Tuareg men wear cotton veils across their faces to shield themselves from desert winds and from evil spirits—the Muslim Tuaregs believe that their breath is the gateway to the soul. "The desert is the Garden of Allah," an Arab saying goes, "from which the Lord of the Faithful removed all superfluous human and animal life, so that there might be one place where he could walk in peace." *(page 64)*

Other Magnificent Deserts

1 *Atacama Desert, Chile:* Where the slopes of the Andes Mountains meet the Pacific Ocean is one of the driest places on Earth. Arica, Chile, receives an average .03 inches (.08 centimeters) of moisture a year, mostly brought by ocean fogs. *(page 92)*

2 *Australian Interior:* In the "Red Heart" interior of the most desertified continent besides Antarctica, enormous expanses of parallel sand ridges shift with the winds and small clumps of porcupine grass survive on 0.4 inches (one centimeter) of rain a year. *(pages 74-75)*

3 *The Empty Quarter, Southwest Asia:* Acclaimed by T. E. Lawrence of Lawrence of Arabia fame, the roughly 250,000 square miles (640,000 square kilometers) of Ar-rub al-Khali on the Arabian Peninsula contain the world's largest continual tract of sand dunes. *(page 56)*

4 *Gobi Desert, Mongolia/China:* This rocky plateau in Central Asia—home of the two-humped Bactrian camel ridden by Mongol nomads—has one of the world's harshest climates, with temperatures ranging from -40 degrees Fahrenheit (-40 degrees Celsius) to 113 degrees Fahrenheit (45 degrees Celsius). *(page 36)*

5 *Mojave Desert, United States:* Mostly a high plateau, 560 square miles (1,450 square kilometers) of this desert are below sea level. In Death Valley, California, soil temperatures get so hot that early natives called the land "Ground Afire." *(page 135)*

6 *Negev Desert, Israel:* The Negev's 4,700 square miles (12,200 square kilometers) of undulating ridges and basins bisected by dry riverbeds was the site of four thousand years of Biblical history, including Moses' exodus out of Egypt. *(page 59)*

7 *White Sands National Monument, United States:* Not technically a desert, this milky white sea of billowing sand represents the world's largest gypsum dune field. *(page 130)*

Antarctica

Antarctica brings to mind endless seas of snow and ice, a vast sheet of frost up to three miles (4,775 meters) thick and deep enough to bury the Alps. This pristine frozen wilderness contains three quarters of the world's fresh water—enough, if melted, to raise all the oceans by 200 feet (61 meters). But Antarctica is also the world's largest desert. Less than two inches (five centimeters) of precipitation fall annually on the continent, and water vapor is literally frozen out of the air by extreme cold temperatures that average -40 degrees Fahrenheit (-40 degrees Celsius).

In the Dry Valleys along the Ross Sea in East Antarctica no rain has fallen at all for more than a million years. The air is too dry in these expansive lowlands for snow and ice to exist; the ice sheet has thinned to expose gigantic areas of rock that absorb radiation from the sun. The strongest winds on Earth—with speeds up to 199 miles per hour (320 kilometers per hour)—sweep dense, colder air down from the polar plateau, sculpting and polishing fantastic rock boulders and fins called "ventrifacts" while essentially freeze-drying any forms of life. Scientists believe this desolately beautiful terrain is quite similar to that of Mars.

Explorer Robert Scott deemed the valleys a "very wonderful place" when he discovered them during a 1903 expedition. "We have seen all the indications of colossal ice action and considerable water action, and yet neither of these agents is now at work," he wrote in *The Voyage of the Discovery.* "It is certainly a valley of the dead; even the great glacier which once pushed through it has withered away." *(page 81)*

In 1933 an American bush pilot scouting Venezuela's Guiana Highlands for a lost cache of gold came upon a treasure greater than he had imagined. Banking his single-engine transport plane around a flat-topped mountain, or *tepuí*, Jimmy Angel saw something incredible: an iridescent column of water 17 times the height of Niagara Falls, plunging in solemn magnificence down the mesa's cliff wall into a dense green jungle shrouded in mist. "Biggest damn waterfall in the world," Angel boasted later to a bartender in Ciudad Bolivar. He was right: The cascade that now bears his name is the tallest on Earth, spanning 3,212 feet (979 meters) from the top of the escarpment to the floor of the gorge.

Angel Falls begins its dramatic descent where the Churun River spills down Auyán-Tepuí (or "Devil's Mountain"), one of many reddish sandstone plateaus that lay like titans' footstools above the high grasslands of the Gran Sabana. Before reaching the plateau's edge, the river disappears underground into a vertical fissure and then springs forth from gashes in the cliff wall, as if emanating from some inner mystical source. It falls in a single unbroken plume for the first 2,648 feet (807 meters) before hitting rock, then tumbles down to a churning plunge pool below.

Tens of thousands of tourists journey to Angel Falls each year, mostly by plane or motorized dugout canoe. But the national park land surrounding the falls is still a wild and remote place where rare species of flora and fauna flourish, red howler monkeys emit plaintive wails, and morpho butterflies dance in slow, jagged serpentines, glinting metallic blue in the sun. *(page 87)*

Angel Falls

Other Wondrous Waterfalls

1 *Iguassu Falls, Argentina/Brazil:* Some 275 dramatic cascades spanning two and a half miles (four kilometers) thunder down from the Iguassu River over the lip of a half-moon-shaped plateau into a lush jungle of bamboos and tree ferns. *(page 93)*

2 *Khone Falls, Laos:* More than six miles (9.6 kilometers) wide, this spectacular chain of waterfalls and islands boasts the greatest volume of all the world's waterfalls. One of its largest cascades, Khong Phapheng Falls, is known as "the voice of the Mekong." *(page 44)*

3 *Mardalsfossen, Norway:* These two-tiered falls crest over a granite ridge and drop more than 2,150 feet (655 meters) down a glacier-carved hanging valley in Norway's breathtaking fjord country. *(page 8)*

4 *Niagara Falls, United States/Canada:* Actually two enormous cataracts flanking a central island, 2,200-foot-wide (670-meter-wide) Horseshoe Falls and 1,060-foot-wide (325-meter-wide) American Falls are slowly devouring the dolomite escarpment and receding upstream from Lake Ontario to Lake Erie. *(page 113)*

5 *Tugela Falls, South Africa:* Descending from the Drakensberg Mountains, the world's second-highest waterfall jumps down several small cataracts, then plunges 2,014 feet (614 meters) in a single cascade for a total drop of 3,110 feet (948 meters). *(page 71)*

Natives called this series of spectacular cataracts Mosi-oa-Tunya, "The Smoke That Thunders." The collective roar of Victoria Falls, located along the border of Zambia and Zimbabwe, clatters window panes a mile away, and its thousand-foot-high (300-meter-high) cloud of vapor refracts rainbows even from the full moon. David Livingstone, the Scottish missionary-explorer escorted down the Zambezi River via dugout canoe by Makololo tribesmen in 1855, named the falls for his queen, concluding that "scenes so lovely must have been gazed upon by angels in their flight."

The breadth of this wall of water—5,500 feet (1,675 meters)—is dramatic, but the narrowness of its gorge is even more astonishing. At the falls, the Zambezi River dives into a steep chasm of black basaltic lava, bottlenecks through a canyon cleft only 200 feet (60 meters) wide, and roils into behemoth Class-V rapids known to kayakers and rafters as the Boiling Pot. From there the river caroms through 45 miles (72 kilometers) of pulse-revving whitewater. Above the falls' crest is an archipelago of palm-shaded islands deemed sacred by tribal chieftains, who, according to Dr. Livingstone's journal, gathered there "with reverential awe" to worship their deities. Here in the flat, hot bushland of southern Africa the mist from the falls nurtures a lush enclave of fig trees, ilala palms, and ferns, and small, striped antelopes called bushbucks live alongside the irascible hippos known to charge Zambezi paddlers above the falls.

The chasm and waterfall were created as erosion enlarged deep fractures in the bedrock of sandstone and basaltic lava. The canyon is growing still larger today as powerful Devil's Cataract at the end of the falls erodes another upstream fracture, which will eventually shift the line of the falls. *(page 68)*

Victoria Falls

Framing a brilliant backdrop of red rock and azure desert sky in southern Utah, the weathered sandstone of the largest natural bridge in the world reflects an earthy rainbow of colors, from rusty reds to deep salmons to burnished golds. Iron oxide has glazed on the span of Rainbow Bridge a patina of dark, vertical streaks, called "desert varnish." The bridge's proportions are massive: 290 feet (88 meters) high—as high as the United States Capitol Building—and 275 feet (84 meters) wide—nearly the length of a football field. At its highest point, the bridge is 42 feet (13 meters) thick and 33 feet (10 meters) wide, awesome in its symmetry as it spans the creek that carved it.

The bridge's formation is linked to the sudden and rapid uplifting of the Colorado Plateau some five million years ago. The land, which had been relatively level, broke and buckled, creating peaks such as Utah's Navajo Mountain. Regional watercourses steepened, and rivers began carving the canyons that today define the U.S. Southwest. One of these rivers, now known as Bridge Creek, rushed down the north flank of Navajo Mountain, cutting a deep canyon and boring its way through a fin of salmon-pink Navajo and reddish-gold Kayenta sandstone to form Rainbow Bridge.

Traces of ancient ceremonial fires indicate that the bridge has been a holy place for hundreds, perhaps thousands of years. The modern Navajo, Hopi, Ute, and Paiute nations continue to regard the awe-inspiring span of rock as a sacred site and a cathedral of nature; pilgrims come to make spiritual offerings and pray in its shadow. The U.S. government designated Rainbow Bridge a national monument in 1910. *(page 132)*

Rainbow Bridge

Along the Antrim coast of Northern Ireland stretches the bizarre and fascinating Giant's Causeway, an uneven 300-yard (275-meter) expanse of vertical, polygonal pillars of rock fitted together as if by a superhuman mason.

Local lore has it that the causeway was indeed the work of a giant. Legendary Irish warrior Finn MacCool assembled the pillars to reach the tiny Scottish island of Staffa, 75 miles (120 kilometers) north, and challenge a rival giant, Finn Gall. After driving the last pillar into place, MacCool went home to nap before the big battle. Finn Gall, however, crossed over the causeway to Ireland, where MacCool's wife convinced him that the snoring form beneath the bedclothes was not her husband but her baby son. Finn Gall, thinking himself no match for the father of such an enormous infant, fled back to Staffa, tearing up the causeway behind him. All that remains is the stretch of shattered pillars on the Antrim coast and similar pillars underpinning Staffa.

In fact, the rock formations were produced 50 to 60 million years ago, when basaltic lava flowed out of great fissures in the Earth's crust, then slowly cooled, shrank, and cracked. At least 40,000 of these mostly hexagonal columns make up the Giant's Causeway. The constant hammering of waves has broken off the columns at varying heights; some groups rise in fantastic formations, others form a surface as smooth as pavement.

There was no easy access to the Giant's Causeway until 1830, when a celebrated coast road was opened. Prior to that, visitors often fortified themselves at the Bushmills distillery before making the difficult journey on horseback to the site. *(page 12)*

Giant's Causeway

Other Fascinating Rock Formations

1 Arches National Park, United States: Shaped by water, ice, and wind, these 2,000 sandstone arches in eastern Utah include breathtaking Delicate Arch and graceful Landscape Arch, at 291 feet (89 meters) the longest natural rock span on Earth. *(page 132)*

2 Ayers Rock, Australia: One of the largest monoliths in the world, Ayers Rock (also known by its aboriginal name, Uluru) rises 1,100 feet (335 meters) above the surrounding plains of central Australia. Its iron-rich sandstone flanks, reflecting the sun in crimson and purple hues, are visible 60 miles (96 kilometers) away. *(page 74)*

3 Cones of Cappadocia, Turkey: Swift streams slicing through a plateau of solidified volcanic ash capped by basalt and limestone created this strange, fairy-tale landscape of 100-foot-tall (30-meter-tall) cones. During the Middle Ages, Christian monks and hermits carved hundreds of churches and monasteries into the cones' soft flanks. *(page 56)*

4 Stolby Nature Reserve, Russia: On the banks of Siberia's Yenisey (Enisej) River lies a rock-climber's paradise: a concentration of granite and syenite pinnacles that tower as high as 300 feet (92 meters) over the surrounding forest and have been sculpted by wind, rain, and ice into fanciful shapes such as "The Feathers" and "The Kiss." *(pages 34-35)*

5 Stone Forests of Guilin, China: The limestone pinnacles of Guangxi province have inspired Chinese artists and poets for centuries. These stone "trees"—the world's prime examples of tower karst—are nearly as spectacular within as without: Hundreds of caverns, shimmering with calcite formations, honeycomb the pinnacles. *(page 43)*

Gaze across the deep, cold, vast waters of Lake Superior and you'll get the sense that you're on the shore of something much more imposing than a lake. Superior seems like an ocean. Towering crags and cliffs, besieged by wind and waves, abut the shore like stone fortresses. Winters are particularly long and severe, but in any season Superior is known for its fierce gales and deadly storms; more than 350 vessels rest at the bottom.

Appropriately, the Ojibwa people called the lake Kitchi Gami, the Great Lake. With a surface area of 31,700 square miles (82,100 square kilometers), it is the largest of the five glacially carved North American inland seas known as the Great Lakes, and the greatest expanse of fresh water on Earth. Scotland could fit neatly within its shores. Superior is also the deepest of the Great Lakes. Its maximum depth of 1,332 feet (406 meters) is not just the work of glaciers: Volcanic rock lining the lake suggests that Superior sits over an ancient rift system, an area where tectonic forces ripped the Earth's crust apart. Molten rock, rising from the planet's fiery mantle and carrying an abundance of minerals, spread across the landscape. Iron, nickel, copper, silver, and gold mined near the lake have long been mainstays of the region's economy.

Scoured out of North America's surface by massive glaciers during the ice ages, the Great Lakes are among the continent's defining features. Lakes Superior, Michigan, Huron, Erie, and Ontario cover an area of 94,450 square miles (244,620 square kilometers) and hold 18 percent of the world's fresh water. They spread across landscapes varying from rolling farmland to unadulterated forests to shifting mountains of sand to the skyscrapered shores of Detroit, Toronto, Cleveland, and Chicago. Since the earliest days of settlement by Europeans, the Great Lakes have been conduits of commerce between the eastern seaboard and the mines and granaries of the central plains. *(pages 108-109)*

Lake Superior & the Great Lakes

Other Wondrous Lakes

1 **Caspian Sea, Europe/Asia:** The largest inland body of water on Earth, the salty Caspian Sea is 750 miles (1,210 kilometers) long and has a surface area of 143,240 square miles (370,900 square kilometers). *(page 32)*

2 **Dead Sea, Israel/Jordan:** The lowest point on the planet's surface, at 1,339 feet (408 meters) below sea level, the Dead Sea is eight times saltier than any ocean, making it extremely buoyant. *(page 59)*

3 **Lake Tanganyika, East Africa:** The longest freshwater lake in the world, Tanganyika is so deep that its water layers do not mix: The cold bottom layers are nearly devoid of life, while the warmer upper layers teem with fish. *(page 67)*

4 **Lake Titicaca, Bolivia/Peru:** Lying on the Andean altiplano at 12,500 feet (3,810 meters), Titicaca is the highest navigable lake on Earth and the birthplace of the pre-Incan Tiahuanaco culture. *(page 84)*

5 **Lake Victoria, East Africa:** Africa's largest lake and the second-largest body of fresh water in the world (after Lake Superior) is situated in a shallow depression between the arms of the Rift Valley. *(page 67)*

Chill, clear, and cradled in a basin of evergreen forests and snowcapped granite peaks in southern Siberia, Lake Baikal is the oldest, deepest, and most voluminous body of fresh water on Earth. Although lakes generally have life spans of less than one million years, Baikal has existed for perhaps 25 million years. It was born of tectonic forces, which tore open a rift in the Earth's crust. As the Baikal Rift grew, so did the lake; the still-active rift widens approximately one inch (2.5 centimeters) per year. Today the lake is 395 miles (636 kilometers) long and an average of 30 miles (48 kilometers) wide.

Lake Baikal reaches a greatest depth of more than a mile (1.6 kilometers). The lake bed sits atop sediment that lies some four miles (6.4 kilometers) thick, the accumulation of 25 million years.

Baikal's tremendous volume—5,500 cubic miles (23,000 cubic kilometers)—represents a fifth of the fresh water in the world, and more than the five Great Lakes combined. It would take all of Earth's rivers together a year to fill Baikal. More than 300 rivers do feed the lake but only one, the Angara, drains it; if all 300 tributaries were suddenly to run dry, it would take Lake Baikal four centuries to empty.

Revered by Russians as "the Pearl of Siberia," and sacred to the local Buryat tribespeople, Baikal shelters more endemic species than any other habitat on Earth. Naturalists come to catch a glimpse of some of these roughly 1,500 species, including a pink, transparent oilfish known as the *golom-yanka* and the Baikal seal, or *nerpa*, prized for its sleek coat of fur. *(page 35)*

Lake Baikal

Crater Lake

Formed in the wake of one of the most powerful volcanic events of the last 10,000 years, Crater Lake is today a serene jewel set high in the mountains of North America's Cascade Range. Circular and stunningly cobalt blue, the lake is fringed with windblown evergreens and surrounded by the steep, sloping sides of the caldera that contains it. Six miles (ten kilometers) wide and 1,932 feet (589 meters) deep, Crater Lake is the deepest lake in the United States and the seventh deepest in the world. The lake has no inlet or outlet; seepage and evaporation keep the water level steady.

Where Crater Lake lies today in southwestern Oregon, a cluster of stratovolcanoes once rose approximately 12,000 feet (3,650 meters) above sea level. Roughly 7,000 years ago, this ancient mountain, now referred to as Mount Mazama, blew its top, spewing ash over much of the continent. Eventually, rainfall and snowmelt filled the caldera that remained, producing Crater Lake. Wizard Island, near the lake's western shore, is the youngest and tallest of three cinder cones that formed after the catastrophic explosion; the other two lie below the surface. Hot spots in the lake's depths and the fact that the water almost never freezes despite huge snowfalls point to continued volcanic activity beneath the lake.

In the legends of the Klamath Indians, Mount Mazama was the throne of Llao, ruler of the underworld; Mount Shasta, a hundred miles south, was the domain of Skell, who ruled the "above world." An ongoing feud manifested itself in thunderous eruptions and rivers of molten lava that destroyed villages. The final battle raged for a week before Llao's ruined mountain collapsed upon him, sealing him forever beneath the Earth.

Crater Lake National Park was established in 1902, and today half a million people come each year to drive around the lake, hike along the rim, cross-country ski, or catch a boat to Wizard Island. *(page 136)*

Within the 2,000-foot-high (610-meter-high) walls of Ngorongoro Crater, a great profusion of animals vie for space and nourishment amidst the swamps, springs, lakes, and low forests that cover the level crater floor. Almost every animal species common to eastern Africa ranges the crater's 100 square miles (260 square kilometers). Whereas wildlife living in other African savanna habitats must migrate with the seasons in search of water, the springs and swamps of Ngorongoro Crater provide water year-round. Lions, elephants, hippos, zebras, gazelles, wildebeests, baboons, leopards, cheetahs, and hyenas—an estimated 25,000 to 30,000 animals in all—make their permanent homes here. The crater is the only remaining habitat of the severely endangered black rhinoceros, and Lake Magadi, an alkaline lake in the middle of the basin, supports thousands of dazzling pink flamingos and throngs of other water birds.

Ngorongoro Crater is the largest volcanic caldera of its type in the world. A volcanic mountain rivaling the height of nearby Kilimanjaro once stood on the site of Ngorongoro. Around 2.5 million years ago, shifting tectonic activity in Africa's Rift Valley caused the huge magma chamber beneath the volcano to drain away, and the mountain caved in upon itself.

Ngorongoro is sacred to the Masai people. Several centuries ago, the tribe took the crater from its original inhabitants, the Datoga, and claimed it as cattle-grazing land. As the Masai made their way down the slopes, bells they were wearing rang out "ngoro, ngoro," and thus the crater was named. Ngorongoro Crater Conservation Area was established in the 1950s, and in 1974 the Tanzanian government ruled that the Masai had to leave. Today Ngorongoro has no permanent human inhabitants. *(page 67)*

Ngorongoro Crater

Other Remarkable Craters and Volcanoes

1 **Kilauea Crater, United States:** The legendary home of the fire goddess Pele and currently Earth's most active volcano, Kilauea has erupted steadily since 1983. Its lava produces a spectacular explosion of steam as it meets the Pacific Ocean. *(page 134)*

2 **Meteor Crater, United States:** This immense crater, 575 feet (176 meters) deep and .8 mile (1.25 kilometers) in diameter, marks the spot in the Arizona desert where a huge meteor slammed into Earth between 5,000 and 50,000 years ago. *(page 133)*

3 **Mount Tambora, Indonesia:** Its cataclysmic 1815 eruption was the most forceful ever recorded. Ash blown into the upper atmosphere screened the sun's rays, lowered temperatures globally for two years, and caused widespread crop failures in 1816, the famous "year without a summer." *(page 51)*

4 **Surtsey, Iceland:** The world's youngest island, tiny one-square-mile (2.5-square-kilometer) Surtsey formed between 1963 and 1967 as magma poured from a volcanic vent on the seafloor off the southern coast of Iceland. *(page 8)*

5 **Vesuvius, Italy:** Vesuvius' eruption in A.D. 79 destroyed Pompeii and Herculaneum, killing more than 3,500 people. Vesuvius is considered one of the most dangerous volcanoes on Earth today: More than 2,000,000 people live in its shadow. *(page 24)*

Great Barrier Reef

The turquoise waters of Australia's 1,250-mile-long (2,010-kilometer-long) Great Barrier Reef teem with life. Schools of brilliant tropical fish shimmer amid forests of anemones, sheltered by multi-hued walls and glowing outcroppings of live coral, while palm-shaded cays of sparkling coral sand are home to myriad birds. In all, some 400 species of coral, 1,500 varieties of vividly colored fish and crustaceans, and more than 200 bird species live in and around the reef.

The largest structure ever built by living creatures, the Great Barrier Reef is the work of countless tiny animals, most no larger than an inch (2.5 centimeters) long. With the symbiotic help of algae, coral polyps secrete skeletons of calcium carbonate, or limestone, to protect themselves and attach themselves to the remains of dead coral. Core samples reveal that the reef has been forming for at least 25 million years: As the continental shelf slowly subsided, the living corals built the reef ever higher to keep within the extent of the sun's rays. Then, during the ice ages when much of Earth's water was frozen, the reef was exposed as limestone cliffs lining the coast of Australia. It's likely that Aborigines lived amidst these cliffs before the ice receded and the reef was again submerged. Today the reef covers an area exceeding 100,000 square miles (270,000 square kilometers) along the continental shelf off Australia's northeastern coast.

Vast portions of the Great Barrier Reef are protected from poachers and oil companies by the Great Barrier Reef Marine Park, the largest marine reserve in the world. Close to five million tourists visit the park annually and take reef excursions ranging from glass-bottom boat rides to hot-air balloon flights. Scuba diving and snorkeling are favorite pastimes on the reef, but they are carefully regulated to keep this exquisite and delicate ecosystem healthy for generations to come. *(page 75)*

Belizean Reef

Other Spectacular Reefs and Sea Caves

1 **Blue Grotto, Italy:** Sunlight streaming in through an underwater aperture casts a brilliant azure reflection on the walls of this marine cave on the island of Capri. The ancient Romans worshiped here, though locals considered the grotto a lair of witches and monsters. *(page 24)*

2 **Blue Holes of Andros, Bahamas:** More than 400 of these circular entrances to submerged limestone caverns dot the continental shelf off the largest island in the Bahamas. The holes appear to "breathe," sucking the sea into ferocious whirlpools, then disgorging it in a roiling frenzy. *(page 104)*

3 **Florida Coral Reef, United States:** Lying about six miles (ten kilometers) offshore, this coral reef parallels the Florida Keys for almost 130 miles (209 kilometers) within a protected marine sanctuary. *(page 117)*

4 **Maldives:** Comprising 26 individual atolls that contain some 1,200 small coral islands—not one larger than five square miles (13 square kilometers)—the Maldives stretch for more than 500 miles (820 kilometers) across the Indian Ocean. *(page 142)*

5 **Racine Formation, United States:** This "reef" in what is now southeastern Wisconsin was alive with coral, sponges, and trilobites about 425 million years ago. Today it has metamorphosed into dolomite; stone quarried from the formation built the cities of Chicago and Milwaukee. *(page 119)*

6 **Red Sea Reefs:** Sheltered from the open ocean, these coral reefs harbor many endemic species, including brilliant butterfly fish. The reefs grow so fast near the Bab el Mandeb strait that they are routinely blasted away to keep the shipping channel clear. *(pages 62-63)*

From the air, the largest barrier reef in the Western Hemisphere—and the second largest on Earth—appears to be a white crest riding the deep blue Caribbean toward mainland Belize. Between the 185-mile-long (296-kilometer-long) reef and the mainland stretch aquamarine waters noted for resplendent red and purple and green corals—colors that are mirrored by fish, anemones, and sponges. At Rocky Point, the northern edge of the reef meets the continental shoreline in one of the only places in the world where a barrier reef and a coastline converge.

Hundreds of cays dot the surface, and on the eastward side of the reef lie three large atolls, circular coral formations common in the South Pacific but extremely rare in the Caribbean. The atolls—Turneffe Islands, Lighthouse Reef, and Glovers Reef—shelter spectacular reef life and are favorite diving destinations due to the extraordinary clarity of their azure waters. Jacques Cousteau's celebrated 1970s exploration of the Blue Hole—a submerged, 300-foot-deep (100-meter-deep) sinkhole in the shallow lagoon of the Lighthouse Reef atoll— revealed that the entire Belizean reef system is riddled with submarine caverns adorned with massive stalactites and stalagmites.

The reef and atolls are also home to large game fish and aquatic mammals such as dolphins and the world's largest population of West Indian manatees. Relics and middens found in the region reveal that the reef served as a Maya fishing ground and transportation and trading corridor, while the cays were used as ceremonial sites and burial places. Once Europeans discovered the reef, it became a favorite hideout for pirates. Today tourism is Belize's economic mainstay, and the reef was recently designated a United Nations World Heritage Site—a move that many hope will protect this beautiful, fragile natural wonder. *(page 102)*

With its steep walls, hanging waterfalls, and Mitre Peak, a 5,551-foot (1,692-meter) sculpted monolith standing perpetual guard, glacier-carved Milford Sound is the northernmost and most spectacular of all of New Zealand's stunning South Island fjords. Only 180 feet (55 meters) deep at its mouth, the fjord plunges to maximum depths exceeding 1,300 feet (396 meters). Some of the highest sea cliffs in the world rise abruptly from the water's edge, soaring nearly a mile (1.6 kilometers) into a sky often shrouded in low mist and rain. One of the rainiest places on Earth, Milford Sound receives in excess of 250 inches (635 centimeters) of precipitation each year.

The aboriginal Maori people knew Milford Sound as Piopiotahi, or "the place of the thrush." According to legend, Maui, the first man, kept a thrush as a companion to sing to him as he wandered the island's coast. After Maui died, the desolate thrush remained beside the sound, its lament ringing off Milford's sheer walls. The Maori came thereafter to hunt, fish, and collect the region's beautiful nephrite jade, which they believed could take on the *mana*, or spiritual power, of its owners. Weapons and ornaments carved from nephrite have passed through families for generations.

Fiordland National Park's 14 fjords, and Milford Sound in particular, harbor a wide range of wildlife, from bottlenose dolphins to the flightless takahe, a blue-plumaged bird once thought to be extinct. Before migrating to Antarctica for the summer, Fiordland crested penguins nest in Milford Sound. The unusual composition of the sound accounts for a stunning variety of sea creatures clinging to the granite walls below the surface: A layer of fresh water, darkened by organic materials leached from the surrounding soil, floats over a deep, clear, warm base of saltwater from the Tasman Sea. Sheltered by the fresh water, colorful reef life—similar to that of Hawaii or the Caribbean—thrives beneath the brackish zone. *(page 80)*

Milford Sound

Other Wondrous Fjords

1 *Desolation Sound and the Fjords of British Columbia, Canada:* Riddled with deep sounds, remote inlets, glacial fjords, and cascading waterfalls, the stunningly rugged coasts of British Columbia and western Vancouver Island were forbidding even to explorer Captain George Vancouver, who gave Desolation Sound its name. *(page 138)*

2 *Fjords of Iceland:* Both the east and west coasts of Iceland are incised by classic fjords with sheer cliffs adorned with lacy ribbons of falling water. The fjords along the east coast are often blanketed in *Austfjardapoka*, the Eastern Fjord Fog. *(page 8)*

3 *Fjords of Southern Chile and Argentina:* Along the heavily glaciated western coast at the southern tip of South America, ice has excavated remote and daunting fjords that reach into the very heart of the Andes and attract adventurous sea kayakers from around the globe. *(page 90)*

4 *Gros Morne National Park, Canada:* The fjords of Newfoundland's Gros Morne are renowned both for beauty and geologic legacy: The strata of their walls harbor volcanic rock and fossils dating back 600 million years. *(page 107)*

5 *Kenai Fjords National Park, United States:* Glaciers once etched steep-sided valleys into the flanks of Alaska's Kenai Mountains; today these valleys are inundated and transformed into breathtaking fjords, framed by the dramatic backdrop of the vast Harding Icefield. *(page 140)*

6 *Scoresby Sund, Greenland:* This sound and its tributaries comprise the world's largest fjord system, extending 196 miles (314 kilometers). Carved into the periphery of granite and basalt mountains, Scoresby presents a strikingly varied cliffside panorama. *(page 141)*

Etched deeply into Norway's western coastline are hundreds of inundated, U-shaped valleys. Farms and tiny hamlets cling to ledges on their nearly vertical walls, and streams plummet into the still waters from hanging valleys hundreds of feet above. The spectacular fjords of Norway are known the world over for their beautiful scenery and their profound depths—positive proof of the power of the ice-age glaciers that sculpted them.

In the last two to three million years, vast ice sheets have advanced and retreated over Northern Europe at least 40 times. On the western coast of present-day Norway, these glaciers followed and filled existing river valleys. So great were the thickness and weight of these glaciers that they scoured the valleys to depths far below sea level. Sogne Fjord, the longest and deepest of Norway's fjords, extends more than 125 miles (200 kilometers) inland and reaches a maximum depth of 4,291 feet (1,308 meters) in Lustra Fjord, its longest branch. For a single glacier to carve such a deep valley, it would have to be approximately 6,000 feet (1,850 meters) thick.

The earliest thriving cultures in Norway's fjord region date back to A.D. 400–600. Nevertheless, the population of the region has always been sparse, due to the scarcity of flat land on which to build and farm. The largest towns are built on river deltas at the heads of the fjords. The most picturesque human habitations, however, are the small farms built on ledges in the sheer valley walls. Farmers who settled on these aeries built systems of ropes and pulleys to bring supplies, building materials, and even farm animals up the cliffs to their homesteads. A series of ladders connected their farms with their boat docks far below. Even today, boats are the best form of fjordland transportation and Sogne Fjord can be crossed only by ferry. *(page 8)*

Fjords of Western Norway

INDEX MAP AND LEGEND

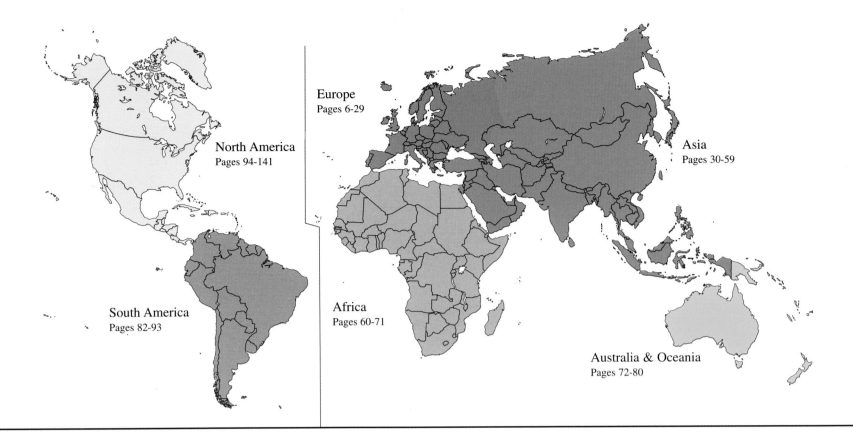

Europe
Pages 6-29

Asia
Pages 30-59

North America
Pages 94-141

South America
Pages 82-93

Africa
Pages 60-71

Australia & Oceania
Pages 72-80

Hydrographic Features

Perennial river

Seasonal river

Aswan High Dam   Dam

Salto Ángel   Falls

Los Angeles Aqueduct   Aqueduct

Lake, reservoir

Seasonal lake

Salt lake

Seasonal salt lake

Dry lake

395   Lake surface elevation

Swamp, marsh

Reef

Glacier/ice sheet

Topographic Features

764 Depth of water

2278 Elevation above sea level

1700 Elevation below sea level

Mountain pass

Huo Shan 1774 Mountain peak/elevation

The highest elevation on each continent is underlined.

The highest elevation in each country is shown in boldface.

Transportation Features

Motorway/special highway

Major road

Other road

Trail

Major railway

Other railway

Navigable canal

Tunnel

Ferry

✈ International airport

✈ Other airport

Political Features

International boundaries (First-order political unit)

Demarcated

Disputed (de facto)

Disputed (de jure)

Indefinite/undefined

Demarcation line

Internal boundaries

State/province

Third-order (counties, oblasts, etc.)

NORMANDIE
(Denmark)
Cultural/historic region
Administering country

Cities and Towns

The size of symbol and type indicates the relative importance of the locality.

■ **LONDON**

▣ **CHICAGO**

◉ **Milwaukee**

◎ Tacna

⊙ Iquitos

○ Old Crow

○ Mettawa

🖤 Urban area

Capitals

MEXICO CITY
Bonn
Country, dependency

RIO DE JANEIRO
Perth
State, province

MANCHESTER
Chester
County

Cultural Features

or ▪ National park, reservation

· Point of interest

Wall

∴ Ruins

Military installation

• Polar research station

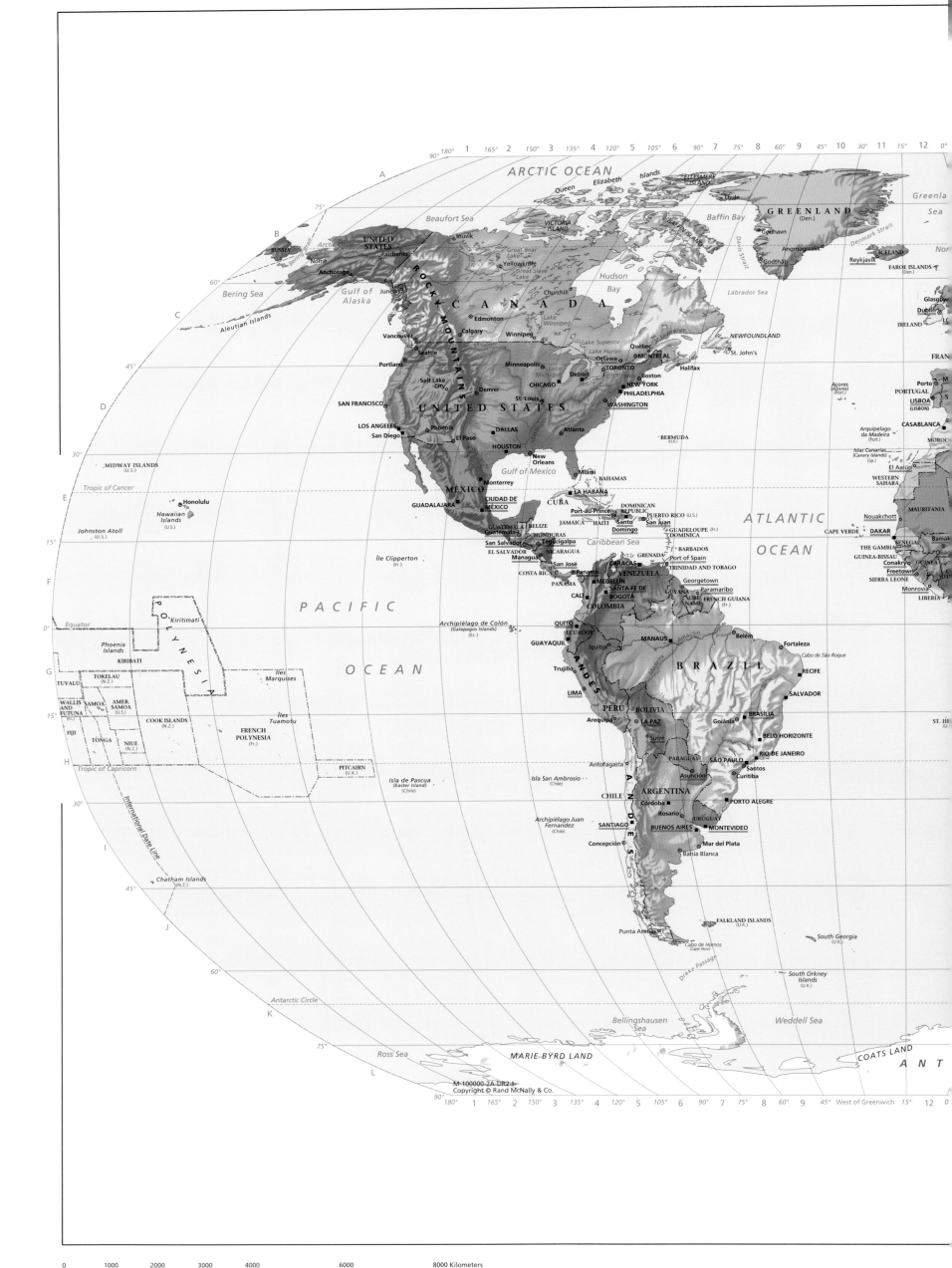

ARCTIC OCEAN

Queen Elizabeth Islands
ELLESMERE ISLAND
GREENLAND (Den.)
Greenla Sea

Beaufort Sea
Baffin Bay
Thule

Inuvik
VICTORIA ISLAND
BAFFIN ISLAND
Godhavn
Angmagssalik
Denmark Strait
ICELAND
Nor

RUSSIA
Bering Strait
Arctic Circle
UNITED STATES
Nome
Fairbanks
Great Bear Lake
Yellowknife
Great Slave Lake
Godthåb
Reykjavík
FAROE ISLANDS (Den.)

Anchorage
CANADA
Glasgow
Dublin
IRELAND
L

Gulf of Alaska
Juneau
ROCKY MOUNTAINS
Edmonton
Calgary
Winnipeg
Lake Winnipeg
Lake Superior
Churchill
Hudson Bay
Labrador Sea
NEWFOUNDLAND
St. John's
FRAN

Aleutian Islands
Vancouver
Seattle
Portland
Lake Huron
Lake Michigan
Ottawa
Quebec
MONTRÉAL
Halifax
FRAN

Minneapolis
TORONTO
Detroit
Lake Erie
Boston
Porto
Açores (Azores) (Port.)
PORTUGAL

Salt Lake City
Denver
CHICAGO
St. Louis
NEW YORK
PHILADELPHIA
WASHINGTON
LISBOA (LISBON)

SAN FRANCISCO
UNITED STATES
CASABLANCA
Arquipélago da Madeira (Port.)

LOS ANGELES
San Diego
Phoenix
El Paso
DALLAS
HOUSTON
Atlanta
BERMUDA (U.K.)
MOROC
Islas Canarias (Canary Islands) (Sp.)

MIDWAY ISLANDS (U.S.)
Tropic of Cancer
New Orleans
Gulf of Mexico
Miami
BAHAMAS
WESTERN SAHARA
El Aaiún

MÉXICO
Monterrey
LA HABANA
CUBA
MAURITANIA
Nouakchott

Honolulu
Hawaiian Islands (U.S.)
GUADALAJARA
CIUDAD DE MÉXICO
Port-au-Prince
DOMINICAN REPUBLIC
Santo Domingo
PUERTO RICO (U.S.)
San Juan
GUADELOUPE (Fr.)
ATLANTIC OCEAN
CAPE VERDE
DAKAR
SENEGAL

Johnston Atoll (U.S.)
GUATEMALA
BELIZE
Guatemala
JAMAICA
HAITI
DOMINICA
THE GAMBIA
GUINEA-BISSAU
Conakry
GUINEA

El Clipperton (Fr.)
San Salvador
HONDURAS
Tegucigalpa
Caribbean Sea
BARBADOS
Port of Spain
GRENADA
TRINIDAD AND TOBAGO
SIERRA LEONE
Freetown
Monrovia
LIBERIA

EL SALVADOR
NICARAGUA
Managua
San José
Panamá
CARACAS
VENEZUELA
Georgetown
Paramaribo
FRENCH GUIANA (Fr.)

PACIFIC
COSTA RICA
PANAMA
MEDELLÍN
SANTA FE DE BOGOTÁ
CALI
COLOMBIA
GUYANA
SURINAME

Equator
Archipiélago de Colón (Galapagos Islands) (Ec.)
QUITO
ECUADOR
MANAUS
Belém
Fortaleza
Cabo de São Roque

GUAYAQUIL
Iquitos
Amazon
BRAZIL
RECIFE

OCEAN
Phoenix Islands
KIRIBATI
Iles Marquises
Trujillo
ANDES
SALVADOR

POLYNESIA
Kiritimati
LIMA
PERÚ
BOLIVIA
Goiânia
BRASÍLIA
ST. HE (U.)

TUVALU
WALLIS AND FUTUNA (Fr.)
SAMOA
AMER. SAMOA (U.S.)
COOK ISLANDS (N.Z.)
Iles Tuamotu
FRENCH POLYNESIA (Fr.)
Arequipa
LA PAZ
Sucre
BELO HORIZONTE
RIO DE JANEIRO

FIJI
TONGA
NIUE (N.Z.)
PITCAIRN (U.K.)
Antofagasta
PARAGUAY
Asunción
SÃO PAULO
Santos
Curitiba

Tropic of Capricorn
Isla de Pascua (Easter Island) (Chile)
Isla San Ambrosio (Chile)
CHILE
ARGENTINA
Córdoba
PORTO ALEGRE

International Date Line
Archipiélago Juan Fernández (Chile)
SANTIAGO
Rosario
URUGUAY
BUENOS AIRES
MONTEVIDEO

Concepción
Mar del Plata
Bahía Blanca

Chatham Islands (N.Z.)

FALKLAND ISLANDS (U.K.)
Punta Arenas
South Georgia (U.K.)

Cabo de Hornos (Cape Horn)
Drake Passage
South Orkney Islands (U.K.)

Antarctic Circle

Ross Sea
MARIE BYRD LAND
Bellingshausen Sea
Weddell Sea
COATS LAND
ANT

M-100000-2A-DR24
Copyright © Rand McNally & Co.

West of Greenwich

0 1000 2000 3000 4000 6000 8000 Kilometers
0 500 1000 1500 2000 3000 4000 5000 Miles
Scale 1 : 80,000,000

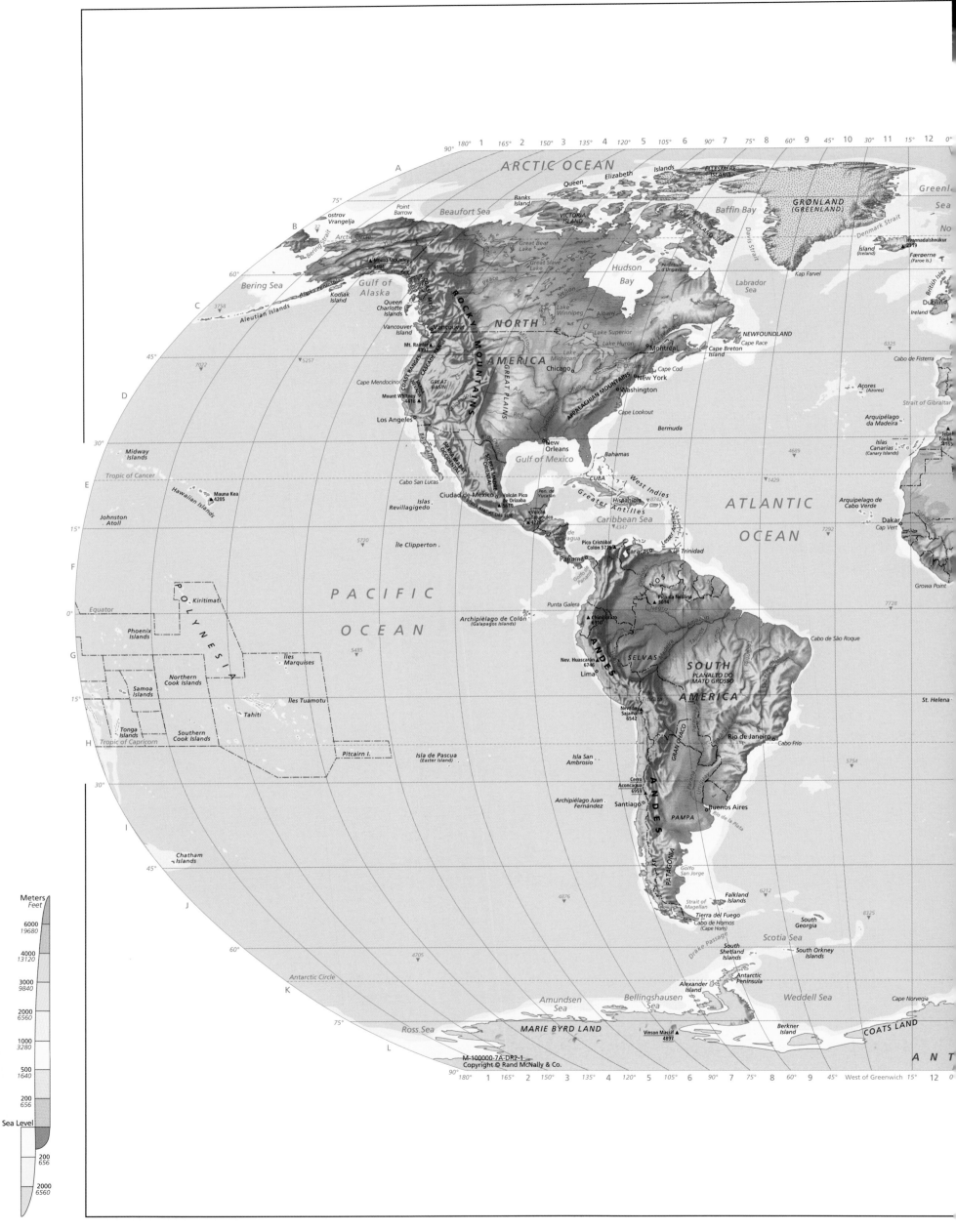

4

ARCTIC OCEAN

Queen Elizabeth Islands
ELLESMERE ISLAND

GRØNLAND (GREENLAND)

Greenland Sea

Point Barrow
Beaufort Sea
Banks Island
VICTORIA ISLAND

Baffin Bay
Davis Strait

Denmark Strait

Hvannadalshnúkur 2119

No

ostrov Vrangelja
Bering Strait
Arctic Circle

Great Bear Lake
Great Slave Lake

Hudson Bay
Peninsule d'Ungava
Kap Farvel

Ísland (Iceland)
Færøerne (Faroe Is.)

British Isles

Bering Sea

Gulf of Alaska
Kodiak Island
Mount McKinley 6194

Peace
Nelson
Albany

Lake Winnipeg
NORTH AMERICA

Labrador Sea

NEWFOUNDLAND
Cape Race

6325

Dublino
Ireland

Aleutian Islands
3758

Queen Charlotte Islands
Vancouver Island
Vancouver

COAST RANGES
CASCADE RANGE
ROCKY MOUNTAINS

Lake Superior
Lake Michigan
Lake Huron
Chicago

Cape Breton Island
Montreal
Lake Ontario

Cabo de Fisterra

7022
5257
Cape Mendocino

Mt. Rainier 4392
GREAT BASIN
GREAT PLAINS
Missouri
Red

New York
Washington
APPALACHIAN MOUNTAINS
Cape Cod

Açores (Azores)

Strait of Gibraltar

Mount Whitney 4418

SIERRA NEVADA

Cape Lookout
Bermuda

Arquipélago da Madeira

Los Angeles

Baja California

New Orleans
Gulf of Mexico
Bahamas

Islas Canarias (Canary Islands)

Tropic of Cancer

SIERRA MADRE OCCIDENTAL
Cabo San Lucas
Ciudad de México
Volcán Pico de Orizaba 5610
Acapulco

CUBA
West Indies
Greater Antilles
Hispaniola
8874
Caribbean Sea

4689
1425

ATLANTIC OCEAN

Arquipélago de Cabo Verde
Dakar
Cap Vert

Midway Islands

Johnston Atoll

Hawaiian Islands
Mauna Kea 4205

Islas Revillagigedo

SIERRA MADRE DEL SUR

de agua

Pico Cristóbal Colón 5775
Caracas
Trinidad

Lesser Antilles

7292

Île Clipperton
5720

Panamá
Golfo de Panamá

ANDES
Pico da Neblina 3014

Growa Point

Equator
Kiritimati

PACIFIC

Punta Galera
Archipiélago de Colón (Galápagos Islands)

NEGRO

SOUTH

7728

POLYNESIA

OCEAN

Chimborazo 6310

SELVAS
AMERICA
PLANALTO DO MATO GROSSO

Cabo de São Roque

Phoenix Islands

5485

Nev. Huascarán 6746
Lima

Íles Marquises

Northern Cook Islands

ANDES
MADEIRA
TAPAJÓS
XINGU

St. Helena

Samoa Islands

Íles Tuamotu
Tahiti

Nevado Sajama 6542

GRAN CHACO

Rio de Janeiro
Cabo Frio

Tonga Islands
Southern Cook Islands
Tropic of Capricorn

Cerro Aconcagua 6959
Santiago

ANDES
PARANÁ
Paraná
PAMPA

5754

Pitcairn I.

Isla de Pascua (Easter Island)

Isla San Ambrosio

Buenos Aires
Rio de la Plata

Archipiélago Juan Fernández

Chatham Islands

PATAGONIA

Golfo San Jorge
4876

Falkland Islands
6212

South Georgia
6325

Strait of Magellan
Tierra del Fuego
Cabo de Hornos (Cape Horn)

Scotia Sea

4705

Drake Passage
South Shetland Islands
South Orkney Islands

Antarctic Circle

Alexander Island
Antarctic Peninsula

Amundsen Sea
Bellingshausen Sea
Weddell Sea
Cape Norvegia

Ross Sea
MARIE BYRD LAND
Vinson Massif 4897

Berkner Island
COATS LAND

ANT

M-100000-7A-DR2-1
Copyright © Rand McNally & Co.

90° 180° 1 165° 2 150° 3 135° 4 120° 5 105° 6 90° 7 75° 8 60° 9 45° West of Greenwich 15° 12

0 1000 2000 3000 4000 6000 8000 Kilometers
0 500 1000 1500 2000 3000 4000 5000 Miles
Scale 1 : 80,000,000   Robinson Projection

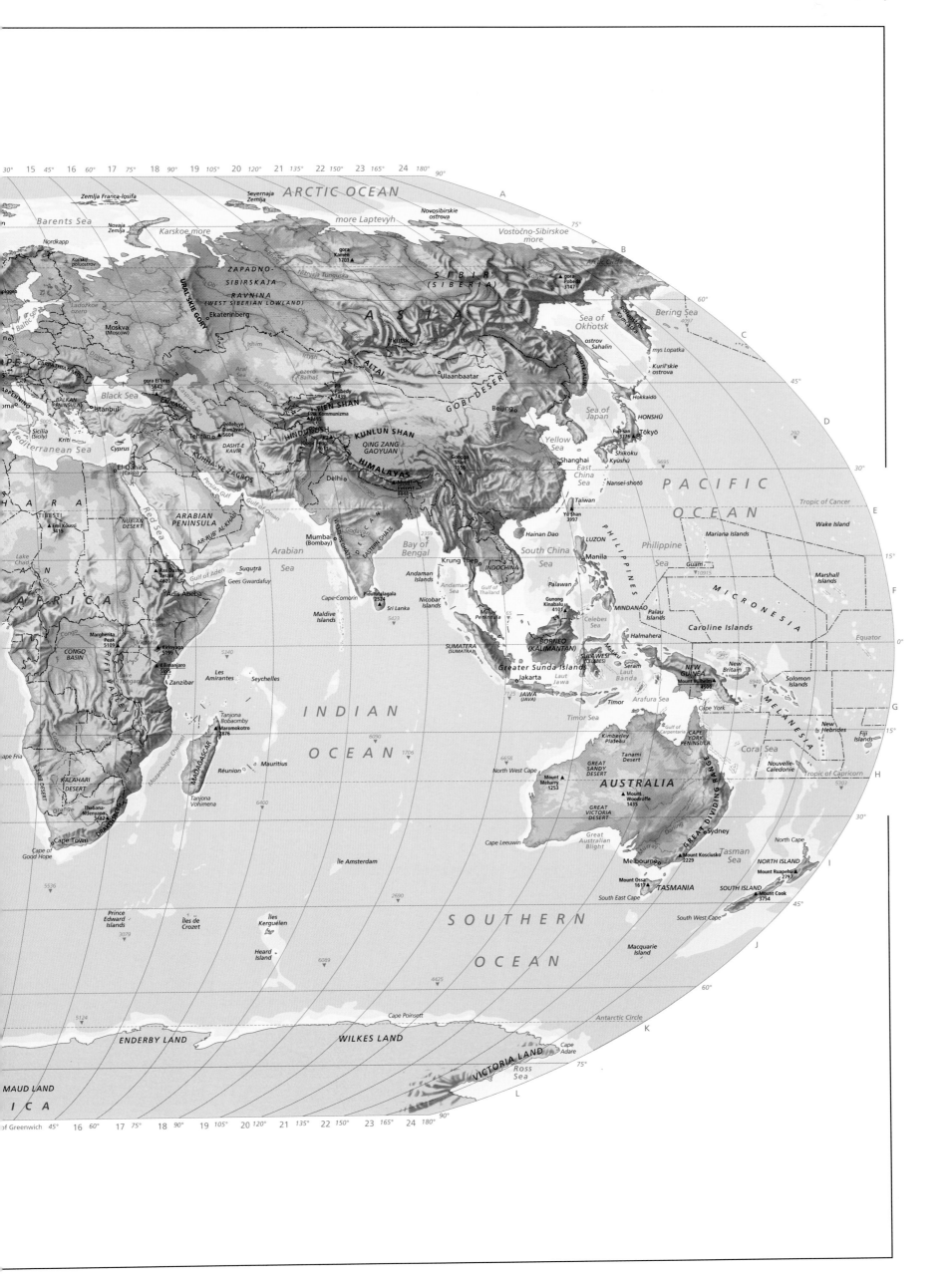

ARCTIC OCEAN

Barents Sea
Zemlja Franca-Iosifa
Severnaja Zemlja
more Laptevyh
Novosibirskie ostrova
Vostočno-Sibirskoe more

Nordkapp
Novaja Zemlja
Karskoe more
gora Kamen 1701 ▲
SIBIR (SIBERIA)
gora Pobeda 3147 ▲
Arctic Circle

Kol'skoj poluostrov
ZAPADNO-SIBIRSKAJA RAVNINA (WEST SIBERIAN LOWLAND)
Nižnaja Tunguska
Kolyma
Bering Sea

Baltic Sea
Ladožskoe ozero
Ekaterinberg
Ob'
ASIA
Sea of Okhotsk

Moskva (Moscow)
URAL'SKIE GORY
Irtyš
ostrov Sahalin
mys Lopatka

PENINO
gora El'brus 5642 ▲
CAUCASUS
Ishim
ALTAI
Kuril'skie ostrova

CARPATHIAN
Black Sea
Aral'sk
Aral Sea
ozero Balhaš
gora Pobedy 7439 ▲
Ulaanbaatar
GOBI DESERT
Beijing
Hokkaidō

Istanbul
BALKAN PENINSULA
Caspian Sea
TIEN SHAN
Pik Kommunizma 7495 ▲
Sea of Japan
HONSHŪ

Sicilia (Sicily)
Kriti
Dollshoye Bianavand
5604
HINDU KUSH
KUNLUN SHAN
Fuji-san 3776 ▲
Tōkyō

Mediterranean Sea
Cyprus
Tehran
DASHT-E KAVIR
QING ZANG GAOYUAN
Shikoku
Kyūshū
292

El Qahira (Cairo)
KŪHHĀ-YE ZAGROS
HIMALAYAS
Gongga Shan 7556 ▲
Shanghai
East China Sea
9695

SAHARA
Persian Gulf
Delhi
Mount Everest 8848 ▲
Huang
Nansei-shotō
PACIFIC

TIBESTI
Emi Koussi 3415 ▲
NUBIAN DESERT
ARABIAN PENINSULA
Gulf of Oman
AR-RUB' AL-KHALI
Taiwan
OCEAN
Tropic of Cancer

Red Sea
DECCAN
2359
Yu Shan 3997
Wake Island

Lake Chad
SUDAN
Mumbai (Bombay)
WESTERN GHATS
EASTERN GHATS
Bay of Bengal
Hainan Dao
LUZON
Mariana Islands

Chari
Arabian Sea
Andaman Islands
INDOCHINA
South China Sea
Manila
Philippine Sea
15°

AFRICA
Gulf of Aden
Ras Dashen Terara 4620 ▲
Gees Gwardafuy
Suquṭrā
Andaman Sea
Gulf of Thailand
Palawan
Guam 10915
Marshall Islands

Adis Abeba
Maldive Islands
Cape Comorin
Pidurutalagala 2524
Sri Lanka
Nicobar Islands
Malay Peninsula
MINDANAO
Palau Islands
MICRONESIA

5140
5423
Krung Thep
Gunong Kinabalu ul. 4101 ▲
Halmahera
Caroline Islands

Margherita Peak 5109 ▲
Lake Victoria
Kirinyaga 5199 ▲
Les Amirantes
Seychelles
SUMATERA (SUMATRA)
BORNEO (KALIMANTAN)
SULAWESI (CELEBES)
Equator
0°

CONGO BASIN
RIFT VALLEY
Kilimanjaro 5895 ▲
Zanzibar
Lake Tanganyika
Greater Sunda Islands
Seram
Laut Banda
NEW GUINEA
Mount Wilhelm 4509 ▲
New Britain
Solomon Islands
8940

Jakarta
JAWA (JAVA)
7125
Laut Jawa
Timor
Arafura Sea
Cape York
MELANESIA

Cape Fria
Tanjona Bobaomby
Maromokotro 2876
INDIAN
6090
1706
Timor Sea
Gulf of Carpentaria
CAPE YORK PENINSULA
New Hebrides
Fiji Islands
15°

NAMIB DESERT
KALAHARI DESERT
MADAGASCAR
Réunion
Mauritius
OCEAN
Kimberley Plateau
Tanami Desert
Coral Sea

Orange
Thabana-Ntlenyana 3482 ▲
Tanjona Vohimena
6400
North West Cape
GREAT SANDY DESERT
Mount Meharry 1253 ▲
Nouvelle-Calédonie
5303
Tropic of Capricorn

DRAKENSBERG
Ile Amsterdam
AUSTRALIA
Mount Woodroffe 1435 ▲
GREAT DIVIDING RANGE
North Cape

Cape Town
Cape of Good Hope
2690
GREAT VICTORIA DESERT
Cape Leeuwin
Great Australian Bight
Murray
Darling
Sydney
NORTH ISLAND
Mount Ruapehu 2797 ▲

5536
Prince Edward Islands
Iles de Crozet
Iles Kerguélen
Melbourne
Mount Kosciusko 2229 ▲
Tasman Sea

3079
Heard Island
6089
Mount Ossa 1617 ▲
TASMANIA
SOUTH ISLAND
Mount Cook 3754 ▲

SOUTHERN
4425
South East Cape
South West Cape
45°

5124
OCEAN
Cape Poinsett
Antarctic Circle
60°

of Greenwich
ENDERBY LAND
WILKES LAND
VICTORIA LAND
Ross Sea
Cape Adare
75°

MAUD LAND
ICA

GREENLAND SEA

NORWEGIAN SEA

Arctic Circle

ATLANTIC OCEAN

ICELAND

Reykjavik

Hvannadalshnúkur
2119

FAROE ISLANDS
(Den.)
Tórshavn

Rockall
(U.K.)

SHETLAND
ISLANDS
(U.K.)

NORWAY

Tromsø

VESTERÅLEN

LOFOTEN

Bodø

Mo i Rana

Namsos

Storuman

SWEDEN

Kristiansund
Trondheim

Ålesund
Dombås
Molde

Galdhøpiggen
2469

Bergen

Haugesund
Stavanger

Oslo

Drammen

Skien

Kristiansand

Östersund

Sundsvall

Harnösand

Hudiksvall

Falun

Gävle

AHVE

Uppsala

Västerås

STOCKHOLM

Norrköping

Linköping

GOTLAND

BALT

ORKNEY
ISLANDS

HEBRIDES

Thurso

Inverness

Aberdeen

GLASGOW
EDINBURGH

Dundee

UNITED
KINGDOM

Londonderry

Sligo
Galway

Belfast
Carlisle

IRELAND

DUBLIN

Limerick

Cork
Mizen
Head

Waterford

IRISH SEA

NEWCASTLE
UPON TYNE

Middlesbrough

LEEDS
LIVERPOOL MANCHESTER
Sheffield

Leicester
Nottingham

BIRMINGHAM

Norwich

Swansea
Cardiff
Bristol

Oxford Ipswich
LONDON

Southampton
Brighton

NORTH SEA

Groningen Bremerhaven

NETHERLANDS
's-Gravenhage
(The Hague)
AMSTERDAM
ROTTERDAM
Utrecht

ANTWERPEN

BRUXELLES
BELGIUM
LILLE
Liège

DENMARK

Holstebro

Esbjerg

Flensburg

Kiel

Lübeck

Odense

Kolding

Århus

Ålborg

Halmstad

KØBENHAVN
(COPENHAGEN)

Bornholm
(Den.)

Helsingborg

Malmö

Karlskrona

Kristiansand

ÖLAND

Kalmar

Växjö

Gdynia

Gdańsk

Kali

HAMBURG

Bremen

Rügen

Stralsund

Rostock

Szczecin

Bydgoszcz

Poznań

POLA

BERLIN

Hannover

Magdeburg

Münster
Dortmund

ESSEN
KÖLN DÜSSELDORF

Bonn

GERMANY

Leipzig

Dresden

Chemnitz

Erfurt

Wrocław

Wałbrzych

Częstochowa

Katowice

Land's End

ISLES OF
SCILLY

Plymouth

Penzance

Cherbourg

Le Havre

English Channel

Strait of Dover

Dover

Calais

Amiens

Reims

FRANKFURT
AM MAIN

Wiesbaden
MANNHEIM

Würzburg

Nürnberg

Plzeň

PRAHA

CZECH REP. Ostrava

Olomouc

Brno

SLOVA

GUERNSEY
(U.K.)
JERSEY
(U.K.)

Pointe de
Saint-Mathieu

Brest

Saint-
Malo

Caen

Rouen

Rennes

Le Mans

Angers

Nantes

Tours

La Rochelle

Poitiers

Loire

Orléans

Bourges

Troyes

PARIS

Metz

Nancy

LUXEMBOURG

Saarbrücken

Strasbourg

STUTTGART

Augsburg

MÜNCHEN
(MUNICH)

Regensburg

Danube

Linz

Salzburg

WIEN
(VIENNA)

Bratislava

Győr

BUDAPEST

HUNG

Dijon

Besançon

Mulhouse

Basel

Zürich

Bern

SWITZ.

Lausanne

Genève

LIECHT.

Innsbruck

AUSTRIA

Klagenfurt

Graz

Balaton

FRANCE

LYON

Clermont-
Ferrand

Limoges

Saint-
Étienne

Grenoble

Mont Blanc
4807

ALPS

Bolzano

SLOVENIA

Ljubljana

Zagreb

CROATIA

A Coruña

Cabo de Fisterra

Gijón

Oviedo

Vigo

Braga

Ourense

Porto

PORTUGAL

Douro

Bay of Biscay

Santander

Bilbao

Bayonne

Burgos

Donostia

PYRENEES

Pamplona

Toulouse

Montpellier

Bordeaux

León

Valladolid

Gasteiz

Zaragoza

Lleida

ANDORRA

Andorra
la-Vella

Perpignan

Nîmes

Avignon

MARSEILLE

Toulon

Nice

MONACO

Brescia

Verona

Padova

TORINO

MILANO

Parma

GENOVA

La Spezia

Bologna

LIGURIAN SEA

Livorno

Firenze

Pisa

Venézia
(Venice)

Trieste

Rijeka

Zadar

APENNINES

ADRIATIC SEA

BOSNIA AND
HERZEGOVINA

Sarajevo

Split

Dubrovnik

Podgorica

LISBOA
(LISBON)

Setúbal

Tagus

Évora

Coimbra

Salamanca

SPAIN

MADRID

Segovia

Toledo

Castelló
de la Plana

Tarragona

BARCELONA

VALÈNCIA

ILLES BALEARS
(BALEARIC ISLANDS)

Menorca

Palma de
Mallorca

MALLORCA

CORSE
(CORSICA)
(Fr.)

Ajaccio

Bastia

SARDEGNA
(SARDINIA)
(It.)

Sassari

Nuoro

Olbia

VATICAN CITY

ROMA
(ROME)

SAN
MARINO

Ancona

Perugia

L'Aquila

Pescara

ITALY

Foggia

Bari

Brindisi

Badajoz

Guadiana

Córdoba

Albacete

Huelva

Faro

Cabo de
São Vicente

Sevilla

Jaén

Granada

Murcia

Elx

Alacant

Cartagena

Eivissa

MEDITERRANEAN

Cágliari

NAPOLI
(NAPLES)

Salerno

Tira

Taranto

Lecce

Cádiz

Málaga

Mulhacén
3487

Strait of Gibraltar

GIBRALTAR
(U.K.)

Tánger

Ceuta (Sp.)

Isla de
Alborán
(Sp.)

Larache

Melilla (Sp.)

Al-Hoceima

Tetouan

EL DJAZAÎR
(ALGIERS)

El Bouïra

TYRRHENIAN
SEA

SICILIA
(SICILY)
(It.)

Trapani

Palermo

Monte Etna
3323

Catania

Messina

Reggio
di Calabria

Cosenza

Catanzaro

IONIAN

SEA

CASABLANCA

Rabat

Salé

El-Jadida

Safi

Essaouira

Agadir

Jebel Toubkal
4165

Marrakech

Meknès

Fès

Khouribga

Taza

MOROCCO

Oujda

Sidi bel
Abbès

Wahran

Mostaganem

Er-Rachidia

Laghouat

ATLAS MOUNTAINS

ALGERIA

Tizi
Ouzou

Béjaïa

Ech Cheliff

Bouïra

Tibert

Chott ech Chergui

Chott el
Hodna

Sétif

Batna

Biskra

Chott
Melrhir

Skikda

Qacentina

Annaba

Bizerte

TUNIS

Béja

Bâb

Cap Bon

Nabeul

Kairouan

Sousse

Sfax

TUNISIA

Gafsa

La Galite

Isola di
Pantelleria
(It.)

Isola
delle Correnti

MALTA

Valletta

ISOLE
PELAGIE
(It.)

SEA

West of Greenwich 0° East of Greenwich

0   200   400   800   1200 Kilometers

0   100   200   400   600   800 Miles

Scale 1 : 12,500,000   Conic Equidistant Projection

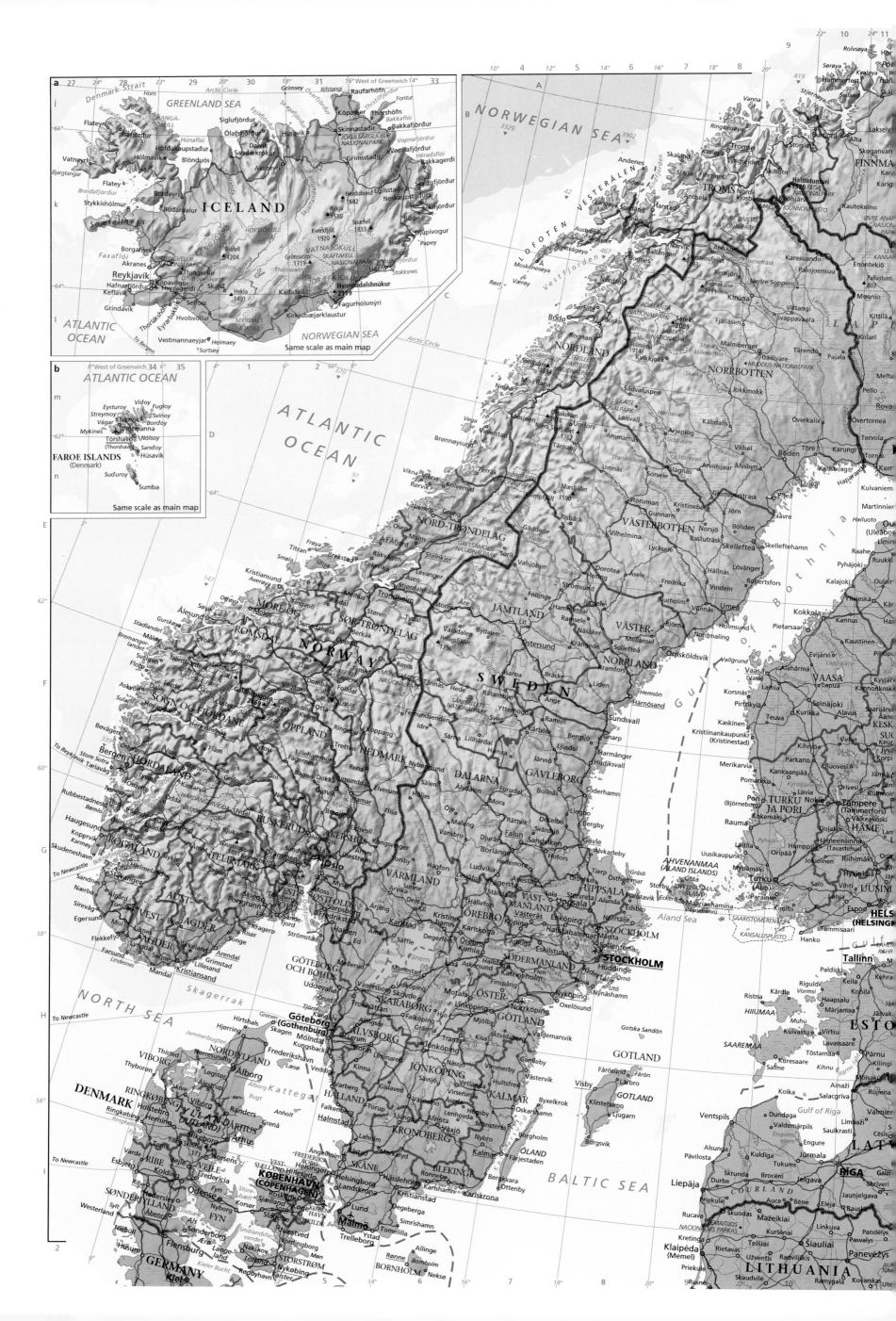

Scale 1 : 2,500,000   Lambert Conformal Conic Projection

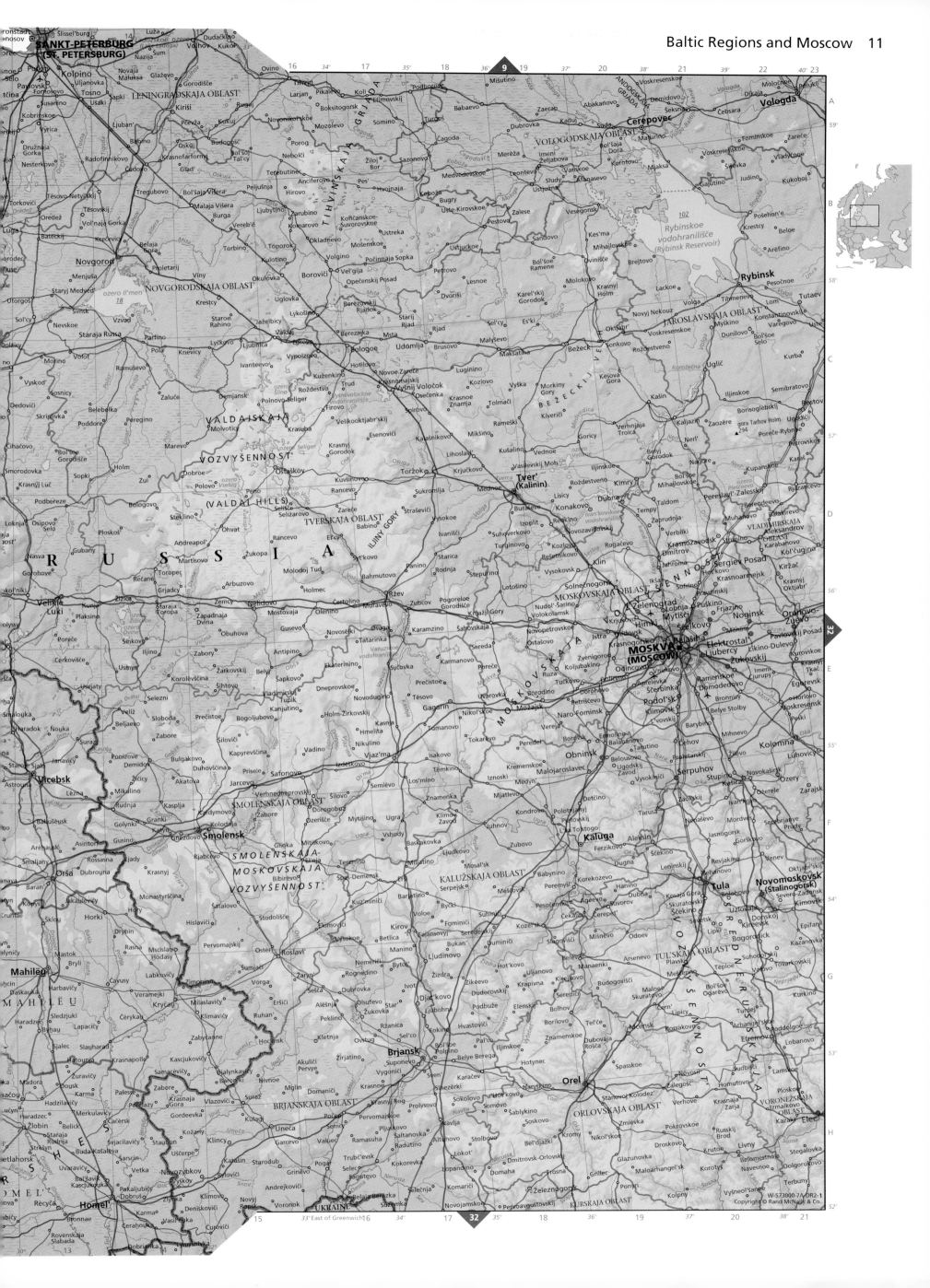

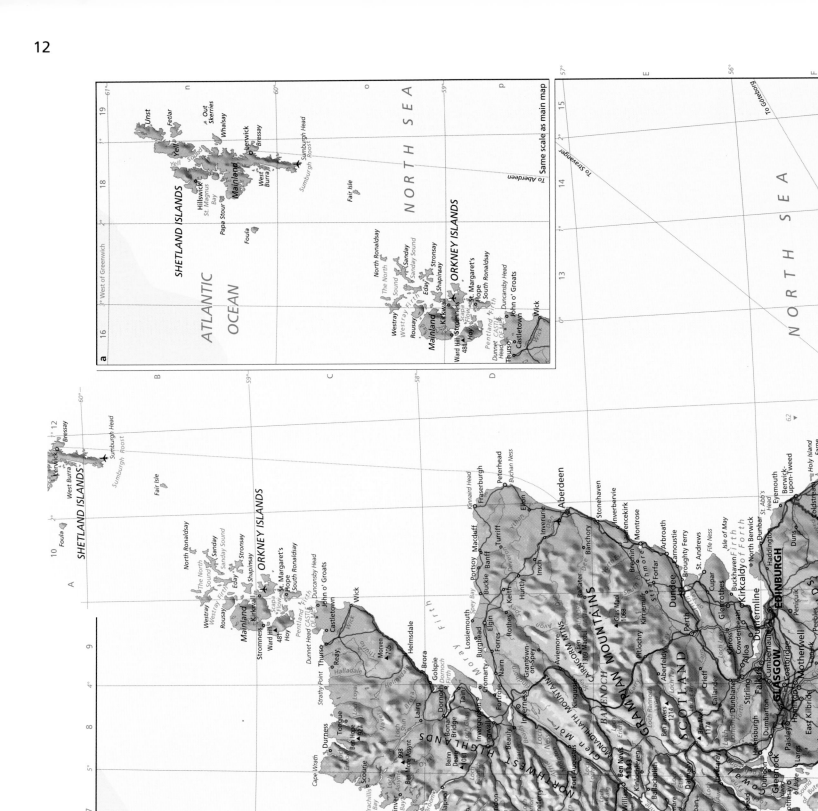

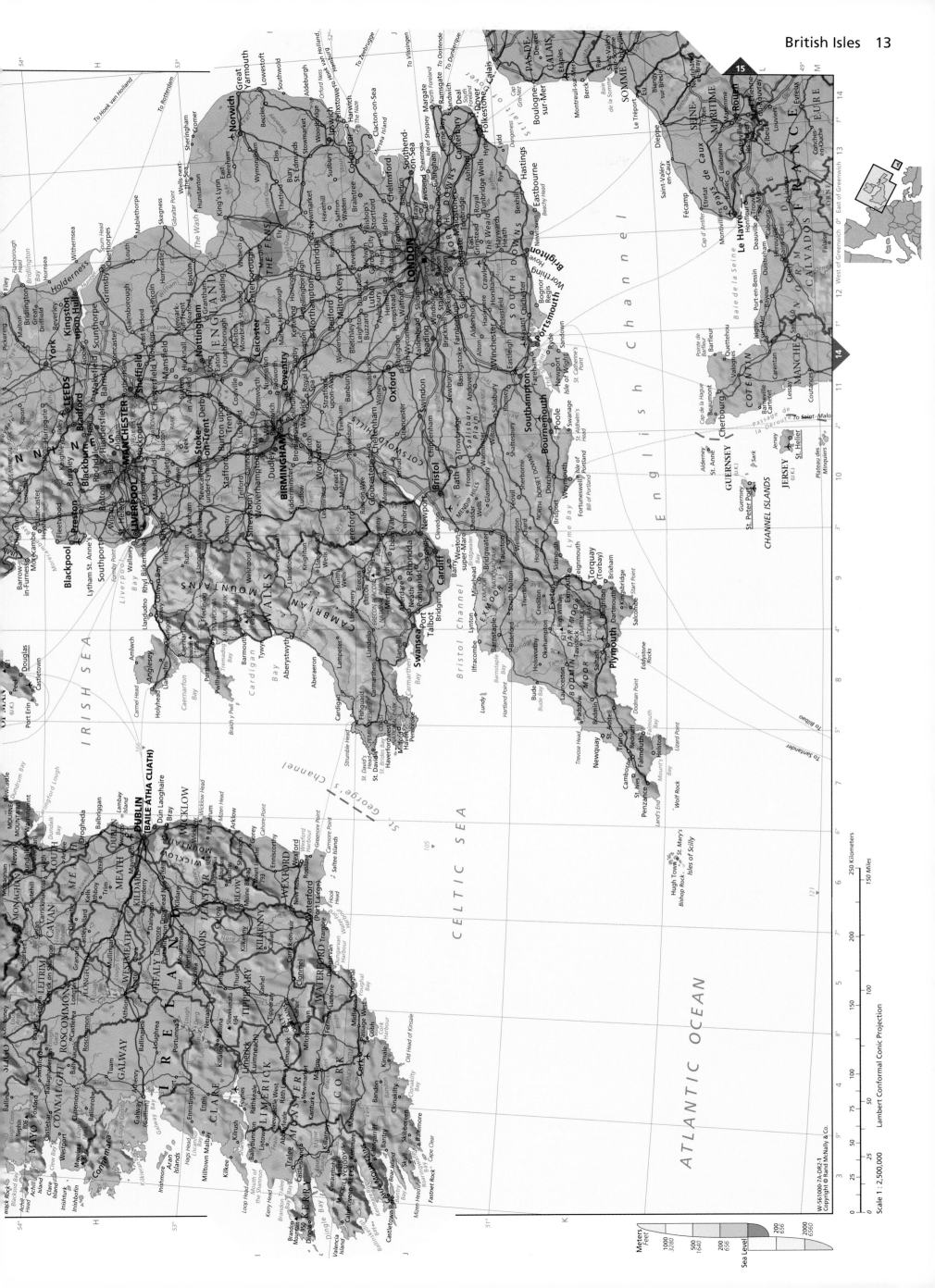

Lambert Conformal Conic Projection

Scale 1 : 2,500,000

ATLANTIC OCEAN

CELTIC SEA

IRISH SEA

IRELAND

WALES

ENGLAND

FRANCE

English Channel

St. George's Channel

Bristol Channel

LONDON

DUBLIN
(BAILE ÁTHA CLIATH)

CHANNEL ISLANDS

Meters / Feet
2000 / 6560
1000 / 3280
500 / 1640
200 / 656
Sea Level
200 / 656

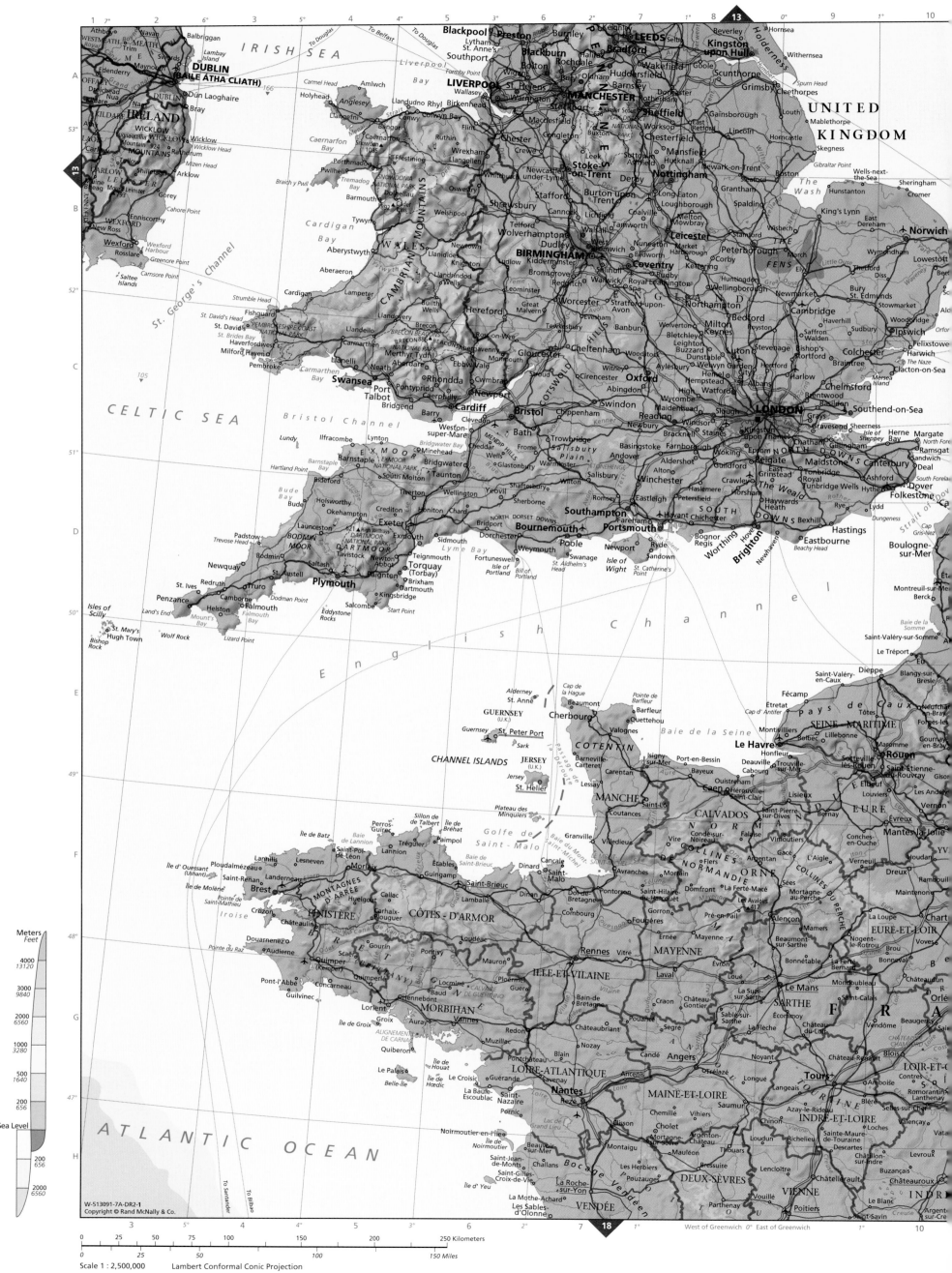

Meters
Feet

4000
13120

3000
9840

2000
6560

1000
3280

500
1640

200
656

Sea Level

200
656

2000
6560

0   25   50   75   100   150   200   250 Kilometers

0   25   50   100   150 Miles

Scale 1 : 2,500,000   Lambert Conformal Conic Projection

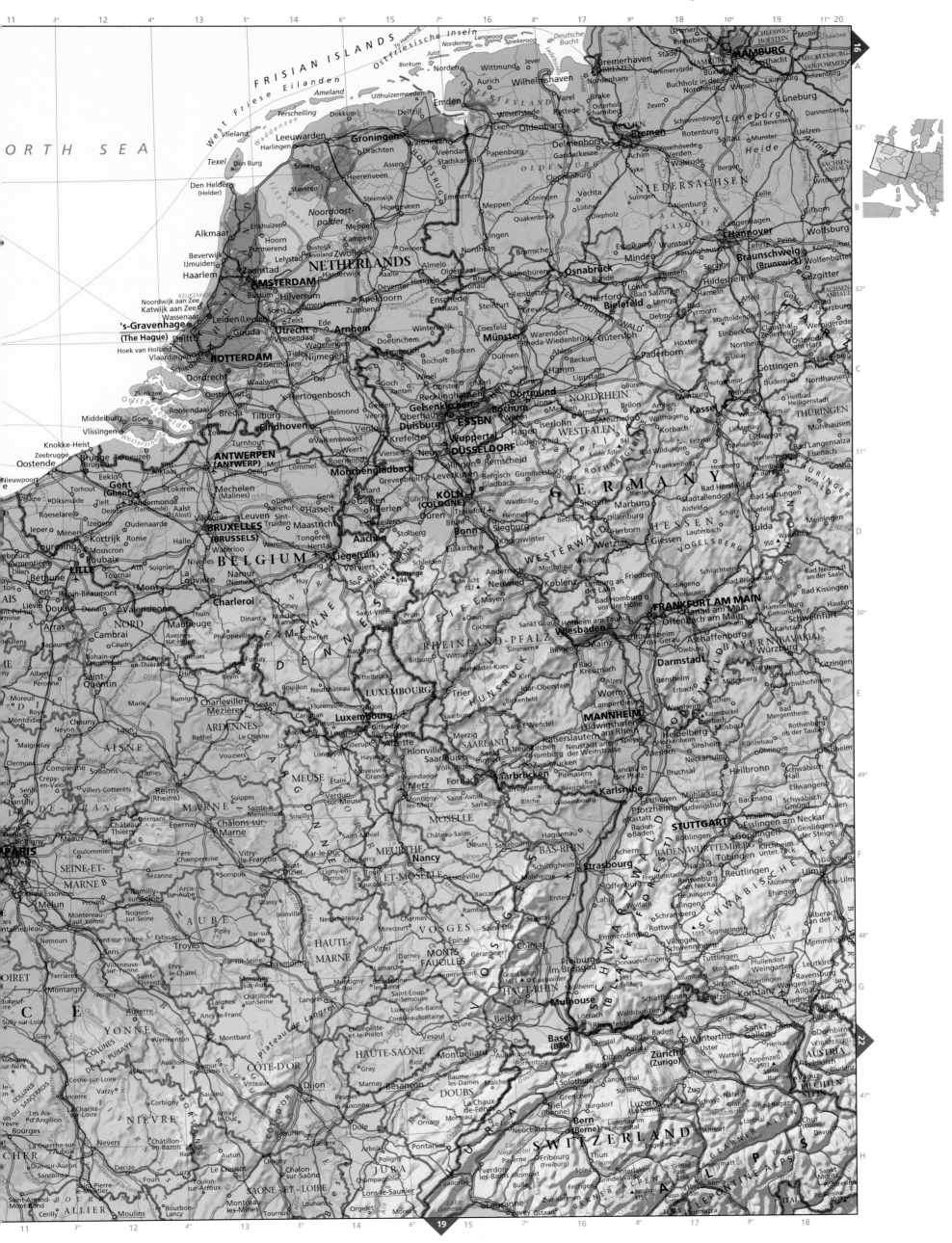

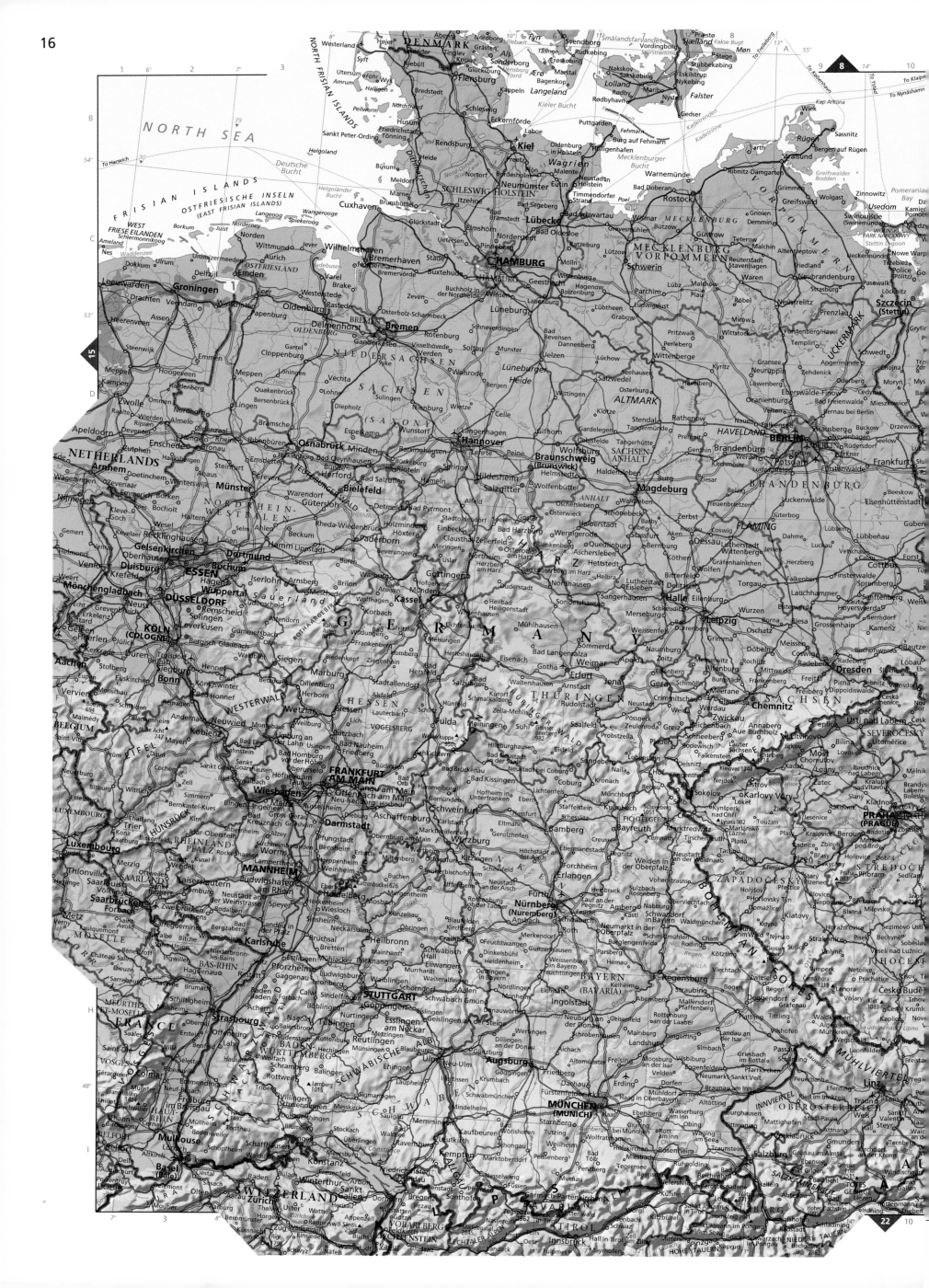

Scale 1 : 2,500,000   Lambert Conformal Conic Projection

MEDITERRANEAN SEA

ILLES BALEARS (BALEARIC ISLANDS)

BALEARS

MALLORCA
(Majorca)

MENORCA
(Minorca)

EIVISSA
(IBIZA)

FORMENTERA

Golfe du Lion

FRANCE

PYRENEES

ARAGÓN

CATALUNYA

BARCELONA

VALÈNCIA

MURCIA

ALGERIAN ATLAS MOUNTAINS

EL DJAZAÏR
(ALGIERS)

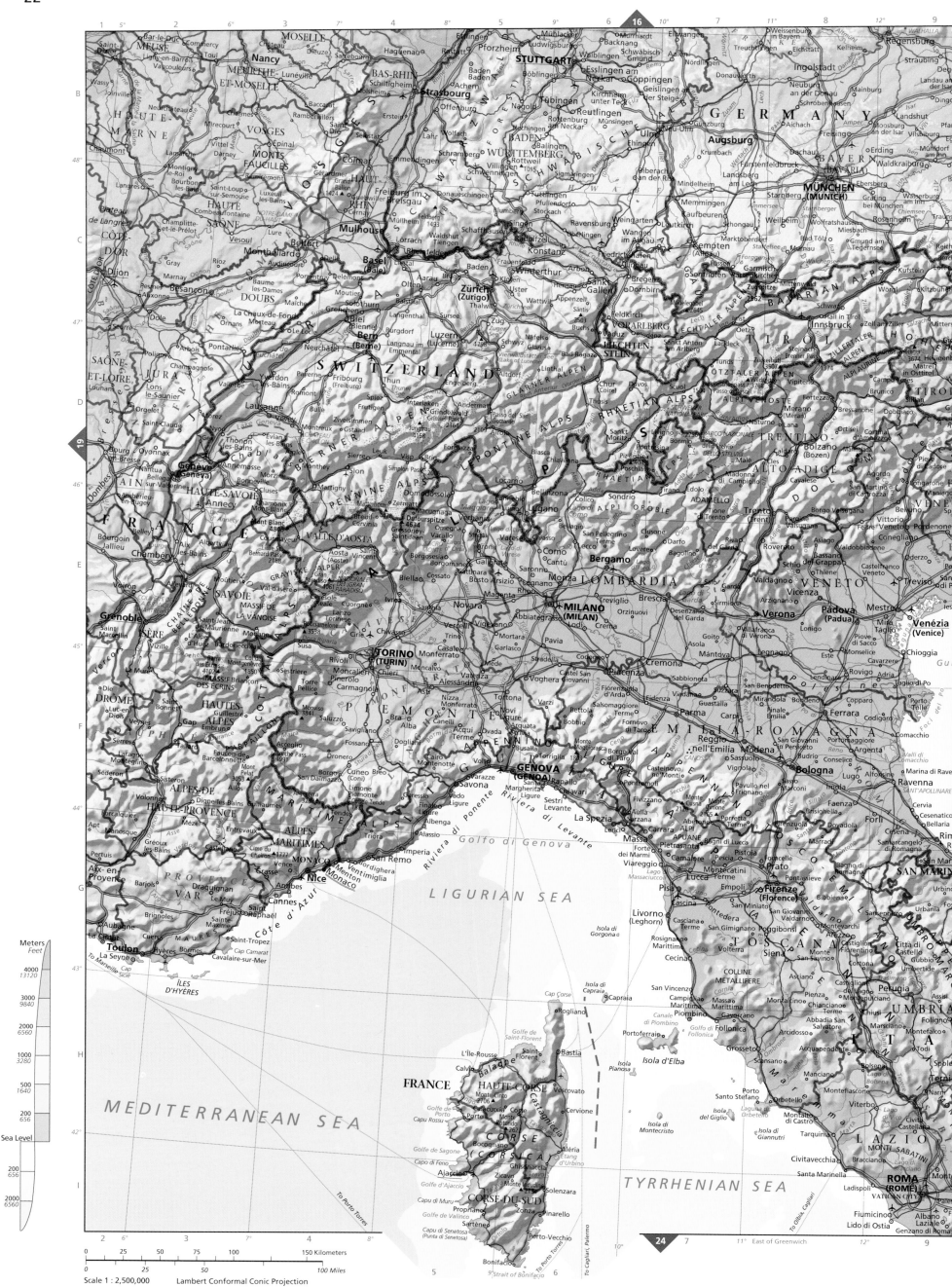

MEDITERRANEAN SEA

LIGURIAN SEA

TYRRHENIAN SEA

Meters
Feet

4000
13120

3000
9840

2000
6560

1000
3280

500
1640

200
656

Sea Level

200
656

2000
6560

0   25   50   75   100   150 Kilometers

0   25   50   100 Miles

Scale 1 : 2,500,000   Lambert Conformal Conic Projection

24

19

22

64

W-520092-7A-DR2-1
Copyright © Rand McNally & Co.

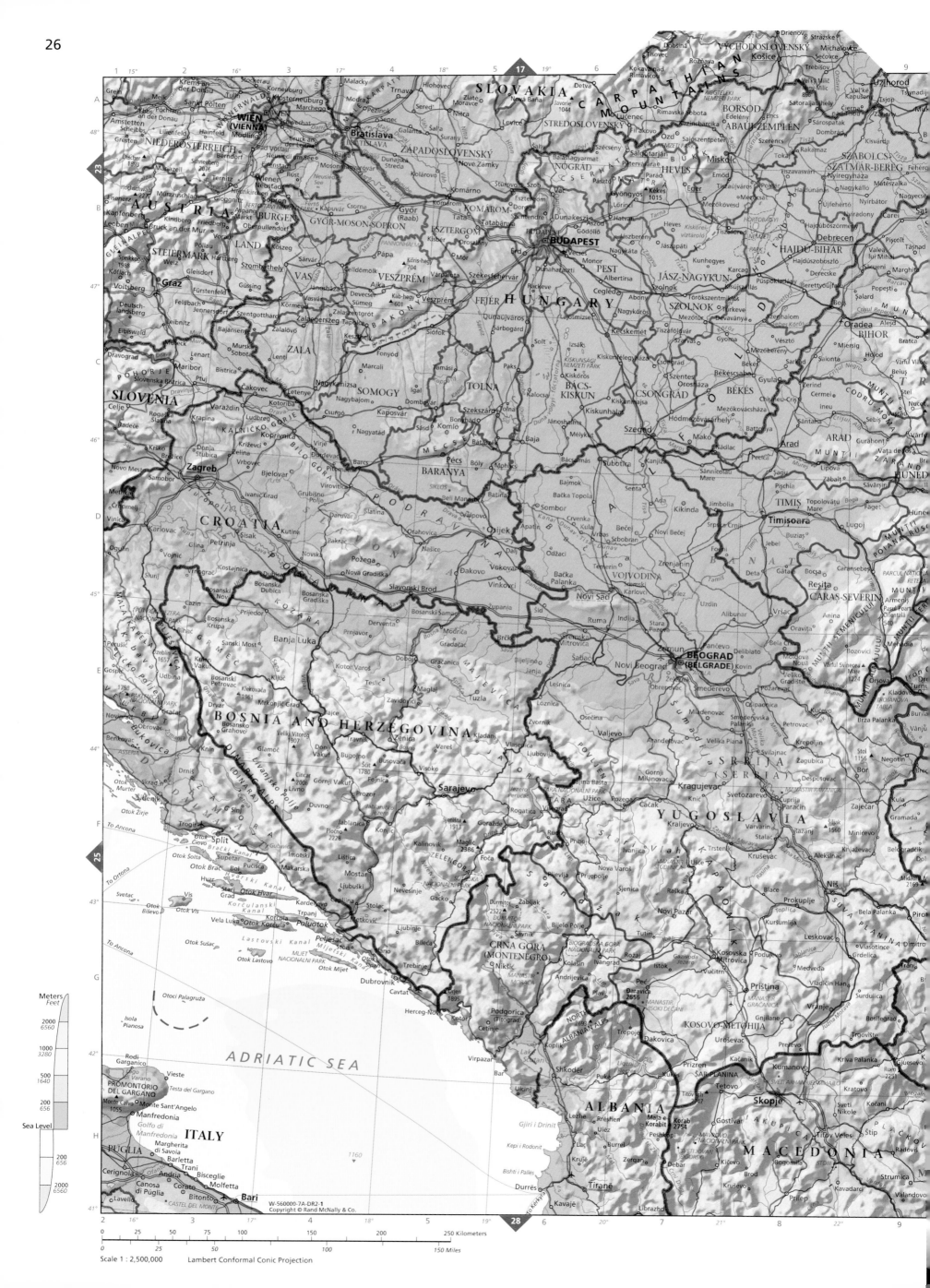

Meters
Feet

3000
9840

2000
6560

1000
3280

500
1640

200
656

Sea Level

200
656

2000
6560

0   25   50   75   100   150   200   250 Kilometers

0   25   50   100   150 Miles

Scale 1 : 2,500,000   Lambert Conformal Conic Projection

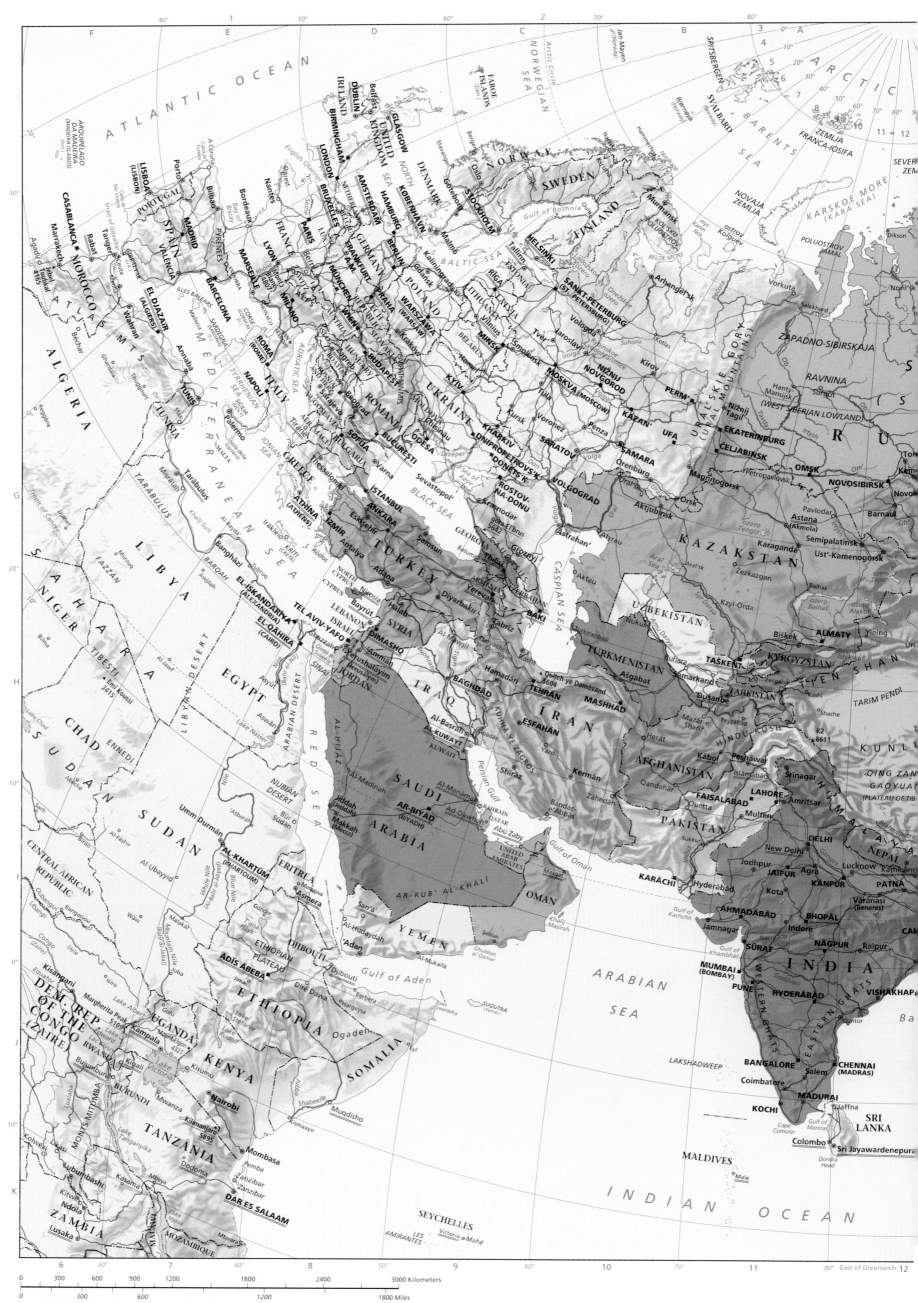

Scale 1 : 30,000,000   Lambert Azimuthal Equal Area Projection

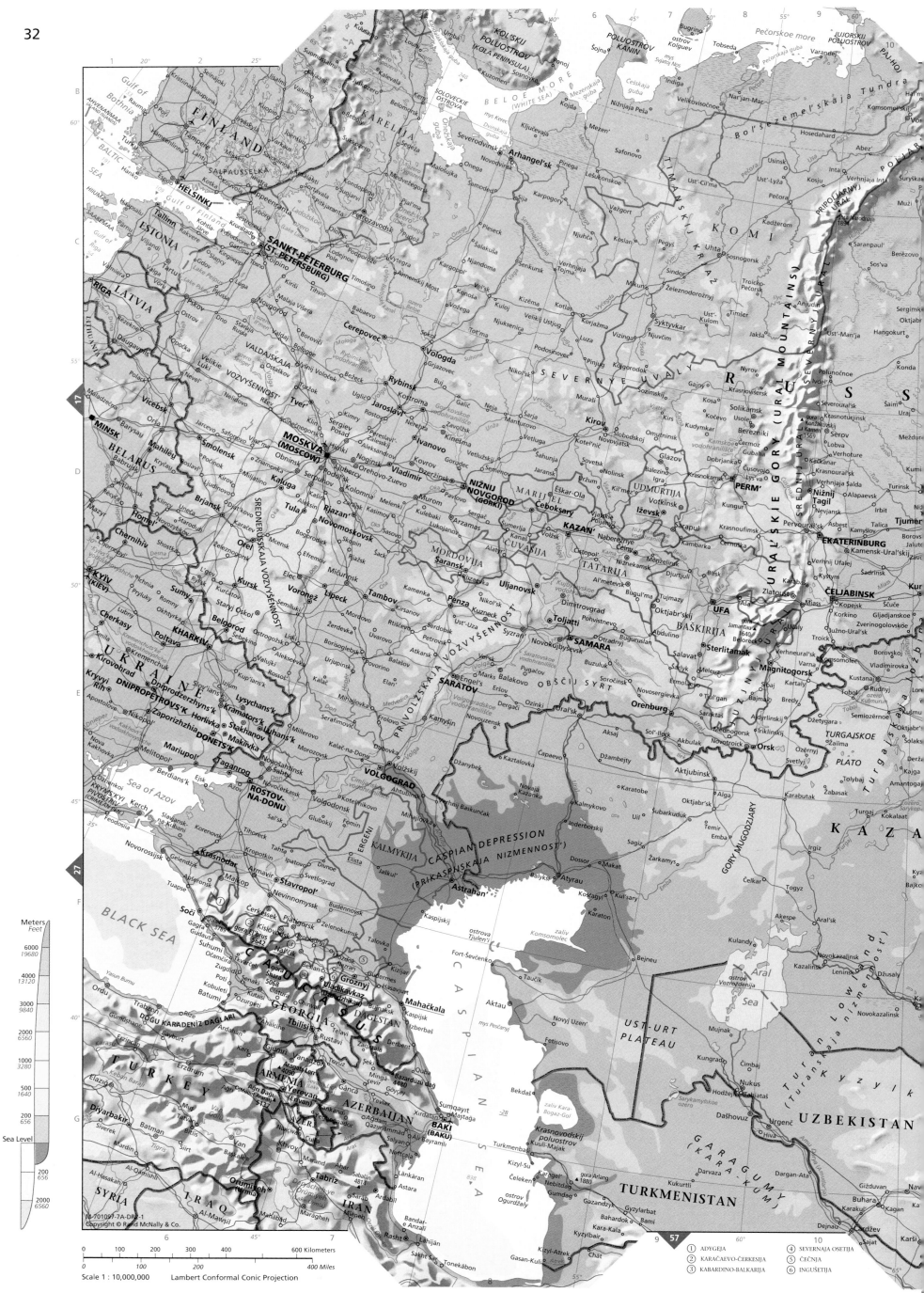

Meters
Feet

6000
19680

4000
13120

3000
9840

2000
6560

1000
3280

500
1640

200
656

Sea Level

200
656

2000
6560

M-701097-7A-DR2-1
Copyright © Rand McNally & Co.

0   100   200   300   400   600 Kilometers

0   100   200   400 Miles

Scale 1 : 10,000,000   Lambert Conformal Conic Projection

① ADYGEJA   ④ SEVERNAJA OSETIJA
② KARAČAEVO-ČERKESIJA   ⑤ ČEČNJA
③ KABARDINO-BALKARIJA   ⑥ INGUŠETIJA

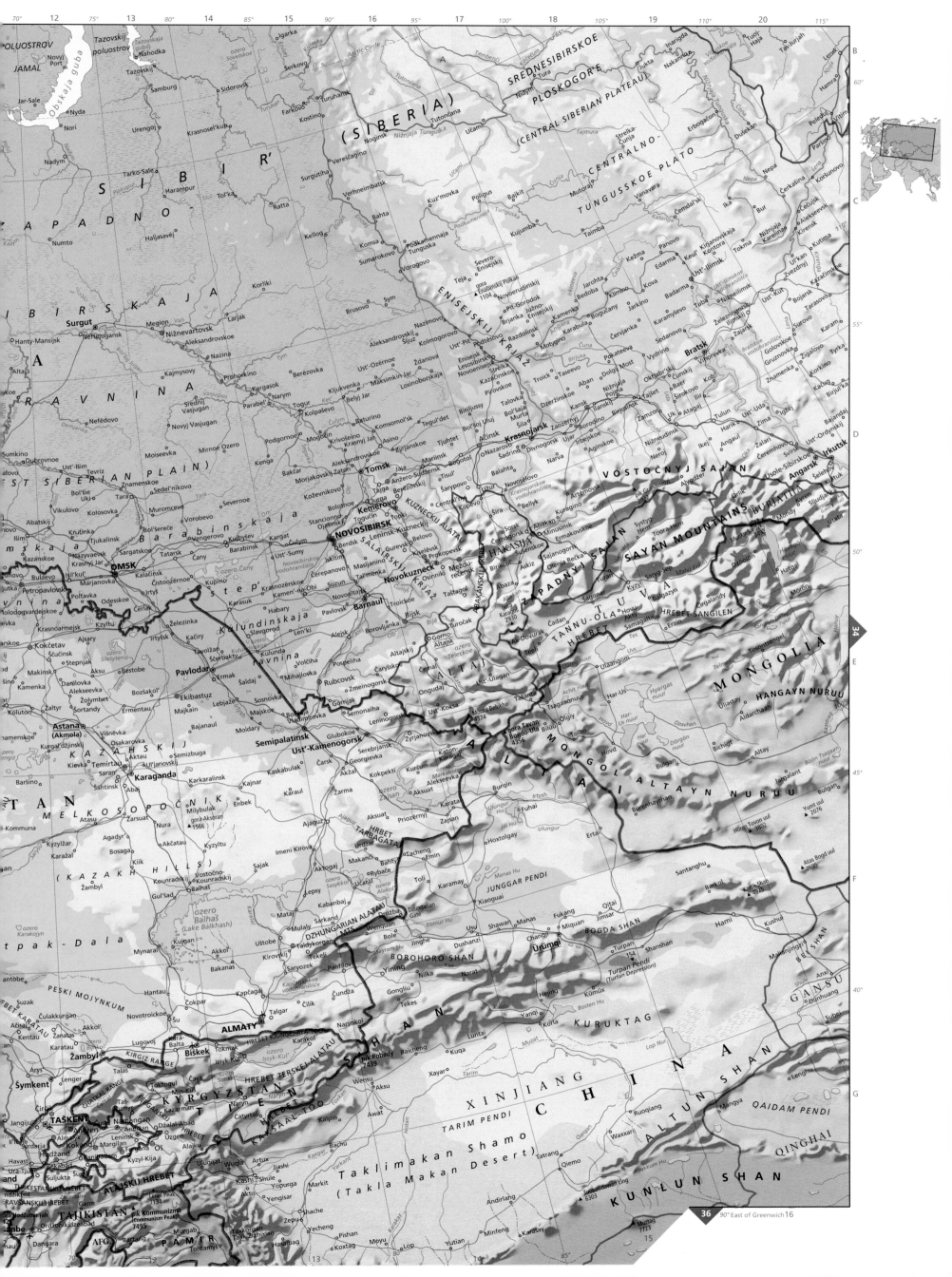

70°   12   75°   13   80°   14   85°   15   90°   16   95°   17   100°   18   105°   19   110°   20   115°

P-OLUOSTROV
JAMAL
Novyj Port
Obskaja guba

Tazovskij
poluostrov
Nahodka

SREDNESIBIRSKOE
PLOSKOGOR'E

(CENTRAL SIBERIAN PLATEAU)

CENTRALNO-
TUNGUSSKOE PLATO

Jar-Sale
Nori
Nyda

Tarko-Sale
Harampur

Arctic Circle

Numto

S I B I R '

(S I B I R ')   (S I B E R I A)

Z A P A D N O -

Surgut
Neftejugansk
Niževartovsk
Aleksandrovskoe

S I B I R S K A J A

R A V N I N A

(WEST SIBERIAN PLAIN)

Hanty-Mansijsk

Megion   Vah

Bratsk

VOSTOČNYJ SAJAN

Krasnojarsk
Angarsk   Irkutsk

Tomsk

Kemerovo
NOVOSIBIRSK

KUZNECKIJ ALATAU

HAKASIA

ZAPADNYJ SAJAN

SAYAN MOUNTAINS   BURJATIA

Novokuzneck

Barnaul

A L T A J

TUVA
TANNU-OLA   HREBET SANGILEN

MONGOLIA

HANGAYN NURUU

OMSK

Pavlodar

Astana
(Akmola)

Karaganda

S t e p'

Kulundinskaja
Ravnina

Semipalatinsk
Ust'-Kamenogorsk

Mount Belukha
4374

gora Tavan-
Bogdo Ula
4356

MONGOL   ALTAYN   NURUU

K A Z A H S K I J

MELKOSOPOČNIK

(KAZAKH HILLS)

HREBET
TARBAGATAJ

JUNGGAR PENDI

BOGDA SHAN

GANSU

ozero
Balhaš
(Lake Balkhash)

DZHUNGARIAN ALATAU
MTS.

BOROHORO SHAN

Ürümqi

Turpan Pendi
(Turfan Depression)

BEI SHAN

PESKI MOJYNKUM

ALMATY

Biškek

KIRGIZ RANGE

HREBET TERSKEJ ALATAU

Pik Pobedy
7439

T I E N   S H A N

KURUKTAG

X I N J I A N G   C H I N A

ALTUN SHAN

Symkent

KYRGYZSTAN

TAŠKENT

Taklimakan Shamo
(Takla Makan Desert)

TARIM PENDI

QAIDAM PENDI

QINGHAI

TAJIKISTAN

PAMIR

KUNLUN SHAN

90° East of Greenwich 16

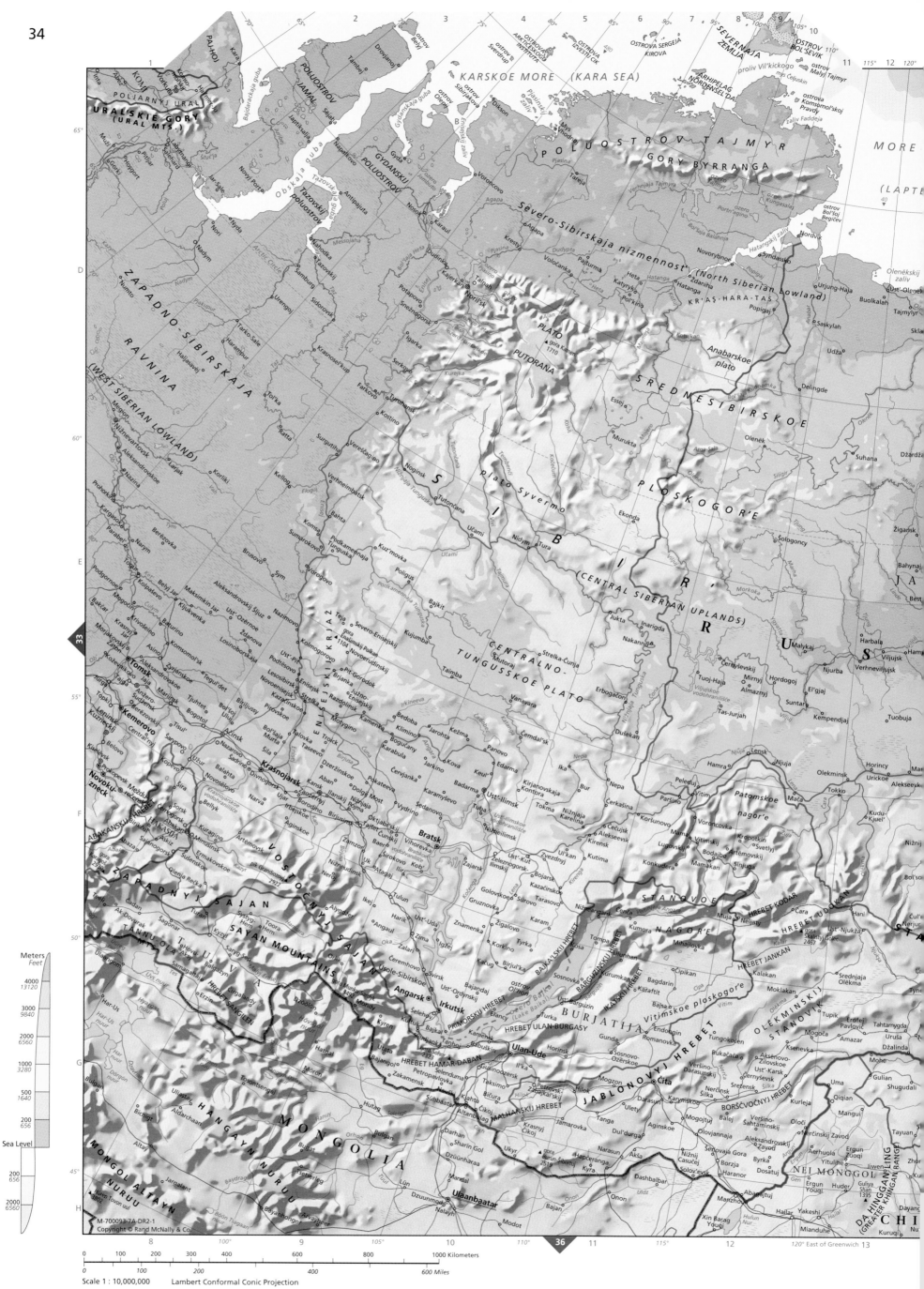

POLJARNYJ URAL
URAL'SKIE GORY
(URAL MTS.)
KOMI

PAJ-HOJ

POLUOSTROV JAMAL

GYDANSKIJ POLUOSTROV

KARSKOE MORE (KARA SEA)

SEVERNAJA ZEMLJA

ARHIPELAG NORDENŠEL'DA

POLUOSTROV TAJMYR

GORY BYRRANGA

MORE

(LAPTE

Severo-Sibirskaja nizmennost' (North Siberian Lowland)

ZAPADNO-SIBIRSKAJA RAVNINA (WEST SIBERIAN LOWLAND)

PLATO PUTORANA

gora Kamen 1710

Anabarskoe plato

KR'AS-HARA-TAS

SREDNESIBIRSKOE PLOSKOGOR'E

plato Syverma

S I B I R'

CENTRALNO-TUNGUSSKOE PLATO

(CENTRAL SIBERIAN UPLANDS)

R U S S

JA

Norilsk

Igarka

Turuhansk

Tomsk

Kemerovo

Krasnojarsk

Novokuznzeck

ZAPADNYJ SAJAN

ABAKANSKIJ HREBET

VOSTOČNYJ SAJAN

SAYAN MOUNTAINS

TANNU-OLA MTS.

T U V A

Angarsk

Irkutsk

Bratsk

Ust'-Ilimsk

PRIMORSKIJ HREBET

BAJKAL'SKIJ HREBET

STANOVOE NAGOR'E

HREBET KODAR

HREBET JANKAN

HREBET UDOKAN

STA

Ulan-Ude

BURJATIJA

Vitimskoe ploskogor'e

HREBET HAMAR-DABAN

HREBET ULAN-BURGASY

JABLONOVYJ HREBET

OLEKMINSKIJ STANOVIK

Čita

MONGOLIA

HANGAYN NURUU

Ulaanbaatar

MONGOL ALTAYN NURUU

MALHANSKIJ HREBET

BORŠČOVOČNYJ HREBET

NEI MONGGOL

CHI

DA HINGGAN LING (GREATER KHINGAN RANGE)

Meters / Feet
4000 / 13120
3000 / 9840
2000 / 6560
1000 / 3280
500 / 1640
200 / 656
Sea Level
200 / 656
2000 / 6560

0 100 200 300 400 600 800 1000 Kilometers
0 100 200 400 600 Miles

NOVOSIBIRSKIE OSTROVA
OSTROVA ANŽU
LJAHOVSKIJE OSTROVA
OSTROV KOTEL'NYJ
OSTROV FADDEEVSKIJ
OSTROV NOVAJA SIBIR'

VOSTOČNO-SIBIRSKOE MORE
(EAST SIBERIAN SEA)

CHUKCHI SEA

ČUKOTSKIJ POLUOSTROV
(CHUKOTSK PEN.)

proliv Longa

OSTROV VRANGELJA
(WRANGEL ISLAND)

Bering Strait

U.S. ALASKA

Anadyrskij zaliv
(Gulf of Anadyr)

Jano-Indigirskaja nizmennost'
Kolymskaja nizmennost'
(Kolyma Plain)

ANADYRSKOE PLOSKOGORE

HREBET PEKUL'NEJ

ANJUJSKIJ HREBET

OLOJSKIJ HREBET

Jukagirskoe ploskogore

KORJAKSKOE NAGORE

VERHOJANSKIJ HREBET
(CHERSKIY MOUNTAINS)
HREBET ČERSKOGO
MOMSKIJ HREBET
(SIBERIA)
HREBET SUNTAR-HAJATA

PENŽINSKIJ HREBET

POLUOSTROV TAJGONOS

zaliv Šelihova

Gižiginskaja guba

BERING SEA

KOMANDORSKIE OSTROVA

ostrov Karaginskij

SREDINNYJ HREBET

KAMČATSKIJ POLUOSTROV

Jakutsk

HREBET SETTE-DABAN

HREBET DŽUGDŽUR

POLUOSTROV KAMČATKA

VOSTOČNYJ HREBET

Petropavlovsk-Kamčatskij

SEA OF OKHOTSK

ŠANTARSKIE OSTROVA

POLUOSTROV SMIDTA

HREBET DŽAGDY

HREBET TURANA

HREBET BUREINSKIJ

BADŽAL'SKIJ HREBET

Komsomol'sk-na-Amure

OSTROV SAHALIN
(SAKHALIN)

ZAPADNYJ HREBET

KURIL'SKIE OSTROVA
(KURIL ISLANDS)

SIHOTE-ALIN'

Habarovsk

TONGJIANG

Scale 1 : 10,000,000   Lambert Conformal Conic Projection

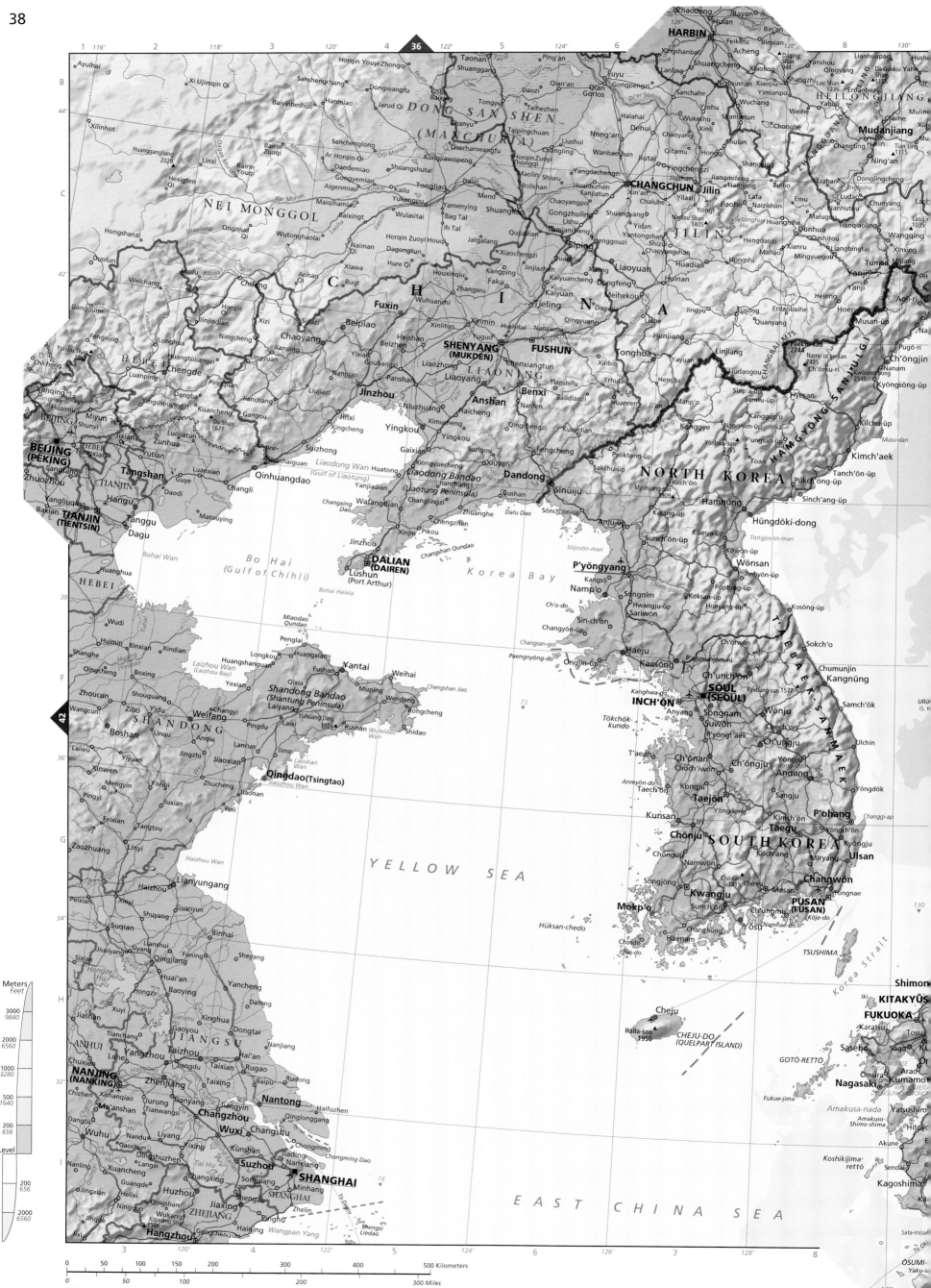

SEA OF OKHOTSK

RUSSIA

KURIL'SKIE OSTROVA (KURIL ISLANDS)

Habomai, Shikotan, Kunashiri and Étorofu, occupied since 1945, are claimed by Japan pending a final peace treaty.

ostrov Iturup (Etorofu-tō)

ostrov Šikotan (Shikotan-tō)
ostrov Kunašir (Kunashiri-tō)
Malaja Kuril'skaja Grjada (Habomai-shotō)

HOKKAIDŌ

RUSSIA

SIHOTÉ ALIN'

Vladivostok
Nahodka

Sapporo

Asahikawa

Hakodate

Aomori
Hirosaki

Akita

SEA OF JAPAN
(EAST SEA)

JAPAN

SADO

Niigata

Sendai

Tok-tō Take-shima
ed by S. Korea and Japan)

Noto-hantō

OKI-SHOTŌ Dōgo

Kanazawa Toyama

Nagano

Utsunomiya

Maebashi

Mito
Hitachi

Matsue Yonago

Gifu

NAGOYA

TŌKYŌ
Chiba
KAWASAKI

YOKOHAMA

Numazu

KYŌTO

Shizuoka

Fuji-san
(Mount Fuji)
3776

HIROSHIMA

Himeji

KŌBE
OSAKA
Wakayama

Nara

Hamamatsu

Toyohashi

HONSHŪ

Takamatsu
Tokushima

Kumano-nada

SHIKOKU

Kōchi

Muroto

PACIFIC OCEAN

KYŪSHŪ

Miyazaki

EAST
CHINA SEA

NANSEI-SHOTŌ (RYUKYU ISLANDS)

Amami-Ō-shima
Naze

JAPAN

PACIFIC OCEAN

OKINAWA-SHOTŌ

Naha Okinawa

Same scale as main map

W-566400-7A-DR2-1
Copyright © Rand McNally & Co.

SEA OF JAPAN (EAST SEA)

JAPA

SOUTH KOREA

NORTH KOREA

EAST CHINA SEA

KYŪSHŪ

SHIKOKU

FUKUOKA

KITAKYŪSHŪ

NAGASAKI

KUMAMOTO

KAGOSHIMA

MIYAZAKI

HIROSHIMA

Matsuyama

Takamatsu

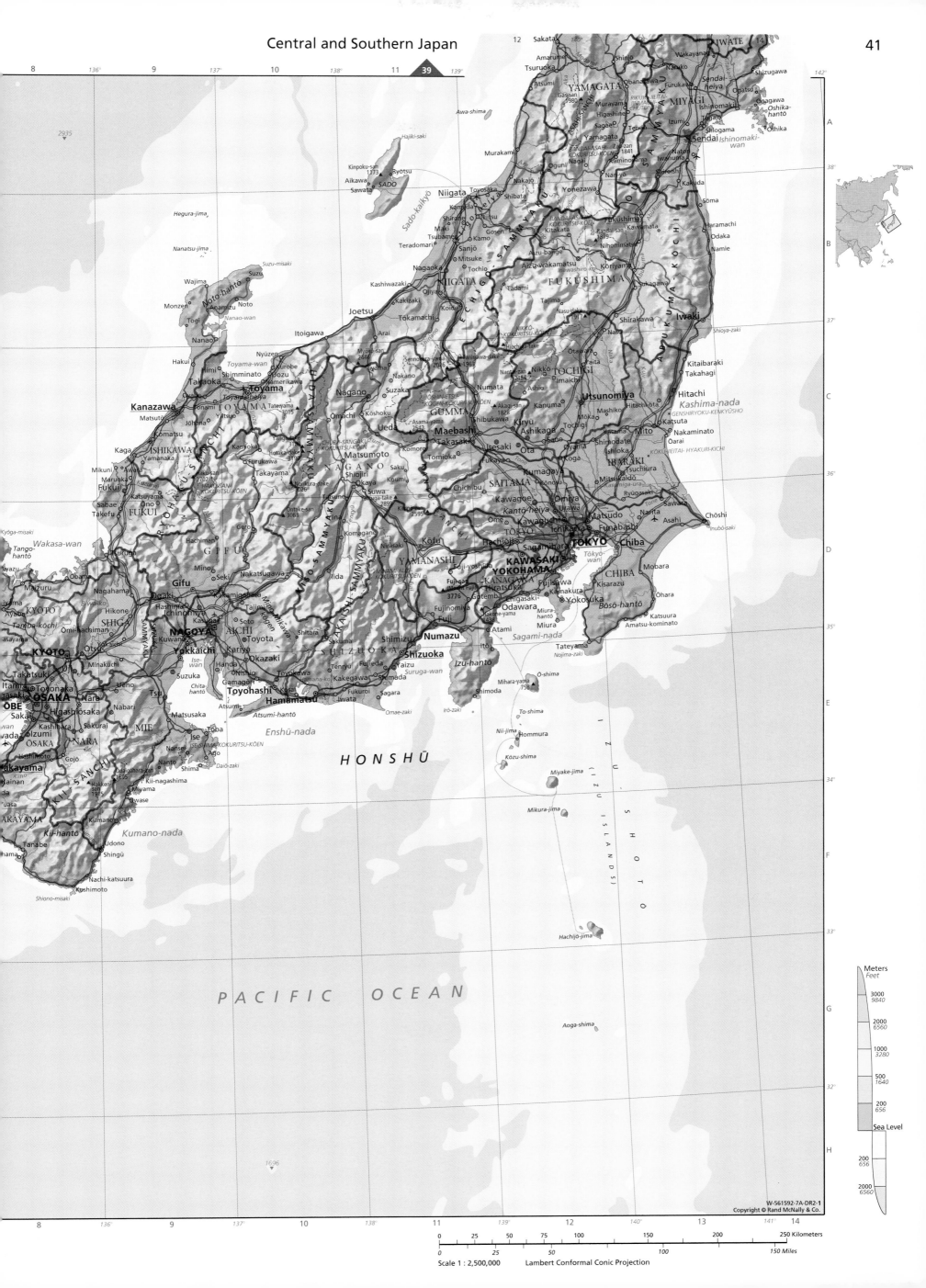

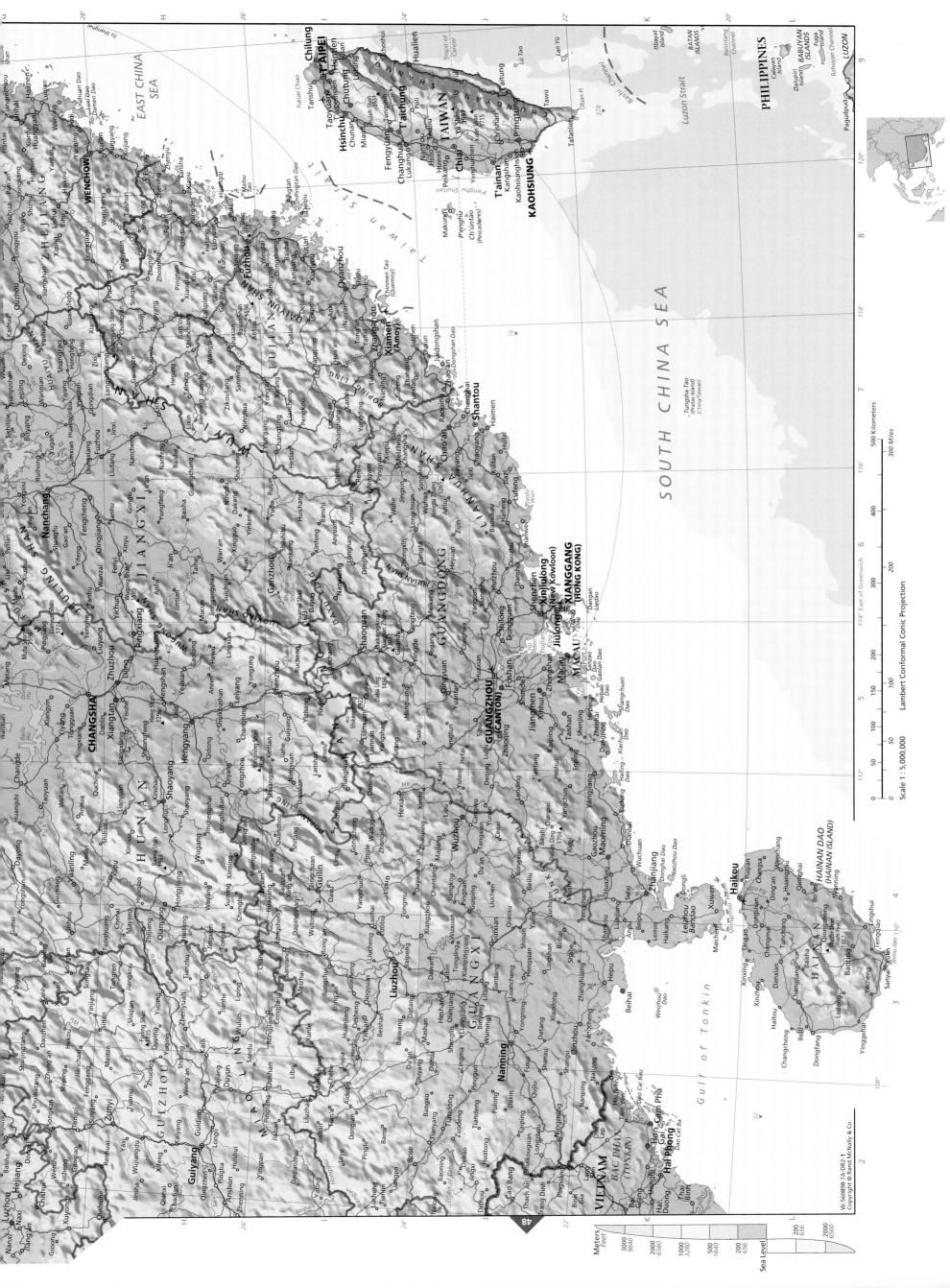

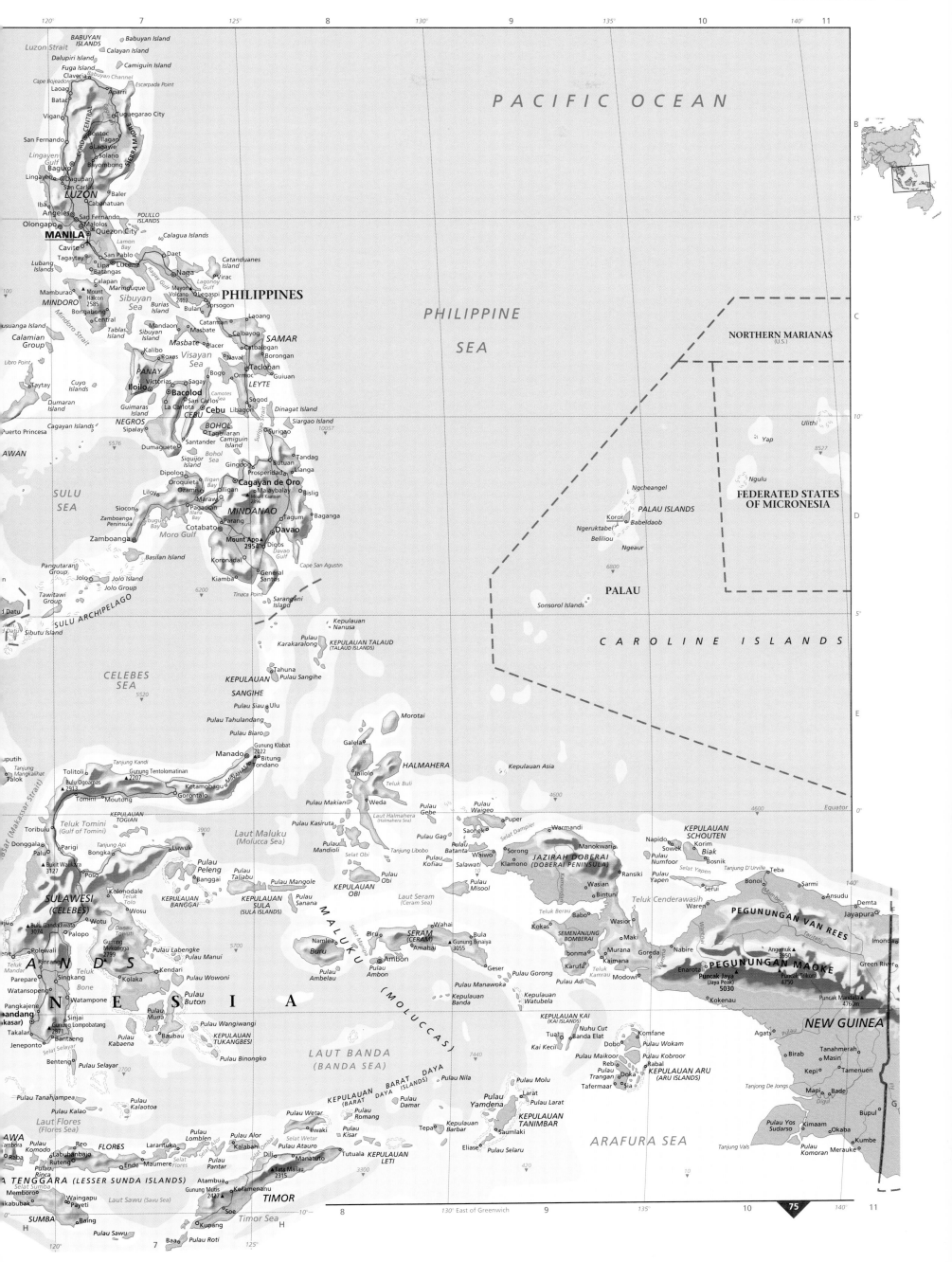

PACIFIC OCEAN

PHILIPPINE SEA

PHILIPPINES

NORTHERN MARIANAS
(U.S.)

FEDERATED STATES OF MICRONESIA

PALAU ISLANDS

PALAU

CAROLINE ISLANDS

LUZON
Luzon Strait
BABUYAN ISLANDS
Babuyan Island
Dalupiri Island
Fuga Island
Calayan Island
Camiguin Island
Babuyan Channel
Claveria
Aparri
Laoag
Batac
Vigan
Escarpada Point
Cape Bojeador
Tuguegarao City
San Fernando
Pontoc
Bangued
Ilagan
Solano
CORDILLERA CENTRAL
SIERRA MADRE
Baguio
Bayombong
Dagupan
San Carlos
Baler
Lingayen
Lingayen Gulf
Iba
Cabanatuan
Angeles
San Fernando
Olongapo
Malolos
Quezon City
MANILA
Cavite
Tagaytay
POLILLO ISLANDS
Lamon Bay
San Pablo
Lucena
Calagua Islands
Lipa
Batangas
Naga
Daet
Calapan
Maringuque
Catanduanes Island
Virac
Mamburao
MINDORO
Mount Halcon
2585
Volcano
2462
Legaspi
Mayon
Sorsogon
Bongabong
Bulan
Calamian Group
Mindoro Strait
Calabanga
Busuanga Island
Sibuyan Sea
Central
Catarman
Laoang
Tablas Island
Sibuyan Island
Mandaon
Masbate
Calbayog
Catbalogan
SAMAR
Libro Point
Cuyo Islands
Roxas
Kalibo
MASBATE
Placer
Naval
Borongan
PANAY
Victorias
Bogo
Tacloban
Ormoc
Guiuan
Iloilo
Sagay
San Carlos
LEYTE
Bacolod
La Carlota
Cebu
Libagon
Sogod
Dinagat Island
Guimaras Island
CEBU
Camotes Sea
Siargao Island
NEGROS
Tagbilaran
BOHOL
Dumaguete
Surigao
Sipalay
Santander
Camiguin Island
Puerto Princesa
Dipolog
Siquijor Island
Bohol Sea
Tandag
PALAWAN
Liloy
Oroquieta
Iligan Bay
Prosperidad
Lianga
Ozamiz
Butuan
Gingoog
SULU SEA
Siocon
Ozamis
Iligan
Cagayan de Oro
Bislig
Zamboanga Peninsula
Marawi
Malaybalay
Mount Kaatoan
2936
Pagadian
Illana Bay
MINDANAO
Zamboanga
Iligan Bay
Parang
Tagum
Baganga
Pangutaran Group
Cotabato
Davao
Jolo
Basilan Island
Koronadal
Mount Apo
2954
Digos
Davao Gulf
SULU ARCHIPELAGO
Jolo Island
Jolo Group
Kiamba
General Santos
Cape San Agustin
Tawitawi Group
Sibutu Island
Datu
Tinaca Point
Sarangani Island
Kepulauan Nanusa

CELEBES SEA

Kepulauan Karakaralong
Pulau
KEPULAUAN TALAUD
(TALAUD ISLANDS)
KEPULAUAN SANGIHE
Tahuna
Pulau Sangihe
Pulau Siau
Ulu
Pulau Tahulandang
Pulau Biaro
Morotai
Galela
Gunung Klabat
2022
Manado
Bitung
Tondano
Jailolo
HALMAHERA
Kepulauan Asia
Tolitoli
Tanjung Kandi
Bulu Ogoamas
Gunung Tentolomatinan
2207
MINAHASA
Kotamobagu
Weda
Gorontalo
Pulau Makian
CELEBES SEA
Pulau Gebe
Tanjung Mangkalihat
Talok
Tomini
Moutong
Pulau Waigeo
Puper
Equator
KEPULAUAN TOGIAN
Laut Halmahera
(Halmahera Sea)
Pulau Gag
Saohek
Warmandi
KEPULAUAN SCHOUTEN
Toribulu
Teluk Tomini
(Gulf of Tomini)
Donggala
Tanjung Api
Bongka
Liuwuk
Pulau Kasiruta
Selat Dampier
Sorong
Manokwari
Napido
Korim
Palu
Parigi
Pulau Mandioli
Tanjung Libobo
Klamono
Sowek
Numfoor
Biak
Poso
Bukit Wandra
3127
Pulau Peleng
Pulau Obi
Waiwo
Salawati
JAZIRAH DOBERAI
(DOBERAI PENINSULA)
Ransiki
Bosnik
Tanjung D'Urville
Teba
SULAWESI
(CELEBES)
Kolonodale
Banggai
Pulau Taliabu
Pulau Misool
Wasian
Serui
Pulau Yapen
Selat Yapen
Bonoi
Sarmi
Ansudu
Wotu
Teluk Tolo
KEPULAUAN BANGGAI
Pulau Mangole
KEPULAUAN OBI
Laut Seram
(Ceram Sea)
Bintuni
Teluk Cenderawasih
Waren
PEGUNUNGAN VAN REES
Demta
Jayapura
Danau Towuti
KEPULAUAN SULA
(SULA ISLANDS)
Pulau Sanana
Wahai
Teluk Berau
Babo
Kokas
Maki
Nabire
Imonda
Gunung Mekongga
2799
MALUKU
Piru
SEMENANJUNG BOMBERAI
Gunung Binaiya
3055
Ibonma
Wasior
PEGUNUNGAN MAOKE
Green River
Palopo
Pulau Labengke
Namlea
Bula
Murana
Goreda
Enarotali
Angemuk
3950
Kendari
Buru
Amahai
SERAM (CERAM)
Karufa
Kaimana
Modowi
Puncak Jaya
(Jaya Peak)
5030
Puncak Trikora
4750
PALU
Kolaka
Pulau Manui
Ambon
Pulau Ambon
Geser
Teluk Kamirau
Kokenau
Puncak Mandala
4760
Parepare
Singkang
Pulau Wowoni
Pulau Ambelau
Pulau Gorong
Pulau Adi
Pandang
Makassar
Watansopeng
Pulau Buton
Pulau Manawoka
KEPULAUAN WATUBELA
NEW GUINEA
Pangkajene
Teluk Bone
Sinjai
Gunung Lompobatang
2871
Pulau Muna
Baubau
Wangiwangi
Kepulauan Banda
KEPULAUAN KAI
(KAI ISLANDS)
Nuhu Cut
Komfane
Agats
Takalar
Bantaeng
Pulau Kabaena
KEPULAUAN TUKANGBESI
Tual
Banda Elat
Dobo
Pulau Wokam
Tanahmerah
Masin
Jeneponto
Benteng
Pulau Selayar
Kai Kecil
Pulau Kobroor
KEPULAUAN ARU
(ARU ISLANDS)
Rebi
Rabal
Birab
LAUT BANDA
(BANDA SEA)
Pulau Binongko
Pulau Trangan
Doka
Sia
Tafermaar
Mapi
Tamenuen
Selat Selayar
Pulau Selayar
Larat
Pulau Molu
Selat Sunda Daya
Tanjong De Jongs
Pulau Tanahjampea
Pulau Nila
Pulau Larat
Pulau Yamdena
Bade
Pulau Kalaotoa
Pulau Kalao
KEPULAUAN BARAT DAYA
(BARAT DAYA ISLANDS)
Pulau Damar
KEPULAUAN TANIMBAR
Digul
Bupul
Laut Flores
(Flores Sea)
Pulau Wetar
Pulau Romang
Saumlaki
Pulau Yos Sudarso
Kimaam
FLORES
Pulau Lomblen
Iwaki
Pulau Kisar
Tepa
Kepulauan Barbar
ARAFURA SEA
Okaba
Reo
Pulau Alor
Kalabahi
Selat Ombai
Dili
Eliase
Pulau Selaru
Tanjung Vals
Kumbe
Merauke
Ruteng
Pulau Pantar
Atauro
Manatuto
KEPULAUAN LETI
Ende
Maumere
Tutuala
Pulau Komoran
Labuhanbajo
Selat Flores
Atambua
Tata Mailau
2315
NUSA TENGGARA (LESSER SUNDA ISLANDS)
Gunung Mutis
2427
TIMOR
Timor Sea
SUMBA
Waingapu
Soe
Payeti
Baing
Kefamenanu
Kupang
Pulau Sawu
Laut Sawu (Savu Sea)
Baa
Pulau Roti

57

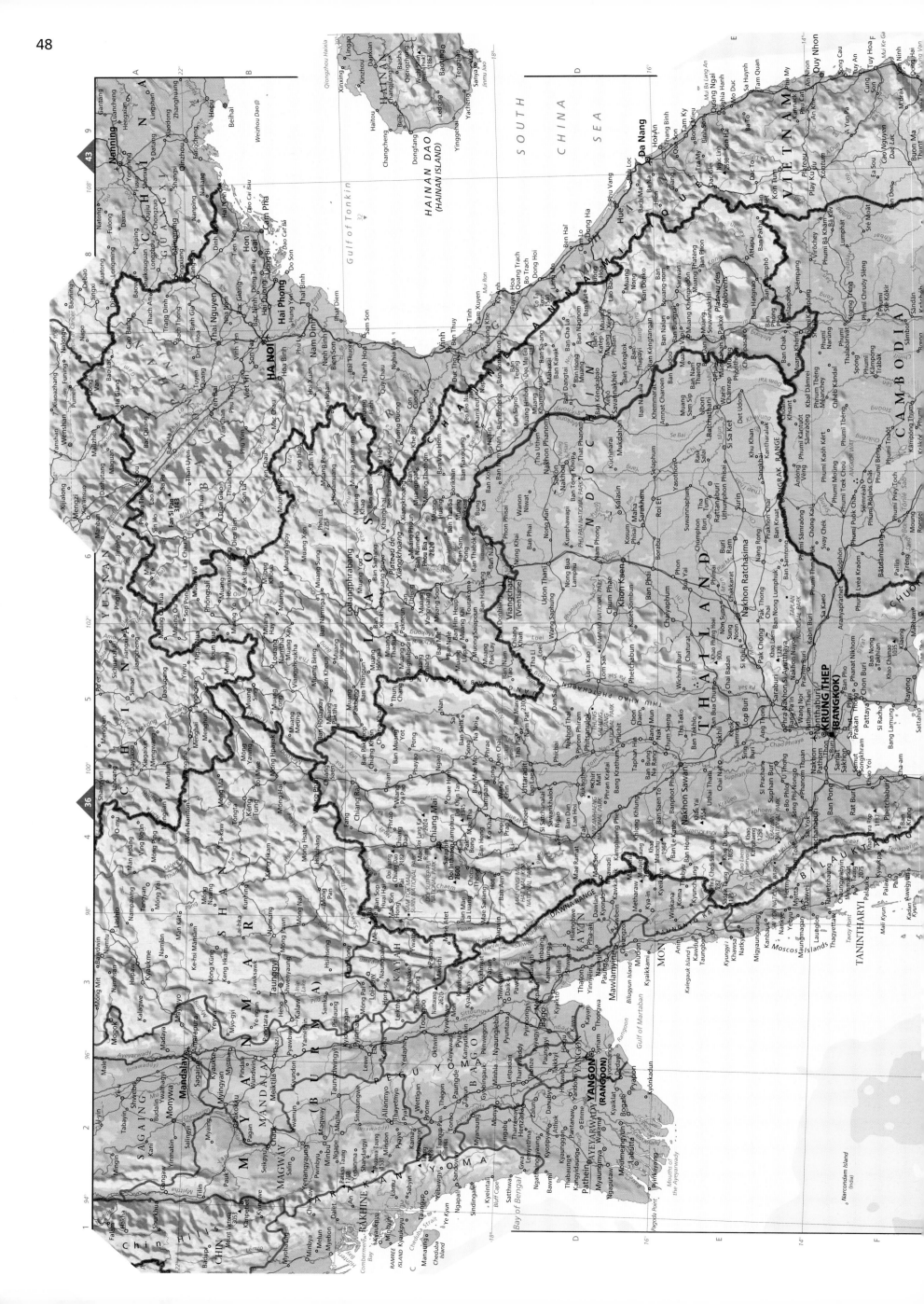

48

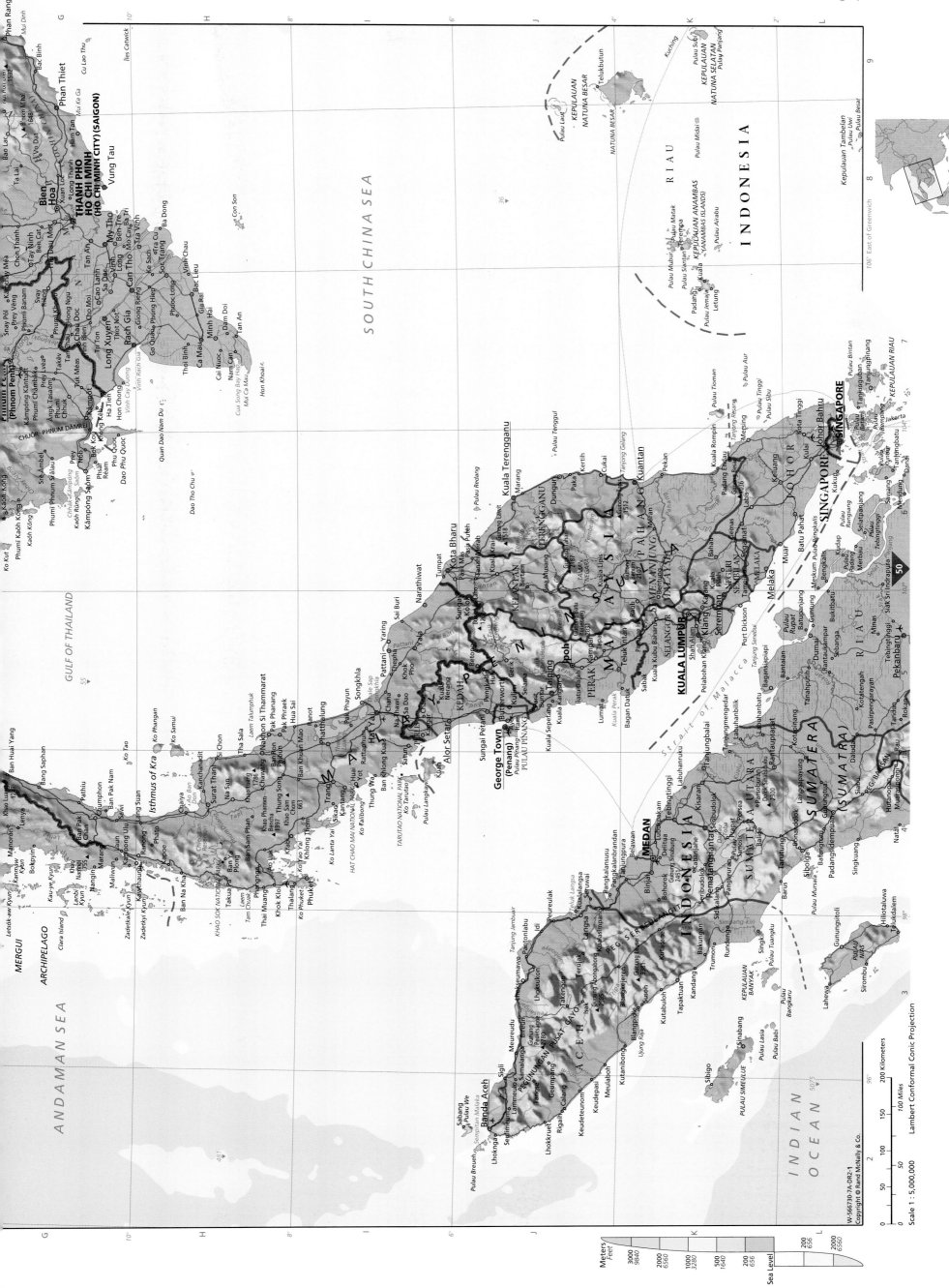

INDONESIA

RIAU

KEPULAUAN
NATUNA BESAR

NATUNA BESAR

KEPULAUAN
NATUNA SELATAN
Pulau Panjang

Kuching

Telukbutun

Pulau Laut

Pulau Siantan
KEPULAUAN ANAMBAS
(ANAMBAS ISLANDS)

Pulau Midai

Pulau Mubur
Pulau Matak

Padang
Pulau Jemaja
Letung

106° East of Greenwich

Kepulauan Tambelan
Pulau Uwi
Pulau Besar

SOUTH CHINA SEA

Con Son

Iles Catwick

Phan Rang

Mui Dinh

Bac Binh

Phan Thiet

Mui Ke Ga
Cu Lao Thu

Vung Tau

THANH PHO
HO CHI MINH
(HO CHI MINH CITY)(SAIGON)

Bien
Hoa

(Phnom Penh)

GULF OF THAILAND

CHUOR PHNUM DAMREI

ANDAMAN SEA

MERGUI
ARCHIPELAGO

Isthmus of Kra

Ko Phangan
Ko Samui
Ko Tao

Gulf of Thailand

INDONESIA

SUMATERA UTARA

ACEH

PEG. BARISAN

MEDAN

SUMATERA
(SUMATRA)

RIAU

INDONESIA

PEG. SERBOLANGIT

KEPULAUAN BANYAK

PULAU NIAS

KUALA LUMPUR

MALAYSIA

George Town
(Penang)
PULAU PINANG

KEDAH

PERAK

SELANGOR

NEGERI
SEMBILAN

PAHANG

TERENGGANU

KELANTAN

Kuala Terengganu

Kota Bharu

SINGAPORE

Johor Bahru

JOHOR

MELAKA

Strait of Malacca

INDIAN
OCEAN

Banda Aceh

Sabang
Pulau We

50

W-566730-7A-DR2-1
Copyright © Rand McNally & Co.

Lambert Conformal Conic Projection

Scale 1 : 5,000,000

200 Kilometers

100 Miles

Meters
Feet

3000
9840

2000
6560

1000
3280

500
1640

200
656

Sea Level

200
656

2000
6560

Meters
Feet

3000
9840

2000
6560

1000
3280

500
1640

200
656

Sea Level

200
656

2000
6560

Scale 1 : 5,000,000   Sinusoidal Projection

0   50   100   150   200   300   400   500 Kilometers

0   50   100   200   300 Miles

SOUTH CHINA SEA

MALAY PENINSULA

MALAYSIA

SINGAPORE

INDIAN

OCEAN

SUMATERA
(SUMATRA)

GREATER

JAWA (JAVA)

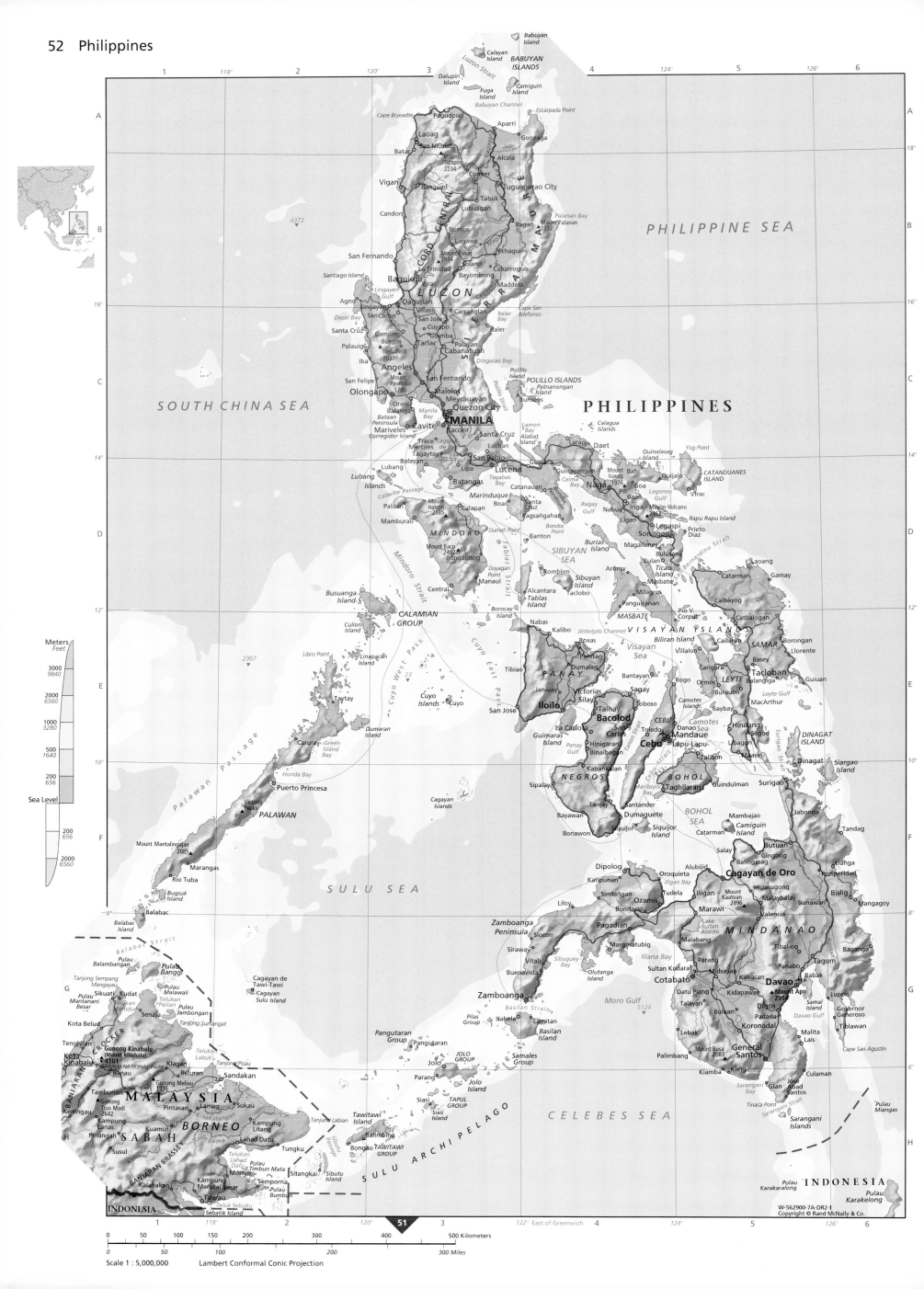

PHILIPPINE SEA

PHILIPPINES

SOUTH CHINA SEA

BABUYAN ISLANDS

LUZON

Babuyan Island
Calayan Island
Dalupiri Island
Fuga Island
Camiguin Island
Luzon Strait

Cape Bojeador
Pagudpud
Laoag
Batac
San Nicolas
Vigan
Candon
San Fernando
Baguio
La Trinidad
Agno
Dagupan
Lingayen
San Carlos
Santa Cruz
Palauig
Iba

Aparri
Gonzaga
Alcala
Tuguegarao City
Ilagan
Echague
Bayombong
Solano
Cabarroguis
Maddela

SIERRA MADRE
CORDILLERA CENTRAL

Mount Sicapoo 2234
Bontoc
Lagawe
Mount Pulog 2934
Bangued
Tabuk
Lubuagan

Escarpada Point
Palanan Bay
Mount Palanan 1212

Cape San Ildefonso

Baler Bay
Baler

Dingalan Bay

Santiago Island
Lingayen Gulf
Dasol Bay

Villasis
San Jose
Cuyapo
Tarlac
Cabanatuan
Palayan

Carranglan
Burgos
Iriga Peak 2037
Angeles
Mount Pinatubo 1780
San Felipe
Olongapo
Orani
Balanga
Bataan Peninsula
Mariveles
Corregidor Island

Malolos
Meycauayan
San Fernando
Quezon City
MANILA
Cavite
Bacoor

Manila Bay

POLILLO ISLANDS
Polillo Island
Patnanongan Island
Burdeos

Lamon Bay

Calauag
Daet

CATANDUANES ISLAND
Virac

Calagua Islands

Trece Martires
Tagaytay
Santa Cruz
Balayan
Lipa
Batangas
Lubang
Lubang Islands

Laguna de Bay
San Pablo
Lucban
Lucena
Tayabas Bay

Catanauan
Marinduque
Boac
Santa Cruz
Pagsanjahan
Calapan
Bongabong

Guinayangan
Guinayan

Guijalo
Naga
Pili
Goa
Baao
Nabua
Iriga
Ligao
Legaspi
Sorsogon

Mount Isarog 1976
Bahi
Mayon Volcano 2462
Rapu Rapu Island
Prieto Diaz

Yog Point
Quinalasag Island
Lagonoy Gulf
Rapu Rapu Island

Mamburao
Mount Halcon 2585
MINDORO
Mount Baco 2497
Dumali Point

Tablas Strait
Duyagan Point

Central
Manaul

Romblon
Tablas Island
Sibuyan Island

Banton
Magallanes
Bulusan
Bulan
Ticao Island
Masbate
Milagros

San Bernardino Strait

Laoang
Catarman
Gamay
Calbayog
Catbalogan

SAMAR
Borongan
Llorente

Arroyo
Pio V.
Corpuz
Panguiranan

Calauit Island
Busuanga Island
CALAMIAN GROUP
Culion Island

Libro Point
Linapacan Island

Cuyo West Pass
Cuyo East Pass

Nabas
Kalibo
Roxas
Pandan
Dumalag
Tibiao
Januauy
Victorias
Silay
Iloilo
Guimaras Island

PANAY
Bantayan
Sagay
Toboso
Bogo
Talisay
La Carlota
Sara
San Carlos
Toledo
Danao
Mandaue
Cebu
Lapu-Lapu

Jintotolo Channel
VISAYAN ISLANDS
Visayan Sea
Biliran Island
Caibiran
Villalon

Camotes Islands
Camotes Sea
CEBU
Ormoc
Burauen
Baybay
Hindang
Sogod
Ubagon
Maasin

LEYTE
Tacloban
Balangiga
MacArthur
Leyte Gulf
Guiuan

Basey
Carigara

DINAGAT ISLAND
Dinagat
Siargao Island

Taytay
Cuyo Islands
Cuyo
San Jose
Caruray
Green Island Bay

Dumaran Island

Honda Bay
Puerto Princesa
Victoria Peaks
PALAWAN

Cagayan Islands

Hinigaran
Binalbagan
Kabankalan
NEGROS
Sipalay

Tanjay
Santander
Tagbilaran
BOHOL

Bayawan
Dumaguete
Bonawon
Squijor
Siquijor Island

Mariboro Bay

Guindulman

BOHOL SEA

Surigao
Jabonga

Mount Mantalingajan 2085
Marangas
Rio Tuba
Bugsuk Island
Balabac
Balabac Island

SULU SEA

Salay
Catarman
Camiguin Island
Mambajao
Butuan
Gingoog
Balingasag
Cagayan de Oro

Tandag
Lianga
Prosperidad

Dipolog
Katipunan
Ozamis
Tudela
Iligan
Iligan Bay
Alubijid
Oroquieta

Impasugong
Malaybalay
Mount Kaatoan 2896
Valencia
Bunawan

Bislig
Mangagoy

Zamboanga Peninsula
Sindangan
Siocon
Liloy
Bonifacio
Pagadian
Marawi
Lake Sultan Alonto

MINDANAO

Siraway
Margosatubig
Vitali
Buenavista
Isabela
Basilan Island

Olutanga Island
Illana Bay

Malabang
Parang

Sultan Kudarat
Cotabato
Datu Piang
Talayan

Midsayap
Kabacan
Kidapawan
Buluan
Lebak

Tibal-og
Panabo
Tagum
Babak
Davao
Mount Apo 2954
Samal Island
Davao Gulf

Baganga
Lupon
Governor Generoso

Balbal
Zamboanga

Moro Gulf
5124

Palimbang
Koronadal
Padada
Digos

Kiamba
Kling
General Santos
Mount Busa 2083
Glan
Malita
Lais
Tiblawan

Cape San Agustin

Jose Abad Santos
Culaman

Sarangani Bay
Tinaca Point
Sarangani Islands

CELEBES SEA

Balabac Strait
Balabac
Balambangan

Tanjong Sempang Mangayau
Pulau Banggi
Pulau Malawali
Kudat
Sikuati
Pulau
Telukan Paitan
Tanjong Jambongan

Kota Belud
Tenghilan
Gunong Kinabalu (Mount Kinabalu) 4101
KINABALU NATIONAL PARK
Ranau
Beluran

Cagayan de Tawi-Tawi
Cagayan Sulu Island

Pulau Mantanani Besar

Kota Kinabalu
Penampang
CROCKER
Tambunan
Gunong Meliau 1336
Keningau

BANJARAN
Gunong Trus Madi 2642
Lanas
Pinangah
Pensiangan

MALAYSIA
BORNEO
SABAH
BANJARAN BRASSEY

Klagan
Sandakan

Sukau
Lamag
Kampung Litang
Kampung Balimbing

Telupid
Tungku
Lahad Datu
Telukan Lahad Datu
Pulau Timbun Mata
Tawau

Pilas Group
Pangutaran Group
Pangutaran

Siasi
Jolo
JOLO GROUP
Jolo Island
Parang

Siasi Island
TAPUL GROUP
Samales Group

SULU ARCHIPELAGO

Bongao
TAWITAWI GROUP
Tawitawi Island

Sitangkai
Sibutu Island

Sibutu Passage

INDONESIA
Pulau Karakalong
Pulau Karakelong
Pulau Miangas

Meters / Feet
3000 / 9840
2000 / 6560
1000 / 3280
500 / 1640
200 / 656
Sea Level
200 / 656
2000 / 6560

W-562900-7A-DR2-1
Copyright © Rand McNally & Co.

0 50 100 150 200 300 400 500 Kilometers
0 50 100 200 300 Miles
Scale 1 : 5,000,000   Lambert Conformal Conic Projection

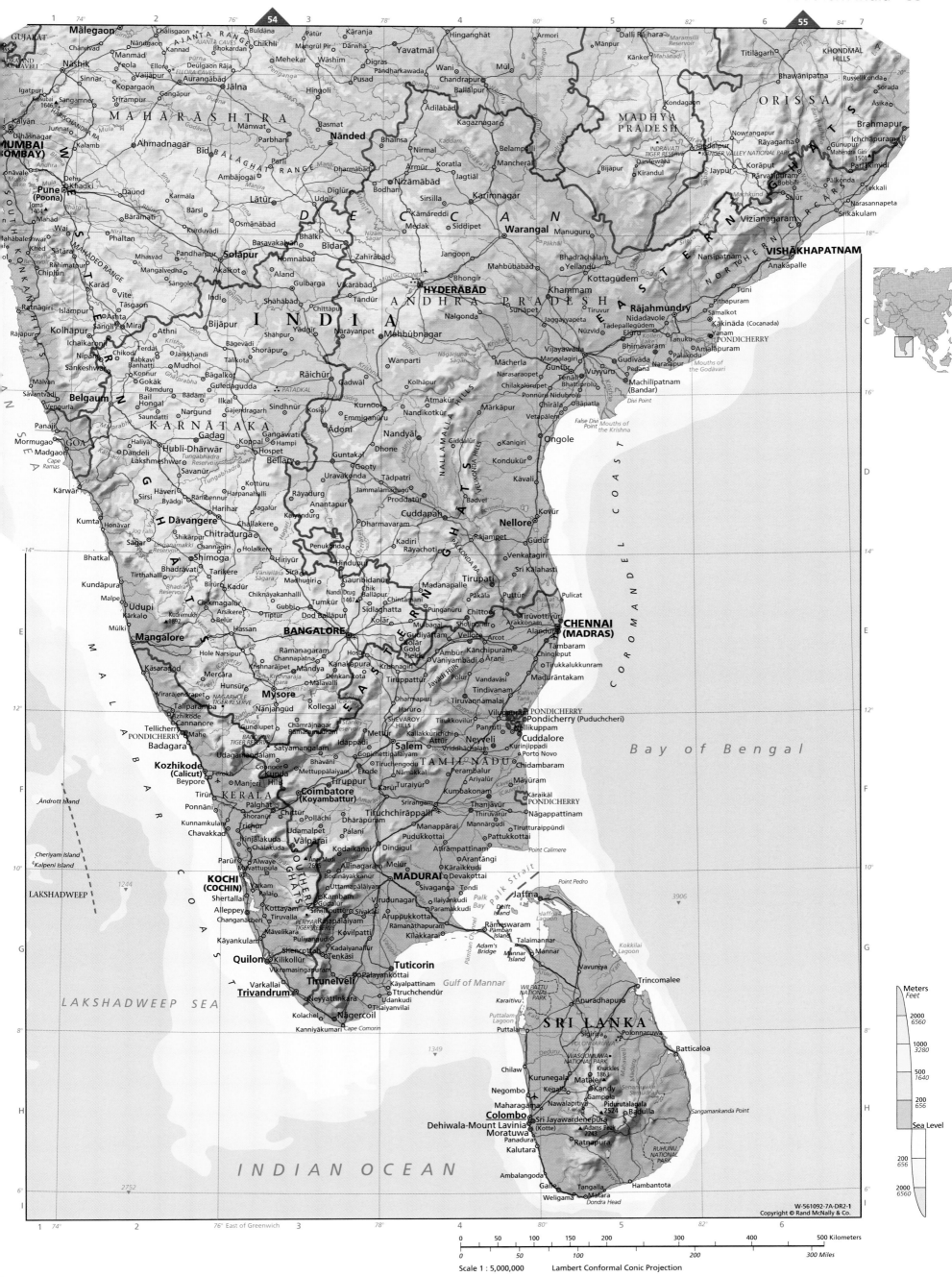

Scale 1 : 5,000,000   Lambert Conformal Conic Projection

Bay of Bengal

Mouths of the Ganges

Ⓐ Area occupied by Pakistan and claimed by India.
Ⓑ Area claimed and occupied by India; status disputed by Pakistan.
Ⓒ Area occupied by China and claimed by India.
Ⓓ Area occupied by India and claimed by China.

W-561091-7A-DR2-1
Copyright © Rand McNally & Co.

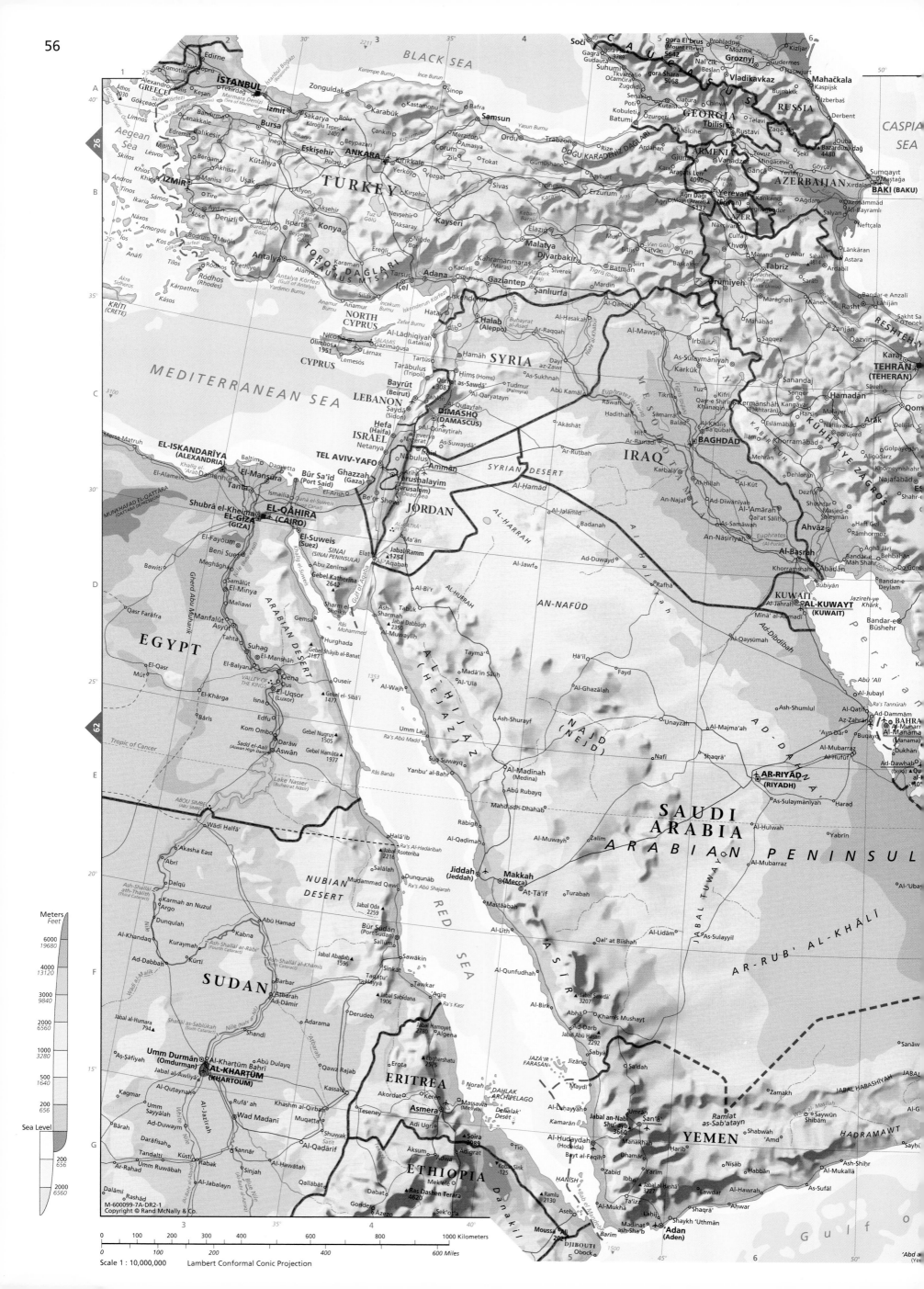

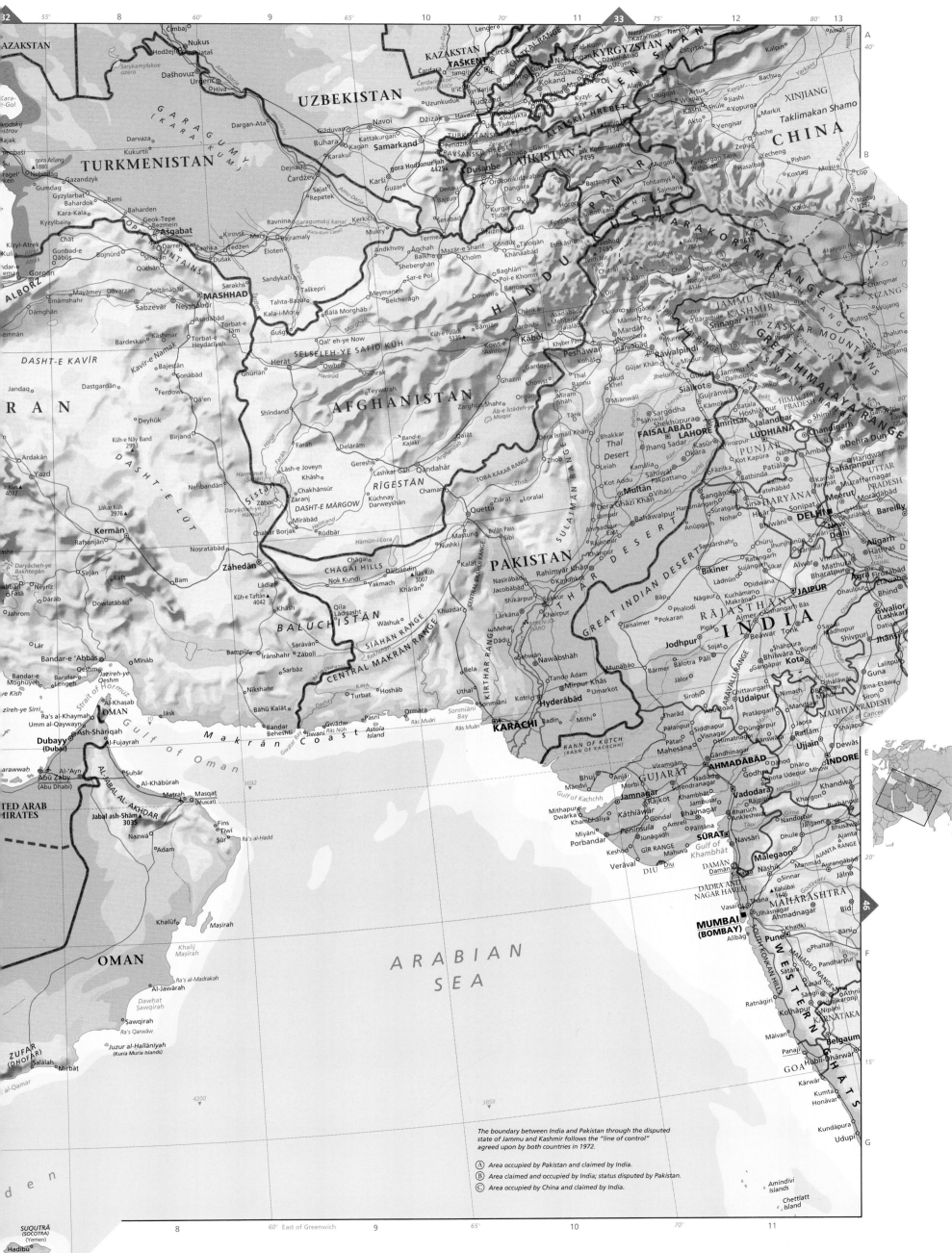

The boundary between India and Pakistan through the disputed
state of Jammu and Kashmir follows the "line of control"
agreed upon by both countries in 1972.

Ⓐ Area occupied by Pakistan and claimed by India.
Ⓑ Area claimed and occupied by India; status disputed by Pakistan.
Ⓒ Area occupied by China and claimed by India.

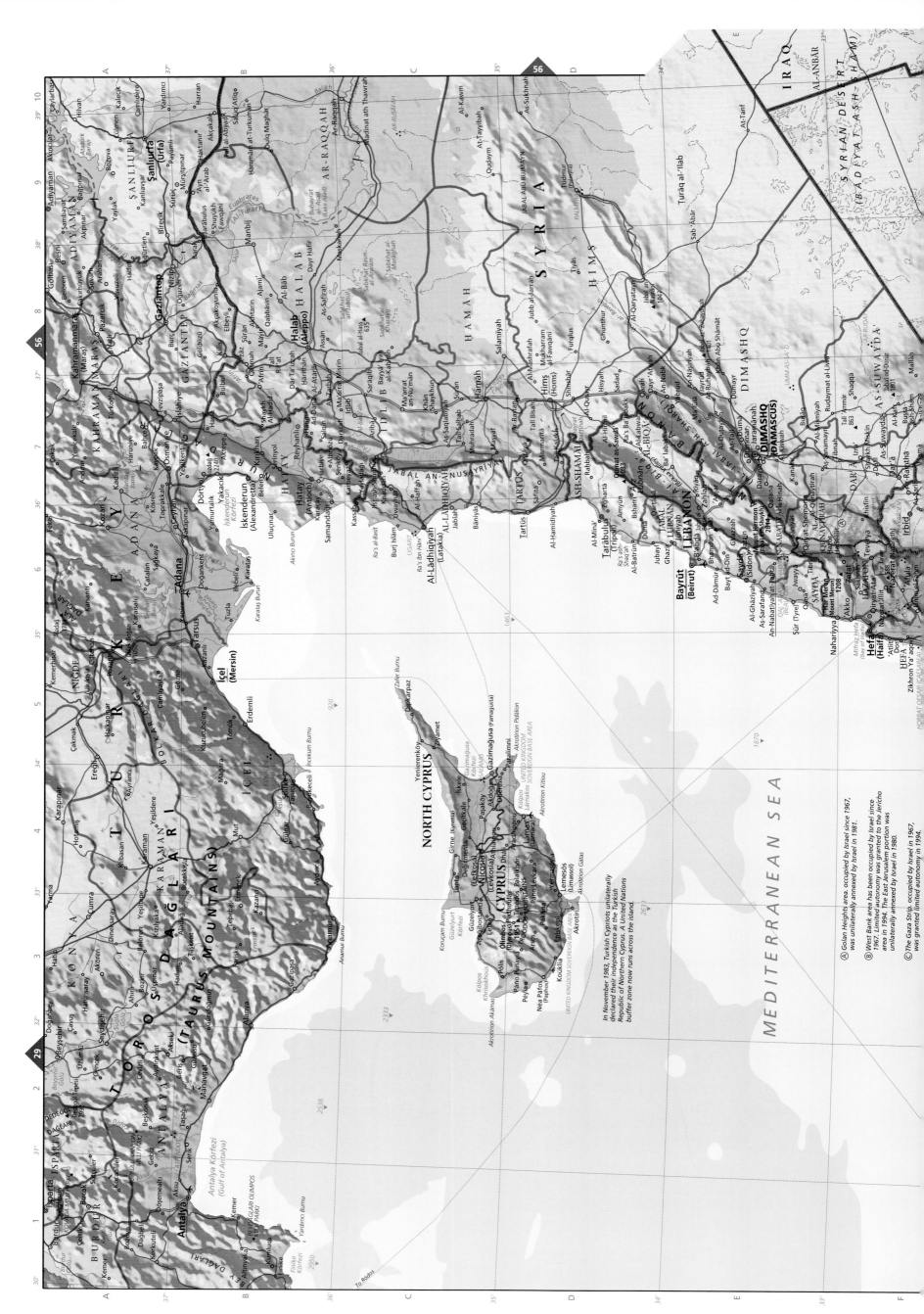

MEDITERRANEAN SEA

NORTH CYPRUS

CYPRUS

In November 1983 Turkish Cypriots unilaterally declared their independence, as the Turkish Republic of Northern Cyprus. A United Nations buffer zone now runs across the island.

Ⓐ Golan Heights area, occupied by Israel since 1967, was unilaterally annexed by Israel in 1981.

Ⓑ West Bank area has been occupied by Israel since 1967. Limited autonomy was granted to the Jericho area in 1994. The East Jerusalem portion was unilaterally annexed by Israel in 1980.

Ⓒ The Gaza Strip, occupied by Israel in 1967, was granted limited autonomy in 1994.

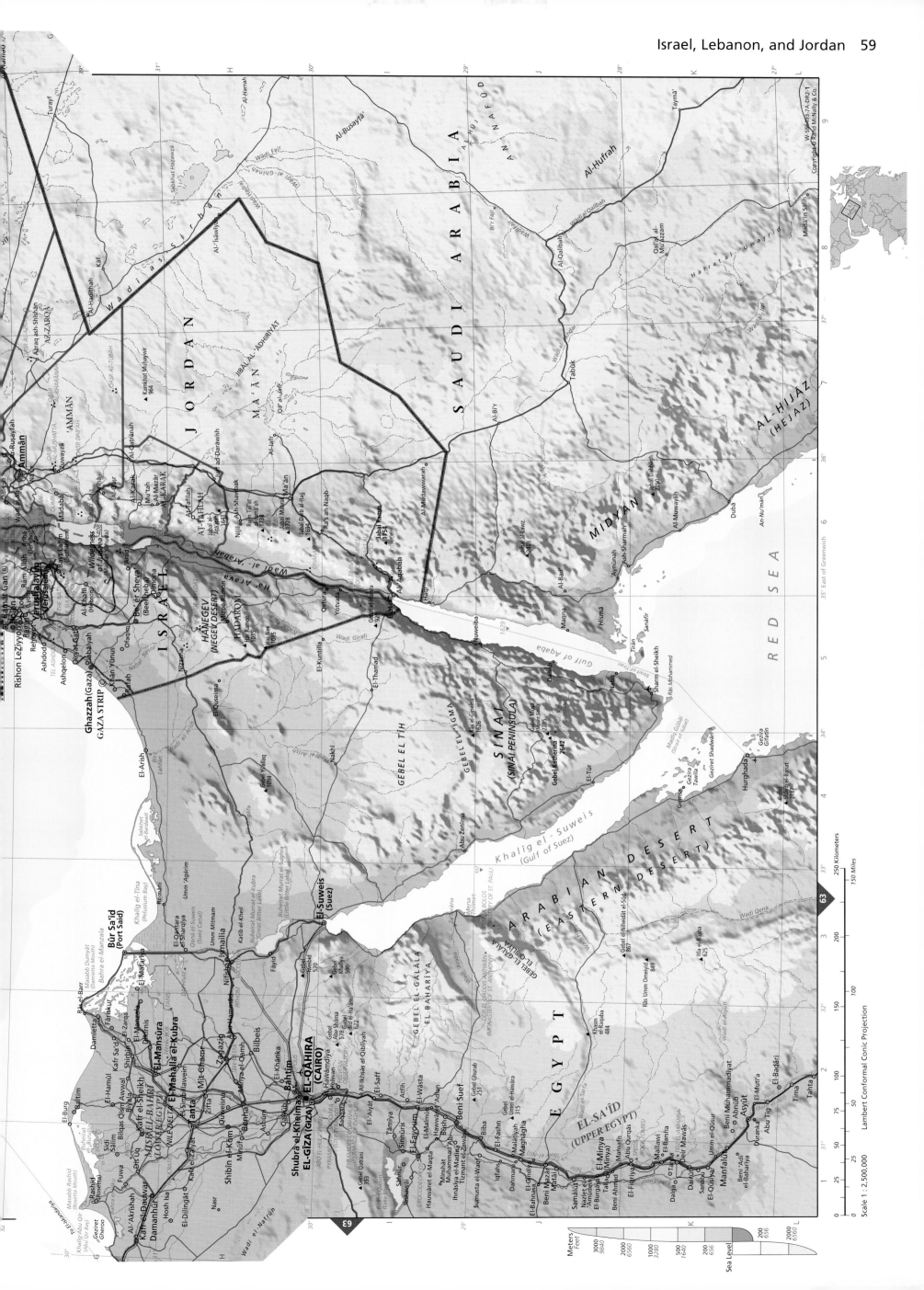

Scale 1 : 2,500,000   Lambert Conformal Conic Projection

Copyright © Rand McNally & Co.

W-594493-7A-DR2-1

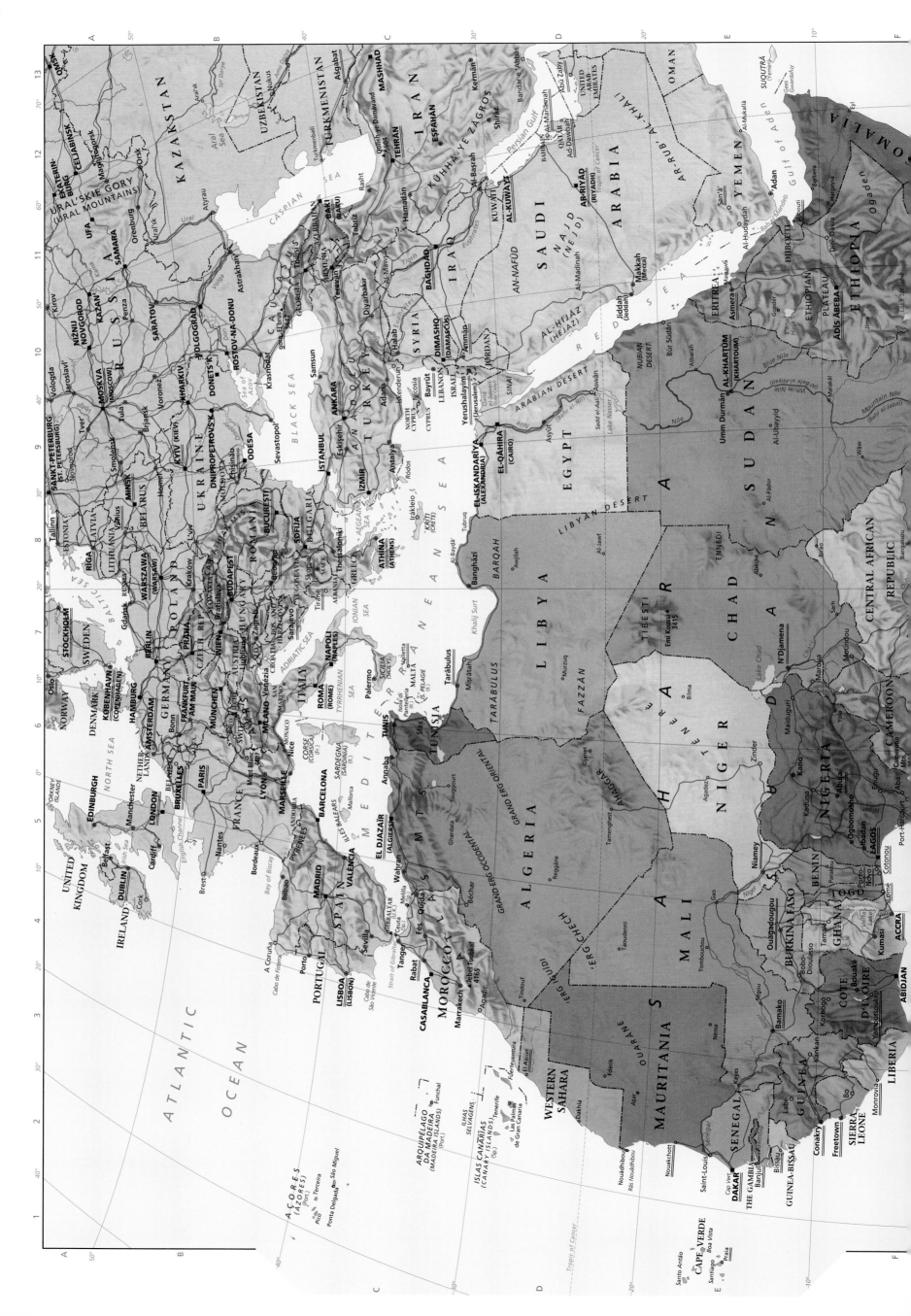

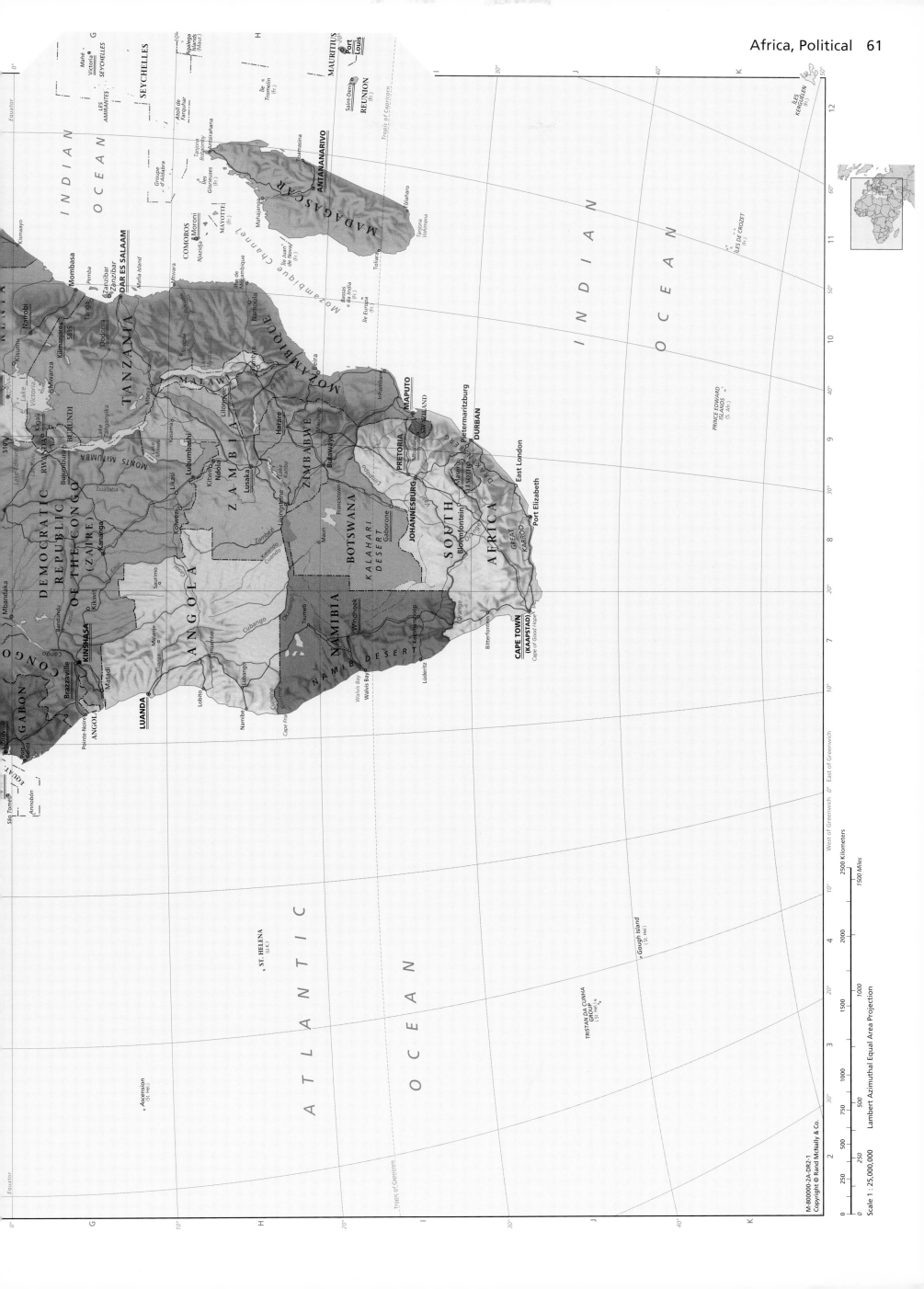

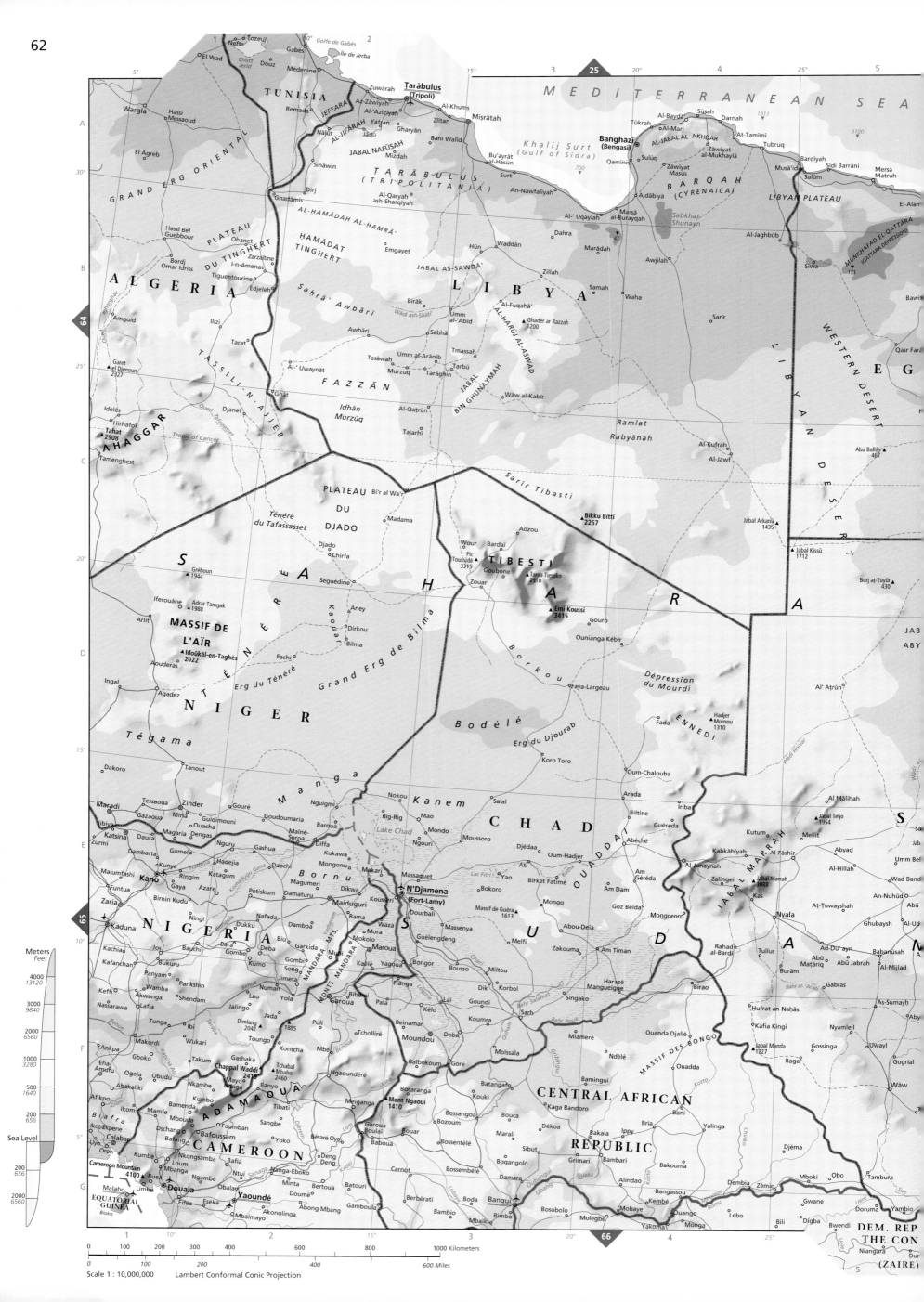

Map Labels

MEDITERRANEAN SEA

TUNISIA
Tozeur
Nefta
El Wad
Douz
Médenine
Golfe de Gabès
Gabès
Île de Jerba
Chott Jerid
Remada
JEFFARA
Zuwārah
Tarābulus (Tripoli)
Al-'Azīzīyah
Al-Khums
Mişrātah
Zlitan
Al-Jifārah
Nālūt
Yafran
Gharyān
JABAL NAFŪSAH
Bani Walid
Mizdah
JABAL NAFŪSAH
Bu'ayrāt al-Ḥasūn
Surt
An-Nawfalīyah
Al-Bayḍā'
Sūsah
Darnah
Tūkrah
Al-Marj
At-Tamīmī
Tubruq
Banghāzī (Bengasi)
AL-JABAL AL-AKHḌAR
Musā'id
Sīdī Barrānī
Mersa Matruh
Salūm
El-Alam
Khalīj Surt (Gulf of Sidra)
Ajdābiyā
BARQAH (CYRENAICA)
Marsā al-Burayqah
Sabkhat Shunayn
Qamīnis
Sulūq
Zāwiyat Masūs
Zāwiyat al-Mukhaylá
Bardīyah

ALGERIA
Wargla
Hassi Messaoud
El Agreb
Hassi Bel Guebbour
PLATEAU DU TINGHERT
Bordj Omar Idriss
Ohanet
Zarzaïtine
I-n-Amenas
Tiguentourine
Edjeleh
Amguid
Ilizi
Tarat
GRAND ERG ORIENTAL
Ghadāmis
Dirj
HAMĀDAT TINGHERT
Al-Ḥamādah al-Ḥamrā'
AL-HAMĀDAH AL-ḤAMRĀ'
Sīnāwin
Emgayet
Waddān
Hūn
Marādah
Dahra
47
Awjilah
Sarir
Waha
Samah
Zillah
JABAL AS-SAWDA'
JABAL AS-SAWDĀ'
Al-Jaghbūb
Siwa
123
MUNKHAFAD EL-QAṬṬĀRA (QATTARA DEPRESSION)

LIBYA
Birāk
Al-Fuqahā'
Umm al-'Abīd
Sabhā
Awbārī
Tasāwah
Umm al-Arānib
Tmassah
Murzuq
Tarāghin
Tarbū
Waha
Ghadér ar Razzah 1200
AL-HARŪJ AL-ASWAD
JABAL BIN GHUNAYMAH
Wāw al-Kabīr
Sarir
Al-Kufrah
Al-Jawf
Qasr Farāfirah

AHAGGAR
Idelès
Hirhafok
Tahat 2908
Tamenghest
Garet el Djenoun 2327
TASSILI-N-AJJER
Ghāt
Djanet
Oued Tin-Tarabine
Tamenghest

FAZZĀN
Sahrā' Awbārī
Al-'Uwaynāt
Tasāwah
Idhān Murzūq
Al-Qaṭrūn
Tajarhi
Tropic of Cancer

WESTERN DESERT
LIBYAN PLATEAU
Qasr Farāfirah
Abu Ballās 467
LIBYAN DESERT
Jabal Kissū 1712
Burj at-Tuyūr 430
Jabal Arkanū 1435

S A H A R A

PLATEAU DU DJADO
Bi'r al Wa'r
Madama
Ténéré du Tafassasset
Djado
Chirfa
Séguédine
Wour
Pic Toussidé 3315
Bardaï
Aozou
Bikkū Bītti 2267
Zouar
Goubone
TIBESTI
Tarso Tieroko 2910
Émi Koussi 3415
Gouro
Ounianga Kébir
Borkou
Faya-Largeau
Dépression du Mourdi
Al' Atrūn

SĀHEL
Gréboun 1944
Iférouâne
Adrar Tamgak 1988
Arlit
MASSIF DE L'AÏR
Idoûkâl-en-Taghès 2022
Aouderas
Aney
Dirkou
Bilma
Fachi
Erg du Ténéré
Grand Erg de Bilma
Ingal
Agadez

NIGER
Tégama
Dakoro
Tanout
Maradi
Tessaoua
Zinder
Gouré
Gazaoua
Mirria
Guidimouni
Ouacha
Goudoumaria
Nguigmi
Manga
Kanem
Ibiya
Katsina
Daura
Magaria
Dengas
Nguru
Gashua
Diffa
Maïné-Soroa
Rig-Rig
Baroua
Lake Chad
Nokou
Mao
Mondo
Ngouri
Salal
Arada
Oum-Chalouba
Koro Toro
Bodélé
Erg du Djourab
Fada
ENNEDI
Hadjer Mornou 1310

Zurmi
Dambarta
Gumel
Kunya
Hadejia
Hadejia
Dapchi
Kukawa
Mongonu
Makari
Massaguet
Djédaa
Oum-Hadjer
Ati
Yao
Biltine
Guéréda
Iriba
Al Māliḩah
Jabal Teljo 1954

CHAD
Moussoro
OUADDAÏ
Abéché
Am-Géréda
Am Dam
Goz Beïda
Kutum
Al-Fāshir
Kabkābīyah
Mellit
Abyaḍ
Al-Hillah
Zalingei
Jabal Marrah 3088
Kas
Nyala
JABAL MARRAH

NIGERIA
Kano
Malumfashi
Ringim
Katagum
Azare
Potiskum
Damaturu
Maiduguri
Dikwa
Kousséri
N'Djamena (Fort-Lamy)
Dourbali
Bokoro
Massaguet
Massenya
Lac Fitri
Birket Fatimé
Mongororo
Abou-Deïa
Melfi
Zakouma
Am Timan
Harazé Mangueigne
Birao
Rahad al-Bardi
Tullus
Ad-Du'ayn
Buram
Abū Maṭāriq
Abū Jabrah
Al-Mijlad
An-Nuhūd
Ghubaysh
Al-Ud
Babanūsah

Zaria
Kaduna
Kachia
Kafanchan
Birnin Kudu
Ningi
Bauchi
Jos
Bukuru
Panyam
Pankshin
Dukku
Nafada
Gombe
Kumo
Deba
Garkida
Biu
Damboa
Bama
Mora
Mokolo
Maroua
Guélengdeng
Bongor
Bousso
Dik
Korbol
Goundi
Koumra
Fianga
Miltou
Laï
Kélo
Bénoué
Sarh
Moïssala
Maro
Singako
Ouanda Djallé
Kafia Kingi
Hufrat an-Nahās
As-Sumayh
Nyamlell
Uwayl
Gossinga
Raga
Gogrial
Wāw

CAMEROON
Keffi
Kafanchan
Wamba
Akwanga
Shendam
Nassarawa
Lafia
Tunga
Ibi
Makurdi
Gboko
Wukari
Takum
Gashaka
Chappal Waddi 2419
Mayo Alim
Maga
Nkambe
Bamenda
Mbouda
Dschang
Bafang
Kumba
Nkongsamba
Bafia
Ntui
Nanga-Eboko
Bertoua
Batouri
Obudu
Ikom
Mamfe
Foumban
Yoko
Deng Deng
Doumé
Meiganga
Bétaré Oya
Garoua Boulaï
Bocaranga
Mont Ngaoui 1410
Bozoum
Bossangoa
Bossentélé
Kaga Bandoro
Bamingui
Ouadda
Massif des Bongo
Jabal Mānda 1227
Ndélé
Bria
Yalinga
Bakouma
Dimlang 2042
Tchabal Mbabo 2460
Poli
Tchollire
Toungo
Kontcha
Jada
Jalingo
Dimlang
Garoua
Pala
Beinamar
Moundou
Doba
Bébédjia
Gore
Baïbokoum
Goundi
ADAMAOUA
Ngaoundéré
Tibati
Banyo
Sangbé
Foumbot
Bafoussam
Bamenda
MAYO Alim
MANDARA MTS
MONTS MANDARA
Mubi
Song
Jimeta
Numan
Yola
Lau
Benue
Kotcha
Gombi
Bara

CENTRAL AFRICAN REPUBLIC
Batangafo
Kaga Bandoro
Kouki
Bossangoa
Bouca
Bozoum
Grimari
Bambari
Ippy
Bakala
Bogangolo
Damara
Sibut
Dékoa
Bogangolo
Bangui
Bimbo
Boda
Mbaïki
Bosobolo
Moboye
Mobaye
Ouango
Kembé
Dembia
Zémio
Mboki
Obo
Tambura
Bangassou
Bakouma
Gwane
Djéma

SUDAN

EQUATORIAL GUINEA
Malabo
Bioko
Cameroon Mountain 4100
Limbe
Buea
Douala
Edéa
Yaoundé
Mbalmayo
Akonolinga
Obala
Eséka
Ngambè
Mbanga
Loum
Kumba
Oron
Calabar
Uyo
Ikot-Ekpene
Afikpo
Eha-Amufu
Ankpa
Ogoja
Abakaliki
Biafra
Onitsha
Sanaga
Bertoua
Abong Mbang
Bali
Gwane
DEM. REP OF THE CONGO (ZAIRE)
Yakoma
Yambio
Doruma
Niangara
Uele
Dungu
Bondo

Elevation Scale

Map Scale

Scale 1 : 10,000,000
Lambert Conformal Conic Projection

0 100 200 300 400 600 800 1000 Kilometers

0 100 200 400 600 Miles

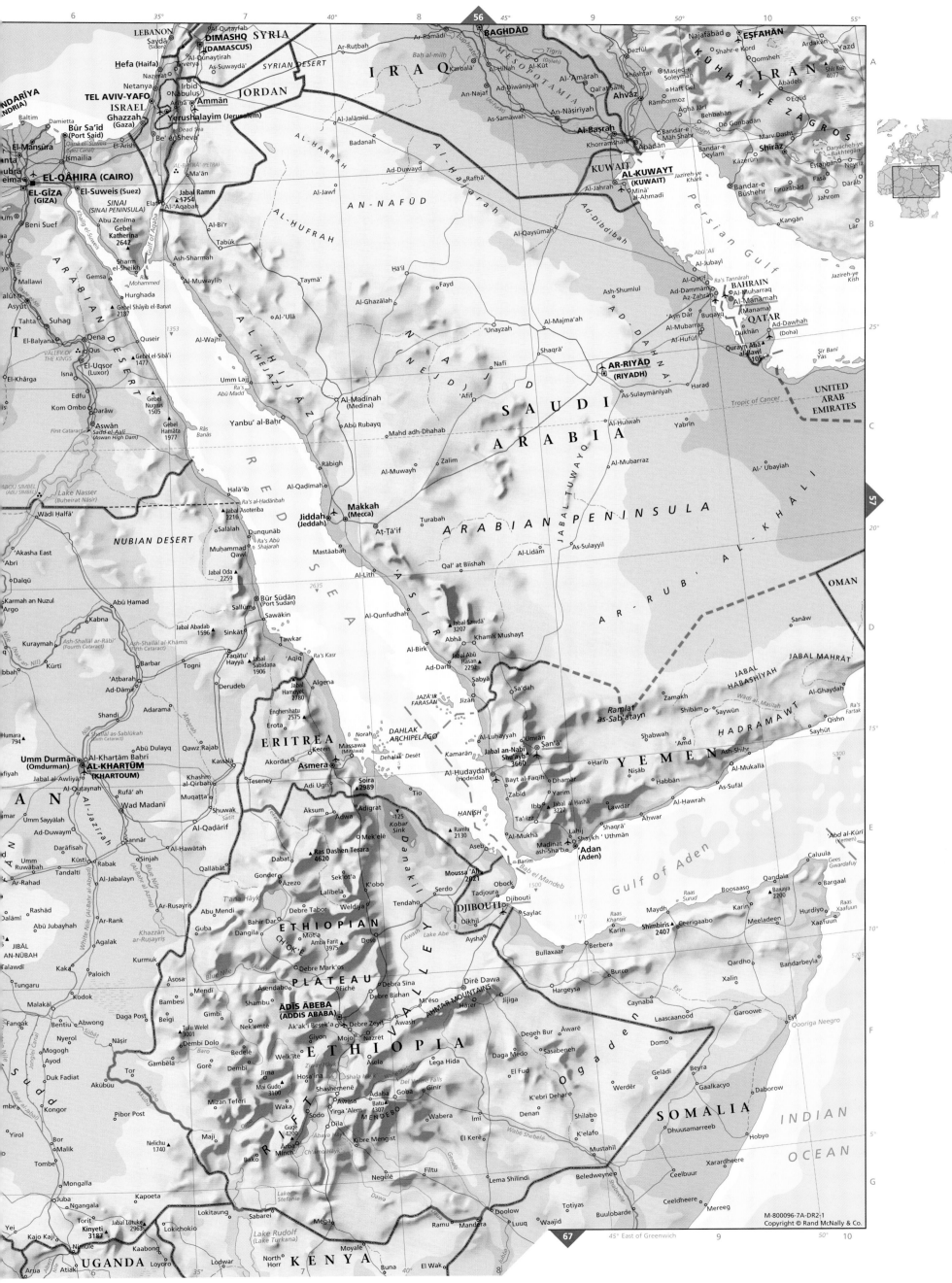

M-800096-7A-DR2-1
Copyright © Rand McNally & Co.

CHAD

N'Djamena

CAMEROON

Yaoundé

MONTS DE CRISTAL

GABON

CONGO

Libreville

EQUATORIAL GUINEA

Malabo

Cameroon Mtn. 4100

Pico de Santa Isabel 3008

BIOKO

Bata

Isla de Corisco

SAO TOME AND PRINCIPE

Principe

Santo Antonio

Pico de São Tomé 2024

SÃO TOMÉ

Porto Alegre

Annobón (Eq. Guineé)

Bight of Biafra

Gulf of Guinea

Niger Delta

Port-Harcourt

Calabar

Douala

NIGER

NIGERIA

Kano

Abuja

Lagos

LAGOS

Ibadan

Ogbomosho

Ilorin

Porto-Novo

Cotonou

BENIN

TOGO

Lomé

Niamey

BURKINA FASO

Ouagadougou

Bobo-Dioulasso

GHANA

ACCRA

Kumasi

Sekondi-Takoradi

Cape Coast

Slave Coast

Gold Coast

Bight of Benin

MALI

Bamako

Tombouctou (Timbuktu)

Gao

NIGER

CÔTE D'IVOIRE

ABIDJAN

Yamoussoukro

Bouaké

Grand-Bassam

Ivory Coast

GUINEA

Conakry

SIERRA LEONE

Freetown

LIBERIA

Monrovia

Grain Coast

SENEGAL

DAKAR

THE GAMBIA

Banjul

GUINEA-BISSAU

Bissau

Saint-Louis

CAPE VERDE

SANTO ANTÃO

SÃO NICOLAU

Mindelo

Sal

Boa Vista

Maio

SANTIAGO

Praia

Pico 2829

Fogo

Brava

ATLANTIC OCEAN

Gulf of Guinea

a   Same scale as main map

M-800097-7A-DR2-1
Copyright © Rand McNally & Co.

Lambert Conformal Conic Projection

Scale 1 : 10,000,000

Meters   Feet
4000 13120
3000 9840
2000 6560
1000 3280
500 1640
200 656
Sea Level
200 656
2000 6560

62

65

68

NIGER

CHAD

SUDAN

NIGERIA

CAMEROON

CENTRAL AFRICAN

REPUBLIC

EQUATORIAL

GUINEA

SAO TOME

AND PRINCIPE

GABON

CONGO

DEMOCRATIC REPUBLIC

OF THE CONGO

(ZAIRE)

ANGOLA

ATLANTIC

OCEAN

Gulf of Guinea

Bight of Biafra

Meters
Feet

4000
13120

3000
9840

2000
6560

1000
3280

500
1640

200
656

Sea Level

200
656

2000
6560

M-80095-7A-DR2-1
Copyright © Rand McNally & Co.

0   100   200   300   400   600   800   1000 Kilometers
0   100   200   400   600 Miles

Scale 1 : 10,000,000   Sinusoidal Projection

ATLANTIC OCEAN

DEMOCRATIC REPUBLIC OF THE CONGO (ZAIRE)

ANGOLA

ZAMBIA

NAMIBIA

BOTSWANA

SOUTH AFRICA

KALAHARI DESERT

NAMIB DESERT

GREAT NAMAQUALAND

Tropic of Capricorn

LUANDA

Windhoek

Walvis Bay

CAPE TOWN (KAAPSTAD)

Port Elizabeth

JOHANNESBURG

Bloemfontein

Lusaka

Gaborone

Kolwezi

Kitwe

Lubumbashi (Élisabethville)

Mbuji-Mayi (Bakwanga)

Meters
Feet
3000 9840
2000 6560
1000 3280
500 1640
200 656
Sea Level
200 656
2000 6560

M-800092-7A-DR2-1
Copyright © Rand McNally & Co.

0   100   200   300   400   600   800   1000 Kilometers
0   100   200   400   600 Miles
Scale 1 : 10,000,000   Lambert Conformal Conic Projection

INDIAN OCEAN

SEYCHELLES

COMOROS

ARCHIPEL DES COMORES

MAYOTTE

Moroni
Kartala
2361
Njazidja
Nzwani
Mwali
Fomboni
Mutsamudu
Dzaoudzi

Groupe
d'Aldabra
Assomption
Atoll de
Cosmoledo
Astove
St. Pierre
Atoll de
Providence
Atoll de
Farquhar

Îles
Glorieuses
(Fr.)

TANZANIA

Dodoma
Mpwapwa
Kilosa
Mikumi
Morogoro
Kidatu
Iringa
Rufiji
Kisiju
Mafia Island
Kilindoni
Utete
Ifakara
Mahenge
Kilwa Kivinje
Kilwa Masoko
Njinjo
Zinga Mulike
Liwale
Nachingwea
Lindi
Mtama
Mikindani
Mtwara
Palma
Diaca
Mueda
Macomia
Mucojo
Quissanga
Pemba
Balama

Zanzibar
Kizimkazi
Bagamoyo
DAR ES SALAAM

MALAWI

Lake Nyasa

MOZAMBIQUE

Lichinga
Niassa
Catur
Maua
Montepuez
Ancuabe
Cuamba
Malema
Ribaué
Mecuburi
Monapo
Nacala
Namapa
Memba
Lúrio
Belém
Marrupa
Mecula
Metangula
Nantulo
Nampula
Lumbo
Ilha de Moçambique
Mogincual
Nametil
Angoche

MADAGASCAR

ANTANANARIVO

Antsiranana
Tanjona
Bobaomby
Ambohitra
1475
Nosy Mitsio
Nosy Be
Andoany
Ambilobe
Iharaña
Ambanja
Maromokotro
2876
TSARATANANA
Sambava
Analalava
Antsohihy
Andapa
Antalaha
Maroantsetra
Bealanana
Mahajanga
Soalala
Marovoay
Mandritsara
Rantabe
Mampikony
Tsaratanana
Andilamena
Ambodifototra
Nosy
Sainte Marie
Besalampy
Madirovalo
Maevatanana
Andriamena
Maintirano
Mahabe
Morafenobe
Kandreho
Farihy
Alaotra
Fenoarivo
Atsinanana
Ankazobe
Ambatondrazaka
Toamasina
Nosy
Barren
Bekopaka
Tsiroanomandidy
Arivonimamo
Ankavandra
Soavinandriana
Ampasimanolotra
Belo-Tsiribihina
Miandrivazo
Tsiafajavona
2643
Ambatolampy
Moramanga
Vatomandry
Morondava
Mahabo
Malaimbandy
Antsirabe
Manjakandriana
Mahanoro
Belo-sur-Mer
Mandabe
Ambatofinandrahana
Ambositra
Nosy-Varika
Manja
Ambohimahasoa
Andranopasy
Fianarantsoa
Mananjary
Morombe
Beroroha
Ifanadiana
Befandriana
Avaratra
Ankazoabo
Ihosy
Ambalavao
Manakara
Boby
2658
Vohipeno
Manombo
Atsimo
Ranohira
Vondrozo
Vohitrafarahana
Sakaraha
Betroka
Vangaindrano
Toliara
Bezaha
Ejeda
Bekily
Beraketa
Midongy Atsimo
Itampolo
Ampanihy
Manantenina
Androka
Amboasary
Tsiombe
Ambovombe
Tôlañaro
Tanjona
Vohimena

INDIAN
OCEAN

Tropic of Capricorn

Mozambique Channel

Île Juan de Nova
(Fr.)

Bassas da India
(Fr.)

Île Europa
(Fr.)

a Same scale as main map

INDIAN OCEAN

Port Louis
MAURITIUS
Curepipe
Piton de la Petite
Rivière Noire
828
Mahébourg
Saint-Denis
Piton des Neiges
3070
Saint-Paul
Saint-Pierre
RÉUNION
(Fr.)

MASCARENE ISLANDS

East of Greenwich

b Same scale as main map

INDIAN OCEAN

SEYCHELLES

Groupe
d'Aldabra
St. Pierre
Atoll de
Providence
Assomption
Atoll de
Cosmoledo
Astove
Atoll de
Farquhar
Agalega
Islands
(Maur.)

East of Greenwich

SEYCHELLES

Praslin
La Digue
Silhouette
Victoria
Mahé
Poivre
Atoll
Desroches
Île Plate
LES
AMIRANTES
Alphonse
Coëtivy

ATLANTIC OCEAN

Meters / Feet

3000 / 9840
2000 / 6560
1000 / 3280
500 / 1640
200 / 656
Sea Level

200 / 656
2000 / 6560

KAOKO VELD
KUNENE
Fransfontein
Khorixas
Outjo
Otjiwarongo
WATERBERG PLATOPARK
OTJOZONDJUPA
Otjozondjou
NGAMILAND
Eiseb
Sehithwa
Lake Ngami
Toteng
MAKGADIKGADI PANS GAME RESE
Khasebake

Sorris-Sorris
Sukses
Kalkfeld
Omatako 2289
Osire Süd
Otjinene
Rooibokiaagte
Groot Laagte
Mabeleapodi
Rakops
Xhur

Brandberg 2579
Uis
Okombahe
Omaruru
Etjo 2085
Onbotozo 1916
Hochfeld
Epukiro Epukiro
Rietfontein
Rietfontein
Ghanzi
Lethiahau
Khomodimo

Erongo 2305
Usakos
Karibib
Wilhelmstal
Okahandja
DAMARALAND
Steinhausen
OMAHEKE
GHANZI
CENTRAL KALAHARI GAME RESERVE

Cape Cross (Kaap Kruis)
Hentiesbaai
ERONGO
Otjimbingwe
Khomas Hochland
Windhoek
Omitara
Witvlei
Gobabis
Tshootsha
Mamuno
Okwa
Tswaane
Buitsivango
BOTS

Skeleton Coast
Arandis
KHOMAS
Seeis
Takachu
Okwa

Swakopmund
Walvis Bay
NAMIBIA
Dordabis
Leonardville
Kule
KALAHARI
Kang
KUTSE GAM RESERVE
KWENEN

Walvis Bay (Walvisbaai)
Rehoboth
Aminuis
KGALAGADI
Kokong
Sekoma

Tropic of Capricorn
Sandwich Bay
Ilhea Point
Uhlenhorst
Aranos
DESERT
Khakhea
SOUTH

Conception Bay
NAMIB-NAUKLUFT PARK
Kalkrand
Stampriet
MABUASEHUBE GAME RESERVE
Werda

214
Meobbaai
Nomtsas
HARDAP
Mariental
Gochas
Aub
GEMSBOK NATIONAL PARK
Maralaleng
Pomfret
Tosca
Tshidil

Hollandsbird Island
GREAT NAMAQUALAND (GROOT NAMALAND)
Maltahöhe
Gibeon
Witbobisvlei
Aub
KALAHARI GEMSBOK NATIONAL PARK
Tshabong
Morokweng

Schwarz-rand
Tses
Koës
Twee Rivieren
Khuis
Van Zylsrus
NOR
Ganyesa
Vryb

Hottentotsbaai
Helmeringhausen
Berseba
Molopo
Askham
Kuruman
Sonstraal
Hotazel
Tsineng
Dibeng
Reivi
Buxt

Diaz Point
Lüderitz
Aus
Bethanien
Keetmanshoop
Aroab
BECHUANALAND
Olifantshoek
Sishen 1855
Kuruman
Jan Keh
Barkly West
War

Possession Island
HUIB-HOCH PLATEAU
Seeheim
Gawachab
Schloffenstein 2202
GROOT KARASBERGE
Molopo
Postmasburg
Danielskuil
Ulco
Delportsh

1654
HUNSBERGE
KARAS
Holoog
Grünau
Kanus
Karasburg
Upington
Keimoes
Kakamas
Grobblershoop
Putsonderwater
GRIQUALAND WEST
Campbell
Ritch
Kimber
Jacob

Sendelingsdrif
Oranjemund
Orange (Oranje)
Noordoewer
Warmbad
AUGRABIES FALLS NATIONAL PARK
Augrabiesvalle
Onseepkans
Bladgrond-Noord
Keimoes
Kenhardt
Marydale
Griekwastad
Douglas
Niekerkshoop
SOUTH A
Belr

Alexander Bay
Vioolsdrif
Goodhouse
Pofadder
Namies
BUSHMAN LAND
Prieska
Hopetown
Luc

LITTLE NAMAQUALAND (KLEIN NAMALAND)
Steinkopf
Aggeneys
Marydale
Strydenburg
Petrusvill

Port Nolloth
Nababeep
Okiep
Springbok
Buffels
Groot vloer
NORTHERN CAPE
Vanwyksvlei
Brandvlei
Carnarvon
Victoria West
Philipstown

150
Gamoep
Kamieskroon
Sak
Sak
Williston
Loxton
Hutchinson
Richmond
De Aar
Hanover
N

Hondeklipbaai
Garies
Loeriesfontein
Sakrivier
Krom
Vosburg
Britstown
Mynfontein

Nieuwoudtville
Calvinia
 ATLANTIC OCEAN

Lutzville
Vanrhynsdorp
Nelspoort
Murraysburg
Graaff-Reinet
Bethes

Vredendal
Klawer
Williston
Fraserburg
Nie

1964
Lambert's Bay
Clanwilliam
Elandsvlei
Bontberg 1922
Sutherland
KAROO NATIONAL PARK
Aberdeen
Kendrew

Wuppertal
To-Wadrif
Merweville
Beaufort West
GREAT KARROO (GROOT KARROO)
Jansenvil

Cape Columbine
Aurora
Citrusdal
Laingsburg
Prince Albert
Willowmore
Klip

Vredenburg
Velddrif
Piketberg
Porterville
WESTERN CAPE
GROOT-SWARTBERGE
Calitzdorp
Oudtshoorn
KOUGABERGE
Uniondale
Joubertina

Saldanha
Hopefield
Moorreesburg
Touwsrivier
Ladismith
Zoar
Steytlerville

Darling
Malmesbury
Tulbagh
Ceres
De Doorns
Montagu
LITTLE KARROO (KLEIN KARROO)
Van Wyksdorp
Herbertsdale
Avontuur
Humar

Wellington
Worcester
Ashton
Riversdale
Groot
Brakrivier
George
Knysna
Cape Seal

CAPE TOWN (KAAPSTAD)
Bellville
Paarl
Robertson
Caledon
Klipdal
BONTEBOK NATIONAL PARK
Witsand
Stilbaai
Mosselbaai (Mossel Bay)
Plettenbergbaai

Somerset West
Stellenbosch
Strand
Swellendam

Simon's Town
Cape of Good Hope (Kaap die Goeie Hoop)
False Bay
Hermanus
Protem
Bredasdorp
Elim
Kaap Agulhas

Walker Bay
Danger Point
Gansbaai
Kaap Agulhas
Krui

0 100 200 300 400 500 600 700 800 900 1000 Kilometer
0 100 200 300 400 500 600 Miles
Scale 1 : 5,000,000   Lambert Conformal Conic Projection

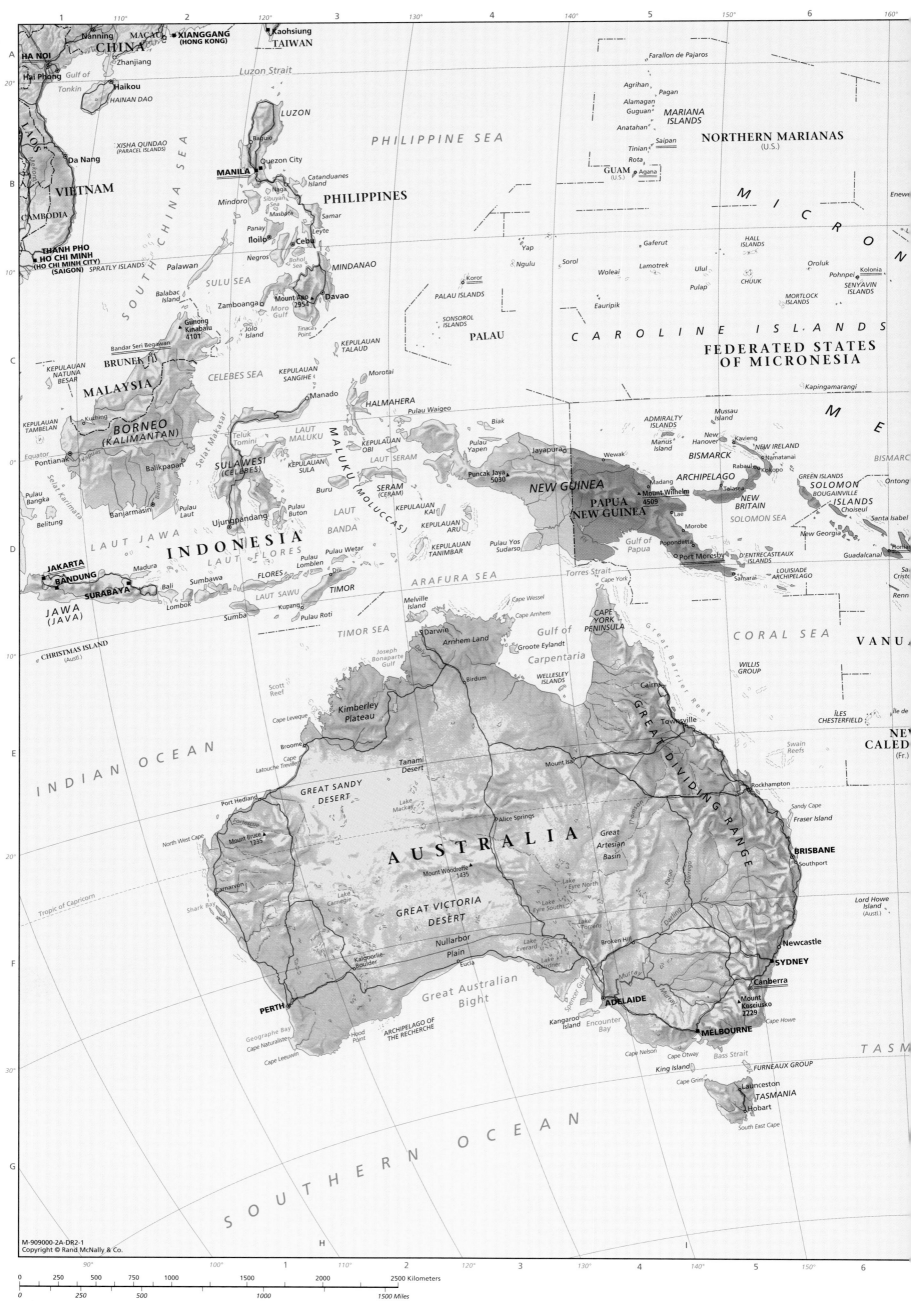

M-909000-2A-DR2-1
Copyright © Rand McNally & Co.

0   250   500   750   1000   1500   2000   2500 Kilometers

0   250   500   1000   1500 Miles

Scale 1 : 25,000,000   Lambert Azimuthal Equal Area Projection

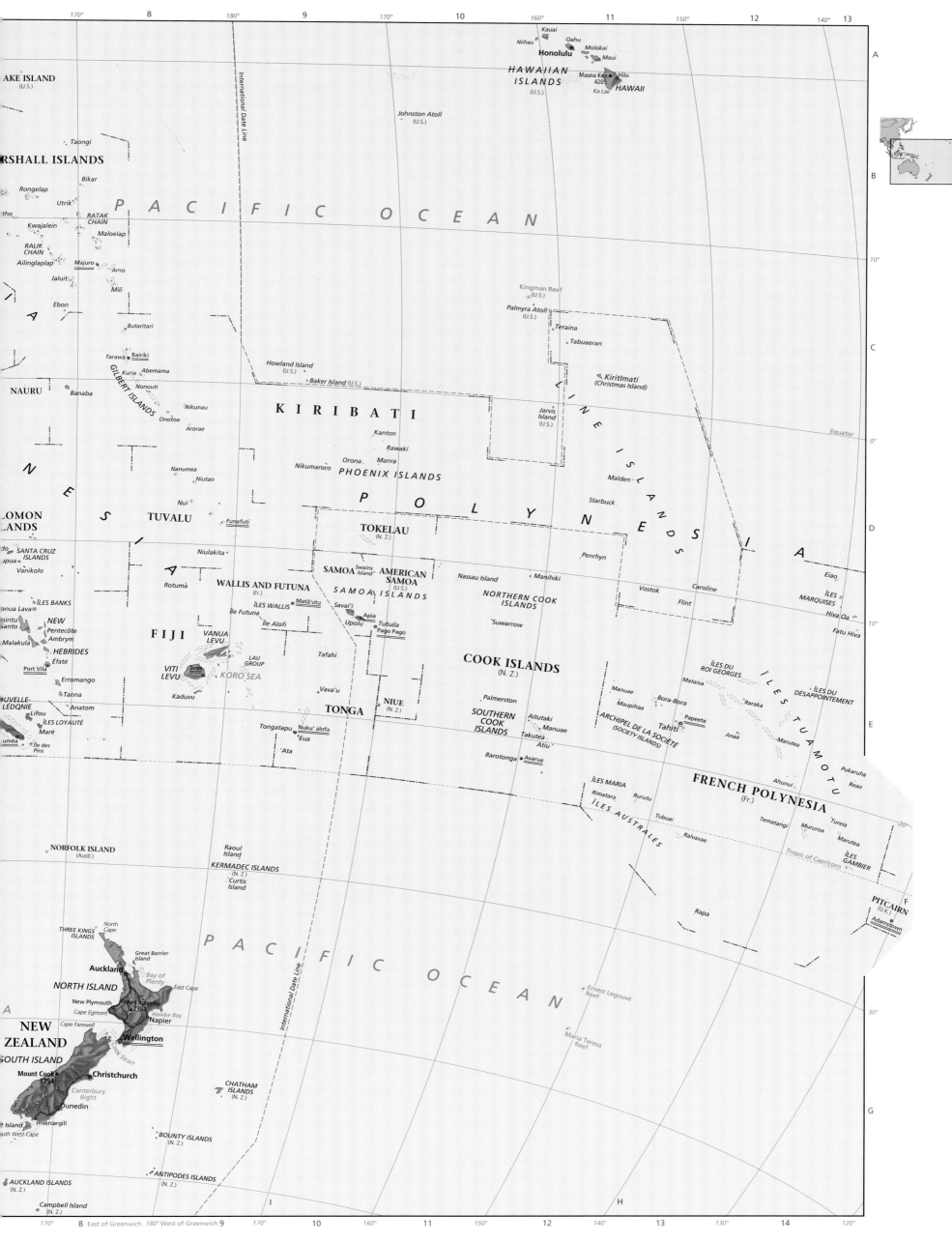

AKE ISLAND
(U.S.)

Taongi

RSHALL ISLANDS

Bikar

Rongelap
Utrik

RATAK
CHAIN

tho
Kwajalein
Maloelap

RALIK
CHAIN
Ailinglaplap
Majuro
Arno

Jaluit
Mili

Ebon

Butaritari

NAURU   Banaba

Tarawa Bairiki
Kuria   Abemama
Nonouti

NAURU   Banaba

Nikunau

Onotoa
Arorae

Nanumea
Niutao

Nui

TUVALU   Funafuti

Niulakita

SANTA CRUZ
ISLANDS
pua
Vanikolo

Rotumà

WALLIS AND FUTUNA
(Fr.)

ÎLES BANKS

anua Lava
piritu
anto
NEW
Pentecôte
Ambrym
Malakula

HEBRIDES

Port Vila
Éfaté
Erromango

UVELLE-
LÉDONIE
Tanna
Anatom

Lifou
ÎLES LOYAUTÉ
Maré

umèa
Île des
Pins

PACIFIC OCEAN

Johnston Atoll
(U.S.)

Kingman Reef
(U.S.)

Palmyra Atoll
(U.S.)
Teraina

Tabuaeran

Howland Island
(U.S.)
Baker Island (U.S.)

KiritImati
(Christmas Island)

Jarvis
Island
(U.S.)

KIRIBATI

Kanton

Rawaki

Orona   Manra
Nikumaroro
PHOENIX ISLANDS

Malden

Starbuck

Vostok
Caroline

Flint

POLYNESIA

TOKELAU
(N. Z.)

Penrhyn

SAMOA Swains
Island
AMERICAN
SAMOA
(U.S.)

Nassau Island   Manihiki

SAMOA ISLANDS

NORTHERN COOK
ISLANDS

ÎLES WALLIS Matà'utu
Île Futuna
Île Alofi

Savai'i
Upolu   Apia
Tutuila
Pago Pago

'Suwarrow

FIJI

VANUA
LEVU

Tafahi

VITI
LEVU   Suva

LAU
GROUP

COOK ISLANDS
(N. Z.)

KORO SEA

Kaduvu

Vava'u

TONGA

NIUE
(N. Z.)

Palmerston

SOUTHERN
COOK
ISLANDS

Aitutaki
Manuae
Takutea
Atiu

Tongatapu Nuku'alofa
'Eua

'Ata

Rarotonga Avarua

Manuae
Maupihaa
Bora-Bora

ÎLES DU
ROI GEORGES

Mataiva

Raraka

ARCHIPEL DE LA SOCIÉTÉ
(SOCIETY ISLANDS)
Tahiti Papeete

Anaa

Marutea

ÎLES DU
DÉSAPPOINTEMENT

Eiao

ÎLES
MARQUISES

Hiva Oa

Fatu Hiva

ÎLES MARIA
Rimatara Rurutu

Ahunui

Pukaruha
Reao

FRENCH POLYNESIA
(Fr.)

ÎLES AUSTRALES

Tubuai
Ralvavae

Tematangi
Mururoa
Tureia

Marutea

ÎLES
GAMBIER

Tropic of Capricorn

NORFOLK ISLAND
(Austl.)

Raoul
Island

KERMADEC ISLANDS
(N. Z.)

Curtis
Island

Rapa

PITCAIRN
(U.K.)
Adamstown

THREE KINGS
ISLANDS
North
Cape

PACIFIC OCEAN

Ernest Legouvé
Reef

Auckland
Great Barrier
Island

NORTH ISLAND
Bay of
Plenty
East Cape

New Plymouth Mount Ruapehu
Cape Egmont 2797
Hawke Bay
Napier

NEW
ZEALAND
Wellington

SOUTH ISLAND

Cook Strait

Mount Cook
3754
Christchurch

Canterbury
Bight

Dunedin

Island
Invercargill
uth West Cape

CHATHAM
ISLANDS
(N. Z.)

Maria Teresa
Reef

BOUNTY ISLANDS
(N. Z.)

AUCKLAND ISLANDS
(N. Z.)

ANTIPODES ISLANDS
(N. Z.)

Campbell Island
(N. Z.)

Kauai
Niihau   Oahu
Molokai
Honolulu   Maui

HAWAIIAN
ISLANDS
(U.S.)   Mauna Kea
4205   Hilo
Ka Lae HAWAII

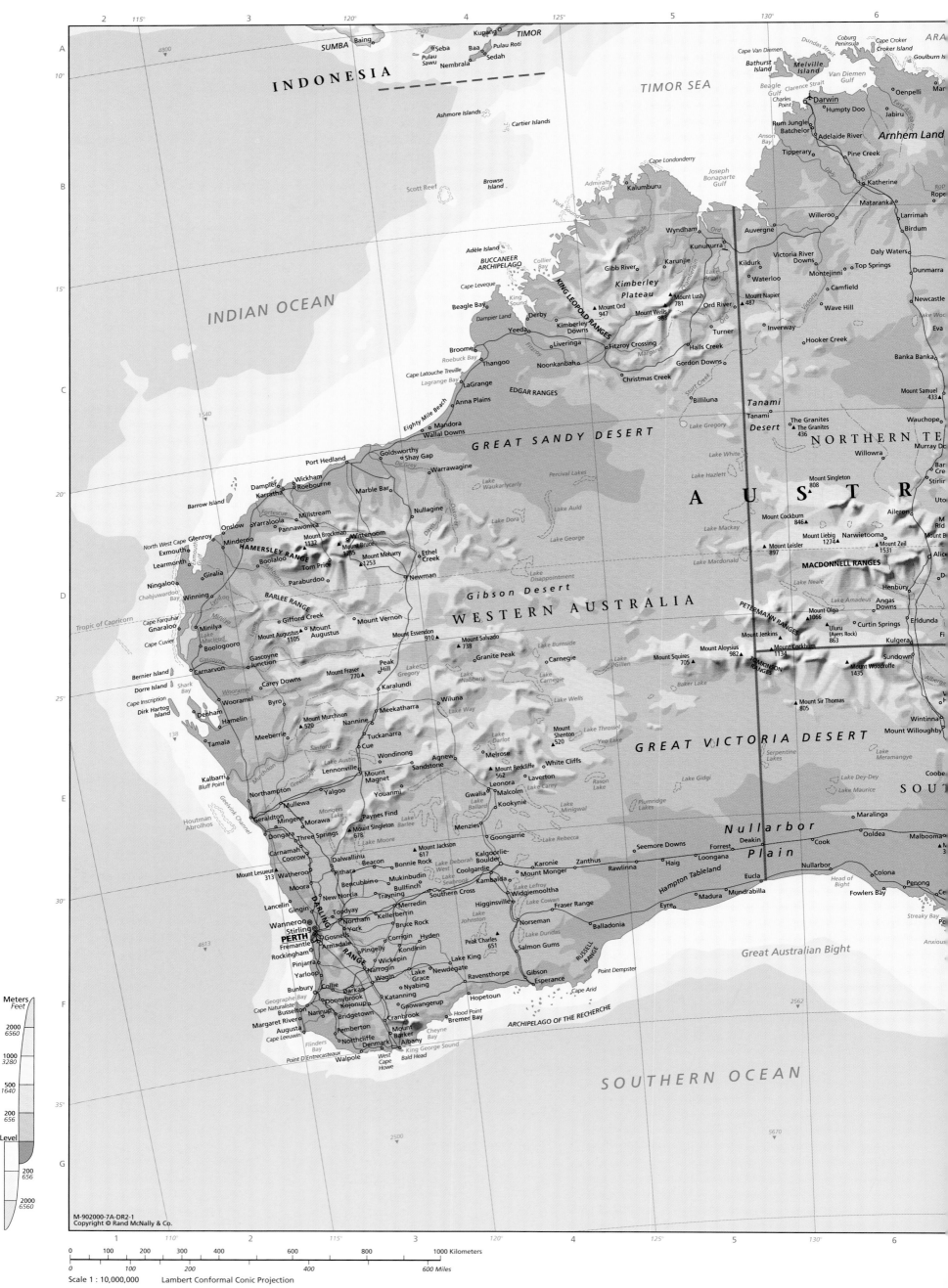

Meters
Feet

2000
6560

1000
3280

500
1640

200
656

Sea Level

200
656

2000
6560

0 100 200 300 400 600 800 1000 Kilometers

0 100 200 400 600 Miles

Scale 1 : 10,000,000   Lambert Conformal Conic Projection

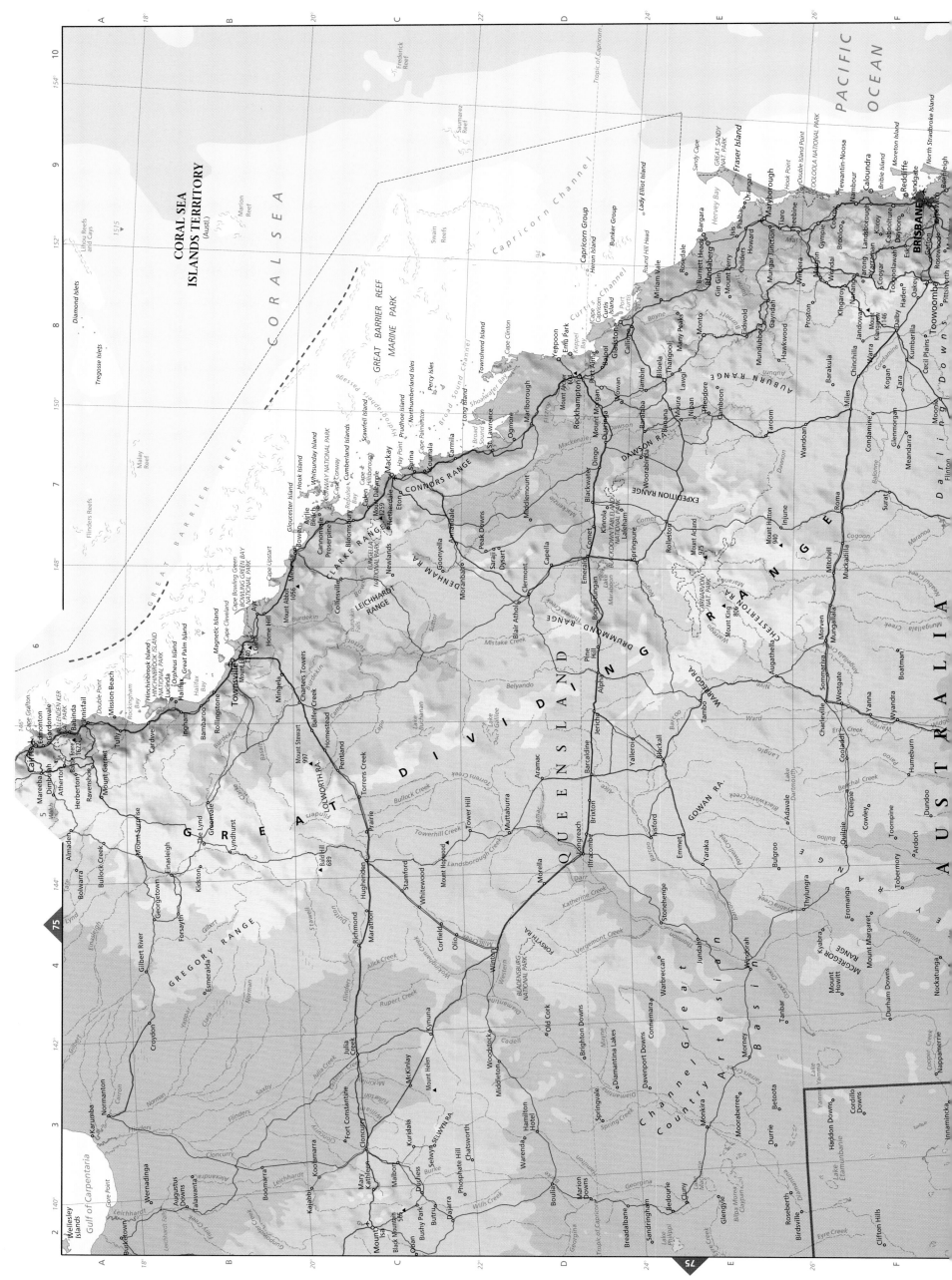

CORAL SEA
ISLANDS TERRITORY
(Austl.)

CORAL SEA

PACIFIC
OCEAN

GREAT BARRIER REEF
MARINE PARK

GREAT DIVIDING RANGE

QUEENSLAND

AUSTRALIA

Gulf of Carpentaria

Townsville

Cairns

Mackay

Rockhampton

Gladstone

Bundaberg

Maryborough

BRISBANE

Toowoomba

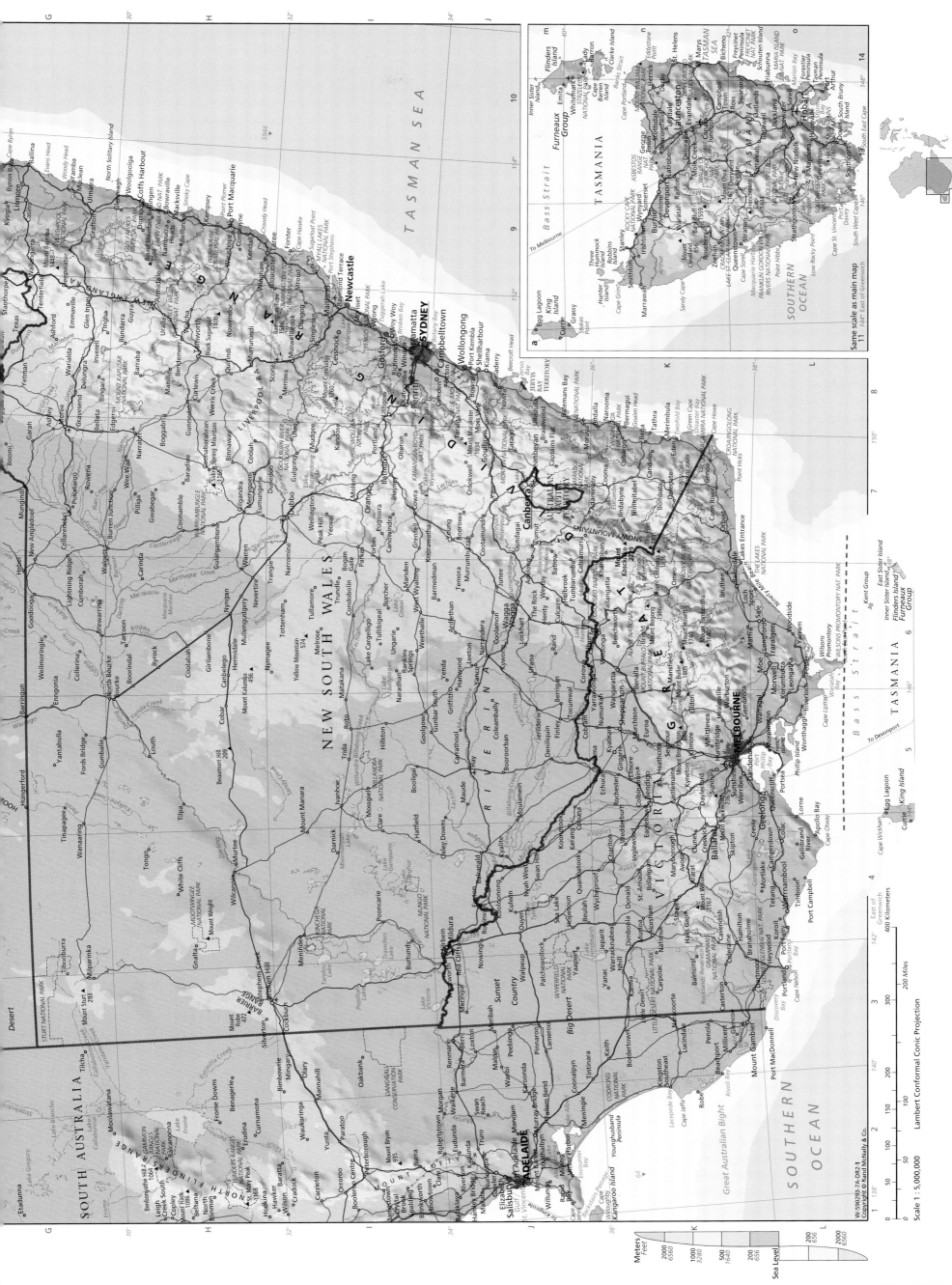

Scale 1 : 5,000,000

Lambert Conformal Conic Projection

TASMAN SEA

SOUTHERN OCEAN

NEW SOUTH WALES

SOUTH AUSTRALIA

VICTORIA

TASMANIA

RIVERINA

SNOWY MOUNTAINS

Bass Strait

Great Australian Bight

SYDNEY

MELBOURNE

ADELAIDE

Canberra

Newcastle

Hobart

Launceston

Same scale as main map

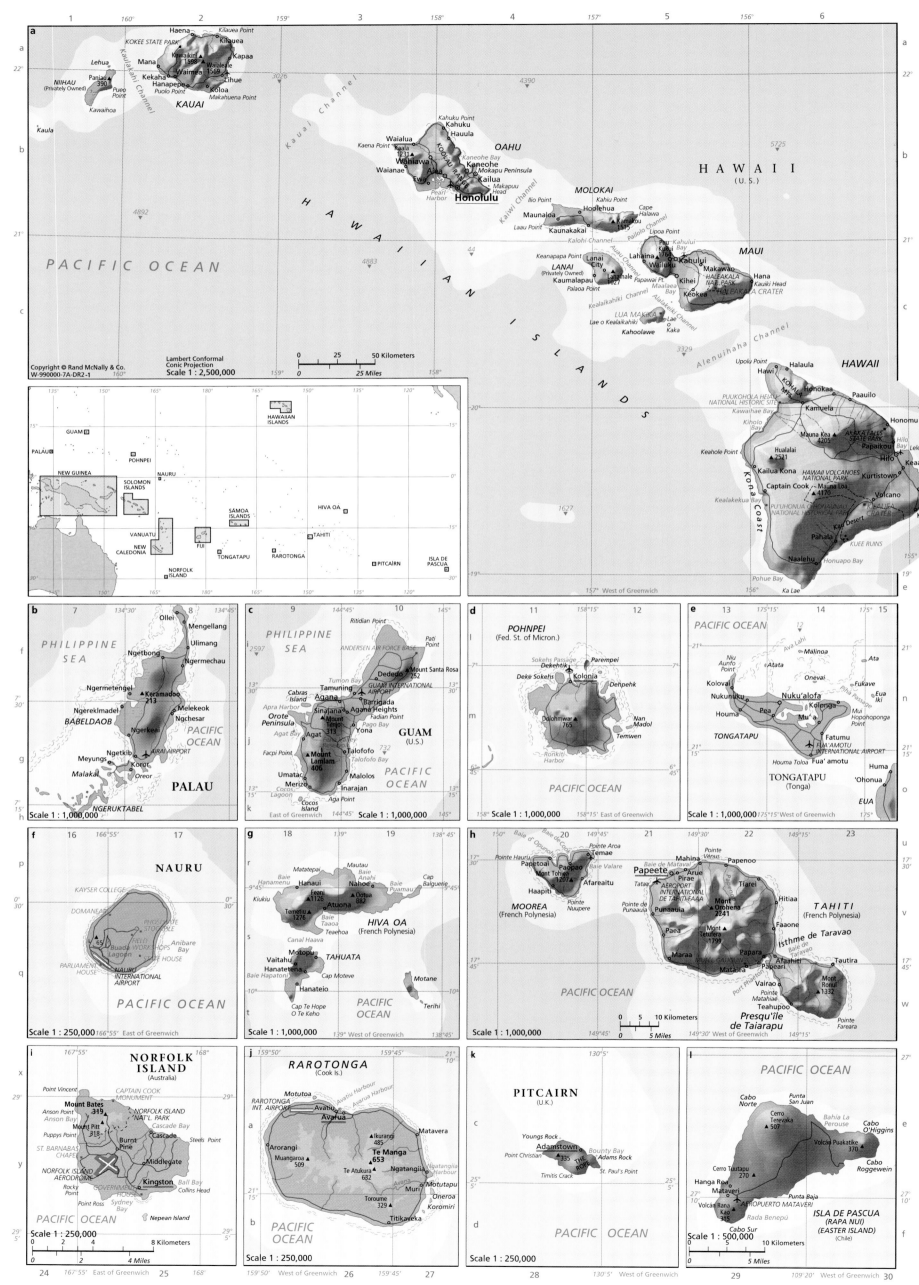

Map labels and features

a (main Hawaii map)

Haena
Kilauea Point
KOKEE STATE PARK
Kilauea
Kawaikini 1598 ▲ Waialeale 1569 ▲ Kapaa
Mana Kekaha Waimea Lihue
NIIHAU (Privately Owned) Paniau 390 ▲ Kaualakahi Channel
Lehua
Kaula
Kawaihoa
Hanapepe Puolo Point Koloa
Makahuena Point
KAUAI
PACIFIC OCEAN
Kauai Channel
3026
4390
4892
4883
5725

OAHU
Waialua Kahuku Point Kahuku Hauula
Kaena Point Kaala 1231 ▲ Kaneohe Bay Mokapu Peninsula
Wahiawa Kaneohe Kailua
Waianae KOOLAU RANGE Makapuu Head
Ewa Aiea Pearl Harbor Honolulu

MOLOKAI
Maunaloa Hoolehua Kahiu Point
Cape Halawa
Kaunakakai 375 ▲
Laau Point Lipoa Point
Kamakou
Ilio Point
Kamalo Channel
44

LANAI (Privately Owned)
Lanai City
Kaumalapau 1027 Palaoa Point
Papawai Pt.
Maalaea Bay
Kealaikahiki Channel
Lae o Kealaikahiki
LUA MAKIKA
KAHOOLAWE
Lae o Kaka
3329

Auau Channel
Pailolo Channel
Kahului Bay Kuau Bay
Wailuku Kahului Makawao
Lahaina Hana
Kihei HALEAKALA NAT'L PARK Kauiki Head
Keokea HALEAKALA CRATER
MAUI
Alalakeiki Channel
Alenuihaha Channel

Lambert Conformal Conic Projection
Scale 1 : 2,500,000
Copyright © Rand McNally & Co.
W-990000-7A-DR2-1

0   25   50 Kilometers
0   25 Miles

HAWAII (U.S.)

HAWAII
Upolu Point Halaula Hawi
Honokaa Paauilo
KOHALA MTS.
PUUKOHOLA HEIAU NATIONAL HISTORIC SITE
Kawaihae Bay Kamuela
Honomu
Kiholo Bay
AKAKA FALLS STATE PARK
Mauna Kea 4205 ▲ Papaikou Hilo
Keahole Point Hualalai 2521 ▲ Hilo Bay Leleiwi
Kailua Kona Mauna Loa Keaau
Captain Cook 4170 ▲ HAWAII VOLCANOES NATIONAL PARK Kurtistown
Kona Coast Volcano
PU'UHONUA O HONAUNAU NATIONAL HISTORICAL PARK KILAUEA CRATER
Kealakekua Bay Kau Desert
Pahala KUEE RUINS
Naalehu Honuapo Bay
Pohue Bay Ka Lae
157° West of Greenwich 156°
1627

(index inset map)
HAWAIIAN ISLANDS
GUAM
PALAU
POHNPEI
NAURU
NEW GUINEA
SOLOMON ISLANDS
HIVA OA
SÁMOA ISLANDS
VANUATU
NEW CALEDONIA
FIJI
TAHITI
NORFOLK ISLAND
TONGATAPU
RAROTONGA
PITCAIRN
ISLA DE PASCUA

b PALAU — Scale 1 : 1,000,000
7   134°30'   8   134°45'
PHILIPPINE SEA
Ollei Mengellang
Ngetbong Ulimang
Ngermetengel Ngermechau
Keramadoo 213 ▲
Ngerekimadel Melekeok
Ngchesar
Meyungs Ngetkib
Malakal Korot Oreor
BABELDAOB
PACIFIC OCEAN
AIRAI AIRPORT
NGERUKTABEL

c GUAM (U.S.) — Scale 1 : 1,000,000
9   144°45'   10   145°
PHILIPPINE SEA
Ritidian Point
Pati Point
ANDERSEN AIR FORCE BASE
2597
Tumon Bay Mount Santa Rosa
Dededo 252 ▲
Cabras Island Tumuning GUAM INTERNATIONAL AIRPORT
Apra Harbor Agana
Orote Peninsula Sinajana Agana Heights Fadian Point
Agat Bay Mount Tenjo 313 ▲ Barrigada
Facpi Point Agat Yona
Umatac Mount Lamlam 406 ▲ Talofofo
Merizo Malolos Talofofo Bay
Cocos Lagoon Inarajan
Cocos Island Aga Point
732
East of Greenwich 144°45'
GUAM
PACIFIC OCEAN

d POHNPEI (Fed. St. of Micron.) — Scale 1 : 1,000,000
11   158°15'   12
Sokehs Passage Ritidian
Deke Sokehs Parempei
Dekehtik Kolonia
Deke Sokehs Dehpehk
Dolohmwar 765 ▲ Nan Madol
Temwen
Ronkiti Harbor
PACIFIC OCEAN
158° 158°15' East of Greenwich

e TONGATAPU (Tonga) — Scale 1 : 1,000,000
13   175°15'   14   175° 15
PACIFIC OCEAN
Niu Aunfo Point Ata Malinoa
Kolovai Onevai Fukave
Nukunuku Nuku'alofa Kolonga Eua Iki
Houma Pea Mu'a Mui Hopohoponga Point
TONGATAPU Fatumu
Houma Toloa Fua'amotu FUA'AMOTU INTERNATIONAL AIRPORT
Huma
'Ohonua
EUA
PACIFIC OCEAN
175°15' West of Greenwich 175°

f NAURU — Scale 1 : 250,000
16   166°55'   17
NAURU
KAYSER COLLEGE
DOMANEAB
PHOSPHATE STOCKPILE
Buada Lagoon 65 ▲ FIELD WORKSHOPS Anibare Bay
PARLIAMENT HOUSE THE HOUSE
NAURU INTERNATIONAL AIRPORT
PACIFIC OCEAN
166°55' East of Greenwich

g HIVA OA (French Polynesia) — Scale 1 : 1,000,000
18   139°   19   138°45'
Matatepai Mautau Baie Anahi
Baie Hanamenu Hanaui Nahoe Cap Puamau
Kiukiu Feani 1126 ▲ Ootua 882 ▲ Baie Balguerie
Temetiu 1276 Atuona
Motopu Baie Taaoa Teaehoa
Canal Haava
HIVA OA
Vaitahu Hanatetena TAHUATA
Baie Hapatoni Cap Moteve Motane
Cap Te Hope Hanateio Terihi
O Te Keho
PACIFIC OCEAN
139° West of Greenwich 138°45'

h TAHITI / MOOREA (French Polynesia) — Scale 1 : 1,000,000
20   149°45'   21   149°30'   22   149°15'   23
Baie d'Opunohu Pointe Aroa
Pointe Hauru Temae Pointe Vénus Papenoo
Papetoai Paopao Mahina
Mont Tohiea 1207 ▲ Papeete Arue Tiarei
Haapiti Afareaitu AÉROPORT INTERNATIONAL DE TAHITI-FAAA Pirae
MOOREA (French Polynesia) Tataa Hitiaa
Pointe Nuupere Punaauia Mont Orohena 2241 ▲
Pointe de Punaauia Paea Faaone
Mont Tetufera 1799 ▲ TAHITI (French Polynesia)
Maraa Mataiea Papara Afaahiti Isthme de Taravao
Baie de Taravao Tautira
Vairao Papeari
Port Phaeton Mont Ronui 1332 ▲
Pointe Matahae Afaahiti
Teahupoo Presqu'île de Taiarapu
Pointe Fareara
PACIFIC OCEAN
0   5   10 Kilometers
0   5 Miles
149°45' West of Greenwich 149°30' 149°15'

i NORFOLK ISLAND (Australia) — Scale 1 : 250,000
24   167°55'   25   168° East of Greenwich
NORFOLK ISLAND
Point Vincent CAPTAIN COOK MONUMENT
Anson Point Mount Bates 319 ▲ NORFOLK ISLAND NAT'L PARK
Anson Bay Cascade Bay
Mount Pitt 318 ▲ Cascade Steels Point
Puppys Point Burnt Pine
ST. BARNABAS CHAPEL Middlegate
NORFOLK ISLAND AERODROME Collins Head
Rocky Point GOVERNMENT HOUSE Ball Bay
Point Ross Kingston
Sydney Bay Nepean Island
PACIFIC OCEAN
167°55' 168°

j RAROTONGA (Cook Is.) — Scale 1 : 250,000
26   159°50'   27   159°45'   21°10'
Motutoa Avatiu Harbor Avarua Harbor
RAROTONGA INT. AIRPORT Avatiu Avarua
Matavera
Arorangi Ikurangi 485 ▲ Ngatangiia
Muangaroa 509 Te Manga 653 ▲ Ngatangiia Harbour
Te Atukura 682 Motutapu
Toroume 329 Avana Oneroa
Titikaveka Muri Koromiri
PACIFIC OCEAN
159°50' West of Greenwich 159°45'

k PITCAIRN (U.K.) — Scale 1 : 250,000
28   130°5'
PITCAIRN
Youngs Rock
Adamstown Bounty Bay
Point Christian 335 ▲ THE ROPE Adams Rock
Timitis Crack St. Paul's Point
PACIFIC OCEAN
130°5' West of Greenwich

l ISLA DE PASCUA (RAPA NUI) (EASTER ISLAND) (Chile) — Scale 1 : 500,000
29   109°20'   30   27°
PACIFIC OCEAN
Cabo Norte Punta San Juan
Cerro Terevaka 507 ▲ Bahia La Perouse
Cabo O'Higgins
Volcán Puakatike 370 ▲
Cerro Tuutapu 270 ▲ Cabo Roggeween
Hanga Roa Punta Baja
Mataveri
Volcán Rana Kao 315 ▲ AEROPUERTO MATAVERI
Rada Benepu
Cabo Sur
ISLA DE PASCUA (RAPA NUI) (EASTER ISLAND) (Chile)
0   5   10 Kilometers
0   5 Miles
109°20' West of Greenwich

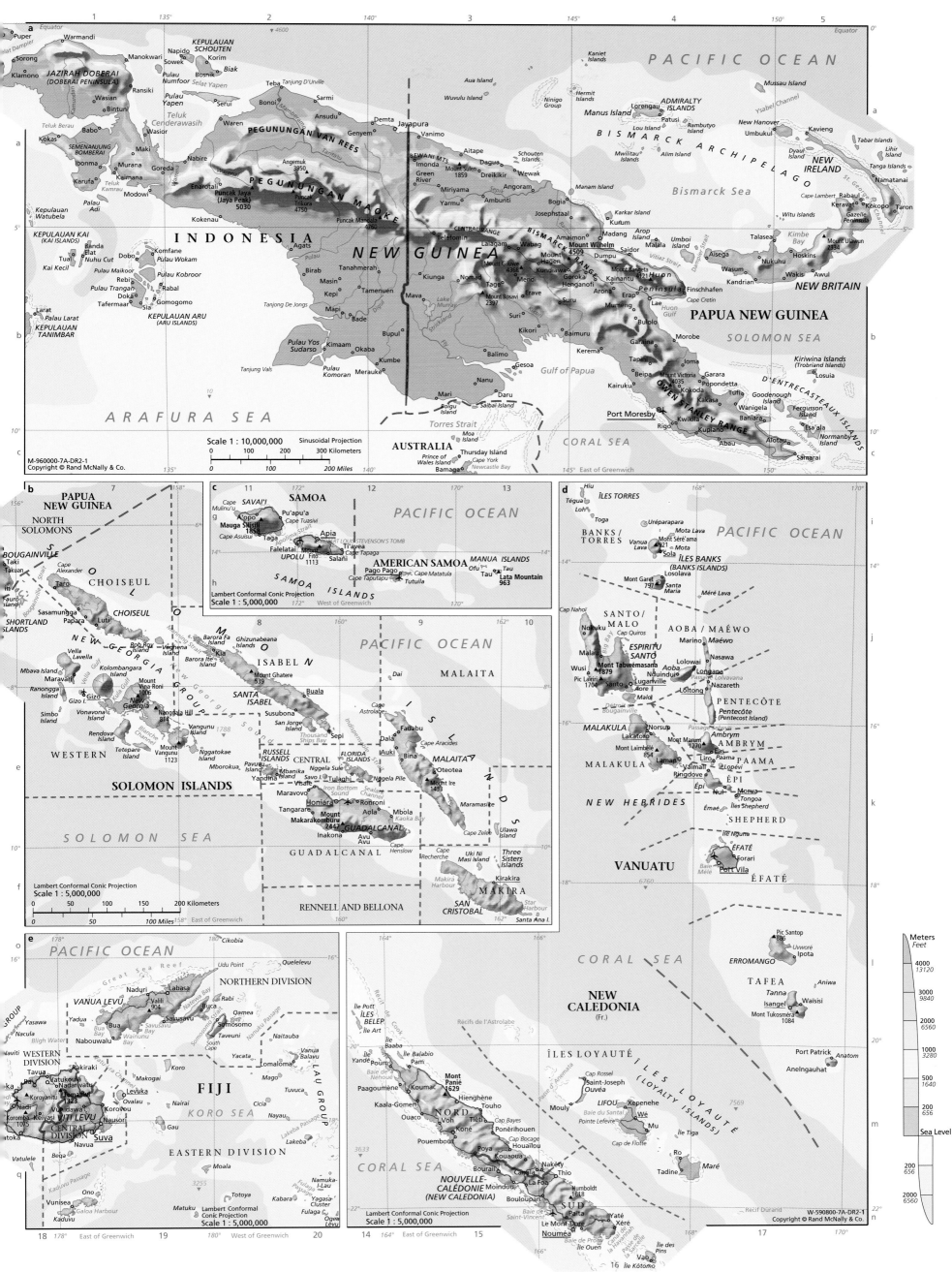

Scale 1 : 10,000,000   Sinusoidal Projection
0   100   200   300 Kilometers
0   100   200 Miles

M-960000-7A-DR2-1
Copyright © Rand McNally & Co.

Lambert Conformal Conic Projection
Scale 1 : 5,000,000
0   50   100   150   200 Kilometers
0   50   100 Miles   158° East of Greenwich

Lambert Conformal Conic Projection
Scale 1 : 5,000,000   172° West of Greenwich

Lambert Conformic Conic Projection
Scale 1 : 5,000,000

Lambert Conformal Conic Projection
Scale 1 : 5,000,000

W-590800-7A-DR2-1
Copyright © Rand McNally & Co.

Meters
Feet
4000
13120
3000
9840
2000
6560
1000
3280
500
1640
200
656
Sea Level
200
656
2000
6560

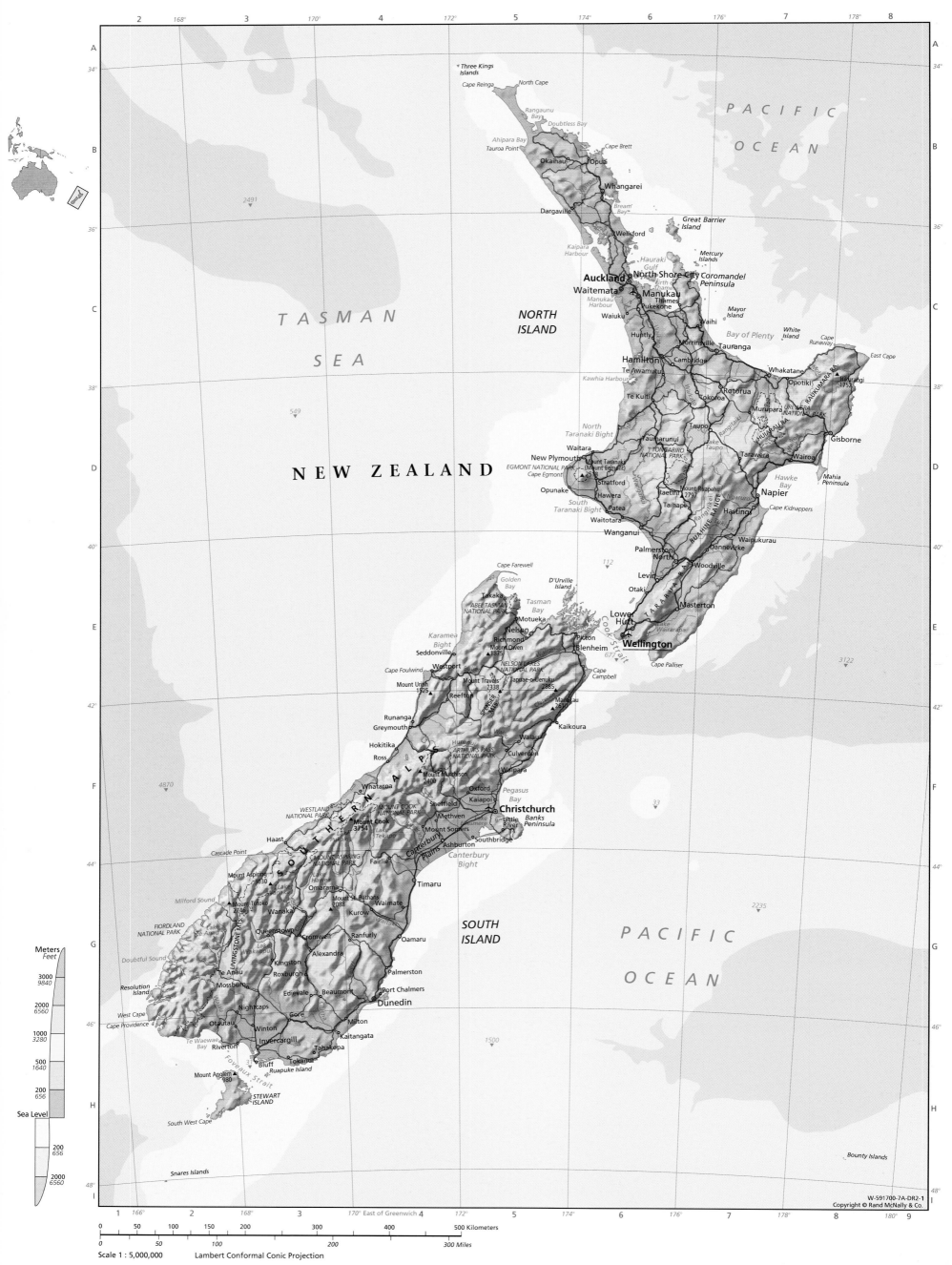

PACIFIC OCEAN

Three Kings Islands
Cape Reinga
North Cape

Rangaunu Bay
Doubtless Bay

Ahipara Bay
Tauroa Point
Cape Brett

Okaihau
Opua
Whangarei

Dargaville
Wellsford
Bream Bay
Great Barrier Island

Kaipara Harbour
Hauraki Gulf
Mercury Islands

Auckland
North Shore City
Coromandel Peninsula

Waitemata
Manukau
Firth of Thames
Thames

Manukau Harbour
Pukekohe
Mayor Island

Waiuku
Waihi

TASMAN SEA

NORTH ISLAND

Huntly
Morrinsville
Tauranga
Bay of Plenty
White Island
Cape Runaway

Hamilton
Cambridge
East Cape

Te Awamutu
Te Puke
Whakatane
Opotiki
Hikurangi 1753

Kawhia Harbour
Rotorua
Tokoroa

Te Kuiti
Taupo
Murupara
UREWERA NATIONAL PARK

North Taranaki Bight
Taumarunui
TONGARIRO NATIONAL PARK
Lake Taupo
Tarawera
Gisborne

NEW ZEALAND

Waitara
New Plymouth
Mount Taranaki (Mount Egmont) 2518
Stratford
Mount Ruapehu 2797
Wairoa

EGMONT NATIONAL PARK
Cape Egmont
Opunake
Hawera
Raetihi
Napier

South Taranaki Bight
Patea
Taihape
Hastings
Hawke Bay
Cape Kidnappers

Waitotara
Mahia Peninsula

Wanganui
Waipukurau
Dannevirke

Palmerston North
Woodville

Levin
Otaki
Masterton

Cape Farewell
Golden Bay
D'Urville Island

Takaka
Lower Hutt
Wellington

ABEL TASMAN NATIONAL PARK
Tasman Bay
Cape Palliser

Karamea Bight
Motueka
Nelson
Richmond
Picton
Cook Strait

Seddonville
Mount Owen 1875
Blenheim

Cape Foulwind
Westport
NELSON LAKES NATIONAL PARK
Cape Campbell

Mount Uriah 1925
Mount Travers 2338
Tapuae-o-Uenuku 2885

Reefton
Manakau 261

Runanga
Kaikoura

Greymouth

Hokitika
ARTHUR'S PASS NATIONAL PARK
Waiau

Ross
Culverden

SOUTHERN ALPS
Mount Murchison 2400
Waipara

Whataroa
Oxford
Pegasus Bay

WESTLAND NATIONAL PARK
Sheffield
Kaiapoi

MOUNT COOK NATIONAL PARK
Methven
Christchurch
Little River
Banks Peninsula

Mount Cook 3754
Mount Somers
Southbridge

Haast
Ashburton
Canterbury Bight

MOUNT ASPIRING NATIONAL PARK
Fairlie
Canterbury Plains

Cascade Point
Timaru

Mount Aspiring 3030
Omarama

Milford Sound
Mount Titoki 2746
Mount St. Bathans 2088
Waimate

FIORDLAND NATIONAL PARK
Wanaka
Kurow

Queenstown
Cromwell
Ranfurly
Oamaru

LIVINGSTONE MTS.
Kingston
Alexandra

SOUTH ISLAND

Doubtful Sound
Te Anau
Palmerston

Resolution Island
Mossburn
Roxburgh
Port Chalmers

Nightcaps
Edievale
Beaumont
Dunedin

West Cape
Gore
Milton

Cape Providence
Otautau
Winton
Kaitangata

Te Waewae Bay
Invercargill
Tahakopa

Riverton
Tokanui

Foveaux Strait
Bluff
Ruapuke Island

Mount Anglem 980

STEWART ISLAND

South West Cape

Snares Islands

PACIFIC OCEAN

Bounty Islands

TASMAN SEA

Meters / Feet
3000 / 9840
2000 / 6560
1000 / 3280
500 / 1640
200 / 656
Sea Level
200 / 656
2000 / 6560

0 50 100 150 200   300   400   500 Kilometers
0   50   100   200   300 Miles

Scale 1 : 5,000,000   Lambert Conformal Conic Projection

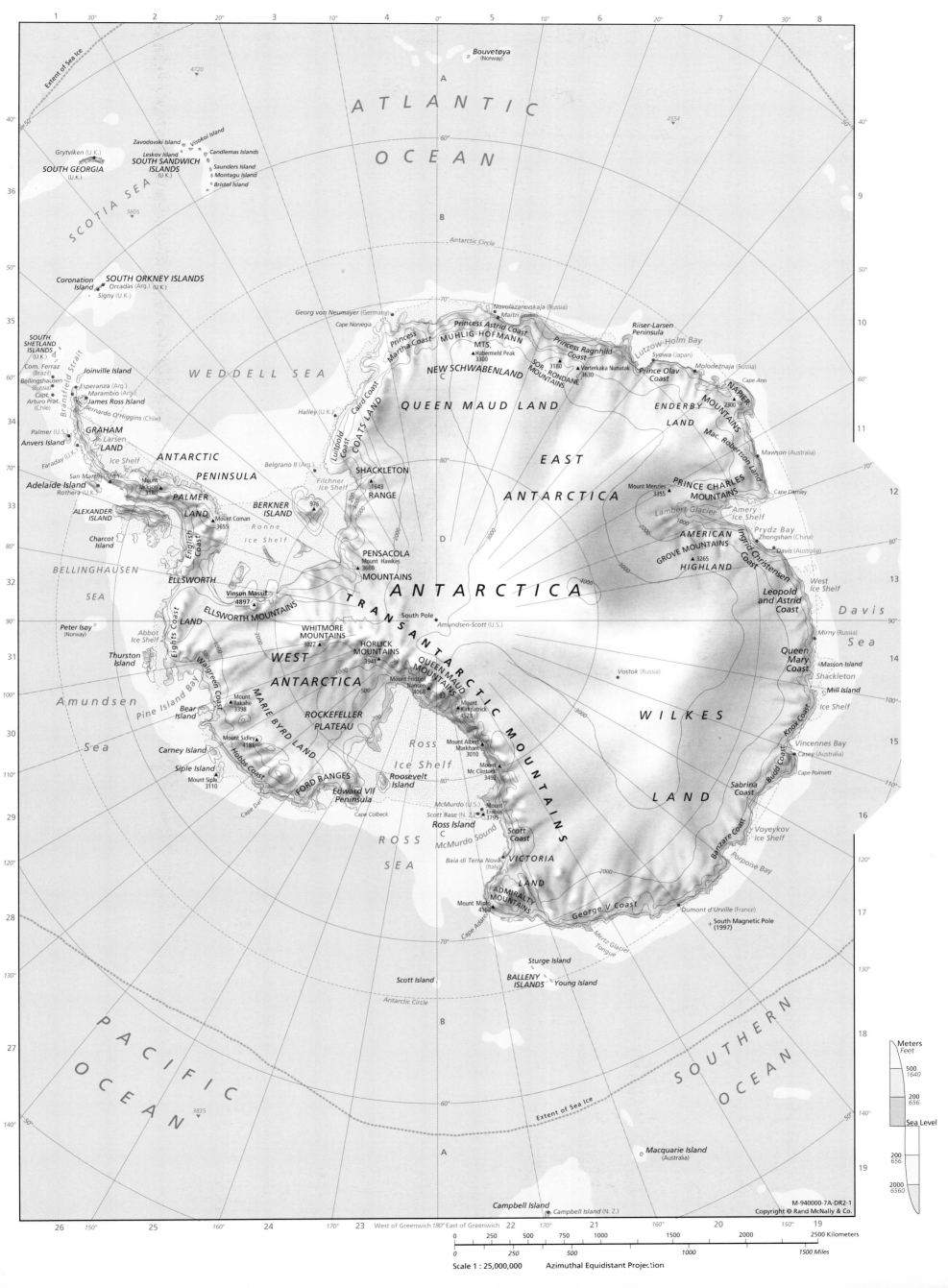

ATLANTIC

OCEAN

Bouvetøya
(Norway)

4720

4554

SCOTIA SEA

Grytviken (U.K.)
SOUTH GEORGIA
(U.K.)

Zavodovski Island
Leskov Island *Visokoi Island*
Candlemas Islands
SOUTH SANDWICH
ISLANDS
(U.K.)
Saunders Island
Montagu Island
Bristol Island

3805

Antarctic Circle

Coronation
Island SOUTH ORKNEY ISLANDS
Orcadas (Arg.) (U.K.)
Signy (U.K.)

Georg von Neumayer (Germany)
Novolazarevskaja (Russia)
Maitri (India)

WEDDELL SEA

Cape Norvegia

Princess Astrid Coast
Princess Martha Coast
MUHLIG-HOFMANN
MTS.
▲Habermehl Peak
3300

Princess Ragnhild
Coast
SØR-
RONDANE 3180
MOUNTAINS 3630 ▲Vorterkaka Nunatak

Riiser-Larsen
Peninsula

Lützow-Holm Bay
Sýowa (Japan)
Molodežnaja (Russia)
Prince Olav
Coast
Cape Ann

SOUTH
SHETLAND
ISLANDS
(U.K.)

Com. Ferraz
(Brazil)
Bellingshausen
(Russia)
Capt.
Arturo Prat
(Chile)

Joinville Island
Esperanza (Arg.)
Marambio (Arg.)
James Ross Island
Bernardo O'Higgins (Chile)

Halley (U.K.)

Caird Coast

NEW SCHWABENLAND

QUEEN MAUD LAND

Luitpold
Coast

COATS LAND

ENDERBY
LAND

NAPIER
2300
MOUNTAINS

EAST

Mac. Robertson Land
Mawson (Australia)

GRAHAM
LAND
Larsen
Ice Shelf

Faraday (U.K.)

ANTARCTIC
PENINSULA

Belgrano II (Arg.)

SHACKLETON
1643
RANGE

ANTARCTICA

Mount Menzies
3355 ▲ PRINCE CHARLES
MOUNTAINS
Cape Darnley

San Martín (Arg.)
Adelaide Island
Rothera (U.K.)

PALMER
LAND

Filchner
Ice Shelf

Lambert Glacier
Amery
Ice Shelf

AMERICAN
HIGHLAND

Ingrid Christensen Coast
Prydz Bay
Zhongshan (China)
Davis (Australia)

Anvers Island

Mount
Jackson▲
3180

BERKNER
ISLAND 976

GROVE
MOUNTAINS ▲ 3265

ALEXANDER
ISLAND

Mount Coman
3655 ▲

Ronne
Ice Shelf

West
Ice Shelf

Charcot
Island

English
Coast

PENSACOLA
Mount Hawkes
3660
MOUNTAINS

3000

Leopold
and Astrid
Coast

Davis

BELLINGHAUSEN
SEA

ELLSWORTH
LAND

ANTARCTICA

4000

Sea

Peter Isøy
(Norway)

Vinson Massif
4897 ▲

ELLSWORTH MOUNTAINS

TRANSANTARCTIC

South Pole
Amundsen-Scott (U.S.)

90°

Mirny (Russia)

90°

Thurston
Island

Abbot
Ice Shelf

Eights Coast

WHITMORE
MOUNTAINS
3022 ▲

HORLICK
MOUNTAINS
3941 ▲

WEST
ANTARCTICA

QUEEN MAUD
MOUNTAINS

Vostok (Russia)

Queen
Mary
Coast

Masson Island
Shackleton
Ice Shelf

Mill Island

Amundsen

Sea

Pine Island Bay

Walgreen Coast

Bear
Island

Mount
Takahe
3398 ▲

MARIE BYRD LAND

Mount Fridtjof
Nansen
4068

ROCKEFELLER
PLATEAU

Mount
Kirkpatrick
4528

WILKES

LAND

Knox Coast

Vincennes Bay
Casey (Australia)
Cape Poinsett

Mount Sidley
4181 ▲

Carney Island

Hobbs Coast

FORD RANGES

500

Ross
Ice Shelf

Roosevelt
Island

Mount
Mc Clintock
3492 ▲

Sabrina
Coast

Siple Island
Mount Siple
3110 ▲

Cape Dart

Edward VII
Peninsula

Cape Colbeck

McMurdo (U.S.)
Scott Base (N.Z.)
Ross Island

Mount
Erebus
3795 ▲

Budd Coast

Banzare Coast

Voyeykov
Ice Shelf

Cape Adare

ROSS

SEA

McMurdo Sound

Scott
Coast

VICTORIA

LAND

George V Coast

Porpoise Bay

Dumont d'Urville (France)

Baia di Terra Nova (Italy)

ADMIRALTY
MOUNTAINS

Mount Minto
4163 ▲

Mertz Glacier
Tongue

South Magnetic Pole
(1997)

Sturge Island

Scott Island

BALLENY
ISLANDS
Young Island

Antarctic Circle

PACIFIC

OCEAN

3835

SOUTHERN

OCEAN

Extent of Sea Ice

Campbell Island
Campbell Island (N.Z.)

Macquarie Island
(Australia)

West of Greenwich 180° East of Greenwich

M-940000-7A-DR2-1
Copyright © Rand McNally & Co.

Meters
Feet

500
1640

200
656

Sea Level

200
656

2000
6560

0   250   500   750   1000   1500   2000   2500 Kilometers

0   250   500   1000   1500 Miles

Scale 1 : 25,000,000   Azimuthal Equidistant Projection

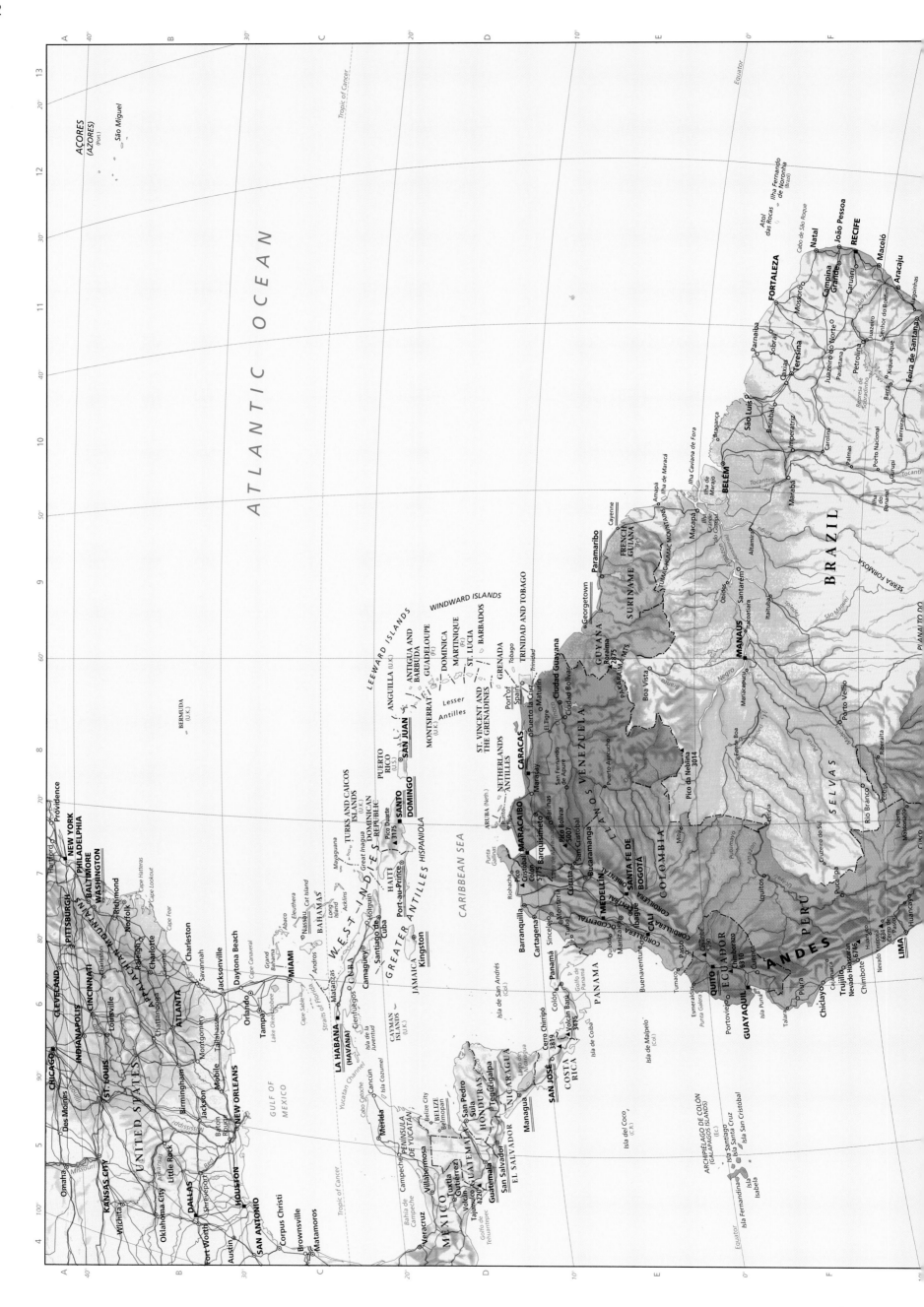

ATLANTIC OCEAN

AÇORES
(AZORES)
(Port.)

São Miguel

BERMUDA
(U.K.)

UNITED STATES

Omaha
Des Moines
CHICAGO
CLEVELAND
KANSAS CITY
INDIANAPOLIS
CINCINNATI
ST. LOUIS
Wichita
Oklahoma City
Little Rock
DALLAS
Fort Worth
Shreveport
Austin
SAN ANTONIO
HOUSTON
Corpus Christi
Brownsville
Matamoros
Baton Rouge
NEW ORLEANS
Jackson
Mobile
Montgomery
Birmingham
ATLANTA
Chattanooga
Louisville
Nashville
Memphis
Tallahassee
Jacksonville
Daytona Beach
Orlando
Tampa
MIAMI
Savannah
Charleston
Charlotte
Raleigh
Columbia
Richmond
Norfolk
Cape Hatteras
Cape Lookout
Cape Fear
PITTSBURGH
Hartford
Providence
NEW YORK
PHILADELPHIA
BALTIMORE
WASHINGTON
APPALACHIAN MOUNTAINS
Arkansas
Missouri
Ohio
Mississippi

Veracruz
MEXICO
Villahermosa
Tuxtla Gutiérrez
Volcán Tajumulco 4220▲
PENÍNSULA DE YUCATÁN
Mérida
Campeche
Cancún
Isla Cozumel
Cabo Catoche
Bahía de Campeche
Golfo de Tehuantepec
GULF OF MEXICO
Cabo San Antonio
Straits of Florida
Cape Canaveral
Grand Bahama
Lake Okeechobee

GUATEMALA
Guatemala
San Salvador
EL SALVADOR
BELIZE
Belize City
Belmopan
San Pedro Sula
HONDURAS
Tegucigalpa
Managua
NICARAGUA
Lago de Nicaragua
Cerro Chirripó 3819▲
Volcán Barú 3475▲
COSTA RICA
SAN JOSÉ
PANAMA
Colón
Panamá
Golfo de Panamá
Isla de Coiba

BAHAMAS
Nassau
Andros
Cat Island
Eleuthera
Abaco
Long Island
Acklins
Mayaguana
Great Inagua
Andros
TURKS AND CAICOS ISLANDS (U.K.)

LA HABANA
(HAVANA)
CUBA
Matanzas
Cienfuegos
Camagüey
Santiago de Cuba
Holguín
CAYMAN ISLANDS (U.K.)
Isla de la Juventud
Yucatan Channel

W E S T   I N D I E S
G R E A T E R   A N T I L L E S
JAMAICA
Kingston
HAITI
Port-au-Prince
HISPANIOLA
DOMINICAN REPUBLIC
SANTO DOMINGO
Pico Duarte 3175▲
PUERTO RICO (U.S.)
SAN JUAN

CARIBBEAN SEA

ARUBA (Neth.)
NETHERLANDS ANTILLES

LEEWARD ISLANDS
ANGUILLA (U.K.)
ANTIGUA AND BARBUDA
MONTSERRAT (U.K.)
GUADELOUPE (Fr.)
DOMINICA
MARTINIQUE (Fr.)
ST. LUCIA
BARBADOS
GRENADA
ST. VINCENT AND THE GRENADINES
Lesser Antilles
WINDWARD ISLANDS
Tobago
Trinidad
TRINIDAD AND TOBAGO
Port of Spain

Barranquilla
Cartagena
Sincelejo
Montería
Riohacha
Punta Gallinas
MARACAIBO
Maracaibo
Barquisimeto
Valencia
CARACAS
Maturín
Puerto la Cruz
Ciudad Bolívar
Ciudad Guayana
El Tigre
San Fernando de Apure
San Cristóbal
Cúcuta
Bucaramanga
Pico Cristóbal Colón 5775▲
Pico Bolívar 5007▲
VENEZUELA
L L A N O S
O R I N O C O
Orinoco
GUYANA
Georgetown
Roraima 2375▲
PAKARAIMA MTS
SURINAME
Paramaribo
FRENCH GUIANA
Cayenne
TUMUC-HUMAC MOUNTAINS
Pico da Neblina 3014▲
Boa Vista
Río Branco
Negro
Branco
Fonte Boa

COLOMBIA
SANTA FE DE BOGOTÁ
MEDELLÍN
CALI
Manizales
Ibagué
Buenaventura
Pasto
Quibdó
Cartago
Armenia
CORDILLERA OCCIDENTAL
CORDILLERA ORIENTAL
CORDILLERA CENTRAL
Putumayo
Mitú
Isla de San Andrés (Col.)
Isla de Malpelo (Col.)

ECUADOR
QUITO
GUAYAQUIL
Portoviejo
Esmeraldas
Cuenca
Chimborazo 6310▲
Punta Galera
ARCHIPIÉLAGO DE COLÓN (GALÁPAGOS ISLANDS) (Ec.)
Isla San Cristóbal
Isla Santa Cruz
Isla Santiago
Isla Fernandina
Isla Isabela
Isla del Coco (C.R.)

PERU
LIMA
Chiclayo
Trujillo
Chimbote
Piura
Talara
Cajamarca
Iquitos
Pucallpa
Nevado Huascarán 6746▲
Nevado Huascarán 6634▲
Cerro Yerupajá 6632▲
Huánuco
Huancayo
A N D E S
S E L V A S
Ucayali
Marañón

BRAZIL
MANAUS
BELÉM
FORTALEZA
RECIFE
Natal
João Pessoa
Campina Grande
Caruaru
Maceió
Aracaju
Feira de Santana
Teresina
São Luís
Parnaíba
Sobral
Mossoró
Juazeiro do Norte
Petrolina
Juazeiro
Caxias
Imperatriz
Carolina
Marabá
Santarém
Óbidos
Itaituba
Altamira
Macapá
Ilha de Maracá
Ilha Caviana de Fora
Ilha de Marajó
Ilha do Bananal
Bragança
Cametá
Tocantins
Xingu
Tapajós
São Francisco
Parnaíba
PLANALTO DO
Porto Velho
Pôrto Nacional
Palmas
Barreiras
Porto Nacional
SERRA FORMOSA
Ilha Fernando de Noronha (Brazil)
Atol das Rocas
Cabo de São Roque
P A K A R A I M A   M T S.
Apaporis
Japurá
Içá
Negro
Solimões
Juruá
Purus
Madeira

Tropic of Cancer
Equator

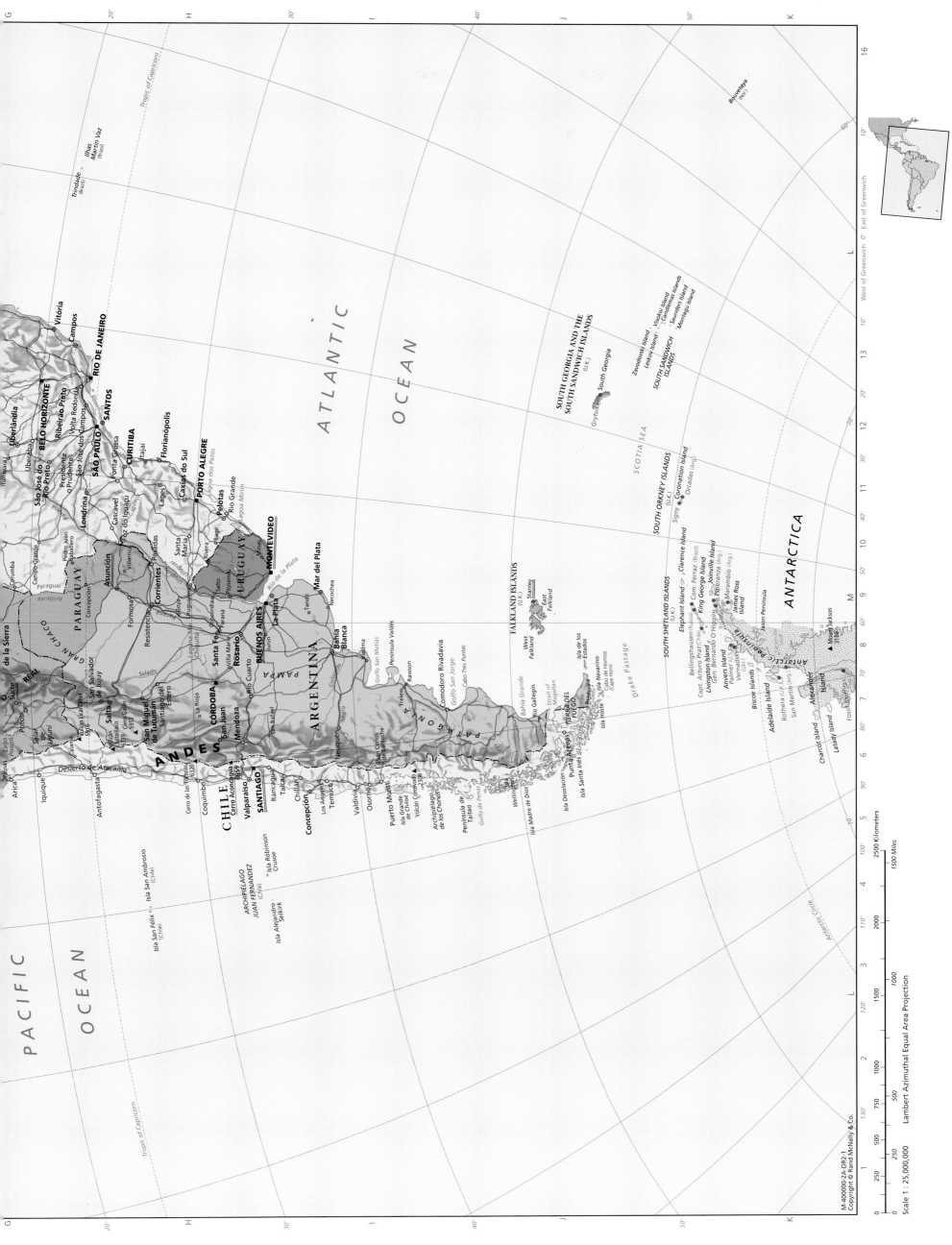

PACIFIC

OCEAN

ATLANTIC

OCEAN

Tropic of Capricorn

Ilhas
Martín Vaz
(Brazil)

Trindade
(Brazil)

Bouvetøya
(Nor.)

SCOTIA SEA

SOUTH GEORGIA AND THE
SOUTH SANDWICH ISLANDS
(U.K.)

Zavodovski Island
Leskov Island · Visokoi Island
Candlemas Islands
Saunders Island
Montagu Island

SOUTH SANDWICH
ISLANDS

Grytviken · South Georgia

Vitória
Campos
RIO DE JANEIRO
SANTOS
SÃO PAULO
BELO HORIZONTE
Ribeirão Preto
Volta Redonda
Uberaba
Uberlândia
São José do
Rio Preto
Presidente
Prudente
Londrina
Cascavel
Foz do Iguaçu
CURITIBA
Ponta Grossa
São José dos Campos
Itajaí
Florianópolis
Lages
Caxias do Sul
PORTO ALEGRE
Rio Grande
Pelotas
Lagoa dos Patos

Campo Grande
Pedro Juan
Caballero
Corumbá
PARAGUAY
Paraguai
Paraguai
GRAN CHACO
Concepción
Villarrica
Asunción
Formosa
Villa María
Resistencia
Corrientes
Posadas
Santa
María
Paraná
Uruguaiana
Salto
Paysandú
Rivera
URUGUAY
MONTEVIDEO
Mar del Plata
Necochea
Tandil
La Plata
BUENOS AIRES
Rosario
Santa Fe
Río de la Plata

de la Sierra
Potosí
Sucre
REAL
San Salvador
de Jujuy
Salta
San Miguel
de Tucumán
Santiago del
Estero
CORDOBA
San Juan
Mendoza
La Rioja
Río Cuarto
Junín
Salado
Salar de
Uyuni
Lago
Poopó
Antofagasta
Iquique
Arica
Desierto de Atacama
Cerro de las Tórtolas
6332
Coquimbo
Valparaíso
SANTIAGO
Rancagua
Talca
Chillán
Concepción
Los Ángeles
Temuco
Valdivia
Osorno
Puerto Montt
CHILE
Cerro Aconcagua
6959
Volcán Ojos del
Salado 6893
ANDES
ARGENTINA
PAMPA
Neuquén
Negro
Colorado
Bahía
Blanca
Golfo San Matías
Península Valdés
Viedma
Carmen de
Patagones
Rawson
Trelew
PATAGONIA
Golfo San Jorge
Comodoro Rivadavia
Cabo Tres Puntas

ARCHIPIÉLAGO
JUAN FERNÁNDEZ
(Chile)
Isla Robinson
Crusoe
Isla Alejandro
Selkirk
Isla San Ambrosio
(Chile)
Isla San Félix
(Chile)

Isla Grande
de Chiloé
Volcán Corcovado
2300
Archipiélago
de los Chonos
Península de
Taitao
Golfo de Penas
San Carlos
de Bariloche
Wellington
Isla Madre de Dios
Isla Desolación
Isla Santa Inés
Punta Arenas
Ushuaia
TIERRA DEL
FUEGO
Isla Navarino
Cabo de Hornos
(Cape Horn)
Isla de los
Estados
Bahía Grande
Río Gallegos
Strait of
Magellan

FALKLAND ISLANDS
(U.K.)
Stanley
East
Falkland
West
Falkland

Drake Passage

ANTARCTICA

SOUTH ORKNEY ISLANDS
(U.K.)
Signy
Coronation Island
Orcadas (Arg.)

SOUTH SHETLAND ISLANDS
(U.K.)
Elephant Island
Clarence Island
Bellingshausen (Russia)
Com. Ferraz (Brazil)
King George Island
Capt. Arturo Prat (Chile)
Livingston Island
Gen. Bernardo O'Higgins
Joinville Island
Esperanza (Arg.)
Anvers Island
Palmer (U.S.)
Vernadsky (U.K.)
Marambio (Arg.)
James Ross
Island
Jason Peninsula
Biscoe Islands
Adelaide Island
Rothera (U.K.)
San Martín (Arg.)
Charcot Island
Alexander
Island
Latady Island
Fossil Bluff

Antarctic Peninsula
Mount Jackson
3180

Antarctic Circle

Tropic of Capricorn

M-400000-2A-DR2-1
Copyright © Rand McNally & Co.

Lambert Azimuthal Equal Area Projection

Scale 1 : 25,000,000

2500 Kilometers
1500 Miles

0   250   500   750   1000   1500   2000

0   250   500   1000

ATLANTIC

OCEAN

SURINAME   FRENCH GUIANA

AMAPÁ

PARÁ

B R A Z I L

MARANHÃO

CEARÁ

PIAUÍ

RIO GRANDE DO NORTE

PARAÍBA

PERNAMBUCO

ALAGOAS

SERGIPE

BAHIA

TOCANTINS

MATO GROSSO

PLANALTO DO MATO GROSSO

GOIÁS

DISTRITO FEDERAL

MINAS GERAIS

MATO GROSSO DO SUL

Paramaribo
BELÉM
São Luís
FORTALEZA
Teresina
Natal
João Pessoa
RECIFE
Maceió
Aracaju
SALVADOR
Feira de Santana
Petrolina
Campina Grande
BRASÍLIA
GOIÂNIA
Cuiabá

M-400091-7A-DR2-1
Copyright © Rand McNally & Co.

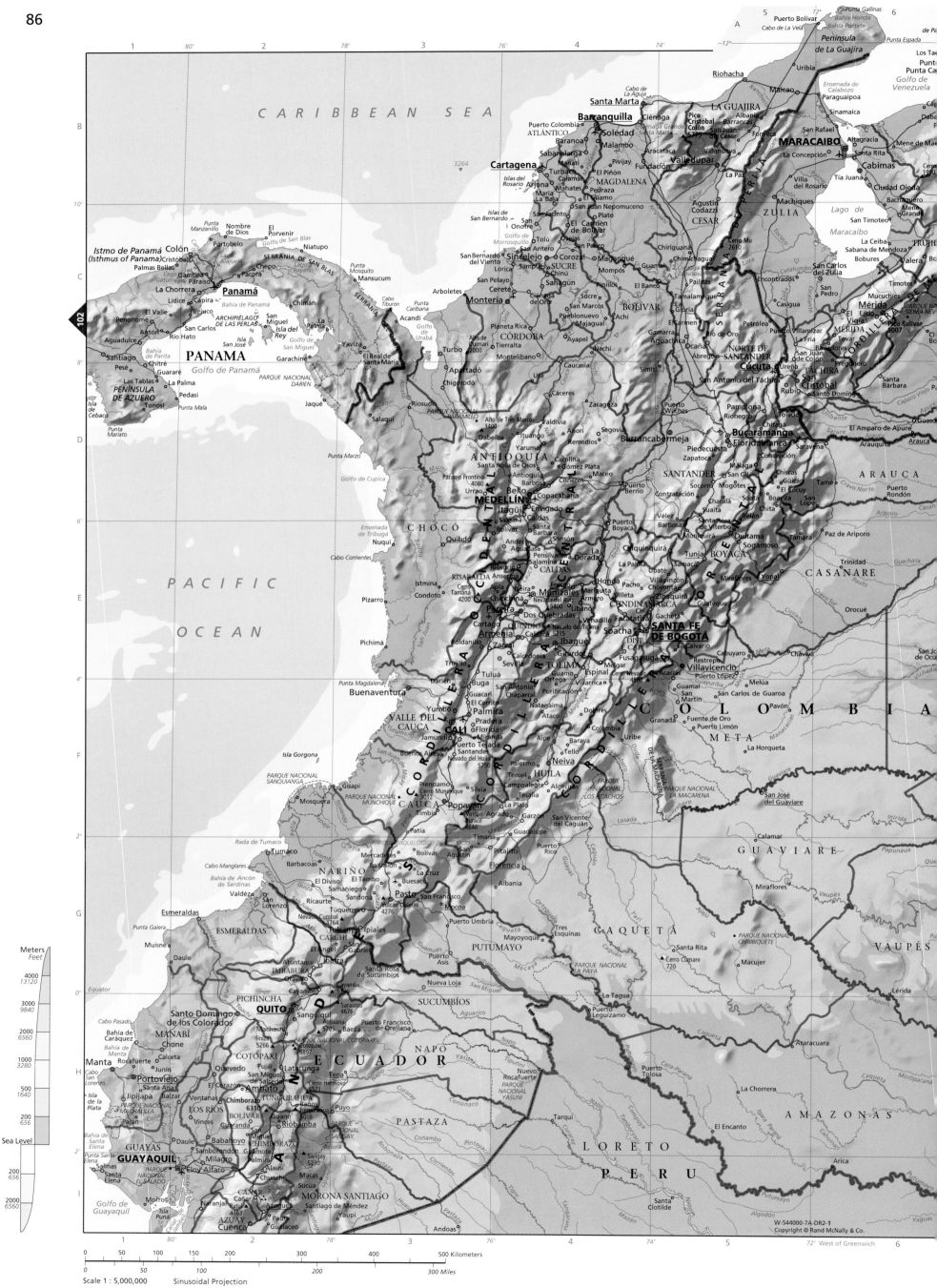

CARIBBEAN SEA

PACIFIC

OCEAN

PANAMA

COLOMBIA

ECUADOR

PERU

Meters
Feet
4000
13120
3000
9840
2000
6560
1000
3280
500
1640
200
656
Sea Level
200
656
2000
6560

Scale 1 : 5,000,000   Sinusoidal Projection

0   50   100   150   200   300   400   500 Kilometers

0   50   100   200   300 Miles

W-544000-7A-DR2-1
Copyright © Rand McNally & Co.

72° West of Greenwich

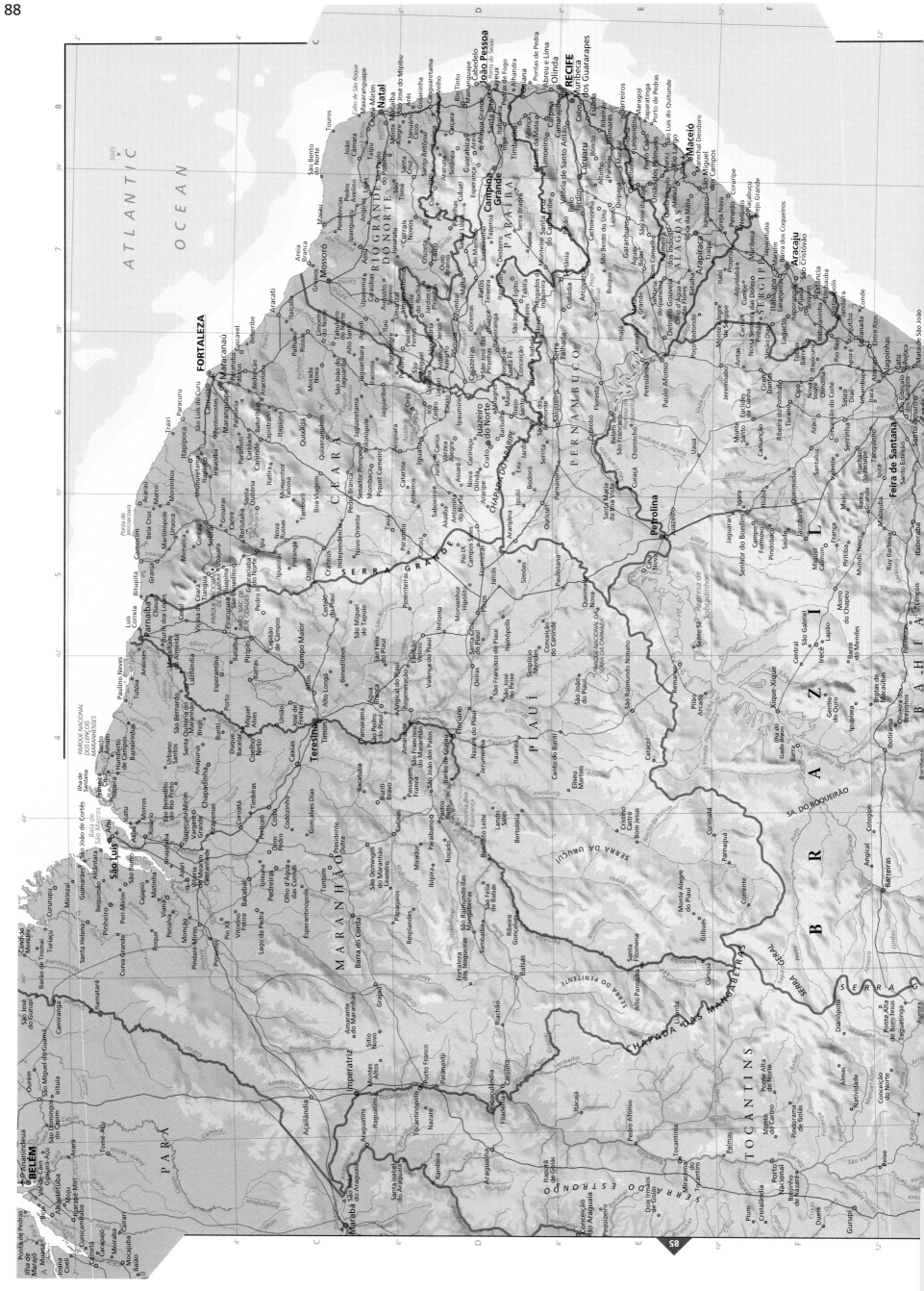

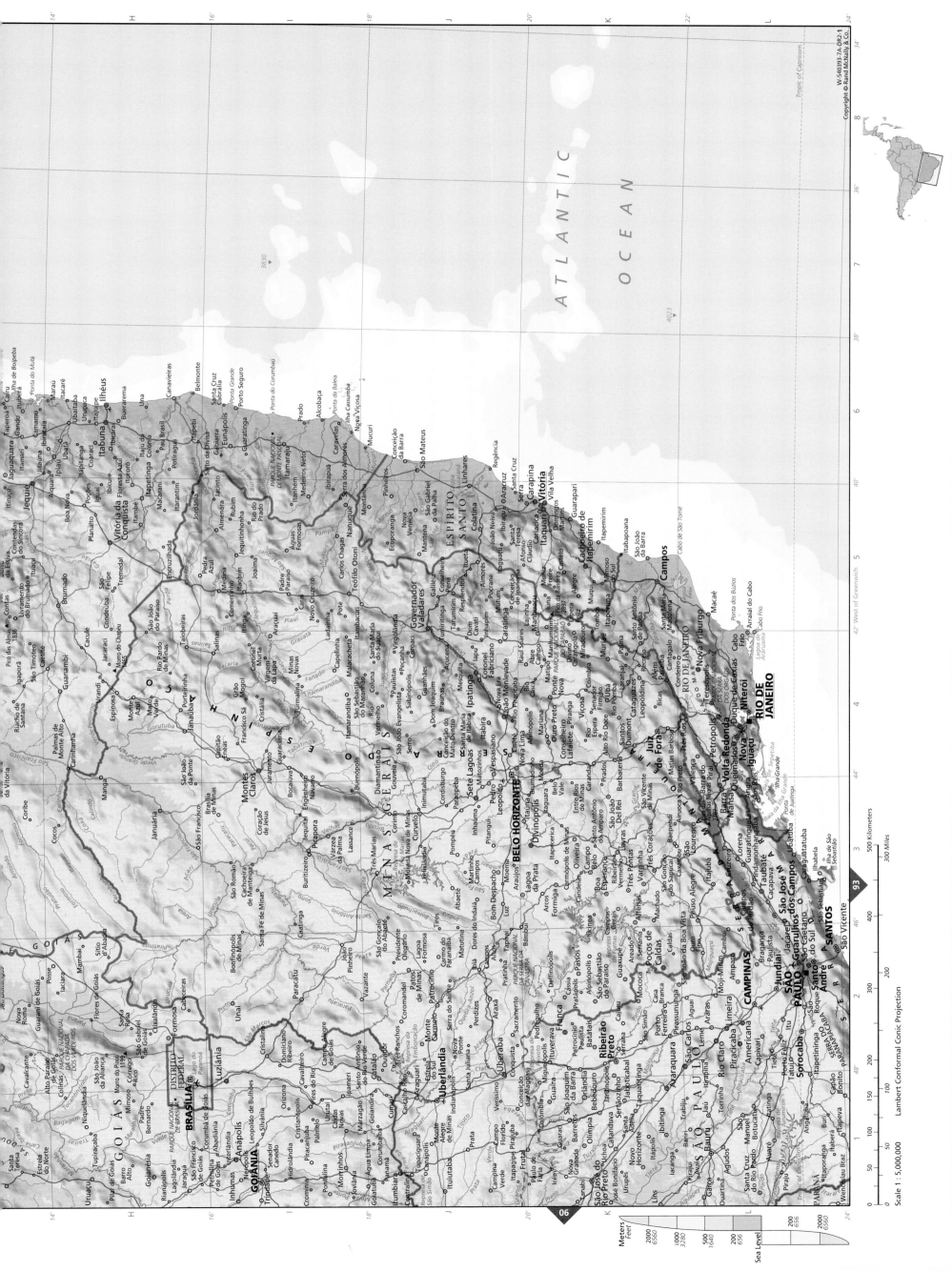

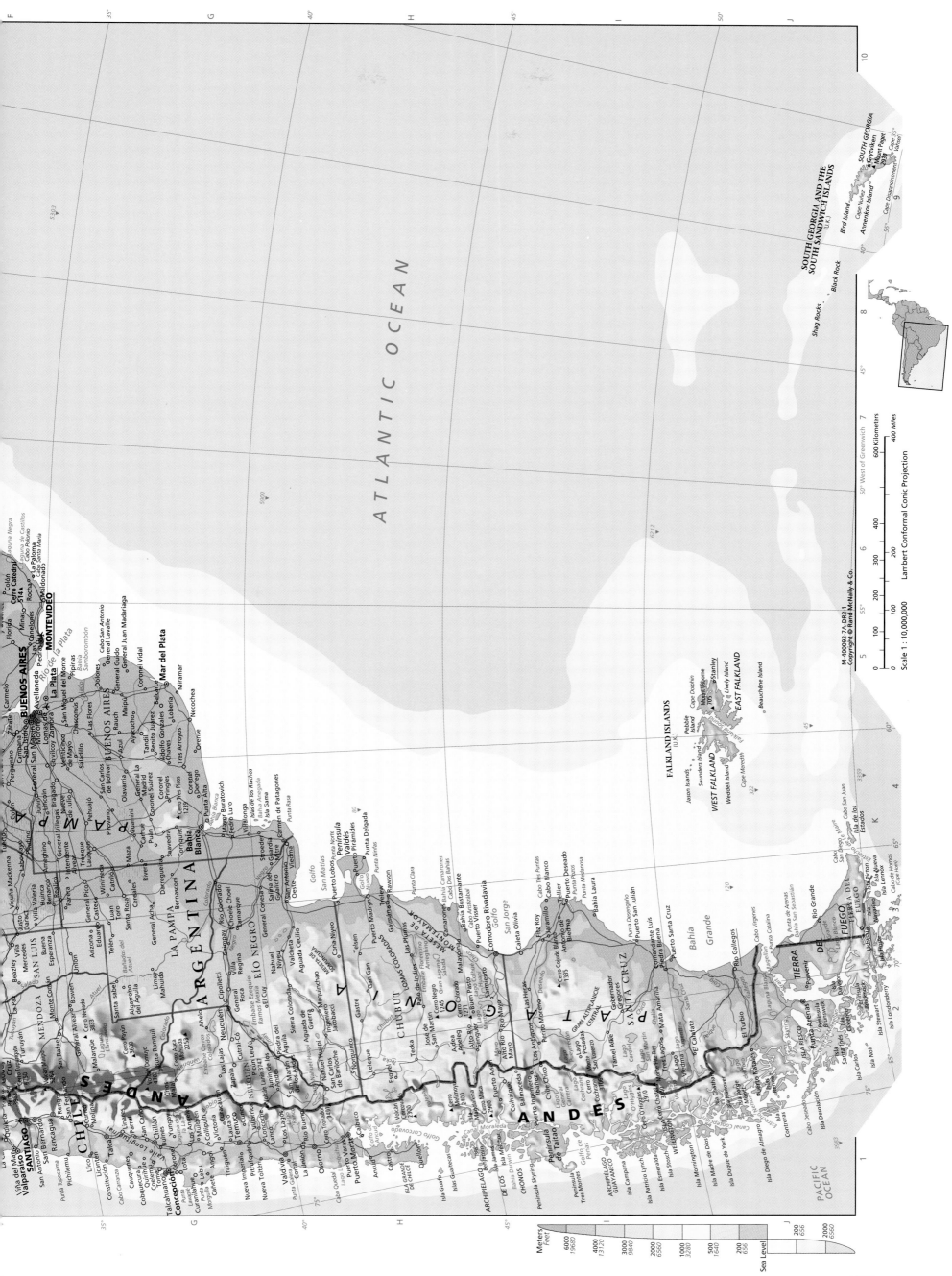

ATLANTIC OCEAN

PACIFIC OCEAN

ANDES

ARGENTINA

PAMPA

CHILE

PATAGONIA

LA PAMPA

RÍO NEGRO

CHUBUT

SANTA CRUZ

NEUQUÉN

BUENOS AIRES

MENDOZA

SAN LUIS

TIERRA DEL FUEGO

CHONOS

ARCHIPIÉLAGO DE LOS CHONOS

ARCHIPIÉLAGO GUAYANECO

BUENOS AIRES

SANTIAGO

MONTEVIDEO

Valparaíso

Concepción

Bahía Blanca

Mar del Plata

FALKLAND ISLANDS
(U.K.)

WEST FALKLAND

EAST FALKLAND

Stanley

SOUTH GEORGIA AND THE
SOUTH SANDWICH ISLANDS
(U.K.)

SOUTH GEORGIA

Bahía Grande

Golfo San Jorge

Península Valdés

50° West of Greenwich

Scale 1 : 10,000,000

Lambert Conformal Conic Projection

M-400092-7A-DR2;1
Copyright © Rand McNally & Co.

Meters / Feet
6000 / 19680
4000 / 13120
3000 / 9840
2000 / 6560
1000 / 3280
500 / 1640
200 / 656
Sea Level
200 / 656
2000 / 6560

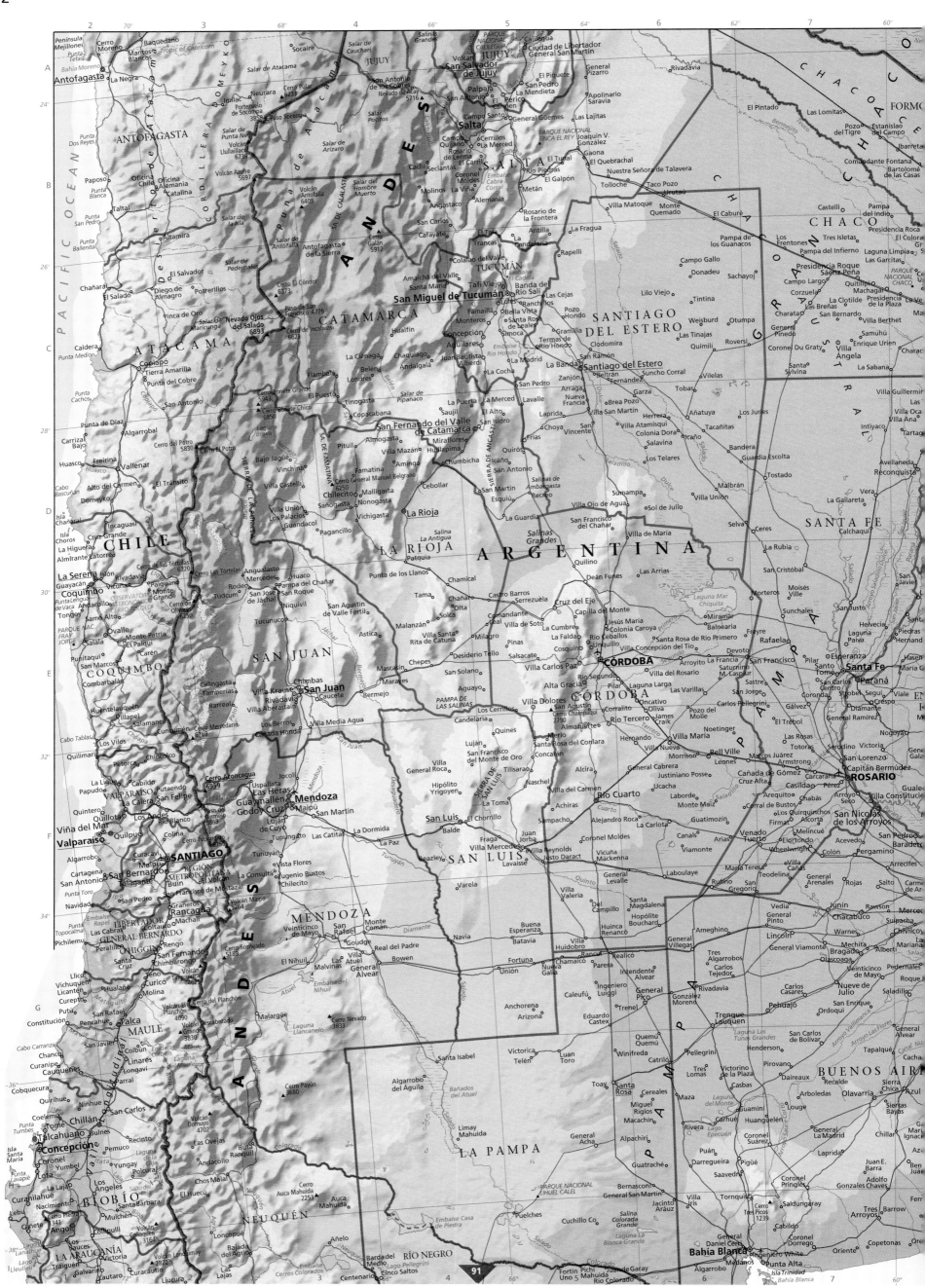

Scale 1 : 5,000,000   Lambert Conformal Conic Projection

0   50   100   150   200   300   400   500 Kilometers

0   50   100   200   300 Miles

Meters
Feet

6000
19680

4000
13120

3000
9840

2000
6560

1000
3280

500
1640

200
656

Sea Level

200
656

2000
6560

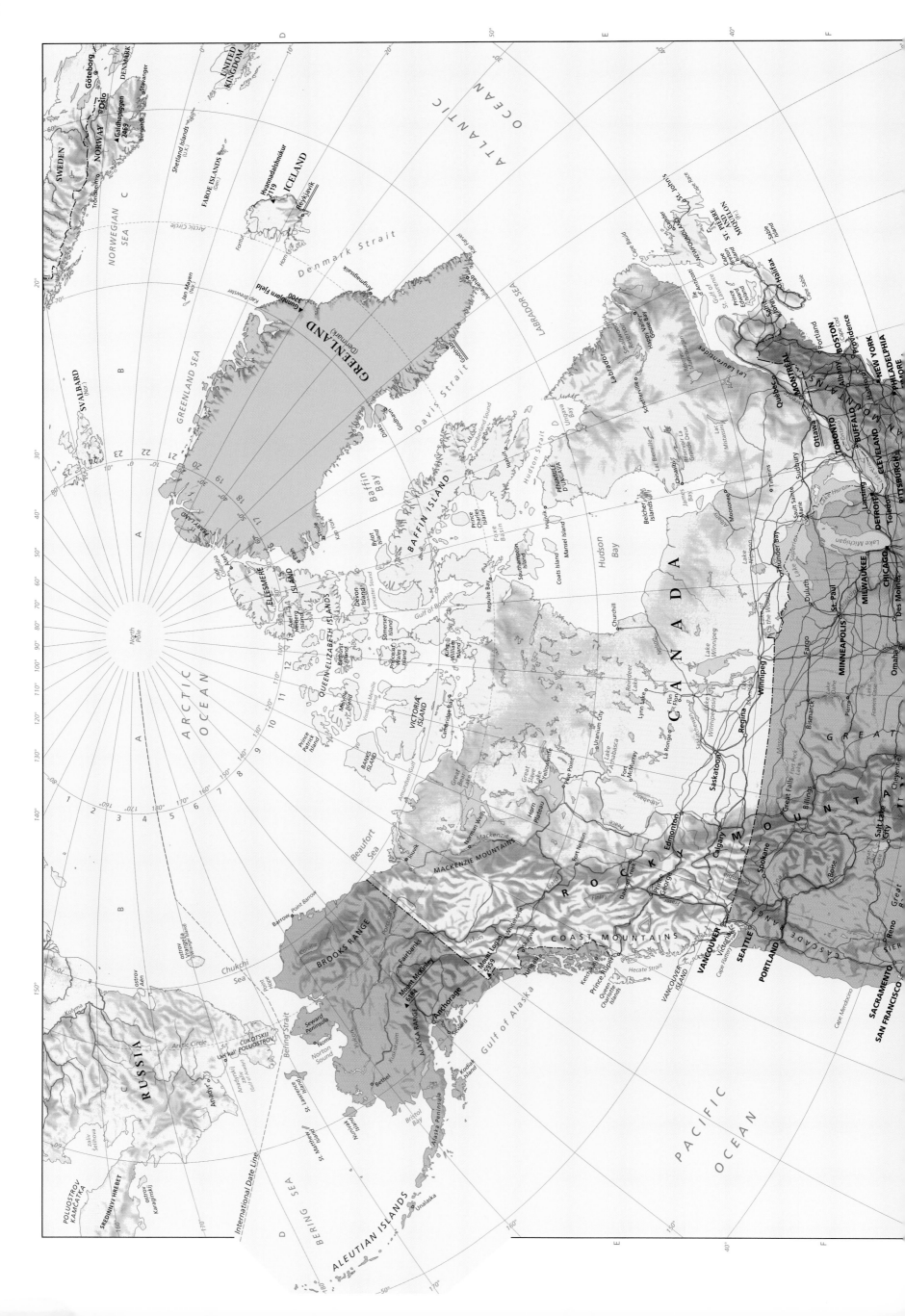

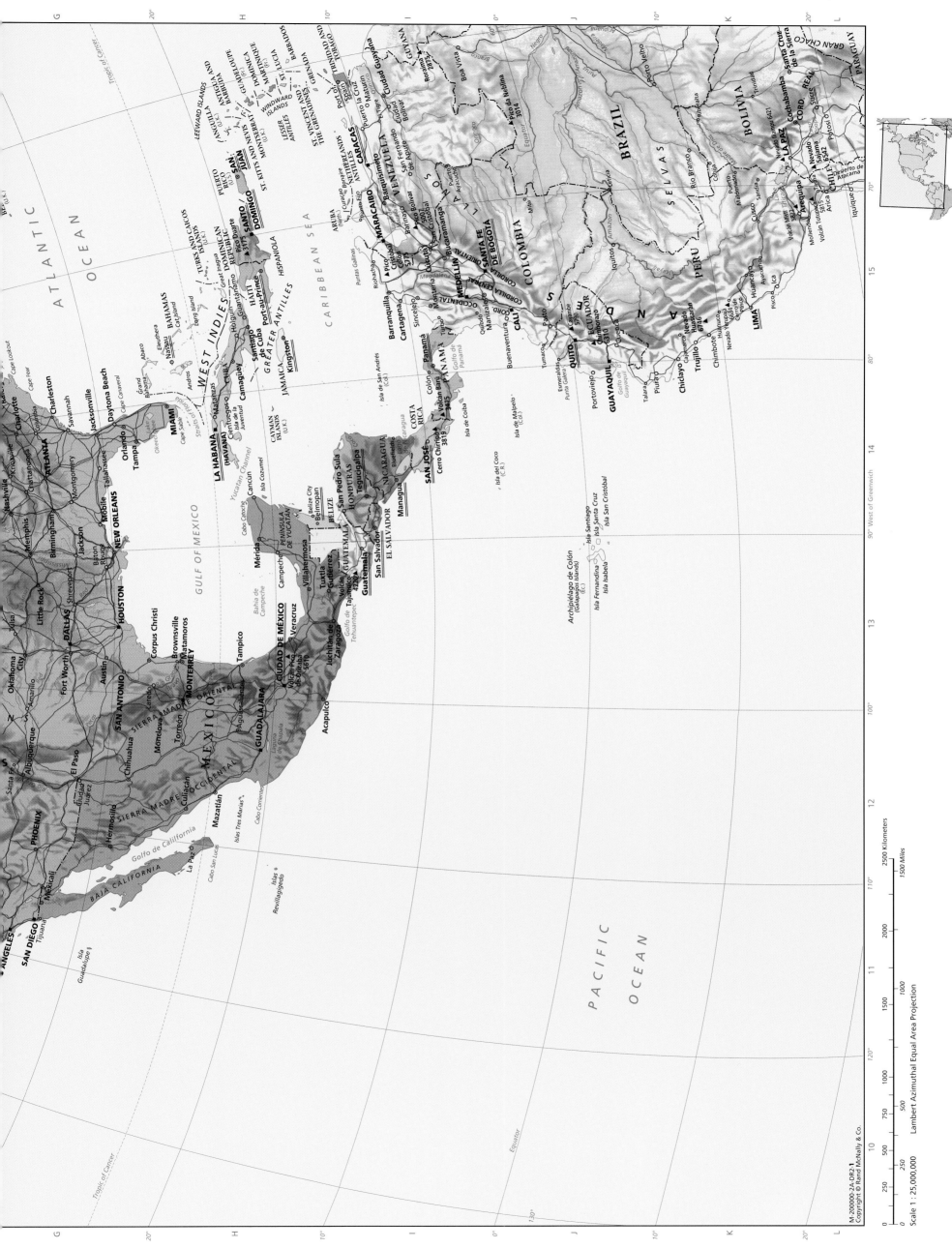

Scale 1 : 25,000,000

Lambert Azimuthal Equal Area Projection

Meters / Feet

4000	13120
3000	9840
2000	6560
1000	3280
500	1640
200	656
Sea Level	
200	656
2000	6560

M-300000-7A-DR2-1
Copyright © Rand McNally & Co.

0 100 200 300 400 500 600 800 1000 Kilometers
0 100 200 400 600 Miles
Scale 1 : 10,000,000   Lambert Conformal Conic Projection

ATLANTIC OCEAN

BERMUDA
(U.K.)
Hamilton

GEORGIA
ALABAMA
MISSISSIPPI
Jackson
Meridian
Mobile
NEW ORLEANS
Biloxi
Gulfport
Pascagoula
Pensacola
Panama City
Tallahassee
FLORIDA
Ocala
Orlando
Tampa
St. Petersburg
Lakeland
Sarasota
Fort Myers
Cape Coral
Naples
Everglades City
MIAMI
Miami Beach
Hialeah
Hollywood
Fort Lauderdale
West Palm Beach
Fort Pierce
Melbourne
Cocoa
Cape Canaveral
Daytona Beach
Jacksonville
Jacksonville Beach
St. Augustine
Gainesville
Homestead
Key Largo
Florida Keys
Key West
Dry Tortugas

Huntsville
Decatur
Gadsden
Anniston
Birmingham
Bessemer
Tuscaloosa
Columbus
Montgomery
Atlanta
Macon
Augusta
Columbia
SOUTH CAROLINA
Charleston
Savannah
Brunswick
Wilmington
N.C.
Myrtle Beach
Cape Fear
Long Bay
Georgetown

BAHAMAS
Little Abaco
Marsh Harbour
Abaco
Freeport
Grand Bahama
Nassau
New Providence
Eleuthera
Governor's Harbour
Cat Island
Mount Alvernia
63
San Salvador
Arthur's Town
Rum Cay
Long Island
Clarence Town
Crooked Island
Acklins
Mayaguana
Great Inagua
Little Inagua

TURKS AND CAICOS
ISLANDS
(U.K.)
Caicos Islands
Grand Turk
Turks Islands

CUBA
LA HABANA
(HAVANA)
Matanzas
Cárdenas
Colón
Pinar del Río
Santa Clara
Cienfuegos
Sancti Spíritus
Ciego de Ávila
Camagüey
Las Tunas
Holguín
Bayamo
Manzanillo
Santiago de Cuba
Pico Turquino
1972
SIERRA MAESTRA
Guantánamo

GREATER
CAYMAN ISLANDS
(U.K.)
George Town
Little Cayman
Cayman Brac
Grand Cayman

JAMAICA
Montego Bay
Savanna-la-Mar
Spanish Town
Kingston
Blue Mountain Peak
2256
Morant Cays

WEST   INDIES

HISPANIOLA
HAITI
Cap-Haïtien
Gonaïves
Port-au-Prince
Morne La Selle
2674
DOMINICAN
REPUBLIC
Santiago de los Caballeros
SANTO DOMINGO
San Pedro de Macorís
La Romana

PUERTO RICO
(U.S.)
Mayagüez

ANTILLES

CARIBBEAN SEA

GUATEMALA
San Pedro Sula
HONDURAS
Tegucigalpa
EL SALVADOR
San Salvador
San Miguel
NICARAGUA
Managua
Granada
León
COSTA RICA
SAN JOSÉ
PANAMA
Panama
Colón

BELIZE
Belmopan
Belize City
Victoria Peak
1120
Gulf of
Honduras
Roatán

Tropic of Cancer

COLOMBIA
Barranquilla
Cartagena
MEDELLÍN
SANTA FE DE BOGOTÁ
CORDILLERA OCCIDENTAL
CORDILLERA CENTRAL
CORDILLERA ORIENTAL

VENEZUELA
MARACAIBO
Barquisimeto
Bucaramanga
Cúcuta
CORD. DE MÉRIDA
Pico Bolívar
5007

ARUBA
(Neth.)
NETH. ANT.

LLANOS

90° West of Greenwich

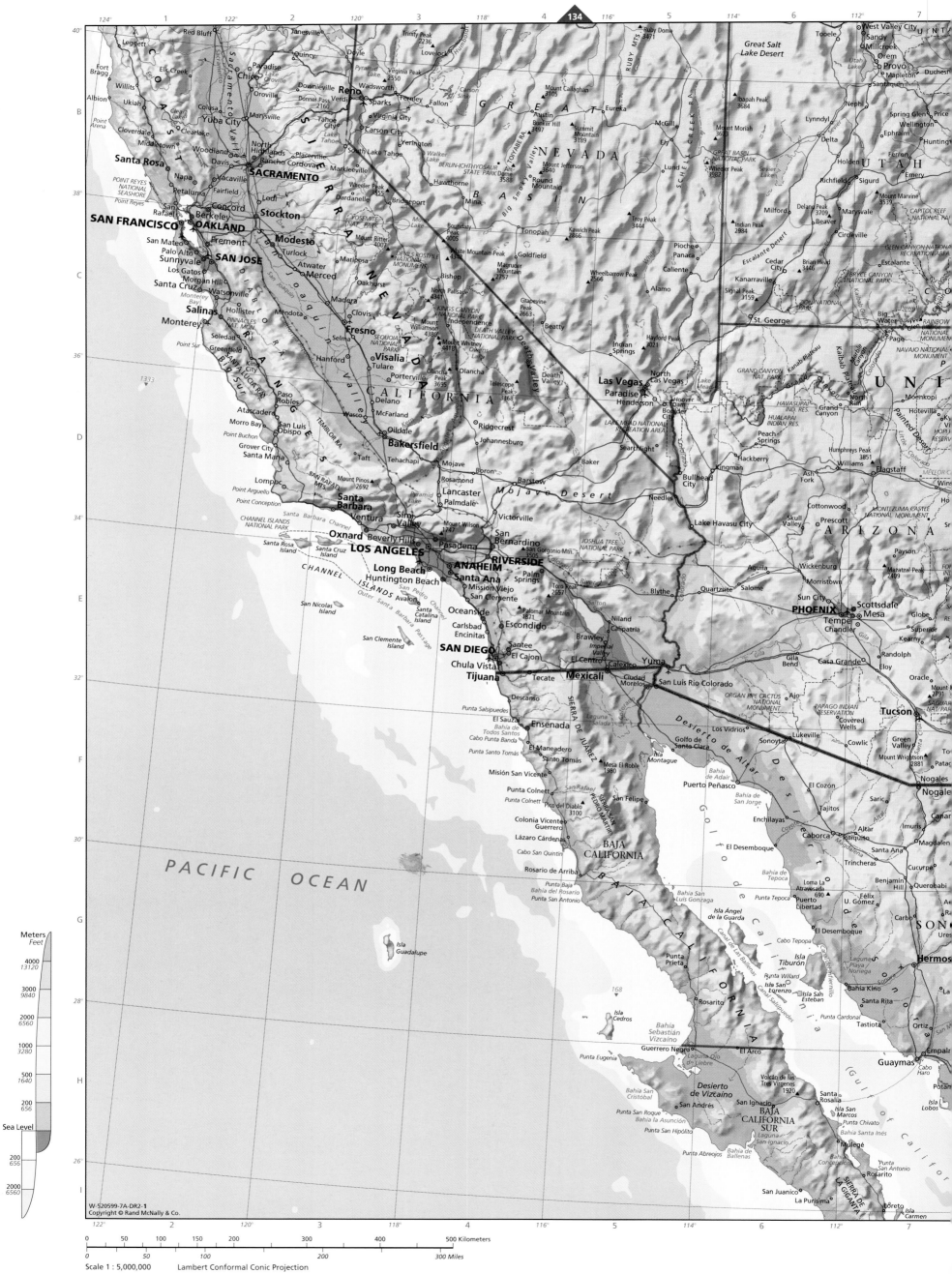

Scale 1 : 5,000,000   Lambert Conformal Conic Projection

Meters
Feet
4000
13120
3000
9840
2000
6560
1000
3280
500
1640
200
656
Sea Level
200
656
2000
6560

0 50 100 150 200 300 400 500 Kilometers
0 50 100 200 300 Miles

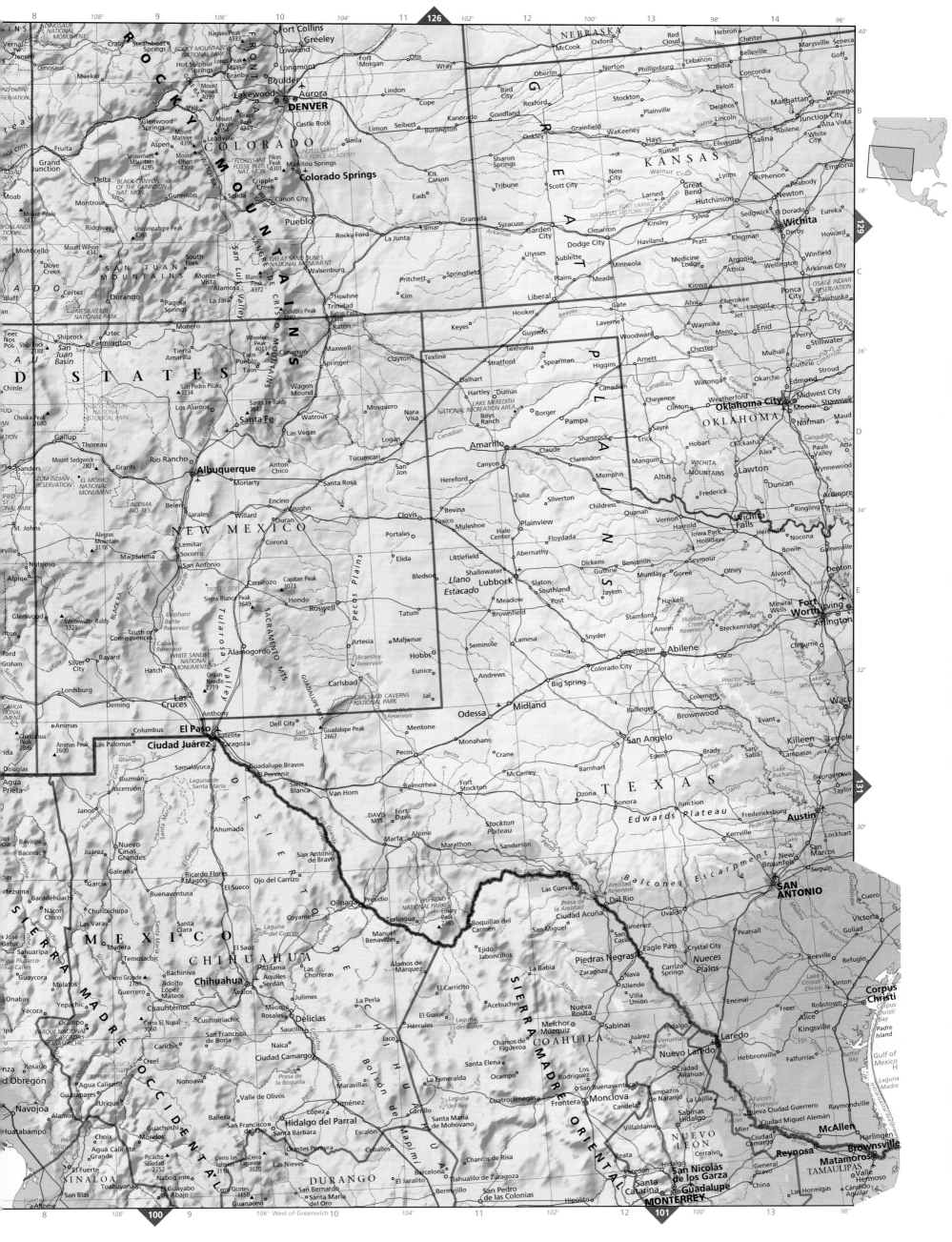

98

BAJA CALIFORNIA / SONORA / CHIHUAHUA

Punta Prieta
Rosarito
Isla Cedros
Bahía Sebastián Vizcaíno
Punta Eugenia
Guerrero Negro
Laguna Ojo de Liebre
Punta San Hipólito
Bahía San Cristóbal
San Andrés
Desierto de Vizcaíno
Punta Abreojos
Bahía de Ballenas
San Juanico
La Purísima

Isla Ángel de la Guarda
Isla Tiburón
Isla San Esteban
Isla San Lorenzo
Punta Cardonal
Canal del Infiernillo
Playa Noriega
Punta Willard

Hermosillo
La Colorada
Tastiota
Guaymas
Cabo Haro
Bahía Kino
Empalme

SONORA
Santa Rita
Ortiz
Potam
Vícam
Esperanza
Ciudad Obregón
Pueblo Yaqui
Villa Juárez
Isla San Lobos
Navojoa
Huatabampo
Yavaros
Etchojoa
Álamos

Gómez Farias
Santa Clara
Madera
Temosachic
Yécora
Guerrero
Onabas
Suaqui Grande
Nácori
Rosario
San José de Batuc
Yepachic
Ocampo
Creel

CHIHUAHUA
Bachíniva
Cuauhtémoc
Aldama
Las Chorreras
Chihuahua
Adolfo López Mateos
Ciudad Camargo
Delicias
Saucillo
Santa Bárbara
Hidalgo del Parral
Escalón
Ceballos
Las Nieves

Volcán de las Tres Vírgenes 1920
Santa Rosalía
San Ignacio
San José de Gracia
Isla San Marcos
Punta Chivato
Bahía Santa Inés
Mulegé
Bahía Concepción

BAJA CALIFORNIA
La Poza Grande
Santo Domingo
Villa Insurgentes
Ciudad Constitución
Cabo San Lázaro
Isla Santa Magdalena
Bahía Magdalena
El Medano
Isla Santa Margarita
Bahía Almejas
Todos Santos

BAJA CALIFORNIA SUR
Loreto
Ligüí
Isla Carmen
Isla Santa Catalina
Punta San Pasqual
Isla San José
San Luis Gonzaga
Isla del Espíritu Santo
Isla Cerralvo
La Paz
Bahía de La Paz
Punta Arena de la Ventana
El Triunfo
Las Casitas 2164
Punta Pescadores
Punta Arena
Santiago
San Lucas
San José del Cabo
Cabo San Lucas

Los Mochis
Higuera de Zaragoza
San Blas
Topolobampo
Guasave
Ahome
El Fuerte
Choix

SINALOA
Culiacán
Navolato
Altata
Mazatlán
Villa Unión
Concordia
Escuinapa de Hidalgo
Teacapán
Laguna del Caimanero
Acaponeta
Tecuala
Rosamorada
Tuxpan
Ruiz

NAYARIT
Tepic
San Blas
Santiago Ixcuintla
Las Varas
Compostela
Ahuacatlán
Ixtlán del Río
San Juan de Abajo
Puerto Vallarta
Bahía de Banderas
Cabo Corrientes
Tomatlán

ISLAS TRES MARÍAS
Isla San Juanito
Isla María Madre
Isla María Magdalena
Isla María Cleofas

DURANGO
El Salto
La Ciudad
Mezquital
Nombre de Dios
Súchil
Vicente Guerrero

COLIMA
Manzanillo
Armería

JALISCO
GUADALAJARA
Zapopan
Tlaquepaque

PACIFIC OCEAN

ISLAS REVILLAGIGEDO
Isla San Benedicto
Isla Roca Partida
Cerro Evermann 1050
Isla Socorro

Tropic of Cancer

Meters / Feet
4000 / 13120
3000 / 9840
2000 / 6560
1000 / 3280
500 / 1640
200 / 656
Sea Level
200 / 656
2000 / 6560

W-532095-7A-DR2-1
Copyright © Rand McNally & Co.

Scale 1 : 5,000,000   Lambert Conformal Conic Projection

0 50 100 150 200 300 400 500 Kilometers
0 50 100 200 300 Miles

Gulf of Mexico

Cayo Arenas

PACIFIC OCEAN

MEXICO

PENÍNSULA DE YUCATÁN
(YUCATAN PENINSULA)

YUCATÁN

QUINTANA ROO

CAMPECHE

CHIAPAS

TABASCO

GUATEMALA

BELIZE

HONDURAS

EL SALVADOR

NICARAGUA

COSTA RICA

SIERRA MADRE

MAYA MOUNTAINS

CORDILLERA DE MORQUITOS

CORDILLERA CHONTALEÑA

CORDILLERA DARIENSE

CORDILLERA ISABELIA

CORDILLERA DE GUANACASTE

Mérida
Campeche
Cancún
Chetumal
Belize City
Belmopan
Guatemala
Tegucigalpa
San Pedro Sula
San Salvador
San Miguel
Managua
Granada
San José

LA HABANA (HAVANA)

CAYMAN ISL.
(U.K.)

George Town
Grand Cayman

Isla de Providencia

Isla de San Andrés

SAN ANDRÉS Y PROVIDENCIA (Col.)

PANA...

Gulf of Honduras

ISLAS DE LA BAHÍA

Meters / Feet
3000 / 9840
2000 / 6560
1000 / 3280
500 / 1640
200 / 656
Sea Level
200 / 656
2000 / 6560

W-536000-7A-DR2-1
Copyright © Rand McNally & Co.

0 50 100 150 200 300 400 500 Kilometers
0 50 100 200 300 Miles
Scale 1 : 5,000,000
Lambert Conformal Conic Projection

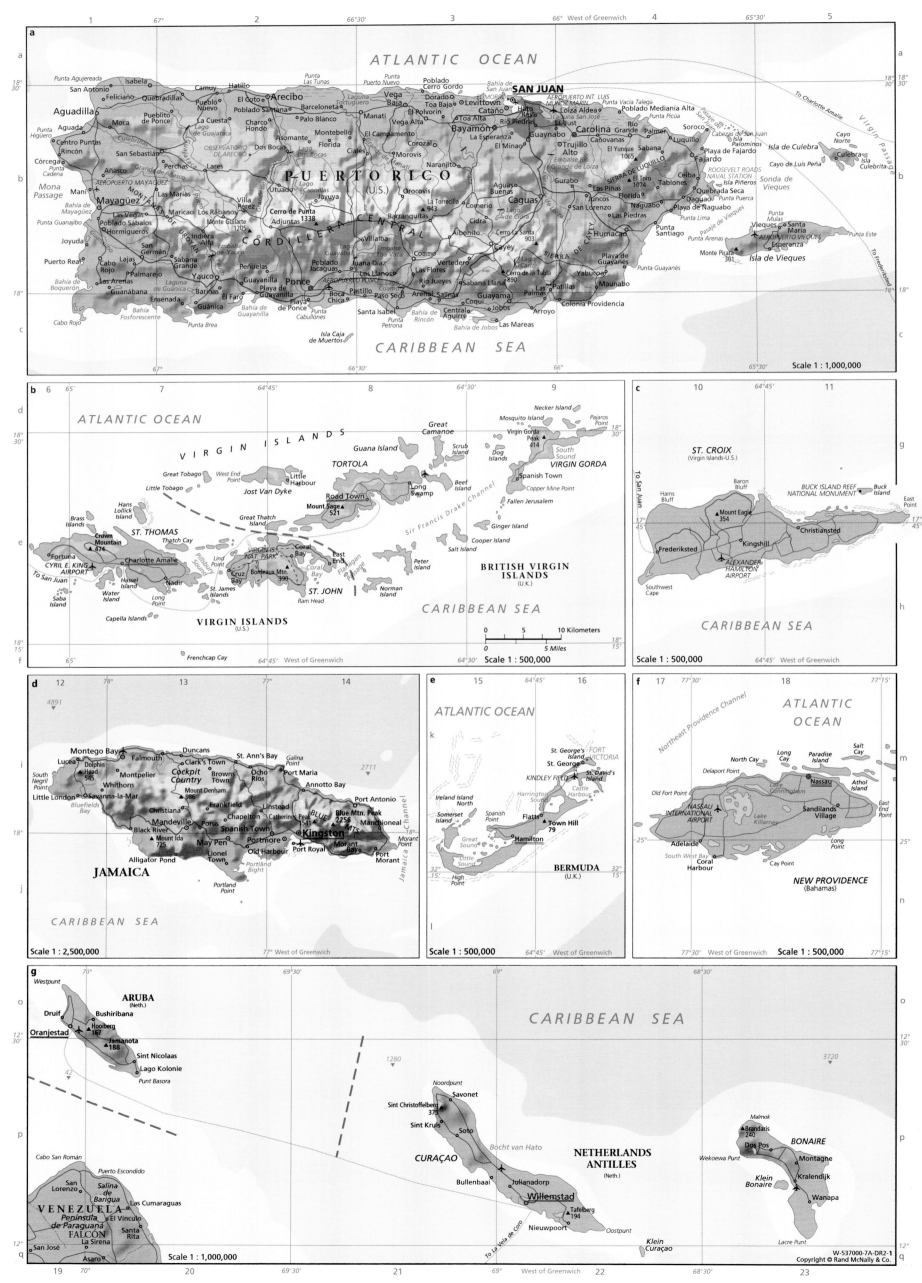

a

ATLANTIC OCEAN

SAN JUAN

PUERTO RICO
(U.S.)

CORDILLERA CENTRAL

Cerro de Punta
Adjuntas 1338

Ponce

CARIBBEAN SEA

Scale 1 : 1,000,000

b VIRGIN ISLANDS

ATLANTIC OCEAN

TORTOLA

VIRGIN GORDA

ST. THOMAS

BRITISH VIRGIN
ISLANDS
(U.K.)

Charlotte Amalie

ST. JOHN

VIRGIN ISLANDS
(U.S.)

CARIBBEAN SEA

0   5   10 Kilometers
0   5 Miles
Scale 1 : 500,000

c

ST. CROIX
(Virgin Islands-U.S.)

BUCK ISLAND REEF
NATIONAL MONUMENT

Mount Eagle
354

Frederiksted   Christiansted

Kingshill

ALEXANDER
HAMILTON
AIRPORT

Southwest
Cape

CARIBBEAN SEA

Scale 1 : 500,000

d

Montego Bay   Duncans
Falmouth   St. Ann's Bay
Lucea   Ocho
Cockpit   Browns   Rios
Country   Town
Montpelier   Port Maria
Mount Denham   Annotto Bay
986
Christiana   Frankfield   Port Antonio
Mandeville   Blue Mtn. Peak
Porus   Chapelton   2256
Spanish Town   BLUE
Mount Ida   May Pen   Kingston   Port
725   Lionel   Old Harbour   Morant
Town   Port Royal
Alligator Pond

JAMAICA

CARIBBEAN SEA

Scale 1 : 2,500,000

e

ATLANTIC OCEAN

St. George's   FORT
Island   VICTORIA
St. George
KINDLEY FIELD
St. David's
Island
Castle
Harbour
Ireland Island
North
Spanish Point   Flatts
Somerset
Island   Town Hill
79
Hamilton

Great
Sound

BERMUDA
(U.K.)

f

ATLANTIC
OCEAN

North Cay   Long   Paradise   Salt
Cay   Island   Cay

Delaport Point

Nassau

Old Fort Point   NASSAU
INTERNATIONAL
AIRPORT   Sandilands
Village

Adelaide
Coral
Harbour   Cay Point

NEW PROVIDENCE
(Bahamas)

Scale 1 : 500,000

g

ARUBA
(Neth.)
Westpunt

Druif   Bushiribana
Oranjestad   Hooiberg
167
Jamanota
188
Sint Nicolaas
Lago Kolonie
Punt Basora

CARIBBEAN SEA

Noordpunt
Savonet
Sint Christoffelberg
375
Sint Kruis
Soto

CURAÇAO

Cabo San Román
Puerto Escondido
San
Lorenzo   Salina
de
Bariqua

VENEZUELA
Peninsula
de Paraguaná
FALCON
La Sirena
San José   Santa
Rita
Asaro

Bonchi van Hato

NETHERLANDS
ANTILLES
(Neth.)

Willemstad

Brandaris
240
Dos Pos
BONAIRE
Montagne
Wekoewa Punt
Klein
Bonaire   Kralendijk
Wanapa
Lacre Punt

Scale 1 : 1,000,000

W-537000-7A-DR2-1
Copyright © Rand McNally & Co.

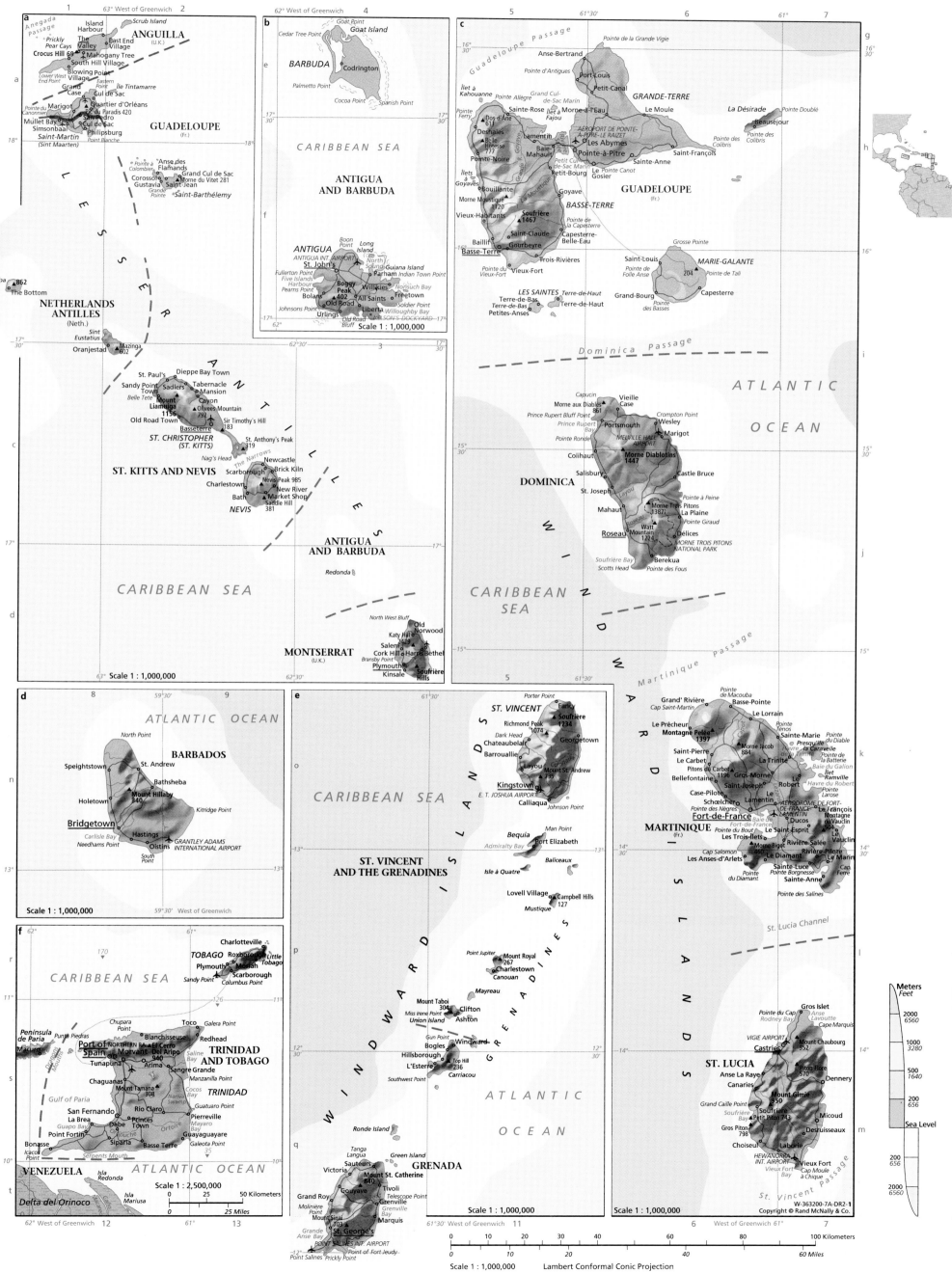

a Anegada Passage

63° West of Greenwich

Scrub Island
Island Harbour
Island Harbour
The Valley • East End Village
Crocus Hill 69 • Mahogany Tree
South Hill Village
Blowing Point
Grand Case
Quartier d'Orléans
du Paradis 420
Marigot
Mullet Bay • Cul de Sac
Simsonbaai • Philipsburg
Saint-Martin
(Sint Maarten)
Point Blanche

ANGUILLA (U.K.)

GUADELOUPE (Fr.)

Pointe à Colombier
Anse des Flamands
Corossol • Grand Cul de Sac
Gustavia • Morne du Vitet 281
Grande Pointe • Saint-Jean
Saint-Barthélemy

862
The Bottom

NETHERLANDS ANTILLES (Neth.)

Sint Eustatius
Mazinga 602
Oranjestad

St. Paul's
Sandy Point Town • Dieppe Bay Town
Sadlers • Tabernacle
Belle Tête • Mansion
Mount • Cayon
Liamuiga 1156
Olivees Mountain 792
Old Road Town • Sir Timothy's Hill 183
Basseterre
ST. CHRISTOPHER (ST. KITTS)
St. Anthony's Peak 919

ST. KITTS AND NEVIS

Nag's Head • The Narrows
Newcastle • Brick Kiln
Scarborough
Charlestown • Nevis Peak 985
New River
Bath • Market Shop
Saddle Hill 381
NEVIS

ANTIGUA AND BARBUDA

Redonda

CARIBBEAN SEA

Scale 1 : 1,000,000

b 62° West of Greenwich

Goat Point
Goat Island
Cedar Tree Point
Scrub Island
BARBUDA
Codrington
Palmetto Point
Cocoa Point • Spanish Point

CARIBBEAN SEA

ANTIGUA AND BARBUDA

Boon Point
Long Island
ANTIGUA
ANTIGUA INT. AIRPORT
North Sound
Fullerton Point
St. John's • Parham • Guiana Island
Five Islands Harbour • Indian Town Point
Pearns Point • Willikies
Boggy • All Saints • Freetown
Bolans Peak 402
Johnsons Point • Liberta • Soldier Point
Urlings • Willoughby Bay
Old Road • NELSON'S DOCKYARD
Bluff

Scale 1 : 1,000,000

c 5 61°30' 6 61° 7

Guadeloupe Passage

Pointe de la Grande Vigie
Anse-Bertrand
Pointe d'Antigues
Îlet à Kahouanne
Pointe Allègre
Grand Cul-de-Sac Marin
Port-Louis
Petit-Canal
Dos d'Âne 611
Sainte-Rose
Îlet à Fajou • Morne-à-l'Eau • Le Moule
GRANDE-TERRE
Deshaies • Belle Hôtesse 777
Lamentin • La Désirade
Pointe-Noire • Baie-Mahault • Les Abymes • Beauséjour
AÉROPORT DE POINTE- • Pointe des Colibris
À-PITRE-LE RAIZET
Pointe-à-Pitre • Pointe Doublé
Le Gosier • Sainte-Anne
Îlets • Saint-François
Goyaves • Le Canot
Bouillante • Petit-Bourg
Goyave
Morne Mazeau • Pointe des Colibris
Morne Mazeau 1120
Vieux-Habitants • **BASSE-TERRE**
Soufrière 1467 • **GUADELOUPE** (Fr.)
Saint-Claude • Pointe de la Capesterre
Baillif • Capesterre • Grosse Pointe
Basse-Terre • Gourbeyre • Belle-Eau
Trois-Rivières • Saint-Louis
Pointe du • MARIE-GALANTE
Vieux-Fort
Pointe de Folle Anse • 204 • Pointe de Tali
LES SAINTES • Terre-de-Haut
Terre-de-Bas • Grand-Bourg • Capesterre
Terre-de-Bas • Terre-de-Haut • Pointe des Basses
Petites-Anses

Dominica Passage

Capucin • Vieille Case
Morne aux Diables 861
Prince Rupert Bluff Point • Crompton Point
Prince Rupert Bay • Wesley
Portsmouth • Marigot
Pointe Ronde • MELVILLE HALL AIRPORT
Colihaut • Morne Diablotins 1447
Salisbury • Castle Bruce
St. Joseph
DOMINICA
Mahaut • Morne Trois Pitons 1387 • Pointe à Peine
Roseau • La Plaine
Watt • Pointe Giraud
Mountain 1224 • Délices
MORNE TROIS PITONS
NATIONAL PARK
Soufrière Bay • Berekua
Scotts Head • Pointe des Fous

CARIBBEAN SEA

ATLANTIC OCEAN

Martinique Passage

d 8 59°30' 9

ATLANTIC OCEAN

North Point
Speightstown • St. Andrew
BARBADOS
Bathsheba
Holetown • Mount Hillaby 340
Kitridge Point
Bridgetown
Hastings
Carlisle Bay • Oistins
Needhams Point • South Point
GRANTLEY ADAMS INTERNATIONAL AIRPORT

Scale 1 : 1,000,000
59°30' West of Greenwich

e 61°30' 11

Porter Point
ST. VINCENT • Fancy
Richmond Peak 1074 • Soufrière 1234
Dark Head • Georgetown
Chateaubelair
Barrouallie • Layou
Mount St. Andrew 735
Kingstown
E. T. JOSHUA AIRPORT • Calliaqua
Johnson Point

Man Point
Bequia • Port Elizabeth
Admiralty Bay
ST. VINCENT AND THE GRENADINES
Isle à Quatre
Baliceaux
Lovell Village • Campbell Hills 127
Mustique

Point Jupiter • Mount Royal 267
Charlestown
Canouan
Mayreau

Mount Taboi 304
Miss Irene Point • Clifton
Union Island • Ashton
Gun Point
Bogles • Windward
Hillsborough
L'Esterre • Top Hill 236
Carriacou
Southwest Point

ATLANTIC OCEAN

Ronde Island

Tanga
Langua • Green Island
Sauteurs
Victoria • Mount St. Catherine 840 • Tivoli
Grand Roy • Gouyave • Telescope Point
Molinière Point • **GRENADA** • Grenville
Mount Sinai 701 • Marquis
St. George's
Anse Bay • POINT SALINES INT. AIRPORT
Point Salines • Point of Fort Jeudy
Prickly Point

Scale 1 : 1,000,000
61°30' West of Greenwich

f 62° 61°

170 • Charlotteville
TOBAGO • Roxborough • Little Tobago
CARIBBEAN SEA
Plymouth • Mason Hall
Scarborough
126 • Sandy Point • Columbus Point

Peninsula de Paria
Punta Piedras • Chupara Point
Macuro • Toco • Galera Point
Blanchisseuse • Redhead
PORT OF • NORTHERN RA. • El Cerro
Port of Spain • Morvant • del Aripo 940
Tunapuna • Saline Bay
Arima • **TRINIDAD AND TOBAGO**
Chaguanas • Sangre Grande
Manzanilla Point
Mount Tamana 308 • *TRINIDAD*
Caroni Swamp
San Fernando • Rio Claro • Cocos Bay
La Brea • Pierreville • Guataro Point
Debe • Princes • Mayaro Point
Point Fortin • Town • Guayaguayare
Siparia • Galeota Point
Bonasse • Basse Terre
Icacos • Guapo Bay
Point • Gulf of Paria
Serpents Mouth

VENEZUELA

ATLANTIC OCEAN

Isla Redonda
Delta del Orinoco
Isla Mariusa

Scale 1 : 2,500,000
0 25 50 Kilometers
0 25 Miles

k Pointe de Macouba
Grand' Rivière • Basse-Pointe
Cap Saint-Martin
Le Prêcheur • Le Lorrain
Montagne Pelée 1397 • Sainte-Marie
Pointe du Diable
Morne Jacob 884 • Pointe de la Batterie
Saint-Pierre • La Trinité
Le Carbet • Presqu'île la Caravelle
Pitons du Carbet 1196 • Baie du Galion
Gros-Morne • Îlet
Bellefontaine • Ramville
Saint-Joseph • Robert • Pointe Larose
Case-Pilote • Havre du Robert
Schoelcher • Le Lamentin • Le François
Fort-de-France • Pointe des Nègres • AÉRODROME DE FORT- • Montagne
DE-FRANCE-LAMENTIN • du Vauclin 504
MARTINIQUE (Fr.) • Ducos • Le Vauclin
Pointe du Bout • Le Saint-Esprit
Les Trois-Îlets • Rivière-Salée • Le Marin
Cap Salomon • Bigot 460 • Rivière-Pilote
Les Anses-d'Arlets • Le Diamant
Sainte-Luce • Cap Ferré
Sainte-Anne • Pointe Borgnesse
Pointe du Diamant • Pointe des Salines

St. Lucia Channel

Pointe du Cap • Gros Islet
Rodney Bay • Anse Lavoutte
VIGIE AIRPORT • Pointe Marquis
Castries • Mount Chaubourg 352
ST. LUCIA
Anse La Raye • Dennery
Canaries
Mount Gimie 950 • Micoud
Grand Caille Point • Soufrière • Petit Piton 743
Soufrière Bay • Gros Piton 798
Choiseul
Laborie
HEWANORRA • Vieux Fort
INT. AIRPORT
Vieux Fort • Cap Moule
Bay • à Chique

St. Vincent Passage

Scale 1 : 1,000,000
West of Greenwich 61°

W-363200-7A-DR2-1
Copyright © Rand McNally & Co.

Meters / Feet
2000 / 6560
1000 / 3280
500 / 1640
200 / 656
Sea Level
200 / 656
2000 / 6560

Scale 1 : 1,000,000
0 10 20 30 40 50 60 70 80 100 Kilometers
0 10 20 30 40 60 Miles
Lambert Conformal Conic Projection

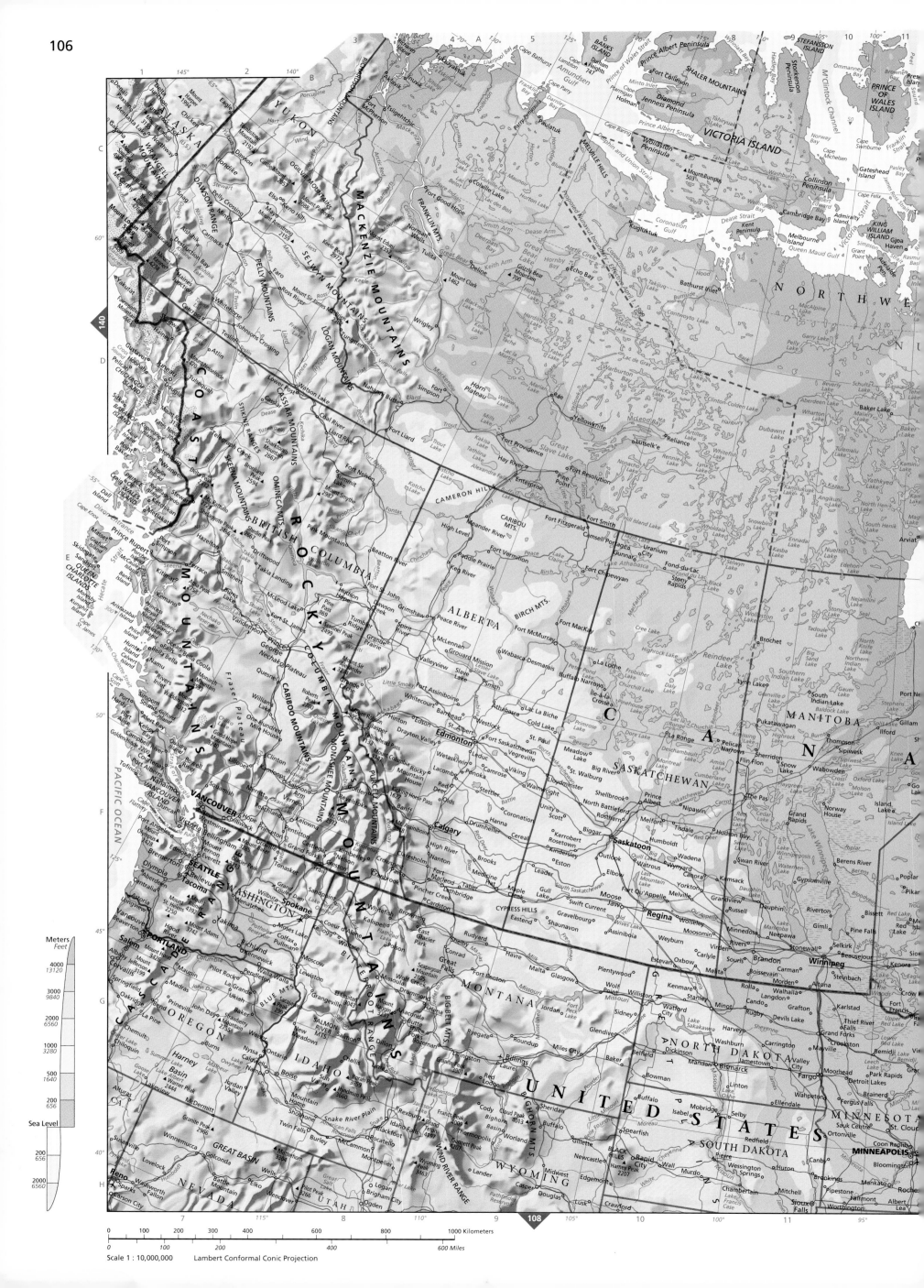

Meters / Feet
3000 / 9840
2000 / 6560
1000 / 3280
500 / 1640
200 / 656
Sea Level
200 / 656
2000 / 6560

M-205000-7A-DR2-1
Copyright © Rand McNally & Co.

0   100   200   300   400   600   800   1000 Kilometers
0   100   200   400   600 Miles
Scale 1 : 10,000,000   Lambert Conformal Conic Projection

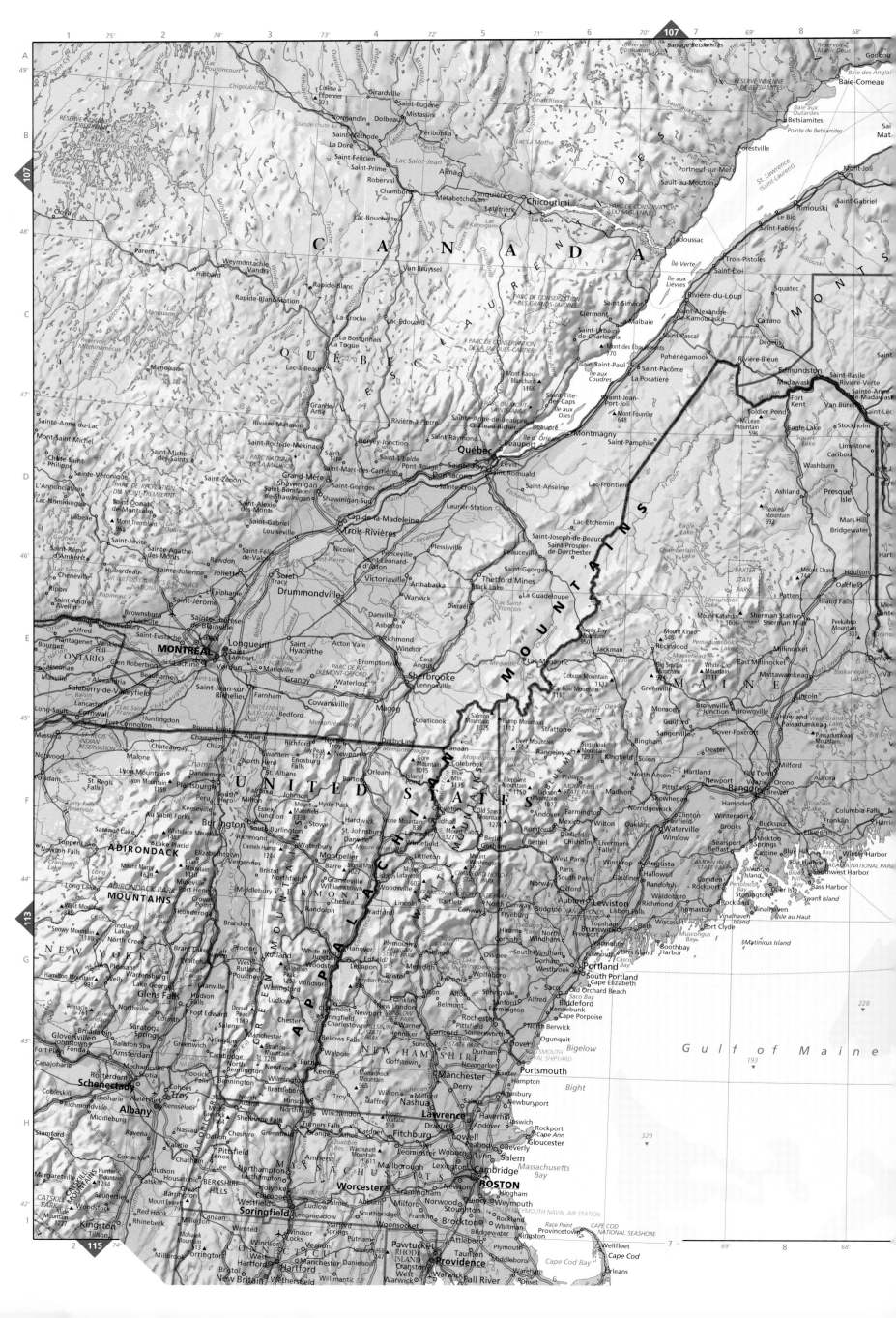

Détroit d'Honguedo

ÎLE D'ANTICOSTI

Pointe du Sud-Ouest
Rivière-de-la-Chaloupe
Pointe de l'Est
Pointe Heath

La Martre   Rivière-à-Claude   Madeleine-Centre   Saint-Yvon
Cap-Chat   Sainte-Anne-des-Monts   Pointe-la-Frégate
Mont Jacques-Cartier 1277
Dartmouth
Fontenelle
PARC NATIONAL DE FORILLON
Gaspé
Cap Gaspé
Baie de Gaspé
Saint-Gabriel-de-Gaspé
Percé
Île Bonaventure
Grande-Rivière
Chandler
Newport
Pointe au Maquereau

Gulf of St. Lawrence

Port au Port Peninsula
Cape St. George

NEWFOUNDLAND

Cape Anguille
Codroy   Doyles
Tompkins
Table Mountain

Cape Ray

Île Brion

La Grosse Île
Grande-Entrée   Île de l' Est
ÎLES DE LA MADELEINE (Que.)
Île du Cap aux Meules
Cap-aux-Meules
Baie de Plaisance
Île du Havre Aubert
Havre-Aubert

St. Paul Island

Cabot Strait

To Channel-Port aux Basques

Cape St. Lawrence   Cape North
Aspy Bay
Dingwall   Long Point
Pleasant Bay
CAPE BRETON HIGHLANDS NATIONAL PARK
Chéticamp   Ingonish
Grand-Étang   Cape Smokey
Margaree Harbour   Margaree   Indian Brook
Inverness   Strathlorne   St. Anns Bay   Boularderie Island
New Waterford
Baddeck   Sydney Mines   Dominion
Mabou   North Sydney   Glace Bay
Iona   Sydney   Port Morien
Port Hood   Whycocomagh   Mira Bay
Judique   Bras d'Or Lake   Scatarie Island
West Bay   LOUISBOURG NAT. HIST. SITE
Pomquet   Louisdale   Louisbourg
St. Georges Bay   Mulgrave   Arichat   Gabarus
Cape George   Port Hawkesbury   St. Peters   Fourchu
   Isle Madame   L'Ardoise   Loch Lomond
Point Michaud

ATLANTIC OCEAN

Sable Island (N.S.)

Meters / Feet
1000 / 3280
500 / 1640
200 / 656
Sea Level
200 / 656
2000 / 6560

W-520298-7A-DR2-1
Copyright © Rand McNally & Co.

0   25   50   75   100   150   200   250 Kilometers
0   25   50   100   150 Miles
Scale 1 : 2,500,000   Lambert Conformal Conic Projection

Scale 1 : 2,500,000   Lambert Conformal Conic Projection

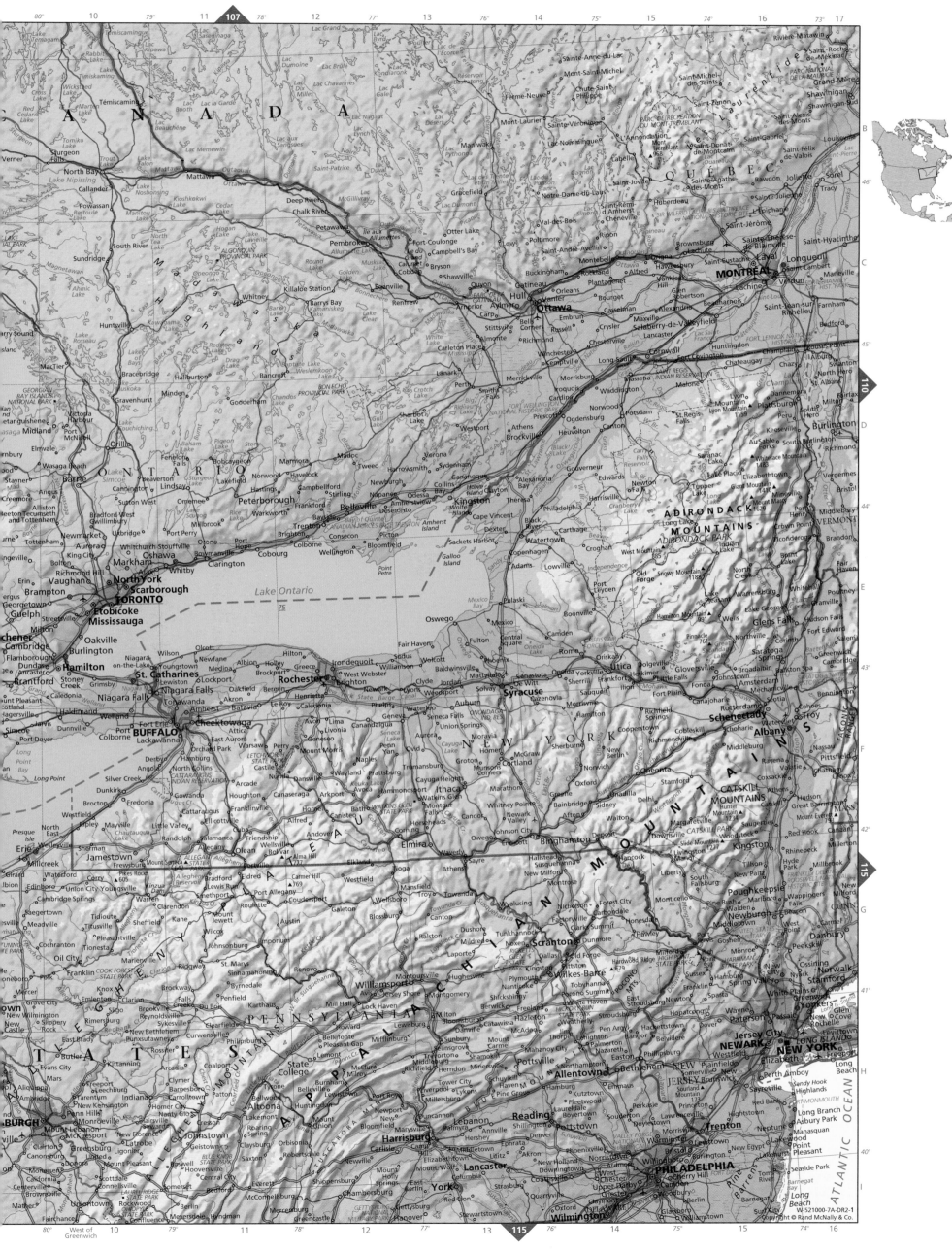

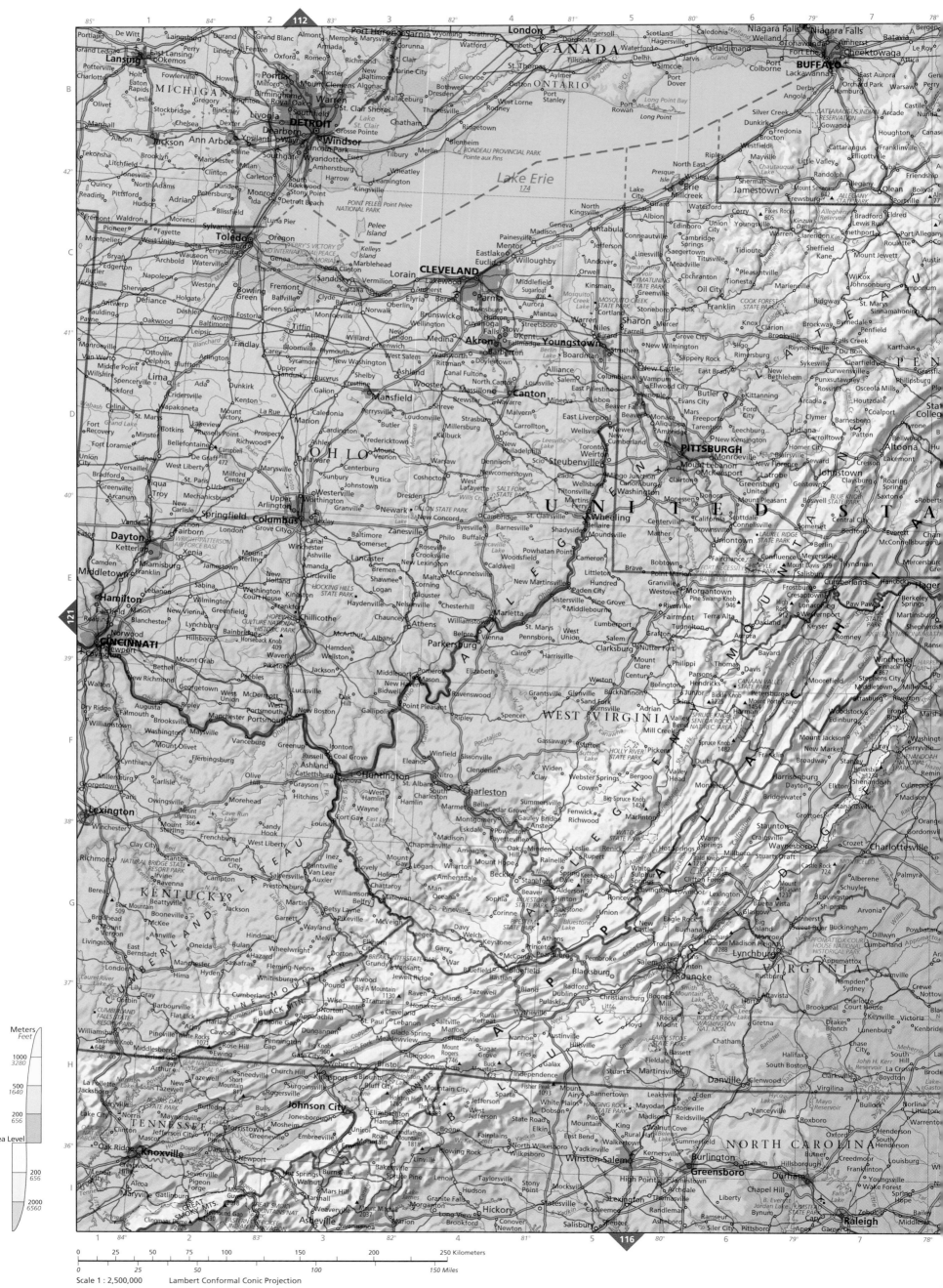

Scale 1 : 2,500,000   Lambert Conformal Conic Projection

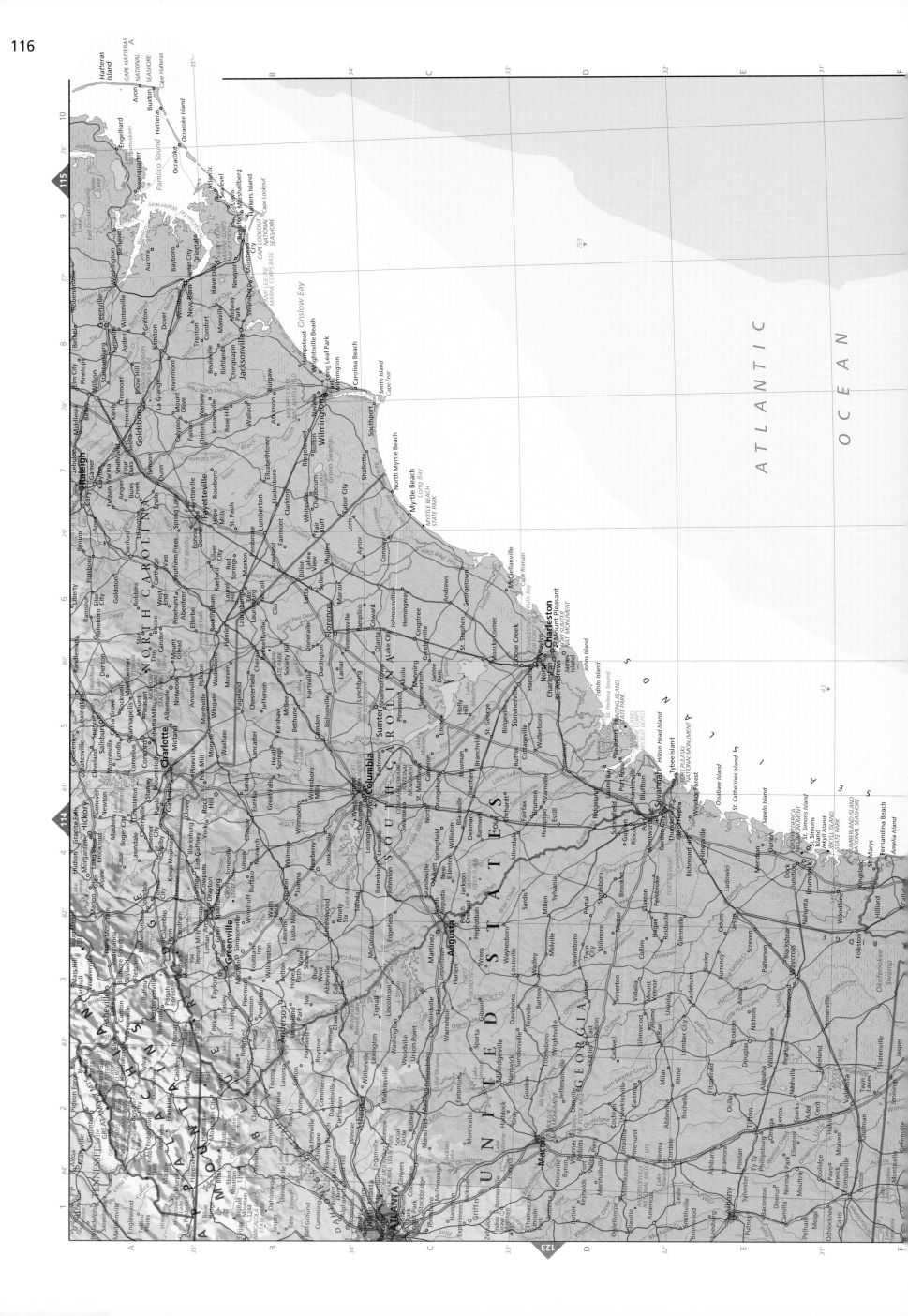

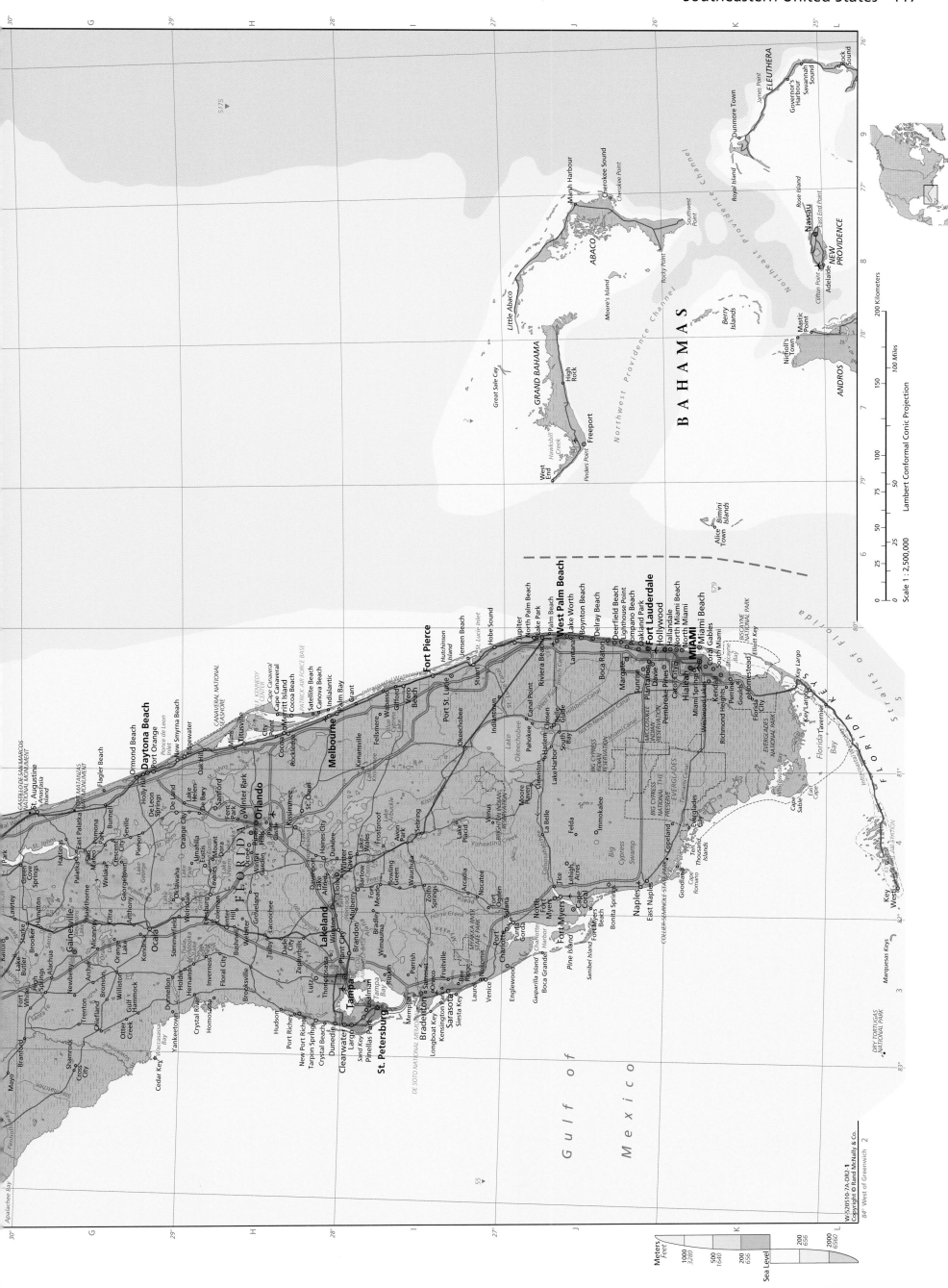

BAHAMAS

ELEUTHERA

ABACO

GRAND BAHAMA

NEW PROVIDENCE

Nassau

Freeport

West End

High Rock

ANDROS

Bimini Islands

Northwest Providence Channel

Northeast Providence Channel

FLORIDA

Jacksonville

St. Augustine

Daytona Beach

Ormond Beach

Port Orange

New Smyrna Beach

Titusville

Orlando

Winter Park

Kissimmee

Cape Canaveral

Cocoa Beach

Melbourne

Palm Bay

Vero Beach

Fort Pierce

Port St. Lucie

Okeechobee

Lake Okeechobee

West Palm Beach

Lake Worth

Boynton Beach

Delray Beach

Boca Raton

Pompano Beach

Fort Lauderdale

Hollywood

Hialeah

MIAMI

Miami Beach

Coral Gables

Kendall

Homestead

Key Largo

Tavernier

Key West

Marathon

Naples

Fort Myers

Cape Coral

Bonita Springs

Bradenton

Sarasota

Venice

Port Charlotte

Punta Gorda

Tampa

St. Petersburg

Clearwater

Lakeland

Ocala

Gainesville

EVERGLADES NATIONAL PARK

BIG CYPRESS NATIONAL PRESERVE

Gulf of Mexico

Straits of Florida

FLORIDA KEYS

DRY TORTUGAS NATIONAL PARK

CANAVERAL NATIONAL SEASHORE

JOHN F. KENNEDY CENTER

PATRICK AIR FORCE BASE

Lambert Conformal Conic Projection

Scale 1 : 2,500,000

200 Kilometers

100 Miles

Sea Level

Meters / Feet

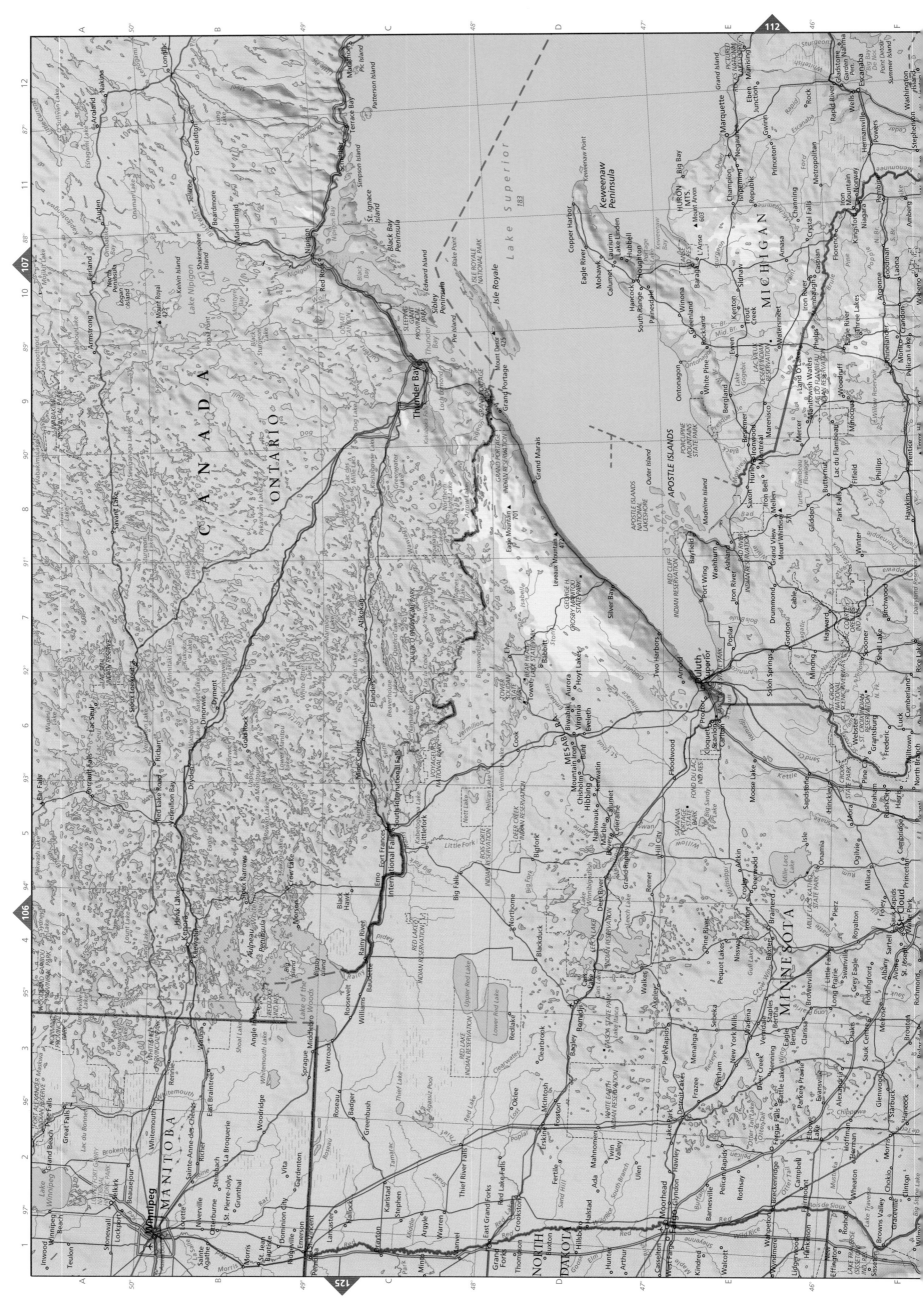

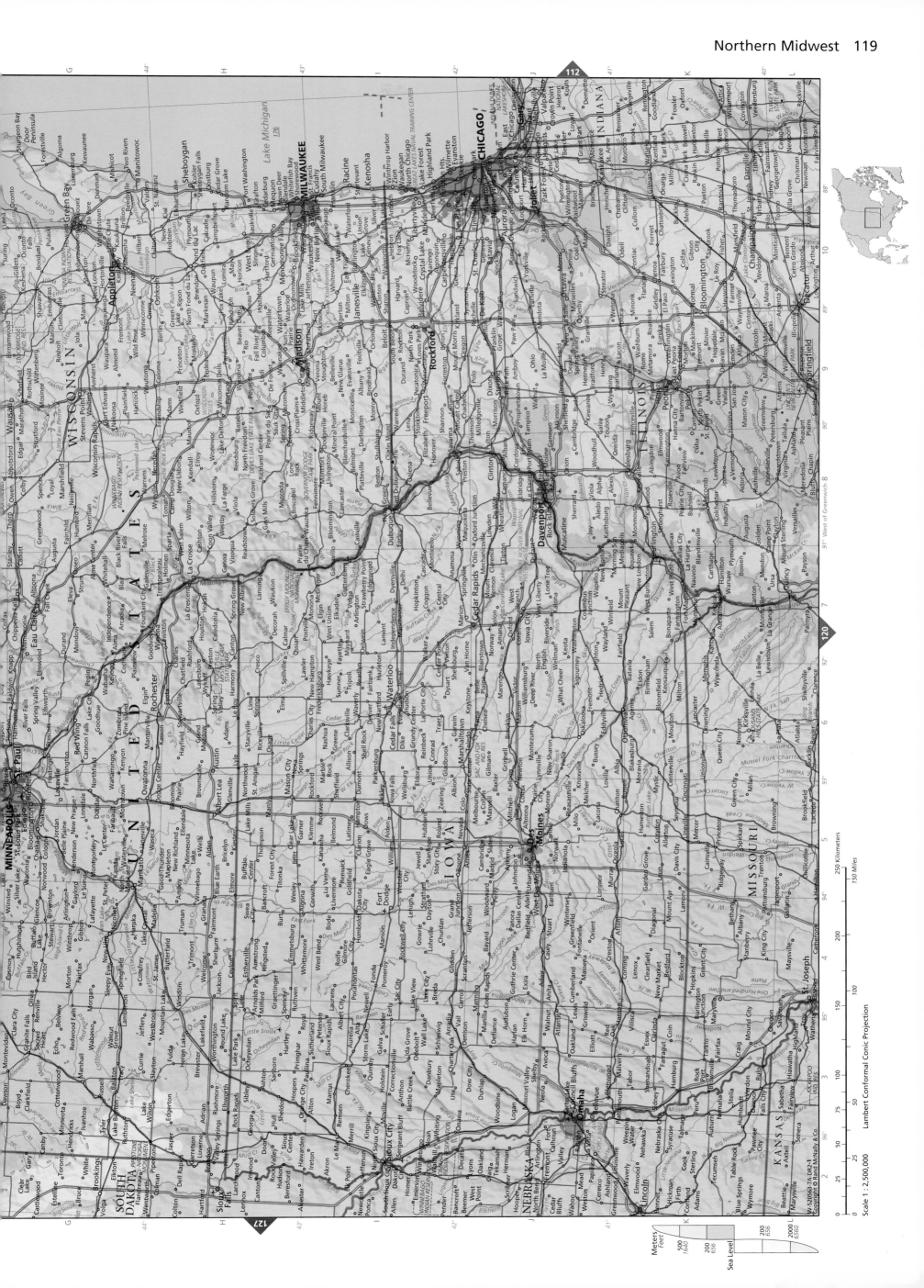

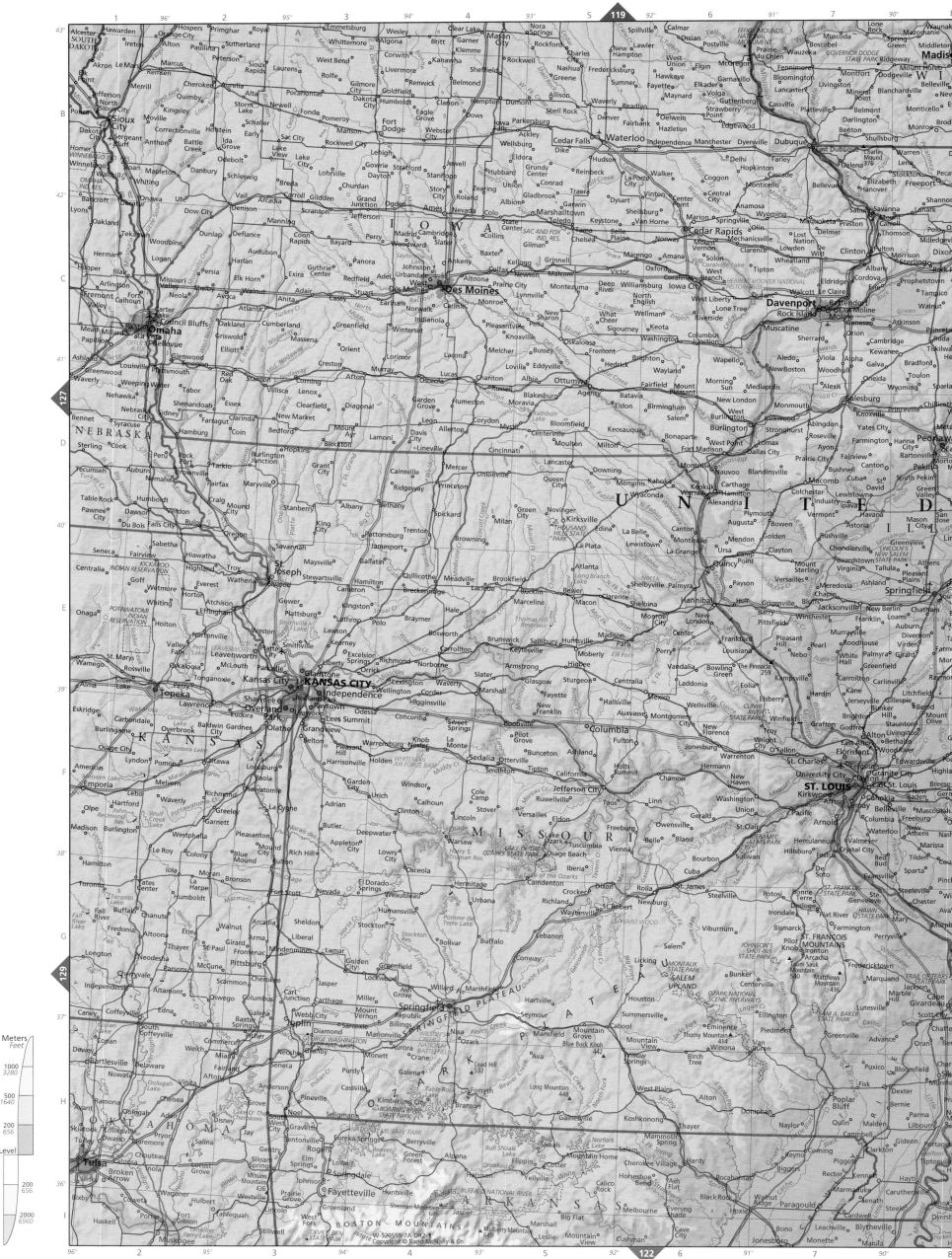

Scale 1 : 2,500,000   Lambert Conformal Conic Projection

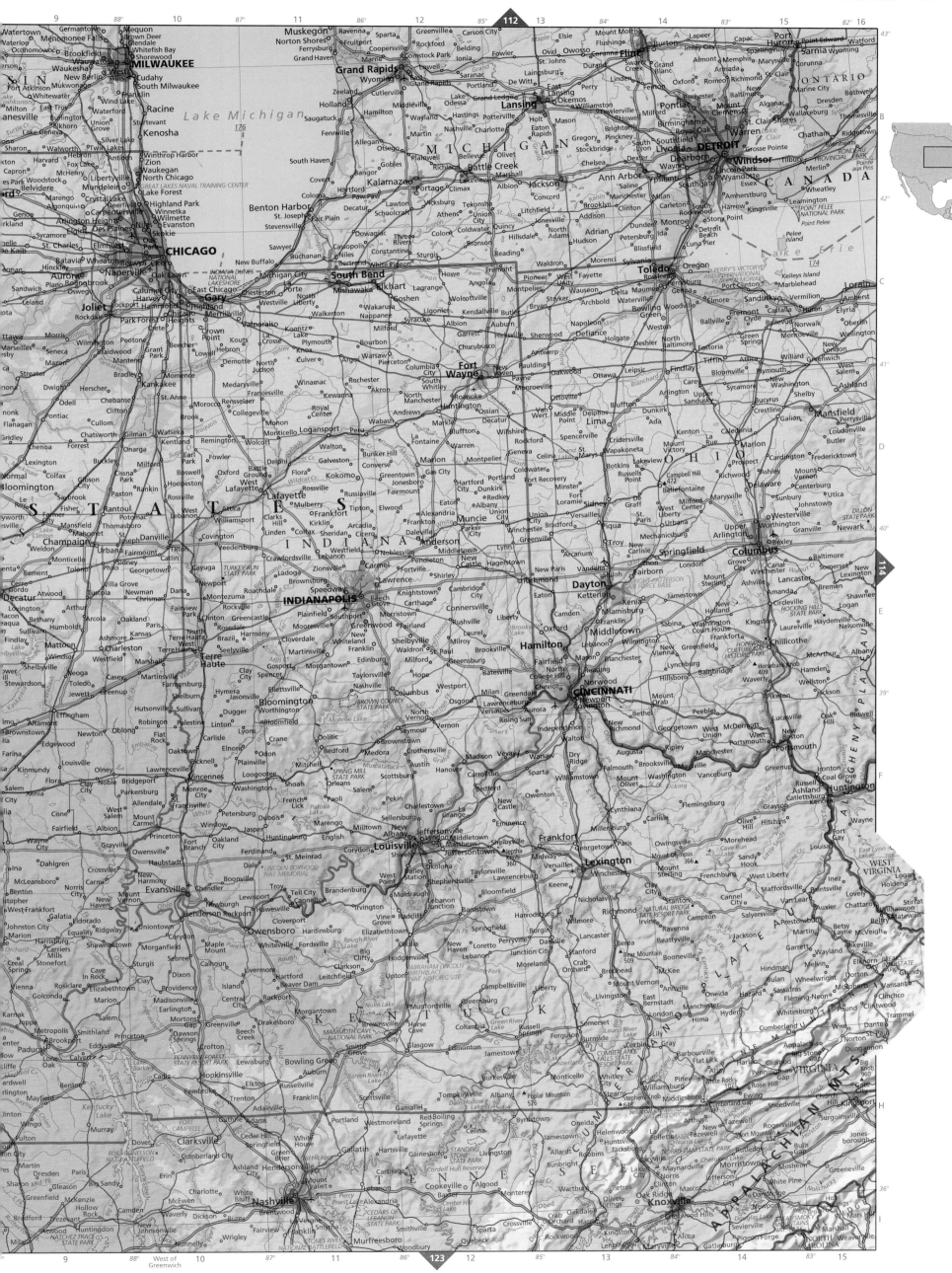

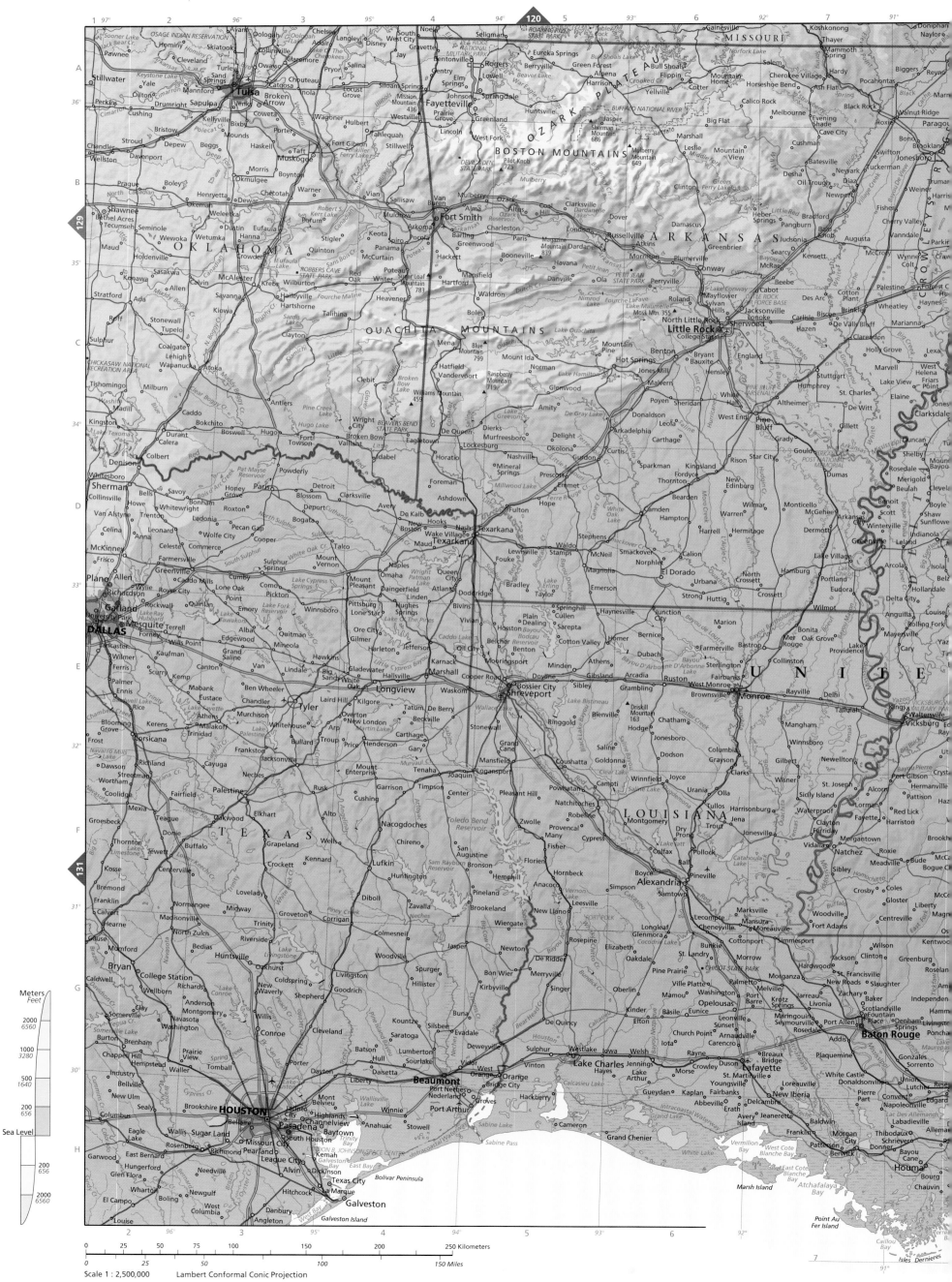

Scale 1 : 2,500,000   Lambert Conformal Conic Projection

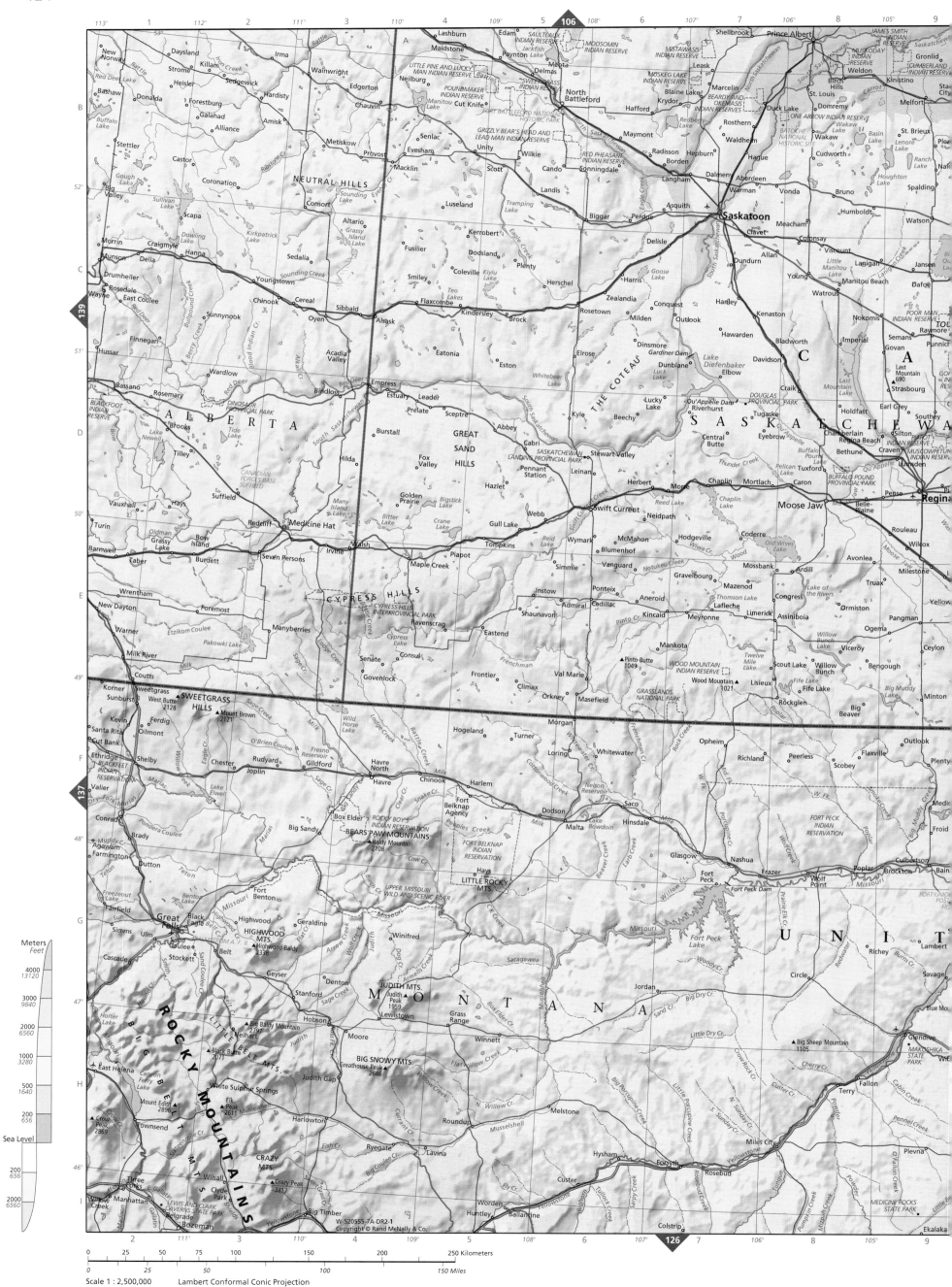

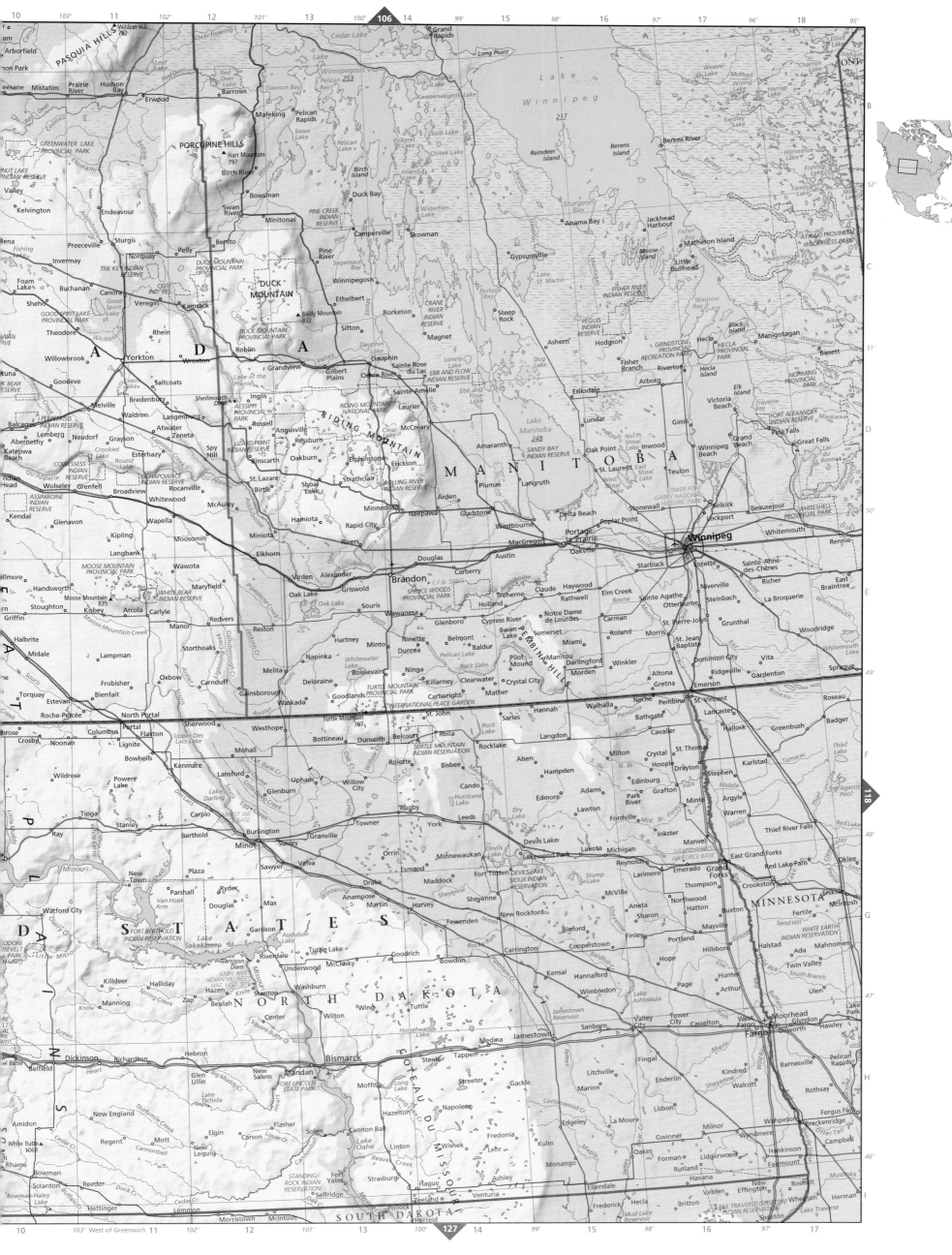

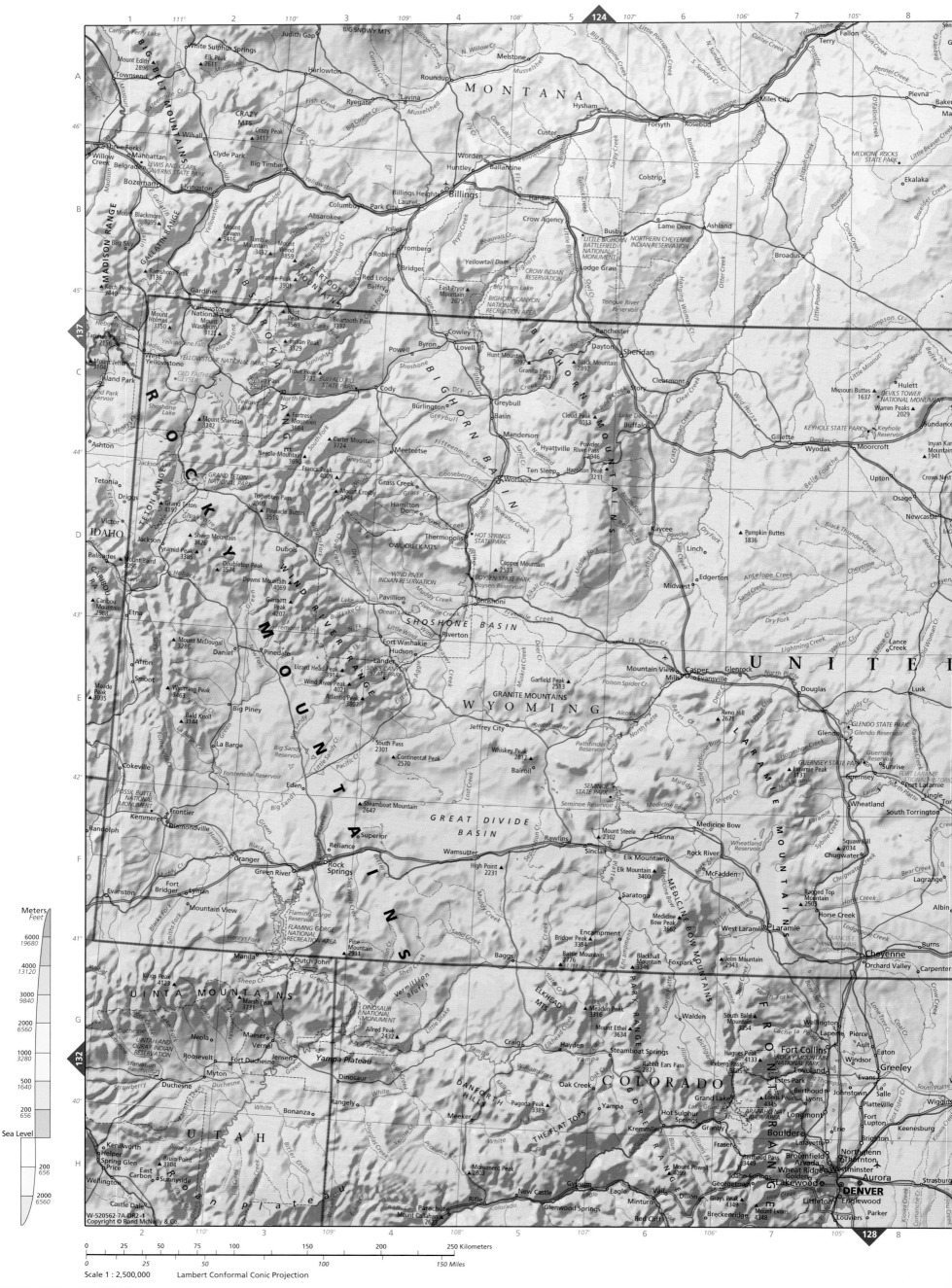

Meters
Feet

6000
19680

4000
13120

3000
9840

2000
6560

1000
3280

500
1640

200
656

Sea Level

200
656

2000
6560

W-520562-7A-DR2-1
Copyright © Rand McNally & Co.

0   25   50   75   100   150   200   250 Kilometers

0   25   50   100   150 Miles

Scale 1 : 2,500,000   Lambert Conformal Conic Projection

128

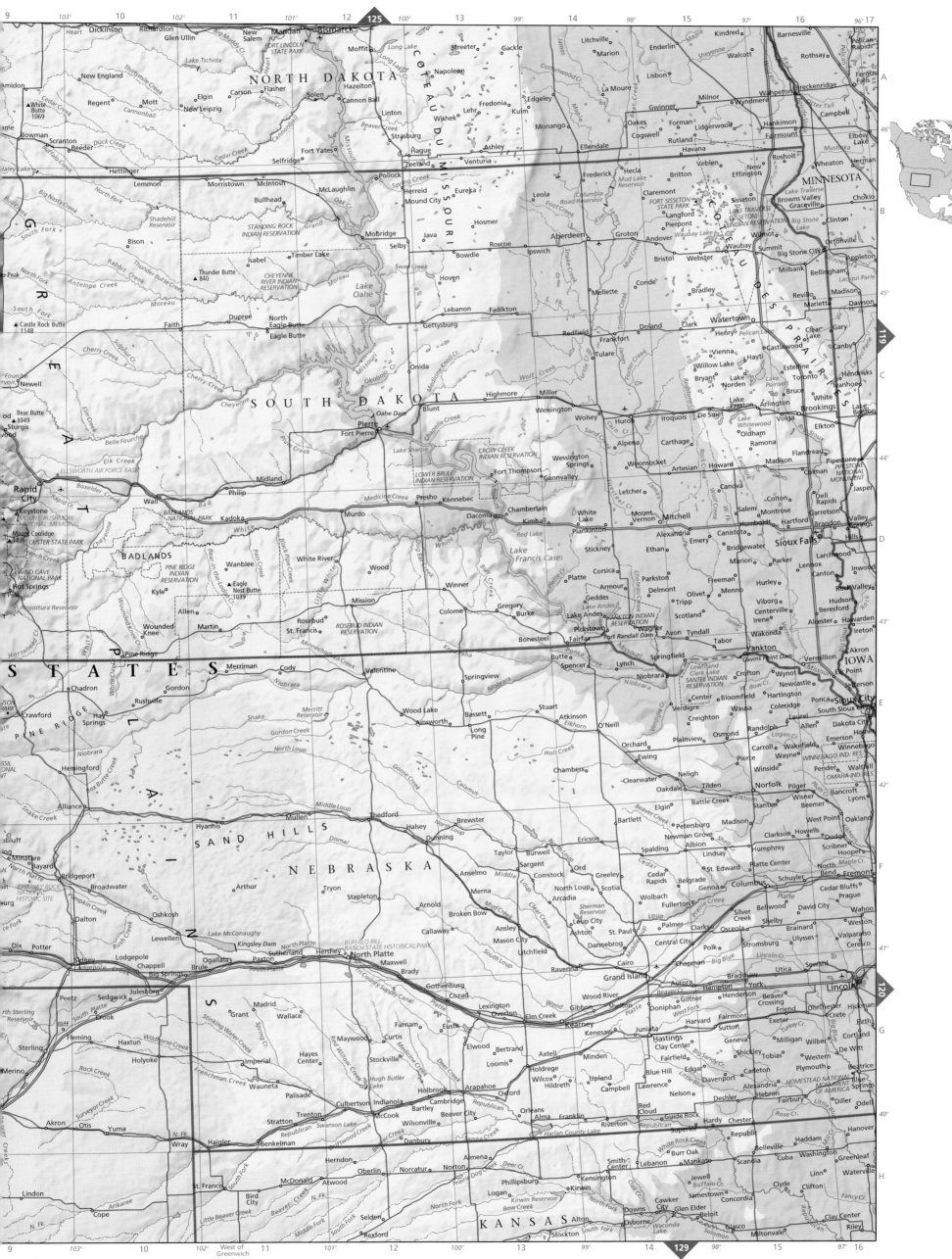

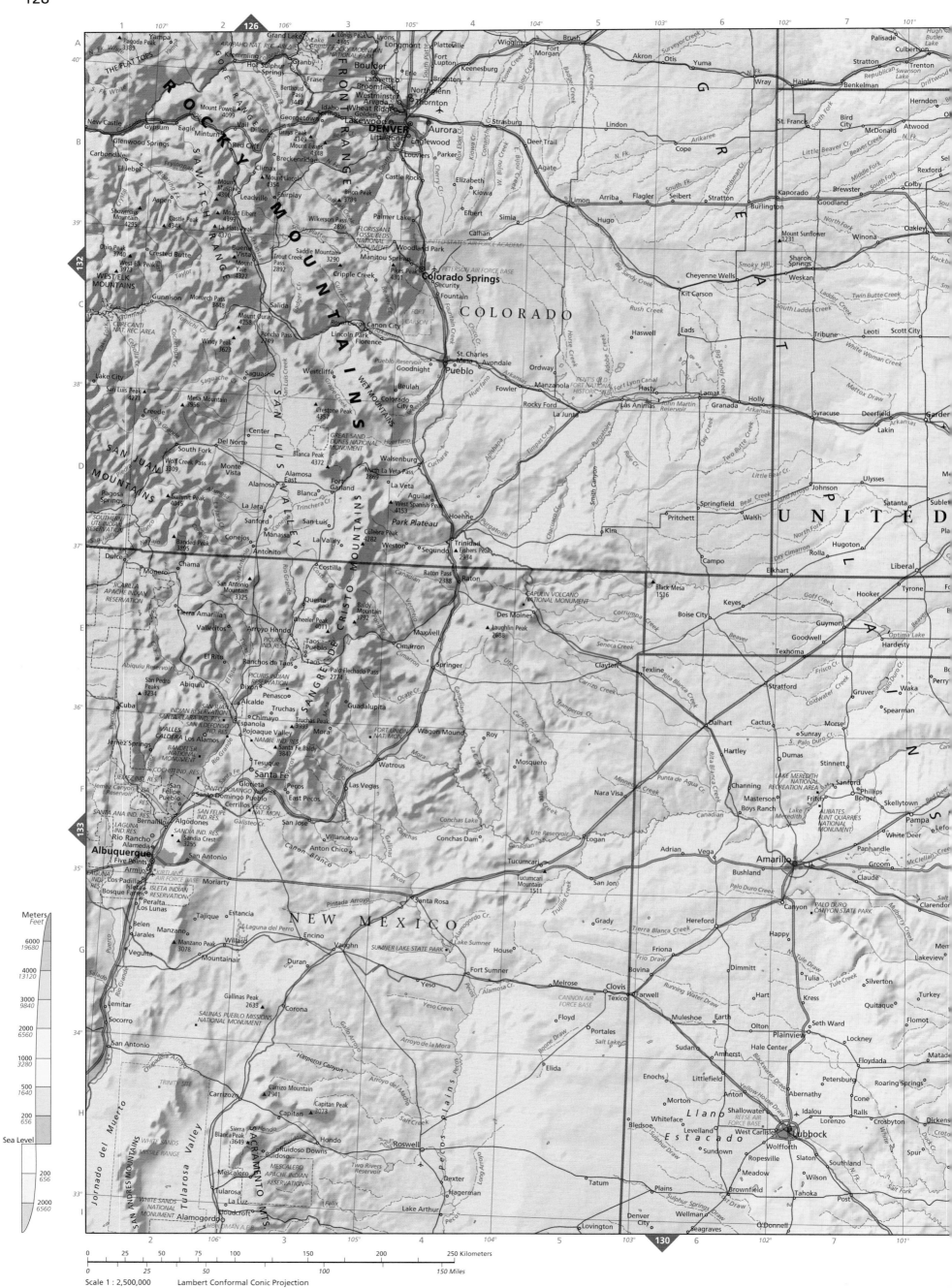

Meters / Feet

6000 / 19680
4000 / 13120
3000 / 9840
2000 / 6560
1000 / 3280
500 / 1640
200 / 656

Sea Level

200 / 656
2000 / 6560

Scale 1 : 2,500,000   Lambert Conformal Conic Projection

0   25   50   75   100   150   200   250 Kilometers

0   25   50   100   150 Miles

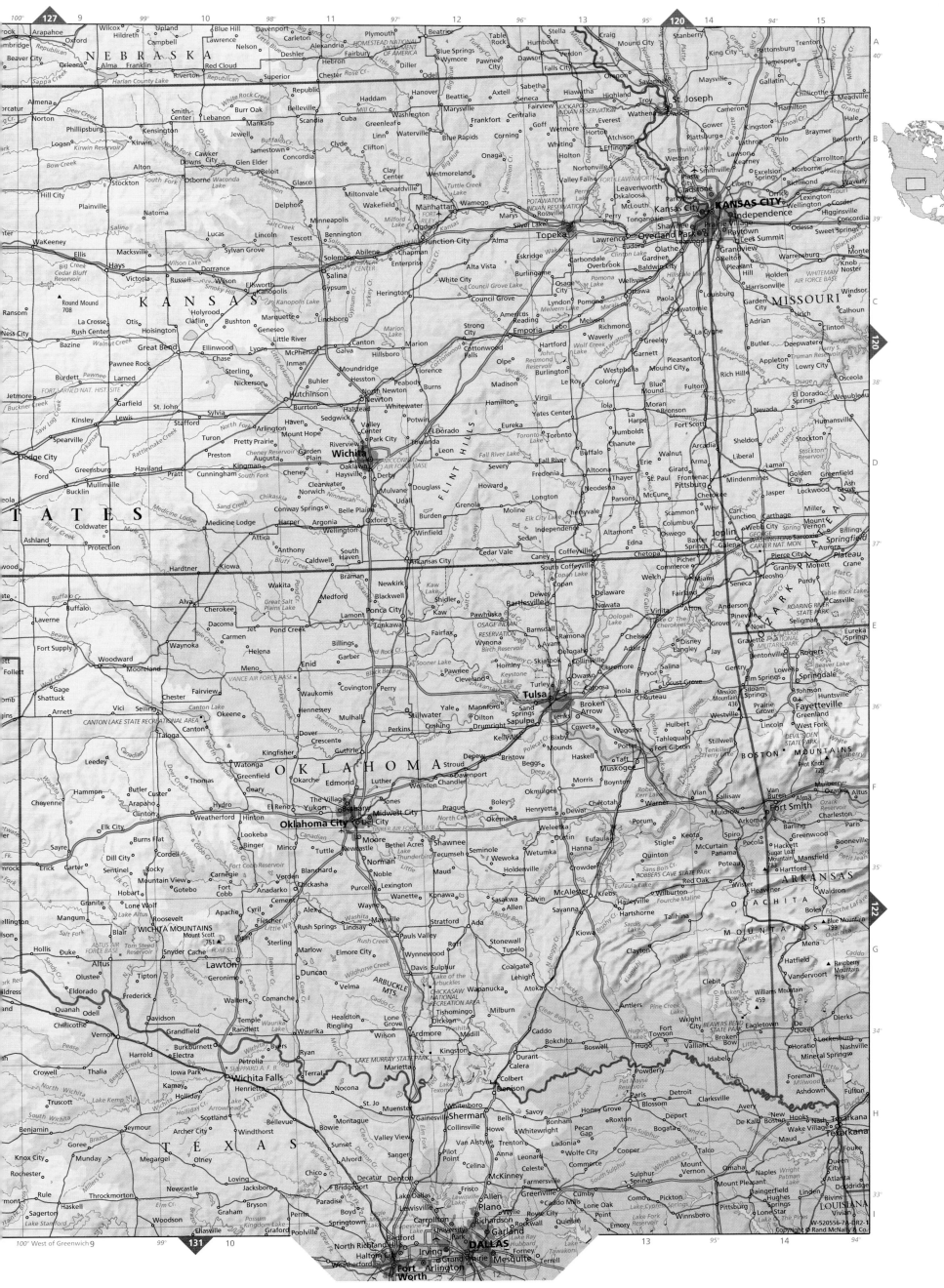

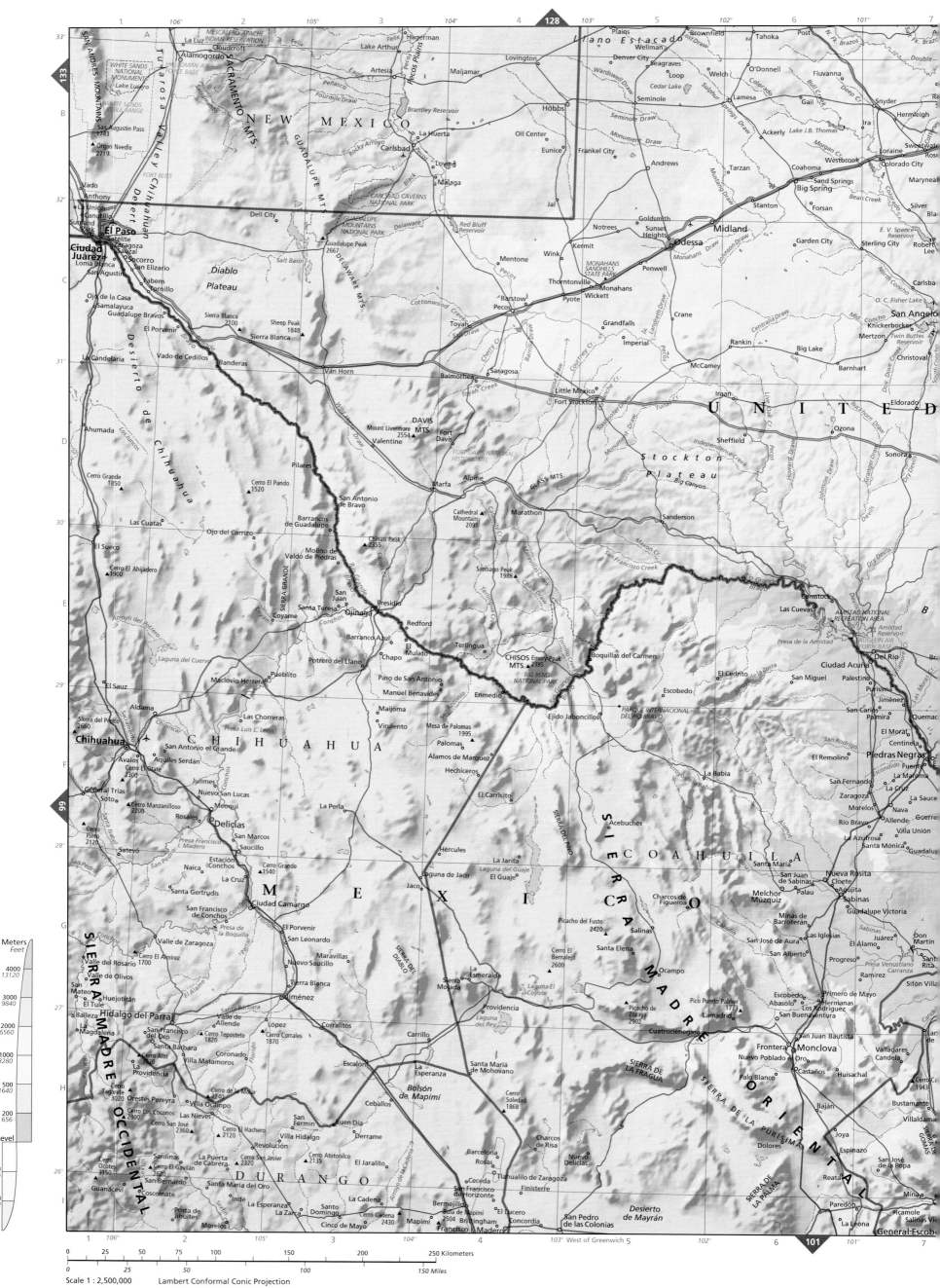

Meters
Feet

4000
13120

3000
9840

2000
6560

1000
3280

500
1640

200
656

Sea Level

200
656

2000
6560

0   25   50   75   100   150   200   250 Kilometers

0   25   50   100   150 Miles

Scale 1 : 2,500,000   Lambert Conformal Conic Projection

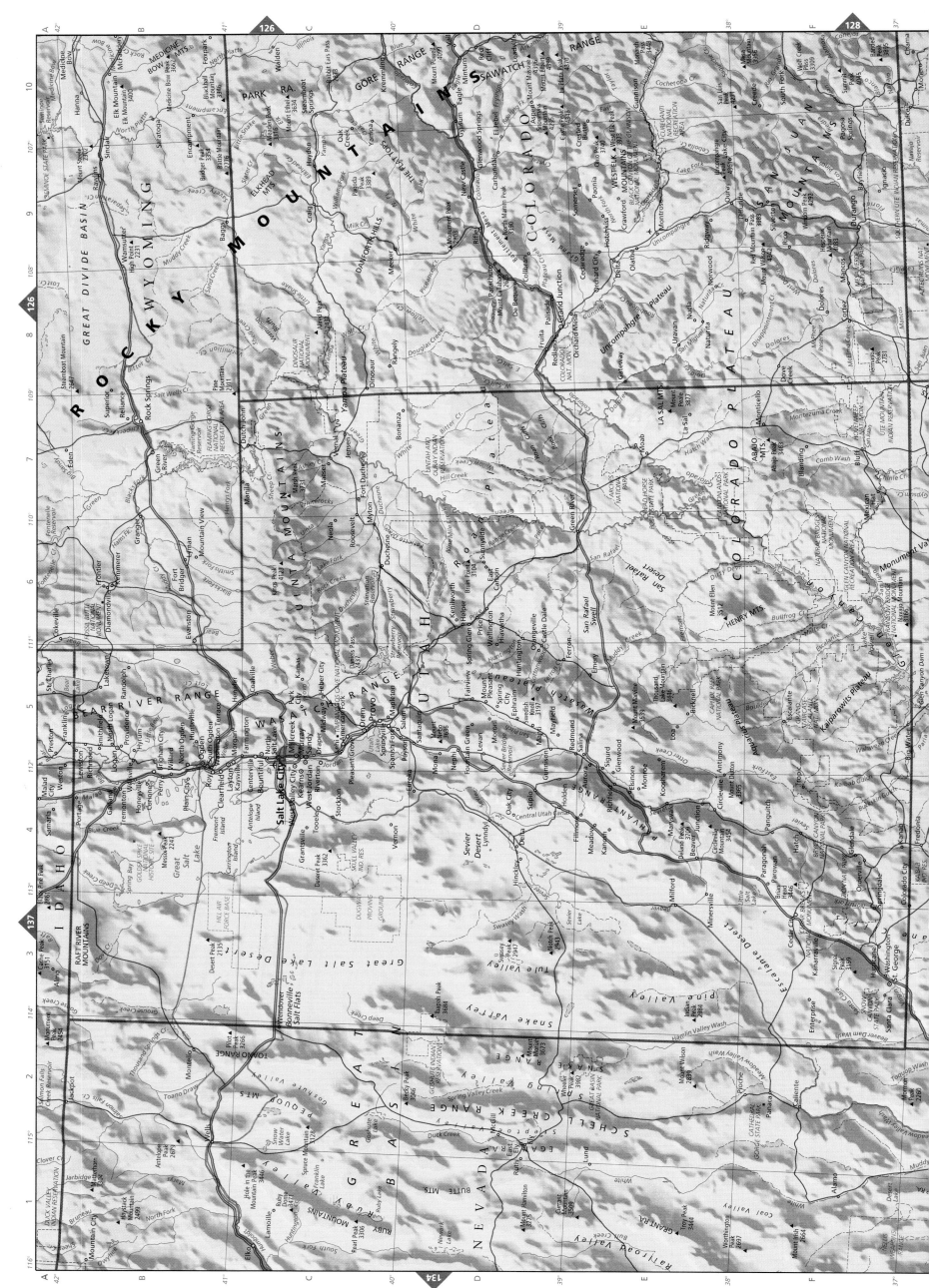

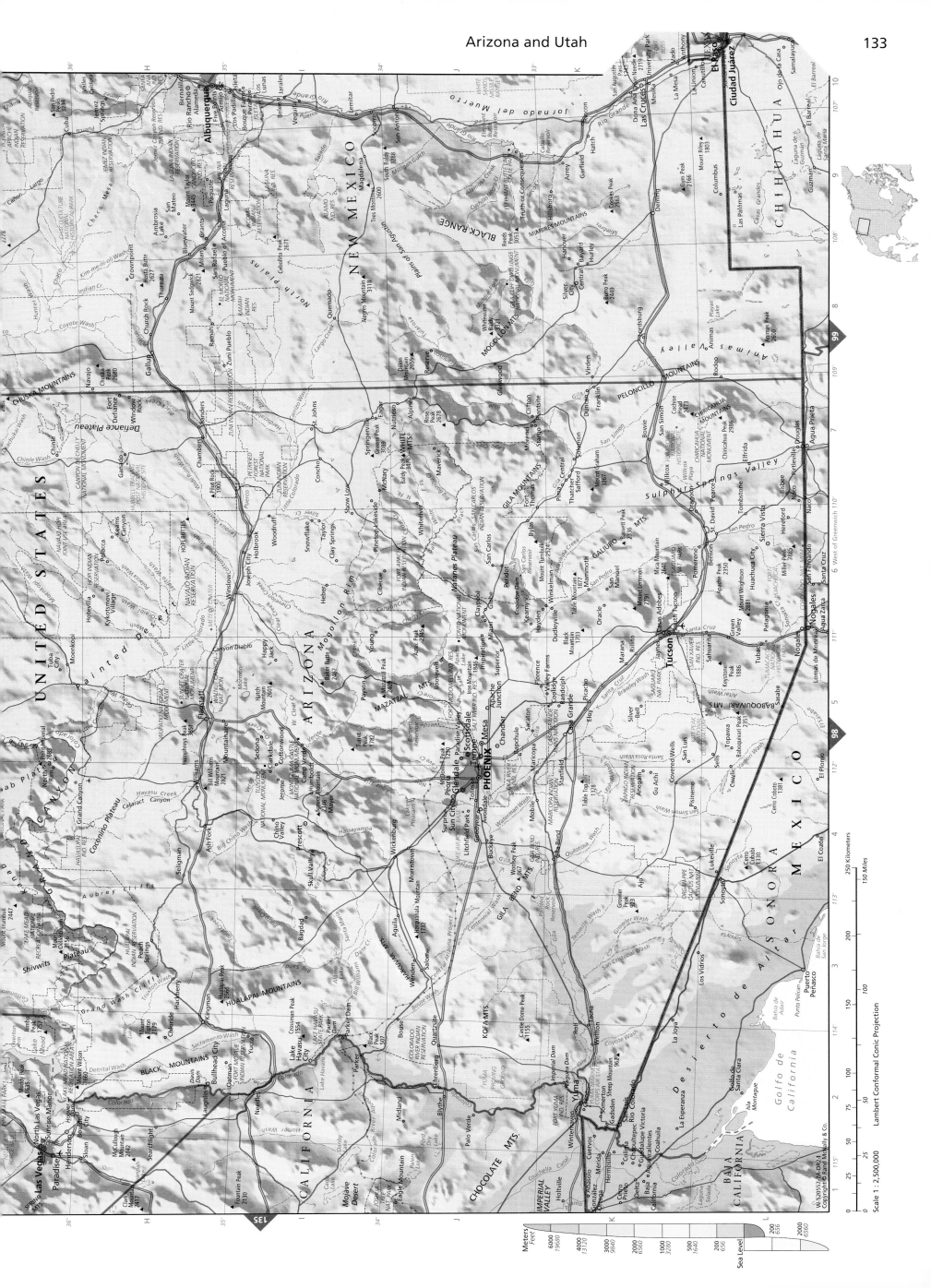

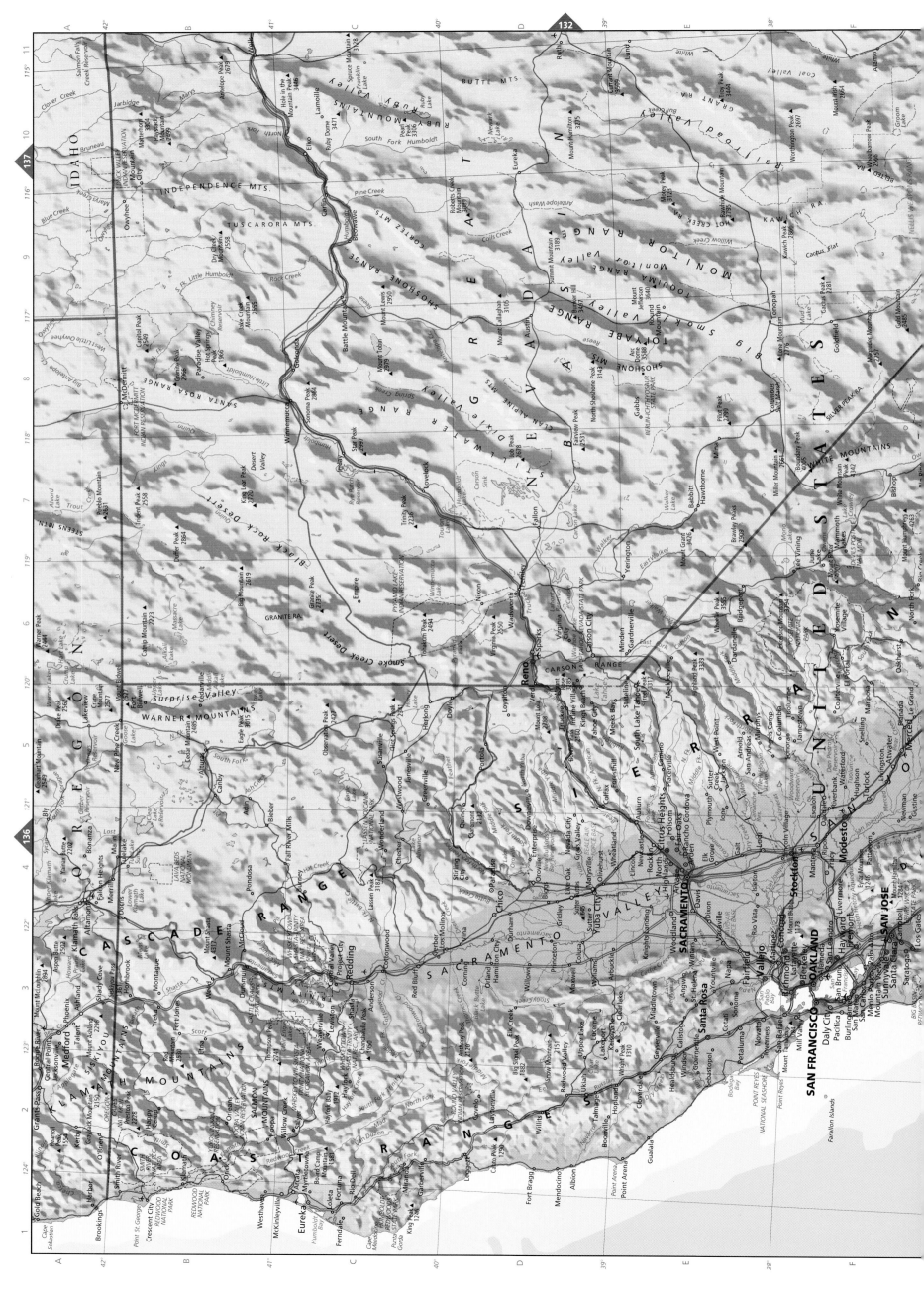

132
137
136

IDAHO

OREGON

NEVADA

UNITED STATES

CALIFORNIA

Reno

Sparks

Carson City

SACRAMENTO

Stockton

Modesto

SAN FRANCISCO

OAKLAND

SAN JOSE

Santa Rosa

Vallejo

Redding

Eureka

Medford

Grants Pass

BUTTE MTS.

RUBY MOUNTAINS

Ruby Valley

INDEPENDENCE MTS.

TUSCARORA MTS.

SANTA ROSA RANGE

SHOSHONE RANGE

CORTEZ MTS.

TOIYABE RANGE

TOQUIMA RANGE

MONITOR RANGE

SHOSHONE MTS.

CLAN ALPINE MTS.

DIXIE VALLEY

STILLWATER RANGE

WHITE MOUNTAINS

Black Rock Desert

Smoke Creek Desert

WARNER MOUNTAINS

CASCADE RANGE

KLAMATH MOUNTAINS

SALMON MOUNTAINS

TRINITY MTS.

COAST RANGE

SIERRA NEVADA

SACRAMENTO VALLEY

Elko

Carlin

Battle Mountain

Winnemucca

Lovelock

Fallon

Fernley

Yerington

Hawthorne

Austin

Eureka

Tonopah

Goldfield

Bishop

Bridgeport

Susanville

Alturas

Klamath Falls

Lakeview

Chico

Red Bluff

Marysville

Auburn

Placerville

South Lake Tahoe

Napa

Fairfield

Santa Cruz

Ukiah

Fort Bragg

Mendocino

Point Arena

Crescent City

Brookings

Gold Beach

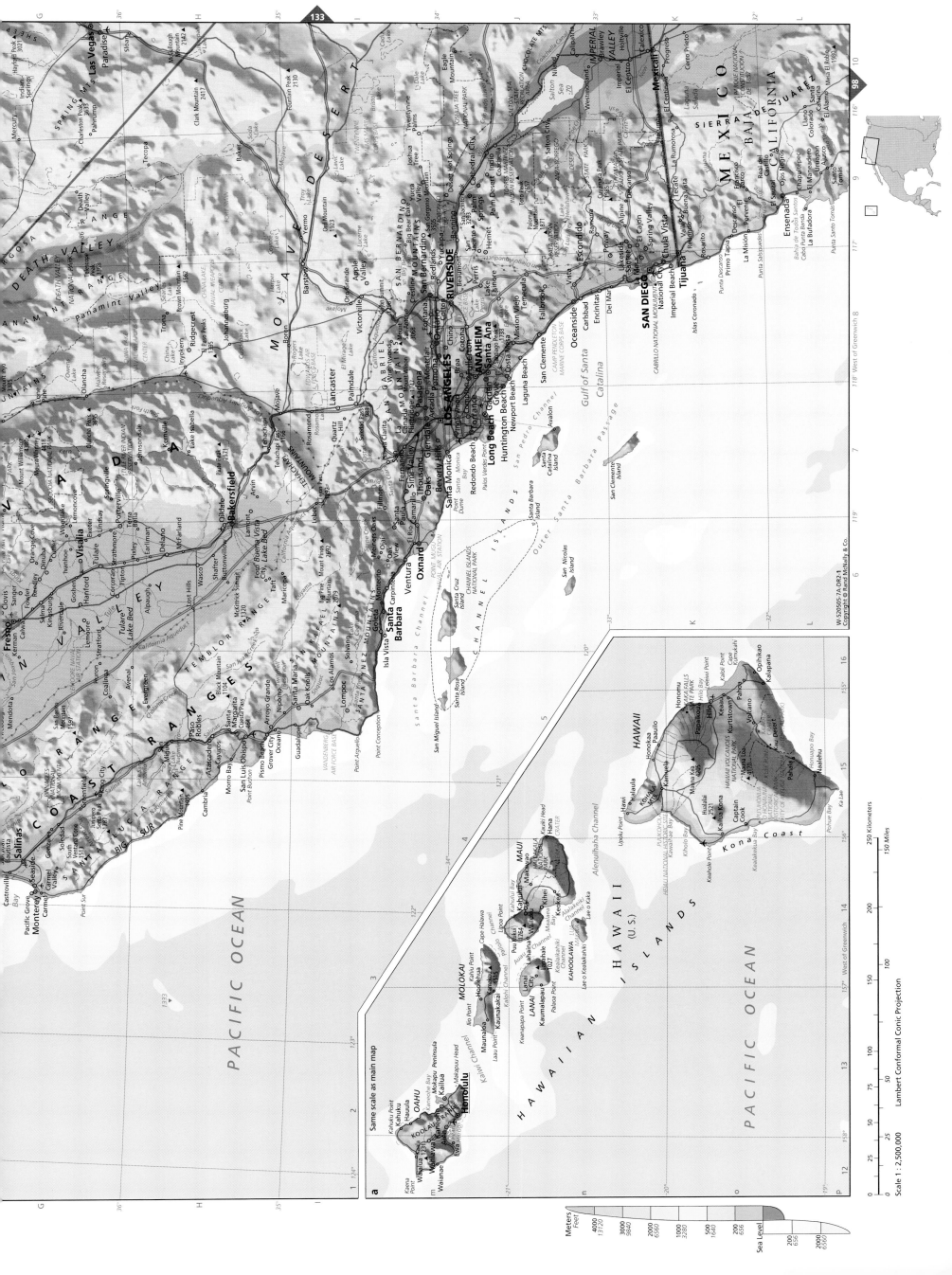

PACIFIC OCEAN

DEATH VALLEY

MOJAVE DESERT

Las Vegas

Paradise

San Bernardino
RIVERSIDE
Los Angeles
ANAHEIM
Santa Ana
Long Beach
Huntington Beach

SAN DIEGO
Tijuana
Mexicali

MEXICO
BAJA CALIFORNIA

Bakersfield
Visalia
Fresno

COAST RANGES

Salinas
Monterey

Santa Barbara
Ventura
Oxnard

CHANNEL ISLANDS

Santa Catalina Island

OAHU
Honolulu

MOLOKAI
LANAI
KAHOOLAWA
MAUI

HAWAIIAN ISLANDS (U.S.)

HAWAII
Hilo

Kona Coast

PACIFIC OCEAN

Same scale as main map

a

W-52050S-7A-DR2-1
Copyright © Rand McNally & Co.

Lambert Conformal Conic Projection

Scale 1 : 2,500,000

Meters / Feet
4000 / 13120
3000 / 9840
2000 / 6560
1000 / 3280
500 / 1640
200 / 656
Sea Level
200 / 656
2000 / 6560

250 Kilometers
150 Miles

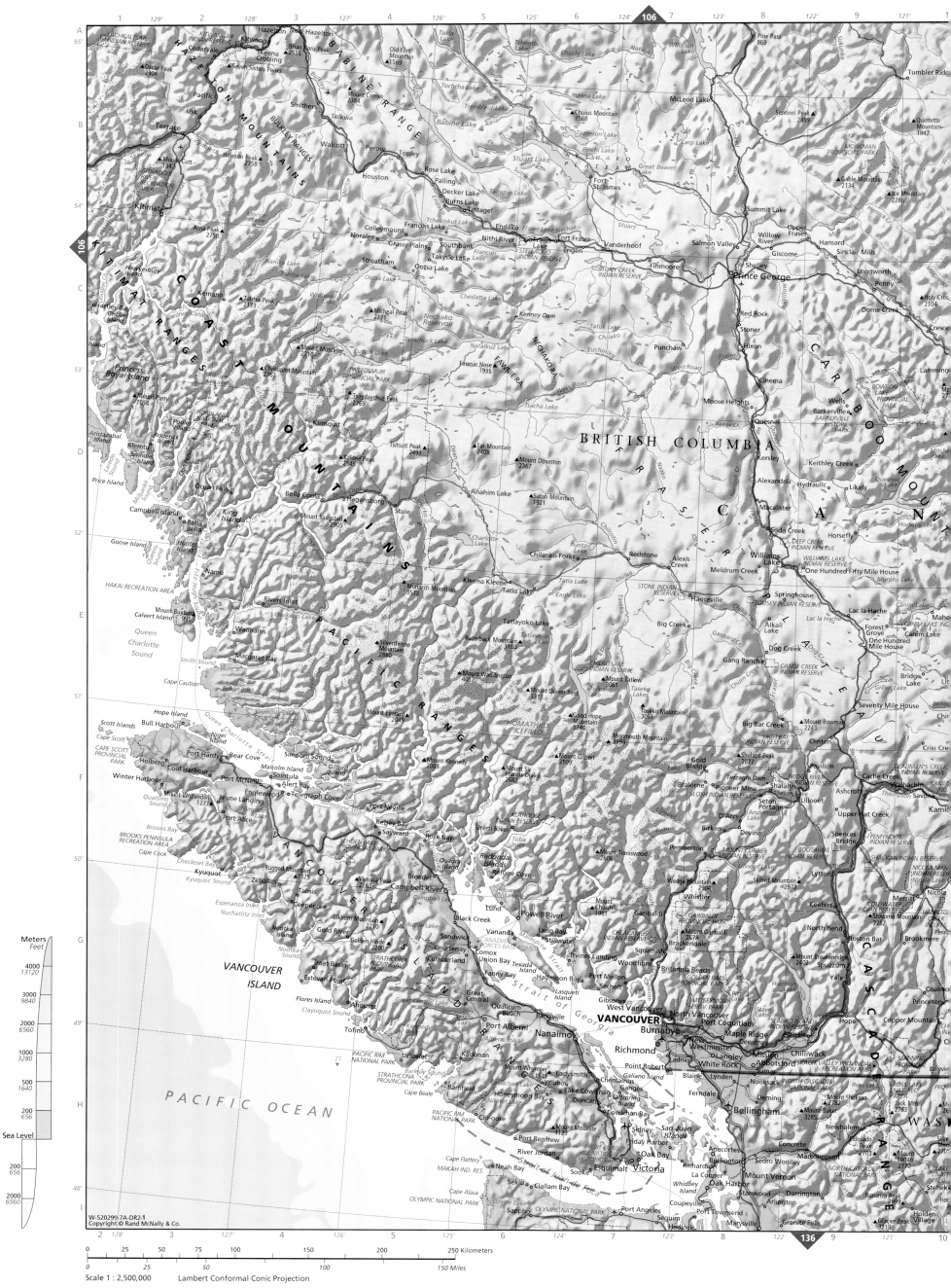

Scale 1 : 2,500,000   Lambert Conformal Conic Projection

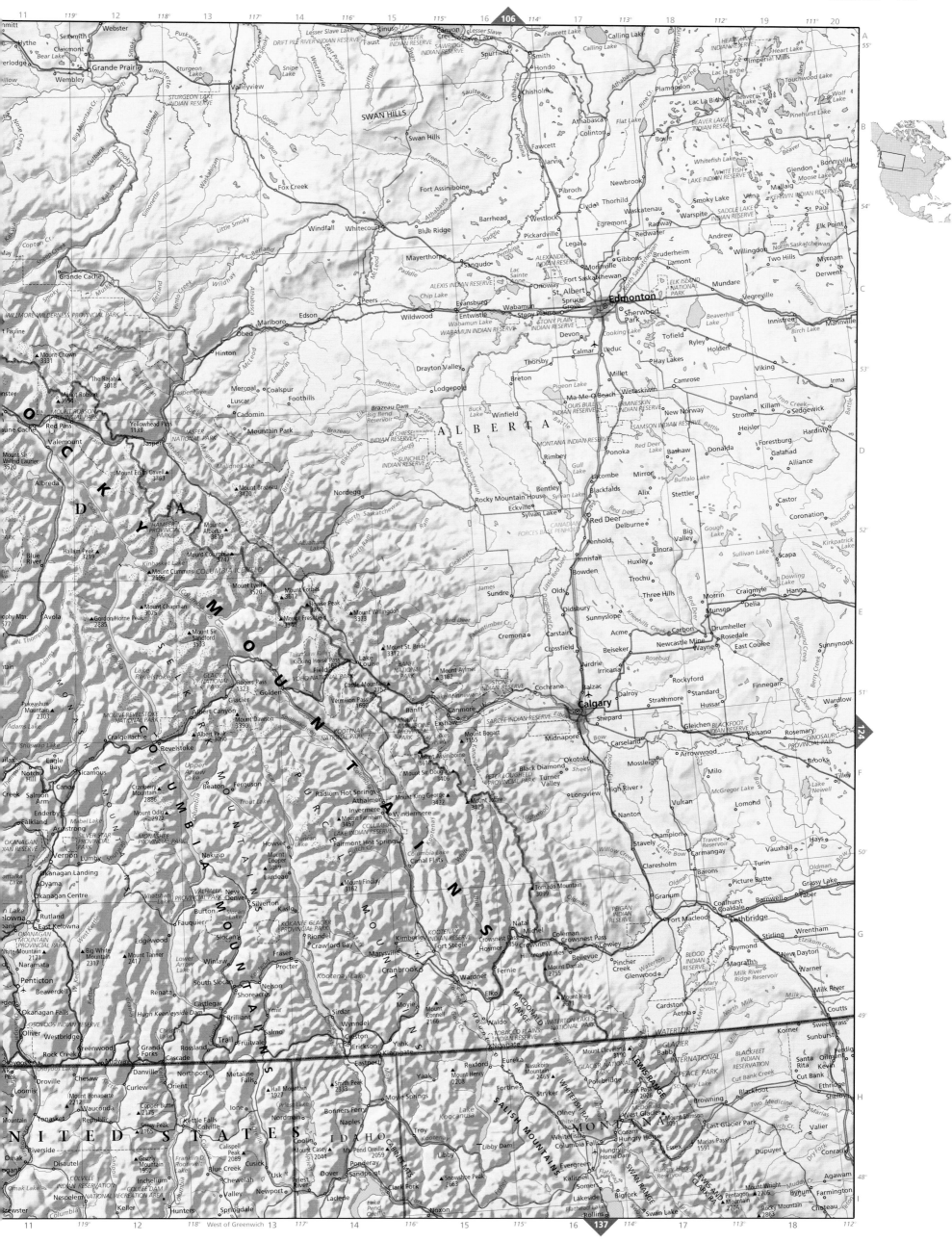

ARCTIC OCEAN

BEAUFORT SEA

CHUKCHI SEA

OSTROV VRANGELJA (WRANGEL ISLAND)
mys Blossom

Meters
Feet
4000
13120
3000
9840
2000
6560
1000
3280
500
1640
200
656
Sea Level
200
656
2000
6560

International Date Line

Vankarem

Point Barrow
Barrow
Wainwright
Icy Cape
Point Hope
Cape Lisburne
Point Hope

Enurmino

RUSSIA
Čukotskij poluostrov
(Chukotski Peninsula)
ostrov Ratmanova

Bering Strait

Providenija

Uelen

Wales
Cape Prince of Wales
Teller
White Mountains
Nome
Cape Rodney

Gambell
ST. LAWRENCE ISLAND
Northeast Cape

St. Matthew Island

BERING SEA

St. Paul Island
Pribilof Islands
St. George Island

Cape Mohican
Mekoryuk
Nunivak Island

Cape Newenham

FOX ISLANDS
Umnak Island
Makushin Volcano 2036
Nikolski
Mount Vsevidof 2109

Smith Bay
Meade
Teshekpuk Lake
Harrison Bay
Prudhoe Bay
Deadhorse
Cape Halkett
Camden Bay
Kaktovik
Mount Michelson 2699
Mount Isto 2761
ROMANZOF MTS.
BRITISH MTS.
Demarcation Point
Herschel Island
Richards Island
Kugmallit Bay
Tuktoyaktuk

BROOKS RANGE
DE LONG MTS.
LOOKOUT RIDGE
BAIRD MTS.
SCHWATKA MTS.
Anaktuvuk Pass
Mount Doonerak 2273
ENDICOTT MOUNTAINS
PHILIP SMITH MTS.
Wiseman
Chandalar
Arctic Village
Old Crow
Aklavik
Inuvik
RICHARDSON MOUNTAINS
NORTHWEST TERRITORIES

Kivalina
Noatak
Kotzebue
Kobuk
Klana
Noorvik
Shungnak
Selawik
Venetie
Yukon Flats
Fort McPherson
Fort Good Hope
FRANKLIN MOUNTAINS

Shishmaref
Kotzebue Sound
Deering
Buckland
Selawik Lake
Bettles Field
Beaver
Fort Yukon
Circle
Old Crow

Seward Peninsula
Koyuk
Moses Point
Golovin

UNITED STATES
Allakaket
Hughes
Huslia
Rampart
Livengood
Eagle
OGILVIE MOUNTAINS
Tombstone Mountain 2192
Castle Mountain 2057
Mount Patterson 2088
SELWYN MOUNTAINS
Mount Eduni 2352

CANADA
YUKON

MACKENZIE MOUNTAINS

Norton Sound
Shaktoolik
Unalakleet
Nulato
Galena
Ruby
Tanana
Manley Hot Springs
Nenana
College Fairbanks
Chicken
Klondike
Dawson
Elsa
Keno Hill
Keele Peak 2972
Mount James 2762
LOGAN MTS.
Tungsten

Stebbins
St. Michael
Stuart Island
Kaltag
KAIYUH MTS.
Mount Harper 1994
Mayo
Mount Armstrong 2159
Macmillan

Emmonak
Sheldon Point
Alakanuk
Mountain Village
Kotlik
Anvik
Shageluk
Von Frank Mountain 1374
KUSKOKWIM
Lake Minchumina
ALASKA
Big Delta
Delta Junction
Mount Hayes 4216
Tanacross
Mount Kimball 3155
Mentasta Lake
Pelly Crossing
Minto
Carmacks
PELLY MOUNTAINS
Faro
Ross River

Scammon Bay
St. Marys
Holy Cross
Flat
McGrath
Ophir
Denali National Park
Mount McKinley 6194
Cantwell
Denali
Paxson
Tok
Northway
DAWSON RANGE
Snag
Aishihik
Carcross

Hooper Bay
Marshall
Crooked Creek
Red Devil
Stony River
Mount Foraker 5302
Farewell
ALASKA RANGE
TALKEETNA MOUNTAINS
Gakona
Gulkana
Glennallen
WRANGELL MOUNTAINS
Mount Sanford 4949
McCarthy
Mount Lucania 5226
Destruction Bay
Johnsons Crossing
Teslin

Chevak
Kalskag
Aniak
KUSKOKWIM
Kwethluk
Sleetmute
Holitna
Mount Gerdine 3431
Skwentna
Talkeetna
Willow
Sutton
Palmer
Copper Center
CHUGACH MOUNTAINS
Blackburn 5036
Mount Blackburn
Mount Kennedy 4238
Haines Junction
Whitehorse
Atlin
Atlin Lake

Bethel
Tuluksak
Eek
Tununak
Kwigillingok
Kipnuk
Quinhagak
Koliganek
New Stuyahok
Iliamna
Nondalton
Iliamna
Mount Redoubt Volcano 3108
Spurr
Mount Spurr 3374
Anchorage
Valdez
Cordova Peak
Cordova
Cape St. Elias
ST. ELIAS MOUNTAINS
Mount Logan 5959
Mount St. Elias 5489
Malaspina Glacier
Yakutat
Dry Bay
Fairweather Mountain 4663
Mount Nesselrode
Haines
Skagway
BRITISH COLUMBIA
Telegraph Creek

Kuskokwim Bay
Goodnews Bay
Togiak
Aleknagik
Dillingham
Igiugig
Naknek
Kenai
Soldotna
Seward
Moose Pass
Whittier
Prince William Sound
Hinchinbrook Island
Montague Island
Kayak Island
Ocean Cape
Gustavus
Juneau
Douglas
Hoonah
CHICHAGOF ISLAND
ADMIRALTY ISLAND

Hagemeister Island
Cape Constantine
Egegik
Becharof Lake
Mount Katmai 2047
Homer
Seldovia
Port Graham
Barren Islands
Shuyak Island
Afognak Island
Kruzof Island
Sitka
BARANOF ISLAND
Kake
Petersburg
Wrangell

BERING SEA

Bristol Bay
Ugashik
Pilot Point
Mount Denison 2304
Stevenson Entrance
KODIAK ISLAND
Kodiak
Karluk
Old Harbor
Cape Alitak
Sitkalidak Island
Chirikof Island
Gulf of Alaska
ALEXANDER ARCHIPELAGO
Sitka
Point Baker
Prince of Wales
WALES ISLAND
Craig
DALL ISLAND
Ketchikan
Cape Ommaney
Christian Sound
Dixon Entrance
Cape Knox
QUEEN
CHARLOTTE
ISLANDS

Port Heiden
Port Moller
Pavlof Volcano 2714
Mount Veniaminof 2507
Chignik
Perryville
ALEUTIAN RANGE
ALASKA PENINSULA
Shumagin Islands
Unga Island
Nagai Island
Sanak Islands
Sand Point
Trinity Islands

Shishaldin Volcano 2852
Cold Bay
False Pass
Unimak Island
Unimak Pass
Tigalda Island
Akutan Island
Unalaska Island

M-250200-7A-DR2-1
Copyright © Rand McNally & Co.
170° 160° 8 155° 9 150° 10 145° 11 140° West of Greenwich 12 135° 13

a

BERING SEA

Cape Wrangell
Attu
Attu Island
Semichi Islands
NEAR ISLANDS
Agattu Island
ALEUTIAN
Buldir Island
Kiska Volcano 1220
Kiska Island
Little Sitkin Island
RAT ISLANDS
Amchitka Island
Delarof Islands
Garaloi Island
Tanaga Island
Adak Island
Kagalaska Island
Kanaga Island
Great Sitkin Island
ANDREANOF ISLANDS
Atka Island
Atka
Korovin Volcano 1478
Amlia Island
Seguam Island
Amukta Pass
Yunaska Island
ISLANDS OF FOUR MOUNTAINS
Chuginadak Island
Samalga Pass
ISLANDS
FOX ISLANDS
Umnak Island
Mount Vsevidof 2109
Nikolski
Unalaska Island
Makushin Volcano 2036
Unalaska
Akutan Island
Akun Island
Tigalda Island
Unimak Pass

International Date Line

PACIFIC OCEAN

Same scale as main map

20 170° 21 22 East of Greenwich 180° West of Greenwich 23 175° 24 170° 25 165° 26 160° 27

0 100 200 300 400 600 800 1000 Kilometers
0 100 200 400 600 Miles
Scale 1 : 10,000,000 Lambert Conformal Conic Projection

ARCTIC OCEAN

GREENLAND SEA

SVALBARD

SPITSBERGEN

Peary Land

Kong Frederik VIII Land

NORDGRØNLAND
(AVANERSUAQ)

Knud Rasmussen Land

ELLESMERE ISLAND

AXEL HEIBERG ISLAND

QUEEN ELIZABETH ISLANDS

SVERDRUP ISLANDS

DEVON ISLAND

NUNAVUT
(Effective April, 1999)

Lauge Koch Kyst

Thule (Qaanaaq)

Melville Bugt

BAFFIN BAY

NORTHWEST TERRITORIES

BAFFIN ISLAND

CANADA

Kong Christian X Land

GREENLAND
(Den.)

ØSTGRØNLAND
(TUNU)

Scoresbysund

Gunnbjørn Field 3700

Kong Christian IX Land

Upernavik

Prøven (Kangersuatsiaq)

DISKO

Godhåvn (Qeqertarsuaq)

Disko Bugt

Jakobshavn (Ilulissat)

Christianshåb (Qasigiannguit)

Egedesminde (Aasiaat)

Kangaatsiaq

Agto

Holsteinsborg (Sisimiut)

Søndre Strømfjord

Kangâmiut

Sukkertoppen (Maniitsoq)

Napasoq

Atangmik

Oqornoq

Kapisigdlit

Godthåb (Nuuk)

J.A.D. Jensens Nunatakker 1680

Frederikshåb (Paamiut)

Ivigtut

Narssaq

Julianehåb (Qaqortoq)

Nanortalik

Frederiksdal

Kap Farvel

VESTGRØNLAND
(KITAA)

Kong Frederik VI Kyst

ICELAND

Reykjavík

Keflavík

Arctic Circle

Denmark Strait

ATLANTIC OCEAN

DAVIS STRAIT

Baffin Bay

Cumberland Peninsula

Pangnirtung

Iqaluit

Hall Peninsula

Frobisher Bay

Hudson Strait

Ungava Bay

Kuujjuaq

QUÉBEC

NEWFOUNDLAND

LABRADOR SEA

M-230000-7A-DR2-1
Copyright © Rand McNally & Co.

Meters	
Feet	
3000	*9840*
2000	*6560*
1000	*3280*
500	*1640*
200	*656*
Sea Level	
200	*656*
2000	*6560*

0   100 200 300 400   600   800 1000 Kilometers

0   100   200   400   600 Miles

Scale 1 : 10,000,000   Lambert Conformal Conic Projection

Meters
Feet

6000
19680

4000
13120

3000
9840

2000
6560

1000
3280

500
1640

200
656

Sea Level

200
656

2000
6560

4000
13120

6000
19680

M-147000-7A-DR2-1
Copyright © Rand McNally & Co.

0   500   1000   2000   3000   4000   5000   6000 Kilometers

0   500   1000   2000   3000   4000 Miles

Scale 1 : 60,000,000   Robinson Projection

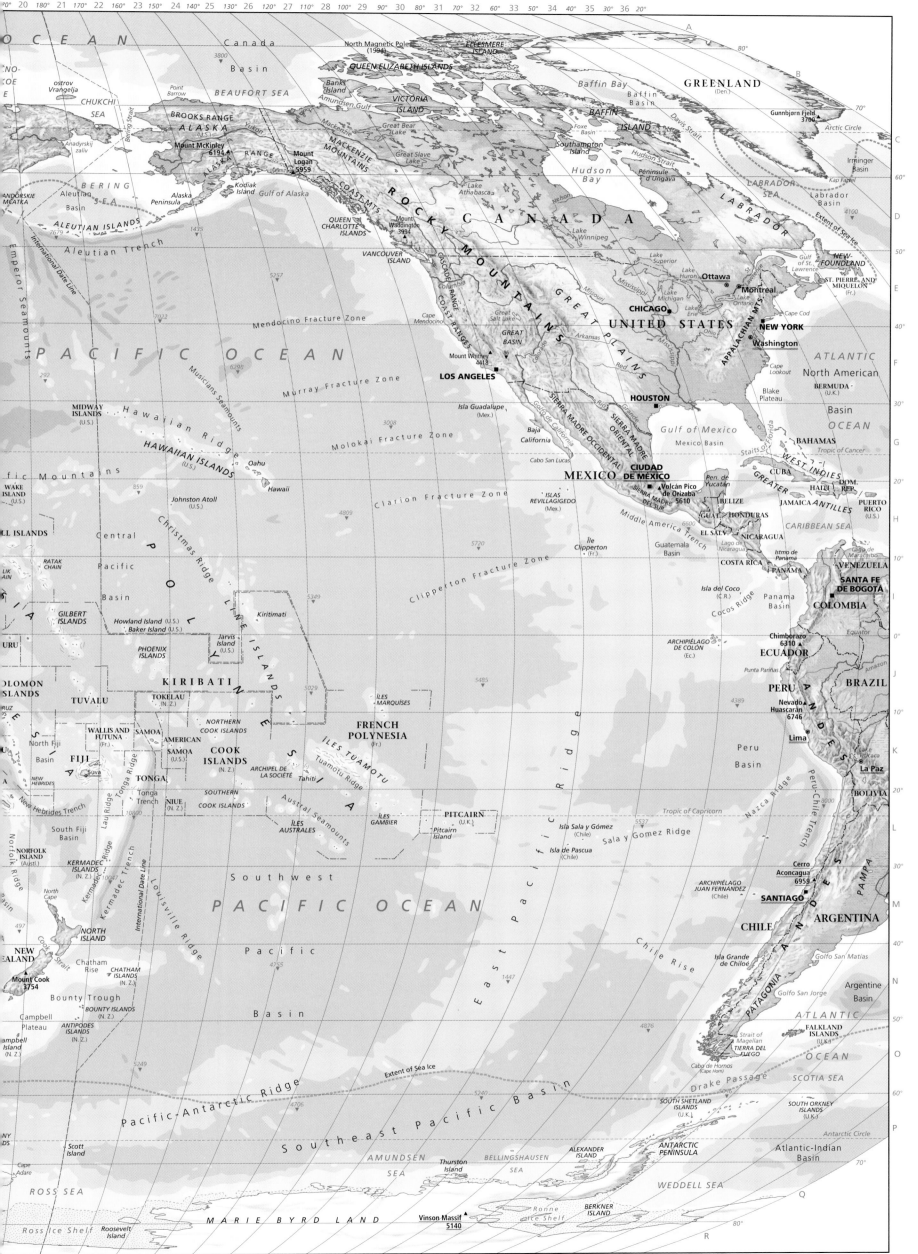

OCEAN

Canada

Basin

OCEAN

NOKOE

ostrov
Vrangelja

CHUKCHI
SEA

Anadyrskij
zaliv

BERING
SEA

ANDORSKIE
MCATKA

Aleutian
Basin

ALEUTIAN ISLANDS

Aleutian Trench

Emperor Seamounts

International Date Line

PACIFIC   OCEAN

Musicians Seamounts

MIDWAY
ISLANDS
(U.S.)

Hawaiian Ridge

HAWAIIAN ISLANDS
(U.S.)

WAKE
ISLAND
(U.S.)

cific Mountains

Johnston Atoll
(U.S.)

LL ISLANDS

Central

RATAK
CHAIN

LIK
AIN

Pacific

Basin

URU

GILBERT
ISLANDS

Howland Island (U.S.)
Baker Island (U.S.)

KIRIBATI

OLOMON
ISLANDS

CRUZ

TUVALU

TOKELAU
(N.Z.)

WALLIS AND
FUTUNA
(Fr.)

SAMOA

AMERICAN
SAMOA
(U.S.)

NORTHERN
COOK ISLANDS
(N.Z.)

North Fiji
Basin

FIJI

Suva

TONGA

COOK
ISLANDS
(N.Z.)

NEW
HEBRIDES

Lau Ridge

Tonga Ridge

Tonga
Trench

NIUE
(N.Z.)

SOUTHERN
COOK ISLANDS

Austral Seamounts

ARCHIPEL DE
LA SOCIÉTÉ

Tahiti

ÎLES TUAMOTU

Tuamotu Ridge

FRENCH
POLYNESIA
(Fr.)

ÎLES
MARQUÍSES

New Hebrides Trench

ÎLES
AUSTRALES

ÎLES
GAMBIER

PITCAIRN
(U.K.)

Pitcairn
Island

Kermadec Trench

KERMADEC
ISLANDS
(N.Z.)

South Fiji
Basin

Norfolk Ridge

NORFOLK
ISLAND
(Austl.)

North
Cape

NORTH
ISLAND

Chatham Rise

CHATHAM
ISLANDS
(N.Z.)

Louisville Ridge

International Date Line

Southwest

PACIFIC OCEAN

Pacific

Basin

East Pacific Ridge

NEW
ZEALAND

Mount Cook
3754

Cook
Strait

Bounty Trough

BOUNTY ISLANDS
(N.Z.)

Campbell

Campbell
Plateau

ANTIPODES
ISLANDS
(N.Z.)

NY
D5

Cape
Adare

Scott
Island

ROSS SEA

Ross Ice Shelf

Roosevelt
Island

MARIE BYRD LAND

Pacific-Antarctic Ridge

Southeast Pacific Basin

Extent of Sea Ice

AMUNDSEN
SEA

Thurston
Island

BELLINGSHAUSEN
SEA

ALEXANDER
ISLAND

ANTARCTIC
PENINSULA

WEDDELL SEA

BERKNER
ISLAND

Ronne
Ice Shelf

Vinson Massif
5140

North Magnetic Pole
(1994)

QUEEN ELIZABETH ISLANDS

ELLESMERE
ISLAND

GREENLAND
(Den.)

BEAUFORT SEA

Point
Barrow

BROOKS RANGE

ALASKA

Mount McKinley
6194

ALASKA

Mount
5959

Banks
Island

Amundsen Gulf

VICTORIA
ISLAND

Mackenzie

RANGE

MACKENZIE
MOUNTAINS

Yukon

Bering Strait

Kodiak
Island

Alaska
Peninsula

Gulf of Alaska

7679

7022

292

Great Bear
Lake

Great Slave
Lake

Lake
Athabasca

ROCKY   MOUNTAINS

CANADA

Nelson

Baffin Bay

Baffin
Basin

BAFFIN

ISLAND

Davis Strait

Southampton
Island

Foxe
Basin

Hudson Strait

Péninsule
d'Ungava

Hudson
Bay

Gunnbjørn Fjeld
3700

Kap Farvel

Irminger
Basin

LABRADOR
SEA

LABRADOR

Labrador
Basin

Extent of Sea Ice

4100

Arctic Circle

1435

COAST MTS.

QUEEN
CHARLOTTE
ISLANDS

3994

Mount
Waddington

VANCOUVER
ISLAND

5757

CASCADE RANGE

COAST RANGES

Columbia

Cape
Mendocino

Mendocino Fracture Zone

6298

Murray Fracture Zone

Molokai Fracture Zone

3008

Oahu

859

Hawaii

Clarion Fracture Zone

4809

5720

5349

5029

5485

Kiritimati

Jarvis
Island
(U.S.)

PHOENIX
ISLANDS

LINE   ISLANDS

POLYNESIA

Christmas Ridge

Île
Clipperton
(Fr.)

Clipperton Fracture Zone

Isla del Coco
(C.R.)

Cocos Ridge

6600

Middle America Trench

Guatemala
Basin

Lago de
Nicaragua

GREAT PLAINS

Lake
Winnipeg

Lake
Superior

Lake
Huron

Lake
Michigan

Lake
Erie

Lake
Ontario

Ottawa

Montreal

CHICAGO

UNITED STATES

Missouri

Mississippi

Arkansas

Red

GREAT
BASIN

Great
Salt Lake

Mount Whitney
4418

LOS ANGELES

Isla Guadalupe
(Mex.)

SIERRA MADRE OCCIDENTAL

Baja
California

Gulf of California

Cabo San Lucas

SIERRA MADRE ORIENTAL

RÍO

Rio Grande

HOUSTON

Mexico Basin

Gulf of Mexico

NEW YORK

Washington

APPALACHIAN MTS.

Cape
Cod

Cape
Lookout

BERMUDA
(U.K.)

Blake
Plateau

ATLANTIC

North American

OCEAN

Basin

St. Lawrence

Gulf of
St.
Lawrence

NEW-
FOUNDLAND

ST. PIERRE AND
MIQUELON
(Fr.)

BAHAMAS

Straits of Florida

Tropic of Cancer

CUBA

WEST INDIES

HAITI

DOM.
REP.

PUERTO
RICO
(U.S.)

MEXICO

CIUDAD
DE MÉXICO

Volcán Pico
de Orizaba
5610

ISLAS
REVILLAGIGEDO
(Mex.)

SIERRA MADRE
DEL SUR

BELIZE

GUAT.

HONDURAS

EL SALV.

NICARAGUA

COSTA RICA

Istmo de
Panamá

PANAMA

Panama
Basin

JAMAICA

GREATER

ANTILLES

CARIBBEAN SEA

Lago de
Maracaibo

VENEZUELA

SANTA FE
DE BOGOTÁ

COLOMBIA

Chimborazo
6310

ECUADOR

Isla Sala y Gómez
(Chile)

Isla de Pascua
(Chile)

Sala y Gomez Ridge

Punta Pariñas

PERU

Nevado
Huascarán
6746

Lima

Peru
Basin

Peru

ANDES

Amazon

BRAZIL

Nazca Ridge

Peru-Chile Trench

BOLIVIA

La Paz

Titicaca

Tropic of Capricorn

4389

5537

ARCHIPIÉLAGO
JUAN FERNÁNDEZ
(Chile)

Cerro
Aconcagua
6959

SANTIAGO

CHILE

3000

ARGENTINA

PAMPA

ANDES

Chile Rise

1447

4755

Isla Grande
de Chiloé

Golfo San Matías

Golfo San Jorge

Argentine
Basin

ATLANTIC

OCEAN

4876

Strait of
Magellan

TIERRA DEL
FUEGO

PATAGONIA

Cabo de Hornos
(Cape Horn)

Drake Passage

SOUTH SHETLAND
ISLANDS
(U.K.)

5240

FALKLAND
ISLANDS
(U.K.)

SCOTIA SEA

SOUTH ORKNEY
ISLANDS
(U.K.)

Antarctic Circle

4706

Atlantic-Indian
Basin

ARCHIPIÉLAGO
DE COLÓN
(Ec.)

Equator

10047

10800

497

New Hebrides Trench

Tonga Trench

497

A

B

C

D

E

F

G

H

I

J

K

L

M

N

O

P

Q

R

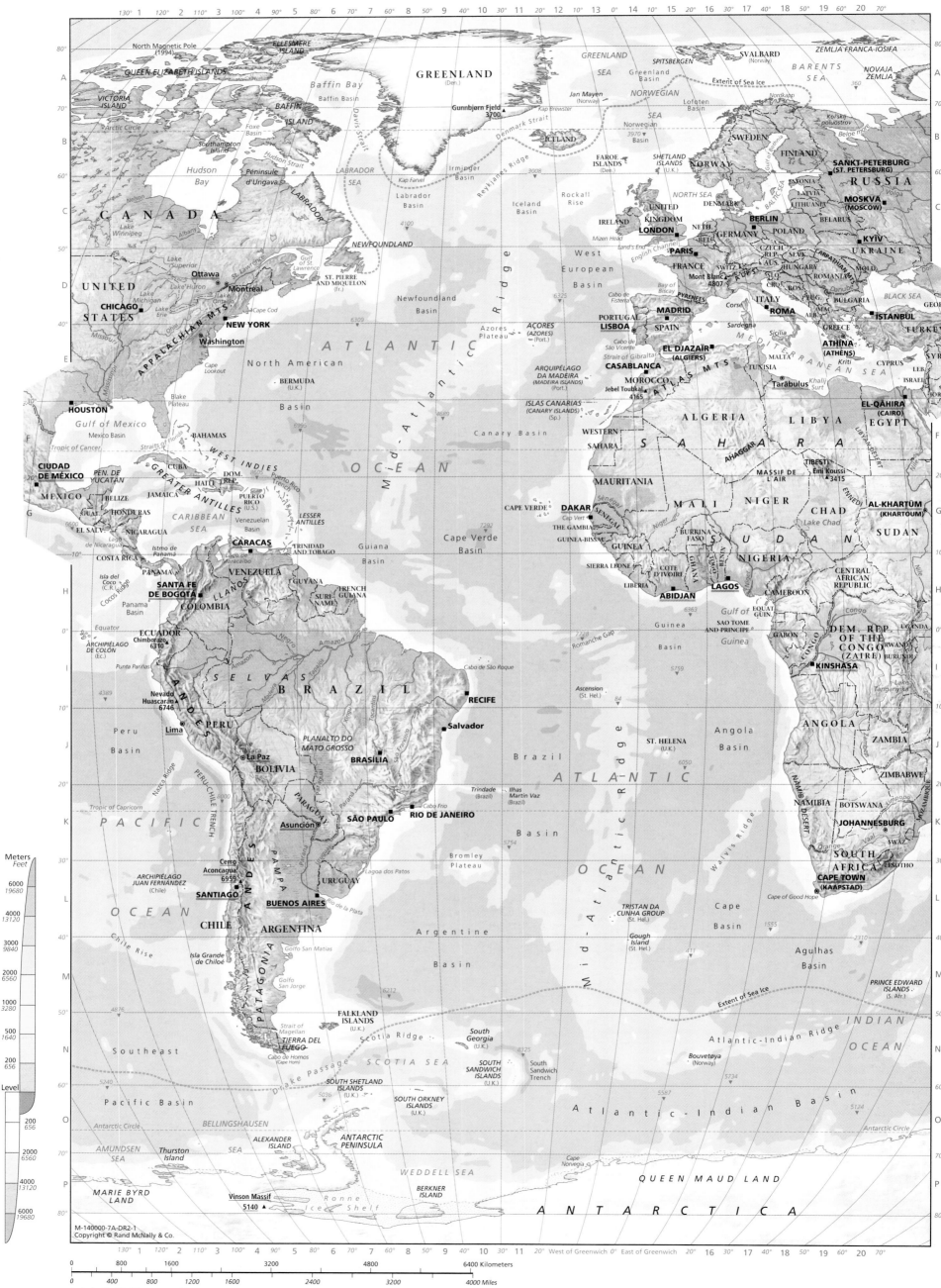

Scale 1 : 60,000,000   Robinson Projection

Index to World Reference Maps

Introduction to the Index

This index includes in a single alphabetical list approximately 54,000 names of places and geographical features that appear on the reference maps. Each name is followed by the name of the country or continent in which it is located, an alpha-numeric map reference key, and a page reference.

Names The names of cities and towns appear in the index in regular type. The names of all other features appear in *italics*, followed by descriptive terms (hill, mtn., state) to indicate their nature.

Abbreviations of names on the maps have been standardized as much as possible. Names that are abbreviated on the maps are generally spelled out in full in the index.

Country names and names of features that extend beyond the boundaries of one country are followed by the name of the continent in which each is located. Country designations follow the names of all other places in the index. The locations of places in the United States, Canada, and the United Kingdom are further defined by abbreviations that indicate the state, province, or other political division in which each is located.

All abbreviations used in the index are defined in the List of Abbreviations to the right.

Alphabetization Names are alphabetized in the order of the letters of the English alphabet. Spanish *ll* and *ch*, for example, are not treated as distinct letters. Furthermore, diacritical marks are disregarded in alphabetization—German or Scandinavian *ä* or *ö* are treated as *a* or *o*.

The names of physical features may appear inverted, since they are always alphabetized under the proper, not the generic, part of the name, thus: "Gibraltar, Strait of". Otherwise every entry, whether consisting of one word or more, is alphabetized as a single continuous entity. "Lakeland", for example, appears after "La Crosse" and before "La Salle". Names beginning with articles (Le Havre, Den Helder, Al-Manāmah) are not inverted. Names beginning "St.", "Ste." and "Sainte" are alphabetized as though spelled "Saint".

In the case of identical names, towns are listed first, then political divisions, then physical features. Entries that are completely identical are listed alphabetically by country name.

Map Reference Keys and Page References The map reference keys and page references are found in the last two columns of each entry.

Each map reference key consists of a letter and number. The letters correspond to letters along the sides of the maps. Lowercase letters refer to inset maps. The numbers correspond to numbers that appear across the tops and bottoms of the maps.

Map reference keys for point features, such as cities and mountain peaks, indicate the locations of the symbols for these features. For other features, such as countries, mountain ranges, or rivers, the map reference keys indicate the locations of the names.

The page number generally refers to the main map for the country in which the feature is located. Page references for two-page maps always refer to the left-hand page.

List of Abbreviations

Ab., Can.	Alberta, Can.
Afg.	Afghanistan
Afr.	Africa
Ak., U.S.	Alaska, U.S.
Al., U.S.	Alabama, U.S.
Alb.	Albania
Alg.	Algeria
Am. Sam.	American Samoa
anch.	anchorage
And.	Andorra
Ang.	Angola
Ant.	Antarctica
Antig.	Antigua and Barbuda
aq.	aqueduct
Ar., U.S.	Arkansas, U.S.
Arg.	Argentina
Arm.	Armenia
at.	atoll
Aus.	Austria
Austl.	Australia
Az., U.S.	Arizona, U.S.
Azer.	Azerbaijan
b.	bay, gulf, inlet, lagoon
B.C., Can.	British Columbia, Can.
Bah.	Bahamas
Bahr.	Bahrain
Barb.	Barbados
bas.	basin
Bdi.	Burundi
Bel.	Belgium
Bela.	Belarus
Ber.	Bermuda
Bhu.	Bhutan
B.I.O.T.	British Indian Ocean Territory
Blg.	Bulgaria
Bngl.	Bangladesh
Bol.	Bolivia
Bos.	Bosnia and Hercegovina
Bots.	Botswana
Braz.	Brazil
Bru.	Brunei
Br. Vir. Is.	British Virgin Islands
Burkina	Burkina Faso
c.	cape, point
Ca., U.S.	California, U.S.
Cam.	Cameroon
Camb.	Cambodia
Can.	Canada
can.	canal
C.A.R.	Central African Republic
Cay. Is.	Cayman Islands
Christ. I.	Christmas Island
C. Iv.	Cote d'Ivoire
clf.	cliff, escarpment
Co., U.S.	Colorado, U.S.
co.	county, district, etc.
Cocos Is.	Cocos (Keeling) Islands
Col.	Colombia
Com.	Comoros
cont.	continent
Cook Is.	Cook Islands
C.R.	Costa Rica
crat.	crater
Cro.	Croatia
cst.	coast, beach
Ct., U.S.	Connecticut, U.S.
ctry.	independent country
C.V.	Cape Verde
cv.	cave
Cyp.	Cyprus
Czech Rep.	Czech Republic
D.C., U.S.	District of Columbia, U.S.
De., U.S.	Delaware, U.S.
Den.	Denmark
dep.	dependency, colony
depr.	depression
des.	desert
Dji.	Djibouti
Dom.	Dominica
Dom. Rep.	Dominican Republic
D.R.C.	Democratic Republic of the Congo
Ec.	Ecuador
El Sal.	El Salvador
Eng., U.K.	England, U.K.
Eq. Gui.	Equatorial Guinea
Erit.	Eritrea
Est.	Estonia
est.	estuary
Eth.	Ethiopia
Eur.	Europe
Falk. Is.	Falkland Islands
Far. Is.	Faroe Islands
Fin.	Finland
Fl., U.S.	Florida, U.S.
for.	forest, moor
Fr.	France
Fr. Gu.	French Guiana
Fr. Poly.	French Polynesia
Ga., U.S.	Georgia, U.S.
Gam.	The Gambia
Gaza	Gaza Strip
Geor.	Georgia
Ger.	Germany
Gib.	Gibraltar
Golan	Golan Heights
Grc.	Greece
Gren.	Grenada
Grnld.	Greenland

Guad.	Guadeloupe
Guat.	Guatemala
Guern.	Guernsey
Gui.	Guinea
Gui.-B.	Guinea-Bissau
Guy.	Guyana
gysr.	geyser
Hi., U.S.	Hawaii, U.S.
hist.	historic site, ruins
hist. reg.	historic region
Hond.	Honduras
Hung.	Hungary
i.	island
Ia., U.S.	Iowa, U.S.
Ice.	Iceland
ice	ice feature, glacier
Id., U.S.	Idaho, U.S.
Il., U.S.	Illinois, U.S.
In., U.S.	Indiana, U.S.
Indon.	Indonesia
I. of Man	Isle of Man
Ire.	Ireland
is.	islands
Isr.	Israel
isth.	isthmus
Jam.	Jamaica
Jer.	Jericho Area
Jord.	Jordan
Kaz.	Kazakhstan
Kir.	Kiribati
Kor., N.	Korea, North
Kor., S.	Korea, South
Ks., U.S.	Kansas, U.S.
Kuw.	Kuwait
Ky., U.S.	Kentucky, U.S.
Kyrg.	Kyrgyzstan
l.	lake, pond
La., U.S.	Louisiana, U.S.
Lat.	Latvia
lav.	lava flow
Leb.	Lebanon
Leso.	Lesotho
Lib.	Liberia
Liech.	Liechtenstein
Lith.	Lithuania
Lux.	Luxembourg
Ma., U.S.	Massachusetts, U.S.
Mac.	Macedonia
Madag.	Madagascar
Malay.	Malaysia
Mald.	Maldives
Marsh. Is.	Marshall Islands
Mart.	Martinique
Maur.	Mauritania
May.	Mayotte
Mb., Can.	Manitoba, Can.
Md., U.S.	Maryland, U.S.
Me., U.S.	Maine, U.S.
Mex.	Mexico
Mi., U.S.	Michigan, U.S.
Micron.	Micronesia, Federated States of
Mid. Is.	Midway Islands
misc. cult.	miscellaneous cultural
Mn., U.S.	Minnesota, U.S.
Mo., U.S.	Missouri, U.S.
Mol.	Moldova
Mon.	Monaco
Mong.	Mongolia
Monts.	Montserrat
Mor.	Morocco
Moz.	Mozambique
Mrts.	Mauritius
Ms., U.S.	Mississippi, U.S.
Mt., U.S.	Montana, U.S.
mth.	river mouth or channel
mtn.	mountain
mts.	mountains
Mwi.	Malawi
Mya.	Myanmar
N.A.	North America
N.B., Can.	New Brunswick, Can.
N.C., U.S.	North Carolina, U.S.
N. Cal.	New Caledonia
N. Cyp.	North Cyprus
N.D., U.S.	North Dakota, U.S.
Ne., U.S.	Nebraska, U.S.
Neth.	Netherlands
Neth. Ant.	Netherlands Antilles
Nf., Can.	Newfoundland, Can.
ngh.	neighborhood
N.H., U.S.	New Hampshire, U.S.
Nic.	Nicaragua
Nig.	Nigeria
N. Ire., U.K.	Northern Ireland, U.K.
N.J., U.S.	New Jersey, U.S.
N.M., U.S.	New Mexico, U.S.
N. Mar. Is.	Northern Mariana Islands
Nmb.	Namibia
Nor.	Norway
Norf. I.	Norfolk Island
N.S., Can.	Nova Scotia, Can.
N.T., Can.	Northwest Territories, Can.
Nv., U.S.	Nevada, U.S.
N.Y., U.S.	New York, U.S.
N.Z.	New Zealand
Oc.	Oceania
Oh., U.S.	Ohio, U.S.

Ok., U.S.	Oklahoma, U.S.
On., Can.	Ontario, Can.
Or., U.S.	Oregon, U.S.
p.	pass
Pa., U.S.	Pennsylvania, U.S.
Pak.	Pakistan
Pan.	Panama
Pap. N. Gui.	Papua New Guinea
Para.	Paraguay
P.E., Can.	Prince Edward Island, Can.
pen.	peninsula
Phil.	Philippines
Pit.	Pitcairn
pl.	plain, flat
plat.	plateau, highland
p.o.i.	point of interest
Pol.	Poland
Port.	Portugal
P.R.	Puerto Rico
Qc., Can.	Quebec, Can.
r.	rock, rocks
reg.	physical region
res.	reservoir
Reu.	Reunion
rf.	reef, shoal
R.I., U.S.	Rhode Island, U.S.
Rom.	Romania
Rw.	Rwanda
S.A.	South America
S. Afr.	South Africa
Samoa	Samoa
sand	sand area
Sau. Ar.	Saudi Arabia
S.C., U.S.	South Carolina, U.S.
sci.	scientific station
Scot., U.K.	Scotland, U.K.
S.D., U.S.	South Dakota, U.S.
Sen.	Senegal
Sey.	Seychelles
S. Geor.	South Georgia
Sing.	Singapore
Sk., Can.	Saskatchewan, Can.
S.L.	Sierra Leone
Slov.	Slovakia
Slvn.	Slovenia
S. Mar.	San Marino
Sol. Is.	Solomon Islands
Som.	Somalia
Sp. N. Afr.	Spanish North Africa
Sri L.	Sri Lanka
state	state, province, etc.
St. Hel.	St. Helena
St. K./N.	St. Kitts and Nevis
St. Luc.	St. Lucia
stm.	stream (river, creek)
S. Tom./P.	Sao Tome and Principe
St. P./M.	St. Pierre and Miquelon
strt.	strait, channel, etc.
St. Vin.	St. Vincent and the Grenadines
Sur.	Suriname
sw.	swamp, marsh
Swaz.	Swaziland
Swe.	Sweden
Switz.	Switzerland
Tai.	Taiwan
Taj.	Tajikistan
Tan.	Tanzania
T./C. Is.	Turks and Caicos Islands
Thai.	Thailand
Tn., U.S.	Tennessee, U.S.
Tok.	Tokelau
Trin.	Trinidad and Tobago
Tun.	Tunisia
Tur.	Turkey
Turkmen.	Turkmenistan
Tx., U.S.	Texas, U.S.
U.A.E.	United Arab Emirates
Ug.	Uganda
U.K.	United Kingdom
Ukr.	Ukraine
unds.	undersea feature
Ur.	Uruguay
U.S.	United States
Ut., U.S.	Utah, U.S.
Uzb.	Uzbekistan
Va., U.S.	Virginia, U.S.
val.	valley, watercourse
Vat.	Vatican City
Ven.	Venezuela
Viet.	Vietnam
V.I.U.S.	Virgin Islands (U.S.)
vol.	volcano
Vt., U.S.	Vermont, U.S.
Wa., U.S.	Washington, U.S.
Wake I.	Wake Island
Wal./F.	Wallis and Futuna
W.B.	West Bank
well	well, spring, oasis
Wi., U.S.	Wisconsin, U.S.
W. Sah.	Western Sahara
wtfl.	waterfall, rapids
W.V., U.S.	West Virginia, U.S.
Wy., U.S.	Wyoming, U.S.
Yk., Can.	Yukon Territory, Can.
Yugo.	Yugoslavia
Zam.	Zambia
Zimb.	Zimbabwe

Index

A

Name	Map Ref.	Page
Angoram, Pap. N. Gui.	a3	79a
Angostura, Presa de la, res., Mex.	H12	100
Angoulême, Fr.	D6	18
Angoumois, hist. reg., Fr.	D5	18
Angra dos Reis, Braz.	L3	88
Angren, Uzb.	F12	32
Angu, D.R.C.	D4	66
Angualasto, Arg.	D3	92
Anguilla, Ms., U.S.	E8	122
Anguilla, dep., N.A.	h15	96a
Anguille, Cape, c., Nf., Can.	C17	110
Anguli Nur, l., China	A6	42
Anguo, China	B6	42
Angus, On., Can.	D10	112
Angusville, Mb., Can.	D13	124
Anhalt, hist. reg., Ger.	D7	16
Anholt, i., Den.	H4	8
Anhua, China	G4	42
Anhui, state, China	F7	42
Anhwei see Anhui, state, China	F7	42
Aniak, Ak., U.S.	D8	140
Anibare Bay, b., Nauru	q17	78f
Anie, Pic d', mtn., Fr.	F5	18
Anil, Braz.	B3	88
Animas, N.M., U.S.	L8	132
Animas, stm., U.S.	G9	132
Animas Valley, val., N.A.	L8	132
Anina, Rom.	D8	26
Anita, Ia., U.S.	C3	120
Anıtkaya, Tur.	E13	28
Aniva, mys, c., Russia	B13	36
Aniva, zaliv, b., Russia	G17	34
Aniwa, i., Vanuatu	I17	79d
Anjangaon, India	H6	54
Anjār, India	G2	54
'Anjar, Leb.	E6	58
Anjou, hist. reg., Fr.	G8	14
Anjouan see Nzwani, i., Com.	C7	68
Anjudin, Russia	B9	32
Anjujsk, Russia	C21	34
Anjujskij hrebet, mts., Russia	C21	34
Anju-ŭp, Kor., N.	E6	38
Anka, Nig.	G6	64
Ankaboa, Tanjona, c., Madag.	E7	68
Ankang, China	E3	42
Ankara, Tur.	D15	28
Ankara, state, Tur.	D15	28
Ankavandra, Madag.	D8	68
Ankazoabo, Madag.	E7	68
Ankazobe, Madag.	D8	68
Ankeny, Ia., U.S.	C4	120
Anking see Anqing, China	F7	42
Ankleshwar, India	H4	54
Ankoro, D.R.C.	F5	66
Anlong, China	F6	36
Ânlóng Vêng, Camb.	E6	48
Anlu, China	F5	42
An Muileann gCearr see Mullingar, Ire.	H5	12
Ånn, l., Swe.	E5	8
Ann, Cape, c., Ant.	B10	81
Ann, Cape, pen., Ma., U.S.	H6	110
Anna, Il., U.S.	G8	120
Anna, Lake, res., Va., U.S.	F8	114
Annaba, Alg.	B6	64
An-Nabaṭīyah, state, Leb.	E6	58
An-Nabaṭīyah at-Taḥtā, Leb.	E6	58
Annaberg-Buchholz, Ger.	F9	16
An-Nabk, Syria	D7	58
An-Nafūd, des., Sau. Ar.	D5	56
An-Najaf, Iraq	C5	56
Annam see Trung Phan, hist. reg., Viet.	D8	48
Annamitique, Chaîne, mts., Asia	D8	48
Annan, Scot., U.K.	G9	12
Annandale, Austl.	C7	76
Annandale, Mn., U.S.	F4	118
Annandale, val., Scot., U.K.	F9	12
Anna Plains, Austl.	C4	74
Annapolis, Md., U.S.	F9	114
Annapolis Royal, N.S., Can.	F11	110
Annapūrṇa, mtn., Nepal	D9	54
Ann Arbor, Mi., U.S.	B2	114
An Nás see Naas, Ire.	H6	12
An-Nāṣirīyah, Iraq	C6	56
An-Nāṣirīyah, Syria	E7	58
An-Nawfalīyah, Libya	A3	62
Annecy, Fr.	D12	18
Annecy, Lac d', l., Fr.	D12	18
Annemasse, Fr.	C12	18
Annenkov Island, i., S. Geor.	J9	90
An Nhon, Viet.	F9	48
Anning, China	G5	36
Anniston, Al., U.S.	D13	122
Annobón, i., Eq. Gui.	J6	64
Annonay, Fr.	D10	18
An-Nuhūd, Sudan	E5	62
Annville, Ky., U.S.	G2	114
Annville, Pa., U.S.	D9	114
Anoka, Mn., U.S.	F5	118
Anori, Braz.	D5	84
Anpu, China	K3	42
Anqing, China	F7	42
Anqiu, China	C8	42
Anren, China	H5	42
Ansai, China	C3	42
Ansbach, Ger.	G6	16
Anse-d'Hainault, Haiti	C10	102
Anse La Raye, St. Luc.	m6	105c
Anselmo, Ne., U.S.	F13	126
Anserma, Col.	E4	86
Anshan, China	D5	38
Anshun, China	H1	42
Ansina, Ur.	E10	92
Ansley, Ne., U.S.	F13	126
Anson Bay, b., Austl.	B5	74
Anson Bay, b., Norf. I.	y24	78i
Ansongo, Mali	F5	64
Ansonville, N.C., U.S.	A5	116
Ansted, W.V., U.S.	F4	114
Antakya see Hatay, Tur.	B7	58
Antalaha, Madag.	C9	68
Antalieptė, Lith.	E8	10
Antalya, Tur.	G13	28
Antalya, state, Tur.	F14	28
Antalya, Gulf of see Antalya Körfezi, b., Tur.	G14	28
Antalya Körfezi (Antalya, Gulf of), b., Tur.	G14	28
Antananarivo, Madag.	D8	68
An tAonach see Nenagh, Ire.	I4	12
Antarctica, cont.	D11	81
Antarctic Peninsula, pen., Ant.	C35	81
Antas, Braz.	F6	88
Antas, stm., Braz.	D12	92
Antelope Island, i., Ut., U.S.	C4	132
Antelope Mine, Zimb.	B9	70
Antelope Peak, mtn., Nv., U.S.	B1	132
Antenor Navarro, Braz.	D6	88
Antequera, Para.	A9	92
Antequera, Spain	H6	20
Anthon, Ia., U.S.	B2	120
Anthony, Ks., U.S.	D10	128
Anthony, N.M., U.S.	K10	132
Anthony, Tx., U.S.	E9	98
Anti-Atlas, mts., Mor.	D3	64
Antibes, Fr.	F13	18
Anticosti, Île d', i., Qc., Can.	F18	106
Antifer, Cap d', c., Fr.	E8	14
Antigonish, N.S., Can.	E14	110
Antigua, i., Antig.	f4	105b
Antigua and Barbuda, ctry., N.A.	h15	96a
Antigua International Airport, Antig.	f4	105b
Antiguo Morelos, Mex.	D9	100
Antikýthira, i., Grc.	H6	28
Anti-Lebanon (Sharqī, Al-Jabal ash-), mts., Asia	E7	58
Antilla, Cuba	B10	102
Antillen, Nederlandse see Netherlands Antilles, dep., N.A.	i14	96a
Antimony, Ut., U.S.	E5	132
Antioch see Hatay, Tur.	B7	58
Antioch, Il., U.S.	F1	112
Antioquia, Col.	D4	86
Antioquia, state, Col.	D4	86
Antipajuta, Russia	C4	34
Antipodes Islands, is., N.Z.	H9	72
Antisana, vol., Ec.	H2	86
Antler, stm., N.A.	E12	124
Antofagasta, Chile	A2	92
Antofagasta, state, Chile	B3	92
Antofagasta de la Sierra, Arg.	C4	92
Antofalla, Salar de, pl., Arg.	C3	92
Antofalla, Volcán, vol., Arg.	B4	92
Antón, Pan.	H7	102
Anton, Tx., U.S.	H6	128
Anton Chico, N.M., U.S.	F3	128
Antongila, Helodrano, b., Madag.	D8	68
Antonina, Braz.	B13	92
Antonina do Norte, Braz.	D5	88
Antônio Prado, Braz.	D12	92
Antonito, Co., U.S.	D2	128
Antón Lizardo, Punta, c., Mex.	F10	100
Antopal', Bela.	H7	10
Antrim, N. Ire., U.K.	G6	12
Antropovo, Russia	G20	8
Antsalova, Madag.	D7	68
Antsirabe, Madag.	D8	68
Antsirañana, Madag.	C8	68
Antsohihy, Madag.	C8	68
Antulai, Gunong, mtn., Malay.	A10	50
Antun', Russia	G16	34
Antung see Dandong, China	D5	38
Antwerp see Antwerpen, Bel.	C13	14
Antwerp, Oh., U.S.	C1	114
Antwerpen (Antwerp), Bel.	C13	14
An Uaimh see Navan, Ire.	H6	12
Anugul, India	H10	54
Anūpgarh, India	D4	54
Anuradhapura, Sri L.	G5	53
Anvers see Antwerpen, Bel.	C13	14
Anvers Island, i., Ant.	B34	81
Anvik, Ak., U.S.	D7	140
Anxi, China	C4	36
Anxi, China	I8	42
Anxiang, China	G5	42
Anxious Bay, b., Austl.	F6	74
Anyang, China	C6	42
Anyang, Kor., S.	F7	38
A'nyêmaqên Shan, mts., China	D4	36
Anyer Kidul, Indon.	G4	50
Anykščiai, Lith.	E7	10
Anyuan, China	I6	42
Anyuanyi see Tianzhu, China	D5	36
Anyue, China	F1	42
Anze, China	C5	42
Anžero-Sudžensk, Russia	C15	32
Anzio, Italy	C6	24
Anzoátegui, state, Ven.	C9	86
Anžu, ostrova, is., Russia	A17	34
Aoba, i., Vanuatu	j16	79d
Aoba / Maéwo, state, Vanuatu	j17	79d
Aoga-shima, i., Japan	G12	40
Aohan Qi, China	C3	38
Aojiang, China	H9	42
Aoji-ri, Kor., N.	C9	38
Ao Luk, Thai.	H4	48
Aomar, Alg.	H14	20
Aomen see Macau, Macau	J5	42
Aomen see Macau, dep., Asia	J5	42
Aomori, Japan	D14	38
Aonla, India	D7	54
Aóös (Vjosës), stm., Eur.	D13	24
A'opo, Samoa	g11	79c
Aôral, Phnum, mtn., Camb.	F7	48
Aore, i., Vanuatu	j16	79d
Aosta (Aoste), Italy	E4	22
Aoste see Aosta, Italy	E4	22
Aouderas, Niger	F6	64
Aouk, Bahr, stm., Afr.	F3	62
Aoukâr, reg., Maur.	F3	64
Aoya, Japan	D7	40
Aozou, Chad	C3	62
Apache Junction, Az., U.S.	J5	132
Apache Peak, mtn., Az., U.S.	L6	132
Apalachee, stm., Ga., U.S.	C2	116
Apalachicola, Fl., U.S.	H13	122
Apalachicola, stm., Fl., U.S.	H14	122
Apalachicola Bay, b., Fl., U.S.	H13	122
Apaporis, stm., S.A.	H7	86
Aparados da Serra, Parque Nacional de, p.o.i., Braz.	D12	92
Aparri, Phil.	A3	52
Apartadó, Col.	D3	86
Apatin, Yugo.	D5	26
Apatity, Russia	C15	8
Apatzingán de la Constitución, Mex.	F7	100
Apaxtla de Castrejón, Mex.	F8	100
Apeldoorn, Neth.	B15	14
Apennines see Appennino, mts., Italy	G11	6
Apex, N.C., U.S.	I7	114
Api, mtn., Nepal	D8	54
Apía, Col.	E4	86
Apia, Samoa	g12	79c
Apiacás, Serra dos, plat., Braz.	E6	84
Apiaí, Braz.	B13	92
Apiaú, stm., Braz.	F11	86
Apishapa, stm., Co., U.S.	D4	128
Apizaco, Mex.	F9	100
Apo, Mount, mtn., Phil.	G5	52
Apodi, Braz.	C7	88
Apodi, stm., Braz.	C7	88
Apolakkiá, Grc.	G10	28
Apolda, Ger.	E7	16
Apolinario Saravia, Arg.	B6	92
Apolo, Bol.	B3	90
Apón, stm., Ven.	B5	86
Aponguao, stm., Ven.	E11	86
Apopka, Lake, l., Fl., U.S.	H4	116
Aporá, Braz.	F6	88
Aporé, Braz.	C6	90
Apostle Islands, is., Wi., U.S.	E8	118
Apostle Islands National Lakeshore, p.o.i., Wi., U.S.	D8	118
Apóstoles, Arg.	C10	92
Apostolove, Ukr.	E4	32
Appalaches, Les see Appalachian Mountains, mts., N.A.	D12	108
Appalachia, Va., U.S.	H3	114
Appalachian Mountains, mts., N.A.	D12	108
Appennino see Apennines, mts., Italy	G11	6
Appennino, Calabro, mts., Italy	E10	24
Appennino Abruzzese, mts., Italy	B7	24
Appennino Ligure, mts., Italy	F6	22
Appennino Lucano, mts., Italy	D9	24
Appennino Tosco-Emiliano, mts., Italy	F8	22
Appennino Umbro-Marchigiano, mts., Italy	G9	22
Appenzell, Switz.	C6	22
Apple Orchard Mountain, mtn., Va., U.S.	G6	114
Appleton, Mn., U.S.	F3	118
Appleton, Wi., U.S.	G10	118
Appleton City, Mo., U.S.	F3	120
Apple Valley, Ca., U.S.	I8	134
Appomattox, Va., U.S.	G7	114
Appomattox, stm., Va., U.S.	G7	114
Aprelevka, Russia	E20	10
Aprilia, Italy	C6	24
Apšeronsk, Russia	F5	32
Apt, Fr.	F11	18
Apucarana, Braz.	A12	92
Apulia see Puglia, state, Italy	C10	24
Apure, state, Ven.	D7	86
Apure, stm., Ven.	D8	86
Apurímac, stm., Peru	F3	84
Apurito, Ven.	D7	86
Aqaba, Gulf of, b.	J5	58
Āqchah, Afg.	B10	56
'Aqīq, Sudan	D7	62
Aqtaū see Aktau, Kaz.	F8	32
Aqtöbe see Aktjubinsk, Kaz.	D9	32
Aquidabã, Braz.	F7	88
Aquidauana, Braz.	D5	90
Aquila, Mex.	F7	100
Aquiles Serdán, Mex.	A6	100
Aquiles Serdán, Mex.	C9	100
Aquin, Haiti	C11	102
Aquio, stm., Col.	F8	86
Ara, India	F10	54
Ara, stm., Japan	D12	40
Arab, Al., U.S.	C12	122
'Arab, Bahr al-, stm., Sudan	E5	62
'Araba, Wadi ('Arabah, Wādī), stm., Egypt	I3	58
'Arabah, Wādī al- (Ha'Arava), val., Asia	H6	58
Arabako, co., Spain	B8	20
Araban, Tur.	A8	58
Arabian Basin, unds.	H9	142
Arabian Desert (Eastern Desert), des., Egypt	B6	62
Arabian Gulf see Persian Gulf, b., Asia	D7	56
Arabian Peninsula, pen., Asia	E6	56
Arabian Sea	F9	56
Araçá, stm., Braz.	G10	86
Aracaju, Braz.	F7	88
Aracataca, Col.	B4	86
Aracati, Braz.	C7	88
Araçatuba, Braz.	D6	90
Aracena, Spain	G4	20
Araci, Braz.	F6	88
Aracides, Cape, c., Sol. Is.	e9	79b
Aracoiaba, Braz.	C6	88
Aracruz, Braz.	J5	88
Araçuaí, Braz.	I4	88
Araçuaí, stm., Braz.	I4	88
'Arad, Isr.	G6	58
Arad, Rom.	C8	26
Arad, state, Rom.	C8	26
Aradhíppou, Cyp.	D4	58
Arafura Sea	J16	142
Arafura Shelf, unds.	K16	142
Aragarças, Braz.	G7	84
Aragats Lerr, mtn., Arm.	A5	56
Aragón, state, Spain	C10	20
Aragón, stm., Spain	B9	20
Aragona, Italy	G7	24
Aragua, state, Ven.	B8	86
Araguacema, Braz.	E8	84
Araguaçu, Braz.	F8	84
Aragua de Barcelona, Ven.	C9	86
Araguaia, stm., Braz.	E8	84
Araguaína, Braz.	D1	88
Araguao, Caño, stm., Ven.	C11	86
Araguari, Braz.	J1	88
Araguari, stm., Braz.	C7	84
Araguari, stm., Braz.	J1	88
Araguatins, Braz.	C1	88
Arahal, Spain	G5	20
Arai, Japan	B11	40
Araioses, Braz.	B4	88
Ârak, Alg.	D5	64
Arāk, Iran	C6	56
Arakan see Rakhine, state, Mya.	C1	48
Arakan Yoma, mts., Mya.	C2	48
Arakkonam, India	E4	53
Araks see Aras, stm., Asia	B6	56
Araks see Araz, stm., Asia	B6	56
Aral Sea, l., Asia	E9	32
Aral'sk, Kaz.	E10	32
Aralsk see Aral'sk, Kaz.	E10	32
Aramac, Austl.	D5	76
Aramac, stm., Austl.	D5	76
Ārāmbāg, India	G11	54
Aramberri, Mex.	C8	100
Ārān, Iran	C7	56
Aranda de Duero, Spain	C7	20
Arandas, Mex.	E7	100
Arandis, Nmb.	C2	70
Arang, India	H8	54
Ārani, India	E4	53
Aran Island, i., Ire.	G4	12
Aran Islands, is., Ire.	H3	12
Aranjuez, Spain	D7	20
Aranos, Nmb.	D4	70
Aransas, stm., Tx., U.S.	F10	130
Arantāngi, India	F4	53
Aranyaprathet, Thai.	F6	48
Arao, Japan	G3	40
Araouane, Mali	F4	64
Arapaho, Ok., U.S.	F9	128
Arapahoe, Ne., U.S.	A9	128
Arapey Grande, stm., Ur.	E9	92
Arapiraca, Braz.	E7	88
Arapongas, Braz.	D6	90
Arapoti, Braz.	B12	92
Araranguá, Braz.	D13	92
Araraquara, Braz.	K1	88
Araras, Braz.	L2	88
Araras, Açude, res., Braz.	C5	88
Ararat, Austl.	K4	76
Ararat, Mount see Ağrı Dağı, mtn., Tur.	B5	56
Arari, Braz.	B3	88
Arāria, India	E11	54
Araripe, Braz.	D5	88
Araripe, Chapada do, plat., Braz.	D6	88
Araripina, Braz.	D5	88
Ararirá, stm., Braz.	H10	86
Araruama, Lagoa de, b., Braz.	L4	88
Araruna, Braz.	D8	88
Aras (Araz), stm., Asia	B6	56
Aratuípe, Braz.	G6	88
Arauca, Col.	D6	86
Arauca, state, Col.	D6	86
Arauca, stm., S.A.	D8	86
Araucária, Braz.	B13	92
Arauquita, Col.	D6	86
Araure, Ven.	C7	86
Arāvalli Range, mts., India	F4	54
Arawa, Pap. N. Gui.	d6	79b
Araxá, Braz.	J2	88
Araya, Ven.	B9	86
Araya, Punta de, c., Ven.	B9	86
Araz (Aras), stm., Asia	B6	56
Ārba Minch', Eth.	F7	62
Arbatax, Italy	E3	24
Arboga, Swe.	G6	8
Arboledas, Arg.	H7	92
Arbon, Switz.	C6	22
Arboréa, Italy	E2	24
Arborea, reg., Italy	E2	24
Arborfield, Sk., Can.	A10	124
Arbroath, Scot., U.K.	E10	12
Arbuckle, Ca., U.S.	D3	134
Arc, stm., Fr.	D12	18
Arcachon, Fr.	E4	18
Arcachon, Bassin d', b., Fr.	E4	18
Arcade, Ca., U.S.	E4	134
Arcade, N.Y., U.S.	B7	114
Arcadia, Ca., U.S.	I7	134
Arcadia, Fl., U.S.	I4	116
Arcadia, Ia., U.S.	B2	120
Arcadia, Ks., U.S.	G3	120
Arcadia, La., U.S.	E6	122
Arcadia, Mi., U.S.	D3	112
Arcadia, Mo., U.S.	G7	120
Arcadia, S.C., U.S.	B3	116
Arcadia, Wi., U.S.	G7	118
Arcanum, Oh., U.S.	D1	114
Arcas, Cayos, is., Mex.	E12	100
Arcata, Ca., U.S.	C1	134
Arc Dome, mtn., Nv., U.S.	E8	134
Arcelia, Mex.	F8	100
Arcevia, Italy	G9	22
Archangel see Arhangel'sk, Russia	D19	8
Archbold, Oh., U.S.	C1	114
Archer, Fl., U.S.	G3	116
Archer, stm., Austl.	B8	74
Archer, Mount, mtn., Austl.	D8	76
Archer City, Tx., U.S.	H10	128
Archer's Post, Kenya	D7	66
Arches National Park, p.o.i., Ut., U.S.	E7	132
Archiac, Fr.	D5	18
Archidona, Spain	G6	20
Arcis-sur-Aube, Fr.	F13	14
Arco, Id., U.S.	G13	136
Arcola, Il., U.S.	E9	120
Arcola, Ms., U.S.	D8	122
Arcos, Braz.	K3	88
Arcos de la Frontera, Spain	H5	20
Arcot, India	E4	53
Arcoverde, Braz.	E7	88
Arctic Bay, N.T., Can.	A14	106
Arctic Ocean	A21	4
Arctic Red, stm., N.T., Can.	B4	106
Arctic Village, Ak., U.S.	C10	140
Arda, stm., Eur.	H12	26
Ardabīl, Iran	B6	56
Ardahan, Tur.	A5	56
Ardakān, Iran	C7	56
Ardatov, Russia	I20	8
Ardèche, state, Fr.	E10	18
Arden, Ca., U.S.	E4	134
Ardennes, state, Fr.	E13	14
Ardennes, reg., Eur.	D14	14
Ardennes, Canal des, can., Fr.	E13	14
Ardestān, Iran	C7	56
Ardila, stm., Eur.	F3	20
Ardill, Sk., Can.	E8	124
Ardlethan, Austl.	J6	76
Ardmore, Al., U.S.	B12	122
Ardmore, Ok., U.S.	G11	128
Ardmore, Pa., U.S.	D10	114
Åre, Swe.	E5	8
Areado, Braz.	K2	88
Arecibo, P.R.	B2	104a
Arecibo, Observatorio de, sci., P.R.	B2	104a
Arecibo Observatory see Arecibo, Observatorio de, sci., P.R.	B2	104a
Arèhausk, Bela.	F13	10
Areia, Braz.	D8	88
Areia, stm., Braz.	H3	88
Areia Branca, Braz.	C7	88
Arena, Point, c., Ca., U.S.	E2	134
Arena, Punta, c., Mex.	D4	100
Arena de la Ventana, Punta, c., Mex.	C4	100
Arenal, P.R.	C3	104a
Arenas, Cayo, i., Mex.	D13	100
Arenas, Punta de, c., Arg.	J3	90
Arenas de San Pedro, Spain	D5	20
Arendal, Nor.	G3	8
Arenys de Mar, Spain	C13	20
Arequipa, Peru	G3	84
Arequito, Arg.	F7	92
Arévalo, Spain	C6	20
Arezzo, Italy	G8	22
Arga, stm., Spain	B9	20
Argadargada, Austl.	D7	74
Argamasilla de Alba, Spain	E7	20
Arganda del Rey, Spain	D7	20
Arga-Sala, stm., Russia	C10	34
Argelès-Gazost, Fr.	F5	18
Argens, stm., Fr.	F12	18
Argent, Côte d', cst., Fr.	F4	18
Argenta, Italy	F8	22
Argentan, Fr.	F8	14
Argentat, Fr.	D7	18
Argenteuil, Fr.	F11	14
Argentina, ctry., S.A.	G3	90
Argentine Basin, unds.	L10	144
Argentino, Lago, l., Arg.	J2	90
Argenton-sur-Creuse, Fr.	H10	14
Argeș, state, Rom.	E11	26
Argeș, stm., Rom.	E13	26
Arghandāb, stm., Afg.	C10	56
Argolikós Kólpos (Argolis, Gulf of), b., Grc.	F6	28
Argolis, Gulf of see Argolikós Kólpos, b., Grc.	F6	28
Argonia, Ks., U.S.	D11	128
Argonne, Wi., U.S.	F10	118
Argonne, reg., Fr.	E14	14
Árgos, Grc.	F5	28
Argos, In., U.S.	G3	112
Argostóli, Grc.	E3	28
Arguello, Point, c., Ca., U.S.	I5	134
Argun' (Ergun), stm., Asia	F12	34
Argungu, Nig.	G5	64
Argyle, Lake, l., Austl.	C5	74
Arhangel'sk, Russia	D19	8
Arhangel'skaja oblast', co., Russia	E20	8
Arhangel'skoe, Russia	G20	10
Arhara, Russia	G15	34
Arhipovo, Russia	C21	8
Århus, Den.	H4	8
Århus, state, Den.	H4	8
Ariake-kai, b., Japan	F3	40
Ariana, Tun.	H4	24
Ariano Irpino, Italy	C9	24
Ariari, stm., Col.	F5	86
Arias, Arg.	F6	92
Ari Atoll, at., Mald.	i12	46a
Arica, Chile	C2	90
Arica, Col.	I6	86
Arichat, N.S., Can.	E16	110
Arichuna, Ven.	D8	86
Arid, Cape, c., Austl.	F4	74
Arida, Japan	E8	40
Aridaía, Grc.	C5	28
Ariège, state, Fr.	G7	18
Ārifwāla, Pak.	C4	54
Ariguaní, stm., Col.	C5	86
Arīḥā (Jericho), Gaza	G6	58
Arīḥā, Syria	C7	58
Arikaree, stm., U.S.	B6	128
Arima, Trin.	s12	105f
Arinos, stm., Braz.	F6	84
Ariogala, Lith.	E6	10
Ariporo, stm., Col.	D6	86
Aripuanã, Braz.	E5	84
Aripuanã, stm., Braz.	E5	84
Ariquemes, Braz.	E5	84
Arisa, stm., Ven.	D9	86
Arish, Wadi el- ('Arīsh, Wādī al-), stm., Egypt	H4	58
Aristazabal Island, i., B.C., Can.	E5	106
Ariton, Al., U.S.	F13	122
Arivonimamo, Madag.	D8	68
Ariyalūr, India	F4	53
Arizaro, Salar de, pl., Arg.	B4	92
Arizgoiti, Spain	A8	20
Arizona, Arg.	G5	92
Arizona, state, U.S.	I5	132
Arizpe, Mex.	F7	98
Arja, Russia	H22	8
Arjasa, Indon.	G9	50
Arjona, Col.	B4	86
Arjona, Spain	G6	20
Arka, Russia	D17	34
Arkadelphia, Ar., U.S.	C5	122
Arkalyk, Kaz.	D11	32
Arkansas, state, U.S.	B6	122
Arkansas, stm., U.S.	E9	108
Arkansas, Salt Fork, stm., U.S.	D7	122
Arkansas City, Ar., U.S.	D7	122
Arkansas City, Ks., U.S.	D11	128
Arkanū, Jabal, mtn., Libya	C4	62
Arkhara see Arhara, Russia	G15	34
Arklow, Ire.	I6	12
Arkoma, Ok., U.S.	B4	122
Arkona, Kap, c., Ger.	B9	16
Arkport, N.Y., U.S.	B8	114
Arktičeskogo Instituta, ostrova, is., Russia	A5	34
Arlanza, stm., Spain	B7	20
Arlanzón, stm., Spain	B7	20
Arles, Fr.	F10	18
Arlington, S. Afr.	E8	70
Arlington, Ga., U.S.	F14	122
Arlington, Ks., U.S.	D10	128
Arlington, Ky., U.S.	H9	120
Arlington, Ne., U.S.	C1	120
Arlington, Oh., U.S.	D2	114
Arlington, Or., U.S.	E6	136
Arlington, Tn., U.S.	B9	122
Arlington, Tx., U.S.	B10	130
Arlington, Vt., U.S.	G3	110
Arlington, Va., U.S.	F8	114
Arlington, Wa., U.S.	B4	136
Arlington Heights, Il., U.S.	F2	112
Arlit, Niger	F6	64
Arlon, Bel.	E14	14
Arm, stm., Sk., Can.	D8	124
Arma, Ks., U.S.	G3	120
Armada, Mi., U.S.	B3	114
Armadale, Austl.	F3	74
Armageddon see Tel Megiddo, hist., Isr.	F6	58
Armagh, N. Ire., U.K.	G6	12
Armançon, stm., Fr.	G13	14
Armavir, Russia	E6	32
Armenia, Col.	E4	86
Armenia, ctry., Asia	A5	56
Armenija see Armenia, ctry., Asia	A5	56
Armenistís, Grc.	F9	28
Armentières, Fr.	D11	14
Armería, Mex.	F6	100
Armero, Col.	E4	86
Armidale, Austl.	H8	76
Armijo, N.M., U.S.	H10	132
Armour, S.D., U.S.	D14	126
Armstrong, Arg.	F7	92
Armstrong, B.C., Can.	F11	138
Armstrong, On., Can.	A9	118
Armstrong, Mo., U.S.	E5	120
Armstrong, Mount, mtn., Yk., Can.	C4	106
Ārmūr, India	B4	53
Armutlu, Tur.	C11	28
Arnarfjörður, b., Ice.	k27	8a
Arnaud, stm., Qc., Can.	D16	106
Arnaudville, La., U.S.	G6	122
Arnay-le-Duc, Fr.	G13	14
Arnedo, Spain	B8	20
Arneiros, Braz.	D5	88
Arnhem, Neth.	B14	14
Arnhem, Cape, c., Austl.	B7	74
Arnhem Bay, b., Austl.	B7	74
Arnhem Land, reg., Austl.	B6	74
Arno, at., Marsh. Is.	C8	72
Arno, stm., Italy	G7	22
Arnold, Ca., U.S.	E5	134
Arnold, Mn., U.S.	E6	118
Arnold, Mo., U.S.	F7	120
Arnold, Ne., U.S.	F12	126
Arnolds Park, Ia., U.S.	H3	118
Arnon, stm., Fr.	C8	18
Arnprior, On., Can.	C13	112
Arnsberg, Ger.	E4	16
Arnstadt, Ger.	F6	16
Aro, stm., Ven.	D9	86
Aroa, Ven.	B7	86
Aroa, Pointe, c., Fr. Poly.	u20	78h
Aroab, Nmb.	E4	70
Aroland, On., Can.	A12	118
Arolsen, Ger.	E5	16
Arona, Italy	E5	22
Arona, Pap. N. Gui.	b4	79a
Aroostook, stm., N.A.	D8	110
Arop Island (Long Island), i., Pap. N. Gui.	b4	79a
Arorae, i., Kir.	D8	72
Aroroy, Phil.	D4	52
Arosa, Ría de see Arousa, Ría de, est., Spain	B1	20
Arousa, Ría de, est., Spain	B1	20
Arp, Tx., U.S.	E3	122
Arqalyq see Arkalyk, Kaz.	D11	32
Arquata Scrivia, Italy	F5	22
Arraga, Arg.	D5	92
Ar-Rahad, Sudan	E6	62
Arraial do Cabo, Braz.	L5	88
Arraias, Braz.	G2	88
Ar-Ramādī, Iraq	C5	56
Ar-Ramthā, Jord.	F7	58
Arran, Island of, i., Scot., U.K.	F7	12
Ar-Rank, Sudan	E6	62
Ar-Raqqah, Syria	B9	58
Ar-Raqqah, state, Syria	B9	58
Arras, Fr.	D11	14
Ar-Rastan, Syria	D7	58
Arrecifes, Arg.	G7	92
Arrey, N.M., U.S.	K9	132
Arriaga, Mex.	G11	100
Ar-Riyāḍ (Riyadh), Sau. Ar.	E6	56
Arroio Grande, Braz.	F11	92
Arrojado, stm., Braz.	G3	88
Arronches, Port.	E3	20
Arros, stm., Fr.	F6	18
Arroux, stm., Fr.	B10	18
Arrowhead, Lake, res., Tx., U.S.	H10	128
Arrowwood, Ab., Can.	F17	138
Arroyito, Arg.	E6	92
Arroyo, P.R.	C3	104a
Arroyo de la Luz, Spain	E4	20
Arroyo Grande, Ca., U.S.	H5	134
Arroyo Hondo, N.M., U.S.	E3	128
Arroyo Seco, Arg.	F7	92
Arroyos y Esteros, Para.	B9	92
Ar-Rub' al-Khālī, des., Asia	E6	56
Ar-Ruqayyah, hist., Syria	F8	58
Ar-Ruṣāfah, hist., Syria	C9	58
Ar-Ruṣayfah, Jord.	F7	58
Ar-Ruṣayriṣ, Sudan	E6	62
Ar-Ruṭbah, Iraq	C5	56
Arsenev, Russia	B10	38
Arsenevka, stm., Russia	B10	38
Arsikere, India	E3	53
Ársos, Cyp.	D3	58
Art, Île, i., N. Cal.	I14	79d
Árta, Grc.	D3	28
Artà, Spain	E14	20
Artá see Artà, Spain	E14	20
Arteaga, Mex.	F7	100
Art'em, Russia	C9	38
Artemisa, Cuba	A6	102
Artëmovsk, Russia	D16	32
Artëmovskij, Russia	E12	34
Artëmovskij, Russia	C10	38
Artesia, Ms., U.S.	D10	122
Artesia, N.M., U.S.	B3	130
Arthabaska, ngh., Qc., Can.	D5	110
Arthal, India	B6	54
Arthur, On., Can.	E9	112
Arthur, Il., U.S.	E9	120
Arthur, N.D., U.S.	D1	118
Arthur, Tn., U.S.	H2	114
Arthur, stm., Austl.	n12	77a
Arthur's Pass National Park, p.o.i., N.Z.	F5	80
Arthur's Town, Bah.	C9	96
Artibonite, stm., Haiti	C11	102
Artigas, Ur.	E9	92
Artillery Lake, l., N.T., Can.	C9	106
Artois, hist. reg., Fr.	D11	14
Artsyz, Ukr.	D16	26
Artyk, Russia	D18	34
Aru, Kepulauan (Aru Islands), is., Indon.	G10	44
Aru, Tanjung, c., Indon.	E10	50
Arua, Ug.	D6	66
Aruanã, Braz.	F7	84
Aruba, dep., N.A.	F12	102
Aru Islands see Aru, Kepulauan, is., Indon.	G10	44
Arunāchal Pradesh, state, India	C7	46
Arun Qi, China	B9	36
Aruppukkottai, India	G4	53
Arurandeua, stm., Braz.	C1	88
Arusha, Tan.	E7	66
Arut, stm., Indon.	E7	50
Aruvi, stm., Sri L.	G5	53
Aruwimi, stm., D.R.C.	D4	66
Arvada, Co., U.S.	B3	128
Arvayheer, Mong.	B5	36
Arvi, India	H7	54
Arviat, N.T., Can.	C12	106
Arvidsjaur, Swe.	D8	8
Arvika, Swe.	G5	8
Arvin, Ca., U.S.	H7	134
Arvon, Mount, mtn., Mi., U.S.	B1	112
Arvorezinha, Braz.	D11	92
Arxan, China	B8	36
Arys', Kaz.	F11	32
Arys, ozero, l., Kaz.	E11	32
Arzachena, Italy	C3	24
Arzamas, Russia	I20	8
Arzignano, Italy	E8	22
Arz Lubnān, for., Leb.	D7	58
Aš, Czech Rep.	F8	16
Aša, Russia	D9	32
Asa, stm., Ven.	D10	86
Asaba, Nig.	H6	64
Asad, Buḥayrat al- (Assad, Lake), res., Syria	B9	58
Asadābād, Afg.	C11	56
Asadābād, Iran	B8	56
Aşağibostancı, N. Cyp.	C3	58
Asahan, stm., Indon.	B1	50
Asahi, Japan	D13	40
Asahi, stm., Japan	E6	40
Asahi-dake, vol., Japan	C15	38
Asahigawa see Asahikawa, Japan	C15	38
Asahikawa, Japan	C15	38
Asama-yama, vol., Japan	C11	40
Asan-man, b., Kor., S.	F7	38
Āsānsol, India	G11	54
Åsarna, Swe.	E6	8
Asaro, Ven.	q20	104g
Asbest, Russia	C10	32
Asbestos, Qc., Can.	E4	110
Asbestos Range National Park, p.o.i., Austl.	n13	77a
Asbury Park, N.J., U.S.	D12	114
Ascensión, Mex.	F9	98
Ascension, i., St. Hel.	G4	60
Aschaffenburg, Ger.	G5	16
Aschersleben, Ger.	E7	16
Ascoli Piceno, Italy	H10	22
Ascoli Satriano, Italy	C9	24
Ascör (Ostër), stm., Eur.	G14	10
Åseb, Erit.	E8	62
Åseda, Swe.	H6	8
Āsela, Eth.	F7	62
Åsele, Swe.	D7	8
Āsendabo, Eth.	F7	62
Asenovgrad, Blg.	G11	26
Aseri, Est.	A9	10
Ašgabat, Turkmen.	B8	56
Ashāqif, Jabal al-, hills, Jord.	F8	58
Ashburton, N.Z.	F4	80
Ashburton, stm., Austl.	D3	74
Ashcroft, B.C., Can.	F9	138
Ashdod, Isr.	G5	58
Ashdod, Tel, hist., Isr.	G5	58
Ashdown, Ar., U.S.	D4	122
Asheboro, N.C., U.S.	I6	114
Ashern, Mb., Can.	C15	124
Asheville, N.C., U.S.	I3	114
Ash Flat, Ar., U.S.	H6	120
Ashford, Eng., U.K.	J13	12
Ashford, Al., U.S.	F13	122
Ash Fork, Az., U.S.	H4	132
Ashgabat see Ašgabat, Turkmen.	B8	56
Ash Grove, Mo., U.S.	G4	120
Ashibe, Japan	F2	40
Ashikaga, Japan	C12	40
Ashington, Eng., U.K.	F11	12
Ashio, Japan	C12	40
Ashizuri-misaki, c., Japan	G6	40
Ashland, Al., U.S.	D13	122
Ashland, Il., U.S.	E7	120
Ashland, Ks., U.S.	D9	128
Ashland, Ky., U.S.	F3	114
Ashland, Mo., U.S.	F5	120
Ashland, Mt., U.S.	B6	126
Ashland, Ne., U.S.	C1	120
Ashland, N.H., U.S.	G5	110
Ashland, Oh., U.S.	D3	114
Ashland, Or., U.S.	A3	134
Ashland, Va., U.S.	G8	114
Ashland, Wi., U.S.	E7	118
Ashland, Mount, mtn., Or., U.S.	A3	134
Ashley, Austl.	G7	76
Ashley, Il., U.S.	F8	120
Ashley, Mi., U.S.	E5	112
Ashley, Oh., U.S.	D3	114
Ashmore, Il., U.S.	E9	120
Ashmore Islands, is., Austl.	B4	74
Ashoknagar, India	F6	54
Ashqelon, Isr.	G5	58
Ash-Shamāl, state, Leb.	D7	58
Ash-Shaqrā' see Shaqrā', Sau. Ar.	D6	56
Ash-Shāriqah, U.A.E.	D8	56
Ash-Shawbak, Jord.	H6	58
Ash-Shiḥr, Yemen	G6	56
Ash-Shurayf, Sau. Ar.	D4	56
Ashta, India	C2	53
Ashta, India	G6	54
Ashtabula, Oh., U.S.	C5	114
Ashtabula, Lake, res., N.D., U.S.	G16	124
Ashton, St. Vin.	p11	105e
Ashton, S. Afr.	H5	70
Ashton, Id., U.S.	F15	136
Ashton, Il., U.S.	C8	120
Ashton, Ne., U.S.	F14	126
Ashuanipi Lake, l., Nf., Can.	E17	106

Ashu-Bala I•5

Name | Map Ref. | Page

Ashuapmushuan, stm., Qc., Can. B3 110
Ashûm, Egypt H1 58
Ashville, Al., U.S. D12 122
Ashwaubenon, Wi., U.S. D1 112
Asi see Orontes, stm., Asia B7 58
Asia, cont. C19 4
Asia, Kepulauan, is., Indon. E9 44
Asia Minor, hist. reg., Tur. E13 28
Āsika, India I10 54
Asinara, Golfo dell', b., Italy D2 24
Asinara, Isola, i., Italy C2 24
Asino, Russia C15 32
Asintorf, Bela. F13 10
Asipovičy, Bela. G11 10
'Asīr, reg., Sau. Ar. F5 56
Askham, S. Afr. E5 70
Askiz, Russia D16 32
Askja, vol., Ice. k31 8a
Aslanapa, Tur. D12 28
Aslantaş Barajı, res., Tur. A7 58
Asmara see Asmera, Erit. D7 62
Asmera, Erit. D7 62
Ašmjany, Bela. F8 10
Asola, Italy E7 22
Asomante, P.R. B2 104a
Āsosa, Eth. E6 62
Asoteriba, Jabal, mtn., Sudan C7 62
Asotin, Wa., U.S. D9 136
Asouf, Oued, stm., Alg. D5 64
Asp, Spain F10 20
Aspe see Asp, Spain F10 20
Aspen, Co., U.S. D10 132
Aspendos, hist., Tur. G14 28
Aspermont, Tx., U.S. A7 130
Aspiring, Mount, mtn., N.Z. G3 80
Assad, Lake see Asad, Buḥayrat al-, res., Syria B9 58
As-Safīrah, Syria B8 58
Aṣ-Ṣāfiyah, Sudan D6 62
As-Salṭ, Jord. F6 58
Assam, state, India C7 46
As-Samāwah, Iraq C6 56
Aṣ-Ṣanamayn, Syria E7 58
Aṣ-Ṣarafand, Leb. E6 58
Assaré, Braz. D6 88
Assateague Island, i., U.S. F10 114
Assateague Island National Seashore, p.o.i., U.S. G10 114
Assemini, Italy E2 24
Assen, Neth. A15 14
Asseria, hist., Cro. F12 22
Assíni, hist., Grc. F5 28
Assiniboia, Sk., Can. E8 124
Assiniboine, stm., Can. E16 124
Assiniboine, Mount, mtn., Can. F15 138
Assis, Braz. D6 90
Assis Chateaubriand, Braz. B11 92
Assisi, Italy G9 22
Assomption, i., Sey. k11 69b
Assu, Braz. C7 88
As-Sudd, reg., Sudan F6 62
As-Sufāl, Yemen G6 56
As-Sulaymānīyah, Iraq B6 56
As-Sulaymānīyah, Sau. Ar. E6 56
As-Sulayyil, Sau. Ar. E6 56
Assumption, Il., U.S. E8 120
As-Suwaydā', Syria F7 58
As-Suwaydā', state, Syria F7 58
Astakós, Grc. E3 28
Astana (Akmola), Kaz. D12 32
Astara, Azer. B6 56
Asti, Italy F5 22
Astica, Arg. E4 92
Astola Island, i., Pak. D9 56
Astorga, Spain B4 20
Astoria, Il., U.S. D7 120
Astoria, Or., U.S. D3 136
Astove, i., Sey. I11 69b
Astrahan', Russia E7 32
Astrakhan see Astrahan', Russia E7 32
Astrašycki Haradok, Bela. F10 10
Astrolabe, Cape, c., Sol. Is. e9 79b
Astrolabe, Récifs de l', rf., N. Cal. I15 79d
Astrolabe Reefs see Astrolabe, Récifs de l', rf., N. Cal. I15 79d
Astrouna, Bela. E12 10
Astudillo, Spain B6 20
Asturias, state, Spain A5 20
Astypálaia, i., Grc. G9 28
Asunción, Para. B9 92
Asunción, Bahía la, b., Mex. B1 100
Asunción Nochixtlán, Mex. G10 100
Åsunden, l., Swe. H5 8
Asveja, Bela. E11 10
Asvejskae, vozero, l., Bela. D10 10
Aswân, Egypt C6 62
Aswan High Dam see Aali, Sadd el-, dam, Egypt C6 62
Asyût, Egypt K2 58
Asyûti, Wadi el- (Asyūṭī, Wādī al-), stm., Egypt K2 58
'Ata, i., Tonga F9 72
Atabapo, stm., S.A. F8 86
Atacama, state, Chile C3 92
Atacama, Desierto de, des., Chile E2 90
Atacama, Puna de, plat., S.A. B4 92
Atacama, Salar de, pl., Chile D3 90
Atacama Desert see Atacama, Desierto de, des., Chile B3 92
Ataco, Col. F4 86
Atagaj, Russia C17 32
Atakpamé, Togo H5 64
Atalaia, Braz. E7 88
Atambua, Indon. G7 44
Atami, Japan D12 40
Atangmik, Grnld. E15 141
Atar, Maur. E2 64
Atascadero, Ca., U.S. H5 134
Atascosa, stm., Tx., U.S. F9 130
Atasu, Kaz. E12 32
Atata, i., Tonga n14 78e
Atatürk Barajı, res., Tur. A9 58
Atauro, Pulau, i., Indon. G8 44
'Aṭbarah, Sudan D6 62
'Aṭbarah, stm., Afr. D7 62
Atbasar, Kaz. D11 32
Atchafalaya, stm., La., U.S. G7 122
Atchafalaya Bay, b., La., U.S. H7 122
Atchison, Ks., U.S. E2 120
Ateca, Spain C9 20
Aterno, stm., Italy H10 22
Atfîh, Egypt I2 58
Ath, Bel. D12 14
Athabasca, Ab., Can. B17 138
Athabasca, stm., Ab., Can. D8 106
Athabasca, Lake, l., Can. D9 106
Athalmer, B.C., Can. F14 138
Athboy, Ire. H6 12
Athena, Or., U.S. E8 136
Athens, On., Can. D14 112
Athens see Athína, Grc. E6 28
Athens, Al., U.S. C11 122
Athens, Ga., U.S. C2 116
Athens, Il., U.S. E8 120
Athens, La., U.S. E5 122
Athens, Mi., U.S. F4 112
Athens, Oh., U.S. E3 114
Athens, Pa., U.S. C9 114
Athens, Tn., U.S. B14 122
Athens, Tx., U.S. E3 122
Athens, W.V., U.S. G5 114
Atherton, Austl. A5 76
Athi, stm., Kenya E7 66
Athiaínou, Cyp. C4 58
Athína (Athens), Grc. E6 28
Athlone, Ire. H4 12
Athni, India C2 53
Athok, Mya. D2 48
Athol, Ma., U.S. B13 114
Áthos, mtn., Grc. C7 28
Athos, Mount see Áthos, mtn., Grc. C7 28
Ati, Chad E3 62
Atiak, Ug. D6 66
Atico, Peru G3 84
Atienza, Spain C8 20
Atikokan, On., Can. C7 118
Atirāmpattinam, India F4 53
Atiu, i., Cook Is. F11 72
Atka, Russia D19 34
Atka Island, i., Ak., U.S. g24 140a
Atkarsk, Russia D6 32
Atkins, Ar., U.S. B6 122
Atkinson, Il., U.S. C8 120
Atkinson, N.C., U.S. B7 116
Atlanta, Ga., U.S. C1 116
Atlanta, Il., U.S. D8 120
Atlanta, Mi., U.S. C5 112
Atlanta, Mo., U.S. E5 120
Atlantic, Ia., U.S. C2 120
Atlantic, N.C., U.S. B9 116
Atlantic Beach, Fl., U.S. F4 116
Atlantic City, N.J., U.S. E11 114
Atlantic-Indian Basin, unds. O5 142
Atlantic-Indian Ridge, unds. N15 144
Atlántico, state, Col. B4 86
Atlantic Ocean E9 144
Atlantic Peak, mtn., Wy., U.S. E3 126
Atlas Mountains, mts., Afr. C4 64
Atlasova, ostrov, i., Russia F20 34
Atlas Saharien, mts., Alg. C4 64
Atlin, B.C., Can. D4 106
Atlin Lake, l., Can. D4 106
'Atlit, Isr. F5 58
Ātmakūr, India D4 53
Atmore, Al., U.S. F11 122
Atnarko, stm., B.C., Can. D5 138
Atocha, Bol. D3 90
Atoka, Ok., U.S. C2 122
Atotonilco, Cerro, mtn., Mex. H3 130
Atoyac, stm., Mex. F9 100
Atoyac de Álvarez, Mex. G8 100
Atrak (Atrek), stm., Asia B7 56
Åtran, stm., Swe. H5 8
Atrato, stm., Col. D3 86
Atrauli, India D7 54
Atrek (Atrak), stm., Asia B7 56
Atri, Italy H10 22
Atsumi, Japan E10 40
Atsumi-hantō, pen., Japan E10 40
Aṭ-Ṭafīlah, Jord. H6 58
Aṭ-Ṭafīlah, state, Jord. H6 58
Aṭ-Ṭā'if, Sau. Ar. E5 56
At-Tall, Syria E7 58
Attalla, Al., U.S. C12 122
Attapu, Laos E8 48
Attawapiskat, On., Can. E14 106
Attawapiskat, stm., On., Can. E13 106
Attawapiskat Lake, l., On., Can. E13 106
Aṭ-Ṭawīl, mts., Sau. Ar. D4 56
Aṭ-Ṭayyibah, Syria C9 58
Attendorn, Ger. E3 16
Attersee, l., Aus. C10 22
Attica, In., U.S. H2 112
Attica, Ks., U.S. D10 128
Attica, N.Y., U.S. B7 114
Attica see Attikí, hist. reg., Grc. E6 28
Attikí, state, Grc. F6 28
Attikí, hist. reg., Grc. E6 28
Attleboro, Ma., U.S. C14 114
Attock, Pak. B4 54
Attu, Ak., U.S. g21 140a
Attu Island, i., Ak., U.S. g21 140a
Āttūr, India F4 53
Aṭ-Ṭuwayshah, Sudan E5 62
Atuel, stm., Arg. G3 92
Atuel, Bañados del, sw., Arg. H4 92
Atuntaqui, Ec. G2 86
Atuona, Fr. Poly. s18 78g
Atwater, Ca., U.S. F5 134
Atwater, Mn., U.S. F4 118
Atwood, Il., U.S. E9 120
Atwood, Ks., U.S. B7 128
Atwood, Tn., U.S. I9 120
Atyrau, Kaz. E8 32
Aua Island, i., Pap. N. Gui. a3 79a
Auari, stm., Braz. F9 86
Auau Channel, strt., Hi., U.S. C5 78a
Aubagne, Fr. F11 18
Aube, state, Fr. F13 14
Aube, stm., Fr. F13 14
Aubigny-sur-Nère, Fr. G11 14
Aubinadong, stm., On., Can. A6 112
Aubrey Cliffs, clf, Az., U.S. H3 132
Aubrey Lake, res., On., Can. A6 112
Aubry Lake, l., N.T., Can. B5 106
Auburn, Al., U.S. E13 122
Auburn, Ca., U.S. E4 134
Auburn, Il., U.S. E8 120
Auburn, In., U.S. G4 112
Auburn, Ky., U.S. H11 120
Auburn, Me., U.S. F6 110
Auburn, Ma., U.S. B14 114
Auburn, Mi., U.S. E5 112
Auburn, N.Y., U.S. B9 114
Auburn, Wa., U.S. C4 136
Auburn, stm., Austl. E8 76
Aubusson, Fr. D8 18
Auca Mahuida, Cerro, mtn., Arg. H3 92
Auce, Lat. D5 10
Auch, Fr. F6 18
Auchi, Nig. H6 64
Aucilla, stm., U.S. F2 116
Auckland, N.Z. C6 80
Auckland Islands, is., N.Z. I7 72
Aude, state, Fr. F8 18
Aude, stm., Fr. F9 18
Auden, On., Can. A11 118
Audenarde see Oudenaarde, Bel. D12 14
Audierne, Fr. F4 14
Audincourt, Fr. G15 14
Audubon Lake, res., N.D., U.S. G12 124
Aue, Ger. F8 16
Augathella, Austl. E6 76
Augrabies Falls National Park, p.o.i., S. Afr. F4 70
Augrabiesvalle, wtfl, S. Afr. F5 70
Augsburg, Ger. H6 16
Augusta, Austl. F2 74
Augusta, Italy G9 24
Augusta, Ar., U.S. B7 122
Augusta, Ga., U.S. C3 116
Augusta, Il., U.S. D6 120
Augusta, Ky., U.S. F1 114
Augusta, Me., U.S. F7 110
Augusta, Mt., U.S. C14 136
Augusta, Wi., U.S. G7 118
Augusto Severo, Braz. C7 88
Augustów, Pol. C18 16
Augustowski, Kanał, can., Eur. C19 16
Augustus, Mount, mtn., Austl. D3 74
Auki, Sol. Is. e9 79b
Aukstaitijos nacionalnis parkas, p.o.i., Lith. E8 10
Aulander, N.C., U.S. H8 114
Auld, Lake, l., Austl. D4 74
Aulla, Italy F6 22
Aulne, stm., Fr. F5 14
Aulneau Peninsula, pen., On., Can. B4 118
Aumale, Fr. E10 14
Auna, Nig. G5 64
Auob, stm., Afr. E5 70
Auraiya, India E7 54
Aurangābād, India B2 53
Aurangābād, India F10 54
Aure, Nor. E3 8
Aurelia, Ia., U.S. B2 120
Aurich, Ger. C3 16
Aurilândia, Braz. G7 84
Aurillac, Fr. E8 18
Aurine, Alpi (Zillertaler Alpen), mts., Eur. C8 22
Aurora, On., Can. D10 112
Aurora, Co., U.S. B4 128
Aurora, Il., U.S. C9 120
Aurora, In., U.S. E13 120
Aurora, Me., U.S. F8 110
Aurora, Mn., U.S. D6 118
Aurora, N.Y., U.S. B9 114
Aurora, N.C., U.S. A9 116
Aurora, Oh., U.S. C4 114
Aurora, Ut., U.S. E4 132
Aurora, W.V., U.S. E6 114
Aurora do Norte, Braz. G2 88
Aursunden, l., Nor. E4 8
Aurukun, Austl. B8 74
Aus, Nmb. E3 70
Ausable, stm., On., Can. E8 112
Au Sable, stm., Mi., U.S. D6 112
Au Sable Forks, N.Y., U.S. F3 110
Au Sable Point, c., Mi., U.S. D6 112
Auschwitz see Oświęcim, Pol. F15 16
Aust-Agder, state, Nor. G3 8
Austin, In., U.S. F12 120
Austin, Mn., U.S. H6 118
Austin, Nv., U.S. D8 134
Austin, Pa., U.S. C7 114
Austin, Tx., U.S. D10 130
Austin, Lake, l., Austl. E3 74
Australes, Îles, is., Fr. Poly. F11 72
Australia, ctry., Oc. D5 74
Australian Capital Territory, state, Austl. J7 76
Austral Islands see Australes, Îles, is., Fr. Poly. F11 72
Austral Seamounts, unds. L24 142
Austria, ctry., Eur. C11 22
Austvågøya, i., Nor. B6 8
Autlán de Navarro, Mex. F6 100
Autun, Fr. H13 14
Auvergne, hist. reg., Fr. D8 18
Auxerre, Fr. G12 14
Auxier, Ky., U.S. G3 114
Auxi-le-Château, Fr. D11 14
Auxvasse, Mo., U.S. E6 120
Auyán Tepuy, mtn., Ven. E10 86
Auzances, Fr. C8 18
Auzangate, Nevado, mtn., Peru F3 84
Ava, Mo., U.S. H5 120
Avai, Braz. L1 88
Avala, hist., Yugo. E7 26
Avallon, Fr. G12 14
Avalon, Ca., U.S. J7 134
Ávalos, Mex. A5 100
Avanersuaq see Nordgrønland, state, Grnld. B14 141
Avant, Ok., U.S. H1 120
Avaré, Braz. L1 88
Avarua, Cook Is. a26 78j
Avarua Harbour, b., Cook Is. a26 78j
Avatiu Harbour, b., Cook Is. a26 78j
'Avedat, Ḥorvot, hist., Isr. H5 58
Aveiro, Port. D2 20
Aveiro, state, Port. D2 20
Aveiro, Ria de, mth., Port. D1 20
Avellaneda, Arg. D8 92
Avellaneda, Arg. G8 92
Avellino, Italy D8 24
Averøya, i., Nor. E2 8
Aversa, Italy D8 24
Avery, Id., U.S. C11 136
Avery, Tx., U.S. D4 122
Avery Island, La., U.S. H6 122
Aves, Islas de, is., Ven. B8 86
Avesnes-sur-Helpe, Fr. D12 14
Avesta, Swe. F6 8
Aveyron, state, Fr. E8 18
Aveyron, stm., Fr. E7 18
Avezzano, Italy H10 22
Avigliano, Italy D9 24
Avignon, Fr. F10 18
Ávila, Spain D6 20
Ávila, co., Spain D6 20
Ávila, Sierra de, mts., Spain D5 20
Avilés, Spain A4 20
Aviño, Spain A2 20
Avinurme, Est. B9 10
Avispa, Cerro, mtn., Ven. G9 86
Avoca, Austl. K4 76
Avoca, Ia., U.S. C2 120
Avoca, N.Y., U.S. B8 114
Avoca, stm., Austl. K4 76
Avola, B.C., Can. E11 138
Avola, Italy H9 24
Avon, Il., U.S. D7 120
Avon, Mn., U.S. F4 118
Avon, N.Y., U.S. B8 114
Avon, N.C., U.S. A10 116
Avon, stm., Eng., U.K. K11 12
Avon, stm., Eng., U.K. I11 12
Avon, stm., Eng., U.K. J10 12
Avondale, Az., U.S. J4 132
Avondale, Co., U.S. C4 128
Avon Downs, Austl. D7 74
Avon Park, Fl., U.S. I4 116
Avontuur, S. Afr. H6 70
Avranches, Fr. F7 14
Awaaso, Ghana H4 64
Awaji, Japan E8 40
Awaji-shima, i., Japan E7 40
Awara, Japan C9 40
Āwarē, Eth. F8 62
Āwasa, Eth. F7 62
Āwash, Eth. F8 62
Āwash, stm., Eth. E8 62
Awa-shima, i., Japan A12 40
Awbārī, Libya B2 62
Awbārī, Ṣaḥrā', reg., Libya B2 62
Awe, Loch, l., Scot., U.K. E7 12
Awegyun, Mya. F4 48
Awjilah, Libya B4 62
Awled Djellal, Alg. C6 64
Awlef, Alg. D5 64
Awul, Pap. N. Gui. b5 79a
Axel Heiberg Island, i., N.T., Can. A7 141
Axim, Ghana I4 64
Axiós (Vardar), stm., Eur. C5 28
Axis, Al., U.S. G10 122
Axixá, Braz. B3 88
Axtell, Ks., U.S. L2 118
Axtell, Ne., U.S. G13 126
Ayabe, Japan D8 40
Ayacucho, Arg. H8 92
Ayacucho, Peru F3 84
Ayakkum Hu, l., China D2 36
Ayakoz see Ajaguz, Kaz. E13 32
Ayam, C. Iv. H4 64
Ayamonte, Spain G3 20
Ayapel, Col. C4 86
Ayaş, Tur. C15 28
Ayaviri, Peru F3 84
Aydın, Tur. F10 28
Aydın, state, Tur. F11 28
Aydınkent, Tur. F14 28
Ayer, Ma., U.S. B14 114
Ayers Rock see Uluru, mtn., Austl. E6 74
Ayeyarwady, state, Mya. D2 48
Ayeyarwady (Irrawaddy), stm., Mya. E8 46
Ayeyarwady, Mouths of the, mth., Mya. E7 46
Ayíou Órous, Kólpos (Singitic Gulf), b., Grc. C6 28
Aylesbury, Eng., U.K. J12 12
Aylmer, On., Can. F8 112
Aylmer, Qc., Can. C14 112
Aylmer Lake, l., N.T., Can. C9 106
Aylsham, Sk., Can. A10 124
'Ayn Dār, Sau. Ar. D6 56
Aynor, S.C., U.S. B6 116
'Aynūnah, Sau. Ar. J6 58
Ayon Island see Aën, ostrov, i., Russia B22 34
Ayora see Aiora, Spain E9 20
Ayorou, Niger G5 64
'Ayoûn el 'Atroûs, Maur. F3 64
Ayr, Austl. B6 76
Ayr, Scot., U.K. F8 12
Ayrancı, Tur. A4 58
Ayre, Point of, c., I. of Man G8 12
Āysha, Eth. E8 62
Aytos see Ajtos, Blg. G14 26
Ayutla, Mex. E6 100
Ayutla de los Libres, Mex. G9 100
Ayvacık, Tur. D9 28
Ayvalık, Tur. D9 28
Azaila, Spain C10 20
Āzamgarh, India E9 54
Azángaro, Peru F3 84
Azaouâd, reg., Mali F4 64
Azare, Nig. G6 64
Azaryčy, Bela. H12 10
A'zāz, Syria B8 58
Azdavay, Tur. B16 28
Azeffâl, sand, Afr. E2 64
Azerbaijan, ctry., Asia A6 56
Azëry, Bela. G7 10
Āzezo, Eth. E7 62
Azhikode, India F2 53
Azilal, Mor. C3 64
Azogues, Ec. I2 86
Azores see Açores, is., Port. C3 60
Azores Plateau, unds. E10 144
Azov, Russia E5 32
Azov, Sea of, Eur. E5 32
Azovskoje more see Azov, Sea of, Eur. E5 32
Azraq, Al-Baḥr al- see Blue Nile, stm., Afr. E6 62
Aztec, N.M., U.S. G9 132
Aztec Peak, mtn., Az., U.S. J5 132
Aztec Ruins National Monument, p.o.i., N.M., U.S. G8 132
Azua, Dom. Rep. C12 102
Azuaga, Spain F5 20
Azuay, state, Ec. I2 86
Azuer, stm., Spain F7 20
Azuero, Península de, pen., Pan. D1 86
Azufre, Volcán, vol., S.A. B3 92
Azuga, Rom. D12 26
Azul, Arg. H8 92
Azur, Côte d', cst., Fr. F13 18
Azurduy, Bol. C4 90
Azure Lake, l., B.C., Can. D10 138
Az-Zahrān, Sau. Ar. D6 56
Az-Zarqā', Jord. F7 58
Az-Zarqā', state, Jord. G8 58
Az-Zāwiyah, Libya A2 62
Azzel Matti, Sebkha, pl., Alg. D5 64

B

Ba, Fiji p18 79e
Ba, stm., China F6 42
Ba, stm., China F2 42
Ba, stm., Viet. F9 48
Baa, Indon. H7 44
Baaba, Île, i., N. Cal. I14 79d
Baao, Phil. D4 52
Baardheere, Som. D8 66
Baba Burnu, c., Tur. D9 28
Babadağ, Tur. F11 28
Babaeski, Tur. B10 28
Babaevo, Russia A18 10
Babahoyo, Ec. H2 86
Babak, Phil. G5 52
Babanango, S. Afr. F10 70
Babanūsah, Sudan E5 62
Babar, Kepulauan, is., Indon. G8 44
Babbitt, Mn., U.S. D7 118
Babbitt, Nv., U.S. E7 134
B'abdā, Leb. E6 58
Babeldaob, i., Palau g7 78b
Bab el Mandeb see Mandeb, Bab el, strt. E8 62
Babia, Arroyo de la, stm., Mex. F5 130
Babian, stm., China A5 48
Babičy, Bela. H12 10
Babīna, India F7 54
Babinda, Austl. A5 76
Babine, stm., B.C., Can. D5 106
Babine Lake, l., B.C., Can. B5 138
Babine Range, mts., B.C., Can. B4 138
Babino, Russia A14 10
Babiogórski Park Narodowy, p.o.i., Pol. G15 16
Babo, Indon. F9 44
Bābol, Iran B7 56
Baboquivari Peak, mtn., Az., U.S. L5 132
Baborów, Pol. F13 16
Babrujsk, Bela. G12 10
Babuškin, Russia F10 34
Babuyan Channel, strt., Phil. A3 52
Babuyan Island, i., Phil. A4 52
Babuyan Islands, is., Phil. A3 52
Bacabal, Braz. C3 88
Bacadéhuachi, Mex. G8 98
Bacatuba, Braz. C4 88
Bacău, Rom. C13 26
Bacău, state, Rom. C13 26
Bac Binh, Viet. G9 48
Baccarat, Fr. F15 14
Bačėjkava, Bela. F12 10
Bac Giang, Viet. B8 48
Bachaquero, Ven. B6 86
Bachiniva, Mex. A5 100
Bach Ma, Viet. D8 48
Bach Thong, Viet. A7 48
Bachu, China B12 56
Back, stm., N.T., Can. B11 106
Bačka, reg., Eur. E16 22
Bačka Palanka, Yugo. D6 26
Bačka Topola, Yugo. D6 26
Back Creek, stm., Va., U.S. F6 114
Backnang, Ger. H5 16
Backstairs Passage, strt., Austl. J1 76
Bac Lieu, Viet. H7 48
Bac Ninh, Viet. B8 48
Baco, Mount, mtn., Phil. D3 52
Bacoachi, Mex. F8 98
Bacolod, Phil. E4 52
Baconton, Ga., U.S. E1 116
Bacoor, Phil. C3 52
Bac Phan, hist. reg., Viet. A7 48
Bács-Kiskun, state, Hung. C6 26
Bâcu, stm., Mol. C15 26
Bacuri, Lago do, l., Braz. B4 88
Bād, Iran C7 56
Bad, stm., Mi., U.S. E5 112
Bad, stm., S.D., U.S. C12 126
Badagara, India F2 53
Badajós, Lago, l., Braz. D5 84
Badajoz, Spain F4 20
Badajoz, co., Spain F4 20
Badalona, Spain C13 20
Bādāmi, India D2 53
Badanah, Sau. Ar. C5 56
Badarīnāth, India C7 54
Badas, Bru. A9 50
Badas, Kepulauan, is., Indon. C5 50
Bad Axe, Mi., U.S. E7 112
Bad Bergzabern, Ger. G3 16
Bad Bevensen, Ger. C6 16
Bad Bramstedt, Ger. C5 16
Baddeck, N.S., Can. D16 110
Bad Doberan, Ger. B7 16
Bad Dürrenberg, Ger. E8 16
Bad Ems, Ger. F3 16
Baden, Switz. C5 22
Baden-Baden, Ger. H4 16
Badenoch, hist. reg., Scot., U.K. E8 12
Badenweiler, Ger. I3 16
Baden-Württemberg, state, Ger. H4 16
Bad Freienwalde, Ger. D9 16
Badgastein, Aus. C10 22
Badger, Mn., U.S. C3 118
Bad Hall, Aus. B11 22
Bad Harzburg, Ger. E6 16
Bad Hersfeld, Ger. F5 16
Bad Homburg vor der Höhe, Ger. F4 16
Bad Honnef, Ger. F3 16
Badin Lake, res., N.C., U.S. A5 116
Bad Ischl, Aus. C10 22
Bad Kissingen, Ger. F6 16
Bad Kreuznach, Ger. G3 16
Badlands, hills, U.S. A9 126
Badlands, hills, S.D., U.S. D10 126
Badlands National Park, p.o.i., S.D., U.S. D10 126
Bad Langensalza, Ger. E6 16
Bad Lauterberg im Harz, Ger. E6 16
Bad Mergentheim, Ger. G5 16
Bad Muskau, Ger. E10 16
Bad Nauheim, Ger. F4 16
Badnera, India H6 54
Bad Neustadt an der Saale, Ger. F6 16
Bad Oeynhausen, Ger. D4 16
Bad Oldesloe, Ger. C6 16
Badong, China F4 42
Bad Orb, Ger. F5 16
Bad Pyrmont, Ger. E5 16
Bad Reichenhall, Ger. I8 16
Bad Salzuflen, Ger. D4 16
Bad Salzungen, Ger. F6 16
Bad Schwalbach, Ger. F3 16
Bad Schwartau, Ger. C6 16
Bad Segeberg, Ger. C6 16
Bādshāhpur, India F9 54
Bad Tölz, Ger. I7 16
Badulla, Sri L. H5 53
Badvel, India D4 53
Bad Vöslau, Aus. C13 22
Bad Waldsee, Ger. I5 16
Bad Wildungen, Ger. E4 16
Bad Wörishofen, Ger. I6 16
Badžalskij hrebet, mts., Russia F15 34
Baena, Spain G6 20
Baependi, Braz. K3 88
Baer, Russia C17 32
Baeza, Spain G7 20
Baezaeko, stm., B.C., Can. D7 138
Bafang, Cam. C1 66
Bafatá, Gui.-B. G2 64
Baffin Basin, unds. A7 144
Baffin Bay, b., N.A. C12 141
Baffin Bay, b., Tx., U.S. G10 130
Baffin Island, i., N.T., Can. B16 106
Bafia, Cam. D2 66
Bafing, stm., Afr. G2 64
Bafoulabé, Mali G2 64
Bafoussam, Cam. C2 66
Bafra, Tur. A4 56
Bāft, Iran D8 56
Bafwaboli, D.R.C. D5 66
Bafwasende, D.R.C. D5 66
Bagaces, C.R. G5 102
Bagagem, stm., Braz. H1 88
Bagaha, India E9 54
Bāgalkot, India C2 53
Bagamoyo, Tan. F7 66
Bagan Datuk, Malay. K5 48
Baganga, Phil. G6 52
Bagansiapiapi, Indon. B2 50
Bagasra, India H3 54
Bagdad, Az., U.S. I3 132
Bagdad, Fl., U.S. G11 122
Bagdarin, Russia F11 34
Bagé, Braz. E10 92
Bagenkop, Den. B6 16
Bāgerhāt, Bngl. G12 54
Bāgevādi, India C2 53
Baghdād, Iraq C5 56
Bagheria, Italy F7 24
Baghlān, Afg. B10 56
Bagley, Mn., U.S. D3 118
Bagnères-de-Luchon, Fr. G6 18
Bagni di Lucca, Italy F7 22
Bagnols-sur-Cèze, Fr. E10 18
Bago (Pegu), Mya. D3 48
Bago, state, Mya. C2 48
Bagodar, India F10 54
Bagoé, stm., Afr. G3 64
Bağpınar, Tur. A9 58
Baguio, Phil. B3 52
Bāh, India E7 54
Bahādurgarh, India D6 54
Bahama, Canal Viejo de, strt., N.A. A8 102
Bahamas, ctry., N.A. C9 96
Baharampur, India F11 54
Bahau, Malay. K6 48
Bahau, stm., Indon. B9 50
Bahāwalnagar, Pak. C4 54
Bahāwalpur, Pak. D3 54
Bahçe, Tur. A7 58
Baheri, India D7 54
Bahi, Phil. D4 52
Bahia see Salvador, Braz. G6 88
Bahia, state, Braz. G4 88
Bahía, Islas de la, is., Hond. D4 102
Bahía Blanca, Arg. I6 92
Bahía Bustamante, Arg. I3 90
Bahía de Caráquez, Ec. H1 86
Bahía Kino, Mex. A3 100
Bahir Dar, Eth. E7 62
Bahraich, India E8 54
Bahrain, ctry., Asia D7 56
Bahta, Russia B15 32
Bahtîm, Egypt H2 58
Bahty, Kaz. E14 32
Bahušėusk, Bela. F13 10
Bai, stm., China A7 42
Bai, stm., China E5 42
Baia de Aramă, Rom. E9 26
Baia di Terra Nova, sci., Ant. C21 81
Baía Farta, Ang. C1 68
Baia Mare, Rom. B10 26
Baião, Braz. B1 88
Baicheng, China F14 32
Baicheng, China B9 36
Baidoa see Baydhabo, Som. D8 66
Baie-Comeau, Qc., Can. A8 110
Baiersbronn, Ger. H4 16
Baie-Saint-Paul, Qc., Can. C6 110
Baie-Trinité, Qc., Can. A9 110
Baie Verte, Nf., Can. j22 107a
Baihe, China B11 46
Baijnāth, India D7 54
Baikal, Lake see Bajkal, ozero, l., Russia F10 34
Baikal Mountains see Bajkal'skij hrebet, mts., Russia F10 34
Baikonur see Bajkonur, Kaz. E11 32
Bailadores, Ven. C6 86
Baile Átha Cliath see Dublin, Ire. H6 12
Baile Átha Luain see Athlone, Ire. H4 12
Băile Govora, Rom. D11 26
Bailén, Spain F7 20
Băilești, Rom. F10 26
Bailey, N.C., U.S. I7 114
Bail Hongal, India D2 53
Bailicun, China I4 42
Bailique, Ilha, i., Braz. C8 84
Baillie Islands, is., N.T., Can. B14 140
Baillif, Guad. h5 105c
Bailong, stm., China E1 42
Bailu Hu, l., China G5 42
Bailundo, Ang. C2 68
Baimamiao, China C2 42
Baima Shan, mtn., China H4 42
Baimuru, Pap. N. Gui. b3 79a
Bainbridge, Ga., U.S. G14 122
Bainbridge, N.Y., U.S. B10 114
Bain-de-Bretagne, Fr. G7 14
Baing, Indon. I12 50
Bainville, Mt., U.S. F9 124
Baio Grande, Spain A2 20
Baiona, Spain B2 20
Baipeng, China I3 42
Baipu, China E9 42
Baiquan, China B10 36
Baird, Tx., U.S. B8 130
Baird Mountains, mts., Ak., U.S. C7 140
Baird Peninsula, pen., N.T., Can. B15 106
Bairiki, Kir. C8 72
Bairin Zuoqi, China C8 36
Bairnsdale, Austl. K6 76
Baïse, stm., Fr. F6 18
Baisha, China G2 42
Baisha, China L3 42
Baisha, China I8 42
Baishe, China H7 42
Baishuijiang, China E2 42
Baisogala, Lith. E6 10
Baiwang, China I3 42
Baixingt, China C4 38
Baixio, Braz. D6 88
Baiyan Shan, mtn., China H8 42
Baiyin, China D5 36
Baiyü, China E4 36
Baja, Hung. C5 26
Baja, Punta, c., Chile e29 78l
Baja California, state, Mex. F5 98
Baja California, pen., Mex. B2 96
Baja California Sur, state, Mex. C2 100
Bajada del Agrio, Arg. I2 92
Baján, Mex. H6 130
Bajan, Mong. B7 36
Bajanaul, Kaz. D13 32
Bajangol, Russia F9 34
Bajánsenye, Hung. C3 26
Bajawa, Indon. H12 50
Bajdarackaja guba, b., Russia C2 34
Bajestān, Iran C8 56
Bajkal, Russia F9 34
Bajkal, ozero (Baikal, Lake), l., Russia F10 34
Bajkal'skij hrebet, mts., Russia F10 34
Bajkit, Russia B17 32
Bajkonur, Kaz. E11 32
Bajmak, Russia D9 32
Bajmok, Yugo. D6 26
Bajo, Indon. H11 50
Bajo Boquete, Pan. H6 102
Bajool, Austl. D8 76
Bajramaly, Turkmen. B9 56
Bajsun, Uzb. G11 32
Bakacak, Tur. C10 28
Bakala, C.A.R. C4 66
Bakanas, Kaz. F13 32
Bake, Indon. E2 50
Bakel, Sen. G2 64
Baker, Ca., U.S. H9 134
Baker, Fl., U.S. G12 122
Baker, La., U.S. G7 122
Baker, Mt., U.S. A8 126
Baker, Or., U.S. F9 136
Baker, Mount, vol., Wa., U.S. B5 136
Baker Butte, mtn., Az., U.S. I5 132
Baker Island, i., Oc. C9 72
Baker Lake, N.T., Can. C11 106
Baker Lake, l., Austl. E5 74
Baker Lake, l., N.T., Can. C11 106
Bakersfield, Ca., U.S. H7 134
Bâ Kêv, Camb. F8 48
Bakharden, Turkmen. B8 56
Bakhardok, Turkmen. B8 56
Bakhtegān, Daryācheh-ye, l., Iran D7 56
Bakı (Baku), Azer. A6 56
Bakkafjörður, Ice. j32 8a
Bakkaflói, b., Ice. j32 8a
Baklan, Tur. F12 28
Bako, C. Iv. H3 64
Bako, Eth. F7 62
Bakony, mts., Hung. C4 26
Bakouma, C.A.R. C4 66
Baku see Bakı, Azer. A6 56
Bakumpai, Indon. D8 50
Bakung, Pulau, i., Indon. C4 50
Bakungan, Indon. K3 48
Bakwanga see Mbuji-Mayi, D.R.C. F4 66
Balâ, Tur. D16 28
Balabac, Phil. F1 52
Balabac Island, i., Phil. G1 52
Balabac Strait, strt., Asia G1 52
Ba'labakk, Leb. D7 58
Balabalagan, Kepulauan, is., Indon. E10 50
Balabanovo, Russia E19 10
Balabio, Île, i., N. Cal. m15 79d
Balad, Iraq C5 56
Baladěk, Russia F15 34
Bālāghāt, India H8 54
Bālāghāt Range, mts., India B3 53
Balagne, reg., Fr. G14 18
Balaguer, Spain C11 20
Balahna, Russia H20 8
Balaikarangan, Indon. C7 50
Balaisepuah, Indon. C7 50
Balakirevo, Russia D21 10
Balaklava, Austl. J2 76
Balakovo, Russia D7 32
Balama, Moz. C6 68
Balambangan, Pulau, i., Malay. G1 52
Bālā Morghāb, Afg. B9 56
Balanga, Phil. C3 52
Balāngīr, India H9 54
Balapulang, Indon. G6 50
Balarāmpur, India G11 54
Balašiha, Russia E20 10

I•6 Bala-Bayo

Name Map Ref. Page

Balašov, Russia D6 32
Balassagyarmat, Hung. A6 26
Balatina, Mol. B14 26
Balaton, Mn., U.S. G3 118
Balaton, l., Hung. C4 26
Balayan, Phil. D3 52
Balbieriškis, Lith. F6 10
Balbina, Represa, res., Braz. H12 86
Balcanoona, Austl. H2 76
Balcarce, Arg. H8 92
Balcarres, Sk., Can. D10 124
Bălcești, Rom. E10 26
Balcones Escarpment, clf, Tx., U.S. D9 130
Balde, Arg. F4 92
Bald Knob, Ar., U.S. B7 122
Bald Knob, mtn., Va., U.S. G6 114
Bald Mountain, mtn., Or., U.S. G5 136
Bald Mountain, mtn., Or., U.S. F3 136
Baldock Lake, l., Mb., Can. D11 106
Baldone, Lat. D7 10
Baldwin, La., U.S. H7 122
Baldwin, Mi., U.S. E4 112
Baldwin, Wi., U.S. G6 118
Baldwinsville, N.Y., U.S. E13 112
Baldwyn, Ms., U.S. C10 122
Baldy Mountain, mtn., Mb., Can. C13 124
Baldy Mountain, mtn., N.M., U.S. E3 128
Baldy Peak, mtn., Az., U.S. J7 132
Bâle see Basel, Switz. C4 22
Baleares see Balears, state, Spain E13 20
Baleares, Islas see Balears, Illes, is., Spain E12 20
Balearic Islands see Balears, state, Spain E13 20
Balearic Islands see Balears, Illes, is., Spain E12 20
Balears, state, Spain E13 20
Balears, Illes (Balearic Islands), is., Spain E12 20
Balease, Gunung, mtn., Indon. E12 50
Baleh, stm., Malay. C8 50
Baleia, Ponta da, c., Braz. I6 88
Baleine, stm., Qc., Can. D17 106
Baleine, Grande rivière de la, stm., Qc., Can. D15 106
Baleine, Petite rivière de la, stm., Qc., Can. D15 106
Balej, Russia F12 34
Baler, Phil. C3 52
Baler Bay, b., Phil. C3 52
Bāleshwar, India H11 54
Balezino, Russia C8 32
Balfate, Hond. E4 102
Balfour, N.C., U.S. A3 116
Balgazyn, Russia D17 32
Balhaš, ozero (Balkhash, Lake), l., Kaz. E13 32
Bāli, India F4 54
Bali, state, Indon. G9 50
Bali, i., Indon. G9 50
Bali, Laut (Bali Sea), Indon. G9 50
Bali, Selat, strt., Indon. H9 50
Bali Barat National Park, p.o.i., Indon. H9 50
Baliceaux, i., St. Vin. p11 105e
Balige, Indon. B1 50
Balıkesir, Tur. D10 28
Balıkesir, state, Tur. D10 28
Balīkh, stm., Syria B10 58
Balikpapan, Indon. D10 50
Balimbing, Indon. F4 50
Balimbing, Phil. H2 52
Balimo, Pap. N. Gui. b3 79a
Balingen, Ger. H4 16
Balingian, Malay. B8 50
Balintang Channel, strt., Phil. K9 42
Bali Sea see Bali, Laut, Indon. G9 50
Bali Strait see Bali, Selat, strt., Indon. H9 50
Baliza, Braz. G7 84
Balkan Mountains, mts., Eur. G11 26
Balkan Peninsula, pen., Eur. B6 28
Balkaria see Kabardino-Balkarija, state, Russia F6 32
Balkh, Afg. B10 56
Balkhash, Lake see Balhaš, ozero, l., Kaz. E13 32
Ballachulish, Scot., U.K. E7 12
Balladonia, Austl. F4 74
Ballālpur, India B4 53
Ballangen, Nor. B7 8
Ballantine, Mt., U.S. B4 126
Ballarat, Austl. K4 76
Ballard, Lake, l., Austl. E4 74
Ballater, Scot., U.K. D9 12
Ball Bay, b., Norf. I. y25 78i
Ballenas, Bahía de, b., Mex. B2 100
Ballenita, Punta, c., Chile B2 92
Balleny Islands, is., Ant. B21 81
Balleza, Mex. B5 100
Balleza, stm., Mex. B5 100
Ball Ground, Ga., U.S. B1 116
Ballia, India F10 54
Ballina, Austl. G9 76
Ballina, Ire. G3 12
Ballina, Ire. I4 12
Ballinrobe, Ire. H3 12
Ballston Spa, N.Y., U.S. G2 110
Ballville, Oh., U.S. C2 114
Ballybunnion, Ire. I3 12
Ballyhaunis, Ire. H4 12
Ballymena, N. Ire., U.K. G6 12
Ballymoney, N. Ire., U.K. F6 12
Ballyrogan, Lake, l., Austl. I6 76
Balmaceda, Chile I2 90
Balmoral, Austl. K3 76
Balmorhea, Tx., U.S. C4 130
Balnearia, Arg. E6 92
Baloda Bāzār, India H9 54
Balombo, Ang. C1 68
Balong, Indon. G7 50
Balonne, stm., Austl. G7 76
Bālotra, India F4 54
Balphakram National Park, p.o.i., India F13 54
Balqash Köli see Balhaš, ozero, l., Kaz. E13 32
Balrāmpur, India E8 54
Balranald, Austl. J4 76
Balș, Rom. E11 26
Balsam Lake, Wi., U.S. F6 118
Balsam Lake, l., On., Can. D11 112
Balsas, Braz. D2 88
Balsas, stm., Braz. F2 88
Balsas, stm., Braz. D3 88
Balsas, stm., Mex. F8 100
Balsas, stm., Pan. C3 86
Balsthal, Switz. C4 22
Balta, Ukr. B16 26
Baltasar Brum, Ur. E9 92
Bălți, Mol. B14 26
Baltic Sea, Eur. D12 6
Baltijsk, Russia F2 10
Baltijskaja kosa, spit, Eur. F2 10
Baltijskoje more see Baltic Sea, Eur. D12 6
Baltim, Egypt G2 58
Baltimore, Ire. J3 12
Baltimore, Md., U.S. E9 114
Baltimore, Oh., U.S. E3 114
Ba Lu, stm., Viet. E9 48
Baluchistān, state, Pak. C2 54
Baluchistan, hist. reg., Asia D9 56
Balui, stm., Malay. B8 50
Bālurghāt, India F12 54
Balvi, Lat. C10 10
Balygyčan, Russia D19 34
Balykši, Kaz. E8 32
Balzac, Ab., Can. E16 138
Balzar, Ec. H2 86
Bam, Iran D8 56
Bama, China I2 42
Bama, Nig. G7 64
Bamaga, Austl. B8 74
Bamako, Mali G3 64
Bamba, Mali F4 64
Bambamarca, Peru E2 84
Bambana, stm., Nic. F6 102
Bambari, C.A.R. C4 66
Bambaroo, Austl. B6 76
Bamberg, Ger. G6 16
Bamberg, S.C., U.S. C4 116
Bambio, C.A.R. D3 66
Bambuí, Braz. K2 88
Bam Co, l., China C13 54
Bamenda, Cam. C1 66
Bami, Turkmen. B8 56
Bāmīān, Afg. C10 56
Bamingui, C.A.R. C4 66
Bampūr, Iran D9 56
Bāmra Hills, hills, India H10 54
Bamumo, China B14 54
Banaba, i., Kir. D7 72
Banabuiú, stm., Braz. C6 88
Banabuiú, Açude, l., Braz. C6 88
Banalia, D.R.C. D5 66
Banamba, Mali G3 64
Banana Islands, is., S.L. H2 64
Bananal, stm., Braz. E1 88
Bananal, Ilha do, i., Braz. F7 84
Banarlı, Tur. B10 28
Banās, stm., India E6 54
Banâs, Râs, c., Egypt C7 62
Banat, hist. reg., Eur. D7 26
Banaz, Tur. E12 28
Ban Ban, Laos C6 48
Ban Bouang-nom, Laos E8 48
Banbridge, N. Ire., U.K. G6 12
Ban Bung Na Rang, Thai. D5 48
Banbury, Eng., U.K. I11 12
Ban Cha La, Laos D7 48
Bancroft, On., Can. C12 112
Bancroft, Id., U.S. H15 136
Bancroft, Ia., U.S. H4 118
Bancroft, Ne., U.S. C1 120
Bānda, India F8 54
Banda, Kepulauan, is., Indon. F9 44
Banda, Laut (Banda Sea), Indon. G8 44
Banda Aceh, Indon. J2 48
Bānda Dāūd Shāh, Pak. B3 54
Banda del Río Salí, Arg. C5 92
Bandai-Asahi-kokuritsu-kōen, p.o.i., Japan B12 40
Bandai-san, vol., Japan B13 40
Bandama, stm., C. Iv. H3 64
Bandama Blanc, stm., C. Iv. H3 64
Ban Dan, Thai. E7 48
Ban Dangtai, Laos D7 48
Bandar Beheshtī, Iran D9 56
Bandarbeyla, Som. C10 66
Bandar-e ʿAbbās, Iran D8 56
Bandar-e Anzalī, Iran B6 56
Bandar-e Būshehr, Iran D7 56
Bandar-e Deylam, Iran D7 56
Bandar-e Lengeh, Iran D7 56
Bandar-e Māh Shahr, Iran C6 56
Bandar-e Moghūyeh, Iran D7 56
Bandar-e Torkeman, Iran B7 56
Bandar Seri Begawan, Bru. A9 50
Banda Sea see Banda, Laut, Indon. G8 44
Bandeira, Pico da, mtn., Braz. K5 88
Bandeirantes, Braz. F7 84
Bandelier National Monument, p.o.i., N.M., U.S. F2 128
Bandera, Arg. D6 92
Bandera, Alto, mtn., Dom. Rep. C12 102
Banderas, Mex. C2 130
Banderas, Bahía de, b., Mex. E6 100
Bandhavgarh National Park, p.o.i., India G8 54
Bāndhi, Pak. E2 54
Bandiagara, Mali G4 64
Bandiantaolehai, China C5 36
Bāndīkūi, India E6 54
Bandipura, India A5 54
Bandipur Tiger Reserve, India F3 53
Bandırma, Tur. C11 28
Bandon, Or., U.S. G2 136
Ban Don, Ao, b., Thai. H4 48
Ban Donhiang, Laos C5 48
Bandundu, D.R.C. E3 66
Bandung, Indon. G5 50
Banes, Cuba B10 102
Banff, Ab., Can. E15 138
Banff, Scot., U.K. D10 12
Banff National Park, p.o.i., Ab., Can. E15 138
Banfora, Burkina G4 64
Banga, D.R.C. F4 66
Banga, India C6 54
Banga, stm., Phil. G5 52
Bangalore, India E3 53
Bangaon, India G12 54
Bangassou, C.A.R. D4 66
Bangdag Co, l., China A8 54
Banggai, Indon. F7 44
Banggai, Kepulauan, is., Indon. F7 44
Banggi, Pulau, i., Malay. G1 52
Banggong Co, l., China B7 54
Banghāzī (Bengasi), Libya A3 62
Banghiang, stm., Laos D7 48
Bangil, Indon. G8 50
Bangka, Pulau, i., Indon. E5 50
Bangka, Selat, strt., Indon. E4 50
Bangkalan, Indon. G8 50
Bangkaru, Pulau, i., Indon. L3 48
Bangkinang, Indon. C2 50
Bangkir, Indon. C12 50
Bangko, Indon. E3 50
Bangkog Co, l., China C12 54
Bangkok see Krung Thep, Thai. F5 48
Bangladesh, ctry., Asia G13 54
Bang Lamung, Thai. F5 48
Bang Mun Nak, Thai. D5 48
Bangor, N. Ire., U.K. G7 12
Bangor, Wales, U.K. H8 12
Bangor, Me., U.S. F8 110
Bangor, Pa., U.S. D10 114
Bangriposi, India G11 54
Bangs, Tx., U.S. C8 130
Bangs, Mount, mtn., Az., U.S. G3 132
Bang Saphan, Thai. G4 48
Bangued, Phil. B3 52
Bangui, C.A.R. D3 66
Bangweulu, Lake, l., Zam. C4 68
Bangweulu Swamps, sw., Zam. C5 68
Bangxu, China J2 42
Ban Hatgnao, Laos E8 48
Ban Hèt, Laos E8 48
Ban Hom, Thai. E4 48
Ban Hong Muang, Laos D7 48
Ban Houayxay, Laos B5 48
Bani, C.A.R. C4 66
Baní, Dom. Rep. C12 102
Bani, Jbel, mts., Mor. D3 64
Baniara, Pap. N. Gui. b4 79a
Bani Bangou, Niger F5 64
Banihāl Pass, p., India B4 46
Banī Walīd, Libya A2 62
Bāniyās, Golan E6 58
Bāniyās, Syria C6 58
Banja Luka, Bos. E4 26
Banjarmasin, Indon. E9 50
Banjul (Bathurst), Gam. G1 64
Bānka, India F11 54
Banka Banka, Austl. C6 74
Ban Katèp, Laos D7 48
Ban Kèngkabao, Laos D7 48
Ban Kèngtangan, Laos D7 48
Ban Kheun, Laos B5 48
Ban Khuan Mao, Thai. I4 48
Ban Kruat, Thai. E6 48
Banks, Al., U.S. F13 122
Banks, Îles (Banks Islands), is., Vanuatu i16 79d
Banks Island, i., B.C., Can. E4 106
Banks Island, i., N.T., Can. B15 140
Banks Islands see Banks, Îles, is., Vanuatu i16 79d
Banks Lake, res., Wa., U.S. C7 136
Banks Peninsula, pen., N.Z. F5 80
Banks Strait, strt., Austl. n13 77a
Banks / Torres, state, Vanuatu i16 79d
Bānkura, India G11 54
Ban Mae La Luang, Thai. C3 48
Ban Mit, Laos C5 48
Ban Muangngat, Laos C6 48
Bann, stm., N. Ire., U.K. F6 12
Ban Nadou, Laos E7 48
Ban Nahin, Laos C7 48
Ban Nalan, Laos E7 48
Ban Nam Chan, Thai. C6 48
Ban Namnga, Laos B6 48
Ban Nam Thaeng, Thai. E7 48
Ban Naxouang, Laos C7 48
Bannertown, N.C., U.S. H5 114
Banning, Ca., U.S. J9 134
Ban Nong Lumphuk, Thai. E6 48
Bannu, Pak. B3 54
Bañolas see Banyoles, Spain B13 20
Baños, Ec. H2 86
Banow, Afg. B10 56
Ban Pak Bong, Thai. C4 48
Ban Pakkhop, Laos C5 48
Ban Pak Nam, Thai. G4 48
Ban Phai, Thai. D6 48
Ban Phai, Thai. D6 48
Ban Pho, Thai. F5 48
Ban Phông Pho, Laos E7 48
Ban Pong, Thai. F4 48
Ban Sa-ang, Laos D7 48
Ban Salik, Thai. C5 48
Ban Sam Pong, Laos C6 48
Ban Samrong, Thai. E6 48
Bānsda, India H4 54
Banshadhāra, stm., India B6 53
Banská Bystrica, Slov. H15 16
Banská Štiavnica, Slov. H14 16
Bansko, Blg. H10 26
Ban Songkhon, Laos C7 48
Bānswāra, India G5 54
Bantaeng, Indon. F11 50
Ban Takhlo, Thai. E5 48
Bantarkawung, Indon. G6 50
Bantayan, Phil. E4 52
Ban Thabôk, Laos C6 48
Ban Thapayi, Laos D7 48
Ban Tian Sa, Laos C6 48
Bantry, Ire. J3 12
Bantry Bay, b., Ire. J3 12
Ban Van Hom, Laos C7 48
Ban Xènkhalôk, Laos C5 48
Banya, Testa de la, c., Spain D11 20
Banyak, Kepulauan, is., Indon. K3 48
Ban Ya Plong, Thai. H4 48
Banyo, Cam. C2 66
Banyoles, Spain B13 20
Banyuwangi, Indon. H9 50
Banzare Coast, cst., Ant. B17 81
Baode, China B4 42
Baoding, China B6 42
Baofeng, China E5 42
Bao Ha, Viet. A7 48
Baoji, China D2 42
Baojing, China G3 42
Bao Lac, Viet. G8 48
Bao Lac, Viet. A7 48
Baolunyuan, China E1 42
Baoqing, China B11 36
Baoshan, China F4 36
Baoting, China L3 42
Baotou, China A4 42
Baoulé, stm., Mali G3 64
Baowei, China A8 48
Baoyi, China E7 42
Baoying, China E8 42
Bāpatla, India D5 53
Bapaume, Fr. D11 14
Baptiste Lake, res., On., Can. C12 112
Bāqa el Gharbiyya, Isr. F6 58
Baqing, China B14 54
Baʿqūbah, Iraq C5 56
Baquedano, Chile A3 92
Bar, Yugo. G6 26
Bara, Nig. G7 64
Baraawe, Som. D8 66
Barabinsk, Russia C13 32
Barabinskaja step', pl., Russia C13 32
Baraboo, Wi., U.S. H9 118
Baraboo, stm., Wi., U.S. H8 118
Baracaldo see Barakaldo, Spain A8 20
Baracoa, Cuba B10 102
Baradero, Arg. F8 92
Baradine, Austl. H7 76
Baraga, Mi., U.S. B1 112
Bārah, Sudan E6 62
Barahona, Dom. Rep. C12 102
Barak, Tur. B8 58
Barāk, stm., India F14 54
Barakaldo, Spain A8 20
Baraki, Afg. B2 54
Barakula, Austl. F8 76
Baralaba, Austl. E7 76
Baram, stm., Malay. A9 50
Barama, stm., Guy. D12 86
Bārāmati, India B2 53
Bārāmūla, India A5 54
Baran', Bela. F13 10
Bārān, India F6 54
Baranagar, India G12 54
Baranavičy, Bela. G9 10
Barangbarang, Indon. G12 50
Baranoa, Col. B4 86
Baranof Island, i., Ak., U.S. E12 140
Barany, Russia C12 10
Baranya, state, Hung. D5 26
Barão de Grajaú, Braz. D4 88
Barão de Melgaço, Braz. G6 84
Barão de Tromaí, Braz. A3 88
Baraški, Russia D24 8
Barataria, La., U.S. H8 122
Barataria Bay, b., La., U.S. H8 122
Barat Daya, Kepulauan (Barat Daya Islands), is., Indon. G8 44
Barat Daya Islands see Barat Daya, Kepulauan, is., Indon. G8 44
Barauana, stm., Braz. G11 86
Barauni, India F10 54
Baraut, India D6 54
Baraya, Col. F4 86
Barbacena, Braz. K4 88
Barbacoas, Col. G2 86
Barbadillo del Mercado, Spain B7 20
Barbados, ctry., N.A. h16 96a
Barbalha, Braz. D6 88
Barbar, Sudan D6 62
Barbaria, Cap de, c., Spain F12 20
Barbas, Cap, c., W. Sah. E1 64
Barbaši, Russia C11 10
Barbastro, Spain B10 20
Barbate, Spain H4 20
Barbeau Peak, mtn., N.T., Can. A10 141
Barberena, Guat. E2 102
Barberton, S. Afr. D10 70
Barberton, Oh., U.S. C4 114
Barbil, India G10 54
Barbosa, Col. E5 86
Barbuda, i., Antig. e4 105b
Barby, Ger. E7 16
Bârca, Rom. F10 26
Barcaldine, Austl. D5 76
Barcău (Berettyó), stm., Eur. B8 26
Barcellona Pozzo di Gotto, Italy F9 24
Barcelona, Mex. B7 100
Barcelona, Spain C13 20
Barcelona, Ven. B9 86
Barcelona, co., Spain C13 20
Barceloneta, P.R. B2 104a
Barcelos, Braz. H10 86
Barcelos, Port. C2 20
Barcin, Pol. D13 16
Barcoo, stm., Austl. E4 76
Barczewo, Pol. C16 16
Barda del Medio, Arg. I3 92
Bardaï, Chad C3 62
Bardawîl, Sabkhet el-, b., Egypt G4 58
Barddhamān, India G11 54
Bardejov, Slov. G17 16
Bardeskan, Iran B8 56
Bardīyah, Libya A5 62
Bardo, Tun. H4 24
Bārdoli, India H4 54
Bardstown, Ky., U.S. G12 120
Bardwell Lake, res., Tx., U.S. E2 122
Bareilly, India D7 54
Barentsburg, Nor. B29 141
Barentsøya, i., Nor. B30 141
Barents Sea, Eur. B7 30
Bareta, India D5 54
Barfleur, Fr. E7 14
Bargaal, Som. B10 66
Bargara, Austl. E9 76
Bargarh, India D5 46
Barguzin, stm., Russia F11 34
Barguzinskij hrebet, mts., Russia F11 34
Bar Harbor, Me., U.S. F8 110
Barharwa, India F11 54
Barhi, India F10 54
Bāri, India E6 54
Bari, Italy C10 24
Baria, stm., Ven. G8 86
Barī Gāv, Afg. B1 54
Barigua, Salina de, pl., Ven. p20 104g
Barillas, Guat. E2 102
Barīm, i., Yemen G5 56
Barima, stm., S.A. C12 86
Barima-Waini, state, Guy. D12 86
Barinas, P.R. B2 104a
Barinas, Ven. C6 86
Barinas, state, Ven. C7 86
Baring, Cape, c., N.T., Can. A7 106
Baringo, Lake, l., Kenya D7 66
Bāripada, India H11 54
Bariri, Braz. L1 88
Bârîs, Egypt C6 62
Bari Sādri, India F5 54
Barisāl, Bngl. G13 54
Barisāl, state, Bngl. G13 54
Barisan, Pegunungan, mts., Indon. E2 50
Barito, stm., Indon. E9 50
Barjols, Fr. F11 18
Barkam, China E5 36
Barkava, Lat. D9 10
Barkerville, B.C., Can. C9 138
Bark Lake, l., On., Can. C12 112
Barkley, Lake, res., U.S. H10 120
Barkley Sound, strt., B.C., Can. H5 138
Barkly East, S. Afr. G8 70
Barkly Tableland, plat., Austl. C7 74
Barkly West, S. Afr. F7 70
Barkol, China C3 36
Bârlad, Rom. C14 26
Bârlad, stm., Rom. D14 26
Bar-le-Duc, Fr. F14 14
Barlee, Lake, l., Austl. E3 74
Barletta, Italy C10 24
Barlinek, Pol. D11 16
Barling, Ar., U.S. B4 122
Barlow, Ky., U.S. G8 120
Barmedman, Austl. J6 76
Bārmer, India F3 54
Barmera, Austl. J3 76
Barnagar, India G5 54
Barnard Castle, Eng., U.K. G11 12
Barnaul, Russia D14 32
Barn Bluff, mtn., Austl. n12 77a
Barnegat, N.J., U.S. E11 114
Barnegat Bay, b., N.J., U.S. E11 114
Barnes Ice Cap, ice, N.T., Can. A16 106
Barnesville, Ga., U.S. C1 116
Barnesville, Mn., U.S. E2 118
Barnesville, Oh., U.S. E4 114
Barneville-Carteret, Fr. E7 14
Barnsdall, Ok., U.S. E12 128
Barnsley, Eng., U.K. H11 12
Barnstable, Ma., U.S. C15 114
Barnstaple, Eng., U.K. J8 12
Barnstaple Bay, b., Eng., U.K. J8 12
Barnwell, Ab., Can. G18 138
Barnwell, S.C., U.S. C4 116
Baro, stm., Afr. F7 62
Baron Bluff, clf, V.I.U.S. g10 104c
Baron'ki, Bela. G15 10
Barora Fa Island, i., Sol. Is. d8 79b
Barora Ite Island, i., Sol. Is. d8 79b
Baroua, Niger G7 64
Barpeta, India E13 54
Barqah (Cyrenaica), hist. reg., Libya A4 62
Barques, Pointe aux, c., Mi., U.S. D7 112
Barquisimeto, Ven. B7 86
Barra, Braz. F4 88
Barra, i., Scot., U.K. D5 12
Barra, Ponta da, c., Moz. C12 70
Barraba, Austl. H8 76
Barra da Estiva, Braz. G5 88
Barra del Colorado, C.R. G6 102
Barra de Rio Grande, Nic. F6 102
Barra do Corda, Braz. C3 88
Barra do Cuanza, Ang. B1 68
Barra do Garças, Braz. G7 84
Barra do Mendes, Braz. F4 88
Barra do Piraí, Braz. L3 88
Barra do Ribeiro, Braz. E12 92
Barra Falsa, Ponta da, c., Moz. C12 70
Barra Mansa, Braz. L3 88
Barranca, Peru F2 84
Barrancabermeja, Col. D4 86
Barrancas, Ven. C10 86
Barrancas, Ven. C7 86
Barrancas, stm., Arg. H2 92
Barranco Azul, Mex. E3 130
Barranco do Velho, Port. G3 20
Barranqueras, Arg. C8 92
Barranquilla, Col. B4 86
Barranquitas, P.R. B3 104a
Barras, Braz. C4 88
Barre, Vt., U.S. F4 110
Barreal, Arg. E3 92
Barreiras, Braz. G3 88
Barreirinha, Braz. D6 84
Barreiro, Port. F1 20
Barreiros, Braz. E8 88
Barren, stm., Ky., U.S. H11 120
Barren, Nosy, is., Madag. D7 68
Barren Islands, is., Ak., U.S. E9 140
Barren River Lake, res., Ky., U.S. H11 120
Barretos, Braz. K1 88
Barrhead, Ab., Can. B16 138
Barrie, On., Can. D10 112
Barrie Island, i., On., Can. C7 112
Barrière, B.C., Can. E10 138
Barrier Range, mts., Austl. H3 76
Barrigada, Guam j10 78c
Barrington, N.S., Can. G11 110
Barrington Tops National Park, p.o.i., Austl. I8 76
Barringun, Austl. G5 76
Barrouallie, St. Vin. o11 105e
Barrow, Arg. I7 92
Barrow, Ak., U.S. B8 140
Barrow, stm., Ire. I5 12
Barrow, Point, c., Ak., U.S. B8 140
Barrow Creek, Austl. D6 74
Barrow-in-Furness, Eng., U.K. G9 12
Barrow Island, i., Austl. D2 74
Barrows, Mb., Can. B12 124
Barrow Strait, strt., N.T., Can. C6 141
Barry, Wales, U.K. J9 12
Barry, Il., U.S. E6 120
Barryton, Mi., U.S. E4 112
Barsalpur, India D4 54
Bārsi, India B2 53
Barsinghausen, Ger. D5 16
Barstow, Ca., U.S. I8 134
Barstow, Tx., U.S. C4 130
Bar-sur-Seine, Fr. F13 14
Bartang, Taj. B11 56
Barth, Ger. B8 16
Barthélemy, Deo, p., Viet. C6 48
Bartholomew, Bayou, stm., U.S. E7 122
Bartibougou, Burkina G5 64
Bartica, Guy. B6 84
Bartın, Tur. B15 28
Bartle Frere, mtn., Austl. A5 76
Bartlesville, Ok., U.S. H2 120
Bartlett, N.H., U.S. F5 110
Bartlett, Tn., U.S. B9 122
Bartlett, Tx., U.S. D10 130
Bartley, Ne., U.S. A8 128
Barton, Vt., U.S. F4 110
Bartoszyce, Pol. B16 16
Bartow, Fl., U.S. I4 116
Bartow, Ga., U.S. D3 116
Barú, Volcán, vol., Pan. H6 102
Bārūk, Jabal al-, mtn., Leb. E6 58
Barumini, Italy E2 24
Barumun, stm., Indon. C2 50
Barung, Nusa, i., Indon. H8 50
Barus, Indon. L4 48
Baruun-Urt, Mong. B7 36
Barvas, Scot., U.K. C6 12
Barview, Or., U.S. G2 136
Barwāh, India G5 54
Barwāni, India H5 54
Barwick, Ga., U.S. F2 116
Barwon, stm., Austl. H6 76
Barybino, Russia E20 10
Barycz, stm., Pol. E13 16
Barysaŭ, Bela. F11 10
Basail, Arg. C8 92
Basalt, stm., Austl. B5 76
Basankusu, D.R.C. D3 66
Basarabeasca, Mol. C15 26
Basatongwula Shan, mtn., China B13 54
Basavakalyān, India C3 53
Basavilbaso, Arg. F8 92
Bascuñán, Cabo, c., Chile D2 92
Basel (Bâle), Switz. C4 22
Basella see Bassella, Spain B12 20
Basey, Phil. E5 52
Bashi Channel, strt., Asia K9 42
Bashkortostan see Baškirija, state, Russia D9 32
Basilan Island, i., Phil. G4 52
Basilan Strait, strt., Phil. G4 52
Basildon, Eng., U.K. J13 12
Basile, La., U.S. G6 122
Basilicata, state, Italy D10 24
Basin, Mt., U.S. D14 136
Basin, Wy., U.S. C4 126
Basingstoke, Eng., U.K. J11 12
Basin Lake, l., Sk., Can. B8 124
Basīrhāt, India G12 54
Baskahegan Lake, l., Me., U.S. E8 110
Baskakovka, Russia F17 10
Başkale, Tur. B5 56
Baskatong, Réservoir, res., Qc., Can. B13 112
Basket Lake, l., On., Can. B6 118
Baškirija, state, Russia D9 32
Baskomutan Milli Parkı, p.o.i., Tur. E13 28
Basmat, India B3 53
Bāsoda, India G6 54
Basoko, D.R.C. D4 66
Basora, Punt, c., Aruba p20 104g
Basque Provinces see Euskal Herriko, state, Spain A8 20
Basra see Al-Baṣrah, Iraq C6 56
Bas-Rhin, state, Fr. F16 14
Bassano, Ab., Can. F18 138
Bassano del Grappa, Italy E8 22
Bassari, Togo H5 64
Bassas da India, rf., Reu. E6 68
Bassein, stm., Mya. D2 48
Bassella, Spain B12 20
Basse Santa Su, Gam. G2 64
Basse-Terre, Guad. i5 105c
Basseterre, St. K./N. C2 105a
Basse Terre, Trin. s12 105f
Basse-Terre, i., Guad. h5 105c
Bassett, Ne., U.S. E13 126
Bassett, Va., U.S. H6 114
Bassfield, Ms., U.S. F9 122
Bassikounou, Maur. F3 64
Bassila, Benin H5 64
Bass River, N.S., Can. E13 110
Bass Strait, strt., Austl. L6 76
Basswood Lake, l., N.A. C6 118
Båstad, Swe. H5 8
Bastenaken see Bastogne, Bel. D14 14
Bastersberge, hill, S. Afr. G5 70
Basti, India E9 54
Bastia, Fr. G15 18
Bastogne, Bel. D14 14
Bastrop, La., U.S. E6 122
Bastrop, Tx., U.S. D10 130
Basu, Pulau, i., Indon. D3 50
Basutoland see Lesotho, ctry., Afr. F9 70
Bata, Eq. Gui. I6 64
Bataan Peninsula, pen., Phil. C3 52
Batabanó, Golfo de, b., Cuba A6 102
Batac, Phil. A3 52
Batagaj, Russia C15 34
Batagaj-Alyta, Russia C15 34
Batak, Blg. H11 26
Batala, India C5 54
Batalha, Braz. E7 88
Batalha, Port. E2 20
Batam, Pulau, i., Indon. C3 50
Batamaj, Russia D14 34
Batang, China E5 36
Batangafo, C.A.R. C3 66
Batangas, Phil. D3 52
Batangtoru, Indon. C1 50
Batan Islands, is., Phil. K9 42
Batanta, Pulau, i., Indon. F9 44
Batatais, Braz. K2 88
Batavia, Arg. G5 92
Batavia see Jakarta, Indon. G5 50
Batavia, Il., U.S. C9 120
Batavia, Ia., U.S. D5 120
Batavia, N.Y., U.S. A7 114
Batchelor, Austl. B6 74
Bătdâmbâng, Camb. F6 48
Bateckij, Russia B13 10
Batemans Bay, Austl. J8 76
Bates, Mount, mtn., Norf. I. y24 78i
Batesburg, S.C., U.S. C4 116
Batesville, Ar., U.S. B7 122
Batesville, Ms., U.S. C9 122
Batesville, Tx., U.S. F8 130
Bath, N.B., Can. D9 110
Bath, Eng., U.K. J10 12
Bath, Me., U.S. G7 110
Bath, N.Y., U.S. B8 114
Batha, stm., Chad E3 62
Bathgate, N.D., U.S. F16 124
Bathinda, India C5 54
Bathsheba, Barb. n8 105d
Bathurst, Austl. I7 76
Bathurst, N.B., Can. C11 110
Bathurst see Banjul, Gam. G1 64
Bathurst, Cape, c., N.T., Can. A5 106
Bathurst Inlet, N.T., Can. B9 106
Bathurst Island, i., Austl. B5 74
Bathurst Island, i., N.T., Can. B5 141
Batlow, Austl. J6 76
Batman, Tur. B5 56
Batna, Alg. B6 64
Ba To, Viet. E9 48
Baton Rouge, La., U.S. G7 122
Batouri, Cam. D2 66
Batsawul, Afg. A3 54
Batson, Tx., U.S. G4 122
Batterie, Pointe de la, c., Mart. k7 105c
Batticaloa, Sri L. H5 53
Battipaglia, Italy D8 24
Battle, stm., Can. D19 138
Battle Creek, Mi., U.S. F4 112
Battle Creek, Ne., U.S. F15 126
Battle Creek, stm., N.A. F4 124
Battle Ground, In., U.S. H3 112
Battle Ground, Wa., U.S. E4 136
Battle Harbour, Nf., Can. i22 107a
Battle Mountain, Nv., U.S. C8 134
Battle Mountain, mtn., Wy., U.S. B9 132
Batu, mtn., Eth. F7 62
Batu, Kepulauan, is., Indon. F2 44
Batu-Batu, Indon. F11 50
Batu Berincang, Gunong, mtn., Malay. J5 48
Batubrok, Bukit, mtn., Indon. C9 50
Batu Gajah, Malay. J5 48
Batukelau, Indon. C9 50
Batumi, Geor. F6 32
Batu Pahat, Malay. L6 48
Batupanjang, Indon. C2 50
Baturaja, Indon. F3 50
Baturino, Russia C15 32
Baturité, Braz. C6 88
Baturusa, Indon. D5 50
Batusangkar, Indon. D2 50
Batz, Île de, i., Fr. F4 14
Bau, Malay. C7 50
Baubau, Indon. G7 44
Bauchi, Nig. G6 64
Bauda, India H10 54
Baudette, Mn., U.S. C4 118
Baudó, stm., Col. E3 86
Bauld, Cape, c., Nf., Can. i22 107a
Bauman Fiord, b., N.T., Can. B8 141
Baume-les-Dames, Fr. G15 14
Baures, Bol. B4 90
Bauru, Braz. L1 88
Bauska, Lat. D7 10
Bautzen, Ger. E10 16
Bauxite, Ar., U.S. C6 122
Bavaria see Bayern, state, Ger. H7 16
Bavarian Alps, mts., Eur. I7 16
Båven, l., Swe. G7 8
Bavispe, Mex. F8 98
Bavispe, stm., Mex. F8 98
Bawang, Indon. G6 50
Bawdwin, Mya. A3 48
Bawean, Pulau, i., Indon. F8 50
Bawiti, Egypt B5 62
Bawmi, Mya. D2 48
Baxaya, mtn., Som. B9 66
Baxian, China G2 42
Baxian, China B7 42
Baxter, Ia., U.S. C4 120
Baxter, Mn., U.S. E4 118
Baxter, Tn., U.S. H12 120
Baxterville, Ms., U.S. F9 122
Bay, Ar., U.S. B8 122
Bay, Laguna de, l., Phil. C3 52
Bayamo, Cuba B9 102
Bayamón, P.R. B3 104a
Bayan, China A7 38
Bayan, Indon. H10 50
Bayāna, India E6 54
Bayan Har Shan, mts., China E4 36
Bayanhongor, Mong. B5 36
Bayannaobao, China B2 42
Bayano, Lago, res., Pan. H8 102
Bayan Obo, China C7 36
Bayard, Ia., U.S. C3 120
Bayard, N.M., U.S. K8 132
Bayard, W.V., U.S. E6 114
Bayawan, Phil. F4 52
Baybay, Phil. E5 52
Bayboro, N.C., U.S. A9 116
Bayburt, Tur. A5 56
Bay City, Mi., U.S. E6 112
Bay City, Or., U.S. E3 136
Bay City, Tx., U.S. F12 130
Baydhabo (Baidoa), Som. D8 66
Baydrag, stm., Mong. B4 36
Bayern (Bavaria), state, Ger. H7 16
Bayeux, Braz. D8 88
Bayeux, Fr. E8 14
Bayfield, Co., U.S. F9 132
Bayfield, Wi., U.S. E8 118
Bayındır, Tur. E10 28
Baykonur see Bajkonur, Kaz. E11 32
Bay Minette, Al., U.S. G11 122
Bayombong, Phil. B3 52
Bayona see Baiona, Spain B2 20
Bayonne, Fr. F4 18
Bayou Bodcau Reservoir, res., La., U.S. E5 122
Bayou Cane, La., U.S. H8 122
Bayou D'Arbonne Lake, res., La., U.S. E6 122

Name	Map Ref.	Page

Name — Map Ref. — Page

Big Lookout Mountain, mtn., Or., U.S. F9 136
Big Lost, stm., Id., U.S. G13 136
Big Muddy, stm., Il., U.S. G8 120
Big Muddy Creek, stm., Mt., U.S. F9 124
Big Nemaha, North Fork, stm., Ne., U.S. K2 118
Bignona, Sen. G1 64
Big Pine, Ca., U.S. F7 134
Big Pine Mountain, mtn., Ca., U.S. I6 134
Big Piney, Wy., U.S. H16 136
Big Piney, stm., Mo., U.S. G6 120
Bigpoint, Ms., U.S. G10 122
Big Porcupine Creek, stm., Mt., U.S. H6 124
Big Prairie Creek, stm., Al., U.S. E11 122
Big Quill Lake, l., Sk., Can. C9 124
Big Raccoon Creek, stm., In., U.S. I2 112
Big Rapids, Mi., U.S. E4 112
Big Rideau Lake, l., On., Can. D13 112
Big River, Sk., Can. E9 106
Big Sable Point, c., Mi., U.S. D3 112
Big Sand Lake, l., Mb., Can. D11 106
Big Sandy, Tn., U.S. H9 120
Big Sandy, Tx., U.S. E3 122
Big Sandy, stm., U.S. F3 114
Big Sandy, stm., Wy., U.S. F3 126
Big Sandy Creek, stm., Co., U.S. C6 128
Bigsby Island, i., On., Can. B4 118
Big Signal Peak, mtn., Ca., U.S. D2 134
Big Sioux, stm., U.S. E16 126
Big Sky, Mt., U.S. E15 136
Big Smoky Valley, val., Nv., U.S. E8 134
Big Spring, Tx., U.S. B6 130
Big Spruce Knob, mtn., W.V., U.S. F5 114
Big Stone City, S.D., U.S. F2 118
Big Stone Gap, Va., U.S. H3 114
Big Stone Lake, l., U.S. F2 118
Big Sunflower, stm., Ms., U.S. D8 122
Big Sur, reg., Ca., U.S. H4 134
Big Timber, Mt., U.S. E16 136
Big Trout Lake, l., On., Can. E12 106
Biguaçu, Braz. C13 92
Big Water, Ut., U.S. F5 132
Big Wells, Tx., U.S. F8 130
Big White Mountain, mtn., B.C., Can. G12 138
Big Wood, stm., Id., U.S. G12 136
Bihać, Bos. E2 26
Bīhar, India F10 54
Bihār, state, India F10 54
Biharamulo, Tan. E6 66
Bihor, state, Rom. C9 26
Bihor, Vârful, mtn., Rom. C9 26
Bihoro, Japan C16 38
Bihosava, Bela. E10 10
Bihu, China G8 42
Bija, stm., Russia D15 32
Bijagós, Arquipélago dos, is., Gui.-B. G1 64
Bijainagar, India F5 54
Bijaipur, India E6 54
Bijāpur, India C2 53
Bījāpur, India B5 53
Bijeljina, Bos. E6 26
Bijelo Polje, Yugo. F6 26
Bijie, China F6 36
Bijlikol', ozero, l., Kaz. F12 32
Bijnor, India D7 54
Bijsk, Russia D15 32
Bīkāner, India D4 54
Bikar, at., Marsh. Is. B8 72
Bikeqi, China A4 42
Bikin, Russia B11 36
Bikini, at., Marsh. Is. B7 72
Bīkkū Bīttī, mtn., Libya C3 62
Bikoro, D.R.C. E3 66
Bilāra, India E4 54
Bilāri, India D7 54
Bilāsipāra, India E13 54
Bilāspur, India C6 54
Bilāspur, India G9 54
Bila Tserkva, Ukr. F15 6
Bilauktaung Range, mts., Asia F4 48
Bilbao, Spain A7 20
Bilbeis, Egypt H2 58
Bilbilis, hist., Spain C9 20
Bileća, Bos. G5 26
Bilecik, Tur. C12 28
Bilecik, state, Tur. C13 28
Biłgoraj, Pol. F18 16
Bilgrām, India E8 54
Bilhorod-Dnistrovs'kyi, Ukr. C17 26
Bili, D.R.C. D5 66
Biliaïvka, Ukr. C17 26
Bilīmora, India H4 54
Bilin, Mya. D3 48
Bilin, stm., Mya. D3 48
Bílina, Czech Rep. F9 16
Biliran Island, i., Phil. E5 52
Billabong Creek, stm., Austl. J5 76
Billings, Mo., U.S. G4 120
Billings, Mt., U.S. B4 126
Billings Heights, Mt., U.S. B4 126
Billiton see Belitung, i., Indon. E5 50
Bill Williams, stm., Az., U.S. I3 132
Billy Chinook, Lake, res., Or., U.S. F5 136
Bilma, Niger F7 64
Biloela, Austl. E8 76
Biloxi, Ms., U.S. G10 122
Bilpa Morea Claypan, l., Austl. E2 76
Bilqas Qism Awwal, Egypt G2 58
Biltine, Chad E4 62
Biltmore Forest, N.C., U.S. A3 116
Bilugyun Island, i., Mya. D3 48
Bimbo, C.A.R. D3 66
Bimbowrie, Austl. H3 76
Bimini Islands, is., Bah. B9 96
Bīna-Etāwa, India F7 54
Binaiya, Gunung, mtn., Indon. F9 44
Binalbagan, Phil. E4 52
Bin'an, China B7 38
Bindki, India E8 54
Bindloss, Ab., Can. D3 124
Bindura, Zimb. D5 68
Binéfar, Spain C11 20
Binford, N.D., U.S. G15 124
Binga, D.R.C. D4 66
Binga, Monte, mtn., Afr. D5 68
Bingara, Austl. G8 76
Bingen, Ger. G3 16
Binger, Ok., U.S. F10 128
Binghamton, N.Y., U.S. B10 114
Bin Ghunaymah, Jabal, mts., Libya B3 62
Binhai, China D8 42
Binh Gia, Viet. B8 48
Binjai, Indon. K4 48
Binnaway, Austl. H7 76
Binongko, Pulau, i., Indon. G7 44
Binscarth, Mb., Can. D12 124
Bintan, Pulau, i., Indon. C4 50
Bintimani, mtn., S.L. H2 64
Bintuhan, Indon. F3 50
Bintulu, Malay. B8 50
Bintuni, Indon. F9 44
Binxian, China B7 38
Binxian, China C7 42
Binxian, China D3 42
Binyang, China J3 42
Bin-Yauri, Nig. G5 64
Biobío, state, Chile H1 92
Biobío, stm., Chile G2 90
Biogradska Gora Nacionalni Park, p.o.i., Yugo. G6 26
Bioko, i., Eq. Gui. I6 64
Bira, Russia G15 34
Birac, Phil. B3 52
Birāk, Libya B2 62
Birakan, Russia G15 34
Bi'r al Wa'r, Libya C2 62
Birao, C.A.R. B4 66
Birch, stm., Ab., Can. D8 106
Birch Creek, stm., Mt., U.S. B14 136
Birch Hills, Sk., Can. B8 124
Birch Island, B.C., Can. E10 138
Birch Island, i., Mb., Can. B13 124
Birch Mountains, hills, Ab., Can. D8 106
Birch Run, Mi., U.S. E6 112
Birch Tree, Mo., U.S. H6 120
Birchwood, Wi., U.S. F7 118
Bird Creek, stm., Ok., U.S. E13 128
Bird Island, Mn., U.S. G4 118
Bird Island, sci., S. Geor. J9 90
Birdsville, Austl. E2 76
Birdtail Creek, stm., Mb., Can. D13 124
Birdum, Austl. C6 74
Birecik, Tur. A9 58
Bireun, Indon. J3 48
Bir Ghbalou, Alg. H14 20
Birigui, Braz. D6 90
Biriljussy, Russia C16 32
Bīrjand, Iran C8 56
Birjul'ka, Russia D19 32
Birjusa, stm., Russia C17 32
Birjusinsk, Russia C17 32
Birken, B.C., Can. F8 138
Birkenfeld, Ger. G3 16
Birkenhead, Eng., U.K. H9 12
Birmingham, Eng., U.K. I10 12
Birmingham, Al., U.S. D11 122
Birmingham, Ia., U.S. D6 120
Birmingham, Mi., U.S. B2 114
Birmitrapur, India G10 54
Bîr Mogreïn, Maur. D2 64
Birnin Gaouré, Niger G5 64
Birnin-Kebbi, Nig. G5 64
Birnin Konni, Niger G5 64
Birnin Kudu, Nig. G6 64
Birobidžan, Russia G15 34
Birrie, stm., Austl. G6 76
Birsk, Russia C9 32
Birštonas, Lith. F7 10
Birtle, Mb., Can. D12 124
Birūr, India E2 53
Biržai, Lith. D7 10
Birżebbuġa, Malta I8 24
Bisaccia, Italy C9 24
Bīsalpur, India D7 54
Bisbee, Az., U.S. L7 132
Bisbee, N.D., U.S. F14 124
Biscarrosse et de Parentis, Étang de, l., Fr. E4 18
Biscay, Bay of, b., Eur. E2 18
Biscayne Bay, b., Fl., U.S. K5 116
Biscayne National Park, p.o.i., Fl., U.S. K5 116
Bisceglie, Italy C10 24
Bischofshofen, Aus. C10 22
Bischofswerda, Ger. E10 16
Biscoe, N.C., U.S. A6 116
Bishnupur, India G11 54
Bisho, S. Afr. H8 70
Bishop, Ca., U.S. F7 134
Bishop, Tx., U.S. G10 130
Bishop Auckland, Eng., U.K. G11 12
Bishop Rock, r., Eng., U.K. L6 12
Bishop's Falls, Nf., Can. j22 107a
Bishop's Stortford, Eng., U.K. J13 12
Bishopville, S.C., U.S. B5 116
Biškek, Kyrg. F12 32
Biskupiec, Pol. C16 16
Bislig, Phil. F6 52
Bismarck, Mo., U.S. G7 120
Bismarck, N.D., U.S. A12 126
Bismarck Archipelago, is., Pap. N. Gui. a4 79a
Bismarck Range, mts., Pap. N. Gui. b3 79a
Bismarck Sea, Pap. N. Gui. a4 79a
Bismark, Kap, c., Grnld. B22 141
Bissa, Djebel, mtn., Alg. H12 20
Bissau, Gui.-B. G1 64
Bissett, Mb., Can. C18 124
Bissikrima, Gui. G2 64
Bistcho Lake, l., Ab., Can. D7 106
Bistineau, Lake, res., La., U.S. E5 122
Bistrica, Slvn. D13 22
Bistrița, Rom. B11 26
Bistrița, stm., Rom. C13 26
Bistrița-Năsăud, state, Rom. B11 26
Biswān, India E8 54
Bitam, Gabon D2 66
Bitburg, Ger. G2 16
Bitche, Fr. E16 14
Bitlis, Tur. B5 56
Bitola, Mac. B4 28
Bitolj see Bitola, Mac. B4 28
Bitonto, Italy C10 24
Bitou, Burkina G4 64
Bitter Creek, stm., Wy., U.S. B8 132
Bitterfeld, Ger. E8 16
Bitterfontein, S. Afr. G4 70
Bitterroot, stm., Mt., U.S. D13 136
Bitterroot, West Fork, stm., Mt., U.S. E12 136
Bitterroot Range, mts., U.S. C11 136
Bitung, Indon. E8 44
Bitupitá, Braz. B5 88
Biu, Nig. G7 64
Bivins, Tx., U.S. E4 122
Biwabik, Mn., U.S. D6 118
Biwa-ko, l., Japan D8 40
Bixby, Ok., U.S. I2 120
Biyala, Egypt G2 58
Biyang, China E5 42
Bizana, S. Afr. G9 70
Bizen, Japan E7 40
Bizerte (Binzert), Tun. G3 24
Bizerte, Lac de, l., Tun. G3 24
Bizkaiko, co., Spain A8 20
Bjahoml', Bela. F10 10
Bjala, Blg. G14 26
Bjala Slatina, Blg. F10 26
Bjalyničy, Bela. F12 10
Bjarèzina, stm., Bela. H13 10
Bjarèzina, stm., Bela. G9 10
Bjaroza, Bela. H7 10
Bjarozauka, Bela. G8 10
Bjelovar, Cro. E13 22
Björna, Swe. E8 8
Björneborg see Pori, Fin. F9 8
Bjorne Peninsula, pen., N.T., Can. B8 141
Bjørnøya, i., Nor. B5 30
Bla, Mali G3 64
Blace, Yugo. F8 26
Black (Da, Song) (Lixian), stm., Asia D9 46
Black, stm., Mb., Can. D18 124
Black, stm., U.S. I6 120
Black, stm., Ak., U.S. C11 140
Black, stm., Az., U.S. J6 132
Black, stm., La., U.S. F7 122
Black, stm., Mi., U.S. E7 112
Black, stm., N.Y., U.S. E14 112
Black, stm., Wi., U.S. G7 118
Blackall, Austl. E5 76
Black Bay, b., On., Can. C10 118
Black Bay Peninsula, pen., On., Can. C10 118
Black Bear Creek, stm., Ok., U.S. E11 128
Blackburn, Eng., U.K. H10 12
Blackburn, Mount, mtn., Ak., U.S. D11 140
Black Butte, mtn., Mt., U.S. D15 136
Black Canyon of the Gunnison National Monument, p.o.i., Co., U.S. E9 132
Black Creek, stm., Ms., U.S. G9 122
Black Creek, stm., S.C., U.S. B6 116
Black Diamond, Ab., Can. F16 138
Black Diamond, Wa., U.S. C5 136
Blackdown Tableland National Park, p.o.i., Austl. D7 76
Blackduck, Mn., U.S. D4 118
Black Eagle, Mt., U.S. C15 136
Blackfoot, Id., U.S. G14 136
Blackfoot, Mt., U.S. B14 136
Blackfoot, stm., Id., U.S. G15 136
Blackfoot, stm., Mt., U.S. D13 136
Blackfoot Reservoir, res., Id., U.S. H15 136
Black Forest see Schwarzwald, mts., Ger. H4 16
Black Hills, mts., U.S. C9 126
Black Island, i., Mb., Can. C17 124
Black Lake, Qc., Can. D5 110
Black Lake, l., Sk., Can. D10 106
Black Lake, l., Mi., U.S. C5 112
Black Lake, l., N.Y., U.S. D14 112
Black Mesa, mtn., U.S. E6 128
Blackmore, Mount, mtn., Mt., U.S. E15 136
Black Mountain, N.C., U.S. A3 116
Black Mountain, mtn., Az., U.S. K5 132
Black Mountain, mtn., Ca., U.S. H5 134
Black Mountain, mtn., Mt., U.S. D14 136
Black Mountain, hill, Austl. C2 76
Black Mountain, mts., U.S. H2 114
Black Nossob, stm., Nmb. C4 70
Black Pine Peak, mtn., Id., U.S. A3 132
Blackpool, Eng., U.K. H9 12
Black Range, mts., N.M., U.S. J9 132
Black River, N.Y., U.S. D14 112
Black River Falls, Wi., U.S. G8 118
Black Rock, Ar., U.S. H6 120
Black Rock, r., Ire. G2 12
Black Rock, r., S. Geor. J8 90
Black Rock Desert, des., Nv., U.S. B7 134
Blacksburg, S.C., U.S. A4 116
Blacksburg, Va., U.S. G5 114
Black Sea G15 6
Blacks Fork, stm., U.S. B7 132
Blackshear, Lake, res., Ga., U.S. D2 116
Blackstone, Va., U.S. G8 114
Black Sturgeon Lake, l., On., Can. B9 118
Blackville, S.C., U.S. C4 116
Black Volta (Volta Noire) (Mouhoun), stm., Afr. H4 64
Blackwater, Austl. D7 76
Blackwater, stm., Ire. I4 12
Blackwater, stm., Mo., U.S. E4 120
Blackwater Creek, stm., Austl. E5 76
Blackwater Draw, stm., Tx., U.S. H7 128
Blackwater Lake, l., N.T., Can. C6 106
Blackwell, Tx., U.S. B7 130
Bladenboro, N.C., U.S. B7 116
Bladensburg National Park, p.o.i., Austl. D4 76
Bladgrond-Noord, S. Afr. F4 70
Bladworth, Sk., Can. C7 124
Bláfell, mtn., Ice. k30 8a
Blagoevgrad, Blg. G10 26
Blagoveščensk, Russia D16 34
Blaine, Mn., U.S. F5 118
Blaine, Wa., U.S. B4 136
Blair, Ne., U.S. C1 120
Blair, Ok., U.S. G9 128
Blair, Wi., U.S. G7 118
Blair Athol, Austl. D6 76
Blairsville, Ga., U.S. B2 116
Blairsville, Pa., U.S. D6 114
Blaj, Rom. C10 26
Blakely, Ga., U.S. F13 122
Blake Plateau, unds. E6 144
Blake Point, c., Mi., U.S. C10 118
Blalock Island, i., Wa., U.S. E7 136
Blanc, Mont, mtn., Eur. D12 18
Blanca, Co., U.S. D3 128
Blanca, Bahía, b., Arg. G4 90
Blanca, Laguna, l., Chile J2 90
Blanca, Punta, c., Chile B2 92
Blanca, Sierra, mtn., Tx., U.S. C2 130
Blanca Peak, mtn., Co., U.S. D3 128
Blanchard, Ok., U.S. F11 128
Blanchard, stm., Oh., U.S. D2 114
Blanche, Lake, l., Austl. G2 76
Blanche Channel, strt., Sol. Is. e7 79b
Blanchester, Oh., U.S. E1 114
Blanchisseuse, Trin. s12 105f
Blanco, Tx., U.S. D9 130
Blanco, stm., Arg. D3 92
Blanco, stm., Ec. G2 86
Blanco, stm., Tx., U.S. E9 130
Blanco, Cabo, c., C.R. H5 102
Blanco, Cañon, val., N.M., U.S. F3 128
Blanco, Cape, c., Or., U.S. H2 136
Blanco, Lago, l., Chile J3 90
Blanc-Sablon, Qc., Can. i22 107a
Bland, Va., U.S. G4 114
Blanda, stm., Ice. k30 8a
Blanding, Ut., U.S. F7 132
Blandinsville, Il., U.S. D7 120
Blanes, Spain C13 20
Blangkejeren, Indon. K3 48
Blangy-sur-Bresle, Fr. E10 14
Blankenburg, Ger. E6 16
Blanquilla, Isla, i., Ven. B9 86
Blansko, Czech Rep. G12 16
Blantyre, Mwi. D6 68
Blarney Castle, hist., Ire. J4 12
Błaszki, Pol. E14 16
Blaubeuren, Ger. H5 16
Blaufelden, Ger. G5 16
Błażowa, Pol. G18 16
Bledsoe, Tx., U.S. H5 128
Blega, Indon. G8 50
Bleik see Andenes, Nor. B6 8
Blekinge, state, Swe. H6 8
Blenheim, On., Can. F8 112
Blenheim, N.Z. E5 80
Blessing, Tx., U.S. F11 130
Bletchley, Eng., U.K. J12 12
Bligh Water, strt., Fiji p18 79e
Blind River, On., Can. B6 112
Blissfield, Mi., U.S. C2 114
Blitar, Indon. H8 50
Block Island, i., R.I., U.S. C14 114
Blockton, Ia., U.S. D3 120
Bloedel, B.C., Can. F5 138
Bloemfontein, S. Afr. F8 70
Bloemhof, S. Afr. E7 70
Bloemhofdam, res., S. Afr. E7 70
Blois, Fr. G10 14
Blönduós, Ice. k29 8a
Bloodvein, stm., Can. E11 106
Bloody Foreland, c., Ire. F4 12
Bloomer, Wi., U.S. F7 118
Bloomfield, On., Can. E12 112
Bloomfield, Ky., U.S. G12 120
Bloomfield, Mo., U.S. H8 120
Bloomfield, Ne., U.S. E15 126
Bloomfield, N.M., U.S. G9 132
Blooming Grove, Tx., U.S. E2 122
Blooming Prairie, Mn., U.S. H5 118
Bloomington, Il., U.S. D9 120
Bloomington, In., U.S. E11 120
Bloomington, Mn., U.S. G5 118
Bloomington, Tx., U.S. F11 130
Bloomington, Wi., U.S. B7 120
Bloomsburg, Pa., U.S. C9 114
Bloomsbury, Austl. C7 76
Bloomville, Oh., U.S. C2 114
Blora, Indon. G7 50
Blosseville Kyst, cst., Grnld. D20 141
Blossom, Tx., U.S. D3 122
Blouberg, mtn., S. Afr. C9 70
Blountstown, Fl., U.S. G13 122
Blountsville, Al., U.S. C12 122
Blowering Reservoir, res., Austl. J6 76
Blowing Point Village, Anguilla A1 105a
Blowing Rock, N.C., U.S. H4 114
Bludenz, Aus. C6 22
Blue, stm., Az., U.S. J7 132
Blue, stm., Ok., U.S. C2 122
Blue Creek, Wa., U.S. B8 136
Blue Cypress Lake, l., Fl., U.S. I5 116
Blue Earth, Mn., U.S. H4 118
Blue Earth, stm., U.S. H4 118
Bluefield, Va., U.S. G4 114
Bluefield, W.V., U.S. G4 114
Bluefields, Nic. F6 102
Blue Hill, Ne., U.S. A10 128
Blue Hill Bay, b., Me., U.S. F8 110
Blue Island, Il., U.S. G2 112
Blue Mound, Ks., U.S. F3 120
Blue Mountain, Ms., U.S. C9 122
Blue Mountain, mtn., Ar., U.S. C4 122
Blue Mountain, mtn., Mt., U.S. G9 124
Blue Mountain, mts., Pa., U.S. D8 114
Blue Mountain Peak, mtn., Jam. i14 104d
Blue Mountains, mts., Jam. i14 104d
Blue Mountains, mts., U.S. E8 136
Blue Mountains, mts., Me., U.S. F6 110
Blue Mountains National Park, p.o.i., Austl. J8 76
Blue Mud Bay, b., Austl. B7 74
Blue Nile (Azraq, Al-Baḥr al-) (Ābay), stm., Afr. E6 62
Bluenose Lake, l., N.T., Can. B6 106
Blue Ridge, Ab., Can. B15 138
Blue Ridge, Ga., U.S. B1 116
Blue Ridge, mts., U.S. H4 114
Blue River, B.C., Can. D11 138
Bluestone Dam, dam, W.V., U.S. G5 114
Bluestone Lake, res., W.V., U.S. G5 114
Bluewater, N.M., U.S. H9 132
Bluff, N.Z. H3 80
Bluff, Ut., U.S. F7 132
Bluff Cape, c., Mya. D2 48
Bluff Creek, stm., U.S. D11 128
Bluff Dale, Tx., U.S. B9 130
Bluff Park, Al., U.S. D12 122
Bluffs, Il., U.S. E7 120
Bluffton, In., U.S. H4 112
Bluffton, S.C., U.S. D5 116
Blumberg, Ger. I4 16
Blumenau, Braz. C13 92
Blumenhof, Sk., Can. D6 124
Bly, Or., U.S. A4 134
Blyth, On., Can. E8 112
Blyth, Eng., U.K. F11 12
Blythe, Ca., U.S. J2 132
Blytheville, Ar., U.S. I7 120
Bø, Nor. G3 8
Bo, S.L. H2 64
Boac, Phil. D3 52
Boaco, Nic. F5 102
Boa Esperança, Braz. K3 88
Boa Esperança, Represa, res., Braz. D3 88
Bo'ai, China D5 42
Boane, Moz. E11 70
Board Camp Mountain, mtn., Ca., U.S. C2 134
Boardman, Oh., U.S. C5 114
Boatman, Austl. F6 76
Boa Viagem, Braz. C5 88
Boa Vista, Braz. F11 86
Boa Vista, i., C.V. k10 65a
Boawai, Indon. H12 50
Boaz, Al., U.S. C12 122
Bobai, China J3 42
Bobaomby, Tanjona, c., Madag. C8 68
Bobbili, India B6 53
Bobcaygeon, On., Can. D11 112
Bobigny, Fr. F11 14
Böblingen, Ger. H4 16
Bobo-Dioulasso, Burkina G4 64
Bobolice, Pol. C12 16
Bobonaza, stm., Ec. H3 86
Bobonong, Bots. B9 70
Bobr, Bela. F12 10
Bobtown, Pa., U.S. E5 114
Bobures, Ven. C6 86
Boby, mtn., Madag. E8 68
Bôca da Mata, Braz. E7 88
Boca do Acre, Braz. E4 84
Boca do Jari, Braz. D7 84
Bocage, Cap, c., N. Cal. m15 79d
Boca Grande, Fl., U.S. J3 116
Bocaiúva, Braz. I3 88
Bocaranga, C.A.R. C3 66
Boca Raton, Fl., U.S. J5 116
Bocas del Toro, Pan. H6 102
Bocay, Nic. E5 102
Bochnia, Pol. G16 16
Bocholt, Ger. E2 16
Bochum, Ger. E3 16
Bocón, Caño, stm., Col. F7 86
Boconó, Ven. C6 86
Bocșa, Rom. D8 26
Boda, C.A.R. D3 66
Bodajbo, Russia E11 34
Bodalla, Austl. K8 76
Bodcau Creek, stm., Ar., U.S. D5 122
Bode, Ia., U.S. I4 118
Bodélé, reg., Chad D3 62
Boden, Swe. D9 8
Bodensee see Constance, Lake, l., Eur. I5 16
Bodhan, India B3 53
Bodh Gaya, India F10 54
Bodināyakkanūr, India G3 53
Bodmin, Eng., U.K. K8 12
Bodø, Nor. C6 8
Bodoquena, Serra da, plat., Braz. D5 90
Bodrum, Tur. F10 28
Bodzentyn, Pol. F16 16
Boende, D.R.C. E4 66
Bœng Lvea, Camb. F7 48
Boeo, Capo, c., Italy G6 24
Boesmans, stm., S. Afr. H7 70
Boeuf, stm., U.S. E7 122
Boffa, Gui. G2 64
Bogale, Mya. D2 48
Bogalusa, La., U.S. G9 122
Bogan, stm., Austl. H6 76
Bogan Gate, Austl. I6 76
Bogangolo, C.A.R. C3 66
Bogata, Tx., U.S. D3 122
Bogcang, stm., China C11 54
Bogda Shan, mts., China C2 36
Bogen, Ger. H8 16
Boger City, N.C., U.S. A4 116
Boggabilla, Austl. G8 76
Boggabri, Austl. H7 76
Boggy Peak, mtn., Antig. f4 105b
Bogles, Gren. p11 105e
Bognor Regis, Eng., U.K. K12 12
Bogo, Phil. E5 52
Bogoljubovo, Russia E15 10
Bogong, Mount, mtn., Austl. K6 76
Bogor, Indon. G5 50
Bogorodick, Russia G21 10
Bogorodsk, Russia H20 8
Bogorodskoe, Russia F17 34
Bogotá see Santa Fe de Bogotá, Col E4 86
Bogotol, Russia C15 32
Bogra, Bngl. F12 54
Bogučany, Russia C17 32
Bogué, Maur. F2 64
Bogue Chitto, stm., U.S. G8 122
Bogue Phalia, stm., Ms., U.S. D8 122
Böğürtlen, Tur. A8 58
Bo Hai (Chihli, Gulf of), b., China B8 42
Bohai Haixia, strt., China B9 42
Bohain-en-Vermandois, Fr. D12 14
Bohai Wan, b., China B8 42
Bohemian Forest, mts., Eur. G8 16
Böhmer Wald see Bohemian Forest, mts., Eur. G8 16
Bohol, i., Phil. F4 52
Bohol Sea, Phil. F5 52
Boiaçu, Braz. H11 86
Boiano, Italy C8 24
Boiestown, N.B., Can. D10 110
Boipeba, Ilha de, i., Braz. G6 88
Bois, stm., Braz. C6 90
Bois, Lac des, l., N.T., Can. B6 106
Bois Blanc Island, i., Mi., U.S. C5 112
Bois de Sioux, stm., U.S. F2 118
Boise, Id., U.S. G10 136
Boise, stm., Id., U.S. G10 136
Boise, Middle Fork, stm., Id., U.S. G11 136
Boise, South Fork, stm., Id., U.S. G11 136
Boise City, Ok., U.S. E6 128
Boissevain, Mb., Can. E13 124
Boistfort Peak, mtn., Wa., U.S. D3 136
Boizenburg, Ger. C6 16
Boja, Indon. G7 50
Bojadła, Pol. E11 16
Bojeador, Cape, c., Phil. A3 52
Bojnūrd, Iran B8 56
Bojonegoro, Indon. G7 50
Bojuru, Braz. E12 92
Bokāro Steel City, India G10 54
Bokchito, Ok., U.S. C2 122
Boké, Gui. G2 64
Bokhara, stm., Austl. G6 76
Bok Koŭ, Camb. G6 48
Boknafjorden, strt., Nor. G1 8
Boko, Congo E2 66
Bokoro, Chad E3 62
Bokote, D.R.C. E4 66
Boksitogorsk, Russia A16 10
Bokungu, D.R.C. E4 66
Bol, Cro. G13 22
Bolama, Gui.-B. G1 64
Bolaños, stm., Mex. E7 100
Bolaños de Calatrava, Spain F7 20
Bolān Pass, p., Pak. D10 56
Bolayır, Tur. C9 28
Bolbec, Fr. E9 14
Bole, China F14 32
Bole, Ghana H4 64
Boles, Ar., U.S. C4 122
Bolesławiec, Pol. E11 16
Boley, Ok., U.S. B2 122
Bolgatanga, Ghana G4 64
Bolhov, Russia G18 10
Bolhrad, Ukr. D15 26
Boli, China B11 36
Boligee, Al., U.S. E10 122
Bolingbrook, Il., U.S. C9 120
Bolishan, China C5 38
Bolívar, Col. G3 86
Bolívar, Col. G3 86
Bolivar, Mo., U.S. G4 120
Bolivar, N.Y., U.S. B7 114
Bolivar, Tn., U.S. B9 122
Bolívar, state, Col. C4 86
Bolívar, state, Ec. H2 86
Bolívar, state, Ven. D10 86
Bolívar, Cerro, mtn., Ven. D10 86
Bolívar, Pico (La Columna), mtn., Ven. C6 86
Bolivar Peninsula, pen., Tx., U.S. H4 122
Bolivia, ctry., S.A. G5 84
Bollnäs, Swe. F7 8
Bollon, Austl. G6 76
Bolmen, l., Swe. H5 8
Bolobo, D.R.C. E3 66
Bologna, Italy F8 22
Bolognesi, Peru F3 84
Bologoe, Russia C17 10
Bologovo, Russia D14 10
Bolohovo, Russia F20 10
Bol'ŏj Anjuj, stm., Russia C21 34
Bolomba, D.R.C. D3 66
Bolon', ozero, l., Russia G16 34
Bolotnoe, Russia C14 32
Bolovens, Plateau des, plat., Laos E8 48
Bol'šaja Balahnja, stm., Russia B9 34
Bol'šaja Heta, stm., Russia C5 34
Bol'šaja Kuonamka, stm., Russia C10 34
Bol'šaja Murta, Russia C16 32
Bol'šaja Ussurka, stm., Russia B11 38
Bol'šaja Višera, Russia B15 10
Bol'šakovo, Russia F4 10
Bolsena, Italy H8 22
Bolsena, Lago di, l., Italy H9 22
Bol'šereče, Russia C13 32
Bol'šereck, Russia F20 34
Bol'ševik, Russia D18 34
Bol'ševik, ostrov, i., Russia A10 34
Bol'šezemel'skaja Tundra, reg., Russia A9 32
Bolshevik see Bol'ševik, ostrov, i., Russia A10 34
Bol'šie Uki, Russia C12 32
Bol'šoe Mihajlovskoe, Russia D20 10
Bol'šoe Polpino, Russia G17 10
Bol'šoe Selo, Russia C21 10
Bol'šoj Begičev, ostrov, i., Russia B11 34
Bol'šoj Jugan, stm., Russia B12 32
Bol'šoj Kamen', Russia C10 38
Bol'šoj Ljahovskij, ostrov, i., Russia B17 34
Bol'šoj Tal'cy, Russia A15 10
Bolton, On., Can. E10 112
Bolton, Eng., U.K. H10 12
Bolton, Ms., U.S. E8 122
Bolton, N.C., U.S. B7 116
Bolu, Tur. C14 28
Bolu, state, Tur. C14 28
Bolva, stm., Russia G17 10
Bolvadin, Tur. E13 28
Bóly, Hung. C5 26
Bolzano (Bozen), Italy D8 22
Boma, D.R.C. F2 66
Bomaderry, Austl. J8 76
Bombala, Austl. K7 76
Bombay see Mumbai, India B1 53
Bomberai, Semenanjung, pen., Indon. F9 44
Bomboma, D.R.C. D3 66
Bom Conselho, Braz. E7 88
Bom Despacho, Braz. J3 88
Bomdila, India E14 54
Bom Jesus, Braz. E3 88
Bom Jesus da Lapa, Braz. G4 88
Bomnak, Russia F14 34
Bomokandi, stm., D.R.C. D5 66
Bomongo, D.R.C. D3 66
Bom Retiro, Braz. C13 92
Bomu, stm., Afr. D4 66
Bon, Cap, c., Tun. G5 24
Bon Air, Va., U.S. G8 114
Bonaire, i., Neth. Ant. p23 104g
Bonampak, hist., Mex. D2 102
Bonandolok, Indon. C1 50
Bonanza, Or., U.S. A4 134
Bonanza, Ut., U.S. C7 132
Bonanza Peak, mtn., Wa., U.S. B5 136
Bonao, Dom. Rep. C12 102
Bonaparte, Ia., U.S. D6 120
Bonaparte, stm., B.C., Can. F9 138
Bonaparte, Mount, mtn., Wa., U.S. B7 136
Bonaparte Lake, l., B.C., Can. E10 138
Bonar Bridge, Scot., U.K. D8 12
Bonasse, Trin. s12 105f
Bonaventure, Qc., Can. B11 110
Bonaventure, stm., Qc., Can. B11 110
Bonaventure, Île, i., Qc., Can. B12 110
Bonavista, Nf., Can. j23 107a
Bonavista Bay, b., Nf., Can. j23 107a
Bondeno, Italy F8 22
Bondo, D.R.C. E4 66
Bondo, D.R.C. D4 66
Bondoc Peninsula, pen., Phil. D4 52
Bondoukou, C. Iv. H4 64
Bondowoso, Indon. G8 50
Bonduel, Wi., U.S. G10 118
Bone, Teluk, b., Indon. F7 44
Bonebone, Indon. E12 50
Boneogeh, Indon. G12 50
Bonerate, Pulau, i., Indon. G12 50
Bonesteel, S.D., U.S. D13 126
Bonete Chico, Cerro, mtn., Arg. D3 92
Bonete Grande, Cerro, mtn., Arg. C3 92
Bongabong, Phil. D3 52
Bongaigaon, India E13 54
Bongandanga, D.R.C. D4 66
Bongka, Indon. F7 44
Bongo, Gabon E2 66
Bongo, Massif des, mts., C.A.R. C4 66
Bongor, Chad E3 62
Bonham, Tx., U.S. D2 122
Bonhomme, Morne, mtn., Haiti C11 102
Bonifacio, Fr. H15 18
Bonifacio, Strait of, strt., Eur. H15 18
Bonifati, Capo, c., Italy E9 24
Bonin Islands see Ogasawara-guntō, is., Japan G18 30
Bonita, La., U.S. E7 122
Bonita Springs, Fl., U.S. J4 116
Bonito, Braz. E8 88
Bonito, Braz. D5 90
Bonito de Santa Fé, Braz. D6 88
Bonn, Ger. F2 16
Bonners Ferry, Id., U.S. B10 136
Bonnet, Lac du, res., Mb., Can. D17 124
Bonnétable, Fr. F9 14
Bonne Terre, Mo., U.S. G7 120
Bonnet Plume, stm., Yk., Can. B3 106
Bonneville, Fr. C12 18
Bonneville Peak, mtn., Id., U.S. H14 136
Bonneville Salt Flats, pl., Ut., U.S. C2 132
Bonney SE, Lake, l., Austl. K3 76
Bonnie Rock, Austl. F3 74
Bonny, Nig. I6 64
Bonnyville, Ab., Can. B20 138
Bono, Ar., U.S. I7 120
Bonoi, Indon. F10 44
Bonshaw, P.E., Can. D13 110
Bontang, Indon. C10 50
Bontebok National Park, p.o.i., S. Afr. I5 70
Bonthe, S.L. H2 64
Bontoc, Phil. B3 52
Bon Wier, Tx., U.S. G5 122
Booker, Tx., U.S. E8 128
Booker T. Washington National Monument, p.o.i., Va., U.S. H6 114
Boola, Gui. H3 64
Boolaloo, Austl. D3 74
Booleroo Centre, Austl. I2 76
Boologooro, Austl. D2 74
Boomarra, Austl. B3 76
Boonah, Austl. F9 76
Boone, Ia., U.S. I5 118
Boone, N.C., U.S. H4 114
Boone, stm., Ia., U.S. B4 120
Booneville, Ar., U.S. B5 122
Booneville, Ky., U.S. G2 114
Booneville, Ms., U.S. C10 122
Böön Tsagaan nuur, l., Mong. B4 36
Boonville, Ca., U.S. D2 134
Boonville, Mo., U.S. F5 120
Boonville, N.Y., U.S. E14 112
Boorindal, Austl. H6 76
Booroorban, Austl. J5 76
Boosaaso, Som. B9 66
Booth, Al., U.S. E12 122
Boothbay Harbor, Me., U.S. G7 110
Boothia, Gulf of, b., N.T., Can. A12 106
Boothia Peninsula, pen., N.T., Can. A12 106
Boothville, La., U.S. H9 122
Booué, Gabon E2 66
Bophuthatswana, hist. reg., S. Afr. E7 70
Boping Ling, mts., China I7 42
Bopolu, Lib. H2 64
Boqueirão, Serra do, hills, Braz. F4 88
Boquilla, Presa de la, res., Mex. B6 100
Boquim, Braz. F7 88
Bor, Russia H20 8
Bor, Russia E20 8
Bor, Sudan F6 62
Bor, Tur. B3 56
Bor, Yugo. E9 26

Bor-Bula I•9

Name	Map Ref.	Page
Bor, Lak, stm., Kenya	D7	66
Bora-Bora, i., Fr. Poly.	E11	72
Borabu, Thai.	E6	48
Borah Peak, mtn., Id., U.S.	F13	136
Borås, Swe.	H5	8
Borba, Braz.	D6	84
Bordeaux, Fr.	E5	18
Bordeaux Mountain, hill, V.I.U.S.	e8	104b
Borden, Sk., Can.	B6	124
Borden Peninsula, pen., N.T., Can.	A14	106
Bordertown, Austl.	K3	76
Bordesholm, Ger.	B6	16
Bordighera, Italy	G4	22
Bordj Menaïel, Alg.	H14	20
Bordj Omar Idriss, Alg.	D6	64
Borđoy, i., Far. Is.	m34	8b
Borgå see Porvoo, Fin.	F11	8
Borgarnes, Ice.	k28	8a
Børgefjell Nasjonalpark, p.o.i., Nor.	D5	8
Borger, Tx., U.S.	F7	128
Borgholm, Swe.	H7	8
Borgne, Lake, b., La., U.S.	G9	122
Borgnesse, Pointe, c., Mart.	I7	105c
Borgomanero, Italy	E5	22
Borgo San Dalmazzo, Italy	F4	22
Borgosesia, Italy	E5	22
Borgo Val di Taro, Italy	F6	22
Borgworm see Waremme, Bel.	D14	14
Borikhan, Laos	C6	48
Borisoglebsk, Russia	D6	32
Borisoglebskij, Russia	C21	10
Borjas Blancas see Les Borges Blanques, Spain	C11	20
Borkavičy, Bela.	E11	10
Borken, Ger.	E2	16
Borkou, reg., Chad	D3	62
Borkum, i., Ger.	C2	16
Borlänge, Swe.	F6	8
Bormes, Fr.	F12	18
Borna, Ger.	E9	16
Borneo (Kalimantan), i., Asia	E5	44
Bornholm, state, Den.	I6	8
Bornholm, i., Den.	I6	8
Borocay Island, i., Phil.	E3	52
Borodino, Russia	C17	32
Borogoncy, Russia	D15	34
Borohoro Shan, mts., China	F14	32
Boromo, Burkina	G4	64
Boron, Ca., U.S.	H8	134
Boronga Islands, is., Mya.	I14	54
Borongan, Phil.	E5	52
Borovan, Blg.	F10	26
Borovići, Russia	B16	10
Borovljanka, Russia	D14	32
Borovsk, Russia	E19	10
Borovskij, Russia	C11	32
Borovskoj, Kaz.	D10	32
Borrachudo, stm., Braz.	J3	88
Borrazópolis, Braz.	A12	92
Borriana, Spain	E10	20
Borroloola, Austl.	C7	74
Borș, Rom.	B8	26
Borșa, Rom.	B11	26
Borsad, India	G4	54
Borščovočnyj hrebet, mts., Russia	F12	34
Borsod-Abaúj-Zemplén, state, Hung.	A8	26
Bort-les-Orgues, Fr.	D8	18
Borūjerd, Iran	C6	56
Borzja, Russia	F12	34
Bosa, Italy	D2	24
Bosanska Dubica, Bos.	D3	26
Bosanska Gradiška, Bos.	D4	26
Bosanska Krupa, Bos.	E3	26
Bosanski Novi, Bos.	D3	26
Bosanski Šamac, Bos.	D5	26
Bosavi, Mount, mtn., Pap. N. Gui.	b3	79a
Boscobel, Wi., U.S.	A7	120
Bose, China	J2	42
Boshan, China	C7	42
Boshof, S. Afr.	F7	70
Bosilegrad, Yugo.	G9	26
Bosna, stm., Bos.	E5	26
Bosnia and Herzegovina, ctry., Eur.	E3	26
Bosnik, Indon.	F10	44
Bošnjakovo, Russia	G17	34
Bosobolo, D.R.C.	D3	66
Bōsō-hantō, pen., Japan	D13	40
Bosporus see İstanbul Boğazı, strt., Tur.	B12	28
Bossangoa, C.A.R.	C3	66
Bossembélé, C.A.R.	C3	66
Bossey Bangou, Niger	G5	64
Bossier City, La., U.S.	E5	122
Bosten Hu, l., China	C2	36
Boston, Eng., U.K.	H12	12
Boston, Ga., U.S.	F2	116
Boston, Ma., U.S.	B14	114
Boston Bar, B.C., Can.	G9	138
Boston Mountains, mts., Ar., U.S.	B5	122
Boswell, In., U.S.	H2	112
Boswell, Ok., U.S.	C3	122
Bosworth, Mo., U.S.	E4	120
Botād, India	G3	54
Botany Bay, b., Austl.	J8	76
Boteti, stm., Bots.	E3	68
Bothaville, S. Afr.	E8	70
Bothnia, Gulf of, b., Eur.	E9	8
Bothwell, On., Can.	F8	112
Boticas, Port.	C3	20
Botna, stm., Mol.	C15	26
Botoșani, Rom.	B13	26
Botoșani, state, Rom.	B13	26
Bo Trach, Viet.	D8	48
Botrange, mtn., Bel.	D15	14
Botswana, ctry., Afr.	E3	68
Botte Donato, Monte, mtn., Italy	E10	24
Bottineau, N.D., U.S.	F13	124
Botucatu, Braz.	L1	88
Botwood, Nf., Can.	j22	107a
Bouaflé, C. Iv.	H3	64
Bouaké, C. Iv.	H3	64
Bouar, C.A.R.	C3	66
Bouârfa, Mor.	C4	64
Bouca, C.A.R.	C3	66
Boucher, stm., Qc., Can.	A7	110
Bouches-du-Rhône, state, Fr.	F11	18
Bouctouche, N.B., Can.	D12	110
Boufarik, Alg.	H13	20
Bou Ficha, Tun.	H4	24
Bougainville, i., Pap. N. Gui.	d7	79b
Bougainville, Détroit de, strt., Vanuatu	j16	79d
Bougainville Strait, strt., Oc.	d7	79b
Bougouni, Mali	G3	64
Bouillante, Guad.	h5	105c
Bouillon, Bel.	E14	14
Bouïra, Alg.	B5	64
Boujdour, Cap, c., W. Sah.	D2	64
Boularderie Island, i., N.S., Can.	D16	110
Boulder, Co., U.S.	A3	128
Boulder, Mt., U.S.	D14	136
Boulder, stm., Mt., U.S.	D15	136
Boulder City, Nv., U.S.	H2	132
Boulia, Austl.	D2	76
Boulogne-sur-Mer, Fr.	D10	14
Bouloupari, N. Cal.	m15	79d
Boulsa, Burkina	G4	64
Bou Medfaa, Alg.	H13	20
Bouna, C. Iv.	H4	64
Boundary Peak, mtn., Nv., U.S.	F7	134
Boundiali, C. Iv.	H3	64
Boun Nua, Laos	B5	48
Bountiful, Ut., U.S.	C4	132
Bounty Bay, b., Pit.	c28	78k
Bounty Islands, is., N.Z.	H8	80
Bounty Trough, unds.	N20	142
Bourail, N. Cal.	m15	79d
Bourbeuse, stm., Mo., U.S.	F6	120
Bourbon, In., U.S.	G3	112
Bourbonnais, hist. reg., Fr.	C9	18
Bourbonne-les-Bains, Fr.	G14	14
Bourem, Mali	F4	64
Bourg, La., U.S.	H8	122
Bourg-en-Bresse, Fr.	C11	18
Bourges, Fr.	G11	14
Bourget, On., Can.	E1	110
Bourget, Lac du, l., Fr.	D11	18
Bourgogne (Burgundy), hist. reg., Fr.	B10	18
Bourgogne, Canal de, can., Fr.	G13	14
Bourgoin-Jallieu, Fr.	D11	18
Bourke, Austl.	H5	76
Bournemouth, Eng., U.K.	K11	12
Bou Saâda, Alg.	B5	64
Bou Salem, Tun.	H2	24
Bouse Wash, stm., Az., U.S.	J3	132
Bou Smail, Alg.	H13	20
Boussac, Fr.	C8	18
Bousso, Chad	E3	62
Boutilimit, Maur.	F2	64
Bouvetøya, i., Ant.	A5	81
Bouza, Niger	G6	64
Bøvågen, Nor.	F1	8
Bovec, Slvn.	D10	22
Bovey, Mn., U.S.	D5	118
Bovill, Id., U.S.	D10	136
Bovina, Tx., U.S.	G6	128
Bow, stm., Ab., Can.	G19	138
Bo-Wadrif, S. Afr.	H4	70
Bowbells, N.D., U.S.	F11	124
Bow Creek, stm., Ks., U.S.	B9	128
Bowden, Ab., Can.	E16	138
Bowdle, S.D., U.S.	B13	126
Bowdon, N.D., U.S.	G14	124
Bowen, Arg.	G4	92
Bowen, Austl.	C7	76
Bowen, Il., U.S.	D7	120
Bowen, stm., Austl.	C6	76
Bowie, Az., U.S.	K7	132
Bowie, Md., U.S.	F9	114
Bowling Green, Fl., U.S.	I4	116
Bowling Green, Ky., U.S.	H11	120
Bowling Green, Mo., U.S.	E6	120
Bowling Green, Oh., U.S.	C2	114
Bowling Green, Va., U.S.	F8	114
Bowling Green, Cape, c., Austl.	B6	76
Bowling Green Bay National Park, p.o.i., Austl.	B6	76
Bowman, N.D., U.S.	A9	126
Bowman, S.C., U.S.	C5	116
Bowman, Mount, mtn., B.C., Can.	E9	138
Bowmanville, On., Can.	E11	112
Bowral, Austl.	J8	76
Bowraville, Austl.	H9	76
Bowron, stm., B.C., Can.	C9	138
Bowsman, Mb., Can.	B12	124
Boxelder Creek, stm., U.S.	B8	126
Box Elder Creek, stm., Mt., U.S.	G5	124
Boxelder Creek, stm., S.D., U.S.	C10	126
Boxing, China	C8	42
Boyacá, state, Col.	E5	86
Boyang, China	G7	42
Boyce, La., U.S.	F6	122
Boyceville, Wi., U.S.	F6	118
Boyd, Tx., U.S.	A10	130
Boyd, stm., Austl.	G9	76
Boydton, Va., U.S.	H7	114
Boyer, stm., Ia., U.S.	C2	120
Boyertown, Pa., U.S.	D10	114
Boykins, Va., U.S.	H8	114
Boyle, Ms., U.S.	D8	122
Boylston, Al., U.S.	E12	122
Boyne, stm., Austl.	E8	76
Boyne, stm., Mb., Can.	E16	124
Boyne, stm., Ire.	H5	12
Boyne City, Mi., U.S.	C5	112
Boynton Beach, Fl., U.S.	J5	116
Boysen Reservoir, res., Wy., U.S.	D4	126
Boys Ranch, Tx., U.S.	F6	128
Bozburun, Tur.	G11	28
Bozburun Yarımadası, pen., Tur.	G11	28
Boz Dağ, mtn., Tur.	E11	28
Boz Dağlar, mts., Tur.	E10	28
Bozdoğan, Tur.	F11	28
Bozeman, Mt., U.S.	E15	136
Bozen see Bolzano, Italy	D8	22
Bozhen, China	B7	42
Bozhou, China	E6	42
Bozkurt, Tur.	F12	28
Bozoum, C.A.R.	C3	66
Bozova, Tur.	A9	58
Bozovici, Rom.	E9	26
Bozšakol', Kaz.	D12	32
Bozüyük, Tur.	D13	28
Bra, Italy	F4	22
Brač, Otok, i., Cro.	G13	22
Bracciano, Italy	H9	22
Bracciano, Lago di, l., Italy	H9	22
Bracebridge, On., Can.	C10	112
Brackendale, B.C., Can.	G7	138
Brackettville, Tx., U.S.	E7	130
Bracknell, Eng., U.K.	J12	12
Braço do Norte, Braz.	D13	92
Brad, Rom.	C9	26
Bradano, stm., Italy	D10	24
Bradenton, Fl., U.S.	I3	116
Bradford, Eng., U.K.	H11	12
Bradford, Ar., U.S.	B7	122
Bradford, Pa., U.S.	C7	114
Bradford, Tn., U.S.	H9	120
Bradford, Vt., U.S.	G4	110
Bradford West Gwillimbury, On., Can.	D10	112
Bradley, Ar., U.S.	D5	122
Bradley, Fl., U.S.	I3	116
Bradley, Il., U.S.	G2	112
Bradley, S.D., U.S.	B15	126
Brady, Mt., U.S.	B15	136
Brady, Ne., U.S.	F12	126
Brady, Tx., U.S.	C8	130
Brady Creek, stm., Tx., U.S.	C8	130
Braga, Port.	C2	20
Braga, state, Port.	C2	20
Bragado, Arg.	G7	92
Bragança, Braz.	D8	84
Bragança, Port.	C4	20
Bragança, state, Port.	C4	20
Bragança Paulista, Braz.	L2	88
Brāhmanbāria, Bngl.	F13	54
Brāhmani, stm., India	H10	54
Brahmapur, India	B7	53
Brahmaputra (Yarlung), stm., Asia	C7	46
Braich y Pwll, c., Wales, U.K.	I8	12
Braidwood, Austl.	J7	76
Braidwood, Il., U.S.	C9	120
Brăila, Rom.	D14	26
Brăila, state, Rom.	D14	26
Brainard, Ne., U.S.	F15	126
Brainerd, Mn., U.S.	E4	118
Braintree, Eng., U.K.	J13	12
Brak, stm., S. Afr.	G6	70
Brake, Ger.	C4	16
Bralorne, B.C., Can.	F8	138
Brampton, On., Can.	E10	112
Bramsche, Ger.	D3	16
Branchville, S.C., U.S.	C5	116
Branco, stm., Braz.	H11	86
Branco, stm., Braz.	F3	88
Brandaris, hill, Neth. Ant.	p23	104g
Brandberg, mtn., Nmb.	B2	70
Brandbu, Nor.	F4	8
Brandenburg, Ger.	D8	16
Brandenburg, Ky., U.S.	G11	120
Brandenburg, state, Ger.	D9	16
Brandfort, S. Afr.	F8	70
Brandon, Mb., Can.	E14	124
Brandon, Fl., U.S.	I3	116
Brandon, Ms., U.S.	E9	122
Brandon, S.D., U.S.	H2	118
Brandon, Vt., U.S.	G3	110
Brandsen, Arg.	G8	92
Brandvlei, S. Afr.	G5	70
Brandy Peak, mtn., Or., U.S.	H3	136
Brandýs nad Labem-Stará Boleslav, Czech Rep.	F10	16
Branford, Fl., U.S.	G2	116
Braniewo, Pol.	B15	16
Bransby, Austl.	G4	76
Bransby Point, c., Monts.	D3	105a
Bransfield Strait, strt., Ant.	B35	81
Branson, Mo., U.S.	H4	120
Brantford, On., Can.	E9	112
Brantley, Al., U.S.	F12	122
Brantley Tank, res., N.M., U.S.	B3	130
Brantôme, Fr.	D6	18
Brantville, N.B., Can.	C12	110
Bras d'Or Lake, l., N.S., Can.	E16	110
Brasiléia, Braz.	F4	84
Brasília, Braz.	H1	88
Brasília, Parque Nacional de, p.o.i., Braz.	H1	88
Brasília de Minas, Braz.	I3	88
Braslau, Bela.	E9	10
Brașov, Rom.	D12	26
Brașov, state, Rom.	D12	26
Brassey, Banjaran, mts., Malay.	A10	50
Brass Islands, is., V.I.U.S.	e7	104b
Brasstown Bald, mtn., Ga., U.S.	B2	116
Bratca, Rom.	C9	26
Bratislava, Slov.	H13	16
Bratislava, state, Slov.	H13	16
Bratsk, Russia	C18	32
Bratskoe vodohranilišče, res., Russia	C18	32
Bratsk Reservoir see Bratskoe vodohranilišče, res., Russia	C18	32
Brattleboro, Vt., U.S.	B13	114
Braulio Carrillo, Parque Nacional, p.o.i., C.R.	G5	102
Braúnas, Braz.	J4	88
Braunau am Inn, Aus.	B10	22
Braunschweig (Brunswick), Ger.	D6	16
Brava, i., C.V.	I10	65a
Brava, Costa, cst., Spain	C14	20
Brava, Laguna, l., Arg.	D3	92
Brava, Punta, c., Ur.	G9	92
Brave, Pa., U.S.	E5	114
Bravo (Rio Grande), stm., N.A.	H13	98
Bravo, Cerro, mtn., Peru	E2	84
Bravo del Norte see Bravo, stm., N.A.	H13	98
Brawley, Ca., U.S.	K10	134
Bray, Ire.	H6	12
Bray Island, i., N.T., Can.	B15	106
Brazeau, stm., Ab., Can.	D15	138
Brazeau, Mount, mtn., Ab., Can.	D13	138
Brazeau Dam, dam, Ab., Can.	C15	138
Brazil, In., U.S.	E10	120
Brazil, ctry., S.A.	F9	82
Brazil Basin, unds.	J11	144
Brazoria, Tx., U.S.	E12	130
Brazos, stm., Tx., U.S.	E8	108
Brazos, Clear Fork, stm., Tx., U.S.	B8	130
Brazos, Double Mountain Fork, stm., Tx., U.S.	H8	128
Brazos, North Fork, stm., Tx., U.S.	H3	122
Brazzaville, Congo	E2	66
Brčko, Bos.	E5	26
Brda, stm., Pol.	C13	16
Bré see Bray, Ire.	H6	12
Brea, Ca., U.S.	J8	134
Bream Bay, b., N.Z.	B6	80
Brea Pozo, Arg.	D6	92
Breaux Bridge, La., U.S.	G7	122
Brebes, Indon.	G6	50
Brechin, Scot., U.K.	E10	12
Breckenridge, Mi., U.S.	E5	112
Breckenridge, Mn., U.S.	E2	118
Breckenridge, Mo., U.S.	E4	120
Brecknock, Península, pen., Chile	J2	90
Břeclav, Czech Rep.	H12	16
Brecon, Wales, U.K.	J9	12
Brecon Beacons, hills, Wales, U.K.	J9	12
Brecon Beacons National Park, p.o.i., Wales, U.K.	J9	12
Breda, Neth.	C13	14
Breda, Ia., U.S.	B3	120
Bredasdorp, S. Afr.	I5	70
Bredenbury, Sk., Can.	D11	124
Bredy, Russia	D9	32
Breë, stm., S. Afr.	I5	70
Breese, Il., U.S.	F8	120
Bregalnica, stm., Mac.	A5	28
Bregenz, Aus.	C6	22
Bregovo, Blg.	E9	26
Bréhat, Île de, i., Fr.	F6	14
Breiđafjörđur, b., Ice.	k28	8a
Brejinho de Nazaré, Braz.	F1	88
Brejo, Braz.	B4	88
Brejo Grande, Braz.	F7	88
Brejo Santo, Braz.	D6	88
Brekstad, Nor.	E3	8
Bremen, Ger.	C4	16
Bremen, Ga., U.S.	D13	122
Bremen, Oh., U.S.	E3	114
Bremen, state, Ger.	C4	16
Bremer Bay, Austl.	F3	74
Bremer Bay, b., Austl.	F3	74
Bremerhaven, Ger.	C4	16
Bremerton, Wa., U.S.	C4	136
Bremervörde, Ger.	C4	16
Bremond, Tx., U.S.	F2	122
Brenham, Tx., U.S.	G2	122
Brenner Pass, p., Eur.	C8	22
Brent, Fl., U.S.	G11	122
Brenta, stm., Italy	D8	22
Brentwood, Eng., U.K.	J13	12
Brentwood, N.Y., U.S.	D12	114
Brentwood, Tn., U.S.	H11	120
Breo, Italy	F4	22
Brescia, Italy	E7	22
Breslau see Wrocław, Pol.	E13	16
Bressanone, Italy	D8	22
Bressay, i., Scot., U.K.	n18	12a
Bresse, reg., Fr.	C11	18
Bressuire, Fr.	H8	14
Brèst, Bela.	H6	10
Brest, Fr.	F4	14
Brèst, state, Bela.	H8	10
Bretagne (Brittany), hist. reg., Fr.	F5	14
Bretenoux, Fr.	E7	18
Breton, Ab., Can.	C16	138
Breton Islands, is., La., U.S.	H9	122
Breton Sound, strt., La., U.S.	H9	122
Brett, Cape, c., N.Z.	B6	80
Bretten, Ger.	G4	16
Breueh, Pulau, i., Indon.	J2	48
Breuil-Cervinia, Italy	E4	22
Brevard, N.C., U.S.	A3	116
Breves, Braz.	D7	84
Brevoort Island, i., N.T., Can.	E13	141
Brewarrina, Austl.	G6	76
Brewer, Me., U.S.	F8	110
Brewster, Mn., U.S.	H3	118
Brewster, Ne., U.S.	F13	126
Brewster, Wa., U.S.	B7	136
Brewster, Kap, c., Grnld.	C21	141
Brewton, Al., U.S.	F11	122
Breyten, S. Afr.	E10	70
Březnice, Czech Rep.	G9	16
Brezno, Slov.	H15	16
Bria, C.A.R.	C4	66
Brian Boru Peak, mtn., B.C., Can.	A3	138
Briançon, Fr.	E12	18
Brian Head, mtn., Ut., U.S.	F4	132
Briare, Canal de, can., Fr.	G11	14
Bribie Island, i., Austl.	F9	76
Bricelyn, Mn., U.S.	H5	118
Briceni, Mol.	A14	26
Briceville, Tn., U.S.	A14	122
Bri Chuallan see Bray, Ire.	H6	12
Bridge, stm., B.C., Can.	F7	138
Bridge City, Tx., U.S.	G5	122
Bridge Lake, B.C., Can.	E10	138
Bridgend, Wales, U.K.	J9	12
Bridgeport, Ca., U.S.	E6	134
Bridgeport, Ct., U.S.	C12	114
Bridgeport, Mi., U.S.	E6	112
Bridgeport, Ne., U.S.	F9	126
Bridgeport, Tx., U.S.	H11	128
Bridgeport, Wa., U.S.	C7	136
Bridgeport, Lake, res., Tx., U.S.	H10	128
Bridger, Mt., U.S.	B4	126
Bridger Peak, mtn., Wy., U.S.	B9	132
Bridgeton, N.J., U.S.	E10	114
Bridgetown, Austl.	F3	74
Bridgetown, Barb.	n8	105d
Bridgetown, N.S., Can.	F11	110
Bridgeville, De., U.S.	F10	114
Bridgewater, N.S., Can.	F12	110
Bridgewater, Ma., U.S.	B15	114
Bridgewater, S.D., U.S.	D15	126
Bridgewater, Va., U.S.	F6	114
Bridgwater, Eng., U.K.	J9	12
Bridgwater Bay, b., Eng., U.K.	J9	12
Bridlington, Eng., U.K.	G12	12
Bridport, Eng., U.K.	K10	12
Brie, reg., Fr.	F12	14
Brier Creek, stm., Ga., U.S.	C4	116
Brig, Switz.	D5	22
Briggs, Tx., U.S.	D10	130
Brigham City, Ut., U.S.	B4	132
Bright, Austl.	K6	76
Brighton, On., Can.	D12	112
Brighton, Eng., U.K.	K12	12
Brighton, Co., U.S.	A4	128
Brighton, Ia., U.S.	C6	120
Brighton, Mi., U.S.	B2	114
Brighton, N.Y., U.S.	E12	112
Brighton Downs, Austl.	D3	76
Brignoles, Fr.	F11	18
Brijuni, i., Cro.	F10	22
Brilliant, B.C., Can.	G13	138
Brilliant, Al., U.S.	C11	122
Brillion, Wi., U.S.	D1	112
Brilon, Ger.	E4	16
Brindisi, Italy	D11	24
Brinkworth, Austl.	I2	76
Brion, Île, i., Qc., Can.	C15	110
Brioude, Fr.	D9	18
Brisbane, Austl.	F9	76
Brisighella, Italy	F8	22
Bristol, Eng., U.K.	J10	12
Bristol, Ct., U.S.	C12	114
Bristol, Fl., U.S.	G14	122
Bristol, N.H., U.S.	G5	110
Bristol, Pa., U.S.	D11	114
Bristol, R.I., U.S.	C14	114
Bristol, Tn., U.S.	H3	114
Bristol, Vt., U.S.	F3	110
Bristol Bay, b., Ak., U.S.	E7	140
Bristol Channel, strt., U.K.	J8	12
Bristol Island, i., S. Geor.	A2	81
Bristol Lake, l., Ca., U.S.	I10	134
Bristow, Ok., U.S.	B2	122
Britannia Beach, B.C., Can.	G7	138
British Columbia, state, Can.	E5	106
British Guiana see Guyana, ctry., S.A.	C6	84
British Honduras see Belize, ctry., N.A.	D3	102
British Indian Ocean Territory, dep., Afr.	G17	2
British Isles, is., Eur.	C12	4
British Mountains, mts., N.A.	C11	140
British Solomon Islands see Solomon Islands, ctry., Oc.	D7	72
British Virgin Islands, dep., N.A.	h15	96a
Brits, S. Afr.	D8	70
Britstown, S. Afr.	G6	70
Britt, Ia., U.S.	A4	120
Brittany see Bretagne, hist. reg., Fr.	F5	14
Britton, S.D., U.S.	B15	126
Brive-la-Gaillarde, Fr.	D7	18
Brixen see Bressanone, Italy	D8	22
Brixham, Eng., U.K.	K9	12
Brixton, Austl.	D5	76
Brjanka, Russia	C16	32
Brjansk, Russia	G17	10
Brjanskaja oblast', co., Russia	H16	10
Brno, Czech Rep.	G12	16
Broa, Ensenada de la, b., Cuba	A6	102
Broad, stm., U.S.	B4	116
Broad, stm., Ga., U.S.	B2	116
Broadalbin, N.Y., U.S.	G2	110
Broad Sound, b., Austl.	D7	76
Broad Sound Channel, strt., Austl.	C8	76
Broadus, Mt., U.S.	B7	126
Broadwater, Ne., U.S.	F10	126
Broadway, Va., U.S.	F7	114
Broceni, Lat.	D5	10
Brochet, Mb., Can.	D10	106
Brock, Sk., Can.	C5	124
Brockman, Mount, mtn., Austl.	D3	74
Brockton, Ma., U.S.	B14	114
Brockton, Mt., U.S.	F9	124
Brockville, On., Can.	D14	112
Brockway, Pa., U.S.	C7	114
Brocton, N.Y., U.S.	B6	114
Brodeur Peninsula, pen., N.T., Can.	A13	106
Brodhead, Wi., U.S.	B8	120
Brodick, Scot., U.K.	F7	12
Brodnax, Va., U.S.	H7	114
Brodnica, Pol.	C15	16
Brogan, Or., U.S.	F9	136
Brok, Pol.	D17	16
Broken Arrow, Ok., U.S.	H2	120
Broken Bay, b., Austl.	I8	76
Broken Bow, Ok., U.S.	C4	122
Broken Bow Lake, res., Ok., U.S.	C4	122
Broken Hill, Austl.	H3	76
Broken Hill see Kabwe, Zam.	C4	68
Broken Ridge, unds.	M12	142
Brokopondo, Sur.	B6	84
Brokopondo Stuwmeer, res., Sur.	C6	84
Bromley Plateau, unds.	K10	144
Bromptonville, Qc., Can.	E4	110
Bromsgrove, Eng., U.K.	I10	12
Bronkhorstspruit, S. Afr.	D9	70
Bronlund Peak, mtn., B.C., Can.	D5	106
Bronnae, Bela.	H13	10
Bronnicy, Russia	E21	10
Bronson, Fl., U.S.	G3	116
Bronson, Ks., U.S.	G2	120
Bronson, Mi., U.S.	G4	112
Bronte, Italy	G8	24
Bronte, Tx., U.S.	C7	130
Brook, In., U.S.	H2	112
Brookeland, Tx., U.S.	F5	122
Brooker, Fl., U.S.	G3	116
Brookfield, N.S., Can.	E13	110
Brookfield, Wi., U.S.	E1	112
Brookford, N.C., U.S.	I4	114
Brookhaven, Ms., U.S.	F8	122
Brookings, Or., U.S.	A1	134
Brookings, S.D., U.S.	G2	118
Brookland, Ar., U.S.	B8	122
Brooklyn, N.S., Can.	F12	110
Brooklyn, Ia., U.S.	J6	118
Brooklyn, Mi., U.S.	B1	114
Brooklyn Center, Mn., U.S.	F5	118
Brookmere, B.C., Can.	G10	138
Brookneal, Va., U.S.	G7	114
Brookport, Il., U.S.	G9	120
Brooks, Ab., Can.	F19	138
Brooks Bay, b., B.C., Can.	F2	138
Brookshire, Tx., U.S.	H3	122
Brooks Range, mts., Ak., U.S.	C8	140
Brooksville, Fl., U.S.	H3	116
Brooksville, Ms., U.S.	D10	122
Brookville, In., U.S.	E12	120
Brookville, Pa., U.S.	C6	114
Brookville Lake, res., In., U.S.	E13	120
Broome, Austl.	C4	74
Broomfield, Co., U.S.	B3	128
Brooten, Mn., U.S.	F3	118
Brora, Scot., U.K.	C9	12
Brosna, stm., Ire.	H5	12
Brotas de Macaúbas, Braz.	G4	88
Brou, Fr.	F10	14
Broughton, Mount, mtn., Austl.	K5	76
Broughty Ferry, Scot., U.K.	E10	12
Browerville, Mn., U.S.	E4	118
Brown, Mount, mtn., Mt., U.S.	B15	136
Brown, Point, c., Wa., U.S.	D2	136
Brown Deer, Wi., U.S.	E2	112
Browne Bay, b., N.T., Can.	A11	106
Brownfield, Tx., U.S.	A5	130
Browning, Mo., U.S.	D4	120
Browning, Mt., U.S.	B13	136
Brownlee Reservoir, res., U.S.	F9	136
Brownsburg, Qc., Can.	E2	110
Brownsburg, In., U.S.	I3	112
Brownsdale, Mn., U.S.	H5	118
Browns Town, Jam.	i13	104d
Brownstown, In., U.S.	F11	120
Brownsville, Ky., U.S.	G11	120
Brownsville, La., U.S.	E6	122
Brownsville, Or., U.S.	F4	136
Brownsville, Tn., U.S.	B9	122
Brownsville, Tx., U.S.	I10	130
Brownton, Mn., U.S.	G4	118
Brownville, Me., U.S.	E7	110
Brownville, Ne., U.S.	D2	120
Brownville Junction, Me., U.S.	E7	110
Brownwood, Tx., U.S.	C8	130
Brownwood, Lake, res., Tx., U.S.	C9	130
Browse Island, i., Austl.	B4	74
Broxton, Ga., U.S.	E3	116
Broža, Bela.	H12	10
Bruay-en-Artois, Fr.	D11	14
Bruce, S.D., U.S.	G2	118
Bruce, Wi., U.S.	F7	118
Bruce, Mount, mtn., Austl.	D3	74
Bruce Mines, On., Can.	B6	112
Bruce Peninsula, pen., On., Can.	C8	112
Bruce Peninsula National Park, p.o.i., On., Can.	C8	112
Bruce Rock, Austl.	F3	74
Bruchsal, Ger.	G4	16
Bruck an der Leitha, Aus.	B13	22
Bruck an der Mur, Aus.	C12	22
Bruges see Brugge, Bel.	C12	14
Brugg, Switz.	C5	22
Brugge (Bruges), Bel.	C12	14
Brühl, Ger.	F2	16
Bruit, Pulau, i., Malay.	B7	50
Brule, Ne., U.S.	F11	126
Brumado, Braz.	H5	88
Brundidge, Al., U.S.	F13	122
Bruneau, Id., U.S.	H11	136
Bruneau, stm., U.S.	H11	136
Bruneck see Brunico, Italy	D8	22
Brunei, ctry., Asia	A9	50
Brunico, Italy	D8	22
Brunsbüttel, Ger.	C4	16
Brunson, S.C., U.S.	D4	116
Brunswick see Braunschweig, Ger.	D6	16
Brunswick, Ga., U.S.	E4	116
Brunswick, Me., U.S.	G6	110
Brunswick, Md., U.S.	E8	114
Brunswick, Mo., U.S.	E4	120
Brunswick, Oh., U.S.	C4	114
Brunswick, Península, pen., Chile	J2	90
Bruntál, Czech Rep.	F13	16
Brus, Laguna de, b., Hond.	E5	102
Brush, Co., U.S.	A5	128
Brusovo, Russia	C18	10
Brusque, Braz.	C13	92
Brussel see Bruxelles, Bel.	D13	14
Brussels see Bruxelles, Bel.	D13	14
Brussels, On., Can.	E8	112
Bruthen, Austl.	K6	76
Bruxelles (Brussels), Bel.	D13	14
Bruzual, Ven.	D7	86
Bryan, Oh., U.S.	C1	114
Bryan, Tx., U.S.	G2	122
Bryan, Mount, mtn., Austl.	I2	76
Bryant, Ar., U.S.	C6	122
Bryce Canyon National Park, p.o.i., Ut., U.S.	F4	132
Bryli, Bela.	G13	10
Bryson, Qc., Can.	C13	112
Bryson, Tx., U.S.	A9	130
Brzeg, Pol.	F13	16
Brześć Kujawski, Pol.	D14	16
Brzesko, Pol.	F16	16
Brzeziny, Pol.	E15	16
Bsharrī, Leb.	D6	58
Bua, Fiji	p19	79e
Bua Bay, b., Fiji	p19	79e
Buada Lagoon, b., Nauru	q17	78f
Buala, Sol. Is.	e8	79b
Bua Yai, Thai.	E6	48
Bubanza, Bdi.	E5	66
Bubaque, Gui.-B.	G1	64
Bubi, stm., Zimb.	B10	70
Būbiyān, i., Kuw.	D6	56
Bubuduo, China	C10	54
Bucak, Tur.	F13	28
Bucaramanga, Col.	D5	86
Buccaneer Archipelago, is., Austl.	C4	74
Buchanan, Sk., Can.	C11	124
Buchanan, Lib.	H2	64
Buchanan, Ga., U.S.	D13	122
Buchanan, Mi., U.S.	G3	112
Buchanan, Lake, l., Austl.	C5	76
Buchanan, Lake, l., Tx., U.S.	D9	130
Buchan Ness, c., Scot., U.K.	D11	12
Buchans, Nf., Can.	j22	107a
Bucharest see București, Rom.	E13	26
Buchen, Ger.	G5	16
Buchholz in der Nordheide, Ger.	C5	16
Buchloe, Ger.	H6	16
Buchon, Point, c., Ca., U.S.	H4	134
Buchs, Switz.	C6	22
Buckatunna, Ms., U.S.	F10	122
Buckatunna Creek, stm., Ms., U.S.	F10	122
Bückeburg, Ger.	D5	16
Buckeye, Az., U.S.	J4	132
Buckeye Lake, Oh., U.S.	I7	112
Buckhaven, Scot., U.K.	E9	12
Buckholts, Tx., U.S.	D10	130
Buckhorn Draw, stm., Tx., U.S.	D7	130
Buckie, Scot., U.K.	D10	12
Buckingham, Qc., Can.	C14	112
Buckingham, Va., U.S.	G7	114
Buckingham Bay, b., Austl.	B7	74
Buck Island, i., V.I.U.S.	g11	104c
Buck Island Reef National Monument, p.o.i., V.I.U.S.	g11	104c
Buck Lake, l., Ab., Can.	D16	138
Buckland, Ak., U.S.	C7	140
Buckley, Wa., U.S.	C4	136
Bucklin, Ks., U.S.	D9	128
Bucklin, Mo., U.S.	E5	120
Buck Mountain, mtn., Wa., U.S.	B7	136
Bucovăț, Mol.	B15	26
Buco Zau, Ang.	A1	68
București (Bucharest), Rom.	E13	26
București, state, Rom.	E13	26
Bucyrus, Oh., U.S.	D3	114
Buda, Il., U.S.	C8	120
Buda, Tx., U.S.	D10	130
Budalin, Mya.	A2	48
Budapest, Hung.	B6	26
Budapest, state, Hung.	B6	26
Budaun, India	D7	54
Budd Coast, cst., Ant.	B16	81
Buddh Gaya see Bodh Gaya, India	F10	54
Buddusò, Italy	D3	24
Bude, Ms., U.S.	F8	122
Bude Bay, b., Eng., U.K.	K8	12
Budënnovsk, Russia	F6	32
Budești, Rom.	E13	26
Büdingen, Ger.	F5	16
Budišov nad Budišovkou, Czech Rep.	G13	16
Budjala, D.R.C.	D3	66
Budogoviščі, Russia	G19	10
Budrio, Italy	F8	22
Budweis see České Budějovice, Czech Rep.	H10	16
Buea, Cam.	D1	66
Buena Esperanza, Arg.	G5	92
Buenaventura, Col.	F3	86
Buenaventura, Mex.	G9	98
Buena Vista, Bol.	C4	90
Buena Vista, Mex.	K9	134
Buenavista, Phil.	G4	52
Buena Vista, Co., U.S.	C2	128
Buena Vista, Ga., U.S.	E14	122
Buena Vista, Va., U.S.	G6	114
Buena Vista Lake Bed, reg., Ca., U.S.	H6	134
Buendía, Embalse de, res., Spain	D8	20
Buenópolis, Braz.	I3	88
Buenos Aires, Arg.	G8	92
Buenos Aires, Col.	F3	86
Buenos Aires, C.R.	H6	102
Buenos Aires, state, Arg.	G5	90
Buenos Aires, Lago see General Carrera, Lago, l., S.A.	I2	90
Buen Pasto, Arg.	I3	90
Buerarema, Braz.	H6	88
Buffalo, Ks., U.S.	G2	120
Buffalo, Mn., U.S.	F5	118
Buffalo, Mo., U.S.	G4	120
Buffalo, N.Y., U.S.	B7	114
Buffalo, Oh., U.S.	E4	114
Buffalo, S.C., U.S.	B4	116
Buffalo, S.D., U.S.	B9	126
Buffalo, Tx., U.S.	F2	122
Buffalo, stm., Can.	C8	106
Buffalo, stm., Ar., U.S.	H4	120
Buffalo, stm., Tn., U.S.	B11	122
Buffalo Creek, stm., Mn., U.S.	G4	118
Buffalo Lake, Mn., U.S.	G4	118
Buffalo Lake, l., Ab., Can.	D18	138
Buffalo Lake, l., N.T., Can.	C7	106
Buffalo Narrows, Sk., Can.	D8	106
Buffalo Pound Lake, l., Sk., Can.	D8	124
Buffels, stm., S. Afr.	F10	70
Buffels, stm., S. Afr.	F3	70
Buford, Ga., U.S.	B2	116
Buford Dam, dam, Ga., U.S.	B1	116
Buftea, Rom.	E12	26
Bug (Buh) (Zakhidnyy Buh), stm., Eur.	D17	16
Buga, Col.	F3	86
Bugala Island, i., Ug.	E6	66
Bugeat, Fr.	D7	18
Bugojno, Bos.	E4	26
Bugrino, Russia	B23	8
Bugsuk Island, i., Phil.	F1	52
Bugt, China	C4	38
Bugul'ma, Russia	D8	32
Buguruslan, Russia	D8	32
Buh, stm., China	D4	36
Buh (Bug) (Zakhidnyy Buh), stm., Eur.	D19	16
Buhara, Uzb.	G10	32
Buhl, Mn., U.S.	D6	118
Buhler, Ks., U.S.	C11	128
Buhuși, Rom.	C13	26
Buies Creek, N.C., U.S.	A7	116
Builth Wells, Wales, U.K.	I9	12
Buin, Chile	F2	92
Buin, Pap. N. Gui.	d6	79b
Buíque, Braz.	E7	88
Buitsivango (Rietfontein), stm., Afr.	B4	70
Buj, Russia	G19	8
Bujalance, Spain	G6	20
Buje, Cro.	E10	22
Bujnaksk, Russia	F7	32
Bujumbura, Bdi.	E5	66
Bukačača, Russia	F12	34
Bukama, D.R.C.	F5	66
Bukan', Russia	G17	10
Bukavu, D.R.C.	E5	66
Bukeya, D.R.C.	G5	66
Bukhara see Buhara, Uzb.	G10	32
Bukittinggi, Indon.	D2	50
Bükki Nemzeti Park, p.o.i., Hung.	A7	26
Bukoba, Tan.	E6	66
Bukovica, reg., Cro.	F12	22
Bukovina, hist. reg., Eur.	B12	26
Bukuru, Nig.	H6	64
Bula, Indon.	F9	44
Bulaevo, Kaz.	C12	32
Bulajevo see Bulaevo, Kaz.	C12	32

Name | Map Ref. | Page

Caney Creek, stm., Tx., U.S. F12 130
Canfranc, Spain B10 20
Cangas de Narcea, Spain A4 20
Cangas de Onís, Spain A5 20
Cangkuang, Tanjung, c., Indon. G4 50
Cangombe, Ang. C2 68
Canguaretama, Braz. D8 88
Canguçu, Braz. E11 92
Cangumbe, Ang. C2 68
Cangxi, China F1 42
Cangzhou, China B7 42
Caniapiscau, stm., Qc., Can. D17 106
Caniapiscau, Lac, res., Qc., Can. E17 106
Canicattì, Italy G7 24
Canim Lake, B.C., Can. E10 138
Canim Lake, l., B.C., Can. E9 138
Canindé, Braz. C6 88
Canindé, stm., Braz. D4 88
Canindeyú, state, Para. B10 92
Canisteo, N.Y., U.S. B8 114
Canistota, S.D., U.S. D15 126
Cañitas de Felipe Pescador, Mex. D7 100
Canjáyar, Spain G8 20
Çankırı, Tur. A3 56
Çankırı, state, Tur. C15 28
Canmore, Ab., Can. E15 138
Cannanore, India F2 53
Cannelton, In., U.S. G11 120
Cannes, Fr. F13 18
Canning, N.S., Can. E12 110
Cannington, On., Can. D10 112
Cannock, Eng., U.K. I10 12
Cannon, stm., Mn., U.S. G5 118
Cannonball, stm., N.D., U.S. A11 126
Cannon Beach, Or., U.S. E2 136
Cannon Falls, Mn., U.S. G6 118
Cannonvale, Austl. C7 76
Cann River, Austl. K7 76
Canoas, Braz. D12 92
Canoas, stm., Braz. C12 92
Canoe, B.C., Can. F11 138
Canoe, stm., B.C., Can. D12 138
Canoinhas, Braz. C12 92
Canon City, Co., U.S. C3 128
Cañon de Río Blanco, Parque Nacional, p.o.i., Mex. F10 100
Canonsburg, Pa., U.S. D5 114
Canoochee, stm., Ga., U.S. E4 116
Canora, Sk., Can. C11 124
Canosa di Púglia, Italy C10 24
Canossa, hist., Italy F7 22
Canouan, i., St. Vin. p11 105e
Canova, S.D., U.S. D15 126
Canova Beach, Fl., U.S. H5 116
Cañovanas, P.R. B4 104a
Canowindra, Austl. I7 76
Canso, N.S., Can. E16 110
Cantabria, state, Spain A6 20
Cantabrian Mountains see Cantábrica, Cordillera, mts., Spain A5 20
Cantábrica, Cordillera, mts., Spain A5 20
Cantagalo, Braz. K4 88
Cantal, state, Fr. D8 18
Cantalejo, Spain C7 20
Cantanhede, Braz. B3 88
Cantaura, Ven. C9 86
Canterbury, Eng., U.K. J14 12
Canterbury Bight, b., N.Z. G4 80
Canterbury Plains, pl., N.Z. G4 80
Can Tho, Viet. G7 48
Canton see Guangzhou, China J5 42
Canton, Il., U.S. D7 120
Canton, Ks., U.S. C11 128
Canton, Mn., U.S. H7 118
Canton, Ms., U.S. E8 122
Canton, Mo., U.S. D6 120
Canton, N.Y., U.S. D14 112
Canton, Oh., U.S. D4 114
Canton, Ok., U.S. E10 128
Canton, Pa., U.S. C9 114
Canton, S.D., U.S. H2 118
Canton, Tx., U.S. E3 122
Canton see Kanton, i., Kir. D9 72
Canton Lake, res., Ok., U.S. E10 128
Cantonment, Fl., U.S. G11 122
Cantù, Italy E6 22
Cantu, stm., Braz. B11 92
Cantwell, Ak., U.S. D10 140
Cañuelas, Arg. G8 92
Canumã, Braz. D6 84
Canutama, Braz. E5 84
Čany, Russia C13 32
Čany, ozero, l., Russia D13 32
Canyon, Tx., U.S. G7 128
Canyon City, Or., U.S. F8 136
Canyon Creek, Ab., Can. A15 138
Canyon de Chelly National Monument, p.o.i., Az., U.S. G7 132
Canyon Ferry Lake, res., Mt., U.S. D15 136
Canyon Lake, res., Tx., U.S. E9 130
Canyonlands National Park, p.o.i., Ut., U.S. E6 132
Canyonville, Or., U.S. H3 136
Cao, stm., China D5 38
Cao Bang, Viet. A7 48
Cao Lanh, Viet. G7 48
Caombo, Ang. B2 68
Caorle, Italy E9 22
Caoxian, China D6 42
Cap, Pointe du, c., St. Luc. I7 105c
Capac, Mi., U.S. E7 112
Čapaevo, Kaz. D8 32
Capanaparo, stm., S.A. D8 86
Capanema, Braz. D8 84
Capão Bonito, Braz. L1 88
Capão Doce, Morro do, mtn., Braz. C12 92
Caparaó, Parque Nacional do, p.o.i., Braz. K4 88
Caparo Viejo, stm., Ven. D6 86
Capatárida, Ven. B6 86
Cap aux Meules, Île du, i., Qc., Can. C14 110
Cap-Chat, Qc., Can. A10 110
Cap-de-la-Madeleine, Qc., Can. D4 110
Cape, stm., Austl. C5 76
Cape Barren Island, i., Austl. n13 77a
Cape Basin, unds. L14 144
Cape Breton Highlands National Park, p.o.i., N.S., Can. D16 110
Cape Breton Island, i., N.S., Can. D16 110
Cape Charles, Va., U.S. G9 114
Cape Coast, Ghana H4 64
Cape Cod Bay, b., Ma., U.S. C15 114
Cape Cod National Seashore, p.o.i., Ma., U.S. B16 114
Cape Coral, Fl., U.S. J4 116
Cape Dorset, N.T., Can. C15 106
Cape Elizabeth, Me., U.S. G6 110
Cape Fear, stm., N.C., U.S. B8 116
Cape Girardeau, Mo., U.S. G8 120
Cape Hatteras National Seashore, p.o.i., N.C., U.S. A10 116
Capelinha, Braz. I4 88
Cape Lisburne, Ak., U.S. C6 140
Capel'ka, Russia B11 10
Capella, Austl. D7 76
Capelongo, Ang. C2 68
Cape Lookout National Seashore, p.o.i., N.C., U.S. B9 116
Cape May, N.J., U.S. F10 114
Cape May Court House, N.J., U.S. E11 114
Cape Porpoise, Me., U.S. G6 110
Capernaum see Kefar Naḥum, hist., Isr. F6 58
Cape Sable Island, i., N.S., Can. G11 110
Capesterre, Guad. i6 105c
Capesterre, Pointe de la, c., Guad. h5 105c
Capesterre-Belle-Eau, Guad. h5 105c
Cape Tormentine, N.B., Can. D12 110
Cape Town (Kaapstad), S. Afr. H4 70
Cape Verde, ctry., Afr. k9 65a
Cape Verde Basin, unds. G10 144
Cape Vincent, N.Y., U.S. D13 112
Cape York Peninsula, pen., Austl. B8 74
Cap-Haïtien, Haiti C11 102
Capilla del Monte, Arg. E5 92
Capim, stm., Braz. A2 88
Capinota, Bol. C3 90
Capira, Pan. H8 102
Capitan, N.M., U.S. H3 128
Capitán Arturo Prat, sci., Ant. B34 81
Capitán Bado, Para. D5 90
Capitán Bermúdez, Arg. F7 92
Capitán Meza, Para. C10 92
Capitão Enéas, Braz. I4 88
Capitola, Ca., U.S. G4 134
Capitol Peak, mtn., Nv., U.S. B8 134
Capitol Reef National Park, p.o.i., Ut., U.S. E5 132
Capivara, Represa de, res., Braz. D6 90
Capivari, Braz. L2 88
Capivari, stm., Braz. G6 88
Cap-Pelé, N.B., Can. D12 110
Cappella Islands, is., V.I.U.S. e7 104b
Capraia, Italy G6 22
Capraia, Isola di, i., Italy G6 22
Caprara, Punta, c., Italy C2 24
Capraròla, Italy B6 24
Capreol, On., Can. B9 112
Caprera, Isola, i., Italy C3 24
Capri, Italy D8 24
Capri, Isola di, i., Italy D8 24
Capricorn Channel, strt., Austl. D9 76
Capricorn Group, is., Austl. D9 76
Caprivi Strip, hist. reg., Nmb. D3 68
Capron, Il., U.S. B9 120
Captain Cook, Hi., U.S. D6 78a
Captain Cook Monument, hist., Norf. I. x25 78i
Captains Flat, Austl. J7 76
Capua, Italy C8 24
Capucapu, stm., Braz. H12 86
Capucin, c., Dom. i5 105c
Capulin Volcano National Monument, p.o.i., N.M., U.S. E5 128
Caquetá, state, Col. G4 86
Caquetá (Japurá), stm., S.A. H7 86
Čara, Russia E12 34
Čara, stm., Russia E12 34
Carabinani, stm., Braz. I10 86
Carabobo, state, Ven. B7 86
Caracal, Rom. E11 26
Caracaraí, Braz. G11 86
Caracas, Ven. B8 86
Caracol, Braz. E4 88
Caraguatatuba, Braz. L3 88
Caraguatay, Para. B9 92
Carajás, Braz. E7 84
Carajás, Serra dos, hills, Braz. E7 84
Carakol, hist., Belize D3 102
Caranavi, Bol. C3 90
Carandaí, Braz. K4 88
Carangola, Braz. K4 88
Caransebeș, Rom. D9 26
Carapá, stm., Para. B10 92
Carapajó, Braz. B1 88
Cara-Paraná, stm., Col. H5 86
Carapina, Braz. K5 88
Caraquet, N.B., Can. C11 110
Caraș-Severin, state, Rom. D8 26
Caratasca, Laguna de, b., Hond. E5 102
Caratinga, Braz. J4 88
Carauari, Braz. D4 84
Caraúbas, Braz. C7 88
Caravaca de la Cruz, Spain F8 20
Caravelas, Braz. I6 88
Caravelí, Peru G3 84
Caravelle, Presqu'île la, pen., Mart. k7 105c
Caraway, Ar., U.S. B8 122
Caraybo, Para. B9 92
Carazinho, Braz. D11 92
Carballiño, Spain B2 20
Carballo, Spain A2 20
Carberry, Mb., Can. E14 124
Carbon, Ab., Can. E17 138
Carbon, Tx., U.S. B9 130
Carbonara, Capo, c., Italy E3 24
Carbondale, Co., U.S. D9 132
Carbondale, Il., U.S. G8 120
Carbondale, Pa., U.S. C10 114
Carbonear, Nf., Can. j23 107a
Carboneras de Guadazaón, Spain E9 20
Carbon Hill, Al., U.S. D11 122
Carbonia, Italy E2 24
Carcagente see Carcaixent, Spain E10 20
Carcaixent, Spain E10 20
Carcajou, stm., N.T., Can. B5 106
Carcans, Lac de, b., Fr. D4 18
Carcarañá, Arg. F7 92
Carcarañá, stm., Arg. F7 92
Carcassonne, Fr. F8 18
Carchi, state, Ec. G3 86
Carcross, Yk., Can. C3 106
Çardak, Tur. F12 28
Čardara, Kaz. F11 32
Čardarinskoe vodohranilišče, res., Asia A10 56
Cárdenas, Cuba A7 102
Cárdenas, Mex. F12 100
Cárdenas, Mex. D9 100
Cárdenas, Bahía de, b., Cuba A7 102
Cardiel, Lago, l., Arg. I2 90
Cardiff, Wales, U.K. J9 12
Cardigan, P.E., Can. D14 110
Cardigan, Wales, U.K. I8 12
Cardigan Bay, b., Wales, U.K. I8 12
Cardinal, On., Can. D14 112
Cardona, Ur. F9 92
Cardonal, Punta, c., Mex. A3 100
Cardoso, Ur. F9 92
Cardston, Ab., Can. G17 138
Cardwell, Austl. B5 76
Cardwell, Mo., U.S. H7 120
Cardwell Mountain, mtn., Tn., U.S. B13 122
Čardžev, Turkmen. B9 56
Carei, Rom. B9 26
Careiro, Braz. I12 86
Careiro, Ilha do, i., Braz. I12 86
Čarėja, Bela. F12 10
Carencro, La., U.S. G6 122
Carey, Oh., U.S. D2 114
Carey, Lake, l., Austl. E4 74
Carey Downs, Austl. E3 74
Cargados Carajos Shoals, is., Mrts. K9 142
Carhaix-Plouguer, Fr. F5 14
Carhué, Arg. H6 92
Cariacica, Braz. K5 88
Cariaco, Golfo de, b., Ven. B9 86
Caribbean Sea D7 82
Cariboo, stm., B.C., Can. D9 138
Cariboo Mountains, mts., B.C., Can. D10 138
Caribou, Me., U.S. D8 110
Caribou Lake, l., On., Can. A9 118
Caribou Mountain, mtn., Me., U.S. E6 110
Caribou Mountains, mts., Ab., Can. D7 106
Carichic, Mex. B5 100
Caridade, Braz. C6 88
Carigara, Phil. E5 52
Carignan, Fr. E14 14
Carinda, Austl. H6 76
Carinhanha, Braz. H4 88
Carinhanha, stm., Braz. H3 88
Carini, Italy F7 24
Carinthia see Kärnten, state, Aus. D10 22
Caripito, Ven. B10 86
Carira, Braz. F7 88
Cariré, Braz. C5 88
Cariús, Braz. D6 88
Carleton, Mi., U.S. B2 114
Carleton, Mount, mtn., N.B., Can. C10 110
Carleton Place, On., Can. C13 112
Carletonville, S. Afr. E8 70
Cârlibaba, Rom. B12 26
Carlin, Nv., U.S. C9 134
Carlingford Lough, b., Eur. H7 12
Carlinville, Il., U.S. E8 120
Carlisle, Eng., U.K. G9 12
Carlisle, In., U.S. F10 120
Carlisle, Ia., U.S. C4 120
Carlisle, Ky., U.S. F1 114
Carlisle, Pa., U.S. D8 114
Carl Junction, Mo., U.S. G3 120
Carlos, Isla, i., Chile J2 90
Carlos Casares, Arg. G7 92
Carlos Chagas, Braz. I5 88
Carlos Pellegrini, Arg. E6 92
Carlow, Ire. I6 12
Carlow, state, Ire. I6 12
Carloway, Scot., U.K. C6 12
Carlsbad see Karlovy Vary, Czech Rep. F8 16
Carlsbad, Ca., U.S. J8 134
Carlsbad, N.M., U.S. B3 130
Carlsbad, Tx., U.S. C7 130
Carlsbad Caverns National Park, p.o.i., N.M., U.S. B3 130
Carlsberg Ridge, unds. I9 142
Carlton, Or., U.S. E3 136
Carlton, Tx., U.S. C9 130
Carlyle, Sk., Can. E11 124
Carlyle Lake, res., Il., U.S. F8 120
Carmacks, Yk., Can. C3 106
Carmagnola, Italy F4 22
Carman, Mb., Can. E16 124
Carmangay, Ab., Can. F17 138
Carmarthen, Wales, U.K. J8 12
Carmarthen Bay, b., Wales, U.K. J8 12
Carmel, Ca., U.S. G3 134
Carmel, In., U.S. I3 112
Carmel, N.Y., U.S. G16 112
Carmel Head, c., Wales, U.K. H8 12
Carmelo, Ur. F8 92
Carmel Valley, Ca., U.S. G4 134
Carmen see Ciudad del Carmen, Mex. F12 100
Carmen, stm., Chile D2 92
Carmen, Isla, i., Mex. C3 100
Carmen, Isla del, i., Mex. F13 100
Carmen de Areco, Arg. G8 92
Carmen de Patagones, Arg. H4 90
Carmi, Il., U.S. F9 120
Carmi, Lake, l., N.A. F4 110
Carmine, Tx., U.S. D11 130
Carmo do Paranaíba, Braz. J2 88
Carmona, Spain G5 20
Carmópolis de Minas, Braz. K3 88
Carnarvon, Austl. D2 74
Carnarvon, S. Afr. G5 70
Carnarvon National Park, p.o.i., Austl. E6 76
Čarnaučycy, Bela. H6 10
Carnduff, Sk., Can. E12 124
Carnegie, Austl. E4 74
Carnegie, Lake, l., Austl. E4 74
Carney Island, i., Ant. C29 81
Carnia, reg., Italy D9 22
Carnic Alps, mts., Eur. D9 22
Car Nicobar Island, i., India G7 46
Carnot, C.A.R. D3 66
Carnoustie, Scot., U.K. E10 12
Carnsore Point, c., Ire. I6 12
Carnwath, stm., N.T., Can. B5 106
Caro, Mi., U.S. E6 112
Carol City, Fl., U.S. K5 116
Carolina, Braz. D2 88
Carolina, P.R. B4 104a
Carolina, S. Afr. E10 70
Carolina Beach, N.C., U.S. B8 116
Caroline, at., Kir. D12 72
Caroline Islands, is., Oc. C5 72
Caron, Sk., Can. D8 124
Caroni, stm., Ven. C10 86
Carora, Ven. B6 86
Carpathian Mountains, mts., Eur. B13 26
Carpații Meridionali (Transylvanian Alps), mts., Rom. D11 26
Carpentaria, Gulf of, b., Austl. B7 74
Carpenter, Wy., U.S. F8 126
Carpenter Lake, res., B.C., Can. F8 138
Carpentersville, Il., U.S. B9 120
Carpentras, Fr. E11 18
Carpi, Italy F7 22
Carpina, Braz. D8 88
Cărpineni, Mol. C15 26
Carpinteria, Ca., U.S. I6 134
Carpio, N.D., U.S. F12 124
Carp Lake, l., B.C., Can. B7 138
Carpolac, Austl. K3 76
Carrabelle, Fl., U.S. H14 122
Carranza, Cabo, c., Chile G1 92
Carrara, Italy F7 22
Carrathool, Austl. J5 76
Carrauntoohil, mtn., Ire. I3 12
Carreta, Punta, c., Peru F2 84
Carriacou, i., Gren. q11 105e
Carrick-on-Shannon, Ire. H4 12
Carrick-on-suir, Ire. I5 12
Carrie, Mount, mtn., Wa., U.S. C3 136
Carriers Mills, Il., U.S. G9 120
Carrieton, Austl. I2 76
Carrillo, Mex. B6 100
Carrington, N.D., U.S. G14 124
Carrión, stm., Spain B6 20
Carrión de los Condes, Spain B6 20
Carrizal Bajo, Chile D2 92
Carrizo Creek, stm., U.S. E5 128
Carrizo Mountain, mtn., N.M., U.S. H3 128
Carrizo Springs, Tx., U.S. F7 130
Carroll, Ia., U.S. B3 120
Carroll, Ne., U.S. E15 126
Carrollton, Al., U.S. D10 122
Carrollton, Ga., U.S. D13 122
Carrollton, Mi., U.S. E5 112
Carrollton, Ms., U.S. D8 122
Carrollton, Mo., U.S. E4 120
Carrollton, Oh., U.S. D4 114
Carrollton, Tx., U.S. A10 130
Carrolltown, Pa., U.S. D7 114
Carron, stm., Austl. A3 76
Carrot, stm., Can. E10 106
Carrot River, Sk., Can. A10 124
Carry Falls Reservoir, res., N.Y., U.S. F2 110
Carseland, Ab., Can. F17 138
Čarsk, Kaz. E14 32
Carson, N.D., U.S. A11 126
Carson, Wa., U.S. E5 136
Carson, East Fork, stm., U.S. E6 134
Carson City, Nv., U.S. D6 134
Carson Lake, res., Nv., U.S. D7 134
Carson Range, mts., U.S. D6 134
Carson Sink, l., Nv., U.S. D7 134
Carstairs, Ab., Can. E16 138
Cartagena, Chile F2 92
Cartagena, Col. B4 86
Cartagena, Spain G9 20
Cartago, Col. E3 86
Cartago, C.R. H6 102
Cartaxo, Port. E2 20
Cartaya, Spain G3 20
Carter, Ok., U.S. F9 128
Carter Lake, Ia., U.S. C2 120
Cartersville, Ga., U.S. C14 122
Carthage, Tun. H4 24
Carthage, Ar., U.S. C6 122
Carthage, Ms., U.S. E9 122
Carthage, Mo., U.S. G3 120
Carthage, N.C., U.S. A6 116
Carthage, S.D., U.S. C15 126
Carthage, Tn., U.S. H11 120
Carthage, Tx., U.S. E4 122
Carthage, hist., Tun. H4 24
Cartier Islands, is., Austl. B4 74
Cartwright, Mb., Can. E14 124
Caruaru, Braz. E8 88
Carúpano, Ven. B10 86
Carutapera, Braz. D8 84
Caruthersville, Mo., U.S. H8 120
Carutu, stm., Ven. E10 86
Carvoeiro, Braz. H10 86
Carvoeiro, Cabo, c., Port. E1 20
Cary, Ms., U.S. E8 122
Cary, N.C., U.S. I7 114
Čaryškoe, Russia D14 32
Caryville, Fl., U.S. G13 122
Casablanca (Dar-el-Beida), Mor. C3 64
Casa Branca, Braz. K2 88
Casa de Piedra, Embalse, res., Arg. I4 92
Casa Grande, Az., U.S. K5 132
Casa Grande Ruins National Monument, p.o.i., Az., U.S. K5 132
Casale Monferrato, Italy E5 22
Casanare, state, Col. E6 86
Casanare, stm., Col. D6 86
Casa Nova, Braz. E5 88
Casar, N.C., U.S. A4 116
Casarano, Italy D12 24
Casar de Cáceres, Spain E4 20
Casas Adobes, Az., U.S. K6 132
Casas Grandes, stm., Mex. F9 98
Casavieja, Spain D6 20
Casca, Braz. D12 92
Cascadas Basaseachic, Parque Nacional, p.o.i., Mex. A4 100
Cascade, B.C., Can. G12 138
Cascade, Norf. I. y25 78i
Cascade, Ia., U.S. B6 120
Cascade, Mt., U.S. C15 136
Cascade, Wi., U.S. E1 112
Cascade Bay, b., Norf. I. y25 78i
Cascade Mountains see Cascade Range, mts., N.A. C3 108
Cascade Range, mts., N.A. C3 108
Cascade Reservoir, res., Id., U.S. F10 136
Cascais, Port. F1 20
Cascapédia, stm., Qc., Can. B10 110
Cascavel, Braz. C6 88
Cascavel, Braz. B11 92
Cascina, Italy G7 22
Case-Pilote, Mart. k6 105c
Caserta, Italy C8 24
Caseville, Mi., U.S. E6 112
Casey, Il., U.S. E9 120
Casey, sci., Ant. B16 81
Casey, Mount, mtn., Id., U.S. B10 136
Cashel, Ire. I5 12
Cashiers, N.C., U.S. A2 116
Cashmere, Wa., U.S. C6 136
Cashton, Wi., U.S. H8 118
Casigua, Ven. C5 86
Casilda, Arg. F7 92
Casino, Austl. G9 76
Casiquiare, stm., Ven. F8 86
Čáslav, Czech Rep. G11 16
Casma, Peru E2 84
Čašniki, Bela. F12 10
Casoli, Italy H11 22
Caspe, Spain C10 20
Casper, Wy., U.S. E6 126
Caspian Depression (Prikaspijskaja nizmennost'), pl. E7 32
Caspian Sea F7 32
Cass, stm., Mi., U.S. E6 112
Cassano allo Ionio, Italy E10 24
Cass City, Mi., U.S. E6 112
Casselman, On., Can. C14 112
Cássia, Braz. K2 88
Cassiar, B.C., Can. D5 106
Cassiar Mountains, mts., Can. D5 106
Cassilândia, Braz. C6 90
Cassinga, Ang. D2 68
Cassino, Italy C7 24
Cass Lake, Mn., U.S. D4 118
Cass Lake, res., Mn., U.S. D4 118
Cassongue, Ang. C1 68
Cassopolis, Mi., U.S. G3 112
Cassumba, Ilha, i., Braz. I6 88
Cassville, Mo., U.S. H4 120
Cassville, Wi., U.S. B7 120
Castagniccia, reg., Fr. G15 18
Castaños, Mex. H6 130
Castelbuono, Italy G8 24
Castelfranco Veneto, Italy E8 22
Castellammare, Golfo di, b., Italy F6 24
Castellammare del Golfo, Italy F6 24
Castellammare di Stabia, Italy D8 24
Castellana Grotte, Italy D11 24
Castellane, Fr. F12 18
Castellaneta, Italy D10 24
Castelli, Arg. B7 92
Castelli, Arg. H9 92
Castelló, co., Spain D10 20
Castelló de la Plana, Spain E11 20
Castellón de la Plana see Castelló de la Plana, Spain E11 20
Castellón de la Plana see Castelló, co., Spain D10 20
Castelnaudary, Fr. F7 18
Castelnau-Montratier, Fr. E7 18
Castelo, Braz. K5 88
Castelo Branco, Port. E3 20
Castelo Branco, state, Port. E3 20
Castelo de Paiva, Port. C2 20
Castel San Giovanni, Italy E6 22
Castelsarrasin, Fr. E6 18
Casteltermini, Italy G7 24
Castelvetrano, Italy G6 24
Casterton, Austl. K3 76
Castets, Fr. F4 18
Castiglione del Lago, Italy G8 22
Castile, N.Y., U.S. B7 114
Castilla, Peru E1 84
Castilla, Playa de, cst., Spain G4 20
Castilla-La Mancha, state, Spain E9 20
Castilla la Nueva, hist. reg., Spain E7 20
Castilla la Vieja (Old Castile), hist. reg., Spain C7 20
Castilla y León, state, Spain C6 20
Castillo de San Marcos National Monument, p.o.i., Fl., U.S. F5 116
Castillo Incaico de Ingapirca, hist., Ec. I2 86
Castillon-la-Bataille, Fr. E5 18
Castillos, Ur. G11 92
Castillos, Laguna de, l., Ur. G11 92
Castine, Me., U.S. F8 110
Castlebar, Ire. H3 12
Castle Bruce, Dom. j6 105c
Castle Dome Peak, mtn., Az., U.S. J2 132
Castlegar, B.C., Can. G13 138
Castle Hills, Tx., U.S. E9 130
Castleisland, Ire. I3 12
Castlemaine, Austl. K5 76
Castle Mountain, mtn., Yk., Can. C3 106
Castle Peak, mtn., Co., U.S. D9 132
Castlerea, Ire. H4 12
Castlereagh, stm., Austl. H7 76
Castle Rock, Co., U.S. B3 128
Castle Rock, Wa., U.S. D3 136
Castle Rock, mtn., Or., U.S. F8 136
Castle Rock Butte, mtn., S.D., U.S. B9 126
Castle Rock Lake, res., Wi., U.S. H8 118
Castletown, I. of Man G8 12
Castlewood, S.D., U.S. G1 118
Castor, Ab., Can. D19 138
Castor, stm., Mo., U.S. G7 120
Castres, Fr. F8 18
Castries, St. Luc. l6 105c
Castro, Braz. B13 92
Castro, Chile H2 90
Castro Barros, Arg. E5 92
Castro Daire, Port. D3 20
Castro del Río, Spain G6 20
Castronuño, Spain C5 20
Castro Verde, Port. G2 20
Castrovillari, Italy E10 24
Castroville, Ca., U.S. G4 134
Catacamas, Hond. E5 102
Catacaos, Peru E1 84
Catacocha, Ec. D2 84
Cataguazes, Braz. K4 88
Catahoula Lake, l., La., U.S. F6 122
Çatalan, Tur. A6 58
Catalão, Braz. J2 88
Çatalca, Tur. B11 28
Catalina, Chile B3 92
Catalina see Santa Catalina Island, i., Ca., U.S. J7 134
Catalina, Punta, c., Chile J3 90
Catalonia see Catalunya, state, Spain C12 20
Cataluña see Catalunya, state, Spain C12 20
Catalunya, state, Spain C12 20
Catamarca, state, Arg. C4 92
Catamayo, Ec. D2 84
Catanauan, Phil. D4 52
Catanduanes Island, i., Phil. D5 52
Catanduva, Braz. K1 88
Catania, Italy G9 24
Catania, Golfo di, b., Italy G9 24
Cataño, P.R. B3 104a
Catanzaro, Italy F10 24
Cataract Canyon, val., Az., U.S. H4 132
Catarina, Braz. C6 88
Catarino Rodriguez, Mex. C8 100
Catarman, Phil. D5 52
Catarman, Phil. F5 52
Catarroja, Spain E10 20
Catatumbo, stm., Ven. C5 86
Catawba, stm., U.S. B5 116
Catawissa, Pa., U.S. D9 114
Cat Ba, Dao, i., Viet. B8 48
Catbalogan, Phil. E5 52
Catedral, Cerro, hill, Ur. G10 92
Catete, Ang. B1 68
Cathcart, S. Afr. H8 70
Cathedral City, Ca., U.S. J9 134
Catherine, Mount see Katherîna, Gebel, mtn., Egypt J4 58
Catherines Peak, mtn., Jam. i14 104d
Cat Island, i., Bah. C9 96
Cat Lake, l., On., Can. E12 106
Catlettsburg, Ky., U.S. F3 114
Catlin, Il., U.S. D10 120
Catoche, Cabo, c., Mex. B4 102
Catolé do Rocha, Braz. D7 88
Catoosa, Ok., U.S. H2 120
Catriló, Arg. H6 92
Catrimani, stm., Braz. G11 86
Catskill, N.Y., U.S. B12 114
Catskill Mountains, mts., N.Y., U.S. B11 114
Catt, Mount, mtn., B.C., Can. B2 138
Cattaraugus, N.Y., U.S. B7 114
Cattolica, Italy G9 22
Catu, Braz. G6 88
Catuane, Moz. E11 70
Catur, Moz. C6 68
Catwick, Îles, is., Viet. G9 48
Čatyrtaš, Kyrg. F13 32
Cau, stm., Viet. A7 48
Cauaburi, stm., Braz. G8 86
Caubvick, Mount, mtn., Can. F13 141
Cauca, state, Col. F3 86
Cauca, stm., Col. D4 86
Caucaia, Braz. B6 88
Caucasia, Col. D4 86
Caucasus, mts. F6 32
Caucete, Arg. E4 92
Cauchari, Salar de, pl., Arg. D3 90
Caudry, Fr. D12 14
Caungula, Ang. B2 68
Čaunskaja guba, b., Russia C22 34
Cauquenes, Chile H1 92
Caura, stm., Ven. D9 86
Caurés, stm., Braz. H10 86
Căușani, Mol. C16 26
Causapscal, Qc., Can. B9 110
Caussade, Fr. E7 18
Cauto, stm., Cuba B9 102
Caux, Pays de, reg., Fr. E9 14
Cávado, stm., Port. C3 20
Cavaillon, Fr. F11 18
Cavalcante, Braz. G2 88
Cavalese, Italy D8 22
Cavalier, N.D., U.S. F16 124
Cavalla (Cavally), stm., Afr. H3 64
Cavalleria, Cap de, c., Spain D15 20
Cavally (Cavalla), stm., Afr. H3 64
Cavan, Ire. G5 12
Cavan, state, Ire. H5 12
Cavarzere, Italy E9 22
Çavdır, Tur. F12 28
Cave City, Ky., U.S. G11 120
Cave In Rock, Il., U.S. G9 120
Caveiras, stm., Braz. C12 92
Cavendish, Austl. K4 76
Cave Run Lake, res., Ky., U.S. F2 114
Cave Spring, Ga., U.S. C13 122
Caviana de Fora, Ilha, i., Braz. C8 84
Cavite, Phil. C3 52
Cavour, Canale, can., Italy E5 22
Çavuş, Tur. A2 58
Čavusy, Bela. G14 10
Cawood, Ky., U.S. H2 114
Cawston, B.C., Can. G11 138
Caxambu, Braz. K3 88
Caxias, Braz. C4 88
Caxias do Sul, Braz. D12 92
Caxito, Ang. B1 68
Çay, Tur. E13 28
Cayambe, Ec. G2 86
Cayambe, vol., Ec. G3 86
Cayce, S.C., U.S. C4 116
Çaycuma, Tur. B15 28
Cay Duong, Vinh, b., Viet. G7 48
Cayenne, Fr. Gu. C7 84
Cayey, P.R. B3 104a
Caylus, Fr. E7 18
Cayman Brac, i., Cay. Is. C8 102
Cayman Islands, dep., N.A. C7 102
Caynaba, Som. C9 66
Cayon, St. K./N. C2 105a
Cayuga, In., U.S. I2 112
Cayuga, Tx., U.S. F3 122
Cayuga Heights, N.Y., U.S. B9 114
Cayuga Lake, res., N.Y., U.S. B9 114
Cazalla de la Sierra, Spain G5 20
Cazaux et de Sanguinet, Étang de, l., Fr. E4 18
Cazères, Fr. F6 18
Cazombo, Ang. C3 68
Cazorla, Spain G7 20
Cea, stm., Spain B5 20
Ceanannas see Kells, Ire. H6 12
Ceará, state, Braz. C6 88
Ceará-Mirim, Braz. C8 88
Ceará-Mirim, stm., Braz. C8 88
Ceatharlach see Carlow, Ire. I5 12
Cebaco, Isla de, i., Pan. I7 102
Ceballos, Mex. B6 100
Čeboksary, Russia C7 32
Cebollar, Arg. D4 92
Cebollas, Mex. D6 100
Cebollatí, Ur. F11 92
Cebollatí, stm., Ur. F10 92
Céboruco, Volcán, vol., Mex. E6 100
Cebu, Phil. E4 52
Cebu, i., Phil. E4 52
Cebu Strait, strt., Phil. F4 52
Ceceda, Mex. H4 130
Čechtice, Czech Rep. G11 16
Čechy, hist. reg., Czech Rep. G10 16
Cecilia, Ky., U.S. G12 120
Cecil Plains, Austl. F8 76
Cecina, Italy G7 22
Čečnja, state, Russia F7 32
Cedar, stm., U.S. J7 118
Cedar, stm., Ne., U.S. F14 126
Cedar Bluffs, Ne., U.S. J2 118
Cedar Breaks National Monument, p.o.i., Ut., U.S. F3 132
Cedarburg, Wi., U.S. E1 112
Cedar City, Ut., U.S. F3 132
Cedar Creek, stm., Id., U.S. B2 132
Cedar Creek, stm., Ia., U.S. C5 120
Cedar Creek, stm., N.D., U.S. A11 126
Cedar Falls, Ia., U.S. B5 120
Cedar Grove, Wi., U.S. E2 112
Cedar Hill, Tn., U.S. H10 120
Cedar Key, Fl., U.S. G2 116
Cedar Lake, In., U.S. J11 118
Cedar Lake, l., On., Can. B11 112
Cedar Lake, res., Mb., Can. E10 106
Cedar Mountain, mtn., Ca., U.S. B5 134
Cedar Rapids, Ia., U.S. C6 120
Cedars of Lebanon see Arz Lubnān, for., Leb. D7 58
Cedar Springs, Mi., U.S. E4 112
Cedartown, Ga., U.S. C13 122
Cedar Tree Point, c., Antig. e4 105b
Cedarvale, B.C., Can. A2 138
Cedar Vale, Ks., U.S. D12 128
Cedarville, Ca., U.S. B5 134
Cedarville, Mi., U.S. B5 112
Cedeira, Spain A2 20
Cedillo, Embalse de, res., Eur. E3 20
Cedro, Braz. D6 88
Cedros, Mex. C8 100
Cedros, Isla, i., Mex. A1 100
Ceduna, Austl. F6 74
Ceelbuur, Som. D9 66
Ceepeecee, B.C., Can. G4 138
Ceerigaabo, Som. B9 66
Cefalonia see Kefallinía, i., Grc. E3 28
Cefalù, Italy F8 24
Cega, stm., Spain C6 20
Čegdomyn, Russia F15 34
Cegléd, Hung. B6 26
Ceglie Messapico, Italy D11 24
Cehegín, Spain F9 20
Čehov, Russia E20 10
Čehov, Russia G17 34
Čekalin, Russia F19 10
Čekuevo, Russia E18 8
Čelákovice, Czech Rep. F10 16
Celano, Italy H10 22
Celaya, Mex. E8 100
Celebes see Sulawesi, i., Indon. F7 44
Celebes Basin, unds. I15 142
Celebes Sea, Asia E7 44
Čeleken, Turkmen. B7 56
Celeste, Tx., U.S. D2 122
Celestún, Mex. B2 102
Celina, Tn., U.S. H12 120
Celina, Tx., U.S. D2 122
Čeljabinsk, Russia C10 32
Čeljahany, Bela. H8 10
Celje, Slvn. D12 22
Čeljuskin, mys, c., Russia A9 34
Čelkar, Kaz. E9 32
Celle, Ger. D6 16
Čelmozero, Russia D14 8
Celtic Sea, Eur. J6 12
Çeltikçi, Tur. A1 58
Čemal, Russia D15 32
Cement, Ok., U.S. G10 128
Cenajo, Embalse del, res., Spain F9 20
Cenderawasih, Teluk, b., Indon. F10 44
Cenovo, Blg. F12 26
Centenario, Arg. I3 92
Center, Co., U.S. D2 128
Center, Mo., U.S. E6 120
Center, N.D., U.S. G12 124
Center, Tx., U.S. F4 122
Centerburg, Oh., U.S. D3 114
Center Hill, Fl., U.S. H3 116

Name	Map Ref.	Page
Chilpancingo de los Bravo, Mex.	G9	100
Chiluage, Ang.	B3	68
Chilumba, Mwi.	C5	68
Chilung, Tai.	I9	42
Chilwa, Lake, l., Afr.	D6	68
Chimaltenango, Guat.	E2	102
Chimán, Pan.	H8	102
Chimayo, N.M., U.S.	E3	128
Chimbarongo, Chile	G2	92
Chimbas, Arg.	E3	92
Chimborazo, state, Ec.	H2	86
Chimborazo, vol., Ec.	H2	86
Chimbote, Peru	E2	84
Chimoio, Moz.	D5	68
Chimpay, Arg.	G3	90
Chin, state, Mya.	B1	48
China, Mex.	C9	100
China, ctry., Asia	B8	46
Chinan see Jinan, China	C7	42
Chinandega, Nic.	F4	102
Chinati Peak, mtn., Tx., U.S.	E3	130
Chincha Alta, Peru	F2	84
Chinchaga, stm., Can.	D7	106
Chinchilla, Austl.	F8	76
Chinchilla de Monte-Aragón, Spain	F9	20
Chinchiná, Col.	E4	86
Chinchou see Jinzhou, China	A9	42
Chinchow see Jinzhou, China	A9	42
Chincolco, Chile	F2	92
Chincoteague, Va., U.S.	G10	114
Chinde, Moz.	D6	68
Chindo, Kor., S.	G7	38
Chin-do, i., Kor., S.	G7	38
Chindong, Kor., S.	D1	40
Chindwinn, stm., Mya.	D7	46
Ch'ingchiang see Qingjiang, China	E8	42
Chingleput, India	E4	53
Chingola, Zam.	C4	68
Chingshih see Jinshi, China	G4	42
Ch'ingtao see Qingdao, China	C9	42
Chingtechen see Jingdezhen, China	G7	42
Chinguetti, Maur.	E2	64
Chinhae, Kor., S.	D1	40
Chin Hills, hills, Mya.	D7	46
Chinhoyi, Zimb.	D5	68
Chinhsien see Jinzhou, China	B9	42
Chinhua see Jinhua, China	G8	42
Ch'inhuangtao see Qinhuangdao, China	B8	42
Chining see Jining, China	D7	42
Chining see Jining, China	A5	42
Chiniot, Pak.	C4	54
Chinit, stm., Camb.	F7	48
Chinjan, Pak.	C1	54
Chinju, Kor., S.	G7	38
Chinkiang see Zhenjiang, China	E8	42
Chinko, stm., C.A.R.	C4	66
Chinle, Az., U.S.	G7	132
Chinle Wash, stm., Az., U.S.	G7	132
Chinmen Tao (Quemoy), i., Tai.	I8	42
Chino, Ca., U.S.	J8	134
Chinon, Fr.	G9	14
Chinook, Ab., Can.	C2	124
Chinook Cove, B.C., Can.	E10	138
Chino Valley, Az., U.S.	I4	132
Chinquapin, N.C., U.S.	B8	116
Chinsali, Zam.	C5	68
Chintāmani, India	E4	53
Chinú, Col.	C4	86
Chinwangtao see Qinhuangdao, China	B8	42
Chioco, Moz.	D5	68
Chioggia, Italy	E9	22
Chíos, Grc.	E9	28
Chíos, i., Grc.	E8	28
Chios see Chíos, i., Grc.	E8	28
Chipata, Zam.	C5	68
Chip Lake, l., Ab., Can.	C15	138
Chiplūn, India	C1	53
Chipman, N.B., Can.	D11	110
Chipola, stm., Fl., U.S.	G13	122
Chippenham, Eng., U.K.	J10	12
Chippewa, stm., Mn., U.S.	F3	118
Chippewa, stm., Wi., U.S.	G6	118
Chippewa, East Fork, stm., Wi., U.S.	F8	118
Chippewa Falls, Wi., U.S.	G7	118
Chiquimula, Guat.	E3	102
Chiquinquirá, Col.	E4	86
Chīrāla, India	D5	53
Chirāwa, India	D5	54
Chiredzi, Zimb.	B10	70
Chireno, Tx., U.S.	F4	122
Chirfa, Niger	E7	64
Chīrgaon, India	F7	54
Chiribiquete, Parque Nacional, p.o.i., Col.	G5	86
Chiricahua Mountains, mts., Az., U.S.	L7	132
Chiricahua National Monument, p.o.i., Az., U.S.	L7	132
Chiricahua Peak, mtn., Az., U.S.	L7	132
Chiriguaná, Col.	C5	86
Chirikof Island, i., Ak., U.S.	E8	140
Chiriquí, Golfo de, b., Pan.	H6	102
Chiriquí, Laguna de, b., Pan.	H6	102
Chiromo, Mwi.	D5	68
Chirpan see Čirpan, Blg.	G12	26
Chirripó, Cerro, mtn., C.R.	H6	102
Chirripó, Parque Nacional, p.o.i., C.R.	H6	102
Chisago City, Mn., U.S.	F5	118
Chisamba, Zam.	C4	68
Chisasibi, Qc., Can.	E15	106
Chisep'o, Kor., S.	E1	40
Ch'ishan, Tai.	J9	42
Chisholm, Ab., Can.	B16	138
Chisholm, Me., U.S.	F6	110
Chisholm, Mn., U.S.	D5	118
Chishtiān Mandi, Pak.	D4	54
Chishui, China	G1	42
Chishui, stm., China	F6	36
Chisimayu see Kismaayo, Som.	E8	66
Chişinău, Mol.	B15	26
Chişineu-Criş, Rom.	C8	26
Chita, Col.	D5	86
Chitado, Ang.	D1	68
Chitagá, Col.	D5	86
Chita-hantō, pen., Japan	E9	40
Chitato, Ang.	B3	68
Chitek Lake, l., Mb., Can.	B14	124
Chitembo, Ang.	C2	68
Chitina, Ak., U.S.	D11	140
Chitina, stm., Ak., U.S.	D11	140
Chitipa, Mwi.	B5	68
Chitokoloki, Zam.	C3	68
Chitose, Japan	C14	38
Chitradurga, India	D3	53
Chitrakūt Dham, India	F8	54
Chitrāl, Pak.	B11	56
Chitrāvati, stm., India	D3	53
Chitré, Pan.	H7	102
Chittagong, Bngl.	G13	54
Chittagong, state, Bngl.	G13	54
Chittāpur, India	C3	53
Chittaurgarh, India	F5	54
Chittoor, India	E4	53
Chittūr, India	F3	53
Chitungwiza, Zimb.	D5	68
Chiuchiang see Jiujiang, China	G6	42
Chiumbe (Tshumbe), stm., Afr.	B3	68
Chiume, Ang.	D3	68
Chiusi, Italy	G8	22
Chiva see Xiva, Spain	E10	20
Chivacoa, Ven.	B7	86
Chivasso, Italy	E4	22
Chivi, Zimb.	B10	70
Chivilcoy, Arg.	G7	92
Chivirira Falls, wtfl, Zimb.	B11	70
Chizu, Japan	D7	40
Chloride, Az., U.S.	H2	132
Chmielnik, Pol.	F16	16
Chŏâm Khsant, Camb.	E7	48
Choapa, stm., Chile	E2	92
Choceň, Czech Rep.	F12	16
Chochis, Cerro, mtn., Bol.	C5	90
Choch'iwŏn, Kor., S.	F7	38
Chociwel, Pol.	C11	16
Chocó, state, Col.	E3	86
Chocolate Mountains, mts., U.S.	J1	132
Chocontá, Col.	E5	86
Chocope, Peru	E2	84
Choctawhatchee, West Fork, stm., Al., U.S.	G13	122
Choctawhatchee Bay, b., Fl., U.S.	G12	122
Chodzież, Pol.	D12	16
Choele Choel, Arg.	G3	90
Choiseul, St. Luc.	m6	105c
Choiseul, state, Sol. Is.	d7	79b
Choiseul, i., Sol. Is.	d7	79b
Chojna, Pol.	D10	16
Chojnice, Pol.	C13	16
Chojnów, Pol.	E11	16
Ch'ok'ē, mts., Eth.	E7	62
Choke Canyon Reservoir, res., Tx., U.S.	F9	130
Chokio, Mn., U.S.	F2	118
Chókwe, Moz.	D11	70
Cholet, Fr.	G8	14
Choluteca, Hond.	F4	102
Choluteca, stm., Hond.	F4	102
Choma, Zam.	D4	68
Chomo Lhāri, mtn., Asia	E12	54
Chomūm, India	E5	54
Chomutov, Czech Rep.	F9	16
Ch'ŏnan, Kor., S.	F7	38
Chon Buri, Thai.	F5	48
Chon Daen, Thai.	D5	48
Chone, Ec.	H1	86
Chong'an, China	H8	42
Ch'ŏngdo, Kor., S.	D1	40
Ch'ŏngjin, Kor., N.	D8	38
Ch'ŏngju, Kor., S.	F7	38
Chŏng Kal, Camb.	E6	48
Chongming, China	I4	38
Chongming Dao, i., China	F9	42
Chongoroi, Ang.	C1	68
Chongqing (Chungking), China	G2	42
Chŏngsŏn, Kor., S.	B1	40
Chŏngŭp, Kor., S.	G7	38
Chongxin, China	D2	42
Chongzuo, China	A8	48
Chŏnju, Kor., S.	G7	38
Chonos, Archipiélago de los, is., Chile	I1	90
Ch'ŏnsu-ri, Kor., N.	D8	38
Chontaleña, Cordillera, mts., Nic.	G5	102
Cho Oyu see Chopu, mtn., Asia	D11	54
Cho Oyu see Qowowuyag, mtn., Asia	D11	54
Chop, Ukr.	A9	26
Chopda, India	H5	54
Chopim, stm., Braz.	C11	92
Chopinzinho, Braz.	B11	92
Chopu (Qowowuyag), mtn., Asia	D11	54
Chorna, Ukr.	B16	26
Chornobyl', Ukr.	D4	32
Choros, Isla, i., Chile	D2	92
Ch'ŏrwŏn, Kor., S.	E7	38
Chorzele, Pol.	C16	16
Chosen, Fl., U.S.	J5	116
Chōshi, Japan	D13	40
Chosica, Peru	F2	84
Chos Malal, Arg.	H2	92
Choszczno, Pol.	C11	16
Choteau, Mt., U.S.	C14	136
Chotila, India	G3	54
Chouchiak'ou see Shangshui, China	E6	42
Chouk'ou see Shangshui, China	E6	42
Choushan Islands see Zhoushan Qundao, is., China	F10	42
Chowchilla, Ca., U.S.	F5	134
Chown, Mount, mtn., Ab., Can.	C11	138
Choya, Arg.	D5	92
Choybalsan, Mong.	B7	36
Choyr, Mong.	B6	36
Chrisman, Il., U.S.	I2	112
Christanshåb (Qasigiannguit), Grnld.	D15	141
Christchurch, N.Z.	F5	80
Christian, Cape, c., N.T., Can.	A17	106
Christian, Point, c., Pit.	c28	78k
Christiana, Jam.	i13	104d
Christiana, S. Afr.	E7	70
Christian Island, i., On., Can.	D9	112
Christiansburg, Va., U.S.	G5	114
Christian Sound, strt., Ak., U.S.	E12	140
Christianstad, V.I.U.S.	h11	104c
Christmas Island, dep., Oc.	K13	142
Christmas Island, i., Christ. I.	E1	72
Christmas Island see Kiritimati, at., Kir.	C11	72
Christmas Ridge, unds.	I22	142
Christoval, Tx., U.S.	C7	130
Chrudim, Czech Rep.	G11	16
Chrzanów, Pol.	F15	16
Chu (Xam), stm., Asia	B7	48
Chuādanga, Bngl.	G12	54
Chuanchou see Quanzhou, China	I8	42
Chubbuck, Id., U.S.	H14	136
Chūbu-Sangaku-kokuritsu-kōen, p.o.i., Japan	C10	40
Chubut, state, Arg.	H3	90
Chubut, stm., Arg.	H3	90
Ch'üchiang see Shaoguan, China	I5	42
Chuchi Lake, l., B.C., Can.	A6	138
Chuchou see Zhuzhou, China	H5	42
Chuchow see Zhuzhou, China	H5	42
Chu Chua, B.C., Can.	E10	138
Chucunaque, stm., Pan.	H9	102
Chugach Mountains, mts., Ak., U.S.	D10	140
Chuginadak Island, i., Ak., U.S.	g25	140a
Chūgoku-sanchi, mts., Japan	D6	40
Chugwater Creek, stm., Wy., U.S.	F8	126
Chuhuichupa, Mex.	G8	98
Chuí, Braz.	F11	92
Chukchi Sea	C5	94
Chuke Hu, l., China	C11	54
Chukotsk Peninsula see Čukotskij poluostrov, pen., Russia	C26	34
Chula Vista, Ca., U.S.	K8	134
Chulucanas, Peru	E1	84
Chumbicha, Arg.	D4	92
Chum Phae, Thai.	D6	48
Chumphon, Thai.	G4	48
Chumphon Buri, Thai.	E6	48
Chum Saeng, Thai.	E5	48
Chumunjin, Kor., S.	B1	40
Chun'an, China	G8	42
Chunan, Tai.	I9	42
Chuncheon see Ch'unch'ŏn, Kor., S.	F7	38
Chunchi, Ec.	I2	86
Ch'unch'ŏn, Kor., S.	F7	38
Chunchula, Al., U.S.	G10	122
Ch'ungch'ŏng-bukto, state, Kor., S.	B1	40
Ch'ungju, Kor., S.	F7	38
Chungking see Chongqing, China	G2	42
Ch'ungmu, Kor., S.	E1	40
Chungshan see Zhongshan, China	J5	42
Chungyang Shanmo, mts., Tai.	J9	42
Chunhua, China	D3	42
Chunhuhux, Mex.	C3	102
Chuquibamba, Peru	G3	84
Chuquicamata, Chile	D3	90
Chur (Coire), Switz.	D6	22
Church Hill, Tn., U.S.	H3	114
Churchill, Mb., Can.	D12	106
Churchill, stm., Can.	D11	106
Churchill, stm., Nf., Can.	E18	106
Churchill, Mount, mtn., B.C., Can.	G7	138
Churchill, Mount, vol., Ak., U.S.	D11	140
Churchill Falls, wtfl, Nf., Can.	E17	106
Churchill Lake, l., Sk., Can.	D9	106
Church Point, La., U.S.	G6	122
Church Rock, N.M., U.S.	H8	132
Chūru, India	D5	54
Churubusco, In., U.S.	G4	112
Churuguara, Ven.	B7	86
Chushul, India	B7	54
Chute-Saint-Philippe, Qc., Can.	D1	110
Chutung, Tai.	I9	42
Chuuk, is., Micron.	C6	72
Chuvashia see Čuvašija, state, Russia	C7	32
Chuxian, China	E8	42
Chuxiong, China	F5	36
Ci, stm., China	B6	42
Ci, stm., China	E6	42
Ciadâr Lunga, Mol.	C15	26
Ciales, P.R.	B3	104a
Ciamis, Indon.	G6	50
Cianjur, Indon.	G5	50
Çianorte, Braz.	A11	92
Čiatura, Geor.	F6	32
Ciawi, Indon.	G5	50
Cibaliung, Indon.	G4	50
Cibatu, Indon.	G6	50
Cibinong, Indon.	G5	50
Cibolo Creek, stm., Tx., U.S.	E3	130
Cibolo Creek, stm., Tx., U.S.	E10	130
Cicero, Il., U.S.	G2	112
Cicero, In., U.S.	H3	112
Cícero Dantas, Braz.	F6	88
Cicurug, Indon.	G5	50
Cidra, P.R.	B3	104a
Ciechanów, Pol.	D16	16
Ciechanów, state, Pol.	C16	16
Ciechanowiec, Pol.	D18	16
Ciego de Ávila, Cuba	B8	102
Ciempozuelos, Spain	D7	20
Ciénaga, Col.	B4	86
Ciénega de Flores, Mex.	H7	130
Cienfuegos, Cuba	A7	102
Cíes, Illas, is., Spain	B1	20
Cies, Islas see Cíes, Illas, is., Spain	B1	20
Cieszanów, Pol.	F19	16
Cieszyn, Pol.	G14	16
Cieza, Spain	F9	20
Çifteler, Tur.	D13	28
Cifuentes, Spain	D8	20
Cigüela, stm., Spain	E7	20
Çihanbeyli, Tur.	E15	28
Čiili, Kaz.	F11	32
Cijara, Embalse de, res., Spain	E6	20
Cijulang, Indon.	G6	50
Cikampek, Indon.	G5	50
Çikobia, i., Fiji	o20	79e
Čikoj, Russia	F10	34
Cilacap, Indon.	G6	50
Cilamaya, Indon.	G5	50
Cilento, reg., Italy	D9	24
Cili, China	G4	42
Cilician Gates see Gülek Boğazı, p., Tur.	A5	58
Čilik, Kaz.	F13	32
Cill Chainnigh see Kilkenny, Ire.	I5	12
Cilleruelo de Bezana, Spain	B7	20
Cil'ma, stm., Russia	D24	8
Cimarron, N.M., U.S.	E4	128
Cimarron, stm., U.S.	F12	128
Cimarron, North Fork, stm., U.S.	D7	128
Čimbaj, Uzb.	F9	32
Cimişlia, Mol.	C15	26
Cimljanskoe vodohranilišče, res., Russia	E6	32
Cimone, Monte, mtn., Italy	F7	22
Cimpu, Indon.	E12	50
Cina, Tanjung, c., Indon.	G4	50
Cinaruco, stm., Ven.	D7	86
Cinaruco-Capanaparo Santos Luzardo, Parque Nacional, p.o.i., Ven.	D8	86
Cinca, stm., Spain	C11	20
Cincinnati, Ia., U.S.	D4	120
Cincinnati, Oh., U.S.	E1	114
Cinco, Canal Numero, can., Arg.	H9	92
Cinco de Mayo, Mex.	I3	130
Cinco Saltos, Arg.	I3	92
Çine, Tur.	F10	28
Ciney, Bel.	D14	14
Cinfães, Port.	C2	20
Cinişeuţi, Mol.	B15	26
Cintalapa, Mex.	G12	100
Cinto, Monte, mtn., Fr.	G14	18
Cintra, Golfe de, b., W. Sah.	E1	64
Ciociaria, reg., Italy	I10	22
Cipa, stm., Russia	F11	34
Cipatujah, Indon.	G5	50
Cipó, Braz.	F6	88
Cipó, stm., Braz.	J4	88
Cipolletti, Arg.	G3	90
Circeo, Parco Nazionale del, p.o.i., Italy	C6	24
Čirčik, Uzb.	F11	32
Circle, Ak., U.S.	C11	140
Circle, Mt., U.S.	G8	124
Circleville, Oh., U.S.	E3	114
Circleville, Ut., U.S.	E4	132
Circleville Mountain, mtn., Ut., U.S.	E4	132
Cirebon, Indon.	G6	50
Ciremay, Gunung, vol., Indon.	G6	50
Cirencester, Eng., U.K.	J11	12
Čirgalandy, Russia	D17	32
Ciriè, Italy	E4	22
Çirò Marina, Italy	E11	24
Čirpan, Blg.	G12	26
Ciskei, hist. reg., S. Afr.	H8	70
Cisnădie, Rom.	D11	26
Cisne, Il., U.S.	F9	120
Cisne, Islas del see Santanilla, Islas, is., Hond.	D6	102
Cisneros, Col.	D4	86
Cisolok, Indon.	G5	50
Çissna Park, Il., U.S.	H2	112
Čistoozërnoe, Russia	D13	32
Čistopol', Russia	C8	32
Čita, Russia	F11	34
Citlaltépetl, Volcán see Pico de Orizaba, Volcán, vol., Mex.	F10	100
Citra, Fl., U.S.	G3	116
Citrus Heights, Ca., U.S.	E4	134
Città di Castello, Italy	G9	22
Cittanova, Italy	F10	24
City of Sunrise see Sunrise, Fl., U.S.	J5	116
City Point, Fl., U.S.	H5	116
Ciudad Acuña, Mex.	A8	100
Ciudad Altamirano, Mex.	F8	100
Ciudad Anáhuac, Mex.	B8	100
Ciudad Bolívar, Ven.	C10	86
Ciudad Bolivia, Ven.	C6	86
Ciudad Camargo, Mex.	B6	100
Ciudad Camargo, Mex.	B9	100
Ciudad Constitución, Mex.	C3	100
Ciudad Cortés, C.R.	H6	102
Ciudad Darío, Nic.	F4	102
Ciudad del Carmen, Mex.	F12	100
Ciudad del Este, Para.	B10	92
Ciudad de Libertador General San Martín, Arg.	A5	92
Ciudad de México (Mexico City), Mex.	F9	100
Ciudad de Nutrias, Ven.	C7	86
Ciudadela see Ciutadella de Menorca, Spain	D14	20
Ciudad Guayana, Ven.	C10	86
Ciudad Hidalgo, Mex.	F8	100
Ciudad Jiménez see Jiménez, Mex.	B6	100
Ciudad Juárez, Mex.	C1	130
Ciudad Lerdo see Lerdo, Mex.	C7	100
Ciudad Madero, Mex.	D10	100
Ciudad Mante, Mex.	D9	100
Ciudad Miguel Alemán, Mex.	B9	100
Ciudad Morelos, Mex.	E5	98
Ciudad Netzahualcóyotl, Mex.	F9	100
Ciudad Obregón, Mex.	B4	100
Ciudad Ojeda, Ven.	B6	86
Ciudad Piar, Ven.	D10	86
Ciudad Real, Spain	F6	20
Ciudad Real, co., Spain	F6	20
Ciudad Rodrigo, Spain	D4	20
Ciudad Valles, Mex.	E9	100
Ciudad Victoria, Mex.	D9	100
Ciutadella de Menorca, Spain	D14	20
Civita Castellana, Italy	H9	22
Civitanova Marche, Italy	G10	22
Civitavecchia, Italy	H8	22
Çivril, Tur.	E12	28
Çixi, China	F9	42
Čiža, Russia	C21	8
Çjaluša, Bela.	G12	10
Čkalovsk, Russia	H20	8
Clackamas, stm., Or., U.S.	E4	136
Clacton-on-Sea, Eng., U.K.	J14	12
Claflin, Ks., U.S.	C10	128
Claiborne, Al., U.S.	F11	122
Clain, stm., Fr.	C6	18
Claire, Lake, l., Ab., Can.	D8	106
Clair Engle Lake, res., Ca., U.S.	C3	134
Clairton, Pa., U.S.	D6	114
Clallam Bay, Wa., U.S.	B2	136
Clanton, Al., U.S.	E12	122
Clanwilliam, S. Afr.	H4	70
Clapperton Island, i., On., Can.	B7	112
Clara, Ire.	H5	12
Clara, Ms., U.S.	F10	122
Clara, stm., Austl.	B4	76
Clara, Punta, c., Arg.	H4	90
Clare, Austl.	I4	76
Clare, Mi., U.S.	E5	112
Clare, state, Ire.	I3	12
Clare Island, i., Ire.	H2	12
Claremont, N.H., U.S.	G4	110
Claremont, S.D., U.S.	B15	126
Claremont, mtn., Ca., U.S.	D4	134
Claremore, Ok., U.S.	H2	120
Clarence, Mo., U.S.	E5	120
Clarence, stm., Austl.	G9	76
Clarence, stm., N.Z.	F5	80
Clarence, Cape, c., N.T., Can.	A13	106
Clarence, Isla, i., Chile	J2	90
Clarence Strait, strt., Austl.	B6	74
Clarence Strait, strt., Ak., U.S.	E13	140
Clarence Town, Bah.	C9	96
Clarendon, Ar., U.S.	C7	122
Clarendon, Tx., U.S.	G8	128
Clarenville, Nf., Can.	j23	107a
Claresholm, Ab., Can.	F17	138
Clarinda, Ia., U.S.	D2	120
Clarines, Ven.	C9	86
Clarington, On., Can.	E11	112
Clarion, Ia., U.S.	B4	120
Clarion, Pa., U.S.	C6	114
Clarion, stm., Pa., U.S.	C6	114
Clarion Fracture Zone, unds.	H25	142
Clarissa, Mn., U.S.	E3	118
Clark, Mount, mtn., N.T., Can.	C6	106
Clarke, stm., Austl.	B5	76
Clarke Island, i., Austl.	n14	77a
Clarkesville, Ga., U.S.	B2	116
Clarkfield, Mn., U.S.	G3	118
Clark Fork, Id., U.S.	B10	136
Clark Fork, stm., U.S.	C11	136
Clarks, La., U.S.	E6	122
Clarksburg, W.V., U.S.	E5	114
Clarksdale, Ms., U.S.	C8	122
Clark's Harbour, N.S., Can.	G11	110
Clarks Hill, In., U.S.	H3	112
Clarkson, Ky., U.S.	G11	120
Clarks Summit, Pa., U.S.	C10	114
Clarkston, Wa., U.S.	D9	136
Clark's Town, Jam.	i13	104d
Clarksville, Ar., U.S.	B5	122
Clarksville, Ia., U.S.	I6	118
Clarksville, Tn., U.S.	H10	120
Clarksville, Va., U.S.	H7	114
Clarkton, Mo., U.S.	H7	120
Clarkton, N.C., U.S.	B7	116
Claro, stm., Braz.	G7	84
Claude, Tx., U.S.	F7	128
Clausthal-Zellerfeld, Ger.	E5	16
Claveria, Phil.	B7	44
Clavering Ø, i., Grnld.	C22	141
Clavet, Sk., Can.	B7	124
Claxton, Ga., U.S.	D4	116
Clay, Ky., U.S.	G10	120
Clay, Tx., U.S.	G2	122
Clay Center, Ne., U.S.	G14	126
Clay City, Il., U.S.	F9	120
Clay City, In., U.S.	E10	120
Clay City, Ky., U.S.	G1	114
Claymont, De., U.S.	E10	114
Claypool, Az., U.S.	J6	132
Claysburg, Pa., U.S.	D7	114
Clayton, Al., U.S.	F13	122
Clayton, Ga., U.S.	B2	116
Clayton, Il., U.S.	D7	120
Clayton, La., U.S.	F7	122
Clayton, Mo., U.S.	F7	120
Clayton, N.M., U.S.	E5	128
Clayton, N.Y., U.S.	D13	112
Clayton, Ok., U.S.	C3	122
Clayton, Wa., U.S.	B9	136
Clear, Cape, c., Ire.	J3	12
Clear Boggy Creek, stm., Ok., U.S.	C2	122
Clearbrook, Mn., U.S.	D3	118
Clear Creek, stm., Wy., U.S.	C6	126
Clearfield, Pa., U.S.	C7	114
Clearfield, Ut., U.S.	B4	132
Clearlake, Ca., U.S.	E3	134
Clear Lake, Ia., U.S.	A4	120
Clear Lake, S.D., U.S.	G2	118
Clear Lake, Wi., U.S.	F6	118
Clear Lake, l., Mb., Can.	D14	124
Clear Lake, l., Ca., U.S.	D3	134
Clear Lake, res., La., U.S.	F5	122
Clear Lake Reservoir, res., Ca., U.S.	B4	134
Clearmont, Wy., U.S.	C6	126
Clearwater, B.C., Can.	E10	138
Clearwater, Mb., Can.	E14	124
Clearwater, Fl., U.S.	I3	116
Clearwater, Ne., U.S.	E14	126
Clearwater, stm., Can.	D8	106
Clearwater, stm., Ab., Can.	D15	138
Clearwater, stm., B.C., Can.	D10	138
Clearwater, stm., Id., U.S.	D10	136
Clearwater, stm., Mn., U.S.	D3	118
Clearwater, stm., Mt., U.S.	C13	136
Clearwater, Middle Fork, stm., Id., U.S.	D11	136
Clearwater, North Fork, stm., Id., U.S.	D11	136
Clearwater Lake, l., B.C., Can.	D10	138
Clearwater Mountains, mts., Id., U.S.	D11	136
Clebit, Ok., U.S.	C4	122
Cleburne, Tx., U.S.	B10	130
Cle Elum, stm., Wa., U.S.	C5	136
Cle Elum Lake, res., Wa., U.S.	C6	136
Cleethorpes, Eng., U.K.	H12	12
Clementsport, N.S., Can.	F11	110
Clemson, S.C., U.S.	B3	116
Clermont, Austl.	D6	76
Clermont, Qc., Can.	C6	110
Clermont, Fr.	E11	14
Clermont-Ferrand, Fr.	D9	18
Clevedon, Eng., U.K.	J10	12
Cleveland, Al., U.S.	D12	122
Cleveland, Ms., U.S.	D8	122
Cleveland, N.C., U.S.	A5	116
Cleveland, Oh., U.S.	C4	114
Cleveland, Ok., U.S.	A2	122
Cleveland, Tn., U.S.	B14	122
Cleveland, Tx., U.S.	G3	122
Cleveland, Va., U.S.	H3	114
Cleveland, Cape, c., Austl.	B6	76
Cleveland, Mount, mtn., Mt., U.S.	B13	136
Clevelândia, Braz.	C11	92
Cleves see Kleve, Ger.	E2	16
Clew Bay, b., Ire.	H3	12
Clewiston, Fl., U.S.	J4	116
Clifton, St. Vin.	p11	105e
Clifton, Az., U.S.	J7	132
Clifton, Tn., U.S.	B11	122
Clifton, Tx., U.S.	C10	130
Clifton Forge, Va., U.S.	G6	114
Clifton Hills, Austl.	F2	76
Climax, Sk., Can.	E5	124
Climax, Co., U.S.	B2	128
Clinch, stm., U.S.	I13	120
Clinchco, Va., U.S.	G15	120
Clingmans Dome, mtn., U.S.	I2	114
Clinton, B.C., Can.	E9	138
Clinton, On., Can.	E8	112
Clinton, Al., U.S.	E11	122
Clinton, Ar., U.S.	B6	122
Clinton, In., U.S.	I2	112
Clinton, Ia., U.S.	C7	120
Clinton, Ky., U.S.	H9	120
Clinton, La., U.S.	G7	122
Clinton, Mi., U.S.	B2	114
Clinton, Mn., U.S.	F2	118
Clinton, Ms., U.S.	E8	122
Clinton, N.C., U.S.	A7	116
Clinton, Ok., U.S.	F9	128
Clinton, S.C., U.S.	B4	116
Clinton, Wi., U.S.	B9	120
Clinton, Cape, c., Austl.	D8	76
Clinton, Lake, res., Il., U.S.	D9	120
Clinton-Colden Lake, l., N.T., Can.	C9	106
Clinton Lake, res., Ks., U.S.	F2	120
Clintonville, Wi., U.S.	G10	118
Clintwood, Va., U.S.	G3	114
Clio, Mi., U.S.	E6	112
Clio, S.C., U.S.	B6	116
Clipperton, Île, at., Oc.	H28	142
Clipperton Fracture Zone, unds.	I25	142
Clipperton Island see Clipperton, Île, at., Oc.	H28	142
Clisson, Fr.	G7	14
Clodomira, Arg.	C5	92
Cloete, Mex.	G6	130
Cloncurry, Austl.	C3	76
Cloncurry, stm., Austl.	B3	76
Clonmel, Ire.	I5	12
Clo-oose, B.C., Can.	H6	138
Cloppenburg, Ger.	D3	16
Cloquet, Mn., U.S.	E6	118
Clorinda, Arg.	B9	92
Cloud Peak, mtn., Wy., U.S.	C5	126
Clova, Qc., Can.	B1	110
Clover, S.C., U.S.	A4	116
Cloverdale, Ca., U.S.	E2	134
Cloverdale, In., U.S.	E11	120
Cloverport, Ky., U.S.	G11	120
Clovis, Ca., U.S.	G6	134
Clovis, N.M., U.S.	G5	128
Cluain Meala see Clonmel, Ire.	I5	12
Cluj, state, Rom.	C10	26
Cluj-Napoca, Rom.	C10	26
Clunes, Austl.	K4	76
Cluny, Austl.	E2	76
Cluny, Fr.	C10	18
Clusone, Italy	E7	22
Clute, Tx., U.S.	E12	130
Clutha, stm., N.Z.	H3	80
Clyde, Ks., U.S.	B11	128
Clyde, N.C., U.S.	A3	116
Clyde, Oh., U.S.	C3	114
Clyde, Tx., U.S.	B8	130
Clyde, stm., Scot., U.K.	F9	12
Clyde, Firth of, b., Scot., U.K.	F7	12
Clyde Inlet, b., N.T., Can.	A17	106
Clyde Park, Mt., U.S.	E16	136
Clyde River, N.T., Can.	A16	106
Çlymer, Pa., U.S.	D6	114
Ćmielów, Pol.	F17	16
Cna, stm., Russia	C17	10
Cna, stm., Russia	D6	32
Cnossus see Knosós, hist., Grc.	H8	28
Côa, stm., Port.	D3	20
Coachella, Ca., U.S.	J9	134
Coachella Canal, can., Ca., U.S.	K1	132
Coahoma, Tx., U.S.	B6	130
Coahuila, state, Mex.	B7	100
Coal City, Il., U.S.	J10	118
Coalcomán de Matamoros, Mex.	F7	100
Coal Creek, stm., Wa., U.S.	C8	136
Coaldale, Ab., Can.	G18	138
Coalgate, Ok., U.S.	C2	122
Coal Grove, Oh., U.S.	F3	114
Coal Hill, Ar., U.S.	B5	122
Coalinga, Ca., U.S.	G5	134
Coalmont, B.C., Can.	G10	138
Coalport, Pa., U.S.	D7	114
Coal River, B.C., Can.	D5	106
Coal Valley, val., Nv., U.S.	F1	132
Coalville, Eng., U.K.	I11	12
Coalville, Ut., U.S.	C5	132
Coamo, P.R.	B3	104a
Coaraci, Braz.	H6	88
Coari, Braz.	D5	84
Coari, stm., Braz.	D5	84
Coast Mountains, mts., N.A.	D4	106
Coast Ranges, mts., U.S.	C2	134
Coatbridge, Scot., U.K.	F9	12
Coatesville, Pa., U.S.	E10	114
Coaticook, Qc., Can.	E5	110
Coats Island, i., N.T., Can.	C14	106
Coats Land, reg., Ant.	C2	81
Coatzacoalcos, Mex.	F11	100
Cobá, hist., Mex.	B4	102
Cobalt, On., Can.	F14	106
Cobán, Guat.	E2	102
Cobar, Austl.	H5	76
Cobberas, Mount, mtn., Austl.	K6	76
Cobden, On., Can.	C13	112
Cobequid Bay, b., N.S., Can.	E13	110
Cobh, Ire.	J4	12
Cobham, stm., Can.	B18	124
Cobija, Bol.	B3	90
Coblence see Koblenz, Ger.	F3	16
Coblenz see Koblenz, Ger.	F3	16
Cobleskill, N.Y., U.S.	B11	114
Cobourg, On., Can.	E11	112
Cobquecura, Chile	H1	92
Cobram, Austl.	J5	76
Cobre, Barranca del (Copper Canyon), misc. cult., Mex.	B5	100
Cóbuè, Moz.	C5	68
Coburg, Ger.	F6	16
Coburg Island, i., N.T., Can.	B10	141
Coburg Peninsula, pen., Austl.	B6	74
Coca, stm., Ec.	H3	86
Cocal, Braz.	B5	88
Cocentaina, Spain	F10	20
Cŏch, stm., Asia	B6	36
Cochabamba, Bol.	C3	90
Coche, Isla, i., Ven.	B10	86
Cochem, Ger.	F3	16
Cochin see Kochi, India	G3	53
Cochin China see Nam Phan, hist. reg., Viet.	G8	48
Cochinos, Bahía de (Pigs, Bay of), b., Cuba	B7	102
Cochise Head, mtn., Az., U.S.	K7	132
Cochrane, Ab., Can.	E16	138
Cochrane, On., Can.	F14	106
Cochrane, Wi., U.S.	G7	118
Cochrane, Lago (Pueyrredón, Lago), l., S.A.	I2	90
Cochranton, Pa., U.S.	C5	114
Cockburn, Austl.	I3	76
Cockburn, Mount, mtn., Austl.	E5	74
Cockburn, Mount, mtn., Austl.	D5	74
Cockburn Island, i., On., Can.	C6	112
Cockermouth, Eng., U.K.	G9	12
Cockpit Country, reg., Jam.	i13	104d
Côco, stm., Braz.	F1	88
Coco, stm., N.A.	E6	102
Coco, Cayo, i., Cuba	A8	102
Coco, Isla del, i., C.R.	F7	96
Cocoa, Fl., U.S.	H5	116
Cocoa Beach, Fl., U.S.	H5	116
Coco Channel, strt., Asia	F7	46
Cocodrie Lake, res., La., U.S.	G6	122
Coco Islands, is., Mya.	F7	46
Coconino Plateau, plat., Az., U.S.	H4	132
Cocos, Braz.	H3	88
Cocos Islands, dep., Oc.	K12	142
Cocos Lagoon, b., Guam	k9	78c
Cocos Ridge, unds.	H5	144
Cocula, Mex.	E7	100
Cod, Cape, pen., Ma., U.S.	C15	114
Codajás, Braz.	D5	84
Codera, Cabo, c., Ven.	B8	86
Coderre, Sk., Can.	D7	124
Codigoro, Italy	F9	22
Cod Island, i., Nf., Can.	F13	141
Codlea, Rom.	D12	26
Codó, Braz.	C3	88
Codogno, Italy	E6	22
Codòzinho, Braz.	C3	88
Codroy, Nf., Can.	C17	110
Cody, Ne., U.S.	E11	126
Cody, Wy., U.S.	C3	126
Coelho Neto, Braz.	C4	88
Coen, Austl.	B8	74
Coëtivy, i., Sey.	k13	69b
Coeur d'Alene, Id., U.S.	C10	136
Coeur d'Alene, stm., Id., U.S.	C10	136
Coeur d'Alene Lake, res., Id., U.S.	C10	136
Coffeeville, Ms., U.S.	D9	122
Coffeyville, Ks., U.S.	G2	120
Coffs Harbour, Austl.	H9	76
Cofre de Perote, Cerro, mtn., Mex.	F10	100
Cofre de Perote, Parque Nacional, p.o.i., Mex.	F10	100
Cofrentes see Cofrents, Spain	E9	20
Cofrents, Spain	E9	20
Cogâlnic (Kohyl'nyk), stm., Eur.	C15	26
Coggon, Ia., U.S.	B6	120
Cognac, Fr.	D5	18
Cogolludo, Spain	D7	20
Cogoon, stm., Austl.	F7	76
Cogswell, N.D., U.S.	A15	126
Cohocton, stm., N.Y., U.S.	F12	112
Cohoes, N.Y., U.S.	B12	114
Cohuna, Austl.	J5	76
Coiba, Isla de, i., Pan.	I6	102
Coig, stm., Arg.	J3	90
Coihaique, Chile	I2	90
Coimbatore (Koyambattur), India	F3	53
Coimbra, Braz.	K4	88
Coimbra, Port.	D2	20
Coimbra, state, Port.	D2	20
Coín, Spain	H6	20
Coipasa, Lago, l., Bol.	C3	90
Coipasa, Salar de, pl., S.A.	C3	90
Coire see Chur, Switz.	D6	22
Cojedes, state, Ven.	C7	86
Cojudo Blanco, Cerro, mtn., Arg.	I3	90
Cojutepeque, El Sal.	F3	102
Cokato, Mn., U.S.	F4	118
Çokeville, Wy., U.S.	A6	132
Çokpar, Kaz.	F12	32
Čokurdah, Russia	B18	34
Colac, Austl.	L4	76
Colatina, Braz.	J5	88
Colbeck, Cape, c., Ant.	C25	81
Colbert, Ok., U.S.	D2	122

I • 14 Colb-Crew

Name | Map Ref. | Page

Colbinabbin, Austl. K5 76
Colbún, Chile G2 92
Colbún, Embalse, res., Chile G2 92
Colby, Ks., U.S. B7 128
Colby, Wi., U.S. G8 118
Colchester, Eng., U.K. J13 12
Colchester, Il., U.S. D7 120
Cold Bay, Ak., U.S. E7 140
Cold Lake, Ab., Can. E8 106
Cold Spring, Mn., U.S. F4 118
Coldstream, Scot., U.K. F10 12
Coldwater, Ks., U.S. D9 128
Coldwater, Mi., U.S. G4 112
Coldwater, Oh., U.S. H5 112
Coldwater, stm., Ms., U.S. C8 122
Coldwater Creek, stm., U.S. E7 128
Coleambally, Austl. J5 76
Colebrook, N.H., U.S. F5 110
Cole Camp, Mo., U.S. F4 120
Coleman, Ab., Can. G16 138
Coleman, Fl., U.S. H3 116
Coleman, Mi., U.S. E5 112
Coleman, Wi., U.S. C1 112
Coleman, stm., Austl. B8 74
Colenso, S. Afr. F9 70
Coleraine, Austl. K3 76
Coleraine, N. Ire., U.K. F6 12
Coleridge, Ne., U.S. E15 126
Coles, Ms., U.S. F7 122
Colesberg, S. Afr. G7 70
Coleville, Sk., Can. C4 124
Colfax, In., U.S. H3 112
Colfax, Ia., U.S. C4 120
Colfax, La., U.S. F6 122
Colfax, Wa., U.S. D9 136
Colfax, Wi., U.S. F7 118
Colgong, India F11 54
Colhué Huapi, Lago, l., Arg. I3 90
Colibris, Pointe des, c., Guad. h6 105c
Colico, Italy D6 22
Coligny, S. Afr. E8 70
Colihaut, Dom. j5 105c
Colima, Mex. F7 100
Colima, state, Mex. F7 100
Colima, Nevado de, vol., Mex. F7 100
Colinas, Braz. D3 88
Colinas, Braz. H1 88
Colinton, Ab., Can. B17 138
Coll, i., Scot., U.K. E6 12
Collarenebri, Austl. G7 76
College, Ak., U.S. D10 140
Collegedale, Tn., U.S. B13 122
College Park, Ga., U.S. D14 122
College Place, Wa., U.S. D8 136
College Station, Ar., U.S. C6 122
College Station, Tx., U.S. G2 122
Collerina, Austl. G6 76
Colleymount, B.C., Can. B4 138
Collie, Austl. F3 74
Collier Bay, b., Austl. C4 74
Collierville, Tn., U.S. B9 122
Collingwood, On., Can. D9 112
Collins, Ga., U.S. D3 116
Collins, Ms., U.S. F9 122
Collins Bay, On., Can. D13 112
Collins Head, c., Norf. I. y25 78i
Collinston, La., U.S. E7 122
Collinsville, Austl. C6 76
Collinsville, Al., U.S. C13 122
Collinsville, Ok., U.S. H2 120
Collinsville, Tx., U.S. D2 122
Collinwood, Tn., U.S. B11 122
Collipulli, Chile H1 92
Colman, S.D., U.S. H2 118
Colmar, Fr. F16 14
Colmenar, Spain H6 20
Colmenar Viejo, Spain D7 20
Colmeneros, Mex. F8 100
Colmesneil, Tx., U.S. G4 122
Colnett, Punta, c., Mex. F4 98
Cologne see Köln, Ger. F2 16
Cologne, Mn., U.S. G5 118
Coloma, Mi., U.S. F3 112
Coloma, Wi., U.S. G9 118
Colomb-Béchar see Béchar, Alg. C4 64
Colombia, Col. F4 86
Colombia, ctry., S.A. C3 84
Colombie-Britannique see British Columbia, state, Can. E5 106
Colombo, Braz. B13 92
Colombo, Sri L. H4 53
Colome, S.D., U.S. D13 126
Colomiers, Fr. F7 18
Colón, Arg. F8 92
Colón, Arg. F7 92
Colón, Cuba A7 102
Colón, Pan. H7 102
Colon, Mi., U.S. G4 112
Colón, Ur. F10 92
Colón, Archipiélago de (Galapagos Islands), is., Ec. h12 84a
Colona, Austl. F6 74
Colonelganj, India E8 54
Colônia, stm., Braz. H6 88
Colonia Alvear Norte see General Alvear, Arg. G3 92
Colonia del Sacramento, Ur. G9 92
Colonia Dora, Arg. D6 92
Colonia Elisa, Arg. C8 92
Colonia Lavalleja, Ur. E9 92
Colonial Heights, Va., U.S. G8 114
Colonia Providencia, P.R. C4 104a
Colonia Suiza, Ur. G9 92
Colonias Unidas, Arg. C8 92
Colonne, Capo, c., Italy E11 24
Colonsay, Sk., Can. B8 124
Colonsay, i., Scot., U.K. E6 12
Colony, Ks., U.S. F2 120
Colorada Grande, Salina, pl., Arg. I5 92
Coloradas, Lomas, hills, Arg. H3 90
Colorado, Hond. E4 102
Colorado, state, U.S. D6 108
Colorado, stm., Arg. G4 90
Colorado, stm., N.A. E5 98
Colorado, stm., Tx., U.S. F11 130
Colorado, Cerro, mtn., Arg. H3 90
Colorado City, Co., U.S. C4 128
Colorado City, Tx., U.S. B7 130
Colorado Kolonie see Lago Kolonie, Aruba p20 104g
Colorado National Monument, p.o.i., Co., U.S. D8 132
Colorado Plateau, plat., U.S. E7 132
Colorado River Aqueduct, aq., Ca., U.S. E5 98
Colorado Springs, Co., U.S. C4 128
Colotlán, Mex. D7 100
Colquechaca, Bol. C3 90
Colstrip, Mt., U.S. B6 126
Colt, Ar., U.S. B8 122
Coltauco, Chile G2 92
Colton, Ca., U.S. I8 134
Colton, S.D., U.S. H2 118
Columbia, Ca., U.S. E5 134
Columbia, Il., U.S. F7 120
Columbia, Ky., U.S. G12 120
Columbia, La., U.S. E6 122
Columbia, Md., U.S. E9 114
Columbia, Mo., U.S. F5 120
Columbia, N.C., U.S. I9 114
Columbia, Pa., U.S. D9 114
Columbia, S.C., U.S. C4 116
Columbia, Tn., U.S. B11 122
Columbia, stm., N.A. D3 136
Columbia, Cape, c., N.T., Can. A11 141
Columbia, Mount, mtn., Ab., Can. D13 138
Columbia Basin, bas., Wa., U.S. C8 136
Columbia City, In., U.S. G4 112
Columbia Falls, Me., U.S. F9 110
Columbia Icefield, ice, Can. D13 138
Columbia Mountains, mts., N.A. G13 138
Columbiana, Al., U.S. D12 122
Columbiana, Oh., U.S. D5 114
Columbine, Cape, c., S. Afr. H3 70
Columbrets, Illes, is., Spain E11 20
Columbus, Ga., U.S. E14 122
Columbus, In., U.S. E12 120
Columbus, Ks., U.S. G3 120
Columbus, Ms., U.S. D10 122
Columbus, Ne., U.S. F15 126
Columbus, N.M., U.S. L9 132
Columbus, N.C., U.S. A3 116
Columbus, N.D., U.S. F11 124
Columbus, Oh., U.S. E2 114
Columbus, Tx., U.S. H2 122
Columbus, Wi., U.S. H9 118
Columbus Point, c., Trin. r13 105f
Columbus Salt Marsh, pl., Nv., U.S. E8 134
Colusa, Ca., U.S. D3 134
Colville, Wa., U.S. B9 136
Colville, stm., Ak., U.S. C9 140
Colville Lake, l., N.T., Can. B5 106
Colwyn Bay, Wales, U.K. H9 12
Comacchio, Italy F9 22
Comacchio, Valli di, l., Italy F9 22
Comala, Mex. F7 100
Comalcalco, Mex. F12 100
Comales, Mex. H9 130
Coman, Mount, mtn., Ant. C34 81
Comana, Rom. F15 26
Comanche, Ok., U.S. G10 128
Comandante Ferraz, sci., Ant. B35 81
Comandante Fontana, Arg. B7 92
Comandante Leal, Arg. E5 92
Comandante Luis Piedra Buena, Arg. I3 90
Comănești, Rom. C13 26
Comayagua, Hond. E4 102
Combarbalá, Chile E2 92
Combermere Bay, b., Mya. C1 48
Combourg, Fr. F7 14
Comboyne, Austl. H9 76
Comendador, Dom. Rep. C12 102
Comer, Ga., U.S. B2 116
Comercinho, Braz. I5 88
Comet, stm., Austl. E7 76
Cometela, Moz. B12 70
Comfort, N.C., U.S. B8 116
Comfort, Tx., U.S. E8 130
Comfort, Cape, c., N.T., Can. B14 106
Comfrey, Mn., U.S. G4 118
Comilla, Bngl. G13 54
Comino see Kemmuna, i., Malta H8 24
Comiso, Italy H8 24
Comitán de Domínguez, Mex. G12 100
Commerce, Ga., U.S. B2 116
Commerce, Ok., U.S. H3 120
Commercy, Fr. F14 14
Comminges, reg., Fr. F6 18
Committee Bay, b., N.T., Can. B13 106
Communism Peak see Kommunizma, pik, mtn., Taj. B11 56
Como, Italy E6 22
Como, Tx., U.S. D3 122
Como, Lago di, l., Italy D6 22
Comodoro Rivadavia, Arg. I3 90
Comores, Archipel des, is., Afr. C7 68
Comorin, Cape, c., India G3 53
Comoros, ctry., Afr. C7 68
Comox, B.C., Can. G6 138
Compiègne, Fr. E11 14
Compostela, Mex. E6 100
Compton, Ca., U.S. J7 134
Comrat, Mol. C15 26
Comstock, Ne., U.S. F13 126
Comstock, Tx., U.S. E6 130
Comstock Park, Mi., U.S. E4 112
Çon, stm., Viet. C7 48
Čona, stm., Russia B19 32
Co Nag, l., China B13 54
Conakry, Gui. H2 64
Conambo, stm., Ec. H3 86
Cona Niyeo, Arg. H3 90
Conasauga, stm., U.S. C14 122
Concarán, Arg. F5 92
Concarneau, Fr. G5 14
Conceição, Braz. D6 88
Conceição da Barra, Braz. J6 88
Conceição das Alagoas, Braz. J1 88
Conceição do Araguaia, Braz. E1 88
Conceição do Canindé, Braz. D5 88
Conceição do Coité, Braz. F6 88
Conceição do Mato Dentro, Braz. J4 88
Conceição do Norte, Braz. G2 88
Concepción, Arg. D9 92
Concepción, Arg. C5 92
Concepción, Bol. C4 90
Concepción, Chile H1 92
Concepción, Col. D5 86
Concepción, Para. D5 90
Concepción, Bahía, b., Mex. B2 100
Concepción, Canal, strt., Chile J2 90
Concepción, Laguna, l., Bol. C4 90
Concepción, Volcán, vol., Nic. G5 102
Concepción de la Sierra, Arg. D10 92
Concepción del Oro, Mex. C8 100
Concepción del Uruguay, Arg. F8 92
Conception, Point, c., Ca., U.S. I5 134
Conception Bay, b., Nf., Can. j23 107a
Conception Bay, b., Nmb. C2 70
Conchas, stm., Arg. B5 92
Conchas Dam, N.M., U.S. F4 128
Conchas Lake, res., N.M., U.S. F4 128
Concho, Az., U.S. I7 132
Concho, stm., Tx., U.S. C8 130
Conchos, stm., Mex. A6 100
Conchos, stm., Mex. C10 100
Conconully, Wa., U.S. B7 136
Concord, Ca., U.S. E4 134
Concord, Ga., U.S. D14 122
Concord, N.H., U.S. G5 110
Concord, N.C., U.S. A5 116
Concordia, Arg. E8 92
Concórdia, Braz. C11 92
Concordia, Mex. D5 100
Concordia, Mex. I4 130
Concordia, Mo., U.S. F4 120
Concrete, Wa., U.S. B5 136
Con Cuong, Viet. C7 48
Conda, Ang. C1 68
Condamine, Austl. F7 76
Condamine, stm., Austl. F8 76
Condat, Fr. D8 18
Conde, S.D., U.S. B14 126
Condeúba, Braz. H5 88
Condobolin, Austl. I6 76
Condom, Fr. F6 18
Condon, Or., U.S. E6 136
Condoto, Col. E3 86
Condroz, hist. reg., Bel. D14 14
Cone, Tx., U.S. H7 128
Conecuh, stm., U.S. F12 122
Conegliano, Italy E9 22
Conejos, Co., U.S. D2 128
Conejos, stm., Co., U.S. D3 128
Confuso, stm., Para. B8 92
Congaree Swamp National Monument, p.o.i., S.C., U.S. C5 116
Congaz, Mol. C15 26
Conghua, China J5 42
Congjiang, China I3 42
Congleton, Eng., U.K. H10 12
Congo, ctry., Afr. E3 66
Congo (Zaïre), stm., Afr. F2 66
Congo, Democratic Republic of the (Zaire), ctry., Afr. E4 66
Congo, République démocratique du see Congo, Democratic Republic of the, ctry., Afr. E4 66
Congo Basin, bas., Afr. E4 66
Congonhinhas, Braz. A12 92
Congress, Sk., Can. E8 124
Conitaca, Mex. C5 100
Conn, Lough, l., Ire. G3 12
Connacht see Connaught, hist. reg., Ire. H3 12
Connaught, hist. reg., Ire. H3 12
Conneaut, Oh., U.S. C5 114
Conneautville, Pa., U.S. C5 114
Connecticut, state, U.S. C13 114
Connecticut, stm., U.S. H4 110
Connellsville, Pa., U.S. D6 114
Connemara, reg., Ire. H3 12
Connersville, In., U.S. E12 120
Conn Lake, l., N.T., Can. A15 106
Connors Range, mts., Austl. C7 76
Cononaco, stm., Ec. H3 86
Conorochite, stm., Ven. F8 86
Conover, N.C., U.S. I4 114
Conquest, Sk., Can. C6 124
Conquista, Braz. J2 88
Conrad, Ia., U.S. B5 120
Conroe, Tx., U.S. G3 122
Conroe, Lake, res., Tx., U.S. G3 122
Consecon, On., Can. D12 112
Conselheiro Lafaiete, Braz. K4 88
Conselheiro Pena, Braz. J5 88
Conselice, Italy F8 22
Consett, Eng., U.K. G10 12
Consolación del Sur, Cuba A6 102
Con Son, is., Viet. H8 48
Consort, Ab., Can. B3 124
Constance see Konstanz, Ger. I4 16
Constance, Lake (Bodensee), l., Eur. I5 16
Constância, Port. E2 20
Constanța, Rom. E15 26
Constanța, state, Rom. E15 26
Constantina, Spain G5 20
Constantine see Qacentina, Alg. B6 64
Constantine, Mi., U.S. G4 112
Constantine, Cape, c., Ak., U.S. E8 140
Constantinople see İstanbul, Tur. B12 28
Constitución, Chile G1 92
Constitución, Ur. E9 92
Constitución de 1857, Parque Nacional, p.o.i., Mex. K10 134
Consuegra, Spain E7 20
Contai, India H11 54
Contas, stm., Braz. H6 88
Contentnea Creek, stm., N.C., U.S. A8 116
Continental Peak, mtn., Wy., U.S. E4 126
Contratación, Col. D5 86
Contreras, Embalse de, res., Spain E9 20
Contreras, Isla, i., Chile J1 90
Contursi, Italy D9 24
Contwoyto Lake, l., N.T., Can. B8 106
Convent, La., U.S. G8 122
Conversano, Italy D10 24
Converse, In., U.S. H4 112
Conway, Ar., U.S. B6 122
Conway, Mo., U.S. G5 120
Conway, N.H., U.S. F5 110
Conway, N.C., U.S. H8 114
Conway, S.C., U.S. C6 116
Conway, Lake, res., Ar., U.S. C6 122
Conway National Park, p.o.i., Austl. C7 76
Conway Springs, Ks., U.S. D11 128
Conwy, Wales, U.K. H9 12
Coober Pedy, Austl. E6 74
Cook, Austl. F6 74
Cook, Mn., U.S. D6 118
Cook, Ne., U.S. D1 120
Cook, Cape, c., B.C., Can. F2 138
Cook, Mount, mtn., N.Z. F4 80
Cook, Récif de, rf., N. Cal. I14 79d
Cookeville, Tn., U.S. H12 120
Cooking Lake, l., Ab., Can. C17 138
Cook Inlet, b., Ak., U.S. D9 140
Cook Islands, dep., Oc. E10 72
Cook Strait, strt., N.Z. E6 80
Cooktown, Austl. C9 74
Coolabah, Austl. H6 76
Cooladdi, Austl. F5 76
Coolamon, Austl. J6 76
Coolangatta, Austl. G9 76
Cooleemee, N.C., U.S. I5 114
Coolgardie, Austl. F4 74
Coolidge, Ga., U.S. E2 116
Coolidge, Tx., U.S. F2 122
Coolidge, Mount, mtn., S.D., U.S. D9 126
Coolidge Dam, dam, Az., U.S. J6 132
Coolin, Id., U.S. B10 136
Cooloola National Park, p.o.i., Austl. F9 76
Cooma, Austl. K7 76
Coonabarabran, Austl. H7 76
Coonalpyn, Austl. J2 76
Coonamble, Austl. H7 76
Coonoor, India F3 53
Coon Rapids, Mn., U.S. F5 118
Coon Valley, Wi., U.S. H8 118
Cooper, Tx., U.S. D3 122
Cooper Creek, stm., Austl. G2 76
Cooper Road, La., U.S. E5 122
Coopers, Al., U.S. E12 122
Cooperstown, N.Y., U.S. B11 114
Coopersville, Mi., U.S. E4 112
Coopracambra National Park, p.o.i., Austl. K7 76
Coorong National Park, p.o.i., Austl. K2 76
Coorow, Austl. E3 74
Cooroy, Austl. F9 76
Coosa, stm., U.S. E12 122
Coos Bay, Or., U.S. G2 136
Cootamundra, Austl. J7 76
Cootehill, Ire. G5 12
Copacabana, Arg. D4 92
Copacabana, Col. D4 86
Copainalá, Mex. G12 100
Copan, Ok., U.S. H2 120
Copán, hist., Hond. E3 102
Copatana, Braz. I8 86
Copeland, Fl., U.S. K4 116
Copenhagen see København, Den. I4 8
Copenhagen, N.Y., U.S. E14 112
Copertino, Italy D11 24
Copiapó, Chile C2 92
Copiapó, stm., Chile C2 92
Copley, Austl. H2 76
Copparo, Italy F8 22
Copper, stm., Ak., U.S. D11 140
Copperas Cove, Tx., U.S. C9 130
Copper Butte, mtn., Wa., U.S. B8 136
Copper Canyon see Cobre, Barranca del, misc. cult., Mex. B5 100
Copper Center, Ak., U.S. D10 140
Copper Harbor, Mi., U.S. D10 118
Coppermine, stm., N.T., Can. B7 106
Copper Mine Point, c., Br. Vir. Is. e9 104b
Copper Mountain, B.C., Can. G10 138
Coquí, P.R. C3 104a
Coquilhatville see Mbandaka, D.R.C. D3 66
Coquimbo, Chile E2 92
Coquimbo, state, Chile E2 92
Corabia, Rom. F11 26
Coração de Jesus, Braz. I3 88
Coradi, Isole see Cheradi, Isole, i., Italy D11 24
Coral Gables, Fl., U.S. K5 116
Coral Harbour, Bah. n18 104f
Coral Harbour, N.T., Can. C14 106
Coral Sea, Oc. E6 72
Coral Sea Basin, unds. K18 142
Coral Sea Islands Territory, dep., Oc. B9 76
Coralville, Ia., U.S. C6 120
Coram, Mt., U.S. B12 136
Corangamite, Lake, l., Austl. K4 76
Corato, Italy C10 24
Corbeil-Essonnes, Fr. F11 14
Corbett National Park, p.o.i., India D7 54
Corbigny, Fr. G12 14
Corbin, Ky., U.S. H1 114
Corbones, stm., Spain G5 20
Corby, Eng., U.K. I12 12
Corcaigh see Cork, Ire. J4 12
Córcega, P.R. B1 104a
Corcoran, Ca., U.S. G6 134
Corcovado, Golfo, b., Chile H2 90
Corcovado, Parque Nacional, p.o.i., C.R. H6 102
Corcovado, Volcán, vol., Chile H2 90
Corcubión, Spain B1 20
Cordeiro, Braz. L4 88
Cordele, Ga., U.S. E2 116
Cordell Hull Reservoir, res., Tn., U.S. H12 120
Corder, Mo., U.S. E4 120
Cordillera, state, Para. B9 92
Cordillo Downs, Austl. F3 76
Córdoba, Arg. E5 92
Córdoba, Mex. F10 100
Córdoba (Cordova), Spain G6 20
Córdoba, state, Arg. E5 92
Córdoba, state, Col. C4 86
Córdoba, co., Spain F6 20
Córdova, Peru F2 84
Cordova see Córdoba, Spain G6 20
Cordova, Al., U.S. D11 122
Cordova, Ak., U.S. D10 140
Cordova, Il., U.S. C7 120
Cordova Peak, mtn., Ak., U.S. D10 140
Coreaú, Braz. B5 88
Coreaú, stm., Braz. B5 88
Corentyne, stm., S.A. C6 84
Corfield, Austl. C4 76
Corfu see Kérkyra, Grc. D2 28
Corfu see Kérkyra, i., Grc. D2 28
Coria, Spain D4 20
Coria del Río, Spain G4 20
Coribe, Braz. G3 88
Coricudgy, Mount, mtn., Austl. I8 76
Corigliano Calabro, Italy E10 24
Corinne, Ut., U.S. B4 132
Corinne, W.V., U.S. G4 114
Corinth see Kórinthos, Grc. F5 28
Corinth, Ms., U.S. C10 122
Corinth, N.Y., U.S. G3 110
Corinth, Gulf of see Korinthiakós Kólpos, b., Grc. E5 28
Corinto, Braz. J3 88
Corisco, Isla de, i., Eq. Gui. I6 64
Corjeuți, Mol. A14 26
Cork, Ire. J4 12
Cork, state, Ire. I4 12
Corleone, Italy G7 24
Çorlu, Tur. B10 28
Cornelia, Ga., U.S. B2 116
Cornélio Procópio, Braz. D6 90
Cornelius, N.C., U.S. A5 116
Cornelius Grinnell Bay, b., N.T., Can. E13 141
Cornell, Wi., U.S. F7 118
Corner Brook, Nf., Can. j22 107a
Cornești, Mol. B14 26
Corneta, Punta, c., Mex. H10 100
Corning, Ar., U.S. H7 120
Corning, Ca., U.S. D3 134
Corning, Ia., U.S. D3 120
Corning, Ks., U.S. B12 128
Corning, N.Y., U.S. B8 114
Cornish, Me., U.S. G6 110
Čornoe more see Black Sea G15 6
Corno Grande, mtn., Italy H10 22
Cornwall, On., Can. E2 110
Cornwallis Island, i., N.T., Can. B7 141
Cornwall Island, i., N.T., Can. B6 141
Coro, Ven. B7 86
Coro, Golfete de, b., Ven. B6 86
Coroaci, Braz. J4 88
Coroatá, Braz. C3 88
Corocoro, Bol. C3 90
Corocoro, Isla, i., S.A. C11 86
Coroico, Bol. C3 90
Coromandel, Braz. J2 88
Coromandel Coast, cst., India E5 53
Coromandel Peninsula, pen., N.Z. C6 80
Corona, Ca., U.S. J8 134
Corona, N.M., U.S. G3 128
Coronado, Mex. D8 100
Coronado, Bahía de, b., C.R. H6 102
Coronado, Islas, is., Mex. K8 134
Coronation, Ab., Can. D19 138
Coronation Gulf, b., N.T., Can. B8 106
Coronation Island, i., Ant. B36 81
Coronda, Arg. E7 92
Coronel, Chile H1 92
Coronel Bogado, Para. C9 92
Coronel Dorrego, Arg. I7 92
Coronel Fabriciano, Braz. J4 88
Coronel Moldes, Arg. B5 92
Coronel Moldes, Arg. F5 92
Coronel Oviedo, Para. B9 92
Coronel Pringles, Arg. H7 92
Coronel Suárez, Arg. H6 92
Coronel Vidal, Arg. H9 92
Coronel Vivida, Braz. C11 92
Corongo, Peru E2 84
Coropuna, Nevado, vol., Peru G3 84
Corossol, Guad. B2 105a
Çorovodë, Alb. D14 24
Čorowa, Austl. J6 76
Corozal, Belize C3 102
Corozal, Col. C4 86
Corozal, P.R. B3 104a
Corpus Christi, Tx., U.S. G10 130
Corpus Christi, Lake, res., Tx., U.S. F9 130
Corpus Christi Bay, b., Tx., U.S. G10 130
Corral, Chile H2 90
Corral de Almaguer, Spain E7 20
Corral de Bustos, Arg. F6 92
Corrales, Cerro, mtn., Mex. H2 130
Corralito, Arg. F5 92
Correctionville, Ia., U.S. B2 120
Corregidor Island, i., Phil. C3 52
Corrente, Braz. F3 88
Corrente, stm., Braz. G4 88
Correntes, Cabo das, c., Moz. D12 70
Correntina, Braz. G3 88
Corrèze, state, Fr. D7 18
Corrib, Lough, l., Ire. H3 12
Corrientes, Arg. C8 92
Corrientes, state, Arg. D9 92
Corrientes, stm., Arg. D8 92
Corrientes, stm., S.A. D2 84
Corrientes, Bahía de, b., Cuba B5 102
Corrientes, Cabo, c., Arg. I9 92
Corrientes, Cabo, c., Col. E3 86
Corrientes, Cabo, c., Mex. E6 100
Corrigan, Tx., U.S. F4 122
Corrigin, Austl. F3 74
Corriverton, Guy. B6 84
Corrumpa Creek, stm., U.S. E5 128
Corry, Pa., U.S. C6 114
Corse (Corsica), i., Fr. G15 18
Corse, Cap, c., Fr. F15 18
Corse-du-Sud, state, Fr. H15 18
Corsica see Corse, i., Fr. G15 18
Corsicana, Tx., U.S. E2 122
Cort Adelaer, Kap, c., Grnld. E17 141
Cortazar, Mex. E8 100
Corte, Fr. G15 18
Cortés, Mar de see California, Golfo de, b., Mex. B2 96
Cortez, Co., U.S. F8 132
Cortez, Sea of see California, Golfo de, b., Mex. B2 96
Cortina d'Ampezzo, Italy D8 22
Cortland, Ne., U.S. K2 118
Cortland, N.Y., U.S. B9 114
Cortland, Oh., U.S. C5 114
Cortona, Italy G8 22
Corubal, stm., Afr. G2 64
Coruche, Port. F2 20
Çorum, Tur. A4 56
Čorumbá, Braz. C5 90
Corumbá, stm., Braz. I1 88
Corumbaíba, Braz. J1 88
Corumbataí, stm., Braz. B11 92
Corumo, stm., Ven. D11 86
Corunna see A Coruña, Spain A2 20
Corunna, Mi., U.S. F5 112
Coruripe, Braz. F7 88
Corvallis, Mt., U.S. D12 136
Corvallis, Or., U.S. F3 136
Corwith, Ia., U.S. B3 120
Corydon, In., U.S. F11 120
Corydon, Ky., U.S. G10 120
Corzu, Rom. E10 26
Corzuela, Arg. C7 92
Cos see Kos, i., Grc. G10 28
Cosamaloapan de Carpio, Mex. F10 100
Coscomate, Mex. I2 130
Cosenza, Italy E10 24
Coshocton, Oh., U.S. D4 114
Cosigüina, Punta, c., Nic. F4 102
Cosigüina, Volcán, vol., Nic. F4 102
Cosmoledo, Atoll de, i., Sey. k11 69b
Cosmos, Mn., U.S. G4 118
Cosne-sur-Loire, Fr. G11 14
Cosquín, Arg. E5 92
Cossato, Italy E5 22
Cossatot, stm., Ar., U.S. C4 122
Costa Mesa, Ca., U.S. J8 134
Costa Rica, Mex. C5 100
Costa Rica, ctry., N.A. H5 102
Coswig, Ger. E9 16
Coswig, Ger. E8 16
Cotabato, Phil. G4 52
Cotahuasi, Peru G3 84
Cotati, Ca., U.S. E3 134
Coteaux, Haiti C10 102
Cote d'Ivoire, ctry., Afr. H3 64
Côte-d'Or, state, Fr. G13 14
Cotegipe, Braz. F3 88
Cotentin, pen., Fr. E7 14
Côtes-d'Armor, state, Fr. F6 14
Cotingo, stm., Braz. E11 86
Cotiujeni, Mol. B15 26
Cotonou, Benin H5 64
Cotopaxi, state, Ec. H2 86
Cotopaxi, vol., Ec. H2 86
Cotopaxi, Parque Nacional, p.o.i., Ec. H2 86
Cotswold Hills, hills, Eng., U.K. J10 12
Cottage Grove, Or., U.S. G3 136
Cottbus, Ger. E10 16
Cotter, Ar., U.S. H5 120
Cottian Alps, mts., Eur. E12 18
Cottondale, Fl., U.S. G13 122
Cotton Plant, Ar., U.S. C7 122
Cottonport, La., U.S. G6 122
Cotton Valley, La., U.S. E5 122
Cottonwood, Az., U.S. I5 132
Cottonwood, Ca., U.S. C3 134
Cottonwood, Mn., U.S. G3 118
Cottonwood, stm., Ks., U.S. C12 128
Cottonwood, stm., Mn., U.S. G3 118
Cottonwood Creek, stm., Mt., U.S. F5 124
Cottonwood Falls, Ks., U.S. C12 128
Coubre, Pointe de la, c., Fr. D4 18
Couchiching, Lake, l., On., Can. D10 112
Coudersport, Pa., U.S. C8 114
Coudres, Île aux, i., Qc., Can. C6 110
Coulee City, Wa., U.S. C7 136
Coulee Dam, Wa., U.S. B8 136
Coulommiers, Fr. F12 14
Coulonge, stm., Qc., Can. C13 112
Coulterville, Il., U.S. F8 120
Counce, Tn., U.S. B10 122
Council, Id., U.S. F10 136
Council Bluffs, Ia., U.S. C2 120
Council Grove, Ks., U.S. C12 128
Coupeville, Wa., U.S. B4 136
Courantyne see Corentyne, stm., S.A. C6 84
Courland (Kurzeme), hist. reg., Lat. C5 10
Courland Lagoon, b., Eur. E3 10
Courmayeur, Italy E3 22
Courtenay, B.C., Can. G5 138
Courtland, Al., U.S. C11 122
Courtland, Va., U.S. H8 114
Courtrai see Kortrijk, Bel. D12 14
Coutras, Fr. D5 18
Coutts, Ab., Can. G19 138
Couture, Lac, l., Qc., Can. C16 106
Covasna, state, Rom. C12 26
Cove, Or., U.S. E9 136
Cove Island, i., On., Can. C8 112
Covelo, Ca., U.S. D2 134
Coventry, Eng., U.K. I11 12
Covert, Mi., U.S. F3 112
Covilhã, Port. D3 20
Covington, Ga., U.S. C2 116
Covington, In., U.S. H2 112
Covington, Ky., U.S. E1 114
Covington, La., U.S. G8 122
Covington, Oh., U.S. H5 112
Covington, Ok., U.S. E11 128
Covington, Tn., U.S. B9 122
Covington, Va., U.S. G5 114
Cowal, pen., Scot., U.K. E7 12
Cowal, Lake, l., Austl. I6 76
Cowan, Tn., U.S. B13 122
Cowan, Lake, l., Austl. F4 74
Cowansville, Qc., Can. E4 110
Cowarie, Austl. E7 74
Cow Creek, stm., Ks., U.S. C10 128
Cow Creek, stm., Or., U.S. H3 136
Cowdenbeath, Scot., U.K. E9 12
Cowell, Austl. F7 74
Cowen, W.V., U.S. F5 114
Coweta, Ok., U.S. I2 120
Cowhouse Creek, stm., Tx., U.S. C10 130
Cowichan Bay, B.C., Can. H7 138
Cowichan Lake, l., B.C., Can. H6 138
Cowley, Austl. F5 76
Cowley, Wy., U.S. C4 126
Cowlic, Az., U.S. L4 132
Cowlitz, stm., Wa., U.S. D4 136
Cowpasture, stm., Va., U.S. F6 114
Cowpens, S.C., U.S. A4 116
Cowra, Austl. I7 76
Coxá, stm., Braz. H3 88
Coxim, Braz. C6 90
Cox's Bāzār, Bngl. H13 54
Coyaguaima, Cerro, mtn., Arg. D3 90
Coyame, Mex. A6 100
Coyle see Coig, stm., Arg. J3 90
Coyote, stm., Mex. F6 98
Coyote Wash, stm., N.M., U.S. G8 132
Coyuca de Benítez, Mex. G8 100
Coyuca de Catalán, Mex. F8 100
Cozad, Ne., U.S. G13 126
Cozumel, Mex. B4 102
Cozumel, Isla, i., Mex. B4 102
Crab Orchard, Tn., U.S. I13 120
Crab Orchard Lake, res., Il., U.S. G9 120
Cradle Mountain-Lake Saint Clair National Park, p.o.i., Austl. n12 77a
Cradock, S. Afr. H7 70
Craig, Co., U.S. C9 132
Craig, Mo., U.S. D2 120
Craig, Ne., U.S. J2 118
Craigellachie, B.C., Can. E12 138
Craigmont, Id., U.S. D10 136
Craigsville, Va., U.S. F6 114
Craik, Sk., Can. C8 124
Crailsheim, Ger. G6 16
Craiova, Rom. E10 26
Cranberry Lake, l., N.Y., U.S. F1 110
Cranbrook, Austl. F3 74
Cranbrook, B.C., Can. G15 138
Crandon, Wi., U.S. F9 118
Crane, Az., U.S. K2 132
Crane, In., U.S. F11 120
Crane, Tx., U.S. C5 130
Crane Lake, l., Sk., Can. D4 124
Crane Mountain, mtn., Or., U.S. A5 134
Crângeni, Rom. E11 26
Cranston, R.I., U.S. C14 114
Crasna, Rom. D13 26
Crasna, stm., Eur. I18 16
Crasnoe, Mol. C16 26
Crater Lake, l., Or., U.S. H4 136
Crater Lake National Park, p.o.i., Or., U.S. H5 136
Craters of the Moon National Monument, p.o.i., Id., U.S. G13 136
Crateús, Braz. C5 88
Crato, Braz. D6 88
Crauford, Cape, c., N.T., Can. A14 106
Cravo Norte, Col. D6 86
Cravo Norte, stm., Col. D6 86
Cravo Sur, stm., Col. E6 86
Crawford, Co., U.S. E9 132
Crawford, Ms., U.S. D10 122
Crawford, Tx., U.S. C10 130
Crawford Bay, B.C., Can. G14 138
Crawfordsville, Ar., U.S. B8 122
Crawfordsville, In., U.S. H2 112
Crawfordville, Ga., U.S. C3 116
Crawley, Eng., U.K. J12 12
Crazy Woman Creek, stm., Wy., U.S. C6 126
Creal Springs, Il., U.S. G9 120
Cree, stm., Sk., Can. D9 106
Creede, Co., U.S. F10 132
Creedmoor, N.C., U.S. H7 114
Cree Lake, l., Sk., Can. D9 106
Creemore, On., Can. D9 112
Creighton, Ne., U.S. E15 126
Creighton Mine, On., Can. B8 112
Creil, Fr. E11 14
Crema, Italy E6 22
Cremona, Italy E7 22
Crenshaw, Ms., U.S. C8 122
Crepori, stm., Braz. E6 84
Crépy-en-Valois, Fr. E11 14
Cres, Cro. E11 22
Cres, Otok, i., Cro. F11 22
Cresaptown, Md., U.S. E7 114
Crescent, Or., U.S. G5 136
Crescent City, Ca., U.S. B1 134
Crescent City, Fl., U.S. G4 116
Crescent Spur, B.C., Can. C10 138
Cresco, Ia., U.S. H6 118
Crespo, Arg. F7 92
Cresson, Tx., U.S. B10 130
Cressy, Austl. K4 76
Crested Butte, Co., U.S. E9 132
Crestline, Ca., U.S. I8 134
Creston, B.C., Can. G14 138
Creston, Ia., U.S. C3 120
Crestone Peak, mtn., Co., U.S. D3 128
Crestview, Fl., U.S. G12 122
Crestwood Hills, Tn., U.S. I1 114
Creswell, Or., U.S. G3 136
Creswell Bay, b., N.T., Can. A12 106
Crete, Il., U.S. G2 112
Crete, Ne., U.S. G16 126
Crete see Kríti, i., Grc. H7 28
Crete, Sea of see Kritikón Pélagos, Grc. H8 28
Créteil, Fr. F11 14
Cretin, Cape, c., Pap. N. Gui. b4 79a
Creus, Cap de, c., Spain B14 20
Creuse, state, Fr. C8 18
Creuse, stm., Fr. C6 18
Creussen, Ger. G7 16
Creve Coeur, Il., U.S. K9 118
Crevillent, Spain F10 20
Crevillente see Crevillent, Spain F10 20
Crewe, Eng., U.K. H10 12
Crewe, Va., U.S. G7 114

Name | Map Ref. | Page

Cricaré, stm., Braz. J5 88
Criciúma, Braz. D13 92
Crikvenica, Cro. E11 22
Crimea see Kryms'kyi pivostriv, pen., Ukr. E4 32
Crimean Peninsula see Kryms'kyi pivostriv, pen., Ukr. E4 32
Crimmitschau, Ger. F8 16
Cripple Creek, Co., U.S. C3 128
Crisfield, Md., U.S. F10 114
Criss Creek, B.C., Can. E10 138
Crissiumal, Braz. C10 92
Cristal, Monts de, mts., Afr. I7 64
Cristalândia, Braz. F1 88
Cristália, Braz. I4 88
Cristalina, Braz. I2 88
Cristinápolis, Braz. F7 88
Cristino Castro, Braz. E3 88
Cristóbal Colón, Pico, mtn., Col. B5 86
Crişul Alb, stm., Eur. C8 26
Crişul Negru, stm., Eur. C8 26
Crişul Repede (Sebes Körös), stm., Eur. B8 26
Crivitz, Wi., U.S. C1 112
Crna, stm., Mac. B4 28
Crna Gora (Montenegro), state, Yugo. G6 26
Crni Drim (Drinit të Zi), stm., Eur. C14 24
Črnomelj, Slvn. E12 22
Croajingolong National Park, p.o.i., Austl. K7 76
Croatia, ctry., Eur. E13 22
Croche, stm., Qc., Can. C4 110
Crocker, Mo., U.S. G5 120
Crocker, Banjaran, mts., Malay. H1 52
Crockett, Tx., U.S. F3 122
Crocodilopilos, hist., Egypt I1 58
Crocus Hill, hill, Anguilla A1 105a
Crofton, Ky., U.S. G10 120
Croghan, N.Y., U.S. E14 112
Croix, Lac la, l., N.A. C6 118
Croker, Cape, c., Austl. B6 74
Croker, Cape, c., On., Can. D9 112
Croker Island, i., Austl. B6 74
Cromer, Eng., U.K. I14 12
Cromínia, Braz. I1 88
Crompton Point, c., Dom. i6 105c
Cromwell, N.Z. G3 80
Cromwell, Al., U.S. E10 122
Crooked, stm., Or., U.S. F5 136
Crooked Creek, Ak., U.S. D8 140
Crooked Creek, stm., U.S. D8 128
Crooked Island, i., Bah. A10 102
Crooked Island Passage, strt., Bah. A10 102
Crooked River, Sk., Can. B10 124
Crookston, Mn., U.S. D2 118
Crooksville, Oh., U.S. E3 114
Crosby, Mn., U.S. E5 118
Crosby, N.D., U.S. F10 124
Crosby, Mount, mtn., Wy., U.S. D3 126
Crosbyton, Tx., U.S. H7 128
Cross, stm., Afr. H6 64
Crossett, Ar., U.S. D7 122
Cross Lake, res., Mb., Can. E11 106
Crossman Peak, mtn., Az., U.S. I2 132
Cross Plains, Tx., U.S. B8 130
Cross Plains, Wi., U.S. H9 118
Cross Sound, strt., Ak., U.S. E12 140
Crossville, Il., U.S. F9 120
Crossville, Tn., U.S. I12 120
Croswell, Mi., U.S. E7 112
Crotone, Italy E11 24
Crow, North Fork, stm., Mn., U.S. F5 118
Crow, South Fork, stm., Mn., U.S. G4 118
Crow Agency, Mt., U.S. B5 126
Crow Creek, stm., U.S. G8 126
Crowder, Ms., U.S. C8 122
Crowduck Lake, l., Mb., Can. A3 118
Crowdy Head, c., Austl. H9 76
Crowell, Tx., U.S. H9 128
Crow Lake, On., Can. B5 118
Crowley, La., U.S. G6 122
Crowleys Ridge, mts., U.S. B8 122
Crown Mountain, mtn., V.I.U.S. e7 104b
Crown Point, In., U.S. G2 112
Crownpoint, N.M., U.S. H8 132
Crown Point, N.Y., U.S. G3 110
Crown Prince Frederik Island, i., N.T., Can. A13 106
Crowsnest Pass, Ab., Can. G16 138
Crowsnest Pass, p., Can. G16 138
Crows Nest Peak, mtn., S.D., U.S. C8 126
Crow Wing, stm., Mn., U.S. E4 118
Croydon, Austl. B4 76
Croydon Station, B.C., Can. C11 138
Crozet, Va., U.S. F7 114
Crozet, Îles, is., Afr. J16 4
Crozet Basin, unds. M9 142
Crucea, Rom. E15 26
Cruces, Cuba A7 102
Cruger, Ms., U.S. D8 122
Crump Lake, l., Or., U.S. A6 134
Cruz, Cabo, c., Cuba C9 102
Cruz Alta, Arg. F6 92
Cruz Alta, Braz. D11 92
Cruz Bay, V.I.U.S. e7 104b
Cruz del Eje, Arg. E5 92
Cruzeiro, Braz. L3 88
Cruzeiro do Oeste, Braz. A11 92
Cruzeiro do Sul, Braz. E3 84
Cruzeta, Braz. D7 88
Cruz Grande, Chile D2 92
Crysler, On., Can. C14 112
Crystal, Mn., U.S. F5 118
Crystal, N.D., U.S. F16 124
Crystal Brook, Austl. I2 76
Crystal City, Mb., Can. E15 124
Crystal City, Mo., U.S. F7 120
Crystal City, Tx., U.S. F8 130
Crystal Falls, Mi., U.S. B1 112
Crystal Lake, Il., U.S. B9 120
Crystal Lake, l., Mi., U.S. D3 112
Crystal Springs, Ms., U.S. E8 122
Csongrád, Hung. C7 26
Csongrád, state, Hung. C7 26
Csorna, Hung. B4 26
Cu, stm., Asia F11 32
Cúa, Ven. B8 86
Cuajinicuilapa, Mex. G9 100
Cuamba, Moz. C6 68
Cuando (Kwando), stm., Afr. D3 68
Cuangar, Ang. D2 68
Cuango, Ang. B2 68
Cuango see Kwango, stm., Afr. F3 66
Cuanza, stm., Ang. C2 68
Cuao, stm., Ven. E8 86
Cuareim (Quaraí), stm., S.A. E9 92
Cuaró, Ur. E9 92
Cuarto, stm., Arg. F5 92
Cuatrociénegas, Mex. B7 100
Cuauhtémoc, Mex. A5 100
Cuautitlán, Mex. F6 100
Cuba, Port. F3 20
Cuba, Al., U.S. E10 122
Cuba, Il., U.S. D7 120
Cuba, Mo., U.S. F6 120
Cuba, N.M., U.S. G10 132
Cuba, ctry., N.A. C9 96
Cubagua, Isla, i., Ven. B9 86
Cubal, Ang. C1 68
Cubango (Okavango), stm., Afr. D2 68
Cubati, Braz. D7 88
Čublas, Russia D21 8
Çubuk, Tur. C15 28
Čuchi, stm., Ang. C2 68
Cuchillo Co, Arg. I5 92
Cuchivero, stm., Ven. D9 86
Cucuí, Braz. G8 86
Cucurpe, Mex. F7 98
Cúcuta, Col. D5 86
Cucuy, Piedra de, hill, Ven. G8 86
Cudahy, Wi., U.S. F2 112
Cuddalore, India F4 53
Cuddapah, India D4 53
Čudovo, Russia A14 10
Cudworth, Sk., Can. B8 124
Čudzin, Bela. H9 10
Cue, Austl. E3 74
Cuemba, Ang. C2 68
Cuenca, Ec. I2 86
Cuenca, Spain D8 20
Cuenca, co., Spain E9 20
Cuencamé de Ceniceros, Mex. C7 100
Cuernavaca, Mex. F9 100
Cuero, Tx., U.S. E10 130
Cuers, Fr. F12 18
Cuervo, Laguna del, l., Mex. A6 100
Cuesta Pass, p., Ca., U.S. H5 134
Cueto, Cuba B9 102
Cugir, Rom. D10 26
Čuguevka, Russia B10 38
Čuhlomskoe, ozero, l., Russia G19 8
Cuiabá, Braz. G6 84
Cuiabá, stm., Braz. G6 84
Cuiari, Braz. G7 86
Cuicatlán, Mex. G10 100
Cuilapa, Guat. E2 102
Cuilco see Grijalva, stm., N.A. G12 100
Cuilo (Kwilu), stm., Afr. F3 66
Cuité, Braz. D7 88
Cuíto, stm., Ang. D2 68
Cuito Cuanavale, Ang. D2 68
Cuitzeo, Lago de, l., Mex. F8 100
Cuiuni, stm., Braz. H10 86
Cukai, Malay. J6 48
Cukas, Indon. D4 50
Čukotskij, mys, c., Russia D26 34
Čukotskij poluostrov (Chukotsk Peninsula), pen., Russia C26 34
Čulakkurgan, Kaz. F11 32
Culbertson, Mt., U.S. F9 124
Cul de Sac, Guad. A1 105a
Cul de Sac, Neth. Ant. A1 105a
Culebra, P.R. B5 104a
Culebra, Isla de, i., P.R. B5 104a
Culebra Peak, mtn., Co., U.S. D3 128
Culfa, Azer. B6 56
Culgoa, stm., Austl. G6 76
Culiacán, Mex. C5 100
Culiacán, Mex. C5 100
Culion Island, i., Phil. E2 52
Cúllar, Spain G8 20
Cullen, La., U.S. E5 122
Culleoka, Tn., U.S. B12 122
Cullera, Spain E10 20
Cullman, Al., U.S. C12 122
Cullom, Il., U.S. D9 120
Čul'man, Russia E13 34
Culpeper, Va., U.S. F7 114
Culpina, Bol. D4 90
Culuene, stm., Braz. F7 84
Culver, In., U.S. G3 112
Culver, Or., U.S. F5 136
Culverden, N.Z. F5 80
Čulym, Russia C14 32
Čulym, stm., Russia C14 32
Čum, Russia C1 34
Cumaná, Ven. B9 86
Cumare, Cerro, hill, Col. G5 86
Cumari, Braz. J1 88
Cumbal, Nevado, vol., Col. G2 86
Cumbe, Braz. F7 88
Cumberland, B.C., Can. G5 138
Cumberland, Ky., U.S. G2 114
Cumberland, Md., U.S. E7 114
Cumberland, Va., U.S. G7 114
Cumberland, Wi., U.S. F6 118
Cumberland, stm., U.S. H2 114
Cumberland, Lake, res., Ky., U.S. H13 120
Cumberland, South Fork, stm., U.S. H13 120
Cumberland Gap, p., U.S. H2 114
Cumberland Island National Seashore, p.o.i., Ga., U.S. F4 116
Cumberland Islands, is., Austl. C7 76
Cumberland Lake, l., Sk., Can. E10 106
Cumberland Peninsula, pen., N.T., Can. B17 106
Cumberland Plateau, plat., U.S. G14 120
Cumberland Sound, strt., N.T., Can. B17 106
Cumbernauld, Scot., U.K. F9 12
Cumbrian Mountains, mts., Eng., U.K. G9 12
Cumby, Tx., U.S. D3 122
Čumikan, Russia F16 34
Cumming, Ga., U.S. B1 116
Cummins, Austl. F7 74
Cumnock, Scot., U.K. F8 12
Cumpas, Mex. F8 98
Çumra, Tur. F15 28
Čumyš, stm., Russia D15 32
Čuna, stm., Russia C17 32
Cunani, Braz. C7 84
Cunaviche, Ven. D8 86
Cunco, Chile G2 90
Cundinamarca, state, Col. E4 86
Čundža, Kaz. F13 32
Cunene (Kunene), stm., Afr. D1 68
Cuneo (Coni), Italy F4 22
Cunha Porã, Braz. C11 92
Čunja, stm., Russia B17 32
Cunnamulla, Austl. G5 76
Cunningham, Ks., U.S. D10 128
Čunskij, Russia C17 32
Cunucunuma, stm., Ven. F9 86
Čuny, Russia G17 8
Cuorgnè, Italy E4 22
Cupar, Sk., Can. D9 124
Cupar, Scot., U.K. E9 12
Cupica, Golfo de, b., Col. D3 86
Čuprovo, Russia D22 8
Cuquenán, stm., Ven. E11 86
Curaçá, Braz. E6 88
Curaçao, i., Neth. Ant. p21 104g
Curacautín, Chile I2 92
Curanilahue, Chile H1 92
Curanipe, Chile G1 92
Čurapča, Russia D15 34
Curaray, stm., S.A. H4 86
Curepipe, Mrts. i10 69a
Curepto, Chile G1 92
Curicó, Chile G2 92
Curicuriari, stm., Braz. H8 86
Curimatá, Braz. E3 88
Curitiba, Braz. B13 92
Curitibanos, Braz. C12 92
Curiuaú, stm., Braz. H11 86
Curiúva, Braz. B12 92
Curlew, Wa., U.S. B8 136
Curnamona, Austl. H2 76
Čurovići, Russia H15 10
Currais Novos, Braz. D7 88
Curralinho, Braz. D8 84
Currant Mountain, mtn., Nv., U.S. E1 132
Current, stm., U.S. H7 120
Currie, Austl. m12 77a
Currituck, N.C., U.S. H9 114
Currituck Sound, strt., N.C., U.S. H10 114
Curtea de Argeş, Rom. D11 26
Curtina, Ur. F9 92
Curtis, Ar., U.S. D5 122
Curtis, Ne., U.S. G12 126
Curtis, Port, b., Austl. D8 76
Curtis Channel, strt., Austl. D8 76
Curtis Island, i., Austl. D8 76
Curtis Island, i., N.Z. G9 72
Curu, stm., Braz. B6 88
Curuá, stm., Braz. D7 84
Curuá, stm., Braz. E7 84
Curuá, Ilha do, i., Braz. C7 84
Curuá-Una, stm., Braz. D7 84
Curuçá, Braz. D8 84
Curumu, Braz. D7 84
Curup, Indon. E3 50
Curupá, Braz. E2 88
Cururupu, Braz. A3 88
Curuzú Cuatiá, Arg. D8 92
Curvelo, Braz. J3 88
Cusco, Peru F3 84
Cushing, Ok., U.S. B2 122
Cushing, Tx., U.S. F4 122
Cushman, Ar., U.S. I6 120
Cusiana, stm., Col. E5 86
Cusihuiriachic, Mex. A5 100
Čusovaja, stm., Russia C9 32
Čusovoj, Russia C9 32
Cusset, Fr. C9 18
Cusseta, Ga., U.S. E14 122
Čust, Uzb. F12 32
Custer, Mi., U.S. E3 112
Custer, Mt., U.S. A5 126
Custer, S.D., U.S. D9 126
Custódia, Braz. E7 88
Cut, Nuhu, i., Indon. G9 44
Cut Bank, Mt., U.S. B14 136
Cutbank, stm., Ab., Can. B12 138
Cut Bank Creek, stm., U.S. F12 124
Cut Bank Creek, stm., Mt., U.S. B14 136
Cutervo, Peru E2 84
Cuthbert, Ga., U.S. F14 122
Cutler, Ca., U.S. G6 134
Cutler, Me., U.S. F9 110
Cutlerville, Mi., U.S. F4 112
Cutral-Có, Arg. G3 90
Cutro, Italy E10 24
Cuttack, India H10 54
Cutzamalá, stm., Mex. F8 100
Čuvašija, state, Russia C7 32
Cuvier, Cape, c., Austl. D2 74
Cuvo, stm., Ang. C1 68
Cuxhaven, Ger. C4 16
Cuyahoga Falls, Oh., U.S. C4 114
Cuyama, stm., Ca., U.S. I6 134
Cuyamaca Peak, mtn., Ca., U.S. J9 134
Cuyarí, stm., S.A. G7 86
Cuyo, Phil. E3 52
Cuyo East Pass, strt., Phil. E3 52
Cuyo Islands, is., Phil. E3 52
Cuyo West Pass, strt., Phil. E3 52
Cuyubini, stm., Ven. D11 86
Cuyuni, stm., S.A. B6 84
Cuyuni-Mazaruni, state, Guy. D11 86
Cwmbran, Wales, U.K. J10 12
Cyclades see Kikládhes, is., Grc. F7 28
Cypress, La., U.S. F5 122
Cypress Hills, hills, Can. E4 124
Cypress River, Mb., Can. E14 124
Cypress Springs, Lake, res., Tx., U.S. D3 122
Cyprus, ctry., Asia C4 58
Cyprus, i., Asia D15 4
Cyprus, North, ctry., Asia C4 58
Cyrenaica see Barqah, hist. reg., Libya A4 62
Cyril, Ok., U.S. G10 128
Cyril E. King Airport, V.I.U.S. e7 104b
Cyrus Field Bay, b., N.T., Can. E13 141
Čyrvonae, vozero, l., Bela. H10 10
Cythera see Kýthira, i., Grc. G5 28
Czaplinek, Pol. C12 16
Czarna Woda, Pol. C14 16
Czarnków, Pol. D12 16
Czechoslovakia see Czech Republic, ctry., Eur. G11 16
Czechowice-Dziedzice, Pol. G15 16
Czech Republic, ctry., Eur. G11 16
Czerniejewo, Pol. D13 16
Czerwieńsk, Pol. D11 16
Częstochowa, Pol. F15 16
Częstochowa, state, Pol. F15 16
Człuchów, Pol. C13 16

D

Da, stm., China G8 42
Da, Song see Black, stm., Asia D9 46
Da'an, China J4 42
Dabajuro, Ven. B6 86
Daba Ling, mtn., China I5 42
Daba Shan, mts., China E3 42
Dabat, Eth. E7 62
Dabeiba, Col. D3 86
Dabhoi, India G4 54
Dąbie, Pol. D14 16
Dabie Shan, mts., China F6 42
Dabnou, Niger G5 64
Dabola, Gui. G2 64
Dabou, C. Iv. H4 64
Daboya, Ghana H4 64
Dabra, India F7 54
Dąbrowa Białostocka, Pol. C19 16
Dabu, China I7 42
Dacca see Dhaka, Bngl. G13 54
Dac Glei, Viet. E8 48
Dachau, Ger. H7 16
Dačice, Czech Rep. G11 16
Dacoma, Ok., U.S. E10 128
Dadanawa, Guy. F12 86
Dade City, Fl., U.S. H3 116
Dadeldhurā, Nepal D8 54
Dadeville, Al., U.S. E13 122
Dādra and Nagar Haveli, state, India I4 54
Dādu, Pak. D10 56
Daegu see Taegu, Kor., S. D1 40
Daejeon see Taejŏn, Kor., S. F7 38
Daerhanwangfu, China B5 38
Daet, Phil. C4 52
Dafang, China F6 36
Dafeng, China E9 42
Dáfni, Grc. F5 28
Dafoe, Sk., Can. C9 124
Dafu, stm., China F5 42
Dagā, stm., Mya. D2 48
Dagana, Sen. F1 64
Daga Post, Sudan F6 62
Dağardı, Tur. D12 28
Dagda, Lat. D10 10
Dagestan, state, Russia F7 32
Daglung, China D13 54
Dagu, China B7 42
Dagua, Pap. N. Gui. a3 79a
Daguan, China F5 36
Daguan Hu, l., China F7 42
Daguao, P.R. B4 104a
Dagujia, China C6 38
Dagupan, Phil. B3 52
Dagzê Co, l., China B11 54
Dahab, Egypt J5 58
Dahei, India H4 54
Daheiding Shan, mtn., China B10 36
Da Hinggan Ling (Greater Khingan Range), mts., China B9 36
Dahlak Archipelago, is., Erit. D8 62
Dahlonega, Ga., U.S. B1 116
Dahlonega Plateau, plat., U.S. C14 122
Dahmani, Tun. I2 24
Dahme, Ger. E9 16
Dāhod, India G5 54
Dahomey see Benin, ctry., Afr. G5 64
Dahra, Libya B3 62
Dahra, mts., Alg. H11 20
Dahshur, Pyramides de (Dashur, Pyramids of), hist., Egypt I1 58
Dai, i., Sol. Is. d9 79b
Daia, Rom. E12 26
Dai Hai, l., China A5 42
Daik-u, Mya. D3 48
Dā'il, Syria F7 58
Daimiel, Spain E7 20
Daingean, Ire. H5 12
Daingerfield, Tx., U.S. D4 122
Dainkog, China E4 36
Daireaux, Arg. H7 92
Dairen see Dalian, China B9 42
Dairût, Egypt K1 58
Dai-sen, vol., Japan D6 40
Daisetta, Tx., U.S. G4 122
Daixian, China B5 42
Daiyun Shan, mts., China I8 42
Dajarra, Austl. C2 76
Dajian Shan, mtn., China F5 36
Dakar, Sen. G1 64
Dakeng, China H6 42
Dakhin Shāhbāzpur Island, i., Bngl. G13 54
Dakhla, W. Sah. E1 64
Dākoānk, India G7 46
Dakoro, Niger G6 64
Dakota City, Ia., U.S. B3 120
Dakota City, Ne., U.S. B1 120
Đakovica, Yugo. G7 26
Đakovo, Cro. E15 22
Dala, Sol. Is. e9 79b
Dalaba, Gui. G2 64
Dalad Qi, China A4 42
Dalälven, stm., Swe. F7 8
Dalaman, stm., Tur. G11 28
Dalāmī, Sudan E6 62
Dalandzadgad, Mong. C5 36
Dalarna, state, Swe. F6 8
Da Lat, Viet. F9 48
Dālbandin, Pak. D9 56
Dalbosjön, b., Swe. G5 8
Dalby, Austl. F8 76
Dale, Nor. F1 8
Dale, In., U.S. F10 120
Dale Hollow Lake, res., U.S. H12 120
Dalet, Mya. B1 48
Daleville, In., U.S. H4 112
Dalga, Egypt K1 58
Dalhart, Tx., U.S. E6 128
Dalhousie, N.B., Can. B10 110
Dalhousie, India B5 54
Dalhousie, Cape, c., N.T., Can. B14 140
Dali, China F5 36
Dali, China D3 42
Dalian (Dairen), China B9 42
Daliang Shan, mts., China F5 36
Dalin, China C5 38
Daling, stm., China D4 38
Dalj, Cro. E15 22
Dālkola, India F11 54
Dallas, Ga., U.S. D14 122
Dallas, Or., U.S. F3 136
Dallas, Pa., U.S. C9 114
Dallas, Tx., U.S. B11 130
Dallas, Wi., U.S. F7 118
Dallas Center, Ia., U.S. J4 118
Dallas City, Il., U.S. D6 120
Dalli Rājhara, India H8 54
Dall Island, i., Ak., U.S. F13 140
Dall Lake, l., Ak., U.S. D7 140
Dalmacija see Dalmatia, hist. reg., Eur. G12 22
Dalmatia, hist. reg., Eur. G12 22
Dalmau, India E8 54
Dal'negorsk, Russia B11 38
Dal'nerečensk, Russia B11 36
Dal'nyk, Ukr. C17 26
Daloa, C. Iv. H3 64
Dalqū, Sudan C6 62
Dalroy, Ab., Can. E17 138
Dalrymple, Mount, mtn., Austl. C7 76
Dalsing Sarai, India F10 54
Dāltenganj, India F10 54
Dalton, Ga., U.S. C13 122
Dalton, Ma., U.S. B12 114
Dalton, Ne., U.S. F10 126
Daludalu, Indon. C2 50
Dalupiri Island, i., Phil. A3 52
Dalwallinu, Austl. F3 74
Daly, stm., Austl. B6 74
Daly Bay, b., N.T., Can. C13 106
Daly City, Ca., U.S. F3 134
Daly Lake, l., Sk., Can. D9 106
Daly Waters, Austl. C6 74
Dam, stm., China B14 54
Damaia, Port. F1 20
Damān, India H4 54
Damān and Diu, state, India H4 54
Damanhûr, Egypt G1 58
Damar, Pulau, i., Indon. G8 44
Damaraland, hist. reg., Nmb. E2 68
Damascus see Dimashq, Syria E7 58
Damascus, Ar., U.S. B6 122
Damascus, Ga., U.S. F14 122
Damascus, Md., U.S. E8 114
Damaturu, Nig. G7 64
Damāvand, Qolleh-ye, vol., Iran B7 56
Damba, Ang. B2 68
Dambarta, Nig. G6 64
Damboa, Nig. G7 64
Dâmboviţa, state, Rom. E12 26
Dâmboviţa, stm., Rom. D12 26
Dam Doi, Viet. H7 48
Damen Dao, i., China H9 42
Dāmghān, Iran B7 56
Damiao, China C1 42
Damietta, Egypt G2 58
Damietta Mouth see Dumyât, Masabb, mth., Egypt G3 58
Daming, China C6 42
Dāmodar, stm., India G11 54
Damoh, India G7 54
Damongo, Ghana H4 64
Dampier, Austl. D3 74
Dampier, Selat, strt., Indon. F9 44
Dampier Land, pen., Austl. C4 74
Dampier Strait, strt., Pap. N. Gui. b4 79a
Dâmrei, Chuŏr Phnum, mts., Camb. G7 48
Damxung, China C13 54
Dan, stm., China E4 42
Dan, stm., U.S. H6 114
Dana, In., U.S. I2 112
Danai, Indon. C3 50
Danakil, reg., Afr. E8 62
Danané, C. Iv. H3 64
Da Nang, Viet. D9 48
Danao, Phil. E5 52
Dānāpur, India F10 54
Danba, China E5 36
Danbury, Ct., U.S. C12 114
Danbury, Ia., U.S. B2 120
Danbury, Ne., U.S. A8 128
Danby Lake, l., Ca., U.S. I1 132
Dandeli, India D2 53
Dandenong, Austl. K5 76
Dandong, China D5 38
Dandridge, Tn., U.S. H2 114
Danfeng, China E4 42
Danforth, Me., U.S. E9 110
Dang, stm., China F16 32
Dangan Liedao, is., China K6 42
Dangara, Taj. B10 56
Dangchang, China E5 36
Danger Point, c., S. Afr. I4 70
Danggali Conservation Park, p.o.i., Austl. I3 76
Dangila, Eth. E7 62
Dangriga, Belize D3 102
Dangshan, China D7 42
Dangtu, China F8 42
Dan-Gulbi, Nig. G6 64
Dangyang, China F4 42
Daniel, Wy., U.S. H16 136
Daniel-Johnson, Barrage, dam, Qc., Can. E17 106
Daniëlskuil, S. Afr. F6 70
Danielson, Ct., U.S. C13 114
Daniels Pass, p., Ut., U.S. C5 132
Danielsville, Ga., U.S. B2 116
Danilov, Russia G18 8
Danilovka, Kaz. D12 32
Daning, China I4 42
Danjiangkou Shuiku, res., China E4 42
Danjo-guntō, is., Japan G1 40
Danlí, Hond. F4 102
Danmark Fjord, b., Grnld. A22 141
Dannebrog, Ne., U.S. F14 126
Dannenberg, Ger. C6 16
Dannevirke, N.Z. E7 80
Danshui, China J6 42
Dansville, N.Y., U.S. B8 114
Dante, Va., U.S. H3 114
Dantewāra, India B5 53
Danube, stm., Eur. F11 6
Danube, Mouths of the, mth., Eur. E16 26
Danubyu, Mya. D2 48
Danvers, Il., U.S. D8 120
Danville, Qc., Can. E4 110
Danville, Ga., U.S. D2 116
Danville, Il., U.S. H2 112
Danville, Ky., U.S. G13 120
Danville, Pa., U.S. D9 114
Danville, Vt., U.S. F4 110
Danville, Va., U.S. H6 114
Danville, Wa., U.S. B8 136
Danxian, China L3 42
Danyang, China F8 42
Danzig see Gdańsk, Pol. B14 16
Danzig, Gulf of see Gdansk, Gulf of, b., Eur. B15 16
Daocheng, China F5 36
Daodi, China B8 42
Daohu, China G7 42
Daosa, India E6 54
Daotiandi, China B10 36
Daoukro, C. Iv. H4 64
Daoxian, China I4 42
Daozhen, China G2 42
Dapaong, Togo G5 64
Dapchi, Nig. G7 64
Daphnae, hist., Egypt H3 58
Daphne, Al., U.S. G11 122
Dapingshan, China I3 42
Da Qaidam, China D4 36
Daqiu, China I8 42
Dara, Sen. F1 64
Dar'ā, Syria F7 58
Dar'ā, state, Syria F7 58
Dārāb, Iran D7 56
Darāban, Pak. C3 54
Darabani, Rom. A13 26
Darasun, Russia F11 34
Đaravica, mtn., Yugo. G7 26
Darâw, Egypt C6 62
Dārayyā, Syria E7 58
Darb al-Ḥajj, Jabal, mtn., Jord. H6 58
Darbhanga, India E10 54
D'Arbonne, Bayou, stm., La., U.S. E6 122
Darby, Mt., U.S. D12 136
Dardanelle, Ar., U.S. B5 122
Dardanelle Lake, res., Ar., U.S. B5 122
Dardanelles see Çanakkale Boğazı, strt., Tur. C9 28
Dar-el-Beida see Casablanca, Mor. C3 64
Dar es Salaam, Tan. F7 66
Darfo, Italy E7 22
Dargai, Pak. A3 54
Dargan-Ata, Turkmen. A9 56
Dargaville, N.Z. B5 80
Dargol, Niger G5 64
Darhan, Mong. B6 36
Darıca, Tur. C12 28
Darién, Col. F3 86
Darien, Ga., U.S. E4 116
Darien, Parque Nacional, p.o.i., Pan. D2 86
Darién, Serranía del, mts. C3 86
Dārjiling, India E12 54
Dark Head, c., St. Vin. o11 105e
Darlag, China E4 36
Darling, S. Afr. H4 70
Darling, Ms., U.S. C8 122
Darling, stm., Austl. I4 76
Darling Downs, reg., Austl. F8 76
Darlingford, Mb., Can. E15 124
Darling Range, mts., Austl. F3 74
Darlington, Eng., U.K. G11 12
Darlington, Wi., U.S. B7 120
Darlington Dam, res., S. Afr. H7 70
Darlot, Lake, l., Austl. E4 74
Darłowo, Pol. B12 16
Darmstadt, Ger. G4 16
Darnah, Libya A4 62
Darnall, S. Afr. F10 70
Darney, Fr. F15 14
Darnley, Cape, c., Ant. B11 81
Darnley Bay, b., N.T., Can. B6 106
Darr, stm., Austl. D4 76
Darregueira, Arg. H6 92
Darreh Gaz, Iran B8 56
Darrington, Wa., U.S. B5 136
Darrouzett, Tx., U.S. E8 128
Dart, Cape, c., Ant. C27 81
Dartmoor, Austl. K3 76
Dartmoor, for., Eng., U.K. K9 12
Dartmoor National Park, p.o.i., Eng., U.K. K9 12
Dartmouth, N.S., Can. F13 110
Dartmouth, Eng., U.K. K9 12
Dartmouth, Lake, l., Austl. E5 76
Dartmouth Reservoir, res., Austl. K6 76
Daru, Pap. N. Gui. b3 79a
Daruvar, Cro. E14 22
Darvaza, Turkmen. A8 56
Dārwha, India H6 54
Darwin, Austl. B6 74
Darwin, Bahía, b., Chile I2 90
Darya Khān, Pak. C3 54
Dashbalbar, Mong. B7 36
Dashitou, China C8 38
Dašhovuz, Turkmen. A8 56
Dasht, stm., Pak. D9 56
Dashur, Pyramids of see Dahshur, Pyramides de, hist., Egypt I1 58
Dashutang, China A6 48
Dasol Bay, b., Phil. C2 52
Dastgardān, Iran C8 56
Datang, China I3 42
Datça, Tur. G10 28
Date, Japan C14 38
Datia, India F7 54
Datian, China I7 42
Datian Ding, mtn., China J4 42
Datong, China D5 36
Datong, China B9 36
Datong, China A5 42
Datong Shan, mts., China D4 36
Datu, Cape, c., Asia E4 44
Datumakuta, Indon. B10 50
Datu Piang, Phil. G5 52
Daua (Dawa), stm., Afr. G8 62
Daudnagar, India F10 54
Daugai, Lith. F7 10
Daugavpils, Lat. E9 10
Dauhinava, Bela. F10 10
Daule, Ec. H2 86
Daule, stm., Ec. H1 86
Daund, India B2 53
Daung Kyun, i., Mya. F3 48
Dauphin, Mb., Can. C13 124
Dauphin, stm., Mb., Can. C15 124
Dauphiné, hist. reg., Fr. E11 18
Dauphin Island, Al., U.S. G10 122
Dauphin Island, i., Al., U.S. G10 122
Dauphin Lake, l., Mb., Can. C13 124
Daura, Nig. G6 64
Dāvangere, India D2 53
Davant, La., U.S. H9 122
Davao, Phil. G5 52
Davao Gulf, b., Phil. G5 52
Dāvarzan, Iran B8 56
Davenport, Fl., U.S. H4 116
Davenport, Ia., U.S. C7 120
Davenport, Ok., U.S. B2 122
Davenport, Wa., U.S. C8 136
Davenport Downs, Austl. E3 76
Davey, Port, b., Austl. o12 77a
David, Pan. H6 102
David City, Ne., U.S. F15 126
Davidson, Sk., Can. C7 124
Davidson Mountains, mts., Ak., U.S. C11 140
Davie, Fl., U.S. J5 116
Davis, Ca., U.S. E4 134
Davis, N.C., U.S. B9 116
Davis, Ok., U.S. G11 128
Davis, W.V., U.S. E6 114
Davis, stm., Austl. D4 74
Davis, sci., Ant. B12 81
Davis, Mount, mtn., Pa., U.S. E6 114
Davisboro, Ga., U.S. C3 116
Davis Dam, dam, U.S. H2 132
Davis Inlet, Nf., Can. D18 106
Davis Mountains, mts., Tx., U.S. D3 130
Davis Sea, Ant. P11 142
Davis Strait, strt., N.A. D14 141
Davos, Switz. D6 22
Davy, W.V., U.S. G4 114
Davyd-Haradok, Bela. H9 10
Dawa (Daua), stm., Afr. G7 62
Dawei (Tavoy), Mya. E4 48
Dawen, stm., China D7 42
Dawlan, Mya. D4 48
Dawna Range, mts., Mya. D4 48
Dawson, Yk., Can. C3 106
Dawson, Ga., U.S. F14 122
Dawson, Ne., U.S. D2 120
Dawson, Tx., U.S. F2 122
Dawson, stm., Austl. D7 76
Dawson, Isla, i., Chile J2 90
Dawson Bay, b., Mb., Can. B13 124
Dawson Creek, B.C., Can. D7 106
Dawson Inlet, b., N.T., Can. C12 106
Dawson Range, mts., Yk., Can. C3 106
Dawsonville, Ga., U.S. B1 116
Dax, Fr. F4 18
Daxian, China F2 42
Daxing, China B7 42
Daxu, China I4 42
Daxue Shan, mts., China F5 36
Dayang, stm., China D5 38
Dayangshu, China B9 36
Dayao, China F5 36
Daye, China F6 42
Daying, China B5 42
Daylesford, Austl. K5 76
Daymán, stm., Ur. E9 92
Dayong, China G4 42
Dayr az-Zawr, Syria B4 56
Dayr Ḥāfir, Syria B8 58
Daysland, Ab., Can. D18 138
Dayton, Oh., U.S. E1 114
Dayton, Or., U.S. E3 136
Dayton, Tn., U.S. B13 122
Dayton, Tx., U.S. G4 122
Dayton, Wa., U.S. D9 136
Dayton, Wy., U.S. C5 126
Daytona Beach, Fl., U.S. G5 116
Dayu, China I6 42
Dayu Ling, mts., China I6 42
Da Yunhe (Grand Canal), can., China E8 42
Dayville, Or., U.S. F7 136
Dazhu, China F2 42
Dazkırı, Tur. F12 28
De Aar, S. Afr. G7 70
Deadhorse, Ak., U.S. B10 140
Deadman's Cay, Bah. A10 102
Dead Sea, l., Asia G6 58
Deadwood, S.D., U.S. C9 126
Deakin, Austl. F5 74
Deal, Eng., U.K. J14 12
Dealesville, S. Afr. F7 70
Deal Island, Md., U.S. F10 114
De'an, China G6 42
Dean, stm., B.C., Can. D4 138
Deán Funes, Arg. E5 92
Deans Dundas Bay, b., N.T., Can. B16 140
Dearborn, Mi., U.S. B2 114
Dearg, Beinn, mtn., Scot., U.K. D8 12
Dease, stm., B.C., Can. D5 106
Dease Arm, b., N.T., Can. B6 106
Dease Strait, strt., N.T., Can. B9 106
Death Valley, Ca., U.S. G9 134
Death Valley, val., Ca., U.S. G9 134
Death Valley National Park, p.o.i., U.S. G8 134
Deatsville, Al., U.S. E12 122
Deauville, Fr. E8 14
Deba, Nig. G7 64
Debao, China J2 42
Debar, Mac. B3 28
De Bary, Fl., U.S. H4 116
Debe, Trin. s12 105f
De Berry, Tx., U.S. E4 122
Dębica, Pol. F17 16
Dęblin, Pol. E17 16
Débo, Lac, l., Mali F4 64
Deborah West, Lake, l., Austl. F3 74
Deboyne Islands, is., Pap. N. Gui. B10 74
Debre Birhan, Eth. F7 62
Debrecen, Hung. B8 26
Debre Mark'os, Eth. E7 62
Debre Tabor, Eth. E7 62

Name	Map Ref.	Page

Dorc-Elag I•17

Name	Map Ref.	Page
Dorchester, N.B., Can.	E12	110
Dorchester, On., Can.	F8	112
Dorchester, Eng., U.K.	K10	12
Dorchester, Ne., U.S.	G15	126
Dorchester, Cape, c., N.T., Can.	B15	106
Dordabis, Nmb.	C3	70
Dordogne, state, Fr.	D6	18
Dordogne, stm., Fr.	D8	18
Dordrecht, Neth.	C13	14
Dordrecht, S. Afr.	G8	70
Dore Lake, l., Sk., Can.	E9	106
Dorena, Or., U.S.	G4	136
Dores do Indaiá, Braz.	J3	88
Dorfen, Ger.	H8	16
Dorgali, Italy	D3	24
Dörgön nuur, l., Mong.	B3	36
Dori, Burkina	G4	64
Doring, stm., S. Afr.	G4	70
Dornbirn, Aus.	C6	22
Dornoch, Scot., U.K.	D8	12
Dorog, Hung.	B5	26
Dorogobuž, Russia	F16	10
Dorohoi, Rom.	A13	26
Dorokempo, Indon.	H11	50
Dorre Island, i., Austl.	E2	74
Dorrigo, Austl.	H9	76
Dorris, Ca., U.S.	B4	134
Dorsale, mts., Tun.	I3	24
Dort see Dordrecht, Neth.	C13	14
Dortmund, Ger.	E3	16
Dorton, Ky., U.S.	G3	114
Dörtyol, Tur.	B7	58
Doruma, D.R.C.	D5	66
Dos, Canal Numero, can., Arg.	H9	92
Dosatuj, Russia	A8	36
Dos Bahías, Cabo, c., Arg.	H3	90
Dos Bocas, P.R.	B2	104a
Döşemealtı, Tur.	F13	28
Dos Hermanas, Spain	G4	20
Do Son, Viet.	B8	48
Dos Pos, Neth. Ant.	p23	104g
Dos Quebradas, Col.	E4	86
Dosso, Niger	G5	64
Dossor, Kaz.	E8	32
Dothan, Al., U.S.	F13	122
Dotnuva, Lith.	E6	10
Dou, stm., China	B8	42
Douai, Fr.	D11	14
Douala, Cam.	D1	66
Douarnenez, Fr.	F4	14
Doublé, Pointe, c., Guad.	h7	105c
Double Island Point, c., Austl.	E9	76
Double Springs, Al., U.S.	C11	122
Doubletop Peak, mtn., Wy., U.S.	G16	136
Doubs, state, Fr.	G15	14
Doubs, stm., Eur.	H14	14
Doubtful Sound, strt., N.Z.	G2	80
Doubtless Bay, b., N.Z.	B5	80
Douentza, Mali	F4	64
Dougga, hist., Tun.	H3	24
Douglas, Mb., Can.	E14	124
Douglas, I. of Man	G8	12
Douglas, S. Afr.	F6	70
Douglas, Ak., U.S.	E13	140
Douglas, Az., U.S.	L7	132
Douglas, Ga., U.S.	E3	116
Douglas, Wy., U.S.	E7	126
Douglas Channel, strt., B.C., Can.	C1	138
Douglas Lake, B.C., Can.	F10	138
Douglas Lake, res., Tn., U.S.	H2	114
Douglasville, Ga., U.S.	D14	122
Doullens, Fr.	D11	14
Dourada, Serra, plat., Braz.	G1	88
Dourados, Braz.	D6	90
Dourbali, Chad	E3	62
Douro (Duero), stm., Eur.	C2	20
Dousk, Bela.	G13	10
Douz, Tun.	C6	64
Dove Bugt, strt., Grnld.	B21	141
Dove Creek, Co., U.S.	F7	132
Dover, Austl.	o13	77a
Dover, Eng., U.K.	J14	12
Dover, De., U.S.	E10	114
Dover, Id., U.S.	B10	136
Dover, N.H., U.S.	G6	110
Dover, N.J., U.S.	D11	114
Dover, N.C., U.S.	A8	116
Dover, Oh., U.S.	D4	114
Dover, Ok., U.S.	E11	128
Dover, Tn., U.S.	H10	120
Dover, Strait of, strt., Eur.	K14	12
Dover-Foxcroft, Me., U.S.	E7	110
Dovrefjell Nasjonalpark, p.o.i., Nor.	E3	8
Dow City, Ia., U.S.	C2	120
Dowlatābād, Iran	D8	56
Downey, Id., U.S.	H14	136
Downieville, Ca., U.S.	D5	134
Downing, Mo., U.S.	D5	120
Downingtown, Pa., U.S.	D10	114
Downpatrick, N. Ire., U.K.	G7	12
Downs, Ks., U.S.	B10	128
Downton, Mount, mtn., B.C., Can.	D6	138
Dows, Ia., U.S.	B4	120
Dowshī, Afg.	B10	56
Doyle, Ca., U.S.	C5	134
Doyles, Nf., Can.	C17	110
Doylestown, Pa., U.S.	D10	114
Doyline, La., U.S.	E5	122
Dōzen, is., Japan	C5	40
Dozier, Al., U.S.	F12	122
Dra, Cap, c., Mor.	D2	64
Dra'a, Hamada du, des., Alg.	D3	64
Drâa, Oued, stm., Afr.	D2	64
Drac, stm., Fr.	E2	22
Dracena, Braz.	D6	90
Drachten, Neth.	A15	14
Dracut, Ma., U.S.	B14	114
Dragalina, Rom.	E14	26
Drăgănești-Vlașca, Rom.	E12	26
Drăgășani, Rom.	E11	26
Dragonera, Sa, i., Spain	E13	20
Dragons Mouths, strt.	s12	105f
Dragoon, Az., U.S.	K6	132
Draguignan, Fr.	F12	18
Drahičyn, Bela.	H8	10
Drake, N.D., U.S.	G13	124
Drakensberg, mts., Afr.	F9	70
Drake Passage, strt.	K8	82
Drakesboro, Ky., U.S.	G10	120
Drakes Branch, Va., U.S.	H7	114
Dráma, Grc.	B7	28
Drammen, Nor.	G3	8
Drang, stm., Asia	F8	48
Drangajökull, ice, Ice.	j28	8a
Dranov, Ostrovul, i., Rom.	E16	26
Drau (Dráva), stm., Eur.	D11	22
Dráva (Drau), stm., Eur.	D14	22
Dravograd, Slvn.	D12	22
Drawsko Pomorskie, Pol.	C11	16
Drayton, N.D., U.S.	C1	118
Drayton, S.C., U.S.	B4	116
Drayton Valley, Ab., Can.	C15	138
Dresden, On., Can.	F7	112
Dresden, Ger.	E9	16
Dresden, Oh., U.S.	D3	114
Drètun', Bela.	E12	10
Dreux, Fr.	F10	14
Drew, Ms., U.S.	D8	122
Drienov, Slov.	H17	16
Driftwood, B.C., Can.	D5	106
Driftwood, stm., In., U.S.	E12	120
Driggs, Id., U.S.	G15	136
Drin, stm., Alb.	C13	24
Drina, stm., Eur.	F16	22
Drinit, Gjiri i, b., Alb.	C13	24
Drinit të Zi (Crni Drim), stm., Eur.	C14	24
Driskill Mountain, hill, La., U.S.	E6	122
Drissa (Drysa), stm., Eur.	E11	10
Drniš, Cro.	G13	22
Drobeta-Turnu Severin, Rom.	E9	26
Drochia, Mol.	A14	26
Drogheda, Ire.	H6	12
Droichead Átha see Drogheda, Ire.	H6	12
Droichead Nua, Ire.	H6	12
Drôme, state, Fr.	E11	18
Dronero, Italy	F4	22
Dronne, stm., Fr.	D6	18
Dronning Louise Land, reg., Grnld.	B20	141
Druc', stm., Bela.	G12	10
Druif, Aruba	o19	104g
Druja, Bela.	E10	10
Drūkšiai, l., Eur.	E9	10
Drumheller, Ab., Can.	E18	138
Drummond, Mt., U.S.	D13	136
Drummond, Wi., U.S.	E7	118
Drummond Island, i., Mi., U.S.	C6	112
Drummondville, Qc., Can.	E4	110
Druskininkai, Lith.	F7	10
Družba, Kaz.	E14	32
Druzhba see Družba, Kaz.	E14	32
Družina, Russia	C18	34
Drvar, Bos.	E3	26
Dry Arm, b., Mt., U.S.	G7	124
Dry Bay, b., Ak., U.S.	E12	140
Dryberry Lake, l., On., Can.	B4	118
Dry Cimarron, stm., U.S.	B2	122
Dry Creek Mountain, mtn., Nv., U.S.	B9	134
Dryden, On., Can.	B6	118
Dry Devils, stm., Tx., U.S.	D7	130
Dry Prong, La., U.S.	F6	122
Dry Ridge, Ky., U.S.	F1	114
Drysdale, stm., Austl.	C5	74
Dry Tortugas, is., Fl., U.S.	G11	108
Dry Tortugas National Park, p.o.i., Fl., U.S.	L3	116
Drzewica, Pol.	E16	16
Dschang, Cam.	C1	66
Du, stm., China	E4	42
Du'an, China	I3	42
Duaringa, Austl.	D7	76
Duarte, Pico, mtn., Dom. Rep.	C12	102
Duartina, Braz.	L1	88
Dubā, Sau. Ar.	K6	58
Dubach, La., U.S.	E6	122
Dubai see Dubayy, U.A.E.	D8	56
Dubăsari, Mol.	B16	26
Dubăsari, Lacul, res., Mol.	B15	26
Dubawnt, stm., N.T., Can.	C10	106
Dubawnt Lake, l., N.T., Can.	C10	106
Dubayy (Dubai), U.A.E.	D8	56
Dubbo, Austl.	I7	76
Dubh Artach, r., Scot., U.K.	E6	12
Dublin (Baile Átha Cliath), Ire.	H6	12
Dublin, Ga., U.S.	D3	116
Dublin, Tx., U.S.	B9	130
Dublin, Va., U.S.	G5	114
Dublin, state, Ire.	H6	12
Dubna, Russia	F19	10
Dubna, Russia	D20	10
Dubna, stm., Russia	D21	10
Dubnica nad Váhom, Slov.	H14	16
Dubois, In., U.S.	F11	120
Du Bois, Ne., U.S.	D1	120
Du Bois, Pa., U.S.	C7	114
Dubois, Wy., U.S.	D3	126
Dubossary Reservoir see Dubăsari, Lacul, res., Mol.	B15	26
Dubovka, Russia	E6	32
Dubrājpur, India	G11	54
Dubréka, Gui.	H2	64
Dubrouna, Bela.	F13	10
Dubrovka, Russia	G16	10
Dubrovnik, Cro.	H15	22
Dubrovnoe, Russia	C11	32
Dubuque, Ia., U.S.	B7	120
Dubysa, stm., Lith.	E6	10
Duchang, China	G7	42
Duchesne, Ut., U.S.	C6	132
Duchesne, stm., Ut., U.S.	C7	132
Duchess, Austl.	C2	76
Duck, stm., Tn., U.S.	B11	122
Duck Creek, stm., Nv., U.S.	D2	132
Duck Hill, Ms., U.S.	D9	122
Duck Lake, Sk., Can.	B7	124
Ducktown, Tn., U.S.	B14	122
Duda, stm., Col.	F4	86
Dudačkino, Russia	A15	10
Duderstadt, Ger.	E6	16
Dudinka, Russia	C6	34
Dudley, Eng., U.K.	I10	12
Dudleyville, Az., U.S.	K6	132
Dudna, stm., India	B2	53
Dudorovskij, Russia	G18	10
Dudwa National Park, p.o.i., India	D8	54
Dueré, stm., Braz.	F1	88
Duero (Douro), stm., Eur.	C2	20
Due West, S.C., U.S.	B3	116
Dufourspitze, mtn., Eur.	D13	18
Dufur, Or., U.S.	E5	136
Duga-Zapadnaja, mys, c., Russia	E18	34
Dugdemona, stm., La., U.S.	F6	122
Dugi Otok, i., Cro.	F11	22
Dugna, Russia	F19	10
Du Gué, stm., Qc., Can.	D16	106
Duhovščina, Russia	E15	10
Duida, Cerro, mtn., Ven.	F9	86
Duisburg, Ger.	E2	16
Duitama, Col.	E5	86
Duiwelskloof, S. Afr.	C10	70
Dujuuma, Som.	D8	66
Duke, Ok., U.S.	G9	128
Duke of York Bay, b., N.T., Can.	B13	106
Duk Fadiat, Sudan	F6	62
Dukhān, Qatar	D7	56
Duki, Pak.	C2	54
Dukla Pass, p., Eur.	G17	16
Dukou, China	F5	36
Dūkštas, Lith.	E9	10
Dulan, China	D4	36
Dulce, N.M., U.S.	G9	132
Dulce, stm., Arg.	D6	92
Dulce, Golfo, b., C.R.	H6	102
Dul'durga, Russia	F11	34
Dulgalah, stm., Russia	C15	34
Dullstroom, S. Afr.	D10	70
Dulovka, Russia	C11	10
Dulq Maghār, Syria	B9	58
Duluth, Ga., U.S.	C14	122
Duluth, Mn., U.S.	E6	118
Dūmā, Syria	E7	58
Dumaguete, Phil.	F4	52
Dumai, Indon.	C2	50
Dumalag, Phil.	E4	52
Dumali Point, c., Phil.	D3	52
Dumaran Island, i., Phil.	E2	52
Dumaresq, stm., Austl.	G8	76
Dumaring, Indon.	C11	50
Dumas, Tx., U.S.	F7	128
Dumbarton, Scot., U.K.	F8	12
Dumbrăveni, Rom.	C11	26
Dume, Point, c., Ca., U.S.	J7	134
Dumfries, Scot., U.K.	F9	12
Dumka, India	F11	54
Dumlupınar, Tur.	E12	28
Dummar, Syria	E7	58
Dumoine, Lac, l., Qc., Can.	B12	112
Dumont, Ia., U.S.	B4	120
Dumont d'Urville, sci., Ant.	B18	81
Dumpu, Pap. N. Gui.	b4	79a
Dumraon, India	F10	54
Dumyât, Masabb (Damietta Mouth), mth., Egypt	G3	58
Duna see Danube, stm., Eur.	F11	6
Dunaharaszti, Hung.	B6	26
Dunaj see Danube, stm., Eur.	F11	6
Dunajec, stm., Eur.	F16	16
Dunajská Streda, Slov.	H13	16
Dunakeszi, Hung.	B6	26
Dunărea Veche, Brațul, stm., Rom.	E15	26
Dunaújváros, Hung.	C5	26
Dunavățu de Sus, Rom.	E16	26
Duna-völgyi-főcsatorna, can., Hung.	C6	26
Dunav-Tisa-Dunav, Kanal, can., Yugo.	D6	26
Dunbar, Scot., U.K.	E10	12
Dunblane, Sk., Can.	C6	124
Duncan, B.C., Can.	H7	138
Duncan, Az., U.S.	K7	132
Duncan, Ok., U.S.	G11	128
Duncan, stm., B.C., Can.	F13	138
Duncan Lake, res., B.C., Can.	F14	138
Duncannon, Pa., U.S.	D8	114
Duncan Passage, strt., India	F7	46
Duncans, Jam.	i13	104d
Duncansby Head, c., Scot., U.K.	C9	12
Dundaga, Lat.	C5	10
Dundalk, On., Can.	D9	112
Dundalk (Dún Dealgan), Ire.	G6	12
Dundalk, Md., U.S.	E9	114
Dundalk Bay, b., Ire.	H6	12
Dundas, On., Can.	E9	112
Dundas, Lake, l., Austl.	F4	74
Dundas Peninsula, pen., N.T., Can.	B17	140
Dundas Strait, strt., Austl.	B6	74
Dún Dealgan see Dundalk, Ire.	G6	12
Dundee, S. Afr.	F10	70
Dundee, Scot., U.K.	E10	12
Dundee, Fl., U.S.	H4	116
Dundee, Mi., U.S.	C2	114
Dundurn, Sk., Can.	C7	124
Dunedin, N.Z.	G4	80
Dunedin, Fl., U.S.	H3	116
Dunedoo, Austl.	I7	76
Dunfermline, Scot., U.K.	E9	12
Dungannon, N. Ire., U.K.	G6	12
Dūngarpur, India	G4	54
Dungarvan, Ire.	I5	12
Dungeness, c., Eng., U.K.	K13	12
Dungog, Austl.	I8	76
Dungu, D.R.C.	D5	66
Dungun, Malay.	J6	48
Dunhua, China	C8	38
Dunhuang, China	C3	36
Dunilovo, Russia	C21	10
Dunkerque (Dunkirk), Fr.	C11	14
Dunkirk see Dunkerque, Fr.	C11	14
Dunkirk, In., U.S.	H4	112
Dunkirk, N.Y., U.S.	B6	114
Dunkirk, Oh., U.S.	D2	114
Dunkwa, Ghana	H4	64
Dún Laoghaire, Ire.	H6	12
Dunlap, Tn., U.S.	B13	122
Dunmore, Pa., U.S.	C10	114
Dunmore Town, Bah.	K9	116
Dunn, N.C., U.S.	A7	116
Dunnellon, Fl., U.S.	G3	116
Dunnet Head, c., Scot., U.K.	C9	12
Dunning, Ne., U.S.	F12	126
Dunnville, On., Can.	F10	112
Dunoon, Scot., U.K.	F8	12
Dunqulah, Sudan	D5	62
Dunqunāb, Sudan	C7	62
Duns, Scot., U.K.	F10	12
Dunseith, N.D., U.S.	F13	124
Dunsmuir, Ca., U.S.	B3	134
Dunstable, Eng., U.K.	J12	12
Dunster, B.C., Can.	C11	138
Dunyāpur, Pak.	D3	54
Duolun, China	C2	38
Duolundabohuer, China	B14	54
Duomula, China	A9	54
Duozhu, China	J6	42
Dupang Ling, mts., China	I4	42
Dupnica, Blg.	G10	26
Dupnitsa see Dupnica, Blg.	G10	26
Dupuyer, Mt., U.S.	B14	136
Duque Bacelar, Braz.	C4	88
Duque de Caxias, Braz.	L4	88
Duque de York, Isla, i., Chile	J1	90
Duran, N.M., U.S.	G3	128
Durance, stm., Fr.	F11	18
Durand, Il., U.S.	B8	120
Durand, Wi., U.S.	G7	118
Durand, Récif, rf., N. Cal.	n17	79d
Durand Reef see Durand, Récif, rf., N. Cal.	n17	79d
Durango, Mex.	C6	100
Durango, Spain	A8	20
Durango, Co., U.S.	F9	132
Durango, state, Mex.	C6	100
Durant, Ia., U.S.	C6	120
Durant, Ms., U.S.	D9	122
Durant, Ok., U.S.	D2	122
Duras, Fr.	E6	18
Durazno, Ur.	F9	92
Durban, S. Afr.	F10	70
Đurđevac, Cro.	D14	22
Düren, Ger.	F2	16
Durg, India	H8	54
Durgāpur, India	G11	54
Durham, On., Can.	D9	112
Durham, Eng., U.K.	G11	12
Durham, Ca., U.S.	D4	134
Durham, N.H., U.S.	G5	110
Durham, N.C., U.S.	H6	114
Durham Downs, Austl.	F3	76
Durham Heights, mtn., N.T., Can.	A6	106
Durlas éile see Thurles, Ire.	I5	12
Durlești, Mol.	B15	26
Durmitor, mtn., Yugo.	F5	26
Durmitor Nacionalni Park, p.o.i., Yugo.	F6	26
Dürnkrut, Aus.	B13	22
Durrës, Alb.	C13	24
Durrësi see Durrës, Alb.	C13	24
Durrie, Austl.	E3	76
Dursunbey, Tur.	D11	28
Duru Gölü, l., Tur.	B11	28
Durūz, Jabal ad-, mtn., Syria	F7	58
D'Urville, Tanjung, c., Indon.	F10	44
D'Urville Island, i., N.Z.	E5	80
Dušak, Turkmen.	B9	56
Dusa Marreb see Dhuusamarreeb, Som.	C9	66
Dušanbe, Taj.	B10	56
Dušekan, Russia	B19	32
Dusetos, Lith.	E8	10
Dushan, China	I2	42
Du Shan, mtn., China	A8	42
Dushanzi, China	C1	36
Duson, La., U.S.	G6	122
Düsseldorf, Ger.	E2	16
Dustin, Ok., U.S.	B2	122
Dutch John, Ut., U.S.	C7	132
Dutton, Mt., U.S.	C15	136
Dutton, stm., Austl.	C4	76
Duvno, Bos.	F4	26
Duxun, China	J7	42
Duyfken Point, c., Austl.	B8	74
Duyun, China	H2	42
Düzce, Tur.	C14	28
Dve Mogili, Blg.	F12	26
Dvine, ozero, l., Russia	D14	10
Dvinskaja guba, b., Russia	D17	8
Dvuh Cirkov, gora, mtn., Russia	C22	34
Dvůr Králové nad Labem, Czech Rep.	F11	16
Dwārka, India	G2	54
Dwight, Il., U.S.	C9	120
Dworshak Reservoir, res., Id., U.S.	D11	136
Dwyka, stm., S. Afr.	H5	70
Dyer, Tn., U.S.	H8	120
Dyer, Cape, c., N.T., Can.	D13	141
Dyer Bay, b., On., Can.	C8	112
Dyersburg, Tn., U.S.	H8	120
Dyje (Thaya), stm., Eur.	H12	16
Dyment, On., Can.	B6	118
Dynów, Pol.	G18	16
Dysart, Sk., Can.	D9	124
Dysart, Ia., U.S.	B5	120
Dysna (Dzisna), stm., Eur.	E9	10
Dytikí Elláda, state, Grc.	E4	28
Dytikí Makedonía, state, Grc.	C4	28
Džagdy, hrebet, mts., Russia	F15	34
Džalal-Abad, Kyrg.	F12	32
Džalinda, Russia	F13	34
Džambejty, Kaz.	D8	32
Džanybek, Kaz.	E7	32
Dzaoudzi, May.	C8	68
Džardžan, Russia	C13	34
Dzavhan, stm., Mong.	B3	36
Dzeržinsk, Russia	H20	8
Dzeržinskoe, Russia	C16	32
Džetygara, Kaz.	D10	32
Dzhankoi, Ukr.	E4	32
Dzhugdzhur Mountains see Džugdžur, hrebet, mts., Russia	E16	34
Dzhungarian Alatau Mountains, mts., Asia	E14	32
Działoszyce, Pol.	F16	16
Dzibilchaltún, hist., Mex.	B3	102
Dzierżoniów, Pol.	F12	16
Dzilam González, Mex.	B3	102
Dzisna, Bela.	E11	10
Dzisna (Dysna), stm., Eur.	E9	10
Dzitbalché, Mex.	B2	102
Dziwnów, Pol.	B10	16
Džizak, Uzb.	F11	32
Dzjarèčyn, Bela.	G7	10
Dzjaršynskaja, hara, hill, Bela.	G9	10
Dzjaržynsk, Bela.	G9	10
Dzjatlavičy, Bela.	H9	10
Dzöölön, Mong.	F8	34
Džugdžur, hrebet, mts., Russia	E16	34
Dzūkijos nacionalinis parkas, p.o.i., Lith.	F7	10
Dzungarian Basin see Junggar Pendi, bas., China	B2	36
Dzungarian Gate, p., Asia	E14	32
Džusaly, Kaz.	E10	32
Dzüünharaa, Mong.	B6	36
Dzuunmod, Mong.	B6	36
Dzyhivka, Ukr.	A15	26

E

Name	Map Ref.	Page
Eads, Co., U.S.	C6	128
Eagle, Ak., U.S.	D11	140
Eagle, Co., U.S.	D10	132
Eagle, stm., Co., U.S.	B2	128
Eagle Bay, B.C., Can.	F11	138
Eagle Butte, S.D., U.S.	C11	126
Eagle Creek, stm., Sk., Can.	B6	124
Eagle Grove, Ia., U.S.	B4	120
Eaglehawk, Austl.	K4	76
Eagle Lake, Tx., U.S.	H2	122
Eagle Lake, l., On., Can.	B5	118
Eagle Lake, l., Ca., U.S.	C5	134
Eagle Lake, l., Me., U.S.	D7	110
Eagle Mountain, Ca., U.S.	J1	132
Eagle Mountain, mtn., Id., U.S.	D11	136
Eagle Mountain, mtn., Mn., U.S.	D8	118
Eagle Mountain Lake, res., Tx., U.S.	A10	130
Eagle Pass, Tx., U.S.	F7	130
Eagle Peak, mtn., Ca., U.S.	B5	134
Eagle River, Mi., U.S.	D10	118
Eagle River, Wi., U.S.	F9	118
Eagletown, Ok., U.S.	C4	122
Ear Falls, On., Can.	A5	118
Earle, Ar., U.S.	B8	122
Earl Grey, Sk., Can.	D9	124
Earlham, Ia., U.S.	C3	120
Earlimart, Ca., U.S.	H6	134
Earlville, Il., U.S.	C8	120
Early, Ia., U.S.	B2	120
Early, Tx., U.S.	C9	130
Eas, Vanuatu	k17	79d
Easley, S.C., U.S.	B3	116
East Alton, Il., U.S.	F7	120
East Angus, Qc., Can.	E5	110
East Antarctica, reg., Ant.	C8	81
East Aurora, N.Y., U.S.	B7	114
East Bay, b., Tx., U.S.	H4	122
East Bend, N.C., U.S.	H5	114
East Bernard, Tx., U.S.	H2	122
East Bernstadt, Ky., U.S.	G1	114
East Borneo see Kalimantan Timur, state, Indon.	C10	50
Eastbourne, Eng., U.K.	K13	12
East Brady, Pa., U.S.	D6	114
East Brewton, Al., U.S.	F11	122
East Cache Creek, stm., Ok., U.S.	G10	128
East Caicos, i., T./C. Is.	B12	102
East Cape, c., N.Z.	C8	80
East Cape, c., Fl., U.S.	K4	116
East Carbon, Ut., U.S.	D6	132
East Caroline Basin, unds.	I17	142
East Chicago, In., U.S.	G2	112
East China Sea, Asia	F9	36
East Cote Blanche Bay, b., La., U.S.	H7	122
East Coulee, Ab., Can.	E18	138
East Dereham, Eng., U.K.	I13	12
East Dismal Swamp, sw., N.C., U.S.	A9	116
East Dubuque, Il., U.S.	B7	120
East Ely, Nv., U.S.	D2	132
East End, V.I.U.S.	e8	104b
Easter Island see Pascua, Isla de, i., Chile	f30	78l
Eastern Cape, state, S. Afr.	G8	70
Eastern Channel see Tsushima-kaikyō, strt., Japan	F2	40
Eastern Creek, stm., Austl.	C3	76
Eastern Desert see Arabian Desert, des., Egypt	B6	62
Eastern Division, state, Fiji	q20	79e
Eastern Ghāts, mts., India	E4	53
Eastern Point, c., Guad.	A1	105a
Eastern Sayans see Vostočnyj Sajan, mts., Russia	D17	32
East Falkland, i., Falk. Is.	J5	90
East Fayetteville, N.C., U.S.	A7	116
East Frisian Islands see Ostfriesische Inseln, is., Ger.	C3	16
East Gaffney, S.C., U.S.	A4	116
East Germany see Germany, ctry., Eur.	E6	16
East Glacier Park, Mt., U.S.	B13	136
East Grand Forks, Mn., U.S.	D2	118
East Grand Rapids, Mi., U.S.	F4	112
East Grinstead, Eng., U.K.	J12	12
Easthampton, Ma., U.S.	B13	114
East Java see Jawa Timur, state, Indon.	G8	50
East Jordan, Mi., U.S.	C4	112
East Kelowna, B.C., Can.	G11	138
East Kilbride, Scot., U.K.	F8	12
Eastlake, Mi., U.S.	D3	112
Eastlake, Oh., U.S.	C4	114
Eastland, Tx., U.S.	B9	130
East Lansing, Mi., U.S.	B1	114
East Laurinburg, N.C., U.S.	B6	116
Eastleigh, Eng., U.K.	K11	12
East Liverpool, Oh., U.S.	D5	114
East London (Oos-Londen), S. Afr.	H9	70
Eastmain, Qc., Can.	E15	106
Eastmain, stm., Qc., Can.	E15	106
Eastmain-Opinaca, Réservoir, res., Qc., Can.	E15	106
Eastman, Ga., U.S.	D2	116
East Mariana Basin, unds.	H18	142
East Matagorda Bay, b., Tx., U.S.	F11	130
East Missoula, Mt., U.S.	D13	136
East Moline, Il., U.S.	C7	120
East Naples, Fl., U.S.	J4	116
East Nishnabotna, stm., Ia., U.S.	C2	120
East Nusa Tenggara see Nusa Tenggara Timur, state, Indon.	H12	50
East Olympia, Wa., U.S.	D3	136
Easton, Md., U.S.	F9	114
Easton, Pa., U.S.	D10	114
East Pacific Rise, unds.	N27	142
East Palatka, Fl., U.S.	G4	116
East Pecos, N.M., U.S.	F3	128
East Peoria, Il., U.S.	D8	120
Eastpoint, Fl., U.S.	H14	122
East Point, Ga., U.S.	D14	122
East Point, c., P.E., Can.	D15	110
East Point, c., V.I.U.S.	g11	104c
Eastport, Id., U.S.	B10	136
Eastport, Me., U.S.	F9	110
East Prairie, Mo., U.S.	H8	120
East Prairie, stm., Ab., Can.	A14	138
East Pryor Mountain, mtn., Mt., U.S.	B4	126
East Retford, Eng., U.K.	H12	12
East Saint Louis, Il., U.S.	F7	120
East Sea (Japan, Sea of), Asia	D11	38
East Shoal Lake, l., Mb., Can.	D16	124
East Siberian Sea see Vostočno-Sibirskoe more, Russia	B20	34
East Sister Island, i., Austl.	L6	76
East Slovakia see Východoslovenský Kraj, state, Slov.	H17	16
East Stroudsburg, Pa., U.S.	D11	114
East Troy, Wi., U.S.	B9	120
Eastville, Va., U.S.	G10	114
East Wenatchee, Wa., U.S.	C6	136
East Wilmington, N.C., U.S.	B8	116
Eaton, In., U.S.	H4	112
Eaton, Oh., U.S.	E1	114
Eaton Rapids, Mi., U.S.	B1	114
Eatonton, Ga., U.S.	C2	116
Eatonville, Wa., U.S.	D4	136
Eau Claire, Wi., U.S.	G7	118
Eau Claire, Lac à l', l., Qc., Can.	D16	106
Eauripik, at., Micron.	C5	72
Eauripik Rise, unds.	I17	142
Eauze, Fr.	F6	18
Ebano, Mex.	D9	100
Ebb and Flow Lake, l., Mb., Can.	D14	124
Ebbw Vale, Wales, U.K.	J9	12
Ebebiyín, Eq. Gui.	I7	64
Eben Junction, Mi., U.S.	B2	112
Ebensee, Aus.	C10	22
Eberbach, Ger.	G4	16
Eber Gölü, l., Tur.	E14	28
Ebern, Ger.	F6	16
Ebersbach, Ger.	E10	16
Eberswalde-Finow, Ger.	D9	16
Ebetsu, Japan	C14	38
Ebino, Japan	G3	40
Ebinur Hu, l., China	F14	32
Eboli, Italy	D9	24
Ebolowa, Cam.	D2	66
Ebon, at., Marsh. Is.	C7	72
Ebre see Ebro, stm., Spain	C11	20
Ebre, Delta de l', Spain	D11	20
Ebro (Ebre), stm., Spain	C11	20
Ebro, Delta del see Ebre, Delta de l', Spain	D11	20
Ebro, Embalse del, res., Spain	B7	20
Eceabat, Tur.	C9	28
Ech Cheliff, Alg.	B5	64
Echeng, China	E7	36
Echínos, Grc.	B7	28
Echt, Neth.	E1	16
Echuca, Austl.	K5	76
Écija, Spain	G5	20
Eckernförde, Ger.	B5	16
Eckerö, i., Fin.	F8	8
Eckville, Ab., Can.	D16	138
Eclectic, Al., U.S.	E12	122
Eclipse Sound, strt., N.T., Can.	A14	106
Ecoporanga, Braz.	J5	88
Écorce, Lac de l', res., Qc., Can.	B13	112
Écrins, Barre des, mtn., Fr.	E12	18
Écrins, Massif des, plat., Fr.	E12	18
Ecru, Ms., U.S.	C9	122
Ecuador, ctry., S.A.	D2	84
Ed, Swe.	G4	8
Edam, Sk., Can.	A5	124
Eddrachillis Bay, b., Scot., U.K.	C7	12
Eddystone Rocks, r., Eng., U.K.	K8	12
Eddyville, Ia., U.S.	C5	120
Eddyville, Ky., U.S.	G9	120
Ede, Neth.	B14	14
Ede, Nig.	H5	64
Edéa, Cam.	D2	66
Edehon Lake, l., N.T., Can.	C11	106
Edelény, Hung.	A7	26
Eden, Austl.	K7	76
Eden, Ms., U.S.	D8	122
Eden, N.C., U.S.	H6	114
Eden, Wy., U.S.	A7	132
Eden, stm., Eng., U.K.	G10	12
Edendale, S. Afr.	F10	70
Eden Valley, Mn., U.S.	F4	118
Edenville, S. Afr.	E8	70
Eder, stm., Ger.	E4	16
Édessa, Grc.	C4	28
Edfu, Egypt	C6	62
Edgar, Ne., U.S.	G14	126
Edgar, Wi., U.S.	G8	118
Edgard, La., U.S.	H8	122
Edgartown, Ma., U.S.	C15	114
Edgeley, N.D., U.S.	A14	126
Edgell Island, i., Grnld.	E13	141
Edgemont, S.D., U.S.	D9	126
Edgeøya, i., Nor.	B30	141
Edgeroi, Austl.	H7	76
Edgerton, Ab., Can.	B3	124
Edgerton, Mn., U.S.	H2	118
Edgerton, Oh., U.S.	C1	114
Edgerton, Wi., U.S.	B8	120
Edgewater, Fl., U.S.	H5	116
Edgewood, Il., U.S.	F9	120
Edgewood, Ia., U.S.	B6	120
Edgewood, Md., U.S.	E9	114
Edgewood, Tx., U.S.	E3	122
Edina, Mn., U.S.	G5	118
Edina, Mo., U.S.	D5	120
Edinburg, Il., U.S.	E8	120
Edinburg, In., U.S.	E11	120
Edinburg, Ms., U.S.	E9	122
Edinburg, Tx., U.S.	H9	130
Edinburg, Va., U.S.	F7	114
Edinburgh, Scot., U.K.	F9	12
Edincik, Tur.	C10	28
Edineț, Mol.	A14	26
Edirne, Tur.	B9	28
Edirne, state, Tur.	B9	28
Edison, Ga., U.S.	F14	122
Edisto, stm., S.C., U.S.	D5	116
Edisto, North Fork, stm., S.C., U.S.	C4	116
Edisto Island, i., S.C., U.S.	D5	116
Edith, Mount, mtn., Mt., U.S.	D15	136
Edith Cavell, Mount, mtn., Ab., Can.	D12	138
Edjeleh, Alg.	D6	64
Edmond, Ok., U.S.	F11	128
Edmonds, Wa., U.S.	C4	136
Edmonton, Austl.	A5	76
Edmonton, Ab., Can.	C17	138
Edmonton, Ky., U.S.	G12	120
Edmore, N.D., U.S.	F15	124
Edmundston, N.B., Can.	C8	110
Edna, Ks., U.S.	G2	120
Edna, Tx., U.S.	E11	130
Edremit, Tur.	D10	28
Edremit Körfezi, b., Tur.	D9	28
Edrovo, Russia	C16	10
Edson, Ab., Can.	C14	138
Eduardo Castex, Arg.	G5	92
Eduni, Mount, mtn., N.T., Can.	C5	106
Edward, stm., Austl.	J5	76
Edward, Lake, l., Afr.	E5	66
Edward Island, i., On., Can.	C10	118
Edwards, Ms., U.S.	E8	122
Edwards Air Force Base, Ca., U.S.	I8	134
Edwards Plateau, plat., Tx., U.S.	D7	130
Edwardsville, Il., U.S.	F8	120
Edward VII Peninsula, pen., Ant.	C25	81
Eek, Ak., U.S.	D7	140
Eeklo, Bel.	C12	14
Eel, stm., Ca., U.S.	D2	134
Eel, stm., In., U.S.	G4	112
Eel, stm., In., U.S.	E10	120
Eems (Ems), stm., Eur.	A16	14
Éfaté, state, Vanuatu	k17	79d
Éfaté, i., Vanuatu	k17	79d
Eferding, Aus.	B10	22
Efes (Ephesus), hist., Tur.	F10	28
Effigy Mounds National Monument, p.o.i., Ia., U.S.	A6	120
Effingham, Il., U.S.	E9	120
Effingham, Ks., U.S.	E2	120
Eflâni, Tur.	B15	28
Eforie Nord, Rom.	E15	26
Eforie Sud, Rom.	F15	26
Efremov, Russia	G20	10
Eg, stm., Mong.	F9	34
Egadi, Isole, is., Italy	G5	24
Egaña, Arg.	H8	92
Egan Range, mts., Nv., U.S.	D2	132
Egedesminde (Aasiaat), Grnld.	D15	141
Egegik, Ak., U.S.	E8	140
Eger, Hung.	B7	26
Egersund, Nor.	G1	8
Eggenfelden, Ger.	H8	16
Egg Harbor City, N.J., U.S.	E11	114
Égletons, Fr.	D7	18
Egmont, Cape, c., N.Z.	D5	80
Egmont, Mount see Taranaki, Mount, vol., N.Z.	D6	80
Egmont Bay, b., P.E., Can.	D12	110
Egmont National Park, p.o.i., N.Z.	D5	80
Egorevsk, Russia	E22	10
Egremont, Ab., Can.	B17	138
Eğridir, Tur.	F13	28
Eğridir Gölü, l., Tur.	E13	28
Éguas, stm., Braz.	G3	88
Egvekinot, Russia	C25	34
Egypt, ctry., Afr.	B5	62
Eha-Amufu, Nig.	H6	64
Ehime, state, Japan	F5	40
Ehingen, Ger.	H5	16
Ehrhardt, S.C., U.S.	C4	116
Eibar, Spain	A8	20
Eibiswald, Aus.	D12	22
Eichstätt, Ger.	H7	16
Eidsvold, Austl.	E8	76
Eifel, mts., Ger.	F2	16
Eigg, i., Scot., U.K.	E6	12
Eight Degree Channel, strt., Asia	h12	46a
Eights Coast, cst., Ant.	C31	81
Eighty Mile Beach, cst., Austl.	C4	74
Eildon, Austl.	K5	76
Eildon, Lake, res., Austl.	K5	76
Eilenburg, Ger.	E8	16
Eiler Rasmussen, Kap, c., Grnld.	A21	141
Einasleigh, Austl.	B5	76
Einasleigh, stm., Austl.	A4	76
Einbeck, Ger.	E5	16
Eindhoven, Neth.	C14	14
Einme, Mya.	D2	48
Eirunepé, Braz.	E4	84
Eiseb, stm., Afr.	B4	70
Eisenach, Ger.	E6	16
Eisenberg, Ger.	F7	16
Eisenerz, Aus.	C11	22
Eisenhüttenstadt, Ger.	D10	16
Eisenstadt, Aus.	C13	22
Eisfeld, Ger.	F6	16
Eišiškės, Lith.	F7	10
Eislingen, Ger.	H5	16
Eitorf, Ger.	F3	16
Eivissa (Iviza), Spain	F12	20
Eivissa (Ibiza), i., Spain	F12	20
Ejea de los Caballeros, Spain	B9	20
Ejeda, Madag.	E7	68
Ejido Jaboncillos, Mex.	A7	100
Ejin Horo Qi, China	B3	42
Ejin Qi, China	C5	36
Ejsk, Russia	E5	32
Ejura, Ghana	H4	64
Ejutla de Crespo, Mex.	G10	100
Ekaterinburg, Russia	C10	32
Ekaterinino, Russia	E16	10
Ekateriny, proliv, strt., Russia	B17	38
Ekenäs see Tammisaari, Fin.	G10	8
Ekibastuz, Kaz.	D13	32
Ekimčan, Russia	F15	34
Ekonda, Russia	C10	34
Ekwan, stm., On., Can.	E14	106
Ela, Mya.	C3	48
El Aaiún (Laayoune), W. Sah.	D2	64
El 'Açâba, plat., Maur.	F2	64
El Affroun, Alg.	H13	20
El Agreb, Alg.	C6	64

Name — Map Ref. — Page

El Ahijadero, Cerro, mtn., Mex. E1 130
Elaine, Ar., U.S. C8 122
El-'Aiyât, Egypt I2 58
El-Alamein, Egypt A5 62
El Álamo, Mex. G7 130
El Álamo, Mex. H8 130
El Álamo, Mex. L9 134
El Alto, Arg. D5 92
Elan', Russia D6 32
Elancy, Russia F10 34
El Ángel, Ec. G2 86
El-Arish, Egypt G4 58
Elat, Isr. I5 58
Elat, Gulf of see Aqaba, Gulf of, b. J5 58
El Ávila, Parque Nacional, p.o.i., Ven. B8 86
Elazığ, Tur. B4 56
Elba, Isola d', i., Italy H7 22
El-Badâri, Egypt K2 58
El-Bahnasa, Egypt J1 58
El-Balyana, Egypt B6 62
El'ban, Russia F16 34
El Banco, Col. C4 86
El Barco de Ávila, Spain D5 20
Elbasan, Alb. C13 24
Elbasani see Elbasan, Alb. C13 24
El Baúl, Ven. C7 86
El Baúl, Cerro, mtn., Mex. G11 100
Elbe (Labe), stm., Eur. C5 16
Elbe-Havel-Kanal, can., Ger. D8 16
Elbert, Co., U.S. B4 128
Elbert, Mount, mtn., Co., U.S. D10 132
Elberta, Mi., U.S. D3 112
Elberton, Ga., U.S. B3 116
Elbeuf, Fr. E10 14
Elbeyli, Tur. B8 58
El Beyyadh, Alg. C5 64
Elbląg, Pol. B15 16
Elbląg, state, Pol. B15 16
El Bluff, Nic. G6 102
El Bonillo, Spain F8 20
El Boulaïda, Alg. B5 64
Elbow, stm., Ab., Can. E16 138
Elbow Lake, Mn., U.S. E3 118
El'brus, gora, mtn., Russia F6 32
Elbrus, Mount see El'brus, gora, mtn., Russia F6 32
El-Burg, Egypt G1 58
El-Burgâya, Egypt J1 58
Elburs see Alborz, Reshteh-ye Kūhhā-ye, mts., Iran B7 56
Elburz Mountains see Alborz, Reshteh-ye Kūhhā-ye, mts., Iran B7 56
El Cadilla, Embalse, res., Arg. C5 92
El Cajon, Ca., U.S. K9 134
El Calafate, Arg. J2 90
El Callao, Ven. D11 86
El Calvario, Ven. C8 86
El Campamento, P.R. B3 104a
El Campo, Tx., U.S. H2 122
El Capitan, mtn., Mt., U.S. D12 136
El Carmen, Arg. B5 92
El Carmen, Col. C5 86
El Carmen, stm., Mex. F9 98
El Carmen de Bolívar, Col. C4 86
El Carricito, Mex. A7 100
El Carril, Arg. B5 92
El Centinela, Mex. K10 134
El Centro, Ca., U.S. K10 134
El Cerrito, Col. F3 86
El Cerro Del Aripo, mtn., Trin. s12 105f
Elche see Elx, Spain F10 20
El Chile, Montaña, mtn., Nic. E4 102
Elcho, Wi., U.S. F9 118
Elcho Island, i., Austl. B7 74
El Cocuy, Col. D5 86
El Colorado, Arg. C8 92
El Cóndor, Cerro, vol., Arg. C3 92
El Corazón, Ec. H2 86
El Corpus, Hond. F4 102
El Coto, P.R. B2 104a
El'cy, Russia D16 10
Elda, Spain F10 20
El Desemboque, Mex. G6 98
El Desemboque, Mex. F6 98
El'dikan, Russia D16 34
El-Dilingât, Egypt H1 58
El Diviso, Col. G2 86
El Djazaïr (Algiers), Alg. B5 64
El Djelfa, Alg. C5 64
Eldon, Ia., U.S. D5 120
Eldora, Ia., U.S. B4 120
Eldorado, Arg. C10 92
Eldorado, Braz. B13 92
El Dorado, Ar., U.S. D6 122
Eldorado, Il., U.S. G9 120
El Dorado, Ks., U.S. D12 128
Eldorado, Ok., U.S. G9 128
El Dorado, Ven. D11 86
El Dorado Springs, Mo., U.S. G3 120
Eldoret, Kenya D7 66
Eldred, Pa., U.S. C7 114
Eldridge, Ia., U.S. C7 120
Eleanor, W.V., U.S. F3 114
Elec, Russia H21 10
Electric City, Wa., U.S. C7 136
Elefantes (Olifants), stm., Afr. D10 70
Elefsína, Grc. E6 28
Eleftheroúpoli, Grc. C7 28
Elektrostal', Russia E21 10
Elena, Blg. G12 26
El Encanto, Col. H5 86
Elephant Butte Reservoir, res., N.M., U.S. J9 132
Elephant Mountain, mtn., Me., U.S. F6 110
Elesbão Veloso, Braz. D4 88
El Estor, Guat. E3 102
Eleuthera, i., Bah. B9 96
Eleva, Wi., U.S. G7 118
Eleven Point, stm., U.S. H6 120
El Fahs, Tun. H3 24
El Faro, P.R. C2 104a
El-Fashn, Egypt J1 58
El-Fayoum, Egypt I1 58
El Ferrol del Caudillo see Ferrol, Spain A2 20
El-Fiqriya, Egypt K1 58
Elfrida, Az., U.S. L7 132
El Fuerte, Mex. B4 100
El Galpón, Arg. B5 92
Elgin, Scot., U.K. D9 12
Elgin, Il., U.S. B9 120
Elgin, Ia., U.S. B6 120
Elgin, Mn., U.S. G6 118
Elgin, Ne., U.S. F14 126
Elgin, N.D., U.S. A11 126
Elgin, Ok., U.S. G10 128
Elgin, Or., U.S. E8 136
El-Gindîya, Egypt J1 58
El-Gîza (Giza), Egypt H1 58
Elgon, Mount, mtn., Afr. D6 66
El Grara, Alg. C5 64
El Grove see O Grove, Spain B2 20
El Guaje, Mex. A7 100
El Guamo, Col. B4 86
El Guapo, Ven. B9 86
El Hachero, Cerro, mtn., Mex. H2 130
El Hammâmi, reg., Maur. E2 64
El-Hamûl, Egypt G2 58
El Hank, clf, Afr. E3 64
El-Hawâmdîya, Egypt I2 58
Elhovo, Blg. G13 26
El Huisache, Mex. D8 100
Eliase, Indon. G9 44
Elida, N.M., U.S. H5 128
Elila, stm., D.R.C. E5 66
Elim, Ak., U.S. D7 140
Elisenvaara, Russia F13 8
Eliseu Martins, Braz. E4 88
El-Iskandarīya (Alexandria), Egypt A6 62
Elista, Russia E6 32
Elizabeth, Austl. J2 76
Elizabeth, Co., U.S. B4 128
Elizabeth, Il., U.S. B7 120
Elizabeth, N.J., U.S. D11 114
Elizabeth, W.V., U.S. E4 114
Elizabeth City, N.C., U.S. H9 114
Elizabethton, Tn., U.S. H3 114
Elizabethtown, Il., U.S. G9 120
Elizabethtown, Ky., U.S. G11 120
Elizabethtown, N.Y., U.S. F3 110
Elizabethtown, Pa., U.S. D9 114
Elizavety, mys, c., Russia F17 34
Elizovo, Russia F20 34
El-Jadida, Mor. C3 64
El Jaralito, Mex. B6 100
El Jebel, Co., U.S. D9 132
Ełk, Pol. C18 16
Elk, stm., B.C., Can. F16 138
Elk, stm., U.S. C12 122
Elk, stm., Ks., U.S. D12 128
Elk, stm., W.V., U.S. F4 114
Elkader, Ia., U.S. B6 120
Elk City, Ok., U.S. F9 128
Elk Creek, Ca., U.S. D3 134
Elk Creek, stm., S.D., U.S. C10 126
El Kef, Tun. H2 24
El-Kelaa-Srarhna, Mor. C3 64
Ēl Kerē, Eth. F8 62
Elk Grove, Ca., U.S. E4 134
El-Khânka, Egypt H2 58
El-Khārga, Egypt B6 62
Elkhart, In., U.S. G4 112
Elkhart, Ks., U.S. D7 128
Elkhart, Tx., U.S. F3 122
El Khnâchîch, clf, Mali E4 64
Elkhorn, Mb., Can. D12 124
Elk Horn, Ia., U.S. C2 120
Elkhorn, Wi., U.S. B9 120
Elkhorn, stm., Ne., U.S. F16 126
Elkhorn City, Ky., U.S. G3 114
Elkhorn Mountain, mtn., B.C., Can. G4 138
Elkhovo see Elhovo, Blg. G13 26
Elkins, W.V., U.S. F6 114
Elk Island, i., Mb., Can. D17 124
Elk Island National Park, p.o.i., Ab., Can. C18 138
Elkland, Pa., U.S. C8 114
Elk Mountain, mtn., Wy., U.S. B10 132
Elko, B.C., Can. G15 138
Elko, Nv., U.S. C1 132
Elk Point, Ab., Can. C19 138
Elk Point, S.D., U.S. B1 120
Elk Rapids, Mi., U.S. D4 112
Elk River, Mn., U.S. F5 118
Elkton, Md., U.S. E10 114
Elkton, Mi., U.S. E6 112
Elkton, S.D., U.S. G2 118
Elkton, Va., U.S. F7 114
Ellaville, Ga., U.S. D1 116
Ellef Ringnes Island, i., N.T., Can. B5 141
Ellen, Mount, mtn., Ut., U.S. E6 132
Ellendale, Mn., U.S. H5 118
Ellendale, N.D., U.S. A14 126
Ellensburg, Wa., U.S. C6 136
Ellenton, Ga., U.S. E2 116
Ellesmere, Lake, l., N.Z. F5 80
Ellesmere Island, i., N.T., Can. B9 141
Ellettsville, In., U.S. E11 120
Ellice, stm., N.T., Can. B10 106
Ellice Islands see Tuvalu, ctry., Oc. D8 72
Ellicottville, N.Y., U.S. B7 114
Ellijay, Ga., U.S. B1 116
Ellinwood, Ks., U.S. C10 128
Elliot, S. Afr. G8 70
Elliot, Mount, mtn., Austl. B6 76
Elliot Lake, On., Can. B7 112
Elliot Lake, l., Mb., Can. B18 124
Elliott, Ia., U.S. C2 120
Elliott, Ms., U.S. D9 122
Ellisras, S. Afr. C8 70
Elliston, Austl. F6 74
Elliston, Mt., U.S. D14 136
Ellisville, Ms., U.S. F9 122
Ellon, Scot., U.K. D10 12
Ellora, India H5 54
Ellora Caves, hist., India A2 53
Elloree, S.C., U.S. C5 116
Ellsworth, Ks., U.S. C10 128
Ellsworth, Me., U.S. F8 110
Ellsworth, Mi., U.S. C4 112
Ellsworth, Mn., U.S. H3 118
Ellsworth, Wi., U.S. G6 118
Ellsworth Land, reg., Ant. C32 81
Ellsworth Mountains, mts., Ant. C32 81
El Lucero, Mex. I4 130
Ellwangen, Ger. H5 16
Ellwood City, Pa., U.S. D5 114
Elm, stm., U.S. B14 126
Elma, Wa., U.S. D3 136
El-Mahalla el-Kubra, Egypt H2 58
El-Maimûn, Egypt I2 58
Elmalı, Tur. G12 28
El Maneadero, Mex. L9 134
El-Mansûra, Egypt G2 58
El Manteco, Ven. D10 86
El-Manzala, Egypt G2 58
El-Matariya, Egypt G3 58
Elm Creek, Mb., Can. E16 124
Elm Creek, Ne., U.S. G13 126
El Médano, Mex. C3 100
El Menia, Alg. C5 64
Elmer, N.J., U.S. E10 114
Elmhurst, Il., U.S. G2 112
El-Minya (Minya), Egypt J1 58
Elmira, On., Can. E9 112
Elmira, P.E., Can. D14 110
Elmira, N.Y., U.S. B9 114
El Moral, Mex. F7 130
Elmore, Austl. K5 76
Elmore, Mn., U.S. H4 118
Elmore, Oh., U.S. C2 114
Elmore City, Ok., U.S. G11 128
El Morro, hist., P.R. B3 104a
El Morro National Monument, p.o.i., N.M., U.S. H8 132
El Mreyyé, reg., Maur. F3 64
Elmshorn, Ger. C5 16
Elm Springs, Ar., U.S. H3 120
El Mulato, Mex. E3 130
El-Mutî'a, Egypt K2 58
Elmvale, On., Can. D10 112
Elmwood, Il., U.S. K8 118
Elmwood, Ne., U.S. K2 118
El Negrito, Hond. E4 102
Elnora, Ab., Can. D17 138
Elnora, In., U.S. F10 120
Eloguj, stm., Russia B15 32
Eloise, Fl., U.S. H4 116
Elora, On., Can. E9 112
Elorza, Ven. D7 86
El Otate, Cerro, mtn., Mex. F1 130
Eloten, Turkmen. B9 56
Eloy, Az., U.S. K5 132
Eloy Alfaro, Ec. I2 86
El Palmar, Ven. D10 86
El Palmar de los Sepúlveda, Mex. C5 100
El Palmito, Mex. I8 130
El Palqui, Chile E2 92
El Pao, Ven. C7 86
El Paso, Il., U.S. D8 120
El Paso, Tx., U.S. L10 132
El Paso de Robles see Paso Robles, Ca., U.S. H5 134
El Paso Peaks, mtn., Ca., U.S. H8 134
El Perú, Ven. D11 86
Elphinstone, Mb., Can. D13 124
El Piñón, Col. B4 86
El Pintado, Arg. B7 92
El Pital, Cerro, mtn., N.A. E3 102
El Planchón, Volcán (Planchón, Cerro del), vol., S.A. G2 92
El Polvorín, P.R. B3 104a
El Portal, Ca., U.S. F6 134
El Porvenir, Mex. G3 130
El Porvenir, Mex. K9 134
El Porvenir, Pan. H8 102
El Potrero, Mex. H7 130
El Potro, Cerro (Potro, Cerro del), mtn., S.A. D3 92
El Prat de Llobregat, Spain C12 20
El Progreso, Hond. E4 102
El Puerto de Santa María, Spain H4 20
El Puesto, Arg. C4 92
El-Qâhira (Cairo), Egypt H2 58
El-Qantara el-Sharqîya, Egypt H3 58
El-Qasr, Egypt B5 62
El Quebrachal, Arg. B5 92
El Quelite, Mex. D5 100
Elqui, stm., Chile D2 92
El-Qûsîya, Egypt K1 58
El Real de Santa María, Pan. H9 102
El Remolino, Mex. F6 130
El Reno, Ok., U.S. F10 128
El Rio, Ca., U.S. I6 134
El Roble, Mesa, mtn., Mex. L10 134
Elroy, Wi., U.S. H8 118
Elsa, Yk., Can. C3 106
Elsa, Tx., U.S. H9 130
El-Saff, Egypt I2 58
El-Sa'îd (Upper Egypt), hist. reg., Egypt J2 58
El Salado, Chile C2 92
El Salado, Parque Nacional, p.o.i., Ec. I1 86
El Salto, Mex. D6 100
El Salvador, Chile C3 92
El Salvador, ctry., N.A. F3 102
El Samán de Apure, Ven. D7 86
El Sauz, Mex. A5 100
El Sauzal, Mex. L9 134
Elsberry, Mo., U.S. E7 120
El Seibo, Dom. Rep. C13 102
Elsen Nur, l., China D3 36
El-Simbillawein, Egypt H2 58
Elsinore see Helsingør, Den. H5 8
Elsinore, Ut., U.S. E4 132
El Sombrero, Ven. C8 86
Elsterwerda, Ger. E9 16
El Sueco, Mex. E1 130
El-Suweis (Suez), Egypt I3 58
El Tajín, hist., Mex. E10 100
El Tala, Arg. C5 92
El Tanque, Mex. H8 130
El Tecuán, Mex. C5 100
El-Thamad, Egypt I5 58
El Tigre, Ven. C9 86
Eltmann, Ger. G6 16
El Toco, Chile D3 90
El Tocuyo, Ven. C7 86
Elton, La., U.S. G6 122
El Tránsito, Chile D2 92
El Trébol, Arg. F7 92
El Tule, Mex. G1 130
El Tuparro, Parque Nacional, p.o.i., Col. E7 86
El-Tûr, Egypt J4 58
El Turbio, Arg. J2 90
El-Uqsor (Luxor), Egypt B6 62
Elūru, India C5 53
El Valle, Pan. H7 102
Elvas, Port. F3 20
El Vendrell, Spain C12 20
Elverum, Nor. F4 8
El Viejo, Nic. F4 102
El Vigía, Ven. C6 86
El Vínculo, Ven. p20 104g
Elvira, Arg. G8 92
El Volcán, Chile F2 92
El Wad, Alg. C6 64
El-Wâsta, Egypt I2 58
Elwell, Lake, res., Mt., U.S. B15 136
Elwood, In., U.S. H4 112
Elwood, Ne., U.S. G13 126
Elx, Spain F10 20
Ely, Eng., U.K. I13 12
Ely, Mn., U.S. D7 118
Ely, Nv., U.S. D2 132
El Yagual, Ven. D7 86
Elyria, Oh., U.S. C3 114
El Yunque, mtn., P.R. B4 104a
El-Zarqa, Egypt G2 58
Émaé, i., Vanuatu k17 79d
Emajõgi, stm., Est. B9 10
Emāmshahr, Iran B8 56
Emba, Kaz. E9 32
Emba, stm., Kaz. E9 32
Embarras, stm., Il., U.S. F10 120
Embarrass, Wi., U.S. G10 118
Emborcação, Represa da, res., Braz. J2 88
Embreeville, Tn., U.S. H3 114
Embrun, Fr. E12 18
Embu, Kenya E7 66
Emca, stm., Russia E19 8
Emden, Ger. C3 16
Emden, Il., U.S. K9 118
Emelle, Al., U.S. E10 122
Emerado, N.D., U.S. G16 124
Emerald, Austl. D6 76
Emerson, Mb., Can. E16 124
Emerson, Ar., U.S. D5 122
Emerson, Ia., U.S. C2 120
Emery, S.D., U.S. D15 126
Emery, Ut., U.S. E5 132
Emet, Tur. D12 28
Emiliano Zapata, Mex. G13 100
Emilia-Romagna, state, Italy F8 22
Emin, China B1 36
Emine, nos, c., Blg. G14 26
Eminence, Mo., U.S. G6 120
Emirdağ, Tur. D14 28
Emır Dağları, mts., Tur. E14 28
Emita, Austl. m13 77a
Emlembe, mtn., Afr. D10 70
Emlenton, Pa., U.S. G10 112
Emmaste, Est. B5 10
Emmaus, Pa., U.S. D10 114
Emmaville, Austl. G8 76
Emmen, Neth. B15 14
Emmendingen, Ger. H3 16
Emmerich, Ger. E2 16
Emmet, Ar., U.S. D5 122
Emmetsburg, Ia., U.S. A3 120
Emmiganūru, India D3 53
Emmitsburg, Md., U.S. E8 114
Emmonak, Ak., U.S. D7 140
Emo, On., Can. C5 118
Emory Peak, mtn., Tx., U.S. E4 130
Empalme, Mex. A3 100
Empangeni, S. Afr. F10 70
Empedrado, Arg. C8 92
Emperor Seamounts, unds. E19 142
Empire, La., U.S. H9 122
Empire, Nv., U.S. C6 134
Empoli, Italy G7 22
Emporia, Ks., U.S. F1 120
Emporia, Va., U.S. H8 114
Emporium, Pa., U.S. C7 114
Empty Quarter see Ar-Rub' al-Khālī, des., Asia E6 56
Ems, stm., Eur. C3 16
Emsdetten, Ger. D3 16
Emu, China C8 38
Emu Park, Austl. D8 76
Enarotali, Indon. F10 44
Enašimskij Polkan, gora, mtn., Russia C16 32
Encampment, Wy., U.S. B10 132
Encantado, Braz. D11 92
Encarnación, Para. C9 92
Enchi, Ghana H4 64
Enchilayas, Mex. F6 98
Encinal, Tx., U.S. F8 130
Encinitas, Ca., U.S. J8 134
Encino, N.M., U.S. G3 128
Encontrados, Ven. C5 86
Encounter Bay, b., Austl. J2 76
Encruzilhada, Braz. H5 88
Encruzilhada do Sul, Braz. E11 92
Encs, Hung. A8 26
Endako, B.C., Can. B5 138
Ende, Indon. G7 44
Endeavor, Wi., U.S. H9 118
Endeavour Strait, strt., Austl. B8 74
Enderby, B.C., Can. F11 138
Enderby Land, reg., Ant. B10 81
Enderlin, N.D., U.S. A15 126
Endicott, N.Y., U.S. B9 114
Endicott, Wa., U.S. D9 136
Endicott Mountains, mts., Ak., U.S. C9 140
Ene, stm., Peru F3 84
Enewetak, at., Marsh. Is. B7 72
Enez, Tur. C9 28
Enfield, N.C., U.S. H8 114
Engaño, Cabo, c., Dom. Rep. C13 102
Engcobo, S. Afr. G9 70
Engelhard, N.C., U.S. A10 116
Engel's, Russia D7 32
Engen, B.C., Can. B6 138
Engenheiro Navarro, Braz. I3 88
Enggano, Pulau, i., Indon. F2 50
England, state, U.K. I12 12
Englefield, Cape, c., N.T., Can. B13 106
Englehart, On., Can. F15 106
Englewood, B.C., Can. F3 138
Englewood, Co., U.S. B4 128
Englewood, Fl., U.S. J3 116
Englewood, Ks., U.S. D8 128
Englewood, Tn., U.S. A1 116
English, stm., On., Can. A4 118
English Channel, strt., Eur. D7 14
English Coast, cst., Ant. C33 81
Engure, Lat. C6 10
Engures ezers, l., Lat. C6 10
Enid, Ok., U.S. E11 128
Enid Lake, res., Ms., U.S. C9 122
Enisej, stm., Russia C6 34
Enisejsk, Russia C16 32
Enisejskij krjaž, mts., Russia C16 32
Enisejskij zaliv, b., Russia B5 34
Eniwetok see Enewetak, at., Marsh. Is. B7 72
Enka, N.C., U.S. A3 116
Enkhuizen, Neth. B14 14
Enköping, Swe. G7 8
Enmedio, Mex. E4 130
Enmedio, Cerro de, mtn., Mex. F8 100
Enna, Italy G8 24
Ennadai Lake, l., N.T., Can. C10 106
Ennedi, plat., Chad D4 62
Ennis, Ire. I3 12
Ennis, Mt., U.S. E15 136
Ennis, Tx., U.S. E2 122
Enniscorthy, Ire. I6 12
Enniskillen, N. Ire., U.K. G5 12
Enns, Aus. B11 22
Enns, stm., Aus. B11 22
Enon, Oh., U.S. E2 114
Enontekiö, Fin. B10 8
Enoree, stm., S.C., U.S. B3 116
Enosburg Falls, Vt., U.S. F4 110
Enping, China J5 42
Enrekang, Indon. E11 50
Enrique Urien, Arg. C7 92
Enriquillo, Dom. Rep. D12 102
Enriquillo, Lago, l., Dom. Rep. C12 102
Enschede, Neth. B15 14
Ensenada, Arg. G9 92
Ensenada, Mex. L9 134
Enshi, China F3 42
Enshū-nada, Japan E10 40
Entebbe, Ug. D6 66
Enterprise, N.T., Can. C7 106
Enterprise, Al., U.S. F13 122
Enterprise, Ca., U.S. D4 134
Enterprise, Ms., U.S. E10 122
Enterprise, Or., U.S. E9 136
Enterprise, Ut., U.S. F3 132
Entrepeñas, Embalse de, res., Spain D8 20
Entre Ríos, Bol. D4 90
Entre Rios, Braz. G7 88
Entre Ríos, state, Arg. F8 92
Entrevaux, Fr. F12 18
Entroncamento, Port. E2 20
Entwistle, Ab., Can. C16 138
Enugu, Nig. H6 64
Enurmino, Russia C26 34
Envalira, Port d', p., And. B12 20
Envigado, Col. D4 86
Envira, stm., Braz. E3 84
Enyamba, D.R.C. E5 66
Enyellé, Congo D3 66
Eolia, Mo., U.S. E6 120
Eolie, Isole (Lipari, Isole), is., Italy F8 24
Epanomí, Grc. C5 28
Epecuén, Lago, l., Arg. H6 92
Épernay, Fr. E12 14
Epes, Al., U.S. E10 122
Ephesus see Efes, hist., Tur. F10 28
Ephraim, Ut., U.S. D5 132
Ephrata, Pa., U.S. D9 114
Ephrata, Wa., U.S. C7 136
Épi, state, Vanuatu k17 79d
Épi, i., Vanuatu k17 79d
Epídavros, hist., Grc. F6 28
Épila, Spain C9 20
Épinal, Fr. F15 14
Epirus see Ípeiros, hist. reg., Grc. D3 28
Epsom, Eng., U.K. J12 12
Epukiro, Nmb. B4 70
Epukiro, stm., Nmb. B4 70
Eqlīd, Iran C7 56
Equatorial Guinea, ctry., Afr. I6 64
Erap, Pap. N. Gui. b4 79a
Erath, La., U.S. H6 122
Erave, Pap. N. Gui. b3 79a
Erawan National Park, p.o.i., Thai. E4 48
Erbach, Ger. G5 16
Erbogačon, Russia B19 32
Ercevo, Russia F18 8
Ercolano, Italy D8 24
Érd, Hung. B5 26
Erdao, stm., China C8 38
Erdaohezi, China B8 38
Erdek, Tur. C10 28
Erdemli, Tur. B5 58
Erding, Ger. H7 16
Erebato, stm., Ven. E9 86
Erebus, Mount, mtn., Ant. C21 81
Erechim, Braz. C11 92
Ereğli, Tur. B14 28
Ereğli, Tur. A4 58
Erenhot, China C7 36
Erepecuru, Lago do, l., Braz. D6 84
Erfoud, Mor. C4 64
Erft, stm., Ger. E2 16
Erfurt, Ger. F7 16
Ergene, stm., Tur. B10 28
Ergeni, hills, Russia E6 32
Ērgli, Lat. D8 10
Ergun Youqi, China A9 36
Ergun Zuoqi, China F13 34
Er Hai, l., China F5 36
Erice, Italy F6 24
Ericeira, Port. F1 20
Erichsen Lake, l., N.T., Can. A14 106
Erick, Ok., U.S. F9 128
Erickson, Mb., Can. D14 124
Ericson, Ne., U.S. F14 126
Erie, Co., U.S. A3 128
Erie, Il., U.S. C7 120
Erie, Pa., U.S. B5 114
Erie, Lake, l., N.A. B4 114
Erie Canal see New York State Barge Canal, can., N.Y., U.S. E12 112
Eriksdale, Mb., Can. D15 124
Erimo-misaki, c., Japan D15 38
Erin, On., Can. E9 112
Erin, Tn., U.S. H10 120
Eriskay, i., Scot., U.K. D5 12
Eritrea, ctry., Afr. D7 62
Erivan see Yerevan, Arm. A5 56
Erkelenz, Ger. E2 16
Erkner, Ger. D9 16
Erlangen, Ger. G7 16
Ermak, Kaz. D13 32
Ermelo, S. Afr. E10 70
Ermenek, Tur. B3 58
Ermenek, stm., Tur. B3 58
Ermentau, Kaz. D12 32
Ermica, Russia C25 8
Ermolaevo, Russia D9 32
Ermolino, Russia E19 10
Ermoúpoli, Grc. F7 28
Erne, Lower Lough, l., N. Ire., U.K. G4 12
Erne, Upper Lough, l., Eur. G5 12
Ernée, Fr. F8 14
Erode, India F3 53
Erofej Pavlovič, Russia F13 34
Eromanga, Austl. F4 76
Erongo, state, Nmb. C2 70
Erongo, mtn., Nmb. B2 70
Eropol, Russia C22 34
Erota, Erit. D7 62
Er-Rachidia, Mor. C4 64
Errego, Moz. D6 68
Errigal Mountain, mtn., Ire. F4 12
Errinundra National Park, p.o.i., Austl. K7 76
Erris Head, c., Ire. G2 12
Errol Heights, Or., U.S. E4 136
Erromango, i., Vanuatu I17 79d
Erši, Russia F17 10
Eršov, Russia D7 32
Erstein, Fr. F16 14
Ertai, China B3 36
Ertix see Irtysh, stm., Asia E15 32
Ertoma, Russia E22 8
Erval, Braz. F11 92
Ervy-le-Châtel, Fr. F12 14
Erwin, N.C., U.S. A7 116
Erwin, Tn., U.S. H3 114
Erwood, Sk., Can. B11 124
Erýmanthos, mtn., Grc. F4 28
Eryuan, China F4 36
Erzhan, China B8 38
Erzin, Russia D17 32
Erzincan, Tur. B4 56
Erzurum, Tur. B5 56
Esa'ala, Pap. N. Gui. b5 79a
Esashi, Japan D13 38
Esbjerg, Den. I3 8
Esbo see Espoo, Fin. F11 8
Escada, Braz. E8 88
Escalante, stm., Ut., U.S. F6 132
Escalante, stm., Ven. C5 86
Escalón, Mex. B6 100
Escalon, Ca., U.S. F5 134
Escambia, stm., Fl., U.S. G11 122
Escanaba, Mi., U.S. C2 112
Escanaba, stm., Mi., U.S. B2 112
Escandón, Puerto, p., Spain D10 20
Escárcega, Mex. C2 102
Escarpada Point, c., Phil. A4 52
Escatawpa, stm., U.S. G10 122
Esch-sur-Alzette, Lux. E15 14
Escobedo, Mex. G6 130
Escocesa, Bahía, b., Dom. Rep. C13 102
Escondido, Ca., U.S. J8 134
Escondido, stm., Mex. F7 130
Escondido, stm., Nic. F6 102
Escuinapa de Hidalgo, Mex. D5 100
Escuintla, Guat. E2 102
Escuintla, Mex. H12 100
Eséka, Cam. D2 66
Eşen, Tur. G12 28
Eşfahān, Iran C7 56
Esgueva, stm., Spain C6 20
Eshkāshem, Afg. B11 56
Eshowe, S. Afr. F10 70
Esil', Kaz. D11 32
Esil see Ishim, stm., Asia C12 32
Esk, Austl. F9 76
Ěškar-Ola, Russia C7 32
Eskdale, W.V., U.S. F4 114
Es'ki, Russia C19 10
Eskilstrup, Den. B7 16
Eskilstuna, Swe. G7 8
Eskimo Lakes, l., N.T., Can. B4 106
Eskimo Point see Arviat, N.T., Can. C12 106
Eskişehir, Tur. D13 28
Eskişehir, state, Tur. D13 28
Eskridge, Ks., U.S. F1 120
Esla, stm., Spain C5 20
Eslāmābād, Iran C6 56
Eşme, Tur. E11 28
Esmeralda, Austl. B4 76
Esmeralda, Cuba B8 102
Esmeralda, Isla, i., Chile I1 90
Esmeraldas, Ec. G2 86
Esmeraldas, state, Ec. G2 86
Esmeraldas, stm., Ec. G2 86
Esnagami Lake, l., On., Can. A11 118
Espada, Punta, c., Col. A6 86
Espalion, Fr. E8 18
Espanola, On., Can. B8 112
Espanola, N.M., U.S. F2 128
Espejo, Spain G6 20
Espelkamp, Ger. D4 16
Espera Feliz, Braz. K5 88
Esperança, Braz. D4 84
Esperança, Braz. D7 88
Esperance, Austl. F4 74
Esperantina, Braz. B4 88
Esperanza, Arg. E7 92
Esperanza, Mex. B4 100
Esperanza, P.R. B5 104a
Esperanza, sci., Ant. B35 81
Espichel, Cabo, c., Port. F1 20
Espinal, Col. E4 86
Espinazo, Mex. H6 130
Espinhaço, Serra do, mts., Braz. I4 88
Espinho, Port. D2 20
Espinillo, Arg. B8 92
Espino, Ven. C9 86
Espinosa, Braz. H4 88
Espírito Santo, state, Braz. J5 88
Espiritu Santo, i., Vanuatu j16 79d
Espíritu Santo, Isla del, i., Mex. C3 100
Espita, Mex. B3 102
Esplanada, Braz. F7 88
Espoo, Fin. F11 8
Espungabera, Moz. B11 70
Esquel, Arg. H2 90
Esquimalt, B.C., Can. H7 138
Esquina, Arg. D8 92
Esquiú, Arg. D5 92
Essaouira, Mor. C3 64
Essej, Russia C9 34
Essen, Ger. E3 16
Essendon, Mount, mtn., Austl. D3 74
Essequibo, stm., Guy. C6 84
Es Sers, Tun. H2 24
Essex, On., Can. F7 112
Essex, Md., U.S. E9 114
Essex, Mt., U.S. B13 136
Essex Junction, Vt., U.S. F3 110
Essexville, Mi., U.S. E6 112
Esslingen am Neckar, Ger. H5 16
Essonne, state, Fr. F11 14
Est, Pointe de l', c., Qc., Can. A15 110
Estacada, Or., U.S. E4 136
Estaca de Bares, Punta da, c., Spain A3 20
Estaca de Bares, Punta de la see Estaca de Bares, Punta da, c., Spain A3 20
Estacado, Llano, pl., U.S. H6 128
Estación Adolfo Rodriguez Sáa see Santa Rosa del Conlara, Arg. F5 92
Estación Colonia Alvear Norte see General Alvear, Arg. G3 92
Estación Foguista J. F. Juárez see El Galpón, Arg. B5 92
Estación Gobernador Vera see Vera, Arg. D7 92
Estación J. J. Castelli see Castelli, Arg. B7 92
Estación Justino Solari see Mariano I. Loza, Arg. D8 92
Estación Manuel F. Mantilla see Pedro R. Fernández, Arg. D8 92
Estación Vela see María Ignacia, Arg. H8 92
Estados, Isla de los, i., Arg. J4 90
Eştahbān, Iran D7 56
Estância, Braz. F7 88
Estancia, N.M., U.S. G2 128
Estanislao del Campo, Arg. B7 92
Estarreja, Port. D2 20
Estats, Pic d' (Estats, Pique d'), mtn., Eur. G7 18
Estats, Pico de see Estats, Pic d', mtn., Eur. G7 18
Estats, Pique d' (Estats, Pic d'), mtn., Eur. G7 18
Estcourt, S. Afr. F9 70
Este, Italy E8 22
Esteio, Braz. D12 92
Estelí, Nic. F4 102
Estella, Spain B8 20
Estelline, S.D., U.S. G2 118
Estelline, Tx., U.S. G8 128
Estepa, Spain G6 20
Estepona, Spain H5 20
Estes Park, Co., U.S. G7 126
Este Sudeste, Cayos del, is., Col. F7 102
Estevan, Sk., Can. E10 124
Estevan Point, B.C., Can. G4 138
Estherville, Ia., U.S. H4 118
Estill, S.C., U.S. D4 116
Estiva, stm., Braz. G3 88
Eston, Sk., Can. C5 124
Estonia, ctry., Eur. G11 8
Estrela, Braz. D11 92
Estrela, mtn., Port. D3 20
Estrela do Sul, Braz. J2 88
Estremadura, hist. reg., Port. E1 20
Estremoz, Port. F3 20
Estrondo, Serra do, plat., Braz. E1 88
Esztergom, Hung. B5 26
Etadunna, Austl. G2 76
Etah, Grnld. B11 141
Etah, India E7 54
Étain, Fr. E14 14
Étampes, Fr. F11 14
Etamunbanie, Lake, l., Austl. F2 76
Étaples, Fr. D10 14
Etāwah, India E7 54
Etchojoa, Mex. B4 100
Ethan, S.D., U.S. D14 126
Ethel, Ms., U.S. D9 122
Ethel, Mount, mtn., Co., U.S. C10 132
Ethiopia, ctry., Afr. F7 62
Ethiopian Plateau, plat., Eth. E7 62
Ethridge, Mt., U.S. B14 136
Ethridge, Tn., U.S. B11 122
Etigo-heiya, pl., Japan B12 40
Etive, Loch, l., Scot., U.K. E7 12
E. T. Joshua Airport, St. Vin. o11 105e
Etna, Ca., U.S. B3 134
Etna, Monte, vol., Italy G8 24
Etobicoke, ngh., On., Can. E10 112
Etolin Island, i., Ak., U.S. E13 140
Etolin Strait, strt., Ak., U.S. D6 140
Etomami, stm., Sk., Can. B11 124
Eton, Austl. C7 76
Etorofu-tō (Iturup, ostrov), i., Russia B17 38
Etosha Pan, pl., Nmb. D2 68
Etoumbi, Congo D2 66
Etowah, Tn., U.S. B14 122
Etowah, stm., Ga., U.S. C14 122
Étretat, Fr. E9 14
Etsch see Adige, stm., Italy E8 22
Et Tîdra, i., Maur. F1 64
Ettlingen, Ger. H4 16
Etzikom Coulee, stm., Ab., Can. E2 124
Etzná, hist., Mex. C2 102
Eu, Fr. D10 14
Eua, i., Tonga F9 72
Eua Iki, i., Tonga n15 78e
Euboea see Évvoia, i., Grc. E6 28
Euboea, Gulf of see Vórios Evvoikós Kólpos, b., Grc. E5 28
Eucla, Austl. F5 74
Euclid, Oh., U.S. C4 114
Euclides da Cunha, Braz. F6 88
Eucumbene, Lake, res., Austl. K7 76
Eudora, Ar., U.S. D7 122
Eudora, Ks., U.S. F2 120
Eufaula, Al., U.S. F13 122
Eufaula Lake, res., Ok., U.S. B3 122
Eugene, Or., U.S. F3 136
Eugenia, Punta, c., Mex. B1 100
Eugenio Bustos, Arg. F3 92
Eugowra, Austl. I7 76
Eumungerie, Austl. H7 76
Eunápolis, Braz. I6 88

Name	Map Ref.	Page
Eungella National Park, p.o.i., Austl.	C7	76
Eunice, La., U.S.	G6	122
Eunice, N.M., U.S.	B4	130
Euphrates (Al-Furāt), stm., Asia	C6	56
Eupora, Ms., U.S.	D9	122
Eure, state, Fr.	E9	14
Eure, stm., Fr.	E10	14
Eure-et-Loir, state, Fr.	F10	14
Eureka, Can.	A8	141
Eureka, Ca., U.S.	C1	134
Eureka, Il., U.S.	K9	118
Eureka, Ks., U.S.	D12	128
Eureka, Mt., U.S.	B11	136
Eureka, Nv., U.S.	D10	134
Eureka, S.C., U.S.	B4	116
Eureka Springs, Ar., U.S.	H4	120
Eurinilla Creek, stm., Austl.	H3	76
Euroa, Austl.	K5	76
Europa, Île, i., Reu.	E7	68
Europa, Picos de, mts., Spain	A6	20
Europa Island see Europa, Île, i., Reu.	E7	68
Europa Point, c., Gib.	H5	20
Europe, cont.	C13	4
Euskal Herriko, state, Spain	A8	20
Euskirchen, Ger.	F2	16
Eustace, Tx., U.S.	E2	122
Eustis, Fl., U.S.	H4	116
Eustis, Lake, l., Fl., U.S.	H4	116
Euston, Austl.	J4	76
Eutaw, Al., U.S.	E11	122
Eutin, Ger.	B6	16
Eutsuk Lake, l., B.C., Can.	C4	138
Eva, Al., U.S.	C12	122
Evadale, Tx., U.S.	G4	122
Evandale, Austl.	n13	77a
Evans, Lac, l., Qc., Can.	E15	106
Evans, Mount, mtn., Co., U.S.	B3	128
Evansburg, Ab., Can.	C15	138
Evans City, Pa., U.S.	D5	114
Evansdale, Ia., U.S.	I6	118
Evans Strait, strt., N.T., Can.	C14	106
Evanston, Il., U.S.	F2	112
Evanston, Wy., U.S.	B6	132
Evansville, In., U.S.	F10	120
Evansville, Mn., U.S.	E3	118
Evansville, Wi., U.S.	B8	120
Evansville, Wy., U.S.	E6	126
Evart, Mi., U.S.	E4	112
Eveleth, Mn., U.S.	D6	118
Evening Shade, Ar., U.S.	H6	120
Evensk, Russia	D20	34
Everard, Lake, l., Austl.	F6	74
Everest, Mount (Qomolangma Feng), mtn., Asia	D11	54
Everett, Pa., U.S.	E7	114
Everett, Wa., U.S.	C4	136
Everett, Mount, mtn., Ma., U.S.	B12	114
Everglades, The, sw., Fl., U.S.	K4	116
Everglades City, Fl., U.S.	K4	116
Everglades National Park, p.o.i., Fl., U.S.	K5	116
Evergreen, Al., U.S.	F12	122
Evergreen, Mt., U.S.	B12	136
Evermann, Cerro, vol., Mex.	F3	100
Evesham, Sk., Can.	B4	124
Evesham, Eng., U.K.	I11	12
Évian-les-Bains, Fr.	C12	18
Evje, Nor.	G2	8
Évora, Port.	F3	20
Évora, state, Port.	F3	20
Evoron, ozero, l., Russia	F16	34
Évreux, Fr.	E10	14
Évry, Fr.	F11	14
E. V. Spence Reservoir, res., Tx., U.S.	C7	130
Évvoia, i., Grc.	E6	28
Ewa, Hi., U.S.	B3	78a
Ewing, Ne., U.S.	E14	126
Ewing, Va., U.S.	H2	114
Ewo, Congo	E2	66
Exaltación, Bol.	B3	90
Excelsior Mountain, mtn., Ca., U.S.	E6	134
Excelsior Springs, Mo., U.S.	E3	120
Exeter, On., Can.	E8	112
Exeter, Eng., U.K.	K9	12
Exeter, Ca., U.S.	G6	134
Exeter, N.H., U.S.	G6	110
Exeter Sound, strt., N.T., Can.	D13	141
Exira, Ia., U.S.	C3	120
Exmoor, plat., Eng., U.K.	J9	12
Exmoor National Park, p.o.i., Eng., U.K.	J9	12
Exmore, Va., U.S.	G10	114
Exmouth, Austl.	D2	74
Exmouth, Eng., U.K.	K9	12
Exmouth Gulf, b., Austl.	D2	74
Exshaw, Ab., Can.	E15	138
Extremadura, state, Spain	E4	20
Exuma Cays, is., Bah.	C9	96
Exuma Sound, strt., Bah.	C9	96
Eyasi, Lake, l., Tan.	E6	66
Eyebrow, Sk., Can.	D7	124
Eyemouth, Scot., U.K.	F10	12
Eye Peninsula, pen., Scot., U.K.	C6	12
Eyjafjördur, b., Ice.	j30	8a
Eyl, Som.	C9	66
Eyl, val., Som.	C9	66
Eylar Mountain, mtn., Ca., U.S.	F4	134
Eyota, Mn., U.S.	H6	118
Eyrarbakki, Ice.	I29	8a
Eyre, Austl.	F5	74
Eyre Creek, stm., Austl.	F2	76
Eyre North, Lake, l., Austl.	E7	74
Eyre Peninsula, pen., Austl.	F7	74
Eyre South, Lake, l., Austl.	E7	74
Ezequiel Ramos Mexía, Embalse, res., Arg.	G3	90
Ežerėlis, Lith.	F6	10
Ezine, Tur.	D9	28

F

Name	Map Ref.	Page
Faaone, Fr. Poly.	v22	78h
Faber Lake, l., N.T., Can.	C7	106
Fabriano, Italy	G9	22
Facatativá, Col.	E4	86
Fachi, Niger	F7	64
Facpi Point, c., Guam	j9	78c
Factoryville, Pa., U.S.	C10	114
Fada, Chad	D4	62
Fada-Ngourma, Burkina	G5	64
Faddeevskij, ostrov, i., Russia	A18	34
Faddeja, zaliv, b., Russia	A10	34
Fadiffolu Atoll, at., Mald.	h12	46a
Faenza, Italy	F8	22
Fafe, Port.	C2	20
Făgăraș, Rom.	D11	26
Fagernes, Nor.	F3	8
Fagersta, Swe.	F6	8
Faguibine, Lac, l., Mali	F4	64
Fagurhólsmýri, Ice.	I31	8a
Fairbank, Ia., U.S.	B5	120
Fairbanks, Ak., U.S.	D10	140
Fairbanks, La., U.S.	E6	122
Fair Bluff, N.C., U.S.	B6	116
Fairborn, Oh., U.S.	E1	114
Fairbury, Il., U.S.	K10	118
Fairbury, Ne., U.S.	A11	128
Fairchance, Pa., U.S.	E6	114
Fairchild, Wi., U.S.	G8	118
Fairfax, Mn., U.S.	G4	118
Fairfax, Mo., U.S.	D2	120
Fairfax, S.C., U.S.	D4	116
Fairfax, S.D., U.S.	D14	126
Fairfax, Vt., U.S.	F3	110
Fairfax, Va., U.S.	F8	114
Fairfield, Al., U.S.	D11	122
Fairfield, Ca., U.S.	E3	134
Fairfield, Id., U.S.	G12	136
Fairfield, Il., U.S.	F9	120
Fairfield, Me., U.S.	F7	110
Fairfield, Ne., U.S.	G14	126
Fairfield, Oh., U.S.	E1	114
Fairfield, Tx., U.S.	F2	122
Fairgrove, Mi., U.S.	E6	112
Fairhaven, Ma., U.S.	C15	114
Fair Haven, N.Y., U.S.	E13	112
Fair Head, c., N. Ire., U.K.	F6	12
Fairhope, Al., U.S.	G11	122
Fair Isle, i., Scot., U.K.	B11	12
Fairland, In., U.S.	E12	120
Fairlie, N.Z.	G4	80
Fairmont, Mn., U.S.	H4	118
Fairmont, Ne., U.S.	G15	126
Fairmont, N.C., U.S.	B6	116
Fairmont, W.V., U.S.	E5	114
Fairmont Hot Springs, B.C., Can.	F14	138
Fairmount, Il., U.S.	H2	112
Fairmount, In., U.S.	H4	112
Fairmount, N.D., U.S.	E2	118
Fair Ness, c., N.T., Can.	C16	106
Fair Oaks, Ca., U.S.	E4	134
Fair Plain, Mi., U.S.	F3	112
Fairplay, Co., U.S.	B3	128
Fairview, Ga., U.S.	C13	122
Fairview, Il., U.S.	D7	120
Fairview, Mi., U.S.	D5	112
Fairview, Mt., U.S.	G9	124
Fairview, Tn., U.S.	I10	120
Fairview, Ut., U.S.	D5	132
Fairview Park, In., U.S.	I2	112
Fairview Peak, mtn., Nv., U.S.	D7	134
Fairweather Mountain, mtn., N.A.	D3	106
Faisalabad (Lyallpur), Pak.	C4	54
Faison, N.C., U.S.	A7	116
Faistós, hist., Grc.	H7	28
Faith, S.D., U.S.	B10	126
Faizābād, India	E9	54
Fajardo, P.R.	B4	104a
Fajou, Îlet à, i., Guad.	h5	105c
Fajr, Bi'r, well, Sau. Ar.	J8	58
Fajr, Wādī, stm., Sau. Ar.	H9	58
Fajr, Wādī, stm., Sau. Ar.	J8	58
Fakse Bugt, b., Den.	A8	16
Faku, China	C5	38
Falaba, S.L.	H2	64
Falaise, Fr.	F8	14
Fālākāta, India	E12	54
Falam, Mya.	A1	48
Falcón, state, Ven.	B7	86
Falcón, Presa (Falcon Reservoir), res., N.A.	H8	130
Falconara Marittima, Italy	G10	22
Falcon Reservoir (Falcón, Presa), res., N.A.	H8	130
Falelatai, Samoa	g11	79c
Falémé, stm., Afr.	G2	64
Fălești, Mol.	B14	26
Falfurrias, Tx., U.S.	G9	130
Falkenberg, Ger.	E9	16
Falkenberg, Swe.	H5	8
Falkensee, Ger.	D9	16
Falkenstein, Ger.	F8	16
Falkirk, Scot., U.K.	E9	12
Falkland, B.C., Can.	F11	138
Falkland Islands, dep., S.A.	J4	90
Falkland Sound, strt., Falk. Is.	J5	90
Falköping, Swe.	G5	8
Falkville, Al., U.S.	C11	122
Fall, stm., Ks., U.S.	D13	128
Fallbrook, Ca., U.S.	J8	134
Fallon, Nv., U.S.	D7	134
Fall River, Ks., U.S.	G1	120
Fall River, Ma., U.S.	C14	114
Fall River, Wi., U.S.	H9	118
Fall River Mills, Ca., U.S.	C4	134
Falls City, Ne., U.S.	D2	120
Falls City, Or., U.S.	F3	136
Falls Creek, Pa., U.S.	C7	114
Falls Lake, res., N.C., U.S.	I7	114
Falmouth, Jam.	i13	104d
Falmouth, Eng., U.K.	K7	12
Falmouth, Me., U.S.	G6	110
Falmouth, Ma., U.S.	C15	114
False Bay, b., S. Afr.	I4	70
False Divi Point, c., India	D5	53
False Pass, Ak., U.S.	F7	140
Falset, Spain	C11	20
Falso, Cabo, c., Dom. Rep.	D12	102
Falster, i., Den.	I4	8
Fălticeni, Rom.	B13	26
Falun, Swe.	F6	8
Famagusta see Gazimağusa, N. Cyp.	C4	58
Famaillá, Arg.	C5	92
Famatina, Sierra de, mts., Arg.	D4	92
Famenne, reg., Bel.	D14	14
Family Lake, l., Mb., Can.	B18	124
Fanchang, China	F8	42
Fanch'eng see Xiangfan, China	F4	42
Fanchon, Pointe, c., Haiti	C10	102
Fancy, St. Vin.	o11	105e
Fang, Thai.	C4	48
Fangak, Sudan	F6	62
Fangcheng, China	E5	42
Fangxian, China	E4	42
Fangzheng, China	B10	36
Fanipal', Bela.	G10	10
Fanjiatun, China	C6	38
Fanny Bay, B.C., Can.	G6	138
Fano, Italy	G10	22
Fan Si Pan, mtn., Viet.	A6	48
Faraday, sci., Ant.	B34	81
Faradje, D.R.C.	D5	66
Farafangana, Madag.	E8	68
Farāh, Afg.	C9	56
Farāh, stm., Afg.	C9	56
Farallon de Pajaros, i., N. Mar. Is.	A5	72
Farallon Islands, is., Ca., U.S.	F2	134
Faranah, Gui.	G2	64
Farasān, Jazā'ir, is., Sau. Ar.	F5	56
Fareham, Eng., U.K.	K11	12
Farewell, Ak., U.S.	D9	140
Farewell, Cape, c., N.Z.	E5	80
Fargo, N.D., U.S.	E2	118
Faribault, Mn., U.S.	G5	118
Faribault, Lac, l., Qc., Can.	D16	106
Farīdābad, India	D6	54
Farīdkot, India	C5	54
Farīdpur, Bngl.	G12	54
Farīdpur, India	D7	54
Farilhões, is., Port.	E1	20
Farim, Gui.-B.	G2	64
Farina, Il., U.S.	F9	120
Farinha, stm., Braz.	D2	88
Fâriskur, Egypt	G2	58
Farit, Amba, mtn., Eth.	E7	62
Färjestaden, Swe.	H7	8
Farley, Ia., U.S.	B7	120
Farmer City, Il., U.S.	D9	120
Farmersville, Il., U.S.	E8	120
Farmersville, Tx., U.S.	D2	122
Farmerville, La., U.S.	E6	122
Farmington, Il., U.S.	D7	120
Farmington, Me., U.S.	F6	110
Farmington, Mn., U.S.	G5	118
Farmington, Mo., U.S.	G7	120
Farmington, Mt., U.S.	C14	136
Farmington, N.H., U.S.	G5	110
Farmington, N.M., U.S.	G8	132
Farmington, Ut., U.S.	C5	132
Far Mountain, mtn., B.C., Can.	D5	138
Farmville, N.C., U.S.	A8	116
Farmville, Va., U.S.	G7	114
Farnborough, Eng., U.K.	J12	12
Farne Islands, is., Eng., U.K.	F11	12
Farnham, Qc., Can.	E3	110
Faro, Braz.	D6	84
Faro, Yk., Can.	C4	106
Faro, Port.	H3	20
Faro, state, Port.	G3	20
Faroe Islands, dep., Eur.	n34	8b
Fårön, i., Swe.	H8	8
Farquhar, Atoll de, i., Sey.	I12	69b
Farquhar, Cape, c., Austl.	D2	74
Farragut, Ia., U.S.	D2	120
Farrars Creek, stm., Austl.	E3	76
Farrell, Pa., U.S.	C5	114
Farrukhābād, India	E7	54
Fársala, Grc.	D5	28
Fartak, Ra's, c., Yemen	F7	56
Farvel, Kap, c., Grnld.	F17	141
Farwell, Mi., U.S.	E5	112
Fasā, Iran	D7	56
Fasano, Italy	D11	24
Fastnet Rock, r., Ire.	J3	12
Fatehābād, India	D5	54
Fatehjang, Pak.	B4	54
Fatehpur, India	F8	54
Fatehpur, India	E5	54
Fatehpur Sīkri, India	E6	54
Fathom Five National Marine Park, p.o.i., On., Can.	C8	112
Fatick, Sen.	G1	64
Fátima, Port.	E2	20
Fatshan see Foshan, China	J5	42
Fatu Hiva, i., Fr. Poly.	E13	72
Fatumu, Tonga	n14	78e
Fatwā, India	F10	54
Fauabu, Sol. Is.	e9	79b
Faucilles, Monts, mts., Fr.	F15	14
Faulkton, S.D., U.S.	B13	126
Fauquier, B.C., Can.	G12	138
Făurei, Rom.	D14	26
Fauresmith, S. Afr.	F7	70
Fauro Island, i., Sol. Is.	d6	79b
Fauske, Nor.	C6	8
Faust, Ab., Can.	A15	138
Favara, Italy	G7	24
Fawcett Lake, l., Ab., Can.	A17	138
Fawn, stm., On., Can.	E13	106
Fawnie Nose, mtn., B.C., Can.	C5	138
Faxaflói, b., Ice.	k28	8a
Faxinal do Soturno, Braz.	D11	92
Faya-Largeau, Chad	D3	62
Fayette, Al., U.S.	D11	122
Fayette, Ia., U.S.	B6	120
Fayette, Ms., U.S.	F7	122
Fayette, Mo., U.S.	E5	120
Fayette, Lake, res., Tx., U.S.	E2	122
Fayetteville, Ar., U.S.	H3	120
Fayetteville, Ga., U.S.	D14	122
Fayetteville, N.C., U.S.	A7	116
Fayetteville, W.V., U.S.	F4	114
Fâyid, Egypt	H3	58
Fāzilka, India	C5	54
Fāzilpur, Pak.	D3	54
Fazzān, hist. reg., Libya	B2	62
Fdérik, Maur.	E2	64
Fear, Cape, c., N.C., U.S.	C8	116
Feather, stm., Ca., U.S.	D4	134
Feather, Middle Fork, stm., Ca., U.S.	D5	134
Feather, North Fork, East Branch, stm., Ca., U.S.	C5	134
Fécamp, Fr.	E9	14
Federación, Arg.	E8	92
Federal, Arg.	E8	92
Federally Administered Tribal Areas, state, Pak.	B2	54
Federal Republic of Germany see Germany, ctry., Eur.	E6	16
Federalsburg, Md., U.S.	F10	114
Federated States of Micronesia see Micronesia, Federated States of, ctry., Oc.	C6	72
Fehérgyarmat, Hung.	A9	26
Fehmarn, i., Ger.	B7	16
Feia, Lagoa, b., Braz.	L5	88
Fei Huang, stm., China	D8	42
Feijó, Braz.	E3	84
Feiketu, China	B7	38
Feira de Santana, Braz.	G6	88
Feixi, China	F7	42
Feixian, China	D7	42
Fejér, state, Hung.	B5	26
Felanitx, Spain	E14	20
Felda, Fl., U.S.	J4	116
Feldbach, Aus.	D12	22
Feldberg, mtn., Ger.	I4	16
Feldkirch, Aus.	C6	22
Feliciano, P.R.	B1	104a
Feliciano, Arroyo, stm., Arg.	E8	92
Felipe Carrillo Puerto, Mex.	C4	102
Felix, Cape, c., N.T., Can.	B11	106
Felixlândia, Braz.	J3	88
Felixstowe, Eng., U.K.	I14	12
Felletin, Fr.	D8	18
Fellsmere, Fl., U.S.	I5	116
Feltre, Italy	E8	22
Femunden, l., Nor.	E4	8
Femundsmarka Nasjonalpark, p.o.i., Nor.	E4	8
Fen, stm., China	D4	42
Fenelon Falls, On., Can.	D11	112
Fengcheng, China	D6	38
Fengcheng, China	G6	42
Fengdu, China	G2	42
Fengfeng, China	C6	42
Fenggang, China	G2	42
Fenghuang, China	H3	42
Fengjiabao, China	C1	42
Fengjie, China	F3	42
Fengning, China	A7	42
Fengqing, China	G4	36
Fengqiu, China	D6	42
Fengtai, China	B7	42
Fengtai, China	E7	42
Fengtien see Shenyang, China	D5	38
Fengxi, China	F3	42
Fengxian, China	D7	42
Fengxiang, China	D2	42
Fengyang, China	E7	42
Fengyüan, Tai.	I9	42
Fengzhen, China	A5	42
Feni, Bngl.	G13	54
Fennimore, Wi., U.S.	B7	120
Fenoarivo Atsinanana, Madag.	D8	68
Fenton, Mi., U.S.	B2	114
Fentress, Tx., U.S.	E10	130
Fenwick, W.V., U.S.	F5	114
Fenyang, China	C4	42
Fenyi, China	H6	42
Feodosiia, Ukr.	F5	32
Fer, Cap de, c., Alg.	B6	64
Ferdinand, In., U.S.	F10	120
Ferdows, Iran	C8	56
Ferentino, Italy	I10	22
Fergana, Uzb.	F12	32
Fergana Mountains see Ferganskij hrebet, mts., Kyrg.	F12	32
Ferganskij hrebet, mts., Kyrg.	F12	32
Fergus, On., Can.	E9	112
Fergus Falls, Mn., U.S.	E2	118
Ferguson, B.C., Can.	F13	138
Ferguson, Ky., U.S.	G13	120
Ferguson, Mo., U.S.	F7	120
Fergusson Island, i., Pap. N. Gui.	b5	79a
Ferkéssédougou, C. Iv.	H4	64
Ferlo, reg., Sen.	F2	64
Ferme-Neuve, Qc., Can.	B14	112
Fermo, Italy	G10	22
Fermont, Qc., Can.	E17	106
Fermoselle, Spain	C4	20
Fernández, Arg.	C6	92
Fernandina, Isla, i., Ec.	i11	84a
Fernandina Beach, Fl., U.S.	F4	116
Fernando de la Mora, Para.	B9	92
Fernando de Noronha, Ilha, i., Braz.	F11	82
Fernandópolis, Braz.	D6	90
Fernando Póo see Bioko, i., Eq. Gui.	I6	64
Fernán-Núñez, Spain	G6	20
Ferndale, Ca., U.S.	C1	134
Fernie, B.C., Can.	G15	138
Fernley, Nv., U.S.	D6	134
Fern Park, Fl., U.S.	H4	116
Fern Ridge Lake, res., Or., U.S.	F3	136
Fernwood, Id., U.S.	C10	136
Ferokh, India	F2	53
Ferrandina, Italy	D10	24
Ferrara, Italy	F8	22
Ferrato, Capo, c., Italy	E3	24
Ferreira Gomes, Braz.	C7	84
Ferreñafe, Peru	E2	84
Ferret, Cap, c., Fr.	E4	18
Ferrières, Fr.	F11	14
Ferris, Tx., U.S.	E2	122
Ferrol, Spain	A2	20
Ferron, Ut., U.S.	D5	132
Ferrysburg, Mi., U.S.	E3	112
Ferto-tavi Nemzeti Park, p.o.i., Hung.	B3	26
Fès, Mor.	C3	64
Feshi, D.R.C.	F3	66
Fessenden, N.D., U.S.	G14	124
Festus, Mo., U.S.	F7	120
Fetești, Rom.	E14	26
Fethiye, Tur.	G12	28
Fetisovo, Kaz.	F8	32
Fetlar, i., Scot., U.K.	n19	12a
Feucht, Ger.	G7	16
Feuchtwangen, Ger.	G6	16
Feuilles, stm., Qc., Can.	D16	106
Feuilles, Baie aux, b., Qc., Can.	D16	106
Feurs, Fr.	D10	18
Feyzābād, Afg.	B11	56
Fez see Fès, Mor.	C3	64
Fezzan see Fazzān, hist. reg., Libya	B2	62
Ffestiniog, Wales, U.K.	I9	12
Fianarantsoa, Madag.	E8	68
Fianga, Chad	F3	62
Fichē, Eth.	F7	62
Fichtelgebirge, mts., Eur.	F7	16
Ficksburg, S. Afr.	F8	70
Fidalgo, stm., Braz.	E5	88
Fidenza, Italy	F7	22
Field, B.C., Can.	E14	138
Fier, Alb.	D13	24
Fieri see Fier, Alb.	D13	24
Fiery Creek, stm., Austl.	B2	76
Fierzës, Liqeni i, res., Alb.	B14	24
Fife Lake, Sk., Can.	E8	124
Fife Lake, Mi., U.S.	D4	112
Fife Lake, l., Sk., Can.	E8	124
Fife Ness, c., Scot., U.K.	E10	12
Fifield, Wi., U.S.	F8	118
Fifth Cataract see Khāmis, Ash-Shallāl al-, wtfl, Sudan	D6	62
Figeac, Fr.	E7	18
Figtree, Zimb.	B9	70
Figueira da Foz, Port.	D1	20
Figueras see Figueres, Spain	B13	20
Figueres, Spain	B13	20
Figuig, Mor.	C4	64
Fiji, ctry., Oc.	E8	72
Filabusi, Zimb.	B9	70
Filadelfia, Italy	F10	24
Filchner Ice Shelf, ice, Ant.	C1	81
Filey, Eng., U.K.	G12	12
Filí, hist., Grc.	E6	28
Filiatrá, Grc.	F4	28
Filingué, Niger	G5	64
Fílippoi, hist., Grc.	B7	28
Fillmore, Sk., Can.	E10	124
Fillmore, Ca., U.S.	I7	134
Fīltu, Eth.	F8	62
Fimi, stm., D.R.C.	E3	66
Finale Emilia, Italy	F8	22
Finale Ligure, Italy	F5	22
Finca El Rey, Parque Nacional, p.o.i., Arg.	B5	92
Findlay, Il., U.S.	E9	120
Findlay, Oh., U.S.	C2	114
Findlay, Mount, mtn., B.C., Can.	F14	138
Fingal, N.D., U.S.	H16	124
Fíngoè, Moz.	D5	68
Finistère, state, Fr.	F5	14
Finisterre, Cabo de see Fisterra, Cabo de, c., Spain	B1	20
Finke, Austl.	E6	74
Finland, ctry., Eur.	C12	8
Finland, Gulf of, b., Eur.	G11	8
Finlay, stm., B.C., Can.	D5	106
Finley, Austl.	J5	76
Finley, N.D., U.S.	G16	124
Finmoore, B.C., Can.	C7	138
Finnegan, Ab., Can.	E18	138
Finnis, Cape, c., Austl.	F6	74
Finnmark, state, Nor.	B11	8
Finnsnes, Nor.	B8	8
Finschhafen, Pap. N. Gui.	b4	79a
Finse, Nor.	F2	8
Finspång, Swe.	G6	8
Finsterwalde, Ger.	E9	16
Fiordland National Park, p.o.i., N.Z.	G2	80
Fiorenzuola d'Arda, Italy	F6	22
Fire Island National Seashore, p.o.i., N.Y., U.S.	D12	114
Firenze (Florence), Italy	G8	22
Firmat, Arg.	F7	92
Firminy, Fr.	D10	18
Firovo, Russia	C16	10
Fīrozābād, India	E7	54
Fīrozpur, India	C5	54
Firozpur Jhirka, India	E6	54
First Cataract, wtfl, Egypt	C6	62
Firth, Ne., U.S.	K2	118
Firth, stm., N.A.	C11	140
Fīrūzābād, Iran	D7	56
Fisher, Ar., U.S.	B7	122
Fisher, Il., U.S.	D9	120
Fisher Bay, b., Mb., Can.	C17	124
Fisher Branch, Mb., Can.	C16	124
Fisher Peak, mtn., Va., U.S.	H5	114
Fishers Island, i., N.Y., U.S.	C14	114
Fisher Strait, strt., N.T., Can.	C14	106
Fishing Creek, Md., U.S.	F9	114
Fishing Creek, stm., N.C., U.S.	H8	114
Fishing Lake, l., Mb., Can.	B18	124
Fisk, Mo., U.S.	H7	120
Fiskárdo, Grc.	E3	28
Fisterra, Cabo de, c., Spain	B1	20
Fitchburg, Ma., U.S.	B14	114
Fito, Mount, vol., Samoa	g12	79c
Fitri, Lac, l., Chad	E3	62
Fitz Roy, Arg.	I3	90
Fitzroy, stm., Austl.	C4	74
Fitzroy, stm., Austl.	D8	76
Fitz Roy, Monte (Chaltel, Cerro), mtn., S.A.	I2	90
Fitzroy Crossing, Austl.	C5	74
Fitzwilliam Island, i., On., Can.	C8	112
Fiuggi, Italy	I10	22
Fiume see Rijeka, Cro.	E11	22
Fiumicino, Italy	I9	22
Five Islands, N.S., Can.	E12	110
Five Islands Harbour, b., Antig.	f4	105b
Fivemile Creek, stm., Wy., U.S.	D4	126
Five Points, N.M., U.S.	H10	132
Fivizzano, Italy	F7	22
Fizi, D.R.C.	E5	66
Fjällåsen, Swe.	C8	8
Flagler, Co., U.S.	B5	128
Flagstaff, Az., U.S.	H5	132
Flagstaff Lake, res., Me., U.S.	E6	110
Flamands, Anse des, Guad.	B2	105a
Flambeau, stm., Wi., U.S.	F8	118
Flamborough, On., Can.	E9	112
Flamborough Head, c., Eng., U.K.	G12	12
Fläming, reg., Ger.	E8	16
Flaming Gorge National Recreation Area, p.o.i., U.S.	B7	132
Flaming Gorge Reservoir, res., U.S.	B7	132
Flanagan, Il., U.S.	D9	120
Flanders, On., Can.	C6	118
Flasher, N.D., U.S.	A11	126
Flåsjön, l., Swe.	D6	8
Flat, Ak., U.S.	D8	140
Flat, Tx., U.S.	C10	130
Flat, stm., N.T., Can.	C5	106
Flat, stm., Mi., U.S.	E4	112
Flatey, Ice.	k28	8a
Flathead (Flathead, North Fork), stm., N.A.	H16	138
Flathead, stm., Mt., U.S.	C12	136
Flathead, Middle Fork, stm., Mt., U.S.	B13	136
Flathead, North Fork (Flathead), stm., N.A.	H16	138
Flathead, South Fork, stm., Mt., U.S.	B13	136
Flathead Lake, l., Mt., U.S.	C12	136
Flat Lake, l., Ab., Can.	B17	138
Flatonia, Tx., U.S.	E10	130
Flat River, P.E., Can.	D13	110
Flat River, Mo., U.S.	G7	120
Flat Rock, Al., U.S.	C13	122
Flattery, Cape, c., Wa., U.S.	B2	136
Flatts, Ber.	k15	104e
Flatwillow Creek, stm., Mt., U.S.	H5	124
Flatwood, U.S.	E11	122
Flaxton, N.D., U.S.	F11	124
Flaxville, Mt., U.S.	F8	124
Fleetwood, Eng., U.K.	H10	12
Fleetwood, Pa., U.S.	D10	114
Flekkefjord, Nor.	G2	8
Fleming-Neon, Ky., U.S.	G3	114
Flemingsburg, Ky., U.S.	F2	114
Flen, Swe.	G7	8
Flensburg, Ger.	B5	16
Fletcher, N.C., U.S.	A3	116
Fletcher Pond, l., Mi., U.S.	D5	112
Fleurance, Fr.	F6	18
Flinders, stm., Austl.	A3	76
Flinders Bay, b., Austl.	F3	74
Flinders Island, i., Austl.	m14	77a
Flinders Ranges National Park, p.o.i., Austl.	H2	76
Flinders Reefs, rf., Austl.	A7	76
Flin Flon, Mb., Can.	E10	106
Flint, Wales, U.K.	H9	12
Flint, Mi., U.S.	E6	112
Flint, i., Kir.	E11	72
Flint, stm., U.S.	C12	122
Flint, stm., Ga., U.S.	G14	122
Flint Lake, l., N.T., Can.	B16	106
Flinton, Austl.	F7	76
Flintville, Tn., U.S.	B12	122
Flippin, Ar., U.S.	H5	120
Flix, Pantà de, res., Spain	C11	20
Flomaton, Al., U.S.	F11	122
Floodwood, Mn., U.S.	E6	118
Flora, Il., U.S.	F9	120
Flora, In., U.S.	H3	112
Florac, Fr.	E9	18
Floral City, Fl., U.S.	H3	116
Floral Park, Mt., U.S.	E14	136
Flora Vista, N.M., U.S.	G8	132
Flore, Piton, mtn., St. Luc.	m7	105c
Florence see Firenze, Italy	G8	22
Florence, Al., U.S.	C11	122
Florence, Az., U.S.	J5	132
Florence, Co., U.S.	C3	128
Florence, Ks., U.S.	C12	128
Florence, S.C., U.S.	B6	116
Florence, Tx., U.S.	D10	130
Florence, Wi., U.S.	C1	112
Florencia, Col.	G4	86
Florentino Ameghino, Embalse, res., Arg.	H3	90
Flores, Braz.	D7	88
Flores, i., Indon.	G7	44
Flores, Laut (Flores Sea), Indon.	G11	50
Flores, Selat, strt., Indon.	G7	44
Flores de Goiás, Braz.	H2	88
Flores Island, i., B.C., Can.	G4	138
Flores Sea see Flores, Laut, Indon.	G11	50
Floresta, Braz.	E6	88
Florești, Mol.	B15	26
Floresville, Tx., U.S.	E9	130
Floriano, Braz.	D4	88
Floriano Peixoto, Braz.	E4	84
Florianópolis, Braz.	C13	92
Florida, Col.	F3	86
Florida, Cuba	B8	102
Florida, P.R.	B4	104a
Florida, Ur.	G9	92
Florida, state, U.S.	F11	108
Florida, Straits of, strt., N.A.	G11	108
Florida Bay, b., Fl., U.S.	K5	116
Floridablanca, Col.	D5	86
Florida City, Fl., U.S.	K5	116
Florida Islands, is., Sol. Is.	e9	79b
Florida Keys, is., Fl., U.S.	L4	116
Floridia, Italy	G9	24
Florido, stm., Mex.	B6	100
Florien, La., U.S.	F5	122
Flórina, Grc.	C4	28
Florissant, Mo., U.S.	F7	120
Florissant Fossil Beds National Monument, p.o.i., Co., U.S.	B3	128
Florø, Nor.	F1	8
Flotte, Cap de, c., N. Cal.	m16	79d
Floyd, N.M., U.S.	G5	128
Floyd, Va., U.S.	H5	114
Floyd, stm., Ia., U.S.	I2	118
Floydada, Tx., U.S.	G7	128
Flumendosa, stm., Italy	E3	24
Fluminimaggiore, Italy	E2	24
Flushing see Vlissingen, Neth.	C12	14
Fluvanna, Tx., U.S.	B6	130
Fly, stm.	b3	79a
Foam Lake, Sk., Can.	C10	124
Foča, Bos.	F5	26
Foça, Tur.	E9	28
Focșani, Rom.	D14	26
Fogang, China	J5	42
Foggaret ez Zoua, Alg.	D5	64
Foggia, Italy	C9	24
Fogo, i., C.V.	k10	65a
Fogo Island, i., Nf., Can.	j23	107a
Foguista J. F. Juárez see El Galpón, Arg.	B5	92
Föhr, i., Ger.	B4	16
Fóia, mtn., Port.	G2	20
Foix, Fr.	G7	18
Foix, hist. reg., Fr.	F7	18
Fojnica, Bos.	F4	26
Fokino, Russia	G17	10
Folda, b., Nor.	C6	8
Foley, Al., U.S.	G11	122
Foleyet, On., Can.	F14	106
Foley Island, i., N.T., Can.	B15	106
Folgefonni, ice, Nor.	G2	8
Foligno, Italy	H9	22
Folkestone, Eng., U.K.	J14	12
Folkston, Ga., U.S.	F3	116
Follett, Tx., U.S.	E8	128
Föllinge, Swe.	E6	8
Follonica, Italy	H7	22
Follonica, Golfo di, b., Italy	H7	22
Folsom, Ca., U.S.	E4	134
Folsom Lake, res., Ca., U.S.	E4	134
Fomboni, Com.	C7	68
Fominiči, Russia	F17	10
Fominskoe, Russia	A22	10
Fonda, N.Y., U.S.	B11	114
Fond-du-Lac, Sk., Can.	D9	106
Fond du Lac, Wi., U.S.	H10	118
Fond du Lac, stm., Sk., Can.	D9	106
Fondi, Italy	C7	24
Fonni, Italy	D3	24
Fonseca, Col.	B5	86
Fonseca, Golfo de, b., N.A.	F4	102
Fontainebleau, Fr.	F11	14
Fontana, Arg.	C8	92
Fontana, Ca., U.S.	I8	134
Fontana Lake, res., N.C., U.S.	A2	116
Fontanelle, Ia., U.S.	J4	118
Fontas, stm., Can.	D6	106
Fonte Boa, Braz.	I8	86
Fontenay-le-Comte, Fr.	C5	18
Fontenelle, Qc., Can.	B12	110
Fontenelle Reservoir, res., Wy., U.S.	A6	132
Fontur, c., Ice.	j32	8a
Fonyód, Hung.	C4	26
Foochow see Fuzhou, China	H8	42
Foothills, Ab., Can.	C14	138
Forari, Vanuatu	k17	79d
Forbach, Fr.	E15	14
Forbach, Ger.	H4	16
Forbes, Austl.	I7	76
Forbes, Mount, mtn., Ab., Can.	E14	138
Forbesganj, India	E11	54
Forchheim, Ger.	G7	16
Ford, Ks., U.S.	D9	128
Ford, stm., Mi., U.S.	B2	112
Ford City, Ca., U.S.	H6	134
Ford City, Pa., U.S.	D6	114
Førde, Nor.	F1	8
Ford Ranges, mts., Ant.	C26	81
Fords Bridge, Austl.	G5	76
Fordville, N.D., U.S.	F16	124
Fordyce, Ar., U.S.	D6	122
Forécariah, Gui.	H2	64
Forel, Mont, mtn., Grnld.	D18	141
Foreman, Ar., U.S.	D4	122
Forest, On., Can.	E8	112
Forest, Ms., U.S.	E9	122
Forest Acres, S.C., U.S.	B4	116
Forestburg, Ab., Can.	D18	138
Forest City, N.C., U.S.	A4	116
Forest City, Pa., U.S.	C10	114
Forest Grove, B.C., Can.	E9	138
Foresthill, Ca., U.S.	D5	134
Forestier Peninsula, pen., Austl.	o14	77a
Forest Lake, Mn., U.S.	F5	118
Forest Park, Ga., U.S.	C1	116
Forestville, Qc., Can.	B7	110
Forgan, Ok., U.S.	E8	128
Forges-les-Eaux, Fr.	E10	14
Forillon, Parc national de, p.o.i., Qc., Can.	B12	110
Forked Deer, stm., Tn., U.S.	I8	120
Forks, Wa., U.S.	C2	136
Forlì, Italy	F9	22
Formby Point, c., Eng., U.K.	H9	12
Formentera, i., Spain	F12	20
Formentor, Cap de, c., Spain	E14	20
Formia, Italy	C7	24
Formiga, Braz.	K3	88
Formosa, Arg.	C8	92
Formosa, Braz.	H2	88
Formosa, state, Arg.	D4	90
Formosa see Taiwan, ctry., Asia	J9	42
Formosa, Serra, plat., Braz.	F6	84
Formosa Strait see Taiwan Strait, strt., Asia	I8	42
Formoso, stm., Braz.	G3	88
Forncelle, Italy	G8	22
Forney, Tx., U.S.	E2	122
Fornosovo, Russia	A13	10
Forres, Scot., U.K.	D9	12
Forrest, Austl.	F5	74
Forrest, Il., U.S.	D9	120
Forrest City, Ar., U.S.	B8	122
Forreston, Il., U.S.	I9	118
Forsayth, Austl.	B4	76
Forst, Ger.	E10	16
Forster, Austl.	I9	76
Forsyth, Ga., U.S.	C2	116
Forsyth, Mo., U.S.	H4	120
Forsyth, Mt., U.S.	A6	126
Fort Abbās, Pak.	D4	54
Fort Albany, On., Can.	E14	106
Fortaleza, Braz.	B6	88
Fortaleza do Ituxi, Braz.	E4	84
Fort Assiniboine, Ab., Can.	B15	138
Fort Atkinson, Wi., U.S.	B9	120
Fort Bayard see Zhanjiang, China	K4	42
Fort Beaufort, S. Afr.	H8	70
Fort Belknap Agency, Mt., U.S.	F5	124
Fort Benton, Mt., U.S.	C16	136
Fort Bragg, Ca., U.S.	D2	134
Fort Branch, In., U.S.	F10	120
Fort Bridger, Wy., U.S.	B6	132
Fort Calhoun, Ne., U.S.	C1	120
Fort Chipewyan, Ab., Can.	D8	106
Fort Collins, Co., U.S.	G7	126
Fort-Coulonge, Qc., Can.	C13	112
Fort Covington, N.Y., U.S.	E2	110
Fort Davis, Al., U.S.	E13	122
Fort Davis, Tx., U.S.	D4	130
Fort-de-France, Mart.	k6	105c
Fort-de-France-Lamentin, Aérodrome de, Mart.	k7	105c
Fort Deposit, Al., U.S.	F12	122
Fort Dodge, Ia., U.S.	B3	120

I • 20 Fort-Gasp

Name	Map Ref.	Page
Fort Duchesne, Ut., U.S.	C7	132
Forte dei Marmi, Italy	G7	22
Fort Edward, N.Y., U.S.	G3	110
Fort Erie, On., Can.	F10	112
Fortescue, stm., Austl.	D3	74
Fortezza, Italy	D8	22
Fort Frances, On., Can.	C5	118
Fort Fraser, B.C., Can.	B6	138
Fort Frederica National Monument, p.o.i., Ga., U.S.	E4	116
Fort Gaines, Ga., U.S.	F13	122
Fort Garland, Co., U.S.	D3	128
Fort Gibson, Ok., U.S.	I2	120
Fort Good Hope, N.T., Can.	B5	106
Forth, Firth of, b., Scot., U.K.	E10	12
Fort Hall, Id., U.S.	G14	136
Fortine, Mt., U.S.	B12	136
Fortín Uno, Arg.	I5	92
Fort Jones, Ca., U.S.	B3	134
Fort Klamath, Or., U.S.	H4	136
Fort Knox, Ky., U.S.	G12	120
Fort-Lamy see N'Djamena, Chad	E3	62
Fort Laramie, Wy., U.S.	E8	126
Fort Lauderdale, Fl., U.S.	J5	116
Fort Liard, N.T., Can.	C6	106
Fort Loramie, Oh., U.S.	D1	114
Fort Loudoun Lake, res., Tn., U.S.	B15	122
Fort Lyon Canal, can., Co., U.S.	C5	128
Fort MacKay, Ab., Can.	D8	106
Fort Macleod, Ab., Can.	G17	138
Fort Madison, Ia., U.S.	D6	120
Fort Matanzas National Monument, p.o.i., Fl., U.S.	G4	116
Fort McMurray, Ab., Can.	D8	106
Fort McPherson, N.T., Can.	B4	106
Fort Meade, Fl., U.S.	I4	116
Fort Mill, S.C., U.S.	A5	116
Fort Morgan, Co., U.S.	A5	128
Fort Myers, Fl., U.S.	J3	116
Fort Myers Beach, Fl., U.S.	J3	116
Fort Nelson, B.C., Can.	D6	106
Fort Nelson, stm., B.C., Can.	D6	106
Fort Ogden, Fl., U.S.	I4	116
Fort Payne, Al., U.S.	C13	122
Fort Peck, Mt., U.S.	F7	124
Fort Peck Dam, dam, Mt., U.S.	G7	124
Fort Peck Lake, res., Mt., U.S.	G7	124
Fort Pierce, Fl., U.S.	I5	116
Fort Plain, N.Y., U.S.	B11	114
Fort Portal, Ug.	D6	66
Fort Providence, N.T., Can.	C7	106
Fort Pulaski National Monument, p.o.i., Ga., U.S.	E5	116
Fort Qu'Appelle, Sk., Can.	D10	124
Fort Randall Dam, dam, S.D., U.S.	D14	126
Fort Recovery, Oh., U.S.	D1	114
Fort Resolution, N.T., Can.	C8	106
Fort Rixon, Zimb.	B9	70
Fort Saint James, B.C., Can.	B6	138
Fort Saint John, B.C., Can.	D6	106
Fort Saskatchewan, Ab., Can.	C17	138
Fort Scott, Ks., U.S.	G3	120
Fort-Ševčenko, Kaz.	F7	32
Fort Severn, On., Can.	D13	106
Fort Simpson, N.T., Can.	C6	106
Fort Smith, N.T., Can.	C8	106
Fort Smith, Ar., U.S.	B4	122
Fort Stockton, Tx., U.S.	D4	130
Fort Sumner, N.M., U.S.	G4	128
Fort Sumter National Monument, p.o.i., S.C., U.S.	D6	116
Fort Supply, Ok., U.S.	E9	128
Fort Thomas, Az., U.S.	J7	132
Fort Totten, N.D., U.S.	G14	124
Fort Towson, Ok., U.S.	D3	122
Fortuna, Arg.	G5	92
Fortuna, C.R.	G5	102
Fortuna, Ca., U.S.	C1	134
Fortuna, V.I.U.S.	e6	104b
Fortune Bay, b., Nf., Can.	j22	107a
Fortuneswell, Eng., U.K.	K10	12
Fort Union National Monument, p.o.i., N.M., U.S.	F3	128
Fort Valley, Ga., U.S.	D2	116
Fort Vermilion, Ab., Can.	D7	106
Fort Victoria, hist., Ber.	k16	104e
Fort Walton Beach, Fl., U.S.	G12	122
Fort Wayne, In., U.S.	G4	112
Fort White, Fl., U.S.	G3	116
Fort William, Scot., U.K.	E7	12
Fort Worth, Tx., U.S.	B10	130
Fort Yates, N.D., U.S.	A12	126
Fort Yukon, Ak., U.S.	C10	140
Foshan, China	J5	42
Fosheim Peninsula, pen., N.T., Can.	B9	141
Foso, Ghana	H4	64
Fossano, Italy	F4	22
Fossil, Or., U.S.	F6	136
Fossil Butte National Monument, p.o.i., Wy., U.S.	B6	132
Fossil Lake, l., Or., U.S.	G6	136
Fossombrone, Italy	G9	22
Fosston, Mn., U.S.	D3	118
Foster, Austl.	L6	76
Foster Bugt, strt., Grnld.	C21	141
Fosters, Al., U.S.	D11	122
Fostoria, Oh., U.S.	C2	114
Fougamou, Gabon	E2	66
Fougères, Fr.	F7	14
Fouhsin see Fuxin, China	C4	38
Fou-kien see Fujian, state, China	I7	42
Foula, i., Scot., U.K.	n17	12a
Fouling see Fuling, China	G2	42
Foulwind, Cape, c., N.Z.	E4	80
Foumban, Cam.	C2	66
Foum-el-Hassan, Mor.	D3	64
Foum-Zguid, Mor.	C3	64
Foundiougne, Sen.	G1	64
Fountain, Co., U.S.	C4	128
Fountain, Fl., U.S.	G13	122
Fountain City, Wi., U.S.	G7	118
Fountain Green, Ut., U.S.	D5	132
Fountain Peak, mtn., Ca., U.S.	I1	132
Fountain Place, La., U.S.	G7	122
Fourche LaFave, stm., Ar., U.S.	C6	122
Fourchu, N.S., Can.	E16	110
Four Corners, Or., U.S.	F4	136
Fourmies, Fr.	D13	14
Four Mountains, Islands of, is., Ak., U.S.	g24	140a
Four Oaks, N.C., U.S.	A7	116
Fourth Cataract see Rābi', Ash-Shallāl ar-, wtfl, Sudan	D6	62
Fous, Pointe des, c., Dom.	j6	105c
Fouta Djalon, reg., Gui.	G2	64
Foux, Cap à, c., Haiti	C11	102
Fouyang see Fuyang, China	E6	42
Foveaux Strait, strt., N.Z.	H3	80
Fowler, Co., U.S.	C4	128
Fowler, In., U.S.	H2	112
Fowler, Mi., U.S.	E5	112
Fowlers Bay, Austl.	F6	74
Fowlerville, Mi., U.S.	B1	114
Fox, stm., U.S.	C9	120
Fox, stm., U.S.	D5	120
Fox, stm., Wi., U.S.	H10	118
Fox Creek, Ab., Can.	B14	138
Foxe Basin, b., N.T., Can.	B15	106
Foxe Channel, strt., N.T., Can.	C15	106
Foxe Peninsula, pen., N.T., Can.	C15	106
Foxford, Ire.	H3	12
Fox Islands, is., Ak., U.S.	g25	140a
Fox Lake, Il., U.S.	B9	120
Foxpark, Wy., U.S.	B10	132
Fox Valley, Sk., Can.	D4	124
Foxworth, Ms., U.S.	F9	122
Foyle, Lough, b., Eur.	F5	12
Foz do Areia, Represa de, res., Braz.	B12	92
Foz do Cunene, Ang.	D1	68
Foz do Iguaçu, Braz.	B10	92
Foz do Jordão, Braz.	E3	84
Foz Giraldo, Port.	E3	20
Fraga, Spain	C11	20
Fraile Muerto, Ur.	F10	92
Framingham, Ma., U.S.	B14	114
França, Braz.	F5	88
Franca, Braz.	K2	88
Franca-Iosifa, Zemlja, is., Russia	B9	30
Francavilla al Mare, Italy	H11	22
Francavilla Fontana, Italy	D11	24
France, ctry., Eur.	C8	18
Frances, stm., Yk., Can.	C5	106
Frances Lake, l., Yk., Can.	C4	106
Francés Viejo, Cabo, c., Dom. Rep.	C13	102
Franceville, Gabon	E2	66
Franche-Comté, hist. reg., Fr.	B12	18
Francis, Sk., Can.	D10	124
Francis Case, Lake, res., S.D., U.S.	D13	126
Francisco Beltrão, Braz.	B11	92
Francisco I. Madero, Mex.	C6	100
Francisco I. Madero, Mex.	I4	130
Francisco Murguía, Mex.	C7	100
Francisco Sá, Braz.	I4	88
Francistown, Bots.	B8	70
Francofonte, Italy	G8	24
François Lake, B.C., Can.	B5	138
François Lake, l., B.C., Can.	C5	138
Francs Peak, mtn., Wy., U.S.	C3	126
Frankel City, Tx., U.S.	B5	130
Franken, hist. reg., Ger.	G6	16
Frankenberg, Ger.	F9	16
Frankenberg, Ger.	E4	16
Frankenmuth, Mi., U.S.	E6	112
Frankford, On., Can.	D12	112
Frankford, Mo., U.S.	E6	120
Frankfort, S. Afr.	E9	70
Frankfort, In., U.S.	H3	112
Frankfort, Ks., U.S.	B12	128
Frankfort, Ky., U.S.	F13	120
Frankfort, N.Y., U.S.	A10	114
Frankfort, Oh., U.S.	E2	114
Frankfort, S.D., U.S.	C14	126
Frankfurt, Ger.	D10	16
Frankfurt am Main, Ger.	F4	16
Franklin, Az., U.S.	K7	132
Franklin, Ga., U.S.	D13	122
Franklin, Id., U.S.	A5	132
Franklin, Il., U.S.	E7	120
Franklin, In., U.S.	E11	120
Franklin, Ma., U.S.	B14	114
Franklin, Ne., U.S.	A9	128
Franklin, N.H., U.S.	G5	110
Franklin, N.J., U.S.	C11	114
Franklin, N.C., U.S.	A2	116
Franklin, Oh., U.S.	E1	114
Franklin, Pa., U.S.	C6	114
Franklin, Tn., U.S.	I11	120
Franklin, Tx., U.S.	F2	122
Franklin, Va., U.S.	H9	114
Franklin, Wi., U.S.	F2	112
Franklin Bay, b., N.T., Can.	B5	106
Franklin D. Roosevelt Lake, res., Wa., U.S.	B4	108
Franklin Gordon Wild Rivers National Park, p.o.i., Austl.	o12	77a
Franklin Grove, Il., U.S.	C8	120
Franklin Lake, l., N.T., Can.	B12	106
Franklin Mountains, mts., N.T., Can.	B5	106
Franklin Strait, strt., N.T., Can.	A11	106
Franklinton, La., U.S.	G8	122
Franklinville, N.Y., U.S.	B7	114
Frankston, Tx., U.S.	E3	122
Frankton, In., U.S.	H4	112
Fransfontein, Nmb.	B2	70
Franzensfeste see Fortezza, Italy	D8	22
Franz Josef Land see Franca-Iosifa, Zemlja, is., Russia	B9	30
Frascati, Italy	I9	22
Fraser, B.C., Can.	G13	138
Fraser, Co., U.S.	B3	128
Fraser, stm., B.C., Can.	G9	138
Fraser, Mount, mtn., Austl.	E3	74
Fraserburgh, Scot., U.K.	D11	12
Fraser Island, i., Austl.	E9	76
Fraser Lake, B.C., Can.	B6	138
Fraser Lake, l., B.C., Can.	B6	138
Fraser Plateau, plat., B.C., Can.	E8	138
Fraser Range, Austl.	F4	74
Frauenfeld, Switz.	C5	22
Fray Bentos, Ur.	F8	92
Fray Jorge, Parque Nacional, p.o.i., Chile	E2	92
Fray Marcos, Ur.	G10	92
Frazer, Mt., U.S.	F7	124
Frederic, Wi., U.S.	F6	118
Frederica, De., U.S.	E10	114
Fredericia, Den.	I3	8
Frederick, Md., U.S.	E8	114
Frederick, S.D., U.S.	B14	126
Frederick Hills, hills, Austl.	B7	74
Frederick Reef, rf., Austl.	C10	76
Fredericksburg, Ia., U.S.	B5	120
Fredericksburg, Tx., U.S.	D9	130
Fredericksburg, Va., U.S.	F8	114
Fredericktown, Oh., U.S.	D3	114
Frederico Westphalen, Braz.	C11	92
Fredericton, N.B., Can.	E10	110
Fredericton Junction, N.B., Can.	E10	110
Frederiksborg, state, Den.	H5	8
Frederiksdal, Grnld.	E17	141
Frederikshåb (Paamiut), Grnld.	E15	141
Frederikshavn, Den.	H4	8
Frederiksted, V.I.U.S.	h10	104c
Fredonia, Ks., U.S.	G2	120
Fredonia, N.Y., U.S.	B6	114
Fredonia, N.D., U.S.	A13	126
Fredrika, Swe.	D8	8
Fredrikstad, Nor.	G4	8
Freeburg, Il., U.S.	F8	120
Freeland, Mi., U.S.	E5	112
Freeland, Pa., U.S.	C9	114
Freel Peak, mtn., Ca., U.S.	E5	134
Freels, Cape, c., Nf., Can.	j23	107a
Freeman, S.D., U.S.	D15	126
Freeport, Bah.	B9	96
Freeport, N.S., Can.	F10	110
Freeport, Fl., U.S.	G12	122
Freeport, Il., U.S.	B8	120
Freeport, N.Y., U.S.	H16	112
Freeport, Pa., U.S.	D6	114
Freeport, Tx., U.S.	F12	130
Free State, state, S. Afr.	F8	70
Freetown, Antig.	f4	105b
Freetown, S.L.	H2	64
Fregenal de la Sierra, Spain	F4	20
Freiberg, Ger.	F9	16
Freiburg see Fribourg, Switz.	D4	22
Freiburg im Breisgau, Ger.	I3	16
Freirina, Chile	D2	92
Freising, Ger.	H7	16
Freistadt, Aus.	B11	22
Freital, Ger.	F9	16
Fréjus, Fr.	F12	18
Fremantle, Austl.	F3	74
Fremont, Ca., U.S.	F4	134
Fremont, In., U.S.	C1	114
Fremont, Ia., U.S.	C5	120
Fremont, Mi., U.S.	E4	112
Fremont, Ne., U.S.	C1	120
Fremont, Oh., U.S.	C2	114
Fremont, Wi., U.S.	G10	118
Fremont, stm., Ut., U.S.	E6	132
French, stm., On., Can.	B9	112
French Broad, stm., U.S.	I3	114
Frenchcap Cay, i., V.I.U.S.	f7	104b
French Guiana, dep., S.A.	C7	84
French Island, i., Austl.	L5	76
French Lick, In., U.S.	F11	120
Frenchman (Frenchman Creek), stm., N.A.	E5	124
Frenchman Creek (Frenchman), stm., N.A.	E5	124
Frenchman Creek, stm., U.S.	G11	126
Frenchmans Cap, mtn., Austl.	o12	77a
French Polynesia, dep., Oc.	K24	142
French Somaliland see Djibouti, ctry., Afr.	E8	62
Fresco, C. Iv.	H3	64
Fresco, stm., Braz.	E7	84
Fresnillo, Mex.	D7	100
Fresno, Ca., U.S.	G6	134
Fresno, stm., Ca., U.S.	F6	134
Fresno Reservoir, res., Mt., U.S.	B16	136
Freu, Cap des, c., Spain	E14	20
Freudenstadt, Ger.	H4	16
Frewena, Austl.	C7	74
Frewsburg, N.Y., U.S.	B6	114
Freycinet National Park, p.o.i., Austl.	o14	77a
Freycinet Peninsula, pen., Austl.	o14	77a
Freyre, Arg.	E6	92
Fria, Gui.	G2	64
Fria, Cape, c., Nmb.	D1	68
Friant, Ca., U.S.	G6	134
Friars Point, Ms., U.S.	C8	122
Frías, Arg.	D5	92
Fribourg (Freiburg), Switz.	D4	22
Fridley, Mn., U.S.	F5	118
Fridtjof Nansen, Mount, mtn., Ant.	D25	81
Friedberg, Aus.	C12	22
Friedberg, Ger.	F4	16
Friedberg, Ger.	H7	16
Friedland, Ger.	C9	16
Friedrichshafen, Ger.	I5	16
Friend, Ne., U.S.	G15	126
Friendship, N.Y., U.S.	B7	114
Friendship, Tn., U.S.	I8	120
Fries, Va., U.S.	H4	114
Friesach, Aus.	D11	22
Frio, stm., Tx., U.S.	F9	130
Frio, Cabo, c., Braz.	L5	88
Frio Draw, stm., U.S.	G6	128
Friona, Tx., U.S.	G6	128
Frisco, Tx., U.S.	D2	122
Frisian Islands, is., Eur.	A14	14
Fritch, Tx., U.S.	F7	128
Fritzlar, Ger.	E5	16
Friuli, hist. reg., Italy	E9	22
Friuli-Venezia Giulia, state, Italy	D9	22
Frjazino, Russia	E21	10
Frobisher, Sk., Can.	E11	124
Frobisher Bay, b., N.T., Can.	C17	106
Frobisher Lake, l., Sk., Can.	D9	106
Froid, Mt., U.S.	F9	124
Frolovo, Russia	E6	32
Frome, Eng., U.K.	J10	12
Frome, stm., Austl.	G2	76
Frome, Lake, l., Austl.	H2	76
Fronteiras, Braz.	D5	88
Frontenac, Ks., U.S.	G3	120
Frontera, Mex.	F12	100
Frontera, Mex.	B8	100
Frontier, Sk., Can.	E5	124
Frontier, Wy., U.S.	B6	132
Frontino, Col.	B2	84
Frontino, Páramo, mtn., Col.	D3	86
Front Range, mts., Co., U.S.	H7	126
Front Royal, Va., U.S.	F7	114
Frosinone, Italy	C7	24
Frostburg, Md., U.S.	E6	114
Frostproof, Fl., U.S.	I4	116
Frøya, i., Nor.	E3	8
Fruges, Fr.	D11	14
Fruita, Co., U.S.	D8	132
Fruitdale, Or., U.S.	H3	136
Fruithurst, Al., U.S.	D13	122
Fruitland, Id., U.S.	F10	136
Fruitport, Mi., U.S.	E3	112
Fruitvale, B.C., Can.	G13	138
Fruitvale, Wa., U.S.	D6	136
Frunzivka, Ukr.	B16	26
Frutal, Braz.	J1	88
Frutigen, Switz.	D4	22
Frýdek-Místek, Czech Rep.	G14	16
Fryeburg, Me., U.S.	G6	110
Fu, stm., China	G7	42
Fu, stm., China	F2	42
Fu, stm., China	G6	42
Fua'amotu International Airport, Tonga	n14	78e
Fu'an, China	H8	42
Fuchou see Fuzhou, China	H8	42
Fuchow see Fuzhou, China	G7	42
Fuchū, Japan	E6	40
Fuchun, stm., China	G8	42
Fuding, China	H9	42
Fuego, Volcán de, vol., Guat.	E2	102
Fuencaliente, Spain	F6	20
Fuengirola, Spain	H6	20
Fuensalida, Spain	D6	20
Fuente, Mex.	F7	130
Fuente de Cantos, Spain	F4	20
Fuente de Oro, Col.	F5	86
Fuentes de Ebro, Spain	C10	20
Fuerte, stm., Mex.	B4	100
Fuerte Olimpo, Para.	D5	90
Fuga Island, i., Phil.	A3	52
Fugou, China	D6	42
Fuhai, China	B2	36
Fuhsien see Wafangdian, China	B9	42
Fuji, Japan	D11	40
Fuji, Mount see Fuji-san, vol., Japan	D11	40
Fujian, state, China	I7	42
Fujieda, Japan	E11	40
Fujin, China	B11	36
Fujinomiya, Japan	D11	40
Fuji-san (Fuji, Mount), vol., Japan	D11	40
Fujisawa, Japan	D12	40
Fujiyama see Fuji-san, vol., Japan	D11	40
Fuji-yoshida, Japan	D11	40
Fukagawa, Japan	C14	38
Fukang, China	C2	36
Fukave, i., Tonga	n14	78e
Fukaya, Japan	C12	40
Fukien see Fujian, state, China	I7	42
Fukuchiyama, Japan	D8	40
Fukue, Japan	G1	40
Fukue-jima, i., Japan	G1	40
Fukui, Japan	C9	40
Fukui, state, Japan	D9	40
Fukuoka, Japan	F3	40
Fukuoka, state, Japan	F3	40
Fukuroi, Japan	E10	40
Fukushima, Japan	B13	40
Fukushima, state, Japan	B12	40
Fukuyama, Japan	E6	40
Fūlādī, Kūh-e, mtn., Afg.	C10	56
Fulaga Passage, strt., Fiji	q20	79e
Fulda, Ger.	F5	16
Fulda, Mn., U.S.	H3	118
Fulda, stm., Ger.	E5	16
Fuling, China	G2	42
Fullarton, stm., Austl.	C3	76
Fullerton, Ca., U.S.	J8	134
Fullerton Point, c., Antig.	f4	105b
Fulong, China	J2	42
Fulton, Al., U.S.	F11	122
Fulton, Ar., U.S.	D5	122
Fulton, Il., U.S.	C7	120
Fulton, Ks., U.S.	F3	120
Fulton, Ky., U.S.	H9	120
Fulton, Mo., U.S.	F5	120
Fulton, N.Y., U.S.	E13	112
Fulton, Tx., U.S.	F10	130
Fumay, Fr.	D13	14
Funabashi, Japan	D12	40
Funafuti, i., Tuvalu	D8	72
Funan, China	E6	42
Funchal, Port.	C1	64
Fundación, Col.	B4	86
Fundão, Port.	D3	20
Fundy, Bay of, b., Can.	F10	110
Fundy National Park, p.o.i., N.B., Can.	E11	110
Funhalouro, Moz.	C12	70
Funing, China	E8	42
Funiu Shan, mts., China	E5	42
Funsi, Ghana	G4	64
Funtua, Nig.	G6	64
Fuping, China	D3	42
Fuqing, China	I8	42
Fuquay-Varina, N.C., U.S.	A7	116
Furculești, Rom.	F12	26
Furmanov, Russia	H19	8
Furnas, Represa de, res., Braz.	K2	88
Furneaux Group, is., Austl.	m13	77a
Furnes see Veurne, Bel.	C11	14
Fürstenberg / Havel, Ger.	C9	16
Fürstenfeld, Aus.	C12	22
Fürstenfeldbruck, Ger.	H7	16
Fürstenwalde, Ger.	D9	16
Fürth, Ger.	G6	16
Furth im Wald, Ger.	G8	16
Furukawa, Japan	C10	40
Furukawa, Japan	A13	40
Fury and Hecla Strait, strt., N.T., Can.	B14	106
Fusagasugá, Col.	E4	86
Fusan see Pusan, Kor., S.	D2	40
Fushan, China	C9	42
Fushan, China	D4	42
Fushih see Yan'an, China	C3	42
Fushun, China	D5	38
Fushun, China	G1	42
Fusilier, Sk., Can.	C4	124
Fusong, China	C7	38
Füssen, Ger.	I6	16
Fuste, Picacho del, mtn., Mex.	G5	130
Fusui, China	J2	42
Futun, stm., China	H7	42
Futuna, Île, i., Wal./F.	E9	72
Futuyu, China	B6	42
Fuwa, Egypt	G1	58
Fuxian Hu, l., China	G5	36
Fuxin, China	C4	38
Fuyang, China	E6	42
Fuyang, stm., China	C6	42
Fuyu, China	B9	36
Fuyu, China	B6	38
Fuyuan see Tongjiang, China	B11	36
Fuyuan, China	F5	36
Fuyuan, China	B11	36
Fuzhou, China	G7	42
Fuzhou, China	H8	42
Fyn, state, Den.	I4	8
Fyn, i., Den.	I4	8
Fyne, Loch, b., Scot., U.K.	E7	12
Fyresvatnet, l., Nor.	G2	8

G

Name	Map Ref.	Page
Gaalkacyo, Som.	C9	66
Gabare, Blg.	F10	26
Gabarus, N.S., Can.	E16	110
Gabela, Ang.	C1	68
Gaberones see Gaborone, Bots.	D7	70
Gabès, Tun.	C7	64
Gabiarra, Braz.	I6	88
Gabon, ctry., Afr.	E2	66
Gaborone, Bots.	D7	70
Gabras, Sudan	E5	62
Gabriel Strait, strt., N.T., Can.	C17	106
Gabriel y Galán, Embalse de, res., Spain	D4	20
Gabrovo, Blg.	G12	26
Gacé, Fr.	F9	14
Gackle, N.D., U.S.	A13	126
Gadag, India	D2	53
Gādarwāra, India	G7	54
Gäddede, Swe.	D6	8
Gado Bravo, Ilha do, i., Braz.	F4	88
Gádor, Spain	H8	20
Gadsden, Al., U.S.	C12	122
Gadsden, Az., U.S.	K2	132
Gadwāl, India	C3	53
Gael Hamke Bugt, b., Grnld.	C22	141
Găești, Rom.	E12	26
Gaeta, Italy	C7	24
Gaeta, Golfo di, b., Italy	C7	24
Gaferut, i., Micron.	C5	72
Gaffney, S.C., U.S.	A4	116
Gafour, Tun.	H3	24
Gafsa, Tun.	C6	64
Gag, Pulau, i., Indon.	F8	44
Gagarin, Russia	E17	10
Gage, Ok., U.S.	E9	128
Gaggenau, Ger.	H4	16
Gagliano del Capo, Italy	E12	24
Gagnoa, C. Iv.	H3	64
Gagra, Geor.	F5	32
Gaibandha, Bngl.	F12	54
Gail, Tx., U.S.	B6	130
Gaillac, Fr.	F7	18
Gaillimh see Galway, Ire.	H3	12
Gaimán, Arg.	H3	90
Gainesboro, Tn., U.S.	H12	120
Gainesville, Fl., U.S.	G3	116
Gainesville, Ga., U.S.	B2	116
Gainesville, Mo., U.S.	H5	120
Gainesville, Tx., U.S.	H11	128
Gainsborough, Eng., U.K.	H12	12
Gainsborough Creek, stm., Can.	E12	124
Gairdner, Lake, l., Austl.	F7	74
Gaithersburg, Md., U.S.	E8	114
Gaixian, China	A10	42
Gaizina Kalns, hill, Lat.	D8	10
Gajendragarh, India	D2	53
Gajny, Russia	B8	32
Gajuapara, stm., Braz.	C2	88
Gajutino, Russia	B21	10
Gakarosa, mtn., S. Afr.	E6	70
Gakona, Ak., U.S.	D10	140
Galahad, Ab., Can.	D19	138
Galâla el Baharîya, Gebel el-, mts., Egypt	I3	58
Galâla el-Qiblîya, Gebel el-, mts., Egypt	J3	58
Galán, Cerro, mtn., Arg.	C4	92
Galana, stm., Kenya	E7	66
Galanta, Slov.	H13	16
Galapagos Islands see Colón, Archipiélago de, is., Ec.	h12	84a
Galashiels, Scot., U.K.	F9	12
Galați, Rom.	D14	26
Galați, state, Rom.	D14	26
Galatia, Il., U.S.	G9	120
Galatina, Italy	D12	24
Galaxídi, Grc.	E5	28
Galdhøpiggen, mtn., Nor.	F2	8
Galeana, Mex.	F9	98
Galeana, Mex.	C8	100
Galela, Indon.	E8	44
Galena, Ak., U.S.	D8	140
Galena, Il., U.S.	B7	120
Galena, Mo., U.S.	H4	120
Galena Park, Tx., U.S.	E12	130
Galeota Point, c., Trin.	s13	105f
Galera, Punta, c., Chile	G2	90
Galera, Punta, c., Ec.	G1	86
Galera Point, c., Trin.	s13	105f
Galeras, Volcán, vol., Col.	G3	86
Galesburg, Il., U.S.	D7	120
Galesville, Wi., U.S.	G7	118
Galeton, Pa., U.S.	C8	114
Galiano Island, i., B.C., Can.	H7	138
Galič, Russia	G20	8
Galicia, state, Spain	B3	20
Galicia, hist. reg., Eur.	G18	16
Galičica Nacionalni Park, p.o.i., Mac.	C3	28
Galičskaja vozvyšennost', hills, Russia	G20	8
Galičskoe, ozero, l., Russia	G20	8
Galilee, Lake, l., Austl.	D5	76
Galilee, Sea of see Kinneret, Yam, l., Isr.	F6	58
Galiléia, Braz.	J5	88
Galina Point, c., Jam.	i14	104d
Galion, Oh., U.S.	D3	114
Galite, Canal de la, strt., Tun.	G3	24
Gallarate, Italy	E5	22
Gallatin, Tn., U.S.	H11	120
Gallatin, stm., U.S.	E15	136
Galle, Sri L.	H5	53
Gállego, stm., Spain	B10	20
Gallegos, stm., Arg.	J3	90
Galliano, La., U.S.	H8	122
Gallinas, stm., N.M., U.S.	F4	128
Gallinas, Punta, c., Col.	A6	86
Gallipoli, Italy	D11	24
Gallipoli see Gelibolu, Tur.	C9	28
Gallipoli Peninsula see Gelibolu Yarımadası, pen., Tur.	C9	28
Gallipolis, Oh., U.S.	F3	114
Gällivare, Swe.	C9	8
Gallo, Capo, c., Italy	F7	24
Gallo Arroyo, stm., N.M., U.S.	G3	128
Galloo Island, i., N.Y., U.S.	E13	112
Galloway, hist. reg., Scot., U.K.	G8	12
Galloway, Mull of, c., Scot., U.K.	G8	12
Gallup, N.M., U.S.	H8	132
Gallura, reg., Italy	C3	24
Galoa Harbour, b., Fiji	q19	79e
Galt, Ca., U.S.	E4	134
Galtat Zemmour, W. Sah.	D2	64
Galty Mountains, mts., Ire.	I4	12
Galva, Il., U.S.	C7	120
Galva, Ks., U.S.	C11	128
Galveston, In., U.S.	H3	112
Galveston, Tx., U.S.	H4	122
Galveston Bay, b., Tx., U.S.	H4	122
Galveston Island, i., Tx., U.S.	E13	130
Gálvez, Arg.	F7	92
Galway (Gaillimh), Ire.	H3	12
Galway, state, Ire.	H4	12
Galway Bay, b., Ire.	H3	12
Gam (Jin), stm., Asia	A7	48
Gama, Isla, i., Arg.	H4	90
Gamagōri, Japan	E10	40
Gamarra, Col.	C5	86
Gamay, Phil.	D5	52
Gamba, China	D12	54
Gambaga, Ghana	G4	64
Gambēla, Eth.	F6	62
Gambell, Ak., U.S.	D5	140
Gambia (Gambie), stm., Afr.	G1	64
Gambia, The, ctry., Afr.	G1	64
Gambie (Gambia), stm., Afr.	G2	64
Gambier, Îles, is., Fr. Poly.	F13	72
Gamboa, Pan.	C2	86
Gamboma, Congo	E3	66
Gamboula, C.A.R.	D2	66
Gamka, stm., S. Afr.	H5	70
Gamlakarleby see Kokkola, Fin.	E10	8
Gamleby, Swe.	H7	8
Gammon Ranges National Park, p.o.i., Austl.	H2	76
Ga-Mogara, stm., S. Afr.	E6	70
Gan, stm., China	B10	36
Gan, stm., China	G6	42
Ganado, Az., U.S.	H7	132
Ganado, Tx., U.S.	E11	130
Gananoque, On., Can.	D13	112
Gäncä, Azer.	A6	56
Gand see Gent, Bel.	C12	14
Ganda, Ang.	C1	68
Gandadiwata, Bulu, mtn., Indon.	E11	50
Gandajika, D.R.C.	F4	66
Gandak (Nārāyani), stm., Asia	E10	54
Gándara, Spain	A2	20
Gander, Nf., Can.	j23	107a
Ganderkesee, Ger.	C4	16
Gandesa, Spain	C11	20
Gandevi, India	H4	54
Gāndhinagar, India	G4	54
Gandhi Reservoir see Gāndhi Sāgar, res., India	F5	54
Gāndhi Sāgar, res., India	F5	54
Gandia, Spain	F10	20
Gandu, Braz.	G6	88
Ganga see Ganges, stm., Asia	F11	54
Gan Gan, Arg.	H3	90
Gangānagar, India	D4	54
Gangāpur, India	B2	53
Gangāpur, India	F5	54
Gangāpur, India	E6	54
Gangārāmpur, India	F12	54
Gangaw, Mya.	A2	48
Gangāwati, India	D3	53
Gangdhār, India	G5	54
Gangdisê Shan, mts., China	C9	54
Ganges, B.C., Can.	H7	138
Ganges (Ganga) (Padma), stm., Asia	G13	54
Ganges, Mouths of the, mth., Asia	H12	54
Ganghu, China	B11	54
Gangmar Co, l., China	B10	54
Gangneung see Kangnŭng, Kor., S.	B1	40
Gangoa, China	D5	36
Gangotri, India	C7	54
Gangotri, India	C7	54
Gangoumen, China	D2	38
Gangtok, India	E12	54
Gangu, China	D1	42
Gangweon see Kangwŏn-do, state, Kor., S.	B1	40
Gannan, China	B9	36
Gannett Peak, mtn., Wy., U.S.	D3	126
Gannvalley, S.D., U.S.	C14	126
Ganquan, China	C3	42
Gansbaai, S. Afr.	I4	70
Gansu, state, China	D5	36
Gantang, China	H8	42
Gantt, Al., U.S.	F12	122
Gantung, Indon.	E6	50
Ganyanchi, China	C1	42
Ganyesa, S. Afr.	E7	70
Ganzê, China	E4	36
Ganzhou, China	I6	42
Gao, Mali	F4	64
Gao'an, China	G6	42
Gaochun, China	F8	42
Gaohebu, China	F7	42
Gaojian, China	F9	36
Gaolan, China	D5	36
Gaolong, China	H5	42
Gaona, Arg.	B5	92
Gaoping, China	D5	42
Gaotan, China	E3	42
Gaotang, China	C7	42
Gaoua, Burkina	G4	64
Gaoual, Gui.	G2	64
Gaoxian, China	F5	36
Gaoyi, China	C6	42
Gaoyou, China	E8	42
Gaoyou Hu, l., China	E8	42
Gaozhou, China	K4	42
Gap, Fr.	E12	18
Gar, China	B8	54
Gar, stm., China	C8	54
Gara, Lough, l., Ire.	H4	12
Garagumskij kanal (Kara-Kum Canal), can., Turkmen.	B9	56
Garagumy (Kara-Kum), des., Turkmen.	A8	56
Garaina, Pap. N. Gui.	b4	79a
Garanhuns, Braz.	E7	88
Garapan, N. Mar. Is.	B5	72
Garara, Pap. N. Gui.	b4	79a
Garber, Ok., U.S.	E11	128
Garberville, Ca., U.S.	C2	134
Gârbovu, Rom.	E10	26
Garça, Braz.	L1	88
García, Mex.	G8	98
García de Sola, Embalse de, res., Spain	E5	20
Gard, state, Fr.	F10	18
Garda, Italy	E7	22
Garda, Lago di, l., Italy	E7	22
Gardelegen, Ger.	D7	16
Garden City, Ks., U.S.	C8	128
Garden City, Mo., U.S.	F3	120
Garden City, Tx., U.S.	C6	130
Gardendale, Al., U.S.	D12	122
Garden Grove, Ca., U.S.	J7	134
Garden Grove, Ia., U.S.	D4	120
Garden Island, i., Mi., U.S.	C4	112
Garden Peninsula, pen., Mi., U.S.	C3	112
Garden Reach, India	G11	54
Gardenton, Mb., Can.	E17	124
Gardey, Arg.	H8	92
Gardeyz, Afg.	C10	56
Gardiner, Mt., U.S.	E16	136
Gardiner, Or., U.S.	G2	136
Gardiner Dam, dam, Sk., Can.	C6	124
Gardner, Ks., U.S.	F2	120
Gardner, Ma., U.S.	B13	114
Gardner Canal, b., B.C., Can.	C2	138
Gardnerville, Nv., U.S.	E6	134
Garessio, Italy	F5	22
Garet, Mont, vol., Vanuatu	j16	79d
Garfield, Ks., U.S.	C9	128
Garfield, N.M., U.S.	K9	132
Garfield Mountain, mtn., Mt., U.S.	F14	136
Gargano, Promontorio del, mts., Italy	I12	22
Gargano, Testa del, c., Italy	I13	22
Gargždai, Lith.	E4	10
Garhākota, India	G7	54
Garibaldi, Braz.	D12	92
Garibaldi, B.C., Can.	G7	138
Garibaldi, Or., U.S.	E2	136
Garibaldi, Mount, vol., B.C., Can.	G8	138
Gariep Dam, res., S. Afr.	G7	70
Garies, S. Afr.	G4	70
Garigliano, stm., Italy	C7	24
Gariglione, Monte, mtn., Italy	E10	24
Garissa, Kenya	E7	66
Garland, Tx., U.S.	E2	122
Garland, Ut., U.S.	B4	132
Garlasco, Italy	E5	22
Garlin, Fr.	F5	18
Garm, Taj.	B11	56
Garmisch-Partenkirchen, Ger.	I7	16
Garnavillo, Ia., U.S.	B6	120
Garner, Ia., U.S.	A4	120
Garner, N.C., U.S.	I7	114
Garnpung Lake, l., Austl.	I4	76
Garona (Garonne), stm., Eur.	E5	18
Garonne (Garona), stm., Eur.	E5	18
Garoowe, Som.	C9	66
Garoua, Cam.	C2	66
Garoua Boulaï, Cam.	C2	66
Garqu Yan, China	B14	54
Garqu Yan, China	A14	54
Garrel, Ger.	D3	16
Garretson, S.D., U.S.	H2	118
Garrett, In., U.S.	G4	112
Garrett, Ky., U.S.	G3	114
Garrison, N.D., U.S.	G12	124
Garrison, Tx., U.S.	F4	122
Garrison Dam, dam, N.D., U.S.	G12	124
Garry Bay, b., N.T., Can.	B13	106
Garry Lake, l., N.T., Can.	B10	106
Garsen, Kenya	E7	66
Garson, On., Can.	B9	112
Garut, Indon.	G5	50
Garwolin, Pol.	E17	16
Garwood, Tx., U.S.	H2	122
Gary, In., U.S.	G2	112
Gary, Tx., U.S.	E4	122
Gary, W.V., U.S.	G4	114
Garyarsa, China	C8	54
Garza, Arg.	D6	92
Garza Ayala, Mex.	H7	130
Garzón, Col.	F4	86
Garzón, Ur.	G10	92
Gasan-Kuli, Turkmen.	B7	56
Gas City, In., U.S.	H4	112
Gascogne (Gascony), hist. reg., Fr.	F6	18
Gasconade, stm., Mo., U.S.	F6	120
Gasconade, Osage Fork, stm., Mo., U.S.	G5	120
Gascony see Gascogne, hist. reg., Fr.	F6	18
Gascoyne, stm., Austl.	D2	74
Gashaka, Nig.	H7	64
Gashua, Nig.	G7	64
Gaspar, Braz.	C13	92

Name	Map Ref.	Page

I•22 Gota-Guay

Name — Map Ref. — Page

Göta, stm., Swe. G5 8
Gotebo, Ok., U.S. F10 128
Göteborg (Gothenburg), Swe. H4 8
Gotemba, Japan D11 40
Gotești, Mol. C15 26
Gotha, Ger. F6 16
Gothenburg see Göteborg, Swe. H4 8
Gothenburg, Ne., U.S. G12 126
Gothèye, Niger G5 64
Gotland, state, Swe. G8 8
Gotland, i., Swe. H8 8
Gotō-rettō, is., Japan F1 40
Gotska Sandön, i., Swe. G8 8
Gōtsu, Japan D5 40
Göttingen, Ger. E5 16
Goubangzi, China D4 38
Gouda, Neth. B13 14
Goudge, Arg. G3 92
Goudiri, Sen. G2 64
Gough Island, i., St. Hel. K5 60
Gough Lake, l., Ab., Can. D18 138
Gouin, Réservoir, res., Qc., Can. B1 110
Goulais, stm., On., Can. B6 112
Goulburn, Austl. J7 76
Goulburn Islands, is., Austl. B6 74
Goulburn River National Park, p.o.i., Austl. I7 76
Gould, Ar., U.S. D7 122
Goulds, Fl., U.S. K5 116
Goumbou, Mali G3 64
Goundam, Mali F4 64
Goundi, Chad F3 62
Gourbeyre, Guad. h5 105c
Gourdon, Fr. E7 18
Gouré, Niger G7 64
Gourma-Rharous, Mali F4 64
Gournay-en-Bray, Fr. E10 14
Gouro, Chad D3 62
Gouverneur, N.Y., U.S. D14 112
Govan, Sk., Can. C9 124
Gove, Ks., U.S. C8 128
Govena, mys, c., Russia E22 34
Govenlock, Sk., Can. E4 124
Governador Valadares, Braz. J5 88
Govind Ballabh Pant Reservoir see Govind Ballabh Pant Sāgar, res., India F9 54
Govind Ballabh Pant Sāgar, res., India F9 54
Govind Reservoir see Govind Sāgar, res., India C6 54
Govind Sāgar, res., India C6 54
Gowanda, N.Y., U.S. B7 114
Gower, Mo., U.S. E3 120
Gowmal (Gumal), stm., Asia B2 54
Gowmal Kalay, Afg. B2 54
Gowrie, Ia., U.S. B3 120
Goya, Arg. D8 92
Goyaves, Îlets à, is., Guad. h5 105c
Göyçay, Azer. A6 56
Goz Beïda, Chad E4 62
Gozdnica, Pol. E11 16
Gozha Co, l., China A5 46
Gozo see Għawdex, i., Malta H8 24
Graaff-Reinet, S. Afr. H7 70
Grabo, C. Iv. I3 64
Grabow, Ger. C7 16
Grabów nad Prosną, Pol. E13 16
Gračac, Cro. F12 22
Gračanica, Bos. E5 26
Grace, Id., U.S. H15 136
Gracefield, Qc., Can. B13 112
Graceville, Fl., U.S. G13 122
Gracias a Dios, Cabo, c., N.A. E6 102
Gradaús, Braz. E7 84
Grado, Italy E10 22
Grado, Spain A4 20
Grad Sofija, state, Blg. G10 26
Grady, Ar., U.S. C7 122
Grady, N.M., U.S. G5 128
Graettinger, Ia., U.S. H4 118
Grafenau, Ger. H9 16
Gräfenhainichen, Ger. E8 16
Grafing bei München, Ger. H7 16
Grafton, Austl. G9 76
Grafton, Il., U.S. F7 120
Grafton, N.D., U.S. F16 124
Grafton, W.V., U.S. E5 114
Grafton, Wi., U.S. E2 112
Grafton, Cape, c., Austl. A5 76
Graham, N.C., U.S. H6 114
Graham, Mount, mtn., Az., U.S. K7 132
Graham Island, i., B.C., Can. E4 106
Graham Island, i., N.T., Can. B7 141
Graham Lake, res., Me., U.S. F8 110
Graham Land, reg., Ant. B34 81
Graham Moore, Cape, c., N.T., Can. A15 106
Grahamstad see Grahamstown, S. Afr. H8 70
Grahamstown, S. Afr. H8 70
Grain Coast, cst., Lib. I3 64
Grainfield, Ks., U.S. B8 128
Grajaú, Braz. C2 88
Grajaú, stm., Braz. B3 88
Grajewo, Pol. C18 16
Gramada, Blg. F9 26
Grambling, La., U.S. E6 122
Gramilla, Arg. C5 92
Grammichele, Italy G8 24
Grampian Mountains, mts., Scot., U.K. E9 12
Grampians National Park, p.o.i., Austl. K3 76
Gramsh, Alb. D14 24
Granada, Col. F5 86
Granada, Nic. G5 102
Granada, Spain G7 20
Granada, Co., U.S. C6 128
Granada, co., Spain G7 20
Granadella see La Granadella, Spain C11 20
Granbury, Tx., U.S. B10 130
Granbury, Lake, res., Tx., U.S. B10 130
Granby, Qc., Can. E4 110
Granby, Co., U.S. A3 128
Granby, Mo., U.S. H3 120
Granby, stm., B.C., Can. G12 138
Granby, Lake, res., Co., U.S. A2 128
Gran Chaco, reg., S.A. D5 90
Grand, stm., On., Can. E9 112
Grand, stm., U.S. E4 120
Grand, stm., Mi., U.S. E3 112
Grand, stm., Oh., U.S. C4 114
Grand, stm., S.D., U.S. B12 126
Grand, East Fork, stm., U.S. D3 120
Grand, Lac, l., Qc., Can. A12 112
Grand, North Fork, stm., U.S. B10 126
Grand, South Fork, stm., S.D., U.S. B9 126
Grandas, Spain A4 20
Grand Bahama, i., Bah. B9 96
Grand Ballon, mtn., Fr. G16 14
Grand Bank, Nf., Can. j22 107a
Grand-Bassam, C. Iv. H4 64
Grand Bay, Al., U.S. G10 122
Grand Beach, Mb., Can. D17 124
Grand Bend, On., Can. E8 112
Grand-Bourg, Guad. i6 105c
Grand Caille Point, c., St. Luc. m6 105c
Grand Calumet, Île du, i., Qc., Can. C13 112
Grand Canal see Da Yunhe, can., China E8 42
Grand Canal, can., Ire. H6 12
Grand Cane, La., U.S. E5 122
Grand Canyon, Az., U.S. G4 132
Grand Canyon, val., Az., U.S. G4 132
Grand Canyon National Park, p.o.i., Az., U.S. G4 132
Grand Case, Guad. A1 105a
Grand Cayman, i., Cay. Is. C7 102
Grand Cess, Lib. I3 64
Grand Chenier, La., U.S. H6 122
Grand Coulee Dam, dam, Wa., U.S. C8 136
Grand Cul de Sac, Guad. B2 105a
Grande, stm., Arg. H3 92
Grande, stm., Arg. A5 92
Grande, stm., Bol. C4 90
Grande, stm., Braz. F4 88
Grande, stm., Braz. C7 90
Grande, stm., S.A. J3 90
Grande, stm., Ven. C11 86
Grande, Arroyo, stm., Ur. F9 92
Grande, Bahía, b., Arg. J3 90
Grande, Boca, mth., Ven. C11 86
Grande, Cerro, mtn., Mex. E7 100
Grande, Cerro, mtn., Mex. G2 130
Grande, Ilha, i., Braz. L3 88
Grande, Ilha, i., Braz. A11 92
Grande, Ponta, c., Braz. I6 88
Grande, Rio see Rio Grande, stm., N.A. H13 98
Grande, Serra, mts., Braz. D5 88
Grande-Anse, Qc., Can. C4 110
Grande Cache, Ab., Can. C11 138
Grande Cayemite, i., Haiti C11 102
Grande de Manacapuru, Lago, l., Braz. I11 86
Grande de Matagalpa, stm., Nic. F6 102
Grande de Santiago, stm., Mex. E6 100
Grande do Gurupá, Ilha, i., Braz. D7 84
Grande-Entrée, Qc., Can. C15 110
Grande Prairie, Ab., Can. A12 138
Grand Erg de Bilma, des., Niger F7 64
Grand Erg Occidental, des., Alg. C5 64
Grand Erg Oriental, des., Alg. C6 64
Grande-Rivière, Qc., Can. B12 110
Grande Rivière, La, stm., Qc., Can. E15 106
Grande Ronde, stm., U.S. E9 136
Grandes, Salinas, pl., Arg. A4 92
Grandes, Salinas, pl., Arg. D5 92
Grand-Étang, N.S., Can. D15 110
Grande-Terre, i., Guad. h6 105c
Grande Vigie, Pointe de la, c., Guad. g6 105c
Grand Falls, N.B., Can. C9 110
Grandfather Mountain, mtn., N.C., U.S. H4 114
Grandfield, Ok., U.S. G10 128
Grand Forks, B.C., Can. G12 138
Grand Forks, N.D., U.S. D1 118
Grand Haven, Mi., U.S. E3 112
Grandin, Lac, l., N.T., Can. C7 106
Grand Island, Ne., U.S. G14 126
Grand Island, i., Mi., U.S. B3 112
Grand Isle, La., U.S. H9 122
Grand Junction, Co., U.S. D8 132
Grand Junction, Ia., U.S. B3 120
Grand Lake, Co., U.S. A3 128
Grand Lake, l., N.B., Can. D11 110
Grand Lake, l., N.A. E9 110
Grand Lake, l., La., U.S. H6 122
Grand Lake, l., Mi., U.S. C6 112
Grand Lake, res., Oh., U.S. D1 114
Grand Ledge, Mi., U.S. B1 114
Grand Manan, N.B., Can. F10 110
Grand Manan Island, i., N.B., Can. F10 110
Grand Marais, Mi., U.S. B4 112
Grand Meadow, Mn., U.S. H6 118
Grand-Mère, Qc., Can. D4 110
Grand Morin, stm., Fr. F12 14
Grand Portage, Mn., U.S. D9 118
Grand Portage National Monument, p.o.i., Mn., U.S. C9 118
Grand Prairie, Tx., U.S. B11 130
Grand Rapids, Mb., Can. A14 124
Grand Rapids, Mi., U.S. F4 112
Grand Rapids, Mn., U.S. D5 118
Grand Rhône, stm., Fr. F10 18
Grand Saline, Tx., U.S. E3 122
Grand Staircase–Escalante National Monument, p.o.i., Ut., U.S. F5 132
Grand Teton, mtn., Wy., U.S. G16 136
Grand Teton National Park, p.o.i., Wy., U.S. F16 136
Grand Tower, Il., U.S. G8 120
Grand Traverse Bay, b., Mi., U.S. C4 112
Grand Turk, T./C. Is. B12 102
Grandview, Mb., Can. C13 124
Grandview, Mo., U.S. F3 120
Grandview, Tx., U.S. B10 130
Grandview, Wa., U.S. D6 136
Grand View, Wi., U.S. E7 118
Grand Wash Cliffs, clf, Az., U.S. H3 132
Grañén, Spain C10 20
Graneros, Chile G2 92
Granger, Wa., U.S. D6 136
Granger, Wy., U.S. B6 132
Granger Draw, stm., Tx., U.S. D7 130
Granger Lake, res., Tx., U.S. D10 130
Granges see Grenchen, Switz. C4 22
Grangeville, Id., U.S. E10 136
Granite City, Il., U.S. F7 120
Granite Falls, Mn., U.S. G3 118
Granite Falls, N.C., U.S. I4 114
Granite Falls, Wa., U.S. B5 136
Granite Pass, p., Wy., U.S. C5 126
Granite Peak, Austl. E4 74
Granite Peak, mtn., Mt., U.S. E14 136
Granite Peak, mtn., Mt., U.S. E17 136
Granite Peak, mtn., Nv., U.S. C6 134
Graniteville, S.C., U.S. C4 116
Granitola, Capo, c., Italy G6 24
Granja, Braz. B5 88
Gran Laguna Salada, l., Arg. H3 90
Gränna, Swe. G6 8
Granollers, Spain C13 20
Gran Paradiso, mtn., Italy E4 22
Gran Paradiso, Parco Nazionale del, p.o.i., Italy E4 22
Gran Rio, stm., Sur. C6 84
Gran Sasso d'Italia, mts., Italy H10 22
Gransee, Ger. C9 16
Grant, Fl., U.S. I5 116
Grant, Mi., U.S. E4 112
Grant City, Mo., U.S. D3 120
Grantham, Eng., U.K. I12 12
Grantley Adams International Airport, Barb. n9 105d
Grant Park, Il., U.S. C10 120
Grant Point, c., N.T., Can. B11 106
Grants, N.M., U.S. H9 132
Grantsburg, Wi., U.S. F6 118
Grants Pass, Or., U.S. A2 134
Grant-Suttie Bay, b., N.T., Can. B15 106
Grantsville, W.V., U.S. F4 114
Grantville, Ga., U.S. D14 122
Granum, Ab., Can. G17 138
Granville, Fr. F7 14
Granville, Il., U.S. J9 118
Granville, N.D., U.S. F13 124
Granville, W.V., U.S. E5 114
Granville Lake, l., Mb., Can. D10 106
Granvin, Nor. F2 8
Grão Mogol, Braz. I4 88
Grapeland, Tx., U.S. F3 122
Grapevine Lake, res., Tx., U.S. B10 130
Grapevine Peak, mtn., Nv., U.S. G8 134
Gras, Lac de, l., N.T., Can. C8 106
Gräsö, i., Swe. F8 8
Grasonville, Md., U.S. F9 114
Grass, stm., N.Y., U.S. D15 112
Grass Creek, Wy., U.S. D4 126
Grasse, Fr. F12 18
Grassflat, Pa., U.S. D7 114
Grasslands National Park, p.o.i., Sk., Can. E6 124
Grass Valley, Ca., U.S. D4 134
Grass Valley, Or., U.S. E6 136
Grassy, Austl. n12 77a
Grassy Plains, B.C., Can. C4 138
Graulhet, Fr. F7 18
Gravelbourg, Sk., Can. E7 124
Gravelines, Fr. D11 14
Gravelotte, S. Afr. C10 70
Gravenhage, 's- see 's-Gravenhage, Neth. B12 14
Gravenhurst, On., Can. D10 112
Gravesend, Eng., U.K. J13 12
Gravette, Ar., U.S. H3 120
Gravina in Puglia, Italy D10 24
Gray, Fr. G14 14
Gray, Ga., U.S. D2 116
Grayback Mountain, mtn., Or., U.S. A2 134
Grayiske alper, mts., Eur. D13 18
Grayling, Mi., U.S. D5 112
Grays, Eng., U.K. J13 12
Grays Harbor, b., Wa., U.S. D2 136
Grays Lake, sw., Id., U.S. G15 136
Grayson, Sk., Can. D11 124
Grayson, Al., U.S. C11 122
Grayson, La., U.S. E6 122
Grays Peak, mtn., Co., U.S. B3 128
Graysville, Tn., U.S. B13 122
Grayville, Il., U.S. F9 120
Graz, Aus. C12 22
Grdelica, Yugo. G9 26
Great Artesian Basin, bas., Austl. E3 76
Great Australian Bight, b., Austl. F5 74
Great Barrier Island, i., N.Z. C6 80
Great Barrier Reef, rf., Austl. C9 74
Great Basin, bas., U.S. C4 108
Great Basin National Park, p.o.i., Nv., U.S. E2 132
Great Bear, stm., N.T., Can. B6 106
Great Bear Lake, l., N.T., Can. B6 106
Great Beaver Lake, l., B.C., Can. B7 138
Great Belt see Storebælt, strt., Den. I4 8
Great Bend, Ks., U.S. C10 128
Great Bitter Lake see Murrat el-Kubra, Buheirat, l., Egypt H3 58
Great Britain see United Kingdom, ctry., Eur. D8 6
Great Camanoe, i., Br. Vir. Is. e8 104b
Great Central, B.C., Can. G6 138
Great Channel, strt., Asia G7 46
Great Dismal Swamp, sw., U.S. H9 114
Great Divide Basin, bas., Wy., U.S. F4 126
Great Dividing Range, mts., Austl. C8 74
Great Driffield, Eng., U.K. G12 12
Greater Antilles, is., N.A. H15 94
Greater Khingan Range see Da Hinggan Ling, mts., China B9 36
Greater Sunda Islands, is., Asia F4 44
Great Exuma, i., Bah. C9 96
Great Falls, Mb., Can. D18 124
Great Falls, Mt., U.S. C15 136
Great Falls, S.C., U.S. B4 116
Great Himalayan National Park, p.o.i., India C6 54
Great Inagua, i., Bah. B11 102
Great Indian Desert (Thar Desert), des., Asia D3 54
Great Karroo (Groot Karroo), plat., S. Afr. H6 70
Great La Cloche Island, i., On., Can. B8 112
Great Lake, res., Austl. n13 77a
Great Malvern, Eng., U.K. I10 12
Great Miami, stm., U.S. E13 120
Great Namaqualand (Groot Namaland), hist. reg., Nmb. D3 70
Great Nicobar, i., India G7 46
Great Ouse, stm., Eng., U.K. I13 12
Great Palm Island, i., Austl. B6 76
Great Pee Dee, stm., S.C., U.S. C6 116
Great Plain of the Koukdjuak, pl., N.T., Can. B16 106
Great Plains, pl., N.A. C4 108
Great Point, c., Ma., U.S. C15 114
Great Ruaha, stm., Tan. F7 66
Great Sacandaga Lake, res., N.Y., U.S. G2 110
Great Sale Cay, i., Bah. I7 116
Great Salt Lake, l., Ut., U.S. B4 132
Great Salt Lake Desert, des., Ut., U.S. C3 132
Great Salt Plains Lake, res., Ok., U.S. E10 128
Great Sand Dunes National Monument, p.o.i., Co., U.S. D3 128
Great Sand Hills, hills, Sk., Can. D4 124
Great Sandy Desert, des., Austl. D4 74
Great Sandy National Park, p.o.i., Austl. E9 76
Great Scarcies, stm., Afr. H2 64
Great Sea Reef, rf., Fiji p19 79e
Great Slave Lake, l., N.T., Can. C8 106
Great Smoky Mountains, mts., U.S. A2 116
Great Smoky Mountains National Park, p.o.i., U.S. A2 116
Great Tenasserim, stm., Mya. F4 48
Great Thatch Island, i., Br. Vir. Is. e7 104b
Great Tobago, i., Br. Vir. Is. e7 104b
Great Victoria Desert, des., Austl. E5 74
Great Wall see Chang Cheng, misc. cult., China D6 36
Great Yarmouth, Eng., U.K. I14 12
Gréboun, mtn., Niger F6 64
Grecco, Ur. F9 92
Gredos, Sierra de, mts., Spain D5 20
Greece, N.Y., U.S. E12 112
Greece, ctry., Eur. H13 6
Greeley, Co., U.S. G8 126
Greeley, Ks., U.S. F2 120
Greeleyville, S.C., U.S. C6 116
Greely Fiord, b., N.T., Can. A9 141
Green, stm., U.S. E7 132
Green, stm., Il., U.S. C8 120
Green, stm., Ky., U.S. G10 120
Green, stm., N.D., U.S. G17 136
Green, stm., Wa., U.S. C5 136
Green Bay, Wi., U.S. D1 112
Green Bay, b., U.S. D2 112
Greenbrier, Ar., U.S. B6 122
Green Brier, Tn., U.S. H11 120
Greenbrier, stm., W.V., U.S. F5 114
Greenburg, La., U.S. G8 122
Greenbush, Mn., U.S. C2 118
Greencastle, In., U.S. E10 120
Greencastle, Pa., U.S. E8 114
Green Cove Springs, Fl., U.S. G4 116
Greendale, In., U.S. E13 120
Greene, Ia., U.S. B5 120
Greeneville, Tn., U.S. H3 114
Greenfield, Ca., U.S. B13 114
Greenfield, Il., U.S. E7 120
Greenfield, Ia., U.S. C3 120
Greenfield, Ma., U.S. H4 110
Greenfield, Mo., U.S. G4 120
Greenfield, Oh., U.S. E2 114
Greenfield, Ok., U.S. F10 128
Green Forest, Ar., U.S. H4 120
Green Island Bay, b., Phil. E2 52
Green Islands, is., Pap. N. Gui. D6 72
Green Lake, Wi., U.S. H10 118
Green Lake, l., B.C., Can. E9 138
Green Lake, l., Wi., U.S. H9 118
Greenland, Ar., U.S. I3 120
Greenland, dep., N.A. B19 94
Greenland Basin, unds. A14 144
Greenland Sea B21 94
Greenleaf, Ks., U.S. B11 128
Green Lookout Mountain, mtn., Wa., U.S. E4 136
Green Mountains, mts., N.A. G4 110
Greenock, Scot., U.K. F8 12
Greenore Point, c., Ire. I6 12
Greenough, stm., Austl. E3 74
Greenport, N.Y., U.S. C13 114
Green River, Pap. N. Gui. a3 79a
Green River, Ut., U.S. D7 132
Green River, Wy., U.S. B7 132
Green River Lake, res., Ky., U.S. G12 120
Greensboro, Fl., U.S. G14 122
Greensboro, Ga., U.S. C2 116
Greensboro, N.C., U.S. H6 114
Greensburg, In., U.S. E12 120
Greensburg, Ks., U.S. D9 128
Greensburg, Pa., U.S. D6 114
Green Springs, Oh., U.S. C2 114
Green Swamp, sw., N.C., U.S. B7 116
Greentown, In., U.S. H4 112
Greenup, Il., U.S. E9 120
Greenup, Ky., U.S. F3 114
Greenvale, Austl. B5 76
Green Valley, Az., U.S. L6 132
Greenville, Lib. H3 64
Greenville, Al., U.S. F12 122
Greenville, Ga., U.S. D14 122
Greenville, Il., U.S. F8 120
Greenville, Ky., U.S. G10 120
Greenville, Me., U.S. E7 110
Greenville, Mi., U.S. E4 112
Greenville, Ms., U.S. D7 122
Greenville, Mo., U.S. G7 120
Greenville, N.C., U.S. A8 116
Greenville, Oh., U.S. D1 114
Greenville, Pa., U.S. C5 114
Greenville, S.C., U.S. B3 116
Greenville, Tx., U.S. D2 122
Greenwater Lake, l., On., Can. C8 118
Greenwich, Ct., U.S. C12 114
Greenwich, Oh., U.S. C3 114
Greenwood, B.C., Can. G12 138
Greenwood, Ar., U.S. B4 122
Greenwood, In., U.S. E11 120
Greenwood, Ms., U.S. D8 122
Greenwood, S.C., U.S. B3 116
Greenwood, Wi., U.S. G8 118
Greenwood, Lake, res., S.C., U.S. B4 116
Greer, S.C., U.S. B3 116
Greers Ferry Lake, res., Ar., U.S. B6 122
Greeson, Lake, res., Ar., U.S. C5 122
Gregório, stm., Braz. E3 84
Gregory, Mi., U.S. B1 114
Gregory, S.D., U.S. D13 126
Gregory, Tx., U.S. G10 130
Gregory, stm., Austl. C7 74
Gregory, Lake, l., Austl. E3 74
Gregory, Lake, l., Austl. D5 74
Gregory, Lake, l., Austl. G2 76
Gregory Range, mts., Austl. B4 76
Greifswald, Ger. B9 16
Greifswalder Bodden, b., Ger. B9 16
Greiz, Ger. F8 16
Gremiha, Russia B18 8
Grenå, Den. H4 8
Grenada, Ms., U.S. D9 122
Grenada, ctry., N.A. q11 105e
Grenada Lake, res., Ms., U.S. D9 122
Grenadines, is., N.A. p11 105e
Grenchen, Switz. C4 22
Grenen, c., Den. H4 8
Grenfell, Austl. I7 76
Grenoble, Fr. D11 18
Grenola, Ks., U.S. D12 128
Grenora, N.D., U.S. F10 124
Grenville, Gren. q10 105e
Gresham, Or., U.S. E4 136
Gresik, Indon. G8 50
Gresik, Indon. E3 50
Gressåmoen Nasjonalpark, p.o.i., Nor. D5 8
Gretna, Mb., Can. E16 124
Gretna, La., U.S. H8 122
Gretna, Va., U.S. H6 114
Gretna Green, Scot., U.K. F9 12
Greven, Ger. D3 16
Grevená, Grc. C4 28
Grevenbroich, Ger. E2 16
Grevesmühlen, Ger. C7 16
Greybull, stm., Wy., U.S. C4 126
Grey Eagle, Mn., U.S. F4 118
Grey Islands, is., Nf., Can. i22 107a
Greylock, Mount, mtn., Ma., U.S. B12 114
Greymouth, N.Z. F4 80
Grey Range, mts., Austl. F4 76
Greytown, S. Afr. F10 70
Gribbel Island, i., B.C., Can. C1 138
Gribingui, stm., C.A.R. C3 66
Gridley, Ca., U.S. D4 134
Gridley, Il., U.S. D9 120
Griesheim, Ger. G4 16
Griffin, Sk., Can. E10 124
Griffin, Ga., U.S. C1 116
Griffin, Lake, l., Fl., U.S. H4 116
Griffith, Austl. J5 76
Griggsville, Il., U.S. E7 120
Grignols, Fr. E5 18
Grigoriopol, Mol. B16 26
Grijalva (Cuilco), stm., N.A. G12 100
Grim, Cape, c., Austl. n12 77a
Grimari, C.A.R. C3 66
Grimma, Ger. E8 16
Grimmen, Ger. B9 16
Grimsby, On., Can. E10 112
Grimsby, Eng., U.K. H12 12
Grimsel Pass, p., Switz. D5 22
Grímsey, i., Ice. j30 8a
Grimshaw, Ab., Can. D7 106
Grimstad, Nor. G3 8
Grímsvötn, vol., Ice. k31 8a
Grindelwald, Switz. D5 22
Grinnell, Ia., U.S. C5 120
Grinnell Peninsula, pen., N.T., Can. B7 141
Grintavec, mtn., Slvn. D11 22
Griqualand East, hist. reg., S. Afr. G9 70
Griqualand West, hist. reg., S. Afr. F6 70
Grise Fiord, N.T., Can. B9 141
Gris-Nez, Cap, c., Fr. D10 14
Griswold, Mb., Can. E13 124
Griswold, Ia., U.S. C2 120
Grizzly Bear Mountain, mtn., N.T., Can. B6 106
Grizzly Mountain, mtn., Id., U.S. C10 136
Grjadcy, Russia D14 10
Grjazovec, Russia G18 8
Groaíras, Braz. B5 88
Groblersdal, S. Afr. D9 70
Grodków, Pol. F13 16
Grodzisk Mazowiecki, Pol. D16 16
Groen, stm., S. Afr. G6 70
Groesbeck, Tx., U.S. F2 122
Grofa, hora, mtn., Ukr. A10 26
Groix, Fr. G5 14
Groix, Île de, i., Fr. G5 14
Grójec, Pol. E16 16
Grombalia, Tun. H4 24
Gronau, Ger. D3 16
Grong, Nor. D5 8
Groningen, Neth. A15 14
Groningen, Sur. B6 84
Groom, Tx., U.S. F7 128
Groot, stm., S. Afr. H7 70
Groot-Berg, stm., S. Afr. H4 70
Groot-Brakrivier, S. Afr. I6 70
Grootdraaidam, res., S. Afr. E9 70
Groote Eylandt, i., Austl. B7 74
Grootfontein, Nmb. D2 68
Grootgeluk, S. Afr. C8 70
Groot Karasberge, mts., Nmb. E4 70
Groot Karroo see Great Karroo, plat., S. Afr. H6 70
Groot-Kei, stm., S. Afr. H9 70
Groot Laagte, stm., Afr. B5 70
Groot Namaland see Great Namaqualand, hist. reg., Nmb. D3 70
Groot-Swartberge, mts., S. Afr. H6 70
Groot-Vis, stm., S. Afr. H8 70
Grootvloer, pl., S. Afr. F5 70
Gros Islet, St. Luc. I7 105c
Gros-Morne, Mart. k6 105c
Gros Morne, mtn., Nf., Can. j22 107a
Gros Piton, vol., St. Luc. m6 105c
Grossenhain, Ger. E9 16
Grosse Pointe, Mi., U.S. B3 114
Grosse Pointe, c., Guad. h6 105c
Grosser Beerberg, mtn., Ger. F6 16
Grosseto, Italy H7 22
Gross-Gerau, Ger. G4 16
Grossglockner, mtn., Aus. C9 22
Grossos, Braz. C7 88
Grossvenediger, mtn., Aus. C9 22
Groton, N.Y., U.S. F13 112
Groton, S.D., U.S. B14 126
Grottaglie, Italy D11 24
Grottammare, Italy G11 22
Grottoes, Va., U.S. F7 114
Grouard Mission, Ab., Can. D7 106
Groundhog, stm., On., Can. F14 106
Grove City, Mn., U.S. F4 118
Grove City, Oh., U.S. E2 114
Grove City, Pa., U.S. C5 114
Grove Hill, Al., U.S. F11 122
Grove Mountains, mts., Ant. C12 81
Grover City, Ca., U.S. H5 134
Groves, Tx., U.S. H5 122
Groveton, N.H., U.S. F5 110
Groveton, Tx., U.S. F3 122
Grovetown, Ga., U.S. C3 116
Growa Point, c., Lib. I3 64
Growler Peak, mtn., Az., U.S. K3 132
Groznyj, Russia F7 32
Grubišno Polje, Cro. E14 22
Grudziądz, Pol. C14 16
Grulla, Tx., U.S. H9 130
Grumo Appula, Italy D10 24
Grundy, Va., U.S. G3 114
Grundy Center, Ia., U.S. B5 120
Grušino, Russia G21 8
Gruver, Tx., U.S. E7 128
Gruznovka, Russia E10 34
Gryfice, Pol. C11 16
Gryfino, Pol. C10 16
Grytviken, S. Geor. J9 90
Guacanayabo, Golfo de, b., Cuba B9 102
Guacara, Ven. B7 86
Guacarí, Col. F3 86
Gu Achi, Az., U.S. K4 132
Guachiría, stm., Col. E6 86
Guachochi, Mex. B5 100
Guadajoz, stm., Spain G6 20
Guadalajara, Mex. E7 100
Guadalajara, Spain D7 20
Guadalajara, co., Spain D8 20
Guadalcanal, state, Sol. Is. f8 79b
Guadalcanal, i., Sol. Is. e9 79b
Guadalete, stm., Spain H4 20
Guadalhorce, stm., Spain G6 20
Guadalimar, stm., Spain F7 20
Guadalmena, stm., Spain F8 20
Guadalope, stm., Spain D10 20
Guadalquivir, stm., Spain H4 20
Guadalquivir, Marismas del, sw., Spain G4 20
Guadalupe, Mex. D7 100
Guadalupe, Mex. C8 100
Guadalupe, Ca., U.S. I5 134
Guadalupe, stm., Tx., U.S. F11 130
Guadalupe, Isla, i., Mex. G3 98
Guadalupe Bravos, Mex. C1 130
Guadalupe Mountains, mts., U.S. B3 130
Guadalupe Mountains National Park, p.o.i., Tx., U.S. C3 130
Guadalupe Peak, mtn., Tx., U.S. C3 130
Guadalupe Victoria, Mex. C6 100
Guadalupe Victoria, Mex. G6 130
Guadarrama, Puerto de, p., Spain D6 20
Guadarrama, Sierra de, mts., Spain D6 20
Guadeloupe, dep., N.A. h15 96a
Guadeloupe Passage, strt., N.A. g5 105c
Guadiana, stm., Eur. G3 20
Guadiana Menor, stm., Spain G7 20
Guadiato, stm., Spain F5 20
Guadiela, stm., Spain D8 20
Guadix, Spain G7 20
Guafo, Isla, i., Chile H1 90
Guaíba, Braz. E12 92
Guaíba, est., Braz. E12 92
Guaimaca, Hond. E4 102
Guainía, state, Col. F7 86
Guainía, stm., S.A. F8 86
Guaiquinima, Cerro, mtn., Ven. E10 86
Guaíra, Braz. K1 88
Guaíra, Braz. B10 92
Guairá, state, Para. B9 92
Guairá, Salto del (Sete Quedas, Salto das), wtfl, S.A. B10 92
Guáitara, stm., Col. G3 86
Guaitecas, Islas, is., Chile H2 90
Guajaba, Cayo, i., Cuba B9 102
Guajará-Açu, Braz. A1 88
Guajará-Mirim, Braz. F4 84
Guaje, Laguna del, l., Mex. B7 100
Gualaca, Pan. H6 102
Gualaceo, Ec. I2 86
Gualala, Ca., U.S. E2 134
Gualdo Tadino, Italy G9 22
Gualeguay, Arg. F8 92
Gualeguay, stm., Arg. F8 92
Gualeguaychú, Arg. F8 92
Gualicho, Salina del, pl., Arg. H4 90
Guam, dep., Oc. j10 78c
Guamá, stm., Braz. A1 88
Guamal, Col. F5 86
Guamal, Col. C4 86
Guaminí, Arg. H6 92
Guam International Airport, Guam i10 78c
Guamote, Ec. H2 86
Guamúchil, Mex. C4 100
Guamués, stm., Col. G3 86
Gua Musang, Malay. J5 48
Guanacaste, Cordillera de, mts., C.R. G5 102
Guanaceví, Mex. C6 100
Guanahacabibes, Golfo de, b., Cuba A5 102
Guana Island, i., Br. Vir. Is. e8 104b
Guanaja, Hond. D5 102
Guanaja, Isla de, i., Hond. D5 102
Guanajuato, Mex. E8 100
Guanajuato, state, Mex. E8 100
Guanambi, Braz. H4 88
Guanaparo, Caño, stm., Ven. C7 86
Guañape, Islas, is., Peru E2 84
Guanare, Ven. C7 86
Guanare, stm., Ven. C7 86
Guanarito, Ven. C7 86
Guandacol, Arg. D3 92
Guandu, China I5 42
Guane, Cuba A5 102
Guang'an, China F2 42
Guangchang, China H7 42
Guangde, China F8 42
Guangdong, state, China J6 42
Guangfeng, China G8 42
Guangji, China G6 42
Guangling, China B6 42
Guangming Ding, mtn., China F7 42
Guangnan, China G5 36
Guangxi, state, China G6 36
Guangxi Zhuangzu Zizhiqu see Guangxi, state, China G6 36
Guangyuan, China E1 42
Guangze, China H7 42
Guangzhou (Canton), China J5 42
Guanhães, Braz. J4 88
Guánica, P.R. C2 104a
Guanipa, stm., Ven. C10 86
Guanta, Ven. B9 86
Guantánamo, Cuba B10 102
Guantao, China C6 42
Guanting Shuiku, res., China A6 42
Guanxian, China E5 36
Guanxian, China C6 42
Guanyun, China D8 42
Guapí, Col. F3 86
Guapiara, Braz. B13 92
Guápiles, C.R. G6 102
Guaporé, Braz. D11 92
Guaporé (Iténez), stm., S.A. F5 84
Guaqui, Bol. C3 90
Guará, stm., Braz. G3 88
Guarabira, Braz. D8 88
Guaraciaba do Norte, Braz. C5 88
Guaraciana, Braz. I4 88
Guaranda, Ec. H2 86
Guaraniaçu, Braz. B11 92
Guarapari, Braz. K5 88
Guarapuava, Braz. B12 92
Guaraqueçaba, Braz. B13 92
Guaratinguetá, Braz. L3 88
Guaratuba, Braz. B13 92
Guarda, Port. D3 20
Guarda, state, Port. D3 20
Guardafui, Cape see Gwardafuy, Gees, c., Som. B10 66
Guardia Escolta, Arg. D6 92
Guardiagrele, Italy H11 22
Guardia Mitre, Arg. H4 90
Guardo, Spain B6 20
Guareña, Spain F4 20
Guarenas, Ven. B8 86
Guárico, state, Ven. C8 86
Guárico, stm., Ven. C8 86
Guárico, Embalse del, l., Ven. C8 86
Guariquito, stm., Ven. C8 86
Guarulhos, Braz. L2 88
Guasare, stm., Ven. B5 86
Guasave, Mex. C4 100
Guasdualito, Ven. D6 86
Guasipati, Ven. D11 86
Guastalla, Italy F7 22
Guatemala, Guat. E2 102
Guatemala, ctry., N.A. E2 102
Guatemala Basin, unds. H29 142
Guateque, Col. E5 86
Guatimozín, Arg. F6 92
Guatopo, Parque Nacional, p.o.i., Ven. B8 86
Guatuaro Point, c., Trin. s13 105f
Guaviare, state, Col. G5 86
Guaviare, stm., Col. E8 86
Guaxupé, Braz. K2 88
Guayabal, Cuba B9 102
Guayabal, Ven. D8 86
Guayabero, stm., Col. F5 86
Guayacán, Chile D2 92
Guayaguayare, Trin. s12 105f
Guayama, P.R. C3 104a
Guayana see Guyana, ctry., S.A. C6 84
Guayana, Macizo de (Guiana Highlands), mts., S.A. E10 86
Guayaneco, Archipiélago, is., Chile I1 90
Guayanilla, P.R. B2 104a
Guayape, stm., Hond. E4 102
Guayapo, stm., Ven. E8 86
Guayaquil, Ec. I1 86
Guayaquil, Golfo de, b., S.A. D1 84
Guayaramerín, Bol. B3 90
Guayas, state, Ec. H1 86
Guayas, stm., Ec. I2 86
Guaymallén, Arg. F3 92
Guaymas, Mex. B3 100
Guaynabo, P.R. B3 104a

Guay-Haut I•23

Name — Map Ref. — Page

Guayquiraró, stm., Arg. E8 92
Guazapares, Mex. B4 100
Guazárachi, Mex. B5 100
Guba, D.R.C. G5 66
Gubaha, Russia C9 32
Gûbâi, Madîq (Jubal, Strait of), strt., Egypt K4 58
Gubavica, wtfl, Cro. G13 22
Gubbi, India E3 53
Gubbio, Italy G9 22
Guben, Ger. E10 16
Gubin, Pol. E10 16
Gucheng, China E4 42
Gūdalūr, India G3 53
Gúdar, Sierra de, mts., Spain D10 20
Gudauta, Geor. F6 32
Gudermes, Russia F7 32
Gudivāda, India C5 53
Gudiyāttam, India E4 53
Güdül, Tur. C15 28
Gūdūr, India D4 53
Guebwiller, Fr. G16 14
Güejar, stm., Col. F5 86
Guékédou, Gui. H2 64
Guélengdeng, Chad E3 62
Guelma, Alg. B6 64
Guelmime, Mor. D2 64
Guelph, On., Can. E9 112
Guérande, Fr. G6 14
Guercif, Mor. C4 64
Guerdjoumane, Djebel, mtn., Alg. H13 20
Güere, stm., Ven. C9 86
Guéréda, Chad E4 62
Guéret, Fr. C7 18
Guerla Mandata Shan, mtn., China C8 54
Guernesey see Guernsey, dep., Eur. L10 12
Guerneville, Ca., U.S. E3 134
Guernica see Gernika, Spain A8 20
Guernica y Luno see Gernika, Spain A8 20
Guernsey, dep., Eur. E6 14
Guernsey, i., Guern. E6 14
Guerrero, Mex. A5 100
Guerrero, Mex. F7 130
Guerrero, state, Mex. G8 100
Guerrero Negro, Mex. B1 100
Gueydan, La., U.S. G6 122
Guga, Russia F16 34
Gugē, mtn., Eth. F7 62
Guguan, i., N. Mar. Is. B5 72
Gui, stm., China I4 42
Guiana Basin, unds. G9 144
Guiana Highlands (Guayana, Macizo de), mts., S.A. E10 86
Güicán, Col. D5 86
Guichi, China F7 42
Guide, China D5 36
Guidimouni, Niger G6 64
Guiding, China H2 42
Guier, Lac de, l., Sen. F1 64
Guijuelo, Spain D5 20
Guilarte, Monte, mtn., P.R. B2 104a
Guildford, Eng., U.K. J12 12
Guildhall, Vt., U.S. F5 110
Guilford, Me., U.S. E7 110
Guilin, China I4 42
Guillaume-Delisle, Lac, l., Qc., Can. D15 106
Guillestre, Fr. E12 18
Guimarães, Braz. B3 88
Guimaras Island, i., Phil. E4 52
Guimba, Phil. C3 52
Guin, Al., U.S. D11 122
Guinan, China D5 36
Guindulman, Phil. F5 52
Guinea, ctry., Afr. G2 64
Guinea, Gulf of, b., Afr. I6 64
Guinea Basin, unds. H13 144
Guinea-Bissau, ctry., Afr. G1 64
Güines, Cuba A7 102
Guingamp, Fr. F5 14
Güinope, Hond. F4 102
Guiping, China J4 42
Guipúzcoa see Gipuzkoako, co., Spain A8 20
Guiratinga, Braz. G7 84
Güiria, Ven. B10 86
Guitry, C. Iv. H3 64
Guiuan, Phil. E5 52
Guixian, China J3 42
Guiyang, China I5 42
Guiyang, China H2 42
Güiza, stm., Col. G2 86
Guizhou, state, China F6 36
Gujarāt, state, India G3 54
Gūjar Khān, Pak. B4 54
Gujrānwāla, Pak. B4 54
Gujrāt, Pak. B4 54
Gukou, China H8 42
Gulargambone, Austl. H7 76
Gulbarga, India C3 53
Gulbene, Lat. C9 10
Güldüzü, Tur. B8 58
Guledagudda, India C2 53
Gülek Boğazı, p., Tur. A5 58
Gulf Islands National Seashore, p.o.i., U.S. G10 122
Gulfport, Ms., U.S. G9 122
Gulf Shores, Al., U.S. G11 122
Gulgong, Austl. I7 76
Gulian, China F13 34
Gulistan, Uzb. F11 32
Gulkana, Ak., U.S. D10 140
Gull, stm., On., Can. B9 118
Gullfoss, wtfl, Ice. k29 8a
Gull Lake, Sk., Can. D5 124
Gull Lake, l., Ab., Can. D17 138
Gull Lake, l., Mn., U.S. E4 118
Güllük, Tur. F10 28
Güllük Körfezi, b., Tur. F10 28
Gülpınar, Tur. D9 28
Gulu, Ug. D6 66
Guluogongba, China A10 54
Gumaca, Phil. D4 52
Gumal (Gowmal), stm., Asia B2 54
Gumbalie, Austl. G5 76
Gumdag, Turkmen. B7 56
Gumel, Nig. G6 64
Gumla, India G10 54
Gumma, state, Japan C11 40
Gummersbach, Ger. E3 16
Gümüşhane, Tur. A4 56
Gümüşsü, Tur. E12 28
Guna, India F6 54
Gundagai, Austl. J7 76
Gundji, D.R.C. D4 66
Gundlupet, India F3 53
Gündoğdu, Tur. C9 28
Güney, Tur. E12 28
Gungu, D.R.C. F3 66
Gunmi, Nig. G6 64
Gunnar, Sk., Can. D9 106
Gunnarn, Swe. D7 8
Gunnbjørn Fjeld, mtn., Grnld. D19 141
Gunnedah, Austl. H7 76
Gunnison, Ut., U.S. D5 132
Gunnison, stm., Co., U.S. E8 132
Gunong Mulu National Park, p.o.i., Malay. A9 50
Gun Point, c., Gren. p11 105e
Gunpowder Creek, stm., Austl. B2 76
Gunsan see Kunsan, Kor., S. F7 38
Guntakal, India D3 53
Guntersville, Al., U.S. C12 122
Guntersville Dam, dam, Al., U.S. C12 122
Guntersville Lake, res., Al., U.S. C12 122
Guntūr, India C5 53
Gunungkencana, Indon. G4 50
Gunungsahilan, Indon. C2 50
Gunungsitoli, Indon. L3 48
Gunupur, India B6 53
Günzburg, Ger. H6 16
Gunzenhausen, Ger. G6 16
Guo, stm., China E7 42
Guoyang, China E7 42
Guoyangzhen, China B5 42
Gupis, Pak. B11 56
Gurabo, P.R. B4 104a
Gura Humorului, Rom. B12 26
Gurais, India A5 54
Gurdāspur, India B5 54
Gurdon, Ar., U.S. D5 122
Güre, Tur. E12 28
Gurevsk, Russia D15 32
Gurgueia, stm., Braz. D4 88
Gurha, India F3 54
Guri, Embalse de, res., Ven. D10 86
Gurskoe, Russia F16 34
Gurskøya, i., Nor. E1 8
Gürsu, Tur. C12 28
Gurupá, Braz. D7 84
Gurupi, Braz. F1 88
Gurupi, stm., Braz. D8 84
Guru Sikhar, mtn., India F4 54
Gurvan Sayhan uul, mts., Mong. C5 36
Gusau, Nig. G6 64
Gusev, Russia F5 10
Gušgy, Turkmen. B9 56
Gushan, China B10 42
Gushi, China E6 42
Gus'-Hrustal'nyj, Russia I19 8
Gusino, Russia F14 10
Gusinoozersk, Russia F10 34
Gus'-Khrustal'nyy see Gus'-Hrustal'nyj, Russia I19 8
Guspini, Italy E2 24
Güssing, Aus. C13 22
Gustav Holm, Kap, c., Grnld. D19 141
Gustavus, Ak., U.S. E12 140
Gustine, Ca., U.S. F5 134
Gustine, Tx., U.S. C9 130
Güstrow, Ger. C8 16
Gütersloh, Ger. E4 16
Guthrie, Ok., U.S. F11 128
Guthrie, Tx., U.S. H8 128
Guthrie Center, Ia., U.S. C3 120
Gutian, China H8 42
Gutiérrez Zamora, Mex. E10 100
Guttenberg, Ia., U.S. B6 120
Guwāhāti, India E13 54
Guxian, China E5 42
Guyana, ctry., S.A. C6 84
Guyang, China A4 42
Guye, China B8 42
Guy Fawkes River National Park, p.o.i., Austl. H9 76
Guymon, Ok., U.S. E7 128
Guyot, Mount, mtn., U.S. I2 114
Guyra, Austl. H8 76
Guyton, Ga., U.S. D4 116
Guyuan, China D2 42
Guzar, Uzb. G11 32
Güzelyurt, N. Cyp. C3 58
Güzelyurt Körfezi, b., N. Cyp. C3 58
Guzhen, China E7 42
Guzmán, Mex. F9 98
Guzmán, Mex. F7 100
Gvardejsk, Russia F4 10
Gwa, Mya. D2 48
Gwaai, Zimb. D4 68
Gwādar, Pak. D9 56
Gwalia, Austl. E4 74
Gwalior (Lashkar), India E7 54
Gwanda, Zimb. B9 70
Gwane, D.R.C. D5 66
Gwangju see Kwangju, Kor., S. G7 38
Gwardafuy, Gees, c., Som. B10 66
Gwātar Bay, b., Asia E9 56
Gwayi, stm., Zimb. D4 68
Gwda, stm., Pol. C12 16
Gweedore, Ire. F4 12
Gweru, Zimb. D4 68
Gwinn, Mi., U.S. B2 112
Gwydir, stm., Austl. G7 76
Gyangtse see Gyangzê, China D12 54
Gyangzê, China D12 54
Gyaring Co, l., China C12 54
Gyaring Hu, l., China E4 36
Gyda, Russia B4 34
Gydanskaja guba, b., Russia B4 34
Gydanskij poluostrov, pen., Russia B4 34
Gyeongju see Kyŏngju, Kor., S. D2 40
Gyirong, China D10 54
Gyldenløves Fjord, b., Grnld. E17 141
Gym Peak, mtn., N.M., U.S. K9 132
Gympie, Austl. F9 76
Gyobingauk, Mya. C2 48
Gyoma, Hung. C7 26
Gyöngyös, Hung. B6 26
Győr (Raab), Hung. B4 26
Győr-Moson-Sopron, state, Hung. B4 26
Gypsum, Co., U.S. D10 132
Gypsum, Ks., U.S. C11 128
Gypsumville, Mb., Can. C15 124
Gyula, Hung. C8 26
Gyulafehérvár see Alba Iulia, Rom. C10 26
Gyzylarbat, Turkmen. B8 56

H

Haag in Oberbayern, Ger. H8 16
Haaksbergen, Neth. D2 16
Haapiti, Fr. Poly. v20 78h
Haapsalu, Est. G10 8
Haar, Ger. H7 16
Ha'Arava ('Arabah, Wādī al-), val., Asia H6 58
Ha'Arava (Jayb, Wādī al-), stm., Asia H6 58
Haarlem, Neth. B13 14
Habaqila, China C6 36
Habarovsk, Russia G16 34
Habary, Russia D13 32
Ḩabashīyah, Jabal, mts., Yemen F7 56
Habbān, Yemen G6 56
Habermehl Peak, mtn., Ant. C6 81
Habiganj, Bngl. F13 54
Habomai Islands see Malaja Kuril'skaja Grjada, is., Russia C17 38
Hachijō-jima, i., Japan F12 40
Hachiman, Japan D9 40
Hachinohe, Japan D14 38
Hachiōji, Japan D12 40
Hackberry, La., U.S. H5 122
Hackberry Creek, stm., Ks., U.S. C8 128
Hackett, Ar., U.S. B4 122
Hackettstown, N.J., U.S. D11 114
Hadāli, Pak. B4 54
HaDarom, state, Isr. H5 58
Ḩadd, Ra's al-, c., Oman E8 56
Haddam, Ks., U.S. B11 128
Haddington, Scot., U.K. F10 12
Haddock, Ga., U.S. C2 116
Haddon Downs, Austl. F3 76
Hadejia, Nig. G7 64
Hadejia, stm., Nig. G6 64
Haden, Austl. F8 76
Ḩadera, Isr. F5 58
Haderslev, Den. I3 8
Hadībū, Yemen G7 56
Ḩadīthah, Iraq C5 56
Hadley Bay, b., N.T., Can. A9 106
Hadlock, Wa., U.S. B4 136
Ha Dong, Viet. B7 48
Ḩaḑramawt, reg., Yemen F6 56
Hadrian's Wall, misc. cult., Eng., U.K. G10 12
Hadzilavičy, Bela. G13 10
Haeju, Kor., N. E6 38
Haenam, Kor., S. G7 38
Haerhpin see Harbin, China B7 38
Haffner Bjerg, mtn., Grnld. B13 141
Hafford, Sk., Can. B6 124
Haffouz, Tun. I3 24
Hāfizābād, Pak. B4 54
Hāflong, India F14 54
Hafnarfjörður, Ice. k28 8a
Haft Gel, Iran C6 56
Hagan, Ga., U.S. D3 116
Hagari, stm., India D3 53
Hagemeister Island, i., Ak., U.S. E7 140
Hagen, Ger. E3 16
Hagenow, Ger. C7 16
Hagensborg, B.C., Can. D4 138
Hagerman, N.M., U.S. A3 130
Hagerstown, In., U.S. I4 112
Hagerstown, Md., U.S. E8 114
Hagersville, On., Can. F9 112
Hagfors, Swe. F5 8
Haggin, Mount, mtn., Mt., U.S. D13 136
Hagi, Japan E4 40
Ha Giang, Viet. A7 48
Hagondange, Fr. E15 14
Hags Head, c., Ire. I3 12
Hague, Sk., Can. B7 124
Hague, Cap de la, c., Fr. E7 14
Haguenau, Fr. F16 14
Hagues Peak, mtn., Co., U.S. G7 126
Hahira, Ga., U.S. F2 116
Hai'an, China E9 42
Haibei, China B10 36
Haicheng, China A10 42
Haichow Bay see Haizhou Wan, b., China D8 42
Haidargarh, India E8 54
Hai Duong, Viet. B8 48
Haifa see Ḩefa, Isr. F5 58
Haifa see Ḩefa, state, Isr. F5 58
Haifeng, China J6 42
Haig, Austl. F5 74
Haigler, Ne., U.S. A7 128
Haikang, China K3 42
Haikou, China K4 42
Haikou, China G9 42
Ḩā'il, Sau. Ar. D5 56
Hailākāndi, India F14 54
Hailar, China B8 36
Hailar, stm., China B8 36
Haileyville, Ok., U.S. C3 122
Hailin, China B8 38
Hailun, China B10 36
Hailuoto, i., Fin. D11 8
Haimen, China J7 42
Haimen, China G9 42
Hainan, state, China L3 42
Hainan Dao (Hainan Island), i., China L4 42
Hainan Island see Hainan Dao, i., China L4 42
Hainan Strait see Qiongzhou Haixia, strt., China K4 42
Haines, Ak., U.S. E12 140
Haines, Or., U.S. F8 136
Haines City, Fl., U.S. H4 116
Haines Junction, Yk., Can. C3 106
Haining, China F9 42
Hai Ninh, Viet. B8 48
Hai Phong, Viet. B8 48
Haiphong see Hai Phong, Viet. B8 48
Haiti, ctry., N.A. C11 102
Haitun, China D4 36
Haivoron, Ukr. A16 26
Haiyuan, China C1 42
Haizhou, China D8 42
Haizhou Wan, b., China D8 42
Hajdú-Bihar, state, Hung. B8 26
Hajdúböszörmény, Hung. B8 26
Hajdúnánás, Hung. B8 26
Hajdúszoboszló, Hung. B8 26
Hājīpur, India F10 54
Hajnówka, Pol. D19 16
Hakasija, state, Russia D16 32
Hakha, Mya. A1 48
Hakken-san, mtn., Japan E8 40
Hakodate, Japan D14 38
Hakone-yama, vol., Japan D12 40
Hakui, Japan C9 40
Haku-san, vol., Japan C9 40
Haku-san-kokuritsu-kōen, p.o.i., Japan C9 40
Hal see Halle, Bel. D13 14
Ḩalab (Aleppo), Syria B8 58
Ḩalab, state, Syria B8 58
Halachó, Mex. B2 102
Halahai, China B6 38
Ḩalā'ib, Sudan C7 62
Halawa, Cape, c., Hi., U.S. B5 78a
Halberstadt, Ger. E7 16
Halbrite, Sk., Can. E10 124
Halcon, Mount, mtn., Phil. D3 52
Halden, Nor. G4 8
Haldensleben, Ger. D7 16
Haldimand, On., Can. F10 112
Haldwāni, India D7 54
Hale, Mo., U.S. E4 120
Haleakala Crater, crat., Hi., U.S. C5 78a
Haleakala National Park, p.o.i., Hi., U.S. C5 78a
Hale Center, Tx., U.S. G7 128
Halenkov, Czech Rep. G14 16
Halfmoon Bay, B.C., Can. G6 138
Halfway, Md., U.S. E8 114
Halfway, Or., U.S. F9 136
Halicarnassus, hist., Tur. F10 28
Halifax, Austl. B6 76
Halifax, N.S., Can. F13 110
Halifax, Eng., U.K. H11 12
Halifax, N.C., U.S. H8 114
Halifax, Va., U.S. H6 114
Halifax Bay, b., Austl. B6 76
Haliyāl, India D2 53
Haljala, Est. A9 10
Halkapınar, Tur. A5 58
Halland, state, Swe. H5 8
Hallandale, Fl., U.S. K5 116
Ḩallānīyah, Juzur al- (Kuria Muria Islands), is., Oman F8 56
Halla-san, mtn., Kor., S. H7 38
Hall Basin, b., N.A. A13 141
Halle, Bel. D13 14
Halle, Ger. E7 16
Hällefors, Swe. G6 8
Hallein, Aus. C10 22
Hallettsville, Tx., U.S. E11 130
Halley, sci., Ant. C2 81
Halligen, is., Ger. B4 16
Hall in Tirol, Aus. C8 22
Hall Islands, is., Micron. C6 72
Hall Lake, l., N.T., Can. B14 106
Hall Land, reg., Grnld. A14 141
Hall Mountain, mtn., Wa., U.S. B9 136
Hallock, Mn., U.S. C2 118
Hallowell, Me., U.S. F7 110
Hall Peninsula, pen., N.T., Can. C17 106
Halls, Tn., U.S. I8 120
Hallsberg, Swe. G6 8
Halls Creek, Austl. C5 74
Hallstahammar, Swe. G7 8
Hallstavik, Swe. F8 8
Hallstead, Pa., U.S. C10 114
Hallsville, Mo., U.S. E5 120
Halmahera, i., Indon. E8 44
Halmahera, Laut (Halmahera Sea), Indon. F8 44
Halmahera Sea see Halmahera, Laut, Indon. F8 44
Hal'mer-Ju, Russia A10 32
Halmstad, Swe. H5 8
Haloučyn, Bela. F12 10
Hal'šany, Bela. F8 10
Halsey, Ne., U.S. F12 126
Halsey, Or., U.S. F3 136
Halstead, Ks., U.S. D11 128
Haltern, Ger. E3 16
Haltiatunturi, mtn., Eur. B9 8
Haltom City, Tx., U.S. B10 130
Halton Hills see Georgetown, On., Can. E9 112
Halvorson, Mount, mtn., B.C., Can. C10 138
Ham, stm., Nmb. F4 70
Hamada, Japan E4 40
Hamadān, Iran C6 56
Ḩamāh, Syria C7 58
Ḩamāh, state, Syria C8 58
Hamamatsu, Japan E10 40
Haman, Kor., S. D1 40
Hamana-ko, l., Japan E10 40
Hamar, Nor. F4 8
Ha Marakabei, Leso. F9 70
Hamar-Daban, hrebet, mts., Russia F9 34
Hamburg, Ger. C6 16
Hamburg, Ar., U.S. D7 122
Hamburg, Ia., U.S. D2 120
Hamburg, N.J., U.S. C11 114
Hamburg, N.Y., U.S. B7 114
Hamburg, state, Ger. C6 16
Hamden, Ct., U.S. C13 114
Hamden, Oh., U.S. E3 114
Häme, state, Fin. F11 8
Hämeenlinna (Tavastehus), Fin. F10 8
Hamelin, Austl. E2 74
Hameln, Ger. D5 16
HaMerkaz, state, Isr. F5 58
Hamersley Range, mts., Austl. D3 74
Hamgyŏng-sanjulgi, mts., Kor., N. D8 38
Hamhŭng, Kor., N. E7 38
Hami, China C3 36
Hamilton, Austl. K4 76
Hamilton, Ber. k15 104e
Hamilton, On., Can. E10 112
Hamilton, N.Z. C6 80
Hamilton, Scot., U.K. F8 12
Hamilton, Al., U.S. C11 122
Hamilton, Ga., U.S. E14 122
Hamilton, Il., U.S. D6 120
Hamilton, Mi., U.S. F4 112
Hamilton, Mo., U.S. E3 120
Hamilton, Mt., U.S. D12 136
Hamilton, N.Y., U.S. B10 114
Hamilton, Oh., U.S. E1 114
Hamilton, stm., Austl. D3 76
Hamilton, Lake, res., Ar., U.S. C5 122
Hamilton, Mount, mtn., Ca., U.S. F4 134
Hamilton City, Ca., U.S. D3 134
Hamilton Dome, Wy., U.S. D4 126
Hamilton Hotel, Austl. D3 76
Hamilton Mountain, mtn., N.Y., U.S. G2 110
Hamina, Fin. F12 8
Hamiota, Mb., Can. D13 124
Hamīrpur, India F7 54
Hamlin, Tx., U.S. B7 130
Hamlin, W.V., U.S. F3 114
Hamlin Valley Wash, stm., U.S. E3 132
Hamm, Ger. E3 16
Hammamet, Tun. H4 24
Hammamet, Golfe de, b., Tun. H4 24
Hammam Lif, Tun. H4 24
Hammelburg, Ger. F5 16
Hammerdal, Swe. E6 8
Hammerfest, Nor. A10 8
Hammon, Ok., U.S. F9 128
Hammond, In., U.S. G2 112
Hammond, La., U.S. G8 122
Hammondsport, N.Y., U.S. F12 112
Hampden, Me., U.S. F8 110
Hampden, N.D., U.S. F15 124
Hampi, India D3 53
Hampshire, Il., U.S. I10 118
Hampstead, N.C., U.S. B8 116
Hampton, N.B., Can. E11 110
Hampton, Ar., U.S. D6 122
Hampton, Fl., U.S. G3 116
Hampton, Ga., U.S. C1 116
Hampton, Ne., U.S. G15 126
Hampton, N.H., U.S. H6 110
Hampton, Tn., U.S. H3 114
Hampton, Va., U.S. G9 114
Hampton Butte, mtn., Or., U.S. G6 136
Hampton Tableland, plat., Austl. F5 74
Hamra, Swe. F6 8
Ḩamrā', Al-Ḩamādah al-, des., Libya B2 62
Hamra, As Saquia al, stm., W. Sah. D2 64
Hamsara, stm., Russia D16 32
Hams Fork, stm., Wy., U.S. F2 126
Hamṭa, Gebel (Ḩamāṭah, Jabal), mtn., Egypt C6 62
Ham Tan, Viet. G8 48
Hāmūn, Daryācheh-ye, l., Iran C9 56
Han, stm., China I7 42
Han, stm., China F6 42
Han, Nong, l., Thai. D7 48
Hana, Hi., U.S. C6 78a
Hanahan, S.C., U.S. D5 116
Hanamaki, Japan E14 38
Hananui see Anglem, Mount, mtn., N.Z. H2 80
Hanapepe, Hi., U.S. B2 78a
Hanateio, Fr. Poly. s18 78g
Hanatetena, Fr. Poly. s18 78g
Hanau am Main, Ger. F4 16
Hanbury, stm., N.T., Can. C9 106
Hancavičy, Bela. H9 10
Hâncești, Mol. C15 26
Hanceville, Al., U.S. C12 122
Hancheng, China D7 36
Hancheng, China D4 42
Hanchung see Hanzhong, China E2 42
Hancock, Md., U.S. E7 114
Hancock, Mi., U.S. D10 118
Hancock, Mn., U.S. F3 118
Hancock, N.Y., U.S. C10 114
Handa, Japan E9 40
Handan, China C6 42
Handlová, Slov. H14 16
Handsworth, Sk., Can. E10 124
Handyga, Russia D16 34
HaNegev (Negev Desert), reg., Isr. H5 58
Hanford, Ca., U.S. G6 134
Hanga Roa, Chile e29 78l
Hangayn nuruu, mts., Mong. B4 36
Hangchou see Hangzhou, China F9 42
Hangchow see Hangzhou, China F9 42
Hangchow Bay see Hangzhou Wan, b., China F9 42
Hanggin Houqi, China A2 42
Hanggin Qi, China B3 42
Hangman Creek, stm., U.S. C9 136
Hangö see Hanko, Fin. G10 8
Hangokurt, Russia B10 32
Hangu, China B7 42
Hangu, Pak. B3 54
Hanguang, China I5 42
Hangzhou, China F9 42
Hangzhou Wan, b., China F9 42
Hanino, Russia F19 10
Ḩanīsh, is., Yemen G5 56
Hanish Islands see Ḩanīsh, is., Yemen G5 56
Hanjiang, China I8 42
Hankinson, N.D., U.S. E2 118
Hanko, Fin. G10 8
Hankow see Wuhan, China F6 42
Hanku see Hangu, China B7 42
Hānle, India B7 54
Hanley, Sk., Can. C7 124
Hanna, Ab., Can. E19 138
Hanna, Ok., U.S. B3 122
Hanna, Wy., U.S. B10 132
Hanna City, Il., U.S. D8 120
Hannah, N.D., U.S. F15 124
Hannah Bay, b., On., Can. E14 106
Hannibal, Mo., U.S. E6 120
Hannover, Ger. D5 16
Ha Noi (Hanoi), Viet. B7 48
Hanoi see Ha Noi, Viet. B7 48
Hanover, On., Can. D8 112
Hanover see Hannover, Ger. D5 16
Hanover, S. Afr. G7 70
Hanover, Il., U.S. B7 120
Hanover, In., U.S. F12 120
Hanover, N.H., U.S. G4 110
Hanover, N.M., U.S. K8 132
Hanover, Pa., U.S. E9 114
Hanover, Va., U.S. G8 114
Hanover, Isla, i., Chile J2 90
Hansdiha, India F11 54
Hānsi, India D5 54
Hanska, Mn., U.S. G4 118
Hantajskoe, ozero, l., Russia C6 34
Hantan see Handan, China C6 42
Hantau, Kaz. F12 32
Hantsport, N.S., Can. E12 110
Hanty-Mansijsk, Russia B11 32
Hantzsch, stm., N.T., Can. B16 106
Hanumāngarh, India C3 46
Hanumangarh, India D4 54
Hanuy, stm., Mong. B5 36
Hanyin, China E3 42
Hanzhong, China E2 42
Hanzhuang, China D7 42
Haojiadian, China F5 42
Haoli see Hegang, China B11 36
Hāora, India G12 54
Haparanda, Swe. D10 8
Hapčeranga, Russia G11 34
Happy, Tx., U.S. G7 128
Happy Jack, Az., U.S. I5 132
Happy Valley-Goose Bay, Nf., Can. E18 106
Hāpur, India D6 54
Ḩaql, Sau. Ar. I5 58
Ḩaraḑ, Sau. Ar. E6 56
Haradok, Bela. E13 10
Haradzec, Bela. H7 10
Haradzec, Bela. G13 10
Haradzišča, Bela. G9 10
Haramachi, Japan B13 40
Haranor, Russia A8 36
Harar see Hārer, Eth. F8 62
Harare, Zimb. D5 68
Harazé Mangueigne, Chad E4 62
Harbala, Russia D13 34
Harbavičy, Bela. G13 10
Harbin, China B7 38
Harbiye, Tur. B7 58
Harbor, Or., U.S. A1 134
Harbor Beach, Mi., U.S. E7 112
Harbour Breton, Nf., Can. j22 107a
Harbourville, N.S., Can. E12 110
Harda, India G6 54
Hardangerfjorden, b., Nor. F2 8
Hardangerjøkulen, ice, Nor. F2 8
Hardangervidda Nasjonalpark, p.o.i., Nor. F2 8
Hardap, state, Nmb. D3 70
Hardeeville, S.C., U.S. D4 116
Harderwijk, Neth. B14 14
Hardin, Il., U.S. E7 120
Hardin, Mt., U.S. B5 126
Harding, S. Afr. G9 70
Harding, Lake, res., U.S. E13 122
Hardinsburg, Ky., U.S. G11 120
Hardisty Lake, l., N.T., Can. C7 106
Hardoi, India E7 54
Hardtner, Ks., U.S. D10 128
Hardwick, Ga., U.S. C2 116
Hardwick, Vt., U.S. F4 110
Hardy, Ar., U.S. H6 120
Hardy, Ne., U.S. G15 126
Hardy Bay, b., N.T., Can. B16 140
Hare Bay, b., Nf., Can. i22 107a
Hare Indian, stm., N.T., Can. B5 106
Hareøen, i., Grnld. C14 141
Hārer, Eth. F8 62
Hargeysa, Som. C8 66
Harghita, state, Rom. C12 26
Har Hu, l., China D4 36
Hari, stm., Indon. D3 50
Ḩarīb, Yemen G6 56
Haridwār, India D7 54
Harihar, India D2 53
Ḩārim, Syria B7 58
Harīpur, Pak. B4 54
Harīrūd (Tedžen), stm., Asia C9 56
Harischandra Range, mts., India B1 53
Haritonovo, Russia F22 8
Harkers Island, N.C., U.S. B9 116
Harlan, Ky., U.S. H2 114
Harlan County Lake, res., Ne., U.S. A9 128
Harlem, Fl., U.S. J5 116
Harlem, Ga., U.S. C3 116
Harleton, Tx., U.S. E4 122
Harlingen, Neth. A14 14
Harlingen, Tx., U.S. H10 130
Harlovka, Russia B17 8
Harlow, Eng., U.K. J13 12
Harlowton, Mt., U.S. D17 136
Harman, W.V., U.S. F6 114
Harmancık, Tur. D12 28
Harmanli, Blg. H12 26
Harmony, In., U.S. E10 120
Harnai, India C1 53
Harney Basin, bas., Or., U.S. G8 136
Harney Lake, l., Or., U.S. G7 136
Harney Peak, mtn., S.D., U.S. D9 126
Härnösand, Swe. E8 8
Har nuur, l., Mong. B3 36
Haro, Spain B8 20
Haro, Cabo, c., Mex. B3 100
Harovsk, Russia F18 8
Harpanahalli, India D3 53
Harper, Lib. I3 64
Harper, Ks., U.S. D10 128
Harper, Tx., U.S. D8 130
Harper, Mount, mtn., Ak., U.S. D11 140
Harqin Qi, China D3 38
Harrai, India G7 54
Harricana, stm., Can. E15 106
Harriman, Tn., U.S. I13 120
Harrington, De., U.S. F10 114
Harrington, Me., U.S. F9 110
Harris, Sk., Can. C6 124
Harris, Monts. D3 105a
Harris, Mn., U.S. F5 118
Harris, reg., Scot., U.K. D6 12
Harris, Lake, l., Fl., U.S. H4 116
Harrisburg, Ar., U.S. B8 122
Harrisburg, Ne., U.S. F9 126
Harrisburg, Or., U.S. F3 136
Harrisburg, Pa., U.S. D8 114
Harrismith, S. Afr. F9 70
Harrison, Ar., U.S. H4 120
Harrison, Mi., U.S. D5 112
Harrison, Ne., U.S. E9 126
Harrison Bay, b., Ak., U.S. B9 140
Harrisonburg, La., U.S. F7 122
Harrisonburg, Va., U.S. F6 114
Harrison Islands, is., N.T., Can. B13 106
Harrison Lake, l., B.C., Can. G9 138
Harriston, On., Can. E9 112
Harriston, Ms., U.S. F7 122
Harrisville, N.Y., U.S. D14 112
Harrisville, W.V., U.S. E4 114
Harrodsburg, Ky., U.S. G13 120
Harrogate, Eng., U.K. H11 12
Harrold, Tx., U.S. G9 128
Harrowsmith, On., Can. D13 112
Harry S. Truman Reservoir, res., Mo., U.S. F4 120
Har Sai Shan, mtn., China D4 36
Harsīn, Iran C6 56
Hârșova, Rom. E14 26
Harstad, Nor. B7 8
Harsūd, India G6 54
Hart, Mi., U.S. E3 112
Hart, Tx., U.S. G6 128
Hart, stm., Yk., Can. B3 106
Hartbees, stm., S. Afr. F5 70
Hartberg, Aus. C12 22
Hartford, Ar., U.S. C4 122
Hartford, Ct., U.S. C13 114
Hartford, Ks., U.S. F2 120
Hartford, Mi., U.S. F3 112
Hartford, S.D., U.S. H2 118
Hartford, Wi., U.S. H10 118
Hartford City, In., U.S. H4 112
Hartland, N.B., Can. D9 110
Hartland, Me., U.S. F7 110
Hartlepool, Eng., U.K. G11 12
Hartley, Ia., U.S. H3 118
Hartley Bay, B.C., Can. C1 138
Hart Mountain, mtn., Mb., Can. B12 124
Hartney, Mb., Can. E13 124
Harts, stm., S. Afr. E7 70
Hartselle, Al., U.S. C12 122
Hartshorne, Ok., U.S. C3 122
Hartsville, S.C., U.S. B5 116
Hartville, Mo., U.S. G5 120
Hartwell, Ga., U.S. B3 116
Hartwell Lake, res., U.S. B2 116
Hartz Mountains National Park, p.o.i., Austl. o13 77a
Hārūnābād, Pak. D4 54
Haruniye, Tur. A7 58
Harūr, India E4 53
Har-Us nuur, l., Mong. B3 36
Hārūt, stm., Afg. C9 56
Harvard, Ne., U.S. G14 126
Harvey, N.B., Can. E12 110
Harvey, Il., U.S. G2 112
Harvey, N.D., U.S. G14 124
Harwich, Eng., U.K. J14 12
Haryāna, state, India D6 54
Haryn', stm., Eur. H10 10
Harz, mts., Ger. E6 16
Hasavjurt, Russia F7 32
Hasdo, stm., India G9 54
Hase, stm., Ger. D3 16
Hasenkamp, Arg. E8 92
Hashima, Japan D9 40
Hashimoto, Japan E8 40
Hāsilpur, Pak. D4 54
Haskell, Ok., U.S. I2 120
Haskell, Tx., U.S. A8 130
Haskovo, Blg. H12 26
Haskovo, state, Blg. G12 26
Haslemere, Eng., U.K. J12 12
Hasperos Canyon, val., N.M., U.S. H3 128
Ḩaşş, Jabal al-, hill, Syria C8 58
Hassa, Tur. B7 58
Hassan, India E3 53
Hassayampa, stm., Az., U.S. J4 132
Hassel Sound, strt., N.T., Can. B6 141
Hasselt, Bel. D14 14
Hassfurt, Ger. F6 16
Hassi Messaoud, Alg. C6 64
Hässleholm, Swe. H5 8
Hastings, Barb. n8 105d
Hastings, On., Can. D11 112
Hastings, N.Z. D7 80
Hastings, Eng., U.K. K13 12
Hastings, Mi., U.S. F4 112
Hastings, Mn., U.S. G6 118
Hastings, Ne., U.S. G14 126
Haswell, Co., U.S. C5 128
Hatanga, Russia B9 34
Hatanga, stm., Russia B9 34
Hatangskij zaliv, b., Russia B10 34
Hatay (Antioch), Tur. B7 58
Hatay, state, Tur. B7 58
Hatch, N.M., U.S. K9 132
Hatch, Ut., U.S. F4 132
Hat Chao Mai National Park, p.o.i., Thai. I4 48
Hatchie, stm., U.S. B9 122
Hatfield, Austl. I4 76
Hatfield, Ar., U.S. C4 122
Hatfield, Ma., U.S. B13 114
Hatgal, Mong. F9 34
Hāthras, India E7 54
Ha Tien, Viet. G7 48
Hatillo, P.R. A2 104a
Ha Tinh, Viet. C7 48
Hatip, Tur. F15 28
Hato, Bocht van, b., Neth. Ant. p21 104g
Hato Mayor del Rey, Dom. Rep. C13 102
Hāt Pīplia, India G6 54
Hatta, India F7 54
Hatteras, N.C., U.S. A10 116
Hatteras, Cape, c., N.C., U.S. A10 116
Hatteras Island, i., N.C., U.S. A10 116
Hattiesburg, Ms., U.S. F9 122
Hatton, Al., U.S. C11 122
Hatton, N.D., U.S. G16 124
Hatunsaray, Tur. A3 58
Hatvan, Hung. B6 26
Hat Yai, Thai. I5 48
Hatyrka, Russia D24 34
Haugesund, Nor. G1 8
Haukeligrend, Nor. G2 8
Haukivesi, l., Fin. E12 8
Hauraki Gulf, b., N.Z. C6 80
Hausach, Ger. H4 16
Haut, Isle au, i., Me., U.S. F8 110
Haut Atlas, mts., Mor. C3 64
Haute-Corse, state, Fr. G15 18

Name	Map Ref.	Page

Horm-Indi I•25

Name	Map Ref.	Page
Hormuz, Strait of, strt., Asia	D8	56
Horn, Aus.	B12	22
Horn, c., Ice.	j28	8a
Horn, stm., N.T., Can.	C7	106
Horn, Cape see Hornos, Cabo de, c., Chile	K3	90
Hornad (Hernád), stm., Eur.	H17	16
Hornaday, stm., N.T., Can.	B6	106
Hornafjörður, b., Ice.	k32	8a
Hornavan, l., Swe.	C7	8
Hornbeck, La., U.S.	F5	122
Hornbrook, Ca., U.S.	B3	134
Hornby Bay, b., N.T., Can.	B7	106
Hornell, N.Y., U.S.	B8	114
Hornepayne, On., Can.	F13	106
Horn Island, i., Ms., U.S.	G10	122
Horn Lake, Ms., U.S.	C8	122
Hornos, Cabo de (Horn, Cape), c., Chile	K3	90
Horn Plateau, plat., N.T., Can.	C6	106
Hornsea, Eng., U.K.	H12	12
Horodkivka, Ukr.	A15	26
Horodok, Ukr.	G19	16
Horog, Taj.	B11	56
Horol', Russia	B10	38
Horqin Youyi Qianqi, China	B9	36
Horqin Youyi Zhongqi, China	B4	38
Horqin Zuoyi Houqi, China	C4	38
Horqin Zuoyi Zhongqi, China	B5	38
Horqueta, Para.	D5	90
Horse Cave, Ky., U.S.	G12	120
Horse Creek, stm., U.S.	F8	126
Horse Creek, stm., Co., U.S.	C5	128
Horsefly, B.C., Can.	D9	138
Horsefly Lake, l., B.C., Can.	D10	138
Horseheads, N.Y., U.S.	B9	114
Horse Islands, is., Nf., Can.	i22	107a
Horsens, Den.	I3	8
Horseshoe Bend, Id., U.S.	G10	136
Horsham, Austl.	K4	76
Horsham, Eng., U.K.	J12	12
Horšovský Týn, Czech Rep.	G8	16
Horten, Nor.	G4	8
Hortobágy, reg., Hung.	B8	26
Hortobágyi Nemzeti Park, p.o.i., Hung.	B8	26
Horton, Ks., U.S.	E2	120
Horton, stm., N.T., Can.	B6	106
Horton Lake, l., N.T., Can.	B6	106
Hortonville, Wi., U.S.	G10	118
Hory, Bela.	F14	10
Hosa'ina, Eth.	F7	62
Hösbach, Ger.	F5	16
Hosedahard, Russia	A9	32
Hosford, Fl., U.S.	G14	122
Hoshāb, Pak.	D9	56
Hoshangābād, India	G6	54
Hoshiārpur, India	C5	54
Hosh Isa, Egypt	H1	58
Hosmer, B.C., Can.	G15	138
Hospers, Ia., U.S.	A2	120
Hospet, India	D3	53
Hospitalet see L'Hospitalet de Llobregat, Spain	C13	20
Hossegor, Fr.	F4	18
Hosston, La., U.S.	E5	122
Hosta Butte, mtn., N.M., U.S.	H8	132
Hoste, Isla, i., Chile	K3	90
Hosūr, India	E3	53
Hotagen, l., Swe.	E5	8
Hotaka-dake, mtn., Japan	C10	40
Hotamış, Tur.	A4	58
Hotan, China	A5	46
Hotazel, S. Afr.	E6	70
Hotevilla, Az., U.S.	H6	132
Hotilovo, Russia	C17	10
Hot'kovo, Russia	G18	10
Hot'kovo, Russia	D21	10
Hot Springs, Ar., U.S.	C5	122
Hot Springs, N.C., U.S.	I3	114
Hot Springs, S.D., U.S.	D9	126
Hot Springs, Va., U.S.	F6	114
Hot Springs National Park see Hot Springs, Ar., U.S.	C5	122
Hot Springs Peak, mtn., Nv., U.S.	B8	134
Hot Sulphur Springs, Co., U.S.	A2	128
Hottah Lake, l., N.T., Can.	B7	106
Hottentotsbaai, b., Nmb.	E2	70
Hotynec, Russia	G18	10
Houaïlou, N. Cal.	m15	79d
Houat, Île de, i., Fr.	G6	14
Houdan, Fr.	F10	14
Houghton, Mi., U.S.	D10	118
Houghton, N.Y., U.S.	B7	114
Houghton Lake, l., Mi., U.S.	D4	112
Houlka, Ms., U.S.	C10	122
Houlton, Me., U.S.	D9	110
Houma, China	D4	42
Houma, Tonga	n13	78e
Houma, La., U.S.	H8	122
Hou-pei see Hubei, state, China	F5	42
Hourtin, Étang d', l., Fr.	D4	18
Housatonic, Ma., U.S.	B12	114
House, N.M., U.S.	G5	128
Houston, B.C., Can.	B4	138
Houston, Mn., U.S.	H7	118
Houston, Mo., U.S.	G6	120
Houston, Tx., U.S.	H3	122
Houston, Lake, res., Tx., U.S.	H3	122
Hout, stm., S. Afr.	C9	70
Houtman Abrolhos, is., Austl.	E2	74
Houxinqiu, China	C5	38
Hovd, Mong.	B3	36
Hovd, Mong.	C5	36
Hovd, stm., Mong.	E16	32
Hove, Eng., U.K.	K12	12
Hoven, S.D., U.S.	B13	126
Hovenweep National Monument, p.o.i., U.S.	F7	132
Hoverla, hora, mtn., Ukr.	A11	26
Hovgaard Ø, i., Grnld.	A22	141
Hövsgöl nuur, l., Mong.	F9	34
Hovu-Aksy, Russia	D16	32
Howar, Wādī, val., Afr.	D5	62
Howard, Austl.	E9	76
Howard, Ks., U.S.	D12	128
Howard, Pa., U.S.	D8	114
Howard, S.D., U.S.	C15	126
Howard City, Mi., U.S.	E4	112
Howard Draw, stm., Tx., U.S.	D6	130
Howard Lake, Mn., U.S.	F4	118
Howe, In., U.S.	G4	112
Howe, Cape, c., Austl.	K7	76
Howe Island, i., On., Can.	D13	112
Howell, Mi., U.S.	B2	114
Howells, Ne., U.S.	F15	126
Howick, S. Afr.	F10	70
Howitt, Mount, mtn., Austl.	K6	76
Howland Island, i., Oc.	C9	72
Howser, B.C., Can.	F13	138
Howson Peak, mtn., B.C., Can.	B3	138
Hoxie, Ar., U.S.	H6	120
Hoxie, Ks., U.S.	B8	128
Höxter, Ger.	E5	16
Hoxtolgay, China	B2	36
Hoy, i., Scot., U.K.	C9	12
Hoyerswerda, Ger.	E10	16
Hoyos, Spain	D4	20
Höytiäinen, l., Fin.	E13	8
Hoyt Lakes, Mn., U.S.	D6	118
Hradec Králové, Czech Rep.	F11	16
Hradzjanka, Bela.	G11	10
Hranice, Czech Rep.	G13	16
Hrèsk, Bela.	G10	10
Hristoforovo, Russia	F22	8
Hrodna, Bela.	G6	10
Hrodna, state, Bela.	G7	10
Hroma, stm., Russia	B17	34
Hron, stm., Slov.	H14	16
Hronov, Czech Rep.	F12	16
Hrubieszów, Pol.	F19	16
Hrustal'nyj, Russia	B11	38
Hsiakuan see Dali, China	F5	36
Hsiamen see Xiamen, China	I7	42
Hsian see Xi'an, China	D3	42
Hsiangt'an see Xiangtan, China	H5	42
Hsiangyang see Xiangfan, China	F4	42
Hsienyang see Xianyang, China	D3	42
Hsi-hseng, Mya.	B3	48
Hsilo, Tai.	J9	42
Hsim, stm., Mya.	B4	48
Hsinchu, Tai.	I9	42
Hsinghua see Xinghua, China	E8	42
Hsingt'ai see Xingtai, China	C6	42
Hsinhailien see Lianyungang, China	D8	42
Hsinhsiang see Xinxiang, China	D5	42
Hsining see Xining, China	D5	36
Hsinking see Changchun, China	C6	38
Hsinp'u see Lianyungang, China	D8	42
Hsintien, Tai.	I9	42
Hsinyang see Xinyang, China	E6	42
Hsipaw, Mya.	A3	48
Hsüanhua see Xuanhua, China	A6	42
Hsüch'ang see Xuchang, China	D5	42
Hsüchou see Xuzhou, China	D7	42
Hua'an, China	I7	42
Huab, stm., Nmb.	B2	70
Huacaraje, Bol.	B4	90
Huacho, Peru	F2	84
Huachuca City, Az., U.S.	L6	132
Huadian, China	C7	38
Huading Shan, mtn., China	G9	42
Hua Hin, Thai.	F4	48
Huai, stm., China	C6	42
Huai, stm., China	E8	42
Huai'an, China	E8	42
Huai'an, China	A6	42
Huaibin, China	E6	42
Huaicheng see Huai'an, China	E8	42
Huaidezhen, China	C6	38
Huaiji, China	I5	42
Huailai, China	A6	42
Huainan, China	E7	42
Huairou, China	A7	42
Huaite see Gongzhuling, China	C6	38
Huaiyang, China	E6	42
Huai Yot, Thai.	I4	48
Huaiyuan, China	E7	42
Huajuapan de León, Mex.	G10	100
Hualahuises, Mex.	C9	100
Hualalai, vol., Hi., U.S.	D6	78a
Hualañé, Chile	G2	92
Hualfín, Arg.	C4	92
Hualien, Tai.	J9	42
Huallaga, stm., Peru	E2	84
Huallanca, Peru	E2	84
Hualong, China	D5	36
Huambo, Ang.	C2	68
Huamei Shan, mtn., China	I5	42
Huan, stm., China	F6	42
Huanan, China	B11	36
Huancabamba, Peru	E2	84
Huancané, Peru	G4	84
Huancavelica, Peru	F2	84
Huancayo, Peru	F2	84
Huang (Yellow), stm., China	D8	36
Huangchuan, China	E6	42
Huanggai Hu, l., China	G5	42
Huanggang, China	F6	42
Huanggangliang, mtn., China	C2	38
Huanghua, China	B7	42
Huangjinbu, China	G7	42
Huangling, China	D3	42
Huanglong, China	D3	42
Huangnihe, China	C7	38
Huangpi, China	F6	42
Huangqi, China	H8	42
Huangshahe, China	H4	42
Huangshan, China	G8	42
Huangshan see Guangming Ding, mtn., China	F7	42
Huangshi, China	F6	42
Huangshi, China	G4	42
Huangtang Hu, l., China	G6	42
Huangtuliangzi, China	A8	42
Huanguelén, Arg.	H6	92
Huangxian, China	C9	42
Huangyan, China	G9	42
Huangyuan, China	D5	36
Huangzhong, China	D5	36
Huangzhu, China	L4	42
Huanjiang, China	I3	42
Huanren, China	D6	38
Huánuco, Peru	E2	84
Huanuni, Bol.	C3	90
Huanxian, China	C2	42
Huara, Chile	C3	90
Huaral, Peru	F2	84
Huaraz, Peru	E2	84
Huariaca, Peru	F2	84
Huarmey, Peru	F2	84
Huarong, China	G5	42
Huasaga, stm., S.A.	I3	86
Hua Sai, Thai.	H5	48
Huascarán, Nevado, mtn., Peru	E2	84
Huasco, Chile	D2	92
Huasco, stm., Chile	D2	92
Huatabampo, Mex.	B4	100
Huating, China	D2	42
Huatong, China	A9	42
Huauchinango, Mex.	E9	100
Huautla, Mex.	C5	96
Huaxian, China	J5	42
Huaxian, China	D3	42
Huaxian, China	D6	42
Huaynamota, stm., Mex.	D6	100
Huazamota, Mex.	D6	100
Huazhou, China	K4	42
Hubbard, Ia., U.S.	B4	120
Hubbard Creek Reservoir, l., Tx., U.S.	B8	130
Hubbard Lake, l., Mi., U.S.	D6	112
Hubbards, N.S., Can.	F12	110
Hubbell, Mi., U.S.	D10	118
Hubei, state, China	F5	42
Huberdeau, Qc., Can.	E2	110
Hubli-Dhārwār, India	D2	53
Hubuleng, China	A4	42
Huchow see Huzhou, China	F9	42
Huckleberry Mountain, mtn., Or., U.S.	G4	136
Hucknall, Eng., U.K.	H11	12
Huddersfield, Eng., U.K.	H11	12
Huddinge, Swe.	G8	8
Huder, China	A9	36
Hudiksvall, Swe.	F7	8
Hudson, Fl., U.S.	H3	116
Hudson, Ia., U.S.	B5	120
Hudson, N.Y., U.S.	H3	110
Hudson, N.C., U.S.	I4	114
Hudson, Oh., U.S.	C4	114
Hudson, S.D., U.S.	H2	118
Hudson, Wy., U.S.	E4	126
Hudson, stm., U.S.	G16	112
Hudson, Baie d' see Hudson Bay, b., Can.	C13	106
Hudson Bay, Sk., Can.	B11	124
Hudson Bay, b., Can.	C13	106
Hudson Falls, N.Y., U.S.	G3	110
Hudson's Hope, B.C., Can.	D6	106
Hudson Strait, strt., Can.	C16	106
Hudžand, Taj.	A10	56
Hue, Viet.	D8	48
Huebra, stm., Spain	D4	20
Huehuetenango, Guat.	E2	102
Huejutla de Reyes, Mex.	E9	100
Huelgoat, Fr.	F5	14
Huelva, Spain	G3	20
Huelva, co., Spain	G4	20
Huentelauquén, Chile	E2	92
Huércal-Overa, Spain	G8	20
Huerfano, stm., Co., U.S.	C4	128
Huerlumada, China	B13	54
Huerva, stm., Spain	C9	20
Huesca, Spain	B10	20
Huesca, co., Spain	B10	20
Huéscar, Spain	G8	20
Huetamo de Núñez, Mex.	F8	100
Hueytown, Al., U.S.	D11	122
Hufrat an-Naḥās, Sudan	F4	62
Hughenden, Austl.	C4	76
Hughes, Ak., U.S.	C9	140
Hughes, Ar., U.S.	C8	122
Hughes Springs, Tx., U.S.	E4	122
Hugh Keenleyside Dam, dam, B.C., Can.	G12	138
Hughson, Ca., U.S.	F5	134
Hugh Town, Eng., U.K.	L6	12
Hugli, stm., India	G12	54
Hugo, Co., U.S.	B5	128
Hugo, Ok., U.S.	C3	122
Hugoton, Ks., U.S.	D7	128
Huhar, stm., China	B4	38
Huhehaote see Hohhot, China	A4	42
Huhehot see Hohhot, China	A4	42
Huichang, China	I6	42
Huicheng see Huilai, China	J7	42
Hŭich'ŏn, Kor., N.	D7	38
Huichou see Huizhou, China	J6	42
Huila, state, Col.	F4	86
Huila, Nevado del, vol., Col.	F3	86
Huilai, China	J7	42
Huili, China	F5	36
Huillapima, Arg.	D4	92
Huimin, China	C7	42
Huinan, China	C7	38
Huisachal, Mex.	H6	130
Huishui, China	H2	42
Huisne, stm., Fr.	F9	14
Huitong, China	H3	42
Huitzo, Mex.	G10	100
Huitzuco de los Figueroa, Mex.	F9	100
Huixian, China	E2	42
Huixian, China	D5	42
Huixtla, Mex.	H12	100
Huize, China	F5	36
Huizhou, China	J6	42
Hŭksan-chedo, is., Kor., S.	G6	38
Hukuntsi, Bots.	D5	70
Hulan, China	B7	38
Hulan Ergi, China	B9	36
Hulbert, Mi., U.S.	B4	112
Hulett, Wy., U.S.	C8	126
Hulga, stm., Russia	B10	32
Hulin, China	B11	36
Hulin, stm., China	B4	38
Huliu, stm., China	A6	42
Hull, Qc., Can.	C14	112
Hull, Il., U.S.	E6	120
Hull, Ia., U.S.	H2	118
Hullo, Est.	A6	10
Hulun see Hailar, China	B8	36
Hulun Nur, l., China	B8	36
Huma, China	F14	34
Huma, Tonga	o15	78e
Humacao, P.R.	B4	104a
Humahuaca, Arg.	D3	90
Humaitá, Braz.	E5	84
Humaitá, Para.	C8	92
Humansdorp, S. Afr.	I7	70
Humansville, Mo., U.S.	G4	120
Humara, Jabal al-, hill, Sudan	D6	62
Humbe, Ang.	D1	68
Humber, stm., Eng., U.K.	H12	12
Humbird, Wi., U.S.	G8	118
Humboldt, Sk., Can.	B8	124
Humboldt, Az., U.S.	I4	132
Humboldt, Il., U.S.	E9	120
Humboldt, Ia., U.S.	B3	120
Humboldt, Ne., U.S.	D2	120
Humboldt, S.D., U.S.	D15	126
Humboldt, stm., Nv., U.S.	C7	134
Humboldt, North Fork, stm., Nv., U.S.	B1	132
Humboldt, South Fork, stm., Nv., U.S.	C1	132
Humboldt Gletscher, ice, Grnld.	B13	141
Humboldt Lake, l., Nv., U.S.	D7	134
Hume, Ca., U.S.	G7	134
Hume, Lake, res., Austl.	J6	76
Humeburn, Austl.	F5	76
Humenné, Slov.	H17	16
Humeston, Ia., U.S.	D4	120
Hummi, ozero, l., Russia	F16	34
Humphrey, Ne., U.S.	F15	126
Humphreys, Mount, mtn., Ca., U.S.	F7	134
Humphreys Peak, mtn., Az., U.S.	H5	132
Humpolec, Czech Rep.	G11	16
Humpty Doo, Austl.	B6	74
Hūn, Libya	B3	62
Hun, stm., China	D5	38
Hun, stm., China	D6	38
Húnaflói, b., Ice.	j29	8a
Hunan, state, China	H4	42
Hunchun, China	C9	38
Hundred, W.V., U.S.	E5	114
Hunedoara, Rom.	D9	26
Hunedoara, state, Rom.	C9	26
Hünfeld, Ger.	F5	16
Hungary, ctry., Eur.	B6	26
Hungchiang see Hongjiang, China	H4	42
Hŭngdŏki-dong, Kor., N.	E7	38
Hungerford, Austl.	G5	76
Hungerford, Tx., U.S.	H2	122
Hungry Horse Dam, dam, Mt., U.S.	B13	136
Hungry Horse Reservoir, res., Mt., U.S.	B12	136
Hung Yen, Viet.	B8	48
Hunjiang, China	C7	38
Hunlen Falls, wtfl, B.C., Can.	D5	138
Hunsberge, mts., Nmb.	E3	70
Hunsrück, mts., Ger.	G3	16
Hunsūr, India	E3	53
Hunte, stm., Ger.	D4	16
Hunter, N.D., U.S.	D1	118
Hunter, stm., Austl.	I8	76
Hunter Island, i., Austl.	n12	77a
Hunter Island, i., B.C., Can.	E2	138
Hunter Mountain, mtn., N.Y., U.S.	B11	114
Hunter River, P.E., Can.	D13	110
Hunters, Wa., U.S.	B8	136
Hunters Bay, b., Mya.	C1	48
Huntingdon, Qc., Can.	E2	110
Huntingdon, Eng., U.K.	I12	12
Huntingdon, Pa., U.S.	D7	114
Huntingdon, Tn., U.S.	I9	120
Huntington, In., U.S.	H4	112
Huntington, Tx., U.S.	F4	122
Huntington, Ut., U.S.	D5	132
Huntington, W.V., U.S.	F3	114
Huntington Beach, Ca., U.S.	J7	134
Huntland, Tn., U.S.	B12	122
Huntley, Mt., U.S.	B4	126
Huntly, N.Z.	C6	80
Huntly, Scot., U.K.	D10	12
Huntsville, On., Can.	C10	112
Huntsville, Al., U.S.	C12	122
Huntsville, Mo., U.S.	E5	120
Huntsville, Tn., U.S.	H13	120
Huntsville, Tx., U.S.	G3	122
Huntsville, Ut., U.S.	B5	132
Hunyuan, China	B5	42
Huong Hoa, Viet.	D8	48
Huon Gulf, b., Pap. N. Gui.	b4	79a
Huon Peninsula, pen., Pap. N. Gui.	b4	79a
Huonville, Austl.	o13	77a
Huoqiu, China	E7	42
Huoshan, China	F7	42
Huoxian, China	C4	42
Hurd, Cape, c., On., Can.	C8	112
Hüren Tovon uul, mtn., Mong.	C4	36
Hure Qi, China	C4	38
Hurghada, Egypt	K4	58
Hurley, N.M., U.S.	K8	132
Hurley, S.D., U.S.	D15	126
Hurley, Wi., U.S.	E8	118
Huron, Ca., U.S.	G5	134
Huron, Oh., U.S.	C3	114
Huron, S.D., U.S.	C14	126
Huron, stm., Mi., U.S.	B2	114
Huron, Lake, l., N.A.	D7	112
Huron Mountains, hills, Mi., U.S.	B2	112
Hurricane, Ut., U.S.	F3	132
Hurstbridge, Austl.	K5	76
Hurtado, stm., Chile	E2	92
Hurtsboro, Al., U.S.	E13	122
Hurunui, stm., N.Z.	F5	80
Husainīwāla, India	C5	54
Húsavík, Far. Is.	n34	8b
Húsavík, Ice.	j31	8a
Hushitai, China	C5	38
Huşi, Rom.	C15	26
Huslia, Ak., U.S.	C8	140
Hussar, Ab., Can.	E18	138
Husum, Ger.	B4	16
Hutag, Mong.	B5	36
Hutanopan, Indon.	C1	50
Hutchinson, S. Afr.	G6	70
Hutchinson, Ks., U.S.	C11	128
Hutchinson, Mn., U.S.	G4	118
Hutch Mountain, mtn., Az., U.S.	I5	132
Hutsonville, Il., U.S.	E10	120
Huttig, Ar., U.S.	D6	122
Hutto, Tx., U.S.	D10	130
Hutuo, stm., China	B5	42
Huwei, Tai.	J9	42
Huxi, China	H6	42
Huxian, China	D3	42
Huxley, Ab., Can.	E17	138
Huy, Bel.	D14	14
Huzhen, China	G9	42
Huzhou, China	F9	42
Hvannadalshnúkur, mtn., Ice.	k31	8a
Hvar, Cro.	G13	22
Hvar, Otok, i., Cro.	G13	22
Hveragerði, Ice.	k29	8a
Hvolsvöllur, Ice.	l29	8a
Hwainan see Huainan, China	E7	42
Hwange, Zimb.	D4	68
Hwang Ho see Huang, stm., China	D8	36
Hwangju-ŭp, Kor., N.	E6	38
Hwangshih see Huangshi, China	F6	42
Hyannis, Ma., U.S.	C15	114
Hyannis, Ne., U.S.	F11	126
Hyargas nuur, l., Mong.	B3	36
Hyattville, Wy., U.S.	C5	126
Hyden, Austl.	F3	74
Hyden, Ky., U.S.	G2	114
Hyde Park, Guy.	B6	84
Hyde Park, N.Y., U.S.	C12	114
Hyde Park, Vt., U.S.	F4	110
Hyderābād, India	C4	53
Hyderābād, Pak.	F2	54
Hydra see Ýdra, i., Grc.	F6	28
Hydraulic, B.C., Can.	D9	138
Hydro, Ok., U.S.	F10	128
Hydrographers Passage, strt., Austl.	C8	76
Hyères, Fr.	F12	18
Hyères, Îles d', is., Fr.	G12	18
Hyesan, Kor., N.	D8	38
Hyland, stm., Can.	C5	106
Hyndman, Pa., U.S.	E7	114
Hyndman Peak, mtn., Id., U.S.	G12	136
Hyōgo, state, Japan	D7	40
Hyrum, Ut., U.S.	B5	132
Hysham, Mt., U.S.	A5	126
Hythe, Eng., U.K.	J13	12
Hyūga, Japan	G4	40
Hyūga-nada, Japan	G4	40
Hyvinge see Hyvinkää, Fin.	F11	8
Hyvinkää, Fin.	F11	8

I

Name	Map Ref.	Page
Iaciara, Braz.	H2	88
Iaco (Yaco), stm., S.A.	F4	84
Iaçu, Braz.	G5	88
Iaeger, W.V., U.S.	G4	114
Ialomița, state, Rom.	E14	26
Ialomița, stm., Rom.	E13	26
Ialomiței, Balta, sw., Rom.	E14	26
Iamonia, Lake, l., Fl., U.S.	F1	116
Iapu, Braz.	J4	88
Iargara, Mol.	C15	26
Iași, Rom.	B14	26
Iași, state, Rom.	B14	26
Iatt, Lake, res., La., U.S.	F6	122
Ib, stm., India	G10	54
Iba, Phil.	C2	52
Ibadan, Nig.	H5	64
Ibagué, Col.	E4	86
Ibaiti, Braz.	A12	92
Ibănești, Rom.	A13	26
Ibapah Peak, mtn., Ut., U.S.	D3	132
Ibar, stm., Yugo.	F7	26
Ibaraki, state, Japan	C13	40
Ibarra, Ec.	G2	86
Ibarreta, Arg.	B8	92
Ibb, Yemen	G5	56
Ibbenbüren, Ger.	D3	16
Ibembo, D.R.C.	D4	66
Iberá, Esteros del, sw., Arg.	D8	92
Iberia, Mo., U.S.	F5	120
Iberian Mountains see Ibérico, Sistema, mts., Spain	D8	20
Iberian Peninsula, pen., Eur.	D12	4
Ibérico, Sistema (Iberian Mountains), mts., Spain	D8	20
Ibiá, Braz.	J2	88
Ibiapina, Braz.	B5	88
Ibicaraí, Braz.	H6	88
Ibicuí, Braz.	H5	88
Ibicuí, stm., Braz.	D9	92
Ibiquera, Braz.	G5	88
Ibiraçu, Braz.	J5	88
Ibirapuã, Braz.	I5	88
Ibirapuitã, stm., Braz.	D10	92
Ibirataia, Braz.	H6	88
Ibirubá, Braz.	D11	92
Ibitiara, Braz.	G4	88
Ibitinga, Braz.	K1	88
Ibiza see Eivissa, Spain	F12	20
Ibiza see Eivissa, i., Spain	F12	20
Ibotirama, Braz.	G4	88
İbriktepe, Tur.	B9	28
Ibshawâi, Egypt	I1	58
Ibusuki, Japan	H3	40
Ica, Peru	F2	84
Içá (Putumayo), stm., S.A.	D4	84
Icabarú, stm., Ven.	E10	86
Icacos Point, c., Trin.	s11	105f
Icamaquã, stm., Braz.	D10	92
Icamole, Mex.	I7	130
Içana, Braz.	G8	86
Içana (Isana), stm., S.A.	G7	86
Icaño, Arg.	D5	92
Icatu, Braz.	B3	88
Iceberg Pass, p., Co., U.S.	G7	126
İçel (Mersin), Tur.	B5	58
İçel, state, Tur.	B4	58
Iceland, ctry., Eur.	k30	8a
Iceland Basin, unds.	C11	144
Ice Mountain, mtn., B.C., Can.	B9	138
Ichaikaronji, India	C2	53
Ichchāpuram, India	B7	53
Ichikawa, Japan	D12	40
Ichinomiya, Japan	D9	40
Ichkeul, Lac, l., Tun.	G3	24
Ichnia, Ukr.	D4	32
Ich'un see Yichun, China	B10	36
Ičinskaja Sopka, vulkan, vol., Russia	E20	34
Icó, Braz.	D6	88
Icy Cape, c., Ak., U.S.	B7	140
Ida, Mount see Ídhi Óros, mtn., Grc.	H7	28
Idabel, Ok., U.S.	D4	122
Ida Grove, Ia., U.S.	B2	120
Idah, Nig.	H6	64
Idaho, state, U.S.	G12	136
Idaho City, Id., U.S.	G11	136
Idaho Falls, Id., U.S.	G14	136
Idaho National Engineering Laboratory, sci., Id., U.S.	G14	136
Idalou, Tx., U.S.	H7	128
Idanha-a-Nova, Port.	E3	20
Idāppādi, India	F3	53
Idar, India	G4	54
Idar-Oberstein, Ger.	G3	16
Idelès, Alg.	E6	64
Ídhi Óros, mtn., Grc.	H7	28
Idi, Indon.	J3	48
Idiofa, D.R.C.	F3	66
Idku, Bahra el-, l., Egypt	G1	58
Idlib, Syria	C7	58
Idlib, state, Syria	C7	58
Ídolo, Isla del, i., Mex.	E10	100
Idoûkâl-en-Taghès, mtn., Niger	F6	64
Idre, Swe.	F5	8
Idrija, Slvn.	D11	22
Idutywa, S. Afr.	H9	70
Iecava, stm., Lat.	D7	10
Ieper, Bel.	D11	14
Ierápetra, Grc.	H8	28
Ierzu, Italy	E3	24
Iesolo, Italy	E9	22
Ifakara, Tan.	F7	66
Ife, Nig.	H5	64
Iferouâne, Niger	F6	64
Iferten see Yverdon-les-Bains, Switz.	D3	22
Ifôghas, Adrar des, mts., Afr.	F5	64
Igan, Malay.	B7	50
Igan, stm., Malay.	B7	50
Iganga, Ug.	D6	66
Igaporã, Braz.	G4	88
Igara, Braz.	F5	88
Igara Paraná, stm., Col.	H5	86
Igarapé-Açu, Braz.	D8	84
Igarapé-Miri, Braz.	B1	88
Igarka, Russia	A15	32
Igatpuri, India	B1	53
Igboho, Nig.	H5	64
Igharghar, Oued, stm., Alg.	D6	64
Igiugig, Ak., U.S.	E8	140
Iglesias, Italy	E2	24
Iglesias, Cerro las, mtn., Mex.	B5	100
Iglesiente, reg., Italy	E2	24
Igloolik, N.T., Can.	B14	106
ʿIgma, Gebel el-, mts., Egypt	I4	58
Ignacio, Co., U.S.	F9	132
Ignalina, Lith.	E9	10
Ignaței, Mol.	B15	26
Igoumenítsa, Grc.	D3	28
Igra, Russia	C8	32
Iguaçu (Iguazú), stm., S.A.	B10	92
Iguaçu, Parque Nacional do, p.o.i., Braz.	B11	92
Iguaí, Braz.	H5	88
Iguala, Mex.	F9	100
Igualada, Spain	C12	20
Iguana, stm., Ven.	D9	86
Iguape, Braz.	B14	92
Iguape, stm., Braz.	B13	92
Iguassu Falls, wtfl, S.A.	B10	92
Iguatemi, stm., Braz.	A10	92
Iguatu, Braz.	D6	88
Iguazú (Iguaçu), stm., S.A.	B10	92
Iguazú, Parque Nacional, p.o.i., S.A.	B10	92
Iguéla, Gabon	E1	66
Iguéla, Lagune, b., Gabon	E1	66
Iguîdi, ʿErg, sand, Afr.	D3	64
Igžej, Russia	D18	32
Iharaña, Madag.	C9	68
Iheya-shima, i., Japan	I18	39a
Ihnâsiya el-Madina, Egypt	I1	58
Ihosy, Madag.	E8	68
Ihtiman, Blg.	G10	26
Iida, Japan	D10	40
Iisalmi, Fin.	E12	8
Iiyama, Japan	C11	40
Iizuka, Japan	F3	40
Ijâfene, des., Maur.	E3	64
Ijebu-Ode, Nig.	H5	64
IJmuiden, Neth.	B13	14
IJssel, stm., Neth.	B15	14
IJsselmeer, l., Neth.	B14	14
Ijuí, Braz.	D11	92
Ijuí, stm., Braz.	D10	92
Ika, Russia	C19	32
Ikali, D.R.C.	E4	66
Ikaría, i., Grc.	F9	28
Ikatskij hrebet, mts., Russia	F11	34
Ikeda, Japan	E6	40
Ikej, Russia	D17	32
Ikeja, Nig.	H5	64
Ikela, D.R.C.	E4	66
Ikerre, Nig.	H6	64
İkizce, Tur.	D15	28
Ikom, Nig.	H6	64
Ikot-Ekpene, Nig.	H6	64
Ikuno, Japan	D7	40
Ikurangi, hill, Cook Is.	a26	78j
Ila, Nig.	H6	64
Ilagan, Phil.	B3	52
Ilaiyānkudi, India	G4	53
Īlām, Iran	C6	56
Ilām, Nepal	E11	54
Ilan, Tai.	I9	42
Ilanskij, Russia	C17	32
Ilaro, Nig.	H5	64
Iława, Pol.	C15	16
Ilbenge, Russia	D13	34
Île-à-la-Crosse, Sk., Can.	D9	106
Ilebo, D.R.C.	E4	66
Île-de-France, hist. reg., Fr.	E11	14
Île de France, i., Grnld.	B22	141
Île-du-Prince-Édouard see Prince Edward Island, state, Can.	D13	110
Ilek, stm., Asia	D8	32
Ilesha, Nig.	H5	64
Îles Loyauté, state, N. Cal.	m16	79d
Île Tintamarre, i., Anguilla	A2	105a
Ilevskij Pogost, Russia	F20	8
Ileza, Russia	F20	8
Ilfracombe, Austl.	D5	76
Ilfracombe, Eng., U.K.	J8	12
Ilhabela, Braz.	L3	88
Ilha Grande, Baía da, b., Braz.	L3	88
Ilha Solteira, Represa de, res., Braz.	D6	90
Ilhea Point, c., Nmb.	C2	70
Ilhéus, Braz.	H6	88
Ilia, Rom.	D9	26
Iliamna, Ak., U.S.	E8	140
Iliamna Lake, l., Ak., U.S.	D9	140
Il'ič, Kaz.	F11	32
Ilicinea, Braz.	K3	88
Iliff, Co., U.S.	G9	126
Iligan, Phil.	F5	52
Iligan Bay, b., Phil.	F4	52
Iliniza, vol., Ec.	H2	86
Ilion, N.Y., U.S.	A10	114
Ilir, Russia	C18	32
Ilizi, Alg.	D6	64
Il'ja, Bela.	F10	10
Iljino, Russia	E14	10
Iljinskij, Russia	G17	34
Iljinskoe, Russia	D19	10
Iljinsko-Podomskoe, Russia	F23	8
Il'iny gory, hills, Russia	D17	10
Ilkal, India	D2	53
Ilkley, Eng., U.K.	H11	12
Illampu, Nevado, mtn., Bol.	C3	90
Illana Bay, b., Phil.	G4	52
Illapel, Chile	E2	92
Ille-et-Vilaine, state, Fr.	F7	14
Illéla, Niger	G6	64
Iller, stm., Ger.	I6	16
Illertissen, Ger.	H6	16
Illescas, Mex.	D7	100
Illichivs'k, Ukr.	C17	26
Illimani, Nevado, mtn., Bol.	C3	90
Illinois, state, U.S.	D8	120
Illinois, stm., U.S.	B3	122
Illinois, stm., Il., U.S.	E7	120
Illinois, stm., Or., U.S.	H3	136
Il'men', ozero, l., Russia	B14	10
Ilo, Peru	G3	84
Iloilo, Phil.	E4	52
Ilomantsi, Fin.	E14	8
Ilorin, Nig.	H5	64
Il'pyrskij, Russia	D21	34
Ilūkste, Lat.	E9	10
Ilulissat see Jakobshavn, Grnld.	D15	141
Ilwaki, Indon.	G8	44
Ilwŏl-san, mtn., Kor., S.	C1	40
Imabari, Japan	E5	40
Imaichi, Japan	C12	40
Imandra, ozero, l., Russia	C14	8
Imari, Japan	F2	40
Imaruí, Braz.	D13	92
Imaruí, Lagoa do, l., Braz.	D13	92
Imatra, Fin.	F13	8
Imavere, Est.	B8	10
Imbabura, state, Ec.	G2	86
Imbituba, Braz.	D13	92
Imeni Cjurupy, Russia	E21	10
Imeni Kirova, Russia	E14	34
Imeni Poliny Osipenko, Russia	F16	34
Imeni Stepana Razina, Russia	I21	8
Imeni Željabova, Russia	A19	10
Īmī, Eth.	F8	62
Imías, Cuba	B10	102
Imilac, Chile	B3	92
Imlay, Nv., U.S.	C7	134
Imlay City, Mi., U.S.	E6	112
Immenstadt, Ger.	I6	16
Immokalee, Fl., U.S.	J4	116
Imnaha, stm., Or., U.S.	E10	136
Imola, Italy	F8	22
Imonda, Pap. N. Gui.	a3	79a
Impasugong, Phil.	F5	52
Imperatriz, Braz.	C2	88
Imperia, Italy	G5	22
Imperial, Sk., Can.	C8	124
Imperial, Ca., U.S.	K10	134
Imperial, Tx., U.S.	C5	130
Imperial Beach, Ca., U.S.	K8	134
Imperial Dam, dam, U.S.	K2	132
Imperial de Aragón, Canal, can., Spain	C9	20
Imperial Valley, val., Ca., U.S.	E5	98
Impfondo, Congo	D3	66
Imphāl, India	D7	46
Imroz, Tur.	C8	28
Imst, Aus.	C7	22
Imuris, Mex.	F7	98
Ina, Japan	D10	40
Ina, Il., U.S.	F9	120
Inajá, Braz.	E7	88
I-n-Amenas, Alg.	D6	64
Iñapari, Peru	F4	84
Inarajan, Guam	j10	78c
Inari, Fin.	B12	8
Inarigda, Russia	B19	32
Inarijärvi, l., Fin.	B12	8
Inawashiro-ko, l., Japan	B12	40
Inca, Spain	E13	20
Inca de Oro, Chile	C3	92
Incahuasi, Cerro de, mtn., S.A.	C3	92
İnce Burun, c., Tur.	C10	28
İncekum Burnu, c., Tur.	B4	58
Inchelium, Wa., U.S.	B8	136
Inch'ŏn, Kor., S.	F7	38
İncirliova, Tur.	F10	28
Incomati (Komati), stm., Afr.	E10	70
Incudine, Monte, mtn., Fr.	H15	18
Incy, Russia	D19	8
Indaiá, stm., Braz.	J3	88
Indalsälven, stm., Swe.	E6	8
Indé, Mex.	I2	130
Independence, Ca., U.S.	G7	134
Independence, Ia., U.S.	B6	120
Independence, Ks., U.S.	G2	120
Independence, Ky., U.S.	F13	120
Independence, La., U.S.	G8	122
Independence, Mo., U.S.	E3	120
Independence, Va., U.S.	H4	114
Independence, Wi., U.S.	G7	118
Independence Fjord, b., Grnld.	A20	141
Independencia, Bol.	C3	90
Independência, Braz.	C5	88
Inderborskij, Kaz.	E8	32
Indi, India	C2	53
India, ctry., Asia	D4	46
Indialantic, Fl., U.S.	H5	116
Indiana, Pa., U.S.	D6	114
Indiana, state, U.S.	D11	120
Indiana Dunes National Lakeshore, p.o.i., In., U.S.	G2	112
Indianapolis, In., U.S.	I3	112
Indian Bayou, stm., Ar., U.S.	C7	122
Indian Church, Belize	D3	102
Indian Head, Sk., Can.	D10	124
Indian Lake, N.Y., U.S.	G2	110
Indian Lake, l., On., Can.	A7	112
Indian Lake, l., Mi., U.S.	B3	112
Indian Ocean	K11	142
Indianola, Ia., U.S.	C4	120

I • 26 Indi-Jark

Name	Map Ref.	Page
Indianola, Ms., U.S.	D8	122
Indianola, Ne., U.S.	A8	128
Indian Peak, mtn., Ut., U.S.	E3	132
Indian River, Mi., U.S.	C5	112
Indian Rock, mtn., Wa., U.S.	E6	136
Indiantown, Fl., U.S.	I5	116
Indiera Alta, P.R.	B2	104a
Indiga, Russia	C23	8
Indigirka, stm., Russia	C18	34
Indin, Mya.	H14	54
Indio, Ca., U.S.	J9	134
Indira Gandhi Canal, can., India	E4	54
Indispensable Strait, strt., Sol. Is.	e9	79b
Indochina, reg., Asia	D7	48
Indonesia, ctry., Asia	J16	30
Indore, India	G5	54
Indragiri, stm., Indon.	D2	50
Indramayu, Indon.	G6	50
Indrāvati, stm., India	B5	53
Indravati Tiger Reserve, p.o.i., India	B5	53
Indre, state, Fr.	C7	18
Indre, stm., Fr.	G10	14
Indre-et-Loire, state, Fr.	G9	14
Indus, stm., Asia	D2	46
Industry, Tx., U.S.	H2	122
İnece, Tur.	B10	28
In Ecker, Alg.	E6	64
İnegöl, Tur.	C12	28
Ineu, Rom.	C8	26
Inez, Ky., U.S.	G3	114
Inez, Tx., U.S.	F11	130
Inferior, Laguna, b., Mex.	G11	100
Infiernillo, Canal del, strt., Mex.	G6	98
Infiernillo, Presa del, res., Mex.	F7	100
Ing, stm., Thai.	C5	48
Ingá, Braz.	D8	88
Ingabu, Mya.	D2	48
Ingal, Niger	F6	64
Ingall Point, c., On., Can.	B10	118
Ingelheim, Ger.	G4	16
Ingende, D.R.C.	E3	66
Ingeniero Jacobacci, Arg.	H3	90
Ingeniero Luiggi, Arg.	G5	92
Ingham, Austl.	B6	76
Inglefield Land, reg., Grnld.	B12	141
Ingleside, Tx., U.S.	G10	130
Inglewood, Austl.	G8	76
Inglewood, Austl.	K4	76
Inglewood, Ca., U.S.	J7	134
Inglis, Mb., Can.	D12	124
Ingolf Fjord, b., Grnld.	A22	141
Ingolstadt, Ger.	H7	16
Ingonish, N.S., Can.	D16	110
Ingrāj Bāzār, India	F12	54
Ingrid Christensen Coast, cst., Ant.	B12	81
In Guezzam, Alg.	F6	64
Ingušetija, state, Russia	F6	32
Ingushetia see Ingušetija, state, Russia	F6	32
Inhaca, Ilha da, i., Moz.	E11	70
Inhambane, Moz.	C12	70
Inhambane, state, Moz.	C12	70
Inhambane, Baía de, b., Moz.	C12	70
Inhambupe, Braz.	F6	88
Inhaminga, Moz.	D5	68
Inhapim, Braz.	J4	88
Inharrime, Moz.	D12	70
Inhassoro, Moz.	B12	70
Inhuma, Braz.	D5	88
Inhumas, Braz.	I1	88
Inimutaba, Braz.	J3	88
Ining see Yining, China	F14	32
Inírida, stm., Col.	F7	86
Inis see Ennis, Ire.	I3	12
Inis Córthaidh see Enniscorthy, Ire.	I6	12
Inishbofin, i., Ire.	H2	12
Inishmore, i., Ire.	H3	12
Inishowen, pen., Ire.	F5	12
Inishturk, i., Ire.	H2	12
Inja, Russia	E17	34
Inja, stm., Russia	D18	34
Injune, Austl.	E7	76
Inkom, Id., U.S.	H14	136
Inkster, N.D., U.S.	F16	124
Inland Lake, l., Mb., Can.	B14	124
Inland Sea see Seto-naikai, Japan	E5	40
Inle Lake, l., Mya.	B3	48
Inman, Ks., U.S.	C11	128
Inman Mills, S.C., U.S.	A3	116
Inn, stm., Eur.	B10	22
Innamincka, Austl.	F3	76
Inner Channel, strt., Belize	D3	102
Inner Hebrides, is., Scot., U.K.	E6	12
Inner Mongolia see Nei Monggol, state, China	C7	36
Inner Sister Island, i., Austl.	m13	77a
Innisfail, Austl.	A6	76
Innisfail, Ab., Can.	D17	138
Innisfree, Ab., Can.	C19	138
Innokentevka, Russia	G16	34
Innoko, stm., Ak., U.S.	D8	140
Innoshima, Japan	E6	40
Innsbruck, Aus.	C8	22
Innviertel, reg., Aus.	B10	22
Inola, Ok., U.S.	H2	120
Inongo, D.R.C.	E3	66
İnönü, Tur.	D13	28
Inowrocław, Pol.	D14	16
In Salah, Alg.	D5	64
Instow, Sk., Can.	E5	124
Inta, Russia	A10	32
Intendente Alvear, Arg.	G6	92
İntepe, Tur.	D9	28
Interlaken, Switz.	D4	22
Interlândia, Braz.	I1	88
International Falls, Mn., U.S.	C5	118
Inthanon, Doi, mtn., Thai.	C4	48
Intiyaco, Arg.	D7	92
Intracoastal Waterway, strt., U.S.	L5	116
Intracoastal Waterway, strt., U.S.	H10	130
Intu, Indon.	D9	50
Inubō-saki, c., Japan	D13	40
Inukjuak, Qc., Can.	D15	106
Inuvik, N.T., Can.	B4	106
Inverbervie, Scot., U.K.	E10	12
Invercargill, N.Z.	H3	80
Inverell, Austl.	G8	76
Inverloch, Austl.	L5	76
Invermay, Sk., Can.	C10	124
Invermere, B.C., Can.	F14	138
Inverness, N.S., Can.	D15	110
Inverness, Scot., U.K.	D8	12
Inverness, Ca., U.S.	E3	134
Inverness, Fl., U.S.	H3	116
Inverurie, Scot., U.K.	D10	12
Inverway, Austl.	C5	74
Investigator Strait, strt., Austl.	G7	74
Inwood, Mb., Can.	D16	124
Inyangani, mtn., Zimb.	D5	68
Inyathi, Zimb.	D4	68
Inyo, Mount, mtn., Ca., U.S.	G8	134
Inyokern, Ca., U.S.	H8	134
Inyo Mountains, mts., Ca., U.S.	G7	134
Inzana Lake, l., B.C., Can.	B6	138
Ioánnina, Grc.	D3	28
Iokanga, stm., Russia	C18	8
Iola, Ks., U.S.	G2	120
Ioma, Pap. N. Gui.	b4	79a
Iona, Ang.	D1	68
Iona, N.S., Can.	D16	110
Iona, Id., U.S.	G15	136
Iona, i., Scot., U.K.	E6	12
Ione, Ca., U.S.	E5	134
Ione, Wa., U.S.	B9	136
Ionia, Mi., U.S.	E4	112
Ionian Islands see Iónioi Nísoi, is., Grc.	E3	28
Ionian Sea, Eur.	F11	24
Iónioi Nísoi, state, Grc.	E3	28
Iónioi Nísoi (Ionian Islands), is., Grc.	E3	28
Iony, ostrov, i., Russia	E17	34
Íos, i., Grc.	G8	28
Iosegun Lake see Fox Creek, Ab., Can.	B14	138
Iowa, La., U.S.	G5	122
Iowa, state, U.S.	I5	118
Iowa, stm., Ia., U.S.	C6	120
Iowa City, Ia., U.S.	C6	120
Iowa Falls, Ia., U.S.	B4	120
Iowa Park, Tx., U.S.	H10	128
Ipameri, Braz.	I1	88
Ipanema, stm., Braz.	E7	88
Ipanguaçu, Braz.	C7	88
Ipatinga, Braz.	J4	88
Ipatovo, Russia	E6	32
Ipaumirim, Braz.	D6	88
Ípeiros, state, Grc.	D3	28
Ípeiros, hist. reg., Grc.	D3	28
Ipel' (Ipoly), stm., Eur.	I14	16
Ipiales, Col.	G3	86
Ipiaú, Braz.	H6	88
Ipin see Yibin, China	F5	36
Ipirá, Braz.	G6	88
Ipixuna, Braz.	C3	88
Ipoh, Malay.	J5	48
Ipojuca, stm., Braz.	E7	88
Ipoly (Ipel'), stm., Eur.	I14	16
Iporã, Braz.	G7	84
Iporã, Braz.	A11	92
Ipota, Vanuatu	I17	79d
Ipsala, Tur.	C9	28
Ipswich, Austl.	F9	76
Ipswich, Eng., U.K.	I14	12
Ipswich, Ma., U.S.	B15	114
Ipswich, S.D., U.S.	B13	126
Ipu, Braz.	C5	88
Ipubi, Braz.	D5	88
Ipuc' (Iput'), stm., Eur.	H14	10
Ipueiras, Braz.	C5	88
Iput' (Ipuc'), stm., Eur.	H14	10
Iqaluit, N.T., Can.	C17	106
Iqfahs, Egypt	J1	58
Iquique, Chile	D2	90
Iquitos, Peru	D3	84
Ira, Tx., U.S.	B7	130
Iracema, Braz.	C6	88
Irákleia, i., Grc.	G8	28
Irákleio, Grc.	H8	28
Iran, ctry., Asia	C7	56
Iran Mountains, mts., Asia	C9	50
Īrānshahr, Iran	D9	56
Irapa, Ven.	B10	86
Irapuato, Mex.	E8	100
Iraq, ctry., Asia	C5	56
Irará, Braz.	F6	88
Irati, Braz.	B12	92
Irazú, Volcán, vol., C.R.	G6	102
Irbejskoe, Russia	C17	32
Irbid, Jord.	F6	58
Irbid, state, Jord.	F6	58
Irbīl, Iraq	B5	56
Irbit, Russia	C10	32
Irdning, Aus.	C11	22
Irebu, D.R.C.	E3	66
Irecê, Braz.	F5	88
Ireland, ctry., Eur.	H4	12
Ireland Island North, i., Ber.	k15	104e
Irene, S.D., U.S.	D15	126
Ireng (Maú), stm., S.A.	F12	86
Ireton, Ia., U.S.	B1	120
Irgiz, Kaz.	E10	32
Iri, Kor., S.	G7	38
Iriba, Chad	E4	62
Iriga, Phil.	D4	52
Irîgui, reg., Afr.	F3	64
Iringa, Tan.	F7	66
Irinjālakuda, India	F3	53
Iriomote-jima, i., Japan	G9	36
Iriri, stm., Braz.	D7	84
Irish, Mount, mtn., Nv., U.S.	F1	132
Irish Sea, Eur.	H7	12
Irituia, Braz.	A2	88
Irkutsk, Russia	D18	32
Irma, Ab., Can.	D19	138
Irminger Basin, unds.	B10	144
Irnijärvi, l., Fin.	D13	8
Iroise, b., Fr.	F4	14
Iron Bottom Sound, strt., Sol. Is.	e8	79b
Iron Bridge, On., Can.	B6	112
Iron City, Tn., U.S.	B11	122
Irondale, Al., U.S.	D12	122
Irondale, Mo., U.S.	G7	120
Irondequoit, N.Y., U.S.	E12	112
Iron Gate, val., Eur.	E9	26
Iron Knob, Austl.	F7	74
Iron Mountain, Mi., U.S.	C1	112
Iron Range, Austl.	B8	74
Iron River, Mi., U.S.	E10	118
Ironton, Mn., U.S.	E4	118
Ironton, Mo., U.S.	G7	120
Ironton, Oh., U.S.	F3	114
Ironwood, Mi., U.S.	E8	118
Iroquois, On., Can.	D14	112
Iroquois, stm., U.S.	H2	112
Iroquois Falls, On., Can.	F14	106
Irō-zaki, c., Japan	E11	40
Irrawaddy see Ayeyarwady, stm., Mya.	E8	46
Irricana, Ab., Can.	E17	138
Irrigon, Or., U.S.	E7	136
Irshava, Ukr.	A10	26
Irsina, Italy	D10	24
Irtyš see Irtysh, stm., Asia	C11	32
Irtysh (Irtyš) (Ertix), stm., Asia	C11	32
Irtyšsk, Kaz.	D12	32
Irún, Spain	A9	20
Iruña see Pamplona, Spain	B9	20
Irurzun, Spain	B9	20
Irú Tepuy, mtn., Ven.	E11	86
Irvine, Ab., Can.	E3	124
Irvine, Scot., U.K.	F8	12
Irvines Landing, B.C., Can.	G6	138
Irving, Tx., U.S.	B10	130
Irvington, Ky., U.S.	G11	120
Isa, Nig.	G6	64
Isaac, stm., Austl.	D7	76
Isaac Lake, l., B.C., Can.	C10	138
Isabel, state, Sol. Is.	d8	79b
Isabela, Phil.	G3	52
Isabela, P.R.	A1	104a
Isabela, Cabo, c., Dom. Rep.	C12	102
Isabela, Isla, i., Ec.	i11	84a
Isabelia, Cordillera, mts., Nic.	F5	102
Isaccea, Rom.	D15	26
Isachsen, N.T., Can.	B5	141
Isachsen, Cape, c., N.T., Can.	B4	141
Ísafjarðardjúp, b., Ice.	j28	8a
Ísafjörður, Ice.	j28	8a
Isahaya, Japan	G3	40
Isak, Indon.	J3	48
Isaka, Tan.	E6	66
Īsa Khel, Pak.	B3	54
Işalniţa, Rom.	E10	26
Isana (Içana), stm., S.A.	G7	86
Isangel, Vanuatu	I17	79d
Isanti, Mn., U.S.	F5	118
Isar, stm., Eur.	H8	16
Isarog, Mount, vol., Phil.	D4	52
İscehisar, Tur.	E13	28
Ischia, Italy	D7	24
Ischia, Isola d', i., Italy	D7	24
Ise, Japan	E9	40
Iseo, Lago d', l., Italy	E6	22
Isère, state, Fr.	D11	18
Isère, stm., Fr.	D11	18
Iserlohn, Ger.	E3	16
Isernia, Italy	C8	24
Isesaki, Japan	C12	40
Ise-shima-kokuritsu-kōen, p.o.i., Japan	E9	40
Ise-wan, b., Japan	E9	40
Iseyin, Nig.	H5	64
Isezaki see Isesaki, Japan	C12	40
Isfahan see Eşfahān, Iran	C7	56
Isfara, Taj.	A11	56
Isherton, Guy.	F12	86
Ishigaki, Japan	G9	36
Ishikari, stm., Japan	C14	38
Ishikari-wan, b., Japan	C14	38
Ishikawa, state, Japan	C9	40
Ishim (Išim), stm., Asia	C12	32
Ishinomaki, Japan	A14	40
Ishioka, Japan	C13	40
Ishizuchi-san, mtn., Japan	F5	40
Ishpeming, Mi., U.S.	B2	112
Ishurdi, Bngl.	F12	54
Isigny-sur-Mer, Fr.	E7	14
Işıklı, Tur.	E12	28
Isil'kul', Russia	C12	32
Išim, Russia	C11	32
Išimskaja ravnina, pl., Asia	C11	32
Isiolo, Kenya	D7	66
Isipingo, ngh., S. Afr.	G10	70
Isiro, D.R.C.	D5	66
Isis, Austl.	E9	76
Iskăr, stm., Blg.	F11	26
Iskăr, Jazovir, res., Blg.	G10	26
İskenderun (Alexandretta), Tur.	B6	58
İskenderun Körfezi, b., Tur.	B6	58
Iskitim, Russia	D14	32
Iskut, stm., B.C., Can.	D4	106
Isla, Mex.	G11	100
Isla, Salar de la, pl., Chile	B3	92
İslâhiye, Tur.	A7	58
Islāmābād, Pak.	B4	54
Islāmkot, Pak.	F3	54
Islāmpur, India	C2	53
Islāmpur, India	F10	54
Islāmpur, India	E12	54
Island, Ky., U.S.	G10	120
Island Falls, Me., U.S.	E8	110
Island Harbour, Anguilla	A1	105a
Island Lake, l., Mb., Can.	E12	106
Island Park, Id., U.S.	F15	136
Island Pond, Vt., U.S.	F5	110
Islands, Bay of, b., Nf., Can.	j22	107a
Isla Patrulla, Ur.	F10	92
Isla Vista, Ca., U.S.	I5	134
Islay, i., Scot., U.K.	F6	12
Isle, Mn., U.S.	E5	118
Isle, stm., Fr.	E5	18
Isle of Man, dep., Eur.	G8	12
Isle of Wight, Va., U.S.	H9	114
Isle Royale National Park, p.o.i., Mi., U.S.	C10	118
Islesboro Island, i., Me., U.S.	F8	110
Isleta, N.M., U.S.	I10	132
Isleton, Ca., U.S.	E4	134
Islón, Chile	D2	92
Ismailia (Al-Ismā'īlīyah), Egypt	H3	58
Isna, Egypt	B6	62
Isny, Ger.	I5	16
Isoka, Zam.	C5	68
Isola del Liri, Italy	I10	22
Isola di Capo Rizzuto, Italy	F11	24
Isonzo, stm., Eur.	E10	22
Isparta, Tur.	F13	28
Isparta, state, Tur.	F13	28
Ispica, Italy	H8	24
Israel, ctry., Asia	G5	58
Isrā'īl see Israel, ctry., Asia	G5	58
Issa, stm., Russia	D11	10
Isser, Oued, stm., Alg.	H14	20
Issia, C. Iv.	H3	64
Issoire, Fr.	D9	18
Issoudun, Fr.	H10	14
Issuna, Tan.	F6	66
Issyk-Kul', Kyrg.	F13	32
Issyk-Kul, Lake see Issyk-Kul', ozero, l., Kyrg.	F13	32
Issyk-Kul', ozero, l., Kyrg.	F13	32
Īstādeh-ye Moqor, Āb-e, l., Afg.	B2	54
İstanbul, Tur.	B12	28
İstanbul, state, Tur.	B11	28
İstanbul Boğazı (Bosporus), strt., Tur.	B12	28
Istiaía, Grc.	E6	28
Istmina, Col.	E3	86
Isto, Mount, mtn., Ak., U.S.	C11	140
Istra, Russia	E19	10
Istria, pen., Eur.	E10	22
Itá, Para.	B9	92
Itabaiana, Braz.	D8	88
Itabaiana, Braz.	F7	88
Itabaianinha, Braz.	F7	88
Itabapoana, Braz.	K5	88
Itaberaba, Braz.	G5	88
Itaberaí, Braz.	G8	84
Itabi, Braz.	F7	88
Itabira, Braz.	J4	88
Itabuna, Braz.	H6	88
Itacajá, Braz.	E2	88
Itacambiruçu, stm., Braz.	I4	88
Itacoatiara, Braz.	D6	84
Itacurubí del Rosario, Para.	B9	92
Itaeté, Braz.	G5	88
Itaguajé, Braz.	D6	90
Itaguara, Braz.	K3	88
Itaguari, stm., Braz.	H3	88
Itagüí, Col.	D4	86
Itaí, Braz.	A13	92
Itaiçaba, Braz.	C7	88
Itaim, stm., Braz.	D5	88
Itainópolis, Braz.	D5	88
Itaipu Reservoir, res., S.A.	B10	92
Itäisen Suomenlahden kansallispuisto, p.o.i., Fin.	F12	8
Itaituba, Braz.	D6	84
Itajaí, Braz.	C13	92
Itajubá, Braz.	L3	88
Itaju do Colônia, Braz.	H6	88
Itajuípe, Braz.	H6	88
Itala Game Reserve, S. Afr.	E10	70
Itálica, hist., Spain	G4	20
Italy, Tx., U.S.	B11	130
Italy, ctry., Eur.	G11	6
Itamaraju, Braz.	I6	88
Itamarandiba, Braz.	I4	88
Itamarandiba, stm., Braz.	I4	88
Itamari, Braz.	G6	88
Itambacuri, Braz.	I5	88
Itambé, Braz.	H5	88
Itami, Japan	E8	40
Itampolo, Madag.	E7	68
Itānagar, India	E14	54
Itanhaém, Braz.	B14	92
Itanhém, Braz.	I5	88
Itaobim, Braz.	I5	88
Itapagipe, Braz.	J1	88
Itapajé, Braz.	B6	88
Itaparica, Ilha de, i., Braz.	G6	88
Itaparica, Represa de, res., Braz.	E6	88
Itapebi, Braz.	H6	88
Itapecerica, Braz.	K3	88
Itapecuru-Mirim, Braz.	B3	88
Itapemirim, Braz.	K5	88
Itaperuna, Braz.	K5	88
Itapetim, Braz.	D7	88
Itapetinga, Braz.	H5	88
Itapetininga, Braz.	L1	88
Itapetininga, stm., Braz.	A14	92
Itapeva, Braz.	L1	88
Itapicuru, Braz.	F6	88
Itapicuru, stm., Braz.	B3	88
Itapicuru, stm., Braz.	F6	88
Itapipoca, Braz.	B6	88
Itapiranga, Braz.	D6	84
Itapirapuã, Braz.	G7	84
Itapiúna, Braz.	C6	88
Itápolis, Braz.	K1	88
Itaporã de Goiás, Braz.	D1	88
Itaporanga, Braz.	D6	88
Itaporanga d'Ajuda, Braz.	F7	88
Itapúa, state, Para.	C10	92
Itaquara, Braz.	G6	88
Itaquari, Braz.	K5	88
Itaqui, Braz.	D9	92
Itarantim, Braz.	H5	88
Itararé, Braz.	B13	92
Itararé, stm., Braz.	A13	92
Itārsi, India	G6	54
Itarumã, Braz.	C6	90
Itasca, Tx., U.S.	B10	130
Itasca, Lake, l., Mn., U.S.	D3	118
Itata, stm., Chile	H1	92
Itatinga, Braz.	L1	88
Itatira, Braz.	C6	88
Itatupã, Braz.	D7	84
Itaueira, Braz.	D4	88
Itaueira, stm., Braz.	D4	88
Itaúna, Braz.	K3	88
Itbayat Island, i., Phil.	K9	42
Itéa, Grc.	E5	28
Iténez (Guaporé), stm., S.A.	F5	84
Ithaca, Mi., U.S.	E5	112
Ithaca, N.Y., U.S.	B9	114
Ithaca see Itháki, i., Grc.	E3	28
Itháki, i., Grc.	E3	28
Itimbiri, stm., D.R.C.	D4	66
Itinga, Braz.	I5	88
Itiquira, stm., Braz.	G6	84
Itiruçu, Braz.	G5	88
Itiúba, Braz.	F5	88
Itla el-Bâsha, hill, Egypt	K3	58
Itō, Japan	E12	40
Itoigawa, Japan	B10	40
Iton, stm., Fr.	F9	14
Itororó, Braz.	H5	88
Itsuki, Japan	G3	40
Ittiri, Italy	D2	24
Ittoqqortoormiit see Scoresbysund, Grnld.	C21	141
Itu, Braz.	L2	88
Itu, stm., Braz.	D10	92
Ituaçu, Braz.	G5	88
Ituango, Col.	D4	86
Ituberá, Braz.	G6	88
Itueta, Braz.	J5	88
Ituí, stm., Braz.	E3	84
Ituiutaba, Braz.	J1	88
Itumbiara, Braz.	J1	88
Ituna, Sk., Can.	C10	124
Itupiranga, Braz.	E8	84
Ituporanga, Braz.	C13	92
Iturama, Braz.	C6	90
Iturbide, Mex.	C3	102
Iturup, ostrov (Etorofu-tō), i., Russia	B17	38
Ituverava, Braz.	K2	88
Ituxi, stm., Braz.	E4	84
Ituzaingó, Arg.	C9	92
Itzehoe, Ger.	C5	16
Iuka, Ms., U.S.	C10	122
Iul'tin, Russia	C25	34
Iúna, Braz.	K5	88
Ivacevičy, Bela.	H8	10
Ivačovo, Russia	F17	8
Ivaí, stm., Braz.	D6	90
Ivaiporã, Braz.	B12	92
Ivalo, Fin.	B12	8
Ivalojoki, stm., Fin.	B12	8
Ivanava, Bela.	H8	10
Ivančice, Czech Rep.	G12	16
Ivangorod, Russia	A11	10
Ivangrad, Yugo.	G6	26
Ivanhoe, Austl.	I5	76
Ivanhoe, Ca., U.S.	G6	134
Ivanhoe, Mn., U.S.	G2	118
Ivanhoe, Va., U.S.	H4	114
Ivanišči, Russia	D18	10
Ivanjica, Yugo.	F7	26
Ivan'kovo, Russia	F20	10
Ivan'kovskoe vodohranilišče, res., Russia	D19	10
Ivano-Frankivs'k, Ukr.	F13	6
Ivano-Frankivs'k, co., Ukr.	A11	26
Ivanovka, Russia	F14	34
Ivanovo, Russia	H19	8
Ivanovskaja oblast', co., Russia	H19	8
Ivanovskoe, Russia	A11	10
Ivanpah Lake, l., Ca., U.S.	H1	132
Ivdel', Russia	B9	32
Ivigtut, Grnld.	E16	141
Ivindo, stm., Gabon	D2	66
Ivinheíma, stm., Braz.	D6	90
Iviza see Eivissa, Spain	F12	20
Ivjanec, Bela.	G9	10
Ivohibe, Madag.	E8	68
Ivory Coast see Cote d'Ivoire, ctry., Afr.	H3	64
Ivory Coast, cst., C. Iv.	I3	64
Ivrea, Italy	E4	22
İvrindi, Tur.	D10	28
Ivujivik, Qc., Can.	C15	106
Iwaki, Japan	B13	40
Iwaki-san, vol., Japan	D14	38
Iwakuni, Japan	E5	40
Iwami, Japan	D7	40
Iwanuma, Japan	A13	40
Iwata, Japan	E10	40
Iwate, state, Japan	A14	40
Iwate-san, vol., Japan	E14	38
'Iweibid, Gebel, mtn., Egypt	H3	58
Iwo, Nig.	H5	64
Ixmiquilpan, Mex.	E9	100
Ixopo, S. Afr.	G10	70
Ixtapa, Mex.	G8	100
Ixtepec, Mex.	G11	100
Ixtlán del Río, Mex.	E6	100
Iyang see Yiyang, China	G5	42
Iyo, Japan	F5	40
Iyo-mishima, Japan	F6	40
Iyo-nada, Japan	F5	40
Izabal, Lago de, l., Guat.	E3	102
Izamal, Mex.	B3	102
Izapa, hist., Mex.	H12	100
Izberbaš, Russia	F7	32
Izbica, Pol.	F19	16
Izegem, Bel.	D12	14
Iževsk, Russia	C8	32
Izium, Ukr.	E5	32
Ižma, stm., Russia	B8	32
Izmail, Ukr.	D15	26
Izmalkovo, Russia	H21	10
İzmayil see Izmail, Ukr.	D15	26
İzmir (Smyrna), Tur.	E10	28
İzmir, state, Tur.	E10	28
İzmir Körfezi, b., Tur.	E9	28
İzmit (Kocaeli), Tur.	C12	28
İzmit Körfezi, b., Tur.	C12	28
İznik, Tur.	C12	28
İznik Gölü, l., Tur.	C12	28
Iznoski, Russia	E18	10
Izozog, Bañados del, sw., Bol.	C4	90
Izra', Syria	F7	58
Izsák, Hung.	C6	26
Iztaccíhuatl, Volcán, vol., Mex.	F9	100
Iztaccíhuatl y Popocatéptl, Parques Nacionales, p.o.i., Mex.	F9	100
Izucar de Matamoros, Mex.	F9	100
Izu-hantō, pen., Japan	E11	40
Izuhara, Japan	E2	40
Izu Islands see Izu-shotō, is., Japan	E12	40
Izumi, Japan	G3	40
Izumi, Japan	A13	40
Izumi, Japan	E8	40
Izumo, Japan	D5	40
Izu-shotō (Izu Islands), is., Japan	E12	40
Izu Trench, unds.	G17	142
Izvestij CIK, ostrova, is., Russia	A5	34
Izvorul Muntelui, Lacul, l., Rom.	C12	26

J

Name	Map Ref.	Page
Jabal, Bahr al- see Mountain Nile, stm., Afr.	F6	62
Jabal al-Awliyā', Sudan	D6	62
Jabal Lubnān, state, Leb.	D6	58
Jabalón, stm., Spain	F7	20
Jabalpur, India	G7	54
Jabālyah, Gaza	G5	58
Jabbūl, Sabkhat al-, l., Syria	C8	58
Jabiru, Austl.	B6	74
Jablah, Syria	C6	58
Jablanica, Bos.	F4	26
Jablaničko jezero, res., Bos.	F4	26
Jablonec nad Nisou, Czech Rep.	F11	16
Jabłonka, Pol.	G15	16
Jablonovyj hrebet, mts., Russia	F11	34
Jablunkov, Czech Rep.	G14	16
Jaboticabal, Braz.	K1	88
Jaca, Spain	B10	20
Jacala, Mex.	E9	100
Jacaré, stm., Braz.	F5	88
Jacareí, Braz.	L2	88
Jacarezinho, Braz.	D7	90
Jáchal, stm., Arg.	E4	92
Jaciara, Braz.	G6	84
Jacinto, Braz.	I5	88
Jacinto Aráuz, Arg.	I6	92
Jacinto City, Tx., U.S.	H3	122
Jackfish Lake, l., Sk., Can.	A5	124
Jackhead Harbour, Mb., Can.	C16	124
Jack Mountain, mtn., Mt., U.S.	D14	136
Jackpot, Nv., U.S.	B2	132
Jacksboro, Tn., U.S.	H1	114
Jacksboro, Tx., U.S.	H10	128
Jackson, Ca., U.S.	E5	134
Jackson, Ky., U.S.	G2	114
Jackson, La., U.S.	G7	122
Jackson, Mi., U.S.	B1	114
Jackson, Mn., U.S.	H4	118
Jackson, Ms., U.S.	E8	122
Jackson, N.C., U.S.	H8	114
Jackson, Oh., U.S.	E3	114
Jackson, S.C., U.S.	C4	116
Jackson, Tn., U.S.	B10	122
Jackson, Wy., U.S.	G16	136
Jackson, stm., Va., U.S.	G6	114
Jackson, Mount, mtn., Ant.	C34	81
Jackson, Mount, mtn., Austl.	F3	74
Jackson Creek, stm., Can.	E12	124
Jackson Lake, l., Wy., U.S.	G16	136
Jacksonville, Al., U.S.	D13	122
Jacksonville, Ar., U.S.	C6	122
Jacksonville, Fl., U.S.	F4	116
Jacksonville, Il., U.S.	E7	120
Jacksonville, N.C., U.S.	B8	116
Jacksonville, Or., U.S.	A2	134
Jacksonville, Tx., U.S.	F3	122
Jacksonville Beach, Fl., U.S.	F4	116
Jacmel, Haiti	C11	102
Jaco, Mex.	B6	100
Jacobābād, Pak.	D2	54
Jacobina, Braz.	F5	88
Jacobsdal, S. Afr.	F7	70
Jacques-Cartier, Mont, mtn., Qc., Can.	A11	110
Jacu, stm., Braz.	D8	88
Jacuí, stm., Braz.	D11	92
Jacuípe, stm., Braz.	F5	88
Jacumba, Ca., U.S.	K9	134
Jacundá, Braz.	D8	84
Jacupiranga, Braz.	B13	92
Jacuriaí, stm., Braz.	F6	88
Jadebusen, b., Ger.	C4	16
J.A.D. Jensens Nunatakker, mtn., Grnld.	E16	141
Jadraque, Spain	D8	20
Jādū, Libya	A2	62
Jaén, Peru	E2	84
Jaén, Spain	G7	20
Jaén, co., Spain	G7	20
Jāfarābād, India	H3	54
Jaffa, Cape, c., Austl.	K2	76
Jaffna, Sri L.	G4	53
Jaffna Lagoon, b., Sri L.	G4	53
Jaffrey, N.H., U.S.	B13	114
Jafr, Qā' al-, depr., Jord.	H7	58
Jagalūr, India	D3	53
Jagannāthganj Ghāt, Bngl.	F12	54
Jagatsingpur, India	H11	54
Jagdalpur, India	B6	53
Jageljurta, gora, hill, Russia	C17	8
Jagersfontein, S. Afr.	F7	70
Jaggayyapeta, India	C5	53
Jagodnoe, Russia	D18	34
Jagraon, India	C5	54
Jagtiāl, India	B4	53
Jaguaquara, Braz.	G6	88
Jaguarão, Braz.	F11	92
Jaguarão (Yaguarón), stm., S.A.	F11	92
Jaguarari, Braz.	F5	88
Jaguari, Braz.	D10	92
Jaguariaíva, Braz.	B13	92
Jaguaribara, Braz.	C6	88
Jaguaribe, Braz.	C6	88
Jaguaribe, stm., Braz.	C7	88
Jaguaruna, Braz.	D13	92
Jagüey Grande, Cuba	A7	102
Jahānābād, India	F10	54
Jahrom, Iran	D7	56
Jahroma, Russia	D20	10
Jaicós, Braz.	D5	88
Jailolo, Indon.	E8	44
Jaintiāpur, Bngl.	F14	54
Jaipur, India	E5	54
Jaipur Hāt, Bngl.	F12	54
Jais, India	E8	54
Jaisalmer, India	E3	54
Jaito, India	C5	54
Jaja, Russia	C15	32
Jājapur, India	H11	54
Jajce, Bos.	E4	26
Jakarta, Indon.	G5	50
Jakarta, Teluk, b., Indon.	F5	50
Jakaulevičy, Bela.	F13	10
Jakhāu, India	G2	54
Jakobshavn (Ilulissat), Grnld.	D15	141
Jakobstad see Pietarsaari, Fin.	E10	8
Jakovlevka, Russia	B10	38
Jakša, Russia	B9	32
Jakutija, state, Russia	C14	34
Jakutsk, Russia	D14	34
Jal, N.M., U.S.	B4	130
Jalaid Qi, China	B9	36
Jalālābād, Afg.	C11	56
Jalālpur, India	E9	54
Jalandhar, India	C5	54
Jalapa, Guat.	E3	102
Jalapa see Xalapa, Mex.	F10	100
Jālaun, India	E7	54
Jales, Braz.	D6	90
Jalesar, India	E7	54
Jaleshwar, India	H11	54
Jālgaon, India	H5	54
Jālgaon, India	H6	54
Jalingo, Nig.	H7	64
Jalisco, state, Mex.	E6	100
Jālna, India	B2	53
Jalón, stm., Spain	C9	20
Jālor, India	F4	54
Jalostotitlán, Mex.	E7	100
Jalpa, Mex.	E7	100
Jalpāiguri, India	E12	54
Jaluit, at., Marsh. Is.	C7	72
Jalutorovsk, Russia	C11	32
Jamaame, Som.	E8	66
Jamaica, ctry., N.A.	D8	102
Jamaica Channel, strt., N.A.	D9	102
Jamal, poluostrov, pen., Russia	B2	34
Jam-Alin', hrebet, mts., Russia	F15	34
Jamālpur, Bngl.	F12	54
Jamālpur, India	F11	54
Jamanota, hill, Aruba	o20	104g
Jamantau, gora, mtn., Russia	D9	32
Jamanxim, stm., Braz.	E6	84
Jamari, stm., Braz.	E5	84
Jamarovka, Russia	F11	34
Jambelí, Canal de, strt., Ec.	I2	86
Jambi, Indon.	D3	50
Jambi, state, Indon.	D3	50
Jamboaye, stm., Indon.	J3	48
Jambol, Blg.	G13	26
Jambongan, Pulau, i., Malay.	G1	52
Jambuair, Tanjung, c., Indon.	J3	48
Jambusar, India	G4	54
James, stm., U.S.	C8	108
James, stm., Mo., U.S.	H4	120
James, stm., Va., U.S.	G8	114
James, Isla, i., Chile	H2	90
James Bay, b., Can.	E14	106
James City, N.C., U.S.	A8	116
James Craik, Arg.	F6	92
James Island, S.C., U.S.	D5	116
James Point, c., Bah.	K9	116
Jamesport, Mo., U.S.	E4	120
James Ross, Cape, c., N.T., Can.	B17	140
James Ross Island, i., Ant.	B35	81
James Ross Strait, strt., N.T., Can.	A11	106
Jamestown, Austl.	I2	76
Jamestown, S. Afr.	G8	70
Jamestown, Ca., U.S.	F5	134
Jamestown, Ky., U.S.	H12	120
Jamestown, N.Y., U.S.	B6	114
Jamestown, N.C., U.S.	I6	114
Jamestown, N.D., U.S.	H15	124
Jamestown, Tn., U.S.	H13	120
Jamestown, misc. cult., Va., U.S.	G9	114
Jām Jodhpur, India	H3	54
Jamkhandi, India	C2	53
Jamm, Russia	B10	10
Jammerbugten, b., Den.	H3	8
Jammu, India	B5	54
Jammu and Kashmir see Kashmir, hist. reg., Asia	B4	46
Jamnagar (Navanagar), India	G3	54
Jampang-kulon, Indon.	G5	50
Jāmpur, Pak.	D3	54
Jämsä, Fin.	F11	8
Jamshedpur, India	G10	54
Jamsk, Russia	E19	34
Jämtland, state, Swe.	E6	8
Jamūi, India	F11	54
Jamuna, stm., Bngl.	F12	54
Jana, stm., Russia	C16	34
Janaúba, Braz.	H4	88
Janaucu, Ilha, i., Braz.	C7	84
Jand, Pak.	B4	54
Jandaia, Braz.	G7	84
Jandiāla, India	C5	54
Jandowae, Austl.	F8	76
Jándula, stm., Spain	F7	20
Janeiro, stm., Braz.	F3	88
Janesville, Ca., U.S.	C5	134
Janesville, Mn., U.S.	G5	118
Janesville, Wi., U.S.	B9	120
Jangamo, Moz.	D12	70
Jangeru, Indon.	E10	50
Jangijul', Uzb.	F11	32
Jangīpur, India	F11	54
Jangoon, India	C4	53
Janīn, W.B.	F6	58
Janisjarvi, ozero, l., Russia	E14	8
Janiuay, Phil.	E4	52
Jankan, hrebet, mts., Russia	E12	34
Jan Kempdorp, S. Afr.	E7	70
Janlohong, Indon.	B10	50
Jan Mayen, i., Nor.	B22	94
Janos, Mex.	F8	98
Jánosháza, Hung.	B4	26
Janowiec Wielkopolski, Pol.	D13	16
Janskij, Russia	C15	34
Janskij zaliv, b., Russia	B16	34
Jantra, stm., Blg.	F12	26
Januária, Braz.	H3	88
Januário Cicco, Braz.	D8	88
Jaora, India	G5	54
Japan, ctry., Asia	E12	38
Japan, Sea of (East Sea), Asia	D11	38
Japan Basin, unds.	E16	142
Japan Trench, unds.	F17	142
Japaratinga, Braz.	E8	88
Japi, Braz.	D7	88
Japonskoje more see East Sea, Asia	D11	38
Japonskoje more see Japan, Sea of, Asia	D11	38
Japtiksalja, Russia	C3	34
Japurá, Braz.	H8	86
Japurá (Caquetá), stm., S.A.	D5	84
Jaqué, Pan.	D2	86
Jarābulus, Syria	B9	58
Jaraguá, Braz.	H1	88
Jaraguá do Sul, Braz.	C13	92
Jaraíz de la Vera, Spain	D5	20
Jarales, N.M., U.S.	I10	132
Jarama, stm., Spain	D7	20
Jaramānah, Syria	E7	58
Jaransk, Russia	C7	32
Jarānwāla, Pak.	C4	54
Jarash, Jord.	F6	58
Jarash, hist., Jord.	F6	58
Jarcevo, Russia	E15	10
Jardim, Braz.	D6	88
Jardim, Braz.	D5	90
Jardim de Piranhas, Braz.	D7	88
Jardín América, Arg.	C10	92
Jardines de la Reina, Archipiélago de los, is., Cuba	B8	102
Jardinópolis, Braz.	K1	88
Jarej-Uliga-Delap, Marsh. Is.	C8	72
Jarenga, Russia	E23	8
Jarensk, Russia	E23	8
Jargalant, Mong.	B4	36
Jari, stm., Braz.	C7	84
Jaridih, India	G11	54
Jarkand see Shache, China	B12	56
Jarkino, Russia	C17	32

Name | Map Ref. | Page

Name	Map Ref.	Page
Kenansville, N.C., U.S.	B7	116
Kenbridge, Va., U.S.	H7	114
Kendal, Sk., Can.	D10	124
Kendal, Indon.	G7	50
Kendal, Eng., U.K.	G10	12
Kendall, Austl.	H9	76
Kendall, Fl., U.S.	K5	116
Kendall, Wi., U.S.	H8	118
Kendall, Cape, c., N.T., Can.	C13	106
Kendari, Indon.	F7	44
Kendawangan, Indon.	E7	50
Kendrāparha, India	H11	54
Kendrew, S. Afr.	H7	70
Kendrick, Fl., U.S.	G3	116
Kendrick, Id., U.S.	D10	136
Kendujhargarh, India	H10	54
Kenedy, Tx., U.S.	F10	130
Kenema, S.L.	H2	64
Kenga, Russia	C14	32
Kenge, D.R.C.	E3	66
Keng Hkam, Mya.	B3	48
Kēng Tung, Mya.	B4	48
Kenhardt, S. Afr.	F5	70
Kenilworth, Ut., U.S.	D6	132
Kénitra, Mor.	C3	64
Kenly, N.C., U.S.	A7	116
Kenmare, Ire.	J3	12
Kenmare, N.D., U.S.	F11	124
Kennard, Tx., U.S.	F3	122
Kennebec, stm., Me., U.S.	F7	110
Kennebecasis Bay, b., N.B., Can.	E11	110
Kennebunk, Me., U.S.	G6	110
Kennedy, Al., U.S.	D11	122
Kennedy, Cape see Canaveral, Cape, c., Fl., U.S.	H5	116
Kennedy, Mount, mtn., B.C., Can.	F5	138
Kennedy, Mount, mtn., Yk., Can.	C3	106
Kennedy Lake, l., B.C., Can.	G5	138
Kenner, La., U.S.	G8	122
Kennetcook, N.S., Can.	E13	110
Kennett, Mo., U.S.	H7	120
Kennewick, Wa., U.S.	D7	136
Kenney Dam, dam, B.C., Can.	C6	138
Kenogami, stm., On., Can.	E13	106
Kénogami, Lac, res., Qc., Can.	B5	110
Keno Hill, Yk., Can.	C3	106
Kenora, On., Can.	B4	118
Kenosha, Wi., U.S.	F2	112
Kenozero, ozero, l., Russia	E18	8
Kensal, N.D., U.S.	G15	124
Kensett, Ar., U.S.	B7	122
Kensington, Ks., U.S.	B9	128
Kensington Park, Fl., U.S.	I3	116
Kent, Oh., U.S.	C4	114
Kent, Wa., U.S.	C4	136
Kentau, Kaz.	F11	32
Kent Group, is., Austl.	L6	76
Kentland, In., U.S.	H2	112
Kenton, Mi., U.S.	E10	118
Kenton, Tn., U.S.	H8	120
Kent Peninsula, pen., N.T., Can.	B9	106
Kentrikí Makedonía, state, Grc.	C6	28
Kentucky, state, U.S.	G12	120
Kentucky, stm., Ky., U.S.	F13	120
Kentucky, Middle Fork, stm., Ky., U.S.	G2	114
Kentucky, North Fork, stm., Ky., U.S.	G2	114
Kentucky Lake, res., U.S.	H9	120
Kentville, N.S., Can.	E12	110
Kentwood, La., U.S.	G8	122
Kenya, ctry., Afr.	D7	66
Kenya, Mount see Kirinyaga, mtn., Kenya	E7	66
Kenyon, Mn., U.S.	G6	118
Keokuk, Ia., U.S.	D6	120
Keoladeo National Park, p.o.i., India	E6	54
Keo Nua, Deo, p., Asia	C7	48
Keosauqua, Ia., U.S.	D5	120
Keota, Ia., U.S.	C6	120
Keota, Ok., U.S.	B4	122
Keowee, Lake, res., S.C., U.S.	B2	116
Kepi, Indon.	G10	44
Kepina, Russia	D19	8
Kępno, Pol.	E13	16
Keppel Bay, b., Austl.	D8	76
Kepsut, Tur.	D11	28
Kerala, state, India	F3	53
Keramadoo, mtn., Palau	f8	78b
Keramian, Pulau, i., Indon.	F9	50
Kerang, Austl.	J4	76
Keratéa, Grc.	F6	28
Keravat, Pap. N. Gui.	a5	79a
Kerch, Ukr.	E5	32
Kerec, mys, c., Russia	D18	8
Kerema, Pap. N. Gui.	b4	79a
Keremeos, B.C., Can.	G11	138
Keren, Erit.	D7	62
Kerens, Tx., U.S.	E2	122
Keret', Russia	C15	8
Keret', ozero, l., Russia	D15	8
Kerewan, Gam.	G1	64
Kerguelen, Îles, is., Afr.	J17	4
Kerguelen Plateau, unds.	O10	142
Keri, Grc.	F3	28
Kericho, Kenya	E7	66
Kerinci, Gunung, vol., Indon.	D2	50
Kerkenna, Îles, is., Tun.	C7	64
Kerkhoven, Mn., U.S.	F3	118
Kerkiči, Turkmen.	B10	56
Kerkrade, Neth.	F2	16
Kérkyra (Corfu), Grc.	D2	28
Kérkyra (Corfu), i., Grc.	D2	28
Kermadec Islands, is., N.Z.	F9	72
Kermadec Ridge, unds.	M20	142
Kermadec Trench, unds.	M21	142
Kermān, Iran	C8	56
Kermānshāh (Bākhtarān), Iran	C6	56
Kerme, Gulf of see Gökova Körfezi, b., Tur.	G10	28
Kermit, Tx., U.S.	C4	130
Kern, stm., Ca., U.S.	H7	134
Kern, South Fork, stm., Ca., U.S.	H7	134
Kernersville, N.C., U.S.	H5	114
Kernville, Ca., U.S.	H7	134
Kérouané, Gui.	H3	64
Kerrobert, Sk., Can.	C4	124
Kerrville, Tx., U.S.	D8	130
Kerry, state, Ire.	I2	12
Kerry Head, c., Ire.	I2	12
Kershaw, S.C., U.S.	B5	116
Kersley, B.C., Can.	D8	138
Kertamulia, Indon.	D6	50
Kerulen, stm., Asia	B7	36
Kesagami Lake, l., On., Can.	E14	106
Keşan, Tur.	C9	28
Kesennuma, Japan	E14	38
Keshan, China	B10	36
Keshod, India	H3	54
Keski-Suomi, state, Fin.	E11	8
Kes'ma, Russia	B20	10
Kesova Gora, Russia	C20	10
Kestell, S. Afr.	F9	70
Keswick, Eng., U.K.	G9	12
Keszthely, Hung.	C4	26
Ket', stm., Russia	C14	32
Keta, Ghana	H5	64
Keta, ozero, l., Russia	C6	34
Ketapang, Indon.	F4	50
Ketapang, Indon.	D6	50
Ketchikan, Ak., U.S.	E13	140
Ketchum, Id., U.S.	G12	136
Kete-Krachi, Ghana	H4	64
Ketoj, ostrov, i., Russia	G19	34
Kętrzyn, Pol.	B17	16
Kettering, Eng., U.K.	I12	12
Kettering, Oh., U.S.	E1	114
Kettle, stm., N.A.	H12	138
Kettle Falls, Wa., U.S.	B8	136
Kęty, Pol.	G15	16
Keudeteunom, Indon.	J2	48
Keuka Lake, l., N.Y., U.S.	B8	114
Keukenhof, misc. cult., Neth.	B13	14
Keul', Russia	C18	32
Kevelaer, Ger.	E2	16
Kevin, Mt., U.S.	B14	136
Kew, T./C. Is.	A12	102
Kewanee, Il., U.S.	C7	120
Kewaunee, Wi., U.S.	D2	112
Keweenaw Bay, b., Mi., U.S.	E10	118
Keweenaw Peninsula, pen., Mi., U.S.	D11	118
Keweenaw Point, c., Mi., U.S.	D11	118
Key, Lough, l., Ire.	G4	12
Keya Paha, stm., U.S.	E13	126
Keyes, Ok., U.S.	E6	128
Keyhole Reservoir, res., Wy., U.S.	C8	126
Key Largo, Fl., U.S.	K5	116
Key Largo, i., Fl., U.S.	K5	116
Keyser, W.V., U.S.	E7	114
Keystone, S.D., U.S.	D9	126
Keystone, W.V., U.S.	G4	114
Keystone Lake, res., Ok., U.S.	A2	122
Keystone Peak, mtn., Az., U.S.	L5	132
Keysville, Va., U.S.	G7	114
Keytesville, Mo., U.S.	E5	120
Key West, Fl., U.S.	L4	116
Kezi, Zimb.	B9	70
Kežma, Russia	C18	32
Kežmarok, Slov.	G16	16
Kgalagadi, state, Bots.	D5	70
Kgatleng, state, Bots.	D8	70
Khadki, India	B1	53
Khadzhybeis'kyi lyman, l., Ukr.	C17	26
Khagaria, India	F11	54
Khairāgarh, India	H8	54
Khairpur, Pak.	E2	54
Khairpur, Pak.	D4	54
Khajrāho, India	F8	54
Khakassia see Hakasija, state, Russia	D16	32
Kha Khaeng, stm., Thai.	E4	48
Khakhea, Bots.	D6	70
Khalatse, India	A6	54
Khālidī, Khirbat al-, hist., Jord.	I6	58
Khalîya, Gebel, mtn., Egypt	I3	58
Khalūf, Oman	E8	56
Khambhāliya, India	G2	54
Khambhāt, India	G4	54
Khambhāt, Gulf of, b., India	H3	54
Khāmgaon, India	H6	54
Khāmis, Ash-Shallāl al- (Fifth Cataract), wtfl, Sudan	D6	62
Khamīs Mushayt, Sau. Ar.	F5	56
Khammam, India	C5	53
Khan, stm., Laos	C6	48
Khan, stm., Nmb.	C2	70
Khānābād, Afg.	B10	56
Khān Abū Shāmāt, Syria	E7	58
Khānaqīn, Iraq	C6	56
Khancoban, Austl.	K7	76
Khandela, India	E5	54
Khandwa, India	H6	54
Khānewāl, Pak.	C3	54
Khāngarh, Pak.	D3	54
Khangchendzonga National Park, p.o.i., India	E12	54
Khangkhai, Laos	C6	48
Khania, Gulf of see Chanión, Kólpos, b., Grc.	H6	28
Khanka, Lake, l., Asia	B10	38
Khanna, India	C6	54
Khānpur, Pak.	D3	54
Khansiir, Raas, c., Som.	B9	66
Khān Yūnus, Gaza	G5	58
Khao Laem Reservoir, res., Thai.	E4	48
Khao Sok National Park, p.o.i., Thai.	H4	48
Khao Yoi, Thai.	F4	48
Kharagpur, India	G11	54
Khārān, Pak.	D10	56
Kharāyij, Sabkhat al-, l., Syria	C8	58
Kharg Island see Khārk, Jazīreh-ye, i., Iran	D7	56
Khargon, India	H5	54
Khāriān Cantonment, Pak.	B4	54
Khārk, Jazīreh-ye, i., Iran	D7	56
Kharkiv, Ukr.	D5	32
Kharmanli see Harmanli, Blg.	H12	26
Khartoum see Al-Kharṭūm, Sudan	D6	62
Khartoum North see Al-Kharṭūm Baḥrī, Sudan	D6	62
Khasebake, Bots.	B7	70
Khāsh, Afg.	C9	56
Khāsh, Iran	D9	56
Khashm al-Qirbah, Sudan	D7	62
Khaskovo see Haskovo, Blg.	H12	26
Khatanga see Hatanga, Russia	B9	34
Khatanga see Hatanga, stm., Russia	B9	34
Khatauli, India	D6	54
Khatt, Oued al, stm., W. Sah.	D2	64
Khavast see Havast, Uzb.	F11	32
Khawsa, Mya.	E3	48
Khayung, stm., Thai.	E7	48
Khed, India	C1	53
Kheil, Katîb el-, sand, Egypt	H3	58
Khemis el Khechna, Alg.	H14	20
Khemis Melyana, Alg.	H13	20
Khemmarat, Thai.	D7	48
Khenchla, Alg.	B6	64
Khenifra, Mor.	C3	64
Kherson, Ukr.	F15	6
Kheta see Heta, stm., Russia	B8	34
Khetia, India	H5	54
Khimki see Himki, Russia	E20	10
Khipro, Pak.	F2	54
Khisfīn, Golan	F6	58
Khiva see Hiva, Uzb.	F10	32
Khlong Thom, Thai.	I4	48
Khlung, Thai.	F6	48
Khok Kloi, Thai.	H4	48
Khok Samrong, Thai.	E5	48
Kholm, Afg.	B10	56
Khomas, state, Nmb.	C3	70
Khomeynīshahr, Iran	C7	56
Khondmāl Hills, hills, India	H10	54
Khong see Mekong, stm., Asia	E10	46
Khon Kaen, Thai.	D6	48
Khordha, India	H10	54
Khorixas, Nmb.	B2	70
Khorog see Horog, Taj.	B11	56
Khorramābād, Iran	C6	56
Khorramshahr, Iran	C6	56
Khotyn, Ukr.	A13	26
Khouribga, Mor.	C3	64
Khowai, India	F13	54
Khowst, Afg.	C10	56
Khrisokhoús, Kólpos, b., Cyp.	C3	58
Khuis, Bots.	E5	70
Khuīyāla, India	E3	54
Khulna, Bngl.	G12	54
Khulna, state, Bngl.	G12	54
Khun Tan, Doi, mtn., Thai.	C4	48
Khunti, India	G10	54
Khurai, India	F7	54
Khurja, India	D6	54
Khushāb, Pak.	B4	54
Khust, Ukr.	A10	26
Khuzdār, Pak.	D10	56
Khvoy, Iran	B6	56
Khwae Noi, stm., Thai.	E4	48
Khyber Pass, p., Asia	A3	54
Khyriv, Ukr.	G18	16
Kiama, Austl.	J8	76
Kiama, D.R.C.	F3	66
Kiamba, Phil.	H5	52
Kiambi, D.R.C.	F5	66
Kiamichi, stm., Ok., U.S.	C3	122
Kiamusze see Jiamusi, China	B11	36
Kian see Ji'an, China	H6	42
Kiangarow, Mount, mtn., Austl.	F8	76
Kiang-si see Jiangxi, state, China	H6	42
Kiangsi see Jiangxi, state, China	H6	42
Kiang-sou see Jiangsu, state, China	E8	42
Kiangsu see Jiangsu, state, China	E8	42
Kiaohsien see Jiaoxian, China	C8	42
Kibangou, Congo	E2	66
Kibombo, D.R.C.	E5	66
Kibondo, Tan.	E6	66
Kibre Mengist, Eth.	F7	62
Kıbrıs see Cyprus, ctry., Asia	C4	58
Kıbrıscık, Tur.	C14	28
Kibuye, Rw.	E5	66
Kičevo, Mac.	B3	28
Kickapoo, stm., Wi., U.S.	H8	118
Kicking Horse Pass, p., Can.	E14	138
Kidal, Mali	F5	64
Kidapawan, Phil.	G5	52
Kidatu, Tan.	F7	66
Kidderminster, Eng., U.K.	I10	12
Kidira, Sen.	G2	64
Kidnappers, Cape, c., N.Z.	D7	80
Kidston, Austl.	B5	76
Kiefersfelden, Ger.	I8	16
Kiel, Ger.	B6	16
Kiel, Wi., U.S.	H10	118
Kiel Bay see Kieler Bucht, b., Ger.	B6	16
Kiel Canal see Nord-Ostsee-Kanal, can., Ger.	B5	16
Kielce, Pol.	F16	16
Kielce, state, Pol.	F16	16
Kieler Bucht, b., Ger.	B6	16
Kiester, Mn., U.S.	H5	118
Kiev see Kyïv, Ukr.	D4	32
Kievka, Kaz.	D12	32
Kiev Reservoir see Kyïvs'ke vodoskhovyshche, res., Ukr.	D4	32
Kiffa, Maur.	F2	64
Kifisiá, Grc.	E6	28
Kigali, Rw.	E6	66
Kigoma, Tan.	E5	66
Kihčik, Russia	F20	34
Kihei, Hi., U.S.	C5	78a
Kihniö, Fin.	E10	8
Kihnu, i., Est.	G10	8
Kii-hantō, pen., Japan	F8	40
Kiik, Kaz.	E12	32
Kii-suidō, strt., Japan	F7	40
Kikerino, Russia	A12	10
Kikinda, Yugo.	D7	26
Kikládhes (Cyclades), is., Grc.	F7	28
Kikori, Pap. N. Gui.	b3	79a
Kikori, stm., Pap. N. Gui.	b3	79a
Kikuchi, Japan	G3	40
Kikwit, D.R.C.	F3	66
Kīlakkarai, India	G4	53
Kilauea, Hi., U.S.	A2	78a
Kilauea Crater, crat., Hi., U.S.	D6	78a
Kılbasan, Tur.	A4	58
Kilbuck Mountains, mts., Ak., U.S.	D8	140
Kilchu-ŭp, Kor., N.	D8	38
Kilcoy, Austl.	F9	76
Kildare, state, Ire.	H6	12
Kildare, Cape, c., P.E., Can.	D13	110
Kildurk, Austl.	C5	74
Kilembe, D.R.C.	F3	66
Kilgore, Tx., U.S.	E4	122
Kilian Island, i., N.T., Can.	B18	140
Kılıç, Tur.	C12	28
Kiliia, Ukr.	D16	26
Kilikollūr, India	G3	53
Kilimanjaro, mtn., Tan.	E7	66
Kilimli, Tur.	B14	28
Kilindoni, Tan.	F7	66
Kilis, Tur.	B8	58
Kilkee, Ire.	I3	12
Kilkenny, Ire.	I5	12
Kilkenny, state, Ire.	I5	12
Kilkís, Grc.	C5	28
Killaloe, Ire.	I4	12
Killaloe Station, On., Can.	C12	112
Killam, Ab., Can.	D19	138
Killarney, Austl.	G9	76
Killarney, Mb., Can.	E14	124
Killarney, On., Can.	C8	112
Killarney, Ire.	I3	12
Killdeer, N.D., U.S.	G11	124
Killeen, Tx., U.S.	C10	130
Killen, Al., U.S.	C11	122
Killington Peak, mtn., Vt., U.S.	G4	110
Killiniq Island, i., Can.	E13	141
Killybegs, Ire.	G4	12
Kilmarnock, Scot., U.K.	F8	12
Kilmarnock, Va., U.S.	G9	114
Kilmore, Austl.	K5	76
Kilo, Indon.	H11	50
Kilombero, stm., Tan.	F7	66
Kilomines, D.R.C.	D5	66
Kilosa, Tan.	F7	66
Kilrush, Ire.	I3	12
Kilttān Island, i., India	F3	46
Kilwa, D.R.C.	F5	66
Kilwa Kivinje, Tan.	F7	66
Kim, Co., U.S.	D5	128
Kimba, Austl.	F7	74
Kimball, Ne., U.S.	F9	126
Kimball, S.D., U.S.	D13	126
Kimbe Bay, b., Pap. N. Gui.	b5	79a
Kimberley, B.C., Can.	G15	138
Kimberley, S. Afr.	F7	70
Kimberley Downs, Austl.	C4	74
Kimberley Plateau, plat., Austl.	C5	74
Kimberling City, Mo., U.S.	H4	120
Kimberly, Id., U.S.	H12	136
Kimberly, Wi., U.S.	G10	118
Kimch'aek, Kor., N.	D8	38
Kimch'ŏn, Kor., S.	F8	38
Kimhae, Kor., S.	D1	40
Kimito, Fin.	F10	8
Kim-me-ni-oli Wash, stm., N.M., U.S.	H8	132
Kimmirut, N.T., Can.	C17	106
Kímolos, i., Grc.	G7	28
Kimovsk, Russia	F21	10
Kimpō-zan, mtn., Japan	D11	40
Kimry, Russia	D20	10
Kinabalu, Gunong (Kinabalu, Mount), mtn., Malay.	G1	52
Kinabalu National Park, p.o.i., Malay.	H1	52
Kinabatangan, stm., Malay.	H2	52
Kinbasket Lake, res., B.C., Can.	D12	138
Kincaid, Sk., Can.	E6	124
Kincardine, On., Can.	D8	112
Kinchafoonee Creek, stm., Ga., U.S.	F14	122
Kinchega National Park, p.o.i., Austl.	I4	76
Kinda, D.R.C.	F4	66
Kinde, Mi., U.S.	E7	112
Kinder, La., U.S.	G6	122
Kindersley, Sk., Can.	C4	124
Kindia, Gui.	G2	64
Kindu, D.R.C.	E5	66
Kinešma, Russia	H19	8
King, N.C., U.S.	H5	114
King and Queen Court House, Va., U.S.	G9	114
Kingaroy, Austl.	F8	76
King City, On., Can.	E10	112
King City, Ca., U.S.	G4	134
Kingfield, Me., U.S.	F6	110
Kingfisher, Ok., U.S.	F10	128
King George, Va., U.S.	F8	114
King George, Mount, mtn., B.C., Can.	F15	138
King George Islands, is., N.T., Can.	D14	106
King George Sound, strt., Austl.	G3	74
King Hill, Id., U.S.	G11	136
Kingisepp, Russia	A11	10
King Island, i., Austl.	m12	77a
King Island, i., B.C., Can.	D3	138
King Leopold Ranges, mts., Austl.	C4	74
Kingman, Az., U.S.	H2	132
Kingman, Ks., U.S.	D10	128
Kingman Reef, rf., Oc.	C10	72
King Mountain, mtn., Or., U.S.	H3	136
Kingombe, D.R.C.	E5	66
Kingoonya, Austl.	F7	74
King Peak, mtn., Ca., U.S.	C1	134
Kings, stm., Ca., U.S.	G6	134
Kings Beach, Ca., U.S.	D5	134
Kingsbridge, Eng., U.K.	K9	12
Kingsburg, Ca., U.S.	G6	134
Kings Canyon National Park, p.o.i., Ca., U.S.	G7	134
Kingsford, Mi., U.S.	C1	112
Kingshill, V.I.U.S.	h10	104c
Kingsland, Ar., U.S.	D6	122
Kingsland, Ga., U.S.	F4	116
Kingsley, S. Afr.	E10	70
Kingsley, Ia., U.S.	B2	120
Kingsley, Mi., U.S.	D4	112
Kingsley Dam, dam, Ne., U.S.	F11	126
King's Lynn, Eng., U.K.	I13	12
Kings Mountain, N.C., U.S.	A4	116
King Solomon's Mines see Mikhrot Timna', hist., Isr.	I5	58
King Sound, strt., Austl.	C4	74
Kings Peak, mtn., Ut., U.S.	C6	132
Kingsport, Tn., U.S.	H3	114
Kingston, N.S., Can.	E11	110
Kingston, On., Can.	D13	112
Kingston, Jam.	i14	104d
Kingston, N.Z.	G3	80
Kingston, Norf. I.	y25	78i
Kingston, Ga., U.S.	C14	122
Kingston, Mo., U.S.	E3	120
Kingston, N.Y., U.S.	C11	114
Kingston, Ok., U.S.	C2	122
Kingston, Pa., U.S.	C9	114
Kingston, Tn., U.S.	I13	120
Kingston Southeast, Austl.	K2	76
Kingston upon Hull, Eng., U.K.	H12	12
Kingston upon Thames, Eng., U.K.	J12	12
Kingstown, St. Vin.	o11	105e
Kingstree, S.C., U.S.	C6	116
Kingsville, On., Can.	G7	112
Kingsville, Tx., U.S.	G10	130
Kingtechen see Jingdezhen, China	G7	42
King William Island, i., N.T., Can.	B11	106
King William's Town, S. Afr.	H8	70
Kinhwa see Jinhua, China	G8	42
Kınık, Tur.	D10	28
Kinira, stm., S. Afr.	G9	70
Kinistino, Sk., Can.	B9	124
Kinkala, Congo	E2	66
Kinlochleven, Scot., U.K.	E8	12
Kinnaird Head, c., Scot., U.K.	D10	12
Kinneret, Yam (Galilee, Sea of), l., Isr.	F6	58
Kinosaki, Japan	D7	40
Kinpoku-san, mtn., Japan	A11	40
Kinross, Scot., U.K.	E9	12
Kinsale, Monts.	D3	105a
Kinsale, Old Head of, c., Ire.	J4	12
Kinsarvik, Nor.	F2	8
Kinshasa (Léopoldville), D.R.C.	E3	66
Kinsley, Ks., U.S.	D9	128
Kinsman, Oh., U.S.	C5	114
Kinston, N.C., U.S.	A8	116
Kintampo, Ghana	H4	64
Kintyre, pen., Scot., U.K.	F7	12
Kintyre, Mull of, c., Scot., U.K.	F7	12
Kinuseo Falls, wtfl, B.C., Can.	B9	138
Kinuso, Ab., Can.	A15	138
Kinyangiri, Tan.	E6	66
Kinyeti, mtn., Sudan	G6	62
Kinzia, D.R.C.	E3	66
Kinzua, Or., U.S.	E7	136
Kinzua Dam, dam, Pa., U.S.	C6	114
Kiowa, Co., U.S.	B4	128
Kiowa, Ok., U.S.	C3	122
Kiowa Creek, stm., Co., U.S.	A4	128
Kipawa, stm., Qc., Can.	B11	112
Kipawa, Lac, res., Qc., Can.	A10	112
Kipembawe, Tan.	F6	66
Kipengere Range, mts., Tan.	F6	66
Kipili, Tan.	F6	66
Kipini, Kenya	E8	66
Kipling, Sk., Can.	D11	124
Kipnuk, Ak., U.S.	E7	140
Kipushi, D.R.C.	G5	66
Kirakira, Sol. Is.	f9	79b
Kirandul, India	B5	53
Kiraųsk, Bela.	G12	10
Kirazlı, Tur.	C9	28
Kirbla, Est.	B6	10
Kirchberg, Ger.	G5	16
Kirchmöser, Ger.	D8	16
Kireevsk, Russia	G20	10
Kirejkovo, Russia	G18	10
Kirenga, stm., Russia	C19	32
Kirensk, Russia	C19	32
Kirghizia see Kyrgyzstan, ctry., Asia	F12	32
Kirgiz Range, mts., Asia	F12	32
Kirgiz Soviet Socialist Republic see Kyrgyzstan, ctry., Asia	F12	32
Kiri, D.R.C.	E3	66
Kiribati, ctry., Oc.	D9	72
Kırıkhan, Tur.	B7	58
Kırıkkale, Tur.	B3	56
Kirillovo, Russia	H21	8
Kirin see Jilin, China	C7	38
Kirin see Jilin, state, China	C10	36
Kirinyaga (Kenya, Mount), mtn., Kenya	E7	66
Kirishima-Yaku-kokuritsu-kōen, p.o.i., Japan	H3	40
Kirishima-yama, vol., Japan	H3	40
Kiriši, Russia	A15	10
Kiritimati (Christmas Island), at., Kir.	C11	72
Kiriwina Islands (Trobriand Islands), is., Pap. N. Gui.	b5	79a
Kırka, Tur.	D13	28
Kırkağaç, Tur.	D10	28
Kirkcaldy, Scot., U.K.	E9	12
Kirkcudbright, Scot., U.K.	G8	12
Kirkenes, Nor.	B14	8
Kirkland, Il., U.S.	B9	120
Kirkland, Tx., U.S.	G8	128
Kirkland, Wa., U.S.	C4	136
Kirkland Lake, On., Can.	F14	106
Kırklareli, Tur.	B10	28
Kırklareli, state, Tur.	B10	28
Kirklin, In., U.S.	H3	112
Kirkpatrick, Mount, mtn., Ant.	D21	81
Kirksville, Mo., U.S.	D5	120
Kirkwall, Scot., U.K.	B9	12
Kirkwood, S. Afr.	H7	70
Kirkwood, Mo., U.S.	F7	120
Kirmir, stm., Tur.	C15	28
Kirn, Ger.	G3	16
Kirov, Russia	F17	10
Kirov, Russia	C7	32
Kirovakan see Vanadzor, Arm.	A5	56
Kirovohrad, Ukr.	E4	32
Kirovohrad, co., Ukr.	A17	26
Kirovsk, Russia	C15	8
Kirovsk, Turkmen.	B9	56
Kirovskaja oblast', co., Russia	F22	8
Kirovskij, Kaz.	F13	32
Kirovskij, Russia	F20	34
Kirovskij, Russia	B10	38
Kirriemuir, Scot., U.K.	E9	12
Kirs, Russia	C8	32
Kirsanov, Russia	D6	32
Kırşehir, Tur.	B3	56
Kīrthar Range, mts., Pak.	D10	56
Kirtland, N.M., U.S.	G8	132
Kiruna, Swe.	C8	8
Kirundu, D.R.C.	E5	66
Kirwin, Ks., U.S.	B9	128
Kiryū, Japan	C12	40
Kiržač, Russia	D21	10
Kisa, Swe.	G6	8
Kisangani (Stanleyville), D.R.C.	D5	66
Kisar, Pulau, i., Indon.	G8	44
Kisaran, Indon.	B1	50
Kisarazu, Japan	D12	40
Kisbey, Sk., Can.	E11	124
Kiselëvsk, Russia	D15	32
Kīsh, Jazīreh-ye, i., Iran	D7	56
Kishanganj, India	E11	54
Kishangarh, India	E3	54
Kishangarh Bās, India	E5	54
Kishi, Nig.	H5	64
Kishinev see Chişinău, Mol.	B15	26
Kishiwada, Japan	E8	40
Kishorganj, Bngl.	F13	54
Kisii, Kenya	E6	66
Kisiju, Tan.	F7	66
Kisiwada see Kishiwada, Japan	E8	40
Kiska Island, i., Ak., U.S.	g22	140a
Kiskatinaw, stm., B.C., Can.	A10	138
Kiska Volcano, vol., Ak., U.S.	g22	140a
Kiskörei-víztároló, res., Hung.	B7	26
Kiskőrös, Hung.	C6	26
Kiskunfélegyháza, Hung.	C6	26
Kiskunhalas, Hung.	C6	26
Kiskunmajsa, Hung.	C6	26
Kiskunsági Nemzeti Park, p.o.i., Hung.	C6	26
Kislovodsk, Russia	F6	32
Kismaayo, Som.	E8	66
Kiso, stm., Japan	D9	40
Kiso-sammyaku, mts., Japan	D10	40
Kissidougou, Gui.	H2	64
Kissimmee, Fl., U.S.	H4	116
Kissimmee, stm., Fl., U.S.	I4	116
Kissimmee, Lake, l., Fl., U.S.	I4	116
Kississing Lake, l., Mb., Can.	D10	106
Kisújszállás, Hung.	B7	26
Kisuki, Japan	D5	40
Kisumu, Kenya	E6	66
Kisvárda, Hung.	A9	26
Kita, Mali	G3	64
Kitaa see Vestgrønland, state, Grnld.	D16	141
Kitaibaraki, Japan	C13	40
Kitakami, stm., Japan	E14	38
Kitakata, Japan	B12	40
Kitakyūshū, Japan	F3	40
Kitale, Kenya	D7	66
Kitami, Japan	C15	38
Kitangiri, Lake, l., Tan.	E6	66
Kitchener, On., Can.	E9	112
Kithārah, Khirbat, hist., Jord.	I6	58
Kitimat, B.C., Can.	B2	138
Kitimat Ranges, mts., B.C., Can.	C2	138
Kitinen, stm., Fin.	C12	8
Kitíou, Akrotírion, c., Cyp.	D4	58
Kitridge Point, c., Barb.	n9	105d
Kitsuki, Japan	F4	40
Kittanning, Pa., U.S.	D6	114
Kittitas, Wa., U.S.	D6	136
Kitt Peak National Observatory, sci., Az., U.S.	K5	132
Kitui, Kenya	E7	66
Kitunda, Tan.	F6	66
Kitwanga, B.C., Can.	A2	138
Kitwe, Zam.	C4	68
Kityang see Jieyang, China	J7	42
Kitzbühel, Aus.	C9	22
Kitzingen, Ger.	G6	16
Kiukiang see Jiujiang, China	G6	42
Kiunga, Pap. N. Gui.	b3	79a
Kiuruvesi, Fin.	E12	8
Kivalina, Ak., U.S.	C7	140
Kivijärvi, l., Fin.	E11	8
Kiviõli, Est.	G12	8
Kivu, Lake, l., Afr.	E5	66
Kıyıköy, Tur.	B11	28
Kiyiu Lake, l., Sk., Can.	C5	124
Kızıl Adalar, is., Tur.	C11	28
Kızılcabölük, Tur.	F11	28
Kızılcahamam, Tur.	C15	28
Kızıldağ Milli Parkı, p.o.i., Tur.	F14	28
Kızılırmak, stm., Tur.	A4	56
Kızılören, Tur.	F15	28
Kizimkazi, Tan.	F7	66
Kızkalesi, hist., Tur.	B4	58
Kizljar, Russia	F7	32
Kizyl-Atrek, Turkmen.	B7	56
Kizyl-Su, Turkmen.	B7	56
Kjahta, Russia	F10	34
Kjungej-Ala-Too, hrebet, mts., Asia	F13	32
Kjusjur, Russia	B14	34
Kjustendil, Blg.	G9	26
Klabat, Gunung, vol., Indon.	E8	44
Kladno, Czech Rep.	F10	16
Kladovo, Yugo.	E9	26
Klagan, Malay.	G1	52
Klagenfurt, Aus.	D11	22
Klaipėda (Memel), Lith.	E3	10
Klakah, Indon.	G8	50
Klamath, stm., U.S.	B2	134
Klamath Falls, Or., U.S.	A3	134
Klamath Marsh, sw., Or., U.S.	H5	136
Klamath Mountains, mts., U.S.	B2	134
Klamono, Indon.	F9	44
Klang, Malay.	K5	48
Klangenan, Indon.	G6	50
Klangenang, Indon.	G6	50
Klangpi, Mya.	G14	54
Klatovy, Czech Rep.	G9	16
Klawer, S. Afr.	G4	70
Kleck, Bela.	G9	10
Kleczew, Pol.	D14	16
Kleena Kleene, B.C., Can.	E5	138
Klein Curaçao, i., Neth. Ant.	q22	104g
Klein Karroo see Little Karroo, plat., S. Afr.	H5	70
Klein Namaland see Little Namaqualand, hist. reg., S. Afr.	F3	70
Klekovača, mtn., Bos.	E3	26
Klemme, Ia., U.S.	A4	120
Klemtu, B.C., Can.	D2	138
Klerksdorp, S. Afr.	E8	70
Kletnja, Russia	G16	10
Kleve, Ger.	E2	16
Klickitat, stm., Wa., U.S.	E5	136
Klimavičy, Bela.	G14	10
Klimino, Russia	C17	32
Klimovo, Russia	H15	10
Klimovsk, Russia	E20	10
Klimpfjäll, Swe.	D6	8
Klin, Russia	D19	10
Klinaklini, stm., B.C., Can.	E5	138
Klincy, Russia	H15	10
Klingenthal, Ger.	F8	16
Klínovec, mtn., Czech Rep.	F8	16
Klintehamn, Swe.	H8	8
Klip, stm., S. Afr.	E9	70
Klipdale, S. Afr.	I4	70
Klipplaat, S. Afr.	H7	70
Klisura, Blg.	G11	26
Kljazma, stm., Russia	E21	10
Ključ, Bos.	E3	26
Ključevskaja Sopka, vulkan, vol., Russia	E21	34
Ključi, Russia	E21	34
Kljukvenka, Russia	C15	32
Kłobuck, Pol.	F14	16
Kłodawa, Pol.	D14	16
Kłodzko, Pol.	F12	16
Klondike, hist. reg., Yk., Can.	C3	106
Klooga, Est.	A7	10
Klosterneuburg, Aus.	B13	22
Kloten, Switz.	C5	22
Klotz, Lac, l., Qc., Can.	C16	106
Klötze, Ger.	D7	16
Kluane Lake, l., Yk., Can.	C3	106
Kluczbork, Pol.	F14	16
Klungkung, Indon.	H9	50
Knaddah, Syria	C7	58
Knapp, Wi., U.S.	G6	118
Kneehills Creek, stm., Ab., Can.	E17	138
Knee Lake, l., Mb., Can.	D12	106
Kneža, Blg.	F11	26
Knić, Yugo.	F7	26
Knickerbocker, Tx., U.S.	C7	130
Knife, stm., N.D., U.S.	G12	124
Knight Inlet, b., B.C., Can.	F4	138
Knights Landing, Ca., U.S.	E4	134
Knin, Cro.	F13	22
Knippa, Tx., U.S.	E8	130
Knittelfeld, Aus.	C11	22
Knjaževac, Yugo.	F9	26
Knob Noster, Mo., U.S.	F4	120
Knokke-Heist, Bel.	C12	14
Knosós, hist., Grc.	H8	28
Knox, Pa., U.S.	C6	114
Knox, Cape, c., B.C., Can.	E4	106
Knox City, Tx., U.S.	H9	128
Knox Coast, cst., Ant.	B15	81
Knoxville, Ga., U.S.	D2	116
Knoxville, Il., U.S.	D7	120
Knoxville, Tn., U.S.	I2	114
Knuckles, mtn., Sri L.	H5	53
Knud Rasmussen Land, reg., Grnld.	A14	141
Knysna, S. Afr.	I6	70
Knyszyn, Pol.	C18	16
Kob', Russia	C18	32
Kobar Sink, depr., Eth.	E8	62
Kobayashi, Japan	H3	40
Kōbe, Japan	E8	40
København (Copenhagen), Den.	I4	8
København, state, Den.	I5	8
Kobjaj, Russia	D14	34
Koblenz, Ger.	F3	16
K'obo, Eth.	E7	62
Koboža, Russia	B18	10
Koboža, stm., Russia	A18	10
Kobroor, Pulau, i., Indon.	G10	44
Kobryn, Bela.	H7	10
Kobuk, Ak., U.S.	C8	140
Kobuk, stm., Ak., U.S.	C8	140
Kobuleti, Geor.	F6	32
Kobylin, Pol.	E13	16
Kocaali, Tur.	B13	28
Kocaavşar, stm., Tur.	D10	28
Kocaeli, state, Tur.	C12	28
Kočani, Mac.	B5	28
Koçarlı, Tur.	F10	28
Kočečum, stm., Russia	C8	34
Kočevje, Slvn.	E11	22
Kočevo, Russia	C8	32
Kŏch'ang, Kor., S.	G7	38
Koch Bihār, India	E12	54
Kocher, stm., Ger.	G5	16
Kochi (Cochin), India	G3	53
Kōchi, Japan	F6	40
Kōchi, state, Japan	F6	40
Koch Island, i., N.T., Can.	B15	106
Kochiu see Gejiu, China	G5	36
Kodaikānal, India	F3	53
Kodar, hrebet, mts., Russia	E12	34
Kodāri, Nepal	E10	54
Kodarma, India	F10	54
Kodiak, Ak., U.S.	E9	140
Kodiak Island, i., Ak., U.S.	E9	140
Kodinār, India	H3	54
Kodok, Sudan	F6	62
Kodyma, Ukr.	A16	26
Kodyma, stm., Ukr.	B17	26
Koës, Nmb.	D4	70
Köflach, Aus.	C11	22
Koforidua, Ghana	H4	64
Kōfu, Japan	D11	40
Koga, Japan	C12	40
Kogaluc, stm., Qc., Can.	D15	106
Kogaluc, Baie, b., Qc., Can.	D15	106
Kogan, Austl.	F8	76
Køge, Den.	I5	8
Kogon, stm., Gui.	G2	64
Kohanava, Bela.	F12	10
Kohāt, Pak.	B3	54
Kohīma, India	C7	46
Kohler, Wi., U.S.	E2	112
Kohtla-Järve, Est.	G12	8
Kohyl'nyk (Cogâlnic), stm., Eur.	C15	26
Koide, Japan	B11	40
Koigi, Est.	B8	10
Koindu, S.L.	H2	64
Koiva (Gauja), stm., Eur.	C7	10
Kojda, Russia	C20	8

Name	Map Ref.	Page
Kŏje-do, i., Kor., S.	E1	40
Kojgorodok, Russia	B8	32
Kojonup, Austl.	F3	74
Kok (Hkok), stm., Asia	B4	48
Kokalaat, Kaz.	E10	32
Kokand, Uzb.	F12	32
Kokas, Indon.	F9	44
Kokčetav, Kaz.	D12	32
Kokemäki, Fin.	F9	8
Kokenau, Indon.	F10	44
Kokhav HaYarden, hist., Isr.	F6	58
Kokiu see Gejiu, China	G5	36
Kokkilai Lagoon, b., Sri L.	G5	53
Kokkola, Fin.	E10	8
Kokoda, Pap. N. Gui.	b4	79a
Kokomo, In., U.S.	H3	112
Kokomo, Ms., U.S.	F8	122
Kokong, Bots.	D6	70
Kokopo, Pap. N. Gui.	a5	79a
Kokorevka, Russia	H17	10
Koksan-ŭp, Kor., N.	E7	38
Kökshetaū see Kokčetav, Kaz.	D12	32
Koksoak, stm., Qc., Can.	D17	106
Kokstad, S. Afr.	G9	70
Kokubu, Japan	H3	40
Kola, Russia	B15	8
Kolachel, India	G3	53
Kolaka, Indon.	F7	44
Kolangār, Afg.	A2	54
Kola Peninsula see Kol'skij poluostrov, pen., Russia	C17	8
Kolār, India	E3	53
Kolāras, India	F6	54
Kolār Gold Fields, India	E4	53
Kolárovo, Slov.	I13	16
Kolašin, Yugo.	G6	26
Kolbio, Kenya	E8	66
Kolbuszowa, Pol.	F17	16
Kol'čugino, Russia	D22	10
Kolda, Sen.	G2	64
Kolding, Den.	I3	8
Kole, D.R.C.	E4	66
Kolea, Alg.	H13	20
Kolguev, ostrov, i., Russia	B18	6
Kolhāpur, India	C4	53
Kolhāpur, India	C1	53
Koli, Russia	A17	10
Kolín, Czech Rep.	F11	16
Koljubakino, Russia	E19	10
Kollam see Quilon, India	G3	53
Kollegāl, India	E3	53
Kolleru Lake, l., India	C5	53
Kolmogorovo, Russia	C16	32
Köln (Cologne), Ger.	E2	16
Kolno, Pol.	C17	16
Koło, Pol.	D14	16
Koloa, Hi., U.S.	B2	78a
Kołobrzeg, Pol.	B11	16
Kolodnja, Russia	F15	10
Kolokani, Mali	G3	64
Kolombangara Island, i., Sol. Is.	d7	79b
Kolomna, Russia	E21	10
Kolomyia, Ukr.	A12	26
Kolonga, Tonga	n14	78e
Kolonia, Micron.	m11	78d
Kolonodale, Indon.	F7	44
Kolosib, India	F14	54
Kolosovka, Russia	C12	32
Kolovai, Tonga	n13	78e
Kolozsvár see Cluj-Napoca, Rom.	C10	26
Kolp', stm., Russia	A19	10
Kolpaševo, Russia	C14	32
Kolpino, Russia	A13	10
Kolpny, Russia	H19	10
Kol'skij poluostrov (Kola Peninsula), pen., Russia	C17	8
Koluton, Kaz.	D11	32
Kolwezi, D.R.C.	G5	66
Kolyma, stm., Russia	C20	34
Kolyma Plain see Kolymskaja nizmennost', pl., Russia	C19	34
Kolymskaja, Russia	C20	34
Kolymskaja nizmennost' (Kolyma Plain), pl., Russia	C19	34
Kom, mtn., Blg.	F10	26
Koma, Mya.	E4	48
Komadugu Gana, stm., Nig.	G7	64
Komagane, Japan	D10	40
Komandorskie ostrova, is., Russia	D20	30
Komandorski Islands see Komandorskie ostrova, is., Russia	D20	30
Komárno, Slov.	I13	16
Komarnyky, Ukr.	G19	16
Komárom, Hung.	B5	26
Komárom-Esztergom, state, Hung.	B5	26
Komati (Incomati), stm., Afr.	E10	70
Komatipoort, S. Afr.	D10	70
Komatsu, Japan	C9	40
Komatsushima, Japan	E7	40
Kome Island, i., Ug.	E6	66
Komering, stm., Indon.	E4	50
Komfane, Indon.	G9	44
Komi, state, Russia	B8	32
Komissarovo, Russia	B9	38
Komló, Hung.	C5	26
Kommunizma, pik, mtn., Taj.	B11	56
Komodo, Pulau, i., Indon.	H11	50
Komodo National Park, p.o.i., Indon.	H11	50
Komoé, stm., Afr.	H4	64
Kom Ombo, Egypt	C6	62
Komoran, Pulau, i., Indon.	G10	44
Komoro, Japan	C11	40
Komotiní, Grc.	B8	28
Kompasberg, mtn., S. Afr.	G7	70
Komsomolec, Kaz.	D10	32
Komsomolec, zaliv, b., Kaz.	E8	32
Komsomol'sk, Russia	H18	8
Komsomol'sk, Russia	C15	32
Komsomol'sk-na-Amure, Russia	F16	34
Komsomol'skoj Pravdy, ostrova, is., Russia	A10	34
Konakovo, Russia	D19	10
Konakpınar, Tur.	D10	28
Konar, stm., Asia	A3	54
Konārak, India	I11	54
Konawa, Ok., U.S.	C2	122
Konch, India	F7	54
Konda, stm., Russia	B10	32
Kondagaon, India	B5	53
Kondega, Russia	F15	8
Kondinin, Austl.	F3	74
Kondoa, Tan.	E7	66
Kondopoga, Russia	E16	8
Kondrovo, Russia	F18	10
Kondukūr, India	D4	53
Kondūz, Afg.	B10	56
Koné, N. Cal.	m15	79d
Kong, stm., Asia	F8	48
Kŏng, Kaôh, i., Camb.	G6	48
Kongcheng, China	F7	42
Kong Christian IX Land, reg., Grnld.	D18	141
Kong Christian X Land, reg., Grnld.	C19	141
Kong Frederik VIII Land, reg., Grnld.	B19	141
Kong Frederik VI Kyst, cst., Grnld.	E17	141
Kongjiawopeng, China	B5	38
Kongju, Kor., S.	F7	38
Kongmoon see Jiangmen, China	J5	42
Kongolo, D.R.C.	F5	66
Kongor, Sudan	F6	62
Kong Oscar Fjord, strt., Grnld.	C21	141
Kongsvinger, Nor.	F5	8
Kongur Shan, mtn., China	G13	32
Kong Wilhelms Land, reg., Grnld.	B21	141
Konice, Czech Rep.	G12	16
Königsberg see Kaliningrad, Russia	F3	10
Königswinter, Ger.	F3	16
Konin, Pol.	D14	16
Konin, state, Pol.	D14	16
Konispol, Alb.	E14	24
Kónitsa, Grc.	C3	28
Konjic, Bos.	F4	26
Konkiep, stm., Nmb.	E3	70
Konkouré, stm., Gui.	G2	64
Konna, Mali	G4	64
Konnevesi, l., Fin.	E12	8
Konnur, India	C2	53
Konoša, Russia	F18	8
Kōnosu, Japan	C12	40
Konotop, Ukr.	E15	6
Końskie, Pol.	E16	16
Konstantinovskij, Russia	C22	10
Konstanz, Ger.	I4	16
Kontagora, Nig.	G5	64
Kontcha, Cam.	C2	66
Kontha, Mya.	C3	48
Kontseba, Ukr.	A16	26
Kon Tum, Viet.	E8	48
Konya, Tur.	F15	28
Konya, state, Tur.	E15	28
Konz, Ger.	G2	16
Konza, Kenya	E7	66
Konžakovskij Kamen', gora, mtn., Russia	C9	32
Koocanusa, Lake, res., N.A.	B11	136
Kookynie, Austl.	E4	74
Koolatah, Austl.	C8	74
Kooloonong, Austl.	J4	76
Koontz Lake, In., U.S.	G3	112
Koorawatha, Austl.	J7	76
Koosa, Est.	B9	10
Kooskia, Id., U.S.	D11	136
Kootenai (Kootenay), stm., N.A.	G13	138
Kootenay (Kootenai), stm., N.A.	G13	138
Kootenay Lake, l., B.C., Can.	G14	138
Kootenay National Park, p.o.i., B.C., Can.	F14	138
Kopāganj, India	E9	54
Kopargaon, India	B2	53
Kópavogur, Ice.	k29	8a
Kopejsk, Russia	C10	32
Koper, Slvn.	E10	22
Kopervik, Nor.	G1	8
Kopet Mountains, mts., Asia	B8	56
Köping, Swe.	G6	8
Koplik, Alb.	B13	24
Koppal, India	D3	53
Koppang, Nor.	F4	8
Koppies, S. Afr.	E8	70
Koprivnica, Cro.	D13	22
Köprü, stm., Tur.	F14	28
Köprülü Kanyon Milli Parkı, p.o.i., Tur.	F14	28
Kopylovo, Russia	F21	8
Korab (Korabit, Maja e), mtn., Eur.	C14	24
Korabit, Maja e (Korab), mtn., Eur.	C14	24
Korāput, India	B6	53
Korarou, Lac, l., Mali	F4	64
Koratla, India	B4	53
Korba, India	G9	54
Korba, Tun.	H4	24
Korbach, Ger.	E4	16
Korça see Korçë, Alb.	D14	24
Korçë, Alb.	D14	24
Korčula, Cro.	H14	22
Korčula, Otok, i., Cro.	H13	22
Korea, North, ctry., Asia	D7	38
Korea, South, ctry., Asia	G8	38
Korea Bay, b., Asia	E5	38
Korea Strait, strt., Asia	E2	40
Korelakša, Russia	D15	8
Korenovsk, Russia	E5	32
Korf, Russia	D22	34
Korhogo, C. Iv.	H3	64
Korientzé, Mali	F4	64
Korim, Indon.	F10	44
Korinthiakós Kólpos (Corinth, Gulf of), b., Grc.	E5	28
Kórinthos, Grc.	F5	28
Kōriyama, Japan	B13	40
Korjakskaja Sopka, vulkan, vol., Russia	F20	34
Korjakskoe nagor'e, mts., Russia	D22	34
Korjažma, Russia	F22	8
Korkino, Russia	D10	32
Korkuteli, Tur.	F13	28
Korla, China	C2	36
Korliki, Russia	B14	32
Körmend, Hung.	C3	26
Kornat, Otok, i., Cro.	G12	22
Kornati, Nacionalni Park, p.o.i., Cro.	G12	22
Korner, Mt., U.S.	A14	136
Korneuburg, Aus.	B13	22
Koro, i., Fiji	p19	79e
Köroğlu Tepesi, mtn., Tur.	C14	28
Korogwe, Tan.	F7	66
Koroleve, Ukr.	H19	16
Koromere see East Cape, c., N.Z.	C8	80
Koronadal, Phil.	G5	52
Koróni, Grc.	G4	28
Korónia, Límni, l., Grc.	C6	28
Korópi, Grc.	F6	28
Koror, Palau	g8	78b
Körös, stm., Hung.	C7	26
Koro Sea, Fiji	p20	79e
Korosten', Ukr.	E14	6
Koro Toro, Chad	D3	62
Korotyš, Russia	H20	10
Korovin Volcano, vol., Ak., U.S.	g24	140a
Korovou, Fiji	p19	79e
Koroyanitu, mtn., Fiji	p18	79e
Korsakov, Russia	G17	34
Korsakovo, Russia	G20	10
Korsør, Den.	I4	8
Koršunovo, Russia	C20	32
Kortrijk, Bel.	D12	14
Korucam, Cape see Koruçam Burnu, c., N. Cyp.	C3	58
Koruçam Burnu, c., N. Cyp.	C3	58
Korucu, Tur.	D10	28
Korumburra, Austl.	L5	76
Koryak Mountains see Korjakskoe nagor'e, mts., Russia	D22	34
Koryŏng, Kor., S.	D1	40
Kos (Cos), i., Grc.	G10	28
Kosa, Russia	C8	32
Kosa, Russia	F10	34
Kosai, Japan	E10	40
Kosaja Gora, Russia	F20	10
Koščagyl, Kaz.	E8	32
Kościan, Pol.	D12	16
Kościerzyna, Pol.	B14	16
Kosciusko, Ms., U.S.	D9	122
Kosciusko, Mount, mtn., Austl.	K6	76
Kosciusko National Park, p.o.i., Austl.	K6	76
Kose, Est.	A8	10
Koshikijima-rettō, is., Japan	H2	40
Koshkonong, Lake, l., Wi., U.S.	B9	120
Kōshoku, Japan	C11	40
Košice, Slov.	H17	16
Kosi Kalan, India	E6	54
Kosimeer, l., S. Afr.	E11	70
Kosiv, Ukr.	A12	26
Köşk, Tur.	F11	28
Koslan, Russia	E23	8
Kosŏng, Kor., S.	E1	40
Kosŏng-ŭp, Kor., N.	E8	38
Kosovo-Metohija, co., Yugo.	G7	26
Kosovska Mitrovica, Yugo.	G7	26
Kosrae, i., Micron.	C7	72
Kösreli, Tur.	A6	58
Kosse, Tx., U.S.	F2	122
Kossou, Lac de, res., C. Iv.	H3	64
Kostenec, Blg.	G10	26
Koster, S. Afr.	D8	70
Kostomukša, Russia	D14	8
Kostonjärvi, l., Fin.	D12	8
Kostroma, Russia	H19	8
Kostroma, stm., Russia	G19	8
Kostromskaja oblast', co., Russia	G20	8
Kostrzyn, Pol.	D10	16
Kosum Phisai, Thai.	D6	48
Koszalin, Pol.	B12	16
Koszalin, state, Pol.	C12	16
Kőszeg, Hung.	B3	26
Kota, India	G9	54
Kota, India	F5	54
Kotaagung, Indon.	F4	50
Kotabangun, Indon.	D10	50
Kotabaru, Indon.	E10	50
Kota Belud, Malay.	G1	52
Kota Bharu, Malay.	I6	48
Kotabumi, Indon.	F4	50
Kotadabok, Indon.	D4	50
Kot Addu, Pak.	C3	54
Kota Kinabalu, Malay.	G1	52
Kotamobagu, Indon.	E7	44
Kotapinang, Indon.	C1	50
Kota Tinggi, Malay.	L6	48
Kotawaringin, Indon.	E7	50
Kotcho Lake, l., B.C., Can.	D6	106
Kot Chutta, Pak.	D3	54
Kotel'nič, Russia	C7	32
Kotel'nikovo, Russia	E6	32
Kotel'nyj, ostrov, i., Russia	A16	34
Kotelnyj, ostrov, i., Russia	B3	34
Köthen, Ger.	E7	16
Kotikovo, Russia	G17	34
Kotka, Fin.	F12	8
Kot Kapūra, India	C5	54
Kotlas, Russia	F22	8
Kotli, Pak.	B4	54
Kotlik, Ak., U.S.	D7	140
Kôtomo, Île, i., N. Cal.	n16	79d
Kotor, Yugo.	G5	26
Kotoriba, Cro.	D13	22
Kotovs'k, Ukr.	B16	26
Kot Pūtli, India	E6	54
Kotri, Pak.	F2	54
Kottagūdem, India	C5	53
Kottayam, India	G3	53
Kotto, stm., C.A.R.	C4	66
Kottūru, India	D3	53
Kotuj, stm., Russia	B9	34
Kotzebue, Ak., U.S.	C7	140
Kotzebue Sound, strt., Ak., U.S.	C7	140
Kötzting, Ger.	G8	16
Kouang-si see Guangxi, state, China	G6	36
Kouang-tong see Guangdong, state, China	J6	42
Kouaoua, N. Cal.	m15	79d
Kouchibouguac National Park, p.o.i., N.B., Can.	D11	110
Koudougou, Burkina	G4	64
Kouei-tcheou see Guizhou, state, China	H2	42
Kouga, stm., S. Afr.	H7	70
Kougaberge, mts., S. Afr.	H6	70
Koukdjuak, stm., N.T., Can.	B16	106
Kouki, C.A.R.	C3	66
Koúklia, Cyp.	D3	58
Koulamoutou, Gabon	E2	66
Koulikoro, Mali	G3	64
Koumala, Austl.	C7	76
Koumbia, Gui.	G2	64
Koumpentoum, Sen.	G2	64
Koumra, Chad	F3	62
Koundâra, Gui.	G2	64
Kounradskij, Kaz.	E12	32
Kourou, Fr. Gu.	B7	84
Kouroussa, Gui.	G3	64
Kousséri, Cam.	B2	66
Koussi, Emi, mtn., Chad	D3	62
Koutiala, Mali	G3	64
Kouts, In., U.S.	G2	112
Kouvola, Fin.	F12	8
Kova, Russia	C18	32
Kovada Milli Parkı, p.o.i., Tur.	F13	28
Kovarskas, Lith.	E7	10
Kovdor, Russia	C14	8
Kovdozero, ozero, res., Russia	C14	8
Kovilpatti, India	G3	53
Kovrov, Russia	H19	8
Kovūr, India	D5	53
Kovža, Russia	F18	8
Kowalewo Pomorskie, Pol.	C14	16
Kowloon see Jiulong, China	J5	42
Kowŏn-ŭp, Kor., N.	E7	38
Kowt-e'Ashrow, Afg.	C10	56
Koxtag, China	A4	46
Köyceğiz Gölü, l., Tur.	G11	28
Koyna Reservoir, res., India	C1	53
Koyuk, Ak., U.S.	D7	140
Koyukuk, Ak., U.S.	D8	140
Koyukuk, stm., Ak., U.S.	C8	140
Kō-zaki, c., Japan	E2	40
Kozan, Tur.	A6	58
Kozáni, Grc.	C4	28
Kožany, Russia	H14	10
Kozel'sk, Russia	F18	10
Koževnikovo, Russia	C14	32
Kozhikode (Calicut), India	F2	53
Kozienice, Pol.	E17	16
Kozlov Bereg, Russia	B10	10
Kozlovo, Russia	D19	10
Kozlu, Tur.	B14	28
Koz'mino, Russia	F22	8
Kožposëlok, Russia	E17	8
Kōzu-shima, i., Japan	E12	40
Kpalimé, Togo	H5	64
Kra, Isthmus of, isth., Asia	H4	48
Kraai, stm., S. Afr.	G8	70
Krabi, Thai.	H4	48
Krâchéh, Camb.	F8	48
Kraeva, Russia	B9	38
Kragan, Indon.	G7	50
Kragujevac, Yugo.	F7	26
Krajenka, Pol.	C13	16
Krakatoa see Rakata, Pulau, i., Indon.	G4	50
Krakovets', Ukr.	G19	16
Kraków, Pol.	F15	16
Kraków, state, Pol.	G15	16
Kralendijk, Neth. Ant.	p23	104g
Kraljevo, Yugo.	F7	26
Kralovice, Czech Rep.	G9	16
Kralupy nad Vltavou, Czech Rep.	F10	16
Kramators'k, Ukr.	E5	32
Kramfors, Swe.	E7	8
Kranídi, Grc.	F6	28
Kranj (Krainburg), Slvn.	D11	22
Kranskop, S. Afr.	F10	70
Krapivna, Russia	G18	10
Krasavino, Russia	F22	8
Krasieo, stm., Thai.	E4	48
Krasivaja Meča, stm., Russia	G20	10
Krāslava, Lat.	E10	10
Krasnae, Bela.	F10	10
Krasnaja Gorbatka, Russia	I19	8
Krasnaja Slabada, Bela.	H9	10
Krasnaluki, Bela.	F11	10
Krasneno, Russia	D23	34
Kraśnik, Pol.	F18	16
Kraśnik Fabryczny, Pol.	F18	16
Krasni Okny, Ukr.	B16	26
Krasnoarmejsk, Russia	D21	10
Krasnoarmejskij, Russia	C23	34
Krasnobród, Pol.	F19	16
Krasnodar, Russia	E5	32
Krasnoe, ozero, l., Russia	D23	34
Krasnoe Selo, Russia	A12	10
Krasnoe Znamja, Russia	C18	10
Krasnogorodskoe, Russia	D11	10
Krasnogorsk, Russia	E20	10
Krasnogorsk, Russia	G17	34
Krasnojarovo, Russia	F14	34
Krasnojarsk, Russia	C16	32
Krasnojarskoe vodohranilišče, res., Russia	D16	32
Krasnokamsk, Russia	C8	32
Krasnomajskij, Russia	C17	10
Krasnoščele, Russia	C17	8
Krasnosel'kup, Russia	A14	32
Krasnoturjinsk, Russia	C10	32
Krasnoufimsk, Russia	C9	32
Krasnoural'sk, Russia	C10	32
Krasnovišersk, Russia	B9	32
Krasnovodskij poluostrov, pen., Turkmen.	A7	56
Krasnozavodsk, Russia	D20	10
Krasnozërskoe, Russia	D14	32
Krasnoznamensk, Russia	F5	10
Krasnoznamenskoe, Kaz.	D11	32
Krasnye Gory, Russia	B12	10
Krasnyj Čikoj, Russia	F10	34
Krasnyj Gorodok, Russia	C16	10
Krasnyj Jar, Russia	C12	32
Krasnyj Luč, Russia	C13	10
Krasnyj Oktjabr', Russia	D21	10
Krasnyj Tkač, Russia	E22	10
Krasnystaw, Pol.	E19	16
Kratovo, Mac.	A5	28
Krâvanh, Chuŏr Phnum, mts., Camb.	F6	48
Krbava, reg., Cro.	F12	22
Krečetovo, Russia	F18	8
Krefeld, Ger.	E2	16
Kremastón, Technití Límni, res., Grc.	E4	28
Kremenchug Reservoir see Kremenchuts'ke vodoskhovyshche, res., Ukr.	E4	32
Kremenchuk, Ukr.	E4	32
Kremenchuts'ke vodoskhovyshche, res., Ukr.	E4	32
Kremenskoe, Russia	E18	10
Kremmling, Co., U.S.	C10	132
Krems an der Donau, Aus.	B12	22
Kress, Tx., U.S.	G7	128
Kresta, zaliv, b., Russia	C25	34
Krestcy, Russia	B22	10
Krestcy, Russia	B15	10
Krest-Maër, Russia	C17	34
Kretinga, Lith.	E4	10
Kribi, Cam.	D1	66
Křimice, Czech Rep.	G9	16
Krishna, stm., India	C5	53
Krishna, Mouths of the, mth., India	D5	53
Krishnagiri, India	E4	53
Krishnanagar, India	G12	54
Krishnarāja Sāgara, res., India	E3	53
Krishnarājpet, India	E3	53
Kristiansand, Nor.	G3	8
Kristianstad, Swe.	I6	8
Kristiansund, Nor.	E2	8
Kristiinankaupunki (Kristinestad), Fin.	E9	8
Kristinehamn, Swe.	G6	8
Kristinestad see Kristiinankaupunki, Fin.	E9	8
Kríti, state, Grc.	H7	28
Kríti (Crete), i., Grc.	H7	28
Kritikón Pélagos (Crete, Sea of), Grc.	H8	28
Kriva Palanka, Mac.	A5	28
Krivodol, Blg.	F10	26
Križevci, Cro.	D13	22
Krjukovo, Russia	E20	10
Krjukovo, Russia	C20	34
Krk, Otok, i., Cro.	E11	22
Krnov, Czech Rep.	F13	16
Krobia, Pol.	E12	16
Krøderen, l., Nor.	F3	8
Krokodil, stm., S. Afr.	D8	70
Krom, stm., S. Afr.	G4	70
Kroměříž, Czech Rep.	G13	16
Kromy, Russia	H18	10
Kronach, Ger.	F7	16
Krŏng Kaôh Kŏng, Camb.	G6	48
Krŏng Kêb, Camb.	G7	48
Kronoberg, state, Swe.	H6	8
Kronockaja Sopka, vulkan, vol., Russia	F21	34
Kronockij zaliv, b., Russia	F21	34
Kronoki, Russia	F21	34
Kronprins Christian Land, reg., Grnld.	A22	141
Kronštadt, Russia	A12	10
Kroonstad, S. Afr.	E8	70
Kropotkin, Russia	E6	32
Kropotkin, Russia	E12	34
Krośniewice, Pol.	D14	16
Krosno, Pol.	G17	16
Krosno, state, Pol.	G17	16
Krotoszyn, Pol.	E13	16
Krotz Springs, La., U.S.	G7	122
Kroya, Indon.	G6	50
Krško, Slvn.	E12	22
Kruger National Park, p.o.i., S. Afr.	C10	70
Krugersdorp, S. Afr.	E8	70
Kruhlae, Bela.	F12	10
Krui, Indon.	F3	50
Kruisfontein, S. Afr.	H7	70
Kruja see Krujë, Alb.	C13	24
Krujë, Alb.	C13	24
Krumbach, Ger.	H6	16
Krumovgrad, Blg.	H12	26
Krung Thep (Bangkok), Thai.	F5	48
Kruså, Den.	B5	16
Kruševac, Yugo.	F8	26
Krušinovka, Bela.	G12	10
Krutcy, Russia	C12	10
Krutoe, Russia	H20	10
Kruzenšterna, proliv, strt., Russia	G19	34
Kruzof Island, i., Ak., U.S.	E12	140
Kryčaŭ, Bela.	G14	10
Kryms'kyi pivostriv (Crimean Peninsula), pen., Ukr.	E4	32
Krynica, Pol.	G16	16
Krynychne, Ukr.	D15	26
Kryve Ozero, Ukr.	B17	26
Kryvošyn, Bela.	H8	10
Kryvyj Rih, Ukr.	E4	32
Kryzhopil', Ukr.	A15	26
Krzeszowice, Pol.	F15	16
Krzyż, Pol.	D11	16
Ksenevka, Russia	F12	34
Kstovo, Russia	H20	8
Kuah, Malay.	I4	48
Kuai, stm., China	E7	42
Kualacenako, Indon.	D3	50
Kuala Kangsar, Malay.	J5	48
Kualakapuas, Indon.	E9	50
Kuala Krai, Malay.	J6	48
Kuala Kubu Baharu, Malay.	K5	48
Kualakurun, Indon.	D8	50
Kualalangsa, Indon.	J4	48
Kuala Lipis, Malay.	J5	48
Kuala Lumpur, Malay.	K5	48
Kuala Nerang, Malay.	I5	48
Kualapesaguan, Indon.	E6	50
Kuala Pilah, Malay.	K6	48
Kuala Rompin, Malay.	K6	48
Kuala Sepetang, Malay.	J5	48
Kualasimpang, Indon.	J3	48
Kuala Terengganu, Malay.	J6	48
Kualu, stm., Indon.	B1	50
Kuamut, stm., Malay.	A10	50
Kuancheng, China	A8	42
Kuandian, China	D6	38
Kuan Shan, mtn., Tai.	J9	42
Kuantan, Malay.	K6	48
Kuanyün see Guanyun, China	D8	42
Kuban', stm., Russia	E6	32
Kubenskoe, ozero, l., Russia	G18	8
Kubokawa, Japan	F6	40
Kubrat, Blg.	F13	26
Kučema, Russia	D20	8
Kuchaiburi, India	G11	54
Kuchāman, India	E5	54
Kuching, Malay.	C7	50
Kūchnay Darweyshān, Afg.	C9	56
Kuchurhan, stm., Eur.	B16	26
Kuçova see Kuçovë, Alb.	D13	24
Kuçovë, Alb.	D13	24
Kūd, India	B5	54
Kudamatsu, Japan	F4	40
Kudat, Malay.	G1	52
Kudever', Russia	D12	10
Kudirkos Naumiestis, Lith.	F5	10
Kudus, Indon.	G7	50
Kudymkar, Russia	C8	32
Kuee Ruins, hist., Hi., U.S.	D6	78a
Kueisui see Hohhot, China	A4	42
Kueiyang see Guiyang, China	H2	42
K'uerhlo see Korla, China	C2	36
Kufstein, Aus.	C9	22
Kugluktuk, N.T., Can.	B8	106
Kugmallit Bay, b., N.T., Can.	C13	140
Kuhësi see Kukës, Alb.	B14	24
Kuhmoinen, Fin.	F11	8
Kuhn Ø, i., Grnld.	C22	141
Kuial'nyts'kyi lyman, l., Ukr.	C17	26
Kuiseb, stm., S. Afr.	C2	70
Kuitan, China	J7	42
Kuito, Ang.	C2	68
Kuiu Island, i., Ak., U.S.	E13	140
Kuivastu, Est.	G10	8
Kuja, Russia	D18	8
Kujang-ŭp, Kor., N.	E7	38
Kujawy, reg., Pol.	D14	16
Kujbyšev, Russia	C13	32
Kujbyševskoe vodohranilišče, res., Russia	D7	32
Kujgan, Kaz.	E12	32
Kujū-san, vol., Japan	F4	40
Kukalaya, stm., Nic.	F6	102
Kukawa, Nig.	G7	64
Kukës, Alb.	B14	24
Kukoboj, Russia	B22	10
Kükong see Shaoguan, China	I5	42
Kukshi, India	G5	54
Kukuj, Russia	A15	10
Kukukus Lake, l., On., Can.	B7	118
Kukurtli, Turkmen.	B8	56
Kula, Blg.	F9	26
Kula, Tur.	E11	28
Kula, Yugo.	D6	26
Kulagi, Russia	H15	10
Kula Gulf, strt., Sol. Is.	e7	79b
Kulai, Malay.	L6	48
Kula Kangri, mtn., Bhu.	E13	54
Kular, Russia	B15	34
Kulaura, Bngl.	F13	54
Kuldīga, Lat.	D5	10
Kuldja see Yining, China	F14	32
Kule, Bots.	C5	70
Kulebaki, Russia	I20	8
Kulen Vakuf, Bos.	E3	26
Kulim, Malay.	J5	48
Kuljab, Taj.	B10	56
Kulkyne Creek, stm., Austl.	H5	76
Kullu, India	B6	54
Kulm, N.D., U.S.	A13	126
Kulmbach, Ger.	F7	16
Kuloj, Russia	D20	8
Kuloj, Russia	F20	8
Kuloj, stm., Russia	D20	8
Kul'sary, Kaz.	E8	32
Kulti, India	G11	54
Kultuk, Russia	D18	32
Kulu, Tur.	D16	28
Kulunda, Russia	D13	32
Kulundinskaja ravnina, pl., Asia	D13	32
Kulundinskoe, ozero, l., Russia	D13	32
Kulwin, Austl.	J4	76
Kumagaya, Japan	C12	40
Kumai, Indon.	E8	50
Kumai, Teluk, b., Indon.	E7	50
Kumajri see Gjumri, Arm.	A5	56
Kumamoto, Japan	G3	40
Kumamoto, state, Japan	G3	40
Kumano, Japan	F9	40
Kumano-nada, Japan	F9	40
Kumanovo, Mac.	A4	28
Kumara, Russia	F14	34
Kumārghāt, India	F14	54
Kumasi, Ghana	H4	64
Kumba, Cam.	D1	66
Kumbakonam, India	F4	53
Kumbarilla, Austl.	F8	76
Kumdanlı, Tur.	E13	28
Kume-jima, i., Japan	I18	39a
Kŭm-gang, stm., Kor., S.	F7	38
Kumla, Swe.	G6	8
Kumluca, Tur.	B15	28
Kumluca, Tur.	G13	28
Kumo, Nig.	H7	64
Kumon Range, mts., Mya.	C8	46
Kumora, Russia	E11	34
Kumta, India	D2	53
Kumu, D.R.C.	D5	66
Kumukahi, Cape, c., Hi., U.S.	o16	135a
Kümüx, China	C2	36
Kŭmya-ŭp, Kor., N.	E7	38
Kuna, Id., U.S.	G10	136
Kunašir, ostrov (Kunashiri-tō), i., Russia	C16	38
Kunda, Est.	G12	8
Kunda Hills, hills, India	F3	53
Kundāpura, India	E2	53
Kundar, stm., Asia	C2	54
Kunderu, stm., India	D4	53
Kundiān, Pak.	B3	54
Kundiawa, Pap. N. Gui.	b3	79a
Kundla, India	H3	54
Kundur, Pulau, i., Indon.	C3	50
Kunene, state, Nmb.	B2	70
Kunene (Cunene), stm., Afr.	D1	68
Kunes, Nor.	A12	8
Kungchuling see Gongzhuling, China	C6	38
Kunggyü Yumco, l., China	C9	54
Kunghit Island, i., B.C., Can.	E4	106
Kungrad, Uzb.	F9	32
Kungsbacka, Swe.	H4	8
Kungur, Russia	C9	32
Kunhegyes, Hung.	B7	26
Kuningan, Indon.	G6	50
Kunisaki, Japan	F4	40
Kunisaki-hantō, pen., Japan	F4	40
Kunja, Russia	D13	10
Kunja, stm., Russia	D13	10
Kunlong, Mya.	D8	46
Kunlun Mountains see Kunlun Shan, mts., China	A5	46
Kunlun Shan, mts., China	A5	46
Kunming, China	F5	36
Kunnamkulam, India	F2	53
Kunsan, Kor., S.	F7	38
Kunshan, China	F9	42
Kunting, China	G9	42
Kununurra, Austl.	C5	74
Kunwi, Kor., S.	C1	40
Kunya, Nig.	G6	64
Künzelsau, Ger.	G5	16
Kuopio, Fin.	E12	8
Kuopio, state, Fin.	E12	8
Kupa, stm., Eur.	E12	22
Kupang, Indon.	H7	44
Kupanskoe, Russia	D21	10
Kup'ians'k, Ukr.	E5	32
Kupino, Russia	D13	32
Kupiškis, Lith.	E7	10
Kupreanof Island, i., Ak., U.S.	E13	140
Kuqa, China	F14	32
Kuqa, China	F14	32
Kuragino, Russia	D16	32
Kuranec, Bela.	F9	10
Kurashiki, Japan	E6	40
Kurasiki see Kurashiki, Japan	E6	40
Kurauli, India	E7	54
Kuraymah, Sudan	D6	62
Kurayoshi, Japan	D6	40
Kurčatov, Russia	D5	32
Kurčum, Kaz.	E14	32
Kurdistān, hist. reg., Asia	B5	56
Kurdistan see Kurdistān, hist. reg., Asia	B5	56
Kurdufān, state, Sudan	E6	62
Kurduvādi, India	B2	53
Kure, Japan	E5	40
Kurejka, stm., Russia	C7	34
Kuresaare, Est.	G10	8
Kurgal'džinskij, Kaz.	D12	32
Kurgan, Russia	C11	32
Kurgan-Tjube, Taj.	B10	56
Kuria, i., Kir.	C8	72
Kuria Muria Islands see Ḩallānīyah, Juzur al-, is., Oman	F8	56
Kuridala, Austl.	C3	76
Kurīgrām, Bngl.	F12	54
Kurikka, Fin.	E10	8
Kuril Islands see Kuril'skie ostrova, is., Russia	E19	30
Kuril'sk, Russia	B14	36
Kuril'skie ostrova (Kuril Islands), is., Russia	E19	30
Kuril Strait see Pervyj Kuril'skij proliv, strt., Russia	F20	34
Kuril Trench, unds.	E18	142
Kurinjippadi, India	F4	53
Kurinwás, stm., Nic.	F5	102
Kurjanovskaja, Russia	F19	8
Kurkliai, Lith.	E8	10
Kurmuk, Sudan	E6	62
Kurnool, India	D3	53
Kurobe, Japan	C10	40
Kurort Schmalkalden, Ger.	F6	16
Kurovskoe, Russia	E21	10
Kurow, N.Z.	G4	80
Kuršėnai, Lith.	D6	10
Kurseong, India	E12	54
Kuršiu nerija (Kuršskaja kosa), spit, Eur.	E3	10
Kursk, Russia	D5	32
Kurskaja oblast', co., Russia	H19	10
Kuršskaja kosa (Kuršiu nerija), spit, Eur.	E3	10
Kuršumlija, Yugo.	F8	26
Kurşunlu, Tur.	C16	28
Kūrtī, Sudan	D6	62
Kurtistown, Hi., U.S.	D6	78a
Kurtoğlu Burnu, c., Tur.	G11	28
Kuruktag, mts., China	C2	36
Kuruman, S. Afr.	E6	70
Kuruman, stm., S. Afr.	E5	70
Kurumanheuwels, mts., S. Afr.	E6	70
Kurume, Japan	F3	40
Kurumkan, Russia	F11	34
Kurunegala, Sri L.	H5	53
Kuruqi, China	B9	36
Kuryongp'o, Kor., S.	C2	40
Kuşadası, Tur.	F10	28
Kuşadası Körfezi, b., Tur.	F9	28
Kusan-ni, Kor., S.	B1	40
Kusawa Lake, l., Yk., Can.	D12	140
Kuş Gölü, l., Tur.	C10	28
Kuş Gölü Milli Parkı, p.o.i., Tur.	C10	28
Kushālgarh, India	G5	54
Kusheriki, Nig.	G6	64
Kushikino, Japan	H3	40
Kushima, Japan	H4	40
Kushiro, Japan	C16	38
Kushnytsia, Ukr.	A10	26
Kushtia, Bngl.	G12	54
Kushui, China	C3	36
Kusiro see Kushiro, Japan	C16	38
Kusiyāra, stm., Bngl.	F13	54
Kuskokwim, stm., Ak., U.S.	D7	140
Kuskokwim Bay, b., Ak., U.S.	E7	140
Kuskokwim Mountains, mts., Ak., U.S.	D8	140
Kuśmā, Nepal	D9	54
Kušmurun, Kaz.	D10	32
Kušmurun, ozero, l., Kaz.	D10	32
Kustanaj, Kaz.	D10	32
Kūstī, Sudan	E6	62
Kusu, Japan	F4	40
Kut, Ko, i., Thai.	G6	48
Kutabaru, Indon.	D3	50
Kutacane, Indon.	K3	48
Kütahya, Tur.	D13	28
Kütahya, state, Tur.	D12	28
Kutaisi, Geor.	F6	32
Kutch, Rann of (Kachchh, Rann of), reg., Asia	D2	46
Kutima, Russia	C19	32
Kutina, Cro.	E13	22
Kutiyāna, India	H3	54
Kutná Hora, Czech Rep.	G11	16
Kutno, Pol.	D15	16
Kutse Game Reserve, Bots.	C7	70
Kutu, D.R.C.	E3	66
Kutubdia Island, i., Bngl.	H13	54
Kutum, Sudan	E4	62
Kúty, Slov.	H13	16
Kuujjuaq, Qc., Can.	D17	106
Kuuli-Majak, Turkmen.	A7	56
Kuusamo, Fin.	D13	8
Kuusankoski, Fin.	F12	8
Kuvango, Ang.	C2	68
Kuvšinovo, Russia	C16	10
Kuwait see Al-Kuwayt, Kuw.	D6	56
Kuwait, ctry., Asia	D6	56
Kuwana, Japan	D9	40
Kuybyshev Reservoir see Kujbyševskoe vodohranilišče, res., Russia	D7	32

Name — Map Ref. — Page

Kuye, stm., China B4 42
Kuženkino, Russia C16 10
Kuz'miniči, Russia F16 10
Kuz'movka, Russia B16 32
Kuzneck, Russia D7 32
Kuzneckij Alatau, mts., Russia D15 32
Kuznecovka, Russia D11 10
Kuznetsk see Kuzneck, Russia D7 32
Kuzomen', Russia C17 8
Kvænangen, b., Nor. A9 8
Kvaløya, i., Nor. B8 8
Kvaløya, i., Nor. A10 8
Kvam, Nor. F3 8
Kvarnbergsvattnet, l., Swe. D5 8
Kvarner, b., Cro. F11 22
Kvarnerić, b., Cro. F11 22
Kverkfjöll, vol., Ice. k31 8a
Kvichak Bay, b., Ak., U.S. E8 140
Kwa, stm., D.R.C. E3 66
Kwai see Khwae Noi, stm., Thai. E4 48
Kwajalein, at., Marsh. Is. C7 72
Kwakoegron, Sur. B6 84
Kwamisa, mtn., Ghana H4 64
Kwamouth, D.R.C. E3 66
Kwando (Cuando), stm., Afr. D3 68
Kwangchow see Guangzhou, China J5 42
Kwangju, Kor., S. G7 38
Kwango (Cuango), stm., Afr. E3 66
Kwangsi Chuang see Guangxi, state, China G6 36
Kwangtung see Guangdong, state, China J6 42
KwaZulu-Natal, state, S. Afr. F10 70
Kweichow see Guizhou, state, China F6 36
Kweihwa see Hohhot, China A4 42
Kweilin see Guilin, China I4 42
Kweisui see Hohhot, China A4 42
Kweiyang see Guiyang, China H2 42
Kwekwe, Zimb. D4 68
Kweneng, state, Bots. C7 70
Kwenge (Caengo), stm., Afr. B2 68
Kwethluk, Ak., U.S. D7 140
Kwidzyn, Pol. C14 16
Kwigillingok, Ak., U.S. E7 140
Kwilu (Cuilo), stm., Afr. F3 66
Kyabra, Austl. F4 76
Kyabra Creek, stm., Austl. E4 76
Kyabram, Austl. K5 76
Kyaikkami, Mya. D3 48
Kyaiklat, Mya. D2 48
Kyaikto, Mya. D3 48
Kya-in, Mya. D4 48
Kyalite, Austl. J4 76
Kyancutta, Austl. F7 74
Ky Anh, Viet. C8 48
Kyaukhnyat, Mya. C3 48
Kyaukme, Mya. A3 48
Kyaukpa, Mya. F4 48
Kyaukpyu, Mya. C1 48
Kyaukse, Mya. B2 48
Kyauktaw, Mya. D7 46
Kyaunggon, Mya. D2 48
Kybartai, Lith. F5 10
Kyebang-san, mtn., Kor., S. B1 40
Kyeikdon, Mya. E4 48
Kyidaunggan, Mya. C3 48
Kyïv (Kiev), Ukr. D4 32
Kyïvs'ke vodoskhovyshche, res., Ukr. D4 32
Kyjov, Czech Rep. G13 16
Kykotsmovi Village, Az., U.S. H6 132
Kyle, Sk., Can. D5 124
Kyle, S.D., U.S. D10 126
Kyle, Lake, res., Zimb. B10 70
Kyllíni, Grc. F4 28
Kymi, state, Fin. F12 8
Kyneton, Austl. K5 76
Kynšperk nad Ohří, Czech Rep. F8 16
Kyoga, Lake, l., Ug. D6 66
Kyogle, Austl. G9 76
Kyŏngju, Kor., S. D2 40
Kyŏngsan, Kor., S. D1 40
Kyŏngsang-bukto, state, Kor., S. C1 40
Kyŏngsang-namdo, state, Kor., S. D1 40
Kyŏngsŏng-ŭp, Kor., N. D8 38
Kyônkadun, Mya. D2 48
Kyonpyaw, Mya. D2 48
Kyōto, Japan D8 40
Kyōto, state, Japan D8 40
Kyparissía, Grc. F4 28
Kyparissiakós Kólpos, b., Grc. F4 28
Kyra, Russia G11 34
Kyren, Russia D18 32
Kyrgyzstan, ctry., Asia F12 32
Kyritz, Ger. D8 16
Kyrönjoki, stm., Fin. E10 8
Kyrösjärvi, l., Fin. F10 8
Kyštym, Russia C10 32
Kýthira, Grc. G5 28
Kýthira, i., Grc. G5 28
Kýthnos, i., Grc. F7 28
Kyundon, Mya. B2 48
Kyungyi, i., Mya. E3 48
Kyuquot, B.C., Can. F3 138
Kyūshū, i., Japan G2 40
Kyushu-Palau Ridge, unds. H16 142
Kyūshū-sanchi, mts., Japan G4 40
Kywong, Austl. J6 76
Kyyjärvi, Fin. E11 8
Kyyvesi, l., Fin. E12 8
Kyzyl, Russia D16 32
Kyzylbair, Turkmen. B8 56
Kyzyl-Kija, Kyrg. F12 32
Kyzylkum, des., Asia F10 32
Kyzyluj, Kaz. E11 32
Kzyl-Orda, Kaz. F11 32
Kzyltu, Kaz. D12 32

L

La Aguja, Cabo de, c., Col. B4 86
La Albuera, Spain F4 20
La Alcarria, reg., Spain D8 20
La Algaba, Spain G4 20
La Almunia de Doña Godina, Spain C9 20
La Antigua, Salina, pl., Arg. D4 92
La Araucanía, state, Chile I1 92
Laascaanood, Som. C9 66
La Ascención, hill, Mex. C8 100
La Asunción, Ven. B10 86
Laau Point, c., Hi., U.S. B4 78a
Laayoune see El Aaiún, W. Sah. D2 64
La Azufrosa, Mex. F7 130
La Babia, Mex. A7 100
Labadieville, La., U.S. H8 122
La Baie, Qc., Can. B6 110
La Banda, Arg. C5 92
La Bandera, Cerro, mtn., Mex. C6 100
La Bañeza, Spain B4 20
La Barca, Mex. E7 100
La Barge, Wy., U.S. H16 136
Labasa, Fiji p19 79e
La Baule-Escoublac, Fr. G6 14
Labé, Gui. G2 64
Labe (Elbe), stm., Eur. C5 16
Labelle, Qc., Can. D2 110
La Belle, Mo., U.S. D5 120
Laberge, Lake, l., Yk., Can. C4 106
Labi, Bru. A9 50
Labian, Tanjong, c., Malay. A11 50
La Biche, stm., Ab., Can. B18 138
Labis, Malay. K6 48
La Bisbal d'Empordà, Spain C13 20
Łabiszyn, Pol. D13 16
La Blanca Grande, Laguna, l., Arg. I5 92
Labná, hist., Mex. B3 102
Laboe, Ger. B6 16
Laborde, Arg. F6 92
Laborie, St. Luc. m7 105c
La Bostonnais, Qc., Can. C4 110
Laboulaye, Arg. G6 92
Labrador, reg., Nf., Can. E18 106
Labrador Basin, unds. C9 144
Labrador City, Nf., Can. E17 106
Labrador Sea, N.A. D17 94
Lábrea, Braz. E5 84
La Brea, Trin. s12 105f
Labuan, Malay. A9 50
Labuan, state, Malay. A9 50
Labuan, Pulau, i., Malay. A9 50
Labuchongshan, mts., China C10 54
La Bufadora, Mex. L9 134
Labuhan, Indon. G4 50
Labuhanbajo, Indon. H11 50
Labuhanbilik, Indon. B2 50
Labuhanpandan, Indon. H10 50
Labuhanruku, Indon. B1 50
Labuk, stm., Malay. H1 52
Labuk, Telukan, b., Malay. G1 52
Labu Kananga, Indon. H10 50
Labutta, Mya. D2 48
Labytnangi, Russia A11 32
Laç, Alb. C13 24
Lača, ozero, l., Russia F18 8
Lac-à-Beauce, Qc., Can. C4 110
La Cadena, Mex. I3 130
La Calera, Chile F2 92
La Campana, Spain G5 20
La Canada Flintridge, Ca., U.S. I7 134
La Candelaria, Arg. C5 92
La Candelaria, Mex. C1 130
Lacantum, stm., Mex. D2 102
La Capelle-en-Thiérache, Fr. D12 14
La Carlota, Arg. F6 92
La Carlota, Phil. E4 52
La Carolina, Spain F7 20
Lacaune, Fr. F8 18
Laccadive Islands see Lakshadweep, is., India F3 46
Lac-Édouard, Qc., Can. C4 110
La Ceiba, Hond. E4 102
Lacepede Bay, b., Austl. K2 76
Lac-Etchemin, Qc., Can. D6 110
Lacey, Wa., U.S. C4 136
Lac-Frontière, Qc., Can. D6 110
La Chapelle-d'Angillon, Fr. G11 14
La Châtaigneraie, Fr. C5 18
La Chaux-de-Fonds, Switz. C3 22
Lachhmangarh Sīkar, India E5 54
Lachine, Qc., Can. E3 110
Lachlan, stm., Austl. J5 76
La Chorrera, Col. H5 86
La Chorrera, Pan. H8 102
Lachute, Qc., Can. E2 110
Laçi see Laç, Alb. C13 24
La Ciénaga, Arg. C4 92
La Ciotat, Fr. F11 18
La Citadelle, hist., Haiti C11 102
La Ciudad, Mex. D6 100
Lackawanna, N.Y., U.S. B6 114
Lac La Biche, Ab., Can. B18 138
Lac la Hache, B.C., Can. E9 138
Laclede, Id., U.S. B10 136
Laclede, Mo., U.S. E4 120
La Clotilde, Arg. C7 92
Lac-Mégantic, Qc., Can. E6 110
La Colorada, Mex. A3 100
La Coma, Mex. C9 100
Lacombe, Ab., Can. D17 138
Lacombe, La., U.S. G9 122
Lacona, Ia., U.S. C4 120
La Concepción, Pan. H6 102
La Concepción, Ven. B5 86
Laconi, Italy E2 24
Laconia, N.H., U.S. G5 110
Laconia, Gulf of see Lakonikós Kólpos, b., Grc. G5 28
La Consulta, Arg. F3 92
Lacoochee, Fl., U.S. H3 116
La Coruña see A Coruña, Spain A2 20
La Coruña see A Coruña, co., Spain A2 20
La Coste, Tx., U.S. E9 130
La Courtine, Fr. D8 18
La Crescent, Mn., U.S. H7 118
La Crosse, Ks., U.S. C9 128
La Crosse, Va., U.S. H7 114
Lacrosse, Wa., U.S. D9 136
La Crosse, Wi., U.S. H7 118
La Cruz, Arg. D9 92
La Cruz, Col. G3 86
La Cruz, C.R. E7 96
La Cruz, Mex. G2 130
La Cruz de Río Grande, Nic. F5 102
Lac Seul, On., Can. A6 118
La Cuesta, P.R. B2 104a
La Cumbre, Arg. E5 92
La Cygne, Ks., U.S. F3 120
Ladākh, hist. reg., Pak. A6 54
Ladākh Range, mts., Asia A6 54
Ladder Creek, stm., Ks., U.S. C7 128
Laddonia, Mo., U.S. E6 120
La Désirade, i., Guad. h6 105c
La Digue, i., Sey. j13 69b
Ladismith, S. Afr. H5 70
Ladispoli, Italy I8 22
Lādīz, Iran D9 56
Ladner, B.C., Can. G7 138
Lādnūn, India E5 54
Ladoga, In., U.S. I3 112
Ladoga, Lake see Ladožskoe ozero, l., Russia F14 8
La Dorada, Col. E4 86
La Dormida, Arg. F4 92
Ladožskoe ozero (Ladoga, Lake), l., Russia F14 8
Laduškin, Russia F3 10
Ladva-Vetka, Russia F15 8
Lady Ann Strait, strt., N.T., Can. B10 141
Lady Barron, Austl. n14 77a
Ladybrand, S. Afr. F8 70
Lady Elliot Island, i., Austl. E9 76
Ladysmith, B.C., Can. H7 138
Ladysmith, S. Afr. F9 70
Ladysmith, Wi., U.S. F7 118
Lae, Pap. N. Gui. b4 79a
La Encantada, Mex. C8 100
La Escondida, Mex. H8 130
La Esmeralda, Mex. B7 100
Læsø, i., Den. H4 8
La Esperanza, Cuba A5 102
La Esperanza, Hond. E3 102
La Esperanza, Mex. H4 130
La Esperanza, P.R. B3 104a
La Estrada see A Estrada, Spain B2 20
Lafa, China C7 38
La Falda, Arg. E5 92
La Farge, Wi., U.S. H8 118
Lafayette, Al., U.S. E13 122
Lafayette, Ca., U.S. F3 134
Lafayette, Co., U.S. A3 128
Lafayette, Ga., U.S. C13 122
Lafayette, In., U.S. H3 112
Lafayette, La., U.S. G6 122
Lafayette, Tn., U.S. H11 120
Lafayette, Mount, mtn., N.H., U.S. F5 110
La Feria, Tx., U.S. H10 130
La Ferté-Bernard, Fr. F9 14
La Ferté-Saint-Aubin, Fr. G10 14
Lafia, Nig. H6 64
Lafiagi, Nig. H6 64
Lafleche, Sk., Can. E7 124
La Flèche, Fr. G8 14
La Florida, Guat. D2 102
La Foa, N. Cal. m15 79d
La Follette, Tn., U.S. H1 114
Lafourche, Bayou, stm., La., U.S. H8 122
La Fragua, Arg. C5 92
La Fría, Ven. C5 86
La Fuente de San Esteban, Spain D4 20
La Galite, i., Tun. G2 24
La Gallareta, Arg. D7 92
Lagan, stm., Swe. E3 8
Lagarto, Braz. F7 88
Lagawe, Phil. B3 52
Lage, China D10 54
Lågen, stm., Nor. F4 8
Lages, Braz. C12 92
Laghmān, state, Afg. A3 54
Laghouat, Alg. C5 64
Lagkadás, Grc. C5 28
Lagoa da Prata, Braz. K3 88
Lagoa Vermelha, Braz. D12 92
Lago da Pedra, Braz. C3 88
Lago Kolonie, Aruba p20 104g
Lagolândia, Braz. H1 88
Lagonegro, Italy D9 24
Lagonoy Gulf, b., Phil. D4 52
Lago Posadas, Arg. I2 90
Lagos, Nig. H5 64
Lagos, Port. G2 20
Lagos de Moreno, Mex. E8 100
La Gouèra, W. Sah. E1 64
La Goulette, Tun. H4 24
Lago Viedma, Arg. I2 90
La Granadella, Spain C11 20
La Grande, Or., U.S. E8 136
La Grande Deux, Réservoir, res., Qc., Can. E15 106
La Grande Quatre, Réservoir, res., Qc., Can. E16 106
LaGrange, Austl. C4 74
La Grange, Ga., U.S. D13 122
La Grange, Ky., U.S. F12 120
La Grange, Mo., U.S. D6 120
La Grange, Tx., U.S. E11 130
Lagrange, Wy., U.S. F8 126
Lagrange Bay, b., Austl. C4 74
La Gran Sabana, pl., Ven. E10 86
La Guadeloupe, Qc., Can. E6 110
La Guajira, state, Col. G11 102
La Guajira, Península de, pen., S.A. A6 86
La Guardia, Arg. D5 92
La Guardia, Bol. C4 90
La Guardia see A Guardia, Spain C1 20
La Guerche-sur-l'Aubois, Fr. G11 14
Laguiole, Fr. E8 18
Laguna, Braz. D13 92
Laguna, N.M., U.S. H9 132
Laguna, Ilha da, i., Braz. D7 84
Laguna Beach, Ca., U.S. J8 134
Laguna Dam, dam, U.S. K2 132
Laguna de Jaco, Mex. G4 130
Laguna Larga, Arg. E6 92
Laguna Paiva, Arg. E7 92
Lagunas, Peru E2 84
Lagunas de Chacagua, Parque Nacional, p.o.i., Mex. H9 100
Lagunillas, Bol. C4 90
Laha, China B9 36
La Habana (Havana), Cuba A6 102
Lahad Datu, Malay. A11 50
Lahad Datu, Telukan, b., Malay. A11 50
La Harpe, Il., U.S. K7 118
La Harpe, Ks., U.S. G2 120
Lahat, Indon. E3 50
Lahdenpohja, Russia F14 8
Lahemaa rahrus, p.o.i., Est. G11 8
Lahewa, Indon. L3 48
Lahfân, Bîr, well, Egypt G4 58
Lahij, Yemen G5 56
Lāhījān, Iran B7 56
Lahnstein, Ger. F3 16
Laholm, Swe. H5 8
Lahontan Reservoir, res., Nv., U.S. D6 134
Lahore, Pak. C5 54
La Horqueta, Col. F5 86
Lahr, Ger. H3 16
Lahti, Fin. F11 8
La Huerta, N.M., U.S. B3 130
Lahva, Bela. H10 10
Laï, Chad F3 62
Laiagam, Pap. N. Gui. b3 79a
Laibin, China J3 42
Lai Chau, Viet. A6 48
Laichow Bay see Laizhou Wan, b., China C8 42
Laifeng, China G3 42
L'Aigle, Fr. F9 14
Laihia, Fin. E9 8
Laïmbélé, Mont, mtn., Vanuatu k16 79d
Laingsburg, S. Afr. H5 70
Laingsburg, Mi., U.S. B1 114
Lainioälven, stm., Swe. C10 8
Lainsitz see Lužnice, stm., Eur. G10 16
Laird Hill, Tx., U.S. E3 122
Lais, Indon. C12 50
Lais, Indon. E3 50
Lais, Phil. G5 52
Laitila, Fin. F9 8
Laiwu, China C7 42
Laixi, China C9 42
Laiyang, China C9 42
Laizhou Bay see Laizhou Wan, b., China C8 42
Laizhou Wan (Laizhou Bay), b., China C8 42
Laja, stm., Chile H2 92
Laja, Laguna de la, l., Chile H2 92
Laja, Salto del, wtfl, Chile H2 92
La Jara, Co., U.S. D2 128
La Jara, reg., Spain E5 20
La Jara Canyon, val., N.M., U.S. G9 132
La Jarita, Mex. F4 130
Lajas, P.R. B1 104a
Laje, Braz. G6 88
Lajeado, Braz. D11 92
Lajedo, Braz. E7 88
Lajes, Braz. C7 88
Lajinha, Braz. K5 88
Laji Shan, mts., China D5 36
Lajosmizse, Hung. B6 26
Lajta (Leitha), stm., Eur. H12 16
La Junta, Co., U.S. D5 128
Lakar Kūh, mtn., Iran C8 56
Lakatoro, Vanuatu k16 79d
Lake, Ms., U.S. E9 122
Lake Alfred, Fl., U.S. H4 116
Lake Andes, S.D., U.S. D14 126
Lake Arthur, La., U.S. G6 122
Lakeba, i., Fiji q20 79e
Lakeba Passage, strt., Fiji q20 79e
Lake Benton, Mn., U.S. G2 118
Lake Brownwood, Tx., U.S. C8 130
Lake Cargelligo, Austl. I6 76
Lake Charles, La., U.S. G5 122
Lake Chelan National Recreation Area, p.o.i., Wa., U.S. B6 136
Lake City, Ar., U.S. B8 122
Lake City, Co., U.S. E9 132
Lake City, Fl., U.S. F3 116
Lake City, Mi., U.S. D4 112
Lake City, Pa., U.S. B5 114
Lake City, S.C., U.S. C6 116
Lake City, Tn., U.S. H1 114
Lake Cowichan, B.C., Can. H6 138
Lake Crystal, Mn., U.S. G4 118
Lake Dallas, Tx., U.S. A10 130
Lake Delton, Wi., U.S. H9 118
Lake District National Park, p.o.i., Eng., U.K. G9 12
Lake Elsinore, Ca., U.S. J8 134
Lakefield, On., Can. D11 112
Lakefield, Mn., U.S. H3 118
Lake Forest, Il., U.S. F2 112
Lake Fork Reservoir, res., Tx., U.S. E3 122
Lake Geneva, Wi., U.S. B9 120
Lake George, N.Y., U.S. G3 110
Lake Harbor, Fl., U.S. J5 116
Lake Havasu City, Az., U.S. I2 132
Lake Helen, Fl., U.S. H4 116
Lakehurst, N.J., U.S. D11 114
Lake Jackson, Tx., U.S. E12 130
Lake King, Austl. F3 74
Lakeland, Fl., U.S. H3 116
Lakeland, Ga., U.S. E2 116
Lake Linden, Mi., U.S. D10 118
Lake Louise, Ab., Can. E14 138
Lake Mead National Recreation Area, p.o.i., U.S. G2 132
Lake Mills, Wi., U.S. A8 120
Lake Minchumina, Ak., U.S. D9 140
Lake Mohawk see Sparta, N.J., U.S. C11 114
Lake Nash, Austl. D7 74
Lake Norden, S.D., U.S. C15 126
Lake Oswego, Or., U.S. E4 136
Lake Ozark, Mo., U.S. F5 120
Lake Park, Fl., U.S. J5 116
Lake Park, Ia., U.S. H3 118
Lake Placid, Fl., U.S. I4 116
Lake Placid, N.Y., U.S. F3 110
Lake Pleasant, N.Y., U.S. G2 110
Lakeport, Ca., U.S. D3 134
Lakeport, Mi., U.S. E7 112
Lake Preston, S.D., U.S. C15 126
Lakes Entrance, Austl. K7 76
Lakeshore, Ms., U.S. G9 122
Lakeside, Ca., U.S. K8 134
Lakeside, Mt., U.S. B12 136
Lake Stevens, Wa., U.S. B4 136
Laketown, Ut., U.S. B5 132
Lake View, Ar., U.S. C8 122
Lake View, Ia., U.S. B2 120
Lakeview, Mi., U.S. E4 112
Lakeview, Mi., U.S. F4 112
Lakeview, Oh., U.S. D2 114
Lakeview, Or., U.S. A5 134
Lake Village, Ar., U.S. D7 122
Lakeville, Mn., U.S. G5 118
Lake Wales, Fl., U.S. I4 116
Lake Wilson, Mn., U.S. G2 118
Lakewood, Co., U.S. B3 128
Lakewood, N.J., U.S. D11 114
Lakewood, Oh., U.S. C4 114
Lakewood, Wa., U.S. C4 136
Lakewood, Wi., U.S. C1 112
Lakewood Park, N.D., U.S. F15 124
Lake Worth, Fl., U.S. J5 116
Lakhdaria, Alg. H14 20
Lākheri, India F5 54
Lakhīmpur, India D8 54
Lakhipur, India F14 54
Lakhnādon, India G7 54
Lakinsk, Russia H18 8
Lakonikós Kólpos (Laconia, Gulf of), b., Grc. G5 28
Lakota, N.D., U.S. F15 124
Laksefjorden, b., Nor. A12 8
Lakshadweep, state, India F3 46
Lakshadweep, is., India F3 46
Lakshadweep Sea, Asia G3 46
Lākshām, Bngl. G13 54
Lakshmeshwar, India D2 53
La Laja, Chile H1 92
Lāla Mūsa, Pak. B4 54
Lâlapaşa, Tur. B9 28
L'Albufera, l., Spain E10 20
Laleham, Austl. D7 76
La Leona, Mex. I6 130
La Leonesa, Arg. C8 92
Lālganj, India F10 54
Lalībela, Eth. E7 62
La Libertad, Guat. D2 102
La Ligua, Chile F2 92
La Lima, Hond. E3 102
Lalin, stm., China B7 38
Lalindi, Indon. I12 50
La Línea de la Concepción, Spain H5 20
Lalitpur, India F7 54
Lalitpur, Nepal E10 54
Lalla Khedidja, Tamgout de, mtn., Alg. H14 20
Lālmanir Hāt, Bngl. F12 54
La Loche, Sk., Can. D9 106
La Lora, plat., Spain B7 20
La Louvière, Bel. D13 14
L'Alpe-d'Huez, Fr. D12 18
Lālpur, India G2 54
Lālsot, India E6 54
La Luz, Mex. C10 100
La Luz, Mex. I10 130
Lama, ozero, l., Russia C7 34
La Macarena, Parque Nacional, p.o.i., Col. F5 86
La Macarena, Serranía de, mts., Col. F5 86
La Maddalena, Italy C3 24
La Madrid, Arg. C5 92
Lamadrid, Mex. G6 130
La Magdalena, Mex. H1 130
Lama-Kara, Togo H5 64
La Malbaie, Qc., Can. C6 110
La Mancha, reg., Spain E8 20
Lamandau, stm., Indon. E7 50
Lamap, Vanuatu k16 79d
Lamar, Co., U.S. C6 128
Lamar, Mo., U.S. G3 120
Lamarche, Fr. F14 14
La Marmora, Punta, mtn., Italy D3 24
La Maroma, Mex. F7 130
La Marque, Tx., U.S. H4 122
La Marsa, Tun. H4 24
La Martre, Qc., Can. A10 110
Lamas, Peru E2 84
Lamballe, Fr. F6 14
Lambaréné, Gabon E1 66
Lambari, stm., Braz. J3 88
Lambayeque, Peru E2 84
Lambay Island, i., Ire. H7 12
Lambert, Ms., U.S. C8 122
Lambert, Mt., U.S. G9 124
Lambert, Cape, c., Pap. N. Gui. a5 79a
Lambert Glacier, ice, Ant. C11 81
Lambert Land, reg., Grnld. B21 141
Lamberton, Mn., U.S. G3 118
Lambertsbaai see Lambert's Bay, S. Afr. H3 70
Lambert's Bay, S. Afr. H3 70
Lambton, Cape, c., N.T., Can. A6 106
Lame Deer, Mt., U.S. B6 126
La Media Luna, Arrecifes de, rf., Hond. E6 102
Lamentin, Guad. h5 105c
Lamèque, N.B., Can. C12 110
Lamèque, Île, i., N.B., Can. C12 110
La Merced, Arg. B5 92
La Merced, Arg. D5 92
Lameroo, Austl. J3 76
La Mesa, Ca., U.S. K8 134
Lamesa, Tx., U.S. B6 130
Lamía, Grc. E5 28
Lamine, stm., Mo., U.S. F5 120
Lamington National Park, p.o.i., Austl. G9 76
La Misión, Mex. K9 134
Lamitan, Phil. G4 52
Lamlam, Mount, hill, Guam j9 78c
Lammeulo, Indon. J2 48
La Moille, Il., U.S. C8 120
Lamoille, Nv., U.S. C1 132
Lamoille, stm., Vt., U.S. F4 110
Lamon Bay, b., Phil. C4 52
Lamone, stm., Italy F9 22
Lamongan, Indon. G8 50
Lamoni, Ia., U.S. D3 120
Lamont, Ca., U.S. H6 134
Lamont, Ia., U.S. I7 118
Lamont, Ok., U.S. E11 128
La Monte, Mo., U.S. F4 120
La Mothe, Lac, l., Qc., Can. B5 110
La Mothe-Achard, Fr. H7 14
Lamotrek, at., Micron. C5 72
Lamotte-Beuvron, Fr. G10 14
Lampang, Thai. C4 48
Lampasas, Tx., U.S. C9 130
Lampasas, stm., Tx., U.S. C9 130
Lampazos de Naranjo, Mex. B8 100
Lampedusa, Isola di, i., Italy I6 24
Lampertheim, Ger. G4 16
Lamphun, Thai. C4 48
Lampman, Sk., Can. E11 124
Lampung, state, Indon. F4 50
Lamskoe, Russia H21 10
Lamu, Kenya E8 66
La Mure, Fr. E11 18
Lan', stm., Bela. H10 10
Lana, Italy D8 22
Lanai, i., Hi., U.S. C4 78a
Lanai City, Hi., U.S. C4 78a
Lanaihale, mtn., Hi., U.S. C5 78a
Lanalhue, Lago, l., Chile I1 92
Lanark, On., Can. C13 112
Lanark, Scot., U.K. F9 12
Lanbi Kyun, i., Mya. G4 48
Lancang, China A4 48
Lancang see Mekong, stm., Asia D9 46
Lancaster, Eng., U.K. G10 12
Lancaster, Ca., U.S. I7 134
Lancaster, Mn., U.S. C2 118
Lancaster, Mo., U.S. D5 120
Lancaster, N.H., U.S. F5 110
Lancaster, Oh., U.S. E3 114
Lancaster, Pa., U.S. D9 114
Lancaster, S.C., U.S. B5 116
Lancaster, Tx., U.S. E2 122
Lancaster, Va., U.S. G9 114
Lancaster, Wi., U.S. B7 120
Lancaster Sound, strt., N.T., Can. C8 141
Lance Creek, Wy., U.S. D8 126
Lancelin, Austl. F2 74
Lanchou see Lanzhou, China D5 36
Lanchow see Lanzhou, China D5 36
Lanciano, Italy H11 22
Lancun, China C9 42
Łańcut, Pol. F18 16
Lândana, Ang. B1 68
Landau an der Isar, Ger. H8 16
Landau in der Pfalz, Ger. G4 16
Landeck, Aus. C7 22
Lander, Wy., U.S. E4 126
Landerneau, Fr. F4 14
Landes, state, Fr. F5 18
Landes, reg., Fr. E5 18
Landete, Spain E9 20
Landis, Sk., Can. B5 124
Lando, S.C., U.S. B4 116
Land O'Lakes, Wi., U.S. E9 118
Landösjön, l., Swe. E5 8
Landri Sales, Braz. D3 88
Landrum, S.C., U.S. A3 116
Landsborough Creek, stm., Austl. D5 76
Land's End, c., Eng., U.K. K7 12
Landshut, Ger. H7 16
Landskrona, Swe. I5 8
Lane, mth., Fr. G9 14
Lanesboro, Mn., U.S. H6 118
Lanett, Al., U.S. E13 122
Lanezi Lake, l., B.C., Can. C10 138
La'nga Co, l., China C8 54
Langa-Langa, D.R.C. E3 66
Langbank, Sk., Can. D11 124
Lang Bay, B.C., Can. G6 138
Langdale, Al., U.S. E13 122
Langdon, N.D., U.S. F15 124
Langeac, Fr. D9 18
Langeberg, mts., S. Afr. H5 70
Langeland, i., Den. I4 8
Langenhagen, Ger. D5 16
Langenthal, Switz. C4 22
Langfang, China B7 42
Langford, S.D., U.S. B15 126
Langgam, Indon. C2 50
Langham, Sk., Can. B6 124
Langhe, hist. reg., Italy F5 22
Langholm, Scot., U.K. F9 12
Langjökull, ice, Ice. k29 8a
Langkawi, Pulau, i., Malay. I4 48
Langley, B.C., Can. G8 138
Langley, Ok., U.S. A3 122
Langlo, stm., Austl. E5 76
Langnau im Emmental, Switz. C4 22
Langogne, Fr. E9 18
Langøya, i., Nor. B6 8
Langping, China F4 42
Langreo, Spain A5 20
Langres, Fr. G14 14
Langruth, Mb., Can. D15 124
Langsa, Indon. J3 48
Langsa, Teluk, b., Indon. J4 48
Langshan, China A2 42
Lang Son, Viet. B8 48
Lang Suan, Thai. H4 48
Languedoc, hist. reg., Fr. F8 18
L'Anguille, stm., Ar., U.S. C8 122
Langxi, China F8 42
Langzhong, China F1 42
Lanigan, Sk., Can. C8 124
Lanigan Creek, stm., Sk., Can. C9 124
Lanín, Volcán, vol., S.A. G2 90
Länkäran, Azer. B6 56
Länkipohja, Fin. F11 8
Lannemezan, Fr. F6 18
Lannion, Fr. F5 14
Lanping, China F4 36
Lansdowne, India D7 54
Lansdowne House, On., Can. E13 106
L'Anse, Mi., U.S. B1 112
Lansing, Ia., U.S. H7 118
Lansing, Mi., U.S. B1 114
Lantana, Fl., U.S. J5 116
Lantau Island, i., China J6 42
Lanta Yai, Ko, i., Thai. I4 48
Lantian, China D3 42
La Nurra, reg., Italy D2 24
Lanusei, Italy E3 24
Lanxi, China G8 42
Lan Yü, i., Tai. J9 42
Lanzhou, China D5 36
Lanzo Torinese, Italy E4 22
Lao, stm., Thai. C4 48
Laoag, Phil. A3 52
Laoang, Phil. D5 52
Lao Cai, Viet. A6 48
Laodao, stm., China G5 42
Laofu, China C3 38
Laoha, stm., China C4 38
Laohekou, China E4 42
Laohokow see Laohekou, China E4 42
Laois, state, Ire. I5 12
Lao Ling, mtn., China C9 38
Laon, Fr. E12 14
Laona, Wi., U.S. F10 118
La Orchila, Isla, i., Ven. B8 86
La Oroya, Peru F2 84
Laos, ctry., Asia C6 48
Laoshan Wan, b., China C9 42
Lapa, Braz. B13 92
Lapai, Nig. H6 64
Lapalisse, Fr. C9 18
La Palma, Col. E4 86
La Palma, Pan. H8 102
La Palma, Pan. I7 102
La Palma del Condado, Spain G4 20
La Paloma, Ur. G10 92
La Pampa, state, Arg. G3 90
La Paragua, Ven. D10 86
La Pasión, stm., Guat. D2 102
La Paya, Parque Nacional, p.o.i., Col. G4 86
La Paz, Arg. E8 92
La Paz, Arg. F4 92
La Paz, Bol. C3 90
La Paz, Col. B5 86
La Paz, Hond. E4 102
La Paz, Mex. C3 100
La Paz, Mex. D8 100
La Paz, Ur. G9 92
La Paz, Bahía de, b., Mex. C3 100
La Perla, Mex. A6 100
La Perouse, Bahía, b., Chile e30 78l
La Perouse Strait, strt., Asia B13 36
La Pesca, Mex. D10 100
La Piedad de Cabadas, Mex. E7 100
La Pine, Or., U.S. G5 136
La Place, La., U.S. G8 122
Lap Lae, Thai. D4 48
Lapland, hist. reg., Eur. C11 8
La Plata, Arg. G8 92
La Plata, Col. F4 86
La Plata, Md., U.S. F9 114
La Plata, Mo., U.S. D5 120
La Plata Peak, mtn., Co., U.S. D10 132
La Pobla de Segur, Spain B11 20
La Pocatière, Qc., Can. C6 110
Lapominka, Russia D19 8
Laporte, Co., U.S. G7 126
La Porte, In., U.S. G3 112
Laporte, Pa., U.S. C9 114
La Porte City, Ia., U.S. B5 120
La Potherie, Lac, l., Qc., Can. D16 106
La Poza Grande, Mex. C2 100
Lappajärvi, l., Fin. E10 8
Lappeenranta, Fin. F12 8
Lappi, state, Fin. C12 8
Laprida, Arg. D5 92
Laprida, Arg. H7 92
La Pryor, Tx., U.S. F8 130
Lapta, N. Cyp. C4 58
Laptev Sea see Laptevyh, more, Russia B4 32
Laptevyh, more, Russia B4 32
La Puebla de Montalbán, Spain E6 20
La Puerta, Arg. D5 92
La Puerta de Cabrera, Mex. H2 130
Lapu-Lapu, Phil. E4 52
La Purísima, Mex. B2 100
Lăpuş, Rom. B11 26
Lapwai, Id., U.S. D10 136
La Quiaca, Arg. D3 90
L'Áquila, Italy H10 22
Lār, Iran D7 56
Lara, state, Ven. B7 86
Laracha, Spain A2 20
Larache, Mor. B3 64
Laramie, Wy., U.S. F7 126
Laramie, stm., U.S. E8 126
Laramie Mountains, mts., Wy., U.S. F7 126
Laramie Peak, mtn., Wy., U.S. E7 126
Laranjal, Braz. K4 88
Laranjeiras, Braz. F7 88
Laranjeiras do Sul, Braz. B11 92
Larantuka, Indon. G7 44
Larap, Phil. C4 52
Larat, Indon. G9 44
Larat, Pulau, i., Indon. G9 44
Larche Pass, p., Eur. E12 18
Larchwood, Ia., U.S. H2 118
Larde, Moz. D6 68
L'Ardoise, N.S., Can. E16 110
Laredo, Spain A7 20
Laredo, Tx., U.S. G8 130
La Reforma, Mex. C4 100
Lares, P.R. B2 104a
Larga, Mol. A13 26
Larga, Laguna, l., Tx., U.S. G10 130
Largo, Fl., U.S. I3 116
Largo, Cañon, val., N.M., U.S. G9 132
Largo, Cayo, i., Cuba B7 102
Largs, Scot., U.K. F8 12
Lariang, stm., Indon. D11 50
Larimore, N.D., U.S. G16 124
Larino, Italy I11 22
Lario see Como, Lago di, l., Italy D6 22
La Rioja, Arg. D4 92
La Rioja, state, Arg. D4 92
La Rioja, state, Spain B8 20
Lárisa, Grc. D5 28
Larjak, Russia B14 32
Lārkāna, Pak. D10 56
Lárnakos, Kólpos, b., Cyp. D4 58
Larne, N. Ire., U.K. G7 12
Larned, Ks., U.S. C9 128
La Robla, Spain B5 20
La Rochefoucauld, Fr. D6 18
La Rochelle, Fr. C4 18
La Roche-sur-Yon, Fr. H7 14
La Roda, Spain E8 20
La Romaine, Qc., Can. i21 107a
La Romana, Dom. Rep. C13 102
La Ronge, Sk., Can. D10 106
Laroquebrou, Fr. D8 18
Larose, Pointe, c., Mart. k7 105c
Larroque, Arg. F8 92
Larrys River, N.S., Can. E15 110
Larsen Ice Shelf, ice, Ant. B34 81
La Rubia, Arg. E7 92
La Rue, Oh., U.S. D2 114
Larvik, Nor. G3 8
Larzac, Causse du, plat., Fr. F9 18
La Sabanilla, Mex. C8 100
La Sal, Ut., U.S. E7 132
La Salle, Co., U.S. G8 126
La Salle, Il., U.S. C8 120
La Salle, stm., Mb., Can. E16 124
Lasan, Indon. C9 50
Las Animas, Co., U.S. C5 128
Las Arenas, P.R. B1 104a
La Sarre, Qc., Can. F15 106

I•32 Lasa-Lind

Name	Map Ref.	Page
Las Arrias, Arg.	E6	92
Las Ballenas, Canal de, strt., Mex.	G6	98
Las Breñas, Arg.	C7	92
Las Cabezas de San Juan, Spain	G5	20
Las Cabras, Chile	G2	92
Lascano, Ur.	F10	92
Las Casitas, mtn., Mex.	D4	100
Las Catitas, Arg.	F3	92
Las Choapas, Mex.	G11	100
Las Chorreras, Mex.	A6	100
Las Cruces, N.M., U.S.	K10	132
Las Cuatas, Mex.	D1	130
Las Cuevas, Mex.	A8	100
Las Cumaraguas, Ven.	p20	104g
La Selle, Morne, mtn., Haiti	C11	102
La Serena, Chile	D2	92
La Serena, reg., Spain	F5	20
La Seu d'Urgell, Spain	B12	20
La Seyne, Fr.	F11	18
La Seyne, Fr.	F11	18
Las Flores, Arg.	G8	92
Las Flores, P.R.	B3	104a
Las Flores, Arroyo, stm., Arg.	H7	92
Las Garcitas, Arg.	C7	92
Las Guayabas, Mex.	C10	100
Lashburn, Sk., Can.	A4	124
Las Heras, Arg.	I3	90
Las Heras, Arg.	F3	92
Lashio, Mya.	A3	48
Lashkar Gāh, Afg.	C9	56
Las Hormigas, Mex.	C9	100
Lasia, Pulau, i., Indon.	K3	48
Łasin, Pol.	C15	16
La Sirena, Ven.	p20	104g
Łaskarzew, Pol.	E17	16
Las Lajas, Arg.	I2	92
Las Lajas, Pan.	H7	102
Las Lomitas, Arg.	B7	92
Las Malvinas, Arg.	G3	92
Las Mareas, P.R.	C3	104a
Las Margaritas, Mex.	G13	100
Las Marianas, Arg.	G8	92
Las Marías, P.R.	B1	104a
Las Minas, Cerro, mtn., Hond.	E3	102
Las Nopaleras, Cerro, mtn., Mex.	C7	100
La Solana, Spain	F7	20
Las Ovejas, Arg.	H2	92
Las Palmas, Arg.	C8	92
Las Palmas, P.R.	C3	104a
Las Palomas, Mex.	F9	98
La Spezia, Italy	F6	22
Las Piedras, P.R.	B4	104a
Las Piedras, Ur.	G9	92
Las Piedras, stm., Peru	F3	84
Las Plumas, Arg.	H3	90
Lasqueti Island, i., B.C., Can.	G6	138
Las Rosas, Arg.	F7	92
Las Rosas, Mex.	G12	100
Lassance, Braz.	I3	88
Lassen Peak, vol., Ca., U.S.	C4	134
Lassen Volcanic National Park, p.o.i., Ca., U.S.	C4	134
L'Assomption, stm., Qc., Can.	D3	110
Las Tablas, Pan.	I7	102
Las Tinajas, Arg.	C6	92
Last Mountain Lake, l., Sk., Can.	C8	124
Las Tórtolas, Cerro (Tórtolas, Cerro de las), mtn., S.A.	D2	92
Lastoursville, Gabon	E2	66
Las Tunas, Cuba	B9	102
Las Tunas Grandes, Laguna, l., Arg.	H6	92
Las Varas, Mex.	G8	98
Las Varas, Mex.	E6	100
Las Varillas, Arg.	E6	92
Las Vegas, P.R.	B1	104a
Las Vegas, Nv., U.S.	G1	132
Las Vegas, N.M., U.S.	F3	128
Las Vegas, Ven.	C7	86
Latacunga, Ec.	H2	86
La Tagua, Col.	H4	86
Latakia see Al-Lādhiqīyah, Syria	C6	58
Lata Mountain, vol., Am. Sam.	h13	79c
Latehar, India	G10	54
La Teste-de-Buch, Fr.	E4	18
Lāthi, India	H3	54
Lathrop, Mo., U.S.	E3	120
Latimer, Ia., U.S.	I5	118
Latina, Italy	C6	24
Latisana, Italy	E10	22
Latium see Lazio, state, Italy	B6	24
Latjuga, Russia	D23	8
La Torrecilla, mtn., P.R.	B3	104a
La Tortuga, Isla, i., Ven.	B9	86
Latouche Treville, Cape, c., Austl.	C4	74
La Tour-d'Auvergne, Fr.	D8	18
La Trimouille, Fr.	C7	18
La Trinidad, Nic.	F4	102
La Trinidad, Phil.	B3	52
La Trinidad de Orichuna, Ven.	D7	86
La Trinité, Mart.	k6	105c
Latrobe, Pa., U.S.	D6	114
Latta, S.C., U.S.	B6	116
La Tuque, Qc., Can.	C4	110
Lātūr, India	B3	53
Latvia, ctry., Eur.	D7	10
Lau, Nig.	H7	64
Lauchhammer, Ger.	E9	16
Lauenburg, Ger.	C6	16
Lauf an der Pegnitz, Ger.	G7	16
Lauge Koch Kyst, cst., Grnld.	B13	141
Laughlin, Nv., U.S.	H2	132
Laughlin Peak, mtn., N.M., U.S.	E4	128
Lau Group, is., Fiji	p20	79e
Lauis see Lugano, Switz.	D5	22
Laukaa, Fin.	E11	8
Laun, Thai.	G4	48
Launceston, Austl.	n13	77a
Launceston, Eng., U.K.	K8	12
La Unión, Chile	H2	90
La Unión, El Sal.	F4	102
La Unión, Mex.	G8	100
La Unión, Spain	G10	20
La Union, N.M., U.S.	L10	132
La Unión, Ven.	C8	86
Laupheim, Ger.	H5	16
Laura, Austl.	C8	74
La Urbana, Ven.	D8	86
Laurel, Fl., U.S.	I3	116
Laurel, In., U.S.	E12	120
Laurel, Md., U.S.	E9	114
Laurel, Ms., U.S.	F9	122
Laurel, Mt., U.S.	B4	126
Laurel, Ne., U.S.	E15	126
Laurel Bay, S.C., U.S.	D5	116
Laureldale, Pa., U.S.	D10	114
Laureles, Ur.	E9	92
Laurel River Lake, res., Ky., U.S.	G1	114
Laurelville, Oh., U.S.	E15	120
Laurencekirk, Scot., U.K.	E10	12
Laurens, S.C., U.S.	B3	116
Laurentides, Les, plat., Qc., Can.	F16	106
Lau Ridge, unds.	L21	142
Laurier, Mb., Can.	D14	124
Laurier-Station, Qc., Can.	D5	110
Laurinburg, N.C., U.S.	B6	116
Laurium, Mi., U.S.	D10	118
Lausanne, Switz.	D3	22
Lausitzer Neisse (Nysa Łużycka), stm., Eur.	F10	16
Laut, Pulau, i., Indon.	A5	50
Laut, Pulau, i., Indon.	E10	50
Laut, Selat, strt., Indon.	E9	50
Lauta, Ger.	E9	16
Lautaro, Chile	I1	92
Lauterbach, Ger.	F5	16
Lauter Sachsen, Ger.	F8	16
Laut Kecil, Kepulauan, is., Indon.	F9	50
Lautoka, Fiji	p18	79e
Lauzerte, Fr.	E7	18
Lava (Łyna), stm., Eur.	B16	16
Lava Beds National Monument, p.o.i., Ca., U.S.	B4	134
Lavaca, stm., Tx., U.S.	E11	130
Laval, Qc., Can.	E3	110
Laval, Fr.	F8	14
La Vall d'Uixó, Spain	E10	20
Lavalle, Arg.	D5	92
Lavalle, Arg.	D8	92
Lavapié, Punta, c., Chile	H1	92
Lavassaare, Est.	G11	8
La Vega, Dom. Rep.	C12	102
La Vela de Coro, Ven.	B7	86
Lavelanet, Fr.	G7	18
Lavello, Italy	C9	24
La Venada, Mex.	I10	130
La Venta, hist., Mex.	F11	100
La Ventura, Mex.	C8	100
La Vera, reg., Spain	D5	20
La Vergne, Tn., U.S.	H11	120
Laverne, Ok., U.S.	E9	128
Laverton, Austl.	E4	74
La Veta, Co., U.S.	D4	128
Lavieille, Lake, l., On., Can.	C11	112
La Vila Joiosa, Spain	F10	20
Lavillette, N.B., Can.	C11	110
La Viña, Arg.	B5	92
Lavina, Mt., U.S.	A4	126
La Vista, Ne., U.S.	C1	120
La Voulte-sur-Rhône, Fr.	E10	18
Lavras, Braz.	K3	88
Lávrio, Grc.	F7	28
Lavumisa, Swaz.	E10	70
Lawang, Indon.	G8	50
Lawas, Malay.	A9	50
Lawdar, Yemen	G6	56
Lawers, Ben, mtn., Scot., U.K.	E8	12
Lawgi, Austl.	E8	76
Lawksawk, Mya.	B3	48
Lawler, Ia., U.S.	A5	120
Lawn, Tx., U.S.	B8	130
Lawndale, N.C., U.S.	A4	116
Lawn Hill, Austl.	C7	74
Lawn Hill Creek, stm., Austl.	C7	74
Lawrence, In., U.S.	I3	112
Lawrence, Ks., U.S.	F2	120
Lawrence, Ma., U.S.	B14	114
Lawrenceburg, In., U.S.	E12	120
Lawrenceburg, Ky., U.S.	F12	120
Lawrenceburg, Tn., U.S.	B11	122
Lawrenceville, Il., U.S.	F10	120
Lawrenceville, N.J., U.S.	D11	114
Lawson, Mo., U.S.	E3	120
Lawtey, Fl., U.S.	F3	116
Lawton, N.D., U.S.	F15	124
Lawton, Ok., U.S.	G10	128
Lawu, Gunung, vol., Indon.	G7	50
Lawz, Jabal al-, mtn., Sau. Ar.	J6	58
Laxå, Swe.	G6	8
Laxe, Spain	A1	20
Lay Lake, res., Al., U.S.	D12	122
Layou, St. Vin.	o11	105e
Layton, Ut., U.S.	B4	132
Laytonville, Ca., U.S.	D2	134
La Zarca, Mex.	C6	100
Lazarev, Russia	F17	34
Lázaro Cárdenas, Mex.	G7	100
Lázaro Cárdenas, Presa, res., Mex.	C6	100
Lazdijai, Lith.	F6	10
Lazio, state, Italy	B6	24
Léach, Camb.	F6	48
Leachville, Ar., U.S.	I7	120
Lead, S.D., U.S.	C9	126
Leadbetter Point, c., Wa., U.S.	D2	136
Leader, Sk., Can.	D4	124
Lead Hill, hill, Mo., U.S.	H4	120
Leadore, Id., U.S.	F13	136
Leadville, Co., U.S.	D10	132
Leaf, stm., Ms., U.S.	F10	122
Leaf Lake, l., Sk., Can.	A11	124
Leaghur, Lake, l., Austl.	I4	76
League City, Tx., U.S.	H3	122
Leakey, Tx., U.S.	E8	130
Leaksville, N.C., U.S.	H5	114
Lealman, Fl., U.S.	I3	116
Leamington, On., Can.	F7	112
Le'an, China	H6	42
Leandro, Braz.	C3	88
Leandro N. Alem, Arg.	C10	92
Leary, Ga., U.S.	F14	122
Leatherman Peak, mtn., Id., U.S.	F13	136
Leavenworth, Ks., U.S.	E2	120
Leavenworth, Wa., U.S.	C6	136
Leawood, Ks., U.S.	F3	120
Lebak, Phil.	G5	52
Lebam, Wa., U.S.	D3	136
Lebanon, In., U.S.	H3	112
Lebanon, Ks., U.S.	B10	128
Lebanon, Ky., U.S.	G12	120
Lebanon, N.H., U.S.	G4	110
Lebanon, Oh., U.S.	E1	114
Lebanon, Or., U.S.	F3	136
Lebanon, Pa., U.S.	D9	114
Lebanon, S.D., U.S.	B13	126
Lebanon, Tn., U.S.	H11	120
Lebanon, Va., U.S.	H3	114
Lebanon, ctry., Asia	E6	58
Lebec, Ca., U.S.	I7	134
Lebesby, Nor.	A12	8
Le Bic, Qc., Can.	B8	110
Lebjaže, Kaz.	D13	32
Le Blanc, Fr.	H10	14
Lebo, D.R.C.	D4	66
Lebo, Ks., U.S.	F2	120
Lębork, Pol.	B13	16
Lebrija, Spain	H4	20
Lebrija, stm., Col.	D5	86
Łebsko, Jezioro, l., Pol.	B13	16
Lebu, Chile	H1	92
Le Carbet, Mart.	k6	105c
Lecce, Italy	D12	24
Lecco, Italy	E6	22
Le Center, Mn., U.S.	G5	118
Lech, stm., Eur.	H6	16
Lechainá, Grc.	F4	28
Lechang, China	I5	42
Le Chesne, Fr.	E13	14
Lechiguanas, Islas de las, is., Arg.	F8	92
Lechuguilla, Cerro, mtn., Mex.	D6	100
Lecompte, La., U.S.	F6	122
Le Creusot, Fr.	H13	14
Le Croisic, Fr.	G6	14
Łęczyca, Pol.	D15	16
Ledesma, Spain	C4	20
Le Diamant, Mart.	I6	105c
Ledjanaja, gora, mtn., Russia	D23	34
Ledo, India	C8	46
Ledo, Indon.	C6	50
Ledong, China	L3	42
Le Dorat, Fr.	C7	18
Ledu, China	D5	36
Leduc, Ab., Can.	C17	138
Leechburg, Pa., U.S.	D6	114
Leech Lake, l., Mn., U.S.	D4	118
Leedey, Ok., U.S.	F9	128
Leeds, Eng., U.K.	H11	12
Leeds, Al., U.S.	D12	122
Leek, Eng., U.K.	H10	12
Leelanau, Lake, l., Mi., U.S.	D4	112
Leelanau Peninsula, pen., Mi., U.S.	C4	112
Leer, Ger.	C3	16
Leesburg, Fl., U.S.	H4	116
Leesburg, Ga., U.S.	E1	116
Leesburg, Va., U.S.	E8	114
Lees Summit, Mo., U.S.	F3	120
Leesville, La., U.S.	F5	122
Leesville, Tx., U.S.	E10	130
Leeton, Austl.	J6	76
Leeu-Gamka, S. Afr.	H6	70
Leeuwarden, Neth.	A14	14
Leeuwin, Cape, c., Austl.	F2	74
Lee Vining, Ca., U.S.	F6	134
Leeward Islands, is., N.A.	h15	96a
Lefkáda, Grc.	E3	28
Lefkáda, i., Grc.	E3	28
Lefke, N. Cyp.	C3	58
Lefkosía see Nicosia, Cyp.	C4	58
Lefors, Tx., U.S.	F8	128
Le François, Mart.	k7	105c
Lefroy, Lake, l., Austl.	F4	74
Legal, Ab., Can.	C17	138
Leganés, Spain	D7	20
Legaspi, Phil.	D4	52
Leggett, Ca., U.S.	D2	134
Leghorn see Livorno, Italy	G7	22
Legion, Zimb.	B9	70
Legionowo, Pol.	D16	16
Legnago, Italy	E8	22
Legnano, Italy	E5	22
Legnica, Pol.	E12	16
Legnica, state, Pol.	E12	16
Le Gosier, Guad.	h6	105c
Le Grand, Ca., U.S.	F5	134
Le Guelta, Alg.	H11	20
Legume, Austl.	G9	76
Leh, India	A6	54
Le Havre, Fr.	E8	14
Lehčevo, Blg.	F10	26
Lehigh, Ia., U.S.	B3	120
Lehigh, Ok., U.S.	C2	122
Lehigh Acres, Fl., U.S.	J4	116
Lehighton, Pa., U.S.	D10	114
Lehrte, Ger.	D5	16
Lehtse, Est.	A8	10
Lehua, i., Hi., U.S.	A1	78a
Lehututu, Bots.	C5	70
Lei, stm., China	H5	42
Leiah, Pak.	C3	54
Leibnitz, Aus.	D12	22
Leicester, Eng., U.K.	I11	12
Leichhardt, stm., Austl.	A2	76
Leichhardt Falls, wtfl, Austl.	B2	76
Leiden (Leyden), Neth.	B13	14
Leigh Creek South, Austl.	H2	76
Leighton, Al., U.S.	C11	122
Leighton Buzzard, Eng., U.K.	J12	12
Leinan, Sk., Can.	D6	124
Leine, stm., Ger.	D5	16
Leinster, hist. reg., Ire.	I6	12
Leinster, Mount, mtn., Ire.	I6	12
Leipalingis, Lith.	F6	10
Leipsic, Oh., U.S.	C2	114
Leipzig, Ger.	E8	16
Leiria, Port.	E2	20
Leiria, state, Port.	E2	20
Leisler, Mount, mtn., Austl.	D6	74
Leitariegos, Puerto de, p., Spain	A4	20
Leitha (Lajta), stm., Eur.	H12	16
Leitrim, Ire.	H4	12
Leitrim, state, Ire.	H5	12
Leivádia, Grc.	E5	28
Leiyang, China	H5	42
Leizhou Bandao, pen., China	K3	42
Lejasciems, Lat.	C9	10
Lekeitio, Spain	A8	20
Leksozero, ozero, l., Russia	E14	8
Le Lamentin, Mart.	k6	105c
Leland, Il., U.S.	C9	120
Leland, Mi., U.S.	C4	112
Leland, Ms., U.S.	D8	122
Leleiwi Point, c., Hi., U.S.	D7	78a
Leleque, Arg.	H2	90
Leles, Indon.	G5	50
Leli Shan, mtn., China	B8	54
Le Locle, Switz.	C3	22
Lelystad, Neth.	B14	14
Le Maire, Estrecho de, strt., Arg.	J4	90
Le Mans, Fr.	G9	14
Le Marin, Mart.	I7	105c
Le Mars, Ia., U.S.	B1	120
Lema Shilindi, Eth.	G8	62
Lemay, Mo., U.S.	F7	120
Lembak, Indon.	C10	50
Lemdiyya, Alg.	H13	20
Leme, Braz.	L2	88
Lemesós (Limassol), Cyp.	D4	58
Lemhi, stm., Id., U.S.	F13	136
Lemhi Pass, p., U.S.	F13	136
Lemhi Range, mts., Id., U.S.	F13	136
Lemieux Islands, is., N.T., Can.	E13	141
Leming, Tx., U.S.	E9	130
Lemitar, N.M., U.S.	I10	132
Lemmatsi, Est.	B9	10
Lemmenjoen kansallispuisto, p.o.i., Fin.	B11	8
Lemmon, S.D., U.S.	B10	126
Lemmon, Mount, mtn., Az., U.S.	K6	132
Lemnos see Límnos, i., Grc.	D8	28
Lemoncove, Ca., U.S.	G7	134
Le Mont-Dore, N. Cal.	n16	79d
Lemoore, Ca., U.S.	G6	134
Le Moule, Guad.	h6	105c
Lempa, stm., N.A.	F3	102
Lempe, Indon.	D12	50
Lemro, stm., Mya.	B1	48
Le Murge, hills, Italy	D10	24
Le Muy, Fr.	F12	18
Lemyethna, Mya.	D2	48
Lena, Il., U.S.	B8	120
Lena, Wi., U.S.	D1	112
Lena, stm., Russia	B14	34
Lenart, Slvn.	D12	22
Lençóis, Braz.	G5	88
Lençoís Maranhenses, Parque Nacional dos, p.o.i., Braz.	B4	88
Lendery, Russia	E14	8
Lendinara, Italy	E8	22
Lenger, Kaz.	F12	32
Lenggor, stm., Malay.	K6	48
Lenghu, China	D3	36
Lengshuitan, China	H4	42
Lenhovda, Swe.	H6	8
Leningrad see Sankt-Peterburg, Russia	A13	10
Leningradskaja oblast', co., Russia	G15	8
Leninogor see Leninogorsk, Kaz.	D14	32
Leninogorsk, Kaz.	D14	32
Lenin Peak, mtn., Asia	B11	56
Leninsk, Kaz.	E10	32
Leninsk, Uzb.	F12	32
Leninskij, Russia	F20	10
Leninsk-Kuzneckij, Russia	D15	32
Leninskoe, Russia	G15	34
Lennonville, Austl.	E3	74
Lennox, S.D., U.S.	H2	118
Lennox, Isla, i., Chile	K3	90
Lennoxville, Qc., Can.	E5	110
Lenoir, N.C., U.S.	I4	114
Lenora, Czech Rep.	H9	16
Lenore Lake, l., Sk., Can.	B9	124
Lenox, Ga., U.S.	E2	116
Lenox, Ia., U.S.	D3	120
Lenox, Tn., U.S.	H8	120
Lens, Fr.	D11	14
Lensk, Russia	B20	32
Lenti, Hung.	C3	26
Lentini, Italy	G9	24
Lentua, l., Fin.	D13	8
Lentvaris, Lith.	F8	10
Lenya, stm., Mya.	G4	48
Léo, Burkina	G4	64
Leoben, Aus.	C12	22
Léogâne, Haiti	C11	102
Leola, Ar., U.S.	C6	122
Leola, S.D., U.S.	B14	126
Leominster, Eng., U.K.	I10	12
Leominster, Ma., U.S.	B14	114
Léon, Fr.	F4	18
León, Mex.	E8	100
León, Nic.	F4	102
León, Spain	B5	20
Leon, Ks., U.S.	D12	128
León, co., Spain	B5	20
Leon, stm., Tx., U.S.	C10	130
León, Montes de, mts., Spain	B4	20
Leona, stm., Tx., U.S.	F8	130
Leonard, Tx., U.S.	D2	122
Leonardtown, Md., U.S.	F9	114
Leonardville, Ks., U.S.	B11	128
Leonberg, Ger.	H4	16
Leones, Arg.	F6	92
Leonforte, Italy	G8	24
Leongatha, Austl.	L5	76
Leoniha, Russia	G18	8
Leonora, Austl.	E4	74
Leopold and Astrid Coast, cst., Ant.	B13	81
Leopoldina, Braz.	K4	88
Leopoldo de Bulhões, Braz.	I1	88
Léopoldville see Kinshasa, D.R.C.	E3	66
Leoti, Ks., U.S.	C7	128
Leova, Mol.	C15	26
Lepanto see Náfpaktos, Grc.	E4	28
Lepanto, Ar., U.S.	B8	122
Lepar, Pulau, i., Indon.	E5	50
Lepe, Spain	G3	20
Lepel', Bela.	F11	10
Leping, China	G7	42
L'Épiphanie, Qc., Can.	E3	110
Lepontine Alps, mts., Eur.	C14	18
Lepreau, Point, c., N.B., Can.	E10	110
Le Prêcheur, Mart.	k6	105c
Lepsi see Lepsy, Kaz.	E13	32
Lepsy, Kaz.	E13	32
Le Puy, Fr.	D9	18
Lequeitio see Lekeitio, Spain	A8	20
Lercara Friddi, Italy	G7	24
Lerdo, Mex.	C7	100
Lerici, Italy	F6	22
Lérida, Col.	G6	86
Lérida see Lleida, Spain	C11	20
Lerma, stm., Mex.	E8	100
Le Roy, Il., U.S.	D9	120
Le Roy, Ks., U.S.	F2	120
Le Roy, N.Y., U.S.	B7	114
Lerum, Swe.	H5	8
Lerwick, Scot., U.K.	n18	12a
Les Abymes, Guad.	h5	105c
Le Saint-Esprit, Mart.	k7	105c
Les Andelys, Fr.	E10	14
Les Anses-d'Arlets, Mart.	I6	105c
Les Borges Blanques, Spain	C11	20
Lesbos see Lésvos, i., Grc.	D9	28
Les Cayes, Haiti	C11	102
Leshan, China	F5	36
Les Herbiers, Fr.	H7	14
Lesina, Lago di, b., Italy	I12	22
Lesko, Pol.	G18	16
Leskovac, Yugo.	F8	26
Leskov Island, i., S. Geor.	K12	82
Les Laurentides see Laurentides, Les, plat., Qc., Can.	F16	106
Leslie, Ar., U.S.	I5	120
Leslie, Mi., U.S.	B1	114
Leslie, W.V., U.S.	F5	114
Lesneven, Fr.	F4	14
Lesnoe, Russia	B18	10
Lesogorsk, Russia	G17	34
Lesosibirsk, Russia	E7	34
Lesotho, ctry., Afr.	F9	70
Lesozavodsk, Russia	B10	38
Lesozavodskij, Russia	C15	8
Les Sables-d'Olonne, Fr.	H7	14
Les Saintes, is., Guad.	i5	105c
Lesser Antilles, is.	D8	82
Lesser Khingan Range see Xiao Hinggan Ling, mts., China	B10	36
Lesser Slave, stm., Ab., Can.	A16	138
Lesser Slave Lake, l., Ab., Can.	D8	106
Lesser Sunda Islands see Tenggara, Nusa, is., Indon.	G6	44
L'Esterre, Gren.	q10	105e
Lestock, Sk., Can.	C9	124
Le Sueur, Mn., U.S.	G4	118
Le Sueur, stm., Mn., U.S.	G5	118
Lešukonskoe, Russia	D21	8
Lésvos (Lesbos), i., Grc.	D9	28
Leszno, Pol.	E12	16
Leszno, state, Pol.	E12	16
Letaba, stm., S. Afr.	C10	70
Letcher, S.D., U.S.	D14	126
Letea, Ostrovul, i., Rom.	D16	26
Letenye, Hung.	C3	26
Lethbridge, Ab., Can.	G18	138
Lethem, Guy.	F12	86
Le Thillot, Fr.	B12	18
Leti, Kepulauan, is., Indon.	G8	44
Leticia, Col.	D4	84
Letlhakane, Bots.	B7	70
Letlhakeng, Bots.	D7	70
Letnjaja Zolotica, Russia	D17	8
Letpadan, Mya.	D2	48
Le Tréport, Fr.	D10	14
Letsôk-aw Kyun, i., Mya.	G3	48
Letung, Indon.	B4	50
Leucas see Lefkáda, i., Grc.	E3	28
Leucate, Étang de, l., Fr.	G9	18
Leuk, Switz.	D4	22
Leuser, Gunung, mtn., Indon.	K3	48
Leutkirch, Ger.	I6	16
Leuven, Bel.	D13	14
Levack, On., Can.	B8	112
Levan, Ut., U.S.	D5	132
Levanger, Nor.	E4	8
Levante, Riviera di, cst., Italy	F6	22
Levanzo, Isola di, i., Italy	F6	24
Le Vauclin, Mart.	k7	105c
Levelland, Tx., U.S.	H6	128
Leveque, Cape, c., Austl.	C4	74
Leverkusen, Ger.	E3	16
Levice, Slov.	H14	16
Levin, N.Z.	E6	80
Lévis, Qc., Can.	D5	110
Levisa Fork, stm., U.S.	G3	114
Levittown, P.R.	B3	104a
Levittown, N.Y., U.S.	D12	114
Levittown, Pa., U.S.	D11	114
Levkosía see Nicosia, Cyp.	C4	58
Levoča, Slov.	H16	16
Levski, Blg.	F12	26
Levuka, Fiji	p19	79e
Lėvuo, stm., Lith.	E7	10
Lewe, Mya.	C2	48
Lewellen, Ne., U.S.	F10	126
Lewer, stm., Nmb.	D3	70
Lewes, De., U.S.	F10	114
Lewin Brzeski, Pol.	F13	16
Lewis, Ia., U.S.	J3	118
Lewis, Butt of, c., Scot., U.K.	C6	12
Lewis, Isle of, i., Scot., U.K.	C6	12
Lewis, Mount, mtn., Nv., U.S.	C8	134
Lewis and Clark Lake, res., U.S.	E15	126
Lewis and Clark Range, mts., Mt., U.S.	C13	136
Lewisburg, Ky., U.S.	H10	120
Lewisburg, Pa., U.S.	D8	114
Lewisburg, Tn., U.S.	B12	122
Lewis Range, mts., N.A.	B13	136
Lewis Run, Pa., U.S.	C7	114
Lewis Smith Lake, res., Al., U.S.	C11	122
Lewiston, Ca., U.S.	C3	134
Lewiston, Id., U.S.	D10	136
Lewiston, Me., U.S.	F6	110
Lewiston, Mi., U.S.	D5	112
Lewiston, Mn., U.S.	H7	118
Lewiston, Ut., U.S.	B5	132
Lewiston Orchards, Id., U.S.	D10	136
Lewistown, Il., U.S.	D7	120
Lewistown, Mt., U.S.	C17	136
Lewistown, Pa., U.S.	D8	114
Lewisville, N.B., Can.	D12	110
Lewisville, Ar., U.S.	D5	122
Lewisville, Tx., U.S.	A10	130
Lewisville Lake, res., Tx., U.S.	H12	128
Lewvan, Sk., Can.	D9	124
Lexa, Ar., U.S.	C8	122
Lexington, Ga., U.S.	C2	116
Lexington, Il., U.S.	D9	120
Lexington, Ky., U.S.	F1	114
Lexington, Ma., U.S.	B14	114
Lexington, Mi., U.S.	E7	112
Lexington, Ms., U.S.	D8	122
Lexington, N.C., U.S.	I5	114
Lexington, Ok., U.S.	F11	128
Lexington, Or., U.S.	E7	136
Lexington, S.C., U.S.	C4	116
Lexington, Tx., U.S.	D10	130
Lexington, Va., U.S.	G6	114
Lexington Park, Md., U.S.	F9	114
Leyden see Leiden, Neth.	B13	14
Leye, China	I2	42
Leyte, i., Phil.	E5	52
Leyte Gulf, b., Phil.	E5	52
Lezhë, Alb.	C13	24
Lezhi, China	F1	42
Lëzna, Bela.	E13	10
L'gov, Russia	D5	32
Lhasa, China	D13	54
Lhasa, stm., China	C13	54
Lhazê, China	D11	54
Lhokng a, Indon.	J2	48
Lhokseumawe, Indon.	J3	48
Lhoksukon, Indon.	J3	48
Lhorong, China	E4	36
L'Hospitalet de Llobregat, Spain	C13	20
Lhuntsi Dzong, Bhu.	E13	54
Li, Thai.	D4	48
Li, stm., China	G4	42
Li, stm., Thai.	D4	48
Liamuiga, Mount, vol., St. K./N.	C2	105a
Lian, stm., China	I5	42
Liancheng, China	I7	42
Lianga, Phil.	F6	52
Liangbao, China	D4	42
Liangbuaya, Indon.	C10	50
Liangdang, China	E1	42
Lianghekou, China	G3	42
Liangmentou, China	G9	42
Liangping, China	F2	42
Liangyuan, China	E7	42
Liangzi Hu, l., China	F6	42
Lianhuapao, China	B8	38
Lianhua Shan, mts., China	J6	42
Lianjiang, China	K4	42
Liannan, China	I5	42
Lianshui, China	E8	42
Lianxian, China	I5	42
Lianyuan, China	H4	42
Lianyungang, China	D8	42
Liao, stm., China	D5	38
Liaocheng, China	C7	42
Liaodong Bandao (Liaotung Peninsula), pen., China	D5	38
Liaodong Wan (Liaotung, Gulf of), b., China	A9	42
Liaoning, state, China	D5	38
Liaotung, Gulf of see Liaodong Wan, b., China	A9	42
Liaotung Peninsula see Liaodong Bandao, pen., China	E5	38
Liaoyang, China	D5	38
Liaoyuan, China	C6	38
Liaozhong, China	D5	38
Liard, stm., Can.	C6	106
Liat, Pulau, i., Indon.	E5	50
Libagon, Phil.	E5	52
Líbano, Col.	E4	86
Libby, Mt., U.S.	B11	136
Libby Dam, dam, Mt., U.S.	B11	136
Libenge, D.R.C.	D3	66
Liberal, Ks., U.S.	D7	128
Liberal, Mo., U.S.	G3	120
Liberec, Czech Rep.	F11	16
Liberia, C.R.	G5	102
Liberia, ctry., Afr.	H3	64
Liberta, Antig.	f4	105b
Libertad, Ven.	C7	86
Libertad, Ven.	C7	86
Libertador General Bernardo O'Higgins, state, Chile	G2	92
Liberty, Ms., U.S.	F8	122
Liberty, Mo., U.S.	E3	120
Liberty, N.Y., U.S.	C11	114
Liberty, N.C., U.S.	I6	114
Liberty, S.C., U.S.	B3	116
Liberty, Tx., U.S.	G4	122
Liberty Center, Oh., U.S.	G5	112
Libertyville, Il., U.S.	B9	120
Libo, China	I2	42
Libobo, Tanjung, c., Indon.	F8	44
Libode, S. Afr.	G9	70
Libourne, Fr.	E5	18
Librazhd, Alb.	C14	24
Libres, Mex.	F10	100
Libreville, Gabon	D1	66
Liburung, Indon.	F12	50
Libya, ctry., Afr.	B3	62
Libyan Desert, des., Afr.	C5	62
Libyan Plateau, plat., Afr.	A4	62
Licancábur, Volcán, vol., S.A.	D3	90
Licantén, Chile	G1	92
Licata, Italy	G7	24
Lich, Ger.	F4	16
Licheng, China	C5	42
Licheng see Liyang, China	F8	42
Lichfield, Eng., U.K.	I11	12
Lichinga, Moz.	C6	68
Lichtenau, Ger.	E5	16
Lichtenburg, S. Afr.	E7	70
Lichtenfels, Ger.	F7	16
Lichuan, China	H7	42
Lichuan, China	F3	42
Licking, Mo., U.S.	G6	120
Licking, stm., Ky., U.S.	F1	114
Ličko Polje, val., Cro.	F12	22
Lida, Bela.	G8	10
Liddon Gulf, b., N.T., Can.	B17	140
Liden, Swe.	E7	8
Lidgerwood, N.D., U.S.	E1	118
Lidköping, Swe.	G5	8
Lido di Ostia, Italy	I9	22
Lidzbark, Pol.	C15	16
Lidzbark Warmiński, Pol.	B16	16
Liebenbergsvlei, stm., S. Afr.	E9	70
Liebig, Mount, mtn., Austl.	D6	74
Liechtenstein, ctry., Eur.	C6	22
Liège (Luik), Bel.	D14	14
Lielais Liepu kalns, hill, Lat.	D10	10
Lielvārde, Lat.	D7	10
Lienchou see Hepu, China	K3	42
Lienz, Aus.	D9	22
Liepāja, Lat.	D3	10
Liepājas ezers, l., Lat.	D4	10
Lier, Bel.	C13	14
Lierre see Lier, Bel.	C13	14
Liestal, Switz.	C4	22
Liești, Rom.	D14	26
Liévin, Fr.	D11	14
Lièvre, stm., Qc., Can.	C14	112
Liezen, Aus.	C11	22
Liffey, stm., Ire.	H6	12
Lifford, Ire.	G5	12
Lifou, i., N. Cal.	m16	79d
Līgatne, Lat.	C7	10
Lighthouse Point, Fl., U.S.	J5	116
Lighthouse Point, c., Fl., U.S.	H14	122
Lighthouse Point, c., Mi., U.S.	C4	112
Lightning Creek, stm., Wy., U.S.	D7	126
Lightning Ridge, Austl.	G6	76
Lignite, N.D., U.S.	F11	124
Ligny-en-Barrois, Fr.	F14	14
Ligonha, stm., Moz.	D6	68
Ligonier, In., U.S.	G4	112
Ligonier, Pa., U.S.	H10	112
Liguria, state, Italy	F5	22
Ligurian Sea, Eur.	G5	22
Lihir Island, i., Pap. N. Gui.	a5	79a
Lihoslavl', Russia	C18	10
Lihou Reefs and Cays, rf., Austl.	A8	76
Lihue, Hi., U.S.	B2	78a
Lihuel Calel, Parque Nacional, p.o.i., Arg.	H5	92
Lihula, Est.	B6	10
Lijiang, China	F5	36
Lik, stm., Laos	C6	48
Likasi (Jadotville), D.R.C.	G5	66
Likati, D.R.C.	D4	66
Likely, B.C., Can.	D9	138
Liki, Indon.	D2	50
Likino-Dulevo, Russia	E21	10
Lilbourn, Mo., U.S.	H8	120
Lilibeo, Capo see Boeo, Capo, c., Italy	G6	24
Lilienfeld, Aus.	B12	22
Liling, China	H5	42
Lille, Fr.	D12	14
Lillebælt, strt., Den.	I3	8
Lillebonne, Fr.	E9	14
Lillehammer, Nor.	F3	8
Lillers, Fr.	D11	14
Lillestrøm, Nor.	F4	8
Lillhärdal, Swe.	F6	8
Lillington, N.C., U.S.	A7	116
Lillooet, B.C., Can.	F9	138
Lillooet, stm., B.C., Can.	G8	138
Lillooet Lake, l., B.C., Can.	F8	138
Lilongwe, Mwi.	C5	68
Liloy, Phil.	F4	52
Lilydale, Austl.	n13	77a
Lim, stm., Eur.	G16	22
Lima, Para.	A9	92
Lima, Peru	F2	84
Lima, Mt., U.S.	F14	136
Lima, N.Y., U.S.	B8	114
Lima, Oh., U.S.	D1	114
Lima (Limia), stm., Eur.	C2	20
Limarí, stm., Chile	E2	92
Limas, Indon.	C4	50
Limassol see Lemesós, Cyp.	D4	58
Limavady, N. Ire., U.K.	F6	12
Limay, stm., Arg.	G3	90
Limay Mahuida, Arg.	H4	92
Limbang, Malay.	A9	50
Limbang, stm., Malay.	A9	50
Līmbdi, India	G3	54
Limbe, Cam.	D1	66
Limbé, Haiti	C11	102
Limbujan see Pio V. Corpuz, Phil.	E5	52
Limburg an der Lahn, Ger.	F4	16
Limeira, Braz.	L2	88
Limerick, Sk., Can.	E7	124
Limerick (Luimneach), Ire.	I4	12
Limerick, state, Ire.	I4	12
Limestone, Me., U.S.	D9	110
Limestone, Lake, res., Tx., U.S.	F2	122
Limfjorden, l., Den.	H3	8
Limia (Lima), stm., Eur.	C2	20
Limingen, l., Nor.	D5	8
Limmared, Swe.	H5	8
Limmen Bight, b., Austl.	B7	74
Límnos, i., Grc.	D8	28
Limoeiro, Braz.	D8	88
Limoeiro do Norte, Braz.	C6	88
Limoges, Fr.	D7	18
Limón, Hond.	E5	102
Limone Piemonte, Italy	F4	22
Limoux, Fr.	F8	18
Limpopo, stm., Afr.	D8	70
Linahamari, Russia	B14	8
Lin'an, China	F8	42
Linapacan Island, i., Phil.	E2	52
Linares, Chile	G2	92
Linares, Mex.	C9	100
Linares, Spain	F7	20
Linch, Wy., U.S.	D6	126
Lincheng, China	C6	42
Linch'ing see Linqing, China	C6	42
Lincoln, Arg.	G7	92
Lincoln, Eng., U.K.	H12	12
Lincoln, Ar., U.S.	I3	120
Lincoln, Ca., U.S.	E4	134
Lincoln, Il., U.S.	D8	120
Lincoln, Mi., U.S.	D6	112
Lincoln, Mo., U.S.	F4	120
Lincoln, Mt., U.S.	D14	136
Lincoln, Ne., U.S.	K2	118
Lincoln, N.H., U.S.	F5	110
Lincoln, Mount, mtn., Co., U.S.	B2	128
Lincoln City, Or., U.S.	F2	136
Lincoln Creek, stm., Ne., U.S.	F15	126
Lincoln Park, Co., U.S.	C3	128
Lincoln Park, Mi., U.S.	B2	114
Lincoln Sea, N.A.	A13	141
Lincolnton, Ga., U.S.	C3	116
Lincolnton, N.C., U.S.	A4	116
Lincoln Village, Ca., U.S.	F4	134
Lindale, Ga., U.S.	C13	122
Lindale, Tx., U.S.	E3	122
Lindau, Ger.	I5	16
Linde, stm., Russia	C13	34
Linden, Guy.	B6	84
Linden, Al., U.S.	E11	122
Linden, In., U.S.	H3	112
Linden, Mi., U.S.	B2	114

Name	Map Ref.	Page
Linden, Tn., U.S.	B11	122
Lindesnes, c., Nor.	H2	8
Lindi, Tan.	F7	66
Lindi, stm., D.R.C.	D5	66
Líndos, hist., Grc.	G10	28
Lind Point, c., V.I.U.S.	e7	104b
Lindsay, On., Can.	D11	112
Lindsay, Ca., U.S.	G6	134
Lindsay, Ne., U.S.	F15	126
Lindsay, Ok., U.S.	G11	128
Line Islands, is., Oc.	D11	72
Linesville, Pa., U.S.	C5	114
Lineville, Al., U.S.	D13	122
Lineville, Ia., U.S.	D4	120
Linfen, China	C4	42
Linganamakki Reservoir, res., India	D2	53
Lingao, China	L3	42
Lingayen, Phil.	B3	52
Lingayen Gulf, b., Phil.	B3	52
Lingbi, China	E7	42
Lingbo, Swe.	F7	8
Lingchuan, China	D5	42
Lingen, Ger.	D3	16
Lingfengwei, China	I6	42
Lingga, Kepulauan, is., Indon.	C4	50
Lingga, Pulau, i., Indon.	D4	50
Lingomo II, D.R.C.	D4	66
Lingqiu, China	B6	42
Lingshan, China	J3	42
Lingshi, China	C4	42
Lingshui, China	L4	42
Linguère, Sen.	F2	64
Lingwu, China	B2	42
Lingxian, China	H5	42
Lingyuan, China	A8	42
Linh, Ngoc, mtn., Viet.	E9	48
Linhai, China	G9	42
Linhares, Braz.	J5	88
Linhe, China	A2	42
Linhsia see Linxia, China	D5	36
Lini see Linyi, China	D8	42
Linjiang, China	D7	38
Linköping, Swe.	G6	8
Linkou, China	B9	38
Linksmakalnis, Lith.	F6	10
Linkuva, Lith.	D6	10
Linn, Ks., U.S.	B11	128
Linn, Mo., U.S.	F6	120
Linnansaaren kansallispuisto, p.o.i., Fin.	E13	8
Linnhe, Loch, b., Scot., U.K.	E7	12
Linqi, China	D5	42
Linqing, China	C6	42
Linqu, China	C8	42
Linquan, China	E6	42
Linru, China	D5	42
Lins, Braz.	K1	88
Linstead, Jam.	i13	104d
Lintan, China	E5	36
Linton, In., U.S.	E10	120
Linton, N.D., U.S.	A12	126
Lintong, China	D3	42
Linwu, China	I5	42
Linxi, China	C8	36
Linxi, China	C3	38
Linxia, China	D5	36
Linxian, China	C4	42
Linxian, China	C5	42
Linyi, China	D8	42
Linyi, China	C7	42
Linyü see Shanhaiguan, China	A8	42
Linz, Aus.	B11	22
Lio Matoh, Malay.	B9	50
Lion, Golfe du, b., Fr.	G10	18
Lion, Gulf of see Lion, Golfe du, b., Fr.	G10	18
Lionel Town, Jam.	j13	104d
Liouesso, Congo	D3	66
Lipa, Phil.	D3	52
Lipan, Tx., U.S.	B9	130
Lipari, Italy	F8	24
Lipari, Isola, i., Italy	F9	24
Lipari, Isole see Eolie, Isole, is., Italy	F8	24
Lipcani, Mol.	A13	26
Lipeck, Russia	D6	32
Lipez, Cerro, mtn., Bol.	D3	90
Lipicy, Russia	G20	10
Liping, China	H3	42
Lipki, Russia	G20	10
Lipník nad Bečvou, Czech Rep.	G13	16
Lipno, Pol.	D15	16
Lipno, údolní nádrž, res., Czech Rep.	H10	16
Lipova, Rom.	C8	26
Lipovcy, Russia	B9	38
Lippe, stm., Ger.	E2	16
Lippstadt, Ger.	E4	16
Lipscomb, Tx., U.S.	E8	128
Lipsoí, i., Grc.	F9	28
Liptovská Teplička, Slov.	G15	16
Liptovský Mikuláš, Slov.	G15	16
Liptrap, Cape, c., Austl.	L5	76
Lipu, China	I4	42
Lira, Ug.	D6	66
Liri, stm., Italy	C7	24
Liria see Llíria, Spain	E10	20
Liro, Vanuatu	k17	79d
Lisala, D.R.C.	D4	66
Lisboa (Lisbon), Port.	F1	20
Lisboa, state, Port.	E1	20
Lisbon see Lisboa, Port.	F1	20
Lisbon, N.H., U.S.	F5	110
Lisbon, N.D., U.S.	A15	126
Lisbon, Oh., U.S.	D5	114
Lisburn, N. Ire., U.K.	G6	12
Lisburne, Cape, c., Ak., U.S.	C6	140
Lishi, China	C4	42
Lishu, China	C6	38
Lishui, China	G8	42
Lishuzhen, China	B9	38
Lisicy, Russia	D19	10
Lisieux, Sk., Can.	E7	124
Lisieux, Fr.	E9	14
Liski, Russia	D5	32
L'Isle-Jourdain, Fr.	C6	18
Lisman, Al., U.S.	E10	122
Lismore, Austl.	G9	76
Lismore, N.S., Can.	E14	110
Lišov, Czech Rep.	G10	16
Listowel, On., Can.	E9	112
Listowel, Ire.	I3	12
Litang, China	F5	36
Litang, China	J3	42
Litchfield, Il., U.S.	E8	120
Litchfield, Mn., U.S.	F4	118
Litchfield, Ne., U.S.	F13	126
Litchville, N.D., U.S.	A14	126
Lithgow, Austl.	I8	76
Líthinon, Ákra, c., Grc.	I7	28
Lithonia, Ga., U.S.	D14	122
Lithuania, ctry., Eur.	E7	10
Litija, Slvn.	D11	22
Lititz, Pa., U.S.	D9	114
Litoměřice, Czech Rep.	F10	16
Litomyšl, Czech Rep.	G12	16
Litovko, Russia	G16	34
Little, stm., U.S.	D5	122
Little, stm., U.S.	B8	122
Little, stm., Ga., U.S.	C3	116
Little, stm., N.C., U.S.	A7	116
Little, stm., Ok., U.S.	F11	128
Little, stm., Tx., U.S.	D11	130
Little, Mountain Fork, stm., U.S.	C4	122
Little Abaco, i., Bah.	B9	96
Little Andaman, i., India	F7	46
Little Arkansas, stm., Ks., U.S.	C11	128
Little Beaver Creek, stm., U.S.	A8	126
Little Beaver Creek, stm., U.S.	B7	128
Little Belt see Lillebælt, strt., Den.	I3	8
Little Belt Mountains, mts., Mt., U.S.	D16	136
Little Bighorn, stm., U.S.	B5	126
Little Bighorn Battlefield National Monument, p.o.i., Mt., U.S.	B5	126
Little Blue, stm., U.S.	G15	126
Little Buffalo, stm., Can.	C8	106
Little Carpathians see Malé Karpaty, mts., Slov.	H13	16
Little Cayman, i., Cay. Is.	C7	102
Little Chute, Wi., U.S.	D1	112
Little Colorado, stm., Az., U.S.	H5	132
Little Current, On., Can.	C8	112
Little Current, stm., On., Can.	A12	118
Little Deep Creek, stm., N.D., U.S.	F12	124
Little Deschutes, stm., Or., U.S.	G5	136
Little Desert, des., Austl.	K3	76
Little Desert National Park, p.o.i., Austl.	K3	76
Little Dry Creek, stm., Mt., U.S.	G7	124
Little Falls, Mn., U.S.	E4	118
Little Falls, N.Y., U.S.	E15	112
Littlefork, Mn., U.S.	C5	118
Little Fork, stm., Mn., U.S.	C5	118
Little Hurricane Creek, stm., Ga., U.S.	E3	116
Little Inagua, i., Bah.	B11	102
Little Kanawha, stm., W.V., U.S.	E4	114
Little Karroo (Klein Karroo), plat., S. Afr.	H5	70
Little Lake, l., La., U.S.	H8	122
Little London, Jam.	i12	104d
Little Lost, stm., Id., U.S.	F13	136
Little Mexico, Tx., U.S.	D4	130
Little Missouri, stm., U.S.	B7	108
Little Missouri, stm., Ar., U.S.	D5	122
Little Namaqualand (Klein Namaland), hist. reg., S. Afr.	F3	70
Little Nicobar, i., India	G7	46
Little Osage, stm., U.S.	G3	120
Little Pee Dee, stm., S.C., U.S.	B6	116
Little Pic, stm., On., Can.	C12	118
Little Powder, stm., U.S.	B7	126
Little Quill Lake, l., Sk., Can.	C10	124
Little Rann of Kachchh, reg., India	G3	54
Little Red, stm., Ar., U.S.	B7	122
Little Red, Middle Fork, stm., Ar., U.S.	B6	122
Little Red Deer, stm., Ab., Can.	E16	138
Little River, Ks., U.S.	C10	128
Little Rock, Ar., U.S.	C6	122
Little Rock, stm., U.S.	H2	118
Little Sable Point, c., Mi., U.S.	E3	112
Little Saint Bernard Pass, p., Eur.	D12	18
Little Sandy Creek, stm., Wy., U.S.	E3	126
Little Sioux, stm., U.S.	J3	118
Little Sioux, West Fork, stm., Ia., U.S.	B2	120
Little Smoky, stm., Ab., Can.	A14	138
Little Snake, stm., U.S.	C8	132
Littlestown, Pa., U.S.	E8	114
Little Tallapoosa, stm., U.S.	D13	122
Little Tennessee, stm., U.S.	A1	116
Little Tobago, i., Trin.	r13	105f
Littleton, Co., U.S.	B3	128
Littleton, N.H., U.S.	F5	110
Littleton, W.V., U.S.	E5	114
Little Valley, N.Y., U.S.	B7	114
Little Wabash, stm., Il., U.S.	F9	120
Little White, stm., S.D., U.S.	D12	126
Little Wood, stm., Id., U.S.	G12	136
Litvínov, Czech Rep.	F9	16
Liu, stm., China	C6	38
Liu, stm., China	C5	38
Liu, stm., China	I3	42
Liuaniua see Ontong Java, at., Sol. Is.	D7	72
Liuba, China	E2	42
Liuboml', Ukr.	E20	16
Liuchen, China	J4	42
Liucheng, China	I3	42
Liuchow see Liuzhou, China	I3	42
Liucura, Chile	I2	92
Liufang, China	H7	42
Liuhe, China	C6	38
Liuheng Dao, i., China	G10	42
Liujiazi, China	A9	42
Liupan Shan, mts., China	D2	42
Liushuquan, China	F16	32
Liuxi, stm., China	J5	42
Liuyang, China	G5	42
Liuyang, stm., China	G5	42
Liuzhou, China	I3	42
Livada, Rom.	B10	26
Livadija, Russia	C10	38
Līvāni, Lat.	D9	10
Livanjsko Polje, val., Bos.	F3	26
Lively, On., Can.	B8	112
Lively Island, i., Falk. Is.	J5	90
Live Oak, Ca., U.S.	D4	134
Live Oak, Fl., U.S.	F2	116
Liveringa, Austl.	C4	74
Livermore, Ca., U.S.	F4	134
Livermore, Ia., U.S.	B3	120
Livermore, Ky., U.S.	G10	120
Livermore, Mount, mtn., Tx., U.S.	D3	130
Livermore Falls, Me., U.S.	F6	110
Liverpool, N.S., Can.	F12	110
Liverpool, Eng., U.K.	H10	12
Liverpool, Cape, c., N.T., Can.	C10	141
Liverpool Bay, b., N.T., Can.	A5	106
Liverpool Bay, b., Eng., U.K.	H9	12
Lívingston, Guat.	E3	102
Livingston, Al., U.S.	E10	122
Livingston, Il., U.S.	F8	120
Livingston, La., U.S.	G8	122
Livingston, Mt., U.S.	E16	136
Livingston, Tn., U.S.	H12	120
Livingston, Tx., U.S.	G4	122
Livingston, Wi., U.S.	B7	120
Livingston, Lake, res., Tx., U.S.	G3	122
Livingstone, Zam.	D4	68
Livingstone Falls, wtfl, Afr.	A1	68
Livingstonia, Mwi.	C5	68
Livingston Manor, N.Y., U.S.	C11	114
Livno, Bos.	F4	26
Livny, Russia	H20	10
Livonia, La., U.S.	G7	122
Livonia, Mi., U.S.	B2	114
Livonia, N.Y., U.S.	B8	114
Livorno (Leghorn), Italy	G7	22
Livramento do Brumado, Braz.	G5	88
Liwale, Tan.	F7	66
Lixi, China	G6	42
Lixian, China	G4	42
Lixian, China	D1	42
Lixian see Black, stm., Asia	D9	56
Lixin, China	E7	42
Lixoúri, Grc.	E3	28
Liyang, China	F8	42
Lizarda, Braz.	E2	88
Lizard Point, c., Eng., U.K.	L7	12
Lizarra see Estella, Spain	B8	20
Ljady, Bela.	F14	10
Ljahavičy, Bela.	G9	10
Ljahovskie ostrova, is., Russia	B17	34
Ljamca, Russia	D17	8
Ljaskavičy, Bela.	H11	10
Ljasnaja, Bela.	G8	10
Ljuban', Bela.	H10	10
Ljuban', Russia	A14	10
Ljubercy, Russia	E20	10
Ljubimec, Blg.	H12	26
Ljubljana, Slvn.	D11	22
Ljubnica, Russia	C15	10
Ljubohna, Russia	G17	10
Ljubuški, Bos.	F4	26
Ljudinovo, Russia	G17	10
Ljudkovo, Russia	F17	10
Ljungan, stm., Swe.	E5	8
Ljungby, Swe.	H5	8
Ljusdal, Swe.	F7	8
Ljusina, Bela.	H9	10
Ljusnan, stm., Swe.	F6	8
Llancanelo, Laguna, l., Arg.	G3	92
Llandeilo, Wales, U.K.	J8	12
Llandrindod Wells, Wales, U.K.	I9	12
Llandudno, Wales, U.K.	H9	12
Llanelli, Wales, U.K.	J8	12
Llangefni, Wales, U.K.	H8	12
Llanidloes, Wales, U.K.	I9	12
Llano, stm., Tx., U.S.	D8	130
Llano Colorado, Mex.	L9	134
Llanos, pl., S.A.	E7	86
Llanquihue, Lago, l., Chile	H2	90
Lleida, Spain	C11	20
Lleida, co., Spain	B12	20
Llera de Canales, Mex.	D9	100
Llerena, Spain	F4	20
Lleulleu, Lago, l., Chile	I1	92
Llico, Chile	G1	92
Llíria, Spain	E10	20
Llivia, Spain	B12	20
Llobregat, stm., Spain	C12	20
Lloydminster, Sk., Can.	E9	106
Llucena, Spain	D10	20
Lluchmayor see Llucmajor, Spain	E13	20
Llucmajor, Spain	E13	20
Llullaillaco, Volcán, vol., S.A.	B3	92
Lo (Panlong), stm., Asia	A7	48
Loa, Ut., U.S.	E5	132
Loa, stm., Chile	D3	90
Loanda, Braz.	D6	90
Loange (Luangue), stm., Afr.	F3	66
Lobamba, Swaz.	E10	70
Lobanovo, Russia	G21	10
Lobatse, Bots.	D7	70
Löbau, Ger.	E10	16
Lobaye, stm., C.A.R.	D3	66
Lobelville, Tn., U.S.	B11	122
Lobería, Arg.	I8	92
Lobnja, Russia	D20	10
Lobos, Arg.	G8	92
Lobos, Cay, i., Bah.	A9	102
Lobos, Isla, i., Mex.	B3	100
Lobskoe, Russia	E16	8
Łobżenica, Pol.	C13	16
Locarno, Switz.	D5	22
Loches, Fr.	G10	14
Loch Garman see Wexford, Ire.	I6	12
Lochinver, Scot., U.K.	C7	12
Lochsa, stm., Id., U.S.	D12	136
Lock, Austl.	F7	74
Lockeport, N.S., Can.	G11	110
Lockerbie, Scot., U.K.	F9	12
Lockesburg, Ar., U.S.	D4	122
Lockhart, Austl.	J6	76
Lock Haven, Pa., U.S.	C8	114
Lockney, Tx., U.S.	G7	128
Lockport, Il., U.S.	C9	120
Lockport, La., U.S.	H8	122
Lockport, N.Y., U.S.	E11	112
Lockwood, Mo., U.S.	G4	120
Locminé, Fr.	G6	14
Loc Ninh, Viet.	G8	48
Locust Creek, stm., U.S.	D4	120
Locust Fork, stm., Al., U.S.	D11	122
Locust Grove, Ok., U.S.	H2	120
Lod (Lydda), Isr.	G5	58
Lodalskåpa, mtn., Nor.	F2	8
Loddon, stm., Austl.	K4	76
Lodejnoe Pole, Russia	F15	8
Lodève, Fr.	F9	18
Lodge Creek, stm., N.A.	F4	124
Lodge Grass, Mt., U.S.	B5	126
Lodgepole, Ab., Can.	C15	138
Lodgepole, Ne., U.S.	F10	126
Lodgepole Creek, stm., U.S.	F10	126
Lodhrān, Pak.	D3	54
Lodi, Italy	E6	22
Lodi, Ca., U.S.	E4	134
Lodi, Wi., U.S.	H9	118
Lodja, D.R.C.	E4	66
Lodwar, Kenya	D7	66
Łódź, Pol.	E15	16
Łódź, state, Pol.	E15	16
Loei, Thai.	D5	48
Loei, stm., Thai.	D5	48
Loeriesfontein, S. Afr.	G4	70
Lofer, Aus.	C9	22
Lofoten, is., Nor.	B5	8
Lofoten Basin, unds.	A14	144
Loga, Niger	G5	64
Logan, Ia., U.S.	C2	120
Logan, Ks., U.S.	B9	128
Logan, Oh., U.S.	E3	114
Logan, Ut., U.S.	B5	132
Logan, W.V., U.S.	G4	114
Logan, Mount, mtn., Yk., Can.	C2	106
Logan Creek, stm., Ne., U.S.	E15	126
Logan Island, i., On., Can.	A10	118
Logan Martin Lake, res., Al., U.S.	D12	122
Logan Mountains, mts., Yk., Can.	C5	106
Logan Pass, p., Mt., U.S.	B13	136
Logansport, In., U.S.	H3	112
Logansport, La., U.S.	F5	122
Loganville, Ga., U.S.	C2	116
Logone, stm., Afr.	F3	62
Logroño, Spain	B8	20
Løgstør, Den.	H3	8
Logudoro, reg., Italy	D2	24
Lohārdaga, India	G10	54
Lohiniva, Fin.	C11	8
Lohne, Ger.	D4	16
Loho see Luohe, China	E6	42
Lohrville, Ia., U.S.	B3	120
Loi (Nanlei), stm., Asia	B4	48
Loi, Phou, mtn., Laos	B6	48
Loi-kaw, Mya.	C3	48
Loi Mwe, Mya.	B4	48
Loing, stm., Fr.	F11	14
Loing, Canal du, can., Fr.	F11	14
Loir, stm., Fr.	G8	14
Loire, state, Fr.	D10	18
Loire, stm., Fr.	B4	18
Loire, Canal latéral à la, can., Fr.	C9	18
Loire-Atlantique, state, Fr.	G7	14
Loiret, state, Fr.	F11	14
Loir-et-Cher, state, Fr.	G10	14
Loja, Ec.	D2	84
Loja, Spain	G6	20
Lokandu, D.R.C.	E5	66
Lokan Reservoir see Lokan tekojärvi, res., Fin.	C12	8
Lokan tekojärvi, res., Fin.	C12	8
Lokeren, Bel.	C13	14
Loket, Czech Rep.	F8	16
Lokichar, Kenya	D7	66
Lokichokio, Kenya	D6	66
Loknja, Russia	D13	10
Lokoja, Nig.	H6	64
Lokolama, D.R.C.	E3	66
Lokot', Russia	H17	10
Loksa, Est.	A8	10
Loks Land, i., N.T., Can.	E13	141
Lola, Gui.	H3	64
Loleta, Ca., U.S.	C1	134
Loliondo, Tan.	E7	66
Lolita, Tx., U.S.	F11	130
Lolland, i., Den.	I4	8
Lolo, Mt., U.S.	D12	136
Lolodorf, Cam.	D2	66
Lolo Pass, p., U.S.	D12	136
Lolowai, Vanuatu	j16	79d
Loltong, Vanuatu	j16	79d
Lolvavana, Passage, strt., Vanuatu	j16	79d
Lom, Blg.	F10	26
Lom, Nor.	F3	8
Lom, stm., Afr.	F2	62
Lomami, stm., D.R.C.	D4	66
Lomas de Zamora, Arg.	G8	92
Lomax, Il., U.S.	D6	120
Łomazy, Pol.	E19	16
Lombardia, state, Italy	E6	22
Lombardy see Lombardia, state, Italy	E6	22
Lomblen, Pulau, i., Indon.	G7	44
Lombok, Indon.	H10	50
Lombok, i., Indon.	H10	50
Lombok, Selat, strt., Indon.	H9	50
Lomé, Togo	H5	64
Lomela, D.R.C.	E4	66
Lomela, stm., D.R.C.	E4	66
Lometa, Tx., U.S.	C9	130
Lomié, Cam.	D2	66
Lomira, Wi., U.S.	H10	118
Lommel, Bel.	C14	14
Lomond, Loch, l., Scot., U.K.	E8	12
Lomonosov, Russia	A12	10
Lomonosovka, Kaz.	D11	32
Lomovoe, Russia	D19	8
Lompobatang, Gunung, mtn., Indon.	F11	50
Lompoc, Ca., U.S.	I5	134
Lom Sak, Thai.	D5	48
Łomża, Pol.	C18	16
Łomża, state, Pol.	C18	16
Lonaconing, Md., U.S.	E7	114
Lonāvale, India	B1	53
Loncoche, Chile	G2	90
Loncopué, Arg.	I2	92
London, On., Can.	F8	112
London, Eng., U.K.	J12	12
London, Ar., U.S.	B5	122
London, Ky., U.S.	G1	114
London, Tx., U.S.	D8	130
Londonderry, N.S., Can.	E13	110
Londonderry (Derry), N. Ire., U.K.	F6	12
Londonderry, Cape, c., Austl.	B5	74
Londonderry, Isla, i., Chile	K2	90
Londrina, Braz.	D6	90
Lone Grove, Ok., U.S.	G11	128
Lone Oak, Ky., U.S.	G9	120
Lone Pine, Ca., U.S.	G7	134
Lone Rock, Wi., U.S.	A7	120
Lone Tree, Ia., U.S.	C6	120
Lone Wolf, Ok., U.S.	G9	128
Long, stm., China	I3	42
Longa, Ang.	C2	68
Longá, stm., Braz.	B5	88
Longa, proliv, strt., Russia	B24	34
Long Akah, Malay.	B9	50
Longana, Vanuatu	j17	79d
Longarone, Italy	D9	22
Longaví, Chile	G2	92
Longbangun, Indon.	C9	50
Long Bay, b., U.S.	C7	116
Long Beach, Ca., U.S.	J7	134
Long Beach, Ms., U.S.	G9	122
Long Beach, N.Y., U.S.	D12	114
Long Beach, Wa., U.S.	D2	136
Long Beach, cst., N.J., U.S.	E11	114
Longboat Key, Fl., U.S.	I3	116
Long Branch, N.J., U.S.	D12	114
Long Cay, i., Bah.	m18	104f
Longchang, China	G1	42
Longchuan, China	I6	42
Long Creek, stm., N.A.	E10	124
Longde, China	D2	42
Long Eaton, Eng., U.K.	I11	12
Longford, Austl.	L6	76
Longford, Ire.	H5	12
Longford, state, Ire.	H5	12
Long Hu, l., China	F6	42
Longhua, China	A7	42
Longhui, China	H4	42
Longiram, Indon.	C9	50
Long Island, i., Antig.	f4	105b
Long Island, i., Austl.	D7	76
Long Island, i., Bah.	A10	102
Long Island, i., N.T., Can.	E14	106
Long Island, i., N.S., Can.	F10	110
Long Island, i., N.Y., U.S.	D12	114
Long Island Sound, strt., U.S.	D12	114
Longitudinal, Valle, val., Chile	H1	92
Longjiang, China	B9	36
Longkou, China	C9	42
Long Lake, N.Y., U.S.	G2	110
Long Lake, l., On., Can.	B11	118
Longleaf, La., U.S.	F6	122
Long Leaf Park, N.C., U.S.	B8	116
Longli, China	H2	42
Longlin, China	G6	36
Longling, China	G4	36
Longmeadow, Ma., U.S.	B13	114
Long Moc, Viet.	C7	48
Longmont, Co., U.S.	A3	128
Long Mountain, mtn., Mo., U.S.	H5	120
Longnan, China	I6	42
Longnawan, Indon.	C9	50
Long Pine, Ne., U.S.	E13	126
Long Point, c., Bah.	n18	104f
Long Point, c., N.S., Can.	D16	110
Long Point, pen., Mb., Can.	A15	124
Long Point, pen., On., Can.	F9	112
Long Point Bay, b., On., Can.	F9	112
Longquan, China	G8	42
Long Range Mountains, mts., Nf., Can.	j22	107a
Longreach, Austl.	D5	76
Long-Sault, On., Can.	E2	110
Longsegah, Indon.	B10	50
Longshan, China	G3	42
Longsheng, China	I3	42
Longs Peak, mtn., Co., U.S.	A3	128
Long Swamp, Br. Vir. Is.	e8	104b
Long Thanh, Viet.	G8	48
Longton, Ks., U.S.	G1	120
Longtown, Eng., U.K.	F10	12
Longueuil, Qc., Can.	E3	110
Longuyon, Fr.	E14	14
Longview, Ab., Can.	F16	138
Long View, N.C., U.S.	I4	114
Longview, Tx., U.S.	E4	122
Longview, Wa., U.S.	D4	136
Longwai, Indon.	C10	50
Longwy, Fr.	E14	14
Longxi, China	E5	36
Longxian, China	D2	42
Long Xuyen, Viet.	G7	48
Longyan, China	I7	42
Longyou, China	G8	42
Longzhen, China	B10	36
Longzhou, China	J2	42
Lonigo, Italy	E8	22
Löningen, Ger.	D3	16
Lonja, stm., Cro.	E13	22
Lonoke, Ar., U.S.	C7	122
Lonquimay, Volcán, vol., Chile	I2	92
Lonsdale, Mn., U.S.	G5	118
Lons-le-Saunier, Fr.	H14	14
Lontra, stm., Braz.	D1	88
Loogootee, In., U.S.	F11	120
Lookout, Cape, c., N.C., U.S.	B9	116
Lookout Mountain, mts., U.S.	C13	122
Lookout Pass, p., U.S.	C11	136
Lookout Ridge, mts., Ak., U.S.	C8	140
Loolmalassin, vol., Tan.	E7	66
Loomis, Ne., U.S.	G13	126
Loomis, Wa., U.S.	B7	136
Loop, Tx., U.S.	B5	130
Loop Head, c., Ire.	I2	12
Lop, China	A5	46
Lop, stm., Viet.	F8	48
Lopatina, gora, mtn., Russia	F17	34
Lopatka, mys, c., Russia	F20	34
Lopatovo, Russia	D12	10
Lop Buri, Thai.	E5	48
Lopévi, i., Vanuatu	k17	79d
Lopez, Cap, c., Gabon	E1	66
Lop Nur, l., China	C3	36
Loptjuga, Russia	E22	8
Lora, Hāmūn-i-, l., Asia	D9	56
Lora del Río, Spain	G5	20
Lorain, Oh., U.S.	C3	114
Loraine, Tx., U.S.	B7	130
Loralai, Pak.	C2	54
Lorca, Spain	G9	20
Lord Howe Island, i., Austl.	G6	72
Lord Howe Rise, unds.	L19	142
Lord Mayor Bay, b., N.T., Can.	B12	106
Lordsburg, N.M., U.S.	K8	132
Loreauville, La., U.S.	G7	122
Loreley, misc. cult., Ger.	F3	16
Lorena, Braz.	L3	88
Lorengau, Pap. N. Gui.	a4	79a
Lorenzo, Tx., U.S.	H7	128
Lorenzo Geyres, Ur.	F9	92
Loreto, Arg.	C9	92
Loreto, Mex.	D8	100
Loreto, Mex.	B3	100
Loreto, state, Peru	H4	86
Loretto, Ky., U.S.	G12	120
Loretto, Tn., U.S.	B11	122
Lorica, Col.	C4	86
Lorient, Fr.	G5	14
Lorimor, Ia., U.S.	C3	120
Loriol-sur-Drôme, Fr.	E10	18
Loris, S.C., U.S.	B7	116
Lorman, Ms., U.S.	F7	122
Lorn, Firth of, b., Scot., U.K.	E7	12
Lorne, Austl.	L5	76
Lorne, N.B., Can.	C10	110
Lörrach, Ger.	I3	16
Lorraine, hist. reg., Fr.	F14	14
Los, Îles de, is., Gui.	H2	64
Losada, stm., Col.	F4	86
Los Alamos, N.M., U.S.	F2	128
Los Aldamas, Mex.	B9	100
Los Andes, Chile	F2	92
Los Angeles, Chile	H1	92
Los Angeles, Ca., U.S.	I7	134
Los Angeles Aqueduct, aq., Ca., U.S.	H7	134
Los Antiguos, Arg.	I2	90
Los Banos, Ca., U.S.	F5	134
Los Blancos, Arg.	D4	90
Los Bolones, Cerro, mtn., Mex.	G12	100
Los Cerrillos, Arg.	E5	92
Los Conquistadores, Arg.	E8	92
Los Fresnos, Tx., U.S.	H10	130
Los Garza, Mex.	H8	130
Los Gatos, Ca., U.S.	F4	134
Loshan see Leshan, China	F5	36
Los Hermanos, Islas, is., Ven.	B9	86
Łosice, Pol.	D18	16
Los Idolos, Parque Arquelógico de, hist., Col.	G3	86
Lošinj, Otok, i., Cro.	F11	22
Losinoborskaja, Russia	C15	32
Los Juríes, Arg.	D6	92
Los Lagos, Chile	G2	90
Los Llanos, P.R.	B3	104a
Los López, Mex.	H8	130
Los Lunas, N.M., U.S.	I10	132
Los Mochis, Mex.	C4	100
Los Nogales, Mex.	H8	130
Losolava, Vanuatu	j16	79d
Los Padillas, N.M., U.S.	I10	132
Los Palacios, Arg.	D3	92
Los Palacios, Cuba	A6	102
Los Palacios y Villafranca, Spain	G4	20
Los Picachos, Parque Nacional, p.o.i., Col.	F4	86
Los Rábanos, P.R.	B2	104a
Los Ríos, state, Ec.	H2	86
Los Roques, Islas, is., Ven.	B8	86
Los Sauces, Chile	H1	92
Lossiemouth, Scot., U.K.	D9	12
Lost, stm., U.S.	A4	134
Los Taques, Ven.	B6	86
Los Teques, Ven.	B8	86
Los Testigos, Islas, is., Ven.	B10	86
Lost Hills, Ca., U.S.	H6	134
Lost Nation, Ia., U.S.	C7	120
Lost River Range, mts., Id., U.S.	F13	136
Lost Trail Pass, p., U.S.	E13	136
Losuia, Pap. N. Gui.	b5	79a
Los Vidrios, Mex.	F6	98
Los Vilos, Chile	E2	92
Los Yébenes, Spain	E6	20
Lot, state, Fr.	E7	18
Lot, stm., Fr.	E7	18
Lota, Chile	H1	92
Lot-et-Garonne, state, Fr.	E6	18
Lothair, S. Afr.	E10	70
Lotošino, Russia	D18	10
Lotsane, stm., Bots.	C8	70
Lotta, stm., Eur.	B13	8
Lotuke, Jabal, mtn., Sudan	G6	62
Lotung, Tai.	I9	42
Louang Namtha, Laos	B5	48
Louangphrabang, Laos	C6	48
Loubomo, Congo	E2	66
Loudon, Tn., U.S.	A1	116
Loudonville, Oh., U.S.	D3	114
Loudun, Fr.	G9	14
Loue, stm., Fr.	H14	14
Louga, Sen.	F1	64
Louge, Arg.	H7	92
Loughborough, Eng., U.K.	I11	12
Loughrea, Ire.	H4	12
Louhi, Russia	C15	8
Louin, Ms., U.S.	E9	122
Louisa, Ky., U.S.	F3	114
Louisbourg, N.S., Can.	E16	110
Louisburg, Ks., U.S.	F3	120
Louisburg, N.C., U.S.	H7	114
Louise, Ms., U.S.	D8	122
Louise, Tx., U.S.	H2	122
Louiseville, Qc., Can.	D3	110
Louisiade Archipelago, is., Pap. N. Gui.	B10	74
Louisiana, Mo., U.S.	E6	120
Louisiana, state, U.S.	F6	122
Louis Trichardt, S. Afr.	C9	70
Louisville, Al., U.S.	F13	122
Louisville, Ga., U.S.	C3	116
Louisville, Ky., U.S.	F12	120
Louisville, Ne., U.S.	D1	120
Louisville, Oh., U.S.	D4	114
Louisville Ridge, unds.	M22	142
Louis-XIV, Pointe, c., Qc., Can.	E14	106
Loulé, Port.	G2	20
Loum, Cam.	D1	66
Lount Lake, l., On., Can.	A4	118
Louny, Czech Rep.	F9	16
Loup, stm., Ne., U.S.	F14	126
Loup City, Ne., U.S.	F14	126
Loups Marins, Lacs des, l., Qc., Can.	D16	106
Lourdes, Fr.	F5	18
Lourenço Marques see Maputo, Moz.	D11	70
Lourinhã, Port.	E1	20
Lousã, Port.	D2	20
Louth, Austl.	H5	76
Louth, Ire.	H6	12
Louth, Eng., U.K.	H13	12
Louth, state, Ire.	H6	12
Loutrá Aidhipsoú, Grc.	E6	28
Louvain see Leuven, Bel.	D13	14
Louviers, Fr.	E10	14
Louviers, Co., U.S.	B4	128
Lovat', stm., Russia	B14	10
Loveč, Blg.	F11	26
Loveč, state, Blg.	F11	26
Loveland, Co., U.S.	G7	126
Lovell, Wy., U.S.	C4	126
Lovell Village, St. Vin.	p11	105e
Lovelock, Nv., U.S.	C7	134
Lovely, Ky., U.S.	G3	114
Lovere, Italy	E6	22
Loves Park, Il., U.S.	B8	120
Loving, N.M., U.S.	B3	130
Loving, Tx., U.S.	H10	128
Lovingston, Va., U.S.	G7	114
Lovington, N.M., U.S.	B4	130
Lovosice, Czech Rep.	F9	16
Lovozero, Russia	D13	8
Lovozero, ozero, l., Russia	C16	8
Lóvua, Ang.	B3	68
Low, Qc., Can.	C14	112
Low, Cape, c., N.T., Can.	C13	106
Lowa, D.R.C.	E5	66
Lowa, stm., D.R.C.	E5	66
Lowden, Ia., U.S.	C7	120
Lowell, Ar., U.S.	H3	120
Lowell, In., U.S.	G2	112
Lowell, Ma., U.S.	B14	114
Lowell, Or., U.S.	G4	136
Lowell, Lake, res., Id., U.S.	G10	136
Löwen, stm., Nmb.	E3	70
Löwenberg, Ger.	D8	16
Lower Arrow Lake, res., B.C., Can.	G12	138
Lower Austria see Niederösterreich, state, Aus.	B12	22
Lower California see Baja California, pen., Mex.	B2	96
Lower Egypt see Misr el-Bahrî, hist. reg., Egypt	G2	58
Lower Glenelg National Park, p.o.i., Austl.	L3	76
Lower Hutt, N.Z.	E6	80
Lower Lake, l., U.S.	B5	134
Lower Manitou Lake, l., On., Can.	B6	118
Lower Post, B.C., Can.	D5	106
Lower Red Lake, l., Mn., U.S.	D3	118
Lower Saxony see Niedersachsen, state, Ger.	D4	16
Lower Trajan's Wall, misc. cult., Eur.	D15	26
Lower West End Point, c., Anguilla	A1	105a
Lower Woods Harbour, N.S., Can.	G10	110
Lowestoft, Eng., U.K.	I14	12
Lowgar, state, Afg.	A2	54
Łowicz, Pol.	D15	16
Lowmoor, Va., U.S.	G6	114
Low Rocky Point, c., Austl.	o12	77a
Lowry City, Mo., U.S.	F4	120
Lowville, N.Y., U.S.	E14	112
Loxton, Austl.	J3	76
Loyal, Wi., U.S.	G8	118
Loyalton, Ca., U.S.	D5	134
Loyalty Islands see Loyauté, Îles, is., N. Cal.	m16	79d
Loyang see Luoyang, China	D5	42
Loyauté, Îles (Loyalty Islands), is., N. Cal.	m16	79d
Loyoro, Ug.	D6	66
Lozère, state, Fr.	E9	18
Loznica, Yugo.	E6	26
Lualaba, stm., Afr.	E5	66
Luama, stm., D.R.C.	E5	66
Lu'an, China	F7	42
Luan, stm., China	E3	38
Luancheng, China	J3	42
Luanda, Ang.	B1	68
Luando, stm., Ang.	C2	68
Luang, Khao (Maw Taung), mtn., Asia	G4	48
Luang, Thale, l., Thai.	I5	48
Luang Chiang Dao, Doi, mtn., Thai.	C4	48
Luanginga, stm., Afr.	G4	66
Luang Prabang see Louangphrabang, Laos	C6	48
Luangue (Loange), stm., Afr.	F3	66
Luangwa, stm., Afr.	C5	68
Luanping, China	A7	42
Luanshya, Zam.	C4	68
Luan Toro, Arg.	H5	92
Luanxian, China	B8	42
Luapula, stm., Afr.	C4	68
Luar, Danau, l., Indon.	C8	50
Luarca, Spain	A4	20
Luba, Eq. Gui.	I6	64
Lubaantun, hist., Belize	D3	102
Lubań, Pol.	E11	16
Lubāna, Lat.	D9	10
Lubang Islands, is., Phil.	D2	52
Lubango, Ang.	C1	68
Lubāns, l., Lat.	D9	10
Lubartów, Pol.	E18	16
Lübben, Ger.	E9	16
Lübbenau, Ger.	E9	16
Lubbock, Tx., U.S.	H7	128
Lübeck, Ger.	C6	16
Lubefu, D.R.C.	E4	66
Lubefu, stm., D.R.C.	E4	66
Lubień Kujawski, Pol.	D15	16
Lubilash, stm., D.R.C.	F4	66
Lubin, Pol.	E12	16
Lublin, Pol.	E18	16
Lublin, state, Pol.	E18	16
Lubliniec, Pol.	F14	16
Lubny, Ukr.	E4	32
Luboń, Pol.	D12	16
Lubsko, Pol.	E10	16
Lübtheen, Ger.	C7	16
Lubuagan, Phil.	B3	52
Lubudi, D.R.C.	G5	66
Lubukbatang, Indon.	F3	50
Lubuklinggau, Indon.	E3	50
Lubukpakam, Indon.	B1	50
Lubuksikaping, Indon.	C1	50

Name	Map Ref.	Page

I•36 Mast-Mhas

Name	Map Ref.	Page
Mastic Point, Bah.	K8	116
Mastung, Pak.	D10	56
Masty, Bela.	G7	10
Masuda, Japan	E4	40
Masurai, Gunung, mtn., Indon.	E2	50
Masuria see Mazury, reg., Pol.	C16	16
Masvingo, Zimb.	E5	68
Masvingo, state, Zimb.	B10	70
Maṣyāf, Syria	C7	58
Mata Amarilla, Arg.	I2	90
Matabeleland North, state, Zimb.	A9	70
Matabeleland South, state, Zimb.	B9	70
Matabuena, Spain	C7	20
Matacuni, stm., Ven.	F9	86
Mata de São João, Braz.	G6	88
Matadi, D.R.C.	F2	66
Matagalpa, Nic.	F5	102
Matagami, Qc., Can.	F15	106
Matagorda, Tx., U.S.	F12	130
Matagorda Island, i., Tx., U.S.	F11	130
Matagorda Peninsula, pen., Tx., U.S.	F11	130
Matahiae, Pointe, c., Fr. Poly.	w22	78h
Matâî, Egypt	J1	58
Mataiea, Fr. Poly.	w22	78h
Mataiva, at., Fr. Poly.	E12	72
Matak, Pulau, i., Indon.	B5	50
Matakana, Austl.	I5	76
Matale, Sri L.	H5	53
Matam, Sen.	F2	64
Matamoros, Mex.	C10	100
Matamoros, Mex.	C7	100
Matan, Indon.	D7	50
Matandu, stm., Tan.	F7	66
Matane, Qc., Can.	B9	110
Matanni, Pak.	B3	54
Matanzas, Cuba	A7	102
Matanzas, Mex.	E8	100
Matapan, Cape see Taínaro, Ákra, c., Grc.	G5	28
Matape, stm., Mex.	A3	100
Matapédia, Qc., Can.	C9	110
Matapédia, Lac, l., Qc., Can.	B9	110
Mataquito, stm., Chile	G2	92
Matara, Sri L.	I5	53
Mataram, Indon.	H9	50
Mataranka, Austl.	B6	74
Mataró, Spain	C13	20
Matasiri, Pulau, i., Indon.	F9	50
Matatiele, S. Afr.	G9	70
Matatula, Cape, c., Am. Sam.	h12	79c
Matâ'utu, Wal./F.	E9	72
Matavera, Cook Is.	a27	78j
Mataveri, Chile	e29	78l
Mataveri, Aeropuerto, Chile	f29	78l
Mataveri Airstrip see Mataveri, Aeropuerto, Chile	f29	78l
Matehuala, Mex.	D8	100
Mateke Hills, hills, Zimb.	B10	70
Matera, Italy	D10	24
Mateur, Tun.	G3	24
Matha, Fr.	D5	18
Mather, Mb., Can.	E14	124
Mather, Pa., U.S.	E5	114
Matheson, On., Can.	F14	106
Mathews, Va., U.S.	G9	114
Mathis, Tx., U.S.	F10	130
Mathura (Muttra), India	E6	54
Matias Barbosa, Braz.	K4	88
Matías Romero, Mex.	G11	100
Matícora, stm., Ven.	B6	86
Matinha, Braz.	B3	88
Matipó, Braz.	K4	88
Matiyure, stm., Ven.	D7	86
Mātli, Pak.	F2	54
Mato, Cerro, mtn., Ven.	D9	86
Mato Grosso, state, Braz.	F6	84
Mato Grosso, Planalto do, plat., Braz.	B5	90
Mato Grosso, Plateau of see Mato Grosso, Planalto do, plat., Braz.	B5	90
Mato Grosso do Sul, state, Braz.	C6	90
Matola Rio, Moz.	D11	70
Matopos, Zimb.	B9	70
Matosinhos, Port.	C2	20
Matouying, China	B8	42
Matozinhos, Braz.	J3	88
Maṭraḥ, Oman	E8	56
Matsudo, Japan	D12	40
Matsue, Japan	D6	40
Matsumoto, Japan	C10	40
Matsusaka, Japan	E9	40
Matsu Tao, i., Tai.	H8	42
Matsutō, Japan	C9	40
Matsuura, Japan	F2	40
Matsuyama, Japan	F5	40
Mattagami, stm., On., Can.	F14	106
Mattamuskeet, Lake, l., N.C., U.S.	A9	116
Mattaponi, stm., Va., U.S.	G8	114
Mattawa, On., Can.	B11	112
Mattawa, Wa., U.S.	D7	136
Mattawamkeag, stm., Me., U.S.	E8	110
Matterhorn, mtn., Eur.	D13	18
Matterhorn, mtn., Nv., U.S.	B1	132
Matthews Mountain, hill, Mo., U.S.	G7	120
Matthew Town, Bah.	C10	96
Mattighofen, Aus.	B10	22
Mattoon, Il., U.S.	E9	120
Mattoon, Wi., U.S.	F9	118
Mattydale, N.Y., U.S.	E13	112
Matua, Indon.	E7	50
Matudo see Matsudo, Japan	D12	40
Matue see Matsue, Japan	D6	40
Matuku, i., Fiji	q19	79e
Matumoto see Matsumoto, Japan	C10	40
Maturín, Ven.	C10	86
Matutina, Braz.	J2	88
Matuzaka see Matsusaka, Japan	E9	40
Maú (Ireng), stm., S.A.	F12	86
Maúa, Moz.	C6	68
Mau Aimma, India	F8	54
Maubeuge, Fr.	D12	14
Maud, Tx., U.S.	D4	122
Maudaha, India	F7	54
Maude, Austl.	J5	76
Maués, Braz.	D6	84
Maués, stm., Braz.	D6	84
Mauganj, India	F8	54
Maui, i., Hi., U.S.	C5	78a
Mauk, Indon.	F5	50
Mauldin, S.C., U.S.	B3	116
Maule, state, Chile	G2	92
Maule, stm., Chile	G1	92
Maule, Laguna del, l., Chile	G2	92
Mauléon-Licharre, Fr.	F5	18
Maumee, Oh., U.S.	G6	112
Maumee, stm., U.S.	G6	112
Maumelle, Lake, res., Ar., U.S.	C6	122
Maumere, Indon.	G7	44
Maun, Bots.	D3	68
Maunabo, P.R.	B4	104a
Mauna Kea, vol., Hi., U.S.	D6	78a
Maunaloa, Hi., U.S.	B4	78a
Mauna Loa, vol., Hi., U.S.	D6	78a
Maunath Bhanjan, India	F9	54
Maungdaw, Mya.	H14	54
Maungmagan, Mya.	E3	48
Maunoir, Lac, l., N.T., Can.	B6	106
Maupihaa, at., Fr. Poly.	E11	72
Mau Rānīpur, India	F7	54
Maurepas, Lake, l., La., U.S.	G8	122
Maurice, Lake, l., Austl.	E6	74
Mauricie, Parc national de la, p.o.i., Qc., Can.	D3	110
Mauritania, ctry., Afr.	F2	64
Mauritanie see Mauritania, ctry., Afr.	F2	64
Mauritius, ctry., Afr.	h10	69a
Mauron, Fr.	F6	14
Mauston, Wi., U.S.	H8	118
Mautau, c., Fr. Poly.	r19	78g
Mauterndorf, Aus.	C10	22
Mauthen, Aus.	D9	22
Mauvais Coulee, stm., N.D., U.S.	F14	124
Mava, Pap. N. Gui.	b3	79a
Maverick, Az., U.S.	J7	132
Mavinga, Ang.	D3	68
Mavrovo Nacionalni Park, p.o.i., Mac.	B3	28
Mavuradonha Mountains, mts., Zimb.	D5	68
Mawchi, Mya.	C3	48
Mawlaik, Mya.	D7	46
Mawlamyine (Moulmein), Mya.	D3	48
Mawson, sci., Ant.	B11	81
Maw Taung (Luang, Khao), mtn., Asia	G4	48
Max, N.D., U.S.	G12	124
Maxaranguape, Braz.	C8	88
Maxcanú, Mex.	B3	102
Maxixe, Moz.	C12	70
Maxville, On., Can.	E2	110
Maxwell, Ca., U.S.	D3	134
Maxwell, Ne., U.S.	F12	126
Maxwell, N.M., U.S.	E4	128
May, Tx., U.S.	B9	130
May, Cape, pen., N.J., U.S.	F11	114
May, Mount, mtn., Ab., Can.	B11	138
Maya, Pulau, i., Indon.	D6	50
Mayaguana, i., Bah.	A11	102
Mayaguana Passage, strt., Bah.	A11	102
Mayagüez, P.R.	B1	104a
Mayang, China	H3	42
Mayarí, Cuba	B10	102
Maybole, Scot., U.K.	F8	12
Maydena, Austl.	o13	77a
Maydh, Som.	B9	66
Mayen, Ger.	F3	16
Mayenne, Fr.	F8	14
Mayenne, state, Fr.	F8	14
Mayenne, stm., Fr.	F8	14
Mayer, Az., U.S.	I4	132
Mayerthorpe, Ab., Can.	C15	138
Mayfield, Ky., U.S.	H9	120
Mayfield, Ut., U.S.	D5	132
Mayflower, Ar., U.S.	C6	122
Māyir, Syria	B8	58
Maykain see Majkain, Kaz.	D13	32
Maymyo, Mya.	A3	48
Maynard, Ia., U.S.	B6	120
Maynardville, Tn., U.S.	H2	114
Mayne, stm., Austl.	D3	76
Mayo, Yk., Can.	C3	106
Mayo, Fl., U.S.	F2	116
Mayo, state, Ire.	H3	12
Mayo, stm., Arg.	I3	90
Mayo, stm., Mex.	B4	100
Mayon Volcano, vol., Phil.	D4	52
Mayor Buratovich, Arg.	G4	90
Mayotte, dep., Afr.	C8	68
Mayoyoque, Col.	G4	86
May Pen, Jam.	j13	104d
Mayreau, i., St. Vin.	p11	105e
Mays Landing, N.J., U.S.	E11	114
Maysville, Ky., U.S.	F2	114
Maysville, Mo., U.S.	E3	120
Maysville, N.C., U.S.	B8	116
Maysville, Ok., U.S.	G11	128
Mayumba, Gabon	E2	66
Māyūram, India	F4	53
Mayville, Mi., U.S.	E6	112
Mayville, N.Y., U.S.	B6	114
Mayville, N.D., U.S.	G16	124
Maywood, Ne., U.S.	G12	126
Maza, Arg.	H6	92
Mazabuka, Zam.	D4	68
Mazagão, Braz.	D7	84
Mazamet, Fr.	F8	18
Mazán, stm., Peru	I4	86
Mazara, Val di, reg., Italy	G7	24
Mazara del Vallo, Italy	G6	24
Mazār-e Sharīf, Afg.	B10	56
Mazarrón, Golfo de, b., Spain	G9	20
Mazaruni, stm., Guy.	D11	86
Mazatenango, Guat.	E2	102
Mazatlán, Mex.	D5	100
Mažeikiai, Lith.	D5	10
Mazenod, Sk., Can.	E7	124
Mazinga, mtn., Neth. Ant.	C2	105a
Mazirbe, Lat.	C5	10
Mazon, Il., U.S.	C9	120
Mazowe, stm., Afr.	D5	68
Mazury (Masuria), reg., Pol.	C16	16
Mazyr, Bela.	D3	32
Mbabane, Swaz.	E10	70
M'bahiakro, C. Iv.	H4	64
Mbaïki, C.A.R.	D3	66
Mbaké, Sen.	G1	64
Mbala, Zam.	B5	68
Mbalabala, Zimb.	B9	70
Mbale, Ug.	D6	66
Mbalmayo, Cam.	D2	66
Mbamba Bay, Tan.	G7	66
Mbandaka (Coquilhatville), D.R.C.	D3	66
Mbanga, Cam.	D1	66
Mbanika Island, i., Sol. Is.	e8	79b
M'banza Congo, Ang.	B1	68
Mbanza-Ngungu, D.R.C.	F3	66
Mbarara, Ug.	E6	66
Mbashe, stm., S. Afr.	H9	70
Mbava Island, i., Sol. Is.	d7	79b
Mbé, Cam.	C2	66
Mberengwa, Zimb.	B9	70
Mbeya, Tan.	F6	66
Mbigou, Gabon	E2	66
Mbinda, Congo	E2	66
Mbini, Eq. Gui.	I6	64
Mbini, stm., Afr.	I6	64
Mboi, D.R.C.	F4	66
Mboki, C.A.R.	C5	66
Mbola, Sol. Is.	e9	79b
Mborokua, i., Sol. Is.	e8	79b
Mborong, Indon.	H12	50
Mbouda, Cam.	C2	66
Mbour, Sen.	G1	64
Mbout, Maur.	F2	64
Mbuji-Mayi (Bakwanga), D.R.C.	F4	66
Mbuluzi, stm., Swaz.	E10	70
Mbwemkuru, stm., Tan.	F7	66
McAdam, N.B., Can.	E9	110
McAdoo, Pa., U.S.	D9	114
McAlester, Ok., U.S.	C3	122
McAllen, Tx., U.S.	H9	130
McArthur, Oh., U.S.	E3	114
McArthur, stm., Austl.	C7	74
McArthur River, Austl.	C7	74
McBain, Mi., U.S.	D4	112
McBee, S.C., U.S.	B5	116
McBeth Fjord, b., N.T., Can.	B17	106
McBride, B.C., Can.	C10	138
McCall Creek, Ms., U.S.	F8	122
McCamey, Tx., U.S.	C5	130
McCammon, Id., U.S.	H14	136
McCauley Island, i., B.C., Can.	E4	106
McCleary, Wa., U.S.	C3	136
McClellan Creek, stm., Tx., U.S.	F8	128
McClellanville, S.C., U.S.	C6	116
McClintock, Mount, mtn., Ant.	D21	81
McCloud, Ca., U.S.	B3	134
McCloud, stm., Ca., U.S.	B3	134
McClure, Il., U.S.	G8	120
Mcclusky, N.D., U.S.	G13	124
McColl, S.C., U.S.	B6	116
McComb, Ms., U.S.	F8	122
McConaughy, Lake, res., Ne., U.S.	F11	126
McConnellsburg, Pa., U.S.	E7	114
McConnelsville, Oh., U.S.	E4	114
McCook, Ne., U.S.	A8	128
McCormick, S.C., U.S.	C3	116
McCreary, Mb., Can.	D14	124
McCullough Mountain, mtn., Nv., U.S.	H1	132
McCune, Ks., U.S.	G2	120
McCurtain, Ok., U.S.	B4	122
McDade, Tx., U.S.	D10	130
McDermitt, Nv., U.S.	B8	134
McDermott, Oh., U.S.	F2	114
McDonald, Ks., U.S.	B7	128
McDonald, Lake, l., Mt., U.S.	B12	136
McDowell Peak, mtn., Az., U.S.	J4	132
Mcensk, Russia	G19	10
McEwen, Tn., U.S.	H10	120
McFadden, Wy., U.S.	B10	132
McFarland, Ca., U.S.	H6	134
McGehee, Ar., U.S.	D7	122
McGill, Nv., U.S.	D2	132
McGrath, Ak., U.S.	D8	140
McGraw, N.Y., U.S.	B9	114
McGregor, Tx., U.S.	C10	130
McGregor, stm., B.C., Can.	B9	138
McGregor Lake, l., Ab., Can.	F18	138
McHenry, Il., U.S.	B9	120
McHenry, Ms., U.S.	G9	122
Mchinji, Mwi.	C5	68
McIntosh, Al., U.S.	F10	122
McIntosh, Mn., U.S.	D3	118
McIntyre Bay, b., On., Can.	B10	118
McKeand, stm., N.T., Can.	C17	106
McKee, Ky., U.S.	G2	114
McKeesport, Pa., U.S.	D6	114
McKenzie, Tn., U.S.	H9	120
McKenzie, stm., Or., U.S.	F4	136
McKenzie Bridge, Or., U.S.	F4	136
McKenzie Island, On., Can.	E12	106
McKinlay, Austl.	C3	76
McKinlay, stm., Austl.	C3	76
McKinley, Mount, mtn., Ak., U.S.	D9	140
McKinleyville, Ca., U.S.	C1	134
McKinney, Tx., U.S.	D2	122
McKittrick Summit, mtn., Ca., U.S.	H6	134
McLain, Ms., U.S.	F10	122
McLaurin, Ms., U.S.	F9	122
McLean, Il., U.S.	D8	120
McLean, Tx., U.S.	F8	128
McLeansboro, Il., U.S.	F9	120
McLennan, Ab., Can.	D7	106
McLeod, stm., Ab., Can.	C15	138
McLeod Bay, b., N.T., Can.	C8	106
McLeod Lake, B.C., Can.	B7	138
M'Clintock Channel, strt., N.T., Can.	A10	106
McLoughlin, Mount, mtn., Or., U.S.	A3	134
McLouth, Ks., U.S.	E2	120
M'Clure Strait, strt., N.T., Can.	B16	140
McMahon, Sk., Can.	D6	124
McMinnville, Or., U.S.	E3	136
McMinnville, Tn., U.S.	B13	122
McMurdo, sci., Ant.	C22	81
McMurdo Sound, strt., Ant.	C22	81
McNary, Az., U.S.	I7	132
McNeil, Ar., U.S.	D5	122
McPherson, Ks., U.S.	C11	128
McQueeney, Tx., U.S.	E9	130
McRae, Ar., U.S.	B7	122
McRae, Ga., U.S.	D3	116
McVeigh, Ky., U.S.	G3	114
McVille, N.D., U.S.	G15	124
McWilliams, Al., U.S.	F11	122
Mdantsane, S. Afr.	H8	70
M'drak, Viet.	F9	48
Mead, Ne., U.S.	C1	120
Mead, Lake, res., U.S.	G2	132
Meade, Ks., U.S.	D8	128
Meaden Peak, mtn., Co., U.S.	C9	132
Meadow, Ut., U.S.	E4	132
Meadow Lake, Sk., Can.	E9	106
Meadow Valley Wash, stm., Nv., U.S.	F2	132
Meadowview, Va., U.S.	H3	114
Meadville, Ms., U.S.	F7	122
Meadville, Mo., U.S.	E4	120
Meadville, Pa., U.S.	C5	114
Meaford, On., Can.	D9	112
Mealhada, Port.	D2	20
Meandarra, Austl.	F7	76
Meander River, Ab., Can.	D7	106
Mearim, stm., Braz.	B3	88
Meath, state, Ire.	H6	12
Meath, hist. reg., Ire.	H6	12
Meaux, Fr.	F11	14
Mecaya, stm., Col.	G4	86
Mecca see Makkah, Sau. Ar.	E4	56
Mechanicsburg, Oh., U.S.	D2	114
Mechanicsville, Ia., U.S.	C6	120
Mechanicsville, Va., U.S.	G8	114
Mechanicville, N.Y., U.S.	B12	114
Mechelen (Malines), Bel.	C13	14
Mecklenburg, hist. reg., Ger.	C7	16
Mecklenburger Bucht, b., Ger.	B7	16
Mecklenburg-Vorpommern, state, Ger.	C8	16
Mecubúri, Moz.	C6	68
Mecula, Moz.	C6	68
Meda, Port.	D3	20
Medak, India	B4	53
Medan, Indon.	B1	50
Medanosa, Punta, c., Arg.	I3	90
Mede, Italy	E5	22
Medeiros Neto, Braz.	I5	88
Medellín, Col.	D4	86
Médenine, Tun.	C6	64
Mederdra, Maur.	F1	64
Medford, Ok., U.S.	E11	128
Medford, Or., U.S.	A2	134
Medford, Wi., U.S.	F8	118
Medgidia, Rom.	E15	26
Mediapolis, Ia., U.S.	C6	120
Mediaș, Rom.	C11	26
Medicine Bow, Wy., U.S.	B10	132
Medicine Bow, stm., Wy., U.S.	A10	132
Medicine Bow Mountains, mts., U.S.	F6	126
Medicine Creek, stm., Mo., U.S.	E4	120
Medicine Hat, Ab., Can.	D3	124
Medicine Lake, Mt., U.S.	F9	124
Medicine Lodge, Ks., U.S.	D10	128
Medicine Lodge, stm., U.S.	D10	128
Medina, Braz.	I5	88
Medina see Al-Madīnah, Sau. Ar.	E4	56
Medina, N.Y., U.S.	E11	112
Medina, Oh., U.S.	C4	114
Medina, Tx., U.S.	E8	130
Medina, stm., Tx., U.S.	E9	130
Medinaceli, Spain	C8	20
Medina del Campo, Spain	C6	20
Medina-Sidonia, Spain	H5	20
Medinīpur, India	G11	54
Medio, Punta, c., Chile	C2	92
Medio Creek, stm., Tx., U.S.	F10	130
Mediterranean Sea	A4	62
Medje, D.R.C.	D5	66
Medjez el Bab, Tun.	H3	24
Medkovec, Blg.	F10	26
Mednogorsk, Russia	D9	32
Médoc, reg., Fr.	D4	18
Medora, N.D., U.S.	H10	124
Médouneu, Gabon	D2	66
Meductic, N.B., Can.	E9	110
Medveđa, Yugo.	G8	26
Medvedica, stm., Russia	C19	10
Medvedica, stm., Russia	D6	32
Medvėgalis, hill, Lith.	E5	10
Medvežegorsk, Russia	E15	8
Medvežji ostrova, is., Russia	B21	34
Medyn', Russia	F18	10
Meekatharra, Austl.	E3	74
Meeker, Co., U.S.	C8	132
Meeks Bay, Ca., U.S.	D5	134
Meeladeen, Som.	B9	66
Meerane, Ger.	F8	16
Meersburg, Ger.	I5	16
Meerut, India	D6	54
Mēga, Eth.	G7	62
Mega, Pulau, i., Indon.	E2	50
Megalópoli, Grc.	F4	28
Mégantic, Lac, l., Qc., Can.	E5	110
Mégara, Grc.	E6	28
Megargel, Tx., U.S.	H9	128
Meghālaya, state, India	F13	54
Meghna, stm., Bngl.	G13	54
Megísti, i., Grc.	G12	28
Megra, Russia	C19	8
Mehakit, Indon.	E9	50
Meharry, Mount, mtn., Austl.	D3	74
Mehedinți, state, Rom.	E10	26
Mehekar, India	H6	54
Meherrin, stm., U.S.	H7	114
Mehidpur, India	G5	54
Mehikoorma, Est.	B10	10
Mehndāwal, India	E9	54
Mehren'ga, Russia	F19	8
Mehrenga, stm., Russia	E19	8
Mehtarlām, Afg.	C11	56
Mehun-sur-Yèvre, Fr.	G11	14
Mei, stm., China	I7	42
Mei, stm., China	H7	42
Meia Meia, Tan.	F7	66
Meia Ponte, stm., Braz.	I1	88
Meichuan, China	F6	42
Meiganga, Cam.	C2	66
Meighen Island, i., N.T., Can.	A5	141
Meigs, Ga., U.S.	E1	116
Meihekou, China	C6	38
Meihsien see Meizhou, China	I7	42
Meikeng, China	J6	42
Meiktila, Mya.	B2	48
Meiners Oaks, Ca., U.S.	I6	134
Meiningen, Ger.	F6	16
Meishan, China	E5	36
Meissen, Ger.	E9	16
Meitan, China	H2	42
Meizhou, China	I7	42
Mejillones, Chile	D2	90
Mejillones, Península, pen., Chile	A2	92
Mejnypil'gyno, Russia	D24	34
Mékambo, Gabon	D2	66
Mek'elē, Eth.	E7	62
Mékhé, Sen.	F1	64
Mekhtar, Pak.	C2	54
Mekka see Makkah, Sau. Ar.	E4	56
Meknès, Mor.	C3	64
Mekong (Mékôngk) (Khong) (Lancang), stm., Asia	F9	46
Mekongga, Gunung, mtn., Indon.	F7	44
Mékôngk see Mekong, stm., Asia	F10	46
Melado, stm., Chile	H2	92
Melaka, Malay.	K6	48
Melaka, state, Malay.	K6	48
Melanesia, is., Oc.	D7	72
Melawi, stm., Indon.	D8	50
Melbourne, Austl.	K5	76
Melbourne, Ar., U.S.	H6	120
Melbourne, Fl., U.S.	H5	116
Melbourne, Ia., U.S.	J5	118
Melbourne Island, i., N.T., Can.	B10	106
Melcher, Ia., U.S.	C4	120
Melchor, Isla, i., Chile	I2	90
Melchor Múzquiz, Mex.	B8	100
Meldorf, Ger.	B4	16
Meldrum Bay, On., Can.	C6	112
Meldrum Creek, B.C., Can.	D8	138
Mélé, Baie, b., Vanuatu	k17	79d
Melekeok, Palau	g8	78b
Melenki, Russia	I19	8
Meleuz, Russia	D9	32
Mélèzes, stm., Qc., Can.	D16	106
Melfi, Chad	E3	62
Melfi, Italy	C9	24
Melfort, Sk., Can.	B9	124
Meliane, Oued, stm., Tun.	H4	24
Meliau, Indon.	D7	50
Meligalás, Grc.	F4	28
Melilla, Sp. N. Afr.	B4	64
Melimoyu, Cerro, vol., Chile	H2	90
Melincué, Arg.	F7	92
Melita, Mb., Can.	E12	124
Melitopol', Ukr.	E5	32
Melívoia, Grc.	D5	28
Mellansel, Swe.	E7	8
Mellen, Wi., U.S.	E8	118
Mellerud, Swe.	G5	8
Mellish Reef, at., Austl.	C11	74
Mellit, Sudan	E5	62
Mělník, Czech Rep.	F10	16
Melo, Ur.	F10	92
Melolo, Indon.	H12	50
Melos see Mílos, i., Grc.	G7	28
Melrhir, Chott, l., Alg.	C6	64
Melrose, Austl.	E4	74
Melrose, Austl.	I6	76
Melrose, Mn., U.S.	F4	118
Melrose, N.M., U.S.	G5	128
Melrose, Wi., U.S.	G8	118
Melsungen, Ger.	E5	16
Meltaus, Fin.	C11	8
Melton Mowbray, Eng., U.K.	I12	12
Melun, Fr.	F11	14
Melūr, India	F4	53
Melvern, Ks., U.S.	F2	120
Melvern Lake, res., Ks., U.S.	F2	120
Melville, Sk., Can.	D11	124
Melville, La., U.S.	G7	122
Melville, Cape, c., Austl.	B9	74
Melville Bugt, b., Grnld.	B12	141
Melville Hall Airport, Dom.	i6	105c
Melville Hills, hills, N.T., Can.	B7	106
Melville Island, i., Austl.	B6	74
Melville Island, i., N.T., Can.	A17	140
Melville Peninsula, pen., N.T., Can.	B14	106
Melvin, Ky., U.S.	G3	114
Melvin, Tx., U.S.	C8	130
Melyana, Alg.	H13	20
Mélykút, Hung.	C6	26
Mêmar Co, l., China	A9	54
Memba, Moz.	C7	68
Membalong, Indon.	E5	50
Memboro, Indon.	H11	50
Memel see Klaipėda, Lith.	E3	10
Memel, S. Afr.	E9	70
Mēmele (Nemunėlis), stm., Eur.	D7	10
Memmingen, Ger.	I5	16
Mempawah, Indon.	C6	50
Memphis, Fl., U.S.	I3	116
Memphis, Mi., U.S.	B3	114
Memphis, Tn., U.S.	B8	122
Memphis, Tx., U.S.	G8	128
Memphrémagog, Lac (Memphremagog, Lake), l., N.A.	E4	110
Memphremagog, Lake (Memphrémagog, Lac), l., N.A.	E4	110
Memramcook, N.B., Can.	D12	110
Mena, Ar., U.S.	C4	122
Menado see Manado, Indon.	E7	44
Ménaka, Mali	F5	64
Menan, Id., U.S.	G15	136
Menard, Tx., U.S.	D8	130
Menasha, Wi., U.S.	G10	118
Menate, Indon.	D8	50
Mendawai, Indon.	E8	50
Mendawai, stm., Indon.	E8	50
Mende, Fr.	E9	18
Mendebo, mts., Eth.	F7	62
Mendenhall, Ms., U.S.	F9	122
Mendī, Eth.	F7	62
Mendi, Pap. N. Gui.	b3	79a
Mendocino, Ca., U.S.	D2	134
Mendocino, Cape, c., Ca., U.S.	C1	134
Mendocino Fracture Zone, unds.	E24	142
Mendon, Il., U.S.	D6	120
Mendota, Ca., U.S.	G5	134
Mendoza, Arg.	F3	92
Mendoza, state, Arg.	G3	92
Mendoza, stm., Arg.	F3	92
Mene de Mauroa, Ven.	B6	86
Mene Grande, Ven.	C6	86
Menemen, Tur.	E9	28
Menen, Bel.	D12	14
Menfi, Italy	G6	24
Mengban, China	A5	48
Mengcheng, China	E7	42
Mengellang, Palau	f8	78b
Menggala, Indon.	F4	50
Menggudai, China	B2	42
Menghai, China	B5	48
Mengjiawan, China	B3	42
Mengla, China	B5	48
Menglian, China	A4	48
Mengxian, China	D5	42
Mengyin, China	D7	42
Mengzi, China	A6	48
Menihek Lakes, l., Nf., Can.	E17	106
Menin see Menen, Bel.	D12	14
Menindee, Austl.	I4	76
Menjuša, Russia	B13	10
Menlo Park, Ca., U.S.	F3	134
Menno, S.D., U.S.	D15	126
Meno, Ok., U.S.	E10	128
Menominee, Mi., U.S.	C2	112
Menominee, stm., U.S.	C2	112
Menomonee Falls, Wi., U.S.	A9	120
Menomonie, Wi., U.S.	G7	118
Menongue, Ang.	C2	68
Menor, Mar, b., Spain	G10	20
Menorca (Minorca), i., Spain	D15	20
Mentasta Lake, Ak., U.S.	D11	140
Mentawai, Kepulauan, is., Indon.	E1	50
Mentawai, Selat, strt., Indon.	D2	50
Menton, Fr.	F13	18
Mentor, Oh., U.S.	C4	114
Menyapa, Gunung, mtn., Indon.	C9	50
Menzel Bourguiba, Tun.	G3	24
Menzel Bou Zelfa, Tun.	H4	24
Menzelinsk, Russia	C8	32
Menzel Temime, Tun.	H5	24
Menzies, Austl.	E4	74
Menzies, Mount, mtn., Ant.	C10	81
Meobbaai, b., Nmb.	D2	70
Meoqui, Mex.	A6	100
Meota, Sk., Can.	A5	124
Meppel, Neth.	B15	14
Meppen, Ger.	D3	16
Meqerghane, Sebkha, pl., Alg.	D5	64
Mequinenza, Embalse de, res., Spain	C10	20
Mequon, Wi., U.S.	E2	112
Merah, Indon.	C10	50
Meramec, stm., Mo., U.S.	F7	120
Meran see Merano, Italy	D8	22
Merangin, stm., Indon.	E3	50
Merano (Meran), Italy	D8	22
Meratus, Pegunungan, mts., Indon.	E9	50
Merauke, Indon.	G11	44
Merbau, Indon.	C3	50
Merbein, Austl.	J4	76
Mercaderes, Col.	G3	86
Mercāra, India	E2	53
Merced, Ca., U.S.	F5	134
Merced, stm., Ca., U.S.	F5	134
Mercedario, Cerro, mtn., Arg.	E2	92
Mercedes, Arg.	D8	92
Mercedes, Arg.	G8	92
Mercedes, Tx., U.S.	H10	130
Mercedes, Ur.	F8	92
Mercer, Mo., U.S.	D4	120
Mercer, Pa., U.S.	C5	114
Mercersburg, Pa., U.S.	E7	114
Merchants Bay, b., N.T., Can.	D13	141
Mercoal, Ab., Can.	C13	138
Mercury, Nv., U.S.	G10	134
Mercury Islands, is., N.Z.	C6	80
Mercy, Cape, c., N.T., Can.	E13	141
Mercy Bay, b., N.T., Can.	B16	140
Meredith, Lake, res., Tx., U.S.	F7	128
Meredosia, Il., U.S.	E7	120
Mereeg, Som.	D9	66
Méré Lava, i., Vanuatu	j17	79d
Merevari, stm., Ven.	E9	86
Merëža, Russia	A19	10
Mergui, Mya.	F4	48
Mergui Archipelago, is., Mya.	G3	48
Meribah, Austl.	J3	76
Mérida, Mex.	B3	102
Mérida, Spain	F4	20
Mérida, Ven.	C6	86
Mérida, state, Ven.	C6	86
Mérida, Cordillera de, mts., Ven.	C6	86
Meridian, Ga., U.S.	E4	116
Meridian, Ms., U.S.	E10	122
Meridian, Tx., U.S.	C10	130
Meridianville, Al., U.S.	C12	122
Mérignac, Fr.	E5	18
Merigold, Ms., U.S.	D8	122
Merikarvia, Fin.	F9	8
Merimbula, Austl.	K7	76
Merín, Laguna (Mirim, Lagoa), b., S.A.	F11	92
Merinda, Austl.	B6	76
Merino, Co., U.S.	G9	126
Merinos, Ur.	F9	92
Merizo, Guam	j9	78c
Merkinė, Lith.	F7	10
Merkys, stm., Lith.	F8	10
Merlin, On., Can.	F7	112
Merlin, Or., U.S.	H3	136
Merna, Ne., U.S.	F13	126
Meron, Har (Meron, Mount), mtn., Isr.	E6	58
Meron, Mount see Meron, Har, mtn., Isr.	E6	58
Merouane, Chott, l., Alg.	C6	64
Merredin, Austl.	F3	74
Merrick, mtn., Scot., U.K.	F8	12
Merrill, Ia., U.S.	B1	120
Merrill, Mi., U.S.	E5	112
Merrill, Or., U.S.	A4	134
Merrillan, Wi., U.S.	G8	118
Merrillville, In., U.S.	G2	112
Merrimack, stm., U.S.	H5	110
Merriman, Ne., U.S.	E11	126
Merritt, B.C., Can.	F10	138
Merritt Island, Fl., U.S.	H5	116
Merriwa, Austl.	I8	76
Mer Rouge, La., U.S.	E7	122
Merrygoen, Austl.	H7	76
Merryville, La., U.S.	G5	122
Mersa Matruh, Egypt	A5	62
Mersea Island, i., Eng., U.K.	J13	12
Merseburg, Ger.	E7	16
Mersey, stm., Austl.	n13	77a
Mersey, stm., N.S., Can.	F12	110
Mersing, Malay.	K6	48
Mērsrags, Lat.	C6	10
Merta, India	E5	54
Merthyr Tydfil, Wales, U.K.	J9	12
Mértola, Port.	G3	20
Mertz Glacier Tongue, ice, Ant.	B19	81
Méru, Fr.	E11	14
Meru, Kenya	D7	66
Meruoca, Braz.	B5	88
Merweville, S. Afr.	H5	70
Merzifon, Tur.	A4	56
Merzig, Ger.	G2	16
Mesa, Az., U.S.	J5	132
Mesabi Range, hills, Mn., U.S.	D6	118
Mesagne, Italy	D11	24
Mesáras, Órmos, b., Grc.	I7	28
Mesa Verde National Park, p.o.i., Co., U.S.	F8	132
Mescalero, N.M., U.S.	H3	128
Meščerino, Russia	G20	10
Meschede, Ger.	E4	16
Meščura, Russia	E24	8
Mesewa see Massawa, Erit.	D7	62
Mesgouez, Lac, l., Qc., Can.	E16	106
Mesick, Mi., U.S.	D4	112
Mesilla, N.M., U.S.	K10	132
Meškuičiai, Lith.	D6	10
Mesolóngi, Grc.	E4	28
Mesopotamia, hist. reg., Asia	C5	56
Mesquite, Tx., U.S.	E2	122
Messalo, stm., Moz.	C6	68
Messina, Italy	F9	24
Messina, S. Afr.	C9	70
Messina, Gulf of see Messiniakós Kólpos, b., Grc.	G5	28
Messina, Stretto di, strt., Italy	F9	24
Messíni, Grc.	F4	28
Messíni, hist., Grc.	F4	28
Messiniakós Kólpos, b., Grc.	G5	28
Messix Peak, mtn., Ut., U.S.	B4	132
Messkirch, Ger.	H5	16
Messojaha, stm., Russia	C4	34
Mesta (Néstos), stm., Eur.	B6	28
Mestghanem, Alg.	B4	64
Mestre, ngh., Italy	E9	22
Mesuji, stm., Indon.	E4	50
Meta, state, Col.	F5	86
Meta, stm., S.A.	D7	86
Métabetchouan, Qc., Can.	B5	110
Métabetchouane, stm., Qc., Can.	B4	110
Meta Incognita Peninsula, pen., N.T., Can.	C17	106
Metairie, La., U.S.	H8	122
Metaline Falls, Wa., U.S.	B9	136
Metamora, Il., U.S.	D8	120
Metán, Arg.	B5	92
Metangula, Moz.	C5	68
Metapán, El Sal.	E3	102
Metaponto, hist., Italy	D10	24
Metapontum see Metaponto, hist., Italy	D10	24
Meteor Crater, crat., Az., U.S.	H6	132
Metharaw, Mya.	D4	48
Methow, Wa., U.S.	B7	136
Methow, stm., Wa., U.S.	B6	136
Methven, N.Z.	F4	80
Metica, stm., Col.	E5	86
Metiskow, Ab., Can.	B3	124
Metlakatla, Ak., U.S.	E13	140
Metlika, Slvn.	E12	22
Meto, Bayou, stm., Ar., U.S.	C7	122
Metropolis, Il., U.S.	G9	120
Metropolitan, Mi., U.S.	C2	112
Metter, Ga., U.S.	D3	116
Mettuppālaiyam, India	F3	53
Mettūr, India	F3	53
Metz, Fr.	E15	14
Metzingen, Ger.	H5	16
Meu, stm., Fr.	F7	14
Meulaboh, Indon.	J2	48
Meureudu, Indon.	J3	48
Meurthe, stm., Fr.	F15	14
Meurthe-et-Moselle, state, Fr.	F15	14
Meuse, state, Fr.	E14	14
Meuse (Maas), stm., Eur.	D14	14
Meuselwitz, Ger.	E8	16
Mexiana, Ilha, i., Braz.	C8	84
Mexicali, Mex.	K10	134
Mexican Hat, Ut., U.S.	F7	132
México see Ciudad de México, Mex.	F9	100
Mexico, Me., U.S.	F6	110
Mexico, Mo., U.S.	E6	120
Mexico, N.Y., U.S.	E13	112
México, state, Mex.	F9	100
Mexico, ctry., N.A.	C4	96
Mexico, Gulf of, b., N.A.	B6	96
Mexico Basin, unds.	F5	144
Mexico Bay, b., N.Y., U.S.	E13	112
Mexico City see Ciudad de México, Mex.	F9	100
Meycauayan, Phil.	C3	52
Meydān Khvolah, Afg.	B2	54
Meyersdale, Pa., U.S.	E6	114
Meymaneh, Afg.	B9	56
Meyronne, Sk., Can.	E7	124
Meyungs, Palau	g7	78b
Mëža (M'oža), stm., Eur.	E14	10
Meẓada, Ḥorvot (Masada), hist., Isr.	G6	58
Mezcala, Mex.	G9	100
Mezcalapa, stm., Mex.	G12	100
Meždurečensk, Russia	D15	32
Meždurečenskij, Russia	C10	32
Mèze, Fr.	F9	18
Mezen', Russia	D21	8
Mezen', stm., Russia	D21	8
Mezenskaja guba, b., Russia	C20	8
Mežica, Slvn.	D11	22
Mezőberény, Hung.	C8	26
Mezőcsát, Hung.	B7	26
Mezőkövesd, Hung.	B7	26
Mezőtúr, Hung.	B7	26
Mezquital, stm., Mex.	D6	100
Mfangano Island, i., Kenya	E6	66
Mgači, Russia	F17	34
M'Goun, Irhil, mtn., Mor.	C3	64
M'hai, B'nom, mtn., Viet.	G8	48
Mhasvād, India	C2	53

Name — Map Ref. — Page

Mhow, India G5 54
Mi, stm., China H5 42
Mi, stm., China C8 42
Mia, Oued, stm., Alg. D5 64
Miahuatlán de Porfirio Díaz, Mex. G10 100
Miajadas, Spain E4 20
Miaméré, C.A.R. C4 66
Miami, Mb., Can. E15 124
Miami, Az., U.S. J6 132
Miami, Fl., U.S. K5 116
Miami, Ok., U.S. H3 120
Miami, Tx., U.S. F8 128
Miami Beach, Fl., U.S. K5 116
Miami Canal, can., Fl., U.S. J5 116
Miamisburg, Oh., U.S. E1 114
Miami Springs, Fl., U.S. K5 116
Miān Channūn, Pak. C4 54
Mianchi, China D4 42
Miandrivazo, Madag. D8 68
Mianduhe, China B9 36
Mīāneh, Iran B6 56
Miang, Phu, mtn., Thai. D5 48
Mianning, China F5 36
Miānwāli, Pak. B3 54
Mianxian, China E2 42
Mianyang, China F1 42
Mianzhu, China E5 36
Miaodao Qundao, is., China B9 42
Miaoli, Tai. I9 42
Miao Ling, mts., China H2 42
Miass, Russia C10 32
Miass, stm., Russia C10 32
Miastko, Pol. B12 16
Micang Shan, mts., China E2 42
Michalovce, Slov. H17 16
Michaud, Point, c., N.S., Can. E16 110
Micheal Peak, mtn., B.C., Can. C4 138
Michel, B.C., Can. G16 138
Miches, Dom. Rep. C13 102
Michigan, N.D., U.S. F15 124
Michigan, state, U.S. C10 108
Michigan, stm., Co., U.S. G6 126
Michigan, Lake, l., U.S. E2 112
Michigan City, In., U.S. G3 112
Michipicoten Island, i., On., Can. F13 106
Michoacán, state, Mex. F8 100
Micoud, St. Luc. m7 105c
Micronesia, is., Oc. B6 72
Micronesia, Federated States of, ctry., Oc. C6 72
Mičurinsk, Russia D6 32
Midai, Pulau, i., Indon. B5 50
Midale, Sk., Can. E10 124
Mid-Atlantic Ridge, unds. F9 144
Middelburg, Neth. C12 14
Middelburg, S. Afr. G7 70
Middelburg, S. Afr. D9 70
Middle, stm., B.C., Can. B5 138
Middle, stm., Ia., U.S. C3 120
Middle, stm., Mn., U.S. C2 118
Middle Alkali Lake, l., Ca., U.S. B5 134
Middle America Trench, unds. H29 142
Middle Andaman, i., India F7 46
Middleboro, Ma., U.S. C15 114
Middlebourne, W.V., U.S. E5 114
Middleburg, N.Y., U.S. B11 114
Middleburg, Pa., U.S. D8 114
Middlebury, Vt., U.S. F3 110
Middle Caicos, i., T./C. Is. B12 102
Middle Fabius, stm., Mo., U.S. D5 120
Middlefield, Oh., U.S. C4 114
Middlegate, Norf. I. y25 78i
Middle Loup, stm., Ne., U.S. F14 126
Middlemount, Austl. D7 76
Middle Musquodoboit, N.S., Can. E13 110
Middleport, Oh., U.S. E3 114
Middle Raccoon, stm., Ia., U.S. J4 118
Middlesboro, Ky., U.S. H2 114
Middlesbrough, Eng., U.K. G11 12
Middlesex, Belize D3 102
Middle Stewiacke, N.S., Can. E13 110
Middleton, N.S., Can. F11 110
Middleton, Mi., U.S. E5 112
Middleton, Wi., U.S. A8 120
Middleton Island, i., Ak., U.S. E10 140
Middleton Reef, at., Austl. E11 74
Middletown, Ca., U.S. E3 134
Middletown, Ct., U.S. C13 114
Middletown, Il., U.S. K9 118
Middletown, In., U.S. H4 112
Middletown, Ky., U.S. F12 120
Middletown, Md., U.S. E8 114
Middletown, N.Y., U.S. C11 114
Middletown, Oh., U.S. E1 114
Middletown, Pa., U.S. D9 114
Middletown, R.I., U.S. C14 114
Middleville, Mi., U.S. F4 112
Midgic, N.B., Can. E12 110
Midi, Canal du, can., Fr. F9 18
Midi de Bigorre, Pic du, mtn., Fr. G5 18
Mid-Indian Basin, unds. J10 142
Mid-Indian Ridge, unds. L10 142
Midland, On., Can. D9 112
Midland, Ca., U.S. J2 132
Midland, Mi., U.S. E5 112
Midland, S.D., U.S. C11 126
Midland, Tx., U.S. C5 130
Midlands, state, Zimb. B10 70
Midleton, Ire. J4 12
Midlothian, Tx., U.S. B11 130
Midnapore, Ab., Can. F16 138
Midongy Atsimo, Madag. E8 68
Mid-Pacific Mountains, unds. G19 142
Midsayap, Phil. G5 52
Midville, Ga., U.S. D3 116
Midway, B.C., Can. G12 138
Midway, Al., U.S. E13 122
Midway, Ky., U.S. F13 120
Midway, Tx., U.S. F3 122
Midway Islands, dep., Oc. G22 30
Midway Park, N.C., U.S. B8 116
Midwest City, Ok., U.S. F11 128
Midyan, reg., Sau. Ar. J6 58
Midžur (Midžor), mtn., Eur. F9 26
Mie, Japan G4 40
Mie, state, Japan E9 40
Międzybórz, Pol. E13 16
Międzylesie, Pol. F12 16
Międzyrzec Podlaski, Pol. D18 16
Międzyrzecz, Pol. D11 16
Miélan, Fr. F6 18
Mielec, Pol. F17 16
Mier, Mex. B9 100
Miercurea-Ciuc, Rom. C12 26
Mieres, Spain A5 20
Mieroszów, Pol. F12 16
Mier y Noriega, Mex. D8 100
Miesbach, Ger. I7 16
Mī'ēso, Eth. F8 62
Mieszkowice, Pol. D10 16
Mifflinburg, Pa., U.S. H12 112
Miguel Alemán, Presa, res., Mex. F10 100
Miguel Alves, Braz. C4 88
Miguel Auza, Mex. C7 100
Miguel Calmon, Braz. F5 88
Miguel Hidalgo, Presa, res., Mex. B4 100
Miguelópolis, Braz. K1 88
Miguel Riglos, Arg. H6 92
Mihăeşti, Rom. D12 26
Mihajlovka, Russia D6 32
Mihajlovka, Russia D14 32
Mihajlovka, Russia C10 38
Mihajlovskij, Russia F20 8
Mihalgazi, Tur. C13 28
Mihanavičy, Bela. G10 10
Mihara, Japan E5 40
Mihara-yama, vol., Japan E12 40
Mihninskaja, Russia F21 8
Mikame, Japan F5 40
Mikasa, Japan C14 38
Mikaševičy, Bela. H10 10
Mikhrot Timna' (King Solomon's Mines), hist., Isr. I5 58
Mikindani, Tan. G8 66
Mikkeli (Sankt Michel), Fin. F12 8
Mikkeli, state, Fin. F12 8
Mikołajki, Pol. C17 16
Mikołów, Pol. F14 16
Mikrá Préspa, Límni, l., Eur. D15 24
Mikšino, Russia C18 10
Mikulino, Russia E14 10
Mikumi, Tan. F7 66
Mikun', Russia E23 8
Mikuni, Japan C9 40
Miladummadulu Atoll, at., Mald. h12 46a
Milagro, Arg. E5 92
Milagro, Ec. I2 86
Milagros, Phil. D4 52
Milan see Milano, Italy E6 22
Milan, Ga., U.S. D2 116
Milan, In., U.S. E12 120
Milan, Mi., U.S. B2 114
Milan, Mn., U.S. F3 118
Milan, Mo., U.S. D4 120
Milan, N.M., U.S. H8 132
Milang, Austl. J2 76
Milange, Moz. D6 68
Milano (Milan), Italy E6 22
Milâs, Tur. F10 28
Milavidy, Bela. H8 10
Milazzo, Italy F9 24
Milazzo, Golfo di, b., Italy F9 24
Milbank, S.D., U.S. F2 118
Milburn, Ok., U.S. C2 122
Milden, Sk., Can. C6 124
Mildmay, On., Can. D8 112
Mildura, Austl. J4 76
Mile, China G5 36
Miles, Austl. F8 76
Miles, Tx., U.S. C7 130
Miles City, Mt., U.S. A7 126
Milestone, Sk., Can. E9 124
Milet, hist., Tur. F10 28
Milford, De., U.S. F10 114
Milford, Ia., U.S. H3 118
Milford, Me., U.S. F8 110
Milford, Ma., U.S. B14 114
Milford, Mi., U.S. B2 114
Milford, N.H., U.S. B14 114
Milford, Pa., U.S. C11 114
Milford, Ut., U.S. E4 132
Milford Center, Oh., U.S. D2 114
Milford Haven, Wales, U.K. J7 12
Milford Lake, res., Ks., U.S. B11 128
Milford Sound, strt., N.Z. G2 80
Mili, at., Marsh. Is. C8 72
Milian, stm., Malay. A10 50
Milicz, Pol. E13 16
Miljatino, Russia F17 10
Milk, stm., N.A. B6 108
Milk, North Fork (North Milk), stm., N.A. B13 136
Mil'kovo, Russia F20 34
Milk River, Ab., Can. G18 138
Millard, Ne., U.S. C1 120
Millau, Fr. E9 18
Millboro, Va., U.S. F6 114
Millbrook, N.Y., U.S. C12 114
Mill City, Or., U.S. F4 136
Millcreek, Pa., U.S. B5 114
Millcreek, Ut., U.S. C5 132
Mill Creek, W.V., U.S. F5 114
Milledgeville, Ga., U.S. C2 116
Milledgeville, Il., U.S. C8 120
Mille Lacs, Lac des, l., On., Can. C8 118
Mille Lacs Lake, l., Mn., U.S. E5 118
Millen, Ga., U.S. D4 116
Miller, Mo., U.S. G4 120
Miller, S.D., U.S. C14 126
Miller Mountain, mtn., Nv., U.S. E7 134
Millerovo, Russia E6 32
Millersburg, Ky., U.S. F1 114
Millersburg, Mi., U.S. C5 112
Millersburg, Oh., U.S. D4 114
Millersport, Oh., U.S. I7 112
Millerton, N.Y., U.S. C12 114
Millet, Ab., Can. C17 138
Millevaches, Plateau de, plat., Fr. D7 18
Millicent, Austl. K3 76
Milligan, Fl., U.S. G12 122
Milligan, Ne., U.S. G15 126
Millington, Mi., U.S. E6 112
Millington, Tn., U.S. B9 122
Millinocket, Me., U.S. E8 110
Mill Island, i., Ant. B15 81
Mill Island, i., N.T., Can. C15 106
Millry, Al., U.S. F10 122
Mills, Wy., U.S. E6 126
Mills Creek, stm., Austl. D4 76
Mills Lake, l., N.T., Can. C7 106
Millstream, Austl. D3 74
Milltown, Mt., U.S. D13 136
Milltown, Wi., U.S. F6 118
Milltown Malbay, Ire. I3 12
Mill Valley, Ca., U.S. F3 134
Millville, N.J., U.S. E10 114
Millwood, Va., U.S. E7 114
Millwood Lake, res., Ar., U.S. D4 122
Milne Land, i., Grnld. C20 141
Milnor, N.D., U.S. A15 126
Milo, Ab., Can. F18 138
Mílos, i., Grc. G7 28
Miłosław, Pol. D13 16
Milparinka, Austl. G3 76
Milroy, In., U.S. E12 120
Milroy, Pa., U.S. D8 114
Miltenberg, Ger. G5 16
Milton, On., Can. E10 112
Milton, N.Z. H4 80
Milton, Fl., U.S. G11 122
Milton, Ia., U.S. D5 120
Milton, Pa., U.S. G13 112
Milton, Wi., U.S. B9 120
Milton-Freewater, Or., U.S. E8 136
Milton Keynes, Eng., U.K. I12 12
Miltonvale, Ks., U.S. B11 128
Miltou, Chad E3 62
Miluo, stm., China G5 42
Milwaukee, Wi., U.S. E2 112
Milwaukee, stm., Wi., U.S. H11 118
Milwaukie, Or., U.S. E4 136
Mimbres, stm., N.M., U.S. K9 132
Mimizan-les-Bains, Fr. E4 18
Mimoň, Czech Rep. F10 16
Mimoso do Sul, Braz. K5 88
Mims, Fl., U.S. H5 116
Min, stm., China F5 36
Min, stm., China I8 42
Mina, Mex. H7 130
Mina, Nv., U.S. E7 134
Mīnā' al-Aḥmadī, Kuw. D6 56
Mīnāb, Iran D8 56
Minahasa, pen., Indon. E7 44
Minakuchi, Japan E9 40
Minamata, Japan G3 40
Minami-Alps-kokuritsu-kōen, p.o.i., Japan D11 40
Minami-Tori-shima, i., Japan G19 30
Minas, Cuba B9 102
Minas, Indon. C2 50
Minas, Ur. G10 92
Minas Basin, b., N.S., Can. E12 110
Minas de Barroterán, Mex. B8 100
Minas de Corrales, Ur. E10 92
Minas de Matahambre, Cuba A5 102
Minas Gerais, state, Braz. C8 90
Minas Novas, Braz. I4 88
Minatare, Ne., U.S. F9 126
Minatitlán, Mex. F11 100
Minbu, Mya. B2 48
Minbya, Mya. B1 48
Minbyin, Mya. C1 48
Mincio, stm., Italy E7 22
Minco, Ok., U.S. F10 128
Minčol, mtn., Slov. G17 16
Mindanao, i., Phil. G5 52
Mindanao, stm., Phil. G5 52
Mindelheim, Ger. H6 16
Mindelo, C.V. k10 65a
Mindemoya, On., Can. C7 112
Minden, On., Can. D11 112
Minden, Ger. D4 16
Minden, La., U.S. E5 122
Minden, Ne., U.S. G14 126
Minden, Nv., U.S. E6 134
Minden City, Mi., U.S. E7 112
Mindoro, i., Phil. D3 52
Mindoro Strait, strt., Phil. D3 52
Mine, Japan E4 40
Mine Centre, On., Can. C6 118
Minehead, Eng., U.K. J9 12
Mineiros, Braz. G7 84
Mineola, Tx., U.S. E3 122
Mineral, Wa., U.S. D4 136
Mineral Point, Wi., U.S. B7 120
Mineral Springs, Ar., U.S. D5 122
Mineral Wells, Tx., U.S. B9 130
Minersville, Pa., U.S. H13 112
Minerva, Oh., U.S. D4 114
Minervino Murge, Italy C9 24
Mineville, N.Y., U.S. F3 110
Minfeng, China A5 46
Minga, D.R.C. G5 66
Mingäçevir, Azer. A6 56
Mingāora, Pak. C11 56
Mingary, Austl. I3 76
Mingene, Austl. E3 74
Mingin, Mya. A2 48
Minglanilla, Spain E9 20
Mingo Junction, Oh., U.S. D5 114
Mingo Lake, l., N.T., Can. C16 106
Mingshui, China B10 36
Mingulay, i., Scot., U.K. E5 12
Mingyuegou, China C8 38
Minhang, China F9 42
Minh Hai, Viet. H7 48
Minhla, Mya. B2 48
Minhla, Mya. C2 48
Minho, hist. reg., Port. C2 20
Minho (Miño), stm., Eur. B2 20
Minićevo, Yugo. F9 26
Minicoy Island, i., India G3 46
Minigwal, Lake, l., Austl. E4 74
Minija, stm., Lith. E4 10
Minilya, Austl. D2 74
Minilya, stm., Austl. D2 74
Miniota, Mb., Can. D12 124
Minitonas, Mb., Can. B12 124
Minle, China D5 36
Minna, Nig. H6 64
Minneapolis, Ks., U.S. B11 128
Minneapolis, Mn., U.S. G5 118
Minnedosa, Mb., Can. D13 124
Minneola, Ks., U.S. D8 128
Minneota, Mn., U.S. G2 118
Minnesota, state, U.S. E4 118
Minnesota, stm., Mn., U.S. G5 118
Minnesota Lake, Mn., U.S. H5 118
Minnewanka, Lake, res., Ab., Can. E15 138
Minnitaki Lake, l., On., Can. B6 118
Mino, Japan D9 40
Miño (Minho), stm., Eur. B2 20
Minocqua, Wi., U.S. F9 118
Minong, Wi., U.S. E7 118
Minonk, Il., U.S. D8 120
Minorca see Menorca, i., Spain D15 20
Minot, N.D., U.S. F12 124
Minqing, China H8 42
Minquan, China D6 42
Minquiers, Plateau des, is., Jersey E6 14
Min Shan, mts., China E5 36
Minsk, Bela. G10 10
Minsk, state, Bela. G10 10
Minskae uzvyšša, plat., Bela. G10 10
Mińsk Mazowiecki, Pol. D17 16
Minta, Cam. D2 66
Minto, Mb., Can. E13 124
Minto, Yk., Can. C3 106
Minto, N.D., U.S. C1 118
Minto, Lac, l., Qc., Can. D16 106
Minto, Mount, mtn., Ant. C22 81
Minto Inlet, b., N.T., Can. A7 106
Minton, Sk., Can. E9 124
Minturn, Co., U.S. D10 132
Minûf, Egypt H1 58
Minusinsk, Russia D16 32
Minvoul, Gabon D2 66
Minxian, China E5 36
Minya see El-Minya, Egypt J1 58
Minya el-Qamh, Egypt H2 58
Mio, Mi., U.S. D5 112
Miquan, China F15 32
Mir, Bela. G9 10
Mira, stm., Col. G2 86
Mīrābād, Afg. C9 56
Mirabella, Gulf of see Mirampéllou, Kólpos, b., Grc. H8 28
Miracema do Tocantins, Braz. E1 88
Mirador, Braz. D3 88
Miradouro, Braz. K4 88
Miraflores, Col. E5 86
Miraflores, Col. G5 86
Miraj, India C2 53
Miramar, Arg. I9 92
Miramar, Moz. C12 70
Miramas, Fr. F10 18
Miramichi Bay, b., N.B., Can. C11 110
Mirampéllou, Kólpos, b., Grc. H8 28
Mīrān, Pak. C3 54
Miranda, Braz. D5 90
Miranda, Col. F3 86
Miranda, state, Ven. B8 86
Miranda, stm., Braz. D5 90
Miranda de Ebro, Spain B7 20
Mirande, Fr. F6 18
Mirando City, Tx., U.S. G8 130
Mirandola, Italy F8 22
Mira Táglio, Italy E9 22
Miravalles, Volcán, vol., C.R. G5 102
Miravete, Puerto de, p., Spain E5 20
Mirbāṭ, Oman F7 56
Mirecourt, Fr. F14 14
Miri, Malay. A9 50
Miria, Niger G6 64
Miriam Vale, Austl. E8 76
Mirim, Lagoa (Merín, Laguna), b., S.A. F11 92
Miriñay, stm., Arg. D9 92
Miritiparaná, stm., Col. H6 86
Miriyama, Pap. N. Gui. a3 79a
Mirnoe Ozero, Russia C13 32
Mirny, sci., Ant. B14 81
Mirnyj, Russia D11 34
Mirnyy, sci., Ant. B14 81
Miroslav, Czech Rep. H12 16
Mirow, Ger. C8 16
Mīrpur, Bngl. G13 54
Mīrpur, Pak. B4 54
Mīrpur Batoro, Pak. F2 54
Mīrpur Khās, Pak. F2 54
Mirror, Ab., Can. D17 138
Mirtóon Pélagos, Grc. G6 28
Miryang, Kor., S. D1 40
Mirzāpur, India F9 54
Misantla, Mex. F10 100
Misawa, Japan D14 38
Miscou Centre, N.B., Can. C12 110
Miscou Island, i., N.B., Can. C12 110
Miscou Point, c., N.B., Can. B12 110
Mishan, China B9 38
Mishawaka, In., U.S. G3 112
Mishicot, Wi., U.S. D2 112
Misima Island, i., Pap. N. Gui. B10 74
Misiones, state, Arg. C10 92
Misiones, state, Para. C9 92
Misión Santa Rosa, Para. D4 90
Misión San Vicente, Mex. F4 98
Miskitos, Cayos, is., Nic. E6 102
Miskolc, Hung. A7 26
Mišnëvo, Russia G19 10
Misool, Pulau, i., Indon. F9 44
Miṣrātah, Libya A3 62
Misr el-Bahrî (Lower Egypt), hist. reg., Egypt G2 58
Misrikh, India E8 54
Missinaibi, stm., On., Can. E14 106
Missinaibi Lake, l., On., Can. F14 106
Mission, B.C., Can. G8 138
Mission, S.D., U.S. D12 126
Mission, Tx., U.S. H9 130
Mission Mountain, hill, Ok., U.S. H3 120
Mission Viejo, Ca., U.S. J8 134
Mississagi, stm., On., Can. B6 112
Mississauga, On., Can. E10 112
Mississinewa, stm., U.S. H4 112
Mississippi, state, U.S. D9 122
Mississippi, stm., On., Can. C13 112
Mississippi, stm., U.S. E9 108
Mississippi Lake, l., On., Can. C13 112
Mississippi River Delta, La., U.S. H9 122
Mississippi Sound, strt., U.S. G10 122
Mississippi State, Ms., U.S. D10 122
Missoula, Mt., U.S. D12 136
Missouri, state, U.S. F5 120
Missouri, stm., U.S. D9 108
Missouri City, Tx., U.S. H3 122
Mistake Creek, stm., Austl. D6 76
Mistassibi, stm., Qc., Can. A4 110
Mistassini, Qc., Can. E16 106
Mistassini, Qc., Can. B4 110
Mistassini, stm., Qc., Can. B4 110
Mistassini, Lac, l., Qc., Can. E16 106
Mistatim, Sk., Can. B10 124
Mistelbach an der Zaya, Aus. B13 22
Misterbianco, Italy G9 24
Misti, Volcán, vol., Peru G3 84
Misumi, Japan E4 40
Mišutino, Russia A19 10
Mita, Punta de, c., Mex. E6 100
Mitchell, Austl. F6 76
Mitchell, On., Can. E8 112
Mitchell, In., U.S. F11 120
Mitchell, Or., U.S. F6 136
Mitchell, S.D., U.S. D14 126
Mitchell, stm., Austl. C8 74
Mitchell, stm., Austl. K6 76
Mitchell, Mount, mtn., N.C., U.S. I3 114
Mitchinamecus, stm., Qc., Can. C2 110
Mitchinamecus, Réservoir, res., Qc., Can. C1 110
Mît Ghamr, Egypt H2 58
Mithapur, India G2 54
Mithi, Pak. F2 54
Mitidja, Plaine de la, pl., Alg. H14 20
Mitiškovo, Russia F16 10
Mitla, hist., Mex. G10 100
Mito, Japan C13 40
Mitsio, Nosy, i., Madag. C8 68
Mitsukaidō, Japan C13 40
Mitsuke, Japan B11 40
Mittellandkanal, can., Ger. D5 16
Mittenwald, Ger. I7 16
Mittersill, Aus. C9 22
Mittweida, Ger. E9 16
Mitú, Col. G6 86
Mitumba, Monts, mts., D.R.C. F5 66
Mitwaba, D.R.C. F5 66
Mitzic, Gabon D2 66
Miura, Japan D12 40
Miura-hantō, pen., Japan D12 40
Mixian, China D5 42
Miyagi, state, Japan A13 40
Miyake-jima, i., Japan E12 40
Miyako, Japan E14 38
Miyako-jima, i., Japan G10 36
Miyakonojō, Japan H4 40
Miyama, Japan E9 40
Miyanojō, Japan H3 40
Miyazaki, Japan H4 40
Miyazaki, state, Japan G4 40
Miyazu, Japan D8 40
Miyoshi, Japan E5 40
Miyun, China A7 42
Miyun Shuiku, res., China A7 42
Mīzan Teferī, Eth. F7 62
Mizdah, Libya A2 62
Mize, Ms., U.S. F9 122
Mizen Head, c., Ire. I6 12
Mizen Head, c., Ire. J3 12
Mizhhir'ia, Ukr. A10 26
Mizhi, China C4 42
Mizil, Rom. E13 26
Mizoram, state, India G14 54
Mizpah Creek, stm., Mt., U.S. A7 126
Mizque, Bol. C3 90
Mizukaidō see Mitsukaidō, Japan C13 40
Mizusawa, Japan E14 38
Mjadzel, Bela. F9 10
Mjakit, Russia D19 34
Mjaksa, Russia B21 10
Mjölby, Swe. G6 8
Mjøsa, l., Nor. F4 8
Mkalama, Tan. E6 66
Mkhondvo, stm., Afr. E10 70
Mkokotoni, Tan. F7 66
Mkomazi, stm., S. Afr. G10 70
Mkulwe, Tan. F6 66
Mkuze, S. Afr. E10 70
Mkuze, stm., S. Afr. E11 70
Mkuze Game Reserve, S. Afr. E11 70
Mladá Boleslav, Czech Rep. F11 16
Mladenovac, Yugo. E7 26
Mlava, stm., Yugo. E8 26
Mława, Pol. C16 16
Mljet, Otok, i., Cro. H14 22
Mljet Nacionalni Park, p.o.i., Cro. H14 22
Mmabatho, S. Afr. D7 70
Mmadinare, Bots. B8 70
Moa, stm., Afr. H2 64
Moab, Ut., U.S. E7 132
Moala, i., Fiji q18 79e
Moama, Austl. K5 76
Moamba, Moz. D11 70
Moanda, Gabon E2 66
Moar Lake, l., Can. C18 124
Moate, Ire. H5 12
Moba, D.R.C. F5 66
Mobara, Japan D13 40
Mobaye, C.A.R. D4 66
Mobeetie, Tx., U.S. F8 128
Moberly, Mo., U.S. E5 120
Mobile, Al., U.S. G10 122
Mobile, Az., U.S. J4 132
Mobile, stm., Al., U.S. G11 122
Mobile Bay, b., Al., U.S. G10 122
Mobridge, S.D., U.S. B12 126
Moca, Dom. Rep. C12 102
Mocajuba, Braz. B1 88
Mo Cay, Viet. G8 48
Mocha see Al-Mukhā, Yemen G5 56
Mochudi, Bots. D8 70
Mocksville, N.C., U.S. I5 114
Moclips, Wa., U.S. C2 136
Môco, Morro de, mtn., Ang. C2 68
Mocoa, Col. G3 86
Mococa, Braz. K2 88
Mocodoene, Moz. C12 70
Mocoretá, Arg. E8 92
Moctezuma, Mex. G8 98
Moctezuma, stm., Mex. G8 98
Moctezuma, stm., Mex. E9 100
Mocuba, Moz. D6 68
Modane, Fr. D12 18
Modāsa, India G4 54
Modder, stm., S. Afr. F7 70
Módena, Italy F7 22
Modeste, Mount, mtn., B.C., Can. H6 138
Modesto, Ca., U.S. F4 134
Modica, Italy H8 24
Mödling, Aus. B13 22
Modowi, Indon. F9 44
Modra, Slov. H13 16
Moe, Austl. L6 76
Moeda, Braz. K3 88
Moei (Thaungyin), stm., Asia D3 48
Moema, Braz. J3 88
Moengo, Sur. B7 84
Moen-jo-Daro, hist., Pak. D10 56
Moenkopi, Az., U.S. G5 132
Moenkopi Wash, stm., Az., U.S. G6 132
Moeris, Lake see Qârûn, Birket, l., Egypt I1 58
Moeskroen see Mouscron, Bel. D12 14
Moffat, Scot., U.K. F9 12
Moga, India C5 54
Mogadiscio see Muqdisho, Som. D9 66
Mogadishu see Muqdisho, Som. D9 66
Mogalakwena, stm., S. Afr. C9 70
Mogami, stm., Japan A13 40
Mogaung, Mya. C8 46
Mogdy, Russia F15 34
Mogilno, Pol. D13 16
Mogincual, Moz. D7 68
Mogoča, Russia F12 34
Mogočin, Russia C14 32
Mogogh, Sudan F6 62
Mogok, Mya. A3 48
Mogollon Rim, clf, Az., U.S. I6 132
Mogor, Afg. B1 54
Mogotes, Col. D5 86
Mogotón, mtn., N.A. F4 102
Moguer, Spain G4 20
Mogzon, Russia F11 34
Mohács, Hung. C5 26
Mohall, N.D., U.S. F12 124
Mohammed, Râs, c., Egypt K5 58
Mohammedia, Mor. C3 64
Mohania, India F9 54
Mohawk, Mi., U.S. D10 118
Mohawk, stm., N.Y., U.S. B11 114
Mohe, China F13 34
Mohéli see Mwali, i., Com. C7 68
Mohnyin, Mya. D8 46
Mohokare (Caledon), stm., Afr. F8 70
Mohyliv-Podil's'kyi, Ukr. A14 26
Moi, Nor. G2 8
Moineşti, Rom. C13 26
Moira, stm., On., Can. D12 112
Moiraba, Braz. B1 88
Mo i Rana, Nor. C5 8
Moiseevka, Russia C13 32
Moisés Ville, Arg. E7 92
Moisie, Qc., Can. E17 106
Moisie, stm., Qc., Can. E17 106
Moitaco, Ven. C9 86
Mojácar, Spain G9 20
Mojave, Ca., U.S. H7 134
Mojave, stm., Ca., U.S. H9 134
Mojave Desert, des., Ca., U.S. D4 98
Mojero, stm., Russia C9 34
Mojiguaçu, stm., Braz. K2 88
Mojikit Lake, res., On., Can. A10 118
Moji-Mirim, Braz. L2 88
Mojo, Eth. F7 62
Moju, Braz. A1 88
Moju, stm., Braz. D8 84
Mōka, Japan C12 40
Mokāma, India F10 54
Mokapu Peninsula, pen., Hi., U.S. B4 78a
Mokau, stm., N.Z. D6 80
Mokelumne, stm., Ca., U.S. E5 134
Moknine, Tun. B7 64
Mokochu, Khao, mtn., Thai. E4 48
Mokokchūng, India C7 46
Mokolo, Cam. B2 66
Mokolo, stm., S. Afr. C8 70
Mokpalin, Mya. D3 48
Mokp'o, Kor., S. G7 38
Mokša, stm., Russia D6 32
Mokwa, Nig. H5 64
Mol, Bel. C14 14
Mola di Bari, Italy C11 24
Molat, Otok, i., Cro. F11 22
Moldary, Kaz. D13 32
Moldau see Vltava, stm., Czech Rep. F10 16
Moldavia, hist. reg., Rom. C13 26
Molde, Nor. E2 8
Moldova, ctry., Eur. B15 26
Moldova, stm., Rom. C13 26
Moldoveanu, Vârful, mtn., Rom. D11 26
Môle, Cap du, c., Haiti C11 102
Mole Creek, Austl. n13 77a
Molega Lake, l., N.S., Can. F12 110
Molène, Île de, i., Fr. F3 14
Molepolole, Bots. D7 70
Molėtai, Lith. E8 10
Molfetta, Italy C10 24
Molina, Chile G2 92
Molina de Aragón, Spain D9 20
Molina de Segura, Spain F9 20
Moline, Il., U.S. C7 120
Moline, Ks., U.S. D12 128
Molino, Fl., U.S. G11 122
Molino de Valdo de Piedras, Mex. E3 130
Molinos, Arg. B4 92
Molise, state, Italy C8 24
Mollendo, Peru G3 84
Mölln, Ger. C6 16
Mölndal, Swe. H4 8
Molodežjnaja, sci., Ant. B9 81
Molodogvardejskoe, Kaz. D11 32
Mologa, stm., Russia B19 10
Molokai, i., Hi., U.S. B5 78a
Molokai Fracture Zone, unds. G24 142
Molokovo, Russia B19 10
Molong, Austl. I7 76
Molopo, stm., Afr. E5 70
Moloundou, Cam. D3 66
Molson Lake, l., Mb., Can. E11 106
Molu, Pulau, i., Indon. G9 44
Moluccas see Maluku, is., Indon. F8 44
Molucca Sea see Maluku, Laut, Indon. F8 44
Molvoticy, Russia C15 10
Moma, Moz. D6 68
Moma, stm., Russia C17 34
Mombaça, Braz. C6 88
Mombasa, Kenya E7 66
Mombetsu, Japan B15 38
Momčilgrad, Blg. H12 26
Momi, Fiji p18 79e
Momotombo, Volcán, vol., Nic. F4 102
Mompono, D.R.C. D4 66
Mompós, Col. C4 86
Momskij hrebet, mts., Russia C18 34
Mon, state, Mya. E3 48
Møn, i., Den. I5 8
Mona, Ut., U.S. D5 132
Mona, Isla de, i., P.R. h14 96a
Mona, Punta, c., C.R. H6 102
Monaca, Pa., U.S. D5 114
Monach Islands, is., Scot., U.K. D5 12
Monaco, Mon. G4 22
Monaco, ctry., Eur. F13 18
Monadnock Mountain, mtn., N.H., U.S. B13 114
Monagas, state, Ven. C10 86
Monaghan, Ire. G6 12
Monaghan, state, Ire. G6 12
Monahans, Tx., U.S. C5 130
Monakino, Russia C10 38
Mona Passage, strt., N.A. C13 102
Monapo, Moz. C7 68
Monarch, S.C., U.S. B4 116
Monarch Mountain, mtn., B.C., Can. E5 138
Monarch Pass, p., Co., U.S. E10 132
Monashee Mountains, mts., B.C., Can. F12 138
Monastir, Tun. I4 24
Moncalieri, Italy F4 22
Moncalvo, Italy E5 22
Monção, Braz. B3 88
Mončegorsk, Russia B15 8
Mönchengladbach, Ger. E2 16
Monchique, Port. G2 20
Moncks Corner, S.C., U.S. C5 116
Monclova, Mex. B8 100
Moncton, N.B., Can. D12 110
Monday, stm., Para. B10 92
Mondego, stm., Port. D3 20
Mondjamboli, D.R.C. D4 66
Mondoubleau, Fr. F9 14
Mondovi, Wi., U.S. G7 118
Mondragone, Italy C7 24
Monemvasía, Grc. G6 28
Monessen, Pa., U.S. D5 114
Monesterio, Spain F4 20
Monett, Mo., U.S. H4 120
Monette, Ar., U.S. I7 120
Monfalcone, Italy E10 22
Monferrato, hist. reg., Italy F5 22
Monforte de Lemos, Spain B3 20
Monga, D.R.C. D4 66
Mongaguá, Braz. B14 92
Mongalla, Sudan F6 62
Mongers Lake, l., Austl. E3 74
Monggon Qulu, China B8 36
Möng Hai, Mya. B4 48
Möng Hsat, Mya. B4 48
Mongibello see Etna, Monte, vol., Italy G8 24
Möng Küng, Mya. B3 48
Möng Ma, Mya. B4 48
Möng Nai, Mya. B3 48
Mongo, Chad E3 62
Mongol Altayn nuruu, mts., Asia E16 32
Mongolia, ctry., Asia E14 30
Mongonu, Nig. G7 64
Möng Pai, Mya. C3 48
Möng Pawn, Mya. B3 48
Mongu, Zam. D3 68
Möng Yai, Mya. A4 48
Monico, Wi., U.S. F9 118
Monida Pass, p., U.S. F14 136
Monino, Russia E21 10
Moniquirá, Col. E5 86
Mõniste, Est. H12 8
Monitor Valley, val., Nv., U.S. E9 134
Mońki, Pol. C18 16
Monkira, Austl. E3 76
Monmouth, Wales, U.K. J10 12
Monmouth, Or., U.S. F3 136
Monmouth Mountain, mtn., B.C., Can. E7 138
Mono, stm., Afr. H5 64
Mono, Caño, stm., Col. E7 86
Mono Island, i., Sol. Is. d6 79b
Mono Lake, l., Ca., U.S. E7 134
Monon, In., U.S. H3 112
Monona, Ia., U.S. H7 118
Monona, Wi., U.S. A8 120
Monongahela, stm., U.S. E6 114
Monopoli, Italy D11 24
Monor, Hung. B6 26
Monreal del Campo, Spain D9 20
Monreale, Italy F7 24
Monroe, La., U.S. E6 122
Monroe, Mi., U.S. C2 114
Monroe, N.Y., U.S. C11 114
Monroe, N.C., U.S. B5 116
Monroe, Or., U.S. F3 136
Monroe, Ut., U.S. E4 132
Monroe, Va., U.S. G6 114
Monroe, Wa., U.S. C4 136
Monroe, Wi., U.S. B8 120
Monroe City, In., U.S. F10 120
Monroe Lake, res., In., U.S. E11 120
Monroeville, Al., U.S. F11 122
Monroeville, In., U.S. D1 114
Monroeville, Oh., U.S. C3 114
Monroeville, Pa., U.S. D6 114
Monrovia, Lib. H2 64
Mons, Bel. D12 14
Monsefú, Peru E2 84
Monselice, Italy E8 22
Monsenhor Hipólito, Braz. D5 88
Monsenhor Tabosa, Braz. C5 88
Mönsterås, Swe. H7 8
Montabaur, Ger. F3 16
Montagne, Neth. Ant. p23 104g
Montagu, S. Afr. H5 70
Montague, P.E., Can. D14 110
Montague, Mi., U.S. E3 112
Montague, Tx., U.S. H11 128
Montague, Isla, i., Mex. F5 98
Montague Island, i., Ak., U.S. E10 140
Montagu Island, i., S. Geor. K12 82
Montaigu, Fr. H7 14
Montalbano Ionico, Italy D10 24
Montalegre, Port. C3 20
Montana, Blg. F10 26
Montana, state, Blg. F10 26
Montana, state, U.S. B6 108

Name | Map Ref. | Page

Munte, Indon. C11 50
Muntok, Indon. E4 50
Munuscong Lake, l., N.A. B5 112
Muong Hinh, Viet. C7 48
Muong Saiapoun, Laos C5 48
Muonio, Fin. C10 8
Muping, China C9 42
Muqdisho (Mogadiscio), Som. D9 66
Muqui, Braz. K5 88
Mur (Mura), stm., Eur. D12 22
Mura (Mur), stm., Eur. D12 22
Murajá, Braz. D8 84
Murakami, Japan A12 40
Murana, Indon. F9 44
Muraši, Russia C7 32
Murat, Fr. D8 18
Murat, stm., Tur. H17 6
Murat Dağı, mtn., Tur. E12 28
Muratlı, Tur. B10 28
Muravera, Italy E3 24
Murayama, Japan A13 40
Murça, Port. C3 20
Murchison, Tx., U.S. E3 122
Murchison, stm., Austl. E2 74
Murchison, Mount, mtn., N.Z. F4 80
Murcia, Spain G9 20
Murcia, state, Spain G9 20
Mur-de-Barrez, Fr. E8 18
Murdo, S.D., U.S. D12 126
Mürefte, Tur. C10 28
Mureș, state, Rom. C11 26
Mureș (Maros), stm., Eur. C7 26
Muret, Fr. F7 18
Murewa, Zimb. D5 68
Murfreesboro, Ar., U.S. C5 122
Murfreesboro, Tn., U.S. I11 120
Murgab, Taj. B11 56
Murgab (Morghāb), stm., Asia B9 56
Murgha Kibzai, Pak. C2 54
Murgon, Austl. F8 76
Muri, Cook Is. a27 78j
Muriaé, Braz. K4 88
Muriaé, stm., Braz. K5 88
Muribeca dos Guararapes, Braz. E8 88
Murici, Braz. E8 88
Muricizal, stm., Braz. D1 88
Murīdke, Pak. C5 54
Muriege, Ang. C3 68
Müritz, l., Ger. C8 16
Murmansk, Russia B15 8
Murmanskaja oblast', co., Russia C16 8
Murnau, Ger. I7 16
Muro Lucano, Italy D9 24
Murom, Russia I19 8
Muromcevo, Russia C13 32
Muroran, Japan C14 38
Muroto, Japan F7 40
Muroto-zaki, c., Japan F7 40
Murowana Goślina, Pol. D13 16
Murphy, Id., U.S. G10 136
Murphy, N.C., U.S. A1 116
Murphys, Ca., U.S. E5 134
Murra Murra, Austl. G6 76
Murrat el-Kubra, Buheirat (Great Bitter Lake), l., Egypt H3 58
Murray, Ia., U.S. C3 120
Murray, Ky., U.S. H9 120
Murray, Ut., U.S. C5 132
Murray, stm., Austl. J2 76
Murray, stm., B.C., Can. B9 138
Murray, Lake, l., Pap. N. Gui. b3 79a
Murray, Lake, res., S.C., U.S. B4 116
Murray Bridge, Austl. J2 76
Murray Fracture Zone, unds. F24 142
Murray Harbour, P.E., Can. E14 110
Murray Maxwell Bay, b., N.T., Can. A14 106
Murray River, P.E., Can. D14 110
Murraysburg, S. Afr. G6 70
Murree, Pak. B4 54
Murrhardt, Ger. H5 16
Murrumbidgee, stm., Austl. J4 76
Murrumburrah, Austl. J7 76
Murrupula, Moz. D6 68
Mursala, Pulau, i., Indon. L4 48
Murshidābād, India F12 54
Murska Sobota, Slvn. D13 22
Murtajāpur, India H6 54
Murtee, Austl. H4 76
Murter, Otok, i., Cro. G12 22
Murtle Lake, l., B.C., Can. D11 138
Murtoa, Austl. K4 76
Murtosa, Port. D2 20
Muru, Capu di, c., Fr. H14 18
Murud, India B1 53
Murud, Gunong, mtn., Malay. B9 50
Murukta, Russia C9 34
Murung, stm., Indon. C9 50
Mururoa, at., Fr. Poly. F13 72
Murwāra (Katni), India G8 54
Murwillumbah, Austl. G9 76
Murzuq, Libya B2 62
Murzūq, Idhān, des., Libya C2 62
Mürzzuschlag, Aus. C12 22
Muş, Tur. B5 56
Mūsa (Mūša), stm., Eur. D6 10
Mūša (Mūsa), stm., Eur. D6 10
Mûsa, Gebel (Sinai, Mount), mtn., Egypt J5 58
Musadi, D.R.C. E4 66
Musā'id, Libya A4 62
Musala, mtn., Blg. G10 26
Musan-ŭp, Kor., N. C8 38
Muscat see Masqaṭ, Oman E8 56
Muscat and Oman see Oman, ctry., Asia F8 56
Muscatine, Ia., U.S. C6 120
Muscle Shoals, Al., U.S. C11 122
Musclow, Mount, mtn., B.C., Can. C3 138
Muscoda, Wi., U.S. A7 120
Musgrave, Austl. B8 74
Mus-Haja, gora, mtn., Russia D17 34
Mushie, D.R.C. E3 66
Mushin, Nig. H5 64
Mūsi, stm., India C4 53
Musi, stm., Indon. E4 50
Musicians Seamounts, unds. F22 142
Muskegon, Mi., U.S. E3 112
Muskegon, stm., Mi., U.S. E4 112
Muskingum, stm., Oh., U.S. E4 114
Muskogee, Ok., U.S. I2 120
Muskoka, Lake, l., On., Can. D10 112
Musoma, Tan. E6 66
Musquodoboit Harbour, N.S., Can. F13 110
Mussau Island, i., Pap. N. Gui. a4 79a
Musselshell, stm., Mt., U.S. G6 124
Mussende, Ang. C2 68
Mussidan, Fr. D6 18
Mussomeli, Italy G7 24
Mussuma, Ang. C3 68
Mustafakemalpaşa, Tur. C11 28
Mustafa Kemal Paşa, stm., Tur. D11 28
Mustahīl, Eth. F8 62
Mustāng, Nepal D9 54
Mustang Draw, stm., Tx., U.S. B5 130
Mustang Island, i., Tx., U.S. G10 130
Musters, Lago, l., Arg. I3 90
Mustla, Est. B8 10
Mustvee, Est. B9 10
Muswellbrook, Austl. I8 76
Mût, Egypt B5 62
Mut, Tur. B4 58
Mutá, Ponta do, c., Braz. G6 88
Mutanchiang see Mudanjiang, China B8 38
Mutankiang see Mudanjiang, China B8 38
Mutare, Zimb. D5 68
Mutlu (Rezovska), stm., Eur. G14 26
Mutoko, Zimb. D5 68
Mutoraj, Russia B17 32
Mutsamudu, Com. C7 68
Mutshatsha, D.R.C. G4 66
Mutsu, Japan D14 38
Mutsu-wan, b., Japan D14 38
Mutton Bay, Qc., Can. i22 107a
Mutuípe, Braz. G6 88
Mutum, Braz. J5 88
Mu Us Shamo (Ordos Desert), des., China B3 42
Mūvattupula, India F3 53
Muxima, Ang. B1 68
Muyinga, Bdi. E6 66
Muyumba, D.R.C. F5 66
Muzaffarābād, Pak. A4 54
Muzaffargarh, Pak. C3 54
Muzaffarnagar, India D6 54
Muzaffarpur, India E10 54
Muzat, stm., China C2 36
Muži, Russia A10 32
Muzillac, Fr. G6 14
Muztag, mtn., China D2 36
Muztag, mtn., China A5 46
Mvolo, Sudan F6 62
Mvoti, stm., S. Afr. F10 70
Mvuma, Zimb. D5 68
Mwadui, Tan. E6 66
Mwali, i., Com. C7 68
Mwanza, Tan. E6 66
Mweelrea, mtn., Ire. H3 12
Mweka, D.R.C. E4 66
Mwene-Ditu, D.R.C. F4 66
Mwenezi, Zimb. B10 70
Mwenezi, stm., Afr. B10 70
Mweru, Lake, l., Afr. B4 68
Mweru Wantipa, Lake, l., Zam. B4 68
Mwilitau Islands (Purdy Islands), is., Pap. N. Gui. a4 79a
Mwinilunga, Zam. C3 68
Myājlār, India E3 54
Myall Lakes National Park, p.o.i., Austl. I9 76
Myanaung, Mya. C2 48
Myanmar (Burma), ctry., Asia D8 46
Myaungmya, Mya. D2 48
Mycenae see Mykínes, hist., Grc. F5 28
Myebon, Mya. B1 48
Myingyan, Mya. B2 48
Myitkyinā, Mya. C8 46
Myitnge, stm., Mya. B3 48
Myitta, Mya. E4 48
Myittha, Mya. B2 48
Myittha, stm., Mya. B2 48
Myjava, Slov. H13 16
Mykines, i., Far. Is. m34 8b
Mykínes, hist., Grc. F5 28
Mykolaïv, Ukr. F15 6
Mykolaïv, co., Ukr. B17 26
Mykolaïvka, Ukr. C16 26
Mýkonos, i., Grc. F8 28
Myla, Russia D24 8
Mymensingh (Nasirābād), Bngl. F13 54
Mynaral, Kaz. E12 32
Mynfontein, S. Afr. G6 70
Myohaung, Mya. B1 48
Myohyang-san, mtn., Kor., N. D7 38
Myōkō-san, vol., Japan C11 40
Myra, hist., Tur. G12 28
Mýrdalsjökull, ice, Ice. I30 8a
Myrskylä, Fin. F11 8
Myrtle Beach, S.C., U.S. C7 116
Myrtle Creek, Or., U.S. G3 136
Myrtle Grove, Fl., U.S. G11 122
Myrtle Point, Or., U.S. G2 136
Myrtletowne, Ca., U.S. C1 134
Myškino, Russia C21 10
Myślenice, Pol. G15 16
Myślibórz, Pol. D10 16
Mysłowice, Pol. F15 16
Mysore, India E3 53
Mysore see Karnātaka, state, India F4 46
Mystic, Ct., U.S. C14 114
Mystrás, hist., Grc. F5 28
Mys Vhodnoj, Russia B6 34
Myszków, Pol. F15 16
Myt, Russia H20 8
My Tho, Viet. G8 48
Mytilíni, Grc. D9 28
Mytišči, Russia E20 10
Myton, Ut., U.S. C6 132
Mývatn, l., Ice. k31 8a
Mzimba, Mwi. C5 68
Mzimvubu, stm., S. Afr. G9 70
Mzintlava, stm., S. Afr. G9 70
Mzuzu, Mwi. C5 68

N

Na (Tengtiao), stm., Asia A6 48
Naab, stm., Ger. G7 16
Naalehu, Hi., U.S. D6 78a
Naas, Ire. H6 12
Nababeep, S. Afr. F3 70
Nabari, Japan E9 40
Nabberu, Lake, l., Austl. E4 74
Nabburg, Ger. G8 16
Naberežnye Čelny, Russia C8 32
Nabeul, Tun. H4 24
Nābha, India C6 54
Nabire, Indon. F10 44
Nabī Shu'ayb, Jabal an-, mtn., Yemen F5 56
Nabouwalu, Fiji p19 79e
Nabq, Egypt J5 58
Nabula, China C7 54
Nābulus, W.B. F6 58
Nacala-a-Velha, Moz. C7 68
Nachingwea, Tan. G7 66
Nāchna, India E3 54
Náchod, Czech Rep. F12 16
Nachvak Fiord, b., Nf., Can. F13 141
Nacimiento, Chile H1 92
Nacimiento, Lake, res., Ca., U.S. H5 134
Naco, Mex. F8 98
Naco, Az., U.S. L6 132
Nacogdoches, Tx., U.S. F4 122
Nácori Chico, Mex. G8 98
Nacozari de García, Mex. F8 98
Ñacunday, Para. B10 92
Nadarivatu, Fiji p18 79e
Nadela, Spain B3 20
Nadiād, India G4 54
Nadi Bay, b., Fiji p18 79e
Nădlac, Rom. C7 26
Naduri, Fiji p19 79e
Nadvoicy, Russia E16 8
Nadym, Russia A12 32
Nadym, stm., Russia A12 32
Naenwa, India F5 54
Nærbø, Nor. G1 8
Næstved, Den. I4 8
Nafada, Nig. G7 64
Nafī, Sau. Ar. D5 56
Náfpaktos, Grc. E4 28
Náfplio, Grc. F5 28
Nafūsah, Jabal, hills, Libya A2 62
Naga, Phil. D4 52
Nagahama, Japan D9 40
Nagahama, Japan F5 40
Naga Hills, mts., Asia C7 46
Nagai, Japan A12 40
Nagai Island, i., Ak., U.S. F7 140
Nāgāland, state, India C7 46
Nagano, Japan C11 40
Nagano, state, Japan C11 40
Nagaoka, Japan B11 40
Nagaon, India E14 54
Nāgappattinam, India F4 53
Nagara, stm., Japan D9 40
Nagarhole Tiger Reserve, India E2 53
Nāgārjuna Sāgar, res., India C4 53
Nagarote, Nic. F4 102
Nagasaki, Japan G2 40
Nagasaki, state, Japan G2 40
Nagato, Japan E4 40
Nāgaur, India E4 54
Nāgāvali, stm., India B6 53
Nagda, India G5 54
Nāgercoil, India G3 53
Nagīna, India D7 54
Nagłowice, Pol. F15 16
Nago, Japan I19 39a
Nagold, Ger. H4 16
Nagornyj, Russia E13 34
Nagoya, Japan D9 40
Nāgpur, India H7 54
Nagqu, China C14 54
Nagua, Dom. Rep. C12 102
Naguabo, P.R. B4 104a
Nagyatád, Hung. C4 26
Nagybánya see Baia Mare, Rom. B10 26
Nagyecsed, Hung. B9 26
Nagykanizsa, Hung. C4 26
Nagykáta, Hung. B6 26
Nagykőrös, Hung. B6 26
Naha, Japan I18 39a
Nahabuan, Indon. C9 50
Nāhan, India C6 54
Nahanni Butte, N.T., Can. C6 106
Nahariyya, Isr. E5 58
Nahāvand, Iran C6 56
Nahe, China B9 36
Nahe, stm., Ger. G3 16
Nahma, Mi., U.S. C3 112
Nahodka, Russia A13 32
Nahodka, Russia C10 38
Nahoe, Fr. Poly. r19 78g
Nahoï, Cap, c., Vanuatu j16 79d
Nahuel Huapi, Lago, l., Arg. H2 90
Nahuel Niyeu, Arg. H3 90
Naica, Mex. B6 100
Naicam, Sk., Can. B9 124
Naila, Ger. F7 16
Naiman Qi, China C4 38
Nā'īn, Iran C7 56
Naini Tāl, India D7 54
Nainpur, India G8 54
Nairai, i., Fiji p19 79e
Nairn, La., U.S. H9 122
Nairobi, Kenya E7 66
Naitauba, i., Fiji p20 79e
Naivasha, Kenya E7 66
Naizishan, China C7 38
Najac, Fr. E8 18
Najafābād, Iran C7 56
Najasa, stm., Cuba B9 102
Najd (Nejd), hist. reg., Sau. Ar. D5 56
Najībābād, India D7 54
Najin, Kor., N. C9 38
Naka, stm., Japan C13 40
Nakajō, Japan A12 40
Nakama, Japan F3 40
Nakaminato, Japan C13 40
Nakamura, Japan G5 40
Nakano, Japan C11 40
Nakano-shima, i., Japan k19 39a
Nakasongola, Ug. D6 66
Nakatsu, Japan F4 40
Nakatsugawa, Japan D10 40
Nakhl, Egypt I4 58
Nakhon Nayok, Thai. E5 48
Nakhon Pathom, Thai. F5 48
Nakhon Phanom, Thai. D7 48
Nakhon Ratchasima, Thai. E6 48
Nakhon Sawan, Thai. E4 48
Nakhon Si Thammarat, Thai. H5 48
Nakhon Thai, Thai. D5 48
Nakina, On., Can. A12 118
Nakło nad Notecią, Pol. C13 16
Nakodar, India C5 54
Nakonde, Zam. B5 68
Nakskov, Den. I4 8
Naktong-gang, stm., Kor., S. C1 40
Nakuru, Kenya E7 66
Nakusp, B.C., Can. F13 138
Nālanda, India F10 54
Nalayh, Mong. B6 36
Nalbāri, India E13 54
Nal'čik, Russia F6 32
Nałęczów, Pol. E18 16
Nalgonda, India C4 53
Nallamalla Hills, mts., India D4 53
Nallıhan, Tur. C14 28
Nalón, stm., Spain A5 20
Nalong, China J2 42
Nālūt, Libya A2 62
Nam (Nan'a), stm., Asia B4 48
Namaacha, Moz. D10 70
Namacurra, Moz. D6 68
Namadgi National Park, p.o.i., Austl. J7 76
Namak, Daryācheh-ye, l., Iran C7 56
Namakan Lake, l., N.A. C6 118
Nāmakkal, India F4 53
Namangan, Uzb. F12 32
Namanyere, Tan. F6 66
Namapa, Moz. C6 68
Namarrói, Moz. D6 68
Namatanai, Pap. N. Gui. a5 79a
Nambour, Austl. F9 76
Nam Co, l., China C13 54
Nam Dinh, Viet. B7 48
Nam Du, Quan Dao, is., Viet. H6 48
Nameh, Indon. B10 50
Namen see Namur, Bel. D13 14
Namerikawa, Japan C10 40
Nametil, Moz. D6 68
Nam-gang, stm., Kor., N. E7 38
Namhae-do, i., Kor., S. G8 38
Namhan-gang, stm., Kor., S. F7 38
Namhkam, Mya. D8 46
Namib Desert, des., Nmb. E1 68
Namibe, Ang. D1 68
Namibia, ctry., Afr. E2 68
Namib Naukluft Park, p.o.i., Nmb. D2 70
Namie, Japan B14 40
Namies, S. Afr. F4 70
Namji-ri, Kor., S. D1 40
Namlea, Indon. F8 44
Namling, China D12 54
Nam Nao National Park, p.o.i., Thai. D5 48
Nam Ngum Reservoir, res., Laos C6 48
Namnoi, Khao, mtn., Mya. G4 48
Namoi, stm., Austl. H7 76
Nampa, Id., U.S. G10 136
Nampala, Mali F3 64
Nam Pat, Thai. D5 48
Nampawng, Mya. A3 48
Nam Phan (Cochin China), hist. reg., Viet. G8 48
Namp'o, Kor., N. E6 38
Nampula, Moz. D6 68
Namsang, Mya. B3 48
Namsen, stm., Nor. D5 8
Namsos, Nor. D4 8
Nam Tok, Thai. E4 48
Nam Tok Mae Surin National Park, p.o.i., Thai. C4 48
Namtu, Mya. A3 48
Namu, B.C., Can. E3 138
Namuka-I-Lau, i., Fiji q20 79e
Namúli, Serra, mts., Moz. D6 68
Namur (Namen), Bel. D13 14
Namutoni, Nmb. D2 68
Namwala, Zam. D4 68
Namwŏn, Kor., S. G7 38
Namysłów, Pol. E13 16
Nan, Thai. C5 48
Nan, stm., Thai. D5 48
Nan'a (Nam), stm., Asia B4 48
Nanaimo, B.C., Can. G6 138
Nanam, Kor., N. D8 38
Nan'an, China I8 42
Nanango, Austl. F8 76
Nanao, Japan B9 40
Nanatsu-jima, is., Japan B9 40
Nanbu, China F1 42
Nancha, China B10 36
Nanchang, China G6 42
Nancheng, China H7 42
Nancheng see Hanzhong, China E2 42
Nanching see Nanjing, China E8 42
Nanchong, China F2 42
Nanchuan, China G2 42
Nanch'ung see Nanchong, China F2 42
Nancowry Island, i., India G7 46
Nancy, Fr. F15 14
Nanda Devi, mtn., India C8 54
Nandaime, Nic. G4 102
Nandan, Japan E7 40
Nānded, India B3 53
Nāndgaon, India H5 54
Nandi Drug, mtn., India E3 53
Nandikotkūr, India D4 53
Nandu, China F8 42
Nandu, stm., China L4 42
Nāndūra, India H6 54
Nandurbār, India H4 54
Nandyāl, India D4 53
Nanfen, China D5 38
Nanfeng, China H7 42
Nanga-Eboko, Cam. D2 66
Nangakelawit, Indon. C8 50
Nangamau, Indon. D7 50
Nangaobat, Indon. C8 50
Nanga Parbat, mtn., Pak. B11 56
Nangapinoh, Indon. D7 50
Nangarhār, state, Afg. A3 54
Nangatayap, Indon. D7 50
Nanggala Hill, mtn., Sol. Is. e7 79b
Nangin, Mya. G4 48
Nangnim-ŭp, Kor., N. D7 38
Nangong, China C6 42
Nang Rong, Thai. E6 48
Nanguan, China C5 42
Nanhua, China F5 36
Nan Hulsan Hu, l., China D4 36
Nanika Lake, l., B.C., Can. C3 138
Nanjangūd, India E3 53
Nanjiang, China E2 42
Nanjing, China I7 42
Nanjing (Nanking), China E8 42
Nankang, China I6 42
Nanking see Nanjing, China E8 42
Nankoku, Japan F6 40
Nankye, Mya. E3 48
Nanle, China C6 42
Nanlei (Loi), stm., Asia A4 48
Nanling, China F8 42
Nan Ling, mts., China I5 42
Nanliu, stm., China J3 42
Nanlou Shan, mtn., China C7 38
Nannine, Austl. E3 74
Nanning, China J3 42
Na Noi, Thai. C5 48
Nanortalik, Grnld. E16 141
Nanpan, stm., China G5 36
Nānpāra, India E8 54
Nanpiao, China A9 42
Nanping, China E5 36
Nanping, China H8 42
Nansei, Japan E9 40
Nansei-shotō (Ryukyu Islands), is., Japan k19 39a
Nan Shan see Qilian Shan, mts., China D4 36
Nanshan Island, i., Asia C6 44
Nantais, Lac, l., Qc., Can. C16 106
Nantai-zan, vol., Japan C12 40
Nanterre, Fr. F11 14
Nantes, Fr. G7 14
Nantes à Brest, Canal de, can., Fr. F5 14
Nanticoke, Pa., U.S. C9 114
Nanto, Japan E9 40
Nanton, Ab., Can. F17 138
Nantong, China E9 42
Nant'ou, Tai. J9 42
Nantucket, Ma., U.S. C15 114
Nantucket Island, i., Ma., U.S. C15 114
Nantucket Sound, strt., Ma., U.S. C15 114
Nantulo, Moz. C6 68
Nantung see Nantong, China E9 42
Nanty Glo, Pa., U.S. H11 112
Nanu, Pap. N. Gui. b3 79a
Nanuku Passage, strt., Fiji p20 79e
Nanumea, at., Tuvalu D8 72
Nanuque, Braz. I5 88
Nanusa, Kepulauan, is., Indon. E8 44
Nanxi, China G1 42
Nanxian, China G5 42
Nanxiang, China F9 42
Nanxiong, China I6 42
Nanyang, China E5 42
Nanyang Hu, l., China D7 42
Nanyi Hu, l., China F8 42
Nan-yō, Japan A13 40
Nanyuki, Kenya D7 66
Nanzamu, China C6 38
Nanzhao, China E5 42
Nao, Cabo de la see Nau, Cap de la, c., Spain F11 20
Naococane, Lac, l., Qc., Can. E16 106
Naogaon, Bngl. F12 54
Naokot, Pak. F2 54
Náousa, Grc. C5 28
Napa, Ca., U.S. E3 134
Napa, stm., Ca., U.S. E3 134
Napaku, Indon. B9 50
Napalkovo, Russia C3 34
Napanee, On., Can. D12 112
Napassoq, Grnld. D15 141
Naperville, Il., U.S. C9 120
Napido, Indon. F10 44
Napier, N.Z. D7 80
Napier, Mount, hill, Austl. C5 74
Napier Mountains, mts., Ant. B10 81
Naples see Napoli, Italy D8 24
Naples, Fl., U.S. J4 116
Naples, Id., U.S. B10 136
Naples, N.Y., U.S. B8 114
Naples, Tx., U.S. D4 122
Napo, state, Ec. H3 86
Napo, stm., S.A. D3 84
Napoleon, N.D., U.S. A13 126
Napoleonville, La., U.S. H7 122
Napoli (Naples), Italy D8 24
Napoli, Golfo di, b., Italy D8 24
Nappamerrie, Austl. F3 76
Nappanee, In., U.S. G4 112
Napu, Indon. H11 50
Nara, Japan E8 40
Nara, Mali F3 64
Nara, state, Japan E8 40
Nāra, stm., Pak. F2 54
Nara, stm., Russia E20 10
Narač, vozero, l., Bela. F9 10
Naracoorte, Austl. K3 76
Naradhan, Austl. I6 76
Naraini, India F8 54
Naramata, B.C., Can. G11 138
Naranjal, Ec. I2 86
Naranjito, P.R. B3 104a
Narasannapeta, India B7 53
Narasapur, India C5 53
Narasaraopet, India C4 53
Narasun, Russia A7 36
Narathiwat, Thai. I5 48
Naraṷ (Narew), stm., Eur. D17 16
Nārāyanganj, Bngl. G13 54
Nārāyani (Gandak), stm., Asia E10 54
Nārāyanpet, India C3 53
Narbonne, Fr. F8 18
Nardò, Italy D11 24
Nares Strait, strt., N.A. B11 141
Narew (Naraṷ), stm., Eur. D17 16
Nargund, India D2 53
Nariño, state, Col. G3 86
Narita, Japan D13 40
Nariva Swamp, sw., Trin. s12 105f
Nar'jan-Mar, Russia C25 8
Narkatiāganj, India E10 54
Narlı, Tur. A8 58
Narmada, stm., India H4 54
Nārnaul, India D6 54
Narodnaja, gora, mtn., Russia B10 32
Narodnaya, Mount see Narodnaja, gora, mtn., Russia B10 32
Naro-Fominsk, Russia E19 10
Narol, Pol. F19 16
Narooma, Austl. K8 76
Nārowāl, Pak. B5 54
Narrabri, Austl. H7 76
Narran, stm., Austl. G7 76
Narrandera, Austl. J6 76
Narraway, stm., Can. B11 138
Narrogin, Austl. F3 74
Narromine, Austl. I6 76
Narsaq see Narssaq, Grnld. E16 141
Narsimhapur, India G7 54
Narsinghgarh, India G6 54
Narsīpatnam, India C6 53
Narssaq, Grnld. E16 141
Naru, Japan G1 40
Naruto, Japan E7 40
Narva, Est. G13 8
Narva, Russia C16 32
Narva, stm., Eur. A11 10
Narvik, Nor. B7 8
Narvskij zaliv, b., Eur. A10 10
Narvskoe vodohranilišče, l., Eur. A10 10
Narwāna, India D6 54
Narwietooma, Austl. D6 74
Narym, Russia C14 32
Naryn, Kyrg. F13 32
Naryn, stm., Asia F13 32
Narynkol, Kaz. F13 32
Näsåker, Swe. E7 8
Na San, Thai. H4 48
Nasawa, Vanuatu j17 79d
Nasbinals, Fr. E9 18
Nasca, Peru F2 84
Nase see Naze, Japan k19 39a
Nash, Tx., U.S. D4 122
Nāshik, India H4 54
Nashua, Ia., U.S. B5 120
Nashua, N.H., U.S. B14 114
Nashville, Ar., U.S. D5 122
Nashville, Il., U.S. F8 120
Nashville, In., U.S. E11 120
Nashville, Mi., U.S. F4 112
Nashville, N.C., U.S. I8 114
Nashville, Tn., U.S. H11 120
Nashwaak, stm., N.B., Can. D10 110
Nashwauk, Mn., U.S. D5 118
Nasielsk, Pol. D16 16
Näsijärvi, l., Fin. F10 8
Nāṣir, Sudan F6 62
Nāṣir, Buheirat see Nasser, Lake, res., Afr. C6 62
Nasīrābād, India E5 54
Nasr, Egypt H1 58
Nass, stm., B.C., Can. E5 106
Nassarawa, Nig. H6 64
Nassau, Bah. m18 104f
Nassau, N.Y., U.S. B12 114
Nassau International Airport, Bah. m18 104f
Nassau Island, i., Cook Is. E10 72
Nassawadox, Va., U.S. G10 114
Nasser, Lake (Nâsir, Buheirat), res., Afr. C6 62
Nässjö, Swe. H6 8
Nastapoka Islands, is., N.T., Can. D15 106
Nasu, Japan B13 40
Nasu-dake, vol., Japan B12 40
Nasukoin Mountain, mtn., Mt., U.S. B12 136
Nasva, Russia D13 10
Nata, Bots. E4 68
Nata, stm., Afr. B8 70
Natal, Braz. C8 88
Natal, B.C., Can. G16 138
Natal, Indon. C1 50
Natal see KwaZulu-Natal, state, S. Afr. F10 70
Natalia, Tx., U.S. E9 130
Natalkuz Lake, res., B.C., Can. C5 138
Natanes Plateau, plat., Az., U.S. J6 132
Natashquan, stm., Can. i21 107a
Natchez, Ms., U.S. F7 122
Natchez Trace Parkway, p.o.i., U.S. E9 122
Natchitoches, La., U.S. F5 122
Natewa Bay, b., Fiji p19 79e
Nāthdwāra, India F4 54
Natimuk, Austl. K3 76
Nation, stm., B.C., Can. A7 138
National City, Ca., U.S. K8 134
Natitingou, Benin G5 64
Native Bay, b., N.T., Can. C14 106
Natividade, Braz. F2 88
Natkyizin, Mya. E3 48
Natoma, Ks., U.S. B9 128
Nator, Bngl. F12 54
Natori, Japan A13 40
Natron, Lake, l., Afr. E7 66
Natrûn, Wadi el-, val., Egypt H1 58
Nattaung, mtn., Mya. C3 48
Natuna Besar, i., Indon. A6 50
Natuna Besar, Kepulauan, is., Indon. A5 50
Natuna Selatan, Kepulauan, is., Indon. B6 50
Natural Bridge, misc. cult., Va., U.S. G6 114
Natural Bridges National Monument, p.o.i., Ut., U.S. F6 132
Naturaliste, Cape, c., Austl. F2 74
Naturno, Italy D7 22
Nau, Cap de la, c., Spain F11 20
Naucelle, Fr. E8 18
Naucratis, hist., Egypt H1 58
Nauen, Ger. D8 16
Naugatuck, Ct., U.S. C12 114
Naughton, On., Can. B8 112
Naujamiestis, Lith. E6 10
Naujan, Lake, l., Phil. D3 52
Naujoji Akmenė, Lith. D5 10
Naumburg, Ger. E7 16
Naunglon, Mya. D3 48
Nā'ūr, Jord. G6 58
Nauru, state, Oc. p17 78f
Nauru International Airport, Nauru q17 78f
Nauški, Russia F10 34
Nausori, Fiji p19 79e
Nauta, Peru D3 84
Nautanwa, India E9 54
Nautla, Mex. E10 100
Nauvoo, Il., U.S. D6 120
Nava, Mex. A8 100
Navadwip, India G12 54
Navael'nja, Bela. G8 10
Navahrudak, Bela. G8 10
Navajo, N.M., U.S. H7 132
Navajo Mountain, mtn., Ut., U.S. F6 132
Navajo National Monument, p.o.i., Az., U.S. G6 132
Navajo Reservoir, res., U.S. G9 132
Naval, Phil. C7 44
Navalmoral de la Mata, Spain E5 20
Navan, Ire. H6 12
Navapolack, Bela. E11 10
Navāpur, India H4 54
Navarin, mys, c., Russia D24 34
Navarino, Isla, i., Chile K3 90
Navarra, state, Spain B9 20
Navarro Mills Lake, res., Tx., U.S. F2 122
Navasëlki, Bela. H7 10
Navasota, Tx., U.S. G2 122
Navasota, stm., Tx., U.S. D11 130
Navassa, N.C., U.S. B7 116
Navassa Island, i., N.A. C10 102
Navesnoe, Russia H20 10
Navia, Arg. G4 92
Navia, stm., Spain A4 20
Navidad, Chile F1 92
Navidad, stm., Tx., U.S. E11 130
Navio, Riacho do, stm., Braz. E6 88
Naviti, i., Fiji p18 79e
Navlja, Russia H17 10
Năvodari, Rom. E15 26
Navoi, Uzb. F11 32
Navojoa, Mex. B4 100
Navolato, Mex. C5 100
Navsāri, India H4 54
Nawa see Naha, Japan I18 39a
Nawābganj, Bngl. F12 54
Nawābganj, India E8 54
Nawābshāh, Pak. E2 54
Nawāda, India F10 54
Nāwah, Afg. B1 54
Nawalgarh, India E5 54
Nawāpāra, India H8 54
Naxçıvan, Azer. B6 56
Naxi, China G1 42
Náxos, i., Grc. F8 28
Nayāgarh, India H10 54
Nayarit, state, Mex. E6 100
Nāy Band, Kūh-e, mtn., Iran C8 56
Naylor, Mo., U.S. H7 120
Nayoro, Japan B15 38
Nazaré, Braz. D2 88
Nazaré, Port. E1 20
Nazaré da Mata, Braz. D8 88
Nazaré do Piauí, Braz. D4 88
Nazareth see Nazerat, Isr. F6 58
Nazarovo, Russia C16 32
Nazas, Mex. C6 100
Nazas, stm., Mex. C6 100
Nazca Ridge, unds. K5 144
Naze, Japan k19 39a
Naze, The see Lindesnes, c., Nor. H2 8
Naẓerat (Nazareth), Isr. F6 58
Naẓerat'Illit, Isr. F6 58
Nazija, Russia A14 10
Nazilli, Tur. F11 28
Nazina, Russia B13 32
Nazko, stm., B.C., Can. D7 138
Nazlet el-'Amûdein, Egypt J1 58
Nazran', Russia F7 32
Nazrēt, Eth. F7 62
Nazwá, Oman E8 56
Nazyvaevsk, Russia C12 32
N'dalatando, Ang. B1 68
Ndali, Benin H5 64
Ndélé, C.A.R. C4 66
Ndendé, Gabon E2 66
N'Djamena (Fort-Lamy), Chad E3 62
Ndjolé, Gabon E2 66
Ndogo, Lagune, l., Gabon E2 66
Ndola, Zam. C4 68
Ndumu Game Reserve, S. Afr. E11 70
Neabul Creek, stm., Austl. F6 76
Neagh, Lough, l., N. Ire., U.K. G6 12
Neah Bay, Wa., U.S. B2 136
Neale, Lake, l., Austl. D6 74
Neamț, state, Rom. B13 26
Néa Páfos (Paphos), Cyp. D3 58
Neápoli, Grc. G6 28
Near Islands, is., Ak., U.S. g21 140a
Neath, Wales, U.K. J9 12
Nebine Creek, stm., Austl. G6 76
Nebitdag, Turkmen. B7 56
Neblina, Cerro de la see Neblina, Pico da, mtn., S.A. G9 86
Neblina, Pico da, mtn., S.A. G9 86
Nebo, Il., U.S. E7 120
Nebo, Mount, mtn., Ut., U.S. D5 132
Nebolči, Russia A16 10
Nebraska, state, U.S. C7 108
Nebraska City, Ne., U.S. D1 120
Necedah, Wi., U.S. G8 118
Nechako, stm., B.C., Can. C7 138
Nechako Reservoir, res., B.C., Can. C5 138
Neches, Tx., U.S. F3 122
Neches, stm., Tx., U.S. G4 122
Nechí, Col. C4 86
Nechí, stm., Col. D4 86
Nechranice, vodní nádrž, res., Czech Rep. F9 16
Neckarsulm, Ger. G5 16
Necker Island, i., Br. Vir. Is. d9 104b
Necochea, Arg. I8 92
Nederland, Tx., U.S. H4 122
Nêdong, China D13 54
Needhams Point, c., Barb. n8 105d
Needle Mountain, mtn., Wy., U.S. F17 136
Needles, Ca., U.S. I2 132
Needville, Tx., U.S. H3 122
Neegro, Qooriga, b., Som. C10 66
Ñeembucú, state, Para. C8 92
Neenah, Wi., U.S. G10 118
Neepawa, Mb., Can. D14 124
Nefëdovo, Russia C12 32
Nefta, Tun. C6 64
Neftçala, Azer. B6 56
Neftejugansk, Russia B12 32
Nefza, Tun. H3 24
Negage, Ang. B2 68

I•40 Nega-Norm

Name — Map Ref. — Page

Negara, Indon. H9 50
Negara, stm., Indon. E9 50
Negaunee, Mi., U.S. B2 112
Negēlē, Eth. F7 62
Negeribatin, Indon. F4 50
Negeri Sembilan, state, Malay. K6 48
Negev Desert see HaNegev, reg., Isr. H5 58
Negombo, Sri L. H4 53
Negra, Laguna, l., Ur. G11 92
Negreira, Spain B2 20
Nègres, Pointe des, c., Mart. k6 105c
Negrești-Oaș, Rom. B10 26
Negritos, Peru D1 84
Negro, stm., Arg. H4 90
Negro, stm., Braz. C13 92
Negro, stm., Col. E4 86
Negro, stm., Para. B9 92
Negro, stm., S.A. I11 86
Negro, stm., S.A. F9 92
Negros, i., Phil. F4 52
Nehalem, stm., Or., U.S. E3 136
Neharèlae, Bela. G9 10
Nehawka, Ne., U.S. D1 120
Nehbandān, Iran C8 56
Nehe see Nahe, China B9 36
Néhoué, Baie de, b., N. Cal. m14 79d
Neiba, Dom. Rep. C12 102
Neichiang see Neijiang, China G1 42
Neidpath, Sk., Can. D6 124
Neiges, Piton des, mtn., Reu. i10 69a
Neijiang, China G1 42
Neikiang see Neijiang, China G1 42
Neilburg, Sk., Can. B4 124
Neillsville, Wi., U.S. G8 118
Nei Monggol, state, China C7 36
Nei Mongol see Nei Monggol, state, China C7 36
Neiqiu, China C6 42
Neira, Col. E4 86
Neisse see Lausitzer Neisse, stm., Eur. F10 16
Neisse see Nysa Łużycka, stm., Eur. E10 16
Neiva, Col. F4 86
Neixiang, China E4 42
Neja, Russia G20 8
Nejapa de Madero, Mex. G11 100
Nejd see Najd, hist. reg., Sau. Ar. D5 56
Nejdek, Czech Rep. F8 16
Nek'emtē, Eth. F7 62
Nelichu, mtn., Sudan F6 62
Nelidovo, Russia D15 10
Neligh, Ne., U.S. E14 126
Neljaty, Russia E12 34
Nel'kan, Russia E16 34
Nellikuppam, India F4 53
Nellore, India D4 53
Nel'ma, Russia G16 34
Nelson, B.C., Can. G13 138
Nelson, N.Z. E5 80
Nelson, Ne., U.S. A10 128
Nelson, stm., Mb., Can. D12 106
Nelson, Cape, c., Austl. L3 76
Nelson, Estrecho, strt., Chile J2 90
Nelson Lakes National Park, p.o.i., N.Z. E5 80
Nelson's Dockyard, hist., Antig. f4 105b
Nelsonville, Oh., U.S. E3 114
Nelspoort, S. Afr. H6 70
Nelspruit, S. Afr. D10 70
Néma, Maur. F3 64
Nemadji, stm., U.S. E6 118
Neman, Russia E4 10
Neman (Nemunas), stm., Eur. E4 10
Nembe, Nig. I6 64
Nemenčinė, Lith. F8 10
Nemeriči, Russia G16 10
Nemours, Fr. F11 14
Nemunas (Neman), stm., Eur. E4 10
Nemunėlis (Mēmele), stm., Eur. D7 10
Nemuro, Japan C16 38
Nemuro Strait, strt., Asia C16 38
Nen, stm., China B9 36
Nenagh, Ire. I4 12
Nenana, Ak., U.S. D10 140
Nenana, stm., Ak., U.S. D10 140
Nendo, i., Sol. Is. E7 72
Nene, stm., Eng., U.K. I13 12
Neneckij avtonomnyj okrug, Russia C23 8
Nenets see Neneckij avtonomnyj okrug, Russia C23 8
Nenetsia see Neneckij avtonomnyj okrug, Russia C23 8
Nenggiri, stm., Malay. J5 48
Neodesha, Ks., U.S. G2 120
Neoga, Il., U.S. E9 120
Néo Karlovási, Grc. F9 28
Neola, Ut., U.S. C6 132
Neopit, Wi., U.S. G10 118
Neosho, Mo., U.S. H3 120
Neosho, stm., U.S. H2 120
Nepa, stm., Russia C19 32
Nepal, ctry., Asia E9 54
Nepālganj, Nepal D8 54
Nepa Nagar, India H6 54
Nepeña, Peru E2 84
Nephin, mtn., Ire. G3 12
Nepisiguit, stm., N.B., Can. C10 110
Nepisiguit Bay, b., N.B., Can. C11 110
Neptune, N.J., U.S. D11 114
Neptune Beach, Fl., U.S. F4 116
Nérac, Fr. E6 18
Nerča, stm., Russia F12 34
Nerčinsk, Russia F12 34
Nerčinskij Zavod, Russia F12 34
Nerehta, Russia H19 8
Neretva, stm., Eur. G15 22
Neriquinha, Ang. D3 68
Neris (Vilija), stm., Eur. F6 10
Nerja, Spain H7 20
Nerjungri, Russia E13 34
Nerl', Russia C20 10
Nerl', stm., Russia D22 10
Nerópolis, Braz. I1 88
Nerussa, stm., Russia H16 10
Nerva, Spain G4 20
Nes, Neth. C1 16
Nesbyen, Nor. F3 8
Neščarda, vozero, l., Bela. E12 10
Neskaupstaður, Ice. k32 8a
Nesna, Nor. C5 8
Nespelem, Wa., U.S. B7 136
Ness, Loch, l., Scot., U.K. D8 12
Ness City, Ks., U.S. C8 128
Nesselrode, Mount, mtn., N.A. D4 106
Nesterkovo, Russia A13 10
Nestoita, Ukr. B16 26
Netanya, Isr. F5 58
Netherdale, Austl. C7 76
Netherlands, ctry., Eur. B14 14
Netherlands Antilles, dep., N.A. i14 96a
Netherlands Guiana see Surinam, ctry., S.A. C6 84
Netrakona, Bngl. F13 54
Nettilling Fiord, b., N.T., Can. B17 106
Nettilling Lake, l., N.T., Can. B17 106
Nett Lake, l., Mn., U.S. C5 118
Nettuno, Italy C6 24
Neubrandenburg, Ger. C9 16
Neuburg an der Donau, Ger. H7 16
Neuchâtel, Switz. D3 22
Neuchâtel, Lac de, l., Switz. D3 22
Neudorf, Sk., Can. D11 124
Neuenburg see Neuchâtel, Switz. D3 22
Neuenhagen, Ger. D9 16
Neuerburg, Ger. F2 16
Neufchâteau, Fr. F14 14
Neufchâtel-en-Bray, Fr. E10 14
Neu-Isenburg, Ger. F4 16
Neumarkt in der Oberpfalz, Ger. G7 16
Neumünster, Ger. B6 16
Neun, stm., Laos C6 48
Neunkirchen, Aus. C13 22
Neuquén, Arg. G3 90
Neuquén, state, Arg. G2 90
Neuquén, stm., Arg. G3 90
Neurara, Chile B3 92
Neuruppin, Ger. D8 16
Neuse, stm., N.C., U.S. A8 116
Neusiedl am See, Aus. C13 22
Neuss, Ger. E2 16
Neustadt, Ger. F7 16
Neustadt an der Aisch, Ger. G6 16
Neustadt an der Weinstrasse, Ger. G3 16
Neustadt bei Coburg, Ger. F6 16
Neustadt in Holstein, Ger. B6 16
Neustrelitz, Ger. C9 16
Neutral Hills, hills, Ab., Can. B3 124
Neu-Ulm, Ger. H6 16
Neuvic, Fr. D8 18
Neuwied, Ger. F3 16
Neva, stm., Russia A13 10
Nevada, Ia., U.S. B4 120
Nevada, Mo., U.S. G3 120
Nevada, state, U.S. D4 108
Nevada, Sierra, mts., Spain G7 20
Nevada, Sierra, mts., Ca., U.S. F6 134
Nevada City, Ca., U.S. D4 134
Nevado, Cerro, mtn., Arg. G3 92
Nevado, Cerro, mtn., Col. E4 86
Nevado de Colima, Parque Nacional del, p.o.i., Mex. F7 100
Nevado de Toluca, Parque Nacional, p.o.i., Mex. F8 100
Neve, Serra da, mts., Ang. C1 68
Nevel', Russia D12 10
Nevel'sk, Russia G17 34
Nevel'skogo, proliv, strt., Russia F17 34
Never, Russia F13 34
Nevers, Fr. G12 14
Nevesinje, Bos. F5 26
Nevinnomyssk, Russia F6 32
Nevis, i., St. K./N. C2 105a
Nevis, Ben, mtn., Scot., U.K. E7 12
Nevis Peak, vol., St. K./N. C2 105a
Nevjansk, Russia C10 32
Nevşehir, Tur. B3 56
New, stm., Belize D3 102
New, stm., Guy. C6 84
New, stm., U.S. F4 114
New, stm., S.C., U.S. D4 116
Newala, Tan. G7 66
New Albany, In., U.S. F12 120
New Albany, Ms., U.S. C9 122
New Amsterdam, Guy. B6 84
New Angledool, Austl. G6 76
Newark, Ar., U.S. B7 122
Newark, De., U.S. E10 114
Newark, N.J., U.S. D11 114
Newark, N.Y., U.S. A8 114
Newark, Oh., U.S. D3 114
Newark Lake, l., Nv., U.S. D1 132
Newark-on-Trent, Eng., U.K. H12 12
Newark Valley, N.Y., U.S. B9 114
New Athens, Il., U.S. F8 120
New Augusta, Ms., U.S. F9 122
New Baden, Il., U.S. F8 120
New Bedford, Ma., U.S. C15 114
Newberg, Or., U.S. E4 136
New Berlin, Il., U.S. E7 120
New Berlin, N.Y., U.S. B10 114
New Berlin, Wi., U.S. F1 112
Newbern, Al., U.S. E11 122
New Bern, N.C., U.S. A8 116
Newbern, Tn., U.S. H8 120
Newberry, Fl., U.S. G3 116
Newberry, S.C., U.S. B4 116
Newberry National Volcanic Monument, p.o.i., Or., U.S. G5 136
New Bethlehem, Pa., U.S. D6 114
New Bloomfield, Pa., U.S. H12 112
New Boston, Oh., U.S. F3 114
New Boston, Tx., U.S. D4 122
New Braunfels, Tx., U.S. E9 130
New Britain, Ct., U.S. C13 114
New Britain, i., Pap. N. Gui. b5 79a
New Brockton, Al., U.S. F12 122
Newbrook, Ab., Can. B17 138
New Brunswick, N.J., U.S. D11 114
New Brunswick, state, Can. D10 110
Newburg, Mo., U.S. G6 120
Newburgh, In., U.S. G10 120
Newburgh, N.Y., U.S. C11 114
Newbury, Eng., U.K. J11 12
Newburyport, Ma., U.S. B15 114
New Caledonia, dep., Oc. F7 72
New Caledonia see Nouvelle-Calédonie, i., N. Cal. m15 79d
New Caledonia Basin, unds. L19 142
New Carlisle, Qc., Can. B11 110
New Carlisle, Oh., U.S. E2 114
New Castille see Castilla la Nueva, hist. reg., Spain E7 20
Newcastle, Austl. I8 76
Newcastle, N.B., Can. C11 110
Newcastle, St. K./N. C2 105a
Newcastle, S. Afr. E9 70
Newcastle, N. Ire., U.K. G7 12
New Castle, Co., U.S. D9 132
New Castle, De., U.S. E10 114
New Castle, In., U.S. I4 112
Newcastle, Ne., U.S. I2 118
Newcastle, Ok., U.S. F11 128
New Castle, Pa., U.S. D5 114
Newcastle, Tx., U.S. A9 130
New Castle, Va., U.S. G5 114
Newcastle, Wy., U.S. D8 126
Newcastle Bay, b., Austl. B8 74
Newcastle-under-Lyme, Eng., U.K. I10 12
Newcastle upon Tyne, Eng., U.K. G10 12
Newcastle Waters, Austl. C6 74
Newcastle West, Ire. I3 12
New City, N.Y., U.S. C11 114
Newcomerstown, Oh., U.S. D4 114
New Concord, Oh., U.S. D4 114
New Cumberland, W.V., U.S. D5 114
Newdegate, Austl. F3 74
New Delhi, India D6 54
New Denver, B.C., Can. F13 138
New Edinburg, Ar., U.S. D6 122
New Effington, S.D., U.S. F1 118
Newell, Ia., U.S. B2 120
Newell, W.V., U.S. D5 114
Newell, Lake, l., Ab., Can. F19 138
New Ellenton, S.C., U.S. C4 116
Newellton, La., U.S. E7 122
New England, N.D., U.S. A10 126
New England National Park, p.o.i., Austl. H9 76
Newfane, N.Y., U.S. E11 112
Newfane, Vt., U.S. A13 114
New Florence, Pa., U.S. D6 114
Newfound Gap, p., U.S. I2 114
Newfoundland, state, Can. j22 107a
Newfoundland, i., Nf., Can. j22 107a
Newfoundland Basin, unds. D9 144
New Franklin, Mo., U.S. E5 120
New Freedom, Pa., U.S. E9 114
New Galloway, Scot., U.K. F8 12
Newgate, B.C., Can. G15 138
New Georgia, i., Sol. Is. e7 79b
New Georgia Group, is., Sol. Is. d7 79b
New Georgia Sound, strt., Sol. Is. e8 79b
New Germany, N.S., Can. F12 110
New Glasgow, N.S., Can. E14 110
New Guinea, i. b3 79a
Newhalem, Wa., U.S. B5 136
New Hamburg, On., Can. E9 112
New Hampshire, state, U.S. G5 110
New Hampton, Ia., U.S. A5 120
New Hanover, S. Afr. F10 70
New Hanover, i., Pap. N. Gui. a4 79a
New Harmony, In., U.S. F10 120
New Hartford, Ia., U.S. I6 118
Newhaven, Eng., U.K. K13 12
New Haven, Ct., U.S. C13 114
New Haven, Il., U.S. G9 120
New Haven, Ky., U.S. G12 120
New Haven, Mo., U.S. F6 120
New Hazelton, B.C., Can. A3 138
New Hebrides see Vanuatu, ctry., Oc. k16 79d
New Hebrides, is., Vanuatu k16 79d
New Hebrides Trench, unds. L20 142
Newhebron, Ms., U.S. F9 122
New Holland, Oh., U.S. E2 114
New Holland, Pa., U.S. D9 114
New Holstein, Wi., U.S. E1 112
New Hope, Al., U.S. C12 122
New Iberia, La., U.S. G7 122
New Ireland, i., Pap. N. Gui. a5 79a
New Jersey, state, U.S. D11 114
New Johnsonville, Tn., U.S. H10 120
New Kensington, Pa., U.S. D6 114
New Kent, Va., U.S. G9 114
Newkirk, Ok., U.S. E11 128
New Kowloon see Xinjiulong, China J6 42
Newlands, Austl. C6 76
New Lexington, Oh., U.S. E3 114
New Lisbon, Wi., U.S. H8 118
New Liskeard, On., Can. F14 106
New Llano, La., U.S. F5 122
New London, Ct., U.S. C13 114
New London, Mo., U.S. E6 120
New London, N.H., U.S. G5 110
New London, Oh., U.S. C3 114
New London, Tx., U.S. E4 122
New London, Wi., U.S. G10 118
New Madrid, Mo., U.S. H8 120
Newman, Austl. D3 74
Newman, Ca., U.S. F4 134
Newman Grove, Ne., U.S. F15 126
Newmarket, On., Can. D10 112
Newmarket, Eng., U.K. I13 12
New Market, Al., U.S. C12 122
New Market, Ia., U.S. D3 120
Newmarket, N.H., U.S. G5 110
New Market, Va., U.S. F7 114
New Martinsville, W.V., U.S. E4 114
New Mexico, state, U.S. D9 98
New Milford, Ct., U.S. C12 114
New Milford, Pa., U.S. C10 114
Newnan, Ga., U.S. D14 122
New Norfolk, Austl. o13 77a
New Norway, Ab., Can. D18 138
New Orleans, La., U.S. G8 122
New Paris, Oh., U.S. I5 112
New Philadelphia, Oh., U.S. D4 114
New Pine Creek, Or., U.S. A5 134
New Plymouth, N.Z. D5 80
New Plymouth, Id., U.S. G10 136
Newport, Eng., U.K. K11 12
Newport, Wales, U.K. J10 12
Newport, Ar., U.S. B7 122
Newport, Ky., U.S. E1 114
Newport, Me., U.S. F7 110
Newport, N.H., U.S. G4 110
Newport, N.C., U.S. B8 116
Newport, Or., U.S. F2 136
Newport, Pa., U.S. D8 114
Newport, R.I., U.S. C14 114
Newport, Tn., U.S. I2 114
Newport, Vt., U.S. F4 110
Newport Beach, Ca., U.S. J7 134
Newport News, Va., U.S. G9 114
New Port Richey, Fl., U.S. H3 116
New Providence, i., Bah. C9 96
Newquay, Eng., U.K. K7 12
New Richland, Mn., U.S. H5 118
New Richmond, Qc., Can. B10 110
New Richmond, Wi., U.S. F6 118
New River, St. K./N. C2 105a
New Road, N.S., Can. F13 110
New Roads, La., U.S. G7 122
New Rochelle, N.Y., U.S. D12 114
New Ross, N.S., Can. F12 110
New Ross, Ire. I6 12
Newry, N. Ire., U.K. G6 12
Newry, S.C., U.S. B3 116
New Salem, N.D., U.S. A11 126
New Schwabenland, reg., Ant. C5 81
New Sharon, Ia., U.S. C5 120
New Siberian Islands see Novosibirskie ostrova, is., Russia A18 34
New Smyrna Beach, Fl., U.S. G5 116
New South Wales, state, Austl. I6 76
New Tazewell, Tn., U.S. H2 114
New Tecumseth, On., Can. D9 112
Newton, Ga., U.S. F14 122
Newton, Il., U.S. F9 120
Newton, Ia., U.S. C4 120
Newton, Ks., U.S. C11 128
Newton, Ma., U.S. B14 114
Newton, Ms., U.S. E9 122
Newton, N.J., U.S. C11 114
Newton, Tx., U.S. G5 122
Newton Falls, N.Y., U.S. F2 110
Newton Stewart, Scot., U.K. G8 12
New Town, N.D., U.S. F11 124
Newtownabbey, N. Ire., U.K. G6 12
Newtownards, N. Ire., U.K. G7 12
New Ulm, Mn., U.S. G4 118
New Ulm, Tx., U.S. H2 122
New Washington, Oh., U.S. D3 114
New Waterford, N.S., Can. D16 110
New Waverly, Tx., U.S. G3 122
New Westminster, B.C., Can. G8 138
New Whiteland, In., U.S. E11 120
New York, N.Y., U.S. D12 114
New York, state, U.S. C12 108
New York Mills, Mn., U.S. E3 118
New York State Barge Canal, can., N.Y., U.S. E12 112
New Zealand, ctry., Oc. D4 80
Neyrīz, Iran D7 56
Neyshābūr, Iran B8 56
Neyveli, India F4 53
Neyyāttinkara, India G3 53
Nezahualcóyotl, Presa, res., Mex. G12 100
Nezavertailovca, Mol. C16 26
Nezperce, Id., U.S. D10 136
Ngabang, Indon. C6 50
Ngabé, Congo E3 66
Ngambé, Cam. D2 66
Ngami, Lake, l., Bots. B6 70
Ngamiland, state, Bots. B6 70
Ngan-chouei see Anhui, state, China F7 42
Ngangla Ringco, l., China C9 54
Nganglong Kangri, mts., China B9 54
Ngangzê Co, l., China C11 54
Nganjuk, Indon. G7 50
Ngao, Thai. C5 48
Ngaoui, Mont, mtn., Afr. F3 62
Ngaoundéré, Cam. C2 66
Ngape, Mya. B2 48
Ngaputaw, Mya. D2 48
Ngara, Tan. E6 66
Ngatangiia, Cook Is. a27 78j
Ngatangiia Harbour, b., Cook Is. a27 78j
Ngawi, Indon. G7 50
Ngay Nua, Laos B5 48
Ngcheangel, is., Palau D9 44
Ngeaur, i., Palau D9 44
Ngereklmadel, Palau g7 78b
Ngerkeai, Palau g8 78b
Ngermetengel, Palau f7 78b
Ngeruktabel, i., Palau h7 78b
Ngetbong, Palau f8 78b
Nggatokae Island, i., Sol. Is. e8 79b
Nggela Pile, i., Sol. Is. e9 79b
Nghia Hanh, Viet. E9 48
Ngiap, stm., Laos C6 48
Ngidinga, D.R.C. F3 66
Ng'iro, mtn., Kenya D7 66
Ngiro, Ewaso, stm., Kenya D7 66
Ngo, Congo E3 66
Ngoko, stm., Afr. D3 66
Ngom, stm., China B8 46
Ngomeni, Ras, c., Kenya E8 66
Ngong, Kenya E7 66
Ngoring Hu, l., China E4 36
Ngounié, stm., Gabon E2 66
Ngouri, Chad E3 62
Nguigmi, Niger G7 64
Ngulu, at., Micron. C4 72
Ngum, stm., Laos C6 48
Nguna, Île, i., Vanuatu k17 79d
Nguru, Nig. G7 64
Nhacoongo, Moz. D12 70
Nhamundá, stm., Braz. D6 84
Nha Trang, Viet. F9 48
Nhill, Austl. K3 76
Nhoma, stm., Afr. D2 68
Niafounké, Mali F4 64
Niagara, Wi., U.S. C1 112
Niagara Falls, On., Can. E10 112
Niagara Falls, N.Y., U.S. A6 114
Niagara Falls, wtfl, N.A. E10 112
Niagara-on-the-Lake, On., Can. E10 112
Niagassola, Gui. G3 64
Niah, Malay. B8 50
Niamey, Niger G5 64
Niangara, D.R.C. D5 66
Niangay, Lac, l., Mali F4 64
Niangoloko, Burkina G4 64
Niangua, stm., Mo., U.S. G5 120
Nia-Nia, D.R.C. D5 66
Niantic, Il., U.S. E8 120
Nianyushan, China G7 42
Nianzishan, China B9 36
Niari, stm., Congo E2 66
Nias, Pulau, i., Indon. L3 48
Nicaragua, ctry., N.A. F5 102
Nicaragua, Lago de, l., Nic. G5 102
Nicaragua, Lake see Nicaragua, Lago de, l., Nic. G5 102
Nicastro, Italy F10 24
Nice, Fr. F13 18
Niceville, Fl., U.S. G12 122
Nichinan, Japan H4 40
Nicholas Channel (San Nicolás, Canal de), strt., N.A. G11 108
Nicholasville, Ky., U.S. G13 120
Nicholls, Ga., U.S. E3 116
Nicholl's Town, Bah. B9 96
Nicholson, Pa., U.S. C10 114
Nickel Centre, On., Can. B8 112
Nickerson, Ks., U.S. C10 128
Nicobar Islands, is., India G7 46
Nicola, B.C., Can. F10 138
Nicola, stm., B.C., Can. F9 138
Nicolae Bălcescu, Rom. B13 26
Nicolet, Qc., Can. D4 110
Nicolet, Lake, l., Mi., U.S. B5 112
Nicolet Sud-Ouest, stm., Qc., Can. E5 110
Nicollet, Mn., U.S. G4 118
Nicosia (Levkosía), Cyp. C4 58
Nicosia, Italy G8 24
Nicoya, Golfo de, b., C.R. H5 102
Nicoya, Península de, pen., C.R. H5 102
Nida, Lith. E3 10
Nida, stm., Pol. F16 16
Nidadavole, India C5 53
Nidzica, Pol. C16 16
Niebüll, Ger. B4 16
Niedere Tauern, mts., Aus. C10 22
Niederösterreich, state, Aus. B12 22
Niedersachsen, state, Ger. D4 16
Niekerkshoop, S. Afr. F6 70
Niemba, D.R.C. F5 66
Niemodlin, Pol. F13 16
Nienburg, Ger. D5 16
Niers, stm., Eur. C15 14
Niesky, Ger. E10 16
Nieszawa, Pol. D14 16
Nieu-Bethesda, S. Afr. G7 70
Nieuport see Nieuwpoort, Bel. C11 14
Nieuw Amsterdam, Sur. B6 84
Nieuw Nickerie, Sur. B6 84
Nieuwpoort, Bel. C11 14
Nieuwpoort, Neth. Ant. p22 104g
Nièvre, state, Fr. G12 14
Nifisha, Egypt H3 58
Niğde, Tur. H15 6
Niğde, state, Tur. A5 58
Nigei Island, i., B.C., Can. F3 138
Nigel, S. Afr. E9 70
Niger, ctry., Afr. F6 64
Niger, stm., Afr. H6 64
Niger Delta, Nig. I6 64
Nigeria, ctry., Afr. H6 64
Nightcaps, N.Z. G3 80
Nighthawk, Wa., U.S. B7 136
Nigríta, Grc. C6 28
Niheidât el-Sûd, Gebel el-, mtn., Egypt J3 58
Nihommatsu, Japan B13 40
Nihuil, Embalse del, res., Arg. G3 92
Niigata, Japan B11 40
Niigata, state, Japan B11 40
Niihama, Japan F6 40
Niihau, i., Hi., U.S. B1 78a
Nii-jima, i., Japan E12 40
Niitsu, Japan B12 40
Níjar, Spain H8 20
Nijmegen, Neth. C14 14
Nijvel see Nivelles, Bel. D13 14
Nikel', Russia B14 8
Nikki, Benin G5 64
Nikkō, Japan C12 40
Nikkō-kokuritsu-kōen, p.o.i., Japan B12 40
Nikolaevo, Russia B12 10
Nikolaevsk-na-Amure, Russia F17 34
Nikol'sk, Russia G21 8
Nikol'sk, Russia C6 32
Nikolski, Ak., U.S. F6 140
Nikol'skij, Russia F15 8
Nikol'skoe, Russia H19 10
Nikol'skoe, Russia E22 34
Nikopol', Ukr. E4 32
Nīkshahr, Iran D9 56
Nikšić, Yugo. G5 26
Nikumaroro, at., Kir. D9 72
Nikunau, i., Kir. D8 72
Nīl, Bahr el- see Nile, stm., Afr. B6 62
Nīl, Nahr an- see Nile, stm., Afr. D6 62
Nila, Pulau, i., Indon. G9 44
Nilakka, l., Fin. E12 8
Nile, stm., Afr. D6 62
Nile Delta, Egypt H1 58
Niles, Il., U.S. B10 120
Niles, Mi., U.S. G3 112
Niles, Oh., U.S. C5 114
Nīlgiri, India H11 54
Nilka, China F14 32
Nilsiä, Fin. E12 8
Nīmach, India F5 54
Nimba, Mount, mtn., Afr. H3 64
Nimbāhera, India F5 54
Nîmes, Fr. F10 18
Nimpkish Lake, l., B.C., Can. F3 138
Nimule, Sudan G6 62
Ninda, Ang. C3 68
Nindigully, Austl. G7 76
Nine Degree Channel, strt., India G3 46
Ninette, Mb., Can. E14 124
Ninetyeast Ridge, unds. K11 142
Ninety Mile Beach, cst., Austl. L6 76
Ninety Six, S.C., U.S. B3 116
Ninfas, Punta, c., Arg. H4 90
Ninga, Mb., Can. E14 124
Ning'an, China B8 38
Ningbo, China G9 42
Ningcheng, China D3 38
Ningde, China H8 42
Ningdu, China H6 42
Ningguo, China F8 42
Ninghai, China G9 42
Ning-hia see Ningxia, state, China D6 36
Ninghua, China H7 42
Ningi, Nig. G6 64
Ningjing Shan, mts., China F4 36
Ningming, China J2 42
Ningnan, China F5 36
Ningpo see Ningbo, China G9 42
Ningqiang, China E2 42
Ningshan, China E3 42
Ningsia see Yinchuan, China B2 42
Ningsia Hui see Ningxia, state, China D6 36
Ningsia Hui Autonomous Region see Ningxia, state, China D6 36
Ningwu, China B4 42
Ningxia, state, China D6 36
Ningxiang, China G5 42
Ningyuan, China I4 42
Ninh Binh, Viet. B7 48
Ninh Hoa, Viet. F9 48
Ninhue, Chile H1 92
Ninigo Group, is., Pap. N. Gui. a3 79a
Ninnescah, North Fork, stm., Ks., U.S. D10 128
Ninnescah, South Fork, stm., Ks., U.S. D10 128
Ninohe, Japan D14 38
Nioaque, Braz. D5 90
Niobrara, stm., U.S. E14 126
Nioghalvfjerdsfjorden, ice, Grnld. B22 141
Nioki, D.R.C. E3 66
Niono, Mali G3 64
Nioro, Mali F3 64
Niort, Fr. C5 18
Niota, Tn., U.S. B14 122
Nipāni, India C2 53
Nipawin, Sk., Can. E10 106
Nipe, Bahía de, b., Cuba B10 102
Nipigon, On., Can. B10 118
Nipigon, Lake, res., On., Can. B10 118
Nipigon Bay, b., On., Can. C10 118
Nipissing, Lake, l., On., Can. B10 112
Nipomo, Ca., U.S. H5 134
Niquelândia, Braz. H1 88
Niquero, Cuba B9 102
Niquivil, Arg. E3 92
Nīra, stm., India B2 53
Nirasaki, Japan D11 40
Nirgua, Ven. B7 86
Nirmal, India B4 53
Nirmāli, India E11 54
Niš, Yugo. F8 26
Nişāb, Yemen G6 56
Nišava, stm., Eur. F9 26
Niscemi, Italy G8 24
Nishio, Japan E10 40
Nishiwaki, Japan E7 40
Nisporeni, Mol. B15 26
Nisqually, stm., Wa., U.S. D4 136
Nisswa, Mn., U.S. E4 118
Nītaure, Lat. C8 10
Niterói, Braz. L4 88
Nith, stm., On., Can. E9 112
Nitinat Lake, l., B.C., Can. H6 138
Nitra, Slov. H14 16
Nitra, stm., Slov. H14 16
Nitro, W.V., U.S. F4 114
Niue, dep., Oc. E10 72
Niulakita, i., Tuvalu E8 72
Niut, Gunung, mtn., Indon. C6 50
Niutao, i., Tuvalu D8 72
Niutoushan, China B7 38
Niutou Shan, i., China G9 42
Niuzhuang, China A10 42
Nive, stm., Austl. E6 76
Nivelles, Bel. D13 14
Nivernais, hist. reg., Fr. G12 14
Niverville, Mb., Can. E16 124
Nixa, Mo., U.S. G4 120
Nixon, Nv., U.S. D6 134
Niža, Russia C20 8
Nizāmābād, India B4 53
Nizām Sāgar, res., India C3 53
Nižegorodskaja oblast', co., Russia H21 8
Nizip, Tur. A8 58
Nízke Tatry, Narodny Park, p.o.i., Slov. H15 16
Nižneangarsk, Russia E10 34
Nižnee Kujto, ozero, l., Russia D14 8
Nižneilimsk, Russia C18 32
Nižnekamsk, Russia C8 32
Nižnekamskoe vodohranilišče, res., Russia C8 32
Nižneudinsk, Russia D17 32
Nižnevartovsk, Russia B13 32
Nižnij Casučej, Russia F12 34
Nižnij Kuranah, Russia E14 34
Nižnij Novgorod (Gorki), Russia H21 8
Nižnij Pjandž, Taj. B10 56
Nižnij Tagil, Russia C10 32
Nižnjaja Peša, Russia C22 8
Nižnjaja Pojma, Russia C17 32
Nižnjaja Tavda, Russia C11 32
Nižnjaja Tunguska, stm., Russia B16 32
Nizza Monferrato, Italy F5 22
Njandoma, Russia F19 8
Njasviž, Bela. G9 10
Njazidja, i., Com. C7 68
Njesuthi, mtn., Afr. F9 70
Njombe, stm., Tan. F7 66
Njuhča, Russia E22 8
Njuja, Russia D12 34
Njuja, stm., Russia B20 32
Njuk, ozero, l., Russia D14 8
Njuksenica, Russia F21 8
Njurba, Russia D12 34
Njuvčim, Russia B8 32
Nkambe, Cam. C2 66
Nkawkaw, Ghana H4 64
Nkayi, Zimb. D4 68
Nkhata Bay, Mwi. C5 68
Nkhotakota, Mwi. C5 68
Nkomi, Lagune, l., Gabon E1 66
Nkongsamba, Cam. D2 66
Nkwalini, S. Afr. F10 70
Nmai, stm., Mya. C8 46
Noākhāli, Bngl. G13 54
Noatak, Ak., U.S. C7 140
Noatak, stm., Ak., U.S. C8 140
Nobeoka, Japan G4 40
Noble, Il., U.S. F9 120
Noblesville, In., U.S. H3 112
Noboribetsu, Japan C14 38
Nobres, Braz. F6 84
Nocatee, Fl., U.S. I4 116
Noce, stm., Italy D8 22
Nocera Inferiore, Italy D8 24
Nockatunga, Austl. F4 76
Nocona, Tx., U.S. H11 128
Nocupétaro, Mex. F8 100
Noetinger, Arg. F6 92
Nogales, Mex. F7 98
Nogales, Az., U.S. L5 132
Nogent-le-Rotrou, Fr. F9 14
Nogent-sur-Seine, Fr. F12 14
Noginsk, Russia E21 10
Nogliki, Russia F17 34
Nogoa, stm., Austl. E6 76
Nogoyá, Arg. F7 92
Nógrád, state, Hung. B6 26
Noguera Pallaresa, stm., Spain B12 20
Noguera Ribagorçana, stm., Spain B11 20
Nohar, India D5 54
Noia, Spain B2 20
Noir, Causse, plat., Fr. E9 18
Noir, Isla, i., Chile J2 90
Noire, stm., Qc., Can. B13 112
Noirmoutier, Île de, i., Fr. H6 14
Noirmoutier-en-l'Île, Fr. H6 14
Nojima-zaki, c., Japan E12 40
Nokha Mandi, India E4 54
Nokia, Fin. F10 8
Nokomis, Sk., Can. C8 124
Nokomis, Fl., U.S. I3 116
Nokomis, Il., U.S. E8 120
Nokou, Chad E2 62
Nokuku, Vanuatu j16 79d
Nola, C.A.R. D3 66
Nola, Italy D8 24
Nolichucky, stm., U.S. H2 114
Nolin, stm., Ky., U.S. G11 120
Nolin Lake, res., Ky., U.S. G11 120
Nolinsk, Russia C8 32
Nólsoy, i., Far. Is. n34 8b
Nombre de Dios, Pan. H8 102
Nome, Ak., U.S. D6 140
Nomozaki, Japan G2 40
Nomtsas, Nmb. D3 70
Nonacho Lake, l., N.T., Can. C8 106
Nonburg, Russia D24 8
Nondalton, Ak., U.S. D8 140
Nong'an, China B6 38
Nong Han, Thai. D6 48
Nong Khai, Thai. D6 48
Nongoma, S. Afr. E10 70
Nongpoh, India F13 54
Nongstoin, India F13 54
Nonoava, Mex. B5 100
Nonogasta, Arg. D4 92
Nonouti, at., Kir. D8 72
Nonsuch Bay, b., Antig. f4 105b
Nonthaburi, Thai. F5 48
Nooksack, Wa., U.S. B4 136
Noonkanbah, Austl. C4 74
Noordoostpolder, reg., Neth. B14 14
Noordpunt, c., Neth. Ant. p21 104g
Noordwijk aan Zee, Neth. B13 14
Noorvik, Ak., U.S. C7 140
Nootka Island, i., B.C., Can. G4 138
Nóqui, Ang. B1 68
Norah, is., Erit. D7 62
Nora Islands see Norah, is., Erit. D7 62
Noralee, B.C., Can. B4 138
Nora Springs, Ia., U.S. A5 120
Norcatur, Ks., U.S. B8 128
Norcia, Italy H10 22
Norcross, Ga., U.S. D14 122
Nord, Grnld. A22 141
Nord, state, Fr. D12 14
Nord, state, N. Cal. m15 79d
Nord, Canal du, can., Fr. D12 14
Nord, Canal du, can., Fr. E11 14
Nordaustlandet, i., Nor. B29 141
Nordborg, Den. A5 16
Nordegg, Ab., Can. D14 138
Nordegg, stm., Ab., Can. D15 138
Norden, Ger. C3 16
Nordenham, Ger. C4 16
Nordenšel'da, arhipelag, is., Russia A8 34
Nordenskjold Archipelago see Nordenšel'da, arhipelag, is., Russia A8 34
Norderstedt, Ger. C6 16
Nordfjord, b., Nor. F1 8
Nordfold, Nor. C6 8
Nordgrønland (Avanersuaq), state, Grnld. B15 141
Nordhausen, Ger. E6 16
Nordhorn, Ger. D2 16
Nordjylland, state, Den. H4 8
Nordkapp (North Cape), c., Nor. A11 8
Nordkinnhalvøya, pen., Nor. A12 8
Nordland, state, Nor. C6 8
Nördlingen, Ger. H6 16
Nordmaling, Swe. E8 8
Nordman, Id., U.S. B9 136
Nordostrundingen, c., Grnld. A23 141
Nord-Ostsee-Kanal (Kiel Canal), can., Ger. B5 16
Nordrhein-Westfalen, state, Ger. E4 16
Nordstrand, i., Ger. B4 16
Nord-Trøndelag, state, Nor. D5 8
Nordvik, Russia B11 34
Norfolk, Ne., U.S. E15 126
Norfolk, Va., U.S. H9 114
Norfolk Island, dep., Norf. I. x25 78i
Norfolk Island National Park, p.o.i., Norf. I. y25 78i
Norfolk Ridge, unds. L19 142
Norfork Lake, res., U.S. H5 120
Norikura-dake, vol., Japan C10 40
Noril'sk, Russia C6 34
Norlina, N.C., U.S. H7 114
Normal, Il., U.S. D9 120
Norman, Ar., U.S. C5 122
Norman, Ok., U.S. F11 128
Norman, stm., Austl. B3 76
Norman, Lake, res., N.C., U.S. A4 116
Normanby Island, i., Pap. N. Gui. c5 79a
Normandes, Îles see Channel Islands, is., Eur. L10 12

Name	Map Ref.	Page
Normandie, hist. reg., Fr.	F8	14
Normandie, Collines de, hills, Fr.	F8	14
Normandin, Qc., Can.	B4	110
Normandy see Normandie, hist. reg., Fr.	F8	14
Normandy, Hills of see Normandie, Collines de, hills, Fr.	F8	14
Normangee, Tx., U.S.	F2	122
Norman Island, i., Br. Vir. Is.	e8	104b
Normanton, Austl.	A3	76
Norman Wells, N.T., Can.	B5	106
Norogachi, Mex.	B5	100
Norquay, Sk., Can.	C11	124
Ñorquinco, Arg.	H2	90
Norra Storfjället, mtn., Swe.	D6	8
Norrbotten, state, Swe.	C9	8
Nørresundby, Den.	H3	8
Norridgewock, Me., U.S.	F7	110
Norris, Tn., U.S.	H1	114
Norris Lake, res., Tn., U.S.	H2	114
Norristown, Pa., U.S.	D10	114
Norrköping, Swe.	G7	8
Norrtälje, Swe.	G8	8
Norseman, Austl.	F4	74
Norsjö, Swe.	D8	8
Norsjø, l., Nor.	G3	8
Norsk, Russia	F15	34
Norske Øer, is., Grnld.	B22	141
Norsup, Vanuatu	k16	79d
Norte, Cabo, c., Braz.	C8	84
Norte, Serra do, plat., Braz.	F6	84
Norte de Santander, state, Col.	C5	86
Nortelândia, Braz.	F6	84
North, S.C., U.S.	C4	116
North, stm., Ia., U.S.	C3	120
North, Cape, c., N.S., Can.	C16	110
North Adams, Ma., U.S.	B12	114
North Adams, Mi., U.S.	C1	114
North Albany, Or., U.S.	F3	136
Northallerton, Eng., U.K.	G11	12
Northam, Austl.	F3	74
North America, cont.	C5	4
North American Basin, unds.	E7	144
Northampton, Austl.	E2	74
Northampton, Eng., U.K.	I12	12
Northampton, Ma., U.S.	B13	114
North Andaman, i., India	F7	46
North Atlanta, Ga., U.S.	C1	116
North Augusta, S.C., U.S.	C4	116
North Aulatsivik Island, i., Nf., Can.	F13	141
North Australian Basin, unds.	K14	142
North Baltimore, Oh., U.S.	C2	114
North Battleford, Sk., Can.	B5	124
North Bay, On., Can.	B10	112
North Bend, B.C., Can.	G9	138
North Bend, Ne., U.S.	J2	118
North Bennington, Vt., U.S.	B12	114
North Berwick, Scot., U.K.	E10	12
North Berwick, Me., U.S.	G6	110
North Borneo see Sabah, state, Malay.	H1	52
North Bourke, Austl.	H5	76
North Branch, Mi., U.S.	E6	112
North Caicos, i., T./C. Is.	B11	102
North Canadian, stm., Ok., U.S.	F12	128
North Canton, Ga., U.S.	C14	122
North Canton, Oh., U.S.	D4	114
North Cape, c., P.E., Can.	C13	110
North Cape, c., N.Z.	B5	80
North Cape see Nordkapp, c., Nor.	A11	8
North Caribou Lake, l., On., Can.	E12	106
North Carolina, state, U.S.	D11	108
North Cascades National Park, p.o.i., Wa., U.S.	B5	136
North Channel, strt., On., Can.	B7	112
North Channel, strt., U.K.	F7	12
North Charleston, S.C., U.S.	D5	116
North Chicago, Il., U.S.	F2	112
North Chungcheong see Ch'ungch'ŏng-bukto, state, Kor., S.	B1	40
Northcliffe, Austl.	F3	74
North College Hill, Oh., U.S.	E13	120
North Collins, N.Y., U.S.	F11	112
North Concho, stm., Tx., U.S.	C7	130
North Conway, N.H., U.S.	F5	110
North Crossett, Ar., U.S.	D6	122
North Cyprus see Cyprus, North, ctry., Asia	C4	58
North Dakota, state, U.S.	G13	124
North Downs, hills, Eng., U.K.	J13	12
North Eagle Butte, S.D., U.S.	B11	126
North East, Md., U.S.	E9	114
North-East, state, Bots.	B8	70
Northeast Cape, Ak., U.S.	D6	140
Northeast Cape Fear, stm., N.C., U.S.	B8	116
North East Point, c., Bah.	A11	102
Northeast Providence Channel, strt., Bah.	B9	96
Northeim, Ger.	E6	16
North English, Ia., U.S.	C5	120
Northern see HaZafon, state, Isr.	F6	58
Northern, state, S. Afr.	C9	70
Northern Cape, state, S. Afr.	G5	70
Northern Cook Islands, is., Cook Is.	E10	72
Northern Division, state, Fiji	p20	79e
Northern Donets, stm., Eur.	F16	6
Northern Dvina see Severnaja Dvina, stm., Russia	E19	8
Northern Indian Lake, l., Mb., Can.	D11	106
Northern Ireland, state, U.K.	G6	12
Northern Marianas, dep., Oc.	B6	72
Northern Sporades see Vórioi Sporádhes, is., Grc.	D6	28
Northern Territory, state, Austl.	D6	74
North Fabius, stm., U.S.	D6	120
Northfield, Ma., U.S.	B13	114
Northfield, Mn., U.S.	G5	118
Northfield, Vt., U.S.	F4	110
North Fiji Basin, unds.	K20	142
North Flinders Range, mts., Austl.	H2	76
North Fond du Lac, Wi., U.S.	H10	118
North Foreland, c., Eng., U.K.	J14	12
North Fork, Ca., U.S.	F6	134
North Fork, stm., U.S.	H5	120
North Fort Myers, Fl., U.S.	J4	116
North Frisian Islands, is., Eur.	B3	16
Northglenn, Co., U.S.	B4	128
North Gulfport, Ms., U.S.	G9	122
North Gyeongsang see Kyŏngsang-bukto, state, Kor., S.	C1	40
North Henik Lake, l., N.T., Can.	C11	106
North Hero, Vt., U.S.	F3	110
North Highlands, Ca., U.S.	E4	134
North Horr, Kenya	D7	66
North Island, i., N.Z.	C5	80
North Judson, In., U.S.	G3	112
North Kent Island, i., N.T., Can.	B7	141
North Kingsville, Oh., U.S.	C5	114
North Knife Lake, l., Mb., Can.	D11	106
North Korea see Korea, North, ctry., Asia	D7	38
North Lakhimpur, India	C7	46
North Las Vegas, Nv., U.S.	G1	132
North La Veta Pass, p., Co., U.S.	D3	128
North Little Rock, Ar., U.S.	C6	122
North Llano, stm., Tx., U.S.	D8	130
North Logan, Ut., U.S.	B5	132
North Loup, Ne., U.S.	F14	126
North Loup, stm., Ne., U.S.	F14	126
North Magnetic Pole, misc. cult.	B4	141
North Mamm Peak, mtn., Co., U.S.	D9	132
North Manchester, In., U.S.	H4	112
North Manitou Island, i., Mi., U.S.	C3	112
North Mankato, Mn., U.S.	G4	118
North Miami, Fl., U.S.	K5	116
North Miami Beach, Fl., U.S.	K5	116
North Milk (Milk, North Fork), stm., N.A.	B13	136
North Myrtle Beach, S.C., U.S.	C7	116
North New River Canal, can., Fl., U.S.	J5	116
North Newton, Ks., U.S.	C11	128
North Ogden, Ut., U.S.	B5	132
North Ossetia see Severnaja Osetija, state, Russia	F6	32
North Palisade, mtn., Ca., U.S.	F7	134
North Palm Beach, Fl., U.S.	J5	116
North Park, Il., U.S.	B8	120
North Peninsula, pen., On., Can.	A10	118
North Plains, pl., N.M., U.S.	I8	132
North Platte, Ne., U.S.	F12	126
North Platte, stm., U.S.	F11	126
North Point, c., Barb.	n8	105d
North Pole, misc. cult.	A4	94
Northport, Al., U.S.	D11	122
Northport, Mi., U.S.	C4	112
Northport, Wa., U.S.	B9	136
North Portal, Sk., Can.	E11	124
North Raccoon, stm., Ia., U.S.	C3	120
North Rhine-Westphalia see Nordrhein-Westfalen, state, Ger.	E4	16
North Richland Hills, Tx., U.S.	B10	130
North Rim, Az., U.S.	G4	132
North Ronaldsay, i., Scot., U.K.	B10	12
North Rustico, P.E., Can.	D13	110
North Salt Lake, Ut., U.S.	C5	132
North Saskatchewan, stm., Can.	E9	106
North Sea, Eur.	D9	6
North Shoal Lake, l., Mb., Can.	D16	124
North Shore City, N.Z.	C6	80
North Shoshone Peak, mtn., Nv., U.S.	D8	134
North Siberain Lowland see Severo-Sibirskaja nizmennost', pl., Russia	B6	34
North Skunk, stm., Ia., U.S.	C5	120
North Solitary Island, i., Austl.	G9	76
North Solomons, state, Pap. N. Gui.	d7	79b
North Spicer Island, i., N.T., Can.	B15	106
North Stradbroke Island, i., Austl.	F9	76
North Sumatra see Sumatera Utara, state, Indon.	K4	48
North Sydney, N.S., Can.	D16	110
North Taranaki Bight, b., N.Z.	D5	80
North Terre Haute, In., U.S.	E10	120
North Thompson, stm., B.C., Can.	F10	138
North Troy, Vt., U.S.	F4	110
North Tunica, Ms., U.S.	C8	122
North Uist, i., Scot., U.K.	D5	12
Northumberland Isles, is., Austl.	C7	76
Northumberland National Park, p.o.i., Eng., U.K.	F10	12
Northumberland Strait, strt., Can.	D12	110
North Umpqua, stm., Or., U.S.	G4	136
North Vancouver, B.C., Can.	G7	138
North Vietnam see Vietnam, ctry., Asia	E9	48
Northville, N.Y., U.S.	G2	110
North-West, state, S. Afr.	E7	70
North West Bluff, c., Monts.	D3	105a
North West Cape, c., Austl.	D2	74
North-West Frontier, state, Pak.	A4	54
Northwest Miramichi, stm., N.B., Can.	C10	110
Northwest Pacific Basin, unds.	F18	142
Northwest Providence Channel, strt., Bah.	m17	104f
Northwest Territories, state, Can.	B10	106
North Wichita, stm., Tx., U.S.	H9	128
North Wilkesboro, N.C., U.S.	H4	114
North Windham, Me., U.S.	G6	110
Northwood, Ia., U.S.	H5	118
Northwood, N.D., U.S.	G16	124
North York, ngh., On., Can.	E10	112
North York Moors National Park, p.o.i., Eng., U.K.	G12	12
North Zulch, Tx., U.S.	G2	122
Norton, Ks., U.S.	B9	128
Norton, Va., U.S.	H3	114
Norton Shores, Mi., U.S.	E3	112
Norton Sound, strt., Ak., U.S.	D6	140
Nortonville, Ks., U.S.	E2	120
Norvegia, Cape, c., Ant.	C3	81
Norwalk, Ct., U.S.	C12	114
Norwalk, Ia., U.S.	C4	120
Norwalk, Oh., U.S.	C3	114
Norway, Ia., U.S.	C6	120
Norway, Me., U.S.	F6	110
Norway, ctry., Eur.	E3	8
Norway Bay, b., N.T., Can.	A10	106
Norway House, Mb., Can.	E11	106
Norwegian Basin, unds.	B13	144
Norwegian Sea, Eur.	C3	30
Norwich, On., Can.	E9	112
Norwich, Eng., U.K.	I14	12
Norwich, Ct., U.S.	C13	114
Norwich, N.Y., U.S.	B10	114
Norwood, On., Can.	D11	112
Norwood, Co., U.S.	E8	132
Norwood, Ma., U.S.	B14	114
Norwood, Mn., U.S.	G5	118
Norwood, N.C., U.S.	A5	116
Norwood, Oh., U.S.	E1	114
Noshiro, Japan	D13	38
Nosop (Nossob), stm., Afr.	D5	70
Nosovaja, Russia	B26	8
Nosovščina, Russia	E17	8
Nossa Senhora das Dores, Braz.	F7	88
Nossob (Nosop), stm., Afr.	D5	70
Nosy-Varika, Madag.	E8	68
Notasulga, Al., U.S.	E13	122
Notch Hill, B.C., Can.	F11	138
Noteć, stm., Pol.	D11	16
Nótio Aigaío, state, Grc.	G9	28
Noto, Italy	H9	24
Noto, Japan	B10	40
Noto, Golfo di, b., Italy	H9	24
Noto-hantō, pen., Japan	B10	40
Notozero, ozero, l., Russia	C14	8
Notre-Dame, N.B., Can.	D12	110
Notre-Dame, Monts, mts., Qc., Can.	B9	110
Notre Dame Bay, b., Nf., Can.	j22	107a
Notre-Dame-du-Laus, Qc., Can.	B14	112
Notrees, Tx., U.S.	C5	130
Nottawasaga, stm., On., Can.	D10	112
Nottawasaga Bay, b., On., Can.	D9	112
Nottaway, stm., Qc., Can.	E15	106
Nottingham, Eng., U.K.	I11	12
Nottingham Island, i., N.T., Can.	C15	106
Nottoway, stm., Va., U.S.	H8	114
Notukeu Creek, stm., Sk., Can.	E6	124
Notwane, stm., Afr.	D8	70
Nouâdhibou, Maur.	E1	64
Nouâdhibou, Râs, c., Afr.	E1	64
Nouakchott, Maur.	F1	64
Nouâmghâr, Maur.	F1	64
Nouméa, N. Cal.	n16	79d
Noupoort, S. Afr.	G7	70
Nouveau-Québec, Cratère du, crat., Qc., Can.	C16	106
Nouvelle, Qc., Can.	B10	110
Nouvelle-Calédonie (New Caledonia), i., N. Cal.	m15	79d
Nouvelle-Écosse see Nova Scotia, state, Can.	G18	106
Nouvelle-France, Cap de, c., Qc., Can.	C16	106
Nova Andradina, Braz.	D6	90
Nová Baňa, Slov.	H14	16
Nova Caipemba, Ang.	B1	68
Nova Era, Braz.	J4	88
Nova Friburgo, Braz.	L4	88
Nova Gorica, Slvn.	D10	22
Nova Gradiška, Cro.	E14	22
Nova Granada, Braz.	K1	88
Nova Iguaçu, Braz.	L4	88
Novaja Kazanka, Kaz.	E7	32
Novaja Ladoga, Russia	F14	8
Novaja Maluksa, Russia	A14	10
Novaja Sibir', ostrov, i., Russia	B19	34
Novaja Zemlja, is., Russia	B8	30
Nova Kakhovka, Ukr.	E4	32
Nova Lamego, Gui.-B.	G2	64
Nova Lima, Braz.	K4	88
Novalukoml', Bela.	F11	10
Nova Mambone, Moz.	B12	70
Nova Olinda, Braz.	D6	88
Nová Paka, Czech Rep.	F11	16
Nova Ponte, Braz.	J2	88
Nova Prata, Braz.	D12	92
Novara, Italy	E5	22
Nova Roma, Braz.	G2	88
Nova Russas, Braz.	C5	88
Nova Scotia, state, Can.	G18	106
Nova Soure, Braz.	F6	88
Novato, Ca., U.S.	E3	134
Nova Venécia, Braz.	J5	88
Nova Vida, Braz.	F5	84
Novaya Zemlya see Novaja Zemlja, is., Russia	B8	30
Nova Zagora, Blg.	G13	26
Nové Hrady, Czech Rep.	H10	16
Novelda, Spain	F10	20
Nové Město nad Váhom, Slov.	H13	16
Nové Město na Moravě, Czech Rep.	G12	16
Nové Zámky, Slov.	I14	16
Novgorod, Russia	B14	10
Novgorodskaja oblast', co., Russia	B15	10
Novi Bečej, Yugo.	D7	26
Novi Beograd, Yugo.	E7	26
Novice, Tx., U.S.	C8	130
Novigrad, Cro.	E10	22
Novikovo, Russia	G17	34
Novi Ligure, Italy	F5	22
Novinger, Mo., U.S.	D5	120
Novi Pazar, Blg.	F14	26
Novi Pazar, Yugo.	F7	26
Novi Sad, Yugo.	D6	26
Novo, Lago, l., Braz.	C7	84
Novo Airão, Braz.	H11	86
Novoaltajsk, Russia	D14	32
Novo Aripuanã, Braz.	E5	84
Novočerkassk, Russia	E6	32
Novodvinsk, Russia	D19	8
Novoe, Russia	C11	32
Novoenisejsk, Russia	C16	32
Novo Hamburgo, Braz.	D12	92
Novo Horizonte, Braz.	K1	88
Novoizborsk, Russia	C10	10
Novokačalinsk, Russia	B10	38
Novokaširsk, Russia	F21	10
Novokazalinsk, Kaz.	F10	32
Novokujbyševsk, Russia	D7	32
Novokuzneck, Russia	D15	32
Novolazarevskaja, sci., Ant.	C6	81
Novo Mesto, Slvn.	E12	22
Novomoskovsk (Stalinogorsk), Russia	F21	10
Novo Oriente, Braz.	C5	88
Novopetrovskoe, Russia	E19	10
Novorossijsk, Russia	F5	32
Novorybnoe, Russia	B10	34
Novoržev, Russia	C12	10
Novošahtinsk, Russia	E6	32
Novošelovo, Russia	E7	34
Novoselytsia, Ukr.	A13	26
Novosergievka, Russia	D8	32
Novosibirsk, Russia	C14	32
Novosibirskie ostrova, is., Russia	A18	34
Novosibirskoe vodohranilišče, res., Russia	D14	32
Novosil's'ke, Ukr.	D15	26
Novosokol'niki, Russia	D12	10
Novotroick, Russia	D9	32
Novotroickoe, Kaz.	F12	32
Novouzensk, Russia	D7	32
Novovjatsk, Russia	C7	32
Novozavidovskij, Russia	D19	10
Novozybkov, Russia	H14	10
Novska, Cro.	E13	22
Nový Bohumín, Czech Rep.	G14	16
Nový Bor, Czech Rep.	F10	16
Novyja Valosavičy, Bela.	F11	10
Nový Jičín, Czech Rep.	G13	16
Novyj Nekouz, Russia	C20	10
Novyj Port, Russia	A12	32
Novyj Uzen', Kaz.	F8	32
Novyj Vasjugan, Russia	C13	32
Novy Pahost, Bela.	E10	10
Nowa Ruda, Pol.	F12	16
Nowa Sól, Pol.	E11	16
Nowe, Pol.	C14	16
Nowe Miasto nad Pilicą, Pol.	E16	16
Nowendoc, Austl.	H8	76
Nowgong, India	F7	54
Nowitna, stm., Ak., U.S.	D9	140
Nowogard, Pol.	C11	16
Nowogrodziec, Pol.	E11	16
Nowood, stm., Wy., U.S.	C5	126
Nowra, Austl.	J8	76
Nowrangapur, India	B6	53
Nowshāk, mtn., Asia	B11	56
Nowshera, Pak.	B4	54
Nowshera, Pak.	C11	56
Nowy Dwór Mazowiecki, Pol.	D16	16
Nowy Sącz, Pol.	G16	16
Nowy Sącz, state, Pol.	G16	16
Nowy Staw, Pol.	B15	16
Nowy Targ, Pol.	G15	16
Noxapater, Ms., U.S.	E9	122
Noxen, Pa., U.S.	C9	114
Noxon, Mt., U.S.	B11	136
Noxubee, stm., U.S.	D10	122
Noy, stm., Laos	D7	48
Noya see Noia, Spain	B2	20
Noyant, Fr.	G9	14
Noyon, Fr.	E11	14
Nsanje, Mwi.	D6	68
Nsawam, Ghana	H4	64
Nsok, Eq. Gui.	I7	64
Nsukka, Nig.	H6	64
Nsuta, Ghana	H4	64
Ntwetwe Pan, pl., Bots.	B7	70
Nu see Salween, stm., Asia	C8	46
Nūbah, Jibāl an-, mts., Sudan	E6	62
Nubian Desert, des., Sudan	C6	62
Ñuble, stm., Chile	H2	92
Nucet, Rom.	C9	26
Nudol'-Šarino, Russia	D19	10
Nueces, stm., Tx., U.S.	G10	130
Nueces Plains, pl., Tx., U.S.	F8	130
Nueltin Lake, l., Can.	C11	106
Nuestra Señora de Talavera, Arg.	B6	92
Nueva, Isla, i., Chile	K3	90
Nueva Antioquia, Col.	D7	86
Nueva Ciudad Guerrero, Mex.	B9	100
Nueva Esparta, state, Ven.	B9	86
Nueva Galia, Arg.	G5	92
Nueva Germania, Para.	A9	92
Nueva Gerona, Cuba	B6	102
Nueva Imperial, Chile	G2	90
Nueva Italia de Ruiz, Mex.	F7	100
Nueva Loja, Ec.	G3	86
Nueva Palmira, Ur.	F8	92
Nueva Rosita, Mex.	A8	100
Nueva San Salvador, El Sal.	F3	102
Nueva Toltén, Chile	G2	90
Nueve, Canal Numero, can., Arg.	H8	92
Nueve de Julio, Arg.	G7	92
Nuevitas, Cuba	B9	102
Nuevo, Bajo, unds., Col.	E8	102
Nuevo, Cayo, i., Mex.	E12	100
Nuevo, Golfo, b., Arg.	H4	90
Nuevo Camarón, Mex.	G8	130
Nuevo Casas Grandes, Mex.	F9	98
Nuevo Delicias, Mex.	B7	100
Nuevo Laredo, Mex.	B9	100
Nuevo León, state, Mex.	B8	100
Nuevo Primero de Mayo, Mex.	H9	130
Nuevo Progreso, Mex.	F12	100
Nuevo Rocafuerte, Ec.	H4	86
Nuevo San Lucas, Mex.	F2	130
Nûgssuaq, pen., Grnld.	C15	141
Nugu, res., India	F3	53
Nui, at., Tuvalu	D8	72
Nuku'alofa, Tonga	n14	78e
Nukuhu, Pap. N. Gui.	b4	79a
Nukus, Uzb.	F9	32
Nul, Vanuatu	k17	79d
Nulato, Ak., U.S.	D8	140
Nullagine, Austl.	D4	74
Nullarbor, Austl.	F6	74
Nullarbor Plain, pl., Austl.	F5	74
Numan, Nig.	H7	64
Numancia (Numantia), hist., Spain	C8	20
Numantia see Numancia, hist., Spain	C8	20
Numata, Japan	C12	40
Numazu, Japan	D11	40
Numfoor, Pulau, i., Indon.	F10	44
Nunavut, state, Canada	B11	106
Nunda, N.Y., U.S.	B7	114
Nuneaton, Eng., U.K.	I11	12
Nuñez, Cape, c., S. Geor.	J9	90
Nunivak Island, i., Ak., U.S.	D6	140
Nunjiang, China	B10	36
Nunkun, mtn., India	A6	54
Nunnelly, Tn., U.S.	I10	120
Nuomin, stm., China	B10	36
Nuoro, Italy	D3	24
Nuquí, Col.	E3	86
Nura, Kaz.	E12	32
Nura, stm., Kaz.	E12	32
Nur Dağları, mts., Tur.	B7	58
Nuremberg see Nürnberg, Ger.	G6	16
Nuremburg see Nürnberg, Ger.	G6	16
Nuriootpa, Austl.	J2	76
Nürnberg (Nuremberg), Ger.	G6	16
Nūrpur, India	B5	54
Nürtingen, Ger.	H5	16
Nusa Tenggara Barat, state, Indon.	G10	50
Nusa Tenggara Timur, state, Indon.	H12	50
Nuṣayrīyah, Jabal an-, mts., Syria	C7	58
Nu Shan, mts., China	F4	36
Nüshan Hu, l., China	E8	42
Nushki, Pak.	D10	56
Nutrioso, Az., U.S.	J7	132
Nutter Fort, W.V., U.S.	E5	114
Nuuk see Godthåb, Grnld.	E15	141
Nuwerus, S. Afr.	G4	70
Nuweveldberge, mts., S. Afr.	H5	70
Nūzvīd, India	C5	53
Nyabéssan, Cam.	D2	66
Nyabing, Austl.	F3	74
Nyack, N.Y., U.S.	C12	114
Nyahanga, Tan.	E6	66
Nyainqêntanglha Feng, mtn., China	C13	54
Nyainqêntanglha Shan, mts., China	C6	46
Nyainrong, China	B14	54
Nyakanazi, Tan.	E6	66
Nyala, Sudan	E5	62
Nyalam, China	D10	54
Nyamlell, Sudan	F5	62
Nyamtumbo, Tan.	G7	66
Nyang, stm., China	D14	54
Nyanga, stm., Afr.	J7	64
Nyasa, Lake, l., Afr.	C5	68
Nyaunglebin, Mya.	C3	48
Nyboe Land, reg., Grnld.	A14	141
Nyborg, Den.	I4	8
Nybro, Swe.	H6	8
Nyda, Russia	A12	32
Nyêmo, China	C7	46
Nyeri, Kenya	E7	66
Nyerol, Sudan	F6	62
Nyimba, Zam.	C5	68
Nyingchi, China	F3	36
Nyírbátor, Hung.	B9	26
Nyíregyháza, Hung.	B8	26
Nykøbing, Den.	I4	8
Nyköping, Swe.	G7	8
Nyland see Uusimaa, state, Fin.	F11	8
Nylstroom, S. Afr.	D9	70
Nymboida, stm., Austl.	G9	76
Nymburk, Czech Rep.	F11	16
Nynäshamn, Swe.	G7	8
Nyngan, Austl.	H6	76
Nyon, Switz.	D3	22
Nyons, Fr.	E11	18
Nýrsko, Czech Rep.	G9	16
Nyš, Russia	F17	34
Nysa, Pol.	F13	16
Nysa Kłodzka, stm., Pol.	F12	16
Nysa Łużycka (Lausitzer Neisse), stm., Eur.	E10	16
Nyslott see Savonlinna, Fin.	F13	8
Nysted, Den.	B7	16
Nyunzu, D.R.C.	F5	66
Nyūzen, Japan	C10	40
Nyvrovo, Russia	F17	34
Nzébéla, Gui.	H3	64
Nzérékoré, Gui.	H3	64
N'zeto, Ang.	B1	68
Nzwani, i., Com.	C7	68
O		
Oahe, Lake, res., U.S.	A12	126
Oahe Dam, dam, S.D., U.S.	C12	126
Oahu, i., Hi., U.S.	B4	78a
Oakbank, Austl.	I3	76
Oak Bay, B.C., Can.	H7	138
Oak Bluffs, Ma., U.S.	C15	114
Oakburn, Mb., Can.	D13	124
Oak City, N.C., U.S.	I8	114
Oak City, Ut., U.S.	D4	132
Oakdale, Ca., U.S.	F5	134
Oakdale, La., U.S.	G6	122
Oakdale, Ne., U.S.	E14	126
Oakes, N.D., U.S.	A14	126
Oakesdale, Wa., U.S.	C9	136
Oakey, Austl.	F8	76
Oakfield, Me., U.S.	D8	110
Oakfield, Wi., U.S.	H10	118
Oak Grove, La., U.S.	E7	122
Oak Harbor, Wa., U.S.	B4	136
Oak Hill, Fl., U.S.	H5	116
Oak Hill, Oh., U.S.	F3	114
Oak Hill, W.V., U.S.	G4	114
Oakhurst, Ca., U.S.	F6	134
Oak Knolls, Ca., U.S.	I5	134
Oak Lake, Mb., Can.	E13	124
Oak Lake, l., Mb., Can.	E13	124
Oak Lake, l., On., Can.	A5	118
Oakland, Ca., U.S.	F3	134
Oakland, Ia., U.S.	C2	120
Oakland, Me., U.S.	F7	110
Oakland, Md., U.S.	E6	114
Oakland, Ms., U.S.	C9	122
Oakland, Ne., U.S.	C1	120
Oakland, Or., U.S.	G3	136
Oakland City, In., U.S.	F10	120
Oakland Park, Fl., U.S.	J5	116
Oak Lawn, Il., U.S.	G2	112
Oakley, Id., U.S.	H13	136
Oakley, Ks., U.S.	B8	128
Oakman, Al., U.S.	D11	122
Oakohay Creek, stm., Ms., U.S.	F9	122
Oakover, stm., Austl.	D4	74
Oak Park, Il., U.S.	G2	112
Oak Ridge, Tn., U.S.	H1	114
Oak Ridge National Laboratory, sci., Tn., U.S.	H1	114
Oaktown, In., U.S.	F10	120
Oak View, Ca., U.S.	I6	134
Oakville, Mb., Can.	E15	124
Oakville, On., Can.	E10	112
Oakwood, Oh., U.S.	C1	114
Oamaru, N.Z.	G4	80
Oancea, Rom.	D14	26
Ōarai, Japan	C13	40
Oatman, Az., U.S.	H2	132
Oaxaca, state, Mex.	G10	100
Oaxaca de Juárez, Mex.	G10	100
Ob', stm., Russia	A11	32
Obabika Lake, l., On., Can.	A9	112
Obal', stm., Bela.	E12	10
Obala, Cam.	D2	66
Obama, Japan	D8	40
Obama, Japan	G3	40
Oban, Austl.	C2	76
Oban, Scot., U.K.	E7	12
Obanazawa, Japan	A13	40
O Barco de Valdeorras, Spain	B3	20
Ob Bay see Obskaja guba, b., Russia	A12	32
Obed, Ab., Can.	C13	138
Obeliai, Lith.	E8	10
Oberá, Arg.	C10	92
Oberhausen, Ger.	E2	16
Oberlin, La., U.S.	G6	122
Oberlin, Oh., U.S.	C3	114
Oberösterreich, state, Aus.	B10	22
Oberpullendorf, Aus.	C13	22
Oberursel, Ger.	F4	16
Oberviechtach, Ger.	G8	16
Ob Gulf see Obskaja guba, b., Russia	A12	32
Obi, Kepulauan, is., Indon.	F8	44
Obi, Pulau, i., Indon.	F8	44
Obi, Selat, strt., Indon.	F8	44
Óbidos, Braz.	D6	84
Obihiro, Japan	C15	38
Obi Islands see Obi, Kepulauan, is., Indon.	F8	44
Obion, Tn., U.S.	H8	120
Obion, stm., Tn., U.S.	H8	120
Obion, Middle Fork, stm., Tn., U.S.	H9	120
Oblačnaja, gora, mtn., Russia	C11	38
Oblong, Il., U.S.	F9	120
Obluče, Russia	G15	34
Obninsk, Russia	E19	10
Obnova, Blg.	F12	26
Obo, C.A.R.	C5	66
Obock, Dji.	E8	62
Obokote, D.R.C.	E5	66
Obozërskij, Russia	E19	8
O'Brien, Or., U.S.	A2	134
Obrovac, Cro.	F12	22
Obša, stm., Russia	E16	10
Obščij syrt, mts., Eur.	D8	32
Obskaja guba, b., Russia	A12	32
Obuasi, Ghana	H4	64
Obudu, Nig.	H6	64
Ocala, Fl., U.S.	G3	116
Ocamo, stm., Ven.	F9	86
Ocampo, Mex.	A4	100
Ocaña, Col.	C5	86
Ocaña, Spain	E7	20
Occhito, Lago di, res., Italy	C8	24
Occidental, Cordillera, mts., Col.	E3	86
Oceana, W.V., U.S.	G4	114
Ocean Cape, c., Ak., U.S.	E12	140
Ocean City, Md., U.S.	F10	114
Ocean City, N.J., U.S.	E11	114
Ocean Falls, B.C., Can.	D3	138
Ocean Island see Banaba, i., Kir.	D7	72
Ocean Park, Wa., U.S.	D2	136
Oceanside, Ca., U.S.	J8	134
Ocean Springs, Ms., U.S.	G10	122
Ocheyedan, Ia., U.S.	H3	118
Ōchi, Japan	E7	40
Ochlocknee, Ga., U.S.	F1	116
Ochlockonee, stm., U.S.	G14	122
Ocho Rios, Jam.	i13	104d
Ochsenfurt, Ger.	G5	16
Ocilla, Ga., U.S.	E2	116
Ockelbo, Swe.	F7	8
Ocmulgee National Monument, p.o.i., Ga., U.S.	D2	116
Ocniţa, Mol.	A14	26
Ocoa, Bahía de, b., Dom. Rep.	C12	102
Ocoee, Fl., U.S.	H4	116
Ocoña, stm., Peru	G3	84
Oconee, stm., Ga., U.S.	D3	116
Oconee, Lake, res., Ga., U.S.	C2	116
Oconomowoc, Wi., U.S.	A9	120
Oconto, Wi., U.S.	D2	112
Oconto Falls, Wi., U.S.	D1	112
Ocosingo, Mex.	G12	100
Ocotal, Nic.	F4	102
Ocotes, Cerro, mtn., Mex.	B5	100
Ocotlán, Mex.	E7	100
Ocotlán de Morelos, Mex.	G10	100
Ocozocuautla, Mex.	G12	100
Ocracoke Island, i., N.C., U.S.	A10	116
Ocumare del Tuy, Ven.	B8	86
Oda, Ghana	H4	64
Ōda, Japan	D5	40
Oda, Jabal, mtn., Sudan	C7	62
Odaka, Japan	B14	40
Ōdate, Japan	D14	38
Odawara, Japan	D12	40
Odebolt, Ia., U.S.	B2	120
Odell, Il., U.S.	D9	120
Odell, Tx., U.S.	G9	128
Odem, Tx., U.S.	G10	130
Odemira, Port.	G2	20
Ödemiş, Tur.	E10	28
Odendaalsrus, S. Afr.	E8	70
Odense, Den.	I3	8
Odenwald, mts., Ger.	G4	16
Oder (Odra), stm., Eur.	D10	16
Oderzo, Italy	E9	22
Odesa, Ukr.	C17	26
Odesa, co., Ukr.	C16	26
Odessa see Odesa, Ukr.	C17	26
Odessa, Mo., U.S.	F3	120
Odessa, Tx., U.S.	C5	130
Odessa, Wa., U.S.	C8	136
Odesskoe, Russia	D12	32
Odiel, stm., Spain	G4	20
Odienné, C. Iv.	H3	64
Odin, Mount, mtn., B.C., Can.	F12	138
Odincovo, Russia	E20	10
Odobeşti, Rom.	D13	26
Odolanów, Pol.	E13	16
Odon, In., U.S.	F11	120
O'Donnell, Tx., U.S.	B6	130
Odorheiu Secuiesc, Rom.	C12	26
Odra (Oder), stm., Eur.	D10	16
Odrzywół, Pol.	E16	16
Odum, Ga., U.S.	E3	116
Odžaci, Yugo.	D6	26
Oebisfelde, Ger.	D6	16
Oeiras, Braz.	D4	88
Oelsnitz, Ger.	F8	16
Oelwein, Ia., U.S.	B6	120
Oenpelli, Austl.	B6	74
Oetz, Aus.	C7	22
O'Fallon, Mo., U.S.	F7	120
Ofanto, stm., Italy	D9	24
Ofaqim, Isr.	G5	58
Offa, Nig.	H5	64
Offaly, state, Ire.	H5	12
Offenbach am Main, Ger.	F4	16
Offenburg, Ger.	H3	16
Oficina Alemania, Chile	B3	92
Ofu, i., Am. Sam.	h13	79c
Ogaden, reg., Afr.	F8	62
Ōgaki, Japan	D9	40
Ogallala, Ne., U.S.	F11	126
Ogan, stm., Indon.	E4	50
Ogasawara-guntō, is., Japan	G18	30
Ogatsu, Japan	A14	40
Ogawa, Japan	G3	40
Ogbomosho, Nig.	H5	64
Ogden, Ks., U.S.	B12	128
Ogden, Ut., U.S.	B5	132
Ogdensburg, N.Y., U.S.	D14	112
Ogeechee, stm., Ga., U.S.	D4	116
Ogema, Sk., Can.	E8	124
Ogidaki Mountain, hill, On., Can.	A6	112
Ogilvie, Mn., U.S.	F5	118
Ogilvie Mountains, mts., Yk., Can.	C3	106
Oglesby, Il., U.S.	C8	120
Oglethorpe, Ga., U.S.	D1	116
Ogliastra, reg., Italy	E3	24
Oglio, stm., Italy	E6	22
Ogmore, Austl.	D7	76
Ognon, stm., Fr.	G15	14
Ogoja, Nig.	H6	64
Ogoki, stm., On., Can.	E13	106
Ogooué, stm., Afr.	I7	64
Ogōri, Japan	E4	40
Ogosta, stm., Blg.	F10	26
Ogre, Lat.	D7	10
Ogre, stm., Lat.	D8	10
O Grove, Spain	B2	20
Ogulin, Cro.	E12	22
Ogunquit, Me., U.S.	G6	110
Ogurdžaly, ostrov, i., Turkmen.	B7	56
Oğuzeli, Tur.	B8	58
Oha, Russia	F17	34
Ohanet, Alg.	D6	64
Ōhara, Japan	D13	40
O'Higgins, Cabo, c., Chile	e30	78l
O'Higgins, Lago (San Martín, Lago), l., S.A.	I2	90
Ohio, state, U.S.	D3	114
Ohio, stm., U.S.	G9	120
Ohio Peak, mtn., Co., U.S.	E9	132
'Ohonua, Tonga	o15	78e
Ohoopee, stm., Ga., U.S.	D3	116
Ohota, stm., Russia	E17	34
Ohotsk, Russia	E17	34
Ohře, stm., Eur.	F9	16
Ohrid, Mac.	B3	28
Ohrid, Lake, l., Eur.	D14	24
Ohrigstad, S. Afr.	D10	70
Öhringen, Ger.	G5	16
Ohuira, Bahía de, l., Mex.	C4	100
Ōi, stm., Japan	E11	40
Oiapoque, Braz.	C7	84
Oiapoque (Oyapok), stm., S.A.	C7	84
Oies, Île aux, i., Qc., Can.	C6	110
Oil Center, N.M., U.S.	B4	130
Oil City, La., U.S.	E4	122
Oil City, Pa., U.S.	C6	114
Oildale, Ca., U.S.	H7	134
Oilton, Ok., U.S.	A2	122
Oilton, Tx., U.S.	G9	130
Oil Trough, Ar., U.S.	B7	122
Oise, state, Fr.	E11	14
Oise, stm., Eur.	E11	14
Oistins, Barb.	n8	105d
Ōita, Japan	F4	40
Ōita, state, Japan	F4	40
Oituz, Pasul, p., Rom.	C13	26
Ojat', stm., Russia	F16	8
Öje, Swe.	F5	8
Ojinaga, Mex.	A6	100
Ojiya, Japan	B11	40
Ojmjakon, Russia	D17	34
Ojocaliente, Mex.	D7	100
Ojo de la Casa, Mex.	C1	130
Ojo del Carrizo, Mex.	E2	130
Ojo de Liebre, Laguna, b., Mex.	B1	100
Ojos del Salado, Nevado, mtn., S.A.	C3	92
Ojos Negros, Mex.	L9	134

Name	Map Ref.	Page
Oxley Wild Rivers National Park, p.o.i., Austl.	H8	76
Oxnard, Ca., U.S.	I6	134
Oxus see Amu Darya, stm., Asia	F10	32
Oya, stm., Malay.	B8	50
Oyabe, Japan	C9	40
Ōyama, Japan	C12	40
Ōyano, Japan	G3	40
Oyapok (Oiapoque), stm., S.A.	C7	84
Oyem, Gabon	D2	66
Oyen, Ab., Can.	C3	124
Oyo, Nig.	H5	64
Oyonnax, Fr.	C11	18
Oyster Creek, mth., Tx., U.S.	E12	130
Ozamis, Phil.	F4	52
Ozark, Al., U.S.	F13	122
Ozark, Ar., U.S.	B5	122
Ozark, Mo., U.S.	G4	120
Ozark Plateau, plat., U.S.	H4	120
Ozarks, Lake of the, res., Mo., U.S.	F5	120
Ózd, Hung.	A7	26
Ožerele, Russia	F21	10
Ozernovskij, Russia	F20	34
Ozërnyj, Russia	D10	32
Ozery, Russia	F21	10
Ozette Lake, l., Wa., U.S.	B2	136
Ozieri, Italy	D2	24
Ozimek, Pol.	F14	16
Ozinki, Russia	D7	32
Ozorków, Pol.	E15	16
Ōzu, Japan	F5	40
Ozuluama, Mex.	E9	100
Ozurgeti, Geor.	F6	32

P

Name	Map Ref.	Page
Paagoumène, N. Cal.	m14	79d
Paama, state, Vanuatu	k17	79d
Paama, i., Vanuatu	k17	79d
Paamiut see Frederikshåb, Grnld.	E15	141
Paarl, S. Afr.	H4	70
Paauilo, Hi., U.S.	C6	78a
Pabbay, i., Scot., U.K.	D5	12
Pabbiring, Kepulauan, is., Indon.	F11	50
Pabean, Indon.	G9	50
Pabellón, Ensenada del, b., Mex.	C4	100
Pabianice, Pol.	E15	16
Pablo, Mt., U.S.	C12	136
Pābna, Bngl.	G12	54
Pabradė, Lith.	F8	10
Pacaás Novos, Serra dos, mts., Braz.	F5	84
Pacajus, Braz.	C6	88
Pacasmayo, Peru	E2	84
Pacatuba, Braz.	C6	88
Pachino, Italy	H9	24
Pachitea, stm., Peru	E3	84
Pachmarhi, India	G7	54
Pāchora, India	H5	54
Pachuca de Soto, Mex.	E9	100
Pacific, B.C., Can.	B2	138
Pacific, Mo., U.S.	F7	120
Pacifica, Ca., U.S.	F3	134
Pacific-Antarctic Ridge, unds.	P22	142
Pacific Grove, Ca., U.S.	G3	134
Pacific Ocean	F20	142
Pacific Ranges, mts., B.C., Can.	E5	138
Pacific Rim National Park, p.o.i., B.C., Can.	H5	138
Paciran, Indon.	G8	50
Pacitan, Indon.	H7	50
Pacora, Pan.	C2	86
Pacov, Czech Rep.	G11	16
Pacuí, stm., Braz.	I3	88
Padada, Phil.	G5	52
Padamo, stm., Ven.	F9	86
Padampur, India	H9	54
Padang, Indon.	D6	50
Padang, Indon.	G12	50
Padang, Indon.	D2	50
Padang, Pulau, i., Indon.	C3	50
Padang Endau, Malay.	K6	48
Padangpanjang, Indon.	D2	50
Padangsidempuan, Indon.	C1	50
Padany, Russia	E15	8
Padas, stm., Malay.	A9	50
Padauari, stm., Braz.	G9	86
Paddle, stm., Ab., Can.	B16	138
Paddle Prairie, Ab., Can.	D7	106
Paderborn, Ger.	E4	16
Padjelanta Nationalpark, p.o.i., Swe.	C7	8
Padloping Island, i., N.T., Can.	D13	141
Padma see Ganges, stm., Asia	G13	54
Pádova (Padua), Italy	E8	22
Pādra, India	G4	54
Padrauna, India	E9	54
Padre Bernardo, Braz.	H1	88
Padre Island, i., Tx., U.S.	G10	130
Padre Island National Seashore, p.o.i., Tx., U.S.	G10	130
Padre Paraíso, Braz.	I5	88
Padstow, Eng., U.K.	K8	12
Padua see Pádova, Italy	E8	22
Paducah, Ky., U.S.	G9	120
Paducah, Tx., U.S.	G8	128
Paea, Fr. Poly.	v21	78h
Paedun, Kor., S.	D1	40
Paektu-san, mtn., Asia	C10	36
Paestum, hist., Italy	D8	24
Páez, stm., Col.	F4	86
Pafúri, Moz.	C10	70
Pag, Otok, i., Cro.	F11	22
Pagadenbaru, Indon.	G5	50
Pagadian, Phil.	G4	52
Pagai Selatan, Pulau, i., Indon.	E2	50
Pagai Utara, Pulau, i., Indon.	E2	50
Pagan, Mya.	B2	48
Pagan, i., N. Mar. Is.	B5	72
Pagaralam, Indon.	E3	50
Pagasitikós Kólpos, b., Grc.	D5	28
Page, Az., U.S.	G5	132
Page, N.D., U.S.	G16	124
Pagėgiai, Lith.	E4	10
Pagerdewa, Indon.	E4	50
Paget, Mount, mtn., S. Geor.	J9	90
Pagoda Peak, mtn., Co., U.S.	C9	132
Pagoda Point, c., Mya.	E2	48
Pagon, Bukit, mtn., Asia	A9	50
Pago Pago, Am. Sam.	h12	79c
Pagosa Springs, Co., U.S.	F9	132
Paguate, N.M., U.S.	H9	132
Pagudpud, Phil.	A3	52
Pahača, Russia	D22	34
Pahala, Hi., U.S.	D6	78a
Pahang, state, Malay.	K6	48
Pahang, stm., Malay.	K6	48
Pahokee, Fl., U.S.	J5	116
Pahost, Bela.	G12	10
Pahrump, Nv., U.S.	G10	134
Pai, Thai.	C4	48
Pai, stm., Asia	C3	48
Paico, Peru	F3	84
Paide, Est.	B8	10
Paige, Tx., U.S.	D10	130
Paignton, Eng., U.K.	K9	12
Paiguano, Chile	E2	92
Päijänne, l., Fin.	F11	8
Paikü Co, l., China	D10	54
Pailolo Channel, strt., Hi., U.S.	B5	78a
Paimpol, Fr.	F5	14
Painan, Indon.	D2	50
Painesdale, Mi., U.S.	D10	118
Painesville, Oh., U.S.	C4	114
Paint, stm., Mi., U.S.	E10	118
Paint Creek, stm., Oh., U.S.	E14	120
Painted Desert, des., Az., U.S.	H5	132
Painted Rock Reservoir, res., Az., U.S.	K3	132
Paintsville, Ky., U.S.	G3	114
Paisley, Scot., U.K.	F8	12
Paisley, Or., U.S.	H6	136
Païta, N. Cal.	n16	79d
Paita, Peru	E1	84
Paitan, Telukan, b., Malay.	G1	52
Paiton, Indon.	G8	50
Pajala, Swe.	C10	8
Paján, Ec.	H1	86
Pajares, Puerto de, p., Spain	B5	20
Pajaros Point, c., Br. Vir. Is.	d9	104b
Pajęczno, Pol.	E14	16
Pajer, gora, mtn., Russia	C1	34
Pajeú, stm., Braz.	E6	88
Paj-Hoj, hills, Russia	A10	32
Paka, Malay.	J6	48
Pākāla, India	E4	53
Pakaraima Mountains, mts., S.A.	E11	86
Pakashkan Lake, l., On., Can.	B8	118
Pākaur, India	F11	54
Pak Chong, Thai.	E5	48
Pākhāl, l., India	C5	53
Pákhna, Cyp.	D3	58
Pakhoi see Beihai, China	K3	42
Pakistan, ctry., Asia	C2	46
Paklenica Nacionalni Park, p.o.i., Cro.	F12	22
Pakokku, Mya.	B2	48
Pakowki Lake, l., Ab., Can.	E2	124
Pākpattan, Pak.	C4	54
Pak Phanang, Thai.	H5	48
Pak Phayun, Thai.	I5	48
Pak Phraek, Thai.	H5	48
Pakrac, Cro.	E14	22
Pakruojis, Lith.	E6	10
Paks, Hung.	C5	26
Paktīā, state, Afg.	B2	54
Paktīkā, state, Afg.	B2	54
Pakwash Lake, l., On., Can.	A5	118
Pakxé, Laos	E7	48
Pala, Chad	F2	62
Pala, Mya.	F4	48
Palacios, Tx., U.S.	F11	130
Palagruža, Otoci, is., Cro.	H13	22
Palai, India	G3	53
Palaiochóra, Grc.	H6	28
Pālakodu, India	C5	53
Palamós, Spain	C14	20
Pālampur, India	B6	54
Palamu National Park, p.o.i., India	G10	54
Palamut, Tur.	D10	28
Palana, Russia	E20	34
Palanan Bay, b., Phil.	B4	52
Palanga, Lith.	E3	10
Palangkaraya, Indon.	E8	50
Palani, India	F3	53
Pālanpur, India	F4	54
Palaoa Point, c., Hi., U.S.	C4	78a
Palapye, Bots.	C8	70
Pālār, stm., India	E4	53
Palas de Rei, Spain	B3	20
Palatka, Russia	D19	34
Palatka, Fl., U.S.	G4	116
Palau, Italy	C3	24
Palau, ctry., Oc.	g8	78b
Palau Islands, is., Palau	D10	44
Palauk, Mya.	F4	48
Palaw, Mya.	F4	48
Palawan, i., Phil.	F2	52
Palawan Passage, strt., Phil.	F1	52
Palayan, Phil.	C3	52
Pālayankottai, India	G3	53
Palembang, Indon.	E4	50
Palena, Italy	I11	22
Palena, stm., S.A.	H2	90
Palencia, Spain	B6	20
Palencia, co., Spain	B6	20
Palen Lake, l., Ca., U.S.	J1	132
Palenque, Mex.	G13	100
Palenque, hist., Mex.	G12	100
Palermo, Col.	F4	86
Palermo, Italy	F7	24
Palermo, Ur.	F10	92
Palestina, Mex.	E6	130
Palestine, Ar., U.S.	B7	122
Palestine, Il., U.S.	E10	120
Palestine, Tx., U.S.	F3	122
Palestine, hist. reg., Asia	G6	58
Palestine, Lake, res., Tx., U.S.	E3	122
Palestrina, Italy	I9	22
Paletwa, Mya.	D7	46
Pālghāt, India	F3	53
Palgrave Point, c., Nmb.	E1	68
Palhano, stm., Braz.	C6	88
Pāli, India	F4	54
Palima, Indon.	F12	50
Palinuro, Capo, c., Italy	D9	24
Palisade, Ne., U.S.	A7	128
Palisades, Id., U.S.	G15	136
Palisades Reservoir, res., U.S.	G15	136
Pālitāna, India	H3	54
Palivere, Est.	A6	10
Palizada, Mex.	F12	100
Palk Bay, b., Asia	G4	53
Palkino, Russia	G20	8
Pālkonda, India	B6	53
Pālkonda Range, mts., India	D4	53
Palk Strait, strt., Asia	G4	53
Pallastunturi, mtn., Fin.	B11	8
Palliser, Cape, c., N.Z.	E6	80
Palma, Braz.	K4	88
Palma, Moz.	C7	68
Palma, stm., Braz.	G2	88
Palma, Badia de, b., Spain	E13	20
Palmácia, Braz.	C6	88
Palma del Río, Spain	G5	20
Palma de Mallorca, Spain	E13	20
Palma di Montechiaro, Italy	G7	24
Palmar, stm., Ven.	B6	86
Palmar, Lago Artificial del, res., Ur.	F9	92
Palmar Camp, Belize	D3	102
Palmarejo, P.R.	B1	104a
Palmares, Braz.	E8	88
Palmarito, Ven.	D6	86
Palmarola, Isola, i., Italy	D6	24
Palmas, Braz.	F1	88
Palmas, Braz.	C12	92
Palmas Bellas, Pan.	H7	102
Palmas de Monte Alto, Braz.	H4	88
Palma Soriano, Cuba	B9	102
Palm Bay, Fl., U.S.	H5	116
Palm Beach, Fl., U.S.	J5	116
Palmdale, Ca., U.S.	I7	134
Palm Desert, Ca., U.S.	J9	134
Palmeira, Braz.	B13	92
Palmeira das Missões, Braz.	C11	92
Palmeira dos Índios, Braz.	E7	88
Palmeiras, stm., Braz.	F2	88
Palmeirinhas, Ponta das, c., Ang.	B1	68
Palmelo, Braz.	I1	88
Palmer, P.R.	B4	104a
Palmer, Ak., U.S.	D10	140
Palmer, Ma., U.S.	B13	114
Palmer, Ne., U.S.	F14	126
Palmer, Tn., U.S.	B13	122
Palmer, sci., Ant.	B34	81
Palmer Lake, Co., U.S.	B3	128
Palmer Land, reg., Ant.	C34	81
Palmerston, N.Z.	G4	80
Palmerston, at., Cook Is.	E10	72
Palmerston, Cape, c., Austl.	C7	76
Palmerston North, N.Z.	E6	80
Palmerton, Pa., U.S.	D10	114
Palmetto, Ga., U.S.	D14	122
Palmetto, La., U.S.	G6	122
Palmetto Point, c., Antig.	e4	105b
Palmi, Italy	F9	24
Palmira, Col.	F3	86
Palmira, Cuba	A7	102
Palmira, Ec.	I2	86
Palmitas, Ur.	F9	92
Palm Springs, Ca., U.S.	J9	134
Palmyra see Tudmur, Syria	D9	58
Palmyra, Il., U.S.	E7	120
Palmyra, Mo., U.S.	E6	120
Palmyra, N.Y., U.S.	A8	114
Palmyra, Va., U.S.	G7	114
Palmyra, hist., Syria	D9	58
Palmyra Atoll, at., Oc.	C10	72
Palo Alto, Mex.	H8	130
Palo Alto, Ca., U.S.	F3	134
Palo Blanco, P.R.	B2	104a
Palo Flechado Pass, p., N.M., U.S.	E3	128
Paloh, Malay.	B7	50
Paloich, Sudan	E6	62
Palojoensuu, Fin.	B10	8
Palomar Mountain, mtn., Ca., U.S.	J9	134
Palomas, Mex.	F4	130
Palo Pinto, Tx., U.S.	B9	130
Palopo, Indon.	E12	50
Palos, Cabo de, c., Spain	G10	20
Palo Santo, Arg.	B8	92
Palos Verdes Point, c., Ca., U.S.	J7	134
Palouse, stm., U.S.	D8	136
Palo Verde, Ca., U.S.	J2	132
Palpa, Peru	F2	84
Palpalá, Arg.	B5	92
Palu, Indon.	D11	50
Palu, Teluk, b., Indon.	D11	50
Paluga, Russia	D21	8
Palwal, India	D6	54
Pama, Burkina	G5	64
Pamanukan, Indon.	G5	50
Pāmban Channel, strt., India	G4	53
Pāmban Island, i., India	G4	53
Pamekasan, Indon.	G8	50
Pamenang, Indon.	E3	50
Pameungpeuk, Indon.	G5	50
Pamiers, Fr.	F7	18
Pamir, mts., Asia	B11	56
Pamlico Sound, strt., N.C., U.S.	A10	116
Pampa, Tx., U.S.	F8	128
Pampã, stm., Braz.	I5	88
Pampa (Pampas), reg., Arg.	G4	90
Pampa Almirón, Arg.	C8	92
Pampa del Chañar, Arg.	E3	92
Pampa del Indio, Arg.	B7	92
Pampanga, stm., Phil.	C3	52
Pampanua, Indon.	F12	50
Pampas, Peru	F3	84
Pampas, stm., Peru	F3	84
Pampas see Pampa, reg., Arg.	F4	90
Pamplico, S.C., U.S.	B6	116
Pamplona, Col.	D5	86
Pamplona, Spain	B9	20
Pamukkale (Hierapolis), hist., Tur.	F12	28
Pamukova, Tur.	C13	28
Pana, Il., U.S.	E8	120
Panabá, Mex.	B3	102
Panabo, Phil.	G5	52
Panacea, Fl., U.S.	G14	122
Panadura, Sri L.	H4	53
Panagjurište, Blg.	G11	26
Panaitan, Pulau, i., Indon.	G4	50
Panaji, India	D1	53
Panamá, Pan.	H8	102
Panama, Ok., U.S.	B4	122
Panama, ctry., N.A.	F9	96
Panamá, Bahía de, b., Pan.	H8	102
Panamá, Canal de (Panama Canal), can., Pan.	H8	102
Panamá, Golfo de, b., Pan.	D2	86
Panama, Gulf of see Panamá, Golfo de, b., Pan.	D2	86
Panama, Isthmus of see Panamá, Istmo de, isth., Pan.	H8	102
Panamá, Istmo de (Panama, Isthmus of), isth., Pan.	H8	102
Panama Basin, unds.	H5	144
Panama Canal see Panamá, Canal de, can., Pan.	H8	102
Panama City, Fl., U.S.	G13	122
Panambi, Braz.	D11	92
Panamint Range, mts., Ca., U.S.	G8	134
Panamint Valley, val., Ca., U.S.	G8	134
Panao, Peru	E2	84
Panarea, Isola, i., Italy	F9	24
Panaro, stm., Italy	F8	22
Panay, i., Phil.	E4	52
Panay Gulf, b., Phil.	E4	52
Pančevo, Yugo.	E7	26
Panciu, Rom.	D14	26
Panda, Moz.	D12	70
Pandaria, India	G8	54
Pan de Azúcar, Ur.	G10	92
Pandėlys, Lith.	D8	10
Pāndharkawada, India	A4	53
Pandharpur, India	C2	53
Pāndhurna, India	H7	54
Pando, Ur.	G10	92
Panevėžys, Lith.	E7	10
Panfilov, Kaz.	F13	32
Pāng, stm., Mya.	B4	48
Panga, D.R.C.	D5	66
Pangala, Congo	E2	66
Pangandaran, Indon.	G6	50
Pangani, Tan.	F7	66
Pangani, stm., Tan.	E7	66
Pangburn, Ar., U.S.	B7	122
Pangfou see Bengbu, China	E7	42
Panghkam, Mya.	D8	46
Pangi, D.R.C.	E5	66
Pangkajene, Indon.	F11	50
Pangkalanbrandan, Indon.	J4	48
Pangkalanbuun, Indon.	E7	50
Pangkalpinang, Indon.	E5	50
Pangnirtung, N.T., Can.	B17	106
Pango Aluquem, Ang.	B1	68
Pangŏjin, Kor., S.	D2	40
Pangong Tso, l., Asia	B7	54
Panguiranan, Phil.	D4	52
Panguitch, Ut., U.S.	F4	132
Pangutaran, Phil.	G3	52
Pangutaran Group, is., Phil.	G3	52
Panhandle, Tx., U.S.	F7	128
Paniau, mtn., Hi., U.S.	B1	78a
Panié, Mont, mtn., N. Cal.	m15	79d
Panīpat, India	D6	54
Panitan, Phil.	E4	52
Panj (Pjandž), stm., Asia	B11	56
Panjang, Indon.	F4	50
Panjang, Selat, strt., Indon.	C3	50
Pankshin, Nig.	H6	64
Panlong (Lo), stm., Asia	A7	48
P'anmunjŏm-ni, Kor., N.	E7	38
Panna, India	F8	54
Panna National Park, p.o.i., India	F7	54
Pannawonica, Austl.	D3	74
Panola, U.S.	E10	122
Páno Lévkara, Cyp.	D4	58
Panopah, Indon.	D7	50
Panorama, Braz.	D6	90
Panovo, Russia	C18	32
Panruti, India	F4	53
Panshan, China	D4	38
Pantanal, reg., S.A.	C5	90
Pantanaw, Mya.	D2	48
Pantar, Pulau, i., Indon.	G7	44
Pantelleria, Isola di, i., Italy	H6	24
Pantonlabu, Indon.	J3	48
Pánuco, Mex.	E10	100
Pánuco, stm., Mex.	E9	100
Panxian, China	F5	36
Panyam, Nig.	H6	64
Panzós, Guat.	E3	102
Pao, stm., Thai.	D6	48
Pao, stm., Ven.	C8	86
Pao, stm., Ven.	C9	86
Paochi see Baoji, China	D2	42
Paoki see Baoji, China	D2	42
Paola, Italy	E9	24
Paola, Ks., U.S.	F3	120
Paoli, In., U.S.	F11	120
Paopao, Fr. Poly.	v20	78h
Paoting see Baoding, China	B6	42
Paotou see Baotou, China	A4	42
Paotow see Baotou, China	A4	42
Pápa, Hung.	B4	26
Papagaio, stm., Braz.	I10	86
Papagaios, Braz.	D3	88
Papagayo, Golfo de, b., C.R.	G4	102
Papaikou, Hi., U.S.	D6	78a
Papantla de Olarte, Mex.	E10	100
Papara, Fr. Poly.	v22	78h
Papa Stour, i., Scot., U.K.	n18	12a
Papeari, Fr. Poly.	w22	78h
Papeete, Fr. Poly.	v21	78h
Papenburg, Ger.	C3	16
Papetoai, Fr. Poly.	v20	78h
Paphos see Néa Páfos, Cyp.	D3	58
Papigochic, stm., Mex.	G8	98
Papillion, Ne., U.S.	C1	120
Paposo, Chile	B2	92
Papua, Gulf of, b., Pap. N. Gui.	D5	72
Papua New Guinea, ctry., Oc.	D5	72
Papulovo, Russia	F23	8
Papun, Mya.	C3	48
Papunáua, stm., Col.	G6	86
Papurí (Papuri), stm., S.A.	G6	86
Papuri (Papurí), stm., S.A.	G6	86
Pará, state, Braz.	D7	84
Pará, stm., Braz.	A1	88
Pará, stm., Braz.	J3	88
Parabel', Russia	C14	32
Paraburdoo, Austl.	D3	74
Paracatu, Braz.	I2	88
Paracatu, stm., Braz.	I3	88
Paracel Islands see Xisha Qundao, is., China	B5	50
Pārachinār, Pak.	B3	54
Paracho de Verduzco, Mex.	F7	100
Parachute, Co., U.S.	D8	132
Paraćin, Yugo.	F8	26
Paracuru, Braz.	B6	88
Parada, Punta, c., Peru	G2	84
Paradise, Ca., U.S.	D4	134
Paradise, Mt., U.S.	C12	136
Paradise, Nv., U.S.	G1	132
Paradise Island, i., Bah.	m18	104f
Paradise Valley, Az., U.S.	J5	132
Paradise Valley, Nv., U.S.	B8	134
Pāradwīp, India	H11	54
Paragonah, Ut., U.S.	F4	132
Paragould, Ar., U.S.	H7	120
Paraguá, stm., Bol.	B4	90
Paragua, stm., Ven.	D10	86
Paraguaçu, stm., Braz.	G6	88
Paraguai (Paraguay), stm., S.A.	D5	90
Paraguaipoa, Ven.	B6	86
Paraguaná, Península de, pen., Ven.	A6	86
Paraguarí, Para.	B9	92
Paraguarí, state, Para.	C9	92
Paraguay, ctry., S.A.	D5	90
Paraguay (Paraguai), stm., S.A.	E5	90
Paraíba, state, Braz.	D7	88
Paraíba do Sul, stm., Braz.	K5	88
Paraibano, Braz.	D3	88
Parainen, Fin.	F9	8
Paraíso, Mex.	F12	100
Paraiso, Pan.	H8	102
Parakou, Benin	H5	64
Paramakkudi, India	G4	53
Paramaribo, Sur.	B6	84
Parambu, Braz.	D5	88
Paramillo, Parque Nacional, p.o.i., Col.	D3	86
Paramirim, Braz.	G4	88
Paramirim, stm., Braz.	F4	88
Páramo de Masa, Puerto de, p., Spain	B7	20
Paramušir, ostrov, i., Russia	F20	34
Paramythiá, Grc.	D3	28
Paran, Nahal (Girafi, Wadi), stm.	I5	58
Paraná, Arg.	E7	92
Paranã, Braz.	G1	88
Paraná, state, Braz.	D6	90
Paranã, stm., Braz.	G1	88
Paraná, stm., S.A.	F5	90
Paranaguá, Braz.	B13	92
Paranaguá, Baía de, b., Braz.	B13	92
Paranaíba, Braz.	C6	90
Paranaíba, stm., Braz.	C6	90
Paranaidji, Braz.	D2	88
Paranapanema, stm., Braz.	D6	90
Paranapiacaba, Serra do, mts., Braz.	B13	92
Paranavaí, Braz.	D6	90
Parang, Phil.	G5	52
Parang, Pulau, i., Indon.	F7	50
Parângu Mare, Vârful, mtn., Rom.	D10	26
Paranhos, Braz.	A10	92
Paranoá, Lago do, res., Braz.	H2	88
Paraopeba, Braz.	J3	88
Parapetí, stm., Bol.	C4	90
Parara, Indon.	E12	50
Paratinga, Braz.	G4	88
Paratoo, Austl.	I2	76
Paray-le-Monial, Fr.	C9	18
Pārbati, stm., India	F6	54
Pārbatipur, Bngl.	F12	54
Parbhani, India	B3	53
Parchim, Ger.	C7	16
Pardeeville, Wi., U.S.	H9	118
Pārdi, India	H4	54
Parding, China	B12	54
Pardo, stm., Braz.	K1	88
Pardo, stm., Braz.	H6	88
Pardo, stm., Braz.	L1	88
Pardo, stm., Braz.	D6	90
Pardo, stm., Braz.	D11	92
Pardubice, Czech Rep.	F11	16
Paredón, Mex.	C8	100
Parelhas, Braz.	D7	88
Paren', Russia	D21	34
Paren', stm., Russia	D21	34
Parent, Qc., Can.	C2	110
Parentis-en-Born, Fr.	E4	18
Parepare, Indon.	E11	50
Parera, Arg.	G5	92
Parfenevo, Russia	F20	8
Párga, Grc.	D3	28
Parham, Antig.	f4	105b
Paria, Gulf of, b.	B10	86
Paria, Península de, pen., Ven.	B10	86
Pariaguán, Ven.	C9	86
Pariaman, Indon.	D1	50
Paricutín, vol., Mex.	F7	100
Parigi, Indon.	D12	50
Parika, Guy.	B6	84
Parikkala, Fin.	F13	8
Parima, stm., Braz.	F10	86
Parima, Serra (Parima, Sierra), mts., S.A.	F9	86
Parima, Sierra (Parima, Serra), mts., S.A.	F9	86
Parima Tapirapecó, Parque Nacional, p.o.i., Ven.	F9	86
Parintins, Braz.	D6	84
Paris, On., Can.	E9	112
Paris, Fr.	F11	14
Paris, Ar., U.S.	B5	122
Paris, Il., U.S.	I2	112
Paris, Ky., U.S.	F1	114
Paris, Mo., U.S.	E5	120
Paris, Tn., U.S.	H9	120
Paris, Tx., U.S.	D3	122
Parisienne, Ile, i., On., Can.	B5	112
Parita, Bahía de, b., Pan.	H7	102
Parit Buntar, Malay.	J5	48
Parkano, Fin.	E10	8
Park City, Mt., U.S.	B3	126
Park City, Ut., U.S.	C5	132
Parkdale, Or., U.S.	E5	136
Parker, Az., U.S.	I2	132
Parker, Co., U.S.	B4	128
Parker, Fl., U.S.	G13	122
Parker, Cape, c., N.T., Can.	B10	141
Parker City, In., U.S.	H4	112
Parker Dam, Ca., U.S.	I2	132
Parker Dam, dam, U.S.	I2	132
Parkersburg, Il., U.S.	F9	120
Parkersburg, Ia., U.S.	B5	120
Parkersburg, W.V., U.S.	E4	114
Parkes, Austl.	I7	76
Park Falls, Wi., U.S.	F8	118
Park Forest, Il., U.S.	G2	112
Parkhill, On., Can.	E8	112
Parkland, Wa., U.S.	C4	136
Park Range, mts., Co., U.S.	C10	132
Park Rapids, Mn., U.S.	E3	118
Parkrose, Or., U.S.	E4	136
Park Rynie, S. Afr.	G10	70
Parksley, Va., U.S.	G10	114
Parkston, S.D., U.S.	D14	126
Parksville, B.C., Can.	G6	138
Parkville, Md., U.S.	E9	114
Parkville, Mo., U.S.	E3	120
Parla, Spain	D7	20
Parlākimidi, India	B7	53
Parli, India	B3	53
Parma, Italy	F7	22
Parma, Mo., U.S.	H8	120
Parma, Oh., U.S.	C4	114
Parnaguá, Braz.	F3	88
Parnaíba, Braz.	B5	88
Parnaíba, stm., Braz.	B5	88
Parnaíbinha, stm., Braz.	E2	88
Parnamirim, Braz.	E6	88
Parnassós, mtn., Grc.	E5	28
Párnitha, mtn., Grc.	E6	28
Pärnu, Est.	G11	8
Pärnu laht, b., Est.	G11	8
Paro, Bhu.	E12	54
Pārola, India	H5	54
Paromaj, Russia	F17	34
Paroo, stm., Austl.	G5	76
Páros, i., Grc.	F8	28
Parowan, Ut., U.S.	F4	132
Parque Nacional da Chapada da Diamantina, p.o.i., Braz.	G4	88
Parral, Chile	H2	92
Parral, stm., Mex.	B6	100
Parramatta, Austl.	I8	76
Parras de la Fuente, Mex.	C7	100
Parrish, Fl., U.S.	I3	116
Parrsboro, N.S., Can.	E12	110
Parry, Cape, c., N.T., Can.	A6	106
Parry Bay, b., N.T., Can.	B14	106
Parry Island, i., On., Can.	C9	112
Parry Peninsula, pen., N.T., Can.	B6	106
Parry Sound, On., Can.	C9	112
Parsberg, Ger.	G7	16
Parsęta, stm., Pol.	B11	16
Parshall, N.D., U.S.	G11	124
Paršino, Russia	C20	32
Parsnip, stm., B.C., Can.	A8	138
Parsons, Ks., U.S.	G2	120
Parsons, Tn., U.S.	B10	122
Pärsti, Est.	B8	10
Partanna, Italy	G6	24
Parthenay, Fr.	H8	14
Partinico, Italy	F7	24
Partizansk, Russia	C10	38
Partizánske, Slov.	H14	16
Paru, stm., Braz.	D7	84
Parú, stm., Ven.	E9	86
Paru de Oeste, stm., Braz.	C6	84
Parūr, India	F3	53
Pārvatīpuram, India	B6	53
Paryang, China	C9	54
Parys, S. Afr.	E8	70
Pasadena, Ca., U.S.	I7	134
Pasadena, Tx., U.S.	H3	122
Pasaje, Ec.	D2	84
Pa Sak, stm., Thai.	E5	48
Paşaköy, N. Cyp.	C4	58
Pasarbantal, Indon.	E2	50
Pasawng, Mya.	C3	48
Pascagoula, Ms., U.S.	G10	122
Pascagoula, stm., Ms., U.S.	G10	122
Paşcani, Rom.	B13	26
Pasco, Wa., U.S.	D7	136
Pascoag, R.I., U.S.	C14	114
Pascua, Isla de (Easter Island) (Rapa Nui), i., Chile	f30	78l
Pas-de-Calais, state, Fr.	D11	14
Pasewalk, Ger.	C10	16
Pasir Mas, Malay.	J6	48
Pasirpengarayan, Indon.	C2	50
Pasir Puteh, Malay.	J6	48
Paškovo, Russia	G15	34
Pasłęka, stm., Pol.	C16	16
Pasley Bay, b., N.T., Can.	A11	106
Pašman, Otok, i., Cro.	G12	22
Pasmore, stm., Austl.	H2	76
Pasni, Pak.	D9	56
Paso de Indios, Arg.	H3	90
Paso del Cerro, Ur.	E9	92
Paso de los Libres, Arg.	D9	92
Paso de los Toros, Ur.	F9	92
Paso de Patria, Para.	C8	92
Paso de San Antonio, Mex.	E3	130
Paso Hondo, Mex.	H13	100
Paso Robles, Ca., U.S.	H5	134
Pašozero, Russia	F16	8
Pasquia Hills, hills, Sk., Can.	A11	124
Pasrūr, Pak.	B5	54
Passadumkeag, Me., U.S.	E8	110
Passadumkeag Mountain, hill, Me., U.S.	E8	110
Passage Point, c., N.T., Can.	B16	140
Passaic, N.J., U.S.	H15	112
Passamaquoddy Bay, b., N.A.	E10	110
Passau, Ger.	H9	16
Passero, Capo, c., Italy	H9	24
Passo Fundo, Braz.	D11	92
Passo Real, Represa do, res., Braz.	D11	92
Passos, Braz.	K2	88
Pastavy, Bela.	E9	10
Pastaza, state, Ec.	H3	86
Pastaza, stm., S.A.	D2	84
Pastillo, P.R.	B3	104a
Pasto, Col.	G3	86
Pastos Bons, Braz.	D3	88
Pasuruan, Indon.	G8	50
Pasvalys, Lith.	D7	10
Pásztó, Hung.	B6	26
Patacamaya, Bol.	C3	90
Patadkal, hist., India	C3	53
Patagonia, Az., U.S.	L6	132
Patagonia, reg., Arg.	I2	90
Pātan, India	G3	54
Patchogue, N.Y., U.S.	D13	114
Patea, N.Z.	D6	80
Pategi, Nig.	H6	64
Pate Island, i., Kenya	E8	66
Patensie, S. Afr.	H7	70
Paterna, Spain	E10	20
Paternion, Aus.	D10	22
Paternò, Italy	G8	24
Paterson, N.J., U.S.	D11	114
Pathānkot, India	B5	54
Pathein, Mya.	D2	48
Pathfinder Reservoir, res., Wy., U.S.	E5	126
Pathiu, Thai.	G4	48
Pathum Thani, Thai.	E5	48
Pati, Indon.	G7	50
Patía, Col.	F3	86
Patía, stm., Col.	F2	86
Patiāla, India	C6	54
Patillas, P.R.	B3	104a
Pati Point, c., Guam	i10	78c
Pativilca, Peru	F2	84
Pātkai Range, mts., Asia	F4	36
Pat Mayse Lake, res., Tx., U.S.	D3	122
Pátmos, i., Grc.	F9	28
Patna, India	F10	54
Patna, India	H11	54
Patnāgarh, India	H9	54
Patnanongan Island, i., Phil.	C4	52
Pato Branco, Braz.	C11	92
Patoka, Il., U.S.	F8	120
Patoka, stm., In., U.S.	F10	120
Patoka Lake, res., In., U.S.	F11	120
Patomskoe nagor'e, plat., Russia	E12	34
Patonga, Ug.	D6	66
Patos, Braz.	D7	88
Patos, stm., Arg.	E3	92
Patos, Lagoa dos, b., Braz.	E12	92
Patos de Minas, Braz.	J2	88
Patquía, Arg.	D4	92
Pátra, Grc.	E4	28
Patrai, Gulf of see Patraikós Kólpos, b., Grc.	E4	28
Patraikós Kólpos, b., Grc.	E4	28
Patricio Lynch, Isla, i., Chile	I1	90
Patrocínio, Braz.	J2	88
Pattani, Thai.	I5	48
Pattaya, Thai.	F5	48
Patten, Me., U.S.	D8	110
Patterson, Ca., U.S.	F4	134
Patterson, Ga., U.S.	E3	116
Patterson, Mount, mtn., Yk., Can.	C4	106
Patti, Golfo di, b., Italy	F9	24
Pattison, Ms., U.S.	F8	122
Pattoki, Pak.	C4	54
Pattonsburg, Mo., U.S.	D3	120
Pattukkottai, India	F4	53
Pattullo, Mount, mtn., B.C., Can.	D5	106
Patuākhāli, Bngl.	G13	54
Patuca, stm., Hond.	E5	102
Pātūr, India	H6	54
Patusi, Pap. N. Gui.	a4	79a
Patuxent, stm., Md., U.S.	F9	114
Pátzcuaro, Mex.	F8	100
Pau, Fr.	F5	18
Pau, Gave de, stm., Fr.	F5	18
Pau Brasil, Braz.	H6	88
Pau dos Ferros, Braz.	D6	88
Pauh, Indon.	E3	50
Pauini, stm., Braz.	E4	84
Pauini, stm., Braz.	H10	86
Pauk, Mya.	B2	48
Pauksa Taung, mtn., Mya.	C2	48
Paul, Id., U.S.	H13	136
Paulding, Ms., U.S.	E9	122
Paulicéia, Braz.	D6	90
Paulina Peak, mtn., Or., U.S.	G5	136
Pauline, Mount, mtn., Can.	C11	138
Paulino Neves, Braz.	B4	88
Paulistana, Braz.	E5	88
Paulistas, Braz.	J4	88
Paullina, Ia., U.S.	B2	120
Paulo Afonso, Braz.	E6	88
Paulo Afonso, Cachoeira de, wtfl, Braz.	E6	88
Paulpietersburg, S. Afr.	E10	70
Pauls Valley, Ok., U.S.	G11	128
Paung, Mya.	D3	48
Paungde, Mya.	C2	48
Pauri, India	C7	54
Paute, Ec.	I2	86
Paute, stm., Ec.	I2	86
Pauto, stm., Col.	E6	86
Pavia, Italy	E6	22
Pavilion, B.C., Can.	F9	138
Pāvilosta, Lat.	D4	10
Pavlikeni, Blg.	F12	26
Pavlodar, Kaz.	D13	32
Pavlof Volcano, vol., Ak., U.S.	E7	140
Pavlovo, Russia	I20	8
Pavlovsk, Russia	A13	10
Pavlovsk, Russia	D14	32
Pavlovskij Posad, Russia	E21	10
Pavo, Ga., U.S.	F2	116
Pavullo nel Frignano, Italy	F7	22
Pavuvu Island, i., Sol. Is.	e8	79b
Pawan, stm., Indon.	D7	50
Pawhuska, Ok., U.S.	E12	128
Pawn, stm., Mya.	C3	48
Pawnee, Il., U.S.	E8	120
Pawnee, Ok., U.S.	A2	122
Pawnee, stm., Ks., U.S.	C9	128
Pawnee Rock, Ks., U.S.	C9	128
Pawni, India	H7	54
Pawota, Mya.	D3	48
Paw Paw, Il., U.S.	C8	120
Paw Paw, Mi., U.S.	F4	112
Pawtucket, R.I., U.S.	C14	114
Paxoí, i., Grc.	D3	28
Paxson, Ak., U.S.	D10	140
Paxton, Ne., U.S.	F11	126
Paya, Hond.	E5	102
Payakumbuh, Indon.	D2	50
Payamlı, Tur.	A9	58
Payerne, Switz.	D3	22
Payeti, Indon.	H12	50
Payette, Id., U.S.	F10	136
Payette, stm., Id., U.S.	G10	136
Payette, North Fork, stm., Id., U.S.	F11	136
Payette, South Fork, stm., Id., U.S.	F11	136
Payne, Oh., U.S.	C1	114
Payne, Lac, l., Can.	D16	106
Paynes Find, Austl.	E3	74
Paynton, Sk., Can.	A5	124
Paysandú, Ur.	F8	92
Payson, Az., U.S.	I5	132
Payson, Il., U.S.	E6	120
Payson, Ut., U.S.	C5	132

Name — Map Ref. — Page

Pineville, Ky., U.S. H2 114
Pineville, La., U.S. F6 122
Pineville, Mo., U.S. H3 120
Pineville, W.V., U.S. G4 114
Pinewood, S.C., U.S. C5 116
Ping, stm., Thai. E5 48
Ping'an, China B5 38
Pingba, China H2 42
Pingchang, China F2 42
Pingding, China C5 42
Pingdingshan, China E5 42
Pingdu, China C8 42
Pingelly, Austl. F3 74
Pinghe, China A6 48
Pinghu, China F9 42
Pingjiang, China G5 42
Pingle, China I4 42
Pingli, China E3 42
Pingliang, China D2 42
Pingluo, China B2 42
Pingnan, China H8 42
Pingnan, China J4 42
Pingquan, China A8 42
Pingshi, China I5 42
Pingtan, China I8 42
Pingtan Dao, i., China I8 42
P'ingtung, Tai. J9 42
Pingwu, China E5 36
Pingxiang, China H5 42
Pingxiang, China J2 42
Pingyang, China H9 42
Pingyao, China C5 42
Pingyi, China D7 42
Pingyin, China C7 42
Pingyuan, China I6 42
Pinhão, Braz. F7 88
Pinheiro, Braz. B3 88
Pinheiros, Braz. J5 88
Pinhel, Port. D3 20
Pini, Pulau, i., Indon. E2 44
Pinillos, Col. C4 86
Pinjarra, Austl. F3 74
Pinjug, Russia F22 8
Pinkiang see Harbin, China B7 38
Pink Mountain, B.C., Can. D6 106
Pinnacle, mtn., Va., U.S. E7 114
Pinnacle Buttes, mtn., Wy., U.S. G17 136
Pinnacles National Monument, p.o.i., Ca., U.S. G4 134
Pinnaroo, Austl. J3 76
Pinneberg, Ger. C5 16
Pinos, Mex. D8 100
Pinos, Isla de see Juventud, Isla de la, i., Cuba B6 102
Pinos, Mount, mtn., Ca., U.S. I6 134
Pinos Puente, Spain G7 20
Pinrang, Indon. E11 50
Pins, Île des, i., N. Cal. n16 79d
Pins, Pointe aux, c., On., Can. F8 112
Pinsk, Bela. H9 10
Pinsk Marshes see Pripet Marshes, reg., Eur. H12 10
Pinson, Al., U.S. D12 122
Pinta, Isla, i., Ec. h11 84a
Pintada Arroyo, stm., N.M., U.S. G3 128
Pintados, Chile D3 90
Pintasan, Malay. A10 50
Pinto Butte, mtn., Sk., Can. E6 124
Pintoyacu, stm., Ec. H3 86
Pin Valley National Park, p.o.i., India C6 54
Pioche, Nv., U.S. F2 132
Piombino, Italy H7 22
Pioneer Mine, B.C., Can. F8 138
Pionerskij, Russia F3 10
Pionki, Pol. E17 16
Piorini, stm., Braz. D5 84
Piorini, Lago, l., Braz. D5 84
Piotrków, state, Pol. E15 16
Piotrków Trybunalski, Pol. E15 16
Pio V. Corpuz, Phil. E5 52
Piove di Sacco, Italy E8 22
Pio XII, Braz. B3 88
Pipanaco, Salar de, pl., Arg. D4 92
Pīpār, India E4 54
Piparia, India G7 54
Pīpar Road, India E4 54
Pipe Spring National Monument, p.o.i., Az., U.S. G4 132
Pipestem Creek, stm., N.D., U.S. G14 124
Pipestone, Mn., U.S. H2 118
Pipestone, stm., On., Can. E12 106
Pipestone Creek, stm., Can. E12 124
Pipestone National Monument, p.o.i., Mn., U.S. G2 118
Pipinas, Arg. G9 92
Piplān, Pak. B3 54
Pipmuacan, Réservoir, res., Qc., Can. A6 110
Piqua, Oh., U.S. D1 114
Piquet Carneiro, Braz. C6 88
Piquiri, stm., Braz. B11 92
Piracanjuba, Braz. I1 88
Piracanjuba, stm., Braz. I1 88
Piracicaba, Braz. L2 88
Piracicaba, stm., Braz. L1 88
Piracuruca, Braz. B5 88
Pirae, Fr. Poly. v21 78h
Piraeus see Peiraiás, Grc. F6 28
Piraí do Sul, Braz. B12 92
Piraju, Braz. L1 88
Pirajuí, Braz. L1 88
Piram Island, i., India H4 54
Piran, Slvn. E10 22
Pirané, Arg. B8 92
Piranga, Braz. K4 88
Piranhas, Braz. G7 84
Piranhas, stm., Braz. E1 88
Piranhas, stm., Braz. C7 88
Piranji, stm., Braz. C6 88
Pirapemas, Braz. B3 88
Pirapora, Braz. I3 88
Piraquara, Braz. B13 92
Pirassununga, Braz. K2 88
Pirata, Monte, hill, P.R. B4 104a
Piratinga, stm., Braz. H2 88
Piratini, Braz. E11 92
Piratini, stm., Braz. D10 92
Piratuba, Braz. C11 92
Pires do Rio, Braz. I1 88
Piriápolis, Ur. G10 92
Pirin, Parki Narodowe, p.o.i., Blg. H10 26
Piripiri, Braz. C5 88
Píritu, Ven. C7 86
Pirmasens, Ger. G3 16
Pirna, Ger. F9 16
Pirojpur, Bngl. G12 54
Pirot, Yugo. F9 26
Pirovano, Arg. H7 92
Pirovskoe, Russia C16 32
Pīr Panjāl Range, mts., Asia B5 54
Pirtleville, Az., U.S. L7 132
Pirttikylä, Fin. E9 8
Piru, Indon. F8 44
Pisa, Italy G7 22
Pisagua, Chile C2 90
Pisco, Peru F2 84
Pişcolt, Rom. B9 26
Písek, Czech Rep. G10 16
Pishan, China A4 46
Pishchanka, Ukr. A15 26
Pisinemo, Az., U.S. K4 132
Pismo Beach, Ca., U.S. H5 134
Pisticci, Italy D10 24
Pistoia, Italy G7 22
Pisuerga, stm., Spain C6 20
Pit, stm., Ca., U.S. B4 134
Pit, North Fork, stm., Ca., U.S. B5 134
Pita, Gui. G2 64
Pitalito, Col. G4 86
Pitanga, Braz. B12 92
Pitangui, Braz. J3 88
Pitcairn, dep., Pit. c28 78k
Piteå, Swe. D9 8
Piteälven, stm., Swe. D8 8
Piteşti, Rom. E11 26
Pithāpuram, India C6 53
Pithiviers, Fr. F11 14
Pithom, hist., Egypt H2 58
Pithorāgarh, India D8 54
Pitinga, stm., Braz. H12 86
Pitiquito, Mex. F6 98
Pitkjaranta, Russia F14 8
Pitljar, Russia C2 34
Pitomača, Cro. D14 22
Pitrufquén, Chile G2 90
Pitt Island, i., B.C., Can. E5 106
Pitt Lake, l., B.C., Can. G8 138
Pittsboro, N.C., U.S. I6 114
Pittsburg, Ks., U.S. G3 120
Pittsburg, Tx., U.S. E4 122
Pittsburgh, Pa., U.S. D6 114
Pittsfield, Il., U.S. E7 120
Pittsfield, Me., U.S. F7 110
Pittsfield, Ma., U.S. B12 114
Pittsford, Mi., U.S. C1 114
Pittston, Pa., U.S. C10 114
Pittsview, Al., U.S. E13 122
Pittsworth, Austl. F8 76
Pituil, Arg. D4 92
Pium, Braz. F1 88
Piura, Peru E1 84
Piute Peak, mtn., Ca., U.S. H7 134
Pivan', Russia F16 34
Pivdennyy Buh, stm., Ukr. A17 26
Pizarro, Col. E3 86
Pizzo, Italy F10 24
Pjakupur, stm., Russia B13 32
Pjalka, Russia C19 8
Pjandž (Panj), stm., Asia B11 56
Pjaozero, ozero, l., Russia C14 8
Pjasina, stm., Russia B6 34
Pjasino, ozero, l., Russia B6 34
Pjasinskij zaliv, b., Russia B5 34
Pjatigorsk, Russia F6 32
Pjatovskij, Russia F19 10
Pjažieva Sel'ga, Russia F16 8
Placentia Bay, b., Nf., Can. j23 107a
Placerville, Ca., U.S. E5 134
Placetas, Cuba A8 102
Plácido Rosas, Ur. F11 92
Plai Mat, stm., Thai. E6 48
Plain City, Ut., U.S. B4 132
Plain Dealing, La., U.S. E5 122
Plainfield, Ct., U.S. C13 114
Plainfield, In., U.S. I3 112
Plainfield, N.J., U.S. D11 114
Plains, Ga., U.S. E14 122
Plains, Ks., U.S. D8 128
Plains, Mt., U.S. C12 136
Plainview, Mn., U.S. G6 118
Plainview, Ne., U.S. E15 126
Plainview, Tx., U.S. G7 128
Plainville, In., U.S. F10 120
Plainwell, Mi., U.S. F4 112
Plakhtiïvka, Ukr. C16 26
Plamondon, Ab., Can. B18 138
Plampang, Indon. H10 50
Planá, Czech Rep. G8 16
Plana, L'Illa, i., Spain F10 20
Planada, Ca., U.S. F5 134
Planalto, Braz. C11 92
Planchón, Cerro del (El Planchón, Volcán), vol., S.A. G2 92
Planeta Rica, Col. C4 86
Plano, Il., U.S. C9 120
Plano, Tx., U.S. D2 122
Plantagenet, On., Can. E2 110
Plantation, Fl., U.S. J5 116
Plant City, Fl., U.S. I3 116
Plantersville, Ms., U.S. C10 122
Plantsite, Az., U.S. J7 132
Plaquemine, La., U.S. G7 122
Plasencia, Spain D4 20
Plaster Rock, N.B., Can. D9 110
Plasy, Czech Rep. G9 16
Plata, Isla de la, i., Ec. H1 86
Plata, Río de la, est., S.A. G9 92
Plato, Col. C4 86
Platte, stm., U.S. E3 120
Platte, stm., Ne., U.S. C7 108
Platte, Île, i., Sey. k13 69b
Platte Center, Ne., U.S. F15 126
Platte City, Mo., U.S. E3 120
Platteville, Co., U.S. A4 128
Platteville, Wi., U.S. B7 120
Plattsburgh, N.Y., U.S. F3 110
Plattsmouth, Ne., U.S. D2 120
Plau, Ger. C8 16
Plauen, Ger. F8 16
Plav, Yugo. G6 26
Plavsk, Russia G20 10
Playa Azul, Mex. G7 100
Playa de Fajardo, P.R. B4 104a
Playa de Guayanilla, P.R. B2 104a
Playa de Naguabo, P.R. B4 104a
Playa de Ponce, P.R. C2 104a
Playa Noriega, Laguna, l., Mex. A3 100
Playa Vicente, Mex. G11 100
Playgreen Lake, l., Mb., Can. E11 106
Play Ku, Viet. F8 48
Plaza, N.D., U.S. F12 124
Pleasant, Mount, hill, N.B., Can. E9 110
Pleasant Bay, N.S., Can. D16 110
Pleasantdale, Sk., Can. B9 124
Pleasant Grove, Ut., U.S. C5 132
Pleasant Hill, Il., U.S. E7 120
Pleasant Hill, La., U.S. F5 122
Pleasant Hill, Mo., U.S. F3 120
Pleasanton, Ks., U.S. F3 120
Pleasanton, Tx., U.S. F9 130
Pleasantville, N.J., U.S. E11 114
Pleasantville, Pa., U.S. C6 114
Pleaux, Fr. D8 18
Plehanovo, Russia F20 10
Plenty, Sk., Can. C5 124
Plenty, Bay of, b., N.Z. C7 80
Plentywood, Mt., U.S. F9 124
Pleščeevo, ozero, l., Russia D21 10
Pleseck, Russia E19 8
Plessisville, Qc., Can. D5 110
Pleszew, Pol. E13 16
Plétipi, Lac, l., Qc., Can. E16 106
Plettenbergbaai, S. Afr. I6 70
Pleven, Blg. F11 26
Plevna, Mt., U.S. A8 126
Plitvička Jezera Nacionalni Park, p.o.i., Cro. F12 22
Pljevlja, Yugo. F6 26
Pljuskovo, Russia H16 10
Pljussa, stm., Russia A11 10
Płock, Pol. D15 16
Płock, state, Pol. D15 16
Ploërmel, Fr. G6 14
Ploieşti, Rom. E12 26
Plomb du Cantal, mtn., Fr. D8 18
Plomer, Point, c., Austl. H9 76
Plön, Ger. B6 16
Płońsk, Pol. D16 16
Ploskoe, Russia H21 10
Plotnica, Bela. H9 10
Ploudalmézeau, Fr. F4 14
Plovdiv, Blg. G11 26
Plovdiv, state, Blg. G11 26
Plumerville, Ar., U.S. B6 122
Plummer, Id., U.S. C9 136
Plumridge Lakes, l., Austl. E5 74
Plumtree, Zimb. B8 70
Plungė, Lith. E4 10
Plutarco Elías Calles, Presa, res., Mex. G8 98
Plymouth, Monts. D3 105a
Plymouth, Eng., U.K. K8 12
Plymouth, Ca., U.S. E5 134
Plymouth, Il., U.S. D6 120
Plymouth, Ma., U.S. C15 114
Plymouth, Ne., U.S. A11 128
Plymouth, N.H., U.S. G5 110
Plymouth, N.C., U.S. I9 114
Plymouth, Oh., U.S. C3 114
Plymouth, Pa., U.S. C10 114
Plzeň, Czech Rep. G9 16
Pô, Burkina G4 64
Po, stm., Italy F8 22
Po, Foci del, mth., Italy F9 22
Po, Mouths of the see Po, Foci del, mth., Italy F9 22
Poarta Orientală, Pasul, p., Rom. D9 26
Pobè, Benin H5 64
Pobeda, gora, mtn., Russia C18 34
Pobedino, Russia G17 34
Pobedy, pik, mtn., Asia F14 32
Poblado Cerro Gordo, P.R. A3 104a
Poblado Jacaguas, P.R. B2 104a
Poblado Medianía Alta, P.R. B4 104a
Poblado Santana, P.R. B2 104a
Pobra de Trives, Spain B3 20
Pocahontas, Ar., U.S. H6 120
Pocahontas, Ia., U.S. B3 120
Poção, Braz. E7 88
Pocatello, Id., U.S. H14 136
Počep, Russia H16 10
Počinok, Russia D4 32
Pocitos, Salar, pl., Arg. B4 92
Poço da Cruz, Açude, res., Braz. E7 88
Poções, Braz. H5 88
Pocola, Ok., U.S. B4 122
Pocomoke City, Md., U.S. F10 114
Poconé, Braz. G6 84
Pocono Mountains, hills, Pa., U.S. C10 114
Pocono Summit, Pa., U.S. C10 114
Poço Redondo, Braz. E7 88
Poços de Caldas, Braz. K2 88
Pocrane, Braz. J5 88
Podbereze, Russia D13 10
Podborove, Russia A18 10
Poddębice, Pol. E14 16
Poddore, Russia C13 10
Poděbrady, Czech Rep. F11 16
Podgorica (Titograd), Yugo. G6 26
Podjuga, Russia F19 8
Podkamennaja Tunguska, Russia B16 32
Podkamennaja Tunguska, stm., Russia B16 32
Podlasie, reg., Pol. D19 16
Podol'sk, Russia E20 10
Podor, Sen. F2 64
Podporože, Russia F16 8
Podravina, reg., Cro. E15 22
Podtësovo, Russia C16 32
Podujevo, Yugo. G8 26
Poel, i., Ger. B7 16
Poelela, Lagoa, l., Moz. D12 70
Pofadder, S. Afr. F4 70
Pogar, Russia H16 10
Poggibonsi, Italy G8 22
Pogoanele, Rom. E13 26
Pogoreloe Gorodišče, Russia D17 10
Pogradec, Alb. D14 24
Pogradeci see Pogradec, Alb. D14 24
Pograničnyj, Russia B9 38
P'ohang, Kor., S. C2 40
Pohjanmaa, reg., Fin. D11 8
Pohjois-Karjala, state, Fin. E14 8
Pohnpei, i., Micron. I11 78d
Pohri, India F6 54
Pohvistnevo, Russia D8 32
Pöide, Est. B6 10
Poinsett, Cape, c., Ant. B16 81
Poinsett, Lake, l., S.D., U.S. C15 126
Point, Tx., U.S. E3 122
Point Arena, Ca., U.S. E2 134
Point Au Fer Island, i., La., U.S. H7 122
Point Baker, Ak., U.S. E13 140
Pointe-à-la-Garde, Qc., Can. B10 110
Pointe a la Hache, La., U.S. H9 122
Pointe-à-Pitre, Guad. h5 105c
Pointe-à-Pitre-le Raizet, Aéroport de, Guad. h5 105c
Pointe du Canonnier, c., Guad. A1 105a
Point Edward, On., Can. E7 112
Pointe-Noire, Congo E2 66
Pointe-Noire, Guad. h5 105c
Point Fortin, Trin. s12 105f
Point Hope, Ak., U.S. C6 140
Point Jupiter, c., St. Vin. p11 105e
Point Lake, l., N.T., Can. B8 106
Point Marion, Pa., U.S. E5 114
Point Pelee National Park, p.o.i., On., Can. G7 112
Point Pleasant, N.J., U.S. D11 114
Point Reyes National Seashore, p.o.i., Ca., U.S. E2 134
Point Roberts, Wa., U.S. B3 136
Point Salines International Airport, Gren. q10 105e
Point Sapin, N.B., Can. D12 110
Poisson Blanc, Lac du, res., Qc., Can. B14 112
Poissy, Fr. F10 14
Poitiers, Fr. H9 14
Poitou, hist. reg., Fr. C5 18
Poivre Atoll, i., Sey. k12 69b
Pojarkovo, Russia G14 34
Pojoaque Valley, N.M., U.S. F2 128
Pojuca, Braz. G6 88
Pojuca, stm., Braz. G6 88
Pokaran, India E3 54
Pokataroo, Austl. G7 76
Pokharā, Nepal D10 54
Poko, D.R.C. D5 66
Pokrovsk, Russia D14 34
Pokrovskoe, Russia H19 10
Pola, stm., Russia C14 10
Polacca Wash, stm., Az., U.S. H6 132
Polack, Bela. E11 10
Pola de Lena, Spain A5 20
Pola de Siero, Spain A5 20
Poland, ctry., Eur. D15 16
Polanów, Pol. B12 16
Polatlı, Tur. D15 28
Polcura, Chile H2 92
Poldnevica, Russia G22 8
Polebridge, Mt., U.S. B12 136
Pol-e Khomrī, Afg. B10 56
Polese see Pripet Marshes, reg., Eur. H12 10
Polesine, reg., Italy E8 22
Polewali, Indon. E11 50
Polgár, Hung. B8 26
Poli, Cam. C2 66
Poli, China D8 42
Policastro, Golfo di, b., Italy E9 24
Police (Pölitz), Pol. C10 16
Polička, Czech Rep. G12 16
Polillo Island, i., Phil. C3 52
Polillo Islands, is., Phil. C4 52
Pólis, Cyp. C3 58
Polist', stm., Russia C14 10
Polistena, Italy F10 24
Poljarnyj, Russia B15 8
Poljarnyj, Russia C24 34
Poljarnyj Ural, mts., Russia A10 32
Polk, Ne., U.S. F15 126
Polk, Pa., U.S. C6 114
Pol'kino, Russia B8 34
Pollāchi, India F3 53
Pöllau, Aus. C12 22
Pollino, Monte, mtn., Italy E10 24
Pollock, La., U.S. F6 122
Pollock, S.D., U.S. B12 126
Polnovo-Seliger, Russia C15 10
Polo, Il., U.S. B8 120
Polomet', stm., Russia C15 10
Polonnaruwa, Sri L. H5 53
Polonnaruwa, hist., Sri L. H5 53
Polotnjanyj, Russia F19 10
Polotsk see Polack, Bela. E11 10
Polski Trămbeš, Blg. F12 26
Polson, Mt., U.S. C12 136
Poltava, Ukr. E4 32
Poltimore, Qc., Can. C14 112
Põltsamaa, Est. G12 8
Poluj, stm., Russia A11 32
Polunočnoe, Russia B10 32
Polur, India E4 53
Polvijärvi, Fin. E13 8
Polýaigos, i., Grc. G7 28
Polynesia, is., Oc. J22 142
Polysajevo, Russia F6 34
Pomarkku, Fin. F9 8
Pombal, Braz. D7 88
Pomerania, hist. reg., Eur. C11 16
Pomeranian Bay, b., Eur. B10 16
Pomerene, Az., U.S. K6 132
Pomerode, Braz. C13 92
Pomeroy, Ia., U.S. B3 120
Pomeroy, Wa., U.S. D9 136
Pomfret, S. Afr. D6 70
Pomi, Rom. B10 26
Pomme de Terre, stm., Mn., U.S. F3 118
Pomme de Terre, stm., Mo., U.S. G4 120
Pomme de Terre Lake, res., Mo., U.S. G4 120
Pomona, Ca., U.S. I8 134
Pomona, Ks., U.S. F2 120
Pomona Lake, res., Ks., U.S. F2 120
Pomorskij proliv, strt., Russia B24 8
Pompano Beach, Fl., U.S. J5 116
Pompei, hist., Italy D8 24
Pompejevka, Russia G15 34
Pompéu, Braz. J3 88
Pomquet, N.S., Can. E15 110
Ponass Lakes, l., Sk., Can. B9 124
Ponazyrevo, Russia G22 8
Ponca, Ne., U.S. B1 120
Ponca City, Ok., U.S. E11 128
Ponca Creek, stm., U.S. E14 126
Ponce, P.R. B2 104a
Ponce, Aeropuerto, P.R. B2 104a
Ponce de Leon, Fl., U.S. G12 122
Poncha Pass, p., Co., U.S. C2 128
Pond Creek, Ok., U.S. E11 128
Ponderay, Id., U.S. B10 136
Pondicherry (Puduchcheri), India F4 53
Pondicherry, state, India E5 53
Pond Inlet, N.T., Can. A15 106
Pond Inlet, b., N.T., Can. A15 106
Pondosa, Ca., U.S. B4 134
Ponente, Riviera di, cst., Italy F5 22
Ponérihouen, N. Cal. m15 79d
Ponferrada, Spain B4 20
Pongolo, stm., S. Afr. E10 70
Poniatowa, Pol. E17 16
Ponizove, Russia E14 10
Ponnaiyār, stm., India E4 53
Ponnāni, India F2 53
Ponnūru Nidubrolu, India C5 53
Ponoj, Russia C19 8
Ponoj, stm., Russia C18 8
Ponoka, Ab., Can. D17 138
Ponorogo, Indon. G7 50
Pons, Fr. D5 18
Ponta Delgada, Port. C3 60
Ponta Grossa, Braz. B12 92
Pontalina, Braz. I1 88
Ponta Porã, Braz. D5 90
Pontarlier, Fr. H15 14
Pontas de Pedra, Braz. D8 88
Pontassieve, Italy G8 22
Pontchartrain, Lake, l., La., U.S. G8 122
Pontchâteau, Fr. G6 14
Pont-de-Vaux, Fr. C10 18
Ponte Alta do Bom Jesus, Braz. G2 88
Ponte-Caldelas, Spain B2 20
Ponte de Lima, Port. C2 20
Pontedera, Italy G7 22
Pontedeume, Spain A2 20
Ponte do Púngoè, Moz. A12 70
Ponteix, Sk., Can. E6 124
Ponte Nova, Braz. K4 88
Ponte Serrada, Braz. C12 92
Pontevedra, Spain B2 20
Pontevedra, co., Spain B2 20
Pontiac, Il., U.S. D9 120
Pontiac, Mi., U.S. B2 114
Pontianak, Indon. C6 50
Pontine Islands see Ponziane, Isole, is., Italy D6 24
Pontivy, Fr. F5 14
Pontoise, Fr. E11 14
Pontotoc, Ms., U.S. C9 122
Pontotoc, Tx., U.S. D9 130
Pontremoli, Italy F6 22
Pontresina, Switz. D6 22
Pont-Rouge, Qc., Can. D5 110
Ponts, Spain C12 20
Pont-sur-Yonne, Fr. F12 14
Pontus Mountains see Doğu Karadeniz Dağları, mts., Tur. A5 56
Pontypridd, Wales, U.K. J9 12
Ponyri, Russia H19 10
Ponziane, Isole (Pontine Islands), is., Italy D6 24
Poole, Eng., U.K. K11 12
Pooley Island, i., B.C., Can. D2 138
Poolville, Tx., U.S. B10 130
Pooncarie, Austl. I4 76
Poopó, Bol. C3 90
Poopó, Lago, l., Bol. C3 90
Popayán, Col. F3 86
Pope, Ms., U.S. C8 122
Popeşti-Leordeni, Rom. E13 26
Popham Bay, b., N.T., Can. C17 106
Popigaj, Russia B11 34
Popigaj, stm., Russia B10 34
Popiltah Lake, l., Austl. I3 76
Poplar, Mt., U.S. F8 124
Poplar, stm., Can. B16 124
Poplar, stm., N.A. F8 124
Poplar, West Fork (West Poplar), stm., N.A. F8 124
Poplar Bluff, Mo., U.S. H7 120
Poplar Hill, On., Can. E12 106
Poplar Point, Mb., Can. D16 124
Poplarville, Ms., U.S. G9 122
Popocatépetl, Volcán, vol., Mex. F9 100
Popoh, Indon. H7 50
Popokabaka, D.R.C. F3 66
Popoli, Italy H10 22
Popondetta, Pap. N. Gui. b4 79a
Popovo, Blg. F13 26
Poprad, Slov. G16 16
Poprad, stm., Eur. G16 16
Popricani, Rom. B14 26
Pŏptong-ŭp, Kor., N. E7 38
Poquoson, Va., U.S. G9 114
Porangatu, Braz. G1 88
Porbandar, India H2 54
Porce, stm., Col. D4 86
Porcher Island, i., B.C., Can. E4 106
Porco, Bol. C3 90
Porcos, stm., Braz. G3 88
Porcuna, Spain G6 20
Porcupine, stm., N.A. B3 106
Pordenone, Italy D9 22
Pordim, Blg. F11 26
Poreče, Russia E18 10
Poreče-Rybnoe, Russia C22 10
Porhov, Russia C12 10
Pori (Björneborg), Fin. F9 8
Porjaguba, Russia C15 8
Porlamar, Ven. B10 86
Porog, Russia E18 8
Poronajsk, Russia G17 34
Poroshkove, Ukr. H18 16
Porpoise Bay, b., Ant. B17 81
Porrentruy, Switz. C3 22
Porretta Terme, Italy F7 22
Porsangen, b., Nor. A11 8
Porsangerhalvøya, pen., Nor. A11 8
Porsgrunn, Nor. G3 8
Porsuk, stm., Tur. D13 28
Portachuelo, Bol. C4 90
Port Adelaide, Austl. J2 76
Portadown, N. Ire., U.K. G6 12
Portage, Mi., U.S. F4 112
Portage, Ut., U.S. B4 132
Portage Bay, b., Mb., Can. C15 124
Portage Lake, l., Mi., U.S. D10 118
Portage la Prairie, Mb., Can. E15 124
Portageville, Mo., U.S. H8 120
Portal, Ga., U.S. D4 116
Portal, N.D., U.S. F11 124
Port Alberni, B.C., Can. G6 138
Portalegre, Port. E3 20
Portalegre, state, Port. E3 20
Portales, N.M., U.S. G5 128
Port Alfred, S. Afr. H8 70
Port Alice, B.C., Can. F3 138
Port Allen, La., U.S. G7 122
Port Alma, Austl. D8 76
Port Angeles, Wa., U.S. B3 136
Port Antonio, Jam. i14 104d
Port Aransas, Tx., U.S. G10 130
Portarlington, Ire. H5 12
Port Arthur, Austl. o13 77a
Port Arthur see Lüshun, China E4 38
Port Arthur, Tx., U.S. H4 122
Port Askaig, Scot., U.K. F6 12
Port Augusta, Austl. F7 74
Port au Port Peninsula, pen., Nf., Can. B17 110
Port-au-Prince, Haiti C11 102
Port-au-Prince, Baie de, b., Haiti C11 102
Port Austin, Mi., U.S. D6 112
Port Blair, India F7 46
Port Borden, P.E., Can. D13 110
Port Byron, Il., U.S. J8 118
Port Canning, India G12 54
Port-Cartier, Qc., Can. E17 106
Port Chalmers, N.Z. G4 80
Port Charlotte, Fl., U.S. J3 116
Port Clinton, Oh., U.S. C3 114
Port Clyde, Me., U.S. G7 110
Port Colborne, On., Can. F10 112
Port Coquitlam, B.C., Can. G8 138
Port-de-Paix, Haiti C11 102
Port Dickson, Malay. K5 48
Porte Crayon, Mount, mtn., W.V., U.S. F6 114
Port Edward see Weihai, China C10 42
Port Edward, S. Afr. G10 70
Port Edwards, Wi., U.S. G9 118
Porteirinha, Braz. H4 88
Portel, Braz. D7 84
Port Elgin, N.B., Can. D12 110
Port Elgin, On., Can. D8 112
Port Elizabeth, S. Afr. H7 70
Port-en-Bessin, Fr. E8 14
Porter, Tx., U.S. G3 122
Port Erin, I. of Man G8 12
Porter Point, c., St. Vin. o11 105e
Porterville, S. Afr. H4 70
Porterville, Ca., U.S. G7 134
Porterville, Ms., U.S. E10 122
Portete, Bahía, b., Col. A6 86
Port Fairy, Austl. L4 76
Port Gamble, Wa., U.S. C4 136
Port-Gentil, Gabon E1 66
Port Gibson, Ms., U.S. F8 122
Port Graham, Ak., U.S. E9 140
Port-Harcourt, Nig. I6 64
Port Hardy, B.C., Can. F3 138
Port Hawkesbury, N.S., Can. E15 110
Port Hedland, Austl. D3 74
Port Heiden, Ak., U.S. E8 140
Port Hill, P.E., Can. D13 110
Porthmadog, Wales, U.K. I8 12
Port Hood, N.S., Can. D15 110
Port Hope, On., Can. E11 112
Port Hope, Mi., U.S. E7 112
Port Huron, Mi., U.S. B3 114
Portimão, Port. G2 20
Port Isabel, Tx., U.S. H10 130
Port Jervis, N.Y., U.S. C11 114
Port Kembla, Austl. J8 76
Port Lairge see Waterford, Ire. I5 12
Portland, Austl. I7 76
Portland, Austl. L3 76
Portland, Ar., U.S. D7 122
Portland, In., U.S. H5 112
Portland, Me., U.S. G6 110
Portland, N.D., U.S. G16 124
Portland, Or., U.S. E4 136
Portland, Tn., U.S. H11 120
Portland, Tx., U.S. G10 130
Portland, Bill of, c., Eng., U.K. K10 12
Portland, Cape, c., Austl. n13 77a
Portland, Isle of, i., Eng., U.K. K10 12
Portland Bay, b., Austl. L3 76
Portland Bight, b., Jam. j13 104d
Portland Point, c., Jam. j13 104d
Portlaoise, Ire. H5 12
Port Lavaca, Tx., U.S. F11 130
Port Leyden, N.Y., U.S. E14 112
Port Lincoln, Austl. F7 74
Port Loko, S.L. H2 64
Port-Louis, Guad. h5 105c
Port Louis, Mrts. h10 69a
Port-Lyautey see Kénitra, Mor. C3 64
Port MacDonnell, Austl. L3 76
Port Macquarie, Austl. H9 76
Port Maria, Jam. i14 104d
Port McNeill, B.C., Can. F3 138
Port McNicoll, On., Can. D10 112
Port Moller, Ak., U.S. E7 140
Port Morant, Jam. j14 104d
Portmore, Jam. j13 104d
Port Moresby, Pap. N. Gui. b4 79a
Port Morien, N.S., Can. D17 110
Port Neches, Tx., U.S. H4 122
Port Nelson, Mb., Can. D12 106
Portneuf, stm., Qc., Can. B7 110
Portneuf, stm., Id., U.S. H14 136
Port Neville, B.C., Can. F4 138
Port Nolloth, S. Afr. F3 70
Port Norris, N.J., U.S. E10 114
Porto, Port. C2 20
Porto, state, Port. C2 20
Porto Acre, Braz. E4 84
Porto Alegre, Braz. E12 92
Porto Alegre, S. Tom./P. J6 64
Porto Amboim, Ang. C1 68
Portobelo, Pan. H8 102
Porto Calvo, Braz. E8 88
Porto de Moz, Braz. D7 84
Porto de Pedras, Braz. E8 88
Porto dos Gaúchos, Braz. F6 84
Porto Empedocle, Italy G7 24
Porto Esperança, Braz. C5 90
Porto Esperidião, Braz. G6 84
Porto Feliz, Braz. L2 88
Portoferraio, Italy H7 22
Porto Ferreira, Braz. K2 88
Port of Ness, Scot., U.K. C6 12
Porto Franco, Braz. D2 88
Port of Spain, Trin. s12 105f
Portogruaro, Italy E9 22
Portola, Ca., U.S. D5 134
Portomaggiore, Italy F8 22
Porto Mendes, Braz. B10 92
Porto Murtinho, Braz. D5 90
Porto Nacional, Braz. F1 88
Porto-Novo, Benin H5 64
Porto Novo, India F4 53
Port Orange, Fl., U.S. G5 116
Port Orchard, Wa., U.S. C4 136
Port Orford, Or., U.S. H2 136
Porto San Giorgio, Italy G10 22
Porto Santana, Braz. D7 84
Porto Santo, i., Port. C1 64
Porto Santo Stefano, ngh., Italy H7 22
Porto Seguro, Braz. I6 88
Porto Tolle, Italy F9 22
Porto Torres, Italy D2 24
Porto União, Braz. C12 92
Porto Válter, Braz. E3 84
Porto-Vecchio, Fr. H15 18
Porto Velho, Braz. E5 84
Portoviejo, Ec. H1 86
Port Patrick, Vanuatu m17 79d
Port Perry, On., Can. D11 112
Port Phillip Bay, b., Austl. L5 76
Port Pirie, Austl. F7 74
Portree, Scot., U.K. D6 12
Port Renfrew, B.C., Can. H6 138
Port Rowan, On., Can. F9 112
Port Royal, Jam. j14 104d
Port Royal, Pa., U.S. D8 114
Port Royal, S.C., U.S. D5 116
Port Said see Bûr Sa'îd, Egypt G3 58
Port Saint Joe, Fl., U.S. H13 122
Port Saint Johns, S. Afr. G9 70
Port Saint Lucie, Fl., U.S. I5 116
Port Sanilac, Mi., U.S. E7 112
Port Saunders, Nf., Can. i22 107a
Portsea, Austl. L5 76
Portsmouth, Dom. i6 105c
Portsmouth, Eng., U.K. K11 12
Portsmouth, N.H., U.S. G6 110
Portsmouth, Oh., U.S. F2 114
Portsmouth, Va., U.S. H9 114
Portsoy, Scot., U.K. D10 12
Port Stanley, On., Can. F8 112
Port Sudan see Būr Sūdān, Sudan D7 62
Port Sulphur, La., U.S. H9 122
Port Talbot, Wales, U.K. J9 12
Porttipahdan tekojärvi, l., Fin. B12 8
Port Townsend, Wa., U.S. B4 136
Portugal, ctry., Eur. D3 20
Portugalete, Spain A7 20
Portuguesa, state, Ven. C7 86
Portuguesa, stm., Ven. C8 86
Portuguese Guinea see Guinea-Bissau, ctry., Afr. G1 64
Port Vila, Vanuatu k17 79d
Portville, N.Y., U.S. B7 114
Port-Vladimir, Russia B15 8
Port Wentworth, Ga., U.S. D4 116
Port Wing, Wi., U.S. E7 118
Porus, Jam. i13 104d
Porvenir, Chile J2 90
Porvoo, Fin. F11 8
Porzuna, Spain E6 20
Posadas, Arg. C9 92
Posadas, Spain G5 20
Posavina, val., Eur. E14 22
Pošehon'e, Russia B22 10
Poseidon, Temple of, hist., Grc. F6 28
Posen, Mi., U.S. C6 112
Poshan see Boshan, China C7 42
Posio, Fin. C12 8
Poso, Indon. D12 50
Poso, Danau, l., Indon. D12 50
Poso, Teluk, b., Indon. D12 50
Pospeliha, Russia D14 32
Posse, Braz. H2 88
Possession Island, i., Nmb. E2 70
Pössneck, Ger. F7 16
Possum Kingdom Lake, res., Tx., U.S. B9 130
Post, Tx., U.S. A6 130
Posta de Jihuites, Mex. I2 130
Postelle, Tn., U.S. A1 116
Postmasburg, S. Afr. F6 70
Postojna, Slvn. E11 22
Postrervalle, Bol. C4 90
Postville, Ia., U.S. A6 120
Potaro, stm., Guy. E12 86
Potaro-Siparuni, state, Guy. E12 86
Potchefstroom, S. Afr. E8 70
Poté, Braz. I5 88
Poteau, Ok., U.S. B4 122
Poteet, Tx., U.S. E9 130
Potenza, Italy D9 24
Potgietersrus, S. Afr. D9 70
Poth, Tx., U.S. E9 130
Potholes Reservoir, res., Wa., U.S. D7 136
Poti, Geor. F6 32
Poti, stm., Braz. C4 88
Potiraguá, Braz. H6 88
Potiskum, Nig. G7 64
Potomac, Il., U.S. H2 112
Potomac, stm., U.S. F9 114
Potomac, North Fork South Branch, stm., U.S. F6 114
Potomac, South Branch, stm., U.S. E7 114
Potomac Heights, Md., U.S. F8 114
Potosí, Bol. C3 90
Potosi, Mo., U.S. G7 120
Potrerillos, Chile C3 92
Potro, Cerro del (El Potro, Cerro), mtn., S.A. D3 92
Potsdam, Ger. D9 16
Potsdam, N.Y., U.S. F2 110
Pott, Île, i., N. Cal. I14 79d
Potter, Ne., U.S. F9 126
Potterville, Mi., U.S. B1 114
Potts Camp, Ms., U.S. C9 122
Pottstown, Pa., U.S. D10 114
Pottsville, Pa., U.S. D9 114
Pouancé, Fr. G7 14
Poughkeepsie, N.Y., U.S. C11 114
Poulan, Ga., U.S. E2 116
Poulsbo, Wa., U.S. C4 136
Poultney, Vt., U.S. G3 110
Poum, N. Cal. m14 79d
Pouso Alegre, Braz. L3 88

Name	Map Ref.	Page
Poŭthĭsăt, Camb.	F6	48
Poŭthĭsăt, stm., Camb.	F6	48
Poutini see Westland National Park, p.o.i., N.Z.	F3	80
Poutrincourt, Lac, l., Qc., Can.	A2	110
Považská Bystrica, Slov.	G14	16
Povenec, Russia	E16	8
Póvoa de Varzim, Port.	C2	20
Povorino, Russia	D6	32
Povorotnyj, mys, c., Russia	C10	38
Povungnituk, Qc., Can.	C15	106
Povungnituk, stm., Qc., Can.	C15	106
Powassan, On., Can.	B10	112
Poway, Ca., U.S.	K9	134
Powder, stm., U.S.	A7	126
Powder, stm., Or., U.S.	F9	136
Powder, South Fork, stm., Wy., U.S.	D6	126
Powderly, Tx., U.S.	D3	122
Powder River Pass, p., Wy., U.S.	C5	126
Powell, Wy., U.S.	C4	126
Powell, stm., U.S.	H2	114
Powell, Lake, res., U.S.	F5	132
Powell Creek, stm., Austl.	E5	76
Powellhurst, Or., U.S.	E4	136
Powell Lake, l., B.C., Can.	F6	138
Powell River, B.C., Can.	G6	138
Powers, Mi., U.S.	C2	112
Powers, Or., U.S.	H2	136
Powers Lake, N.D., U.S.	F11	124
Powhatan, Va., U.S.	G7	114
Powhatan Point, Oh., U.S.	E4	114
Poxoréu, Braz.	G7	84
Poya, N. Cal.	m15	79d
Poyang Hu, l., China	G7	42
Poyen, Ar., U.S.	C6	122
Poygan, Lake, l., Wi., U.S.	G9	118
Požarevac, Yugo.	E8	26
Poza Rica de Hidalgo, Mex.	E10	100
Požega, Cro.	E14	22
Požega, Yugo.	F7	26
Poznań, Pol.	D12	16
Poznań, state, Pol.	D12	16
Pozoblanco, Spain	F6	20
Pozo-Cañada, Spain	F9	20
Pozo del Molle, Arg.	F6	92
Pozo del Tigre, Arg.	B7	92
Pozuelos, Ven.	B9	86
Pozzallo, Italy	H8	24
Pozzuoli, Italy	D8	24
Prachatice, Czech Rep.	G10	16
Prachin Buri, Thai.	E5	48
Prachuap Khiri Khan, Thai.	G4	48
Pradera, Col.	F3	86
Prado, Braz.	I6	88
Prados, Braz.	K3	88
Præstø, Den.	A8	16
Prague see Praha, Czech Rep.	F10	16
Prague, Ne., U.S.	F16	126
Prague, Ok., U.S.	B2	122
Praha (Prague), Czech Rep.	F10	16
Praha, state, Czech Rep.	F10	16
Praha, mtn., Czech Rep.	G9	16
Prahova, state, Rom.	D13	26
Prahova, stm., Rom.	E13	26
Praia, C.V.	I10	65a
Praia Grande, Braz.	D13	92
Prainha Nova, Braz.	E5	84
Prairie, Austl.	C5	76
Prairie, stm., Mi., U.S.	G4	112
Prairie City, Il., U.S.	D7	120
Prairie City, Ia., U.S.	C4	120
Prairie Creek, stm., Ne., U.S.	F15	126
Prairie Dog Creek, stm., Ks., U.S.	B8	128
Prairie du Chien, Wi., U.S.	A6	120
Prairie du Sac, Wi., U.S.	H9	118
Prairie River, Sk., Can.	B11	124
Prairies, Coteau des, hills, U.S.	C16	126
Prairies, Lake of the, res., Can.	C12	124
Prairie View, Tx., U.S.	G3	122
Prairie Village, Ks., U.S.	B14	128
Pran Buri, Thai.	F4	48
Pran Buri, stm., Thai.	F4	48
Prānhita, stm., India	B5	53
Praslin, i., Sey.	j13	69b
Prasonísi, Ákra, c., Grc.	H10	28
Praszka, Pol.	E14	16
Prata, Braz.	J1	88
Prata, stm., Braz.	J1	88
Prata, stm., Braz.	I2	88
Pratāpgarh, India	F5	54
Pratápolis, Braz.	K2	88
Pratas Island see Tungsha Tao, i., Tai.	K7	42
Prat de Llobregat see El Prat de Llobregat, Spain	C12	20
Prato, Italy	G8	22
Pratt, Ks., U.S.	D10	128
Prattville, Al., U.S.	E12	122
Pratudão, stm., Braz.	H3	88
Pravdinskij, Russia	D20	10
Pravia, Spain	A4	20
Praya, Indon.	H10	50
Preajba, Rom.	E12	26
Prečistoe, Russia	G19	8
Predeal, Rom.	D12	26
Preeceville, Sk., Can.	C11	124
Preetz, Ger.	B6	16
Pregolja, stm., Russia	F3	10
Pregonero, Ven.	D6	86
Preguiças, stm., Braz.	B4	88
Preila, Lith.	E4	10
Prĕk Poŭthĭ, Camb.	G7	48
Prelate, Sk., Can.	D4	124
Premnitz, Ger.	D8	16
Premont, Tx., U.S.	G9	130
Premuda, Otok, i., Cro.	F11	22
Prenjasi see Prrenjas, Alb.	C14	24
Prentiss, Ms., U.S.	F9	122
Prenzlau, Ger.	C9	16
Preobraženie, Russia	C10	38
Preparis Island, i., Mya.	F7	46
Preparis North Channel, strt., Mya.	E7	46
Preparis South Channel, strt., Mya.	F7	46
Přerov, Czech Rep.	G13	16
Prescott, On., Can.	D14	112
Prescott, Az., U.S.	I4	132
Prescott, Ar., U.S.	D5	122
Prescott, Wi., U.S.	G6	118
Prescott Island, i., N.T., Can.	A11	106
Presidencia de la Plaza, Arg.	C7	92
Presidencia Roca, Arg.	C8	92
Presidencia Roque Sáenz Peña, Arg.	C7	92
Presidente Dutra, Braz.	C3	88
Presidente Epitácio, Braz.	D6	90
Presidente Hayes, state, Para.	B8	92
Presidente Prudente, Braz.	D6	90
Presidio, Tx., U.S.	E3	130
Presidio, stm., Mex.	D6	100
Presnogor'kovka, Kaz.	D11	32
Prešov, Slov.	H17	16
Prespa, Lake, l., Eur.	D14	24
Presque Isle, Me., U.S.	D8	110
Presque Isle, pen., Pa., U.S.	B5	114
Prestea, Ghana	H4	64
Preston, Eng., U.K.	H10	12
Preston, Id., U.S.	A5	132
Preston, Ia., U.S.	B7	120
Preston, Ks., U.S.	D10	128
Preston, Mn., U.S.	H6	118
Prestonsburg, Ky., U.S.	G3	114
Prestwick, Scot., U.K.	F8	12
Preto, stm., Braz.	I9	86
Preto, stm., Braz.	I2	88
Preto, stm., Braz.	F3	88
Preto, stm., Braz.	B4	88
Preto, stm., Braz.	G1	88
Preto, stm., Braz.	K1	88
Preto, stm., Braz.	L4	88
Preto do Igapó-açu, stm., Braz.	E5	84
Pretoria, S. Afr.	D9	70
Pretty Prairie, Ks., U.S.	D10	128
Préveza, Grc.	E3	28
Prey Lvéa, Camb.	G7	48
Prey Vêng, Camb.	G7	48
Pribilof Islands, is., Ak., U.S.	E5	140
Priboj, Yugo.	F6	26
Příbram, Czech Rep.	G10	16
Price, Ut., U.S.	D6	132
Price, stm., Ut., U.S.	D6	132
Price Island, i., B.C., Can.	D2	138
Prichard, Al., U.S.	G10	122
Prickly Pear Cays, is., Anguilla	A1	105a
Priddy, Tx., U.S.	C9	130
Priego de Córdoba, Spain	G6	20
Priekule, Lat.	D4	10
Priekule, Lith.	E4	10
Prieska, S. Afr.	F6	70
Priest, stm., Id., U.S.	B10	136
Priest Lake, res., Id., U.S.	B9	136
Priest River, Id., U.S.	B10	136
Prieta, Peña, mtn., Spain	A6	20
Prieto Diaz, Phil.	D5	52
Prievidza, Slov.	H14	16
Prijedor, Bos.	E3	26
Prilep, Mac.	B4	28
Priluki, Russia	A22	10
Primeira Cruz, Braz.	B4	88
Primera, Tx., U.S.	H10	130
Primero, stm., Arg.	E6	92
Primghar, Ia., U.S.	A2	120
Primorsk, Russia	F13	8
Primorskij, Russia	C9	38
Primorskij hrebet, mts., Russia	F10	34
Primo Tapia, Mex.	K8	134
Primrose Lake, l., Can.	E9	106
Prince Albert, Sk., Can.	A8	124
Prince Albert, S. Afr.	H6	70
Prince Albert Sound, strt., N.T., Can.	A7	106
Prince Alfred, Cape, c., N.T., Can.	B15	140
Prince Charles Island, i., N.T., Can.	B15	106
Prince Charles Mountains, mts., Ant.	C11	81
Prince Edward Island, state, Can.	D13	110
Prince Edward Island, i., P.E., Can.	F18	106
Prince Edward Island National Park, p.o.i., P.E., Can.	D13	110
Prince Frederick, Md., U.S.	F9	114
Prince George, B.C., Can.	C8	138
Prince George, Va., U.S.	G8	114
Prince Gustaf Adolf Sea, N.T., Can.	B4	141
Prince of Wales Island, i., Austl.	B8	74
Prince of Wales Island, i., N.T., Can.	A11	106
Prince of Wales Island, i., Ak., U.S.	E13	140
Prince of Wales Strait, strt., N.T., Can.	B15	140
Prince Olav Coast, cst., Ant.	B9	81
Prince Patrick Island, i., N.T., Can.	A16	140
Prince Regent Inlet, b., N.T., Can.	A12	106
Prince Rupert, B.C., Can.	E4	106
Prince Rupert Bluff Point, c., Dom.	i5	105c
Princes Islands see Kızıl Adalar, is., Tur.	C11	28
Princess Anne, Md., U.S.	F10	114
Princess Astrid Coast, cst., Ant.	C6	81
Princess Charlotte Bay, b., Austl.	B8	74
Princess Martha Coast, cst., Ant.	C4	81
Princess Ragnhild Coast, cst., Ant.	C7	81
Princess Royal Island, i., B.C., Can.	C1	138
Princes Town, Trin.	s12	105f
Princeton, B.C., Can.	G10	138
Princeton, Ca., U.S.	D3	134
Princeton, In., U.S.	F10	120
Princeton, Ky., U.S.	G9	120
Princeton, Me., U.S.	E9	110
Princeton, Mi., U.S.	B2	112
Princeton, N.J., U.S.	D11	114
Princeton, N.C., U.S.	A7	116
Princeton, W.V., U.S.	G4	114
Princeton, Wi., U.S.	H9	118
Princeville, Qc., Can.	D4	110
Princeville, Il., U.S.	D8	120
Prince William Sound, strt., Ak., U.S.	D10	140
Príncipe, i., S. Tom./P.	I6	64
Príncipe da Beira, Braz.	F5	84
Prineville, Or., U.S.	F6	136
Pringsewu, Indon.	F4	50
Prinses Margrietkanaal, can., Neth.	A14	14
Prins Karls Forland, i., Nor.	B27	141
Prinzapolka, stm., Nic.	F5	102
Priozërnyj, Kaz.	E14	32
Priozersk, Russia	F14	8
Pripet (Prypjac'), stm., Eur.	H10	10
Pripet Marshes, reg., Eur.	H12	10
Pripoljarnyj Ural, mts., Russia	A9	32
Priština, Yugo.	G8	26
Pritchett, Co., U.S.	D6	128
Pritzwalk, Ger.	C8	16
Privas, Fr.	E10	18
Priverno, Italy	C7	24
Privodino, Russia	F22	8
Prizren, Yugo.	G7	26
Prjaža, Russia	F15	8
Probolinggo, Indon.	G8	50
Probstzella, Ger.	F7	16
Procida, Isola di, i., Italy	D7	24
Procter, B.C., Can.	G13	138
Proctor, Mn., U.S.	E6	118
Proctor Lake, res., Tx., U.S.	C9	130
Proddatūr, India	D4	53
Proença-a-Nova, Port.	E2	20
Progreso, Mex.	B8	100
Progreso, Mex.	B3	102
Progreso, Mex.	K10	134
Progreso, Ur.	G9	92
Prohladnyj, Russia	F6	32
Project City, Ca., U.S.	C3	134
Prokopevsk, Russia	D15	32
Prokuplje, Yugo.	F8	26
Prokuševo, Russia	G16	8
Proletarskij, Russia	E20	10
Prome (Pye), Mya.	C2	48
Pronja, stm., Bela.	G14	10
Pronja, stm., Russia	F21	10
Prony, Baie de, b., N. Cal.	n16	79d
Prophet, stm., B.C., Can.	D6	106
Prophetstown, Il., U.S.	C8	120
Propriá, Braz.	F7	88
Propriano, Fr.	H14	18
Proserpine, Austl.	C7	76
Prosna, stm., Pol.	E14	16
Prospect, Oh., U.S.	D2	114
Prosperidad, Phil.	F5	52
Prosser, Wa., U.S.	D7	136
Prostějov, Czech Rep.	G12	16
Prostki, Pol.	C18	16
Proston, Austl.	F8	76
Proszowice, Pol.	F16	16
Protection, Ks., U.S.	D9	128
Protem, S. Afr.	I5	70
Protva, stm., Russia	F20	10
Provadija, Blg.	F14	26
Prøven (Kangersuatsiaq), Grnld.	C14	141
Provence, hist. reg., Fr.	F12	18
Providence, Ky., U.S.	G10	120
Providence, R.I., U.S.	C14	114
Providence, Ut., U.S.	B5	132
Providence, Atoll de, i., Sey.	k12	69b
Providence, Cape, c., N.Z.	H2	80
Providencia, Mex.	G4	130
Providencia, Isla de, i., Col.	F7	102
Providenciales, i., T./C. Is.	B11	102
Providenija, Russia	D26	34
Provincetown, Ma., U.S.	B15	114
Provins, Fr.	F12	14
Provo, Ut., U.S.	C5	132
Provo, stm., Ut., U.S.	C5	132
Provost, Ab., Can.	B3	124
Prrenjas, Alb.	C14	24
Prudentópolis, Braz.	B12	92
Prudhoe Bay, Ak., U.S.	B10	140
Prudhoe Island, i., Austl.	C7	76
Prudnik, Pol.	F13	16
Pruszków, Pol.	D16	16
Prut, stm., Eur.	D15	26
Pružany, Bela.	H7	10
Prydz Bay, b., Ant.	B12	81
Pryluky, Ukr.	D4	32
Pryor, Ok., U.S.	H2	120
Przasnysz, Pol.	D16	16
Przedbórz, Pol.	E15	16
Przemyśl, Pol.	G18	16
Przemyśl, state, Pol.	F18	16
Przeworsk, Pol.	F18	16
Psachná, Grc.	E6	28
Pskov, Russia	C11	10
Pskov, Lake, l., Eur.	B11	10
Pskovskaja oblast', co., Russia	C11	10
Pszczyna, Pol.	G14	16
Ptarmigan, Cape, c., N.T., Can.	A7	106
Ptolemaïda, Grc.	C4	28
Ptuj, Slvn.	D12	22
Puakatike, Volcán, vol., Chile	e30	78l
Puán, Arg.	H6	92
Pucallpa, Peru	E3	84
Pucará, Bol.	C4	90
Pučeveem, stm., Russia	C23	34
Pučež, Russia	H20	8
Pucheng, China	H8	42
Pucheng, China	D3	42
Púchov, Slov.	G14	16
Pučišća, Cro.	G13	22
Pudasjärvi, Fin.	D12	8
Pudož, Russia	F17	8
Puduari, stm., Braz.	I11	86
Puduchcheri see Pondicherry, India	F4	53
Pudukkottai, India	F4	53
Puebla, state, Mex.	F10	100
Puebla de Don Fadrique, Spain	G8	20
Puebla de Sanabria, Spain	B4	20
Puebla de Zaragoza, Mex.	F9	100
Pueblito, Mex.	E2	130
Pueblito de Ponce, P.R.	B1	104a
Pueblo, Co., U.S.	C4	128
Pueblonuevo, Col.	C4	86
Pueblo Nuevo, P.R.	B2	104a
Pueblo Nuevo, Ven.	B7	86
Pueblo Viejo, Laguna, l., Mex.	D10	100
Pueblo Yaqui, Mex.	B4	100
Puente-Caldelas see Ponte-Caldelas, Spain	B2	20
Puente del Arzobispo, Spain	E5	20
Puentedeume see Pontedeume, Spain	A2	20
Puente Genil, Spain	G6	20
Puerca, Punta, c., P.R.	B4	104a
Puerco, stm., U.S.	I7	132
Puerco, stm., N.M., U.S.	I10	132
Puerto Acosta, Bol.	C3	90
Puerto Adela, Para.	B10	92
Puerto Aisén, Chile	I2	90
Puerto Alegre, Bol.	B4	90
Puerto Ángel, Mex.	H10	100
Puerto Arista, Mex.	H11	100
Puerto Armuelles, Pan.	H6	102
Puerto Asís, Col.	G3	86
Puerto Ayacucho, Ven.	E8	86
Puerto Baquerizo Moreno, Ec.	i12	84a
Puerto Barrios, Guat.	E3	102
Puerto Bermúdez, Peru	F3	84
Puerto Berrío, Col.	D4	86
Puerto Bolívar, Col.	A5	86
Puerto Boyacá, Col.	E4	86
Puerto Cabello, Ven.	B7	86
Puerto Cabezas, Nic.	F6	102
Puerto Carreño, Col.	D8	86
Puerto Chicama, Peru	E2	84
Puerto Colombia, Col.	B4	86
Puerto Cortés, Hond.	E3	102
Puerto Cumarebo, Ven.	B7	86
Puerto Deseado, Arg.	I3	90
Puerto Escondido, Mex.	H10	100
Puerto Escondido, c., Ven.	p20	104g
Puerto Esperanza, Arg.	B10	92
Puerto Fonciere, Para.	D5	90
Puerto Francisco de Orellana, Ec.	H3	86
Puerto Heath, Bol.	B3	90
Puerto Iguazú, Arg.	B10	92
Puerto Ingeniero Ibáñez, Chile	I2	90
Puerto Inírida, Col.	F7	86
Puerto Juárez, Mex.	B4	102
Puerto la Cruz, Ven.	B9	86
Puerto Leguízamo, Col.	H4	86
Puerto Libertad, Mex.	G6	98
Puerto Limón, Col.	F5	86
Puerto Limón, C.R.	G6	102
Puertollano, Spain	F6	20
Puerto Lobos, Arg.	H4	90
Puerto López, Col.	E5	86
Puerto Madero, Mex.	H12	100
Puerto Madryn, Arg.	H3	90
Puerto Maldonado, Peru	F4	84
Puerto Montt, Chile	H2	90
Puerto Morelos, Mex.	B4	102
Puerto Natales, Chile	J2	90
Puerto Padre, Cuba	B9	102
Puerto Páez, Ven.	D8	86
Puerto Palmer, Pico, mtn., Mex.	G6	130
Puerto Peñasco, Mex.	F6	98
Puerto Pinasco, Para.	D5	90
Puerto Pirámides, Arg.	H4	90
Puerto Piray, Arg.	C10	92
Puerto Píritu, Ven.	B9	86
Puerto Plata, Dom. Rep.	C12	102
Puerto Princesa, Phil.	F2	52
Puerto Real, P.R.	B1	104a
Puerto Real, Spain	H4	20
Puerto Rico, Arg.	C10	92
Puerto Rico, Bol.	B3	90
Puerto Rico, Col.	G4	86
Puerto Rico, dep., N.A.	b3	104a
Puerto Rico Trench, unds.	G7	144
Puerto Rondón, Col.	D6	86
Puerto San José, Guat.	F2	102
Puerto San Julián, Arg.	I3	90
Puerto Santa Cruz, Arg.	J3	90
Puerto Sastre, Para.	D5	90
Puerto Suárez, Bol.	C5	90
Puerto Tejada, Col.	F3	86
Puerto Tolosa, Col.	H4	86
Puerto Umbría, Col.	G3	86
Puerto Vallarta, Mex.	E6	100
Puerto Varas, Chile	H2	90
Puerto Victoria, Arg.	C10	92
Puerto Viejo, C.R.	G5	102
Puerto Villamil, Ec.	i11	84a
Puerto Villamizar, Col.	C5	86
Puerto Wilches, Col.	D5	86
Puerto Ybapobó, Para.	D5	90
Pueyrredón, Lago (Cochrane, Lago), l., S.A.	I2	90
Pugačov, Russia	D7	32
Puget Sound, strt., Wa., U.S.	C4	136
Puglia, state, Italy	C10	24
Pugŏ-ri, Kor., N.	D9	38
Puhi-waero see South West Cape, c., N.Z.	H2	80
Puhja, Est.	B9	10
Puiești, Rom.	C14	26
Puigcerdá, Spain	B12	20
Puigmal d' Err (Puigmal), mtn., Eur.	G8	18
Pujiang, China	G8	42
Pujilí, Ec.	H2	86
Puka see Pukë, Alb.	B13	24
Pukaki, Lake, l., N.Z.	F3	80
Pukch'ŏng-ŭp, Kor., N.	D8	38
Pukë, Alb.	B13	24
Pukekohe, N.Z.	C6	80
Pukhrāyān, India	E7	54
Pukou, China	H8	42
Puksoozero, Russia	E19	8
Pula, Cro.	F10	22
Pula, Italy	F3	24
Pulacayo, Bol.	D3	90
Pulantien see Xinjin, China	B9	42
Pulap, at., Micron.	C5	72
Púlar, Cerro, vol., Chile	B3	92
Pulaski, N.Y., U.S.	E13	112
Pulaski, Tn., U.S.	B11	122
Pulaski, Va., U.S.	G5	114
Pulau, stm., Indon.	G10	44
Pulaukida, Indon.	E3	50
Pulau Pinang, state, Malay.	J5	48
Puławy, Pol.	E18	16
Pulgaon, India	H7	54
Puli, Tai.	J9	42
Pulicat, India	E5	53
Pulicat Lake, l., India	E4	53
Puliyangudi, India	G3	53
Pullman, Wa., U.S.	D9	136
Pulog, Mount, mtn., Phil.	B3	52
Pulon'ga, Russia	C18	8
Pułtusk, Pol.	D16	16
Puma Yumco, l., China	D13	54
Pumei, China	A7	48
Pumpkin Buttes, mtn., Wy., U.S.	D7	126
Pumpkin Creek, stm., Mt., U.S.	B7	126
Pumpkin Creek, stm., Ne., U.S.	F10	126
Puná, Isla, i., Ec.	I1	86
Punaauia, Fr. Poly.	v21	78h
Punakha, Bhu.	E12	54
Punan, Indon.	B10	50
Punata, Bol.	C3	90
Pūnch, India	B5	54
Punchaw, B.C., Can.	C7	138
Pune (Poona), India	B1	53
Punganūru, India	E4	53
P'ungsan-ŭp, Kor., N.	D7	38
Pungué, stm., Afr.	A12	70
Punia, D.R.C.	E5	66
Punilla, Sierra de la, mts., Arg.	D3	92
Punitaqui, Chile	E2	92
Punjab, state, India	C5	54
Punjab, state, Pak.	C4	54
Punnichy, Sk., Can.	C9	124
Puno, Peru	G3	84
Punta, Cerro de, mtn., P.R.	B2	104a
Punta Alta, Arg.	I6	92
Punta Arenas, Chile	J2	90
Punta Banda, Cabo, c., Mex.	L9	134
Punta Cardón, Ven.	B6	86
Punta Colnett, Mex.	F4	98
Punta de Agua Creek (Tramperos Creek), stm., U.S.	E5	128
Punta de Díaz, Chile	C2	92
Punta del Cobre, Chile	C2	92
Punta del Este, Ur.	G10	92
Punta Delgada, Arg.	H4	90
Punta de los Llanos, Arg.	E4	92
Punta de Piedras, Ven.	B9	86
Punta Gorda, Nic.	G6	102
Punta Gorda, Fl., U.S.	J3	116
Punta Gorda, Bahía de, b., Nic.	G6	102
Punta Negra, Salar de, pl., Chile	B3	92
Punta Prieta, Mex.	A1	100
Puntarenas, C.R.	G5	102
Punta Santiago, P.R.	B4	104a
Punto Fijo, Ven.	B6	86
Punung, Indon.	H7	50
Puper, Indon.	F9	44
Puppy's Point, c., Norf. I.	y24	78i
Puqi, China	G5	42
Puqian, China	L4	42
Puquio, Peru	F3	84
Pur, stm., Russia	A13	32
Puracé, Volcán, vol., Col.	F3	86
Pūranpur, India	D7	54
Purcell, Ok., U.S.	F11	128
Purcell Mountains, mts., N.A.	F14	138
Purcellville, Va., U.S.	E8	114
Purdy, Mo., U.S.	H3	120
Puré (Puruí), stm., S.A.	I6	86
Purgatoire, stm., Co., U.S.	D5	128
Puri, India	I10	54
Purificación, Col.	F4	86
Purificación, stm., Mex.	C9	100
Purísima, Mex.	E7	130
Purmerend, Neth.	B13	14
Pūrna, stm., India	H5	54
Pūrna, stm., India	H6	54
Pūrnia, India	F11	54
Puronga, Russia	F19	8
Puruí (Puré), stm., S.A.	I6	86
Puruliya, India	G11	54
Puruni, stm., Guy.	D12	86
Purús, stm., S.A.	E4	84
Puruvesi, l., Fin.	F13	8
Purvis, Ms., U.S.	F9	122
Purwakarta, Indon.	G5	50
Purwodadi, Indon.	G6	50
Purwodadi, Indon.	G7	50
Purwokerto, Indon.	G6	50
Purworejo, Indon.	G6	50
Pusa, Malay.	C7	50
Pusad, India	B3	53
Pusan (Fusan), Kor., S.	D2	40
Pusan-jikhalsi, state, Kor., S.	D2	40
Pusat Gayo, Pegunungan, mts., Indon.	J3	48
Pushkar, India	E5	54
Puškin, Russia	A13	10
Puškino, Russia	D20	10
Püspökladány, Hung.	B8	26
Püssi, Est.	A10	10
Pustozersk, Russia	C25	8
Putaendo, Chile	F2	92
Putao, Mya.	C8	46
Putian, China	G6	42
Putian, China	I8	42
Putignano, Italy	D10	24
Puting, Tanjung, c., Indon.	E7	50
Putla de Guerrero, Mex.	D5	96
Putnam, Ct., U.S.	C14	114
Putney, Ga., U.S.	E1	116
Putney, Vt., U.S.	B13	114
Putorana, plato, plat., Russia	C7	34
Puttalam, Sri L.	G4	53
Puttalam Lagoon, b., Sri L.	G4	53
Puttūr, India	E4	53
Putú, Chile	G1	92
Putumayo, state, Col.	G4	86
Putumayo (Içá), stm., S.A.	D3	84
Putuo, China	F10	42
Putussibau, Indon.	C8	50
Putyla, Ukr.	B12	26
Puula, l., Fin.	F12	8
Puurmani, Est.	B9	10
Puyallup, Wa., U.S.	C4	136
Puyang, China	D6	42
Puy-de-Dôme, state, Fr.	D9	18
Puymorens, Col de, p., Fr.	G7	18
Puyo, Ec.	H3	86
Pweto, D.R.C.	F5	66
Pwinbyu, Mya.	B2	48
Pyalo, Mya.	C2	48
Pyapon, Mya.	D2	48
Pyawbwe, Mya.	B3	48
Pyhäjärvi, l., Fin.	E11	8
Pyhäjärvi, l., Fin.	F9	8
Pyhäjoki, Fin.	D10	8
Pyhäjoki, stm., Fin.	D11	8
Pyhäselkä, l., Fin.	E13	8
Pyhätunturi, mtn., Fin.	C12	8
Pyinbongyi, Mya.	D3	48
Pyinmana, Mya.	C3	48
Pyin Oo Lwin see Maymyo, Mya.	A3	48
Pýlos, Grc.	G4	28
Pymatuning Reservoir, res., U.S.	C5	114
Pyŏktong-ŭp, Kor., N.	D6	38
P'yŏngch'ang, Kor., S.	B1	40
P'yonghae, Kor., S.	C2	40
P'yŏngt'aek, Kor., S.	F7	38
P'yŏngyang, Kor., N.	E6	38
Pyote, Tx., U.S.	C4	130
Pyramid Lake, l., Nv., U.S.	D6	134
Pyramid Peak, mtn., Wy., U.S.	G16	136
Pyrenees, mts., Eur.	G6	18
Pyrénées-Atlantiques, state, Fr.	F5	18
Pyrénées Occident, Parc National des, p.o.i., Fr.	G5	18
Pyrénées-Orientales, state, Fr.	G8	18
Pýrgos, Grc.	F4	28
Pytalovo, Russia	C10	10
Pyu, Mya.	C3	48
Pyūṭhān, Nepal	D9	54

Q

Name	Map Ref.	Page
Qaanaaq see Thule, Grnld.	B12	141
Qabbāsīn, Syria	B8	58
Qacentina (Constantine), Alg.	B6	64
Qā'en, Iran	C8	56
Qagan Moron, stm., China	C3	38
Qagan Nur, l., China	C7	36
Qahar Youyi Zhongqi, China	A5	42
Qaidam, stm., China	D4	36
Qaidam Pendi, bas., China	D3	36
Qalāt, Afg.	C10	56
Qal'at ash-Shaqīf (Beaufort Castle), hist., Leb.	E6	58
Qal'at Bīshah, Sau. Ar.	E5	56
Qal'at Ṣāliḥ, Iraq	C6	56
Qal'eh-ye Now, Afg.	C9	56
Qallābāt, Sudan	E7	62
Qalyûb, Egypt	H2	58
Qamar, Ghubbat al-, b., Yemen	F7	56
Qamdo, China	E4	36
Qamea, i., Fiji	p20	79e
Qamīnis, Libya	A3	62
Qānā, Leb.	E6	58
Qandahār, Afg.	C10	56
Qandala, Som.	B9	66
Qaqortoq see Julianehåb, Grnld.	E16	141
Qārah, Syria	D7	58
Qarazhal see Karažal, Kaz.	E12	32
Qardho, Som.	C9	66
Qarqan, stm., China	G15	32
Qârûn, Birket (Moeris, Lake), l., Egypt	I1	58
Qarwāw, Ra's, c., Oman	F8	56
Qasigiannguit see Christianshåb, Grnld.	D15	141
Qaṣr al-Azraq, hist., Jord.	G7	58
Qaṣr al-Kharānah, hist., Jord.	G7	58
Qaṣr al-Mushattá, hist., Jord.	G7	58
Qaṣr aṭ-Ṭūbah, hist., Jord.	G7	58
Qaṣr Ḍab'ah, hist., Jord.	G7	58
Qaṣr-e Shīrīn, Iran	C6	56
Qasr Farâfra, Egypt	B5	62
Qaṭanā, Syria	E6	58
Qatar, ctry., Asia	D7	56
Qatrani, Gebel, hill, Egypt	I1	58
Qattâra, Munkhafad el- (Qattara Depression), depr., Egypt	B5	62
Qattara Depression see Qattâra, Munkhafad el-, depr., Egypt	B5	62
Qaṭṭīnah, Buḥayrat, res., Syria	D7	58
Qāzigund, India	B5	54
Qazımämmäd, Azer.	B6	56
Qazvīn, Iran	B6	56
Qena, Egypt	B6	62
Qena, Wadi (Qinā, Wādī), stm., Egypt	K3	58
Qeqertarsuaq see Godhavn, Grnld.	D15	141
Qesari, Ḥorbat (Caesarea), hist., Isr.	F5	58
Qeshm, Jazīreh-ye, i., Iran	D8	56
Qetura, Isr.	I5	58
Qezel Owzan, stm., Iran	B6	56
Qian, stm., China	J3	42
Qian'an, China	B6	38
Qian Gorlos, China	B6	38
Qianning, China	E5	36
Qianshan, China	F7	42
Qianwei, China	F5	36
Qianxi, China	H1	42
Qianyang, China	H3	42
Qiaolima, China	A8	54
Qiaowan, China	C4	36
Qidong, China	H5	42
Qiemo, China	G15	32
Qigong, China	F5	36
Qijiang, China	G2	42
Qila Saifullāh, Pak.	C2	54
Qilian Shan, mtn., China	D4	36
Qilian Shan, mts., China	D4	36
Qimen, China	G7	42
Qin, stm., China	D5	42
Qing, stm., China	F4	42
Qingcheng, China	C7	42
Qingchengzi, China	D5	38
Qingdao (Tsingtao), China	C9	42
Qingfeng, China	D6	42
Qinggang, China	B10	36
Qinghai, state, China	D4	36
Qinghai Hu, l., China	D5	36
Qingjiang, China	G6	42
Qingjiang, China	E8	42
Qinglong, China	F6	36
Qinglonggang, China	F9	42
Qingshen, China	F5	36
Qingshui, China	D4	36
Qingshui, China	D2	42
Qingshui, stm., China	H3	42
Qingshui, stm., China	C2	42
Qingtang, China	I5	42
Qingyang, China	B8	38
Qingyang, China	F7	42
Qingyang, China	C2	42
Qingyuan, China	C6	38
Qingyuan, China	J5	42
Qingyuan, China	H8	42
Qingyuan, China	I3	42
Qing Zang Gaoyuan (Tibet, Plateau of), plat., China	B6	46
Qingzhen, China	H2	42
Qinhuangdao, China	B8	42
Qin Ling, mts., China	E3	42
Qinshihuang Mausoleum (Terra Cotta Army), hist., China	D3	42
Qinshui, China	D5	42
Qinxian, China	C5	42
Qinyang, China	D5	42
Qinyuan, China	C5	42
Qinzhou, China	J3	42
Qionghai, China	L4	42
Qionglai, China	E5	36
Qionglaishan, mts., China	E5	36
Qiongzhong, China	L3	42
Qiongzhou Haixia, strt., China	K4	42
Qiqian, China	F13	34
Qiqihar, China	B9	36
Qira, China	A5	46
Qiryat Ata, Isr.	F6	58
Qiryat Gat, Isr.	G5	58
Qiryat Shemona, Isr.	E6	58
Qishn, Yemen	F7	56
Qitai, China	C2	36
Qitaihe, China	B11	36
Qitamu, China	B7	38
Qixia, China	C9	42
Qixian, China	D6	42
Qiyang, China	H4	42
Qizhou, China	F6	42
Qizil Jilga, China	A7	54
Qom, Iran	C7	56
Qomsheh, Iran	C7	56
Qonggyai, China	D13	54
Qôrnoq, Grnld.	E15	141
Qostanay see Kustanaj, Kaz.	D10	32
Qowowuyag (Chopu), mtn., Asia	D11	54
Qu, stm., China	F2	42
Qu, stm., China	G8	42
Quabbin Reservoir, res., Ma., U.S.	B13	114
Quadra Island, i., B.C., Can.	F5	138
Quadros, Lagoa dos, l., Braz.	D12	92
Quakenbrück, Ger.	D3	16
Qualicum Beach, B.C., Can.	G6	138
Quambatook, Austl.	J4	76
Quang Ngai, Viet.	E9	48
Quang Trach, Viet.	D8	48
Quantico, Va., U.S.	F8	114
Quanyang, China	C7	38
Quanzhou, China	I8	42
Qu'Appelle, Sk., Can.	D10	124
Qu'Appelle, stm., Can.	D12	124
Qu'Appelle Dam, dam, Sk., Can.	D7	124
Quaraí, Braz.	E9	92
Quaraí (Cuareim), stm., S.A.	E9	92
Quarles, Pegunungan, mts., Indon.	E11	50
Quarryville, Pa., U.S.	E9	114
Quartier d'Orléans, Guad.	A1	105a
Quartu Sant'Elena, Italy	E3	24
Quartz Lake, l., N.T., Can.	A14	106
Quartz Mountain, mtn., Or., U.S.	G4	136
Quartzsite, Az., U.S.	J2	132
Quba, Azer.	A6	56
Qūchān, Iran	B8	56
Quchijie, China	G4	42
Queanbeyan, Austl.	J7	76
Québec, Qc., Can.	D5	110
Québec, state, Can.	E16	106
Quebeck, Tn., U.S.	I12	120
Quebra-Anzol, stm., Braz.	J2	88
Quebracho, Ur.	E9	92
Quebrada Seca, P.R.	B4	104a
Quedal, Cabo, c., Chile	H2	90
Quedlinburg, Ger.	E7	16
Queen Charlotte Islands, is., B.C., Can.	E4	106
Queen Charlotte Sound, strt., B.C., Can.	E2	138
Queen Charlotte Strait, strt., B.C., Can.	F3	138
Queen City, Mo., U.S.	D5	120
Queen City, Tx., U.S.	D4	122
Queen Elizabeth Islands, is., N.T., Can.	B13	94
Queen Mary Coast, cst., Ant.	B14	81
Queen Maud Gulf, b., N.T., Can.	B10	106
Queen Maud Land, reg., Ant.	C4	81
Queen Maud Mountains, mts., Ant.	D23	81
Queenscliff, Austl.	L5	76
Queensland, state, Austl.	D8	74
Queensport, N.S., Can.	E15	110
Queenstown, Austl.	o12	77a
Queenstown, N.Z.	G3	80
Queenstown, S. Afr.	G8	70
Queguay Grande, stm., Ur.	F9	92
Queimada Nova, Braz.	E5	88
Queimadas, Braz.	F6	88
Queimados, Braz.	L4	88
Quela, Ang.	B2	68
Quelelevu, i., Fiji	p20	79e
Quelimane, Moz.	D6	68
Quelpart Island see Cheju-do, i., Kor., S.	H7	38
Quemado, Tx., U.S.	F7	130
Quemado, Punta de, c., Cuba	B10	102
Quemoy see Chinmen Tao, i., Tai.	I8	42
Quemú Quemú, Arg.	H6	92
Quequén, Arg.	I8	92
Querary, stm., Col.	G6	86
Quercy, hist. reg., Fr.	E7	18
Querétaro, Mex.	E8	100
Querétaro, state, Mex.	E8	100
Querobabi, Mex.	F7	98
Quesada, C.R.	E8	96
Quesada, Spain	G7	20
Queshan, China	E5	42
Quesnel, B.C., Can.	C8	138
Quesnel, stm., B.C., Can.	D8	138
Quesnel Lake, l., B.C., Can.	D9	138
Que Son, Viet.	E9	48
Questa, N.M., U.S.	E3	128
Quetico Lake, l., On., Can.	C7	118
Quetta, Pak.	C10	56
Quetzaltenango, Guat.	E2	102

Name | Map Ref. | Page

I•48 Rich-Ruwe

Name | Map Ref. | Page

Richland Center, Wi., U.S. H8 118
Richland Creek, stm., Tx., U.S. C11 130
Richlands, Va., U.S. G4 114
Richland Springs, Tx., U.S. C9 130
Richmond, Austl. C4 76
Richmond, Austl. I8 76
Richmond, B.C., Can. G7 138
Richmond, On., Can. C14 112
Richmond, Qc., Can. E4 110
Richmond, N.Z. E5 80
Richmond, S. Afr. G6 70
Richmond, S. Afr. F10 70
Richmond, Eng., U.K. G11 12
Richmond, Ca., U.S. F3 134
Richmond, In., U.S. I5 112
Richmond, Ky., U.S. G1 114
Richmond, Me., U.S. F7 110
Richmond, Mi., U.S. B3 114
Richmond, Mn., U.S. F4 118
Richmond, Mo., U.S. E4 120
Richmond, Tx., U.S. H3 122
Richmond, Ut., U.S. B5 132
Richmond, Va., U.S. G8 114
Richmond Heights, Fl., U.S. K5 116
Richmond Highlands, Wa., U.S. C4 136
Richmond Hill, On., Can. E10 112
Richmond Hill, Ga., U.S. E4 116
Richmond Peak, mtn., St. Vin. o11 105e
Richton, Ms., U.S. F9 122
Richwood, Oh., U.S. D2 114
Richwood, W.V., U.S. F5 114
Ricobayo, Embalse de, res., Spain C4 20
Riddle, Or., U.S. H3 136
Rideau, stm., On., Can. C14 112
Ridgecrest, Ca., U.S. H8 134
Ridgedale, Sk., Can. A9 124
Ridgeland, Ms., U.S. E8 122
Ridgeland, S.C., U.S. D4 116
Ridgetown, On., Can. F8 112
Ridgeville, Mb., Can. E16 124
Ridgeville, S.C., U.S. C5 116
Ridgeway, Mo., U.S. D4 120
Ridgway, Co., U.S. E9 132
Ridgway, Il., U.S. G9 120
Ridgway, Pa., U.S. C7 114
Riding Mountain National Park, p.o.i., Mb., Can. D13 124
Riegelwood, N.C., U.S. B7 116
Riesa, Ger. E9 16
Riesco, Isla, i., Chile J2 90
Riesi, Italy G8 24
Riet, stm., S. Afr. F7 70
Riet, stm., S. Afr. H5 70
Rietavas, Lith. E4 10
Rietfontein (Buitsivango), stm., Afr. B4 70
Rieti, Italy H9 22
Rif, mts., Mor. C4 64
Riffe Lake, res., Wa., U.S. D4 136
Rifle, Co., U.S. D9 132
Rifstangi, c., Ice. j31 8a
Rift Valley, val., Afr. F7 62
Rīga, Lat. D7 10
Riga, Gulf of, b., Eur. C6 10
Rigaih, Indon. J2 48
Rigby, Id., U.S. G14 136
Rīgestān, reg., Afg. C9 56
Riggins, Id., U.S. E10 136
Rigi, mtn., Switz. C5 22
Rigo, Pap. N. Gui. b4 79a
Rig-Rig, Chad E2 62
Riihimäki, Fin. F11 8
Riiser-Larsen Peninsula, pen., Ant. B8 81
Riječki Zaljev, b., Cro. E11 22
Rijeka (Fiume), Cro. E11 22
Rijssen, Neth. D2 16
Rillito, Az., U.S. K5 132
Rimatara, i., Fr. Poly. F11 72
Rimavská Sobota, Slov. H15 16
Rimbey, Ab., Can. D16 138
Rimersburg, Pa., U.S. C6 114
Rimini, Italy F9 22
Rimouski, Qc., Can. B8 110
Rimouski, stm., Qc., Can. B8 110
Rinbung, China C7 46
Rinca, Pulau, i., Indon. H11 50
Rincon, Ga., U.S. D4 116
Rincon, N.M., U.S. K9 132
Rinconada, Arg. D3 90
Rincón del Bonete, Lago Artificial de, res., Ur. F9 92
Rincón de Romos, Mex. D7 100
Rīngas, India E5 54
Ringdove, Vanuatu k16 79d
Ringebu, Nor. F4 8
Ringgold, Ga., U.S. C13 122
Ringim, Nig. G6 64
Ringkøbing, Den. H2 8
Ringkøbing, state, Den. H3 8
Ringkøbing Fjord, b., Den. H2 8
Ringling, Ok., U.S. G11 128
Ringsted, Ia., U.S. H4 118
Ringvassøya, i., Nor. A8 8
Rinjani, Gunung, vol., Indon. H10 50
Rinteln, Ger. D5 16
Rio, Wi., U.S. H9 118
Riobamba, Ec. H2 86
Río Blanco, Chile F2 92
Rio Branco, Braz. E4 84
Río Branco, Ur. F11 92
Río Bravo, Mex. C9 100
Río Bravo, Parque Internacional del, p.o.i., Mex. F5 130
Rio Brilhante, Braz. D6 90
Río Bueno, Chile H2 90
Rio Casca, Braz. K4 88
Río Ceballos, Arg. E5 92
Río Chico, Ven. B9 86
Rio Claro, Braz. L2 88
Rio Claro, Trin. s12 105f
Río Colorado, Arg. I5 92
Río Cuarto, Arg. F5 92
Rio das Pedras, Moz. C12 70
Rio de Janeiro, Braz. L4 88
Rio de Janeiro, state, Braz. L4 88
Rio Dell, Ca., U.S. C1 134
Río de Oro, Col. C5 86
Rio do Sul, Braz. C13 92
Rio Espera, Braz. K4 88
Rio Felix, stm., N.M., U.S. H3 128
Río Gallegos, Arg. J3 90
Río Grande, Arg. J3 90
Rio Grande, Braz. F11 92
Río Grande, Mex. D7 100
Río Grande, Nic. F4 102
Río Grande, P.R. B4 104a
Rio Grande (Bravo), stm., N.A. H13 98
Rio Grande do Norte, state, Braz. C7 88
Rio Grande do Sul, state, Braz. D11 92
Ríohacha, Col. B5 86
Río Hato, Pan. H7 102
Rio Hondo, Tx., U.S. H10 130
Rio Hondo, stm., N.M., U.S. H3 128
Río Hondo, Embalse, res., Arg. C5 92
Río Jueyes, P.R. B3 104a
Riolândia, Braz. D6 90
Rio Largo, Braz. E8 88
Riom, Fr. D9 18
Río Mayo, Arg. I2 90
Río Mulatos, Bol. C3 90
Riondel, B.C., Can. G14 138
Rio Negro, Braz. C13 92
Ríonegro, Col. D5 86
Río Negro, state, Arg. G3 90
Rio Negro, Pantanal do, sw., Braz. C5 90
Rionero in Vulture, Italy D9 24
Riópar, Spain F8 20
Rio Pardo, Braz. E11 92
Rio Pardo de Minas, Braz. H4 88
Río Piedras, P.R. B3 104a
Rio Piracicaba, Braz. J4 88
Rio Pomba, Braz. K4 88
Rio Preto, Braz. L3 88
Rio Rancho, N.M., U.S. H10 132
Rio Real, Braz. F6 88
Río Segundo, Arg. E5 92
Ríosucio, Col. E4 86
Río Tercero, Arg. F5 92
Rio Tinto, Braz. D8 88
Rio Verde, Braz. G7 84
Ríoverde, Mex. E8 100
Rio Verde de Mato Grosso, Braz. C6 90
Rio Vista, Ca., U.S. E4 134
Riozinho, stm., Braz. D4 84
Riozinho, stm., Braz. E3 88
Ripley, N.Y., U.S. B6 114
Ripley, Oh., U.S. F2 114
Ripley, Tn., U.S. B9 122
Ripoll, Spain B13 20
Ripon, Qc., Can. E1 110
Ripon, Eng., U.K. G11 12
Ripon, Ca., U.S. F4 134
Ripon, Wi., U.S. H10 118
Riposto, Italy G9 24
Risaralda, state, Col. E3 86
Risbäck, Swe. D6 8
Rishīkesh, India C7 54
Rishiri-suidō, strt., Japan B14 38
Rishiri-tō, i., Japan B14 38
Rishon LeZiyyon, Isr. G5 58
Rising Star, Tx., U.S. B9 130
Rising Sun, In., U.S. F12 120
Rising Sun, Md., U.S. E9 114
Risle, stm., Fr. E9 14
Risnjak, mtn., Cro. E11 22
Risti, Est. A7 10
Ristna, Est. G9 8
Rita Blanca Creek, stm., Tx., U.S. F6 128
Ritchie, S. Afr. F7 70
Ritidian Point, c., Guam i10 78c
Ritter, Mount, mtn., Ca., U.S. F6 134
Rittman, Oh., U.S. D4 114
Ritzville, Wa., U.S. C8 136
Rivadavia, Arg. E3 92
Rivadavia, Arg. G6 92
Rivadavia, Chile D2 92
Riva del Garda, Italy E7 22
Rivas, Nic. G5 102
Rive-de-Gier, Fr. D10 18
Rivera, Arg. H6 92
Rivera, Ur. E10 92
River Cess, Lib. H3 64
Riverdale, Ca., U.S. G6 134
Riverdale, N.D., U.S. G12 124
River Falls, Al., U.S. F12 122
River Falls, Wi., U.S. G6 118
Riverhead, N.Y., U.S. D13 114
Riverhurst, Sk., Can. D7 124
Riverina, reg., Austl. J5 76
River John, N.S., Can. E13 110
River Jordan, B.C., Can. H6 138
River Road, Or., U.S. F3 136
Rivers, Mb., Can. D13 124
Riversdale, S. Afr. I5 70
Riverside, Ca., U.S. J8 134
Riverside, Ia., U.S. C6 120
Riverside, Tx., U.S. G3 122
Riverside, Wa., U.S. B7 136
Rivers Inlet, B.C., Can. E3 138
Riversleigh, Austl. C7 74
Riverton, N.Z. H2 80
Riverton, Il., U.S. E8 120
Riverton, Ne., U.S. A10 128
Riverton, Ut., U.S. C4 132
Riverton, Va., U.S. F7 114
Riverton, Wy., U.S. D4 126
Riverton Heights, Wa., U.S. C4 136
River View, Al., U.S. E13 122
Rives, Tn., U.S. H8 120
Rivesville, W.V., U.S. E5 114
Riviera, Tx., U.S. G10 130
Riviera Beach, Fl., U.S. J5 116
Rivière-à-Pierre, Qc., Can. C5 110
Rivière-Bleue, Qc., Can. C7 110
Rivière-de-la-Chaloupe, Qc., Can. A14 110
Rivière-du-Loup, Qc., Can. C7 110
Rivière-Matawin, Qc., Can. D3 110
Rivière-Pilote, Mart. I7 105c
Rivière-Salée, Mart. k7 105c
Rivne, Ukr. E14 6
Rivoli, Italy E4 22
Rivoli Bay, b., Austl. K2 76
Riyadh see Ar-Riyāḍ, Sau. Ar. E6 56
Rīyāq, Leb. E7 58
Rize, Tur. A5 56
Rizzuto, Capo, c., Italy F11 24
Rjad, Russia C18 10
Rjazan', Russia D5 32
Rjazancevo, Russia D22 10
Rjazanskaja oblast', co., Russia I19 8
Rjažsk, Russia D6 32
Rjukan, Nor. G3 8
Ro, N. Cal. m16 79d
Roachdale, In., U.S. I3 112
Road Town, Br. Vir. Is. e8 104b
Roan Mountain, Tn., U.S. H3 114
Roanne, Fr. C9 18
Roanoke, Al., U.S. D13 122
Roanoke, Il., U.S. D8 120
Roanoke, Va., U.S. G6 114
Roanoke, stm., U.S. H8 114
Roanoke Island, i., N.C., U.S. I10 114
Roanoke Rapids, N.C., U.S. H8 114
Roanoke Rapids Lake Dam, dam, N.C., U.S. H8 114
Roan Plateau, plat., U.S. D7 132
Roaring Spring, Pa., U.S. D7 114
Roaring Springs, Tx., U.S. H7 128
Roatán, Isla de, i., Hond. D4 102
Robbins, N.C., U.S. A6 116
Robbins, Tn., U.S. H13 120
Robbins Island, i., Austl. n12 77a
Robbinsville, N.C., U.S. A2 116
Robe, Austl. K2 76
Robe, Mount, hill, Austl. H3 76
Röbel, Ger. C8 16
Robersonville, N.C., U.S. I8 114
Roberta, Ga., U.S. D1 116
Robert Lee, Tx., U.S. C7 130
Robert Louis Stevenson's Tomb, hist., Samoa g12 79c
Roberts, Id., U.S. G14 136
Roberts, Mt., U.S. B3 126
Robertsdale, Al., U.S. G11 122
Robertsfors, Swe. D9 8
Robert S. Kerr Lake, res., Ok., U.S. B3 122
Robertson, S. Afr. H4 70
Roberts Peak, mtn., B.C., Can. D10 138
Roberts Port, Lib. H2 64
Roberval, Qc., Can. B4 110
Robinson, Il., U.S. E10 120
Robinson, Tx., U.S. C10 130
Róbinson Crusoe, Isla, i., Chile I7 82
Robinvale, Austl. J4 76
Robledo, Spain F8 20
Roblin, Mb., Can. C12 124
Roboré, Bol. C5 90
Rob Roy Island, i., Sol. Is. d7 79b
Robson, Mount, mtn., B.C., Can. C11 138
Robstown, Tx., U.S. G10 130
Roby, Tx., U.S. B7 130
Roca, Cabo da, c., Port. F1 20
Roçado, Braz. D3 88
Rocafuerte, Ec. H1 86
Roca Partida, Isla, i., Mex. F2 100
Rocas, Atol das, at., Braz. F11 82
Rocciamelone, mtn., Italy E4 22
Rocha, Ur. G10 92
Rochdale, Eng., U.K. H10 12
Rochechouart, Fr. D6 18
Rochefort, Fr. D5 18
Rochelle, Ga., U.S. E2 116
Rochelle, Il., U.S. C8 120
Roche-Percée, Sk., Can. E10 124
Rochester, In., U.S. G3 112
Rochester, Mi., U.S. B2 114
Rochester, Mn., U.S. G6 118
Rochester, N.H., U.S. G5 110
Rochester, N.Y., U.S. E12 112
Rochester, Tx., U.S. H9 128
Rochlitz, Ger. E8 16
Rock, stm., U.S. H2 118
Rock, stm., U.S. J8 118
Rockall, i., Scot., U.K. D6 6
Rockall Rise, unds. C12 144
Rock Bay, B.C., Can. F5 138
Rock Creek, B.C., Can. G11 138
Rock Creek, stm., N.A. F7 124
Rock Creek, stm., Mt., U.S. D13 136
Rock Creek, stm., Nv., U.S. C9 134
Rock Creek Butte, mtn., Or., U.S. F8 136
Rockdale, Il., U.S. C9 120
Rockdale, Tx., U.S. D11 130
Rockefeller Plateau, plat., Ant. D27 81
Rockenhausen, Ger. G3 16
Rock Falls, Il., U.S. C8 120
Rockford, Il., U.S. B8 120
Rockford, Ia., U.S. A5 120
Rockford, Oh., U.S. D1 114
Rockford, Tn., U.S. B15 122
Rockglen, Sk., Can. E8 124
Rockhampton, Austl. D8 76
Rockhampton Downs, Austl. C7 74
Rock Hill, S.C., U.S. B4 116
Rockingham, N.C., U.S. B6 116
Rockingham Bay, b., Austl. B6 76
Rock Island, Il., U.S. C7 120
Rocklake, N.D., U.S. F14 124
Rockland, On., Can. C14 112
Rockland, Id., U.S. H14 136
Rockland, Me., U.S. F7 110
Rockland, Ma., U.S. B15 114
Rocklands Reservoir, l., Austl. K3 76
Rockledge, Fl., U.S. H5 116
Rocklin, Ca., U.S. E4 134
Rockmart, Ga., U.S. D13 122
Rockport, In., U.S. G10 120
Rockport, Ky., U.S. G11 120
Rockport, Me., U.S. F7 110
Rockport, Ma., U.S. B15 114
Rock Port, Mo., U.S. D2 120
Rock Rapids, Ia., U.S. H2 118
Rock River, Wy., U.S. F6 126
Rocksprings, Tx., U.S. E7 130
Rock Springs, Wy., U.S. B7 132
Rockstone, Guy. B6 84
Rock Tombs see Speos, hist., Egypt K1 58
Rock Valley, Ia., U.S. H2 118
Rockville, In., U.S. I2 112
Rockville, Md., U.S. E8 114
Rockwall, Tx., U.S. E2 122
Rockwell, Ia., U.S. B4 120
Rockwell, N.C., U.S. A5 116
Rockwood, Me., U.S. E7 110
Rockwood, Pa., U.S. I10 112
Rockwood, Tn., U.S. I13 120
Rocky Cape National Park, p.o.i., Austl. n12 77a
Rockyford, Ab., Can. E17 138
Rocky Ford, Co., U.S. C5 128
Rocky Mount, N.C., U.S. I8 114
Rocky Mount, Va., U.S. H5 114
Rocky Mountain, mtn., Mt., U.S. C14 136
Rocky Mountain House, Ab., Can. D16 138
Rocky Mountain National Park, p.o.i., Co., U.S. G7 126
Rocky Mountains, mts., N.A. D6 106
Rocky Mountain Trench, val., N.A. G15 138
Rocky Point, c., Bah. K8 116
Rodalben, Ger. G3 16
Rødbyhavn, Den. I4 8
Rodeo, Arg. E3 92
Rodeo, Mex. C6 100
Rodeo, N.M., U.S. L7 132
Roderick Island, i., B.C., Can. D2 138
Rodewisch, Ger. F8 16
Rodez, Fr. E8 18
Roding, Ger. G8 16
Rodino, Russia G21 8
Rodney, On., Can. F8 112
Rodney, Cape, c., Ak., U.S. D6 140
Rodniki, Russia H19 8
Ródos (Rhodes), Grc. G11 28
Ródos (Rhodes), i., Grc. G10 28
Rodrigues, i., Mrts. K9 142
Roebourne, Austl. D3 74
Roebuck Bay, b., Austl. C4 74
Roeland Park, Ks., U.S. E3 120
Roermond, Neth. C14 14
Roeselare, Bel. D11 14
Roes Welcome Sound, strt., N.T., Can. C13 106
Roff, Ok., U.S. C2 122
Rogačevo, Russia D20 10
Rogagua, Laguna, l., Bol. B3 90
Rogaguado, Laguna, l., Bol. B3 90
Rogaland, state, Nor. G2 8
Rogaška Slatina, Slvn. D12 22
Rogers, Ar., U.S. H3 120
Rogers, Tx., U.S. D10 130
Rogers, Mount, mtn., Va., U.S. H4 114
Rogers Lake, l., Ca., U.S. I8 134
Rogers Pass, p., B.C., Can. E13 138
Rogersville, N.B., Can. D11 110
Rogersville, Al., U.S. C11 122
Rogersville, Tn., U.S. H3 114
Roggewein, Cabo, c., Chile e30 78l
Rogliano, Fr. G15 18
Rognedino, Russia G16 10
Rogue, stm., Or., U.S. H2 136
Rohri, Pak. E2 54
Rohtak, India D6 54
Roi Et, Thai. E6 48
Roi Georges, Îles du, is., Fr. Poly. E12 72
Roilianka, Ukr. C16 26
Rojas, Arg. G7 92
Rojo, Cabo, c., Mex. E10 100
Rojo, Cabo, c., P.R. C1 104a
Rokan, Indon. C2 50
Rokan, stm., Indon. C2 50
Rokel, stm., S.L. H2 64
Rokiškis, Lith. E8 10
Rokycany, Czech Rep. G9 16
Roland, Mb., Can. E16 124
Roland, Ar., U.S. C6 122
Roland, Ia., U.S. B4 120
Rolândia, Braz. D6 90
Roldanillo, Col. E3 86
Rolfe, Ia., U.S. B3 120
Roll, Az., U.S. K2 132
Rolla, Mo., U.S. G6 120
Rolla, N.D., U.S. F14 124
Rolling Fork, Ms., U.S. E8 122
Rolling Fork, stm., Ky., U.S. G12 120
Rollingstone, Austl. B6 76
Rollins, Mt., U.S. C12 136
Rolvsøya, i., Nor. A10 8
Roma, Austl. F7 76
Roma (Rome), Italy I9 22
Roma, Leso. F8 70
Roma, Tx., U.S. H8 130
Romagna, hist. reg., Italy F9 22
Roman, Rom. C13 26
Romanche Gap, unds. I12 144
Romang, Pulau, i., Indon. G8 44
Romania, ctry., Eur. D11 26
Roman Nose Mountain, mtn., Or., U.S. G3 136
Romano, Cape, c., Fl., U.S. K4 116
Romano, Cayo, i., Cuba A9 102
Romans-sur-Isère, Fr. D10 18
Romanzof Mountains, mts., Ak., U.S. C11 140
Romblon, Phil. D4 52
Rome see Roma, Italy I9 22
Rome, Ga., U.S. C13 122
Rome, N.Y., U.S. E14 112
Romeo, Mi., U.S. B2 114
Romilly-sur-Seine, Fr. F12 14
Romney, W.V., U.S. E7 114
Romny, Ukr. D4 32
Romont, Switz. D3 22
Romorantin-Lanthenay, Fr. G10 14
Rompin, stm., Malay. K6 48
Romsey, Eng., U.K. J11 12
Ron, Mui, c., Viet. C8 48
Rona, i., Scot., U.K. D7 12
Rona, i., Scot., U.K. B7 12
Ronan, Mt., U.S. C12 136
Roncador, Banco see Roncador, Cayos de, unds., Col. F7 102
Roncador, Cayos de, unds., Col. F7 102
Roncador, Serra do, plat., Braz. F7 84
Roncador Bank see Roncador, Cayos de, unds., Col. F7 102
Ronda, Spain H5 20
Ronda, Serranía de, mts., Spain H5 20
Rondane Nasjonalpark, p.o.i., Nor. F3 8
Ronde, Pointe, c., Dom. i5 105c
Rondônia, state, Braz. F5 84
Rondonópolis, Braz. G7 84
Rong, stm., China I3 42
Rong'an, China I3 42
Rongcheng, China C10 42
Ronge, Lac la, l., Sk., Can. D10 106
Rongelap, at., Marsh. Is. B7 72
Rongjiang, China I3 42
Rongkop, Indon. H7 50
Rongshui, China I3 42
Rongxian, China J4 42
Rønne, Den. I6 8
Ronneby, Swe. H6 8
Ronne Ice Shelf, ice, Ant. C34 81
Ronse, Bel. D12 14
Ronuro, stm., Braz. F7 84
Roodhouse, Il., U.S. E7 120
Roof Butte, mtn., Az., U.S. G7 132
Rooiboklaagte, stm., Nmb. B5 70
Roorkee, India D6 54
Roosendaal, Neth. C13 14
Roosevelt, Mn., U.S. C3 118
Roosevelt, Ok., U.S. G9 128
Roosevelt, Ut., U.S. C6 132
Roosevelt, stm., Braz. E5 84
Roosevelt Campobello International Park, p.o.i., N.B., Can. F10 110
Roosevelt Island, i., Ant. C24 81
Root, stm., Mn., U.S. H7 118
Ropaži, Lat. C7 10
Roper, N.C., U.S. I9 114
Roper, stm., Austl. B6 74
Roper Valley, Austl. B6 74
Ropesville, Tx., U.S. H6 128
Roque, Braz. B3 88
Roquefort, Fr. E5 18
Roraima, state, Braz. C5 84
Roraima, Mount, mtn., S.A. E11 86
Røros, Nor. E4 8
Rosa, Lake, l., Bah. B11 102
Rosales, Mex. A6 100
Rosalia, Wa., U.S. C9 136
Rosamond, Ca., U.S. I7 134
Rosamond Lake, l., Ca., U.S. I7 134
Rosario, Arg. F7 92
Rosário, Braz. B3 88
Rosario, Mex. B4 100
Rosario, Mex. D5 100
Rosario, Para. B9 92
Rosario, Ur. G9 92
Rosario, stm., Arg. B5 92
Rosario, Bahía del, b., Mex. G4 98
Rosario, Islas del, is., Col. B4 86
Rosario de Arriba, Mex. F4 98
Rosario de la Frontera, Arg. B5 92
Rosario de Lerma, Arg. B5 92
Rosario del Tala, Arg. F8 92
Rosário do Sul, Braz. E10 92
Rosário Oeste, Braz. F6 84
Rosarito, Mex. A2 100
Rosarito, Mex. K8 134
Rosarno, Italy F9 24
Rosas, Mex. H4 130
Roscoe, S.D., U.S. B13 126
Roscoe, Tx., U.S. B7 130
Roscommon, Ire. H4 12
Roscommon, state, Ire. H4 12
Roscrea, Ire. I5 12
Rose, Mount, mtn., Nv., U.S. D5 134
Roseau, Dom. j6 105c
Roseau, Mn., U.S. C3 118
Roseau, stm., N.A. C2 118
Roseberth, Austl. E2 76
Rosebery, Austl. n12 77a
Roseboro, N.C., U.S. B7 116
Rosebud, Mt., U.S. A6 126
Rosebud, S.D., U.S. D12 126
Rosebud, Tx., U.S. C11 130
Rosebud, stm., Ab., Can. E17 138
Rosebud Creek, stm., Mt., U.S. A6 126
Roseburg, Or., U.S. G3 136
Rosebush, Mi., U.S. E5 112
Rose City, Mi., U.S. D5 112
Rosedale, Austl. E8 76
Rosedale, Ab., Can. E18 138
Rosedale, La., U.S. G7 122
Rosedale, Ms., U.S. D7 122
Rose Hill, N.C., U.S. B7 116
Rose Hill, Va., U.S. H2 114
Rose Island, i., Bah. K8 116
Rosemary, Ab., Can. F18 138
Rosenberg, Tx., U.S. H3 122
Rosenheim, Ger. I8 16
Rosepine, La., U.S. G5 122
Roses, Golf de, b., Spain B14 20
Roses, Golfo de see Roses, Golf de, b., Spain B14 20
Roseto degli Abruzzi, Italy H11 22
Rosetown, Sk., Can. C6 124
Rosetta see Rashid, Egypt G1 58
Rosetta Mouth see Rashid, Masabb, mth., Egypt G1 58
Rose Valley, Sk., Can. B10 124
Roseville, Il., U.S. D7 120
Roseville, Mi., U.S. F7 112
Roseville, Mn., U.S. F5 118
Rosholt, S.D., U.S. F2 118
Rosholt, Wi., U.S. G9 118
Rosica, stm., Blg. F12 26
Rosiclare, Il., U.S. G9 120
Rosignol, Guy. B6 84
Roșiori de Vede, Rom. E12 26
Roskilde, Den. I4 8
Roskilde, state, Den. I5 8
Roslavl', Russia G15 10
Rosman, N.C., U.S. A3 116
Rosmead, S. Afr. G7 70
Ros Mhic Thriúin see New Ross, Ire. I6 12
Ross, Austl. o13 77a
Ross, stm., Yk., Can. C4 106
Rossano, Italy E10 24
Rossasna, Bela. F13 10
Rossburn, Mb., Can. D13 124
Rosseau, Lake, l., On., Can. C10 112
Rossel, Cap, c., N. Cal. m16 79d
Rossell y Rius, Ur. F10 92
Rossford, Oh., U.S. C2 114
Ross Ice Shelf, ice, Ant. D23 81
Rossignol, Lake, l., N.S., Can. F11 110
Ross Island, i., Ant. C22 81
Ross Lake, res., N.A. B5 136
Rossland, B.C., Can. G13 138
Rosslau, Ger. E8 16
Rosso, Maur. F1 64
Ross-on-Wye, Eng., U.K. J10 12
Rossoš', Russia D5 32
Ross R. Barnett Reservoir, res., Ms., U.S. E9 122
Ross River, Yk., Can. C4 106
Ross Sea, Ant. C23 81
Røssvatnet, l., Nor. D5 8
Rossville, Ga., U.S. C13 122
Rossville, Il., U.S. H2 112
Rossville, Ks., U.S. E2 120
Røst, is., Nor. C4 8
Rosthern, Sk., Can. B7 124
Roštkala, Taj. B11 56
Rostock, Ger. B7 16
Rostov, Russia C22 10
Rostov-na-Donu, Russia E6 32
Rosvinskoe, Russia C24 8
Roswell, Ga., U.S. B1 116
Roswell, N.M., U.S. H4 128
Rota, i., N. Mar. Is. B5 72
Rotan, Tx., U.S. B7 130
Rotenburg, Ger. C5 16
Roth, Ger. G7 16
Rothenburg ob der Tauber, Ger. G6 16
Rothera, sci., Ant. B34 81
Rotherham, Eng., U.K. H11 12
Rothesay, N.B., Can. E11 110
Rothesay, Scot., U.K. F7 12
Rothsay, Mn., U.S. E2 118
Rothwell, N.B., Can. D10 110
Roti, Pulau, i., Indon. H7 44
Roto, Austl. I5 76
Rotondella, Italy D10 24
Rotorua, N.Z. D7 80
Rottenburg, Ger. H4 16
Rottenburg an der Laaber, Ger. H8 16
Rotterdam, Neth. C13 14
Rotterdam, N.Y., U.S. B11 114
Rottweil, Ger. H4 16
Rotuma, i., Fiji E8 72
Roubaix, Fr. D12 14
Roudnice nad Labem, Czech Rep. F9 16
Rouen, Fr. E10 14
Rouge, stm., Qc., Can. E2 110
Rough, stm., Ky., U.S. G11 120
Rough River Lake, res., Ky., U.S. G11 120
Rouleau, Sk., Can. D9 124
Roulers see Roeselare, Bel. D11 14
Roulette, Pa., U.S. C7 114
Round Hill Head, c., Austl. E8 76
Round Lake, Mn., U.S. H3 118
Round Lake, l., On., Can. C12 112
Round Mound, hill, Ks., U.S. C9 128
Round Mountain, Nv., U.S. E8 134
Round Mountain, mtn., Austl. H9 76
Round Rock, Tx., U.S. D10 130
Roundup, Mt., U.S. A4 126
Rousay, i., Scot., U.K. B9 12
Rouses Point, N.Y., U.S. E3 110
Roussillon, hist. reg., Fr. G8 18
Routhierville, Qc., Can. B9 110
Rouyn-Noranda, Qc., Can. F15 106
Rovaniemi, Fin. C11 8
Rovenskaja Slabada, Bela. H13 10
Rovereto, Italy E8 22
Roversi, Arg. C6 92
Rovigo, Italy E8 22
Rovuma (Ruvuma), stm., Afr. C6 68
Rowan Lake, l., On., Can. B5 118
Rowena, Austl. G7 76
Rowland, N.C., U.S. B6 116
Rowley, stm., N.T., Can. A15 106
Rowley Island, i., N.T., Can. B14 106
Roxas, Phil. E4 52
Roxboro, N.C., U.S. H7 114
Roxborough, Trin. r13 105f
Roxburgh, N.Z. G3 80
Roxton, Tx., U.S. D3 122
Roy, N.M., U.S. F4 128
Roy, Ut., U.S. B4 132
Roy, Wa., U.S. C4 136
Royal Bardiyā Wild Life Reserve, India D8 54
Royal Canal, can., Ire. H6 12
Royal Center, In., U.S. H3 112
Royal Chitwan National Park, p.o.i., Nepal E10 54
Royal City, Wa., U.S. D7 136
Royale, Isle, i., Mi., U.S. D10 118
Royal Gorge, val., Co., U.S. C3 128
Royal Leamington Spa, Eng., U.K. I11 12
Royal Natal National Park, p.o.i., S. Afr. F9 70
Royal Oak, Mi., U.S. B2 114
Royalton, Mn., U.S. F4 118
Royal Tunbridge Wells, Eng., U.K. J13 12
Royan, Fr. D5 18
Roye, Fr. E11 14
Royston, Eng., U.K. I12 12
Royston, Ga., U.S. B2 116
Różan, Pol. D17 16
Roždestveno, Russia C20 10
Rozdil'na, Ukr. C17 26
Rozewie, Przylądek, c., Pol. B14 16
Rožňava, Slov. H16 16
Roznov, Rom. C13 26
Rożnów, Pol. G16 16
Roztocze, hills, Eur. F19 16
Roztoky, Czech Rep. F10 16
Rrogozhina see Rrogozhinë, Alb. C13 24
Rrogozhinë, Alb. C13 24
Rtiščevo, Russia D6 32
Ru, stm., China E6 42
Ruacana Falls, wtfl, Afr. D1 68
Ruahine Range, mts., N.Z. D7 80
Ruapehu, Mount, vol., N.Z. D6 80
Ruapuke Island, i., N.Z. H3 80
Rubbestadneset, Nor. G1 8
Rubcovsk, Russia D14 32
Rubi, stm., D.R.C. D5 66
Rubio, Ven. D5 86
Rubondo Island, i., Tan. E6 66
Ruby, Ak., U.S. D8 140
Ruby, stm., Mt., U.S. E14 136
Ruby Dome, mtn., Nv., U.S. C1 132
Ruby Lake, sw., Nv., U.S. C1 132
Ruby Mountains, mts., Nv., U.S. C1 132
Ruby Valley, val., Nv., U.S. C1 132
Rucheng, China I5 42
Ruciane-Nida, Pol. C17 16
Ruda Śląska, Pol. F14 16
Rudauli, India E8 54
Rūdbār, Afg. C9 56
Rüdersdorf, Ger. D9 16
Rudkøbing, Den. B6 16
Rudnaja Pristan', Russia B11 38
Rudnja, Russia F14 10
Rudnyj, Kaz. D10 32
Rudnyj, Russia B11 38
Rūdnyy see Rudnyj, Kaz. D10 32
Rudo, Bos. F6 26
Rudolf, Lake (Turkana, Lake), l., Afr. D7 66
Rudolf Hāyk' see Rudolf, Lake, l., Afr. D7 66
Rudolstadt, Ger. F7 16
Rudong, China E9 42
Rudozem, Blg. H11 26
Rudyard, Mi., U.S. B5 112
Rue, Fr. D10 14
Rufā'ah, Sudan E6 62
Ruffin, S.C., U.S. C5 116
Rufiji, stm., Tan. F7 66
Rufino, Arg. G6 92
Rufisque, Sen. G1 64
Rufunsa, Zam. D4 68
Rufus, Or., U.S. E6 136
Rugāji, Lat. D10 10
Rugao, China E9 42
Rugby, Eng., U.K. I11 12
Rugby, N.D., U.S. F14 124
Rügen, i., Ger. B9 16
Rugged Mountain, mtn., B.C., Can. F4 138
Ruhan', Russia G15 10
Ruhengeri, Rw. E5 66
Ruhpolding, Ger. I8 16
Ruhr, stm., Ger. E3 16
Ruhunu National Park, p.o.i., Sri L. H5 53
Rui'an, China H9 42
Ruidoso, N.M., U.S. H3 128
Ruidoso, stm., N.M., U.S. H3 128
Ruihong, China G7 42
Ruijin, China I6 42
Ruiz, Mex. D6 100
Ruiz, Nevado del, vol., Col. E4 86
Ruiz de Montoya, Arg. C10 92
Ruki, stm., D.R.C. E3 66
Rukwa, Lake, l., Tan. F6 66
Rule, Tx., U.S. A8 130
Ruleville, Ms., U.S. D8 122
Rulo, Ne., U.S. D2 120
Rúm, i., Scot., U.K. D6 12
Rum, stm., Mn., U.S. F5 118
Ruma, Yugo. D6 26
Rumbek, Sudan F5 62
Rum Cay, i., Bah. C10 96
Rumia, Pol. B14 16
Rumigny, Fr. E13 14
Rum Jungle, Austl. B6 74
Rumoi, Japan B14 38
Runan, China E6 42
Runanga, N.Z. F4 80
Runde, stm., Zimb. B10 70
Rundēni, Lat. D10 10
Rundu, Nmb. D2 68
Rŭng, Kaôh, i., Camb. G6 48
Runge, Tx., U.S. F10 130
Rungwa, Tan. F6 66
Rungwa, stm., Tan. F6 66
Running Water Draw, stm., U.S. G6 128
Ruo, stm., China C4 36
Ruoqiang, China D2 36
Ruoxi, China G6 42
Rupat, Pulau, i., Indon. C2 50
Rupert, Id., U.S. H13 136
Rupert, W.V., U.S. G5 114
Rupert, stm., Qc., Can. E15 106
Rupert Creek, stm., Austl. C4 76
Rupununi, stm., Guy. F12 86
Rur, stm., Eur. D15 14
Rural Retreat, Va., U.S. H4 114
Rurrenabaque, Bol. B3 90
Rurutu, i., Fr. Poly. F11 72
Rusape, Zimb. D5 68
Ruṣayriṣ, Khazzān ar-, res., Afr. E6 62
Ruse, Blg. F12 26
Ruse, state, Blg. F13 26
Rusera, India F11 54
Rushan, China C9 42
Rush Center, Ks., U.S. C9 128
Rush City, Mn., U.S. F5 118
Rush Creek, stm., Co., U.S. C5 128
Rushford, Mn., U.S. H7 118
Rushmore, Mn., U.S. H3 118
Rushville, Il., U.S. D7 120
Rushville, In., U.S. E12 120
Rusinga Island, i., Kenya E6 66
Rusizi, stm., Afr. E5 66
Rusk, Tx., U.S. F3 122
Ruskin, Fl., U.S. I3 116
Rusnė, Lith. E4 10
Russas, Braz. C6 88
Russell, Mb., Can. D12 124
Russell, Ia., U.S. D4 120
Russell, Ks., U.S. C10 128
Russell, Ky., U.S. F3 114
Russell, Cape, c., N.T., Can. A16 140
Russell Cave National Monument, p.o.i., Al., U.S. C13 122
Russell Islands, is., Sol. Is. e8 79b
Russellkonda, India I10 54
Russells Point, Oh., U.S. D2 114
Russell Springs, Ky., U.S. G12 120
Russellville, Al., U.S. C11 122
Russellville, Ar., U.S. B5 122
Russellville, Ky., U.S. H11 120
Rüsselsheim, Ger. G4 16
Russia, ctry., Eur. B18 2
Russian, stm., Ca., U.S. E2 134
Russiaville, In., U.S. H3 112
Russkij, Russia C9 38
Rust, Aus. C13 22
Rustavi, Geor. F7 32
Rustburg, Va., U.S. G6 114
Rustenburg, S. Afr. D8 70
Ruston, La., U.S. E6 122
Rutana, Bdi. E6 66
Rute, Spain G6 20
Ruteng, Indon. H12 50
Ruth, Nv., U.S. D1 132
Rutherford, Tn., U.S. H8 120
Rutherfordton, N.C., U.S. A3 116
Ruthin, Wales, U.K. H9 12
Ruthven, Ia., U.S. H4 118
Rutland, B.C., Can. G11 138
Rutland, N.D., U.S. A15 126
Rutland, Vt., U.S. G4 110
Rutledge, Ga., U.S. C2 116
Rutog, China B7 54
Rutshuru, D.R.C. E5 66
Rutter, On., Can. B9 112
Ruvuma (Rovuma), stm., Afr. C6 68
Ruwenzori, mts., Afr. D6 66
Ruwenzori Range see Ruwenzori, mts., Afr. D6 66

Name	Map Ref.	Page

Name	Map Ref.	Page
Shoshone Lake, l., Wy., U.S.	F15	136
Shoshone Mountains, mts., Nv., U.S.	E8	134
Shoshone Peak, mtn., Nv., U.S.	G9	134
Shoshone Range, mts., Nv., U.S.	C9	134
Shoshong, Bots.	C8	70
Shostka, Ukr.	D4	32
Shouchang, China	G8	42
Shouguang, China	C8	42
Shouning, China	H8	42
Shouxian, China	E7	42
Shouyang, China	C5	42
Show Low, Az., U.S.	I6	132
Shqipëria see Albania, ctry., Eur.	C14	24
Shreve, Oh., U.S.	D4	114
Shreveport, La., U.S.	E5	122
Shrewsbury, Eng., U.K.	I10	12
Shri Dūngargarh, India	D4	54
Shri Mohangarh, India	E3	54
Shū see Šu, Kaz.	F12	32
Shū see Ču, stm., Asia	F11	32
Shu, stm., China	D8	42
Shuajingsi, China	B9	46
Shuangcheng, China	B7	38
Shuangfeng, China	H5	42
Shuanggou, China	E5	42
Shuanggou, China	D7	42
Shuangji, stm., China	D5	42
Shuangjiang, China	G4	36
Shuangliao, China	C5	38
Shuangpai, China	I4	42
Shuangshutai, China	C4	38
Shuangyang, China	C6	38
Shuangyashan, China	B11	36
Shubrâ el-Kheima, Egypt	H1	58
Shubuta, Ms., U.S.	F10	122
Shucheng, China	F7	42
Shuibatang, China	G2	42
Shuiji, China	H8	42
Shuijingtang, China	G2	42
Shuikoushan, China	H5	42
Shuitou, China	I8	42
Shuiye, China	C5	42
Shujāābād, Pak.	D3	54
Shujālpur, India	G6	54
Shuksan, Mount, mtn., Wa., U.S.	B5	136
Shulan, China	B7	38
Shulaps Peak, mtn., B.C., Can.	F8	138
Shule, China	B12	56
Shule, stm., China	C4	36
Shumagin Islands, is., Ak., U.S.	F7	140
Shunchang, China	H7	42
Shunde, China	J5	42
Shungnak, Ak., U.S.	C8	140
Shunyi, China	A7	42
Shuqualak, Ms., U.S.	E10	122
Shurkhua, Mya.	A1	48
Shurugwi, Zimb.	D5	68
Shūshtar, Iran	C6	56
Shuswap, stm., B.C., Can.	F12	138
Shuswap Lake, l., B.C., Can.	F11	138
Shuwak, Sudan	E7	62
Shuyak Island, i., Ak., U.S.	E9	140
Shuyang, China	D8	42
Shwangliao see Liaoyuan, China	C6	38
Shwebo, Mya.	A2	48
Shwegun, Mya.	D3	48
Shwegyin, Mya.	D3	48
Shymkent see Šymkent, Kaz.	F11	32
Shyok, India	A7	54
Shyok, stm., Asia	B4	46
Si, stm., China	D7	42
Sia, Indon.	G9	44
Siāhān Range, mts., Pak.	D9	56
Siak, stm., Indon.	C2	50
Siak Sri Indrapura, Indon.	C3	50
Siālkot, Pak.	B5	54
Siam see Thailand, ctry., Asia	E5	48
Siam, Gulf of see Thailand, Gulf of, b., Asia	G5	48
Sian see Xi'an, China	D3	42
Siangtan see Xiangtan, China	H5	42
Sianów, Pol.	B12	16
Siantan, Pulau, i., Indon.	B4	50
Siapa, stm., Ven.	G9	86
Siargao Island, i., Phil.	F6	52
Siasconset, Ma., U.S.	C15	114
Siasi, Phil.	H3	52
Siasi Island, i., Phil.	H3	52
Siaškotan, ostrov, i., Russia	G19	34
Siau, Pulau, i., Indon.	E7	44
Šiauliai, Lith.	E6	10
Sibaj, Russia	D9	32
Sibayi, Lake, l., S. Afr.	E11	70
Šibenik, Cro.	G12	22
Siberia see Sibir', reg., Russia	C12	34
Siberut, Pulau, i., Indon.	D1	50
Sibi, Pak.	D10	56
Sibigo, Indon.	K2	48
Sibir', reg., Russia	C12	34
Sibircevo, Russia	B10	38
Sibirjakova, ostrov, i., Russia	B4	34
Sibiti, Congo	E2	66
Sibiu, Rom.	D11	26
Sibiu, state, Rom.	D11	26
Sibley, Ia., U.S.	H3	118
Sibley, La., U.S.	E5	122
Sibley, Ms., U.S.	F7	122
Sibley Peninsula, pen., On., Can.	C10	118
Sibolga, Indon.	C1	50
Sibsāgar, India	C7	46
Sibu, Malay.	B7	50
Sibuguey Bay, b., Phil.	G4	52
Sibut, C.A.R.	C3	66
Sibutu Island, i., Phil.	H2	52
Sibutu Passage, strt., Asia	H2	52
Sibuyan Island, i., Phil.	D4	52
Sibuyan Sea, Phil.	D4	52
Sicapoo, Mount, mtn., Phil.	B3	52
Siccus, stm., Austl.	H2	76
Sichang see Xichang, China	F5	36
Si Chon, Thai.	H4	48
Sichuan, state, China	E5	36
Sichuan Pendi, bas., China	F1	42
Sichuanzhai, China	A5	48
Sicilia, state, Italy	F8	24
Sicilia (Sicily), i., Italy	G7	24
Sicily see Sicilia, state, Italy	F8	24
Sicily see Sicilia, i., Italy	G7	24
Sicily, Strait of, strt.	G5	24
Sicily Island, La., U.S.	F7	122
Sicuani, Peru	F3	84
Sidareja, Indon.	G6	50
Sidas, Indon.	C6	50
Siddhapur, India	G4	54
Siddipet, India	B4	53
Sidéradougou, Burkina	G4	64
Siderno, Italy	F10	24
Siderópolis, Braz.	D13	92
Síderos, Ákra, c., Grc.	H9	28
Sidhauli, India	E8	54
Sidhi, India	F8	54
Sîdi Barrâni, Egypt	A5	62
Sidi bel Abbès, Alg.	B4	64
Sidi-Ifni, Mor.	D2	64
Siding Spring Mountain, mtn., Austl.	H7	76
Sidirókastro, Grc.	B6	28
Sidi Sâlim, Egypt	G1	58
Sidlaghatta, India	E3	53
Sidley, Mount, mtn., Ant.	C28	81
Sidmouth, Eng., U.K.	K9	12
Sidnaw, Mi., U.S.	E10	118
Sidney, B.C., Can.	H7	138
Sidney, Il., U.S.	D9	120
Sidney, Mt., U.S.	G9	124
Sidney, Ne., U.S.	F10	126
Sidney, N.Y., U.S.	B10	114
Sidney, Oh., U.S.	D1	114
Sidney Lanier, Lake, res., Ga., U.S.	B2	116
Sidon see Şaydā, Leb.	E6	58
Sidon, Ms., U.S.	D8	122
Sidorovsk, Russia	A14	32
Sidra, Gulf of see Surt, Khalīj, b., Libya	A3	62
Sidrolândia, Braz.	D6	90
Siedlce, Pol.	D18	16
Siedlce, state, Pol.	D17	16
Siegburg, Ger.	F3	16
Siegen, Ger.	F4	16
Siemianowice Śląskie, Pol.	F15	16
Siĕmpang, Camb.	E8	48
Siĕmréab, Camb.	F6	48
Siena, Italy	G8	22
Sienyang see Xianyang, China	D3	42
Sieradz, Pol.	E14	16
Sieradz, state, Pol.	E14	16
Sieraków, Pol.	D12	16
Sierpc, Pol.	D15	16
Sierra Blanca, Tx., U.S.	C2	130
Sierra Blanca Peak, mtn., N.M., U.S.	H3	128
Sierra Chica, Arg.	H7	92
Sierra Colorada, Arg.	H3	90
Sierra Gorda, Chile	D3	90
Sierra Leone, ctry., Afr.	H2	64
Sierra Mojada, Mex.	G4	130
Sierra Nevada see Nevada, Sierra, mts., Ca., U.S.	F6	134
Sierra Nevada, Parque Nacional, p.o.i., Ven.	C6	86
Sierra Vista, Az., U.S.	L6	132
Sierre, Switz.	D4	22
Siesta Key, Fl., U.S.	I3	116
Sífnos, i., Grc.	F7	28
Sifón Villanueva, Mex.	G7	130
Sig, Russia	D16	8
Sigatoka, Fiji	q18	79e
Sigep, Indon.	D1	50
Sighetu Marmației, Rom.	B10	26
Sighișoara, Rom.	C11	26
Siglan, Russia	E19	34
Sigli, Indon.	J2	48
Siglufjörður, Ice.	j30	8a
Sigmaringen, Ger.	H5	16
Signal Mountain, Tn., U.S.	B13	122
Signal Mountain, mtn., Vt., U.S.	F4	110
Signy, sci., Ant.	B36	81
Sigourney, Ia., U.S.	C5	120
Sigsig, Ec.	D2	84
Siguanea, Ensenada de la, b., Cuba	B6	102
Siguatepeque, Hond.	E3	102
Sigüenza, Spain	C8	20
Siguiri, Gui.	G3	64
Sigulda, Lat.	C7	10
Sigurd, Ut., U.S.	E5	132
Siguri Falls, wtfl, Tan.	F7	66
Sihabuhabu, Dolok, mtn., Indon.	B1	50
Sihanoukville see Kâmpóng Saôm, Camb.	G6	48
Sihor, India	H3	54
Sihorā, India	G8	54
Sihote-Alin', mts., Russia	E17	30
Sihtovo, Russia	E15	10
Sihui, China	J5	42
Siirt, Tur.	B5	56
Sija, Russia	E19	8
Sijunjung, Indon.	D2	50
Sikandarābād, India	D6	54
Sikanni Chief, stm., B.C., Can.	D6	106
Sikao, Thai.	I4	48
Sīkar, India	E5	54
Sikasso, Mali	G3	64
Sikeston, Mo., U.S.	H8	120
Sikhote-Alin Mountains see Sihote-Alin', mts., Russia	E17	30
Sikiang see Xi, stm., China	J5	42
Siking see Xi'an, China	D3	42
Síkinos, i., Grc.	G8	28
Sikkim, state, India	E12	54
Sikonge, Tan.	F6	66
Sikotan, ostrov (Shikotan-tō), i., Russia	C17	38
Siktjah, Russia	B13	34
Sikuati, Malay.	G1	52
Sikyón, hist., Grc.	F5	28
Sil, stm., Spain	B3	20
Šila, Russia	E7	34
Šilalė, Lith.	E5	10
Silao, Mex.	E8	100
Silas, Al., U.S.	F10	122
Silaut, Indon.	E2	50
Silay, Phil.	E4	52
Silchar, India	F14	54
Şile, Tur.	B12	28
Siler City, N.C., U.S.	I6	114
Sileru, stm., India	C5	53
Silesia, hist. reg., Eur.	F13	16
Siletyteniz, ozero, l., Kaz.	D12	32
Siletz, Or., U.S.	F3	136
Siletz, stm., Or., U.S.	F3	136
Silgadhī, Nepal	D8	54
Silghāt, India	E14	54
Silhouette, i., Sey.	j13	69b
Siliana, Tun.	H3	24
Siliana, Oued, stm., Tun.	I3	24
Silifke, Tur.	B4	58
Siling Co, l., China	C12	54
Silistra, Blg.	E14	26
Silivri, Tur.	B11	28
Siljan, l., Swe.	F6	8
Šilka, Russia	F12	34
Šilka, stm., Russia	F12	34
Silkeborg, Den.	H3	8
Sillamäe, Est.	A10	10
Sillem Island, i., N.T., Can.	A16	106
Sillian, Aus.	D9	22
Sillon de Talbert, pen., Fr.	F5	14
Šiloviči, Russia	E15	10
Silsbee, Tx., U.S.	G4	122
Silton, Sk., Can.	D9	124
Siluas, Indon.	C6	50
Šilutė, Lith.	E4	10
Silvânia, Braz.	I1	88
Silvassa, India	H4	54
Silver, Tx., U.S.	B7	130
Silver Bank Passage, strt., N.A.	B12	102
Silver Bell, Az., U.S.	K5	132
Silver City, N.M., U.S.	K8	132
Silver City, N.C., U.S.	B6	116
Silver Creek, Ms., U.S.	F9	122
Silver Creek, Ne., U.S.	F15	126
Silver Creek, stm., Az., U.S.	I6	132
Silver Creek, stm., Or., U.S.	G7	136
Silverdale, Wa., U.S.	C4	136
Silver Lake, Ks., U.S.	E2	120
Silver Lake, Mn., U.S.	G4	118
Silver Lake, Wi., U.S.	F1	112
Silver Lake, l., Or., U.S.	G7	136
Silver Lake, l., Or., U.S.	G5	136
Silver Spring, Md., U.S.	E8	114
Silver Star Mountain, mtn., Wa., U.S.	B6	136
Silverthrone Mountain, vol., B.C., Can.	E4	138
Silverton, Austl.	H3	76
Silverton, B.C., Can.	G13	138
Silverton, Co., U.S.	F9	132
Silverton, Tx., U.S.	G7	128
Silvi, Italy	H11	22
Silvia, Col.	F3	86
Silvies, stm., Or., U.S.	G7	136
Šimanovsk, Russia	F14	34
Simao, China	A5	48
Simão Dias, Braz.	F6	88
Simav, Tur.	D11	28
Simav, stm., Tur.	C11	28
Simbach, Ger.	H8	16
Simbo Island, i., Sol. Is.	e7	79b
Simcoe, On., Can.	F9	112
Simcoe, Lake, l., On., Can.	D10	112
Simdega, India	G10	54
Simeria, Rom.	D10	26
Simeulue, Pulau, i., Indon.	K2	48
Simferopol', Ukr.	G15	6
Simikot, Nepal	C8	54
Similkameen, stm., N.A.	G10	138
Simití, Col.	D4	86
Simi Valley, Ca., U.S.	I7	134
Simizu see Shimizu, Japan	D11	40
Simla, Co., U.S.	B4	128
Simmern, Ger.	G3	16
Simmie, Sk., Can.	E5	124
Simms, Mt., U.S.	C15	136
Simnas, Lith.	F6	10
Simoca, Arg.	C5	92
Simões, Braz.	D5	88
Simojärvi, l., Fin.	C12	8
Simojovel, Mex.	G12	100
Simon, Lac, l., Qc., Can.	E1	110
Simonette, stm., Ab., Can.	A12	138
Simonoseki see Shimonoseki, Japan	F3	40
Simonstad see Simon's Town, S. Afr.	I4	70
Simon's Town, S. Afr.	I4	70
Simoom Sound, B.C., Can.	F4	138
Simpang, Indon.	D3	50
Simpang-kiri, stm., Indon.	K3	48
Simplon Pass, p., Switz.	D4	22
Simpson Desert, des., Austl.	D7	74
Simpson Island, i., On., Can.	C11	118
Simpson Peninsula, pen., N.T., Can.	B13	106
Simpson Strait, strt., N.T., Can.	B11	106
Simpsonville, S.C., U.S.	B3	116
Simrishamn, Swe.	I6	8
Simsonbaai, Neth. Ant.	A1	105a
Simunjan, Malay.	C7	50
Simušir, ostrov, i., Russia	G19	34
Sīna, stm., India	B2	53
Sinabang, Indon.	K3	48
Sinabung, Gunung, vol., Indon.	K4	48
Sinai (Sinai Peninsula), pen., Egypt	J4	58
Sinai, Mount see Mûsa, Gebel, mtn., Egypt	J5	58
Sinai, Mount, vol., Gren.	q10	105e
Sinaia, Rom.	D12	26
Sinai Peninsula see Sinai, pen., Egypt	J4	58
Sinajana, Guam	j10	78c
Sinaloa, state, Mex.	C5	100
Sinaloa, stm., Mex.	C5	100
Sinamaica, Ven.	B6	86
Sinan, China	H3	42
Sinanpaşa, Tur.	E13	28
Sīnāwin, Libya	A2	62
Sincan, Tur.	D15	28
Sincé, Col.	B2	84
Sincelejo, Col.	C4	86
Sinch'ang-ŭp, Kor., N.	D8	38
Sin-ch'on, Kor., N.	E6	38
Sinclair, Wy., U.S.	B9	132
Sinclair, Lake, res., Ga., U.S.	C2	116
Sinclair Mills, B.C., Can.	B9	138
Sind, state, Pak.	F2	54
Sind, stm., India	F7	54
Sindañgan, Phil.	F4	52
Sindangbarang, Indon.	G5	50
Sindara, Gabon	E2	66
Sindari, India	F3	54
Sindelfingen, Ger.	H4	16
Sindhnūr, India	D3	53
Sindhulī Mādi, Nepal	E10	54
Sindingale, Mya.	C2	48
Sindor, Russia	B8	32
Sines, Port.	G2	20
Sinfra, C. Iv.	H3	64
Singalamwe, Nmb.	D3	68
Singapore, Sing.	C3	50
Singapore, ctry., Asia	L6	48
Singapore, Strait of, strt., Asia	C4	50
Singaraja, Indon.	H9	50
Sing Buri, Thai.	E5	48
Singen, Ger.	I4	16
Singida, Tan.	E6	66
Singitic Gulf see Ayíou Órous, Kólpos, b., Grc.	C6	28
Singkaling Hkāmti, Mya.	C8	46
Singkang, Indon.	F11	50
Singkawang, Indon.	C6	50
Singkep, Pulau, i., Indon.	D4	50
Singkil, Indon.	K3	48
Singkuang, Indon.	C1	50
Singleton, Austl.	I8	76
Singleton, Mount, mtn., Austl.	E3	74
Singuédeze (Shingwidzi), stm., Afr.	C10	70
Sining see Xining, China	D5	36
Sinj, Cro.	G13	22
Sinjah, Sudan	E6	62
Sinjai, Indon.	F12	50
Sinjaja, stm., Eur.	D11	10
Sinjaja, stm., Russia	D14	34
Sinjuga, Russia	E12	34
Sinkāt, Sudan	D7	62
Sinkiang see Xinjiang, state, China	A5	46
Sinnamahoning, Pa., U.S.	C7	114
Sinnamary, Fr. Gu.	B7	84
Sinnar, India	B2	53
Sinnûris, Egypt	I1	58
Sinnyŏng, Kor., S.	C1	40
Sinoie, Lacul, l., Rom.	E15	26
Sinop, Tur.	A4	56
Sinsheim, Ger.	G4	16
Sinsiang see Xinxiang, China	D5	42
Sinskoe, Russia	D14	34
Sintang, Indon.	C7	50
Sint Christoffelberg, hill, Neth. Ant.	p21	104g
Sint Eustatius, i., Neth. Ant.	B1	105a
Sint Helenabaai, b., S. Afr.	H3	70
Sint Kruis, Neth. Ant.	p21	104g
Sint Maarten (Saint-Martin), i., N.A.	A1	105a
Sint Nicolaas, Aruba	p20	104g
Sint-Niklaas, Bel.	C12	14
Sintra, Port.	F1	20
Sint-Truiden, Bel.	D14	14
Sinú, stm., Col.	C4	86
Sinŭiju, Kor., N.	D6	38
Sió, stm., Hung.	C5	26
Siocon, Phil.	G4	52
Siófok, Hung.	C5	26
Sion, Switz.	D4	22
Siorapaluk, Grnld.	B12	141
Sioux Center, Ia., U.S.	H2	118
Sioux City, Ia., U.S.	B1	120
Sioux Falls, S.D., U.S.	H2	118
Sioux Lookout, On., Can.	A6	118
Sioux Narrows, On., Can.	B4	118
Sioux Rapids, Ia., U.S.	B2	120
Sipalay, Phil.	F4	52
Šipan, Otok, i., Cro.	H14	22
Sipapo, stm., Ven.	E8	86
Siparia, Trin.	s12	105f
Šipčenski Prohod (Shipka Pass), p., Blg.	G12	26
Šipicyno, Russia	F22	8
Siping, China	C6	38
Sipiwesk Lake, l., Mb., Can.	D11	106
Siple, Mount, mtn., Ant.	C28	81
Siple Island, i., Ant.	C28	81
Si Prachan, Thai.	E4	48
Sipsey, stm., Al., U.S.	D10	122
Šipunskij, mys, c., Russia	F21	34
Sipura, Pulau, i., Indon.	E1	50
Siqueira Campos, Braz.	A12	92
Siquia, stm., Nic.	F5	102
Siquijor, Phil.	F4	52
Siquijor Island, i., Phil.	F4	52
Siquirres, C.R.	G6	102
Şīra, India	E3	53
Šira, Russia	D16	32
Sira, stm., Nor.	G2	8
Si Racha, Thai.	F5	48
Siracusa, Italy	G9	24
Sirāhā, Nepal	E11	54
Sirājganj, Bngl.	F12	54
Şīr Banī Yās, i., U.A.E.	E7	56
Sirdar, B.C., Can.	G14	138
Sir Douglas, Mount, mtn., Can.	F15	138
Sir Edward Pellew Group, is., Austl.	C7	74
Siret, Rom.	B12	26
Siret (Seret), stm., Eur.	A12	26
Sirhān, Wādī as-, val., Sau. Ar.	H8	58
Sirik, Tanjong, c., Malay.	B7	50
Sirikit Reservoir, res., Thai.	D5	48
Sirino, Monte, mtn., Italy	D9	24
Sir James MacBrien, Mount, mtn., N.T., Can.	C4	106
Sīrjān, Iran	D8	56
Sirkeli, Tur.	C15	28
Sirocina, Bela.	E12	10
Şirohi, India	F4	54
Širokovo, Russia	C17	32
Sironj, India	F6	54
Sırpsındığı, Tur.	B9	28
Sīrrī, Jazīreh-ye, i., Iran	D7	56
Sirsa, India	D5	54
Sir Sandford, Mount, mtn., B.C., Can.	E13	138
Sirsi, India	D2	53
Sirsilla, India	B4	53
Sirte, Gulf of see Surt, Khalīj, b., Libya	A3	62
Sir Timothy's Hill, hill, St. K./N.	C2	105a
Şirupa, stm., Mex.	G8	98
Širvintos, Lith.	E7	10
Sir Wilfrid Laurier, Mount, mtn., B.C., Can.	D11	138
Sisaba, mtn., Tan.	F6	66
Sisak, Cro.	E13	22
Si Sa Ket, Thai.	E7	48
Sishen, S. Afr.	E6	70
Sishilijie, China	G7	42
Sishui, China	D7	42
Sisib Lake, l., Mb., Can.	B14	124
Sisimiut see Holsteinsborg, Grnld.	D15	141
Siskiyou Pass, p., Or., U.S.	A3	134
Sisseton, S.D., U.S.	F1	118
Sīstān, reg., Asia	C9	56
Sister Bay, Wi., U.S.	C2	112
Sisteron, Fr.	E11	18
Sisters, Or., U.S.	F5	136
Sistersville, W.V., U.S.	E5	114
Sit', stm., Russia	B20	10
Sītāmarhi, India	E10	54
Sītāpur, India	E8	54
Siteia, Grc.	H9	28
Siteki, Swaz.	E10	70
Si Thep, hist., Thai.	E5	48
Sithoniá, pen., Grc.	C6	28
Sitidgi Lake, l., N.T., Can.	B4	106
Sítio d'Abadia, Braz.	H2	88
Sitka, Ak., U.S.	E12	140
Sitkalidak Island, i., Ak., U.S.	E9	140
Sittard, Neth.	C14	14
Sitten see Sion, Switz.	D4	22
Sittoung, stm., Mya.	C3	48
Sittwe, Mya.	D7	46
Siuri, India	G11	54
Siuslaw, stm., Or., U.S.	G3	136
Sivaganga, India	G4	53
Sivakāsi, India	G3	53
Sivaki, Russia	F14	34
Sivas, Tur.	B4	56
Šiveluč, vulkan, vol., Russia	E21	34
Siverek, Tur.	B4	56
Siverskij, Russia	A12	10
Sivrihisar, Tur.	D14	28
Siwa, Egypt	B5	62
Siwalik Range, mts., India	C6	54
Siwān, India	E10	54
Sixian, China	E7	42
Sixth Cataract see Sablūkah, Shallāl as-, wtfl, Sudan	D6	62
Siyang, China	E8	42
Sizuoka see Shizuoka, Japan	E11	40
Sjælland, i., Den.	I4	8
Sjalec, Bela.	G13	10
Sjamža, Russia	F19	8
Sjarheevičy, Bela.	G10	10
Sjas', stm., Russia	A15	10
Sjas'stroj, Russia	F15	8
Sjenica, Yugo.	F7	26
Sjuzikozero, Russia	F17	8
Skærfjorden, b., Grnld.	B22	141
Skaftafell Nasjonalpark, p.o.i., Ice.	k31	8a
Skagafjörður, b., Ice.	j31	8a
Skagen, Den.	H4	8
Skagerrak, strt., Eur.	H3	8
Skagit, stm., N.A.	H8	138
Skagway, Ak., U.S.	E12	140
Skaistkalne, Lat.	D7	10
Skalbmierz, Pol.	F16	16
Skalino, Russia	G18	8
Skalistyj Golec, gora, mtn., Russia	E12	34
Skalka, l., Swe.	C8	8
Skåne, state, Swe.	H5	8
Skārdu, Pak.	B12	56
Skarszewy, Pol.	B14	16
Skarżysko-Kamienna, Pol.	E16	16
Skaudvilė, Lith.	E5	10
Skawina, Pol.	F15	16
Skeena, stm., B.C., Can.	B1	138
Skeena Crossing, B.C., Can.	A3	138
Skeena Mountains, mts., B.C., Can.	D5	106
Skegness, Eng., U.K.	H13	12
Skei, Nor.	F2	8
Skeleton Coast, cst., Nmb.	B1	70
Skellefteå, Swe.	D9	8
Skellefteälven, stm., Swe.	D8	8
Skellytown, Tx., U.S.	F7	128
Skerryvore, r., Scot., U.K.	E5	12
Ski, Nor.	G4	8
Skiatook, Ok., U.S.	H1	120
Skibbereen, Ire.	J3	12
Skidal', Bela.	G7	10
Skiddaw, mtn., Eng., U.K.	G9	12
Skidmore, Tx., U.S.	F10	130
Skien, Nor.	G3	8
Skierniewice, Pol.	E16	16
Skierniewice, state, Pol.	D16	16
Skikda, Alg.	B6	64
Skilak Lake, l., Ak., U.S.	D9	140
Skillet Fork, stm., Il., U.S.	F9	120
Skinnastaðir, Ice.	j31	8a
Skipton, Austl.	K4	76
Skipton, Eng., U.K.	H10	12
Skive, Den.	H3	8
Skjálfandafljót, stm., Ice.	k31	8a
Şklad, Russia	B13	34
Šklou, Bela.	F13	10
Škofja Loka, Slvn.	D11	22
Skoganvarre, Nor.	B11	8
Skoganvarri see Skoganvarre, Nor.	B11	8
Skokie, Il., U.S.	F2	112
Skón, Camb.	F7	48
Skópelos, i., Grc.	D6	28
Skopin, Russia	D5	32
Skopje, Mac.	A4	28
Skoplje see Skopje, Mac.	A4	28
Skórcz, Pol.	C14	16
Skövde, Swe.	G5	8
Skowhegan, Me., U.S.	F7	110
Skownan, Mb., Can.	C14	124
Skriplivka, Russia	C13	10
Skrudaliena, Lat.	E9	10
Skudeneshavn, Nor.	G1	8
Skukuza, S. Afr.	D10	70
Skull Valley, Az., U.S.	I4	132
Skuna, can., Ms., U.S.	D9	122
Skunk, stm., Ia., U.S.	D6	120
Skuodas, Lith.	D4	10
Skuratovskij, Russia	F20	10
Skwierzyna, Pol.	D11	16
Skye, Island of, i., Scot., U.K.	D6	12
Skyland, N.C., U.S.	A3	116
Skyring, Península, pen., Chile	I1	90
Skyring, Seno, strt., Chile	J2	90
Skýros, i., Grc.	E7	28
Slabada, Bela.	G11	10
Slagelse, Den.	I4	8
Slagnäs, Swe.	D8	8
Slamet, Gunung, vol., Indon.	G6	50
Slancy, Russia	A11	10
Slaney, stm., Ire.	H6	12
Slănic, Rom.	D12	26
Slano, Cro.	H14	22
Slaný, Czech Rep.	F10	16
Slater, Ia., U.S.	C4	120
Slater, Mo., U.S.	E4	120
Slatina, Cro.	E14	22
Slatina, Rom.	E11	26
Slaughter, La., U.S.	G7	122
Slaunae, Bela.	F12	10
Slautnoe, Russia	D22	34
Slave, stm., Can.	C8	106
Slave Coast, cst., Afr.	H5	64
Slave Lake, Ab., Can.	A16	138
Slavgorod, Russia	D13	32
Slavjanka, Russia	C9	38
Slavjansk-na-Kubani, Russia	E5	32
Slavkoviči, Russia	C12	10
Slavonia see Slavonija, hist. reg., Cro.	E14	22
Slavonija, hist. reg., Cro.	E14	22
Slavonski Brod, Cro.	E15	22
Slavsk, Russia	E4	10
Sławno, Pol.	B12	16
Slayton, Mn., U.S.	G3	118
Sleaford, Eng., U.K.	H12	12
Sledge, Ms., U.S.	C8	122
Sledzjuki, Bela.	G13	10
Sleeper Islands, is., N.T., Can.	D14	106
Sleeping Bear Dunes National Lakeshore, p.o.i., Mi., U.S.	D3	112
Sleepy Eye, Mn., U.S.	G4	118
Ślesin, Pol.	D14	16
Slidell, La., U.S.	G9	122
Slide Mountain, mtn., N.Y., U.S.	B11	114
Sliema, Malta	I8	24
Slievekimalta, mtn., Ire.	I4	12
Sligeach see Sligo, Ire.	G4	12
Sligo, Ire.	G4	12
Sligo, Pa., U.S.	C6	114
Sligo, state, Ire.	G4	12
Sligo Bay, b., Ire.	G4	12
Slinger, Wi., U.S.	H10	118
Šlino, ozero, l., Russia	C16	10
Slippery Rock, Pa., U.S.	C5	114
Šlissel'burg, Russia	A13	10
Slīteres Rezervāts, Lat.	C5	10
Sliven, Blg.	G13	26
Sljudjanka, Russia	D18	32
Sloan, Nv., U.S.	H1	132
Slobidka, Ukr.	B16	26
Slobodskoj, Russia	C8	32
Slobozia, Mol.	C16	26
Slobozia, Rom.	E14	26
Slobozia, Rom.	F12	26
Slocan, B.C., Can.	G13	138
Slocan Lake, l., B.C., Can.	G13	138
Slocomb, Al., U.S.	F13	122
Słomniki, Pol.	F15	16
Slonim, Bela.	G8	10
Slough, Eng., U.K.	J12	12
Slovakia, ctry., Eur.	H14	16
Slovenia, ctry., Eur.	E11	22
Slovenija see Slovenia, ctry., Eur.	E11	22
Slovenské rudohorie, mts., Slov.	H15	16
Slov'ians'k, Ukr.	E5	32
Slovinka, Russia	G20	8
Słowiński Park Narodowy, p.o.i., Pol.	B13	16
Słubice, Pol.	D10	16
Sluč, stm., Bela.	H10	10
Sluck, Bela.	G10	10
Šluknov, Czech Rep.	E10	16
Słupca, Pol.	D13	16
Słupia, stm., Pol.	B13	16
Słupsk (Stolp), Pol.	B13	16
Słupsk, state, Pol.	B13	16
Slutsk see Sluck, Bela.	G10	10
Smålandsfarvandet, b., Den.	I4	8
Smalininkai, Lith.	E5	10
Smaljavičy, Bela.	F10	10
Smallwood Reservoir, res., Nf., Can.	E18	106
Smalouka, Bela.	E13	10
Smarhon', Bela.	F9	10
Smederevo, Yugo.	E7	26
Smeralda, Costa, cst., Italy	C3	24
Smethport, Pa., U.S.	C7	114
Şmidovič, Russia	G15	34
Šmidta, poluostrov, pen., Russia	F17	34
Śmigiel, Pol.	D12	16
Smila, Ukr.	E4	32
Smiley, Sk., Can.	C4	124
Smiley, Tx., U.S.	E10	130
Smiltene, Lat.	C8	10
Smith, Ab., Can.	A16	138
Smith, stm., U.S.	H5	114
Smith, stm., Ca., U.S.	B2	134
Smith, stm., Mt., U.S.	C15	136
Smith, stm., Or., U.S.	G2	136
Smith Arm, b., N.T., Can.	B6	106
Smith Bay, b., N.T., Can.	B10	141
Smith Bay, b., Ak., U.S.	B9	140
Smith Canyon, val., Co., U.S.	D5	128
Smithers, B.C., Can.	B3	138
Smithfield, S. Afr.	G8	70
Smithfield, N.C., U.S.	A7	116
Smithfield, Va., U.S.	G9	114
Smith Island see Sumisu-jima, i., Japan	E13	36
Smith Island, i., N.C., U.S.	C8	116
Smithland, Ky., U.S.	G9	120
Smith Mountain Lake, res., Va., U.S.	G6	114
Smith Point, c., N.S., Can.	E13	110
Smith River, Ca., U.S.	B1	134
Smiths, Al., U.S.	E13	122
Smiths Falls, On., Can.	D13	112
Smiths Grove, Ky., U.S.	G11	120
Smithton, Austl.	n12	77a
Smithville, Ga., U.S.	E1	116
Smithville, Ms., U.S.	C10	122
Smithville, Tn., U.S.	I12	120
Smithville, Tx., U.S.	D10	130
Smithville Lake, res., Mo., U.S.	E3	120
Smoke Creek Desert, des., Nv., U.S.	C6	134
Smokey, Cape, c., N.S., Can.	D16	110
Smoky, stm., Ab., Can.	A12	138
Smoky Cape, c., Austl.	H9	76
Smoky Dome, mtn., Id., U.S.	G12	136
Smoky Hill, stm., U.S.	B12	128
Smoky Hill, North Fork, stm., U.S.	B7	128
Smoky Lake, Ab., Can.	B18	138
Smøla, i., Nor.	E2	8
Smolensk, Russia	F15	10
Smolenskaja-Moskovskaja vozvyšennost', plat., Eur.	F16	10
Smolenskaja oblast', co., Russia	F15	10
Smoljan, Blg.	H11	26
Smoot, Wy., U.S.	H16	136
Smoothrock Lake, l., On., Can.	A9	118
Smorodovka, Russia	C12	10
Smyrna see İzmir, Tur.	E10	28
Smyrna, De., U.S.	E10	114
Smyrna, Ga., U.S.	D14	122
Smyrna, Tn., U.S.	I11	120
Smythe, Mount, mtn., B.C., Can.	D6	106
Snæfell, mtn., Ice.	k32	8a
Snaefell, mtn., I. of Man	G8	12
Snæfellness, pen., Ice.	k28	8a
Snag, Yk., Can.	C3	106
Snake, stm., Yk., Can.	B4	106
Snake, stm., U.S.	D8	136
Snake, stm., Mn., U.S.	E5	118
Snake, stm., Ne., U.S.	E11	126
Snake Creek, stm., S.D., U.S.	B14	126
Snake River Plain, pl., Id., U.S.	G13	136
Snake Valley, val., U.S.	D3	132
Snares Islands, is., N.Z.	H2	80
Snåsavatnet, l., Nor.	D4	8
Sneads, Fl., U.S.	G13	122
Sneedville, Tn., U.S.	H2	114
Sneek, Neth.	A14	14
Sněžka, mtn., Czech Rep.	F11	16
Śniardwy, Jezioro, l., Pol.	C17	16
Sniatyn, Ukr.	A12	26
Snina, Slov.	G18	16
Snipe Lake, l., Ab., Can.	A14	138
Snjadin, Bela.	H11	10
Snøhetta, mtn., Nor.	E3	8
Snohomish, Wa., U.S.	C4	136
Snoqualmie Pass, p., Wa., U.S.	C5	136
Snøtinden, mtn., Nor.	C5	8
Snov, stm., Eur.	H15	10
Snover, Mi., U.S.	E7	112
Snowbird Lake, l., N.T., Can.	C10	106
Snowdon, mtn., Wales, U.K.	H8	12
Snowdonia National Park, p.o.i., Wales, U.K.	I8	12
Snowflake, Az., U.S.	I6	132
Snow Hill, Md., U.S.	F10	114
Snow Hill, N.C., U.S.	A8	116
Snow Lake, Mb., Can.	E10	106
Snowmass Mountain, mtn., Co., U.S.	D9	132
Snow Mountain, mtn., Ca., U.S.	D3	134
Snowtown, Austl.	I2	76
Snowy, stm., Austl.	K7	76
Snowy Mountain, mtn., N.Y., U.S.	G2	110
Snowy Mountains, mts., Austl.	K7	76
Snowy River National Park, p.o.i., Austl.	K6	76
Snuŏl, Camb.	F8	48
Snyder, Ok., U.S.	G10	128
Snyder, Tx., U.S.	B7	130
Soacha, Col.	E4	86
Soalala, Madag.	D8	68
Soap Lake, Wa., U.S.	C7	136
Soavinandriana, Madag.	D8	68
Sobaek-sanmaek, mts., Kor., S.	C1	40
Soběslav, Czech Rep.	G10	16
Sobinka, Russia	I19	8
Sobradinho, Braz.	D11	92
Sobradinho, Represa de, res., Braz.	E5	88
Sobral, Braz.	B5	88
Sobrance, Slov.	H18	16
Sobrarbe, hist. reg., Spain	B10	20
Sochaczew, Pol.	D16	16
Soch'e see Shache, China	B12	56
Soči, Russia	F5	32
Société, Archipel de la (Society Islands), is., Fr. Poly.	E11	72
Society Hill, S.C., U.S.	B6	116
Society Islands see Société, Archipel de la, is., Fr. Poly.	E11	72
Soco, stm., Dom. Rep.	C13	102
Socompa, Paso (Socompa, Portezuelo de), p., S.A.	B3	92
Socompa, Portezuelo de (Socompa, Paso), p., S.A.	B3	92
Soconusco, Sierra de see Madre de Chiapas, Sierra, mts., N.A.	G12	100
Socorro, Col.	D5	86
Socorro, N.M., U.S.	I10	132
Socorro, Tx., U.S.	C1	130
Socorro, Isla, i., Mex.	F3	100
Socotra see Suquṭrā, i., Yemen	G7	56
Soc Trang, Viet.	H8	48
Socuéllamos, Spain	E8	20
Soda Creek, B.C., Can.	D8	138
Soda Lake, l., Ca., U.S.	H9	134
Sodankylä, Fin.	C12	8
Soda Springs, Id., U.S.	H15	136
Söderhamn, Swe.	F7	8
Södermanland, state, Swe.	G7	8
Södertälje, Swe.	G7	8
Sodo, Eth.	F7	62
Sodom see Sedom, hist., Isr.	G6	58
Sodus, N.Y., U.S.	E12	112
Sodwana Bay National Park, p.o.i., S. Afr.	E11	70
Soe, Indon.	G7	44
Soekmekaar, S. Afr.	C9	70
Soest, Ger.	E4	16
Soest, Neth.	B14	14
Sofala, Moz.	B12	70
Sofala, state, Moz.	B12	70
Sofia see Sofija, Blg.	G10	26
Sofija (Sofia), Blg.	G10	26

Name | Map Ref. | Page

Stey-Tabu I•55

Name | Map Ref. | Page

Steytlerville, S. Afr. H7 70
Stickney, S.D., U.S. D14 126
Stiene, Lat. C7 10
Stif, Alg. B6 64
Stigler, Ok., U.S. B3 122
Stih, hora, mtn., Ukr. A10 26
Stikine, stm., N.A. D4 106
Stikine Ranges, mts., B.C., Can. D4 106
Stilbaai, S. Afr. I5 70
Stilfontein, S. Afr. E8 70
Stilís, Grc. E5 28
Stillhouse Hollow Lake, res., Tx., U.S. D10 130
Stillwater, B.C., Can. G6 138
Stillwater, Mn., U.S. F6 118
Stillwater, Ok., U.S. A1 122
Stillwell, Ok., U.S. I3 120
Stînca-Costeşti, Lacul, res., Eur. B14 26
Stine Mountain, mtn., Mt., U.S. E13 136
Stinking Water Creek, stm., Ne., U.S. G11 126
Ştinnett, Tx., U.S. F7 128
Štip, Mac. B5 28
Stirling, Austl. F3 74
Stirling, On., Can. D12 112
Stirling, Scot., U.K. E8 12
Stirling City, Ca., U.S. D4 134
Stirrat, W.V., U.S. G15 120
Stjernøya, i., Nor. A9 8
Stobi, hist., Mac. B4 28
Stockach, Ger. I5 16
Stockbridge, Ga., U.S. C1 116
Stockbridge, Mi., U.S. B1 114
Stockdale, Tx., U.S. E9 130
Stockerau, Aus. B13 22
Stockholm, Swe. G8 8
Stockholm, Me., U.S. C8 110
Stockholm, state, Swe. G8 8
Stockport, Eng., U.K. H10 12
Stockton, Al., U.S. G11 122
Stockton, Ca., U.S. F4 134
Stockton, Il., U.S. B8 120
Stockton, Ks., U.S. B9 128
Stockton, Mo., U.S. G4 120
Stockton-on-Tees, Eng., U.K. G11 12
Stockton Plateau, plat., Tx., U.S. D5 130
Stockton Reservoir, res., Mo., U.S. G4 120
Stockton Springs, Me., U.S. F8 110
Stoczek Łukowski, Pol. D18 16
Stœng Trĕng, Camb. F8 48
Stoffberg, S. Afr. D9 70
Stojba, Russia F15 34
Stoke-on-Trent, Eng., U.K. I11 12
Stokes Point, c., Austl. n11 77a
Stolberg, Ger. F2 16
Stolbovo, Russia H17 10
Stolbovoj, ostrov, i., Russia B16 34
Stoneboro, Pa., U.S. C5 114
Stone Harbor, N.J., U.S. E11 114
Stonehaven, Scot., U.K. E10 12
Stonehenge, Austl. E4 76
Stonehenge, hist., Eng., U.K. J11 12
Stone Mountain, Ga., U.S. C1 116
Stone Mountain, mtn., Vt., U.S. F5 110
Stoner, B.C., Can. C8 138
Stoneville, N.C., U.S. H6 114
Stonewall, Mb., Can. D16 124
Stonewall, Ms., U.S. E10 122
Stonewall, Ok., U.S. C2 122
Stoney Creek, On., Can. E10 112
Stonington, Il., U.S. E8 120
Stonington, Me., U.S. F8 110
Stony Creek, stm., Ca., U.S. D3 134
Stony Lake, l., Mb., Can. D11 106
Stony Lake, l., On., Can. D11 112
Stony Plain, Ab., Can. C16 138
Stony Point, N.C., U.S. I4 114
Stony Rapids, Sk., Can. D9 106
Stony River, Ak., U.S. D8 140
Stopnica, Pol. F16 16
Stora Lulevatten, l., Swe. C8 8
Storavan, l., Swe. D8 8
Stord, i., Nor. G1 8
Storebælt, strt., Den. I4 8
Store Koldewey, i., Grnld. B22 141
Støren, Nor. E4 8
Store Sotra, i., Nor. F1 8
Storkerson Bay, b., N.T., Can. B14 140
Storkerson Peninsula, pen., N.T., Can. A9 106
Storlien, Swe. E5 8
Storm Bay, b., Austl. o13 77a
Storm Lake, Ia., U.S. B2 120
Stornoway, Scot., U.K. C6 12
Storozhynets', Ukr. A12 26
Storrs, Ct., U.S. C13 114
Storsjøen, l., Nor. F4 8
Storsjön, l., Swe. E5 8
Storstrøm, state, Den. I5 8
Storthoaks, Sk., Can. E12 124
Storuman, Swe. D7 8
Storuman, l., Swe. D6 8
Storvindeln, l., Swe. D7 8
Storvreta, Swe. F7 8
Story City, Ia., U.S. B4 120
Stosch, Isla, i., Chile I1 90
Stoubcy, Bela. G9 10
Stoughton, Sk., Can. E10 124
Stoughton, Ma., U.S. B14 114
Stoughton, Wi., U.S. B8 120
Stoung, stm., Camb. F7 48
Stow, Oh., U.S. C4 114
Stowe, Vt., U.S. F4 110
Stowell, Tx., U.S. H4 122
Stowmarket, Eng., U.K. I14 12
Stoyoma Mountain, mtn., B.C., Can. G9 138
Stradella, Italy E6 22
Stradzečy, Bela. I6 10
Strahan, Austl. o12 77a
Strakonice, Czech Rep. G9 16
Stralsund, Ger. B9 16
Strand, S. Afr. I4 70
Stranraer, Scot., U.K. G8 12
Strasbourg, Sk., Can. C9 124
Strasbourg, Fr. F16 14
Strasburg, Ger. C9 16
Strasburg, N.D., U.S. A12 126
Strasburg, Oh., U.S. D4 114
Strasburg, Pa., U.S. E9 114
Străşeni, Mol. B15 26
Stratford, On., Can. E8 112
Stratford, N.Z. D6 80
Stratford, Ca., U.S. G6 134
Stratford, Ct., U.S. C12 114
Stratford, Ia., U.S. B4 120
Stratford, Ok., U.S. C2 122
Stratford, Wi., U.S. G8 118
Stratford-upon-Avon, Eng., U.K. I11 12
Strathalbyn, Austl. J2 76
Strathclair, Mb., Can. D13 124
Strathgordon, Austl. o12 77a
Strathlorne, N.S., Can. D15 110
Strathmore, Ab., Can. E17 138
Strathmore, val., Scot., U.K. E9 12
Strathroy, On., Can. F8 112
Strathy Point, c., Scot., U.K. C8 12
Stratton, Co., U.S. B6 128
Stratton, Me., U.S. E6 110
Stratton, Ne., U.S. A7 128
Straubing, Ger. H8 16
Strausberg, Ger. D9 16
Strawberry, stm., Ar., U.S. H6 120
Strawberry, stm., Ut., U.S. C6 132
Strawberry Mountain, mtn., Or., U.S. F8 136
Strawberry Reservoir, res., Ut., U.S. C5 132
Strawn, Tx., U.S. B9 130
Strážnice, Czech Rep. H13 16
Streaky Bay, b., Austl. F6 74
Streatham, B.C., Can. C4 138
Streator, Il., U.S. C9 120
Středočeský, state, Czech Rep. G10 16
Stredoslovenský Kraj, state, Slov. H15 16
Streeter, N.D., U.S. A13 126
Streetsboro, Oh., U.S. C4 114
Streetsville, On., Can. E10 112
Strehaia, Rom. E10 26
Strelka-Čunja, Russia B18 32
Strel'na, stm., Russia C18 8
Strel'skaja, Russia G22 8
Strenči, Lat. C8 10
Strèšyn, Bela. H13 10
Strickland, stm., Pap. N. Gui. b3 79a
Strimon, Gulf of see Strymonikós Kólpos, b., Grc. C6 28
Strjama, stm., Blg. G11 26
Stroeder, Arg. H4 90
Strofádes, is., Grc. F3 28
Stromboli, Isola, i., Italy F9 24
Strome, Ab., Can. D18 138
Stromeferry, Scot., U.K. D7 12
Stromsburg, Ne., U.S. F15 126
Strömstad, Swe. G4 8
Strömsund, Swe. E6 8
Strong City, Ks., U.S. C12 128
Stronghurst, Il., U.S. D7 120
Stronsay, i., Scot., U.K. B10 12
Stropkov, Slov. G17 16
Stroud, Austl. I8 76
Stroud, Eng., U.K. J10 12
Stroud, Ok., U.S. B2 122
Stroudsburg, Pa., U.S. D10 114
Struga, Mac. B3 28
Struma, stm., Eur. H10 26
Strumble Head, c., Wales, U.K. I7 12
Strumica, Mac. B5 28
Strunino, Russia D21 10
Struthers, Oh., U.S. C5 114
Stryi, stm., Ukr. H19 16
Stryker, Mt., U.S. B12 136
Stryker, Oh., U.S. G5 112
Stryków, Pol. E15 16
Strymonikós Kólpos (Strimon, Gulf of), b., Grc. C6 28
Strzegom, Pol. F12 16
Strzelce Krajeńskie, Pol. D11 16
Strzelce Opolskie, Pol. F14 16
Strzelecki Creek, stm., Austl. G3 76
Strzelecki Desert, des., Austl. F3 76
Strzelecki National Park, p.o.i., Austl. n13 77a
Strzelin, Pol. F12 16
Strzyżów, Pol. G17 16
Stuart, Fl., U.S. I5 116
Stuart, Ia., U.S. C3 120
Stuart, Va., U.S. H5 114
Stuart, stm., B.C., Can. B7 138
Stuart Island, i., Ak., U.S. D7 140
Stuart Lake, l., B.C., Can. B5 138
Stuarts Draft, Va., U.S. G6 114
Studen Kladenec, Jazovir, res., Blg. H12 26
Stuie, B.C., Can. D4 138
Stupino, Russia F20 10
Stura di Demonte, stm., Italy F4 22
Sturge Island, i., Ant. B21 81
Sturgeon, stm., On., Can. B9 112
Sturgeon, stm., Mi., U.S. E10 118
Sturgeon Bay, Wi., U.S. D2 112
Sturgeon Bay, b., Mb., Can. B15 124
Sturgeon Falls, On., Can. B10 112
Sturgeon Lake, l., Ab., Can. A13 138
Sturgeon Lake, l., On., Can. D11 112
Sturgeon Lake, l., On., Can. A7 118
Sturgis, Sk., Can. C11 124
Sturgis, Ky., U.S. G10 120
Sturgis, Mi., U.S. G4 112
Şturgis, S.D., U.S. C9 126
Štúrovo, Slov. I14 16
Sturt, Mount, mtn., Austl. G3 76
Sturtevant, Wi., U.S. F2 112
Sturt National Park, p.o.i., Austl. G3 76
Sturt Stony Desert, des., Austl. G3 76
Stutterheim, S. Afr. H8 70
Stuttgart, Ger. H5 16
Stuttgart, Ar., U.S. C7 122
Styr, stm., Eur. H9 10
Styria see Steiermark, state, Aus. C11 22
Šu, Kaz. F12 32
Suaçuí Grande, stm., Braz. J4 88
Suai, Malay. B8 50
Suaita, Col. D5 86
Suapure, stm., Ven. D8 86
Suaqui Grande, Mex. A4 100
Subah, Indon. G6 50
Subang, Indon. G5 50
Şubansiri, stm., Asia D14 54
Šubarkuduk, Kaz. E9 32
Subarnarekha, stm., India G11 54
Sūbāṭ, stm., Sudan F6 62
Subate, Lat. D8 10
Subei, China D3 36
Subeita see Shivta, Horvot, hist., Isr. H5 58
Subiaco, Italy I10 22
Sublette, Ks., U.S. D8 128
Sublett Range, mts., Id., U.S. H14 136
Subotica, Yugo. C6 26
Sucarnoochee, stm., U.S. E10 122
Succotah, hist., Egypt H3 58
Suceava, Rom. B13 26
Suceava, state, Rom. B12 26
Suchań, Pol. C11 16
Suchou see Suzhou, China F9 42
Süchow see Xuzhou, China D7 42
Sucio, stm., Col. D3 86
Sucre, Bol. C3 90
Sucre, Col. C4 86
Sucre, state, Col. C4 86
Sucre, state, Ven. B10 86
Sucuaro, Col. E7 86
Sucumbíos, state, Ec. H3 86
Sucuriju, Braz. C8 84
Sucuriú, stm., Braz. C6 90
Sud, state, N. Cal. m16 79d
Sud, Canal du, strt., Haiti C11 102
Suda, Russia A20 10
Suda, stm., Russia A20 10
Sudan, Tx., U.S. G6 128
Sudan, ctry., Afr. E5 62
Sudan, reg., Afr. E4 62
Sudbišči, Russia H20 10
Sudbury, On., Can. B8 112
Sudbury, Eng., U.K. I13 12
Sudd see As-Sudd, reg., Sudan F6 62
Sudetes, mts., Eur. F11 16
Sudogda, Russia H19 8
Sudomskaja vozvyšennost', plat., Russia C12 10
Sudost', stm., Eur. H16 10
Südtirol see Trentino-Alto Adige, state, Italy D8 22
Suđuroy, i., Far. Is. n34 8b
Sue, stm., Sudan F5 62
Sueca, Spain E10 20
Suez see El-Suweis, Egypt I3 58
Suez, Gulf of see Suweis, Khalîg el-, b., Egypt J4 58
Suez Canal see Suweis, Qanâ el-, can., Egypt H3 58
Suffield, Ab., Can. D2 124
Suffolk, Va., U.S. H9 114
Sufu see Kashi, China B12 56
Sugar City, Id., U.S. G15 136
Sugar Hill, Ga., U.S. B1 116
Sugar Island, i., Mi., U.S. B5 112
Sugar Land, Tx., U.S. H3 122
Sugarloaf, hill, Oh., U.S. C4 114
Sugarloaf Mountain, mtn., Me., U.S. E6 110
Sugarloaf Point, c., Austl. I9 76
Suğla Gölü, l., Tur. F14 28
Sugoj, stm., Russia D20 34
Sugut, stm., Malay. G1 52
Suhag, Egypt B6 62
Suhai Hu, l., China G16 32
Suhana, Russia C12 34
Şuhār, Oman E8 56
Sühbaatar, Mong. A6 36
Suhindol, Blg. F12 26
Suhiniči, Russia F18 10
Suhl, Ger. F6 16
Suhodol'skij, Russia G21 10
Suhona, stm., Russia F22 8
Suhoverkovo, Russia D18 10
Suhumi, Geor. F6 32
Şuhut, Tur. E13 28
Suiá-Miçu, stm., Braz. F7 84
Suichuan, China H6 42
Suide, China C4 42
Suifu see Yibin, China F5 36
Suihua, China B10 36
Suijiang, China F5 36
Suileng, China B10 36
Suining, China E7 42
Suining, China F1 42
Suipacha, Arg. G8 92
Suiping, China E5 42
Suippes, Fr. E13 14
Suir, stm., Ire. I5 12
Suixi, China E7 42
Suiyang, China B9 38
Suiyang, China H2 42
Suiyangdian, China E5 42
Suizhong, China A9 42
Şuizhou, China F5 42
Šuja, Russia H19 8
Šuja, stm., Russia E15 8
Sujāngarh, India E5 54
Sujāwal, Pak. F2 54
Sukabumi, Indon. G5 50
Sukadana, Indon. D6 50
Sukadana, Indon. F4 50
Sukadana, Teluk, b., Indon. D6 50
Sukagawa, Japan B13 40
Sukamara, Indon. E7 50
Sukaraja, Indon. E7 50
Sukau, Malay. A11 50
Sukhothai, Thai. D4 48
Sukhumi see Suhumi, Geor. F6 32
Sukkertoppen (Maniitsoq), Grnld. D15 141
Sukkozero, Russia E14 8
Sukkur, Pak. E2 54
Sukoharjo, Indon. G7 50
Sukromlja, Russia D17 10
Sukses, Nmb. B3 70
Sukumo, Japan G5 40
Sukunka, stm., B.C., Can. A9 138
Sul, Baía, b., Braz. C13 92
Sula, i., Nor. F1 8
Sula, stm., Russia C23 8
Sula, Kepulauan (Sula Islands), is., Indon. F8 44
Sulaimān Range, mts., Pak. C3 54
Sula Islands see Sula, Kepulauan, is., Indon. F8 44
Sulawesi (Celebes), i., Indon. F7 44
Sulawesi Selatan, state, Indon. E11 50
Sulawesi Tengah, state, Indon. D12 50
Sulawesi Tenggara, state, Indon. E12 50
Sulaymān, Birak (Solomon's Pools), hist., W.B. G5 58
Sulcis, reg., Italy E2 24
Sulechów, Pol. D11 16
Sulęcin, Pol. D11 16
Sulejówek, Pol. D17 16
Sulen, Mount, mtn., Pap. N. Gui. a3 79a
Sulina, Rom. D16 26
Sulina, Bratul, stm., Rom. D16 26
Sulingen, Ger. D4 16
Sulitelma, mtn., Eur. C7 8
Sullana, Peru D1 84
Sulligent, Al., U.S. D10 122
Sullivan, Il., U.S. E9 120
Sullivan, In., U.S. E10 120
Sullivan Lake, l., Ab., Can. E18 138
Sulmona, Italy H10 22
Sulphur, La., U.S. G5 122
Sulphur, Ok., U.S. C2 122
Sulphur, stm., U.S. D5 122
Sulphur Springs, Tx., U.S. D3 122
Sulphur Springs Draw, stm., U.S. H6 128
Sulphur Springs Valley, val., Az., U.S. L7 132
Sultan, Wa., U.S. C5 136
Sultan Alonto, Lake, l., Phil. G5 52
Sultandağı, Tur. E14 28
Sultanhisar, Tur. F11 28
Sultan Kudarat, Phil. G4 52
Sultānpur, India E8 54
Sulu Archipelago, is., Phil. H3 52
Sulu Chi, l., China C11 54
Sulūq, Libya A4 62
Sulu Sea, Asia F2 52
Şulzbach-Rosenberg, Ger. G7 16
Šum, Russia A14 10
Šumadija, reg., Yugo. E7 26
Sumangat, Tanjong, c., Malay. G1 52
Sumatera (Sumatra), i., Indon. E3 44
Sumatera Barat, state, Indon. D2 50
Sumatera Selatan, state, Indon. E4 50
Sumatera Utara, state, Indon. K4 48
Sumatra see Sumatera, i., Indon. E3 44
Sumba, Far. Is. n34 8b
Sumba, i., Indon. H11 50
Sumba, Selat, strt., Indon. H11 50
Sumbawa, i., Indon. H10 50
Sumbawa Besar, Indon. H10 50
Sumbawanga, Tan. F6 66
Sumbe, Ang. C1 68
Sumburgh Head, c., Scot., U.K. o18 12a
Sumé, Braz. D7 88
Sumedang, Indon. G5 50
Şümeg, Hung. B4 26
Šumen, Blg. F13 26
Şumenep, Indon. G8 50
Šumerlja, Russia C7 32
Sumisu-jima (Smith Island), i., Japan E13 36
Šumjači, Russia G15 10
Summerfield, Fl., U.S. G3 116
Summerfield, N.C., U.S. H6 114
Summer Lake, l., Or., U.S. H6 136
Summerland, B.C., Can. G11 138
Summerside, P.E., Can. D13 110
Summersville, Mo., U.S. G6 120
Summerton, S.C., U.S. C5 116
Summerville, Ga., U.S. C13 122
Summerville, S.C., U.S. C5 116
Summit, S.D., U.S. F1 118
Summit Lake, B.C., Can. B8 138
Summit Mountain, mtn., Nv., U.S. D9 134
Sumner, Ia., U.S. B5 120
Sumner, Ms., U.S. D8 122
Sumner, Wa., U.S. C4 136
Sumoto, Japan E7 40
Şumpangbinangae, Indon. F11 50
Šumperk, Czech Rep. G13 16
Sumpiuh, Indon. G6 50
Şumqayıt, Azer. A6 56
Šumšu, ostrov, i., Russia F20 34
Sumter, S.C., U.S. C5 116
Sumusta el-Waqf, Egypt J1 58
Sumy, Ukr. D4 32
Sumzom, China F4 36
Sun, stm., Mt., U.S. C14 136
Sunāmganj, Bngl. F13 54
Sunbright, Tn., U.S. H13 120
Sunburst, Mt., U.S. B14 136
Sunbury, Austl. K5 76
Sunbury, Oh., U.S. D3 114
Sunbury, Pa., U.S. D9 114
Sunchales, Arg. E7 92
Suncho Corral, Arg. C6 92
Sunch'ŏn, Kor., S. G7 38
Sunch'ŏn-ŭp, Kor., N. E6 38
Sun City, Az., U.S. J4 132
Suncook, N.H., U.S. G5 110
Sunda, Selat (Sunda Strait), strt., Indon. G4 50
Sundance, Wy., U.S. C8 126
Sundarbans, reg., Asia H12 54
Sundargarh, India G9 54
Sunda Shelf, unds. I13 142
Sunda Strait see Sunda, Selat, strt., Indon. G4 50
Sundays, stm., S. Afr. H7 70
Sunde, Nor. G1 8
Sunderland, Eng., U.K. G11 12
Sundown, Tx., U.S. H6 128
Sundridge, On., Can. C10 112
Sundsvall, Swe. E7 8
Sunflower, Ms., U.S. D8 122
Sunflower, Mount, mtn., Ks., U.S. B7 128
Sungaianyar, Indon. E10 50
Sungaibuntu, Indon. F5 50
Sungaidareh, Indon. D2 50
Sungaiguntung, Indon. C3 50
Sungai Kolok, Thai. I5 48
Sungailangsat, Indon. D2 50
Sungailimau, Indon. D1 50
Sungaipenuh, Indon. E2 50
Sungai Petani, Malay. J5 48
Sungaipinang, Indon. D8 50
Sungairotan, Indon. E4 50
Sungaiselan, Indon. E5 50
Sungari see Songhua, stm., China B11 36
Sungari Reservoir see Songhua Hu, res., China C7 38
Sungchiang see Songjiang, China F9 42
Sungguminasa, Indon. F11 50
Sungsang, Indon. E4 50
Sunland Park, N.M., U.S. L10 132
Sunne, Swe. G5 8
Sunnynook, Ab., Can. E19 138
Sunnyside, Ut., U.S. D6 132
Sunnyside, Wa., U.S. D7 136
Sunnyslope, Ab., Can. E17 138
Sunnyvale, Ca., U.S. F3 134
Sun Prairie, Wi., U.S. A8 120
Sunrise, Fl., U.S. J5 116
Sunrise, Wy., U.S. E8 126
Sunrise Manor, Nv., U.S. G1 132
Sunset, La., U.S. G6 122
Sunset, Tx., U.S. H11 128
Sunset Country, reg., Austl. J3 76
Sunset Crater National Monument, p.o.i., Az., U.S. H5 132
Sunshine, Austl. K5 76
Suntar, Russia D12 34
Suntar-Hajata, hrebet, mts., Russia D17 34
Sun Valley, Id., U.S. G12 136
Sunwu, China B10 36
Sunwui see Jiangmen, China J5 42
Sunyani, Ghana H4 64
Suojarvi, Russia E15 8
Suomussalmi, Fin. D13 8
Suō-nada, Japan F4 40
Suordah, Russia C15 34
Supamo, stm., Ven. D10 86
Supaul, India E11 54
Superí see La Merced, Arg. D5 92
Superior, Az., U.S. J5 132
Superior, Mt., U.S. C12 136
Superior, Wi., U.S. E6 118
Superior, Wy., U.S. B7 132
Superior, Laguna, b., Mex. G11 100
Superior, Lake, l., N.A. B10 108
Supetar, Cro. G13 22
Suphan Buri, Thai. E4 48
Suphan Buri, stm., Thai. E5 48
Suponevo, Russia G17 10
Supung Reservoir, res., Asia D6 38
Suqian, China E8 42
Sūq Suwayq, Sau. Ar. E4 56
Suquṭrā (Socotra), i., Yemen G7 56
Şūr (Tyre), Leb. E6 58
Şūr, Oman E8 56
Sur, Point, c., Ca., U.S. G4 134
Sura, stm., Russia C7 32
Surabaya, Indon. G8 50
Surakarta, Indon. G7 50
Şūrān, Syria C7 58
Šurany, Slov. H14 16
Surat, Austl. F7 76
Sūrat, India H4 54
Sūratgarh, India D4 54
Surat Thani, Thai. H4 48
Surаž, Bela. E13 10
Surаž, Russia G15 10
Surendranagar, India G3 54
Surf City, N.J., U.S. E11 114
Surfers Paradise, Austl. G9 76
Surgères, Fr. C5 18
Surgoinsville, Tn., U.S. H3 114
Surgut, Russia B12 32
Suriāpet, India C4 53
Surigao, Phil. F5 52
Surin, Thai. E6 48
Surinam, ctry., S.A. C6 84
Suring, Wi., U.S. D1 112
Surprise Valley, val., U.S. B5 134
Surrency, Ga., U.S. E3 116
Surrey, N.D., U.S. F12 124
Surry, Va., U.S. G9 114
Sursee, Switz. C5 22
Surt, Libya A3 62
Surt, Khalīj (Sidra, Gulf of), b., Libya A3 62
Surtanāhu, Pak. E2 54
Surtsey, i., Ice. I29 8a
Suru, Pap. N. Gui. b3 79a
Sürüç, Tur. A9 58
Suruga-wan, b., Japan E11 40
Surulangun, Indon. E3 50
Şurumu, stm., Braz. F11 86
Šuryškary, Russia A10 32
Susa, Italy E4 22
Sušac, Otok, i., Cro. H13 22
Sūsah, Libya A4 62
Susaki, Japan F6 40
Susanino, Russia G19 8
Susanino, Russia F17 34
Şusanville, Ca., U.S. C5 134
Šušenskoe, Russia D16 32
Susitna, stm., Ak., U.S. D9 140
Susleni, Mol. B15 26
Susoh, Indon. K3 48
Susong, China F7 42
Suspiro del Moro, Puerto, p., Spain G7 20
Susquehanna, Pa., U.S. C10 114
Susquehanna, stm., U.S. E9 114
Susquehanna, West Branch, stm., Pa., U.S. C8 114
Susques, Arg. D3 90
Sussex, N.B., Can. E11 110
Sussex, N.J., U.S. C11 114
Sussex, Va., U.S. H8 114
Susuman, Russia D18 34
Susurluk, Tur. D11 28
Şusuzmüsellim, Tur. B9 28
Šušvė, stm., Lith. E6 10
Sutak, India B6 54
Sutherland, S. Afr. H5 70
Sutherland, Ia., U.S. A2 120
Sutherlin, Or., U.S. G3 136
Sutjeska Nacionalni Park, p.o.i., Bos. F5 26
Sutlej (Langqên) (Satluj), stm., Asia D3 54
Sutter, Ca., U.S. D4 134
Sutter Buttes, mtn., Ca., U.S. D4 134
Sutter Creek, Ca., U.S. E5 134
Sutton, Ak., U.S. D10 140
Sutton, W.V., U.S. F5 114
Sutton, Monts see Green Mountains, mts., N.A. G4 110
Sutton in Ashfield, Eng., U.K. H11 12
Sutton West, On., Can. D10 112
Suttor, stm., Austl. C6 76
Sutwik Island, i., Ak., U.S. E8 140
Suure-Jaani, Est. B8 10
Suur Munamägi, hill, Est. C9 10
Suur Pakri, i., Est. A6 10
Suva, Fiji q19 79e
Suvadiva Atoll, at., Mald. i12 46a
Suvarlı, Tur. A8 58
Suvasvesi, l., Fin. E12 8
Suvorov, Russia F19 10
Suwa, Japan C11 40
Suwałki, Pol. B18 16
Suwałki, state, Pol. C18 16
Suwannaphum, Thai. E6 48
Suwannee, stm., U.S. G2 116
Suwanose-jima, i., Japan k19 39a
Suwarrow, at., Cook Is. E10 72
Suweis, Khalîg el- (Suez, Gulf of), b., Egypt J4 58
Suweis, Qanâ el- (Suez Canal), can., Egypt H3 58
Suwŏn, Kor., S. F7 38
Suzak, Kaz. F11 32
Suzaka, Japan C11 40
Suzdal', Russia H19 8
Suzhou, China F9 42
Suzhou, China E7 42
Suzigou, China A10 42
Suzuka, Japan E9 40
Suzuka-sammyaku, mts., Japan D9 40
Suzu-misaki, c., Japan B10 40
Suzun, Russia D14 32
Suzzara, Italy F7 22
Svalbard, dep., Eur. B6 30
Svaliava, Ukr. A10 26
Svapa, stm., Russia H18 10
Svappavaara, Swe. C9 8
Svärdsjö, Swe. F6 8
Svartenhuk, pen., Grnld. C15 141
Svartisen, ice, Nor. C5 8
Svataj, Russia C19 34
Svay Riĕng, Camb. G7 48
Svėdasai, Lith. E8 10
Şvegssjön, l., Swe. E5 8
Švėkšna, Lith. E4 10
Şvelvik, Nor. G4 8
Švenčionėliai, Lith. E8 10
Švenčionys, Lith. E9 10
Şvendborg, Den. A6 16
Šventoji, Lith. D3 10
Šventoji, stm., Lith. E7 10
Sverdlovsk see Ekaterinburg, Russia C10 32
Sverdrup, ostrov, i., Russia B4 34
Sverdrup Channel, strt., N.T., Can. A6 141
Sverdrup Islands, is., N.T., Can. B5 141
Sveti Nikole, Mac. B4 28
Svetlahorsk, Bela. H12 10
Svetlaja, Russia B12 36
Svetlogorsk, Russia F2 10
Svetlograd, Russia E6 32
Svetlyj, Russia F3 10
Svetlyj, Russia D10 32
Svetlyj, Russia E12 34
Svetogorsk, Russia F13 8
Svetozarevo, Yugo. F8 26
Svidník, Slov. G17 16
Svilengrad, Blg. H13 26
Svínoy, i., Far. Is. m34 8b
Svir, Bela. F9 10
Svir', stm., Russia F16 8
Svirica, Russia F15 8
Svirsk, Russia D18 32
Svislač, stm., Bela. G11 10
Svištov, Blg. F12 26
Svit, Slov. G16 16
Svitavy, Czech Rep. G12 16
Svjacilavičy, Bela. H14 10
Svjatoj Nos, mys, c., Russia B18 8
Svjatoj Nos, mys, c., Russia B17 34
Svobodnyj, Russia F14 34
Svolvær, Nor. B6 8
Svratka, stm., Czech Rep. G12 16
Swabia see Schwaben, hist. reg., Ger. H5 16
Swain Reefs, rf., Austl. C9 76
Swainsboro, Ga., U.S. D3 116
Swains Island, at., Am. Sam. E9 72
Swakop, stm., Nmb. C2 70
Swakopmund, Nmb. C2 70
Swale, stm., Eng., U.K. G11 12
Swan, stm., Can. B13 124
Swan, stm., Ab., Can. A15 138
Swan, stm., Mt., U.S. C13 136
Swanage, Eng., U.K. K11 12
Swanee see Suwannee, stm., U.S. G2 116
Swan Hill, Austl. J4 76
Swan Hills, Ab., Can. B15 138
Swan Islands see Santanilla, Islas, is., Hond. D6 102
Swan Lake, Mb., Can. E15 124
Swan Lake, l., Mb., Can. B13 124
Swan Lake, l., Mn., U.S. G4 118
Swannanoa, N.C., U.S. I3 114
Swan Peak, mtn., Mt., U.S. C13 136
Swanquarter, N.C., U.S. A9 116
Swan Range, mts., Mt., U.S. C13 136
Swan Reach, Austl. J2 76
Swan River, Mb., Can. B12 124
Swansboro, N.C., U.S. B8 116
Swansea, Austl. o13 77a
Swansea, Wales, U.K. J8 12
Swanton, Vt., U.S. F3 110
Swanville, Mn., U.S. F4 118
Swart-Mfolozi, stm., S. Afr. F10 70
Swartz Creek, Mi., U.S. F6 112
Swarzędz, Pol. D13 16
Swāt, stm., Pak. A3 54
Swatow see Shantou, China J7 42
Swaziland, ctry., Afr. E10 70
Sweden, ctry., Eur. E6 8
Swedish Knoll, mtn., Ut., U.S. D5 132
Swedru, Ghana H4 64
Sweeny, Tx., U.S. E12 130
Sweet Briar, Va., U.S. G6 114
Sweetgrass, Mt., U.S. A15 136
Sweet Grass Hills, hills, Mt., U.S. B15 136
Sweet Home, Tx., U.S. E10 130
Sweet Springs, Mo., U.S. F4 120
Sweetwater, Tn., U.S. A1 116
Sweetwater, Tx., U.S. B7 130
Sweetwater, stm., Wy., U.S. E5 126
Şwellendam, S. Afr. H5 70
Świdnica, Pol. F12 16
Świdnik, Pol. E18 16
Świdwin, Pol. C11 16
Świebodzice, Pol. F12 16
Świebodzin, Pol. D11 16
Świecie, Pol. C14 16
Świerzawa, Pol. E11 16
Świętokrzyski Park Narodowy, p.o.i., Pol. F16 16
Swift Current, Sk., Can. D6 124
Swift Current Creek, stm., Sk., Can. D6 124
Swinburne, Cape, c., N.T., Can. A11 106
Swindle Island, i., B.C., Can. D2 138
Swindon, Eng., U.K. J11 12
Şwinford, Ire. H4 12
Świnoujście (Swinemünde), Pol. C9 16
Switzerland, ctry., Eur. C14 18
Swords, Ire. H6 12
Syalah, Russia C13 34
Syan (San), stm., Eur. F18 16
Sycamore, Ga., U.S. E2 116
Sycamore, Il., U.S. C9 120
Sycamore, Oh., U.S. D2 114
Syčovka, Russia E17 10
Sydenham, stm., On., Can. F7 112
Sydney, Austl. I8 76
Sydney, N.S., Can. D16 110
Sydney Bay, b., Norf. I. y25 78i
Sydney Lake, l., On., Can. A4 118
Şydney Mines, N.S., Can. D16 110
Şyičy, Bela. H12 10
Syke, Ger. D4 16
Sykesville, Pa., U.S. C7 114
Syktyvkar, Russia B8 32
Sylacauga, Al., U.S. D12 122
Sylhet, Bngl. F13 54
Syloga, Russia E20 8
Sylt, i., Ger. B4 16
Sylva, N.C., U.S. A2 116
Sylvan Grove, Ks., U.S. C10 128
Sylvania, Ga., U.S. D4 116
Sylvania, Oh., U.S. C2 114
Sylvan Lake, Ab., Can. D16 138
Sylvan Lake, l., Ab., Can. D16 138
Sylvan Pass, p., Wy., U.S. F16 136
Sylvester, Ga., U.S. E2 116
Sylvester, Tx., U.S. B7 130
Sym, Russia B15 32
Syme see Sými, i., Grc. G10 28
Şými, i., Grc. G10 28
Šymkent, Kaz. F11 32
Synevir, Ukr. A10 26
Syowa, sci., Ant. C9 81
Syracuse, In., U.S. G4 112
Syracuse, Ks., U.S. C7 128
Syracuse, Ne., U.S. D1 120
Syracuse, N.Y., U.S. A9 114
Syrdarja, Uzb. A10 56
Syr Darya (Syrdar'ja), stm., Asia F11 32
Syria, ctry., Asia B4 56
Syriam, Mya. D3 48
Syrian Desert (Shām, Bādiyat ash-), des., Asia C4 56
Sýrna, i., Grc. G9 28
Sýros, i., Grc. F7 28
Sysmä, Fin. F11 8
Sysola, stm., Russia B8 32
Syt'kovo, Russia D16 10
Syväri, l., Fin. E13 8
Syzran', Russia D7 32
Szabolcs-Szatmár-Bereg, state, Hung. A9 26
Szamos (Someş), stm., Eur. B9 26
Szamotuły, Pol. D12 16
Szarvas, Hung. C7 26
Szczawnica, Pol. G16 16
Szczecin (Stettin), Pol. C10 16
Szczecin, state, Pol. C11 16
Szczecinek, Pol. C12 16
Szczuczyn, Pol. C18 16
Szczytno, Pol. C17 16
Szechwan see Sichuan, state, China E5 36
Szechwan Basin see Sichuan Pendi, bas., China F1 42
Szeged, Hung. C7 26
Szeghalom, Hung. B8 26
Székesfehérvár, Hung. B5 26
Szekszárd, Hung. C5 26
Szentendre, Hung. B5 26
Szentes, Hung. C7 26
Szeping see Siping, China C6 38
Szerencs, Hung. A8 26
Szob, Hung. B5 26
Szolnok, Hung. B7 26
Szombathely, Hung. B3 26
Szprotawa, Pol. E11 16
Szubin, Pol. C13 16
Szypliszki, Pol. B19 16

T

Taal, Lake, l., Phil. D3 52
Tábara, Spain C5 20
Tabar Islands, is., Pap. N. Gui. a5 79a
Tabarka, Tun. H2 24
Tabasco, state, Mex. D6 96
Tabelbala, Alg. D4 64
Taber, Ab., Can. G18 138
Tabernes de Valldigna see Tavernes de la Valldigna, Spain E10 20
Tabira, Braz. D7 88
Tablas de Daimiel, Parque Nacional de las, p.o.i., Spain E7 20
Tablas Island, i., Phil. D4 52
Tablas Strait, strt., Phil. D3 52
Tablat, Alg. H14 20
Table Mountain, mtn., Az., U.S. K6 132
Table Rock, Ne., U.S. D1 120
Table Rock Lake, res., U.S. H4 120
Table Top, mtn., Az., U.S. K4 132
Tablones, P.R. B4 104a
Taboi, Mount, hill, St. Vin. p11 105e
Tábor, Czech Rep. G10 16
Tabor, Russia B19 34
Tabor, Ia., U.S. D2 120
Tabora, Tan. E6 66
Tabor City, N.C., U.S. B7 116
Tabou, C. Iv. I3 64
Tabrīz, Iran B6 56
Tabuaeran, at., Kir. C11 72
Tabu-dong, Kor., S. C1 40
Tabuk, Phil. B3 52

Name	Map Ref.	Page
Tekonsha, Mi., U.S.	B1	114
Te Kuiti, N.Z.	D6	80
Tel, stm., India	A6	53
Tela, Hond.	E4	102
Telaopengsha Shan, mtn., China	C11	54
Telavi, Geor.	F7	32
Tel Aviv-Jaffa see Tel Aviv-Yafo, Isr.	F5	58
Tel Aviv-Yafo, Isr.	F5	58
Telč, Czech Rep.	G11	16
Teleckoe, ozero, l., Russia	D15	32
Telefomin, Pap. N. Gui.	b3	79a
Telegraph Creek, B.C., Can.	D4	106
Telêmaco Borba, Braz.	B12	92
Telemark, state, Nor.	G3	8
Telembí, stm., Col.	G2	86
Telén, Arg.	H5	92
Telen, stm., Indon.	C10	50
Teleneşti, Mol.	B15	26
Teleno, mtn., Spain	B4	20
Teleorman, state, Rom.	E12	26
Teleorman, stm., Rom.	E12	26
Telescope Point, c., Gren.	q10	105e
Telese, Italy	C8	24
Telford, Eng., U.K.	I10	12
Télimélé, Gui.	G2	64
Telire, stm., C.R.	H6	102
Teljo, Jabal, mtn., Sudan	E5	62
Telkwa, B.C., Can.	B3	138
Tell Basta, hist., Egypt	H2	58
Tell City, In., U.S.	G11	120
Tell El-Amarna, hist., Egypt	K1	58
Tellel Rub, hist., Egypt	H2	58
Teller, Ak., U.S.	C6	140
Tellicherry, India	F2	53
Tellier, Arg.	I3	90
Tello, Col.	F4	86
Telluride, Co., U.S.	F9	132
Tel Megiddo, hist., Isr.	F6	58
Telmen nuur, l., Mong.	B4	36
Teloloapan, Mex.	F8	100
Telos see Tílos, i., Grc.	G10	28
Telsen, Arg.	H3	90
Telšiai, Lith.	E5	10
Teltow, Ger.	D9	16
Telukbayur, Indon.	D2	50
Telukbayur, Indon.	B10	50
Telukdalem, Indon.	L3	48
Teluk Intan, Malay.	K5	48
Tema, Ghana	H5	64
Temagami, Lake, l., On., Can.	A9	112
Temaju, Pulau, i., Indon.	C6	50
Te Manga, mtn., Cook Is.	a26	78j
Temangga, Indon.	C7	50
Tematangi, at., Fr. Poly.	F12	72
Temax, Mex.	B3	102
Tembeling, stm., Malay.	J6	48
Tembenči, stm., Russia	A17	32
Tembesi, stm., Indon.	D3	50
Tembilahan, Indon.	D3	50
Temblador, Ven.	C10	86
Temblor Range, mts., Ca., U.S.	H6	134
Teme, stm., Eng., U.K.	I10	12
Temecula, Ca., U.S.	J8	134
Temelli, Tur.	D15	28
Temengor, Tasik, res., Malay.	J5	48
Temetiu, mtn., Fr. Poly.	s18	78g
Temir, Kaz.	E9	32
Temirtau, Kaz.	D12	32
Témiscaming, Qc., Can.	B10	112
Témiscamingue, Lac (Timiskaming, Lake), res., Can.	B10	112
Témiscouata, Lac, l., Qc., Can.	C7	110
Tëmkino, Russia	E17	10
Temora, Austl.	J6	76
Temosachic, Mex.	A5	100
Tempe, Az., U.S.	J5	132
Tempe, Danau, l., Indon.	F12	50
Tempino, Indon.	D3	50
Tempio Pausania, Italy	D2	24
Temple, Tx., U.S.	C10	130
Templi, Valle dei, hist., Italy	G7	24
Templin, Ger.	C9	16
Tempoal, stm., Mex.	E9	100
Tempoal de Sánchez, Mex.	E9	100
Tempy, Russia	D20	10
Temuco, Chile	G2	90
Temwen, i., Micron.	m12	78d
Tena, Ec.	H3	86
Tenabo, Mex.	B2	102
Tenaha, Tx., U.S.	F4	122
Tena Kourou, mtn., Burkina	G4	64
Tenāli, India	C5	53
Tenasserim, Mya.	F4	48
Tendaho, Eth.	E8	62
Tende, Col de, p., Eur.	E13	18
Ten Degree Channel, strt., India	G7	46
Tendō, Japan	A13	40
Ténenkou, Mali	G3	64
Ténéré, des., Niger	F7	64
Ténès, Alg.	H12	20
Ténès, Cap, c., Alg.	H12	20
Teng, stm., Mya.	B3	48
Tengah, Kepulauan, is., Indon.	G10	50
Tengchong, China	G4	36
Tenggara, Nusa (Lesser Sunda Islands), is., Indon.	G6	44
Tenggara Celebes see Sulawesi Tenggara, state, Indon.	E12	50
Tenggarong, Indon.	D10	50
Tengger Shamo, des., China	D5	36
Tenghilan, Malay.	G1	52
Tengiz, ozero, l., Kaz.	D11	32
Tengréla, C. Iv.	G3	64
Tengtiao (Na), stm., Asia	A6	48
Tengxian, China	J4	42
Tengxian, China	D7	42
Tenkāsi, India	G3	53
Tenke, D.R.C.	G5	66
Tenkeli, Russia	B17	34
Tenkiller Ferry Lake, res., Ok., U.S.	B4	122
Tenkodogo, Burkina	G4	64
Tennant Creek, Austl.	C6	74
Tennessee, state, U.S.	D10	108
Tennessee, stm., U.S.	A11	122
Tennille, Ga., U.S.	D3	116
Teno, Chile	G2	92
Teno (Tana), stm., Eur.	B12	8
Tenom, Malay.	A9	50
Tenos see Tínos, Grc.	F8	28
Tenos see Tínos, i., Grc.	F8	28
Tenosique, Mex.	D2	102
Tenryū, Japan	E10	40
Tenryū, stm., Japan	E10	40
Tensas, stm., La., U.S.	F7	122
Tensed, Id., U.S.	C10	136
Ten Sleep, Wy., U.S.	C5	126
Tenterfield, Austl.	G8	76
Ten Thousand Islands, is., Fl., U.S.	K4	116
Tentolomatinan, Gunung, mtn., Indon.	E7	44
Teocaltiche, Mex.	E7	100
Teodelina, Arg.	G7	92
Teófilo Otoni, Braz.	I5	88
Teo Lakes, l., Sk., Can.	C4	124
Teotihuacán, hist., Mex.	F9	100
Tepa, Indon.	G8	44
Tepalcatepec, Mex.	F7	100
Tepebaşı, Tur.	B3	58
Tepehuanes, Mex.	C6	100
Tepehuanes, stm., Mex.	C6	100
Tepeji de Ocampo, Mex.	F9	100
Tepelenë, Alb.	D13	24
Tepic, Mex.	E6	100
Teplice, Czech Rep.	F9	16
Tepoca, Bahía de, b., Mex.	F6	98
Tepoca, Punta, c., Mex.	G6	98
Ter, stm., Spain	B14	20
Téra, Niger	G5	64
Tera, stm., Spain	C4	20
Teradomari, Japan	B11	40
Teraina, i., Kir.	C11	72
Teramo, Italy	H10	22
Terbuny, Russia	H21	10
Terceira, i., Port.	C3	60
Tercero, stm., Arg.	F6	92
Terdal, India	C2	53
Terek, stm., Russia	G18	6
Terempa, Indon.	B5	50
Terengganu, state, Malay.	J6	48
Terengganu, stm., Malay.	J6	48
Terenos, Braz.	D6	90
Teresina, Braz.	C4	88
Teresópolis, Braz.	L4	88
Terespol, Pol.	D19	16
Terevaka, Cerro, mtn., Chile	e29	78l
Tergüün Bogd uul, mtn., Mong.	C5	36
Teriang, stm., Malay.	K6	48
Teriberka, Russia	B16	8
Terihi, i., Fr. Poly.	t19	78g
Terlingua, Tx., U.S.	E4	130
Terlingua Creek, stm., Tx., U.S.	E4	130
Termas del Arapey, Ur.	E9	92
Termas de Río Hondo, Arg.	C5	92
Termez, Uzb.	B10	56
Termini Imerese, Italy	G7	24
Termini Imerese, Golfo di, b., Italy	F7	24
Terminillo, Monte, mtn., Italy	H9	22
Términos, Laguna de, b., Mex.	C2	102
Termoli, Italy	H11	22
Termonde see Dendermonde, Bel.	C12	14
Ternej, Russia	B12	38
Terneuzen, Neth.	C12	14
Terni, Italy	H9	22
Ternitz, Aus.	C12	22
Ternopil', Ukr.	F14	6
Terpenija, mys, c., Russia	G17	34
Terpenija, zaliv, b., Russia	G17	34
Terra Alta, W.V., U.S.	E6	114
Terra Bella, Ca., U.S.	H6	134
Terrace, B.C., Can.	B2	138
Terracina, Italy	C7	24
Terra Cotta Army (Qinshihuang Mausoleum), hist., China	D3	42
Terral, Ok., U.S.	H11	128
Terralba, Italy	E2	24
Terra Santa, Braz.	D6	84
Terrassa, Spain	C13	20
Terrebonne Bay, b., La., U.S.	H8	122
Terre-de-Bas, Guad.	i5	105c
Terre-de-Haut, Guad.	i5	105c
Terre-de-Haut, i., Guad.	i5	105c
Terre Haute, In., U.S.	E10	120
Terrell, Tx., U.S.	E2	122
Terre-Neuve see Newfoundland, state, Can.	B17	110
Territoire du Yukon see Yukon, state, Can.	B3	106
Territoires du Nord-Ouest see Northwest Territories, state, Can.	B10	106
Terry, Ms., U.S.	E8	122
Terry, Mt., U.S.	A7	126
Terschelling, i., Neth.	A14	14
Terskej-Alatau, hrebet, mts., Kyrg.	F13	32
Teruel, Col.	F4	86
Teruel, Spain	D9	20
Teruel, co., Spain	D10	20
Terujak, Indon.	J3	48
Tervola, Fin.	C11	8
Terzaghi Dam, dam, B.C., Can.	F8	138
Tes, stm., Asia	D16	32
Tescott, Ks., U.S.	B11	128
Teseney, Erit.	D7	62
Teshekpuk Lake, l., Ak., U.S.	B9	140
Teshio, Japan	B14	38
Teshio, stm., Japan	B15	38
Teslin, Yk., Can.	C4	106
Teslin, stm., Can.	C4	106
Teslin Lake, l., Can.	C4	106
Tësovo, Russia	E17	10
Tësovo-Netyl'skij, Russia	B13	10
Tësovskij, Russia	B13	10
Tessalit, Mali	E5	64
Tessaoua, Niger	G6	64
Testa, Capo, c., Italy	C3	24
Testour, Tun.	H3	24
Tetachuck Lake, res., B.C., Can.	C4	138
Tete, Moz.	D5	68
Tête Jaune Cache, B.C., Can.	D11	138
Tetepare Island, i., Sol. Is.	e7	79b
Teterow, Ger.	C8	16
Tetica, mtn., Spain	G8	20
Teton, Id., U.S.	G15	136
Teton, stm., Id., U.S.	G15	136
Teton, stm., Mt., U.S.	C15	136
Tetonia, Id., U.S.	G15	136
Teton Range, mts., Wy., U.S.	G16	136
Tetouan, Mor.	B4	64
Tetovo, Mac.	A4	28
Tetufera, Mont, mtn., Fr. Poly.	v22	78h
Teuco, stm., Arg.	D4	90
Teulada, Italy	F2	24
Teulada, Capo, c., Italy	F2	24
Teulon, Mb., Can.	D16	124
Teutoburger Wald, hills, Ger.	D4	16
Teuva, Fin.	E9	8
Tevere (Tiber), stm., Italy	H9	22
Teverya, Isr.	F6	58
Te Waewae Bay, b., N.Z.	H2	80
Tewah, Indon.	D8	50
Tewantin-Noosa, Austl.	F9	76
Tewkesbury, Eng., U.K.	I11	12
Texada Island, i., B.C., Can.	G6	138
Texana, Lake, res., Tx., U.S.	F11	130
Texarkana, Ar., U.S.	D4	122
Texarkana, Tx., U.S.	D4	122
Texas, Austl.	G8	76
Texas, state, U.S.	E8	108
Texas City, Tx., U.S.	H4	122
Texel, i., Neth.	A13	14
Texhoma, Ok., U.S.	E7	128
Texico, N.M., U.S.	G5	128
Texoma, Lake, res., U.S.	H11	128
Teyateyaneng, Leso.	F8	70
Teywarah, Afg.	C9	56
Teziutlán, Mex.	F10	100
Tezpur, India	E14	54
Tezzeron Lake, l., B.C., Can.	B6	138
Tha, stm., Laos	B5	48
Tha-anne, stm., N.T., Can.	C11	106
Thabana-Ntlenyana, mtn., Leso.	F9	70
Thabaung, Mya.	D2	48
Thabazimbi, S. Afr.	D8	70
Thabyu, Mya.	E4	48
Thagyettaw, Mya.	F3	48
Thai Binh, Viet.	B8	48
Thailand, ctry., Asia	E5	48
Thailand, Gulf of, b., Asia	G5	48
Thai Nguyen, Viet.	B7	48
Thak, Pak.	C3	54
Thal, Pak.	B3	54
Thala, Tun.	I2	24
Thal Desert, des., Pak.	C3	54
Thalfang, Ger.	G2	16
Tha Li, Thai.	D5	48
Thalia, Tx., U.S.	H9	128
Thālith, Ash-Shallāl ath- (Third Cataract), wtfl, Sudan	D6	62
Thalwil, Switz.	C5	22
Thames, N.Z.	C6	80
Thames, stm., On., Can.	F8	112
Thames, stm., Eng., U.K.	J13	12
Thames, Firth of, b., N.Z.	C6	80
Thamesford, On., Can.	E8	112
Thamesville, On., Can.	F7	112
Thāna, India	B1	53
Thandaung, Mya.	C3	48
Thangoo, Austl.	C4	74
Thangool, Austl.	E8	76
Thanh Hoa, Viet.	C7	48
Thanh Pho Ho Chi Minh (Saigon), Viet.	G8	48
Thanjāvūr, India	F4	53
Thann, Fr.	B12	18
Thap Than, stm., Thai.	E6	48
Tharabwin West, Mya.	F4	48
Tharād, India	F3	54
Thar Desert (Great Indian Desert), des., Asia	D3	54
Thargomindah, Austl.	F5	76
Tharrawaddy, Mya.	D2	48
Tha Sala, Thai.	H4	48
Thásos, Grc.	C7	28
Thásos, i., Grc.	C7	28
Thásos, hist., Grc.	C7	28
Thaton, Mya.	D3	48
Tha Tum, Thai.	E6	48
Thau, Bassin de, l., Fr.	F9	18
Thaungyin (Moei), stm., Asia	D3	48
Thaya (Dyje), stm., Eur.	H12	16
Thayawthadangyi Kyun, i., Mya.	F3	48
Thayer, Ks., U.S.	G2	120
Thayer, Mo., U.S.	H6	120
Thayetchaung, Mya.	F4	48
Thayetmyo, Mya.	C2	48
Thazi, Mya.	B3	48
Thebes see Thíva, Grc.	E6	28
The Bottom, Neth. Ant.	B1	105a
The Cheviot, mtn., Eng., U.K.	F10	12
The Dalles, Or., U.S.	E5	136
Thedford, Ne., U.S.	E12	126
The Father see Ulawun, Mount, vol., Pap. N. Gui.	b5	79a
The Fens, reg., Eng., U.K.	I12	12
The Fishing Lakes, l., Sk., Can.	D10	124
The Granites, hill, Austl.	D6	74
The Hague see 's-Gravenhage, Neth.	B12	14
The Heads, c., Or., U.S.	H2	136
Theinkun, Mya.	G4	48
The Lakes National Park, p.o.i., Austl.	L6	76
The Little Minch, strt., Scot., U.K.	D6	12
Thelon, stm., N.T., Can.	C11	106
The Lynd, Austl.	B5	76
The Minch, strt., Scot., U.K.	D6	12
Thenia, Alg.	H14	20
Theodore, Austl.	E8	76
Theodore, Sk., Can.	C10	124
Theodore, Al., U.S.	G10	122
Theodore Roosevelt National Park North Unit, p.o.i., N.D., U.S.	G10	124
Theodore Roosevelt National Park South Unit, p.o.i., N.D., U.S.	G10	124
The Pas, Mb., Can.	E10	106
Thepha, Thai.	I5	48
The Pinnacle, hill, Mo., U.S.	E6	120
The Rand see Witwatersrand, mts., S. Afr.	D8	70
Theresa Creek, stm., Austl.	D6	76
The Rhins, pen., Scot., U.K.	G7	12
Thermaikós Kólpos (Salonika, Gulf of), b., Grc.	C6	28
Thermopolis, Wy., U.S.	D4	126
Thermopylae see Thermopýles, hist., Grc.	E5	28
Thermopýles (Thermopylae), hist., Grc.	E5	28
The Rock, Austl.	J6	76
The Rockies, mtn., Wa., U.S.	D4	136
The Rope, clf, Pit.	c28	78k
Thesiger Bay, b., N.T., Can.	B15	140
The Slot see New Georgia Sound, strt., Sol. Is.	e8	79b
Thessalía, state, Grc.	D5	28
Thessalía, hist. reg., Grc.	D5	28
Thessalon, On., Can.	B6	112
Thessaloníki (Salonika), Grc.	C6	28
Thessaly see Thessalía, hist. reg., Grc.	D5	28
Thetford, Eng., U.K.	I13	12
Thetford Mines, Qc., Can.	D5	110
Theunissen, S. Afr.	F8	70
The Valley, Anguilla	A1	105a
The Village, Ok., U.S.	F11	128
The Wash, b., Eng., U.K.	I13	12
The Weald, reg., Eng., U.K.	J13	12
Thibodaux, La., U.S.	H8	122
Thief Lake, l., Mn., U.S.	C3	118
Thief River Falls, Mn., U.S.	C2	118
Thiene, Italy	E8	22
Thiers, Fr.	D9	18
Thiès, Sen.	G1	64
Thika, Kenya	E7	66
Thimphu, Bhu.	E12	54
Thingvallavatn, l., Ice.	k29	8a
Thingvellir, Ice.	k29	8a
Thingvellir Nasjonalpark, p.o.i., Ice.	k29	8a
Thio, N. Cal.	m16	79d
Thionville, Fr.	E15	14
Thíra, Grc.	G8	28
Thíra (Santorini), i., Grc.	G8	28
Third Cataract see Thālith, Ash-Shallāl ath-, wtfl, Sudan	D6	62
Thiruvananthapuram see Trivandrum, India	G3	53
Thiruvārūr, India	F4	53
Thistilfjörður, b., Ice.	j32	8a
Thíva, Grc.	E6	28
Thiviers, Fr.	D6	18
Thjórsá, stm., Ice.	k30	8a
Thohoyandou, S. Afr.	C10	70
Thoi Binh, Viet.	H7	48
Thomas, Ok., U.S.	F10	128
Thomas, W.V., U.S.	E6	114
Thomaston, Al., U.S.	E11	122
Thomaston, Ga., U.S.	D1	116
Thomaston, Me., U.S.	F7	110
Thomasville, Ga., U.S.	F2	116
Thomasville, N.C., U.S.	I5	114
Thompson, Mb., Can.	D11	106
Thompson, Ia., U.S.	H5	118
Thompson, N.D., U.S.	D1	118
Thompson, stm., B.C., Can.	F9	138
Thompson, stm., U.S.	E4	120
Thompson Falls, Mt., U.S.	C11	136
Thompson Peak, mtn., Ca., U.S.	B3	134
Thomsen, stm., N.T., Can.	B16	140
Thomson, Ga., U.S.	C3	116
Thomson, Il., U.S.	C7	120
Thomson, stm., Austl.	E4	76
Thongwa, Mya.	D3	48
Thonon-les-Bains, Fr.	C12	18
Thonotosassa, Fl., U.S.	H3	116
Thonze, Mya.	D2	48
Thorhild, Ab., Can.	B17	138
Thórisvatn, l., Ice.	k30	8a
Thorlákshöfn, Ice.	I29	8a
Thornaby-on-Tees, Eng., U.K.	G11	12
Thornbury, On., Can.	D9	112
Thorndale, Tx., U.S.	D10	130
Thornton, Co., U.S.	B4	128
Thornton, Tx., U.S.	F2	122
Thorntonville, Tx., U.S.	C4	130
Thorp, Wi., U.S.	G8	118
Thorsby, Ab., Can.	C16	138
Thorshavn see Tórshavn, Far. Is.	n34	8b
Thórshöfn, Ice.	j32	8a
Thouars, Fr.	H8	14
Thoune see Thun, Switz.	D4	22
Thousand Lake Mountain, mtn., Ut., U.S.	E5	132
Thousand Oaks, Ca., U.S.	I7	134
Thousand Ships Bay, b., Sol. Is.	e8	79b
Thousand Springs Creek, stm., U.S.	B2	132
Thrace, hist. reg., Eur.	H13	26
Thrakikó Pélagos, Grc.	C8	28
Three Forks, Mt., U.S.	E15	136
Three Gorges Dam, dam, China	F4	42
Three Hills, Ab., Can.	E17	138
Three Hummock Island, i., Austl.	n12	77a
Three Kings Islands, is., N.Z.	B5	80
Three Mile Plains, N.S., Can.	F12	110
Three Points, Cape, c., Ghana	I4	64
Three Rivers, Mi., U.S.	G4	112
Three Rivers, Tx., U.S.	F9	130
Three Sisters, mtn., Or., U.S.	F5	136
Three Sisters Islands, is., Sol. Is.	f10	79b
Three Springs, Austl.	E3	74
Thrissur see Trichūr, India	F3	53
Throssel, Lake, l., Austl.	E4	74
Thu, Cu Lao, i., Viet.	G9	48
Thuan Chau, Viet.	B6	48
Thu Dau Mot, Viet.	G8	48
Thuin, Bel.	D13	14
Thule (Qaanaaq), Grnld.	B12	141
Thun, Switz.	D4	22
Thun Chang, Thai.	C5	48
Thunder Bay, On., Can.	C9	118
Thunder Bay, b., On., Can.	C9	118
Thunderbird, Lake, res., Ok., U.S.	F11	128
Thunderbolt, Ga., U.S.	D4	116
Thunder Butte Creek, stm., S.D., U.S.	B10	126
Thunder Creek, stm., Sk., Can.	D7	124
Thuner See, l., Switz.	D4	22
Thung Salaeng Luang National Park, p.o.i., Thai.	D5	48
Thung Wa, Thai.	I4	48
Thüringen, state, Ger.	F7	16
Thüringer Wald, mts., Ger.	F6	16
Thuringia see Thüringen, state, Ger.	F7	16
Thurles, Ire.	I5	12
Thurmont, Md., U.S.	E8	114
Thursday Island, Austl.	B8	74
Thurso, Scot., U.K.	C9	12
Thurston Island, i., Ant.	C31	81
Thusis, Switz.	D6	22
Thylungra, Austl.	F4	76
Thyolo, Mwi.	D5	68
Thysville see Mbanza-Ngungu, D.R.C.	F3	66
Tiachiv, Ukr.	A10	26
Tianchang, China	E8	42
Tiandeng, China	J2	42
Tiandong, China	J2	42
Tian'e, China	I2	42
Tiangang, China	C7	38
Tianguá, Braz.	B5	88
Tianjin (Tientsin), China	B7	42
Tianjin, state, China	B7	42
Tianjun, China	D4	36
Tianlin, China	I2	42
Tian Ling, mtn., China	B8	38
Tianmen, China	F5	42
Tianqiaoling, China	C8	38
Tianshifu, China	D6	38
Tianshui, China	D1	42
Tiantai, China	G9	42
Tiantang, China	J4	42
Tianwangsi, China	F8	42
Tianyang, China	J2	42
Tianzhen, China	A6	42
Tianzhu, China	D5	36
Tianzhu, China	H3	42
Tiarei, Fr. Poly.	v22	78h
Tiaro, Austl.	E9	76
Tiassalé, C. Iv.	H4	64
Ti'avea, Samoa	g12	79c
Tibaji, stm., Braz.	A12	92
Tibal-og, Phil.	G5	52
Tibasti, Sarīr, des., Libya	C3	62
Tibati, Cam.	C2	66
Tibbie, Al., U.S.	F10	122
Tiber see Tevere, stm., Italy	H9	22
Tiberias, Lake see Kinneret, Yam, l., Isr.	F6	58
Tibesti, mts., Afr.	C3	62
Tibet see Xizang, state, China	B5	46
Tibet, Plateau of see Qing Zang Gaoyuan, plat., China	B6	46
Tiblawan, Phil.	G6	52
Tibnīn, Leb.	E6	58
Tibooburra, Austl.	G4	76
Tiburón, Cabo, c.	C3	86
Tiburón, Isla, i., Mex.	G6	98
Tiča, Jazovir, res., Blg.	F13	26
Ticao Island, i., Phil.	D4	52
Tîchît, Maur.	F3	64
Ticino, stm., Eur.	D14	18
Tickfaw, stm., U.S.	G8	122
Ticonderoga, N.Y., U.S.	G3	110
Ticul, Mex.	B3	102
Tidioute, Pa., U.S.	C6	114
Tidiquin, Jbel, mtn., Mor.	C4	64
Tidjikja, Maur.	F2	64
Tiébissou, C. Iv.	H3	64
T'iehling see Tieling, China	C5	38
Tiel, Neth.	C14	14
Tieli, China	B10	36
Tieling, China	C5	38
Tielt, Bel.	C12	14
Tiémé, C. Iv.	H3	64
T'ienching see Tianjin, China	B7	42
Tien Giang see Mekong, stm., Asia	F9	46
Tien Shan, mts., Asia	F13	32
T'ienshui see Tianshui, China	D1	42
Tientsin see Tianjin, China	B7	42
Tientsin see Tianjin, state, China	B7	42
Tien Yen, Viet.	B8	48
Tie Plant, Ms., U.S.	D9	122
Tierp, Swe.	F7	8
Tierra Amarilla, Chile	C2	92
Tierra Blanca, Mex.	F10	100
Tierra Blanca, Mex.	G3	130
Tierra Blanca Creek, stm., U.S.	G6	128
Tierra de Campos, reg., Spain	C5	20
Tierra del Fuego, Arg.	J3	90
Tierra del Fuego, i., S.A.	J3	90
Tiétar, stm., Spain	E5	20
Tietê, Braz.	L2	88
Tietê, stm., Braz.	D6	90
Tiéti, N. Cal.	m15	79d
Tiffany Mountain, mtn., Wa., U.S.	B7	136
Tiffin, Oh., U.S.	C2	114
Tifton, Ga., U.S.	E2	116
Tiga, Île, i., N. Cal.	m16	79d
Tigalda Island, i., Ak., U.S.	F7	140
Tigapuluh, Pegunungan, mts., Indon.	D3	50
Tighina, Mol.	C16	26
Tigil', Russia	E20	34
Tignall, Ga., U.S.	C3	116
Tignish, P.E., Can.	D12	110
Tigoda, stm., Russia	A14	10
Tigre, Col.	F7	86
Tigre, stm., Peru	D2	84
Tigre, stm., Ven.	C10	86
Tigris (Dicle) (Dijlah), stm., Asia	C5	56
Tiguentourine, Alg.	D6	64
Tihany, hist., Hung.	C4	26
Tihert, Alg.	B5	64
Tihon, Russia	G22	8
Tihookeanskij, Russia	C10	38
Tihoreck, Russia	E6	32
Tihua see Ürümqi, China	C2	36
Tihuatlán, Mex.	E10	100
Tihvin, Russia	A16	10
Tijuana, Mex.	K8	134
Tijuana, stm., N.A.	K9	134
Tijucas, Braz.	C13	92
Tijucas do Sul, Braz.	B13	92
Tijuco, stm., Braz.	J1	88
Tikal, hist., Guat.	D3	102
Tikal, Parque Nacional, p.o.i., Guat.	D3	102
Tikrīt, Iraq	C5	56
Tikša, Russia	D15	8
Tikšeozero, ozero, l., Russia	C14	8
Tiksi, Russia	B14	34
Tiladummati Atoll, at., Mald.	h12	46a
Tilburg, Neth.	C14	14
Tilbury, On., Can.	F7	112
Tilcha, Austl.	G3	76
Tilden, Il., U.S.	F8	120
Tilden, Ne., U.S.	E15	126
Tilden, Tx., U.S.	F9	130
Tilhar, India	D7	54
Tilimsen, Alg.	C4	64
Tilin, Mya.	B2	48
Tillabéri, Niger	G5	64
Tilley, Ab., Can.	F19	138
Tillia, Niger	F5	64
Tillmans Corner, Al., U.S.	G10	122
Tillson, N.Y., U.S.	C11	114
Tillsonburg, On., Can.	F9	112
Tílos, i., Grc.	G10	28
Tilpa, Austl.	H5	76
Tilton, N.H., U.S.	G5	110
Tiltonsville, Oh., U.S.	D5	114
Tima, Egypt	L2	58
Timaná, Col.	G3	86
Timanskij krjaž, hills, Russia	B8	32
Timaru, N.Z.	G4	80
Timbalier Bay, b., La., U.S.	H8	122
Timbaúba, Braz.	D8	88
Timbavati Game Reserve, S. Afr.	D10	70
Timbedgha, Maur.	F3	64
Timber Lake, S.D., U.S.	B11	126
Timbiras, Braz.	C4	88
Timbó, Braz.	C13	92
Timbo, Lib.	H3	64
Timbuktu see Tombouctou, Mali	F4	64
Timétrine, Mali	F4	64
Timétrine, mts., Mali	F4	64
Timimoun, Alg.	D5	64
Timirist, Râs, c., Maur.	F1	64
Timirjazevo, Russia	E4	10
Timiș, state, Rom.	D8	26
Timiș (Tamiš), stm., Eur.	D7	26
Timiskaming, Lake (Témiscamingue, Lac), res., Can.	B10	112
Timișoara, Rom.	D8	26
Timmendorfer Strand, Ger.	B7	16
Timmins, On., Can.	F14	106
Timmonsville, S.C., U.S.	B6	116
Timms Hill, mtn., Wi., U.S.	F8	118
Timna' see Mikhrot Timna', hist., Isr.	I5	58
Timok, stm., Eur.	E9	26
Timon, Braz.	C4	88
Timor, i., Indon.	G8	44
Timor Sea	K15	142
Timošino, Russia	H21	8
Timotes, Ven.	C6	86
Timpanogos Cave National Monument, p.o.i., Ut., U.S.	C5	132
Timpton, stm., Russia	E14	34
Timšer, Russia	B9	32
Tims Ford Lake, res., Tn., U.S.	B12	122
Tina, stm., S. Afr.	G9	70
Tîna, Khalîg el- (Pelusium Bay), b., Egypt	G3	58
Tinaca Point, c., Phil.	H5	52
Tinambung, Indon.	E11	50
Tinapagee, Austl.	G5	76
Tinaquillo, Ven.	C7	86
Tindivanam, India	E4	53
Tindouf, Alg.	D3	64
Tineba, Pegunungan, mts., Indon.	D12	50
Tineg, stm., Phil.	B3	52
Ting, stm., China	I7	42
Tinggi, Pulau, i., Malay.	K7	48
Tingha, Austl.	G8	76
Tinghert, Ḥamādat (Tinghert, Plateau du), plat., Afr.	D7	64
Tinghert, Plateau du (Tinghert, Ḥamādat), plat., Afr.	D6	64
Tinghsien see Dingxian, China	B6	42
Tinglev, Den.	B5	16
Tingo María, Peru	E2	84
Tingri, China	D11	54
Tingri see Dinggyê, China	D11	54
Tinguiririca, Volcán, vol., Chile	G2	92
Tinharé, Ilha de, i., Braz.	G6	88
Tinh Bien, Viet.	G7	48
Tinian, i., N. Mar. Is.	B5	72
Tinjar, stm., Malay.	B9	50
Tínos, Grc.	F8	28
Tínos, i., Grc.	F8	28
Tinsley, Ms., U.S.	E8	122
Tinsukia, India	C8	46
Tintagel, B.C., Can.	B5	138
Tintina, Arg.	C6	92
Tintinara, Austl.	J3	76
Tio, Erit.	E8	62
Tiobrad Árann see Tipperary, Ire.	I4	12
Tioga, N.D., U.S.	F11	124
Tiojala, Fin.	F10	8
Tioman, Pulau, i., Malay.	K7	48
Tionesta, Pa., U.S.	C6	114
Tipasa, Alg.	H13	20
Tipitapa, Nic.	F4	102
Tippecanoe, stm., In., U.S.	H3	112
Tipperary, Ire.	I4	12
Tipperary, state, Ire.	I5	12
Tipton, Ca., U.S.	G6	134
Tipton, Ia., U.S.	C6	120
Tipton, Mo., U.S.	F5	120
Tipton, Ok., U.S.	G9	128
Tipton, Mount, mtn., Az., U.S.	H2	132
Tiptonville, Tn., U.S.	H8	120
Tip Top Mountain, mtn., On., Can.	F13	106
Tiptūr, India	E3	53
Tiputini, stm., Ec.	H4	86
Tīra, Isr.	F5	58
Tīrān, i., Sau. Ar.	K5	58
Tiran, Strait of, strt.	K5	58
Tirana see Tiranë, Alb.	C13	24
Tiranë, Alb.	C13	24
Tirano, Italy	D7	22
Tiraspol, Mol.	C16	26
Tire, Tur.	E10	28
Tiree, i., Scot., U.K.	E6	12
Tirich Mīr, mtn., Pak.	B11	56
Tirna, stm., India	B3	53
Tírnavos, Grc.	D5	28
Tirodi, India	H7	54
Tirol, state, Aus.	C8	22
Tiros, Braz.	J3	88
Tirso, stm., Italy	E2	24
Tīrthahalli, India	E2	53
Tiruchchirāppalli, India	F4	53
Tiruchengodu, India	F3	53
Tirukkalukkunram, India	E5	53
Tirukkovilūr, India	F4	53
Tiruliai, Lith.	E6	10
Tirunelveli, India	G3	53
Tirupati, India	E4	53
Tiruppattūr, India	E4	53
Tiruppur, India	F3	53
Tirūr, India	F2	53
Tirutturaippūndi, India	F4	53
Tiruvalla, India	G3	53
Tiruvannāmalai, India	E4	53
Tirūvottiyūr, India	E5	53
Tiruvur, India	C5	53
Tisa (Tisza) (Tysa), stm., Eur.	D7	26
Tisaiyanvilai, India	G3	53
Tisdale, Sk., Can.	B9	124
Tishomingo, Ok., U.S.	C2	122
Tisīyah, Syria	F7	58
Tiskilwa, Il., U.S.	C8	120
Tisovec, Slov.	H15	16
Tīsta, stm., Asia	F12	54
Tisza (Tisa) (Tysa), stm., Eur.	C7	26
Tiszaföldvár, Hung.	C7	26
Tiszaújváros, Hung.	B7	26
Tiszavasvári, Hung.	A8	26
Titaf, Alg.	D4	64
Tit-Ary, Russia	B14	34
Titicaca, Lake, l., S.A.	G4	84
Titilāgarh, India	H9	54
Titonka, Ia., U.S.	H4	118
Titov Veles, Mac.	B4	28
Titran, Nor.	E2	8
Tittabawassee, stm., Mi., U.S.	E5	112
Tittmoning, Ger.	H8	16
Titule, D.R.C.	D5	66
Titusville, Fl., U.S.	H5	116
Titusville, Pa., U.S.	C6	114
Tiuni, India	C6	54
Tivaouane, Sen.	F1	64
Tiverton, Eng., U.K.	K9	12
Tivoli, Italy	I9	22
Tivoli, Tx., U.S.	F11	130
Tiyās, Syria	D8	58
Tizimín, Mex.	B3	102
Tizi-Ouzou, Alg.	B5	64
Tizmant el-Zawâya, Egypt	I1	58
Tiznados, stm., Ven.	C8	86
Tiznit, Mor.	D3	64
Tjörn, i., Swe.	G4	8
Tjukalinsk, Russia	C12	32
Tjul'gan, Russia	D9	32
Tjumen', Russia	C10	32
Tjung, stm., Russia	D13	34
Tjuva-Guba, Russia	B15	8
Tlacotalpan, Mex.	F11	100
Tlacotepec, Mex.	G9	100
Tlahualilo de Zaragoza, Mex.	B7	100
Tlalnepantla, Mex.	F9	100
Tlaltenango de Sánchez Román, Mex.	E7	100
Tlapaneco, stm., Mex.	G9	100
Tlaquepaque, Mex.	E7	100
Tlaxcala, state, Mex.	F9	100
Tlaxcala de Xicohténcatl, Mex.	F9	100
Tłuszcz, Pol.	D17	16
Tmassah, Libya	B3	62
Tnâot, stm., Camb.	G7	48
Toa Alta, P.R.	B3	104a
Toa Baja, P.R.	B3	104a
Toachi, stm., Ec.	H2	86
Toahayana, Mex.	B5	100
Toamasina, Madag.	D8	68
Toba, Japan	E9	40
Toba, Danau, l., Indon.	K4	48
Tobago, i., Trin.	r13	105f
Toba Inlet, b., B.C., Can.	F6	138
Toba Kākar Range, mts., Pak.	C10	56
Tobarra, Spain	F9	20
Tobas, Arg.	D6	92
Toba Tek Singh, Pak.	C4	54
Tobejuba, Isla, i., Ven.	C11	86
Tobermorey, Austl.	D7	74
Tobermory, On., Can.	C8	112
Tobermory, Scot., U.K.	E6	12
Tobias, Ne., U.S.	G15	126
Tobias Barreto, Braz.	F6	88
Tobin, Mount, mtn., Nv., U.S.	C8	134
Tobique, stm., N.B., Can.	C9	110
Toboali, Indon.	E5	50
Tobol, Kaz.	D10	32
Tobol, stm., Asia	C11	32
Toboli, Indon.	D12	50
Tobol'sk, Russia	C11	32
Toboso, Phil.	E4	52
Tobruk see Ṭubruq, Libya	A4	62
Tobseda, Russia	B25	8
Tobyhanna, Pa., U.S.	C10	114
Tobyš, stm., Russia	C24	8
Tocantínia, Braz.	E1	88
Tocantinópolis, Braz.	D2	88
Tocantins, state, Braz.	F8	84
Tocantins, stm., Braz.	D8	84
Tocantins, stm., Braz.	F1	88
Tocantinzinho, stm., Braz.	H1	88
Tochcha Lake, l., B.C., Can.	B5	138
Tochigi, Japan	C12	40
Tochigi, state, Japan	C12	40
Tochio, Japan	B12	40
Toco, Trin.	s13	105f
Tocoa, Hond.	E5	102
Toconao, Chile	D3	90
Tocopilla, Chile	D2	90
Tocuco, stm., Ven.	C5	86
Tocumwal, Austl.	J5	76
Tocuyo, stm., Ven.	B7	86
Tocuyo de la Costa, Ven.	B7	86
Toda Rāisingh, India	E5	54
Todi, Italy	H9	22
Todos os Santos, Baia de, b., Braz.	G6	88
Todos Santos, Bol.	C3	90
Todos Santos, Mex.	D3	100

Name / Map Ref. / Page

Tungabhadra Reservoir, res., India D2 53
Tungaru, Sudan E6 62
T'ungchou see Tongxian, China B7 42
T'ungch'uan see Tongchuan, China D3 42
Tung Hai see East China Sea, Asia F9 36
T'unghsien see Tongxian, China B7 42
T'unghua see Tonghua, China D6 38
Tunghwa see Tonghua, China D6 38
Tungkal, stm., Indon. D3 50
Tungku, Malay. A11 50
Tungla, Nic. F5 102
T'ungliao see Tongliao, China C4 38
Tungsha Tao (Pratas Island), i., Tai. K7 42
Tungshih, Tai. I9 42
Tungsten, N.T., Can. C5 106
Tungurahua, state, Ec. H2 86
Tungurahua, vol., Ec. H2 86
Tuni, India C6 53
Tunia, stm., Col. G5 86
Tunis, Tun. H4 24
Tunis, Golfe de, b., Tun. G4 24
Tunis, Gulf of see Tunis, Golfe de, b., Tun. G4 24
Tunisia, ctry., Afr. C6 64
Tunisie see Tunisia, ctry., Afr. C6 64
Tunja, Col. E5 86
Tunkhannock, Pa., U.S. C9 114
Tunliu, China C5 42
Tunnel Hill, Ga., U.S. C13 122
Tunnelton, W.V., U.S. E6 114
Tunnsjøen, l., Nor. D5 8
Tuntum, Braz. C3 88
Tunu see Østgrønland, state, Grnld. C18 141
Tununak, Ak., U.S. D6 140
Tunuyán, Arg. F3 92
Tunuyán, stm., Arg. F4 92
Tunxi, China G8 42
Tuo, stm., China G1 42
Tuo, stm., China E7 42
Tuobalage, China C12 54
Tuobuja, Russia D13 34
Tuoj-Haja, Russia B20 32
Tuokusidawan Ling, mtn., China A6 46
Tuolumne, can., Ca., U.S. F5 134
Tuong Duong, Viet. C7 48
Tuotuo, stm., China A13 54
Tupã, Braz. D6 90
Tupaciguara, Braz. J1 88
Tupanciretã, Braz. D10 92
Tuparro, stm., Col. E7 86
Tupelo, Ms., U.S. C10 122
Tupelo, Ok., U.S. C2 122
Tupik, Russia F13 34
Tupinambarana, Ilha, i., Braz. D6 84
Tupiraçaba, Braz. H1 88
Tupiza, Bol. D3 90
Tupper Lake, N.Y., U.S. F2 110
Tupungato, Cerro, mtn., S.A. F2 92
Tuquan, China B9 36
Túquerres, Col. G3 86
Tura, India F13 54
Tura, Russia B18 32
Tura, stm., Russia C11 32
Turabah, Sau. Ar. E5 56
Turaiyūr, India F4 53
Turan, Russia D16 32
Turāq al-'Ilab, hills, Syria E9 58
Turaŭ, Bela. H10 10
Turbaco, Col. B4 86
Turbat, Pak. D9 56
Turbo, Col. C3 86
Turčasovo, Russia E18 8
Turda, Rom. C10 26
Turek, Pol. D14 16
Turfan see Turpan, China C2 36
Turfan Depression see Turpan Pendi, depr., China C2 36
Turgaj, Kaz. E10 32
Turgaj, stm., Kaz. E10 32
Turgajskaja ložbina, reg., Kaz. D10 32
Turgajskoe plato, plat., Kaz. D10 32
Turgay see Turgaj, stm., Kaz. E10 32
Turginovo, Russia D18 10
Turgoš, Russia A18 10
Turgutlu, Tur. E10 28
Türi, Est. B8 10
Túria (Túria), stm., Spain D9 20
Túria (Turia), stm., Spain D9 20
Turiaçu, Braz. A3 88
Turiaçu, stm., Braz. B3 88
Turimiquire, Cerro, mtn., Ven. B10 86
Turin, Ab., Can. F18 138
Turin see Torino, Italy E4 22
Turinsk, Russia C10 32
Turka, Ukr. G19 16
Turkana, Lake see Rudolf, Lake, l., Afr. D7 66
Turkestan, Kaz. F11 32
Turkestanskij hrebet, mts., Asia B10 56
Túrkeve, Hung. B7 26
Turkey, ctry., Asia B3 56
Turkey, stm., Ia., U.S. I7 118
Turkey Creek, stm., Ne., U.S. K2 118
Turkish Republic of Northern Cyprus see Cyprus, North, ctry., Asia C4 58
Turkmenbaši, Turkmen. B7 56
Turkmenia see Turkmenistan, ctry., Asia B8 56
Turkmenistan, ctry., Asia B8 56
Türkoğlu, Tur. A7 58
Turks and Caicos Islands, dep., N.A. A12 102
Turks Island Passage, strt., T./C. Is. B12 102
Turks Islands, is., T./C. Is. B12 102
Turku (Åbo), Fin. F9 8
Turku ja Pori, state, Fin. F10 8
Turkwel, stm., Kenya D7 66
Turley, Ok., U.S. H2 120
Turlock, Ca., U.S. F5 134
Turmalina, Braz. I4 88
Turmantas, Lith. E9 10
Turnagain, stm., B.C., Can. D5 106
Turneffe Islands, is., Belize D4 102
Turner, Mt., U.S. F5 124
Turner, Or., U.S. F4 136
Turners Falls, Ma., U.S. B13 114
Turnhout, Bel. C13 14
Turnov, Czech Rep. F11 16
Turnu Măgurele, Rom. F11 26
Turnu Roşu, Pasul, p., Rom. D11 26
Turočak, Russia D15 32
Turon, Ks., U.S. D10 128
Turpan, China C2 36
Turpan Pendi (Turfan Depression), depr., China C2 36
Turquino, Pico, mtn., Cuba C9 102
Turrell, Ar., U.S. B8 122
Turret Peak, mtn., Az., U.S. I5 132
Turtle, stm., Mb., Can. D14 124
Turtle-Flambeau Flowage, res., Wi., U.S. E8 118
Turtle Islands, is., S.L. H2 64
Turtle Lake, N.D., U.S. G13 124
Turtle Lake, Wi., U.S. F6 118
Turu, stm., Russia B18 32
Turuhan, stm., Russia A14 32
Turuhansk, Russia C6 34
Turvo, Braz. D13 92
Turvo, stm., Braz. K1 88
Turwi, stm., Zimb. B10 70
Turzovka, Slov. G14 16
Tuscaloosa, Al., U.S. D11 122
Tuscaloosa, Lake, res., Al., U.S. D11 122
Tuscany see Toscana, state, Italy G8 22
Tuscarora Mountain, mts., Pa., U.S. D8 114
Tuscola, Tx., U.S. B8 130
Tuscumbia, Al., U.S. C11 122
Tuscumbia, Mo., U.S. F5 120
Tuskegee, Al., U.S. E13 122
Tustumena Lake, l., Ak., U.S. D9 140
Tutaev, Russia C22 10
Tuticorin, India G4 53
Tutin, Yugo. F7 26
Tutóia, Braz. B4 88
Tutoko, Mount, mtn., N.Z. G3 80
Tutrakan, Blg. E13 26
Tuttle, N.D., U.S. G14 124
Tuttle Creek Lake, res., Ks., U.S. B12 128
Tutuala, Indon. G8 44
Tutuila, i., Am. Sam. h12 79c
Tutupaca, Volcán, vol., Peru G3 84
Tutwiler, Ms., U.S. C8 122
Tutzing, Ger. I7 16
Tuul, stm., Mong. B6 36
Tuva, state, Russia D16 32
Tuvalu, ctry., Oc. D8 72
Tuvuca, i., Fiji p20 79e
Ţuwayq, Jabal, mts., Sau. Ar. E6 56
Tuxford, Sk., Can. D8 124
Tuxpan, Mex. E6 100
Tuxpan de Rodríguez Cano, Mex. E10 100
Tuxtepec, Mex. F10 100
Tuxtla Gutiérrez, Mex. G12 100
Túy see Tui, Spain B2 20
Tuy, stm., Ven. B8 86
Tuyen Hoa, Viet. D8 48
Tuyen Quang, Viet. B7 48
Tuy Hoa, Viet. F9 48
Tuyün see Duyun, China H2 42
Tuyūr, Burj aţ-, hill, Sudan C5 62
Tuz, Iraq C5 56
Tuz Gölü, l., Tur. B3 56
Tuzigoot National Monument, p.o.i., Az., U.S. I4 132
Tuzla, Bos. E5 26
Tuzly, Ukr. D17 26
Tvardiţa, Mol. C15 26
Tver' (Kalinin), Russia D18 10
Tverca, stm., Russia D18 10
Tverskaja oblast', co., Russia D16 10
Tweed, On., Can. D12 112
Tweed, stm., U.K. F10 12
Tweed Heads, Austl. G9 76
Twee Rivieren, S. Afr. E5 70
Twelve Mile Lake, l., Sk., Can. E7 124
Twenthekanaal, can., Neth. B15 14
Twentynine Palms, Ca., U.S. I9 134
Twin Buttes, mtn., Or., U.S. F4 136
Twin Buttes Reservoir, res., Tx., U.S. C7 130
Twin City, Ga., U.S. D3 116
Twin Falls, Id., U.S. H12 136
Twin Lakes, Ga., U.S. F2 116
Twin Lakes, Wi., U.S. B9 120
Twinsburg, Oh., U.S. C4 114
Twisp, Wa., U.S. B6 136
Twitchell Reservoir, res., Ca., U.S. H5 134
Twitya, stm., N.T., Can. C5 106
Two Butte Creek, stm., Co., U.S. D6 128
Twofold Bay, b., Austl. K7 76
Two Harbors, Mn., U.S. D7 118
Two Medicine, stm., Mt., U.S. B14 136
Two Rivers, Wi., U.S. D2 112
Tybee Island, Ga., U.S. D5 116
Tychy, Pol. F14 16
Tyczyn, Pol. G18 16
Tye, Tx., U.S. B8 130
Tygda, Russia F14 34
Tyler, Mn., U.S. G2 118
Tyler, Tx., U.S. E3 122
Tylertown, Ms., U.S. F8 122
Tylihul, stm., Ukr. B17 26
Tylihul's'kyi lyman, l., Ukr. B17 26
Tym, stm., Russia C14 32
Tymovskoe, Russia F17 34
Tynda, Russia E13 34
Tyndall, S.D., U.S. D15 126
Tyndaris, hist., Italy F8 24
Tynemouth, Eng., U.K. F11 12
Tynset, Nor. E4 8
Tyre see Şūr, Leb. E6 58
Tyrifjorden, l., Nor. F3 8
Tyrma, Russia F15 34
Tyrma, stm., Russia F15 34
Tyrone, Ok., U.S. E7 128
Tyrrell, Lake, l., Austl. J4 76
Tyrrhenian Sea, Eur. G11 6
Tysa (Tisza) (Tisza), stm., Eur. A10 26
Tysnesøya, i., Nor. F1 8
Tysse, Nor. F1 8
Tytuvėnai, Lith. E6 10
Ty Ty, Ga., U.S. E2 116
Tyva see Tuva, state, Russia D16 32
Tzaneen, S. Afr. C9 70
Tzekung see Zigong, China F5 36
Tzeliutsing see Zigong, China F5 36
Tzucacab, Mex. B3 102
Tzukung see Zigong, China F5 36
Tzupo see Boshan, China C7 42
Tzupo see Zibo, China C8 42

U

Uatumã, stm., Braz. D6 84
Uauá, Braz. E6 88
Uaupés, Braz. H8 86
Uaupés (Vaupés), stm., S.A. G7 86
Uaxactún, hist., Guat. D3 102
Ubá, Braz. K4 88
Ubagan, stm., Kaz. D10 32
Ubaidullaganj, India G6 54
Ubaitaba, Braz. H6 88
Ubajara, Parque Nacional de, p.o.i., Braz. B5 88
Ubangi (Oubangui), stm., Afr. E3 66
Ubatã, Braz. H6 88
Ubaté, Col. E5 86
Ubatuba, Braz. L3 88
Ube, Japan F4 40
Úbeda, Spain F7 20
Uberaba, Braz. J2 88
Uberlândia, Braz. J1 88
Überlingen, Ger. I5 16
Ubiña, Peña, mtn., Spain B5 20
Ubl'a, Slov. H18 16
Ubly, Mi., U.S. E7 112
Ubombo, S. Afr. E11 70
Ubon Ratchathani, Thai. E7 48
Ubrique, Spain H5 20
Ubundu, D.R.C. E5 66
Učaly, Russia D9 32
Učami, Russia B17 32
Učaral, Kaz. E14 32
Ucayali, stm., Peru D3 84
Uchinoura, Japan H4 40
Uchiura-wan, b., Japan C14 38
Uchiza, Peru E2 84
Uchoa, Braz. K1 88
Uckermark, reg., Ger. C9 16
Ucon, Id., U.S. G15 136
Učur, stm., Russia E15 34
Uda, stm., Russia C17 32
Uda, stm., Russia F15 34
Udagamandalam, India F3 53
Udaipur, India F4 54
Udalguri, India E13 54
Udall, Ks., U.S. D11 128
Udamalpet, India F3 53
Udankudi, India G4 53
Udaquiola, Arg. H8 92
Udaypur, Nepal E11 54
Uddevalla, Swe. G4 8
Uddjaur, l., Swe. D8 8
Udgīr, India B3 53
Udhampur, India B5 54
Udimskij, Russia F21 8
Udine, Italy D10 22
Udmurtia see Udmurtija, state, Russia C8 32
Udmurtija, state, Russia C8 32
Udokan, hrebet, mts., Russia E12 34
Udomlja, Russia C17 10
Udon Thani, Thai. D6 48
Udskaja guba, b., Russia F16 34
Udskoe, Russia F15 34
Udupi, India E2 53
Udža, Russia B12 34
Ueckermünde, Ger. C10 16
Ueda, Japan C11 40
Uele, stm., D.R.C. D4 66
Uelen, Russia C26 34
Uel'kal', Russia C25 34
Uelzen, Ger. C6 16
Ueno, Japan E9 40
Uere, stm., D.R.C. D5 66
Uetersen, Ger. C5 16
Ufa, Russia D9 32
Ufa, stm., Russia C9 32
Uffenheim, Ger. G6 16
Ugab, stm., Nmb. E2 68
Uganda, ctry., Afr. D6 66
Uğarčin, Blg. F11 26
Ugarit, hist., Syria C6 58
Ugashik, Ak., U.S. E8 140
Uglegorsk, Russia G17 34
Uglekamensk, Russia C10 38
Uglič, Russia C21 10
Ugljan, Otok, i., Cro. F12 22
Ugodiči, Russia C22 10
Ugodskij Zavod, Russia E19 10
Ugra, stm., Russia F18 10
Uherské Hradiště, Czech Rep. G13 16
Uherský Brod, Czech Rep. H13 16
Uhlenhorst, Nmb. C3 70
Uhra, stm., Russia B22 10
Uhta, Russia F18 8
Uhta, Russia B8 32
Uige, Ang. B1 68
Uil, Kaz. E8 32
Uinebona, stm., Ven. E10 86
Uinta Mountains, mts., Ut., U.S. C6 132
Uiraúna, Braz. D6 88
Uisŏng, Kor., S. C1 40
Uitenhage, S. Afr. H7 70
Uithuizermeeden, Neth. A15 14
Uj, stm., Asia D10 32
Ujandina, stm., Russia C17 34
Ujar, Russia C16 32
Ujelang, at., Marsh. Is. C7 72
Újfehértó, Hung. B8 26
Ujhāni, India D7 54
Uji, Japan E8 40
Uji-guntō, is., Japan H2 40
Ujiji, Tan. E5 66
Ujjain, India G5 54
Ujung, Indon. G12 50
Ujunggenteng, Indon. G5 50
Ujungkulon National Park, p.o.i., Indon. G4 50
Ujungpandang (Makasar), Indon. F11 50
Uk, Russia C17 32
Uka, Russia E21 34
Ukerewe Island, i., Tan. E6 66
Ukiah, Ca., U.S. D2 134
Uki Ni Masi Island, i., Sol. Is. f9 79b
Ukmergė, Lith. E7 10
Ukraine, ctry., Eur. F15 6
Ukui, Indon. D3 50
Ukyr, Russia G10 34
Ula, Bela. E12 10
Ulaanbaatar, Mong. B6 36
Ulaangom, Mong. G7 34
Ulan, Austl. I7 76
Ulan Bator see Ulaanbaatar, Mong. B6 36
Ulan Buh Shamo, des., China A2 42
Ulan-Burgasy, hrebet, mts., Russia F10 34
Ulanów, Pol. F18 16
Ulansuhai Nur, l., China A3 42
Ulan-Ude, Russia F10 34
Ulawa Island, i., Sol. Is. e9 79b
Ulawun, Mount (The Father), vol., Pap. N. Gui. b5 79a
Ulchin, Kor., S. B2 40
Ulcinj, Yugo. H6 26
Ulco, S. Afr. F7 70
Uldz, stm., Asia B8 36
Uleåborg see Oulu, Fin. D11 8
Ulen, Mn., U.S. D2 118
Ulety, Russia F11 34
Ulëz, Alb. C13 24
Ulhāsnagar, India B1 53
Ul'ianovka, Ukr. A17 26
Uliastay, Mong. B4 36
Ulindi, stm., D.R.C. E5 66
Ulja, Russia E17 34
Uljanovo, Russia G18 10
Uljanovsk, Russia D7 32
Ul'kan, Russia C19 32
Ulla, stm., Spain B2 20
Ulladulla, Austl. J8 76
Ullin, Il., U.S. G8 120
Ullŭng-do, i., Kor., S. B3 40
Ulm, Ger. H5 16
Ulm, Mt., U.S. C15 136
Ulmarra, Austl. G9 76
Ulmeni, Rom. D13 26
Ulongué, Moz. C5 68
Ulricehamn, Swe. H5 8
Ulsan, Kor., S. D2 40
Ulster, hist. reg., Eur. G5 12
Ulster Canal, can., Eur. G5 12
Ulu, Indon. E8 44
Ulu, Russia D14 34
Ulúa, stm., Hond. E3 102
Ulubat Gölü, l., Tur. C11 28
Uluborlu, Tur. E13 28
Uluçınar, Tur. B7 58
Uludağ, mtn., Tur. C12 28
Uludağ Yarımdası Milli Parkı, p.o.i., Tur. C12 28
Ulukışla, Tur. A5 58
Ulul, i., Micron. C5 72
Ulungur, stm., China B2 36
Ulungur Hu, l., China B2 36
Ulunhan, Russia F11 34
Uluru (Ayers Rock), mtn., Austl. E6 74
Ulutau, gory, mts., Kaz. E11 32
Ulverston, Eng., U.K. G9 12
Ulverstone, Austl. n12 77a
Ulysses, Ks., U.S. D7 128
Uma, China F13 34
Umán, Mex. B3 102
Umanak, Grnld. C15 141
Umanak Fjord, b., Grnld. C15 141
Umaria, India G8 54
Umarizal, Braz. D7 88
Umarkot, Pak. F2 54
Umatac, Guam j9 78c
Umatilla, Fl., U.S. H4 116
Umatilla, Or., U.S. E7 136
Umatilla, stm., Or., U.S. E7 136
Umatilla, Lake, res., U.S. E6 136
Umba, Russia C16 8
Umbertide, Italy G9 22
Umboi Island, i., Pap. N. Gui. b4 79a
Umbria, state, Italy G9 22
Umbukul, Pap. N. Gui. a4 79a
Umbuzero, ozero, l., Russia C16 8
Umeå, Swe. E9 8
Umeälven, stm., Swe. D8 8
Umfolozi Game Reserve, S. Afr. F10 70
Umfors, Swe. C6 8
Umfreville Lake, res., On., Can. A3 118
Umkomaas, S. Afr. G10 70
Umm al-Arānib, Libya B2 62
Umm al-Jimāl, Khirbat, hist., Jord. F7 58
Umm al-Qaywayn, U.A.E. D8 56
Umm as-Sa'd, hist., Syria E7 58
Umm Bel, Sudan E5 62
Umm Durmān (Omdurman), Sudan D6 62
Umm el Fahm, Isr. F6 58
Umm Lajj, Sau. Ar. D4 56
Umm Mitmam, sand, Egypt H3 58
Umm Omeiyid, Rās, mtn., Egypt K3 58
Umm Ruwābah, Sudan E6 62
Umm Sayyālah, Sudan E6 62
Umnak Island, i., Ak., U.S. g25 140a
Umpqua, stm., Or., U.S. G3 136
Umpulo, Ang. C2 68
'Umrān, Yemen F5 56
Umraniye, Tur. D14 28
Umred, India H7 54
Umreth, India G4 54
Umtata, S. Afr. G9 70
Umuarama, Braz. A11 92
Umzingwani, stm., Zimb. B9 70
Umzinto, S. Afr. G10 70
Una, Braz. H6 88
Una, India H3 54
Una, stm., Eur. E13 22
Unac, stm., Bos. E3 26
Unadilla, Ga., U.S. D2 116
Unadilla, N.Y., U.S. B10 114
Unaí, Braz. I2 88
Unalakleet, Ak., U.S. D7 140
Unalaska, Ak., U.S. F6 140
Unalaska Island, i., Ak., U.S. F6 140
Unare, stm., Ven. C9 86
'Unayzah, Sau. Ar. D5 56
Uncia, Bol. C3 90
Uncompahgre Peak, mtn., Co., U.S. E9 132
Uncompahgre Plateau, plat., Co., U.S. E8 132
Unden, l., Swe. G5 8
Underberg, S. Afr. F9 70
Undva nina, c., Est. B4 10
Uneča, Russia H15 10
Uneiuxi, stm., Braz. H9 86
Unga Island, i., Ak., U.S. E7 140
Ungava, Péninsule d', pen., Qc., Can. D16 106
Ungava Bay, b., Can. D17 106
Ungava Peninsula see Ungava, Péninsule d', pen., Qc., Can. D16 106
Ungch'ŏn, Kor., S. D1 40
Unggi-ŭp, Kor., N. C9 38
Ungheni, Mol. B14 26
União, Braz. C4 88
União dos Palmares, Braz. E7 88
Unicoi, Tn., U.S. H3 114
Uniejów, Pol. D14 16
Unimak Island, i., Ak., U.S. E7 140
Unimak Pass, strt., Ak., U.S. F6 140
Unini, stm., Braz. H11 86
Unión, Arg. G5 92
Unión, Para. B9 92
Union, Ia., U.S. B4 120
Union, La., U.S. G8 122
Union, N.J., U.S. D11 114
Union, Or., U.S. E9 136
Union, S.C., U.S. B4 116
Union, Wa., U.S. C3 136
Union, W.V., U.S. G5 114
Union Bay, B.C., Can. G6 138
Union City, Ga., U.S. D14 122
Union City, Mi., U.S. F4 112
Union City, Oh., U.S. D1 114
Union City, Pa., U.S. C6 114
Union City, Tn., U.S. H8 120
Unión de Reyes, Cuba A7 102
Unión de Tula, Mex. E6 100
Union Flat Creek, stm., U.S. D9 136
Union Grove, Wi., U.S. F1 112
Union Island, i., St. Vin. p10 105e
Union Point, Ga., U.S. C2 116
Union Springs, Al., U.S. E13 122
Uniontown, Al., U.S. E11 122
Uniontown, Ky., U.S. G10 120
Uniontown, Pa., U.S. E6 114
Unionville, Mi., U.S. E6 112
United, Pa., U.S. D6 114
United Arab Emirates, ctry., Asia E7 56
United Arab Republic see Egypt, ctry., Afr. B5 62
United Kingdom, ctry., Eur. D8 6
United States, ctry., N.A. C10 102
Unity, Sk., Can. B4 124
Universal City, Tx., U.S. E9 130
University, Ms., U.S. C9 122
University City, Mo., U.S. F7 120
University Park, N.M., U.S. K10 132
University Park, Tx., U.S. E2 122
Unjha, India G4 54
Unnão, India E8 54
Uno, Canal Numero, can., Arg. H9 92
Unquillo, Arg. E5 92
Unst, i., Scot., U.K. n19 12a
Unstrut, stm., Ger. E7 16
Unža, stm., Russia G21 8
Unzen-dake, vol., Japan G3 40
Uong Bi, Viet. B8 48
Uozu, Japan C10 40
Upa, stm., Russia G20 10
Upanema, Braz. C7 88
Upata, Ven. C10 86
Upemba, Lac, l., D.R.C. F5 66
Upernavik, Grnld. C14 141
Upía, stm., Col. E5 86
Upington, S. Afr. F5 70
Upland, Ne., U.S. A10 128
Upleta, India H3 54
Upolu, i., Samoa h11 79c
Upolu Point, c., Hi., U.S. C6 78a
Upper Arlington, Oh., U.S. D2 114
Upper Arrow Lake, l., B.C., Can. F13 138
Upper Austria see Oberösterreich, state, Aus. B10 22
Upper Blackville, N.B., Can. D10 110
Upper Darby, Pa., U.S. E10 114
Upper Egypt see El-Sa'īd, hist. reg., Egypt J2 58
Upper Fraser, B.C., Can. B8 138
Upper Ganga Canal (Upper Ganges Canal), can., India D6 54
Upper Iowa, stm., U.S. H7 118
Upper Kapuas Mountains, mts., Asia C8 50
Upper Klamath Lake, l., Or., U.S. H5 136
Upper Lake, Ca., U.S. D3 134
Upper Lake, l., Ca., U.S. B5 134
Upper Manitou Lake, l., On., Can. B5 118
Upper Musquodoboit, N.S., Can. E14 110
Upper Red Lake, l., Mn., U.S. C4 118
Upper Sandusky, Oh., U.S. D2 114
Upper Takutu-Upper Essequibo, state, Guy. F12 86
Upper Trajan's Wall, misc. cult., Mol. C15 26
Upper Volta see Burkina Faso, ctry., Afr. G4 64
Uppsala, Swe. G7 8
Uppsala, state, Swe. F7 8
Upshi, India B6 54
Upton, Ky., U.S. G12 120
Urabá, Golfo de, b., Col. C3 86
Uracoa, Ven. C10 86
Uraj, Russia B10 32
Urakawa, Japan C15 38
Ural, stm. E8 32
Ural Mountains see Ural'skie gory, mts., Russia C9 32
Ural'sk, Kaz. D8 32
Ural'skie gory (Ural Mountains), mts., Russia C9 32
Urana, Austl. J6 76
Urandangi, Austl. D7 74
Urangan, Austl. E9 76
Urania, La., U.S. F6 122
Uranium City, Sk., Can. D9 106
Uraricaá, stm., Braz. F10 86
Uraricoera, Braz. F11 86
Uraricoera, stm., Braz. F11 86
Ura-Tjube, Taj. B10 56
Uravakonda, India D3 53
Uravan, Co., U.S. E8 132
Urawa, Japan D12 40
Urbana, Ar., U.S. D6 122
Urbana, Il., U.S. D9 120
Urbana, Oh., U.S. D2 114
Urbandale, Ia., U.S. C4 120
Urbania, Italy G9 22
Urbino, Italy G9 22
Urcos, Peru F3 84
Urdinarrain, Arg. F8 92
Urdžar, Kaz. E14 32
Ure, stm., Eng., U.K. G11 12
Urèčča, Bela. H10 10
Uren', Russia H21 8
Ureña, Ven. D5 86
Ures, Mex. G7 98
Ureshino, Japan F2 40
Urewera National Park, p.o.i., N.Z. D7 80
Urgenč, Uzb. F10 32
Urho Kekkosen kansallispuisto, p.o.i., Fin. B12 8
Uriah, Al., U.S. F11 122
Uriah, Mount, mtn., N.Z. E4 80
Uribante, stm., Ven. D5 86
Uribe, Col. F4 86
Uribia, Col. B5 86
Urich, Mo., U.S. F4 120
Urickij, Kaz. D11 32
Urique, stm., Mex. B5 100
Urjung-Haja, Russia B11 34
Urjupinsk, Russia D6 32
Urla, Tur. E9 28
Urlaţi, Rom. D13 26
Urlings, Antig. f4 105b
Urmia see Orūmīyeh, Iran B6 56
Urmia, Lake see Orūmīyeh, Daryācheh-ye, l., Iran B6 56
Uromi, Nig. H6 64
Uroševac, Yugo. G8 26
Urrao, Col. D3 86
Ursa, Il., U.S. D6 120
Uruaçu, Braz. H1 88
Uruapan, Mex. L9 134
Uruapan del Progreso, Mex. F7 100
Urubamba, Peru F3 84
Urubamba, stm., Peru F3 84
Urubaxi, stm., Braz. H9 86
Urubu, stm., Braz. D6 84
Urubu, stm., Braz. F1 88
Uruburetama, Braz. B6 88
Urucará, Braz. D6 84
Urucu, stm., Braz. D5 84
Uruçuca, Braz. H6 88
Uruçuí, Serra da, hills, Braz. E3 88
Urucuia, stm., Braz. I3 88
Uruçuí-preto, stm., Braz. E3 88
Uruguai (Uruguay), stm., S.A. F8 92
Uruguaiana, Braz. D9 92
Uruguay, ctry., S.A. F10 92
Uruguay (Uruguai), stm., S.A. F8 92
Urumchi see Ürümqi, China C2 36
Ürümqi, China C2 36
Urup, ostrov, i., Russia G19 34
Urupês, Braz. K1 88
Urutaí, Braz. I1 88
Uruwira, Tan. F6 66
Urziceni, Rom. E13 26
Uržum, Russia C7 32
Usa, Japan F4 40
Usa, stm., Russia A9 32
Uşak, Tur. E12 28
Uşak, state, Tur. E12 28
Ušaki, Russia A13 10
Usakos, Nmb. B2 70
Usborne, Mount, mtn., Falk. Is. J5 90
Uščerpe, Russia H14 10
U.S. Department of Energy Hanford Site, sci., Wa., U.S. D7 136
Usedom, i., Ger. B10 16
Ushant see Ouessant, Île d', i., Fr. F3 14
Ushashi, Tan. E6 66
Ushtobe see Uštobe, Kaz. E13 32
Ushuaia, Arg. J3 90
Usingen, Ger. F4 16
Usinsk, Russia A9 32
Usk, Wa., U.S. B9 136
Usk, stm., Wales, U.K. J9 12
Uslar, Ger. E5 16
Usmas ezers, l., Lat. C4 10
Usole, Russia C9 32
Usole-Sibirskoe, Russia D18 32
Uspallata, Arg. F3 92
Uspanapa, stm., Mex. G11 100
Ussuri (Wusuli), stm., Asia C11 36
Ussurijsk, Russia C10 38
Ust'-Barguzin, Russia F10 34
Ust'-Belaja, Russia C23 34
Ust'-Bol'šereck, Russia F20 34
Ust'-Čaun, Russia C23 34
Ust'-Chorna, Ukr. A10 26
Ust'-Cil'ma, Russia D25 8
Uste, Russia G18 8
Uster, Switz. C5 22
Ustica, Isola di, i., Italy F7 24
Ust'-Ilimsk, Russia C18 32
Ust'-Ilimskoe vodohranilišče, res., Russia C18 32
Ústí nad Labem, Czech Rep. F10 16
Ústí nad Orlicí, Czech Rep. G12 16
Ust'-Išim, Russia C12 32
Ustja, stm., Russia F21 8
Ust'-Javron'ga, Russia E21 8
Ustjuckoe, Russia B18 10
Ustjužna, Russia B19 10
Ustka, Pol. B12 16
Ust'-Kamčatsk, Russia E21 34
Ust'-Kamenogorsk, Kaz. E14 32
Ust'-Koksa, Russia D15 32
Ust'-Kujda, Russia B16 34
Ust'-Kulom, Russia B8 32
Ust'-Kut, Russia C19 32
Ust'-Lyža, Russia A9 32
Ust'-Maja, Russia D15 34
Ust'-Man'ja, Russia B10 32
Ust'-Nera, Russia D17 34
Ust'-Njukža, Russia E13 34
Uštobe, Kaz. E13 32
Ust'-Omčug, Russia D18 34
Ust'-Ordynskij, Russia D18 32
Ust'-Ozërnoe, Russia C15 32
Ust'-Pinega, Russia D19 8
Ust'-Reki, Russia E22 8
Ustroń, Pol. G14 16
Ust'-Sumy, Russia D14 32
Ust'-Tym, Russia D24 6
Ust'-Ulagan, Russia D15 32
Ust'-Urgal, Russia F15 34
Ust-Urt Plateau, plat., Asia F9 32
Ust-Vyjskaja, Russia E22 8
Usu, China C1 36
Usuki, Japan F4 40
Usulután, El Sal. F3 102
Usumacinta, stm., N.A. D2 102
Usumbura see Bujumbura, Bdi. E5 66
Ušumun, Russia F14 34
Usvjaty, Russia E13 10
Utah, state, U.S. D5 132
Utah Lake, l., Ut., U.S. C5 132
Utata, Russia D18 32
Ute, Ia., U.S. B2 120
Ute Creek, stm., N.M., U.S. F5 128
Utegi, Tan. E6 66
Utena, Lith. E8 10
Utete, Tan. F7 66
Uthai Thani, Thai. E4 48
Uthal, Pak. D10 56
U Thong, Thai. E4 48
Utiariti, Braz. F6 84
Utica, Ks., U.S. C8 128
Utica, Mi., U.S. F6 112
Utica, Ms., U.S. E8 122
Utica, N.Y., U.S. E14 112
Utica, Oh., U.S. D3 114
Utica see Utique, hist., Tun. G3 24
Utiel, Spain E9 20
Utila, Isla de, i., Hond. D4 102
Utinga, stm., Braz. G5 88
Utique (Utica), hist., Tun. G3 24
Uto, Japan G3 40
Utopia, Tx., U.S. E8 130
Utorgoš, Russia B13 10
Utraula, India E9 54
Utrecht, Neth. B14 14
Utrecht, S. Afr. E10 70
Utrera, Spain G5 20
Utrik, at., Marsh. Is. B7 72
Utroja, stm., Eur. D10 10
Utsunomiya, Japan C12 40
Uttamapālaiyam, India G3 53
Uttaradit, Thai. D5 48
Uttarkāshi, India C7 54
Uttar Pradesh, state, India E7 54
Utuado, P.R. B2 104a
Utukok, stm., Ak., U.S. C7 140
Utupua, i., Sol. Is. E7 72
Uulu, Est. B7 10
Uusimaa, state, Fin. F11 8
Uvá, stm., Col. F7 86
Uvalda, Ga., U.S. D3 116
Uvalde, Tx., U.S. E8 130
Uvaravičy, Bela. H13 10
Uvarovo, Russia D6 32
Uvdal, Nor. F3 8
Uvinza, Tan. F6 66
Uvira, D.R.C. E5 66
Uvs Lake see Uvsu-Nur, ozero, l., Asia F7 34
Uvsu-Nur, ozero, l., Asia F7 34
Uvworé, c., Vanuatu I17 79d
Uwa, Japan F5 40
Uwajima, Japan F5 40
Uwayl, Sudan F5 62
Uxbridge, On., Can. D10 112
Uxmal, hist., Mex. B3 102
Uyo, Nig. H6 64
Uyuni, Bol. D3 90
Uyuni, Salar de, pl., Bol. D3 90
Uzbekistan, ctry., Asia E10 30
Uzda, Bela. G10 10
Uzerche, Fr. D7 18
Uzgen, Kyrg. F12 32
Uzhhorod, Ukr. A9 26
Užice, Yugo. F6 26
Uzlovaja, Russia F20 10
Üzümlü, Tur. G12 28
Uzun Ada, i., Tur. E9 28
Uzunköprü, Tur. B9 28
Uzunkuduk, Uzb. F11 32
Užur, Russia C16 32
Užventis, Lith. E5 10

V

Vaal, stm., S. Afr. F7 70
Vaaldam, res., S. Afr. E8 70
Vaalwater, S. Afr. D8 70
Vaasa (Vasa), Fin. E9 8
Vaasa, state, Fin. E10 8
Vabalninkas, Lith. D7 10
Vác, Hung. B6 26
Vacacaí, stm., Braz. E11 92
Vacaria, Braz. D12 92
Vacaria, stm., Braz. I4 88
Vacaville, Ca., U.S. E4 134
Vaccarès, Étang de, l., Fr. F10 18
Vache, Île à, i., Haiti C11 102
Vad, Russia I21 8
Vadakara see Badagara, India F2 53
Vădeni, Rom. D14 26
Vadnagar, India G4 54
Vado, N.M., U.S. K10 132
Vadodara (Baroda), India G4 54
Vado Ligure, Italy F5 22
Vadsø, Nor. A13 8
Vaduz, Liech. C6 22
Vaga, stm., Russia F20 8
Vågåmo, Nor. F3 8
Vágar, i., Far. Is. m34 8b
Vaghena Island, i., Sol. Is. d7 79b
Vah, stm., Russia B13 32
Váh, stm., Slov. H13 16
Vahsel, Cape, c., S. Geor. J9 90
Vaiden, Ms., U.S. D9 122
Vaigai, stm., India G4 53
Vaigat, strt., Grnld. C15 141
Vaijāpur, India B2 53
Vaikam, India G3 53
Väike-Maarja, Est. A9 10

Name — Map Ref. — Page

Viola, Il., U.S. C7 120
Vioolsdrif, S. Afr. F3 70
Vipiteno, Italy D8 22
Vir, Otok, i., Cro. F11 22
Virac, Phil. D5 52
Viramgām, India G3 54
Vīrarājendrapet, India E2 53
Virbalis, Lith. F5 10
Virden, Mb., Can. E13 124
Virden, Il., U.S. E8 120
Virden, N.M., U.S. K8 132
Vire, Fr. F8 14
Virgem da Lapa, Braz. I4 88
Vírgenes, Cabo, c., S.A. J3 90
Virgil, Ks., U.S. C13 128
Virgin, stm., U.S. G2 132
Virgin Gorda, i., Br. Vir. Is. e9 104b
Virginia, S. Afr. F8 70
Virginia, Il., U.S. E7 120
Virginia, Mn., U.S. D6 118
Virginia, state, U.S. G7 114
Virginia Beach, Va., U.S. H10 114
Virginia City, Mt., U.S. E14 136
Virginia City, Nv., U.S. D6 134
Virginia Falls, wtfl, N.T., Can. C5 106
Virginia Peak, mtn., Nv., U.S. D6 134
Virgin Islands, dep., N.A. h14 96a
Virgin Islands, is., N.A. e7 104b
Virgin Islands National Park, p.o.i., V.I.U.S. e7 104b
Virgin Passage, strt., N.A. B5 104a
Virihaure, l., Swe. C7 8
Virje, Cro. D13 22
Virojoki, Fin. F12 8
Viroqua, Wi., U.S. H7 118
Virovitica, Cro. E14 22
Virrat, Fin. E10 8
Virtaniemi, Fin. B13 8
Virtsu, Est. G10 8
Virú, Peru E2 84
Virudunagar, India G3 53
Virunga, Parc National de, p.o.i., D.R.C. D5 66
Viru-Nigula, Est. A9 10
Virvytė, stm., Lith. D5 10
Vis see Visrivier, stm., Nmb. E3 70
Vis, stm., S. Afr. G5 70
Vis, Otok, i., Cro. G13 22
Visale, Sol. Is. e8 79b
Visalia, Ca., U.S. G6 134
Visayan Islands, is., Phil. E4 52
Visayan Sea, Phil. E4 52
Visby, Swe. H8 8
Viscount, Sk., Can. C8 124
Viscount Melville Sound, strt., N.T., Can. B11 94
Višegrad, Bos. F6 26
Viseu, Port. D3 20
Viseu, state, Port. D3 20
Vishākhapatnam, India C6 53
Visnagar, India G4 54
Višneva, Bela. F9 10
Visoko, Bos. E5 26
Visokoi Island, i., S. Geor. K12 82
Visp, Switz. D4 22
Visrivier, stm., Nmb. E3 70
Vista, Ca., U.S. J8 134
Vistina, Russia A11 10
Vistula see Wisła, stm., Pol. B14 16
Vistula Lagoon, b., Eur. B16 16
Vita, Mb., Can. E17 124
Vita, stm., Col. E7 86
Vitarte, Peru F2 84
Vite, India C2 53
Viterbo, Italy H8 22
Viti see Fiji, ctry., Oc. E8 72
Vitiaz Strait, strt., Pap. N. Gui. b4 79a
Vitigudino, Spain C4 20
Viti Levu, i., Fiji p19 79e
Vitim, Russia E11 34
Vitim, stm., Russia E12 34
Vitimskoe ploskogor'e, plat., Russia F11 34
Vitinja, p., Blg. G10 26
Vítkov, Czech Rep. G13 16
Vitória, Braz. D7 84
Vitória, Braz. K5 88
Vitoria see Gasteiz, Spain B8 20
Vitória da Conquista, Braz. H5 88
Vitória de Santo Antão, Braz. E8 88
Vitória do Mearim, Braz. B3 88
Vitorino Freire, Braz. C3 88
Vitré, Fr. F7 14
Vitry-le-François, Fr. F13 14
Vitteaux, Fr. G13 14
Vittoria, Italy H8 24
Vittorio Veneto, Italy D9 22
Viveiro, Spain A3 20
Viver, Spain E10 20
Vivero see Viveiro, Spain A3 20
Vivi, stm., Russia D8 34
Vivian, La., U.S. E4 122
Vizcaíno, Desierto de, des., Mex. B2 100
Vizcaya see Bizkaiko, co., Spain A8 20
Vize, Tur. B10 28
Vizianagaram, India B6 53
Vizille, Fr. D11 18
Vizinga, Russia B7 32
Vjalikaja Maščanica, Bela. G12 10
Vjalikija Radvaničy, Bela. H7 10
Vjaseja, Bela. G10 10
Vjatka, stm., Russia C8 32
Vjatskie Poljany, Russia C8 32
Vjazemskij, Russia G15 34
Vjaz'ma, Russia E17 10
Vjazniki, Russia H20 8
Vjazyn', Bela. F10 10
Vjosës (Aóös), stm., Eur. D13 24
Vlaardingen, Neth. C13 14
Vlădeasa, Vârful, mtn., Rom. C9 26
Vladičin Han, Yugo. G8 26
Vladikavkaz, Russia F6 32
Vladimir, Russia H18 8
Vladimirskaja oblast', co., Russia I19 8
Vladimirskij Tupik, Russia E16 10
Vladivostok, Russia C9 38
Vlasenica, Bos. E5 26
Vlasotince, Yugo. G9 26
Vlasovo, Russia B16 34
Vlieland, i., Neth. A13 14
Vlissingen, Neth. C12 14
Vlora see Vlorë, Alb. D13 24
Vlorë, Alb. D13 24
Vltava (Moldau), stm., Czech Rep. F10 16
Vnukovo, Russia E20 10
Vöcklabruck, Aus. C10 22
Vo Dat, Viet. G8 48
Vodla, stm., Russia F17 8
Vodlozero, ozero, l., Russia E16 8
Vodosalma, Russia D14 8
Voël, stm., S. Afr. H7 70
Voghera, Italy F6 22
Voh, N. Cal. m15 79d
Vohimena, Tanjona, c., Madag. F8 68
Vohipeno, Madag. E8 68
Võhma, Est. G11 8
Voi, Kenya E7 66
Voinești, Rom. B14 26
Voinjama, Lib. H3 64
Voiron, Fr. D11 18
Voitsberg, Aus. C12 22
Vojmsjön, l., Swe. D6 8
Vojnica, Russia D14 8
Vojvodina, co., Yugo. D7 26
Volcán, Pan. H6 102
Volcano, Hi., U.S. D6 78a
Volcano Islands see Kazan-rettō, is., Japan G18 30
Volčiha, Russia D14 32
Volda, Nor. E2 8
Volga, S.D., U.S. G2 118
Volga, stm., Russia E7 32
Volga-Baltic Canal see Volgo-Baltijskij kanal, can., Russia G17 8
Volgino, Russia B16 10
Volgo, ozero, l., Russia C16 10
Volgo-Baltijskij kanal, can., Russia G17 8
Volgodonsk, Russia E6 32
Volgograd, Russia E6 32
Volgograd Reservoir see Volgogradskoe vodohranilišče, res., Russia E7 32
Volgogradskoe vodohranilišče, res., Russia D7 32
Volhov, Russia A15 10
Volhov, stm., Russia G14 8
Volissós, Grc. E8 28
Völkermarkt, Aus. D11 22
Völklingen, Ger. G2 16
Volksrust, S. Afr. E9 70
Voločanka, Russia B7 34
Volodarskoe, Kaz. D11 32
Voloe, Russia F17 10
Vologda, Russia A22 10
Vologda, stm., Russia A22 10
Vologodskaja oblast', co., Russia G19 8
Volokolamsk, Russia D18 10
Volonga, Russia C22 8
Vólos, Grc. D5 28
Volos, Gulf of see Pagasitikós Kólpos, b., Grc. D5 28
Vološka, Russia F19 8
Volosovo, Russia A12 10
Volot, Russia C13 10
Volovo, Russia G21 10
Vol'sk, Russia D7 32
Volta, stm., Ghana H5 64
Volta Blanche (White Volta), stm., Afr. G4 64
Volta Lake, res., Ghana H4 64
Volta Noire (Black Volta) (Mouhoun), stm., Afr. G4 64
Volta Redonda, Braz. L3 88
Volterra, Italy G7 22
Vol'teva, Russia D21 8
Voltri, ngh., Italy F5 22
Volturno, stm., Italy C8 24
Vólvi, Límni, l., Grc. C6 28
Volyn', co., Ukr. E20 16
Volžsk, Russia C7 32
Volžskij, Russia E6 32
Vonavona Island, i., Sol. Is. e7 79b
Vonda, Sk., Can. B7 124
Vondanka, Russia G22 8
Vondrozo, Madag. E8 68
Von Frank Mountain, mtn., Ak., U.S. D8 140
Vopnafjörđur, Ice. k32 8a
Vopnafjörđur, b., Ice. k32 8a
Vorarlberg, state, Aus. C6 22
Vorau, Aus. C12 22
Vorderrhein see Rein Anteriur, stm., Switz. D6 22
Vordingborg, Den. I4 8
Vóreio Aigaío, state, Grc. D8 28
Vórioi Sporádhes, is., Grc. D6 28
Vórios Évvoikós Kólpos, b., Grc. E5 28
Vorkuta, Russia A10 32
Vormsi, i., Est. G10 8
Vorobevo, Russia C13 32
Voroncov, Mol. B16 26
Voroncovo, Russia C11 10
Voronež, Russia D5 32
Voronežskaja oblast', co., Russia H21 10
Voronja, stm., Russia B16 8
Voronok, Russia H15 10
Voronovo, Russia E5 34
Vorpommern, hist. reg., Ger. C9 16
Vorsma, Russia H20 8
Vørterkaka Nunatak, mtn., Ant. C8 81
Võrtsjärv, l., Est. G12 8
Võru, Est. H12 8
Vosburg, S. Afr. G6 70
Vosges, state, Fr. F15 14
Vosges, mts., Fr. F15 14
Voskresensk, Russia E21 10
Voskresenskoe, Russia C20 10
Voskresenskoe, Russia B21 10
Voss, Nor. F2 8
Vostočno-Kounradskij, Kaz. E13 32
Vostočno-Sibirskoe more, Russia B20 34
Vostočnyj Sajan, mts., Russia D17 32
Vostok, i., Kir. E11 72
Vostok, sci., Ant. C15 81
Votice, Czech Rep. G10 16
Votkinsk, Russia C8 32
Votuporanga, Braz. D7 90
Vouga, stm., Port. D2 20
Vouziers, Fr. E13 14
Voyageurs National Park, p.o.i., Mn., U.S. C6 118
Voyeykov Ice Shelf, ice, Ant. B17 81
Vože, ozero, l., Russia F18 8
Vožega, Russia F19 8
Voznesene, Russia F16 8
Vozroždenija, ostrov, i., Asia E9 32
Vraca, Blg. F10 26
Vradyïvka, Ukr. B17 26
Vrancea, state, Rom. D13 26
Vrangelja, ostrov (Wrangel Island), i., Russia B24 34
Vranje, Yugo. G8 26
Vratsa see Vraca, Blg. F10 26
Vrbas, Yugo. D6 26
Vrbas, stm., Bos. E4 26
Vrbovec, Cro. E13 22
Vrchlabí, Czech Rep. F11 16
Vrede, S. Afr. E9 70
Vredenburg, S. Afr. H3 70
Vredenburgh, Al., U.S. F11 122
Vredenburg-Saldanha see Vredenburg, S. Afr. H3 70
Vredendal, S. Afr. G4 70
Vriddhāchalam, India F4 53
Vrindāvan, India E6 54
Vršac, Yugo. D8 26
Vrútky, Slov. G14 16
Vryburg, S. Afr. E7 70
Vryheid, S. Afr. E10 70
Vselug, ozero, l., Russia C14 10
Vsetín, Czech Rep. G13 16
Vsevidof, Mount, mtn., Ak., U.S. F6 140
Vučitrn, Yugo. G7 26
Vukovar, Cro. E16 22
Vulcan, Ab., Can. F17 138
Vulcan, Rom. D10 26
Vulcănești, Mol. D15 26
Vulcano, Isola, i., Italy F8 24
Vulsino see Bolsena, Lago di, l., Italy H9 22
Vung Tau, Viet. G8 48
Vunidawa, Fiji p19 79e
Vunisea, Fiji q18 79e
Vuohijärvi, l., Fin. F11 8
Vuyyūru, India C5 53
Vyāra, India H4 54
Vyborg (Viipuri), Russia F13 8
Vyčegda, stm., Russia B7 32
Vyčegodskij, Russia F22 8
Východočeský, state, Czech Rep. F11 16
Východoslovenský Kraj, state, Slov. H17 16
Vygoniči, Russia G16 10
Vygozero, ozero, l., Russia E16 8
Vyksa, Russia I20 8
Vylkove, Ukr. D16 26
Vynohradiv, Ukr. A10 26
Vypolzovo, Russia C16 10
Vyrica, Russia A13 10
Vyšgorodok, Russia C11 10
Vyskod', Russia C13 10
Vyškov, Czech Rep. G12 16
Vyšneol'šanoe, Russia H20 10
Vyšnevolockoe vodohranilišče, res., Russia C16 10
Vyšnij Voločok, Russia C17 10
Vysoké Mýto, Czech Rep. G12 16
Vysokiniči, Russia F19 10
Vysokoe, Russia D17 10
Vysokogornyj, Russia G16 34
Vysokovsk, Russia D19 10
Vytebet', stm., Russia G18 10
Vytegra, Russia F17 8
Vyzhnytsia, Ukr. A12 26

W

Wa, Ghana G4 64
Waal, stm., Neth. C14 14
Waalwijk, Neth. C14 14
Wabag, Pap. N. Gui. b3 79a
Wabakimi Lake, l., On., Can. A8 118
Wabamun, Ab., Can. C16 138
Wabamun Lake, l., Ab., Can. C15 138
Wabana, Nf., Can. j23 107a
Wabasca, stm., Ab., Can. D7 106
Wabasca-Desmarais, Ab., Can. D8 106
Wabash, In., U.S. H4 112
Wabash, stm., U.S. F9 120
Wabasha, Mn., U.S. G6 118
Wabasso, Mn., U.S. G3 118
Wabeno, Wi., U.S. F10 118
Wabera, Eth. F8 62
Wabowden, Mb., Can. E11 106
Wąbrzeźno, Pol. C14 16
Wabu Hu, l., China E7 42
Waccamaw, stm., U.S. C7 116
Waccamaw, Lake, l., N.C., U.S. B7 116
Wachapreague, Va., U.S. G10 114
Wachau, reg., Aus. B12 22
Wacissa, Fl., U.S. F2 116
Waco, Tx., U.S. C10 130
Waco Lake, res., Tx., U.S. C10 130
Waconda Lake, res., Ks., U.S. B10 128
Wadayama, Japan D7 40
Wad Bandah, Sudan E5 62
Wadbilliga National Park, p.o.i., Austl. K7 76
Waddenzee, strt., Neth. A14 14
Waddington, N.Y., U.S. D14 112
Waddington, Mount, mtn., B.C., Can. E5 138
Wadena, Sk., Can. C10 124
Wadena, Mn., U.S. E3 118
Wadesboro, N.C., U.S. B5 116
Wādī as-Sīr, Jord. G6 58
Wādī Ḥalfā', Sudan C6 62
Wadley, Al., U.S. D13 122
Wadley, Ga., U.S. D3 116
Wad Madanī, Sudan E6 62
Wadowice, Pol. G15 16
Wadsworth, Nv., U.S. D6 134
Wadsworth, Oh., U.S. C4 114
Wafangdian, China B9 42
Wageningen, Neth. C14 14
Wager Bay, b., N.T., Can. B13 106
Wagga Wagga, Austl. J6 76
Wagin, Austl. F3 74
Waging am See, Ger. I8 16
Wagner, S.D., U.S. D14 126
Wagoner, Ok., U.S. I2 120
Wagon Mound, N.M., U.S. F4 128
Wagontire Mountain, mtn., Or., U.S. G7 136
Wagrien, reg., Ger. B6 16
Wągrowiec, Pol. D13 16
Waha, Libya B4 62
Wahai, Indon. F8 44
Wāh Cantonment, Pak. B4 54
Wahiawa, Hi., U.S. B3 78a
Wahpeton, N.D., U.S. E2 118
Wahran (Oran), Alg. B4 64
Wai, India B1 53
Waialua, Hi., U.S. B3 78a
Waianae, Hi., U.S. B3 78a
Waiau, N.Z. F5 80
Waiau, stm., N.Z. G2 80
Waiau, stm., N.Z. F5 80
Waiblingen, Ger. H5 16
Waidhofen an der Thaya, Aus. B12 22
Waidhofen an der Ybbs, Aus. C11 22
Waigeo, Pulau, i., Indon. E9 44
Waihi, N.Z. C6 80
Waikabubak, Indon. H11 50
Waikato, stm., N.Z. C6 80
Waikelo, Indon. H11 50
Waikerie, Austl. J2 76
Wailuku, Hi., U.S. C5 78a
Waimate, N.Z. G4 80
Waimea, Hi., U.S. A2 78a
Wainganga, stm., India H7 54
Waingapu, Indon. H12 50
Waini, stm., Guy. D12 86
Wainunu Bay, b., Fiji p19 79e
Wainwright, Ab., Can. B3 124
Wainwright, Ak., U.S. B7 140
Waipukurau, N.Z. E7 80
Wairarapa, Lake, l., N.Z. E6 80
Wairau, stm., N.Z. E5 80
Wairoa, N.Z. D7 80
Wairoa, stm., N.Z. B6 80
Waïsisi, Vanuatu I17 79d
Waitaki, stm., N.Z. G4 80
Waitara, N.Z. D6 80
Waitemata, N.Z. C6 80
Waite Park, Mn., U.S. F4 118
Waitotara, N.Z. D6 80
Waitsburg, Wa., U.S. D8 136
Waiwo, Indon. F9 44
Wajima, Japan B9 40
Wajir, Kenya D8 66
Waka, D.R.C. D4 66
Waka, Eth. F7 62
Wakarusa, In., U.S. G3 112
Wakasa-wan, b., Japan D8 40
Wakatipu, Lake, l., N.Z. G3 80
Wakaw, Sk., Can. B8 124
Wakayama, Japan E8 40
Wakayama, state, Japan F8 40
WaKeeney, Ks., U.S. B9 128
Wakefield, Eng., U.K. H11 12
Wakefield, Ks., U.S. B11 128
Wakefield, Ne., U.S. E15 126
Wakefield, Va., U.S. H8 114
Wake Forest, N.C., U.S. I7 114
Wake Island, dep., Oc. B7 72
Wake Island, at., Wake I. H19 142
Wakema, Mya. D2 48
Waki, Japan E7 40
Wakis, Pap. N. Gui. b5 79a
Wakita, Ok., U.S. E10 128
Wakkanai, Japan B14 38
Wakomata Lake, l., On., Can. B6 112
Wakonda, S.D., U.S. E15 126
Waku Kungo, Ang. C2 68
Walachia, hist. reg., Rom. E11 26
Walanae, stm., Indon. F12 50
Walawe, stm., Sri L. H5 53
Wałbrzych, Pol. F12 16
Wałbrzych, state, Pol. F12 16
Walcha, Austl. H8 76
Walcott, Ia., U.S. C7 120
Walcott, N.D., U.S. E1 118
Walcott, Lake, res., Id., U.S. H13 136
Wałcz, Pol. C12 16
Waldbröl, Ger. F3 16
Walden, On., Can. B8 112
Walden, Co., U.S. C10 132
Waldheim, Sk., Can. B7 124
Waldkirchen, Ger. H9 16
Waldmünchen, Ger. G8 16
Waldo, B.C., Can. G15 138
Waldoboro, Me., U.S. F7 110
Waldorf, Md., U.S. F9 114
Waldport, Or., U.S. F2 136
Waldron, Sk., Can. D11 124
Waldron, Ar., U.S. C4 122
Waldron, In., U.S. E12 120
Waldshut-Tiengen, Ger. I4 16
Waldviertel, reg., Aus. B12 22
Wales, state, U.K. I9 12
Wales Island, i., N.T., Can. B13 106
Walewale, Ghana G4 64
Walgett, Austl. G6 76
Walgreen Coast, cst., Ant. C30 81
Walhachin, B.C., Can. F10 138
Walhalla, N.D., U.S. F15 124
Walhalla, S.C., U.S. B2 116
Walhalla, hist., Ger. G8 16
Walker, Ia., U.S. B6 120
Walker, stm., Nv., U.S. D7 134
Walker Bay, b., S. Afr. I4 70
Walker Lake, l., Nv., U.S. E7 134
Walkerton, On., Can. D8 112
Walkerton, In., U.S. G3 112
Walkertown, N.C., U.S. H5 114
Walkerville, Mt., U.S. D14 136
Wall, S.D., U.S. D10 126
Wallace, Id., U.S. C11 136
Wallace, Ne., U.S. G11 126
Wallace, N.C., U.S. B7 116
Wallaceburg, On., Can. F7 112
Wallal Downs, Austl. C4 74
Wallam Creek, stm., Austl. G6 76
Wallangarra, Austl. G8 76
Wallaroo, Austl. F7 74
Wallasey, Eng., U.K. H9 12
Walla Walla, Wa., U.S. D8 136
Wallingford, Ct., U.S. C13 114
Wallingford, Vt., U.S. G4 110
Wallis, Tx., U.S. H2 122
Wallis, Îles, is., Wal./F. E9 72
Wallis and Futuna, dep., Oc. E9 72
Wallisville Lake, res., Tx., U.S. H4 122
Wall Lake, Ia., U.S. I3 118
Wallowa, Or., U.S. E9 136
Wallowa, stm., Or., U.S. E9 136
Walls of Jericho National Park, p.o.i., Austl. n13 77a
Walnut, Il., U.S. C8 120
Walnut, Ia., U.S. C2 120
Walnut, Ms., U.S. C10 122
Walnut, N.C., U.S. I3 114
Walnut, stm., Ks., U.S. D11 128
Walnut Canyon National Monument, p.o.i., Az., U.S. H5 132
Walnut Cove, N.C., U.S. H5 114
Walnut Creek, stm., Ks., U.S. C9 128
Walnut Grove, Mn., U.S. G3 118
Walnut Grove, Ms., U.S. E9 122
Walnut Ridge, Ar., U.S. H7 120
Walnut Springs, Tx., U.S. B10 130
Walpole, Austl. G3 74
Walpole, N.H., U.S. G4 110
Walsall, Eng., U.K. I11 12
Walsenburg, Co., U.S. D4 128
Walsh, Austl. C8 74
Walsh, Ab., Can. E3 124
Walsh, stm., Austl. A5 76
Walsrode, Ger. D5 16
Walterboro, S.C., U.S. D5 116
Walters, Ok., U.S. G10 128
Waltershausen, Ger. F6 16
Walthall, Ms., U.S. D9 122
Walthill, Ne., U.S. B1 120
Walton, N.S., Can. E13 110
Walton, In., U.S. H3 112
Walton, N.Y., U.S. B10 114
Walvisbaai see Walvis Bay, Nmb. C2 70
Walvis Bay (Walvisbaai), Nmb. C2 70
Walvis Bay, b., Nmb. C2 70
Walvis Ridge, unds. K14 144
Walworth, Wi., U.S. B9 120
Wamba, D.R.C. D5 66
Wamba, Nig. H6 64
Wamba (Uamba), stm., Afr. F3 66
Wampsville, N.Y., U.S. A10 114
Wampú, Hond. E5 102
Wampú, stm., Hond. E5 102
Wampum, Pa., U.S. D5 114
Wamsutter, Wy., U.S. B9 132
Wanaka, N.Z. G3 80
Wanaka, Lake, l., N.Z. G3 80
Wan'an, China H6 42
Wanapa, Neth. Ant. p23 104g
Wanapitei, stm., On., Can. B9 112
Wanapitei Lake, l., On., Can. B8 112
Wanbaoshan, China B6 38
Wanbi, Austl. J3 76
Wanblee, S.D., U.S. D11 126
Wanchese, N.C., U.S. I10 114
Wandel Hav, Grnld. A22 141
Wandering, stm., Ab., Can. A18 138
Wanfoxia, China C4 36
Wang, stm., Thai. D4 48
Wanganui, N.Z. D6 80
Wanganui, stm., N.Z. D6 80
Wangaratta, Austl. K6 76
Wangcun, China C7 42
Wangdu Phodrang, Bhu. E12 54
Wangiwangi, Pulau, i., Indon. G7 44
Wang Noi, Thai. E5 48
Wangpan Yang, b., China F9 42
Wangqing, China C8 38
Wangtai, China H7 42
Wangyehmiao see Horqin Youyi Qianqi, China B9 36
Wanhedian, China E5 42
Wanhsien see Wanxian, China F3 42
Wani, India A4 53
Wanie-Rukula, D.R.C. D5 66
Wanigela, Pap. N. Gui. b4 79a
Wanipigow, stm., Can. C18 124
Wānkāner, India G3 54
Wanneroo, Austl. F3 74
Wannian, China G7 42
Wanning, China L4 42
Wanparti, India C4 53
Wantan, China F4 42
Wanxian, China F3 42
Wanyuan, China E3 42
Wanzai, China G6 42
Wanzleben, Ger. D7 16
Wapakoneta, Oh., U.S. D1 114
Wapanucka, Ok., U.S. C2 122
Wapato, Wa., U.S. D6 136
Wapello, Ia., U.S. C6 120
Wāpi, India H4 54
Wapiti, stm., Can. A12 138
Wappingers Falls, N.Y., U.S. C12 114
Wapsipinicon, stm., U.S. J8 118
War, W.V., U.S. G4 114
Warangal, India B4 53
Wārāseoni, India H7 54
Waratah, Austl. n12 77a
Waratah Bay, b., Austl. L5 76
Warburg, Ger. E4 16
Warburton, Austl. K5 76
Warburton Bay, b., N.T., Can. C8 106
Ward, stm., Austl. E6 76
Warden, S. Afr. E9 70
Wardha, India H7 54
Wardha, stm., India H7 54
Ward Hill, hill, Scot., U.K. C9 12
Wardlow, Ab., Can. F19 138
Wardner, B.C., Can. G15 138
Wardswell Draw, stm., U.S. B5 130
Waremme, Bel. D14 14
Waren, Ger. C8 16
Waren, Indon. F10 44
Warenai, stm., Indon. F10 44
Warenda, Austl. D3 76
Warendorf, Ger. E3 16
Ware Shoals, S.C., U.S. B3 116
Wargla, Alg. C6 64
Warialda, Austl. G8 76
Warin Chamrap, Thai. E7 48
Warkworth, On., Can. D11 112
Warman, Sk., Can. B7 124
Warmandi, Indon. F9 44
Warmbad, Nmb. F4 70
Warmbad, S. Afr. D9 70
Warm Baths see Warmbad, S. Afr. D9 70
Warminster, Eng., U.K. J10 12
Warminster, Pa., U.S. D10 114
Warm Springs, Ga., U.S. E14 122
Warm Springs, Mt., U.S. D14 136
Warm Springs, Or., U.S. F5 136
Warnemünde, ngh., Ger. B7 16
Warner, Ab., Can. G18 138
Warner, N.H., U.S. G5 110
Warner Lakes, l., Or., U.S. H6 136
Warner Mountains, mts., U.S. B5 134
Warner Peak, mtn., Or., U.S. A6 134
Warner Robins, Ga., U.S. D2 116
Warnow, stm., Ger. B8 16
Warra, Austl. F8 76
Warracknabeal, Austl. K4 76
Warragul, Austl. L5 76
Warrawagine, Austl. D4 74
Warrego, stm., Austl. G5 76
Warren, Ar., U.S. D6 122
Warren, In., U.S. H4 112
Warren, Mi., U.S. B2 114
Warren, Mn., U.S. C2 118
Warren, Oh., U.S. C5 114
Warren, Pa., U.S. C6 114
Warrens, Wi., U.S. G8 118
Warrensburg, Mo., U.S. F4 120
Warrensburg, N.Y., U.S. G3 110
Warrenton, S. Afr. F7 70
Warrenton, Mo., U.S. F6 120
Warrenton, N.C., U.S. H7 114
Warrenton, Or., U.S. D2 136
Warri, Nig. H6 64
Warrington, Eng., U.K. H10 12
Warrington, Fl., U.S. G11 122
Warrior, Al., U.S. D12 122
Warrnambool, Austl. L4 76
Warroad, Mn., U.S. C3 118
Warrumbungle National Park, p.o.i., Austl. H7 76
Warsaw see Warszawa, Pol. D16 16
Warsaw, Il., U.S. D6 120
Warsaw, In., U.S. G4 112
Warsaw, Ky., U.S. F13 120
Warsaw, Mo., U.S. F4 120
Warsaw, N.Y., U.S. B7 114
Warsaw, N.C., U.S. A7 116
Warspite, Ab., Can. B18 138
Warszawa (Warsaw), Pol. D16 16
Warszawa, state, Pol. D16 16
Warta, Pol. E14 16
Warta, stm., Pol. D11 16
Wartburg, Tn., U.S. H13 120
Wartrace, Tn., U.S. B12 122
Warud, India H7 54
Warwick, Austl. G9 76
Warwick, Eng., U.K. I11 12
Warwick, R.I., U.S. C14 114
Warwick Channel, strt., Austl. B7 74
Wasaga Beach, On., Can. D10 112
Wasagu, Nig. G6 64
Wasatch Range, mts., Ut., U.S. C5 132
Wasbank, S. Afr. F10 70
Wascana Creek, stm., Sk., Can. D9 124
Wasco, Ca., U.S. H6 134
Wasco, Or., U.S. E6 136
Waseca, Mn., U.S. G5 118
Wasgomuwa National Park, p.o.i., Sri L. H5 53
Washademoak Lake, l., N.B., Can. E11 110
Washburn, Il., U.S. D8 120
Washburn, N.D., U.S. G12 124
Washburn, Wi., U.S. E7 118
Washburn, Mount, mtn., Wy., U.S. F16 136
Washburn Lake, l., N.T., Can. A9 106
Wāshīm, India H6 54
Washington, D.C., U.S. F8 114
Washington, Ga., U.S. C3 116
Washington, Il., U.S. D8 120
Washington, In., U.S. F10 120
Washington, Ia., U.S. C6 120
Washington, La., U.S. G6 122
Washington, Mo., U.S. F6 120
Washington, N.C., U.S. A8 116
Washington, Pa., U.S. D5 114
Washington, Tx., U.S. G2 122
Washington, Ut., U.S. F3 132
Washington, Va., U.S. F7 114
Washington, state, U.S. C6 136
Washington, Mount, mtn., N.H., U.S. F5 110
Washington Court House, Oh., U.S. E2 114
Washington Island, i., Wi., U.S. C3 112
Washington Land, reg., Grnld. A12 141
Washington Terrace, Ut., U.S. B5 132
Washita, stm., U.S. G12 128
Washow Bay, b., Mb., Can. C17 124
Washpool National Park, p.o.i., Austl. G9 76
Washtucna, Wa., U.S. D8 136
Wasian, Indon. F9 44
Wasilków, Pol. C19 16
Wasior, Indon. F9 44
Waskada, Mb., Can. E13 124
Waskaganish, Qc., Can. E15 106
Waskahigan, stm., Ab., Can. B13 138
Waskom, Tx., U.S. E4 122
Waspam, Nic. E5 102
Wassenaar, Neth. B13 14
Wasseralfingen, Ger. H6 16
Wassy, Fr. F13 14
Watampone, Indon. F12 50
Watansopeng, Indon. F11 50
Watatic, Mount, mtn., Ma., U.S. B14 114
Waterberge, mts., S. Afr. D8 70
Waterbury, Ct., U.S. C12 114
Wateree Lake, res., S.C., U.S. B5 116
Waterford (Port Lairge), Ire. I5 12
Waterford, Ca., U.S. F5 134
Waterford, Pa., U.S. C6 114
Waterford, Wi., U.S. B9 120
Waterford, state, Ire. I5 12
Waterhen Lake, l., Mb., Can. B14 124
Water Island, i., V.I.U.S. e7 104b
Waterloo, Austl. C5 74
Waterloo, Bel. D13 14
Waterloo, On., Can. E9 112
Waterloo, Qc., Can. E4 110
Waterloo, Al., U.S. C10 122
Waterloo, Il., U.S. F7 120
Waterloo, Ia., U.S. B5 120
Waterloo, N.Y., U.S. B8 114
Waterloo, Wi., U.S. A9 120
Waterman, Il., U.S. C9 120
Waterproof, La., U.S. F7 122
Watersmeet, Mi., U.S. E9 118
Waterton-Glacier International Peace Park, p.o.i., N.A. B13 136
Waterton Lakes National Park, p.o.i., Ab., Can. G16 138
Watertown, N.Y., U.S. E14 112
Watertown, S.D., U.S. C15 126
Watertown, Wi., U.S. A9 120
Waterval Boven, S. Afr. D10 70
Water Valley, Ms., U.S. C9 122
Waterville, N.S., Can. E12 110
Waterville, Ks., U.S. B12 128
Waterville, Me., U.S. F7 110
Waterville, Oh., U.S. C2 114
Waterville, Wa., U.S. C6 136
Watervliet, N.Y., U.S. B12 114
Watford, Eng., U.K. J12 12
Watford City, N.D., U.S. G10 124
Wathena, Ks., U.S. E2 120
Watkins Glen, N.Y., U.S. B9 114
Watkinsville, Ga., U.S. C2 116
Watling Island see San Salvador, i., Bah. C10 96
Watonga, Ok., U.S. F10 128
Watrous, Sk., Can. C8 124
Watsa, D.R.C. D5 66
Watseka, Il., U.S. H2 112
Watsikengo, D.R.C. E4 66
Watson, Sk., Can. B9 124
Watson Lake, Yk., Can. C5 106
Watsonville, Ca., U.S. G4 134
Watt Mountain, vol., Dom. j6 105c
Watts Bar Lake, res., Tn., U.S. B14 122
Watts Mills, S.C., U.S. B4 116
Wattwil, Switz. C5 22
Watubela, Kepulauan, is., Indon. F9 44
Watzmann, mtn., Ger. I8 16
Waubay Lake, l., S.D., U.S. B15 126
Wauchope, Austl. D6 74
Wauchula, Fl., U.S. I4 116
Wauconda, Wa., U.S. B7 136
Waugh, Mb., Can. B3 118
Waukara, Bukit, mtn., Indon. D11 50
Waukaringa, Austl. I2 76
Waukarlycarly, Lake, l., Austl. D4 74
Waukegan, Il., U.S. F2 112
Waukesha, Wi., U.S. A9 120
Waukon, Ia., U.S. H7 118
Waunakee, Wi., U.S. A8 120
Wauneta, Ne., U.S. G11 126
Waupun, Wi., U.S. H10 118
Waurika, Ok., U.S. G11 128
Waurika Lake, res., Ok., U.S. G10 128
Wausa, Ne., U.S. E15 126
Wausau, Wi., U.S. G9 118
Wauseon, Oh., U.S. C1 114
Wautoma, Wi., U.S. G9 118
Wauwatosa, Wi., U.S. E1 112
Wauzeka, Wi., U.S. A7 120
Wave Hill, Austl. C6 74
Waverly, Ia., U.S. B5 120
Waverly, Mo., U.S. E4 120
Waverly, Ne., U.S. D1 120
Waverly, N.Y., U.S. B9 114
Waverly, Oh., U.S. E2 114
Waverly, Tn., U.S. H10 120
Waverly, Va., U.S. G8 114
Waverly Hall, Ga., U.S. E14 122
Wāw, Sudan F5 62
Wawa, On., Can. F14 106
Wawa, Nig. H5 64
Wawa, stm., Nic. E5 102
Wāw al-Kabīr, Libya B3 62
Wawanesa, Mb., Can. E14 124
Waxahachie, Tx., U.S. B11 130
Waxhaw, N.C., U.S. B5 116
Way, Lake, l., Austl. E4 74
Waya, i., Fiji p18 79e
Waycross, Ga., U.S. E3 116
Wayland, Ia., U.S. C6 120
Wayland, Ky., U.S. G3 114
Wayland, Mi., U.S. F4 112
Waylyn, S.C., U.S. D6 116
Wayne, Ab., Can. E18 138
Wayne, Mi., U.S. B2 114
Wayne, Ne., U.S. E15 126
Wayne, N.J., U.S. D11 114
Wayne, W.V., U.S. F3 114
Wayne City, Il., U.S. F9 120
Waynesboro, Ms., U.S. F10 122
Waynesboro, Tn., U.S. B11 122
Waynesboro, Va., U.S. F6 114
Waynesville, Il., U.S. D8 120
Waynesville, N.C., U.S. A3 116
Waynoka, Ok., U.S. E10 128
Wāzah Khwāh, Afg. B2 54
Wazīrābād, Pak. B5 54
Wda, stm., Pol. C14 16
Wé, N. Cal. m16 79d
We, Pulau, i., Indon. J2 48
Weatherford, Ok., U.S. F10 128
Weatherford, Tx., U.S. B10 130
Weatherly, Pa., U.S. D10 114
Weaubleau, Mo., U.S. G4 120
Weaver Lake, l., Mb., Can. B17 124
Weaverville, Ca., U.S. C3 134
Weaverville, N.C., U.S. I3 114
Webb, Sk., Can. D5 124
Webb, Ms., U.S. D8 122
Webbwood, On., Can. B7 112
Weber, stm., Ut., U.S. B5 132
Weber City, Va., U.S. H3 114
Webster, Ab., Can. A12 138
Webster, Fl., U.S. H3 116
Webster, Ma., U.S. B14 114
Webster, Wi., U.S. F6 118
Webster City, Ia., U.S. B4 120
Weda, Indon. E8 44
Weddell Island, i., Falk. Is. J4 90
Weddell Sea, Ant. B36 81
Wedderburn, Austl. K4 76
Wedgeport, N.S., Can. G11 110
Wedowee, Al., U.S. D13 122
Weed, Ca., U.S. B3 134
Weems, Va., U.S. G9 114
Weenen, S. Afr. F10 70
Weeping Water, Ne., U.S. D1 120
Weert, Neth. C14 14
Wee Waa, Austl. H7 76
Węgorzewo, Pol. B17 16
Węgrów, Pol. D17 16